The Regulatory and Administrative State

THE REGULATORY AND ADMINISTRATIVE STATE

MATERIALS, CASES, COMMENTS

Lisa Heinzerling

Professor of Law
Georgetown University Law Center

Mark V. Tushnet

William Nelson Cromwell Professor of Law
Harvard Law School

OXFORD
UNIVERSITY PRESS

2006

OXFORD

UNIVERSITY PRESS

Oxford University Press, Inc., publishes works that further
Oxford University's objective of excellence
in research, scholarship, and education.

Oxford   New York
Auckland   Cape Town   Dar es Salaam   Hong Kong   Karachi
Kuala Lumpur   Madrid   Melbourne   Mexico City   Nairobi
New Delhi   Shanghai   Taipei   Toronto

With offices in
Argentina   Austria   Brazil   Chile   Czech Republic   France   Greece
Guatemala   Hungary   Italy   Japan   Poland   Portugal   Singapore
South Korea   Switzerland   Thailand   Turkey   Ukraine   Vietnam

Published by Oxford University Press, Inc.
198 Madison Avenue, New York, New York 10016

www.oup.com

Oxford is a registered trademark of Oxford University Press

Library of Congress Cataloging-in-Publication Data
Heinzerling, Lisa.
The regulatory and administrative state : materials, cases, comments /
Lisa Heinzerling, Mark V. Tushnet.
   p. cm. — (21st century legal education series)
Includes index.

ISBN-13 978-0-19-518931-5

1. Police power—United States—Cases.   2. Administrative agencies—United States—Cases.
3. Administrative procedure—United States—Cases.   4. Risk—Case studies.
I. Tushnet, Mark V., 1945–   II. Title.   III. Series.
KF5407.A4H45 2006
342.73'0664—dc22   2006003073

9 8 7 6 5 4 3 2

Printed in the United States of America
on acid-free paper

21st Century Legal Education Series

To our students

Preface

This casebook is an introduction to the reasons for regulation, the ways in which regulation can go awry, the choice of legal institutions for regulation, the choice of regulatory instruments, and the theory and practice of statutory interpretation. Often, these subjects are introduced in separate courses, sometimes late in law school. We think that students coming to regulatory issues for the first time—whether in the first year of law school, as upper-class students, or others—will learn more by seeing the subjects in a unified course.

We use several substantive subject areas as the vehicle for introducing students to the modern regulatory state: workplace health and safety, environmental protection, and food and drug law. All three areas involve regulation of "risk." The topic of risk is relevant not only for its intrinsic importance but also because preserving a continuous theme throughout the casebook allows students to focus on the pertinent theoretical, empirical, and doctrinal issues in a specific, concrete setting. Regulatory issues, whether about policy choices or statutory interpretation, never arise in a vacuum. Seeing how they are addressed in their "natural habitat," that is, in the context of specific problems and statutes dealing with risk, will allow students to generalize what they learn from these materials to other areas of regulation and statutory interpretation. The issues that arise in the context of risks to human life and health in the workplace, the environment, and consumer products—about matters such as institutional choice, statutory interpretation, and regulatory failure—arise in many other fields where questions of whether and how to regulate come up. Moreover, much of the interdisciplinary work we examine in this book—the work of economists, cognitive psychologists, sociologists, and others—has been done with reference to risk and then has been applied in other regulatory fields. The focal point of our discussion, risks to human life and health in a variety of settings, though a natural choice, is not at all a confining one.

For that reason, the book is also appropriate for courses addressing more specific subject areas. In this case, the course instructor would supplement the book with other materials, while maintaining the book's basic "spine." Courses in employment relations, housing policy, consumer law, natural resources law, or welfare law all could take the general outline of the book and adapt it to the more targeted course's own specific substantive purposes. Indeed, virtually any subject bordering significantly on the modern regulatory state could be used as a vehicle for introducing the basic concepts presented in this book: rationales for regulation, choices among institutions, choices of regulatory instruments, regulatory failures, and statutory interpretation. These are general topics and require general skills, yet they are most effectively introduced by reference to specific social problems. We have chosen one set of "ribs"—workplace health and safety, environmental protection, and food and drug law—to fit the spine of this book but many alternatives are possible.

Lawyers in the twenty-first century need course materials of this sort. They are deeply involved in public law and the regulatory state, and need the skills—including the ability to read and understand statutes—associated with the modern regulatory state. In recognition of the centrality of materials on regulatory and administrative law to the law school curriculum, proposals to reform the first-year law school curriculum have for perhaps twenty years routinely included a course on statutory interpretation and the regulatory state. Here we present what contemporary lawyers need to know—*both* an understanding of statutory interpretation *and* an understanding of the reasons for regulation—in a casebook that can be used in first-year courses designed to introduce students to the role of statutes and administrative regulation in the modern state.

What follows is an overview of the casebook's conceptualization. Chapters 1 and 2 begin with an examination of the justifications for the characteristic regulatory focus of the modern regulatory state, using a problem—justifying regulation when parties have a contract with each other—that poses the most difficult questions about justifying regulation. Chapter 1 uses two classic cases to focus discussion on the argument that contracts between affected parties are sufficient to deal with risk, here of workplace injury (which we present as a form of environmental risk as well). Chapter 2 then develops in more detail the economic perspective that underlies the analysis we have presented.

Chapter 3 raises questions about the economic perspective introduced in Chapter 2: Should some goods be barred from becoming subject to market transactions? The chapter concludes with consideration of unequal bargaining power as a justification for regulation; the materials attempt to explain why unequal bargaining power has a more limited range of application than they might think.

The second part of the materials deals with the choice of legal institutions, the types of regulatory instruments, and the choices involved in selecting which instrument to use. We begin in chapter 4 by moving from contract as a regulatory system to criminal law and tort law and identifying the doctrinal problems arising in efforts to use these techniques to deal with environmental and workplace injury. Chapter 5 presents three analytic approaches to the choice of regulatory instruments, which focus on the different characteristics of different institutions for regulation. The materials then turn to questions of sociology and history. Does the economic perspective require that people be aware of, and claim, their legal rights? And, finally, why are some things regarded as appropriate subjects for regulation and others not?

Chapter 6 takes up the evolution of the regulation of safety and health risks in the workplace through an examination of the development of the workers' compensation system. The aim of these materials is to introduce the range of problems that arise in connection with *any* regulatory instrument, such as rigidity and the development of efforts to evade the instrument's restrictions.

Just as workers' compensation laws were inspired by the perceived inadequacy of the traditional tort system in addressing workplace injuries, many more contemporary statutes—such as environmental laws—also have come about at least partly because of the inadequacy of the tort system. Part III introduces modern statutory regulation. It begins with an overview of problems of statutory interpretation in chapters 7 and 8. Chapter 9 examines the ways in which regulation can fail, including a discussion of so-called regulatory paradoxes, for example, that intensive regulation may produce *less* protection for health or the environment than less intensive but more extensive regulation. It concludes with two sections on the value of and the problems with cost-benefit analysis. Succeeding chapters take up information provision as a form of regulation and then different standards used in regulation (zero-risk, public health, and the like). Chapter 13 concludes this part by moving from law to political science, and then back, to provide students with some tools for understanding the real-world processes that lead to choices of one or another regulatory technique (or of no statutory regulation at all). This chapter provides the basics of public choice analysis of the legislative process and criticisms of that approach, so that students can evaluate the possibility that the legislature will actually choose the regulatory instrument suggested by the normative analysis they have just gone through. The section then invites students to apply the political analysis to the topics of administrative and presidential setting of regulatory priorities and of congressional adoption of federal occupational safety and health legislation.

The book's fourth and final part offers what we call "new perspectives" on regulatory issues. The materials use information about regulatory styles in Great Britain and Japan as a vehicle for introducing possible reforms in the U.S. regulatory system, which are developed in some detail in chapter 15.

This book emerges out of a decade of experience in teaching courses by using predecessor versions of these materials, and we are grateful to the students who helped us develop the materials. We believe that these materials provide the right kind of introduction to the legal issues associated with the regulatory and administrative state in the twenty-first century. We hope that you agree.

Acknowledgments

We are grateful to many people for their help in bringing this book together. Dedi Feldman at Oxford University Press saw the curricular niche this book would fill and has been energetically pursuing a casebook series that would remake the outdated first-year law curriculum. Lori Wood was a careful and thoughtful editor. Robert Rosing, David Tarr, and Justin Wade provided Professor Heinzerling with excellent research assistance. Other research assistants helped Professor Tushnet with his portion of the materials, over a long enough period when he was not anticipating publication of the materials that he is unable to thank them individually, a fact that he deeply regrets. Students at several different law schools used these materials over the years and offered valuable guidance.

We would also like to single out the Georgetown Law Center and our colleagues there for special praise, as the course around which these materials were initially built was developed as part of Georgetown's forward-thinking alternative first-year curriculum.

Summary of Contents

Contents

Part II
Doctrinal and Institutional Limits of the Common Law   *109*

Chapter 4
Doctrinal Limits   *111*

Chapter 10
Information Provision   547

Justifying Regulation
When Parties Contract

I

This casebook takes a problem—risks to human life and health—and explores the potential justifications for, and contours of, legal responses to that problem. We begin, in this part, with justifications for legal intervention.

When a risk is imposed on one person by another person in the absence of any agreement between the parties, some form of legal response is at least presumptively justifiable. Philosophers going all the way back to Hobbes have argued that the predominant reason for giving authority to the government to manage human affairs was to attain some degree of security against private violence. Even economists, who are generally more resistant to the notion of government intervention, have long held that in the case of "negative externalities"—such as harms imposed by one person upon another without his or her consent—government action is warranted. As we will see, the case for intervention of some kind when one party harms another in the absence of an agreement between the parties is fairly well accepted, even though there is disagreement about what form government action should take.

The appropriateness of government intervention is less obvious when the parties' relationship is governed by a private contract, such as in relationships between employers and employees, manufacturers and consumers, and doctors and patients. Such cases raise the following questions: Should the risks associated with the relationship be regulated exclusively by the terms of the parties' agreement? When, if at all, should legislatures or courts adopt rules that change the allocation of risks found in the parties' agreement?

In the discussion that follows, chapter 1 will use two classic cases to introduce the legal responses to these questions. Chapter 2 will consider the economic perspective on this issue, and chapter 3 will explore alternative perspectives that are critical of the economic point of view.

Legal Responses to the Problem
of Allocating Risk

1

This chapter begins by presenting background material on the presence of risk in the environment and the workplace. One question you should keep in mind throughout this book is whether the "problem" of risk—whether allocated by contract or imposed without consent—is "big" or "small." Why would answering that question—or, more precisely, developing some perspectives on how to answer it—matter? Perhaps because "doing something" about risks, in a world with limited political resources, may mean not doing something about something else.

The chapter then presents two classic cases on workplace safety to consider the regulation of risk at common law and the constitutional restrictions on the power of legislatures to alter the allocation of risk in contracts between private parties. Those restrictions have now been abandoned, but the Supreme Court's rationale for imposing them remains instructive.

A Background: Risk in the Modern United States

It may seem obvious that people in the United States are exposed to risks every day. We drive cars and risk accidents; we buy products and run the risk that they will malfunction and injure us. As background to the extended treatment of risk in this book, we present some basic information about risk in contemporary society. (Consider both the information presented and the differing ways in which the authors present the information, because recurrently we suggest that you think about the different rhetorics used in policy and legal discussions of risk.)

- *Environmental Regulation: Law, Science, and Policy*
  ROBERT V. PERCIVAL ET AL.
  3d ed., pp. 3–7 (Aspen Law & Business, 2000). Reprinted with permission of Aspen Law & Business

In its most comprehensive formulation, the range of environmental concerns potentially extends to any place where earth is modified by human action. As such, environmental concerns have been with humankind for a long time. The Ancestral Pueblo peoples of the American Southwest, for example, apparently migrated from their mesa and cliff dwellings after a period of residency from approximately A.D.

500 to 1300 because the mesas had succumbed to centuries of intensive land use and deforestation.

Still, one can trace a progression in the complexity and severity of environmental concerns as civilization has moved through various periods of development. Speaking again at the most comprehensive level, two elements of human development have been regularly linked to increasing environmental concerns: population growth and technological change. The Ancestral Pueblos may have overused their mesa habitats, but on a broader ecological scale, relocation was a readily available option to them, given the sparse population of the region, and the mesa ecosystems could recover from the damage they sustained. We live in an age in which our consumptive uses of the earth may not be so benign. In the past 40 years more people and more pollutants have been added to the planet than in the preceding 10,000 years. Modern technology creates some problems that were literally unknown 75 years ago. Synthetic organic compounds and nuclear power are prominent examples. In other cases, such as our use of fossil fuels as an energy source, the scale of use links our activity to environmental degradation in qualitatively new ways. Not only are a significant portion of the environmental problems we face new, but a good number of them are truly global in scope. Thus the scale of cooperation needed to manage some of these problems constitutes another dimension in which contemporary environmental problems differ from historical antecedents.

No single list of characteristics can capture all of the topics that fall within the category of environmental concerns. Some enumeration of characteristics is still useful as a device to begin thinking about their general nature and the difficulties that must be faced in addressing those concerns. Here, then, are some characteristics more common to modern environmental problems than to historical environmental concerns.

>*Uncertainty of mechanism and effect.* For many environmental problems, we lack sufficient knowledge about some significant aspect of how they present risks to the environment. We may be uncertain as to how much of a pollutant is being discharged, how it travels once in the environment, how much of it reaches some object of concern, or how it affects humans or other living things once they are exposed to it. Effects of concern may be latent rather than obvious, chronic rather than acute. We may concentrate on certain effects, such as carcinogenicity, and remain ignorant of other serious impacts, such as ecosystem effects. Indeed, we may be entirely unaware that a problem exists or may be in disagreement over whether we have sufficient evidence to draw firm conclusions one way or another. This was the case with respect to the problem of global warming as recently as ten years ago.

>*Potentially catastrophic effects.* Ozone depletion, global warming, a nuclear disaster, and other modern environmental concerns have the potential for adverse effects on a scale and of a duration heretofore unknown. (Not all modern environmental problems present potentially catastrophic effects, however. Isolated exposures to organic chemicals can be considered modern problems because organics are themselves a product of post World War II technology, but the issues raised by such exposures are rather similar to those raised by exposures to trace metals, which have been occurring for centuries.)

Collective risks. Traditional environmental problems, typified by the profile of a two-party nuisance lawsuit, were problems for a relatively circumscribed set of people. Modern problems are more likely to present risks for large numbers of people, often spanning traditional political jurisdictional lines.

Irreversibility. Changes wrought by modern environmental risks have the potential for altering ecosystems and perhaps even the biosphere for an extremely long period of time. Even if no effect is truly forever, plutonium's half-life of 24,000 years is effectively forever. The fact that mammals in remote regions of the world are still being found with concentrations of DDT in their tissue decades after that pesticide was banned also demonstrates the longevity of adverse effects that modern environmental hazards can have.

Controllability. Technological, political, and economic issues pertaining to how readily a perceived problem can be controlled have always been highly germane in society's attempt to address environmental problems. Efforts to grapple with truly pervasive problems, such as urban smog or global warming, confront particularly difficult issues of how control can be achieved because so many interests are affected, reliance on present patterns of behavior is deep, and the benefits of control are often highly in dispute (in part because of uncertainty of mechanism and effect). The difficult issues of control do not arise solely when confronting concentrated and financially powerful interests. Some of the most difficult issues arise when control seems to require alterations in customary modes of living, such as the issues involved in decreasing the volume of emissions coming from automobiles.

In the past 30 years, the United States has enacted a wide variety of laws to address environmental concerns, both the modern-day manifestations of problems that have been known for some time and also the newer phenomena. . . .

There can be little question that our responses to environmental problems have had beneficial effects. For example, EPA reports that emissions of carbon monoxide, over 75 percent of which come from automobiles, nearly tripled between 1940 and 1970, but since then have fallen by 32 percent from 1970 to 1997 (and by 60 percent between 1978 and 1997, the time frame in which federal controls on auto emissions were most strongly in effect), even though vehicle miles traveled actually increased by 127 percent during the same 1970–1997 time period. EPA, National Air Quality and Emissions Trends Report 9–12 (1999). Controls on the use of lead additives have been even more successful: Emissions of lead fell 97 percent between 1978 and 1997. Id. at 9. . . .

While progress in some areas has been made, there are ample reasons to be cautious, consumers of environmental progress report. Even when environmental policy has generated significant reductions in pollution, the reductions often have been insufficient to achieve health-based goals. Despite substantial progress in reducing air pollutants, more than 107 million Americans still live in areas where air pollutants exceed at least one national health-based standard. Even after new releases of a pollutant are curtailed, the residues from prior emissions can continue to cause harm. The phaseout of lead additives from gasoline has reduced average levels of lead in children's blood dramatically, but an estimated 1.7 million children still have lead levels high enough to be of medical concern. Environmental releases of lead from products that now have been banned or severely restricted—lead-based paint, gasoline lead additives, lead plumbing—continue to be sources of lead exposure through soil, dust, air, or drinking water. A cautionary note is raised by those who argue that the progress made so far cannot be read as a harbinger of future successes. They suggest that early successes came because we had created an economy that did so much environmental harm that easy targets of opportunity for cleanup abounded. Remaining problems may be much more intractable.

> The first wave of environmental legislation was directed at the problems that were easiest to see and resolve. Burning rivers and lakes suffocating from massive algal blooms were obvious targets for remediation. The smog covering the nation's urban areas and the odors emanating from open solid waste dumps cried out for attention. In the face of these conspicuous ills, Congress enunciated broad declarations of intent to "protect and enhance" the nation's resources and to eliminate pollutant discharges. Just as the problems seemed obvious, so did the most effective solutions. The early legislation required EPA and the states to prohibit or control industrial and municipal discharges from both stationary and mobile sources, typically by imposing end-of-pipe controls. A direct cause and effect relationship between compliance with these limitations on pollutant discharges and a cleaner environment was simply assumed.
>
> Twenty years later, these early assessments of the nature of both environmental problems and their resolution seem naive. First, the problems recognized and addressed in the early 1970s have proven more obstinate than they first appeared. For example, despite the realization of significant tailpipe emissions reductions by automobile manufacturers, emissions of some automobile pollutants actually increased between 1970 and 1987. Discharges of other such pollutants have been reduced, yet national health standards remain unmet in many urban areas. The Clean Water Act's system of point source controls undoubtedly has improved the quality of the nation's rivers and lakes, but it is now clear that non-point sources, which are harder to control both technologically and politically, continue to contribute heavily to surface water pollution. Second, problems undiscovered or ignored twenty years ago have since attracted attention, and they promise to be even more intractable than the first targets of environmental concern. Some, like groundwater pollution, are difficult to locate and control because of the physical inaccessibility of the resource. Others, like . . . toxic waste sites . . . , are resistant to rapid amelioration because available resources are insufficient to determine the responsible parties and to carry out cleanup operations. Still other problems, like acid rain, cross both state and international boundaries, creating obstacles to either state or national resolution. Finally, controversy embroils the issue of whether conditions like global warming are even the subject of legitimate concern. Effective steps to redress such difficulties seem years away at best. [R. Glicksman and C. H. Schroeder, *EPA and the Courts: Twenty Years of Law and Politics*, 54 Law and Contemporary Problems 249, 252–253 (1991)]

A second reason to be skeptical about claims that environmental problems have largely been conquered is the continuing expansion of the environmental agenda in light of emerging scientific knowledge. (Compared with the more cautious statement concerning global warming in the Glicksman and Schroeder excerpt, the emergence in the past ten years of global warming as a preeminent issue of international concern provides an excellent example of this phenomenon. . . .) We now know that contamination of the environment is far more pervasive, and vastly more difficult to remediate, than first thought. For example, it is now estimated that contamination around the handful of the nation's nuclear weapons production facilities is so serious that it will cost substantially more than $100 billion to clean up; cleanup of the thousands of toxic dump sites throughout the country will be vastly more costly. Scientific advances also are revealing that some health-based environmental standards are insufficiently protective. For example, scientists have discovered that children suffer permanent neurological damage from exposure to low levels of lead that previously were thought to be safe; tests on other pollutants such as ozone and sulfur dioxide suggest that adverse health effects may occur at lower levels than known when the initial standards were set. . . .

- *A Trench Caves In; a Young Worker Is Dead. Is It a Crime?*
  DAVID BARSTOW
  New York Times, Dec. 21, 2003. Reprinted with permission
  of the *New York Times*

As the autopsy confirmed, death did not come right away for Patrick M. Walters. On June 14, 2002, while working on a sewer pipe in a trench 10 feet deep, he was buried alive under a rush of collapsing muck and mud. A husky plumber's apprentice, barely 22 years old, Mr. Walters clawed for the surface. Sludge filled his throat. Thousands of pounds of dirt pressed on his chest, squeezing and squeezing until he could not draw another breath.

His mother, Michelle Marts, was the first in his family to hear.

"You just stand there like you're suspended in blank space," she said of that moment. She remembers being enveloped by a paralyzing numbness. He was her only child. She could not hear or breathe or move. Was this, she found herself wondering, what Patrick felt?

She called Patrick's father, her ex-husband, Jeff. "It literally knocked me off my feet," he said. "I lay there, right there on the floor, screaming and crying."

Mrs. Marts next called Patrick's wife, Crystal. "I remember running upstairs and just hugging my kid and thinking, 'How am I going to tell her,'" Ms. Walters said.

Soon after, an investigator from the coroner's office called Mrs. Marts. He could not have been nicer. Such a tragedy, he said. But by then, the first insistent questions had begun to form. Her son had often spoken about his fear of being buried alive. He had described being sent into deep trenches without safety equipment, like the large metal boxes placed in excavations to create a sheltered workspace.

"Was there a trench box?" she asked the investigator. He paused, she recalled. "He says, 'Ma'am, no safety procedures were followed. None.'

"He was just so disgusted."

Other officials shared his disgust, starting with the federal safety investigator who stood over the trench that night as Patrick Walters's body was pulled from the mud. Only two weeks before, the same investigator had caught men from the same company—Moeves Plumbing—working unprotected in a 15-foot-deep trench, a blatant violation of federal safety laws.

One of the men was Patrick Walters, who, when questioned by the investigator, had described a host of unsafe work practices.

"They don't like me on these jobs a lot," Mr. Walters had volunteered, according to a tape recording of the interview.

"Why is that?"

"Because, I don't like getting in the holes—even with a box."

The inspector's boss, the federal Occupational Safety and Health Administration's top official in Cincinnati, was angry too. He knew Moeves Plumbing well. In 1989, he had confronted the company over another death. The circumstances were nearly identical: a deep trench, no box, a man buried alive.

But their professional disgust could not touch the pure rage of Patrick Walters's parents. A veteran plumber himself, Jeff Walters knew the treachery of trench walls. Moeves Plumbing would deny any wrongdoing and tell OSHA it was trying to do the right thing on safety. But to Jeff Walters, sending an untrained, unskilled apprentice into an unprotected, unstable, rain-saturated, 10-foot-deep trench was flat-out criminal.

"You done killed my boy!" he recalls screaming that night on the phone to Moeves Plumbing.

His first instinct was revenge by shotgun. His wife and members of his church intervened. They prayed and wept, and then they resolved to seek their justice from the authorities instead....

To the Walters family, ... it seemed like such a small thing to ask for—a simple request ... to take a look, consider the evidence and decide whether to prosecute. That was it.

"It looked like an open-and-shut case," Mrs. Marts said. "No box. Put down in a hole. Buried alive."

An Apprentice Looking to Please

There was still mud in his ears.

Patrick Walters was laid out in his coffin for the visitation, his face puffy and bruised, his ears still flecked with dried bits of clay. They all noticed.

"Mom, can I put this in with Dad?" Crystal Walters's 4-year-old daughter, Christen, asked, holding up one of her drawings.

Patrick Walters was not Christen's father, but he had raised her as his own. Young, financially pressed and prone to quarrel, Patrick and Crystal Walters had married in 2000; they were separated at the time of his death, but still trying. "I loved him," Ms. Walters, 22, said. "Still do."

Looking at him there that day, Ms. Walters found the whole thing incomprehensible, she said. With his linebacker build and nonstop motor, her husband had seemed so indestructible.

But it was dangerous work, and he had known it. He told his mother of being buried to his waist in one trench. He told his father of being lowered into trenches on the bucket of a backhoe, leaving him no ladder to escape a collapse. "I just ask God never to let me die that way," he said to his wife.

His family urged him to put up a fuss. But he pointed out that he was only an apprentice, easily replaced. If he was seen as a troublemaker, he worried, his bosses would find an excuse to get rid of him. Their attitude, he told his father, was "either do it or go home."

And in truth, he did not have many better alternatives. His troubles in school had begun when he was 10, the same year his parents' marriage broke up. By 16, he was running afoul of the law. An episode involving stolen guns and then a police chase resulted in a stretch in juvenile detention.

"The best thing that ever happened to him," his father said.

Still, an arrest record and a G.E.D. earned him only dead-end temporary jobs in factories. He cleaned animal cages. Whatever the dangers, he saw Moeves Plumbing as his big break.

Small and family owned, about 50 employees, Moeves (pronounced MAY-vis) had agreed to pay for his four-year apprentice program. That would mean a plumber's license and $25 an hour and a decent middle-class life for him and Crystal and Christen.

"He was looking at Moeves like this is my road, my way forward," his father said. There was even talk of them one day forming Walters & Son Plumbing.

It was a hard road for $8.50 an hour. But he stuck with it. He put in hard days on the job, then went to school three nights a week. School records show that he missed only three classes. His grades were good.

"A miracle," his mother said.

His father saw a boy becoming a man.

The Physics of the Trench

On May 31, 2002, a local fire chief called the Cincinnati OSHA office to complain that men were installing a storm drain in an unsafe trench. Charles Shelton, a veteran OSHA compliance officer, was at the scene in less than an hour.

Every trench is a potential death trap. Trench walls give way at any time, often without warning. The deeper the trench the greater the risk, which is magnified further if the soil is loose or wet. Hundreds are killed or injured in trenches each year.

That is why federal safety laws require employers to take special precautions for trenches deeper than five feet. The walls must be sloped back at a safe angle or shored up with bracing. If a trench box is used instead, it must be big and sturdy enough to withstand the tremendous forces of a collapse. A "competent person"— someone trained in excavation safety—must inspect the trench before work begins and then daily thereafter.

From a parking lot, Mr. Shelton watched the workers from Moeves Plumbing. One was Patrick Walters. Mr. Shelton approached with a video camera. The trench, about 15 feet deep, was neither sloped nor shored. There was a box, but it was far too small—only eight feet tall—to be effective. And Mr. Shelton had seen men working outside even that undersize shelter.

He shut the job down on a Friday afternoon. On Monday, at 9:22 a.m., he turned on his tape recorder to interview Patrick Walters. "Employees were working in an excavation that was unprotected," Mr. Shelton began, "and I've got this young man, he was exposed to the trench."

His voice was noticeably nervous, but Patrick Walters described a company that did not follow the basic requirements of trench safety. He told of supervisors who tolerated dangerous shortcuts and made little effort to enforce safety rules.

Mr. Shelton asked about safety meetings.

"We've had a couple," Mr. Walters said. "They don't do it regularly anymore." He then volunteered that the company no longer had a safety manager.

"How long has he been gone?"

"I can't remember. It's been a while since we had one."

It had been more than three months.

The safety manager, Robert W. Schum, who left Moeves Plumbing with his son and formed his own company, said in a recent interview that his duties had actually involved "very little safety." His main job, he explained, was managing the warehouse. Sometimes he would check toolboxes for frayed power cords. That was about it. In some two years as safety manager, he said, he could not recall giving any training on trench safety.

The month after he left, Moeves Plumbing sent three supervisors to a training course on trench safety. Two of them—including the field supervisor for all Moeves trench crews—subsequently supervised the digging of the very trench that now so troubled Charles Shelton.

In his inspection report, Mr. Shelton wrote that he had recommended several immediate changes. Moeves Plumbing needed "someone competent in trenching" to train workers or "at least to identify good and bad trenches and to provide trench protection and enforce compliance," he told a senior company official.

His advice went unheeded. But the company's owner, Linda Moeves, did take one step. She called the OSHA director in Cincinnati, William M. Murphy, to complain.

"She was agitated," Mr. Murphy recalled. Mr. Shelton had asked for records to show that she was training employees in trench safety and seeking to enforce safety rules. "Why does he need to be asking to see these records?" Mr. Murphy recalled her asking.

He remembers telling her she would do well to show that she had trained her employees properly. "And she said, 'You know that since that last case we've been trying to do the right thing.'"

Same Company, Another Death

Bill Murphy had not forgotten that last case, 13 years before.

Over more than two decades as the agency's chief in Cincinnati, Mr. Murphy had become a legendary figure within OSHA. He and his office had repeatedly received OSHA's highest awards for aggressive enforcement. His personal history gave him an appreciation for the lives of men like Patrick Walters. He was raised in Scott County, Tenn., one of the poorest counties in the country. The son of a coal miner and farmer who fathered 22 children, he was the first in his family to graduate from high school.

"None of us are smart," Mr. Murphy, 61, said in an interview. "We just work harder."

He knew about death on the job firsthand. One of his half brothers had been electrocuted on a power line; another had fallen to his death erecting steel decking. In one of his first jobs, in an aircraft plant, an explosion killed two men in his work area. Soon after, he went to work for OSHA.

When Mr. Shelton told him about the problems at Moeves Plumbing, Mr. Murphy's mind reeled back to 1989, to that last case and to how afterward Linda Moeves had pledged to do the right thing.

Clint Daley, an inexperienced laborer just like Patrick Walters, had been digging a sewer line with a backhoe operator named Dan Callahan. The trench, 12 feet deep, was neither sloped nor shored. There was no trench box. Mr. Daley was in the trench when the walls cracked. Mr. Callahan shouted a warning.

"By the time he got turned around, it caved in," he said later in a deposition.

What made Clint Daley's death particularly outrageous to Mr. Murphy was that his inspectors had three times before warned Moeves Plumbing's crews about trench safety—in 1984, 1985 and 1986. They had issued safety pamphlets, and a $700 fine.

Yet Moeves Plumbing had not bought any trench safety equipment. Nor had it provided any safety training, on trenches or anything else.

Mr. Murphy might have referred the Daley case to the Justice Department for prosecution. He had, after all, concluded that Clint Daley died because Moeves Plumbing willfully violated safety rules. But Mr. Murphy's response was tempered by his assessment of Linda Moeves.

Her husband, the company's founder, had died in 1987, and though she had helped out in the office, it was not clear she had the skills to run a plumbing business. Her prior job was social director of a racket club.

Mr. Murphy admired the way she had hung tough in the cutthroat contracting world. And when she was interviewed by OSHA about Mr. Daley's death, she pleaded ignorance—about the prior OSHA warnings, about the $700 fine, even about there being federal safety rules for trenches.

"She was too willing to trust her employees to do the right thing," Mr. Murphy said.

Mrs. Moeves promised deep changes. She quickly enrolled in a trenching safety seminar. She bought hydraulic shoring equipment. She saw that her supervisors and backhoe crews learned trench safety. There would be regular safety meetings, a new safety director and a safety committee to correct hazards.

She also established a written safety policy. Trenches deeper than four feet would be sloped or shored "as required by OSHA standards," the policy said. What's more, trenches would be inspected daily by either Mrs. Moeves or a field supervisor. Employees who broke the rules would be disciplined, and even fired after a fourth offense.

Ultimately, Mr. Murphy fined Moeves Plumbing $13,700 for the violations that killed Mr. Daley.

Over the next three years, Moeves Plumbing was inspected five times and cited for seven relatively minor violations. Mr. Murphy concluded that Mrs. Moeves had learned a painful lesson.

Now, Mr. Shelton's inspection raised some pointed questions about the permanence of that lesson. Court records show that Moeves Plumbing's safety committee had not existed for years. Nor were there records of any trench inspections or of employees being disciplined for safety violations. Several Moeves workers said they could not recall Mrs. Moeves or her supervisors ever directing them to take precautions against trench collapses.

"I was unpleasantly surprised," Mr. Murphy said. "I had thought she had gotten her act together."

Wet, Deep and Deadly

About a week after Charles Shelton's inspection, Moeves Plumbing received a work order for a routine job running sewer and water lines into new homes about 40 miles north of Cincinnati.

The job was assigned to John F. Kehrer, 49, an experienced backhoe operator. Patrick Walters typically worked as Mr. Kehrer's helper, doing the dirty work of laying, cutting and connecting pipes after Mr. Kehrer dug the trench. In a recent deposition given to lawyers for the Walters family, Mr. Kehrer described Patrick Walters as a hard worker who had never refused an instruction.

On the first day of this job, though, Patrick Walters was unavailable. He had gone for treatment after being hit in the back by a backhoe bucket. A doctor prescribed painkillers and cleared him for work.

With another helper, Mr. Kehrer started to dig. In his deposition, he said seeping water had made him worried.

"It's never safe when there is water in there," he explained.

"Why?"

"Because everything is so unstable."

The trench was at least eight feet deep. Still, he said, they took no precautions.

Mr. Kehrer insisted in his deposition that he was not competent to assess the hazards. Yes, he had taken a 10-hour trench safety class with a prior employer. But he also said that he had forgotten most of what he learned, and had received no safety training in six years at Moeves Plumbing.

The next day, Mr. Kehrer returned to finish the job with Patrick Walters. There had been more rain overnight, a downpour that filled the trench. It took hours to pump the water out. Then he started to dig.

Moeves Plumbing's safety policy—the one instituted after Clint Daley's death—called for a field supervisor to inspect trenches daily. According to Mr. Kehrer, though, no supervisor inspected this trench.

By early afternoon the trench was 10 feet deep. Its walls—saturated with rainwater—were neither shored nor sloped. There was no trench box, no ladder. It was time to cut a sewer pipe, the helper's job.

Mr. Kehrer said he did not actually order Patrick Walters into the trench. "He knew what to do," he said. But he acknowledged doing nothing to stop him, though he knew enough to recognize that the trench violated federal safety laws.

"I just did not think anything was going to happen, plain and simple," he said.

Mr. Kehrer told an investigator that he felt his backhoe start to shift. It slid toward the trench as the walls began to collapse. He barely had time to yell a warning.

In one great whoosh of mud, Patrick Walters was gone. . . .

Angry, Unsatisfied, Determined

Patrick Walters's family has a new plan.

Step 1 is to use the civil courts to put Linda Moeves out of business. Step 2 is to use any money won from Moeves Plumbing to mount a campaign against OSHA. . . .

Their chances of winning are remote.

Ohio's workers' compensation laws broadly shield Moeves Plumbing from civil liability, even if its negligence caused Patrick Walters's death. To win the suit, filed in state court, the family must prove that Moeves Plumbing committed an "intentional tort"—that it sent Patrick Walters into that trench knowing death or injury was "substantially certain to occur." . . .

But [a family acquaintance] says there is no dissuading Jeff Walters from his plan.

"This man will be a bitter man for the rest of his life," he said. "No. 1 because his son was killed. And No. 2 because his government betrayed him, and like so many others out there the anger just continues to build and build."

If her former husband is focused on changing the system, Mrs. Marts, 45, confesses that she is still battling fantasies of revenge. One involves Linda Moeves buried to her neck in mud. For months, Mrs. Marts has lived on the brink of breakdown.

What eats at her, she said, is that she cannot stop thinking about how her boy died. When she gets into an elevator, she holds her breath as long as she can. She imagines him under all that mud, holding his breath.

She still has not washed his pillow cases or his old clothes, clinging to his fading scent as long as she can. She listens often to his interview with Charles Shelton, to his smoker's cough and his nervous laugh. She visits the cemetery nearly every day, tidying up, rearranging the flowers.

It was a lot of money, but after Patrick died the family agreed that his final resting place would have to be in a mausoleum, not six feet under.

"There's no way I was going to put him in the ground again," his mother said.

B The Traditional Framework at Common Law

We begin our examination of legal responses to the risks associated with contractual relationships with a classic case from 1842. Although it is framed as a tort case, one might treat *Farwell* as the first in a line of "contract" remedies because, as you will see, Chief Justice Shaw argues that the injured worker should not recover because the employment contract provides a better mechanism for compensating for the risk of injury.

■ Farwell v. The Boston and Worcester Rail Road Corporation
   45 Mass. 49 (1842)

In an action of trespass upon the case, the plaintiff alleged in his declaration, that he agreed with the defendants to serve them in the employment of an engineer in the management and care of their engines and cars running on their rail road between Boston and Worcester, and entered on said employment, and continued to perform his duties as engineer till October 30th 1837, when the defendants, at Newton, by their servants, so carelessly, negligently and unskillfully managed and used, and put and placed the iron match rail, called the short switch, across the rail or track of their said rail road, that the engine and cars, upon which the plaintiff was engaged and employed in the discharge of his said duties of engineer, were thrown from the track of said rail road, and the plaintiff, by means thereof, was thrown with great violence upon the ground; by means of which one of the wheels of one of said cars passed over the right hand of the plaintiff, crushing and destroying the same.

The case was submitted to the court on the following facts agreed by the parties: "The plaintiff was employed by the defendants, in 1835, as an engineer, and went at first with the merchandize cars, and afterwards with the passenger cars, and so continued till October 30th 1837, at the wages of two dollars per day; that being the usual wages paid to engine-men, which are higher than the wages paid to a machinist, in which capacity the plaintiff formerly was employed.

"On the 30th of October 1837, the plaintiff, then being in the employment of the defendants, as such engine-man, and running the passenger train, ran his engine off at a switch on the road, which had been left in a wrong condition (as alleged by the plaintiff, and, for the purposes of this trial, admitted by the defendants), by one Whitcomb, another servant of the defendants, who had been long in their employment, as a switch-man or tender, and had the care of switches on the road, and was a careful and trustworthy servant, in his general character, and as such servant was well known to the plaintiff. By which running off, the plaintiff sustained the injury complained of in his declaration.

"The said Farwell (the plaintiff) and Whitcomb were both appointed by the superintendent of the road, who was in the habit of passing over the same very frequently in the cars, and often rode on the engine.

"If the court shall be of opinion that, as matter of law, the defendants are not liable to the plaintiff, he being a servant of the corporation, and in their employment, for the injury he may have received from the negligence of said Whitcomb, another servant of the corporation, and in their employment, then the plaintiff shall become nonsuit; but if the court shall be of opinion, as matter of law, that the defendants may be liable in this case, then the case shall be submitted to a jury upon the facts which may be proved in the case; the defendants alleging negligence on the part of the plaintiff." . . .

Shaw, C. J. This is an action of new impression in our courts, and involves a principle of great importance. It presents a case, where two persons are in the service and employment of one company, whose business it is to construct and maintain a rail road, and to employ their trains of cars to carry persons and merchandize for hire. They are appointed and employed by the same company to perform separate duties and services, all tending to the accomplishment of one and the same purpose—that of the safe and rapid transmission of the trains; and they are paid for their respective services according to the nature of their respective duties, and the labor and skill required for their proper performance. The question is, whether, for damages sustained by one of the persons so employed, by means of the carelessness and negligence of another, the party injured has a remedy against the common employer. It is an argument against such an action, though certainly not a decisive one, that no such action has before been maintained.

It is laid down by Blackstone, that if a servant, by his negligence, does any damage to a stranger, the master shall be answerable for his neglect. But the damage must be done while he is actually employed in the master's service; otherwise, the servant shall answer for his own misbehavior. 1 Bl. Com. 431. *M'Manus v. Crickett*, 1 East, 106. This rule is obviously founded on the great principle of social duty, that every man, in the management of his own affairs, whether by himself or by his agents or servants, shall so conduct them as not to injure another; and if he does not, and another thereby sustains damage, he shall answer for it. If done by a servant, in the course of his employment, and acting within the scope of his authority, it is considered, in contemplation of law, so far the act of the master, that the latter shall be answerable *civiliter*. But this presupposes that the parties stand to each other in the relation of strangers, between whom there is no privity; and the action, in such case, is an action sounding in tort. . . . The maxim *respondeat superior* is adopted in that case, from general considerations of policy and security.

But this does not apply to the case of a servant bringing his action against his own employer to recover damages for an injury arising in the course of that employment, where all such risks and perils as the employer and the servant respectively intend to assume and bear may be regulated by the express or implied contract between them, and which, in contemplation of law, must be presumed to be thus regulated. . . .

. . . The claim, therefore, is placed, and must be maintained, if maintained at all, on the ground of contract. As there is no express contract between the parties, applicable to this point, it is placed on the footing of an implied contract of indemnity, arising out of the relation of master and servant. It would be an implied promise, arising from the duty of the master to be responsible to each person employed by him, in the conduct of every branch of business, where two or more persons are employed, to pay for all damage occasioned by the negligence of every other person employed in the same service. If such a duty were established by law—like that of a common carrier, to stand to all losses of goods not caused by the act of God or of a public enemy—or that of an innkeeper, to be responsible, in like manner, for the baggage of his guests; it would be a rule of frequent and familiar occurrence, and its existence and application, with all its qualifications and restrictions, would be settled by judicial precedents. But we are of opinion that no such rule has been established, and the authorities, as far as they go, are opposed to the principle. *Priestley v. Fowler,* 3 Mees. & Welsb. 1. *Murray v. South Carolina Rail Road Company,* 1 McMullan 385.

The general rule, resulting from considerations as well of justice as of policy, is, that he who engages in the employment of another for the performance of specified duties and services, for compensation, takes upon himself the natural and ordinary risks and perils incident to the performance of such services, and in legal presumption, the compensation is adjusted accordingly. And we are not aware of any principle which should except the perils arising from the carelessness and negligence of those who are in the same employment. These are perils which the servant is as likely to know, and against which he can as effectually guard, as the master. They are perils incident to the service, and which can be as distinctly foreseen and provided for in the rate of compensation as any others. To say that the master shall be responsible because the damage is caused by his agents, is assuming the very point which remains to be proved. They are his agents to some extent, and for some purposes; but whether he is responsible, in a particular case, for their negligence, is not decided by the single fact that they are, for some purposes, his agents. . . .

If we look from considerations of justice to those of policy, they will strongly lead to the same conclusion. In considering the rights and obligations arising out of particular relations, it is competent for courts of justice to regard considerations of policy and general convenience, and to draw from them such rules as will, in their practical application, best promote the safety and security of all parties concerned. This is, in truth, the basis on which implied promises are raised, being duties legally inferred from a consideration of what is best adapted to promote the benefit of all persons concerned, under given circumstances. To take the well known and familiar cases already cited; a common carrier, without regard to actual fault or neglect in himself or his servants, is made liable for all losses of goods confided to him for carriage, except those caused by the act of God or of a public enemy, because he can best guard them against all minor dangers, and because, in case of actual loss, it would be extremely difficult for the owner to adduce proof of embezzlement, or other actual fault or neglect on the part of the carrier, although it may have been the real cause of the loss. The risk is therefore thrown upon the carrier, and he receives, in the form of payment for the carriage, a premium for the risk which he thus assumes. So of an innkeeper; he can best secure the attendance of honest and faithful servants, and guard his house against thieves. Whereas, if he were responsible only upon proof of actual negligence, he might connive at the presence of dishonest inmates and retainers, and even participate in the embezzlement of the property of the guests, during the hours of their necessary sleep, and yet it would be difficult, and often impossible, to prove these facts. . . .

We are of opinion that these considerations apply strongly to the case in question. Where several persons are employed in the conduct of one common enterprise or undertaking, and the safety of each depends much on the care and skill with which each other shall perform his appropriate duty, each is an observer of the conduct of the others, can give notice of any misconduct, incapacity or neglect of duty, and leave the service, if the common employer will not take such precautions, and employ such agents as the safety of the whole party may require. By these means, the safety of each will be much more effectually secured, than could be done by a resort to the common employer for indemnity in case of loss by the negligence of each other. Regarding it in this light, it is the ordinary case of one sustaining an injury in the course of his own employment, in which he must bear the loss himself, or seek his remedy, if he have any, against the actual wrong-doer.*

In applying these principles to the present case, it appears that the plaintiff was employed by the defendants as an engineer, at the rate of wages usually paid in that employment, being a higher rate than the plaintiff had before received as a machinist. It was a voluntary undertaking on his part, with a full knowledge of the risks incident to the employment; and the loss was sustained by means of an ordinary casualty, caused by the negligence of another servant of the company. Under these circumstances, the loss must be deemed to be the result of a pure accident, like those to which all men, in all employments, and at all times, are more or less exposed; and like similar losses from accidental causes, it must rest where it first fell, unless the plaintiff has a remedy against the person actually in default; of which we give no opinion.

It was strongly pressed in the argument, that although this might be so, where two or more servants are employed in the same department of duty, where each can exert some influence over the conduct of the other, and thus to some extent provide for his own security; yet that it could not apply where two or more are employed in different departments of duty, at a distance from each other, and where one can in no degree control or influence the conduct of another. But we think this is founded upon a supposed distinction, on which it would be extremely difficult to establish a practical rule. When the object to be accomplished is one and

* See *Winterbottom v. Wright*, 10 Mees. & Welsb. 109. *Milligan v. Wedge*, 12 Adolph. & Ellis 737.

the same, when the employers are the same, and the several persons employed derive their authority and their compensation from the same source, it would be extremely difficult to distinguish, what constitutes one department and what a distinct department of duty. It would vary with the circumstances of every case. If it were made to depend upon the nearness or distance of the persons from each other, the question would immediately arise, how near or how distant must they be, to be in the same or different departments. In a blacksmith's shop, persons working in the same building, at different fires, may be quite independent of each other, though only a few feet distant. In a ropewalk, several may be at work on the same piece of cordage, at the same time, at many hundred feet distant from each other, and beyond the reach of sight and voice, and yet acting together.

Besides, it appears to us, that the argument rests upon an assumed principle of responsibility which does not exist. The master, in the case supposed, is not exempt from liability, because the servant has better means of providing for his safety, when he is employed in immediate connexion with those from whose negligence he might suffer; but because the *implied contract* of the master does not extend to indemnify the servant against the negligence of any one but himself; and he is not liable in tort, as for the negligence of his servant, because the person suffering does not stand towards him in the relation of a stranger, but is one whose rights are regulated by contract express or implied. The exemption of the master, therefore, from liability for the negligence of a fellow servant, does not depend exclusively upon the consideration, that the servant has better means to provide for his own safety, but upon other grounds. Hence the separation of the employment into different departments cannot create that liability, when it does not arise from express or implied contract, or from a responsibility created by law to third persons, and strangers, for the negligence of a servant.

A case may be put for the purpose of illustrating this distinction. Suppose the road had been owned by one set of proprietors whose duty it was to keep it in repair and have it at all times ready and in fit condition for the running of engines and cars, taking a toll, and that the engines and cars were owned by another set of proprietors, paying toll to the proprietors of the road, and receiving compensation from passengers for their carriage; and suppose the engineer to suffer a loss from the negligence of the switch-tender. We are inclined to the opinion that the engineer might have a remedy against the rail road corporation; and if so, it must be on the ground, that as between the engineer employed by the proprietors of the engines and cars, and the switch-tender employed by the corporation, the engineer would be a stranger, between whom and the corporation there could be no privity of contract; and not because the engineer would have no means of controlling the conduct of the switch-tender. The responsibility which one is under for the negligence of his servant, in the conduct of his business, towards third persons, is founded on another and distinct principle from that of implied contract, and stands on its own reasons of policy. The same reasons of policy, we think, limit this responsibility to the case of strangers, for whose security alone it is established. Like considerations of policy and general expediency forbid the extension of the principle, so far as to warrant a servant in maintaining an action against his employer for an indemnity which we think was not contemplated in the nature and terms of the employment, and which, if established, would not conduce to the general good.

In coming to the conclusion that the plaintiff, in the present case, is not entitled to recover, considering it as in some measure a nice question, we would add a caution against any hasty conclusion as to the application of this rule to a case not fully within the same principle. It may be varied and modified by circumstances not appearing in the present case, in which it appears, that no wilful wrong or actual negligence was imputed to the corporation, and where suitable means were furnished and suitable persons employed to accomplish the object in view. We are far from intending to say that there are no implied warranties and undertakings arising out of the relation of master and servant. Whether, for instance, the employer would be responsible to an engineer for a loss arising from a defective or illconstructed steam engine: Whether this would depend upon an implied warranty of its goodness and sufficiency, or upon the fact of wilful misconduct, or gross negligence on the part of the employer, if a natural person, or of the superintendent or immediate representative and managing agent, in case of an incorporated company—are questions on which we give no opinion. In the present case, the claim of the plaintiff is not put on the ground that the defendants did not furnish a sufficient engine, a proper rail road track, a well constructed switch, and a person of suitable skill and experience to attend it; the gravamen of the complaint is, that that person was chargeable with negligence in not changing the switch, in the particular instance, by means of which the accident occurred, by which the plaintiff sustained a severe loss. It ought, perhaps, to be stated, in justice to the person to whom this negligence is imputed, that the fact is strenuously denied by the defendants, and has not been tried by the jury. By consent of the parties, this fact was assumed without trial, in order to take the opinion of the whole court upon the question of law, whether, if such was the fact, the defendants, under the circumstances, were liable. Upon this question, supposing the accident to have occurred, and the loss to have been caused, by the negligence of the person employed to attend to and change the switch, in his not doing so in the particular case, the court are of opinion that it is a loss for which the defendants are not liable, and that the action cannot be maintained.

Plaintiff nonsuit.

COMMENTS AND QUESTIONS

1. Shaw begins the opinion with a paragraph noting, among other things, that this type of action has not "before been maintained." Why hadn't it been?

2. The next paragraph identifies some similar cases, but Shaw ends up distinguishing them. What are his distinctions?

3. Why don't the "considerations of policy and security" that justify the rule of *respondeat superior* justify imposing liability in *Farwell*?

4. Shaw appears to distinguish between considerations of justice and considerations of policy. What, to him, are the former? How are they different, in your view, from his understanding of the latter?

5. Farwell pointed to cases in which courts imposed liability, even though there was a contract between the plaintiff and the defendant. These are the

innkeeper and common carrier cases. How does Shaw distinguish them from *Farwell*?

6. Farwell suggested a "different departments" rule. Why does Shaw reject it? What is the point (or points) Shaw makes in his two examples of the blacksmith's shop and the ropewalk?

7. What point is made in Shaw's discussion of liability where responsibility for maintenance is divided between two sets of proprietors?

8. For a contemporary invocation of *Farwell*-like ideas, see Judge Easterbrook's opinion in *Reich v. Interstate Brands Corp.*, 57 F.3d 574 (7th Cir. 1995):

> Shoppers make their largest purchases of baked goods on Saturday and Monday. To supply fresh products, bakeries are open on Friday and Sunday. Bakery workers' traditional work week has been Monday, Wednesday, Thursday, Friday, and Sunday. In 1972 the bakery workers' union staged a nationwide strike to back up its demand for weekly schedules with two consecutive days off. The employers were unyielding, fearing that a change would impair the freshness of the products on the main shopping days and thus dampen consumer demand. The strike ended with a compromise: workers got higher wages, and employers retained their right to require work without consecutive days off—but employers have to pay a price for exercising the privilege. An employer who gives any worker a schedule that does not include two consecutive days off in a given week must pay $12 per worker per week into a fund. In November of each year the employer distributes these "earned work credits" (as the collective bargaining agreement calls them) to all workers still on the payroll, according to the number of weeks each went without two-day breaks.
>
> Ever since 1972 the collective bargaining agreement has provided that these $12 credits are not compensation for work performed but are "penalties" designed to induce employers to provide consecutive days off. The agreements say that the payments are not part of the base wage on which overtime pay is calculated. For two decades the Secretary of Labor apparently accepted that understanding; federal audits came and went without any challenge to the implementation of the program. In 1991, however, the Secretary reversed course and filed this suit, contending that the $12 payments are part of the employees' "regular rate" for purposes of § 7(a)(1) of the Fair Labor Standards Act, 29 U.S.C. § 207(a)(1). . . . The Secretary did not seek an award of back pay; the relief is entirely prospective, which makes us wonder why anyone is excited. In the long run the parties can adjust the collective bargaining agreement to provide a little lower hourly rate (or a lower rate of increase at the next reopening) so that both employees and employers are indifferent between the current system and treating the $12 payments as part of the "regular rate." This litigation therefore appears to be about formal rather than functional issues. Nonetheless, we plow ahead because adjustment may be delayed or the employees themselves may sue for back wages; substance may lurk behind the form. . . .

9. For a recent but already-classic article setting *Farwell* in its historical context, see Christopher Tomlins, *A Mysterious Power: Industrial Accidents and the Legal Construction of Employment Relations in Massachusetts, 1800–1850*, 6 Law & Hist. Rev. 375 (1988). A follow-up is Jonathan Simon, *For the Government of Its Servants: Law and Disciplinary Power in the Work Place, 1870–1906*, 13 Studies in Law, Politics, and Society 105 (1993).

10. Chief Justice Shaw was Herman Melville's father-in-law, and scholars have suggested that Melville's view of the law in his short story "Bartleby the Scrivener" was influenced by his contacts with Shaw. If you are familiar with the story, do you think that *Farwell* supports that suggestion? Shaw also decided one of the most famous "slave rendition" cases, directing that a fugitive slave be sent back South. Robert Cover, in *Justice Accused*, argued that anti-slavery judges faced a "moral-formal" dilemma in which the dictates of the formal law conflicted with their moral judgments. Some scholars, again noting Melville's connection to Shaw, have suggested that Melville's short story "Benito Cereno," and even more his short novel *Billy Budd*, were influenced by that connection. *Billy Budd* is, they point out, precisely about the moral-formal dilemma.

11. You might want to make a list of the issues the Walters story seems to raise about the analysis presented in *Farwell*, and consult that list as you proceed through the materials, to see how or whether we deal with those issues.

⊂ The Traditional Framework in Constitutional Law

By the late nineteenth century, legislative regulation of workplace risks had begun to supplement common-law regulation. (For a brief discussion of some reasons, see the Comments and Questions on *Lochner*.) Courts continued to have some degree of control over the content of legislatively enacted rules, though, because all such rules had to be consistent with the restrictions imposed by the state and federal constitutions.

One such restriction is the Due Process Clause of the Fourteenth Amendment, which provides that no state shall "deprive any person of life, liberty, or property without due process of law." In *Lochner*, the U.S. Supreme Court held that this clause limited legislative authority to "restrict" the liberty of contract by setting limits on the terms to which workers and employers could agree. You will study the doctrinal justification for this holding in your constitutional law class. Here we use *Lochner* as the basis for exploring additional questions about the justifications for, and limitations of, regulation of risk.

■ Lochner v. New York
198 U.S. 45 (1905)

THIS is a writ of error to the County Court of Oneida County, in the State of New York . . . to review the judgment of the Court of Appeals of that State, affirming the judgment of the Supreme Court...convicting the defendant of a misdemeanor on an indictment under a statute of that State....The section of the statute under which the indictment was found is section 110, and is reproduced in the margin[1] (together with the other sections of the labor law upon the subject of bakeries, being sections 111 to 115, both inclusive).

---

[1] "§ 110. *Hours of labor in bakeries and confectionery establishments.*—No employé shall be required or permitted to work in a biscuit, bread or cake bakery or confectionery establishment more than sixty hours in any one week, or more than ten hours in any one day, unless for the purpose of making a shorter work day on the last day of the week; nor more hours in any one week than will make an average of ten hours per day for the number of days during such week in which such employé shall work.

"§111. *Drainage and plumbing of buildings and rooms occupied by bakeries.*—All buildings or rooms occupied as biscuit, bread, pie or cake bakeries, shall be drained and plumbed in a manner conducive to the proper and healthful sanitary condition thereof, and shall be constructed with air shafts, windows or ventilating pipes, sufficient to insure ventilation. The factory inspector may direct the proper drainage, plumbing and ventilation of such rooms or buildings. No cellar or basement, not now used for a bakery shall hereafter be so occupied or used, unless the proprietor shall comply with the sanitary provisions of this article.

"§112. *Requirements as to rooms, furniture, utensils and manufactured products.*—Every room used for the manufacture of flour or meal food products shall be at least eight feet in height and shall have, if deemed necessary by the factory inspector, an impermeable floor constructed of cement, or of tiles laid in cement, or an additional flooring of wood properly saturated with linseed oil. The side walls of such rooms shall be plastered or wainscoted. The factory inspector may require the side walls and ceiling to be whitewashed, at least once in three months. He may also require the wood work of such walls to be painted. The furniture and utensils shall be so arranged as to be readily cleansed and not prevent the proper cleaning of any part of a room. The manufactured flour or meal food products shall be kept in dry and airy rooms, so arranged that the floors, shelves and all other facilities for storing the same can be properly cleaned. No domestic animals, except cats, shall be allowed to remain in a room used as a biscuit, bread, pie, or cake bakery, or any room in such bakery where flour or meal products are stored.

"§113. *Wash-rooms and closets; sleeping places.*—Every such bakery shall be provided with a proper wash-room and water-closet or water-closets apart from the bake-room, or rooms where the manufacture of such food product is conducted, and no water-closet, earth-closet, privy or ash-pit shall be within or connected directly with the bake-room of any bakery, hotel or public restaurant.

"No person shall sleep in a room occupied as a bake-room. Sleeping places for the persons employed in the bakery shall be separate from the rooms where flour or meal food products are manufactured or stored. If the sleeping places are on the same floor where such products are manufactured, stored or sold, the factory inspector may inspect and order them put in a proper sanitary condition.

"§114. *Inspection of bakeries.*—The factory inspector shall cause all bakeries to be inspected. If it be found upon such inspection that the bakeries so inspected are constructed and conducted in compliance with the provisions of this chapter, the factory inspector shall issue a certificate to the persons owning or conducting such bakeries.

"§115. *Notice requiring alterations.*—If, in the opinion of the factory inspector, alterations are required in or upon premises occupied and used as bakeries, in order to comply with the provisions of this article, a written notice shall be served by him upon the owner, agent or lessee of such premises, either personally or by mail, requiring such alterations to be made within sixty days after such service, and such alterations shall be made accordingly."

The indictment averred that the defendant "wrongfully and unlawfully required and permitted an employé working for him in his biscuit, bread and cake bakery and confectionery establishment, at the city of Utica, in this county, to work more than sixty hours in one week." . . . The plaintiff in error demurred to the indictment on several grounds, one of which was that the facts stated did not constitute a crime. The demurrer was overruled, and the plaintiff in error having refused to plead further, a plea of not guilty was entered by order of the court and the trial commenced, and he was convicted of misdemeanor, second offense, as indicted, and sentenced to pay a fine of $50 and to stand committed until paid, not to exceed fifty days in the Oneida County jail. . . .

Mr. Justice Peckham, after making the foregoing statement of the facts, delivered the opinion of the court.

The indictment, it will be seen, charges that the plaintiff in error violated the one hundred and tenth section of article 8, chapter 415, of the Laws of 1897, known as the labor law of the State of New York, in that he wrongfully and unlawfully required and permitted an employé working for him to work more than sixty hours in one week. There is nothing in any of the opinions delivered in this case, either in the Supreme Court or the Court of Appeals of the State, which construes the section, in using the word "required," as referring to any physical force being used to obtain the labor of an employé. It is assumed that the word means nothing more than the requirement arising from voluntary contract for such labor in excess of the number of hours specified in the statute. There is no pretense in any of the opinions that the statute was intended to meet a case of involuntary labor in any form. All the opinions assume that there is no real distinction, so far as this question is concerned, between the words "required" and "permitted." The mandate of the statute that "no employé shall be required or permitted to work," is the substantial equivalent of an enactment that "no employé shall contract or agree to work," more than ten hours per day, and as there is no provision for special emergencies the statute is mandatory in all cases. It is not an act merely fixing the number of hours which shall constitute a legal day's work, but an absolute prohibition upon the employer, permitting, under any circumstances, more than ten hours work to be done in his establishment. The employé may desire to earn the extra money, which would arise from his working more than the prescribed time, but this statute forbids the employer from permitting the employé to earn it.

The statute necessarily interferes with the right of contract between the employer and employés, concerning the number of hours in which the latter may labor in the bakery of the employer. The general right to make a contract in relation to his business is part of the liberty of the individual protected by the Fourteenth Amendment of the Federal Constitution. *Allgeyer v. Louisiana*, 165 U.S. 578. Under that provision no State can deprive any person of life, liberty or property without due process of law. The right to purchase or to sell labor is part of the liberty protected by this amendment, unless there are circumstances which exclude the right. There are, however, certain powers, existing in the sovereignty of each State in the Union, somewhat vaguely termed police powers, the exact description and limitation of which have not been attempted by the courts. Those powers, broadly stated and without, at present, any attempt at a more specific limitation, relate to the safety, health, morals and general welfare of the public. Both property and liberty are held on such reasonable conditions as may be imposed by the governing power of the State in the exercise of those powers, and with such conditions the Fourteenth Amendment was not designed to interfere.

The State, therefore, has power to prevent the individual from making certain kinds of contracts, and in regard to them the Federal Constitution offers no protection. If the contract be one which the State, in the legitimate exercise of its police power, has the right to prohibit, it is not prevented from prohibiting it by the Fourteenth Amendment. Contracts in violation of a statute, either of the Federal or state government, or a contract to let one's property for immoral purposes, or to do any other unlawful act, could obtain no protection from the Federal Constitution, as coming under the liberty of person or of free contract. Therefore, when the State, by its legislature, in the assumed exercise of its police powers, has passed an act which seriously limits the right to labor or the right of contract in regard to their means of livelihood between persons who are *sui juris* (both employer and employé), it becomes of great importance to determine which shall prevail—the right of the individual to labor for such time as he may choose, or the right of the State to prevent the individual from laboring or from entering into any contract to labor, beyond a certain time prescribed by the State.

This court has recognized the existence and upheld the exercise of the police powers of the States in many cases which might fairly be considered as border ones, and it has, in the course of its determination of questions regarding the asserted invalidity of such statutes, on the ground of their violation of the rights secured by the Federal Constitution, been guided by rules of a very liberal nature, the application of which has resulted, in numerous instances, in upholding the validity of state statutes thus assailed. Among the later cases where the state law has been upheld by this court is that of *Holden v. Hardy*, 169 U.S. 366. A provision in the act of the legislature of Utah was there under consideration, the act limiting the employment of workmen in all underground mines or workings, to eight hours per day, "except in cases of emergency, where life or property is in imminent danger." It also limited the hours of labor in smelting and other institutions for the reduction or refining of ores or metals to eight hours per day, except in like cases of emergency. The act was held to be a valid exercise of the police powers of the State. . . . It was held that the kind of employment, mining, smelting, etc., and the character of the employés in such kinds of labor, were such as to make it reasonable and proper for the State to interfere to prevent the employés from being constrained by the rules laid down by the proprietors in regard to labor. The following citation from the observations of the Supreme Court of Utah in that case was made by the judge writing the opinion of this court, and approved: "The law in question is confined to the protection of that class of people engaged in labor in underground mines, and in smelters and other works wherein ores are reduced and refined. This law applies only to the classes subjected by their employment to the peculiar conditions and effects attending underground mining and work in smelters, and other works for the reduction and refining of ores. Therefore it is not necessary to discuss or decide whether the legislature can fix the hours of labor in other employments."

It will be observed that, even with regard to that class of labor, the Utah statute provided for cases of emergency wherein the provisions of the statute would not apply. The statute now before this court has no emergency clause in it, and, if the statute is valid, there are no circumstances and no emergencies under which the slightest violation of the provisions of the act would be innocent. There is nothing in *Holden v. Hardy* which covers the case now before us. . . . *Knoxville Iron Co. v. Harbison*, 183 U.S. 13, is equally far from an authority for this legislation. The employés in that case were held to be at a disadvantage with the employer in matters of wages, they being miners and coal workers, and the act simply provided for the cashing of coal orders when presented by the miner to the employer.

The latest case decided by this court, involving the police power, is that of *Jacobson v. Massachusetts*, decided at this term and reported in 197 U.S. 11. It related to compulsory vaccination, and the law was held valid as a proper exercise of the police powers with reference to the public health. It was stated in the opinion that it was a case "of an adult who, for aught that appears, was himself in perfect health and a fit subject for vaccination, and yet, while remaining in the community, refused to obey the statute and the regulation adopted in execution of its provisions for the protection of the public health and the public safety, confessedly endangered by the presence of a dangerous disease." That case is also far from covering the one now before the court. . . .

It must, of course, be conceded that there is a limit to the valid exercise of the police power by the State. There is no dispute concerning this general proposition. Otherwise the Fourteenth Amendment would have no efficacy and the legislatures of the States would have unbounded power, and it would be enough to say that any piece of legislation was enacted to conserve the morals, the health or the safety of the people; such legislation would be valid, no matter how absolutely without foundation the claim might be. The claim of the police power would be a mere pretext—become another and delusive name for the supreme sovereignty of the State to be exercised free from constitutional restraint. This is not contended for. In every case that comes before this court, therefore, where legislation of this character is concerned and where the protection of the Federal Constitution is sought, the question necessarily arises: Is this a fair, reasonable and appropriate exercise of the police power of the State, or is it an unreasonable, unnecessary and arbitrary interference with the right of the individual to his personal liberty or to enter into those contracts in relation to labor which may seem to him appropriate or necessary for the support of himself and his family? Of course the liberty of contract relating to labor includes both parties to it. The one has as much right to purchase as the other to sell labor.

This is not a question of substituting the judgment of the court for that of the legislature. If the act be within the power of the State it is valid, although the judgment of the court might be totally opposed to the enactment of such a law. But the question would still remain: Is it within the police power of the State? and that question must be answered by the court.

The question whether this act is valid as a labor law, pure and simple, may be dismissed in a few words. There is no reasonable ground for interfering with the liberty of person or the right of free contract, by determining the hours of labor, in the occupation of a baker. There is no contention that bakers as a class are not equal in intelligence and capacity to men in other trades or manual occupations, or that they are not able to assert their rights and care for themselves without the protecting arm of the State, interfering with their independence of judgment and of action. They are in no sense wards of the State. Viewed in the light of a purely labor law, with no reference whatever to the question of health, we think that a law like the one before us involves neither the safety, the morals nor the welfare of the public, and that the interest of the public is not in the slightest degree affected by such an act. The law must be upheld, if at all, as a law pertaining to the health of the individual engaged in the occupation of a baker. It does not affect any other portion of the public than those who are engaged in that occupation. Clean and wholesome bread does not depend upon whether the baker works but ten hours per day or only sixty hours a week. The limitation of the hours of labor does not come within the police power on that ground.

It is a question of which of two powers or rights shall prevail—the power of the State to legislate or the right of the individual to liberty of person and freedom of contract. The mere assertion that the subject relates though but in a remote degree to the public health does not necessarily render the enactment valid. The act must have a more direct relation, as a means to an end, and the end itself must be appropriate and legitimate, before an act can be held to be valid which with the general right of an individual to be free in his person and in his power to contract in relation to his own labor. . . .

We think the limit of the police power has been reached and passed in this case. There is, in our judgment, no reasonable foundation for holding this to be necessary or appropriate as a health law to safeguard the public health or the health of the individuals who are following the trade of a baker. If this statute be valid, and if, therefore, a proper case is made out in which to deny the right of an individual, *sui juris*, as employer or employé, to make contracts for the labor of the latter under the protection of the provisions of the Federal Constitution, there would seem to be no length to which legislation of this nature might not go. The case differs widely, as we have already stated, from the expressions of this court in regard to laws of this nature, as stated in *Holden v. Hardy* and *Jacobson v. Massachusetts, supra.*

We think that there can be no fair doubt that the trade of a baker, in and of itself, is not an unhealthy one to that degree which would authorize the legislature to interfere with the right to labor, and with the right of free contract on the part of the individual, either as employer or employé. In looking through statistics regarding all trades and occupations, it may be true that the trade of a baker does not appear to be as healthy as some other trades, and is also vastly more healthy than still others. To the common understanding the trade of a baker has never been regarded as an unhealthy one. Very likely physicians would not recommend the exercise of that or of any other trade as a remedy for ill health. Some occupations are more healthy than others, but we think there are none which might not come under the power of the legislature to supervise and control the hours of working therein, if the mere fact that the occupation is not absolutely and perfectly healthy is to confer that right upon the legislative department of the Government. It might be safely affirmed that almost all occupations more or less affect the health. There must be more than the mere fact of the possible existence of some small amount of unhealthiness to warrant legislative interference with liberty. It is unfortunately true that labor, even in any department, may possibly carry with it the seeds of unhealthiness. But are we all, on that account, at the mercy of legislative majorities? A printer, a tinsmith, a locksmith, a carpenter, a cabinetmaker, a dry goods clerk, a bank's, a lawyer's or a physician's clerk, or a clerk in almost any kind of business, would all come under the power of the legislature, on this assumption. No trade, no occupation, no mode of earning one's living, could escape this all-pervading power, and the acts of the legislature in limiting the hours of labor in all employments would be valid, although such limitation might seriously cripple the ability of the laborer to support himself and his family. In our large cities there are many buildings into which the sun penetrates for but a short time in each day, and these buildings are occupied by people carrying on the business of bankers, brokers, lawyers, real estate, and many other kinds of business, aided by many clerks, messengers, and other employés. Upon the assumption of the validity of this act under review, it is not possible to say that an act, prohibiting lawyers' or bank clerks, or others, from contracting to labor for their employers more than eight hours a day, would be invalid. It might be said that it is unhealthy to work more than that number of hours in an apartment lighted by artificial light during the working hours of the day; that the occupation of the bank clerk, the lawyer's clerk, the real estate clerk, or the broker's clerk in such offices is therefore unhealthy, and the legislature in its paternal wisdom must, therefore, have the right to legislate on the subject of and to limit the hours for such labor, and if it exercises that power and its validity be questioned, it is sufficient to say, it has reference to the public health; it has reference to the health of the employés condemned to labor day after day in buildings where the sun never shines; it is a health law, and therefore it is valid, and cannot be questioned by the courts.

It is also urged, pursuing the same line of argument, that it is to the interest of the State that its population should be strong and robust, and therefore any legislation which may be said to tend to make people healthy must be valid as health laws, enacted under the police power. If this be a valid argument and a justification for this kind of legislation, it follows that the protection of the Federal Constitution from undue interference with liberty of person and freedom of contract is visionary, wherever the law is sought to be justified as a valid exercise of the police power. Scarcely any law but might find shelter under such assumptions, and conduct, properly so called, as well as contract, would come under the restrictive sway of the legislature. Not only the hours of employés, but the hours of employers, could be regulated, and doctors, lawyers, scientists, all professional men, as well as athletes and artisans, could be forbidden to fatigue their brains and bodies by prolonged hours of exercise, lest the fighting strength of the State be impaired. We mention these extreme cases because the contention is extreme. We do not believe in the soundness of the views which uphold this law. On the contrary, we think that such a law as this, although passed in the assumed exercise of the police power, and as relating to the public health, or the health of the employés named, is not within that power, and is invalid. The act is not, within any fair meaning of the term, a health law, but is an illegal interference with the rights of individuals, both employers and employés, to make contracts regarding labor upon such terms as they may think best, or which they may agree upon with the other parties to such contracts. Statutes of the nature of that under review, limiting the hours in which grown and intelligent men may labor to earn their living, are mere meddlesome interferences with the rights of the individual, and they are not saved from condemnation by the claim that they are passed in the exercise of the police power and upon the subject of the health of the individual whose rights are interfered with, unless there be some fair ground, reasonable in and of itself, to say that there is material danger to the public health or to the health of the employés, if the hours of labor are not curtailed. If this be not clearly the case the individuals, whose rights are thus made the subject of legislative interference, are under the protection of the Federal Constitution regarding their liberty of contract as well as of person; and the legislature of the State has no power to limit their right as proposed in this statute. All that it could properly do has been done by it with regard to the conduct of bakeries, as provided for in the other sections of the act, above set forth. These several sections provide for the inspection of the premises where the bakery is carried on, with regard to furnishing proper wash-rooms and water-closets, apart from the bake-room, also with regard to providing proper drainage, plumbing and painting; the sections, in addition, provide for the height of the ceiling, the cementing or tiling of floors, where necessary in the opinion of the factory inspector, and for other things of that nature; alterations are also provided for and are to be made where necessary in the opinion of the inspector, in order to comply with the provisions of the statute. These various sections may be wise and valid regulations, and they certainly go to the full extent of providing for the cleanliness and the healthiness, so far as possible, of the quarters in which bakeries are to be conducted. Adding to all these requirements, a prohibition to enter into any contract of labor in a bakery for more than a certain number of hours a week, is, in our judgment, so wholly beside the matter of a proper, reasonable and fair provision, as to run counter to that liberty of person and of free contract provided for in the Federal Constitution.

It was further urged on the argument that restricting the hours of labor in the case of bakers was valid because it tended to cleanliness on the part of the workers, as a man was more apt to be cleanly when not overworked, and if cleanly then his "output" was also more likely to be so. What has already been said applies with equal force to this contention. We do not admit the reasoning to be sufficient to justify the claimed right of such interference. The State in that case would assume the position of a supervisor, or *pater familias*, over every act of the individual, and its right of governmental interference with his hours of labor, his hours of exercise, the character thereof, and the extent to which it shall be carried would be recognized and upheld. In our judgment it is not possible in fact to discover the connection between the number of hours a baker may work in the bakery and the healthful quality of the bread made by the workman. The connection, if any exists, is too shadowy and thin to build any argument for the interference of the legislature. If the man works ten hours a day it is all right, but if ten and a half or eleven his health is in danger and his bread may be unhealthful, and, therefore, he shall not be permitted to do it. This, we think, is unreasonable and entirely arbitrary. When assertions such as we have adverted to become necessary in order to give, if possible, a plausible foundation for the contention that the law is a "health law," it gives rise to at least a suspicion that there was some other motive dominating the legislature than the purpose to subserve the public health or welfare.

This interference on the part of the legislatures of the several States with the ordinary trades and occupations of the people seems to be on the increase. . . .

It is impossible for us to shut our eyes to the fact that many of the laws of this character, while passed under what is claimed to be the police power for the purpose of protecting the public health or welfare, are, in reality, passed from other motives. We are justified in saying so when, from the character of the law and the subject upon which it legislates, it is apparent that the public health or welfare bears but the most remote relation to the law. . . .

It is manifest to us that the limitation of the hours of labor as provided for in this section of the statute under which the indictment was found, and the plaintiff in error convicted, has no such direct relation to and no such substantial effect upon the health of the employé, as to justify us in regarding the section as really a health law. It seems to us that the real object and purpose were simply to regulate the hours of labor between the master and his employés (all being men, *sui juris*), in a private business, not dangerous in any degree to morals or in any real and substantial degree, to the health of the employés. Under such circumstances the freedom of master and employé to contract with each other in relation to their employment, and in defining the same, cannot be prohibited or interfered with, without violating the Federal Constitution.

The judgment of the Court of Appeals of New York as well as that of the Supreme Court and of the County Court of Oneida County must be reversed and the case remanded to the County Court for further proceedings not inconsistent with this opinion.

Reversed.

Mr. Justice Harlan, with whom Mr. Justice White and Mr. Justice Day concurred, dissenting.

While this court has not attempted to mark the precise boundaries of what is called the police power of the State, the existence of the power has been uniformly recognized, both by the Federal and state courts.

All the cases agree that this power extends at least to the protection of the lives, the health and the safety of the public against the injurious exercise by any citizen of his own rights. . . .

Speaking generally, the State in the exercise of its powers may not unduly interfere with the right of the citizen to enter into contracts that may be necessary and essential in the enjoyment of the inherent rights belonging to every one, among which rights is the right "to be free in the enjoyment of all his faculties; to be free to use them in all lawful ways; to live and work where he will; to earn his livelihood by any lawful calling; to pursue any livelihood or avocation." This was declared in *Allgeyer v. Louisiana*, 165 U.S. 578, 589. But in the same case it was conceded that the right to contract in relation to persons and property or to do business, within a State, may be "regulated and sometimes prohibited, when the contracts or business conflict with the policy of the State as contained in its statutes" (p. 591).

So, as said in *Holden v. Hardy*, 169 U.S. 366, 391: "This right of contract, however, is itself subject to certain limitations which the State may lawfully impose in the exercise of its police powers. While this power is inherent in all governments, it has doubtless been greatly expanded in its application during the past century, owing to an enormous increase in the number of occupations which are dangerous, or so far detrimental to the health of the employés as to demand special precautions for their well-being and protection, or the safety of adjacent property. While this court has held, notably in the cases of *Davidson v. New Orleans*, 96 U.S. 97, and *Yick Wo v. Hopkins*, 118 U.S. 356, that the police power cannot be put forward as an excuse for oppressive and unjust legislation, it may be lawfully resorted to for the purpose of preserving the public health, safety or morals, or the abatement of public nuisances, and a large discretion 'is necessarily vested in the legislature to determine not only what the interests of the public require, but what measures are necessary for the protection of such interests.' *Lawton v. Steele*, 152 U.S. 133, 136." Referring to the limitations placed by the State upon the hours of workmen, the court in the same case said (p. 395): "These employments, when too long pursued, the legislature has judged to be detrimental to the health of the employés, and, so long as there are reasonable grounds for believing that this is so, its decision upon this subject cannot be reviewed by the Federal courts." . . .

The authorities on the same line are so numerous that further citations are unnecessary.

I take it to be firmly established that what is called the liberty of contract may, within certain limits, be subjected to regulations designed and calculated to promote the general welfare or to guard the public health, the public morals or the public safety. "The liberty secured by the Constitution of the United States to every person within its jurisdiction does not import," this court has recently said, "an absolute right in each person to be, at all times and in all circumstances, wholly freed from restraint. There are manifold restraints to which every person is necessarily subject for the common good." *Jacobson v. Massachusetts*, 197 U.S. 11.

Granting then that there is a liberty of contract which cannot be violated even under the sanction of direct legislative enactment, but assuming, as according to settled law we may assume, that such liberty of contract is subject to such regulations as the State may reasonably prescribe for the common good and the well-being of society, what are the conditions under which the judiciary may declare such regulations to be in excess of legislative authority and void? Upon this point there is no room for dispute; for, the rule is universal that a legislative enactment, Federal or state, is never to be disregarded or held invalid unless it be, beyond question, plainly and palpably in excess of legislative power. In *Jacobson v. Massachusetts, supra*, we said that the power of the courts to review legislative action in respect of a matter affecting the general welfare exists *only* "when that which the legislature has done comes within the rule that if a statute purporting to have been enacted to protect the public health, the public morals or the public safety, has no real or substantial relation to those objects, or is, beyond all question, a plain, palpable invasion of rights secured by the fundamental law"—citing *Mugler v. Kansas*, 123 U.S. 623, 661; *Minnesota v. Barber*, 136 U.S. 313, 320; *Atkin v. Kansas*, 191 U.S. 207, 223. If there be doubt as to the validity of the statute, that doubt must therefore be resolved in favor of its validity, and the courts must keep their hands off, leaving the legislature to meet the responsibility for unwise legislation. If the end which the legislature seeks to accomplish be one to which its power extends, and if the means employed to that end, although not the wisest or best, are yet not plainly and palpably unauthorized by law, then the court cannot interfere. In other words, when the validity of a statute is questioned, the burden of proof, so to speak, is upon those who assert it to be unconstitutional. *McCulloch v. Maryland*, 4 Wheat. 316, 421. . . .

It is plain that this statute was enacted in order to protect the physical well-being of those who work in bakery and confectionery establishments. It may be that the statute had its origin, in part, in the belief that employers and employés in such establishments were not upon an equal footing, and that the necessities of the latter often compelled them to submit to such exactions as unduly taxed their strength. Be this as it may, the statute must be taken as expressing the belief of the people of New York that, as a general rule, and in the case of the average man, labor in excess of sixty hours during a week in such establishments may endanger the health of those who thus labor. Whether or not this be wise legislation it is not the province of the court to inquire. Under our systems of government the courts are not concerned with the wisdom or policy of legislation. So that in determining the question of power to interfere with liberty of contract, the court may inquire whether the means devised by the State are germane to an end which may be lawfully accomplished and have a real or substantial relation to the protection of health, as involved in the daily work of the persons, male and female, engaged in bakery and confectionery establishments. But when this inquiry is entered upon I find it impossible, in view of common experience, to say that there is here no real or substantial relation between the means employed by the State and the end sought to be accomplished by its legislation. *Mugler v. Kansas, supra.* Nor can I say that the statute has no appropriate or direct connection with that protection to health which each State owes to her citizens, *Patterson v. Kentucky, supra;* or that it is not promotive of the health of the employés in question, *Holden v. Hardy, Lawton v. Steele, supra;* or that the regulation prescribed by the State is utterly unreasonable and extravagant or wholly arbitrary. Still less can I say that the statute is, beyond question, a plain, palpable invasion of rights secured by the fundamental law. *Jacobson v. Massachusetts, supra.* Therefore I submit that this court will transcend its functions if it assumes to annul the statute of New York. It must be remembered that this statute does not apply to all kinds of business. It applies only to work in bakery and confectionery establishments, in which, as all know, the air constantly breathed by workmen is not as pure and healthful as that to be found in some other establishments or out of doors.

Professor Hirt in his treatise on the "Diseases of the Workers" has said: "The labor of the bakers is among the hardest and most laborious imaginable, because it has to be performed under conditions injurious to the health of those engaged in it. It is hard, very hard work, not only because it requires a great deal of physical exertion in an overheated workshop and during unreasonably long hours, but more so because of the erratic demands of the public, compelling the baker to perform the greater part of his work at night thus depriving him of an opportunity to enjoy the necessary rest and sleep, a fact which is highly injurious to his health." Another writer says: "The constant inhaling of flour dust causes inflammation of the lungs and of the bronchial tubes. The eyes also suffer through this dust, which is responsible for the many cases of running eyes among the bakers. The long hours of toil to which all bakers are subjected produce rheumatism, cramps and swollen legs. The intense heat in the workshops induces the workers to resort to cooling drinks, which together with their habit of exposing the greater part of their bodies to the change in the atmosphere, is another source of a number of diseases of various organs. Nearly all bakers are pale-faced and of more delicate health than the workers of other crafts, which is chiefly due to their hard work and their irregular and unnatural mode of living, whereby the power of resistance against disease is greatly diminished. The average age of a baker is below that of other workmen; they seldom live over their fiftieth year, most of them dying between the ages of forty and fifty. During periods of epidemic diseases the bakers are generally the first to succumb to the disease, and the number swept away during such periods far exceeds the number of other crafts in comparison to the men employed in the respective industries. When, in 1720, the plague visited the city of Marseilles, France, every baker in the city succumbed to the epidemic, which caused considerable excitement in the neighboring cities and resulted in measures for the sanitary protection of the bakers."

In the Eighteenth Annual Report by the New York Bureau of Statistics of Labor it is stated that among the occupations involving exposure to conditions that interfere with nutrition is that of a baker (p. 52). In that Report it is also stated that "from a social point of view, production will be increased by any change in industrial organization which diminishes the number of idlers, paupers and criminals. Shorter hours of work, by allowing higher standards of comfort and purer family life, promise to enhance the industrial efficiency of the wage-working class—improved health, longer life, more content and greater intelligence and inventiveness" (p. 82).

Statistics show that the average daily working time among workingmen in different countries is, in Australia, 8 hours; in Great Britain, 9; in the United States, 9¾; in Denmark, 9¾; in Norway, 10; Sweden, France and Switzerland, 10½; Germany, 10¼; Belgium, Italy and Austria, 11; and in Russia, 12 hours.

We judicially know that the question of the number of hours during which a workman should continuously labor has been, for a long period, and is yet, a subject of serious consideration among civilized peoples, and by those having special knowledge of the laws of health. Suppose the statute prohibited labor in bakery and confectionery establishments in excess of eighteen hours each day. No one, I take it, could dispute the power of the State to enact such a statute. But the statute before us does not embrace extreme or exceptional cases. It may be said to occupy a middle ground in respect of the hours of labor. What is the true ground for the State to take between legitimate protection, by legislation, of the public health and liberty of contract is not a question easily solved, nor one in respect of which there is or can be absolute certainty. There are very few, if any, questions in political economy about which entire certainty may be predicated. One writer on relation of the State to labor has well said: "The manner, occasion, and degree in which the State may interfere with the industrial freedom of its citizens is one of the most debatable and difficult questions of social science." Jevons, 33.

We also judicially know that the number of hours that should constitute a day's labor in particular occupations involving the physical strength and safety of workmen has been the subject of enactments by Congress and by nearly all of the States. Many, if not most, of those enactments fix eight hours as the proper basis of a day's labor.

I do not stop to consider whether any particular view of this economic question presents the sounder theory. What the precise facts are it may be difficult to say. It is enough for the determination of this case, and it is enough for this court to know, that the question is one about which there is room for debate and for an honest difference of opinion. There are many reasons of a weighty, substantial character, based upon the experience of mankind, in support of the theory that, all things considered, more than ten hours' steady work each day, from week to week, in a bakery or confectionery establishment, may endanger the health, and shorten the lives of the workmen, thereby diminishing their physical and mental capacity to serve the State, and to provide for those dependent upon them.

If such reasons exist that ought to be the end of this case, for the State is not amenable to the judiciary, in respect of its legislative enactments, unless such enactments are plainly, palpably, beyond all question, inconsistent with the Constitution of the United States. We are not to presume that the State of New York has acted in bad faith. Nor can we assume that its legislature acted without due deliberation, or that it did not determine this question upon the fullest attainable information, and for the common good. We cannot say that the State has acted without reason nor ought we to proceed upon the theory that its action is a mere sham. Our duty, I submit, is to sustain the statute as not being in conflict with the Federal Constitution, for the reason—and such is an all-sufficient reason—it is not shown to be plainly and palpably inconsistent with that instrument. Let the State alone in the management of its purely domestic affairs, so long as it does not appear beyond all question that it has violated the Federal Constitution. This view necessarily results from the principle that the health and safety of the people of a State are primarily for the State to guard and protect.

I take leave to say that the New York statute, in the particulars here involved, cannot be held to be in conflict with the Fourteenth Amendment, without enlarging the scope of the Amendment far beyond its original purpose and without bringing under the supervision of this court matters which have been supposed to belong exclusively to the legislative departments of the several States when exerting their conceded power to guard the health and safety of their citizens by such regulations as they in their wisdom deem best. Health laws of every description constitute, said Chief Justice Marshall, a part of that mass of legislation which "embraces everything within the territory of a State, not surrendered to the General Government; all which can be most advantageously exercised by the States themselves." *Gibbons v. Ogden*, 9 Wheat. 1, 203. A decision that the New York statute is void under the Fourteenth Amendment will, in my opinion, involve consequences of a far-reaching and mischievous character; for such a decision would seriously cripple the inherent power of the States to care for the lives, health and well-being of their citizens. Those are matters which can be best controlled by the States. The preservation of the just powers of the States is quite as vital as the preservation of the powers of the General Government.

When this court had before it the question of the constitutionality of a statute of Kansas making it a criminal offense for a contractor for public work to permit or require his employés to perform labor upon such work in excess of eight hours each day, it was contended that the statute was in derogation of the liberty both of employés and employer. It was further contended that the Kansas statute was mischievous in its tendencies. This court, while disposing of the question only as it affected public work, held that the Kansas statute was not void under the Fourteenth Amendment. But it took occasion to say what may well be here repeated: "The responsibility therefor rests upon legislators, not upon the courts. No evils arising from such legislation could be more far-reaching than those that might come to our system of government if the judiciary, abandoning the sphere assigned to it by the fundamental law, should enter the domain of legislation, and upon grounds merely of justice or reason or wisdom annul statutes that had received the sanction of the people's representatives. We are reminded by counsel that it is the solemn duty of the courts in cases before them to guard the constitutional rights of the citizen against merely arbitrary power. That is unquestionably true. But it is equally true—indeed, the public interests imperatively demand—that legislative enactments should be recognized and enforced by the courts as embodying the will of the people, unless they are plainly and palpably, beyond all question, in violation of the fundamental law of the Constitution." *Atkin v. Kansas,* 191 U.S. 207, 223.

The judgment in my opinion should be affirmed.

Mr. Justice Holmes dissenting.

I regret sincerely that I am unable to agree with the judgment in this case, and that I think it my duty to express my dissent.

This case is decided upon an economic theory which a large part of the country does not entertain. If it were a question whether I agreed with that theory I should desire to study it further and long before making up my mind. But I do not conceive that to be my duty, because I strongly believe that my agreement or disagreement has nothing to do with the right of a majority to embody their opinions in law. It is settled by various decisions of this court that state constitutions and state laws may regulate life in many ways which we as legislators might think as injudicious or if you like as tyrannical as this, and which equally with this interfere with the liberty to contract. Sunday laws and usury laws are ancient examples. A more modern one is the prohibition of lotteries. The liberty of the citizen to do as he likes so long as he does not interfere with the liberty of others to do the same, which has been a shibboleth for some well-known writers, is interfered with by school laws, by the Post Office, by every state or municipal institution which takes his money for purposes thought desirable, whether he likes it or not. The Fourteenth Amendment does not enact Mr. Herbert Spencer's Social Statics. The other day we sustained the Massachusetts vaccination law. *Jacobson v. Massachusetts,* 197 U.S. 11. . . . The decision sustaining an eight hour law for miners is still recent. *Holden v. Hardy,* 169 U.S. 366. Some of these laws embody convictions or prejudices which judges are likely to share. Some may not. But a constitution is not intended to embody a particular economic theory, whether of paternalism and the organic relation of the citizen to the State or of *laissez faire.* It is made for people of fundamentally differing views, and the accident of our finding certain opinions natural and familiar or novel and even shocking ought not to conclude our judgment upon the question whether statutes embodying them conflict with the Constitution of the United States.

General propositions do not decide concrete cases. The decision will depend on a judgment or intuition more subtle than any articulate major premise. But I think that the proposition just stated, if it is accepted, will carry us far toward the end. Every opinion tends to become a law. I think that the word liberty in the Fourteenth Amendment is perverted when it is held to prevent the natural outcome of a dominant opinion, unless it can be said that a rational and fair man necessarily would admit that the statute proposed would infringe fundamental principles as they have been understood by the traditions of our people and our law. It does not need research to show that no such sweeping condemnation can be passed upon the statute before us. A reasonable man might think it a proper measure on the score of health. Men whom I certainly could not pronounce unreasonable would uphold it as a first instalment of a general regulation of the hours of work. Whether in the latter aspect it would be open to the charge of inequality I think it unnecessary to discuss.

COMMENTS AND QUESTIONS

1. The constitutional law in *Lochner*. We begin, again, with some basic questions about the Court's analysis.

    (a) What is the *constitutional* interest the employer (and the worker) has, the liberty adversely affected by the Ten Hour Law?

    (b) Why is there a violation of due *process* of law? The legislature held hearings before the statute was enacted, and Lochner had a full opportunity to present his case to the jury. Does the Court explain why the term *process* nonetheless places some *substantive* limitations on what the legislature can do? (We note that the tradition of what has come to be called *substantive due process* goes back quite a long way, with some scholars tracing it to Magna Carta. The terminology is of course awkward—Judge Richard Posner calls it a "durable oxymoron"—but the *Lochner* Court was following a well-established path in using the Due Process Clause as a means of imposing substantive limitations on legislative power.)

    (c) Suppose that an employer sued a worker for breaching an unwritten contract to work for a term longer than one year. Such a contract would be unenforceable because of the Statute of Frauds. (For present purposes, you should consider the Statute of Frauds to be a judicially developed limitation on the power to contract.) This implies that (some) legislative restrictions on liberty of contract are unconstitutional but that (some?) common law restrictions on that same liberty are not. Why do common law restrictions not violate the liberty of contract? One possibility is that the common law restrictions that existed in 1868, when the Due Process Clause was adopted, are somehow "built into" the liberty of contract the clause protects. (The argument could be extended back to 1791 so that the Fifth Amendment's Due Process Clause would also have a substantive component.)

    (d) Suppose a state court held that contracts for employment for more than ten hours a day were void as against public policy. A constitutional violation?

    (e) Does the *legislature* have any power to alter such common law restrictions? What implications does the Court's discussion of *Holden v. Hardy* have for this question?

2. Justifying the Ten-Hour Law: What are the justifications for denying workers the power to agree to work for longer than ten hours per shift?

    (a) Negative externalities for the public: One possibility is that bakers who work long hours impose risks on the public, for example, by becoming sloppy and allowing health-damaging bacteria to be incorporated in the bread they bake, which they would not do were they working shorter hours. What response, if any, does the Court make to this argument? Suppose the employers challenged Section 112, requiring, among other things, that the walls of bakeries be whitewashed periodically. How would the majority analyze that challenge?

    (b) Negative consequences for the workers: Perhaps those who work long hours are more susceptible to illness or disease than those who work shorter hours. Why wouldn't workers take this risk into account when bargaining for wages by asking for a wage premium for each hour over eight that they agreed to work? Consider the possibility that workers would not know of the increased risk. Should the regulatory response to that lack of knowledge be mandatory provision of information, a restriction on hours, or something else (including doing nothing, on the theory that though workers might not know the risks to which they are being exposed, they know that they are not receiving information about those risks)?

(c) A "labor law, pure and simple": The law is aimed at increasing the wealth of workers relative to employers. How can it do so? Why won't an employer unable to employ workers for more than ten hours reduce workers' per-hour wages, leaving the workers with less income? In what sense might it be said that workers are "forced" to accept employment on terms including long shifts? These are quite complex questions, and we will address them in more detail later in the course. For now, note only that the Court rejects the argument that the Ten Hour Law serves to increase the wealth of workers relative to employers not because the argument is empirically false but because the goal itself is impermissible, at least in the absence of evidence that the bargaining position of bakery workers is different from that of workers in any other ordinary occupation. Does that imply that the problem with the statute is more in the domain of equality (in the differential treatment of different classes of workers) than in the domain of liberty of contract?

3. The opinions: On what questions does Justice Harlan differ from the majority? Is Harlan's disagreement with the majority's evaluation of the evidence supporting the statute, with the majority's allocation of the burden of persuasion in a situation where the evidence is conflicting and its meaning uncertain, or more? On what questions does Justice Holmes differ from the majority? How does Holmes's position differ from Harlan's?

4. The political background of the Ten Hour Law: David E. Bernstein, *The Story of* Lochner v. New York: *Impediment to the Growth of the Regulatory State*, in Constitutional Law Stories (Michael Dorf ed., 2004), gives the case's background. The Ten Hour Law was the result of a sustained political effort by the union representing bakery workers at relatively large bakeries. (The union's chief lobbyist and public spokesperson, Henry Weismann, was himself a bakery worker—until he opened his own bakery and then became a lawyer, ultimately serving as one of Lochner's cocounsels in the U.S. Supreme Court.) For reasons related to the technical details of bread making, large bakeries found it less difficult to operate with workers on ten-hour shifts than smaller bakeries. In addition, the bakery workers' union had found it easier to organize workers at larger bakeries, in part because the workers' union was dominated by German immigrants and their descendants, whereas smaller bakeries were staffed by workers from other countries. As a result, many contracts between large bakeries and their workers already provided for ten-hour shifts when the Ten Hour Law was enacted. The statute's effect fell primarily on small bakeries. Does this information affect your views on the Court's analysis, particularly of the "labor law" justification?

5. The modern position: The Supreme Court overruled *Lochner* in *West Coast Hotel v. Parrish*, 300 U.S. 379 (1937), after a series of decisions in which the Court became more accepting of regulatory statutes premised on health and risk concerns while remaining (until 1937) hostile to statutes whose sole justification appeared to be benefiting workers relative to employers. In general, questions about regulatory legislation today are questions of policy wisdom, not constitutionality. Yet, as you will see, constitutional concerns occasionally crop up in connection with modern regulatory statutes and may exert a subterranean influence on the interpretation of regulatory statutes—as indeed may the policy questions themselves.

An Economic Perspective

We have two objectives in this chapter. Both are tied to economics, and both ultimately have to do with the possibility of allowing private bargains to shape the allocation of risks to human health.

Our first objective is to introduce you, through the Easterbrook article excerpted here, to the argument that courts should, in deciding cases and developing legal rules, have in mind the incentives they are creating for future conduct. The idea is that courts should not be concerned with promoting "fairness" (a problematic term, in Easterbrook's view) after the fact but with shaping forward-looking incentives. Here we also first confront the work of the economist Ronald Coase, who cautioned that no matter what legal result common-law courts might deliver, the parties will bargain to the result they most desire unless they are inhibited from doing so by "transaction costs" arising out of the numerousness of parties, difficulties in communicating, and other such factors.

Our second objective is to consider whether the government's role in addressing health risks should be limited to the enforcement of private contracts allocating the burden of these risks. We will not discuss legal doctrines concerning the enforcement of such contracts. Rather, we discuss the theoretical and empirical support for the proposition that people do indeed allocate the burdens of risks to human health through contract. In particular, we examine some of the vast literature on the existence (or nonexistence) of a "wage premium" or "compensating wage differential" for risky work—that is, the provision of an increased wage to an employee in exchange for the employee's agreement to accept health or safety risks in the workplace. If private individuals do indeed strike bargains regarding risk, then perhaps the government's role in addressing risks should be limited.

■ *The Supreme Court, 1983 Term—Foreword: The Court and the Economic System*
FRANK EASTERBROOK
98 Harv. L. Rev. 4 (1984). Reprinted by permission of the Harvard Law Review Association and William S. Hein Company from the Harvard Law Review

. . .

1. *Ex ante and ex post perspectives.*—The nature of litigation invites judges to treat the parties' circumstances as fixed and to apportion gains and losses. Often the application of legal rules requires no more than that. By the time the judges see the case,

it may be too late for the parties to do anything in response to a decision. Once ships have collided, the court may see nothing to do except tote up the losses and order each ship-owner to pay half (the rule in admiralty). Once a manufacturer has fired a dealer, causing the dealer to lose profits, it may appear best to require the deep-pocket firm to make whole the loss. Once a firm possesses a patent and tries to extract royalties, it may seem wise to restrict the devices available to that end; the royalties lead to less use of the invention and consequent social loss, while restricting the collection of royalties has no visible social costs. Once a firm makes a tender offer for the stock of another, the investors in the target can gain if a court stops the bid long enough for an auction to develop. A party who has agreed in advance to arbitrate a dispute may contend that the particular dispute in question nonetheless should be resolved by a court; he seeks relief from the adverse consequences of his choice. Similar situations are common in commercial litigation, and the tendency to take the situation as given and divide the gains or losses is common too.

When judges take the positions of the parties as given, however, they forfeit any opportunity to create gains through the formulation of the legal rule. The principles laid down today will influence whether similar parties will be in similar situations tomorrow. Indeed, judges who look at cases merely as occasions for the fair apportionment of gains and losses almost invariably ensure that there will be fewer gains and more losses tomorrow. When a court divides the damages between shipowners, it sends the message that one may as well be careless; it is costly to take care, yet the careful and the careless are treated alike. When a court restricts the patent holder's ability to collect royalties, it reduces the rewards anticipated from patents and thus the incentive for other people to invent. When a court declines to enforce the arbitration agreement, it makes others situated similarly to the one who avoided arbitration worse off. These people no longer can strike one kind of bargain; because they cannot agree to arbitrate, they cannot receive any compensation for their forbearance. A right that cannot be the subject of bargaining is worth less, just as eagle feathers that cannot be sold are worth less to their owners. . . .

Often, discovering the correct balance between promised rewards and realized ones is exceptionally difficult. In the patent case, for example, it may be impossible to discover the 'right' system of rules that gives incentives to invent yet preserves the optimal use of things that already have been invented. There is a great tension between optimal creation and optimal use of information. My point is not that creating incentives for future conduct should be the Court's sole objective in adjudicating legal disputes, but that the Court is bound to send the wrong signals to the economic system unless the Justices appreciate the consequences of legal rules for future behavior.

This may appear obvious. Our legal culture favors utilitarian arguments. Lawyers routinely make 'policy' arguments to courts; legislatures invoke instrumental claims to show that their statutes are 'rationally related' to some objective that they attain by changing people's incentives. It is nonetheless startling how often these arguments collapse to claims about 'fairness,' which in the law almost always means some appeal to an equitable division of the gains or losses among existing parties given that certain events have come to pass. Fairness arguments are ex post arguments, and few lawyers or judges are comfortable arguing about or deciding a case without invoking the ideal of fairness. Who is for unfairness?

The degree to which fairness or other ex post arguments dominate in legal decision making is directly related to the court's assumptions about the nature of the economic system. Judges who see economic transactions as zero-sum games are likely to favor 'fair' divisions of the gains and losses. If the stakes are established in advance and will not be altered by courts, why should judges harshly require one party to bear the whole loss or allow another to take the gain? Yet if legal rules can create larger gains (or larger losses), the claim from fairness becomes weaker. The judge will pay less attention to today's unfortunates and more attention to the effects of the rules.

Often only this form of attention protects the interest of increased productivity. The people who might be affected by the rules are not before the court and may not even be in the affected business (yet). The interests of prospective consumers and producers are diffuse, too much so for any one person or group to participate in the litigation. The judge is the representative of these future interests.

The first line of inquiry, then, is whether the Justices take an ex ante or an ex post perspective in analyzing issues. Which they take will depend, in part, on the extent to which they appreciate how the economic system creates new gains and losses; those who lack this appreciation will favor 'fair' treatment of the parties. . . .

2. *Incentives work on many margins.*—Setting out to influence future conduct is not very useful unless you know how people respond to incentives. Judges and other public figures understand the Law of Demand—if you increase the price of something, people will buy less. Judges also appreciate its generality. Write a tedious opinion (one that is more 'costly' to read), and people will read less of it. But judges do not always remember why this happens: at the margin people substitute one product for another. Raise the price of beef, and people will eat less beef and more chicken. Raise the price of automobiles, and even people who 'need' an automobile to get to work will buy fewer. Some will switch to other jobs and travel by bus or train; others will use a car for six years instead of three before trading it in, effectively substituting repair services for a new car this year.

Decisions that appear to be dichotomous (car versus no car) turn out not to be, and even a small change in the price will induce people to change their behavior ever so slightly. On the other hand, effects that seem to be large may have no effect on behavior. If the state suddenly requires every owner of a car to pay a tax of $1,000, but makes a believable promise never to levy the tax again, the ownership of cars will be unaffected. People will hold their cars and trade them in as if the tax had never been levied. Similarly, when the demand for air travel suddenly falls, so that air carriers no longer can charge enough to pay the indebtedness on their planes, they do not take the planes out of service. They may go on operating the planes for an indefinite period, 'losing' money all the while according to their annual reports, so long as the marginal revenues from carrying a load of passengers exceed the marginal costs (crew, maintenance, and fuel) of doing so. If they grounded their fleets, they would lose even more money.

These points are not controversial; they are part of the elementary kit of economic ideas with which every college student (and thus every judge) is supplied. Yet the dynamics of litigation often hide marginal effects from judges. The court sees only the gross effects—averages rather than the margins on which people are trading. In a copyright dispute the person who seeks to make 'fair use' of the work in question inevitably argues that even if he can use the work for free, the copyright holder will be left with 'enough' reward. The would-be user invites attention to the average return rather than to the marginal effects of the decision. If the lawyer for the copyright holder simply replies that there is a legal entitlement to a particular royalty, the point about marginal effects will be obscured. A lawyer opposing a request for attorneys' fees will argue that the prevailing counsel makes a very good living, that the fees in this case would be a windfall, and that they therefore should be reduced. Again the litigant is inviting attention to the average rather than the margin. Finally, think of a dispute under the takings clause. The government argues that after the rights in question have been appropriated or extinguished, the complainant retains many valuable rights. The government is inviting attention to average effects, while the private party's future conduct will be influenced by the change at the margin that makes investments less valuable. Litigation focuses judges' attention on the division of given stakes, on average rather than marginal costs.

When the Court misses these marginal effects, the rules it designs may have unanticipated or perverse consequences. And the marginal effects may be subtle. A prohibition of tie-in sales may lead manufacturers to redesign their products so that the new products combine the elements of the formerly separate items. This response may have the same economic effects as tying arrangements, but it may be more costly in real resources. Private rearrangements undo the legal rule, with losses all around. A decision by the Interstate Commerce Commission to regulate certain conduct may lead railroads to do something else that is worse than the previously unregulated conduct. If the Civil Aeronautics Board regulates the price of air travel, attempting to ensure higher profits for air carriers, it may achieve nothing of the sort. Carriers will compete for custom by offering wider seats, better meals, more frequent flights. The marginal substitution among methods of competition thus may obliterate the profits.

There are substitute ways to do almost anything. Ronald Coase showed that as long as people may bargain and adapt to legal rules, and the costs of transacting are negligible, people will go on adjusting and substituting until they reproduce the situation that would have prevailed in the absence of regulation.[13] If the purpose of the rule was to affect behavior, this is intolerable. Thus regulation abhors a vacuum—once you start to control some aspects of an industry, you must control all, else the subjects of regulation will evade the controls at potentially substantial costs to all. Rules, unless designed to accommodate the outcome of bargaining, must restrict bargains and other adaptations. This is as true of rules established by courts as of rules promulgated by agencies. If a court holds that owners of vessels absolutely warrant the safety of the ship, the owners will reduce seamen's wages (substituting health insurance for salary), install more gear (substituting capital for

---

[13] See Coase, *The Problem of Social Cost*, 3 J. L. & Econ. 1 (1960). The caveat on transaction costs is quite important. Often people cannot transact around a rule without incurring costs exceeding the gains to be had from the new arrangement. When transaction costs are high, legal rules produce efficient results only if they prescribe the result the parties would have arrived at, had they been able to reach a bargain.

labor), and so on. The supposed beneficiaries of the warranty may not like the result. The court must either choose the optimal rule to start with or be prepared to deal with the adaptations. . . .

COMMENTS AND QUESTIONS

1. What are the ex ante and ex post perspectives in *Farwell*, discussed in chapter 1?

2. Make sure that you understand Easterbrook's point about incentives working on margins. For example, what's wrong with the argument that an attorney's fee request should be reduced because the attorney already makes a good living? The argument about copyright and fair use?

3. Easterbrook's argument is in part based on the work of Ronald Coase and the Coase theorem, which, as Easterbrook explains, concludes that in the absence of transaction costs people will bargain to the economically efficient result, regardless of where the court places the legal entitlement. A simple example of the Coase theorem works as follows: Say a court grants an entitlement to party A, perhaps the right to be free from a nuisance. If party B values the right to create the nuisance more than party A values the right to be free from the nuisance, then party B will buy the entitlement to create the nuisance from party A. Therefore, regardless of whether the court finds for party A or party B, in the absence of transaction costs, the party who values the entitlement more highly, party B in our example, will ultimately end up with the entitlement. The implicit assumption of the Coase theorem is that people can and will bargain unless stopped by transaction costs, which typically include such things as the costs associated with organization of numerous parties, free riders, and collecting information.

   But what if, even in the absence of these economic transaction costs, people still refuse to bargain with one another for arguably irrational reasons—because one party just does not like the other party, for example, or because the parties refuse to see their legal rights in terms of marketable commodities? Law professor Ward Farnsworth examined a number of standard nuisance cases, which are typically used as examples of the Coase theorem in action because transaction costs are assumed to be low, to see if people really bargained after the fact to change the outcome of their legal disputes. Farnsworth found that in all of the nuisance cases he considered (a set of twenty), there was no bargaining whatsoever. If the court had awarded the entitlement to the correct side, this is the expected result. However, lawyers for both sides universally agreed that if the court had awarded the entitlement to the losing side, there would still have been no bargaining. The real reasons the parties did not bargain after judgment were that animosity between the parties precluded bargaining and the parties did not see the legal judgment as a marketable commodity. Ward Farnsworth, *Do Parties to Nuisance Cases Bargain after Judgment? A Glimpse inside the Cathedral*, 66 U. Chi. L. Rev. 373 (1999).

   Is animosity just another transaction cost, to be assumed away in Coasian analysis? What about resistance to commodification? We discuss the latter possibility in chapter 3.

■ *Risk by Choice: Regulating Health and Safety in the Workplace*

W. KIP VISCUSI

pp. 37–44 (Harvard University Press, 1983). Reprinted with permission
of Harvard University Press

Exposure to various risks is an intrinsic aspect of many daily activities. Car travel
may lead to accidents and even death, plane flights raise the risk of cancer and pose
the risk of a crash, and the foods we eat create a seemingly endless variety of
carcinogenic hazards. If we wished to ensure minimal risk to our lives, we would
avoid all of these activities, especially those that increase our average risk exposure.
Risk-seeking behavior would have the opposite effect. Our actual behavior lies
somewhere between these extremes. We do not incur risks simply to endanger our
lives, but we are willing to incur additional hazards in return for some offsetting
advantage. Participating in sports is an enjoyable form of recreation despite the risk
of injury. Other risks are incurred for financial reasons, as in the case of the five
hundred people who are electrocuted each year installing their own TV and CB
radio antennas in an effort to avoid professional installation charges.

Workers make similar choices. If a worker takes a job he knows is risky, there
must be some other aspect to compensate for the risk. If the other nonmonetary
aspects of the job are equivalent to those for less risky jobs, this compensation will
take the form of a higher wage rate. The need to pay higher wages in turn provides
a financial incentive for the employer to reduce the risk. This relationship between
worker wages and the risks of the job, which is the central component of the classic
economic theory of compensating wage differentials, is the principal foundation of
most analyses of market-traded risk.

Provided certain minimal assumptions are satisfied, a firm must pay a premium to attract a worker to a risky job. So long as a worker prefers more money to
less and would rather be healthy than injured, ill, or dead, he will necessarily
require more compensation to work at a job he believes is more hazardous. This
applies to all workers, not simply those who are risk-averse, that is, those who are
willing to gamble only at sufficiently favorable odds. This extra compensation may
involve higher wages, greater fringe benefits, more convenient work hours, or
enhanced occupational prestige. Since wages are measured in readily manipulable
units and are monitored for most classes of workers, economists can focus on the
wage premium for risk, holding constant other job characteristics. . . .

If providing a safe work environment were no more costly than providing an
unsafe environment, all workers would hold risk-free jobs, and no risk premiums
would be paid. However, making the workplace safer typically involves substantial
costs. Guards on punch presses, exhaust hoods to remove noxious fumes, and slow
assembly line speeds entail either direct financial outlays or reduced output. A firm
has two principal choices. It can simply pay the workers for incurring the risks, or it
can reduce its wage costs by making greater investments in the safety of the work
environment. Typically these mechanisms are interrelated. The firm increases its
expenditures on safety until the incremental wage reductions generated by improved safety no longer exceed the added costs of these improvements. Worker
welfare enters the firm's calculations through the influence of the risk level on
wages. The worker's own valuations of risk in effect determine the price the firm
must pay if it does not find it financially worthwhile to diminish the risk.

The interaction of these decisions by workers and firms determines the number of people who are exposed to different levels of risk and the premiums these hazards command. The outcomes are not completely capricious and in many instances are not too dissimilar from other market processes. To characterize the risks facing firemen, those in the military, and professional athletes as being essential to these pursuits, while at the same time viewing as unnecessary the black lung risks faced by coal miners, is to neglect the common economic elements in these situations. If the market is functioning properly, the level of risk will reflect both the costs of ameliorating the hazard and the benefits to workers of doing so. Differences in technologies and in individual attitudes toward risk will result in a variety of risk levels in the economy, but this disparity in no way implies that some risks are less necessary than others.

The most meaningful approach to assessing market deficiencies is to examine the ways in which the risk premium analysis fails to reflect the inadequacies of functioning labor markets. A particularly lucid critique was offered in Engels's *The Condition of the Working Class in England*. Engels not only examined the health and safety hazards in detail but also identified pivotal shortcomings of the market—the inadequacy of compensation for injured workers, the lack of worker education and knowledge concerning the risks, and falsification of accident records by mill owners to present an overoptimistic portrayal of conditions at their firm.

These themes overlap with the three critical ingredients of the compensating differential analysis. First, the theory assumes that workers are fully cognizant of the risks and their implications. In many instances, the worker does not have complete information about the risks, and even if he does, he may not fully understand the implications of the risks for his welfare. Particularly for carcinogenic hazards with time lags of a decade or more before a health problem is observed, there may be considerable difficulty in assessing the implications.

Market outcomes also will be optimal only if the insurance arrangements function in an effective (actuarially fair) manner. The shortcomings of private insurance have contributed to the establishment of a comprehensive workers' compensation system. Some of these inadequacies, such as adverse selection (meaning that only the bad risks purchase insurance), are problems associated with the behavior of workers and their employers rather than deficiencies of the insurance industry.

The final critical feature of the compensating differential theory is the assumption that the worker's valuation of the health risks fully reflects the value of the risk to society as a whole. This assumption would be violated if, for example, other people had a major altruistic concern with the worker's well-being. To the extent that the worker takes the preferences of other family members into account when determining the premium he requires to accept the risk, these concerns will be reflected at least in part in labor market outcomes....

Although there are clearly major deviations from the smoothly functioning world of the compensating differential theory, one should not dismiss the legitimate insights of the analysis. Many of the theory's shortcomings are difficult to quantify, so one cannot ascertain whether the inadequacies of the analysis are critical or of only technical interest. Moreover, even in the case of clearly important deviations from the classical analysis, such as the lack of perfect information, complementary market responses may work to promote the desired outcomes....

Advocates of government regulation of risks typically do not believe there is widespread, significant compensation for job risks. Risk premiums are presumably limited to special cases, such a professional athletes, for whom the presence of risk compensation is well known. As former New York Jet quarterback Joe Namath observed in discussing his permanent knee injuries, "We got paid pretty good. Nobody was twisting our arms." But professional athletes are not [the only] workers who receive risk premiums. In some cases, the level of hazard pay is specified precisely in contract provisions. Elephant handlers at the Philadelphia Zoo receive an annual premium of $1,000 because "elephants will work only with people they like, and if they don't like them, the handlers face extra risk." Formal specification of risk premiums is not the norm, however, as the discussion below of collective bargaining agreements will indicate. More typically, job hazards are a component of a job evaluation system that gives each job a rating, which in turn affects the wage that is paid.

The most meaningful test for the presence of risk premiums is to utilize conventional statistical techniques to assess the incremental effect of risks on worker earnings, taking into account other determinants of wages such as the worker's education and experience, the type of job, and regional economic conditions. A large number of studies of risk premiums have followed this approach, and the consensus view is that workers who incur risks are paid substantial rewards. . . .

Studies of risk premiums should be interpreted with some caution, however, since none of them has been ideal. The theory addresses the presence of premiums for risks perceived by workers. To measure these premiums, one would like to have information regarding workers' perceptions of the probabilities of particular types of risk, such as death, injury, or illnesses of differing severity. Instead, the only available data pertain to workers' perceptions about whether their jobs expose them to dangerous or unhealthy conditions. Although this risk measure captures the importance of subjective beliefs, it does not distinguish different gradations of risk.

An alternative approach is to use average risk measures, such as average injury rates, for the worker's industry or occupation. Although this index captures differing degrees of risk, it does not necessarily reflect the worker's beliefs about the risk of his particular job, which is what is relevant for the analysis. Moreover, if workers understand the industry-wide risk but not the risk posed by their own jobs, we will observe wage premiums for the industry even though the worker may substantially misassess the risk of his job. . . .

Workers who believed that they were exposed to dangerous or unhealthy conditions received over $900 annually (1980 prices) in hazard pay. . . .

Unfortunately, these results do not enable us to conclude that markets work perfectly. Is the premium less or more than would prevail if workers and employers were fully cognizant of the risks? The size of the premium only implies that compensating differentials are one element of market behavior. A more meaningful index is the wage premium per unit of risk. If it is very likely that a worker will be killed or injured, a $900 risk premium can be seen as a signal that the compensating differential process is deficient. The average blue-collar worker, however, faces an annual occupational death risk of only about $1/10,000$ and a less than $1/25$ risk of an injury severe enough to cause him to miss a day or more of work. Consequently, the observed premium per unit of risk is quite substantial, with the implicit value of life being on the order of $2 million or more for many workers. . . .

The safety incentives created by market mechanisms are much stronger than those created by [Occupational Safety and Health Administration (OSHA)] standards; a conservative estimate of the total job risk premiums for the entire private sector is $69 billion, or almost 3,000 times the total annual penalties now levied by OSHA. Whereas OSHA penalties are only 34 cents per worker, market risk premiums per worker are $925 annually. This figure would be even higher if we added in the premiums that are displaced by the workers' compensation system, which provides an additional $11.8 billion in compensation to workers.

COMMENTS AND QUESTIONS

1. Are you persuaded that the *theory* of compensating wage premiums is sound? Note the "critical ingredients" of the theory, as Viscusi puts them: worker awareness of risks, fair insurance, and equivalence of worker evaluation of risk with the social value of risk. The internal critiques we will take up later examine these ingredients in detail. As we proceed through these materials, consider whether any legal response can adequately address deficiencies in these critical ingredients and whether the *particular* legal responses we examine address those deficiencies (and if so, which ones, and how adequately). What would follow if you concluded that no legal response could adequately alleviate the deficiencies in the critical ingredients?

2. Note that Viscusi measures the existence of risk premiums with respect to worker perception of job risk. Is that the right measure, or should the measure be how much more workers are paid to compensate for the actual increase in risk? Which "critical ingredient" is that question directed toward?

3. If workplace injuries impose costs on someone other than the worker—create "externalities"—then the wage premium the worker will insist on will fail to take into account all the costs injuries impose. What, though, might those externalities be? Richard Zeckhauser and Albert Nichols argue that "financial" externalities are most important: "The family of a worker killed on the job . . . is likely to qualify for survivor benefits under Social Security. More generally, the whole medical care system is laced with subsidies, so that when a worker seeks medical care, a substantial portion of the cost is borne by taxpayers as a whole." Zeckhauser and Nichols, *OSHA after a Decade: A Time for Reason, in* Case Studies in Regulation, Revolution and Reform 208–209 (Leonard W. Weiss and Michael W. Klass, eds. Little, Brown, 1981). They caution against "rushing to accept government intervention on the basis of financial externalities," though: "(1) What is the relative importance of such externalities for job-related injuries and illnesses? . . . (2) Might some other mechanism, such as . . . merit rating for medical insurance based on behavior, be a better way to reduce the externality? (3) How well can we expect government intervention to perform?" They point out that this argument "applies to a broad range of human activity" that increases health risks, such as smoking and overeating. Consider the possibility that contracts of insurance can adequately address the financial externality.

   Zeckhauser and Nichols suggest that the financial externality is relatively more important for health risks than for safety risks. As you will see in more detail later, compensating workers for job-related illnesses with long latency periods is difficult, which makes job-based compensation through the workers' compensation system equally difficult. They also suggest that there are distinctions even within the class of health impairments; hearing loss, they suggest, is rarely disabling, which means that "workers bear most of the costs in the form of reduced function and enjoyment," whereas asbestos-related illnesses are likely to require costly care. "Note also that the problem of inadequate information provides stronger support for intervention with asbestos than with noise. The presence of noise is obvious, and its link to hearing loss is easy to comprehend. By contrast, substances such as asbestos are carcinogenic at levels too low to detect with the unaided senses, and the ultimate link to health loss may well be too obscure or too delayed for an individual worker to notice."

What if an injured worker (particularly a skilled one) is replaced, perhaps only temporarily, by a less skilled one? Is the effect of this replacement on production a negative externality (in the sense of a cost that is unlikely to be dealt with by the employment contract or some other contract)?

4. In theory, workers can use the compensating wage premium to purchase insurance to compensate them if risk is realized. Of course, if workers misperceive risks, they will underinsure themselves. "The available insurance arrangements also may be inadequate. Problems of adverse selection (only the bad risks join, threatening the viability of the plan) affect most types of insurance to some degree and serve as a rationale for a mandatory workers' compensation system. Under a voluntary . . . system, workers in high-risk jobs would be most likely to join, raising the average premium charged and consequently discouraging workers in lower-risk jobs from joining. As the pool of covered workers became increasingly risky, the fraction of the workforce insured by the program would steadily decline." Viscusi, *Risk by Choice*, pp. 78–79. How does the problem of adverse selection affect proposals for reforming health care financing?

5. Here is a take on Viscusi by Mark Kelman:

> At best, Viscusi shows that workers on jobs grossly classified as "dangerous" rather than "not dangerous" receive more pay, all else being equal. But he doesn't even purport to show any marginal increase in wages for shifts in danger within a dangerous occupation; the idea that, say, miners may get some premiums for hazard as compared to shoe salesmen tells us very close to nothing about whether particular employees receive compensatory wage hikes because their workplace is abnormally dangerous. Since, at the political level, controversy would center on regulations of already hazardous activity (for example, bringing all mines up to a safer, though still "dangerous" level), the study hardly implies that in the absence of regulation workers are already compensated for, or choose, desired safety levels, given the objective cost of greater safety.
>
> Mark Kelman, *A Guide to Critical Legal Studies* 170–71
> (Harvard University Press, 1987)

6. Research on compensating wage differentials continues. Recently, economists have examined how the pay rate for nurses and other medical practitioners

from 1987 to 2001 correlated to the rise and fall of AIDS rates. Because a small but known number of medical practitioners contracted AIDS while working in hospitals, the risk of contracting AIDS is assumed to be known by medical practitioners, who, under the theory, will then demand a greater wage in response to the risk of possible exposure. The researchers found that a ten percent increase in the local AIDS rate resulted in an almost one percent wage increase for registered nurses, relative to non–health care workers, and a slightly smaller increase for other types of health care workers who were less exposed to AIDS patients relative to non–health care workers. The authors also noted that as AIDS rates fell after 1993, registered nurses' wage rates began to fall in line with similarly educated non–health care workers. One percent may seem small, but consider that one percent of a registered nurse's income is about twenty cents an hour, and with more than two million registered nurses in the United States, that is a yearly difference of more than $800 million. Jeff DeSimone and Edward Schumacher, *Compensating Wage Differentials and AIDS Risk*, Nat'l Bureau of Econ. Research, Working Paper No. 10861 (2004), available at http://www.nber.org/papers/w10861.

For a meta-analysis of the major studies on compensating wage differentials over the past several decades, see W. Kip Viscusi and Joseph E. Aldy, *The Value of a Statistical Life: A Critical Review of Market Estimates throughout the World*, 27 J. Risk and Uncertainty 5 (2003). For studies estimating trade-offs between price and health or safety in contexts outside the workplace, see, for example, T. Gayer, J. T. Hamilton, and W. K. Viscusi, *Private Values of Risk Tradeoffs at Superfund Sites: Housing Market Evidence on Learning about Risk*, 82 Rev. Econ. & Stats. 439 (2000) (estimating trade-offs between increased cancer risk and housing prices); and M. K. Dreyfus and W. K. Viscusi, *Rates of Time Preference and Consumer Valuations of Automobile Safety and Fuel Efficiency*, 38 J. L. & Econ. 79 (1995) (estimating trade-offs between automobile safety and price).

- ### Hazard Pay for Workers: Risk and Reward
  JULIE GRAHAM AND DON SHAKOW
  23 Env't 62 (Oct. 1981). Reprinted with permission of Heldref Publications

. . .

Those who claim that the compensation principle operates as an active force for equity in our society argue that, "other things being equal," workers are compensated for accepting risky jobs. In other words, where two workers of equal skill and bargaining power, in the same job location, work at occupations with different levels of risk, their respective wages will differ by a small but discernible magnitude. The higher risk job will command a compensatory "risk premium." Where workers differ in aspects other than their job-related risk, the risk premium will be one of the factors underlying the overall difference in their wages. . . .

The view that these nonmonetary inequities are redressed by wages reflects a belief in the inherent beneficence of the market as an instrument of equality; whereas it is not technically feasible to eliminate differences in the work environment, the market will insure that these differences are reflected in equivalent differences in worker compensation. Holders of the more unpleasant, inconvenient, boring, stressful, or dangerous jobs receive higher wages than workers at safer, more stimulating, and enjoyable jobs. In the words of Adam Smith, who devoted considerable attention to the hypothesis of "equalizing differences," "the whole of the advantages and disadvantages of the different employments of labor and stock must, in the same neighborhood, be either perfectly equal or continually tending toward equality."

More recent economists have greatly expanded the notion of equalizing differences. It has been observed that the extra compensation for workers assuming additional risks reflects only one aspect of the "market for safety." Employers can choose, instead of compensating workers, to expend additional amounts on changing the work environment in order to make it safer. The incentive to employers is that they can avoid the payment of an additional risk premium to their workers by reducing risks. From the standpoint of a profit-oriented employer, it does not matter whether the money is spent on improving the workplace or on paying workers more for accepting risk.

From the standpoint of a social well-being, however, it does matter. A society that favors monetary compensation for differential risk has a conception of human welfare and social justice which is significantly different from that of a society favoring the elimination of risk differentials altogether. By requiring employers to institute safety measures designed to reduce or eliminate risk, society is choosing to emphasize worker health and safety as a social priority. By advocating wage compensation for risk, on the other hand, society is valuing worker choice over worker health. Workers who do not mind being exposed to risk have an opportunity to earn higher wages and to spend the extra income on the goods and services of their choice....

All the economists who have attempted to establish the existence of compensating wages rely on a common model of market behavior. This model assumes that job safety is a marketable good subject to market forces similar to those affecting purchase and sale of potatoes, roller skates, or any other commodity. Of course, job safety is not a real commodity but is rather an aspect or quality of another commodity, jobs.

The idea that the purchase of a tangible commodity can be regarded as the purchase of a bundle of both tangible and intangible qualities has become a popular notion among economists. Studies of demand for automobiles, for example, have partitioned the automobile into a series of qualities such as curb-weight, horsepower, and interior space, calculating separately the consumer demand for each one.

The demand for the commodity, labor, can be divided into similar pieces. A given laborer shows strength, agility, intelligence—and a characteristic propensity to get killed on the job. The demand for each of these qualities by employers and, alternatively, the demand by workers for the various good and bad qualities of a job can be calculated separately. In particular, we can use this framework to analyze the demand for and supply of job safety.

As with any marketable commodity, the separate qualities are each associated with a price. Economists term this price a "shadow price" because it is always combined with other prices and the consumer cannot separate it out. For example, the price of taste as opposed to alcohol content never actually appears explicitly in the beer market. Job safety has its shadow price as well. It is no more nor less than our now familiar risk premium.

Although the market for job safety cannot be identified in the real world like the stock market or the Chicago commodities market but is rather an invention of economists, it is nonetheless assumed to behave like an ordinary market. In particular employers and jobseekers are assumed to have *perfect information* about each other. In other words, people looking for work are supposedly aware of all prospective employment opportunities and fully apprised of the risks associated with prospective jobs; these risks, moreover, can be specified as measurable probabilities. Workers are also assumed to be *perfectly mobile*. Whenever there is a vacancy, an unemployed worker with suitable skills and talents is assumed to have a genuine opportunity to migrate over from his present job and to be taken seriously as an applicant. Furthermore, workers are held to be completely *economically rational*. In choosing among alternative jobs, workers are always expected to try to maximize their personal welfare and to select a proper combination of wages and risk. Firms are assumed to design jobs and to determine appropriate wage levels with a view toward maximizing profits. . . .

The majority of economists testing the doctrine of equalizing differences for workplace risk claim to have confirmed the hypothesis in some essential way. Nonetheless, upon closer examination, we find that many of the issues associated with risk compensation are still unresolved. There are three major reasons why the debate and ambiguity persist:

Economists cannot fully endorse the compensating wage thesis. Their statistical confirmations apply in most cases only to a specific, highly qualified version of risk compensation: while statistical validation of the compensating wage thesis has been obtained for the risk of death, job risk has many other facets. Only one study confirms the existence of compensation for risk of injury. Most attempts to demonstrate the presence of compensating differentials for job-related injuries have yielded negative results, leading one author to conclude, in regard to occupational risks other than risk of death, that the presence of compensating wages is yet to be demonstrated empirically: "In all, one must conclude that the empirical testing of the theory is still in its infancy."

The methodologies and statistical results are problematic in a number of essential respects. The measures of risk employed in many studies are inaccurate or misleading. The Society of Actuaries data show high risk among waiters and bartenders. . . . [T]his may be due as much to a statistically significant incidence of smoking among such workers, for instance, as to the death-dealing hazards of the job. Another problem is the omission of long-term chronic effects from the measurement of risk. Where the risk of death is measured as mortality due to industrial accidents, as in Bureau of Labor Statistics data, mortality due to chronic illness or to the cumulative effects of job-related stress is neglected. . . .

Tests for the existence of compensating wages do not address a number of questions which are particularly relevant to social equality. We need to know the answers to such questions as: Is compensation for job-related risk adequate? Are workers compensated for all risks, or just for certain risks? Are workers compensated uniformly or are there some workers who are not compensated for the risks they take? The first and second questions have been addressed to some extent by economists, but results to date are inconclusive. The third question has not been addressed at all. . . .

Our first and third questions can be addressed more readily and directly by dropping a number of assumptions currently in vogue among economists. It is particularly instructive to consider why taxidrivers and bartenders do not extricate themselves from undesirable occupations with the twin disadvantages of low wages and high risk and offer their services as boilermakers. The answer is that they cannot, for a variety of familiar reasons. They may lack the requisite skills; they may be too old to enter the apprenticeship programs; or they may be victims of some form of discrimination.

Even if workers were apprised of the occupational risks associated with their jobs, they would not be entirely free to migrate from job to job, contrary to the assumption of "perfect labor mobility." Furthermore, workers and employers are often ignorant of job-related threats to worker health, contrary to the neoclassical assumption of "perfect information."

The assertion that compensation mechanisms operate weakly or not at all for certain subgroups in the labor force accords with a recent view of labor market structure termed "labor market segmentation theory" (or alternatively, "dual labor market theory"). Labor economists have long recognized that the labor market is segmented (that is, broken into a multitude of small markets) rather than perfectly mobile, often attributing the source of segmentation to geographic and institutional factors which restrict labor mobility. Recently, however, theorists have posited the existence within the American labor force of two broad groups, structurally distinct "segments" which experience different levels of reward and security in the labor market. The *primary* workforce is characterized, among other attributes, by job permanence and high wages; the *secondary* workforce, by contrast, is characterized by unstable or insecure employment and low income levels. Because of discrimination and a shortage of high-wage employment, secondary workers experience restricted access to primary jobs; it is estimated that as much as one-third of the total labor force is trapped in the secondary segment. . . .

Until now, students of the labor market have not undertaken an empirical investigation of job-related risk as an aspect of the segmented labor market structure. We would like to suggest, however, that secondary workers may be subject to different compensation mechanisms than their counterparts in the primary labor force. Secondary workers experience restricted job mobility and job protection; they are likely to be employed in low-wage competitive industries that must economize on safety and other costly aspects of production.

Since they are generally not unionized, they have little leverage against their employers: it is well known that unorganized workers experience heightened vulnerability to occupational risk. In fact, they may bear risk for other members of society. The documented practice of subcontracting hazardous work to non-union shops is a mechanism by which risk is displaced from organized primary workers onto secondary workers. Such a practice protects employers of primary workers from expenditures in the form of wages or safety-enhancing improvements and puts the burden of risk on workers who are not in a strong position to demand higher wages or a safer working environment. It is common, for instance, in the automobile industry for large firms to subcontract to small independent shops that manufacture components ranging from ball bearings to seat covers. Such shops employ secondary workers.

If valid, labor market segmentation theory could help us determine the quantitative structure of the risk premium and answer the question of whether compensation for risk of death is provided uniformly to all workers. Two possible alternatives suggest themselves: (1) a compensating wage differential may exist for the primary segment but not for the secondary segment; (2) a compensating differential may exist for both segments but the magnitude of the risk premium may be different.

These alternatives raise an ironic possibility. The Adam Smith principle of equalizing differences may play a role in determining wages, but not in the straightforward fashion conceived by traditional economists. Contrary to the moral presuppositions of the neoclassical economists, the existence of compensating wages may not imply that the market operates in the direction of greater social equity. In fact, the hypothesis that compensation is present in one segment and absent in another would imply that compensating wages are an instrument of greater inequity rather than equity. . . .

- ### *Regulating Safety: A Political and Economic Analysis of OSHA*
  JOHN M. MENDELOFF
  pp. 10–11 (MIT Press, 1979). Reprinted with permission of MIT Press

The small body of empirical work on risk premiums, while far from conclusive, offers some weak evidence that, other things being equal, workers do tend to get paid something for accepting extra risks. Existing studies rely mainly on econometric analyses of samples of workers in different occupations or industries. Occasionally they cite the "hazard pay" provisions found in over 5 percent of all union contracts, but they have overlooked a much more pervasive practice among unionized and nonunionized firms which builds risk premiums directly into the wage structure. That practice is "job evaluation," the determination of relative wages within a firm or industry by giving points based on a set of factors including experience, education, and working conditions. Probably most larger firms in the U.S., especially in manufacturing, use some form of job evaluation.

Two of the twelve factors used in many job evaluation plans are relevant here: "hazards" and "surroundings." Significantly, health hazards like dusts, fumes, and noise are not included in the "hazard" ratings but rather in the "surroundings" ratings, where they are considered only as disamenities. Thus this common job evaluation formula does not account for the risks of occupational disease. However, it is apparent that within firms or industries using job evaluation, some sort of risk premium is paid for danger. Yet even here, it is difficult to believe that job evaluation ratings produce risk premiums that fully compensate the worker for two reasons. The first is that compensating differentials can run afoul of management's need to provide incentives for workers to climb the firm's job ladders. Strauss and Sayles give an excellent description of this problem:

> According to worker logic, clean jobs are better than dirty ones. A new man should start at the bottom, at the hardest, dirtiest, least desirable job. Then, as he acquires seniority, he should move up to better, easier, higher-paying jobs. But this is contradictory to the logic of job evaluation, which says that more points should be given for hard work and dirty conditions. Yet people will resist being "promoted" into a higher-paying job that has lower status. In practice, this problem is solved by giving very low point values to the factors of physical effort and job conditions—or by socially separating the two kinds of jobs so that there will be little invidious comparison. At times management disregards the

logic of job evaluation almost completely; dirty jobs are paid less than clean jobs. But the dirty job is a starting job through which all employees must move. As a man gets promoted, he moves by the ordinary process of seniority from a dirty, low-paid, low-status job to a cleaner, higher-paid, higher-status job.

A second and related reason is that the risk premiums appear to be extremely "sticky." For example, a comparison of the 1963 and 1971 job classification manuals for the steel industry indicates that the hazard and surroundings ratings had not changed for even one of the more than 600 jobs described. It seems unlikely that no major changes occurred in any of those jobs during that time. A better explanation relies on the strong disinclination of management (and union officials) to disturb old and familiar relativities.

In summary, although risk premiums apparently do exist—both within firms and industries through job evaluation and among occupations through more direct market forces—there are important reasons to doubt that they fully compensate the worker, much less that they reflect the concerns of all those who value his or her safety. Furthermore, as Robert Smith observes, "because so many injury-related losses are of a psychic nature ('pain and suffering'), we cannot begin to tell if the wage premiums are in fact fully compensating."

COMMENTS AND QUESTIONS

1. Graham and Shakow went on, in later work, to find that secondary workers faced higher risks on the job and received lower compensation for risks than primary workers did. Many economists, however, are not convinced by the segmented labor market theory espoused by Graham and Shakow. In addition to raising technical issues with their empirical conclusions, labor economist Peter Dorman casts doubt on their theory: "Analytically, each segment [of the labor market] could be viewed as its own mini-economy. . . . We might decry the injustice of making one whole category of workers better off than another, but within each group the same [economic] properties would apply. . . ." Peter Dorman, Markets and Mortality: Economics, Dangerous Work, and the Value of Human Life 155 (Cambridge University Press, 1996). Nevertheless, Dorman acknowledges that "[d]angerous working conditions are most likely to arise in secondary jobs, but these are also the least likely to provide adequate wage compensation. . . . Secondary jobs pay lower wages, offer more hazardous working conditions, and use a wage-determination mechanism that further diminishes the well-being of workers in high-risk jobs. Moreover, since employment in most secondary jobs is unstable, workers face much higher barriers to collective action and are therefore poorly placed to agitate for greater safety." Id. at 185.

2. Injury without contract: In this chapter we have been dealing with situations in which risks to human health might be an explicit (or implicit) bargaining chip in private contracts. But in many settings, risks are imposed without any prior agreement. Recall that the absence of such third-party effects was one of Viscusi's "critical ingredients" for an adequate theory of compensating wage differentials. In part II, we will begin discussing potential responses of the legal system to situations in which private contracts cannot, even in theory, take care of problems of risk.

Alternative Perspectives   3

In chapter 2, we explored the economic approach to allocating risks to human health and life in considering the appropriateness of some ways in which the government—including both courts and legislatures—can displace or alter private agreements. In this chapter, we examine two important challenges to the economic perspective: the idea of market-inalienability and the reality of unequal bargaining power. We also consider paternalism as a possible justification for government interference with private agreements.

We use workplace health and safety as our focal point here. In the context of workplace health and safety, the clash between the economic view and the alternative perspectives is especially vivid, and the arguments have been well developed. Keep in mind, though, that the basic problem of justifying government interference with private markets for risk applies well beyond the workplace setting to consumer products, health care, disputes over harmful uses of land, and the like.

A Market-Inalienability

Students often are bothered by the proposition that people should be allowed to trade risks to their arms, legs, lungs, and even lives for higher wages or other financial gain—that freedom from such risks is alienable. In fact, some types of health and safety regulations make the right to be free of such risks inalienable. For example, the pesticide DDT has been banned in the United States; the ban makes the right to be free from risks posed by DDT inalienable. Indeed, at some level, all government-prescribed regulations make something inalienable (even regulations that are designed to ensure that parties to a bargain have particular items of information available to them).

In this section, we will consider the theory of market-inalienability—which generally recognizes that aspects of personhood should not be commodified—and whether it is appropriate for any rights, including the right to be free of harms to health and safety. You will read an important modern defense of making some rights inalienable by Margaret Radin, but as you do so, keep in mind the standard economic critique of inalienability, as offered by Susan Rose-Ackerman:

> Inalienability is supported by those who take an interest in workers' health but not in their overall level of well-being, and by those who do not wish

to acknowledge that base wages are so low that people are willing to sacrifice health for income. Imposing costs on workers because of the squeamishness of others, however, hardly seems like good public policy, especially for a program ostensibly designed to benefit workers. A better response would be a program of redistributive taxation and subsidy that leads most people to choose improvements in health over marginal improvements in income. Susan Rose-Ackerman, *Progressive Law and Economics*, 98 Yale L.J. 341, 357 (1988)

We will return to critiques of market-inalienability later in the chapter, but even now, make sure that you understand why inalienability "is supported by those who take an interest in workers' health *but not in their overall level of well-being.*" How does Radin respond to the kinds of arguments Rose-Ackerman makes?

■ *Market Inalienability*

MARGARET JANE RADIN

100 Harv. L. Rev. 1849 (1987). Reprinted by permission of the Harvard Law Review Association and William S. Hein Company from the Harvard Law Review

... Two theories about freedom are central to the ideological framework in which we view inalienability: the notion that freedom means negative liberty, and the notion that (negative) liberty is identical with, or necessarily connected to, free alienability of everything in markets. The conception of freedom as negative liberty gives rise to the view that all inalienabilities are paternalistic limitations on freedom. The idea that liberty consists in alienability of everything in markets clashes with substantive requirements of personhood, making it difficult, for example, to argue against human commodification. In general, the commitment to negative liberty, like the commitment to the Kantian structure of persons versus objects, has caused confusion in liberal pluralism and has exerted a pull toward universal commodification.*

Inalienabilities are often said to be paternalistic. Paternalism usually means to substitute the judgment of a third party or the government for that of a person on the ground that to do so is in that person's best interests. For advocates of negative liberty, to substitute someone else's choice for my own is a naked infringement of

---

*[Editors' Note: Earlier, Radin defines liberal pluralists as "those who see a normatively appropriate but limited realm for commodification coexisting with one or more nonmarket realms. Pluralists often see one other normative realm besides that of the market, and partition the world into markets and politics, markets and rights, or markets and families; but pluralists may also envision multiple nonmarket realms. For a pluralist, the crucial question is how to conceive of the permissible scope of the market." Radin also asserts that "universal commodification is characterized by universal market rhetoric and universal market methodology. In universal market rhetoric—the discourse of complete commodification—everything that is desired or valued is spoken of as a 'good.' Everything that is desired or valued is an object that can be possessed, that can be thought of as equivalent to a sum of money, and that can be alienated. The person is conceived of and spoken of as the possessor and trader of these goods, and hence all human interactions are sales."]

my liberty. Freedom means doing (or not doing) whatever I as an individual prefer at the moment, as long as I am not harming other people. To think of inalienability as paternalism assumes that freedom is negative liberty—that people would choose to alienate certain things if they could, but are restrained from doing so by moral or legal rules saying, in effect, that they are mistaken about what is good for them.

To say that inalienabilities involve a loss of freedom also assumes that alienation itself is an act of freedom, or is freedom-enhancing. Someone who holds this view and conceives of alienation as sale through free contract is deeply committed to commodification as expressive of—perhaps necessary for—human freedom. Insofar as theories of negative freedom are allied to universal commodification, so are traditional discussions of inalienability in terms of paternalism. If we reject the notion that freedom means negative liberty, and the notion that liberty and alienation in markets are identical or necessarily connected, then inalienability will cease to seem inherently paternalistic. If we adopt a positive view of liberty that includes proper self-development as necessary for freedom, then inalienabilities needed to foster that development will be seen as freedom-enhancing rather than as impositions of unwanted restraints on our desires to transact in markets. . . .

V. Toward an Evolutionary Pluralism

In this Part, I develop a pluralist view that differs in significant respects from liberal pluralism. My central hypothesis is that market-inalienability is grounded in noncommodification of things important to personhood. In an ideal world markets would not necessarily be abolished, but market-inalienability would protect all things important to personhood. But we do not live in an ideal world. In the nonideal world we do live in, market-inalienability must be judged against a background of unequal power. In that world it may sometimes be better to commodify incompletely than not to commodify at all. Market-inalienability may be ideally justified in light of an appropriate conception of human flourishing, and yet sometimes be unjustifiable because of our nonideal circumstances.

A. *Noncommodification and the Ideal of Human Flourishing*

1. Rethinking Personhood: Freedom, Identity, Contextuality

Because of the ideological heritage of the subject/object dichotomy, we tend to view things internal to the person as inalienable and things external as freely alienable. Because of the ideological heritage of negative liberty, we also tend to think of inalienabilities as paternalistic. A better view of personhood, one that does not conceive of the self as pure subjectivity standing wholly separate from an environment of pure objectivity, should enable us to discard both the notion that inalienabilities relate only to things wholly subjective or internal and the notion that inalienabilities are paternalistic.

In searching for such a better view, it is useful to single out three main, overlapping aspects of personhood: freedom, identity, and contextuality. The freedom aspect of personhood focuses on will, or the power to choose for oneself. In order to be autonomous individuals, we must at least be able to act for ourselves through free will in relation to the environment of things and other people. The identity aspect of personhood focuses on the integrity and continuity of the self required for individuation. In order to have a unique individual identity, we must have selves that are integrated and continuous over time. The contextuality aspect of personhood focuses on the necessity of self-constitution in relation to the environment of things and other people. In order to be differentiated human persons, unique individuals, we must have relationships with the social and natural world.

A better view of personhood—a conception of human flourishing that is superior to the one implied by universal commodification—should present more satisfactory views of personhood in each of these three aspects. I am not seeking here to elaborate a complete view of personhood. Rather, I focus primarily on a certain view of contextuality and its consequences: the view that connections between the person and her environment are integral to personhood. I also suggest that to the extent we have already accepted certain views of freedom, identity, and contextuality, we are committed to a view of personhood that rejects universal commodification. . . .

Universal commodification undermines personal identity by conceiving of personal attributes, relationships, and philosophical and moral commitments as monetizable and alienable from the self. A better view of personhood should understand many kinds of particulars—one's politics, work, religion, family, love, sexuality, friendships, altruism, experiences, wisdom, moral commitments, character, and personal attributes—as integral to the self. To understand any of these as monetizable or completely detachable from the person—to think, for example, that the value of one person's moral commitments is commensurate or fungible with those of another, or that the 'same' person remains when her moral commitments are subtracted—is to do violence to our deepest understanding of what it is to be human. . . .

2. Protecting Personhood: Noncommodification of Personal Rights, Attributes, and Things

. . . We are now in a better position to understand how conceiving of personal things as commodities does violence to personhood, and to explore the problem of knowing what things are personal.

To conceive of something personal as fungible assumes that the person and the attribute, right, or thing, are separate. This view imposes the subject/object dichotomy to create two kinds of alienation. If the discourse of fungibility is partially made one's own, it creates disorientation of the self that experiences the distortion of its own personhood. For example, workers who internalize market rhetoric conceive of their own labor as a commodity separate from themselves as persons; they dissociate their daily life from their own self-conception. To the extent the discourse is not internalized, it creates alienation between those who use the discourse and those whose personhood they wrong in doing so. For example, workers who do not conceive of their labor as a commodity are alienated from others who do, because, in the workers' view, people who conceive of their labor as a commodity fail to see them as whole persons.

To conceive of something personal as fungible also assumes that persons cannot freely give of themselves to others. At best they can bestow commodities. At worst—in universal commodification—the gift is conceived of as a bargain. Conceiving of gifts as bargains not only conceives of what is personal as fungible, it also endorses the picture of persons as profit-maximizers. A better view of personhood should conceive of gifts not as disguised sales, but rather as expressions of the interrelationships between the self and others. To relinquish something to someone else by gift is to give of yourself. Such a gift takes place within a personal relationship with the recipient, or else it creates one. Commodification stresses separateness both between ourselves and our things and between ourselves and other people. To postulate personal interrelationship and communion requires us to postulate people who can yield personal things to other people and not have them instantly become fungible. Seen this way, gifts diminish separateness. This is why (to take an obvious example) people say that sex bought and paid for is not the same 'thing' as sex freely shared. Commodified sex leaves the parties as separate individuals and perhaps reinforces their separateness; they only engage in it if each individual considers it worthwhile. Noncommodified sex ideally diminishes separateness; it is conceived of as a union because it is ideally a sharing of selves.

Not everything with which someone may subjectively identify herself should be treated legally or morally as personal. Otherwise the category of personal things might collapse into 'consumer surplus': anything to which someone attached high subjective value would be personal. The question whether something is personal has a normative aspect: whether identifying oneself with something—constituting oneself in connection with that thing—is justifiable. What makes identifying oneself with something justifiable, in turn, is an appropriate connection to our conception of human flourishing. More specifically, such relationships are justified if they can form part of an appropriate understanding of freedom, identity, and contextuality. A proper understanding of contextuality, for example, must recognize that, although personhood is fostered by relations with people and things, it is possible to be involved too much, or in the wrong way, or with the wrong things.

To identify something as personal, it is not enough to observe that many people seem to identify with some particular kind of thing, because we may judge such identification to be bad for people. An example of a justifiable kind of relationship is people's involvement with their homes. This relationship permits self-constitution within a stable environment. An example of an unjustifiable kind of relationship is the involvement of the robber baron with an empire of 'property for power.' The latter is unjustified because it ties into a conception of the person we can recognize as inferior: the person as self-interested maximizer of manipulative power.

There is no algorithm or abstract formula to tell us which items are (justifiably) personal. A moral judgment is required in each case. . . . I am suggesting that we relinquish the subject/object dichotomy and rely instead on our best moral judgment in light of the best conception of personhood as we now understand it.

B. Methods of Justifying Market-Inalienabilities

If some people wish to sell something that is identifiably personal, why not let them? In a market society, whatever some people wish to buy and others wish to sell is deemed alienable. Under these circumstances, we must formulate an affirmative case for market-inalienability, so that no one may choose to make fungible—commodify—a personal attribute, right, or thing. In this Section, I propose and evaluate three possible methods of justifying market-inalienability based on personhood: a prophylactic argument, assimilation to prohibition, and a domino theory.

The method of justification that correlates most readily with traditional liberal pluralism is a prophylactic argument. For the liberal it makes sense to countenance both selling and sharing of personal things as the holder freely chooses. If an item of property is personal, however, sometimes the circumstances under which the holder places it on the market might arouse suspicion that her act is coerced. Given that we cannot know whether anyone really intends to cut herself off from something personal by commodifying it, our suspicions might sometimes justify banning sales. The risk of harm to the seller's personhood in cases in which coerced transactions are permitted (especially if the thing sought to be commodified is normally very important to personhood), and the great difficulties involved in trying to scrutinize every transaction closely, may sometimes outweigh the harm that a ban would impose on would-be sellers who are in fact uncoerced. A prophylactic rule aims to ensure free choice—negative liberty—by the best possible coercion-avoidance mechanism under conditions of uncertainty. This prophylactic argument is one way for a liberal to justify, for example, the ban on selling oneself into slavery. We normally view such commodification as so destructive of personhood that we would readily presume all instances of it to be coerced. We would not wish, therefore, to have a rule creating a rebuttable presumption that such transactions are uncoerced (as with ordinary contracts), nor even a rule that would scrutinize such transactions case-by-case for voluntariness, because the risk of harm to personhood in the coerced transactions we might mistakenly see as voluntary is so great that we would rather risk constraining the exercise of choice by those (if any) who really wish to enslave themselves.

A liberal pluralist might use a prophylactic justification to prevent poor people from selling their children, sexual services, or body parts. The liberal would argue that an appropriate conception of coercion should, with respect to selling these things, include the desperation of poverty. Poor people should not be forced to give up personal things because the relinquishment diminishes them as persons, contrary to the liberal regime of respect for persons. We should presume that such transactions are not the result of free choice.

When thus applied to coercion by poverty, the prophylactic argument is deeply troubling. If poverty can make some things nonsalable because we must prophylactically presume such sales are coerced, we would add insult to injury if we then do not provide the would-be seller with the goods she needs or the money she would have received. If we think respect for persons warrants prohibiting a mother from selling something personal to obtain food for her starving children, we do not respect her personhood more by forcing her to let them starve instead. To the extent it equates poverty with coercion, the prophylactic argument requires a corollary in welfare rights. Otherwise we would be forcing the mother to endure a devastating loss in her primary relationship (with her children) rather than in the secondary one (with the personal thing) she is willing to sacrifice to protect the primary one. It is as if, when someone is coerced at gunpoint, we were to direct our moral opprobrium at the victim rather than the gun-wielder, and our enforcement efforts at preventing the victim from handing over her money rather than at preventing the gun-wielder from placing her in the situation where she must. Thus, this aspect of liberal prophylactic pluralism is hypocritical without a large-scale redistribution of wealth and power that seems highly improbable. Although we may neverthe[le]ss decide to ban sales of certain personal things, the prophylactic argument, insofar as it rests on equating poverty with coercion, cannot be the reason.

A second method of justifying market-inalienability assimilates it to prohibition. If we accept that the commodified object is different from the 'same' thing noncommodified and embedded in personal relationships, then market-inalienability is a prohibition of the commodified version, resting on some moral requirement that it not exist. What might be the basis of such a moral requirement? Something might be prohibited in its market form because it both creates and exposes wealth- and class-based contingencies for obtaining things that are critical to life itself—for example, health care—and thus undermines a commitment to the sanctity of life. Another reason for prohibition might be that the use of market rhetoric, in conceiving of the 'good' and understanding the interactions of people respecting it, creates and fosters an inferior conception of human flourishing. For example, we accept an inferior conception of personhood (one allied to the extreme view of negative freedom) if we suppose people may freely choose to commodify themselves.

The prohibition argument—that commodification of things is bad in itself, or because these things are not the 'same' things that would be available to people in nonmarket relationships—leads to universal noncommodification. If commodification is bad in itself it is bad for everything. Any social good is arguably 'different' if not embedded in a market society. To restrict the argument in order to permit pluralism, we have to accept either that certain things are the 'same' whether or not they are bought and sold, and others are 'different,' or that prohibiting the commodified version morally matters only for certain things, but not for all of them. At present we tend to think that nuts and bolts are pretty much the 'same' whether commodified or not, whereas love, friendship, and sexuality are very 'different'; we also tend to think that trying to keep society free of commodified love, friendship, and sexuality morally matters more than trying to keep it free of commodified nuts and bolts.

A third method of justifying market-inalienability, the domino theory, envisions a slippery slope leading to market domination. The domino theory assumes that for some things, the noncommodified version is morally preferable; it also assumes that the commodified and noncommodified versions of some interactions cannot coexist. To commodify some things is simply to preclude their noncommodified analogues from existing. Under this theory, the existence of some commodified sexual interactions will contaminate or infiltrate everyone's sexuality so that all sexual relationships will become commodified. If it is morally required that noncommodified sex be possible, market-inalienability of sexuality would be justified. This result can be conceived of as the opposite of a prohibition: there is assumed to exist some moral requirement that a certain 'good' be socially available. The domino theory thus supplies an answer (as the prohibition theory does not) to the liberal question why people should not be permitted to choose both market and nonmarket interactions: the noncommodified version is morally preferable when we cannot have both.

We can now see how the prohibition and domino theories are connected. The prohibition theory focuses on the importance of excluding from social life commodified versions of certain 'goods'—such as love, friendship, and sexuality—whereas the domino theory focuses on the importance for social life of maintaining the noncommodified versions. The prohibition theory stresses the wrongness of commodification—its alienation and degradation of the person—and the domino theory stresses the rightness of noncommodification in creating the social context for the proper expression and fostering of personhood. If one explicitly adopts both prongs of this commitment to personhood, the prohibition and domino theories merge. . . .

Rather than merely assuming that money is at the core of every transaction in 'goods,' thereby making commodification inevitable and phasing out the noncommodified version of the 'same' thing (or the nonmarket aspects of sale transactions), we should evaluate the domino theory on a case-by-case basis. We should assess how important it is to us that any particular contested thing remain available in a noncommodified form and try to estimate how likely it is that allowing market transactions for those things would engender a domino effect and make the nonmarket version impossible. This might involve judging how close to universal commodification our consciousness really is, and how this consciousness would affect the particular thing in question.

C. The Problem of Nonideal Evaluation

One ideal world would countenance no commodification; another would insist that all harms to personhood are unjust; still another would permit no relationships of oppression or disempowerment. But we are situated in a nonideal world of ignorance, greed, and violence; of poverty, racism, and sexism. In spite of our ideals, justice under nonideal circumstances, pragmatic justice, consists in choosing the best alternative now available to us. In doing so we may have to tolerate some things that would count as harms in our ideal world. Whatever harms to our ideals we decide we must now tolerate in the name of justice may push our ideals that much farther away. How are we to decide, now, what is the best transition toward our ideals, knowing that our choices now will help to reconstitute those ideals?

The possible avenues for justifying market-inalienability must be reevaluated in light of our nonideal world. In light of the desperation of poverty, a prophylactic market-inalienability may amount merely to an added burden on would-be sellers; under some circumstances we may judge it, nevertheless, to be our best available alternative. We might think that both nonmarket and market interactions can exist in some situations without a domino effect leading to a more commodified order, or we might think it is appropriate to risk a domino effect in light of the harm that otherwise would result to would-be sellers. We might find prohibition of sales not morally warranted, on balance, in some situations, unless there is a serious risk of a domino effect. These will be pragmatic judgments.

1. The Double Bind

Often commodification is put forward as a solution to powerlessness or oppression, as in the suggestion that women be permitted to sell sexual and reproductive services. But is women's personhood injured by allowing or by disallowing commodification of sex and reproduction? The argument that commodification empowers women is that recognition of these alienable entitlements will enable a needy group—poor women—to improve their relatively powerless, oppressed condition, an improvement that would be beneficial to personhood. If the law denies women the opportunity to be comfortable sex workers and baby producers instead of subsistence domestics, assemblers, clerks, and waitresses—or pariahs (welfare recipients) and criminals (prostitutes)—it keeps them out of the economic mainstream and hence the mainstream of American life.

The rejoinder is that, on the contrary, commodification will harm personhood by powerfully symbolizing, legitimating, and enforcing class division and gender oppression. It will create the two forms of alienation that correlate with commodification of personal things. Women will partly internalize the notion that their persons and their attributes are separate, thus creating the pain of a divided self. To the extent that this self-conception is not internalized, women will be alienated from the dominant order that, by allowing commodification, sees them in this light. Moreover, commodification will exacerbate, not ameliorate, oppression and powerlessness, because of the social disapproval connected with marketing one's body.

But the surrejoinder is that noncommodification of women's capabilities under current circumstances represents not a brave new world of human flourishing, but rather a perpetuation of the old order that submerges women in oppressive status relationships, in which personal identity as market-traders is the prerogative of males. We cannot make progress toward the noncommodification that might exist under ideal conditions of equality and freedom by trying to maintain noncommodification now under historically determined conditions of inequality and bondage.

These conflicting arguments illuminate the problem with the prophylactic argument for market-inalienability. If we now permit commodification, we may exacerbate the oppression of women—the suppliers. If we now disallow commodification—without what I have called the welfare-rights corollary, or large-scale redistribution of social wealth and power—we force women to remain in circumstances that they themselves believe are worse than becoming sexual commodity-suppliers. Thus, the alternatives seem subsumed by a need for social progress, yet we must choose some regime now in order to make progress. This dilemma of transition is the double bind.

The double bind has two main consequences. First, if we cannot respect personhood either by permitting sales or by banning sales, justice requires that we consider changing the circumstances that create the dilemma. We must consider wealth and power redistribution. Second, we still must choose a regime for the meantime, the transition, in nonideal circumstances.** To resolve the double bind, we have to investigate particular problems separately; decisions must be made (and remade) for each thing that some people desire to sell. . . .

** [Editors' Note: Radin earlier describes incomplete commodification as a way of mediating the dilemma of the double bind: "Under nonideal circumstances the question whether market-inalienability can be justified is more complicated than a binary decision between complete commodification and complete noncommodification. Rather, we should understand there to be a continuum reflecting degrees of commodification that will be appropriate in a given context. An incomplete commodification—a partial market-inalienability—can sometimes substitute for a complete noncommodification that might accord with our ideals but cause too much harm in our nonideal world."]

VI. Conclusion

Market-inalienability is an important normative category for our society. Economic analysis and traditional liberal pluralism have failed to recognize and correctly understand its significance because of the market orientation of their premises. In attempting to free our conceptions from these premises in order to see market-inalienability as an important countercurrent to our market orientation, I have created an archetype, universal commodification, and tried to show how it underlies both economic analysis and more traditional liberal thinking about inalienability. As an archetype, universal commodification is too uncomplicated to describe fully any actual thinker or complex of ideas, but I believe consideration of the archetype and what it entails is a necessary corrective. The rhetoric of commodification has led us into an unreflective use of market characterizations and comparisons for almost everything people may value, and hence into an inferior conception of personhood. . . .

To the extent that we must not assimilate our conception of personhood to the market, market-inalienabilities are justified. But market-inalienabilities are unjust when they are too harmful to personhood in our nonideal world. Incomplete commodification can help us mediate this kind of injustice. To see the world of exchange as shot through with incomplete commodification can also show us that inalienability is not the anomaly that economics and more traditional liberalism conceive it to be. This perspective can also help us begin to decommodify things important to personhood—like work and housing—that are now wrongly conceived of in market rhetoric.

Market-inalienability ultimately rests on our best conception of human flourishing, which must evolve as we continue to learn and debate. Likewise, market-inalienabilities must evolve as we continue to learn and debate; there is no magic formula that will delineate them with utter certainty, or once and for all. In our debate, there is no such thing as two radically different normative discourses reaching the 'same' result. The terms of our debate will matter to who we are.

COMMENTS AND QUESTIONS

1. What criteria does Radin offer for determining whether some right should be inalienable? Do "risks to health and safety"—for workers, for consumers—satisfy those criteria?

2. Radin offers three arguments for market-inalienability with respect to specific aspects of personhood: the prophylactic argument, prohibition, and the domino theory. Which, if any, of these are applicable in the context of workplace health and safety?

3. Are workers faced with the kind of double bind Radin describes? Does she offer a cogent way of resolving the double bind?

4. What if workers face competing inalienabilities? Within Radin's framework, for example, one might say that gender equality within the workplace should be inalienable because of its close relationship with human flourishing, uncontroversially understood. One might also say, for the same reason, that the

entitlement to a workplace that will not cause serious and permanent damage to one's offspring should be inalienable. But what if a "healthy" workplace is achieved by excluding women of childbearing age from it? Which inalienability should trump—gender equality or workplace safety? For the Supreme Court's answer (gender equality trumps) in the context of a case challenging an employer's requirement that women of childbearing age either show proof of sterilization or transfer out of jobs that expose them to lead levels exceeding federally recommended standards, see *International Union v. Johnson Controls, Inc.*, 499 U.S. 187 (1991).

5. Radin's examples of inalienabilities include selling oneself into slavery, selling sex, and selling body parts. Decisions whether to "sell" in these contexts involve a kind of on-off switch; either one does or does not sell oneself into slavery. But decisions about risks to health and safety seldom have this character. They lie on a continuum, rather than at the extremes of certain life or certain death. Does this characteristic make it more problematic to assert "rights against risks"? For an argument that it does, see Christopher H. Schroeder, *Rights against Risks*, 86 Colum. L. Rev. 495 (1986).

6. The Construction of Consent: Can we make sense of the idea of consent independent of the social circumstances under which consent is exercised? If we cannot, is the entire idea of alienability cast into doubt? Why or why not?

Courts are often called on, for example, to decide whether a worker or consumer consented to "assume the risk of" dangerous conditions in the workplace or dangerous features of consumer products. Typically, the worker or consumer will have manifested "consent," if at all, only by staying in the workplace or buying the product despite its risk. Thus the courts must infer from the overall circumstances of the case whether the worker or consumer actually consented to the risk. In thinking about whether consent is meaningful independent of social circumstances, consider whether the gender of the worker or consumer is, or should be, relevant to the conclusion about consent. Is it fair to say that men are more willing to take on physical risks than women are? Is it fair to argue that when women take on such risks, they are more likely to do so because of economic duress? Would you feel comfortable if courts explicitly recognized such a gender difference? For decisions coming to different conclusions about consent, possibly though not expressly based on the different genders of the injured parties, see *Orfield v. International Harvester Co.*, 535 F.2d 959 (6th Cir. 1976) (finding male worker had assumed the risk of an obvious on-the-job risk), and *Downs v. Gulf & Western Mfg. Co.*, 677 F. Supp. 661 (D. Mass. 1987) (finding female worker had not assumed the risk of an obvious on-the-job risk).

B Unequal Bargaining Power

Here we consider whether employees in fact make free and deliberate choices about accepting a level of risk or are essentially compelled to do so based on their lack of bargaining power. As one commentator observes:

While jet test pilots may in fact be risk preferrers, the ability of many working people to make "free choices" in their selection of jobs is highly questionable. . . .

Fear of job loss and unavailability of alternative employment opportunities by reason of occupational or geographic immobility or lack of training often make hazard pay an unconscionable bargain to those individuals who are forced by circumstances beyond their control to place an inordinately low implicit valuation upon their own lives. Nor is it appropriate to rely upon hazard pay if the distribution of income and opportunities is inequitable to begin with. Individual decisions about the amount of job-related risk to assume are not independent of society's distribution of nonhuman wealth and such associated factors as home environment, educational opportunities, "connections," etc. An individual in need of $100 per week to support his family, when choosing between two jobs, one paying $125 but with high risk of illness or death, another paying $75 per week but safe, may choose differently if he has wealth bearing $50 interest per week than if he has no wealth at all. Hazard pay is too attractive to such individuals from society's point of view, and in any case doesn't come close, typically, to compensating them for the true costs of the assumption of risks involved. Nicholas Ashford, Crisis in the Workplace 363, 365 (MIT Press, 1976).

What is the proper legal response, if any, to the dilemma faced by the worker Ashford describes? Would requiring the employer to offer an even larger compensating wage premium do any good? (Would the job be available if the wage had to be raised?) How about providing the worker with "wealth bearing $50 interest per week"? We will return shortly to the question of whether the legal system should intervene in market arrangements due to unequal bargaining power. But first, we offer excerpts from two articles that argue that the bargaining power of employers and employees is indeed unequal.

- ### *Responses to Occupational Disease: The Role of Markets, Regulation, and Information*
  ELINOR P. SCHROEDER AND SIDNEY A. SHAPIRO
  72 Geo. L.J. 1231, 1241–44 (1984). Reprinted with the permission
  of the publisher, Georgetown Law Journal © 1984

Researchers have offered various explanations for the apparent failure of the wage premium theory. One explanation is that wage premiums will be paid only if some workers are mobile and can easily take less risky jobs if their employers do not pay adequate premiums. With high unemployment, a change in jobs is not a realistic alternative for many people. Further, the transaction costs associated with switching jobs, such as loss of pension rights and seniority, the necessity of becoming familiar with a new employer, and the expense of moving, may be too high for many workers. These factors may explain in part the results in [a study failing to find wage premiums among asbestos insulation workers]. As a practical matter, long-time asbestos insulation workers may have been unwilling to surrender seniority and other job rights and may have been unable to acquire new job skills. In addition, the most mobile workers have traditionally been the young, who would be the most likely to underestimate or ignore the risk of contracting a work-related disease. . . .

For organized workers, collective bargaining between employer and union could be, but is not, a powerful vehicle for achieving changes in the workplace to decrease risks. Unions traditionally have not shown much interest in bargaining over health and safety issues. There was very little union political interest in health and safety before the passage of the Occupational Safety and Health Act in 1970 and occupational disease did not become a union bargaining concern until the late 1970s. Although there is some evidence that union concern with workplace dangers has increased in recent years, it is not clear that union bargaining activity has had any significant effect in promoting the health and safety of workers.

A recent analysis of 400 collective bargaining agreements revealed that eighty-two percent contained occupational safety and health provisions but these provisions seldom provided workers with significant rights they would not have had anyway. For instance, twenty-seven percent of the contracts studied contained provisions that merely required the employer to comply with federal, state, and local safety and health laws, and forty-six percent had provisions concerning safety equipment, such as machine guards and safety glasses, which OSHA regulations required in most instances anyway. On the other hand, only twenty-five percent of the contracts addressed hazardous work, and, of those, only twenty-four percent guaranteed employees the right to refuse hazardous work, a right which is protected under federal law only in certain instances. Further, only five percent of the hazardous work provisions provided for wage rate retention when employees were temporarily transferred because of hazardous conditions or injury. Such rights generally are not guaranteed by existing law. Forty-five percent of the contracts established joint management-union safety committees, but one recent study has shown that such safety and health committees make "little difference" in workplace health and safety. Moreover, the overwhelming emphasis of these contract provisions appeared to be on injury-related matters.

There may be several reasons for labor's seeming failure to make health concerns a major issue in collective bargaining. First, unions generally do not possess the technical and financial resources necessary to determine hazardous exposure levels, to offer feasible alternatives to current methods of operation, and to monitor compliance with any agreement reached with an employer. Second, some unions apparently fear potential liability to their members if they assume any role in assuring workplace safety. Third, because most employers feel that safety and health concerns are intertwined with management of the production process, they may be reluctant even to discuss these issues with the union, much less to agree to change their production methods. Finally, a union will be successful in negotiating only if it is able and willing to enforce its demands with economic action. Many unions may not be strong enough to sustain a strike against the employer, particularly if the employees are relatively unskilled and therefore easily replaced. Even if the union could gain important concessions through striking, its members may not be willing to strike over a noneconomic issue which they view as less crucial than increased wages and fringe benefits. . . .

■ *Coercion, Contract, and Free Labor in the Nineteenth Century*
ROBERT J. STEINFELD
pp. 19–24 (Cambridge University Press, 2001). Reprinted
with the permission of Cambridge University Press

Today, in cases in which wage workers are not subject to contractual liability but to
a different kind of pecuniary pressure, the ordinary economic pressures of a market
society, we classify these workers as free. Two implicit assumptions are usually
made about economic pressure. First, it is supposed to have a different source and
different characteristics than nonpecuniary pressure typically does. Law is supposed to be the main source of the nonpecuniary pressure used in unfree labor. It is
law, normally, that authorizes or permits individuals and state officials to use
physical violence or confinement to extract labor. By contrast, market forces are
supposed to be the source of economic pressure and to operate impersonally and
indirectly. They are supposed to exert pressure only in the way nature exerts
pressure: If you do not work you starve. No one controls market forces. By contrast, law is manufactured and controlled by people. Second, these different kinds
of pressure are supposed to operate with radically different degrees of harshness.
Physical violence and imprisonment are viewed as much severer than economic
pressures.

The simple opposition, economic (pecuniary) versus legal (nonpecuniary) coercion, which places labor subject to one in one category and labor subject to the
other in an opposite category, operates to obscure the common sources and characteristics of the two. Economic coercion always has its source in a set of legal
rights, privileges, and powers that place one person in a position to force another
person to choose between labor and some more disagreeable alternative to the
labor, just as so-called legal compulsion does. The exercise of economic power
is also quite personal and direct. Consider economic coercion in the bargaining
relationship between employers and employees. Robert Hale showed that law was
the ultimate source of an employer's power to force a worker to choose between
wage work and a more disagreeable alternative to work. His argument is worth
quoting at length:

> The owner [of private property] can remove the legal duty under which the
> non-owner labors [not to consume or otherwise use that property]. He can
> remove it, or keep it in force, at his discretion. To keep it in force may or may
> not have unpleasant consequences to the non-owner—consequences which
> spring from the law's creation of a legal duty. To avoid these consequences, the
> non-owner may be willing to obey the will of the owner, provided that the
> obedience is not in itself more unpleasant than the consequences to be avoided.
> Such obedience may take the trivial form of paying five cents for legal per-
> mission to eat a particular bag of peanuts, or it may take the more significant
> form of working for [a factory] owner at disagreeable toil for a slight wage.
> In either case the conduct is motivated . . . by a desire to escape a more
> disagreeable alternative. . . . In the case of the labor what would be the conse-
> quence of refusal to comply with the owner's terms? It would be either absence
> of wages, or obedience to the terms of some other employer. . . . Suppose, now,
> the worker were to refuse to yield to the coercion of any employer, but were to
> choose instead to remain under the legal duty to abstain from the use of any of

the money which anyone owns. He must eat. While there is no law against eating in the abstract, there is a law which forbids him to eat any of the food which actually exists in the community—and that law is the law of property. It can be lifted as to any specific food at the discretion of its owner, but if the owners unanimously refuse to lift the prohibition, the non-owner will starve unless he can himself produce food. And there is every likelihood that the owners will be unanimous in refusing, if he has no money. . . . Unless, then, the non-owner can produce his own food, the law compels him to starve if he has not wages, and compels him to go without wages unless he obeys the behests of some employer. It is the law that coerces him into wage-work under penalty of starvation—unless he can produce food. Can he? Here again there is no law to prevent the production of food in the abstract; but in every settled country there is a law which forbids him to cultivate any particular piece of ground unless he happens to be an owner. This again is the law of property. And this again will not be likely to be lifted unless he already has money. That way of escape from the law-made dilemma of starvation or obedience is closed to him. . . . In short, if he be not a property owner, the law which forbids him to produce with any of the existing equipment, and the law which forbids him to eat any of the existing food, will be lifted *only* in case he works for an employer. It is the law of property which coerces people into working for factory owners. . . .[41] (emphasis original)

So-called "economic" coercion is an artifact of law, not of nature. Organized markets and economic coercion within markets have their origins in an act of the state to restrict liberty, the liberty to use and consume resources, by establishing the law of private property.

There is, however, a crucial respect in which economic compulsion differs from what we normally think of as legal compulsion. Legal compulsion normally confronts a party with a narrow set of unpleasant alternatives from which to choose. The choices, for example, might be between confinement at hard labor, becoming a fugitive from justice, or remaining at work, as they were in the case of one of the main legal remedies used to enforce nineteenth-century English wage labor agreements. In most cases if economic compulsion, the universe of alternatives is, at least in theory, much wider. A worker thinking about leaving an employer can try to find another employer, apply for food stamps and Section 8 housing, open a small business repairing cars in the back yard, homestead in Alaska, move to Georgia where there are more jobs, emigrate to Australia, go back to school to retrain, join the army, move in with relatives, play guitar in the subway, and so forth. What is different about economic compulsion is that it is often difficult to evaluate the universe of alternatives that an individual faces. If all the above options are unfeasible, as they often are, and if unemployment is high, the real choices may be much narrower: remain at work and follow orders, apply for welfare, become homeless. The degree of coercion operating in this situation may be as great as the degree of coercion operating when the threat is a mere fourteen-day sentence in the house of correction.

---

[41] [Robert] Hale, "Coercion and Distribution in a Supposedly Non-Coercive State," [38 Pol. Sci. Q. 470], 472–73 [(1923)].

On the other hand, if Australia is desperate for workers and is willing to subsidize passage, provide housing, and guarantee a good paying job, and the unemployment rate in the United States is 2 percent, then the degree of coercion operating in this situation may be practically nonexistent. Therefore it is difficult to characterize this worker's situation in the abstract, because the feasibility and unpleasantness of all the potential alternatives involve highly context-specific information. It is difficult even to compile a definitive list of what all the "real" options may or may not be. It is much easier to evaluate degrees of coercion when the alternatives confronting a party are clearly defined and strictly circumscribed. This is why economic coercion is such a slippery and contestable concept.

But this difference does not make economic coercion natural. The background conditions that constitute the options available to individuals and determine the degree of economic pressure operating in any situation are pervasively shaped by law. Whether welfare is a good, bad, or impossible option depends on welfare law, eligibility rules, and payment standards. It also depends on how welfare rules are administered. Emigrating to Australia may be difficult or easy depending on Australian immigration rules, but it is only an option because American workers enjoy a background legal privilege of leaving the country whenever they wish to work elsewhere. Alaska may be a better or worse option depending on whether the state government has a homestead program, but it is an option because Americans enjoy a legal privilege of settling in any state in the union. Playing guitar in the subway may be more or less feasible depending on vagrancy rules and their enforcement. Taking another job may be a better or worse option depending on how great the demand for labor is. It is only because a worker possesses a background legal privilege of selling or withholding labor in the first place, however, that increased demand for labor can make this a better or worse option. Looking for other work might not be as good an option even when demand for labor is high if immigration restrictions are relaxed or eliminated. If a preparatory course and a license are required to repair other people's automobiles, opening a small shop in one's yard may be more or less feasible. Let's not even mention nuisance law and zoning rules. How desperate workers as a group may be for work depends in good part on how widely liberty is distributed. Even this situation is conditioned to a great extent by a larger set of taken-for-granted background legal rules. Property is so unevenly distributed in part because inheritance laws make it possible for accumulations of property to be preserved over the generations, and so forth.

Law pervasively conditions the universe of possibilities that determine the degree of economic compulsion individuals confront in all market societies. It has long been recognized that governing elites in certain polities self-consciously used restrictions on property ownership and enforcement of vagrancy legislation to drive workers into wage labor, as, for example, in South Africa. What is true about these extreme cases is that in these situations law-conditioned (created) economic compulsion could produce outcomes very similar to those achievable under slave regimes of direct legal compulsion. But in all market societies, an extensive set of background legal rules establishes to a significant degree the real alternatives working people have available, as they decide whether to enter or to re-main at a job. In most market societies, these numerous background rules are not adopted to promote a single end. They are put in place for many different reasons. Regardless of the reasons for their adoption, however, they affect the universe of possibilities open to working people, creating a systematic field of effects. "To govern," Michel Foucault has written, "is to structure the possible field of action of others." In many cases, at least certain of these rules have consciously been adopted with an eye toward inducing laboring people to enter into or remain in wage work. Because these rules can differ significantly in detail from country to country, the magnitude of the pressures facing ordinary people to enter into a particular laboring relationship or to remain in such a relationship can be quite different in different free market societies.

COMMENTS AND QUESTIONS

1. In their article, Schroeder and Shapiro ultimately argue that good information is key to achieving safe and healthy workplaces and that the government should be actively involved in ensuring that good information is provided by employers. Why wouldn't unions bargain for better *information* about workplace risks, even if—as Schroeder and Shapiro conclude—they do not effectively bargain over the risks themselves? As we will see in chapter 10, however, there can be problems here, too. People often have difficulty processing information about risk and may overreact or underreact, depending on how the information is framed (and depending on the perspectives of the person judging whether the reaction is excessive or inadequate).

2. Consider Richard Epstein's response to Hale:

> One way to see the error of Hale's argument is to ask who is coercing whom in any particular negotiation. When a worker does not get a job, he either has received no offer that he finds satisfactory or has been turned down by all the firms to which he has applied. To which firm do we attach our strong sense of disapprobation, and why? When a manufacturer is unable to sell any of its wares, which of the millions of consumers is guilty of coercion, and why? Surely a firm is not coercive because it does not hire every applicant for a given position. Nor are consumers coercive when they do not purchase every different brand of breakfast cereal. So long as scarcity is a constraint on human behavior, it is just wrong for Hale...to treat ordinary refusals to deal...as tantamount to the use of force. Hale's all-encompassing definition of coercion saps the term of both its analytical use and its moral opprobrium.
>
> Nor is there anything inexorable about the outcomes Hale posits. It may be inevitable that people have to make choices as to what to buy and sell, where to work, and whom to hire; but it is not inevitable for people to rob and steal. Only confusion is sowed when the term "coercion" is applied to the two situations indiscriminately. Indeed, to treat market transactions as coercive deprives that term of its necessary and proper sting in cases of aggression and force.
>
> Richard Epstein, *Imitations of Libertarian Thought*,
> 15 Soc. Phil. & Pol'y 412, 433–34 (1998)

Is Epstein's objection that Hale redefines coercion in a way that eliminates a useful pejorative term from our vocabulary? Or is it that Hale's analysis is somehow wrong, even given Hale's (re)definition of coercion?

■ *Progressive Law and Economics and the New Administrative Law*
SUSAN ROSE-ACKERMAN
98 Yale L.J. 341, 357–58 (1988). Reprinted with permission
of Yale Law Journal

The efficiency arguments for risk regulation are powerful, and suggest the need for federal regulation which emphasizes the establishment of minimum standards and the provision of information. The more familiar distributive justifications for regulation (which presume that workers always benefit from stringent rules) are, however, deeply flawed. They are based on a distorted view of the way labor markets can be expected to respond to health and safety regulations. . . .

If . . . relative status matters to workers, and if status is measured by one's position in the ranking of money incomes, then workers may favor direct regulation. In the absence of regulation, workers are caught in a "prisoners' dilemma" and may agree to higher pay in return for accepting greater risks. If everyone does this, no one ultimately benefits. Relative positions remain unchanged. Given this possibility, most workers might wish to bind themselves not to make such deals. While this argument for inalienability is provocative, it requires more empirical testing. Do workers only care about relative money income? Might not workplace conditions also affect relative status? Do highly paid construction workers have higher status than more poorly paid white collar workers?

Second, however one resolves the inalienability issue, one must assess the value of the right to a safe workplace, in the absence of a right to one's job or to a particular wage. As it stands, if a person holds a job with a particular employer, then he or she may not be subjected to certain hazards. Wages, however, can be adjusted to take account of these hazards, and the size of the workforce can be reduced. In a prosperous industry, unionized workers may obtain real short-term gains if firms spend more on health and safety and cannot adjust wages under the contract. Over the long term, however, government regulation of workplace health and safety is unlikely to cause much redistribution. In order for workers to obtain all the benefits, regulation must impose a fixed cost on the firm that is not large enough to cause it to shut down. This will occur, however, only if the firm was earning monopoly profits before regulation was imposed and if marginal costs are unaffected. In more general cases regulation is likely to reduce employment levels and the real value of take-home pay, and to raise product prices even if workers who retain their jobs are better off. Regulation may still be desirable because workers benefit from better health and fewer accidents, but it should not be lightly presumed that the costs of regulation will be primarily borne by owners of capital and consumers. . . .

COMMENTS AND QUESTIONS

1. Rose-Ackerman observes that a "prisoners' dilemma" arises if workers are concerned with relative status. In the classic prisoners' dilemma, it is in the rational self-interest of two or more people to cooperate with each other, but because they lack information about the likely actions of the other people involved, their tendency will be to avoid cooperating. As a result, they will not reap the advantages they would have gained through cooperation. Why does this kind of dilemma arise if workers are worried about relative status?

2. Rose-Ackerman introduces a standard argument that regulation cannot achieve distributional goals. This is the "landlord will raise the rent" problem. (If you impose a warranty of habitability, the only effect will be that landlords will raise the rent to pay for the improvements the warranty requires, thereby making rental housing unavailable to those able to pay for only relatively bad housing.) The following article addresses that problem in some detail. In this article—which is long, difficult, and important—Duncan Kennedy:

   (a) describes an efficiency argument for compulsory contract terms;

   (b) discusses the "landlord will raise the rent" problem, fleshing out the argument that compulsory terms and/or regulation can serve distributive goals (consider for a moment why Kennedy uses the term "distributive" rather than "redistributive"); and

   (c) comments on the relative "appealing-ness" of efficiency, distributive, and paternalist defenses of compulsory terms and/or regulation—roughly, that efficiency defenses are the most appealing in our culture and paternalist ones the least, that paternalist motives actually motivate people much more often, and that it would be a good thing openly to acknowledge that paternalist motives are present and defensible.

■ *Distributive and Paternalist Motives in Contract and Tort Law, with Special Reference to Compulsory Terms and Unequal Bargaining Power*
DUNCAN KENNEDY
41 Md. L. Rev. 563 (1982). Reprinted with permission of Duncan Kennedy

Introduction

The goal of this article is to get at two generally unacknowledged motives that lie behind legislative, judicial and administrative choices about what kind of law of agreements we should have. These are my most important points: First, distributive and paternalist motives play a central role in explaining the rules of the contract and tort systems with respect to agreements. Second, these motives explain far better than any notion of rectifying unequal bargaining power the widespread legal institution of compulsory contract terms in areas such as the allocation of risk. Third, the notion that paternalist intervention can be justified only by the "incapacity" of the person the decision maker is trying to protect is wrong–the basis of paternalism is empathy or love, and its legitimate operation cannot be constricted to situations in which its object lacks "free will.". . .

The decision maker acts out of distributive motives when he changes a rule (or refuses to change a rule) because he wants to increase the success of some group in the struggle for welfare, expecting and intending that this increase will be at the expense of another group (the groups may overlap). The decision maker acts out of paternalist motives when he changes a rule in order to improve someone's welfare by getting them to behave in their "own real interests," rather than in the fashion they would have adopted under the previous legal regime. The decision maker acts out of efficiency motives when he changes a rule so as to induce people to reach agreements that correspond to those they would have reached under the previous legal regime had it not been for the existence of transaction costs.

1. *Distributive Motives*—The first hallmark of distributive motive is that the decision maker accepts the beneficiary's definition of what will make the beneficiary better off. The notion is that the decision maker finds two people engaged in a struggle over the distribution of something that each values. They are operating under the previous regime. He changes the regime in a way that helps one. The second hallmark is that the decision maker sees the situation as zero sum: helping one means hurting the other. Some examples of issues that get discussed in distributive terms are: should secondary boycotts by labor unions be tortious? Should there be a minimum wage? Should issuers of securities have to give potential investors more, or more accurate information than was required by the common law of fraud as it stood in 1929? . . .

2. *Paternalist Motives*—By contrast, where motives are paternalist the issue is false consciousness. As in the distributive case, the decision maker changes a rule because he believes that under the new regime the objects of his benevolence will end up with a set of experiences that will be "better for them" than those they would have ended up with under the previous regime. What makes this change paternalist rather than distributive is, first, that those who have supposedly benefited do not agree that they are better off, and would return to the previous regime if given a choice in the matter. Second, if there are good or bad consequences for others through the paternalist change, these are seen as side effects, rather than as part and parcel of the decision maker's program. . . .

3. *Efficiency Motives*—A decision maker acting from efficiency motives accepts the rules of the previous regime as legitimate from the point of view of fairness, morality, rights, distribution or whatever. His goal is to modify one of these rules so as to make everyone affected better off by their own criteria of better-offness, than they would have been under the old dispensation. This will be possible where transaction costs of one kind or another have prevented parties under the previous regime from making an exchange. If the decision maker knows that this exchange would have occurred, he may be able to induce the parties to perform it by the right modification of the background rules. . . .

Efficiency motives differ from paternalist motives because their premise is that the affected parties will prefer the new situation to the old, so they would not choose to "waive" the benefits the decision maker has attempted to confer on them. The decision maker is not trying to decide what is "really" best for them, without regard to their own views of the matter. On the other hand, an intervention grounded in efficiency concerns will always involve speculation about what the parties "would have done" had they not been prevented by transaction costs.

This is a form of second-guessing that goes considerably beyond what is required when a decision maker acting from distributive motives tips the scales in favor of one combatant and against the other. It falls short of paternalism because the decision maker sees second-guessing as an unfortunate expedient necessary only because of market imperfections, and will abandon an intervention if convinced that the supposed beneficiaries don't want it. By contrast, the paternalist is identified precisely by his willingness to persist when it's clear his contribution is not wanted.

We might distinguish between efficiency and distributive motives on the ground that the first involve making both parties better off, while the second involve helping one at the expense of the other. However, I want to fudge this distinction, and treat as motivated by efficiency some interventions that have negative effects on some actors. In particular, I will treat as motivated by efficiency the following type of action: the decision maker imposes a term in a contract in the belief that if the parties had full information almost all sellers would offer it at a price that almost all buyers would accept. In this case, there are some negative distributive impacts, on those who wouldn't have offered the term and on those who wouldn't have paid for it had we not changed the rule to make them do so. But the motive of the intervention is to make the great mass of buyers and sellers better off by facilitating the deal they would have made absent transaction costs. The negative distributive impact is a side effect like the side effects of paternalist intervention, rather than the whole point of the enterprise. . . .

II. The Three Motives in Context

This part describes the process by which it has gradually come to be expected, if not accepted, within our social context that decision makers will take account of distributive but not paternalist consequences when they make choices about the law of agreements. The first section describes a (perhaps mythical) earlier situation in which the idea of freedom of contract was supposed to provide an exhaustive guide to decision making, resolving in itself all distributive and paternalist issues. The second section describes the breakdown of confidence, again, within this particular milieu, that implementation of freedom of contract could be the single motive for legal action. The third section describes the situation "after the fall" in which we now live, comparing efficiency (proxy for the old regime) and paternalism (still a pariah) with the semi-legitimate status of the distributive motive.

A. Freedom of Contract as the Sole Motive in Decision Making

There is a strand of social and legal theory that argues for freedom of contract as a coherent guide to decision making about the law of agreements, and as the sole legitimate basis for such decision making. The opponents of this position have tended to represent it as having once been the dominant ideology, to castigate it as the conventional wisdom of an earlier period. It is not important for our purposes whether such an earlier period actually existed. The position itself certainly exists; albeit as the view of a minority, and proponents of other views tend to treat it as polar—as one of the extreme or pure cases with respect to which they define themselves. (The other polar position is that thought to be held by "communists" who believe in the collectivization of everything.)

The view I am talking about asserts that it is possible to decide cases involving the law of agreements by reference to the basic principles of free contract. . . . When there is a gap, inconsistency, or ambiguity in the specific rules of agreement, the decision maker can refer to the idea that people don't have to contract, to the idea that they can bind themselves if they want to, and to the idea that they can pick the terms of their contracts, and come up with a solution that will implement freedom of contract by applying it to these particular circumstances. If, for example, the authorities conflict with respect to contract damages, we can consult the underlying notion that people can make binding promises and come up with expectation damages as the presumptively appropriate measure, since the expectancy is the closest we can get to actually carrying out the intention of the parties (short of specific performance, of course).

Supposing that it is possible to resolve all disputes about the law of agreements by applying the basic principles of free contract, there are, in the view I am describing, quite a number of different reasons why we ought to. (One might accept one of these and quite emphatically reject the others.) One might believe that people have a natural right to the outcomes of a free contract regime (with or without a proviso that someone should make sure the initial distribution of property is fair) or that it is immoral to break promises. One might believe that free contract is presumptively (or analytically) efficient, and that the goal of all decision making should be efficiency. Or that the people (through the Constitution or otherwise) have stated their will that freedom of contract be the rule for all decision makers.

It is common when attacking this polar position to assert that it is blind to the distributive consequences of letting people agree to anything they want, and also insensitive to the need to protect people against their natural propensities to error or weakness. But for a believer, one of the greatest strengths of the free contract position is that it takes these objectives explicitly into account, and claims to accomplish them in a manner far more rational than that proposed by the critics. Remember that the exceptions to the enforcement of agreements made for cases of fraud, duress and incapacity are constitutive of the model of free contract. This means that before we decide to enforce an agreement, we have to make a judgment that neither party was overborne by the other, nor tricked by the other, nor so weak or immature in judgment that he lacked free will. To claim that freedom of contract doesn't take into account unequal bargaining power or possible monopoly of information or the congenital folly of some types of contracting parties is just wrong. Allowance for these situations is part of the very definition of the institution.

But it is also part of this polar position that the judgments about coercion, fraud and capacity to contract that are built into the free contract regime should be the *only* judgments on these subjects made by a decision maker administering the law of agreements. The test of legitimacy is voluntariness. If the transaction is voluntary, the decision maker ought not to bring to bear any further criteria of distributive justice or paternalist concern. Once he has made the distributive and paternalist judgments implicit in the constitutive exceptions, he should let well enough alone.

B. Critiques of Freedom of Contract

I think it is fair to say that all the critiques of freedom of contract within our social context are motivated either by objections to the distributive outcomes of nineteenth and twentieth century economic life or by the sense that the masses under capitalism have used what freedom they have against their own best interests. The first idea is that the inequalities all around us, both between racial, class, sexual and regional groups and within those groups, are unjust, irrational and repulsive. But the critical intelligentsia has had to concede a measure of freedom from naked coercion in the choices of the mass of people. There is a sense in which there has never been a culture more the conscious and intelligent product of the mass of people—a more democratic culture—than that of late capitalism. It just isn't plausible to attribute the spiritual vacuity and desolation of that culture (or its vitality, openness and heroic quality) solely to "the profit motive," or even to the "cultural hegemony of the ruling class." There is as well a problem of mass error, of cultural error as judged against an asserted transcendent standard of the true, good and beautiful (a standard that aspires to be free of racist, sexist and class blindness). . . .

The real problem with freedom of contract is that neither its principles, nor its principles supplemented by common moral understanding, nor its principles supplemented by historical practice are definite enough to tell the decision maker what to do when asked to change or even just to elaborate the existing law of agreements. This is not to say the principles or the actual elaborated body of law have no meaning and no influence. Of course they have both. But of course there are also gaps, conflicts, and ambiguities, and in an area like that of the law of agreements the parties themselves will often have a motive for drafting themselves into these areas of uncertainty.

Confronted with a choice, the decision maker will have available two sets of stereotypical policy arguments. One "altruist" set of arguments suggests that he should resolve the gap, conflict, or ambiguity by requiring a party who injures the other to pay compensation, and also that he should allow a liberal law of excuse when the injuring party claims to be somehow not really responsible. The other "individualist" set of arguments emphasizes that the injured party should have looked out for himself, rather than demanding that the other renounce freedom of action, and that the party seeking excuse should have avoided binding himself to obligations he couldn't fulfill.

The arguments on each side take different forms—some are utilitarian, others appeal to rights or fairness, still others work by evoking stylized images of the social world, or by appealing to common moral sentiments, like self-sacrifice and self-reliance. Because the arguments are symmetrical, few in number, and repeated endlessly in different legal contexts, the legally sophisticated decision maker is unlikely to see them as *in themselves* powerful determinants of his own views about proper outcomes.

The experience of gaps, conflicts, and ambiguities within the institution of freedom of contract, and of the availability of two rhetorical modes for arguing about proper resolution of such situations, puts in question the whole structure of rules. Our decision maker has the power to modify the law of agreements as well as to specify it when there is doubt. The same problem of being "unmoored" that exists when all agree the case is one of first impression exists as well whenever someone asks him to look at a *settled* rule as open to question and objection. There will be arguments in favor of changing the status quo in the direction of more altruism, and others in favor of restricting the range of duty to give actors more freedom. The system as a whole is radically underdetermined at least when viewed as the product of a rational decision process rather than of the brute facts of economic or social or political power. . . .

For example, without doing violence to the notion of voluntariness as it has been worked out in the law, the decision maker could adopt a hard-nosed, self-reliant, individualist posture that shrinks the defenses of fraud and duress almost to nothing. At the other extreme, he could require the slightly stronger or slightly better-informed party to give away all his advantage if he doesn't want to see the agreement invalidated when he tries to enforce it later. If we cut back the rules far enough, we would arrive at something like the state of nature—legalized theft. If we extended them far enough, we would jeopardize the enforceability of the whole range of bargains that define a mixed capitalist economy (capital/labor, business/

consumer, and small/large business deals). In either extreme case, we would have departed from freedom of contract—the concept has some meaning and imposes some loose limits. But staying well within those limits, the decision maker's choices in the definition of voluntariness can have substantial distributive effects.....

C. The Hierarchy of Motives "After the Fall"

One might think from the gradual emergence of arguments that *sound* distributive that the milieu of the decision maker had become sharply politicized, at least by contrast to the situation a hundred years ago. This impression would be false. The acceptance of the distributive motive into the discussion of what rules of agreement should be in force has never been more than partial and oblique. This will become clearer when we consider the limited correspondence between an altruist bias in setting the rules and an egalitarian program for the redistribution of wealth. We will then be in a position to compare the status in legal discourse of our three "post-contractual" motives.

1. Altruism Does Not Equal Egalitarianism

Over the whole spectrum of rule changes that have distributive consequences, advocates will argue in terms of the rhetorics of individualism and altruism. This is true for fraud and duress, for the question of how hard or easy it should be to bind another party, for all the issues about the structure of combinations, and for compulsory terms and price fixing. Moreover, this same rhetoric gets applied to lots of other contract issues that are distributive as between the two parties to the dispute, even if they have no obvious long term significance for distribution between social groups. For example, people argue about whether it should be easy or hard to establish excuses for performance by appealing to ideas like sharing, forbearance and forgiveness, as well as to ideas like self-reliance, the right to be let alone, and so forth.

In all these cases, it is easy to confuse the question whether the decision leads to a more equal distribution of income between two groups with the question whether it intensifies duties of mutual regard, sharing, and sacrifice as between contractual partners. That the change in the rule is in the direction of greater altruistic duty does not mean that the rule promotes more equal distribution between groups, nor does the fact that the change in the rule eliminates or reduces people's obligations to look out for one another mean that it will make the distribution of income less equal. The person invoking altruistic rhetoric may be the stronger party, begging the court to make the weaker disclose the few bits of "inside" information that allow him to survive in the face of an otherwise overpowering adversary. When the court goes ahead and honors the ideal of altruism by imposing a duty on the weaker party to disclose, the weaker party may be forced to the wall.

Some disputes about the rules appear to the participants and to observers to have enormous consequences for the system. The parties pour large quantities of resources into the battle, and the rhetoric of the advocates suggests the most exalted principles and the vastest stakes. For many participants in legal culture, these cases provide emblematic instances of the inescapably distributive character of law making. Yet they often involve questions which, when looked at in terms of the long term structure of the game, are close to meaningless. The focus on these "great" cases is, paradoxically, a sign that the decision making process is only superficially politicized. People see law as occasionally, if dramatically distributive, but as in the main an almost invisible neutral background.

Take, for example, the question whether a sale of land in which the seller reserves a right to a share of the profits from every future sale of the land is void as a restraint on alienation. It is obvious that if such clauses are void, sellers who previously used them will no longer use them, but will find some other way, marginally less satisfying perhaps, to extract a share of the long term appreciation of the value of the land. Perhaps they will merely lease rather than sell. If, on the other hand, such clauses are upheld, it is conceivable that there will be an effect on the rapidity of land turnover somewhat analogous to that of the capital gains tax, and equally difficult to assess empirically. Certainly the future of capitalism is not at stake.

Nonetheless, the case in which the question of the validity of the lease is decided, and a series of other cases like it, may have large distributive effects, just because of their one-shot impact on the wealth of the parties. Such decisions are retroactive. It may be that *after* the decision, landlords will quickly find a new way to exploit their tenants. But all those tenants only bound through this particular clause are now free, and the landlords are impoverished by legal disaster just as they might be by a flood. It is little comfort that they will return to the fray with only the most marginal legal disadvantage. What they care about is that a part of their capital has been handed over to the tenants. A series of such decisions can have an effect on distribution not because it "stacks" the rules in favor of the underdog, but because it enriches underdogs who use their gains to avoid finding themselves again on the bottom.

On the other hand, the most widely heralded victory of this type may do the underdogs no good at all if the actual one-shot transfer is small, or if they don't know how to use it effectively in playing the game under rules that are only marginally different than they were before. Even a long string of such victories will be to no avail if each successive accretion of wealth is inadequate to make the subordinate group truly independent, or if the long-run terms of trade are against it, or if it fails to find a way to profit from striking innovations or if there are no guarantees of success in the struggles of civil society.

But what if the rules were changed in such a way as to deliberately bring about an egalitarian outcome? It is clear that it is possible to change the rules to such an extent that distributive outcomes are changed not just casually, but decisively. Such a set of changes would systematically eliminate all altruistic duty of the weaker groups to the stronger, while increasing the duties of the strong to the weak to the point of actually impoverishing them. Where gaps, conflicts, and ambiguities in the rule system had left the relative wealth of groups uncertain, such a policy would settle the rules to enrich the poor. Where this wasn't enough, systematic imposition of compulsory contracts and price controls would reduce the wealth of the rich to meaninglessness by depriving them of legal backing for its effective use. The mere statement of this alternative should make it clear how limited has been the acceptance of the distributive motive.

2. The Partial Legitimation of the Distributive Motive

The demise of freedom of contract has been accompanied by a distinct increase in self-consciousness about the various kinds of consequences of choosing basic rules about agreements. In our social context, actual power to make decisions about the rules usually belongs either to moderate conservatives or to moderate liberals. The liberals have embraced, in a qualified and ambivalent way, the distributive motive, while the conservatives, with equal qualifications and ambivalence, tend to reject it. By contrast, both liberals and conservatives accept efficiency as a good reason for setting a rule one way or another (though they argue about how to define it, and about whether and how to "trade it off" against other goals). Also by way of contrast, neither liberals nor conservatives acknowledge that paternalism (beyond that implicit in the constitutive exceptions to the enforcement of agreements) is a legitimate goal in setting the rules. The distributive motive falls between the general acceptance of efficiency and the general rejection of paternalism. In order to understand this hierarchy of motives, one must relate it to the social context described in Part I.

The appeal of efficiency rhetoric is that it recreates the aura of unproblematic legitimacy that once characterized freedom of contract. The goal of the decision maker is to make everyone better off. He can therefore claim that he is not taking sides in the desperate struggles between social groups. However things were distributed before he acts, he has no intention of disturbing that distribution. Second, the whole basis of his action is figuring out how people would have contracted had they not been prevented by the altogether nonpolitical impediment of transaction costs. The decision maker can present himself as a mere facilitator of what everyone wanted all along, like a motorist giving a ride to a hitchhiker or a neighbor helping out in a flood. No one likes transaction costs: everyone would like to eliminate their effects; if the parties would have made an agreement, there can be no objection to the decision maker forcing them to that outcome, and the upshot is that everyone is happier than they were before.

Efficiency was initially a liberal slogan, with some of the same "radical" overtones that distribution has today. But as the liberals developed it and the conservatives argued against it in contexts like the battle for workmen's compensation or for strict products liability, it became clear that it could be given a capacious definition useful to either side. And each side had reason to exploit it, since it allowed the proponents and opponents of changes to deny that they had any distributive or paternalist motives at all. One can formulate efficiency as, say, "wealth maximization." This concept is so manipulable as to permit the analyst complete leeway to smuggle distributive and paternalist (or anti-paternalist) motives into the analysis without acknowledging them.

There are some negative overtones to its acknowledged pursuit as a goal. It is associated with a preference for the "technical" (or "quantitative" or "mechanical" or "material" or "individualist") over the "human" and the "communal." It is on the side of the engineers and against the poets in the *kulturkampf* of modernity. Poetry vs. engineering easily becomes the worker vs. the factory owner, the farmer vs. the railroad. Nonetheless, it is striking how little strong negative connotation efficiency carries, at least by contrast with distributive and paternalist motives.

Distributive motives are more or less suspect depending on how they are put, but they are always more suspect than efficiency motives. The decision maker operates against a background of class, sexual, racial and regional division and hierarchy: there is some (though never perfect) correspondence between economic interests at stake in rule changes and these group interests; and all groups conceive themselves as engaged in competitive struggle with all other groups. The decision maker is tipping the scales, when he acts distributively, between these groups. But he himself is a member of groups, and has economic interests. Those who don't see him as "one of us" will suspect the minute he begins to speak of distribution, that he is more of a player than a referee, and those of his group begin to worry that he will go over to the enemy.

These are not minor concerns. In the society of which we speak, the unequal distribution of rewards, with its clear though never perfect correspondence to the historical system of class, sexual and racial hierarchy, is the subject of passionate dispute. Peace and happiness seem to require that most of the time we not think at all about the justice of distributive shares. Otherwise, we risk falling into depression, or into a rage, and, in either case, out of sympathy with one another. Or worse yet, we may fall into the kind of sympathy—intense but selective—that leads to civil war. There is therefore a taboo on the explicit consideration of distributive consequences, let alone distributive goals. Law students blush if asked to discuss these matters in the publicity of the classroom.

While these implications of open discussion of distribution make it seem more prudent to put one's decisions on grounds of efficiency (or fairness, or rights, or morality), they also influence the manner in which distribution is mentioned when there's no way to avoid it. On the one hand, the distributive motive is always egalitarian, at least so far as one can tell from the overt discussion. No one advocates a change on the ground that it's regressive. On the other hand, no one advocates a change just because it takes money away from one group and gives it to another less well off. It is much preferable to find a way to describe what one is doing that refers to formal legal equality, or to equality of bargaining power between people identified in terms of their market roles (buyer vs. seller), rather than to the concrete facts of group membership.

My sense is that paternalism is if anything more taboo than distribution as a subject for open discussion in the literature of decisions about rules. And again this is rooted in the realities of group identity and hierarchy. It is not hard to imagine a society in which everybody agreed that there were particular classes of people who were likely to make choices not in their best interests, and that the legal system should protect them from themselves. Indeed, with respect to children and the insane, this is the condition of our society (though the consensus is beginning to break down). The objects of this protection might be in complete agreement that it was necessary. Or imagine a society in which everyone agreed that in particular situations or states of mind, everyone was likely to make mistakes and needed to be protected from themselves. The category of paternalism might come up mainly with strong positive connotations of loving care for others.

What makes it such a hot issue for us is that the system of class, sexual and racial hierarchy derives from an earlier historical experience in which it was not only material rewards but also knowledge, honor and virtue that seemed to be distributed according to the hierarchy. In this earlier system, upper class males believed (and so did most everyone else) that they had superior knowledge, honor and virtue to those below them. They also believed they had a duty to educate those below them to accept the hierarchical system. There was apparently a hierarchical distribution of true consciousness as well as of material welfare, and an element in true consciousness was acceptance of the legitimacy of hierarchy. Upper class males designed the legal order to preserve both the hierarchy of wealth and power and that of true consciousness, all the while claiming that they acted in the true interests of those subordinated.

The decision maker operates in a state of society in which the submerged groups have achieved juridical equality as citizens of the nation, and in which the official ideology proclaims moral equality as a fact, political equality as a goal attained, and economic equality as a possibility open to all. But the situation with respect to knowledge, honor, and virtue is much more complex. Formerly subordinate and still hierarchically inferior groups have asserted through the course of their struggles that the claim of the old elites to true consciousness was a lie. They (or their self-appointed representatives among the intelligentsia) have argued that all groups have equal access to the enlightenment once claimed exclusively by the elite. Or that there are different forms of enlightenment, corresponding to the consciousnesses of different groups, and that all are equally true. Or that the whole notion of true consciousness is wrong, so that there just isn't any way to compare the relative levels of enlightenment of groups. Running throughout is the theme that the consciousness of the old elites was in fact particular to them, rather than universal, and at least as distorted, at least as false, as the modes of consciousness they once rejected (and perhaps still silently reject) as worthless.

When a decision maker explains his action by pointing to the false consciousness of a purported beneficiary, who needs her choices controlled in her own best interests, many people who identify with historically oppressed groups will feel a chill, likely to be followed with a flush of rage, at what looks at least potentially like the repetition of historic injustice. The injustice was (is) twofold, consisting at once of denying practical freedom to the members of the supposedly beneficiary group and denying the validity of their psychic being, their particular experience of intersubjectivity. The word paternalism directly evokes patriarchy, but calling this kind of intervention "parental" or "maternal" wouldn't make anything but a cosmetic difference.

Should the decision maker turn to those who identify with earlier elites, or who see themselves as the elites of the moment, he will find no support at all for paternalist rhetoric. Modern elites rest their claim to an unequal share of wealth and power on the supposed neutrality as between groups of the groundrules of economic struggle. They would doubly undermine that claim were they to applaud the introduction of paternalist motives into legal justification. Paternalism would suggest that they lacked a proper respect for those they dominate. And the rhetoric of paternalism, while focused on the true interests of the beneficiary, is, in the context of agreements, a rhetoric of the restraint of power—the power of the contractual partner of the beneficiary to exploit the beneficiary's incapacity for his own advantage. It suggests the validity of interventions with distributive consequences that would be directly contrary to the interests of the elites. . . .

III. Compulsory Terms: Definition and Typology

This part presents a description and analysis of a particular type of rule change—the imposition of compulsory terms or nondisclaimable duties—which is far more prevalent and more central to contract/tort ideology than any of the types of changes discussed thus far.

A. Contract vs. Tort Duties

Compulsory terms are duties (or sometimes exposure) that come into existence for a legal actor as a consequence of entering some kind of relationship with another legal actor. The other legal actor cannot waive the benefit of these duties. . . .

Compulsory terms also get imposed through tort law, without explicit relation to the provisions of a contract, i.e., without any pretense that the court is merely interpreting the will of the parties or engaging in the mysterious operation of making "necessary implications.". . .

B. Statutory Schemes

There is a body of legislation going back to the progressive period, and now undergoing a revival, that imposes all kinds of compulsory terms in all kinds of specific contracts. The following list is meant to show that the general idea of fixing terms and conditions (while leaving parties free to adjust the price any way they want to) is as fundamental to legislative as it is to judicial policy.

Legislatures have regulated the safety features of food and drugs, airplanes, railroads and boats, automobiles, fabrics for children's clothing, and building materials. They have regulated the design of residential buildings, and of public buildings, in each case indirectly controlling what arrangements the owners of property could make with willing paying customers. They have regulated interest rates, the sale of securities, the structure of financial intermediaries and the contracts between corporations and their shareholders (both in and out of bankruptcy). They have developed whole panoplies of required terms for insurance contracts, the wages and hours of employment, occupational safety and health, occupational licensing, conditions of rental housing, terms of payment and non-payment of rent, consumer credit (truth in lending), security arrangements, door-to-door sales, franchising, sales of condominiums, condominium conversion, mine safety, pension and annuity contracts, union pension funds. They have required workers, as a condition of employment, to lay aside money for their old age, and required employers to join workmen's compensation schemes. This isn't meant to be an all-inclusive list: it's just what comes to mind by free association.

These regulatory schemes are similar, for our purposes, to the contract and tort schemes I discussed above. (Sometimes there is a direct overlap, as where an activist judiciary has reformed landlord/tenant law in partnership with the legislature.) The crucial similar features are: (i) the transaction is regulated rather than prohibited, (ii) the duties imposed are nondisclaimable, (iii) either party remains free not to contract, and (iv) the parties are free to fix the price at which the regulated transaction will occur.

The differences are likely to be the following. Legislative schemes sometimes look to a public agency using mild criminal sanctions to enforce the compulsory terms, rather than relying on the sanction of private lawsuits for damages, or on the sanction of nullification of contracts containing illegal terms. Legislative schemes are more likely to fix quantitatively specific solutions (forty-eight hours to renege on a door-to-door purchase) rather than rely on ad hoc tests of "reasonableness." Legislative schemes are often restricted to a particular transaction type, whereas judicial schemes supposedly have as much analogical scope as they have analogical validity. For our purposes, the similarities are all-important and the differences

inconsequential, and I will hereafter take examples indiscriminately from the two
bodies of law. . . .

IV. Efficiency and Distributive Motives for Compulsory Terms

It is possible to make sense of many regimes of compulsory terms by reference to
efficiency and distributive motives. This part shows how one does this, taking up,
first, efficiency arguments based on the presence of transaction costs and, second,
the various ways in which the distributive consequences of interference with
freedom of contract might appeal to the decision maker. The role of this Part in the
paper as a whole is to provide a perspective for assessing the "unequal bargaining
power" argument which I will criticize in Part V, and to suggest that while there
are good efficiency and distributive reasons for some compulsory terms, there is a
lot left to explain even when these rationales have been stretched to their limits. I
hope this will make Part VI's argument for an ad hoc paternalist explanation of this
type of intervention more plausible than it would be otherwise.

A. The Efficiency Motive for Compulsory Terms under Transaction Costs

Assume it is costly to bargain. Further assume that there are great disparities of
information among parties, and that it costs money to disseminate information.
Assume that it is possible in any given bargaining situation for holdouts and free-
loaders, each acting in their narrow self-interest, to cause negotiations to collapse
altogether, so a deal that would have benefited everyone doesn't come off. It may
now be plausible to explain particular regimes of nondisclaimable duties as motivated by the desire to reduce the efficiency losses these costs create. I will illustrate the way such arguments are constructed, suggest that they depend on easily
manipulable factual assertions, and then argue that the efficiency rationale is very
often no more than a screen for other motives.

1. Two Classic Efficiency Arguments for Compulsory Terms

By now you must be tired of my style, so just for variety I'll introduce the efficiency
argument with excerpts from other peoples' treatments. Perhaps the single most
familiar argument that the imposition of a compulsory term can lead the parties to
the outcome they would have achieved in the absence of transaction costs is the
following:

> [C]onsumers may lack knowledge of product safety. Criticisms of market
> processes based on the consumer's lack of information are often superficial,
> because they ignore the fact that competition among sellers generates infor-
> mation about the products sold. There is however a special consideration in
> the case of safety information: the firm that advertises that its product is safer
> than a competitor's may plant fears in the minds of potential consumers where
> none existed before. If a product hazard is small, or perhaps great but for some
> reason not widely known (e.g., cigarettes, for a long time), consumers may not
> be aware of it. In these circumstances a seller may be reluctant to advertise a
> safety improvement, because the advertisement will contain an implicit rep-
> resentation that the product is hazardous (otherwise, the improvement would
> be without value). He must balance the additional sales that he may gain from

his rivals by convincing consumers that his product is safer than theirs against the sales that he may lose by disclosing to consumers that the product contains hazards of which they may not have been aware, or may have been only dimly aware. If advertising and marketing a safety improvement are thus discouraged, the incentive to adopt such improvements is reduced. But make the producer liable for the consequences of a hazardous product, and no question of advertising safety improvements to consumers will arise. He will adopt cost-justified precautions not to divert sales from competitors but to minimize liability to injured consumers.[14]

This argument is so familiar in the products liability context that it seems obvious. But it is trickier than it seems. In order for it to make sense, we have to assume the following. First, we must be able to determine that the reason for the failure to offer a safety feature is indeed fear of loss of sales to competitors rather than that buyers won't pay the cost of the precaution. This would make out the type of market failure associated with "freeloading": all sellers, and also all buyers, would be better off if they all together added the precaution, but no seller will do so for fear that none of the others will, so that if one goes ahead he will lose sales to the others. Second, we have to decide how we feel about the differential impact on buyers of the compulsory term. Some of them might have preferred the product without the precaution even under conditions of perfect information. These buyers will now either stop buying, or find themselves forced to take something they really and truly don't want. Moreover, there may be some sellers who could have stayed in business just by selling to those buyers, but who are forced out when the decision maker in effect outlaws sale of this product without the precaution. Third, there are distributive consequences for buyers and sellers who stay in the market: it is very possible that sellers will be able to pass along only part of the new cost, so that buyers get the improvement for less than it costs sellers.

It is in the nature of the efficiency motive as I have been defining it that it will require the making of these judgments about the factual situation (what the parties "would have done absent transaction costs") and about the significance of the distributive side effects of the initiative. To get an idea of how much leeway they create for the decision maker, consider the following extension of the argument from products liability to the law of wrongful discharge of an at-will employee:

> [H]igh information costs may be responsible for the failure of parties to establish job security terms. Employees may for a variety of reasons misperceive their best interests at the outset of the employment relationship. For example, employees may tend to discount substantially the risk of wrongful discharge, and as a result systematically undervalue job security. This reflects a common psychological response; since most people prefer not to think about the possibility of disaster, employees understandably tend to disregard the possibility of job loss. In addition, most employees have only limited access to information about personnel relations in a firm and are unable to "shop around" by comparing the firm's relative turnover rate and firing histories. Companies

---

[14] Posner, *Strict Liability: A Comment*, 2 J. Leg. Stud. 205, 211 (1971).

further contribute to the employee's predicament by promoting an image of job security that is not completely accurate. Either a false sense of security or a failure to realize the risks involved may therefore lead employees to seek wage increases rather than forgo some immediate benefits in return for an appropriate level of job protection. Thus, the employees' situation is comparable to the situation of consumers facing a complex product market without adequate information about safety hazards from defective products. In that context, because consumers systematically fail to obtain protection against these risks, products liability law provides them the protection they would purchase were sufficient information available.

The argument here is that there should be a nondisclaimable duty not to discharge wrongfully an employee hired at will, with wrongfulness defined in terms of "bad faith." While a change from the current American law to such a rule would do no more than bring this country into line with the rest of the industrialized world, it seems implausible that anyone would make such a momentous intervention on the basis of speculation about what workers "would have" bargained for if better informed. The author's flat denial of distributive or paternalist intent seems implausible if not downright disingenuous. Nonetheless, there is no *formal* problem with the argument. It is a matter of empirical and normative judgment whether it is valid in this case. . . .

3. General Reflections on the Appeal of Efficiency Arguments

Once they have at least somewhat mastered the technical apparatus, people just love to argue for their favorite proposals on efficiency grounds. For years, it was mainly a liberal fad, then it fell into favor with the conservatives, and the liberals are now trying to reappropriate it. Given a choice, almost everyone seems to prefer to cast a difficult rule change proposal in these terms rather than in those of paternalism or redistribution. The paradox is that the standard objection to paternalism and distribution as motives is that they are intrinsically "subjective," "uncertain," and therefore political and controversial. What this means is that they evoke the unresolved conflicts between groups within civil society about who deserves how much and what is the nature of true consciousness. Regimes of compulsory terms are part of that battle, no matter how carefully we refer to efficiency as the only motive for imposing them, and efficiency arguments are if anything, even more subjective, uncertain, and therefore potentially controversial than the other kinds. Why is it that the patent manipulability of efficiency arguments does not impair their attractiveness, while distributive and paternalist arguments, which are actually easier to grasp and to apply, seem excessively fuzzy?

At least part of the answer, I think, is that the move to efficiency transposes a conflict between groups in civil society from the level of a dispute about justice and truth to a dispute about *facts*—about probably unknowable social science data that no one will ever actually try to collect but which provides ample room for fanciful hypotheses.

Such a transposition from one level to another makes everyone, just about, feel better about the dispute. The move from a conflict of interests or consciousnesses to a conflict about facts makes it seem—quite falsely—that the whole thing is less intense and less explosive. That it is *imaginable* that someone could one day actually produce the factual data makes it seem irrelevant that no one is practically engaged in that task or ever will be. In this sense, the transposition to the cognitive level allows efficiency to act as a mediator of the intensely contradictory feelings aroused by disputes about the shares of groups and the validity of their choices—a mediator that defuses rather than resolves conflict.

It seems obvious to me, but maybe I'm just wrong, that efficiency is also attractive because it legitimates the pretensions to power of a particular subset of the ruling class—the liberal and conservative policy analysts, most of whom are lawyers, economists or "planners" by profession. Efficiency analysis like many another mode of professional discourse, is an obscure mix of the normative and the merely descriptive; it requires training to master, it provides a basis for an internal hierarchy of the profession that crosscuts political alignments. Its high value in legitimating the outcomes of group conflict in "nonideological" terms is the basis for the professional group's claim to special rewards and a secure niche in the good graces of the ruling class as a whole.

B. The Effects of the Imposition of Compulsory Terms

When one first begins to think about what difference it would make if the decision maker imposed a compulsory term in some type of contract (say, a nondisclaimable tenant right to withhold rent if the landlord breached a nondisclaimable warranty of habitability), it is tempting to take at face value the rhetoric of altruism in which such duties are almost always justified. The duty runs from the landlord to the tenant; law has imposed it in order to benefit the tenant, and the expense will fall on the landlord. It seems to follow that the imposition of the duty helps the tenant and hurts the landlord.

For many years, this initial, oversimplified picture of what's going on has been countered by an equally oversimplified response, often called by the shorthand tag, "the landlord will raise the rent and evict the grandmother." By this it is meant that in our case of compulsory duty, the parties remain free not to deal, and free to deal at any price they choose. The critic of compulsory terms will likely claim that their only effects will be (a) to raise the price of the commodity as the seller "passes along" his increased cost (from having to fulfill the new duty) to buyers, and (b) a reduction in supply as sellers realize that it has become more costly and therefore less profitable to provide the commodity in question.

Neither the position that the compulsory term benefits the beneficiary at the expense of the obligor, nor the position that compulsory terms simply raise the price to the beneficiary and reduce the supply, is correct. Each is far too broad. In fact, it is not possible to predict a priori what consequences will follow when the decision maker imposes a nondisclaimable duty. It all depends on the particular conditions of the market for the commodity in question, and its relation to other related markets. . . .

2. Why Don't Buyers Bargain for the Duty?

. . . But if the compulsory term was worth more to buyers as a group than it would cost sellers to provide why didn't the market produce the desired outcome without the help of coercion by the decision maker? . . .

People often object at this point that the reason why the term was not included in contracts prior to its imposition by the decision maker was that buyers as a group lacked enough bargaining power to force sellers to agree to it. This kind of argument is particularly frequent in the area of landlord/tenant: isn't it obvious that the reason landlords didn't provide a warranty of habitability was that they controlled the housing market and tenants were helpless to impose the warranty on them? Or in the case of products liability, it may seem obvious that consumers have always wanted strict products liability, but lacked the bargaining power necessary to impose it on oligopolistic sellers.

At least in the form stated, this argument is just wrong. If tenants were willing to pay the cost to landlords of a warranty of habitability, why would landlords, operating in a capitalist economy in which profit is supposedly the motive of economic activity, refuse to provide it? It seems clear that in the actual housing market, *some* tenants, in exchange for very high luxury rents, obtain levels of landlord service far in excess of those required by any nondisclaimable warranties. If landlords are just perversely, or cruelly, or irrationally unwilling to provide these terms even though tenants will pay for them, how can the luxury rental market exist? I think the conclusion is inescapable that under the assumption that there are no problems of information or other transaction costs, the beneficiaries of compulsory duties could have those duties written into contracts, if they were willing to pay the obligors what they cost (plus a "normal" profit). Under these circumstances, the decision maker makes the duties compulsory or nonwaivable precisely because he believes that people value them so little they won't buy them of their own accord.

It is no answer to protest that landlords or automobile manufacturers have market power, or even that the industry in question is a monopoly. It is no answer to protest that a single buyer of a product, or a single worker dealing with a large employer, can't haggle over the terms and will be told simply to take it or leave it. It is no answer that the seller's lawyers write the contracts. These points are all true, but they are simply irrelevant to the only question here: is it or is it not the case that consumers (under the assumptions) would get the terms if they were willing to pay for them? To take the hardest point first, even a monopolist has an interest in providing contract terms if buyers will pay him their cost, plus as much in profit as he can make for alternate uses of his capital. The presence of a monopoly will generally mean that consumers get less of the product and must pay more for it than would be the case under competition, and this will be true for contract duties as well as for the underlying commodity. But this is not an argument that the unavailability of the term reflects any peculiar unwillingness of sellers to give buyers what they want.

The basic point is that if both sides have good information, it makes no difference that consumers can't haggle in particular transactions, and it makes no difference that the sellers' lawyers draft the contracts. The profit motive will induce them to provide *any* legal duty consumers will pay for. Consumers exercise power in the market not through their conduct during individual transactions, but through the mechanism of *demand*, backed by dollars. They can control according to their desires what is offered for sale even if each of them is individually powerless in every single transaction.

But demand, of course, is limited by income. If buyers had a lot more income, they might well demand all the duties the decision maker is now requiring them to purchase. Buyers as a group may regard a transaction without these duties as a moral horror. They may buy only with deep regret, believing that they have a right to the commodity-plus-the-duty rather than just the commodity. They may believe that a just society would allocate them enough purchasing power so that it was open to them to buy the commodity-plus-the-duty without having to sacrifice some other good they regard as a necessity. In all these senses, it is true that consumers lack the bargaining power to make the sellers provide the duty. *Consumers are too poor*, given the other things they want to do or have to do with their money, to induce sellers to provide something that, under the free contract model, sellers don't have to provide unless the price is right. . . .

C. *Compulsory Terms and the Rectification of Inequality*

The imposition of a regime of nondisclaimable duties on contractual parties will have a host of distributive effects. For example, to the extent that the term is unwanted, its cost will be distributed between the parties, impoverishing sellers and buyers differentially according to the elasticities of supply and demand curves and according to the competitive structure of the market. There will also be distributive effects on third parties. There are third party strangers, for example, who are better off as a consequence of compulsory safety precautions because those precautions reduce the risk of injury to bystanders as well as to buyers.

Then there are third parties who pay into social insurance funds that would compensate injured buyers had the decision makers not forced buyers to insure against injury through the sales contract. There are those dependent on the beneficiaries of nondisclaimable duties such as children whose housing situation is determined by parents. When sales of the regulated commodity fall, there will be workers (and their dependents) in the industry who will lose their jobs or take pay cuts, as well as owners who lose profits. When buyers are priced out of the market, they spend their money on other things, and owners and workers in those industries benefit at the expense of those in the regulated industry.

At least as a general matter, people don't favor or oppose compulsory terms because of these tax-like or third-party effects. What the decision maker really cares about, probably, is the possibility that the class of buyers will get something they want without having to pay the full price, with the difference made up by sellers who are impoverished for their benefit.

A first case in which it is intuitively plausible that a compulsory term can work such a real redistribution is that in which the beneficiaries are so desperately impoverished that they cannot—simply cannot—pay more for the commodity with the term than they did for the commodity without the term, and sellers have some significant surplus from transacting with this impoverished group. Suppose the seller is an employer offering a starvation wage and that the decision maker compels him to improve working conditions or go out of business. If the business is profitable, he may not fire many (or any) workers, and they may end up substantially better off.

A second case is that in which sellers pass along no price increase at all because they are able to modify their own or their employees' behavior, in response to the term, in a way that has no impact on their costs. Take the cost of the firing of at-will employees for refusal of a supervisor's sexual advances. The employer who is liable in tort for "abusive discharge" or "bad faith" is unlikely to increase the price of his product, or demand that workers take a wage cut, to compensate for a lost privilege. He is much more likely just to order supervisors to desist.

In this case, the redistribution is between two classes of workers. But in other cases, there may be a weakening of the sellers' position, but one that they can correct by changes that end up not increasing costs. Where there is periodic product redesign, the addition of a safety feature may have a negligible impact on price. The reason why the feature was not included before was not that it was expensive but that the seller simply didn't care about safety, and had no motive to figure out how it could be incorporated at minimal cost. While in pure theory the seller has devised the minimum-cost way to produce his product, so any modification must increase his costs, in fact there is always a large element of the random and the sloppy in production. This means that even quite large benefits for the buyer may be effected at minimal cost. These cases are only barely redistributive under our definition.

My fourth case is the most important and most interesting because most clearly at odds both with the standard economists' treatment and with the usual formulation of inequality of bargaining power. It is the case in which the condition of the market is such that the imposition of compulsory terms leaves (most) buyers better off in their own view (so that once it is imposed they would not waive the new regime) and this improvement is directly at the expense of sellers as a class. This case was first developed in Bruce Ackerman's important article about enforcement of housing codes. Here I abstract it to compulsory terms in general. Suppose that a significant part of the demand for the product comes from buyers who don't care much about it—who would switch to other things if its price increased only a little. Suppose further that these marginal buyers don't put much value at all on the benefits of the compulsory term. In the housing market case, suppose that there are a number of tenants who tend to double up or move away in response to small variations in local rents, and that these tenants just don't care much about housing amenity—they'll pay close to the same rent for good housing and bad. Now suppose as well that there are a large number of highly competitive sellers who have a large fixed investment in what they sell, so the supply of the good won't change much with moderate increases or decreases in price. Under these conditions it may not be possible for sellers as a group to pass on much of the cost of the compulsory terms. . . .

My conclusion is that a regime of compulsory terms may make perfect sense as a distributively motivated intervention, but that in order for it to do so the decision maker will have to deal (at a minimum) with the following questions:

1. Are the shapes of the curves and the competitive structure of the market such that sellers will have to absorb a large part of the cost of the term?
2. Would buyers willingly buy the term at the price they will have to pay after compulsion?
3. How do we assess the negative distributive impact on the group of buyers priced out of the market, whose loss is necessary if the other buyers are to gain?
4. Are there transaction/information costs that prevent buyers from making an accurate advance judgment about how much good the term will do them?
5. Could the distributive objective be accomplished more cheaply in some other way?

My own belief is that it will often make sense for a decision maker to make rough intuitive assessments of all these factors and then go ahead and act on distributive grounds. It is also possible that he will feel that there is a good chance that he will either accomplish a purely efficient change, making everyone better off, or that he will bring about a desirable redistribution on the model of this subsection. If he thinks the chances are small that he will actually make buyers worse off, he may be happy to proceed on the ground that the only people he is likely to hurt are sellers. When we add the factor of paternalism, considered below, there may be a strong case for intervention even with sketchy information and a lot of uncertainty about just how the effects will play themselves out.

V. Inequality of Bargaining Power

The most common justification for compulsory terms—in tort law as well as in contract—is that there was inequality of bargaining power between the parties. This simple phrase has been used in dozens (perhaps hundreds) of judicial opinions as though it quite fully explained disallowing contract language so as to restore the background regime, or interpolating a term the parties most definitely did not agree to.

There are two disparate strands to the rhetoric of unequal bargaining power. First, because the parties were not equal in power there was no "real" assent—the terms of the contract were dictated by the stronger party—and it is therefore not legitimate to sanctify the bargain by appealing to the idea of free contract. This point is purely negative: now we know there was no real assent, but what follows from that? The decision maker could respond by throwing out the agreement, leaving the parties to their non-contractual remedies, as may happen when a contract is invalidated because of fraud or duress or illegality. But the second element to this body of thought is that what the decision maker does is to rectify the balance not by throwing out the contract as a whole, but by throwing out the offending term, and reading in a term that is more favorable to the weaker party.

What this means is that there is an ambivalence in the way people assert unequal bargaining power to justify compulsory terms. On the one hand, they usually sound as though they were committed to the system of freedom of contract, and to the market system in general. If the objection to this contract is lack of "real assent," it seems to be implied that there is nothing wrong with contracts between people who are on an equal footing. On the other hand, the advocate of compulsory terms will almost always indicate a clear desire to help the weaker party at the expense of the stronger. The rhetoric of unequal bargaining power is distributionist in that it asserts the desirability of intervention in favor of the weaker party in situations where there is nothing like common law fraud, duress or incapacity.

The first section below examines critically the notion that unequal bargaining power is an appropriate test for deciding when to impose compulsory terms. The second speculates about the ideological significance of the rhetoric of unequal bargaining power in a society divided by class, sex and race.

A. Inequality of Bargaining Power in Light of the Distributive Consequences of Compulsory Terms

There are a number of different things people seem to be referring to when they identify a situation as involving unequal bargaining power. What I will do here is to show in very summary fashion that none of these subtests is likely to help us pick out situations in which compulsory terms will help the weak at the expense of the strong. In other words, I want to show that if you just went about finding all the situations that, according to these subtests, represent unequal bargaining power, and in each case imposed on the stronger party the duty the weaker party is asking for in the lawsuit, you would act more or less at random from the point of view of the distributive interests of the beneficiary class ("buyers")....

Neither the drafting of the terms by the seller, nor the seller's offering them on a take-it-or-leave-it basis, nor the absolute size of the seller affects the buyer's power in any sense we should care about. If there is competition among sellers, and good information about buyer preferences, sellers will offer whatever terms they think buyers will pay for. We cannot test the ability of buyers to influence the content of the bargain by the ability of an individual buyer to dicker with an individual seller. There may be no bargaining because bargaining is expensive, and buyers as a group are unwilling to pay the increased cost of individualized transactions. Further, in a truly competitive market, no one gets to negotiate terms with anyone else. You can't argue that market power skews bargains and then object in those very situations where, because of competition, no one gets any individualized say at all.

The notion that size, the knowledge necessary to draft the contract, and the practice of imposing take-it-or-leave-it terms give sellers the power to dictate to buyers is belied by recent experience all over American industry, from automobiles to typewriters. It is ironic that path-breaking cases like *Henningsen v. Bloomfield Motors* justified compulsory terms for auto warranties by emphasizing that the customer was helpless in the face of gigantic bargaining opponents. Those helpless buyers have somehow induced a proliferation of seller warranty experiments, and then more or less destroyed the auto industry by their preference for foreign cars. Detroit can no longer serve as the textbook case of seller omnipotence. While there is a powerful subjective experience of impotence for most buyers in the market for most goods, it is irrational to translate that experience, *without more*, into a preference for intervention.

But what about the distributive effects of using a test of seller size combined with seller dictation of contract terms? Would such a test lead us to impose compulsory terms in those cases where they would redistribute wealth from sellers to buyers? Or would the test lead to higher prices, impoverishing both groups, or even to the enrichment of sellers at the expense of buyers? There's no way to know. The test has no obvious relation to the presence of marginal buyers, quick to get out of the market in response to price hikes and also indifferent to the things the state usually offers in the way of compulsory terms. Size and dictation of terms tell us nothing about whether sellers can easily reduce supply in response to an attempt to stick them with the cost of nondisclaimable duties. Systematically applied, a test of this kind would have random distributional effects between buyers and sellers....

B. The Ideological Significance of the Doctrine of Unequal Bargaining Power

It seems a reasonable conclusion from the above that the notion of unequal bargaining power is of little use to a person seriously committed to achieving distributive objectives through law. I would go further: there is little behind the idea in the way of an intelligent analysis of the general problem of equality, let alone the problem of the quality of life under our form of capitalism. It is nonetheless the case that the idea has great appeal. Why?

The notion of unequal bargaining power is unintelligible except in the context of the perennial conflict between liberalism and conservatism, the center-left and center-right positions within the politics of welfare-state capitalism. In the center-right version of private law, inequality of bargaining power has no place because problems of power are adequately dealt with by the law of fraud and duress—power issues reduce to issues of voluntariness, and are settled by the late nineteenth century formalization of contract law.

Liberals, on the other hand, argue for a dual law of voluntariness. They agree that fraud and duress should be treated as a stable background regime, but argue for ad hoc legislative and judicial intervention outside their bounds. The liberal position is...phrased in terms of freedom of contract (inequality of bargaining power vitiates consent) but quite overtly distributively intended. When, but only when, the test is met, judges should intervene to help the weak against the strong. It is understood that "weak" and "strong" in terms of bargaining power are stand-ins for rich and poor, privileged and oppressed, within civil society.

To understand the doctrine of unequal bargaining power, one must understand that the liberal position is *center*-left, rather than left. Its essence is that reform of exceptional cases and intelligent response to abuses are all that is needed to meet the just demands of the disadvantaged and thereby to relegitimate the overall system of distribution and the overall quality of life. This is a left position in so much as it acknowledges a problem of justice between groups and a problem of the quality of existence, and denies that these problems are solved simply by the neutral administration of the free contract regime. But it is centrist in that it insists (a) that consent (achieved when bargaining power is equal) is the only criterion of the justice of social arrangements (as opposed, say, to actual equality, or the idea of a virtuous life for the citizenry), and (b) that consent in fact validates the overarching structure of our form of capitalism. It follows that whatever one may think of this or that transaction, one sees the basic allocation of power between capitalists, workers, managers, and government bureaucrats, along with the basic cultural underpinnings of family and social life, as beyond the scope of political action.

In this context, the doctrine of unequal bargaining power has the appeal that it presupposes that most of the time there is equal bargaining power, so that freedom of contract is the appropriate norm. It is an exceptional doctrine, unthreatening to basic arrangements, however critical of particular cases. Indeed, the existence of a doctrine that courts will impose compulsory terms where bargaining power is unequal has, along with its left message, a strong centrist message as well. It says that so long as the liberals don't let the idiot conservatives *exaggerate*, it is possible to make a market system like ours work well. When judges and legislatures have corrected the abuses caused by inequality of bargaining power, everything will be OK.

This implicit message of equality conveyed by appealing to inequality is a classic example of the apologetic functions of doctrine. The equality is of "power," so that though we willingly interpolate terms favoring the buyer into an insurance contract, we don't see that as committing us in any way to equalizing people's actual enjoyment of the material things everyone is struggling over. Eliminating inequality of bargaining power, as liberals conceive it, has nothing to do with eliminating factual inequalities. It has no direct reference either to equality in the actual division of transaction surplus between buyer and seller, or to the actual division of social product among the warring groups of civil society. It nonetheless gives a very good feeling.

In this sense, it resembles efficiency: it transposes the deadly fights of social groups to a plane where the issue is merely formal (for efficiency, merely factual). It is not that people are trying to take things away from one another because they think they have been unjustly distributed, or that people are destroying themselves by making wrong choices. It's just that the rules of the game of bargaining have not worked in this particular case, and the outcome is therefore outside the otherwise automatic legitimation of the bargain principle. Given this state of affairs, liberals can be quite unequivocally on the side of the weaker group against the stronger, without abandoning a stance of benevolence or tolerance toward the social order as a whole. . . .

Second, the doctrine minimizes conscious recognition of the distributive motive in private law. It refers only to the "procedural" aspects of the relationship between a buyer and seller. Thus it points us to facts that are quite removed from the real political motive of the liberal decision maker. He doesn't care about "bargaining power" or even about the distribution of transaction surplus between buyer and seller except as a way to shift income between the warring groups of civil society. But for all the doctrine tells us, it is equally applicable to rich and poor, white and black, men and women. It is only in its ad hoc applications that it turns out to be a way for the liberals to help the oppressed (a little bit) against their oppressors.

Third, the doctrine justifies compulsory terms without any reference at all to paternalism. The squabble within the center about whether even a tiny modicum of distributive motive is acceptable distracts attention from what is probably the most consistent and important effect of these regimes: the overruling of preferences on the basis of a particular substantive moral vision of how people should deal with risk in their lives. As we saw earlier, the paternalist motive is even more difficult to acknowledge, and prima facie even less legitimate than the distributive. Inequality of bargaining power masks it by presenting as a defense of the weak what is often in fact a critique of their spending habits.

Finally, I should say something positive about the motives of the liberal lawyers, judges and legislators who developed the doctrine of unequal bargaining power. The doctrine exists not in a vacuum but as a weapon in the war against the conservative program of reinforcing all kinds of social hierarchy. It may be internally incoherent, and it may achieve only rather randomly good results even when used skillfully. But it is a weapon on the side of equality, of the left and not of the right, however imperfect. . . .

VI. Paternalism

A. Paternalism and Compulsory Terms

1. How Compulsory Terms Work as Paternalism

In a sense, paternalism is the most obvious of motives for compulsory terms, though because of its pariah status it is usually mentioned last, if at all. A compulsory term requires people to make particular contracts when they would rather make different ones. Because the term typically creates a duty for one party that, on its face, helps the other party, the situation bears at least a superficial similarity to classic protective relationships. And because the seller/promisor/obligor is allowed to raise the price in response to imposition of the nondisclaimable duty, there may be no redistributive effects between buyer and seller, so that a distributive motive is not necessarily present.

Paternalism involves compelling a decision on the ground that it is in the beneficiary's best interest. Regimes of compulsory terms typically involve duties that fit easily into this general conception: people often say that it is in your best interests to take the warranty rather than a lower price; to insist on a lease with a landlord's duty to maintain the premises, rather than just signing whatever he hands you; to demand full disclosure before consenting to surgery; to get yourself some job security rather than working on an at-will basis; and so forth.

For an intervention to be paternalist, the distributive effects have to be "side effects" rather than the purpose of the initiative. It may not be obvious whether a particular change following intervention should or should not count as a side effect. For example, the intervention means, in the typical case where the term reduces or insures against a risk, that those who get compensated (or saved from injuries that would otherwise have befallen them) because they were compelled to buy protection gain at the expense of those who, it turns out, don't need the protection but had to pay for it anyway. In other words, if we analogize the term to insurance, those who wouldn't have self-insured but are injured gain at the expense of those compelled to insure against things that never happen to them. But we have to subtract from this distributive effect the benefits to the uninjured in the way of psychic security that come from knowing they are covered (even though the coverage is compelled).

A second distributive effect is that some buyers are priced out of the market now that sellers have raised their price in an attempt to recoup the cost of the compulsory term. From a paternalist perspective, this may not be an undesirable side effect, but a part of the paternalist program. If we really believe that those buyers were not acting in their best interest when they bought the commodity without the term, then they may be better off priced out of the market than they were when we let them stay in it. . . .

2. Varieties of False Consciousness "Cured" by Compulsory Terms

To say that an intervention is paternalist doesn't explain it beyond identifying the problem as a mistake on the part of the beneficiary about his real interests, or as false consciousness. Decision makers in our society impose compulsory terms because they think buyers suffer from a number of quite specific kinds of false consciousness. For example, buyers underestimate the seriousness of risks of injury from products or situations. The tendency to underestimate risk goes far enough beyond mere misinformation so that when we intervene we can't claim to be achieving an efficient outcome blocked by transaction costs. It amounts to a cognitive bias, a systematic tendency to misinterpret or ignore information, to generate fantasies of safety, to repress unwanted information. It has to do with babyishness, not ignorance. When the decision maker makes the buyer pay for protection against the non-negligent injury, or makes the buyer buy a safety precaution that will prevent injury happening at all, he may be doing so in response to a judgment about this kind of misperception.

But it may be that he is concerned not with a misperception of risk, but with willingness to take risks—with recklessness rather than with babyishness about the facts. He may decide that looking at the buyer as a person with a continuous existence in time, as a life rather than as an instant, he can make the buyer better off by forcing him to give up a little now in order to avoid catastrophe later on. That the buyer doesn't think so may be a mistake that seems just a matter of character, or it may be possible to develop an interpretation of the buyer's situation that makes the mistake easy to understand. For example, the buyer may appear to the decision maker to be suffering from addiction, not in the narrower opiate sense, but in the larger sense of needing a continuous flow of commodity fixes in order to keep at bay the pain of being dominated at work or in the family.

Buyers make a third kind of mistake when they fail to obtain guarantees of nonarbitrary treatment. Take the case of consumer remedies and consumer defenses waived by contract, or of extremely favorable creditor remedies written into contracts, or of clauses by which one party determines the venue of any lawsuit favorably to himself, or sets liquidated damages or conditions that create real risks of forfeiture. We have once again the two distinct errors of misperceiving the risk that the terms will be invoked, and of placing too high a discount on the possibility of future loss. But this case also involves a willingness to trust one's present partner to treat one fairly further down the road, when what now seem like congruent interests have begun to diverge. The buyer allows the seller to con him—to make it seem unlikely that there will ever be an occasion to which the terms would be relevant, and that if there were, the seller can be trusted to act reasonably in the circumstances, rather than standing on a legal right to treat the buyer unfairly.

A fourth type of mistake has to do with the long term consequences of choosing a particular structure for a relationship. Recall the example of the buyers who agreed to give the seller a percentage of the appreciation any time they sold the land, a term struck down by a very conservative New York court. This clause, along with the others in a purported "sale" in fee simple, was designed to, and to some extent did, bind the buyers to the land as though they had been (though, of course, in fact they were not) the feudal serfs of the great landlord patron sellers. Or think of the systems of criminal penalties for violating a labor contract that the courts have from time to time struck down as peonage. And why is it that, even before the fourteenth amendment, courts wouldn't enforce a contract of enslavement, though it met the most extreme tests of voluntariness? In all these cases, the objection is not to running a specific risk of loss, or to running a specific risk that the seller will treat the buyer unfairly. The objection is to the whole relationship—it is an objection to *feudalism*, a way of life, or to *slavery*, a way of life. It makes no difference that if we apply to their actions the same tests of voluntariness we apply to our own, some people may sometimes want to be peons. We won't let them be.

The false consciousness involved is in part that people who agree to work a whole lifetime for the same employer on an at-will contract without any provision for their retirement have underestimated how seriously dependent they will be. Had they not been mistaken, they would have risen in revolt, or they would have scrimped and saved. It is no answer to say that they just couldn't scrimp and save. Social Security made them, and then it turned out that they could in fact survive with a deduction that was (more or less) enough to provide for retirement. The problem was not that it was impossible to demand and win job security or a pension plan, but that the social world of day labor, for example, was based on the unspoken assumption that these things couldn't be had. It was based on a consciousness in which a higher wage in the short run was preferred to what the middle-class decision maker saw as the slighted human need for security, which would be in turn the necessary practical basis for the affirmation of equality with an otherwise all-powerful employer....

2. Critique of Principled Anti-Paternalism

The principled anti-paternalist admits readily that one sometimes has to overrule another's choice in his best interest, but argues that those cases are explained by incapacity, or perhaps by another similar principled exception to the general idea that people are autonomous. (Likewise, the principled paternalist will argue that there are some cases in which people should be allowed to choose on their own—the two positions are indistinguishable for the purposes of my argument here.) The plausibility of principled anti-paternalism is therefore linked to the ability to dismiss or explain away cases in which one wants to act paternalistically but can't rationalize the action in terms of incapacity. My basic argument is that when one collects the cases of paternalist intervention that can't be plausibly explained by a notion like capacity, it becomes clearer that we can't be any more than ad hoc in our opposition to intervention....

Suppose that you are spending the weekend at the house of an old woman— perhaps but not necessarily your mother, perhaps but not necessarily someone you love deeply—who is in the terminal stages of cancer. She has an attack of breathlessness. Gasping, she tells the people present that she doesn't want to go to the hospital, but to stay put and die "with dignity" in her own bed. The others are simply paralyzed by this demand, and by the tone of building hysterical fear in which she expresses it (you think; you may be wrong). You want to take the woman to the hospital. You tell her you are going to do so, whether or not she agrees. She looks you carefully in the eye, and then, without any positive indication of assent, begins giving instructions about what she wants taken along with her in the car. She goes to the hospital, but is back at home in a day or two, and some weeks later she does die with dignity in her own bed.

After it was over, you might tell the story this way: the old woman had thought about that moment a lot in advance, and she was much less upset by her breathlessness than any of those around her. I felt a cold band of panic around my chest. I was on the phone to the ambulance service while the others were trying gently to persuade her. Then they started yelling at each other. She looked at us with contempt and resignation as her death worked its infantilizing effect on us. I intervened forcefully. In the car, she was silent, already in the grip of the humiliation and fear she knew she would feel in the emergency room and then in her private room after they hooked her up to the machines. She came home a few days later, but her spirit was sort of broken (not completely) and she didn't really trust us that much any more. She let us have our way with her death.

The problem with the notion of capacity in a setting like this one is not that it's positively wrong—just that it doesn't help. The strategy is to divide the decision into two parts, hoping that will make it easier than if the question whether to act is treated as a single whole. First, we try to decide whether the other possesses a trait or quality called "ability to determine her own best interests." If she does, we accede to her wishes even if in that particular case we are convinced that her action is *not* in her best interests. If it were truly easier to decide the presence or absence of the quality of capacity than to decide on balance whether we should intervene, treating that question all together, then capacity would be useful. But the question of capacity is hopelessly intertwined with the question of what the other wants to do in this particular case.

First, there is no such "thing" as capacity, and there can be no such thing as its "absence" either. We ask the question of capacity already oriented to the further question whether we will have to let the person do something injurious to herself. There is no other reason to ask the question. Now, if you ask me to *answer* the question without knowing what the potentially injurious thing is, it seems to me I should refuse. I don't believe that capacity exists except as capacity-to-make-this-decision. But as soon as I am deciding the issue of capacity-to-make-this-decision, I find myself considering all the factors, testing my intuition of the other's false consciousness, the severity of the consequences, the possibility that I want to render the other dependent through paternalism, just as I would if I frankly admitted at the beginning that it's just a big mess, with no principled way to find your way through.

I come back to ad hoc paternalism, by which I mean that in fear and trembling you approach each case determined to act if that's the best thing to do, recognizing that influencing another's choice—another's life—in the wrong direction, or so as to reinforce their condition of dependence, is a crime against them. Of course, I haven't proved the impossibility of a principled anti-paternalist stance. I think I've undermined the idea that we can decide when to act and when not to act through a notion like: "Do not overrule the choice of a person who has the capacity to choose on their own," but that doesn't prove there aren't other principles, or that someone won't soon discover other principles even if none are currently extant. My strategy is not one of proof, but of offering a lot of material to make it plausible that principled anti-paternalism is a shallow view. This seems a good point at which to bring all that material together.

First of all, it is impossible for a decision maker operating within a regime of freedom of contract to adopt a stance of neutrality in the conflict between paternalist and anti-paternalist tendencies. The paternalist notion that contracts shouldn't be enforced if one party lacks capacity is constitutive of the institution of freedom of contract. We don't have a system based on voluntariness without it. In other words, for the decision maker to do his job of applying the background regime, even supposing he has no desire to change the rules of free contract, he will have to decide whether any given case falls within the constitutive exception that exempts agreements from enforcement on paternalist grounds, or within the part of the doctrine that insists people have the right to make any contract they want to. If it turns out the decision maker can't be either a principled anti-paternalist or a principled paternalist, he will have to be an ad hoc paternalist, just in order to carry out his job of filling gaps, resolving ambiguities and settling conflicts about the rules of the free contract regime. . . .

The single most important piece in the quilt of arguments in favor of ad hoc paternalism is the pervasiveness of compulsory terms, in contract, in tort and in statutory schemes. These make up a large part of our whole legal order. So long as one can see them as responsive to unequal bargaining power, they don't raise any issue of paternalism. But unequal bargaining power is of little use in understanding why we like them. They may redistribute income in a desirable direction. But given the peculiarity of the conditions that must obtain if they are to have this effect, and given the hopeless fluidity of the efficiency arguments on their behalf, it seems clear that a large part of the burden of justifying them fails on the general notion of paternalism. The principled anti-paternalist will have to give an account of each nondisclaimable duty in terms of incapacity, or of some other principled exception, or restore freedom of contract.

My hope is that the accumulating weight of the examples will drive the principled anti-paternalist at last into the camp of the ad hoc. Paternalism everywhere, coming out of the woodwork, suggests that the satisfying clarity of one's initial anti-paternalist reaction is made possible only by excluding most of the problem from consideration. Principled anti-paternalism is a defense mechanism. One way to deal with the pain and fear of having to make an ad hoc paternalist decision— one way to deny the pain and fear—is to claim that you "had" to do what you did because principle (say, the principle of incapacity) required it. That the principle doesn't really work is less important than that it anesthetizes.

There are some cases we can't seem to decide the way we want so long as we adhere to our principled anti-paternalism, even given the manipulability of the notion of capacity. We decide these cases paternalistically, to our credit, but then bury them under other rubrics, such as protection from "unequal bargaining power," so we won't have to confront their challenge to our supposed consistency. The truth of the matter is that what we need when we make decisions affecting the well-being of other people is correct intuition about their needs and an attitude of respect for their autonomy. Nothing else will help. And even intuition and respect may do no good at all. There isn't any guarantee that you'll get it right, but when it's wrong you're still responsible.

3. Paternalism in Public vs. Private Life

When issues of paternalism arise in the context of "private life," the actor is likely to know the other, even to know the other well, and to have a claim to intuitive understanding based on common experience. But the decision maker whose dilemmas we have been examining throughout this essay is a state official deciding cases for people in the abstract, people situated each in his or her particular way in a society divided by class, race, and sex. One might concede that in the private context of intimate knowledge of the other, ad hoc paternalism is unavoidable, but still favor a rule against it in this more complicated situation. . . .

The farther apart they are culturally, the more likely it is that the actor will perceive "mistakes" or false consciousness on the part of the others that they won't recognize as such no matter how much data he lays on them, because they involve basic premises about the world, truth, and the good. Paternalist intervention based on a strong intuition that the supposed beneficiary is wrong on this level—say, in believing that the way to mourn her husband is to throw herself on his funeral pyre—has the unfortunate property of being simultaneously the most imperatively required (when it is required) and the most imperatively forbidden (when it's wrong or officious). In other words, as we move from the personal, private level into the area of relations between large groups that are parts of a single society, the stakes get higher—both for action and for inaction.

It is that the risks escalate *on both sides* that for me ultimately undermines the case for anti-paternalism in public life. This is a difficult point: I want to put it tentatively. It seems to me that the decision maker setting the groundrules as a state actor in a society such as ours, riven by group divisions that are divisions of consciousness, is one of the few people of whom we can demand that he represent our collective commitment to the transcendence of pluralism in the name of truth. . . .

A decision maker who will not take the risk of imposing housing codes and then enforcing them through tenant remedies—just on the grounds that people are wrong to submit to these conditions—because he doesn't feel confident about what the poor "really want," has let a constituent group slip outside his capacity for intimate intuitive knowledge. Since refusing to act paternalistically involves him in applying state force to execute the law of contracts or torts against those who would have been the beneficiaries of paternalism, he can't claim he's practicing benign neglect. What he's doing, if he tries to be a systematic anti-paternalist in public life, is denying his knowledge of the relative incapacity of groups, of their characteristic mistakes. He is acting to deepen their incapacity by treating them as entitled to their mistakes, and then bringing to bear the apparatus of the state to evict them from their subcode apartments, exclude them under the law of trespass from power over the means of production they created through their labor, and leave them to beg for crumbs when accidents they didn't provide for befall them after all.

COMMENTS AND QUESTIONS

1. Consider Kennedy's translation into the employment-at-will context of Posner's efficiency argument for regulation, and translate it once again into the context of workplace safety and health by developing a parallel efficiency argument for banning the use of a particularly hazardous chemical in the workplace. Kennedy argues that Posner's argument, his, and presumably yours (if you have done it right) are all formally correct, but that they do not capture the true motivations people have for supporting regulation. Do you agree? Kennedy also argues that the apparent preference for formally correct efficiency justifications has ideological significance. Again, do you agree?

2. Kennedy's analysis of how regulation can achieve distributive ends identifies two kinds of distributive effects, one among classes of buyers and workers and another between buyers and sellers (or workers and employers). Note the conditions Kennedy identifies as necessary for the latter type of effect to occur. [Kennedy's analysis is confirmed by a more mainstream economic analysis in Richard Craswell, *Passing on the Costs of Legal Rules: Efficiency and Distribution in Buyer-Seller Relationships*, 43 Stan. L. Rev. 361 (1991).] Do you have any sense of how often those conditions are likely to be satisfied? After thinking about the preceding question, consider Kennedy's observation that policy decisions on these matters are likely to be based on empirical judgments that are rarely backed up by empirical evidence.

3. Is it possible to reconcile libertarian and paternalist impulses? Consider the following argument, offered by Cass Sunstein and Richard Thaler:

> Libertarian paternalism is a relatively weak and nonintrusive type of paternalism, because choices are not blocked or fenced off. In its most cautious forms, libertarian paternalism imposes trivial costs on those who seek to depart from the planner's preferred option. But the approach we recommend nonetheless counts as paternalistic, because private and public planners are not trying to track people's anticipated choices, but are self-consciously attempting to move people in welfare-promoting directions. . . . [O]ne of our principal targets is the dogmatic anti-paternalism of numerous analysts of law, including many economists and economically oriented lawyers. We believe that this dogmatism is based on a combination of a false assumption and two misconceptions.
>
> The false assumption is that almost all people, almost all of the time, make choices that are in their best interest or at the very least are better, by their own lights, than the choices that would be made by third parties. This claim is either tautological, and therefore uninteresting, or testable. We claim that it is testable and false, indeed obviously false. In fact, we do not think that anyone believes it on reflection. Suppose that a chess novice were to play against an experienced player. Predictably the novice would lose precisely because he made inferior choices—choices that could easily be improved by some helpful hints. More generally, how well people choose is an empirical question, one whose answer is likely to vary across domains. As a first approximation, it seems reasonable to say that people make better choices in contexts in which they have experience and good information (say, choosing ice cream flavors) than in contexts in which they are inexperienced and poorly informed (say, choosing among medical treatments or investment options). So long as people are not choosing perfectly, it is at least possible that some policy could make them better off by improving their decisions.
>
> The first misconception is that there are viable alternatives to paternalism. In many situations, some organization or agent must make a choice that will affect the behavior of some other people. There is, in those situations, no alternative to a kind of paternalism—at least in the form of an intervention that affects what people choose. We are emphasizing, then, the possibility that people's preferences, in certain domains and across a certain range, are influenced by the choices made by planners. The point applies to both private and public actors, and hence to those who design legal rules as well as to those who serve consumers. As a simple example, consider the cafeteria at some organization. The cafeteria must make a multitude of decisions, including which foods to serve, which ingredients to use, and in what order to arrange the choices. Suppose that the director of the cafeteria notices that customers have a tendency to choose more of the items that are presented earlier in the line. How should the director decide in what order to present the items? To simplify, consider some alternative strategies

that the director might adopt in deciding which items to place early in the line:

(1) She could make choices that she thinks would make the customers best off, all things considered.
(2) She could make choices at random.
(3) She could choose those items that she thinks would make the customers as obese as possible.
(4) She could give customers what she thinks they would choose on their own.

Option 1 appears to be paternalistic, but would anyone advocate options 2 or 3? Option 4 is what many anti-paternalists would favor, but it is much harder to implement than it might seem. Across a certain domain of possibilities, consumers will often lack well-formed preferences, in the sense of preferences that are firmly held and preexist the director's own choices about how to order the relevant items. If the arrangement of the alternatives has a significant effect on the selections the customers make, then their true "preferences" do not formally exist. . . .

The second misconception is that paternalism always involves coercion. As the cafeteria example illustrates, the choice of the order in which to present food items does not coerce anyone to do anything, yet one might prefer some orders to others on grounds that are paternalistic in the sense that we use the term. Would anyone object to putting the fruit and salad before the desserts at an elementary school cafeteria if the result were to increase the consumption ratio of apples to Twinkies? Is this question fundamentally different if the customers are adults? Since no coercion is involved, we think that some types of paternalism should be acceptable to even the most ardent libertarian. . . . To those anti-libertarians who are suspicious of freedom of choice and would prefer to embrace welfare instead, we urge that it is often possible for paternalistic planners to make common cause with their libertarian adversaries by adopting policies that promise to promote welfare but that also make room for freedom of choice. To confident planners, we suggest that the risks of confused or ill-motivated plans are reduced if people are given the opportunity to reject the planner's preferred solutions.

The thrust of our argument is that the term "paternalistic" should not be considered pejorative, just descriptive. Once it is understood that some organizational decisions are inevitable, that a form of paternalism cannot be avoided, and that the alternatives to paternalism (such as choosing options to make people worse off) are unattractive, we can abandon the less interesting question of whether to be paternalistic or not, and turn to the more constructive question of how to choose among the possible choice-influencing options. . . .

Cass R. Sunstein and Richard H. Thaler, Libertarian Paternalism
Is Not an Oxymoron, 70 U. Chi. L. Rev. 1159 (2003)

Sunstein and Thaler propose that people be allowed to opt out of arrangements set by planners, whereas Kennedy argues in favor of compulsory terms. But on a broader level, is Sunstein and Thaler's "libertarian paternalism" any different from Kennedy's paternalism?

4. Should we be as comfortable with paternalist motives as Kennedy urges? (How comfortable does he urge us to be?) The specter in all this is Stalinism— the imposition by an elite of its views of what people "ought" to want, in the face of people's real desires. To what extent are workers' compensation systems best understood as expressions of paternalism? The last lines of Rose-Ackerman's article—presented earlier in this chapter—suggest that regulation can be defended on paternalist grounds. The next reading describes and to some extent defends the proposition that paternalism is morally permissible. It is followed by a brief reading on international paternalism and some notes that raise questions about the defensibility of paternalism.

■ *Paternalism and Public Policy*
BILL NEW
15 Econ. & Phil. 63, 77–81 (1999). Reprinted with permission
of Cambridge University Press

...First, the state could be argued to be more *impartial*, or 'phlegmatic', than an individual. This justification relates to the 'weakness of will' and 'emotional' categories of failure of rationality....Unlike individuals, the state is not swayed by immediate gratification. The choice between a luxurious holiday now and provision for retirement in the future does not involve a difficulty of temptation for the state. It can consider the evidence of decisions made by a large number of individuals who do take out insurance, and on the experience of those people who may regret not doing so. Because it is not swayed by difficulties of weakness of the will, the state may be in the best position to judge that the minority who would otherwise choose to forgo the long-term benefit should be compelled to provide for their future.

Clearly public officials are confronted with temptation to abuse or further their own interests. However, the point in this context is that they do not suffer from temptation in relation to the particular form of immediate gratification faced by the citizen, when they make certain decisions on the citizen's behalf. The public official may be in an advantageous position whenever the good in question involves a significantly delayed 'payoff', that is, its benefits accrue at some point in the future, such as pensions, health care and education.

Second, the state could be argued to have a wider *perspective* than individuals. This relates to the 'lack of experience' failure of rationality....In its position of ultimate responsibility for the welfare of its citizens, the state will typically respond when claims are made on it by those in severe hardship....[I]ll-health and death may be the result of some aspect of personal behavior such as not wearing a seatbelt. The state and its employees are presented with the consequences of this kind of behavior in a way that many individuals will not be (or not until it is too late). Although public employees have not necessarily experienced being in a car crash without a seat belt—no one but the unfortunate crash victim can claim that—they are in a position which makes it possible to empathize more accurately with this unfortunate experience than the car driver who has never suffered an accident. The state is therefore in a better position to make a judgment on the prudence of seat belt wearing than those simply presented with information on abstract possibilities.

It is not that the costs of rescuing individuals who fail to wear seat belts fall on the state, thus providing an incentive for the state to coerce them into doing so (after all, a consistent state which opposed paternalistic policies would not rescue and pay for the individual's treatment). This particular justification rests on a belief that the state is actually in a better position to weigh up the costs and benefits (of not wearing a seat belt) than an individual who at any point in time will only see one side of the picture.

Finally, the state is at an advantage in being able to dedicate able people to consider certain questions, if necessary over long periods of time. This justification relates to the 'technical inability' failure of rationality. . . . Thus, where a decision is subject to particularly complex, technical or large-scale information difficulties, the state has the resources to employ those best able to devote themselves to the problem full time. For example, in the case of airline safety there may be only a few people who are technically able to assess what would be the outcome of certain standards of safety specification; the rest of us could simply never make more than a guess. Clearly, the 'state' will need to make a judgment which then applies to everyone—in this case on the particular level of safety which is deemed a minimum acceptable. This would not be what everyone would choose, given different degrees of risk-aversion. But it seems reasonable, under conditions of complex information, that by removing the possibility of significantly mistaken calculation of risk, welfare will be improved by state paternalism. Note that this is not simply a matter of 'imperfect' information and therefore a question of market failure. Ensuring that all the relevant details relating to safety were made public to all potential consumers, and monitoring the information for its accuracy, would not be sufficient. The ordinary consumer would simply not be able to assess the implications of this information even if he or she had unlimited time in which to scrutinize it.

Where decisions based on probabilities or statistical assessments are concerned, even when the nature of the decision appears to be of no great complexity, people very often make erroneous judgments. Again, the information provided to citizens may be 'perfect'—they need no extra or qualitatively improved information— but the experimental evidence suggests that individuals commonly display inadequate reasoning power to make the correct calculations (Tversky and Kahneman, 1982).

So the state, via the actions of its public officials, may have an advantage over the 'private' citizen in judging what is in that individual's best interests in the following circumstances: when there is significant temptation to satisfy immediate wants above those with long-term benefits; when the individual is not likely to have had first-hand experience of the consequence of a decision; and where an unusual degree of technical expertise is required. Some goods and services seem to be particularly problematic with reference to these conditions:

- goods or services with long-term rather than immediate effects (which require phlegmatic decision making, such as providing for one's pension in old age);
- goods or services for which there is a small chance of seriously harmful consequences occurring for any one individual (which require a wide perspective, such as wearing a seat belt);

- goods or services which involve complex or large quantities of information to be processed before a judgment is possible on the likely impact on welfare (which require technical ability, such as assessing airline safety standards).

Goods which satisfy more than one of these characteristics may provide a particularly strong case for paternalistic intervention by the state. Providing for health care services is a case in point. The first two categories clearly apply: buying health insurance provides delayed welfare for an occurrence which is relatively unlikely but has extremely serious consequences. Thus, the state is justified in compelling some form of health insurance.[6]

There are at least two sets of criticisms of this approach to justifying paternalistic state intervention. The first asks: why the state and not some other organization or individual? Why is it that other institutions, such as unions or family members and friends, are not able to undertake this role? They certainly seem to act in a paternalistic fashion in many cases. An individual can hide the keys of his brother's car because he thinks he is too tired to drive. A health farm can withhold certain items of food from what is on offer in its restaurant. Trade unions and employers can agree that anyone who works at a firm must be a member of the union. An insurer may require that a seat belt is worn (in the absence of a legal requirement) for the insurance to be valid. Some of these agencies display the characteristics described above for the state. Others, particularly friends and family, may have a more intimate knowledge of the paternalized individual.

These acts of 'paternalism', however, are constrained by the need to acquire a degree of consent from the individual concerned. Only the state has a monopoly of legitimate coercive power. If interference in the decision-making autonomy of an individual is necessary to increase welfare, then state action is the only means to ensure its application. Furthermore, since such interferences are inherently controversial it is important that they are debated publicly and that those enforcing the interference are publicly accountable. Simply allowing one individual to impose their will on another allows scope for abuse.

A second set of criticisms of the approach described above is that it paints an unrealistically sanguine picture of the motivation of the state and its agents. The state as portrayed here is an effortlessly neutral institution, with nothing other than the good of its citizens to complicate the decisions it makes. This is certainly simplistic, and ignores the criticisms of the public choice school and in particular those of Niskanen (1971) who argued that the 'selfish' motivations of those who worked in the state would, in general, mean that state agencies over-provide services and try to maximize budgets. Such theories, which have gained much credibility over the last twenty years, clearly throw doubt on the above model, because a paternalistic policy might simply be a means of budget maximization rather than a genuine attempt to improve welfare. However, the objective of this paper has

---

[6] There is also the problem of highly technical and complex medical information, often involving probabilities, being hard to process. This requires technical 'experts' (doctors) to assist in making these decisions. Given the power this offers the doctor in controlling the consumption decision, there is a case for the state regulating the provision of medical services, such that only professionally qualified and controlled clinicians are allowed to practice—thus disallowing the individual from 'taking a chance' with a cheaper doctor.

been to discuss the potential for the state to act in a justifiably paternalistic way; the intention has been to establish why, in certain circumstances, the state has particular characteristics which might enable it to make decisions better than an individual. Other problems of state intervention do, of course, remain.

■ *Risk by Choice: Regulating Health and Safety in the Workplace*
W. KIP VISCUSI
pp. 46, 49–53 (Harvard University Press, 1983). Reprinted with permission of Harvard University Press

Lower-paid workers differ from those at the top in two principal ways. First, even if these individuals took the riskiest and most unpleasant jobs available, they would not be able to earn as much as those at the top of the income scale. Second, their greater willingness to accept risks in return for financial compensation has boosted their income status above what it would otherwise have been. If all jobs were required to be as safe as the most highly paid white-collar positions, the income status of those at the bottom of the income scale would be lowered further. Wage premiums for risk do exist, but they are not sufficient to offset all of the other factors generating the low-income status of the workers who receive them.

Consideration of wealth effects enables one to resolve the apparent paradox that the most attractive jobs in society are also the highest paid. Any person will require a premium for taking a job with a greater perceived risk. However, the confounding of variations in work opportunities for people having different income status (because of educational differences, perhaps) with risk preference variations arising from differences in wealth makes it impossible to distinguish the role of compensating differentials based on a broad overview of income patterns....

As society has become richer, there has been a widespread decline in accidents both at home and at work. Although the general trend is clear, the particular mechanism of influence is not. Two types of effects are most instrumental. First, increased wealth and the associated decreased willingness to incur risks may change people's choices. A richer worker may choose a safer job, firms in a more affluent society will adopt less risky technologies, and wealthier consumers will be more likely to buy safer cars. A second effect is that, especially over long periods of time, increased wealth alters the options available. Wealthier societies have a greater incentive to develop airbags, more durable products, and other technological innovations that decrease the risk of particular activities. The extent to which the wealth-risk relationship arises because greater wealth induces a change in technology or a change in choices within a technology cannot be ascertained. For our purposes, disentangling the components of the mechanism of influence is less important than understanding the overall relationship....

One would expect to find similar differences across countries. More affluent nations, such as the United States, should choose safer technologies and display greater risk-avoiding behavior than less developed countries. Available international accident data, however, yields the opposite relationship, with risks and per capita income positively correlated. One reason for this departure from expected behavior is the differences in individual activities in more and less developed countries; the high auto accident death rates in the United States, Austria, and West Germany are principal contributors to these countries' relatively high accident rates. A second factor is that in advanced countries the mortality rate from illnesses (adjusted for demographic mix) is lower, so the proportion of healthy individuals who might be accident victims is greater. Finally, and perhaps most important, the reporting of accidents is more meticulous in more affluent countries because of greater sensitivity to risk and individual health. Four countries ranked among the safest on the basis of reported fatal accidents are the Dominican Republic, Singapore, Hong Kong, and Chile. In contrast, the advanced countries of Western Europe and the United States have very high accident rates even when motor vehicle deaths are excluded. Differences in record keeping are perhaps the most plausible explanation for these somewhat surprising patterns.

The more affluent countries are characterized by a greater emphasis on policies to reduce risks, as one would expect. As the United States has become richer, the social regulation of risk has escalated. Earlier in this century risk regulations were confined primarily to standards for food processing and drug safety. The same shift in attitudes toward risk that led to the proliferation of risk regulation agencies in the 1970s has also contributed to the influence of Ralph Nader and to a variety of risk-oriented efforts, such as the movement to promote the safety of nuclear power plants. These developments have been interdependent; for example, Ralph Nader's influence has contributed to the public sensitivity to hazards. In the absence of the effect of greater affluence on our willingness to incur risks, however, it is unlikely that these political efforts would have met with much success.

A potential pitfall for policy design is that the individuals who wield the greatest influence over the structuring of policies tend to be richer than those who are exposed to the risks. The disparity in wealth between those who formulate policies and those affected by the policies could provide the impetus for regulations that would reduce the risk exposures of broad segments of the population. If the need for regulation is based simply on a difference in risk preferences, arising from disparities in wealth, it is inappropriate for the government to regulate the risks. To be sure, policy choices usually compound concerns arising from differences in wealth with more compelling rationales for intervention, such as inadequate risk information. However, if differences in risk preferences are the primary determinant of public policies, the resulting regulations will be especially misguided. If coke-oven workers are willing to endanger their lives in return for substantial salaries, or if India chooses to develop nuclear energy as the most promising energy source for its long-term development, government efforts to interfere with these decisions will reduce the welfare of those whose choices are regulated. An ethical issue that invariably arises in these instances is the extent to which policymakers are simply imposing their risk preferences on others.

Among the more extreme manifestations of this interventionist mentality are proposals to impose risk standards on activities in foreign countries that have no direct effect on the risks incurred by U.S. citizens. Some analysts have urged a ban on importation of unsafely produced goods. A broader variant is the suggestion that uniform standards for health and safety be developed and applied internationally. Policies of this type are fundamentally ill conceived. The profound differences in wealth and economic development across countries necessarily lead to quite disparate attitudes toward risk. Penalizing workers in less-developed countries by not buying their products will not boost their welfare.

More generally, insistence on uniform hazard regulations will inevitably lead to the types of compromises that are detrimental to all concerned. More affluent countries, such as the United States, and the industrial European nations, would prefer tighter standards than those reached by international consensus, while less-developed nations would prefer looser standards. The inherent shortcoming of standardization is that uniformity is not desirable. Variations in financial resources give rise to quite valid differences in risk preferences that should not be overridden. The greater danger from wealth differences is not that the poor will choose to incur risks, but that the rich will take interventionist actions.

Wealth-related concerns are also at the forefront of policies to regulate the riskiness of U.S. exports. Should the State Department ban the export of aerosol sprays, Tris-coated sleepwear, or pesticides that are banned in this country? Many of the countries that would receive these goods are poorer and at a stage of economic advancement not too unlike that of the United States before the advent of most risk regulations. Banning products for export may diminish the welfare of these people, impede their economic development, and even result in decreased longevity as resources are reallocated in response to the ban.

A more appropriate basis for export restrictions would be linked to clearly legitimate economic concerns. If the United States does not impose safety standards on its exports, overseas consumers of American products may expect that the same standards are applied to exports as to domestic outputs, thus leading them to misperceive the risk. Moreover, without export restrictions, U.S. producers and the U.S. government may be culpable. If an American-made nuclear reactor that is not subjected to U.S. safety standards leads to a major catastrophe, people in foreign countries may reject U.S. products in general. This response is not simply a political matter. A major change in foreign consumers' assessments of the risks of U.S. goods could have profound implications through market forces alone.

Legitimate economic influences such as these should be mustered to provide a rationale for export restrictions and other regulatory actions. What is important is that these motivations be made clear so that differences in attitudes toward risk do not dominate the policy process.

COMMENTS AND QUESTIONS

1. What precisely is the "wealth effect" that Viscusi identifies? (Note the way he treats empirical evidence inconsistent with the theoretical model.) Should regulatory responses be sensitive to wealth-based differences in preferences about risk? How would you answer Viscusi's question about a ban on exporting products banned in this country? Why does Viscusi say that such a ban "may diminish the welfare" of potential consumers abroad? Do you agree that it does? (That's a question about what you think the appropriate definition of welfare is.)

2. Consider this response, from a student who commented on an earlier version of this book, to a proposal that the "problem" of an inadequate supply of child care workers could be "solved" by eliminating restrictions on immigration and the minimum wage:

> While admitting that the supply of child care workers is limited because of poor wages, you propose that we could solve the problem by substituting foreign low-wage workers. Presumably this is because those

workers are willing to accept substandard pay, minimal or no benefits and low social regard.

While convenient for working parents, this solution is unlikely to result in quality child care. Certainly these foreign workers will be women, and certainly they will be able to provide basic care. But with limited English and education, it is unlikely they will be able to provide the stimulating environment that benefits children in their development—to say nothing of the disturbing idea of working parents exploiting third world women by paying them wages that would be unacceptable to an American worker.

(Note that there is no such thing as an "inadequate" supply in the abstract; there is just a number of workers willing to work at the wages offered that is too small to satisfy everyone seeking such workers. Another response to the problem, of course, would be for those seeking child care workers to offer higher wages.)

What precisely is the nature of the objection to the proposal? Is it an efficiency-based objection (that parents will not, in fact, get the services they think they are buying, because they won't be purchasing a "stimulating environment" and the like)? What reasons are there to think that parents will misunderstand the nature of the services available at the wages they are willing to pay? Is the objection paternalist? Vis-à-vis the parents? The potential employees? With respect to them, consider whether they are better off in not having these jobs available to them, and reconsider Radin's comments on the double-bind.

3. Obviously, questions about paternalism arise in settings beyond the regulation of the workplace. One particularly important area of inquiry involves consumer products. Should the government be involved in limiting consumer choices? If so, what kinds of concerns warrant government intervention? We close this chapter with a case raising these questions in the context of food regulation under the federal Food, Drug, and Cosmetic Act. The case involves asparagus alleged to be "unfit for food" in violation of the act. *United States v. 298 Cases ... Ski Slide Brand Asparagus,* 88 F. Supp. 450 (D. Or. 1949):

> Defendant is an asparagus packer. One of his products is the center cut of the asparagus. This retails for 20 cents per can (1 lb. 3 oz.) containing 95 to 100 cuts, as compared with 40 to 45 cents per can for the choicier tips.
>
> The Government contends that defendant's center cuts are fibrous and woody beyond the permissible limits set up by the Federal Food, Drug and Cosmetic Administration. Three witnesses for the Government said that they had each eaten a can (or attempted to) of defendant's cuts. The composite of their testimony was that 25% or more of the cuts were inedible, ... and the Government's witnesses condemned them as a food product.
>
> On the other hand, the Director of Mary Cullen's Cottage found only 5 or 6 pieces out of 100 that she had to lay aside. Confronted with this conflict in testimony, I obtained counsels' consent to eat a can. This I have done, although I confess had I understood all the difficulties of the undertaking, I might not have been so bold.

To eat a can of asparagus, hand-running, as the saying is, is quite a chore. I took three days to eat the can. That, I can now state, is as much as an old protein user should attempt on his first venture into herbalism. I suspect the Government witnesses tried to eat their cans all at one time, and that may explain the severity of their judgment about defendant's asparagus. I can see where after 50 or 60 cuts, eaten without spelling oneself, one might become very particular.

My test more than confirmed Miss Laughton's good opinion of the cuts. She found 5 or 6 per cent inedible, whereas I ate all of my can, and felt that I was helped by it. There was one runty, tough piece and two or three slivers, but I treated them as de minimis.

I agree with the Director of Mary Cullen's Cottage that this is an excellent product, particularly considering its low price. Not everybody in this country can "keep up with the Joneses" and eat only asparagus tips. Indeed it seems strange to me that the Government should be interested in keeping from the market a moderately priced, wholly nutritious food product. I should think in this period of declining income the Government's interest would be the other way. If [counsel for the company] will prepare appropriate findings, I will give his client's center cuts a clean bill of health. They deserve it.

What arguments might be made in favor of prohibiting food that is "unfit for food" in the sense involved here? How would the arguments in favor of regulation change if the asparagus were alleged to be not just tough but dangerous?

Doctrinal and Institutional Limits of the Common Law

II

P art I introduced you to how and why the legal system allocates risk and compensates people when risk turns into injury. Throughout that discussion, we touched on the distinction between the *common law* and *legislative regulation* as methods of allocating risk. In Part II, we examine in greater depth whether each method (necessarily?) has distinctive doctrinal and institutional characteristics. For example, it might be said that the common law relies on the courts to develop the rules for allocating risk and for determining when and how much compensation is due, whereas regulation uses the legislature for that task. In addition, it might be said that legislatures are able to devise rules that are out of the reach of courts using common law methods of reasoning. This part begins an examination of those contentions, with a particular focus on the characteristics of common law to manage risk. We will also begin to consider whether, or the extent to which, such doctrinal (and, in passing, the institutional) characteristics make it necessary to supplement the common law with legislative regulation.

Doctrinal Limits

4

So far we have examined aspects of contract law that may be used to manage risk. We considered parts of contract *doctrine*—for example, ideas associated with "informed choice" as a predicate for imposing contractual liability—that affect the normative case for and against using contract law to allocate risk. In this chapter, we will examine other common law doctrines of criminal law and tort law that do so as well.

In dealing with criminal law, we focus primarily on the (distinctive?) requirements of a so-called mental element (*mens rea*) for imposing certain kinds of criminal liability, especially on corporations and their officers, and secondarily on the (distinctive?) role of public officials in enforcing the criminal law. In dealing with tort law, we focus primarily on the kinds of risks that tort law traditionally addresses. The chapter concludes with a brief examination of some of the ethical issues that arise in legal practices dealing with corporate risk management practices.

A ■ Criminal Law: The Role of *Mens Rea*

Can corporations and/or their officers be prosecuted for serious criminal offenses arising out of exposure to risk? Suppose the relevant criminal offense requires that the defendant "intend" that injury result. How can a corporation form such an intent? What about the officers of corporations? Do they "intend" that injury result when they choose to operate their businesses in a way that exposes people to risk? As demonstrated by the materials that immediately follow, corporate criminal liability for risk may exist under the common law (today, largely located in penal codes) in some cases. However, as will be discussed at the end of this section, modern regulatory statutes impose criminal liability on corporations and their officers when traditional common law doctrines dealing with the mental element would not.

1 ■ Murder and Cost-Benefit Analysis

a ■ Statutory Definitions

Here are two illustrative (statutory) definitions of murder, which track the main elements of the common law of murder.

California Penal Code section 187. Murder Defined

(a) Murder is the unlawful killing of a human being . . . with malice aforethought. . . .

Section 188. Malice Defined: Express and Implied Murder

Such malice may be express or implied. It is expressed when there is manifested a deliberate intention unlawfully to take away the life of a fellow creature. It is implied, when no considerable provocation appears, or when the circumstances attending the killing show an abandoned and malignant heart.

When it is shown that the killing resulted from the intentional doing of an act with express or implied malice as defined above, no other mental state need be shown to establish the mental state of malice aforethought. Neither an awareness of the obligation to act within the general body of laws regulating society nor acting despite such awareness is included within the definition of malice.

Pennsylvania Criminal Code section 2502. Murder

(a) Murder of the First Degree. A criminal homicide constitutes murder of the first degree when it is committed by an intentional killing. [Punishable by death or life imprisonment.] . . .

(d) Definitions. . . . "Intentional killing." Killing by means of poison, or by lying in wait, or by any other kind of wilful, deliberate and premeditated killing.

b ■ The "Ivey" Memorandum

The following document was written in 1973 by an engineer employed by General Motors. It evaluates the risks associated with different ways of locating gas tanks in automobiles:

Value Analysis of Auto Fuel Fed Fire Related Fatalities

Accident statistical studies indicate a range of 550–1,000 fatalities per year in accidents with fuel fed fires where the bodies were burnt. There has been no real determination of the percent of these people which were killed by the violence of the accidents rather than by fire. The condition of the bodies almost precludes making this determination.

. . .

Based on this statistic and making several assumptions, it is possible to do a value analysis of automotive fire related fatalities as they relate to General Motors.
The following assumptions can be made:
1. In G.M. automobiles there are a maximum of 500 fatalities per year in accidents with fuel fed fires where the bodies were burnt.
2. Each fatality has a value [of] $200,000.
3. There are approximately 41,000,000 G.M. automobiles currently operating on U.S. highways.

Analyzing these figures indicates that fatalities related to accidents with fuel fed fires are costing General Motors $2.40 per automobile in current operation.

$$\frac{500 \text{ fatalities} \times \$200,000/\text{fatality}}{41,000,000 \text{ automobiles}} = \$2.40/\text{automobile}$$

This cost will be with us until a way of preventing all crash related fuel fed fires is developed.

...If we assume that all crash related fuel fed fires can be prevented commencing with a specific model year another type analysis can be made.

Along with the assumptions numbered above the following assumptions are necessary:

1. G.M. builds approximately 5,000,000 automobiles per year.
2. Approximately 11% of the automobiles on the road are of the current model year at the end of that model year.

This analysis indicates that for G.M. it would be worth approximately $2.20 per new model auto to prevent a fuel fed fire in all accidents.

$$500 \text{ fatalities} \times 11\% \text{ new model autos} = 55 \text{ fatalities in new model autos}$$

$$\frac{55 \text{ fatalities} \times \$200,000/\text{fatality}}{5,000,000 \text{ new model autos}} = \$2.20/\text{new model auto}$$

This analysis must be tempered with two thoughts. First, it is really impossible to put a value on human life. This analysis tried to do so in an objective manner but a human fatality is really beyond value, subjectively. Secondly, it is impossible to design an automobile where fuel fed fires can be prevented in all accidents unless the automobile has a non-flammable fuel.

(Signed)
E. C. Ivey
Advance Design

COMMENTS AND QUESTIONS

1. Other internal General Motors documents showed that it would cost at least $8.59 per vehicle to install a safer design.

2. Assume that there was a single General Motors official responsible for choosing which design to put into production and that the official chose the design with the higher risk and lower cost. Could that official be found criminally liable for murder under the California or Pennsylvania murder statutes? The officials to whom Ivey reported? The General Motors board of directors? General Motors? Who, if anyone, had the requisite "intent"? Consider the proposition that the memo demonstrates that someone within General Motors knew what the risks were and that someone (else?) made a decision whose import was that the company was prepared to accept the deaths that resulted from the design choice, even if that person or the company might have preferred that the deaths not occur. Does that proposition show that the deaths resulted from a "wilful, deliberate and premeditated" choice, as required by the Pennsylvania statute?

3. In 1999, a jury awarded $4.9 billion, most of it in punitive damages, in a civil action against General Motors brought by six people who were severely burned when a drunk driver crashed into the back of the 1979 Chevrolet Malibu in which they were traveling. The Ivey memo was introduced in support of the plaintiffs' claims, over General Motors' objection. Consider the argument that such awards irrationally punish corporations that do what the legal formula for

negligence encourages them to do—undertake cost-benefit analysis of the risks their products pose, by comparing the burden of taking precautions to the probability and magnitude of the harm that could be averted through those precautions. *See* W. Kip Viscusi, *Corporate Risk Analysis: A Reckless Act?*, 52 Stan. L. Rev. 547 (2000). Would you advise a client to forgo doing a cost-benefit analysis of alternative designs? For a related discussion, see the material on professional ethics at the conclusion of this chapter.

c ■ Indictment Based on Faulty Automobile Design

Consider this indictment against Ford Motor Company by the grand jury of Elkhart Superior Court, State of Illinois, for three counts of reckless homicide and one count of criminal recklessness.

■ Indictment of Ford Motor Company

Count I

That Ford Motor Company, a corporation, on or about the 10th day of August, 1978, in the County of Elkhart, State of Indiana, did then and there through the acts and omissions of its agents and employees acting within the scope of their authority with said corporation recklessly cause the death of Judy Ann Ulrich, a human being, to-wit: that the Ford Motor Company, a corporation, did recklessly authorize and approve the design, and did recklessly design and manufacture a certain 1973 Pinto automobile, Serial Number F3T10X298722F, in such a manner as would likely cause said automobile to flame and burn upon rear-end impact; and the said Ford Motor Company permitted said Pinto automobile to remain upon the highways and roadways of Elkhart County, State of Indiana, to-wit: U.S. Highway Number 33, in said County and State; and the said Ford Motor Company did fail to repair and modify said Pinto automobile; and thereafter on said date as a proximate contributing cause of said reckless disregard for the safety of other persons within said automobile, including, the said Judy Ann Ulrich, a rear-end impact involving said Pinto automobile did occur creating fire and flame which did then and there and thereby inflict mortal injuries upon the said Judy Ann Ulrich, and the said Judy Ann Ulrich did then languish and die by incineration in Allen County, State of Indiana, on or about the 11th day of August, 1978.

And so the Grand Jurors aforesaid, upon their oaths aforesaid, do say and charge that the said Ford Motor Company, a corporation, did recklessly cause the death of the said Judy Ann Ulrich, a human being, in the manner and form aforesaid, and contrary to the form of the statutes in such cases made and provided, to-wit: Burns Indiana Statutes, Indiana Code Sections 35-42-1-5;* and against the peace and dignity of the State of Indiana.

---

*[Editor's note: This section provides: "A person who recklessly kills another human being commits reckless homicide, a Class C felony. . . ." Section 35-40-2-2(c) defines *recklessly* as follows: "A person engages in conduct 'recklessly' if he engages in the conduct in plain, conscious, and unjustifiable disregard of harm that might result and the disregard involves a substantial deviation from acceptable standards of conduct."]

[Counts II and III repeat the above allegations in connection with the deaths of Donna M. Ulrich and Lynn M. Ulrich, respectively.]

Count IV

That Ford Motor Company, a corporation, on or about the 10th day of August, 1978, and diverse days prior thereto, in the County of Elkhart, State of Indiana, did through the acts and omissions of its agents and employees acting within the scope of their authority with said corporation, recklessly create a substantial risk of bodily injury to the persons of Judy Ann Ulrich, Donna M. Ulrich and Lynn M. Ulrich, human beings, and did recklessly permit a certain 1973 Pinto automobile, Serial Number F3T10X298722F, designed and manufactured by the said Ford Motor Company to remain upon the highways and roadways of Elkhart County, State of Indiana, to-wit: U.S. Highway Number 33 in said County and State; and said Pinto automobile being recklessly designed and manufactured in such a manner as would likely cause said automobile to flame and burn upon rear-end impact; and that the said Ford Motor Company had a legal duty to warn the general public and certain occupants of said Pinto automobile, namely: Judy Ann Ulrich, Donna M. Ulrich and Lynn M. Ulrich of the dangerous tendency of said Pinto automobile to flame and burn upon rear-end impact; and the said Ford Motor Company did fail to repair and modify said Pinto automobile; and that as a proximate contributing cause of said Ford Motor Company's acts, omissions and reckless disregard for the safety of other persons within said Pinto automobile, including the said Judy Ann Ulrich, Donna M. Ulrich and Lynn M. Ulrich, a rear-end impact involving said Pinto automobile did occur on or about August 10, 1978, in Elkhart County, Indiana, creating fire and flame which did then and there and thereby inflict bodily injury upon the persons of the said Judy Ann Ulrich, Donna M. Ulrich and Lynn M. Ulrich, human beings, and each of them.

And so the Grand Jurors aforesaid, upon their oaths aforesaid, do say and charge that the said Ford Motor Company, a corporation, did recklessly create a substantial risk of bodily injury to the persons of Judy Ann Ulrich, Donna M. Ulrich and Lynn M. Ulrich, human beings, and each of them, in the manner and form aforesaid, and contrary to the form of the Statutes in such cases made and provided, to-wit: Burns Indiana Statutes, Indiana Code Section 35-42-2-2,** and against the peace and dignity of the State of Indiana.

COMMENTS AND QUESTIONS

1. If you were prosecuting this case, what evidence would you look for? How would the evidence you would need to convict Ford of reckless homicide differ from the evidence you would need to convict it of criminal recklessness?

_____

** [Editor's note: This section provides: "(a) A person who recklessly, knowingly, or intentionally performs an act that creates a substantial risk of bodily injury to another person commits criminal recklessness, a Class B misdemeanor. However, the offense is a Class A misdemeanor if the conduct includes the use of a vehicle or deadly weapon. (b) A person who recklessly, knowingly, or intentionally inflicts serious bodily injury on another person commits criminal recklessness, a Class D felony."]

2. Viscusi, at 569–70, provides the following description of the cost-benefit analysis Ford engaged in prior to selecting the design used in the Pinto:

> The engineering analysis undertaken by Ford pertained not to rear impact crashes but to rollover risks and a regulation that had been proposed by the NHTSA.* Nevertheless, the analysis demonstrates how corporate engineers undertake safety studies. . . .
>
> . . . Ford estimated potential risks as 180 burn deaths, 180 serious burn injuries, and 2100 burned vehicles. The unit values applied to these injuries were similar to the value of court awards in product liability cases at that time, as well as to the values used by the NHTSA in its regulatory analyses. Each of these values was based on estimates of the present value of lost earnings. Based on Ford's analysis, the total cost of not fixing the gas tank design would be $49.6 million. In contrast, . . . the cost of increased safety would be $137.5 million. By this tally, the expected benefits from improved safety were smaller than the costs; consequently, undertaking the design change was not worthwhile.

To what statutory elements of the crimes related to serious injury and/or death might this analysis be relevant? Should we answer the question, "Was the behavior a plain, conscious, and unjustifiable disregard of harm that might result that involved a substantial deviation from acceptable standards of conduct?" by comparing: (a) the cost per car of making the change to the individual harm, (b) the total cost of making the change to the total harm, or (c) the cost to each individual ($11) to the *risk* (relatively small) to which each individual was exposed?

3. How would you evaluate Ford's criminal liability if Ford had marketed two models that differed in price by the $11 cost of locating the gas tank differently, making it clear to consumers that the price differential existed because the cheaper car posed a slightly greater risk of death by fire in a rear-end crash? (Do you think that anyone would buy the cheaper model? Would you?) What if Ford marketed only one model but made it clear to consumers that it had made the design choice to reduce the car's price by $11 while slightly increasing the risk of death in a crash?

4. Note that Ford calculated the cost of life by using the "human capital" method described in part I rather than the "willingness to pay" method. Is the choice of valuation method relevant to the question of criminal liability? (The "willingness to pay" method was less well established when Ford engineers made their calculations than it is today.)

5. Ford was acquitted after the jury deliberated for approximately twenty-five hours. Several jurors explained that they believed that the Pinto was unsafe because the fuel tank could not withstand a rear-end collision, but they also had concluded that there was insufficient evidence to prove the charges in this case. In light of the cost-benefit analysis, how can you account for the combination of these judgments?

---

* [Editors' Note: The National Highway Traffic Safety Administration (NHTSA) is the federal agency responsible for setting safety standards for automobiles.]

2 ■ Deliberate Indifference?

■ The People of the State of Illinois v. O'Neil
194 Ill. App. 3d 79 (1990)

Justice Lorenz delivered the opinion of the court.

Following a joint bench trial, individual defendants Steven O'Neil, Charles Kirschbaum, and Daniel Rodriguez, agents of Film Recovery Systems, Inc. (Film Recovery), were convicted of murder in the death of Stefan Golab, a Film Recovery employee, from cyanide poisoning stemming from conditions in Film Recovery's plant in Elk Grove Village, Illinois. Corporate defendants Film Recovery and its sister corporation Metallic Marketing Systems, Inc. (Metallic Marketing), were convicted of involuntary manslaughter in the same death. O'Neil, Kirschbaum, Rodriguez, Film Recovery, and Metallic Marketing were also convicted of 14 counts of reckless conduct involving 14 other Film Recovery employees. . . .

Individual defendants O'Neil, Kirschbaum, and Rodriguez each received sentences of 25 years' imprisonment for murder and 14 concurrent 364-day imprisonment terms for reckless conduct. O'Neil and Kirschbaum were also each fined $10,000 with respect to the murder convictions and $14,000 with respect to the convictions for reckless conduct. Corporate defendants Film Recovery and Metallic Marketing were each fined $10,000 with respect to the convictions for involuntary manslaughter and $14,000 with respect to the convictions for reckless conduct.

On appeal, defendants urge that their convictions must be reversed and the cause remanded for retrial because the judgments rendered were inconsistent. . . .

We conclude that the judgments rendered are legally inconsistent. Therefore, we now reverse those convictions as to both the individual and corporate defendants and remand the matter for retrial. We summarize below those facts, as they appear in the record, which are pertinent to our disposition.

In 1982, Film Recovery occupied premises at 1855 and 1875 Greenleaf Avenue in Elk Grove Village. Film Recovery was there engaged in the business of extracting, for resale, silver from used X-ray and photographic film. Metallic Marketing operated out of the same premises on Greenleaf Avenue and owned 50% of the stock of Film Recovery. The recovery process was performed at Film Recovery's plant located at the 1855 address and involved "chipping" the film product and soaking the granulated pieces in large, open, bubbling vats containing a solution of water and sodium cyanide. The cyanide solution caused silver contained in the film to be released. A continuous flow system pumped the silver-laden solution into polyurethane tanks which contained electrically charged stainless steel plates to which the separated silver adhered. The plates were removed from the tanks to another room where the accumulated silver was scraped off. The remaining solution was pumped out of the tanks and the granulated film, devoid of silver, shovelled out.

On the morning of February 10, 1983, shortly after he disconnected a pump on one of the tanks and began to stir the contents of the tank with a rake, Stefan Golab became dizzy and faint. He left the production area to go rest in the lunchroom area of the plant. Plant workers present on that day testified Golab's body had trembled and he had foamed at the mouth. Golab eventually lost consciousness and was taken outside of the plant. Paramedics summoned to the plant were unable to revive him. Golab was pronounced dead upon arrival at Alexian Brothers Hospital.

The Cook County medical examiner performed an autopsy on Golab the following day. Although the medical examiner initially indicated Golab could have died from cardiac arrest, he reserved final determination of death pending examination of results of toxicological laboratory tests on Golab's blood and other body specimens. After receiving the toxicological report, the medical examiner determined Golab died from acute cyanide poisoning through the inhalation of cyanide fumes in the plant air.

Defendants were subsequently indicted by a Cook County grand jury. The grand jury charged defendants O'Neil, Kirschbaum, Rodriguez, Pett, and Mackay with murder, stating that, as individuals and as officers and high managerial agents of Film Recovery, they had, on February 10, 1983, knowingly created a strong probability of Golab's death. Generally, the indictment stated the individual defendants failed to disclose to Golab that he was working with substances containing cyanide and failed to advise him about, train him to anticipate, and provide adequate equipment to protect him from attendant dangers involved. The grand jury charged Film Recovery and Metallic Marketing with involuntary manslaughter stating that, through the reckless acts of their officers, directors, agents, and others, all acting within the scope of their employment, the corporate entities had, on February 10, 1983, unintentionally killed Golab. Finally, the grand jury charged both individual and corporate defendants with reckless conduct as to 20 other Film Recovery employees based on the same conduct alleged in the murder indictment, but expanding the time of that conduct to "on or about March 1982 through March 1983."

Proceedings commenced in the circuit court in January 1985 and continued through the conclusion of trial in June of that year. In the course of the 24-day trial, evidence from 59 witnesses was presented, either directly or through stipulation of the parties. That testimony is contained in over 2,300 pages of trial transcript. The parties also presented numerous exhibits including photographs, corporate documents and correspondence, as well as physical evidence.

On June 14, 1985, the trial judge pronounced his judgment of defendants' guilt. The trial judge found that "the mind and mental state of a corporation is the mind and mental state of the directors, officers and high managerial personnel because they act on behalf of the corporation for both the benefit of the corporation and for themselves." Further, "if the corporation's officers, directors and high managerial personnel act within the scope of their corporate responsibilities and employment for their benefit and for the benefit of the profits of the corporation, the corporation must be held liable for what occurred in the work place."

. . .

[D]efendants argue that the judgments for murder and reckless conduct against individual defendants O'Neil, Kirschbaum, and Rodriguez are inconsistent because, while the offense of murder requires a knowing and intentional act, reckless conduct does not. Defendants argue both convictions, however, arose from the same acts of the individual defendants. Defendants reason O'Neil, Kirschbaum, and Rodriguez could not be responsible for intentional and unintentional conduct at the same time and, therefore, the judgments for murder and reckless conduct against them are inconsistent.

. . .

We find it helpful to set out the pertinent statutory language of the offenses for which the defendants were convicted. The Criminal Code of 1961 defines "murder" as follows:

> "A person who kills an individual without lawful justification commits murder if, in performing the acts which cause the death: . . . He *knows* that such acts create a strong probability of death or great bodily harm to that individual[.]" (Emphasis added.) (Ill. Rev. Stat. 1981, ch. 38, par. 9-1(a)(2).)

"Involuntary manslaughter" is defined as:

> "A person who *unintentionally* kills an individual without lawful justification commits involuntary manslaughter if his acts whether lawful or unlawful which cause the death are such as are likely to cause death or great bodily harm to some individual, and he performs them *recklessly*[.]" (Emphasis added.) (Ill. Rev. Stat. 1981, ch. 38, par. 9-3(a).)

"Reckless conduct" is defined as:

> "A person who causes bodily harm to or endangers the bodily safety of an individual by any means, commits reckless conduct if he performs *recklessly* the acts which cause the harm or endanger safety, whether they otherwise are lawful or unlawful." (Emphasis added.) Ill. Rev. Stat. 1981, ch. 38, par. 12-5(a).

The supreme court, in *People v. Spears* (1986), 112 Ill. 2d 396, and *People v. Hoffer* (1985), 106 Ill. 2d 186, has addressed issues with respect to consistency of verdicts rendered for the above offenses in light of the mental states required to sustain each.

In *Hoffer*, defendant Donald Hoffer was indicted on three counts of murder in the shooting death of Harold (Ed) Peters. In a trial before a jury, the State presented evidence that Hoffer shot Peters with a shotgun after a heated exchange of words outside Hoffer's home. Hoffer testified that he thought Peters was reaching for a gun at the time of the shooting. Hoffer stated the shotgun discharged as he lowered it with one hand and reached with his other hand to grab the gunstock.

Pursuant to Illinois Pattern Jury Instructions, the trial judge instructed the jury that the offense of murder included the offenses of voluntary and involuntary manslaughter. Definitional and issues instructions were tendered to the jury on murder, voluntary manslaughter (unreasonable belief that the killing was justified), and involuntary manslaughter. The jurors, however, were not informed that they could return a guilty verdict on only one of the offenses.

On appeal, the appellate court vacated all three convictions and remanded the cause for a new trial.

The supreme court affirmed the reversal, rejecting the State's argument that the verdicts could be reconciled because the mental state required for murder "subsumed the lesser mental states required for voluntary manslaughter and involuntary manslaughter." After noting the three offenses differed only in the particular mental culpability required to sustain each, the court concluded the mental states involved are mutually inconsistent. Thus, "[w]here a determination is made that one [of the mental states] exists, the others, to be legally consistent, must be found not to exist."

Subsequently, in *People v. Spears* (1986), 112 Ill. 2d 396, the supreme court applied the *Hoffer* rule despite the State's contention that *Spears* involved separable acts and conduct toward multiple victims and, therefore, the rationale in *Hoffer* did not apply.

Defendant Henry Spears was charged with attempted murder (Ill. Rev. Stat. 1983, ch. 38, par. 8-4(a)) and armed violence (based on the great-bodily-harm form of aggravated battery) (Ill. Rev. Stat. 1983, ch. 38, par. 33A-2) in the shooting of his estranged wife, Barbara. Spears was also charged with armed violence in the shooting of Annette Keys. In his jury trial, the State presented evidence that Spears was at his estranged wife's apartment where she, Keys, and two other women had been playing cards. At some point, Spears and Barbara scuffled. Spears drew a gun from a shoulder holster and aimed it at Barbara as she tried to scramble to a side wall. The defendant fired a shot which struck Barbara before she reached the wall. Although Spears was grabbed from behind, he fired a second shot, striking both Barbara and Keys. Spears fired a third shot at Barbara's head, but missed her.

In his defense, Spears testified that Barbara had pushed him and he had stumbled. When someone then grabbed him from behind, he panicked and pulled the gun from the holster. In the ensuing struggle, the gun accidentally fired.

Pattern jury definitional and issues instructions were tendered for attempted murder, armed violence, and two uncharged counts of reckless conduct (Ill. Rev. Stat. 1983, ch. 38, par. 12-5(a)), which, at defendant's request, the jury was instructed to consider as a lesser included offense of the two armed-violence counts. Five verdict forms were provided: one for the attempted murder of Barbara, two for armed violence, and two for reckless conduct as to Barbara and Annette Keys.

The jury found defendant guilty on all five counts. However, the court entered judgment only on the attempted-murder count and one armed-violence count. The appellate court, with one justice dissenting, determined the verdicts were inconsistent and remanded the cause for a new trial.

The supreme court affirmed the reversal. The court agreed, generally, that where a claim of inconsistent guilty verdicts involves multiple shots or victims, the question is whether the trier of fact could rationally find separable acts accompanied by mental states to support all of the verdicts as legally consistent. However, the court noted that that principle found no application where the State was attempting to justify guilty verdicts in direct conflict with both its theory of the case at trial and evidence it presented in support of that theory. The court stated:

> "It would be manifestly unfair to allow the State, with the benefit of hindsight, to be able to create separable acts on appeal, neither alleged nor proved at trial. Such an inquiry does not operate in a vacuum. The manner by which a defendant is charged, and the jury is instructed, provides the essential framework for analyzing the consistency of jury verdicts in the troublesome context of multiple shots or victims. We believe that the substance of the allegations charging the defendant, as an unequivocal expression of prosecutorial intent [citation], and what the evidence showed in relation to those charges, are of particular importance in determining whether guilty verdicts could rationally and consistently be based upon separable acts accompanied by the requisite mental states."

The court examined the information and observed that the State had not charged a separate offense for each action or shot fired by defendant. As to conduct toward Barbara, the State had based each of its three charges on the two shots which actually struck her. Because the same conduct was used as the basis for those charges, the court found the contention of separate acts untenable. More importantly the court noted, even assuming defendant's acts were separable, evidence in the record did not support the State's argument that the defendant's mental state changed during the shootings to support the State's hypothesis. Neither the State nor the defense had presented any evidence to suggest defendant's state of mind had varied during his acts. Because the jury's verdicts as to defendant's conduct toward Barbara for offenses requiring otherwise mutually inconsistent mental states could not be reconciled based on separable acts or a change in defendant's mental state, the supreme court determined the verdicts were legally inconsistent under *Hoffer*.

The supreme court further noted that the *Hoffer* rule also controlled the guilty verdicts for defendant's conduct toward Keys. By its guilty verdict, the jury found, in effect, that defendant had acted both recklessly (reckless conduct) and knowingly (armed violence predicated on aggravated battery) in firing the single shot which struck Keys. Based on that single act, the verdicts were legally inconsistent.

Under the rule in *Hoffer*, the judgments rendered by the circuit court in the instant case appear inconsistent as based on mutually exclusive mental states. However, we must consider whether, under similar analysis used by the supreme court in *Spears*, the judgments are supported by separable acts occurring at different times against different victims by legally different defendants. We therefore begin with a review of the indictments, as they represent the State's prosecutorial intentions in charging defendants, and proceed to evaluate the record of evidence in light of those charges.

The murder indictment states that on February 10, 1983, defendants O'Neil, Kirschbaum, Rodriguez, Pett, and Mackay, acting as individuals and as officers and high managerial agents of Film Recovery, committed murder in that they knowingly created a strong probability of Stefan Golab's death. Specifically, the grand jury charged those individuals had "failed to disclose and make known to [Golab] that he was working with cyanide and substances containing cyanide and failed to instruct him as to matters involving safety procedures and proper handling of said chemicals[.]" Further, those individuals "failed to provide . . . Golab with appropriate and necessary safety and first-aid equipment and sundry health-monitoring systems for his protection while working with and handling cyanide and substances containing cyanide[.]" The murder indictment also states O'Neil, Kirschbaum, Rodriguez, Pett, and Mackay failed to "properly provide for the storage, detoxification and disposition of . . . cyanide and substances containing cyanide . . . [and] failed to advise . . . Golab of the dangerous nature of his work, and the conditions under which he engaged in it[.]"

The involuntary manslaughter indictment against Film Recovery and Metallic Marketing states that, on February 10, 1983, they "unintentionally killed Stefan Golab by authorizing, requesting, commanding and performing certain acts of commission and acts of omission[] by its [sic] officers, board of directors and high managerial agents, to wit: Steven J. O'Neil, Michael T. Mackay, Gerald Pett, Charles Kirschbaum, Daniel Rodriguez, and others, who acting within the scope of their employment . . . performed the said acts recklessly in such manner as was likely to cause death and great bodily harm to some individual and . . . caused the death of Stefan Golab[.]" The indictment did not otherwise specify the nature of the acts.

The indictments against all defendants for reckless conduct contain identical charges made in the murder indictment against the individual defendants as summarized above, save for stating that the conduct occurred "on or about March 1982 through March 1983."

With regard to the consistency of the judgments for murder and reckless conduct against defendants O'Neil, Kirschbaum, and Rodriguez, acting solely in their individual capacities, we note the corresponding indictments differ only in one respect. The murder indictment is limited to the individual defendants' conduct on February 10, 1983, while the reckless conduct indictments concern conduct over a period of time from March 1982 through March 1983, which would include the date of Golab's death. In all other respects, the same conduct is used as the foundation for the indictments for both offenses against the individual defendants. Although the indictments for both offenses are therefore based on identical acts of the individual defendants, it is conceivable the apparent inconsistency in the convictions for those offenses, due to the mutual exclusiveness of the mental states required to sustain each, might be reconciled by evidence in the record. After carefully reviewing the record, however, we do not conclude that, as to the individual defendants, evidence existed to establish, separately, defendants' mental states to support separate offenses of murder and reckless conduct.

A total of four witnesses testified exclusively as to events which might establish defendants' mental states on February 10, 1983. Michael W. Lackman, an Elk Grove fireman and paramedic who responded to the emergency call on February 10, 1983, did not testify as to any condition of the plant at Film Recovery and stated only that someone told him cyanide was used at Film Recovery's plant. Kenneth Kvidera, an Elk Grove Village police officer who assisted in the ambulance call, stated that when he went into the plant on February 10, 1983, he smelled a strong, foul odor which made him gag and experienced a burning sensation in his throat. Kvidera also noted that a "yellowish-orange" haze was visible in the plant. Kenneth Kryzywicki, another Elk Grove Village police officer who responded to the emergency call from Film Recovery on February 10, 1983, also testified to experiencing a burning sensation in his throat when inside the plant. He stated he had difficulty breathing, that his chest hurt, and his eyes teared. Kryzywicki also noted the mist in the plant air and observed that workers present wore paper masks over their faces but did not wear any other protective clothing or equipment. Gordon Hollywood, an Elk Grove Village police investigator, testified to substantially the same facts as Kryzywicki.

The only other witness to testify exclusively with respect to events of February 10, 1983, was Mohammed Hassan, the emergency room physician at Alexian Brothers Hospital who treated Golab. Hassan did not testify as to any facts which might establish defendants' states of mind on February 10, 1983.

Several other plant workers testified to being in the plant on February 10, 1983, but their testimony does not establish what the conditions were in the plant on that particular day. Roman Guzowski testified that he was working with Golab when Golab became faint. Antonio Roman and Juan Fuentes testified they were working nearby and saw Golab trembling and begin to foam at the mouth. The parties stipulated that Elevterio Salinas would testify to similar facts. Through other

stipulations, the parties agreed Mario Rodriquez and Juan Hernandez would testify they were present when Golab died. In addition, Debra Sadzeck, a bookkeeper,
stated she was in the plant on February 10, 1983, retrieving payroll cards, when she
saw Golab "slumped over" in the lunchroom.

None of the above testimony in any way substantially differs from that otherwise contained in the record regarding conditions in the plant, generally. Thus,
we cannot conclude the record supports a determination that the individual defendants possessed different mental states on February 10, 1983, as distinguished
from the period of March 1982 to March 1983, such as might support separate
offenses of murder and reckless conduct. While we do not believe it helpful to
summarize the considerable amount of that testimony in detail here, those who
testified as to working conditions in the plant established the following: workers
were not told that they were working with cyanide or that the compound put into
the vats could be harmful when inhaled; although ceiling fans existed above the
vats, ventilation in the plant was poor; workers were not informed they were
working with cyanide and were given no safety instruction; workers were given no
goggles to protect their eyes; workers were given no protective clothing and, as a
result, workers' clothing would become wet with the solution used in the vats;
there were small puddles of that solution as well as film chips on the plant floor
around the vats; the solution burned exposed skin; a strong and foul odor per-
meated the plant; the condition of air in the plant made breathing difficult and
painful; and, finally, workers experienced dizziness, nausea, headaches, and bouts
of vomiting.

Because the offenses of murder and reckless conduct require mutually exclusive mental states, and because we conclude the same evidence of the individual
defendants' conduct is used to support both offenses and does not establish, separately, each of the requisite mental states, we conclude that the convictions are
legally inconsistent.

. . .

In *Hoffer*, the supreme court affirmed its earlier pronouncement that, where
judgments are legally inconsistent, as they are when rendered for offenses requiring mutually exclusive mental states, reversal and retrial must follow. We are
mindful, however, the supreme court has also directed that, where, as in the instant
case, defendants challenge the sufficiency of evidence at the first trial, it is necessary
to address that issue to avoid the risk of subjecting defendants to double jeopardy.
Our review of the record does not lead us to conclude that the evidence, as first
adduced, was so insufficient as to bar retrial.

Evidence at trial indicated Golab died after inhaling poisonous cyanide fumes
while working in a plant operated by Film Recovery and its sister corporation
Metallic Marketing where such fumes resulted from a process employed to remove
silver from used X-ray and photographic film. The record contains substantial
evidence regarding the nature of working conditions inside the plant. Testimony
established that air inside the plant was foul smelling and made breathing difficult
and painful. Plant workers experienced dizziness, nausea, headaches, and bouts of
vomiting. There is evidence that plant workers were not informed they were
working with cyanide. Nor were they informed of the presence of, or danger of
breathing, cyanide gas. Ventilation in the plant was poor. Plant workers were given
neither safety instruction nor adequate protective clothing. Finally, testimony

established that defendants O'Neil, Kirschbaum, and Rodriguez were responsible for operating the plant under those conditions. For purposes of our disposition, we find further elaboration on the evidence unnecessary. Moreover, although we have determined evidence in the record is not so insufficient as to bar retrial, our determination of the sufficiency of the evidence should not be in any way interpreted as a finding as to defendants' guilt that would be binding on the court on retrial.

COMMENTS AND QUESTIONS

1. *O'Neil* was the first prominent prosecution of corporate officials for the death of an employee. After the court of appeals decision, the defendants pleaded guilty to involuntary manslaughter. Steven O'Neil served three years in prison, Charles Kirschbaum two years; Daniel Rodriguez received two years' probation.

2. The court of appeals reversed the convictions because the judge verdicts were inconsistent in finding that the defendants committed a single act both knowingly and recklessly. Do you agree with the court's analysis and application of the *Hoffer* and *Spears* precedents? Is the problem that the defendants knew that there was a strong probability of death (required for conviction for murder) and therefore could not have also believed that death was likely (required for conviction for manslaughter)? Is the problem that the defendants did not know that Stefan Golab—or any other *individual*—would be the one to die? Consider the proposition that the elements of homicide make it an unsuitable vehicle for dealing with the liability of people who hope that others will not die as a result of their actions but do not do much to prevent such deaths. Call this state of mind "indifference," rather than intent. Should there be criminal liability when a defendant has an "indifferent" state of mind?

3. Note that the judge also convicted the corporate defendants, based on the fact that their officers—"high managerial agents"—acted criminally, with (in the judge's view) the requisite criminal mental state.

4. Consider this variant on the facts: Golab is exposed to benzene or asbestos, not cyanide, and dies of cancer twenty years after he started work at the company. Expert testimony is available to support the proposition that his cancer was caused by exposure to benzene or asbestos at work. What are the legal and practical obstacles to a criminal prosecution for murder? Note that there is no statute of limitations for murder.

3 ■ Battery and "Force"

Gunnell v. Metrocolor Laboratories, 92 Cal. App. 4th 710 (2nd Dist. 2001), considered whether the criminal law of battery covered exposure to environmental hazards. The case was brought by employees against their employer for damages. Ordinarily, the workers' compensation system provides the exclusive remedy for employees against their employer, but California provides an exception to the exclusivity of the remedy when workers sustain injuries as a result of the employer's commission of a criminal battery. California Penal Code

§ 242 defines a "battery" as "any willful and unlawful use of force or violence upon the person of another," which must involve a "touching" of the victim.

These are the facts of *Gunnell*:

Gunnell, Walters, and Cohen were unskilled laborers who belonged to Local 724 of the Studio Utility Employees Union. The union supplied laborers to film studios in the Los Angeles area. Union laborers customarily performed work assisting carpenters as they built sets, dismantling sets after filming was completed, performing maintenance (such as gardening and moving furniture), moving lumber, tools, and construction materials, and cleaning. In 1989, Gunnell, Walters, and Cohen worked for four and one-half months at Metrocolor Laboratories, Inc., which owned a facility to process and develop television and movie film. The laborers' assignment was to clean walls, pipes, and other parts of the interior of the film lab. Gerald House, the Safety and Engineer Project Coordinator and Program Manager of Metrocolor's Hazard Communication Program, generally supervised the cleaning of the Metrocolor film lab, the project on which Gunnell, Walters, and Cohen worked. David Carrasco, Metrocolor's Head of Labor, directly supervised work done by Gunnell, Walters, Cohen, and other Union Local 724 workers.

Metrocolor directed Gunnell, Walters, and Cohen to clean the interior of the film lab with a blue-green substance they then believed to be cleaning soap. They filled mop buckets and sprayers with the blue-green solution from 55-gallon barrels. Metrocolor provided no hazard training, posted no signs about chemical hazards, and never told the laborers what the 55-gallon barrels contained. None of the barrels of blue-green solution had labels warning of a chemical hazard or identifying the contents of the barrels. During delivery of the 55-gallon barrels of blue-green solution, Gunnell observed his supervisor, Carrasco, removing labels from each barrel before offloading them from a truck for use by Gunnell and his coworkers in cleaning the facility. The barrels provided to the workers had no labels by the time the workers used them. At that time, Gunnell believed the blue-green substance was harmless. Charles Bracey, who supervised Gunnell's work crew, testified that the blue-green substance in the barrels was referred to at Metrocolor as "green or blue strong soap."

Cleaning the interior walls and ceiling of the Metrocolor film lab exposed Gunnell, Walters, and Cohen to the blue-green cleaning substance. Gunnell transferred undiluted blue-green liquid from the barrels to buckets and sprayers. The workers sometimes did not dilute the substance before using it. Gunnell sprayed the ceiling with the blue-green solution, causing dirt to bead. He then used a mop to remove the cleaner and dirt from the ceiling, usually repeating the procedure several times to clean each area. After cleaning the ceiling, he cleaned the walls, and finally cleaned floors and pipes. As he worked on the ceiling, the blue-green cleaning liquid "rained" down on him, making contact with his skin, running down his back and chest, and getting inside his gloves. Pressing the mop against the ceiling and walls caused liquid to squeeze out of the mop and run down the handle into his sleeves, down his arms, and into his shirt. Gunnell used several gallons of solution every day. After a day's work, the blue-green solution soaked his clothing and feet. He remained wet until he arrived home. He worked in street clothes. Metrocolor provided no protective gear except for rubber gloves, which disintegrated after about a half-hour of use, and a paper suit that did not protect Gunnell from being soaked.

While working at Metrocolor, Gunnell did not recall ever being told what the blue-green cleaning substance was inside the barrels. No one told him about or required him to attend a safety program or a "right to know" program. No one trained him on how to handle chemicals. Gunnell testified that on one occasion when he was working in clothing soaked with the blue-green substance, he saw House, Carrasco, and Fuhrmann (director of facilities at Metrocolor) observe as he cleaned a room. Gunnell asked if the blue-green substance was safe. House responded, "Yes, sir. Yes, it is safe." Walters's foreman told him several times the cleaner was safe.

After finishing his work at Metrocolor, Gunnell learned that the blue-green substance provided for cleaning the film-processing lab was Absorb, an organic solvent/degreaser. Absorb contains sodium hydroxide and 2-butoxyethanol, known as 2BE. Sodium hydroxide and 2BE appear on the OSHA Director's list of hazardous substances. 2BE is one of a class of chemicals known to cause brain and nervous system damage. 2BE absorbs readily through the skin and into the bloodstream. Diluting 2BE causes it to absorb through skin more readily. Once in the bloodstream, 2BE targets the liver, kidneys, respiratory tract, and central nervous system. Its effects on the central nervous system include headaches, nausea, dizziness, confusion, loss of consciousness, and possible death. Breathing vapor, combined with skin exposure, significantly increases exposure. Workers using 2BE should avoid skin contact and wear chemical-resistant gloves and possibly a respirator.

There was no dispute that there had been a "touching" here as required by California Penal Code section 242. Why? The court of appeals found, however, that "Metrocolor used no force to cause chemicals to touch Gunnell's body. On plaintiffs' facts, it was Metrocolor's fraud or deceit—calling the Absorb solvent a 'green or blue strong soap,' failing to identify the chemical hazards in Absorb or to warn workers about those hazards, assuring Gunnell the blue-green cleaning liquid was safe to use, and removing warning labels from containers of the chemical—which led Gunnell to use the harmful chemicals. Even if those chemicals caused a 'touching,' Metrocolor did not accomplish that touching by using 'physical force' against Gunnell." Is the court's reasoning persuasive?

4 ■ Appropriateness of Common Law Crimes to Address Corporate Risk Creation

The preceding materials raise the question, What's distinctive about criminal law as compared with contract or tort? In thinking about that question, consider that the state of Indiana prosecuted the Ford Pinto case, with the help of volunteer lawyers and law students, on a budget of approximately $20,000. Ford spent approximately $1 million in its defense. The maximum penalty under Indiana law for a corporation convicted of reckless homicide was $10,000. Given this fact, what did the state stand to gain if it had won the case? What did Ford stand to lose?

As you have seen, conviction of common law criminal offenses typically requires a culpable state of mind. For individuals, but not corporations, criminal law involves the distinctive "remedy" of imprisonment upon conviction. For individuals and corporations, a criminal conviction may be distinctively stigmatizing. Consider whether very large damage awards might have a similar stigmatizing effect, particularly if the awards include amounts specifically identified as "punitive damages."

Are these distinctive characteristics appropriately applied to cases involving risk? Unlike liability in tort, which ordinarily requires that risk be "realized," criminal liability is, at least in principle, available to penalize those who engage in risky behavior regardless of whether harm actually occurs. For example, the common law offense of reckless endangerment does not require that the danger actually have come to pass. But is the knowledge that risk will be realized with a known probability sufficient to impose criminal liability? When, if at all, does that sort of knowledge demonstrate a sufficiently culpable state of mind to justify the imposition of criminal penalties? As the cost-benefit analyses performed by Ford and General Motors suggest, don't all employers and manufacturers have that sort of knowledge? Does that mean that imposing criminal liability is inappropriate—or does it mean that there is a large unaddressed problem with corporate behavior? Put another way, is (mere) indifference to the fact that small risks will be realized with certainty in a small number of cases the kind of culpable state of mind to which the criminal sanction should be attached?

There are special procedures associated with criminal prosecutions, including a higher burden of proof on the prosecution. (If punitive damage awards have effects similar to those of criminal convictions, should the procedures associated with criminal prosecutions be adapted for application in civil cases seeking such damages?) Probably most important, criminal prosecutions are brought by public officials. (Note, though, that in the *Gunnell* case, the court addressed the substance of the criminal law in a civil case. How, if at all, might that have affected the court's approach to the criminal law question?)

5 ■ Criminal Liability under Regulatory Statutes

This section describes the limited role of common law crimes (despite their current location in statutes), such as murder and criminal battery, in addressing the problem of modern risk creation, particularly by corporations. Today many regulatory statutes—including the federal Clean Air Act, Clean Water Act, and laws on hazardous waste handling and disposal—provide criminal penalties for statutory violations, although criminal liability under these regulatory statutes has been controversial.

The Clean Air Act, for example, provides for criminal penalties against any person who knowingly releases a hazardous air pollutant into the ambient air, if that person "knows at the time that he thereby places another person in imminent danger of death or serious bodily injury." 42 U.S.C. § 7413(c)(5)(A).

Penalties include fines of up to $1 million and imprisonment for up to fifteen years for each violation. In 2005, the company W. R. Grace and several of its top corporate officials were indicted by a federal grand jury under this provision, based on their activities in Libby, Montana. Among other things, the indictment alleges that W. R. Grace and its officials violated the Clean Air Act by knowingly exposing the citizens of Libby to asbestos-contaminated vermiculite ore without the citizens' knowledge or consent. One vivid example of how W. R. Grace and its officials allegedly treated the citizens of Libby is the company's provision of asbestos-contaminated vermiculite ore to the high school to serve as the foundation for its running track. Another equally arresting example is the alleged provision of such ore to the elementary school to use as the foundation for a skating rink.

The latency period (the period between exposure to a harmful substance and the manifestation of physical illness) for asbestos-related diseases is often measured in decades. In light of this fact, how will the prosecutors in the W. R. Grace case show "imminent danger of death or serious bodily injury" based on the events in Libby?

The federal Occupational Safety and Health Act (OSHA) also provides for criminal penalties. An employer who willfully violates a standard or rule under the act, and who thereby causes an employee's death, may be fined up to $10,000 and imprisoned for up to six months. A repeat conviction raises these maximum penalties to $20,000 and one year. Why do you suppose these penalties are so much less strict than the Clean Air Act's penalties? Note that following a series of articles in the *New York Times* in 2003 on workplace deaths and injuries at facilities owned by McWane Inc., the company and several of its executives were indicted for environmental crimes at several different plants. The penalties available under the environmental laws far exceeded those available under the OSHA.

If the penalties are bigger under the environmental laws, does it matter whether a defendant that has a terrible workplace safety record is charged with hurting employees or with harming the environment?

B. Tort: Recovery for (Pure?) Risk and Fear

You are already familiar with the classic examples of tort recovery for physical injuries resulting from intentional or negligent misconduct. Here we consider whether the tort system can be used to compensate for "injuries" resulting from mere exposure to workplace or environmental risk. The basic problem is this: Almost by definition, mere exposure to risk inflicts no current injury. What "risk" *means* is that there is an increased likelihood that something bad will happen at some point in the future—and "likelihood" doesn't mean "certainty."

The cases in this section deal with several kinds of (present) injuries resulting from mere exposure to risk, including a reduction in life expectancy and the fear thereof. These cases raise issues of legal doctrine and of institutional design. You should read the cases with these two concerns in mind, noting the places where the doctrinal questions play a larger role and those where the design questions do. Regarding the latter, consider whether you think that judges *allowing* recovery have exceeded the bounds of proper judicial behavior and whether judges *denying* recovery have failed to respect the fundamental principles that courts are designed to enforce. (Later in the section, as well as in chapter 5, we'll examine the institutional characteristics of courts, legislatures, and administrative agencies in more detail so you'll understand what kinds of arguments might be developed to support your conclusions.)

1 ■ Recovery for Mere Exposure to Risk and Reduction in Life Expectancy

The cases in this section and the next raise issues of legal doctrine and of institutional design (that is, the role of courts, legislatures, and administrative agencies in devising responses to risk). Initially, we examine the *doctrinal* questions the cases pose. Then, in the third section, we take up some aspects of the issues of institutional design.

■ Ayers v. Township of Jackson
106 N.J. 557 (1987)

Stein, J.:

In this case we consider the application of the New Jersey Tort Claims Act (the Act), N.J.S.A. 59:1-1 to 12-3, to the claims asserted by 339 residents of Jackson Township against that municipality.

The litigation involves claims for damages sustained because plaintiffs' well water was contaminated by toxic pollutants leaching into the Cohansey Aquifer from a landfill established and operated by Jackson Township. After an extensive trial, the jury found that the township had created a "nuisance" and a "dangerous condition" by virtue of its operation of the landfill, that its conduct was "palpably unreasonable"—a prerequisite to recovery under N.J.S.A. 59:4-2—and that it was the proximate cause of the contamination of plaintiffs' water supply. The jury verdict resulted in an aggregate judgment of $15,854,392.78, to be divided among the plaintiffs in varying amounts. The jury returned individual awards for each of the plaintiffs that varied in accordance with such factors as proximity to the landfill, duration and extent of the exposure to contaminants, and the age of the claimant.

The verdict provided compensation for three distinct claims of injury: $2,056,480 was awarded for emotional distress caused by the knowledge that they had ingested water contaminated by toxic chemicals for up to six years; $5,396,940 was awarded for the deterioration of their quality of life during the twenty months when they were deprived of running water; and $8,204,500 was awarded to cover the future cost of annual medical surveillance that plaintiffs' expert testified would be necessary because of plaintiffs' increased susceptibility to cancer and other diseases. The balance of the verdict, approximately $196,500, represented miscellaneous expenses not involved in this appeal.

The Appellate Division upheld that portion of the judgment awarding plaintiffs damages for impairment of their quality of life. . . .

In addition, the Appellate Division affirmed the trial court's dismissal of plaintiffs' claim for damages for their enhanced risk of disease. . . .

I

The evidence at trial provided ample support for the jury's conclusion that the township had operated the Legler landfill in a palpably unreasonable manner, a finding that the township did not contest before the Appellate Division. Briefly summarized, the proof showed that prior to 1971 the township operated another landfill that was the subject of complaints by neighboring residents and at least one citation for violation of state regulations. When the prior landfill's capacity was exhausted, the township opened the Legler landfill in 1972. The Department of Environmental Protection (DEP) granted a conditional permit for the new landfill, excluding liquid or soluble industrial wastes and limiting the depth of waste deposits to a specific grade above the level of the groundwater. The evidence indicated that, from the inception of the landfill's operation, the township failed to monitor the quantity and types of liquid waste dumped at the landfill, and ignored its duty to control and limit the depth of the trenches in which wastes were deposited. There was substantial evidence that the township disregarded the conditions imposed by DEP, and that the township's negligent operation of the landfill resulted in chemical contamination of the groundwater in the area and the underlying aquifer.

At trial plaintiffs offered expert testimony to prove that the chemical contamination of their wells was caused by the township's improper operation of the landfill. The testimony established that, in varying concentrations, the following chemical substances had infiltrated various wells used by plaintiffs as a water source: acetone; benzene; chlorobenzene; chloroform; dichlorofluoromethane; ethyl benzene; methylene chloride; methyl isobutyl ketone; 1,1,2,2-tetrachloroethane; tetrahydrofuran; 1,1,1-trichloroethane; and trichloroethylene. A groundwater expert described the probable movement and concentration of the chemicals as they migrated from the landfill toward plaintiffs' wells. A toxicologist summarized the known hazardous characteristics of the chemical substances. He testified that of the twelve identified chemicals, four were known carcinogens. Other potential toxic effects identified by the toxicologist included liver and kidney damage, mutations and alterations in genetic material, damage to blood and reproductive systems, neurological damage and skin irritations. The toxicologist also testified about differences in the extent of the chemical exposure experienced by various plaintiffs. An expert in the diagnosis and treatment of diseases caused by exposure to toxic substances testified that the plaintiffs required annual medical examinations to afford the earliest possible diagnosis of chemically induced illnesses. Her opinion was that a program of regular medical surveillance for plaintiffs would improve prospects for cure, treatment, prolongation of life, and minimization of pain and disability.

A substantial number—more than 150—of the plaintiffs gave testimony with respect to damages, describing in detail the impairment of their quality of life during the period that they were without running water, and the emotional distress they suffered. With regard to the emotional distress claims, the plaintiffs' testimony detailed their emotional reactions to the chemical contamination of their wells and the deprivation of their water supply, as well as their fears for the health of their family members. Expert psychological testimony was offered to document plaintiffs' claims that they had sustained compensable psychological damage as a result of the contamination of their wells.

We now consider each of the plaintiffs' damage claims in the context of the evidence adduced at trial and the legal principles that should inform our application of the Tort Claims Act.

Quality of Life

In November 1978, the residents of the Legler area of Jackson Township were advised by the local Board of Health not to drink their well water, and to limit washing and bathing to avoid prolonged exposure to the water. This warning was issued by the Board after tests disclosed that a number of wells in the Legler area of the township were contaminated by toxic chemicals. Initially, the township provided water to the affected residents in water tanks that were transported by tank trucks to various locations in the neighborhood. Plaintiffs brought their own containers, filled them with water from the tanks, and transported the water to their homes.

This water-supply system was soon discontinued and replaced by a home-delivery system. Residents in need of water tied a white cloth on their mailbox and received a 40 gallon barrel containing a plastic liner filled with water. The filled barrels weighed in excess of 100 pounds and were dropped off, as needed, on the properties of the Legler-area residents. The family-members frequently were required to move the barrels to a protected area, either inside a garage or inside the residence. Residents who stored the barrels in garages testified that the water froze in cold weather. Other residents rolled or dragged their barrels into their homes. In order to use the water for drinking, cooking, washing or bathing, the residents filled containers with water from the barrels to meet the varying needs of their households. On occasion, there was dirt or debris in the water and the township would be requested to provide a replacement barrel.

The Appellate Division opinion described the inconvenience experienced by one resident: One witness, who suffered from arthritis, testified to hauling her water for drinking, cooking and bathing up nine steps because, as she said,

> [t]here was no way that I could get the water upstairs except by hauling pot after pot out of the containers, . . . which was a considerable amount of hauling everyday just to use for drinking and bathing the children and cooking.

As the Appellate Division noted, the lack of running water was an understandable source of tension and friction among members of the plaintiffs' households, who for nearly two years were compelled to obtain water in this primitive manner.

The trial court charged the jury that plaintiffs' claim for "quality of life" damages encompassed "inconveniences, aggravation, and unnecessary expenditure of time and effort related to the use of the water hauled to their homes, as well as to other disruption in their lives, including disharmony in the family unit." The aggregate jury verdict on this claim was $5,396,940. This represented an average award of slightly over $16,000 for each plaintiff; thus, a family unit consisting of four plaintiffs received an average award of approximately $64,000.

In the Appellate Division and before this Court, defendant argues that this segment of the verdict is barred by the New Jersey Tort Claims Act, which provides:

> No damages shall be awarded against a public entity or public employee for pain and suffering resulting from any injury; provided, however, that this limitation on the recovery of damages for pain and suffering shall not apply in cases of permanent loss of a bodily function, permanent disfigurement or dismemberment where the medical treatment expenses are in excess of $1,000.00. [N.J.S.A. 59:9-2(d).]

Defendant contends that the legislative intent in restricting damages for "pain and suffering" was to encompass claims for all "non-objective" injuries, unless the statutory threshold of severity of injury or expense of treatment is met. The township asserts that the inconvenience, aggravation, effort and disruption of the family unit that resulted from the loss of plaintiffs' water supply was but a form of "pain and suffering" and therefore uncompensable under the Act.

The Appellate Division rejected the township's contention, concluding that there was a clear distinction between

> the subjectively measured damages for pain and suffering, which are not compensable by the Tort Claims Act, and those which objectively affect quality of life by causing an interference with the use of one's land through inconvenience and the disruption of daily activities.

We agree with the Appellate Division's conclusion. The Tort Claims Act's ban against recovery of damages for "pain and suffering resulting from any injury" is intended to apply to the intangible, subjective feelings of discomfort that are associated with personal injuries. It was not intended to bar claims for inconvenience associated with the invasion of a property interest. As the trial court's charge explained, plaintiffs sought damages to compensate them for the multiple inconveniences associated with a lack of running water. Although the disruption of plaintiffs' water supply is an "injury" under the Act, N.J.S.A. 59:1-3, the interest invaded here, the right to obtain potable running water from plaintiffs' own wells, is qualitatively different from "pain and suffering" related to a personal injury.

As the Appellate Division acknowledged, plaintiffs' claim for quality of life damages is derived from the law of nuisance. It has long been recognized that damages for inconvenience, annoyance, and discomfort are recoverable in a nuisance action. . . .

Accordingly, we conclude that the quality of life damages represent compensation for losses associated with damage to property, and agree with the Appellate Division that they do not constitute pain and suffering under the Tort Claims Act. We therefore sustain the judgment for quality of life damages.

Claims for Enhanced Risk

No claims were asserted by plaintiffs seeking recovery for specific illnesses caused by their exposure to chemicals. Rather, they claim damages for the enhanced risk of future illness attributable to such exposure. . . .

Before trial, the trial court granted defendant's motion for summary judgment dismissing the enhanced risk claim. It held that plaintiffs' proofs, with the benefit of all favorable inferences, would not establish a "reasonable probability" that plain-tiffs would sustain future injury as a result of chemical contamination of their water supply. The trial court also observed that recognition of the enhanced risk claim would cause the jury to "speculate . . . [as] to the future health of each plaintiff," and raise "the spectre of potential claims . . . increasing in boundless proportion." How-ever, the court specifically noted that future claims for injury attributable to expo-sure to contaminants in the water supply would not be barred by the statute of limitations. The Appellate Division affirmed the dismissal of the enhanced risk claim, but characterized the trial court's observation that future claims for physical injury would not be barred by the statute of limitations as "dictum only," having "no controlling significance to the future rights of the parties."

. . .

As a result of the trial court's and Appellate Division's rulings, plaintiffs are left to await actual manifestation of physical injury attributable to their exposure to toxic chemicals before they can institute and sustain a damage claim for personal injuries against the defendant. Although the trial court observed that any such future suits could avoid the bar of the statute of limitations by virtue of our "discovery rule," the Appellate Division's characterization of that statement as nonbinding dictum defers to this or another court the task of determining whether subsequent personal injury suits against this defendant may indeed be maintained. In the interim, under the Appellate Division ruling, any plaintiff who obtains regular or periodic medical surveillance for the express purpose of detecting adverse physical conditions at-tributable to exposure to toxic chemicals must personally bear the expense of that evaluation to the extent its cost is not covered by plaintiffs' own health insurance.

In our view, these decisions fall short of effectuating the policies of the Tort Claims Act where claims are asserted against a public entity for wrongful exposure to toxic chemicals. . . . We also deem it appropriate to clarify the effect of the statute of limitations, and the single controversy doctrine on future claims for personal injuries.

1

Our evaluation of the enhanced risk . . . claims requires that we focus on a critical issue in the management of toxic tort litigation: at what stage in the evolution of a toxic injury should tort law intercede by requiring the responsible party to pay damages?

At the outset, we must recognize that the issues presented by this case and others like it will be recurring. We note the difficulty that both law and science experience in attempting to deal with the emerging complexities of industrialized society and the consequent implications for human health. One facet of that problem is represented here, in the form of years of inadequate and improper waste disposal practices. However dimly or callously the consequences of those waste management practices may have been perceived, those consequences are now upon us. According to the Senate Committee on Environment and Public Works, more than ninety percent of all hazardous chemical wastes produced in the United States have been disposed of improperly.

In addition to the staggering problem of removing—or at least containing—the hazardous remnants of past practices, there remains the moral and legal problem of compensating the human victims of past misuse of chemical products.

Governmental response to the problem of compensation has been slow. In enacting the Comprehensive Environmental Response, Compensation and Liability Act of 1980 (CERCLA), 42 U.S.C.A. §§ 9601–9657, more commonly called the Superfund legislation, Congress deliberately made no provision for the recovery of damages for personal injury and property damage resulting from exposure to hazardous waste. . . .

In the absence of statutory or administrative mechanisms for processing injury claims resulting from environmental contamination, courts have struggled to accommodate common-law tort doctrines to the peculiar characteristics of toxic-tort litigation. The overwhelming conclusion of the commentators who have evaluated the result is that the accommodation has failed, that common-law tort doctrines are ill-suited to the resolution of such injury claims, and that some form of statutorily-authorized compensation procedure is required if the injuries sustained by victims of chemical contamination are to be fairly redressed.

A variety of factors are cited to demonstrate that judicial resolution of mass exposure claims is unworkable. Among the obstacles cited are practical difficulties endemic to mass exposure litigation, including the identification of the parties responsible for environmental damage; the risk that responsible parties are judgment-proof; the expense of compensating expert witnesses in specialized fields such as toxicology and epidemiology; and the strong temptation for premature settlement because of the cost and complexity of protracted multi-party litigation.

Although state statutes of limitations are invariably identified as procedural obstacles to mass exposure litigation, the extent of the problem posed by such statutes varies widely among jurisdictions. Because of the long latency period typical of illnesses caused by chemical pollutants, victims often discover their injury and the existence of a cause of action long after the expiration of the personal-injury statute of limitations, where the limitations period is calculated from the date of the exposure. Most jurisdictions have remedied this problem by adopting a version of the "discovery rule" that tolls the statute until the injury is discovered. Few states follow New Jersey's discovery rule that tolls the statute until the victim discovers both the injury and the facts suggesting that a third party may be responsible. However, we note that CERCLA now pre-empts state statutes of limitation where they provide that the limitations period for personal-injury or property-damage suits prompted by exposure to hazardous substances starts on a date earlier than the "federally required commencement date." That term is defined as "the date plaintiff knew (or reasonably should have known) that the personal injury or property damages . . . were caused or contributed to by the hazardous substance . . . concerned." Superfund Amendments and Authorization Act of 1986, 42 U.S.C.A. § 9658.

The single controversy rule "requires that a party include in the action all related claims against an adversary and its failure to do so precludes the maintenance of a second action." The doctrine may bar recovery where, as here, suit is instituted to recover damages to compensate for the immediate consequences of toxic pollution, but the initiation of additional litigation depends upon when, if ever, physical injuries threatened by the pollution are manifested.

As the Appellate Division implied, we need not resolve such issues for the litigants in this case. Nevertheless, it is appropriate that all of the parties in interest understand that neither the single controversy doctrine nor the statute of limitations, will preclude a timely-filed cause of action for damages prompted by the future "discovery" of a disease or injury related to the tortious conduct at issue in this litigation. The bar of the statute of limitations is avoided because, under New Jersey's discovery rule, the cause of action does not accrue until the victim is aware of the injury or disease and of the facts indicating that a third party is or may be responsible. Moreover, the single controversy rule, intended "to avoid the delays and wasteful expense of the multiplicity of litigation which results from the splitting of a controversy," cannot sensibly be applied to a toxic-tort claim filed when disease is manifested years after the exposure, merely because the same plaintiff sued previously to recover for property damage or other injuries. In such a case, the rule is literally inapplicable since, as noted, the second cause of action does not accrue until the disease is manifested; hence, it could not have been joined with the earlier claims.

Accordingly, we concur with the principle advanced by the trial court, and endorsed by other federal and state courts, that neither the statute of limitations nor the single controversy rule should bar timely causes of action in toxic-tort cases instituted after discovery of a disease or injury related to tortious conduct, although there has been prior litigation between the parties of different claims based on the same tortious conduct.

Another commonly identified obstacle to judicial resolution of mass exposure tort claims is the difficulty encountered by plaintiffs in proving negligence. Although causes of action for trespass and nuisance may be available to redress property injuries, most personal injury actions in toxic tort litigation seek recovery on the basis of the defendant's negligence. It is frequently argued that a negligence standard unfairly imposes on plaintiffs the difficult burden of establishing by a cost-benefit analysis that the cost to defendant of taking precautionary measures is outweighed by the probability and gravity of harm. A frequent proposal involves the substitution of strict liability doctrine in place of a negligence standard.

By far the most difficult problem for plaintiffs to overcome in toxic tort litigation is the burden of proving causation. In the typical tort case, the plaintiff must prove tortious conduct, injury and proximate cause. Ordinarily, proof of causation requires the establishment of a sufficient nexus between the defendant's conduct and the plaintiff's injury. In toxic tort cases, the task of proving causation is invariably made more complex because of the long latency period of illnesses caused by carcinogens or other toxic chemicals. The fact that ten or twenty years or more may intervene between the exposure and the manifestation of disease highlights the practical difficulties encountered in the effort to prove causation. Moreover, the fact that segments of the entire population are afflicted by cancer and other toxically-induced diseases requires plaintiffs, years after their exposure, to counter the argument that other intervening exposures or forces were the "cause" of their injury. The thoughtful analysis by District Judge Jenkins in *Allen v. United States*, 588 F. Supp. 247 (D. Utah 1984), a case involving the causal relationship between nuclear fallout and cancer, graphically explains the causation problem in mass exposure litigation:

> In most cases, the factual connection between defendant's conduct and plaintiff's injury is not genuinely in dispute. Often, the cause-and-effect is obvious: A's vehicle strikes B, injuring him; a bottle of A's product explodes, injuring B; water impounded on A's property flows onto B's land, causing immediate damage.

In this case, the factual connection singling out the defendant as the source of the plaintiffs' injuries and deaths is very much in genuine dispute. Determination of the cause-in-fact, or factual connection, issue is complicated by the nature of the injuries suffered (various forms of cancer and leukemia), the nature of the causation mechanism alleged (ionizing radiation from nuclear fallout . . .), the extraordinary time factors and other variables involved in tracing any causal relationship between the two.

At this point, there appears to be no question whether or not ionizing radiation causes cancer and leukemia. It does. Once more, however, it seems important to clarify what is meant by "cause" in relation to radiation and cancer.

When we refer to radiation as a cause, we do not mean that it causes every case of cancer or leukemia. Indeed, the evidence we have indicating radiation in the causation of cancer and leukemia shows that not all cases of cancer are caused by radiation. Second, when we refer to radiation as a cause of cancer, we do not mean that every individual exposed to a certain amount of radiation will develop cancer. We simply mean that a population exposed to a certain dose of radiation will show a greater incidence of cancer than that same population would have shown in the absence of the added radiation.

The question of cause-in-fact is additionally complicated by the long delay, known often as the latency period, between the exposure to radiation and the observed cancer or leukemia. Assuming that cancer originates in a single cell, or a few cells, in a particular organ or tissue, it may take years before those cells multiply into the millions or billions that comprise a detectable tumor. . . .

The problem of the latency period is one factor distinguishing . . . cancer causation questions from the cause-in-fact relationships found in most tort cases; normally "cause" is far more direct, immediate and observable, e.g., A fires a gun at B, seriously wounding him. The great length of time involved . . . allows the possible involvement of "intervening causes," sources of injury wholly apart from the defendant's activities, which obscure the factual connection between the plaintiff's injury and the defendant's purportedly wrongful conduct. The mere passage of time is sufficient to raise doubts about "cause" in the minds of a legal system accustomed to far more immediate chains of events.

These difficulties forced the *Allen* court to invoke analogies to other cases that have relied upon factual connections between plaintiffs and defendants as a basis for liability, where proof of causation was unavailable. Id. at 407 (citing *Summers v. Tice*, 33 Cal.2d 80 (1948) (during a hunting accident, two defendants acted negligently, but only one caused plaintiff's injury; since plaintiff could not prove which defendant was responsible for the injury, burden of proof shifted to each defendant to disprove causation), and *Ybarra v. Spangard*, 25 Cal.2d 486 (1944) (application of doctrine of res ipsa loquitur to a "foreign-instrument" medical-malpractice case where several physicians and nurses participated in an operation)). The same difficulties encountered in *Allen* have also troubled commentators assessing the application of common-law doctrines to toxic tort litigation. Hence, recommendations have been made for a legislative response to the problem of causation when the injury has been manifested.

Although we acknowledge, as we must, the array of complex practical and doctrinal problems that confound litigants and courts in toxic-tort mass-exposure litigation, we are confronted in this case with fairly narrow and manageable issues. A legally and financially responsible defendant has been identified and a jury has determined fault under the "palpably unreasonable" standard of the Tort Claims Act, N.J.S.A. 59:4-2, a standard more difficult to satisfy than ordinary negligence. No statute of limitations questions are raised in this litigation. Nor are we confronted with insurmountable issues of causation: the testimony of plaintiffs' experts has persuasively established the relationship between defendant's wrongful conduct and the contamination of plaintiffs' wells; and plaintiffs do not seek damages for presently-existing illness or disease attributable to defendant's wrongful conduct. The legal issue we must resolve, in the context of the jury's determination of defendant's liability under the Act, is whether the proof of an unquantified enhanced risk of illness or a need for medical surveillance is sufficient to justify compensation under the Tort Claims Act. In view of the acknowledged difficulties of proving causation once evidence of disease is manifest, a determination of the compensability of post-exposure, pre-symptom injuries is particularly important in assessing the ability of tort law to redress the claims of plaintiffs in toxic-tort litigation.

2

Much of the same evidence was material to both the enhanced risk and medical surveillance claims. Dr. Dan Raviv, a geohydrologist, testified as to the movements and concentrations of the various chemical substances as they migrated from the landfill toward plaintiffs' wells. Dr. Joseph Highland, a toxicologist, applied Dr. Raviv's data and gave testimony concerning the level of exposure of various plaintiffs. Dr. Highland also compiled toxicity profiles of the chemical substances found in the wells, and testified concerning the health hazards posed by the chemicals and the exposure levels at which adverse health effects had been experimentally observed. According to Dr. Highland, four of the chemicals were known to be carcinogenic, and at least four of the chemicals were capable of adversely affecting the reproductive system or causing birth defects. Most of the chemical substances could produce adverse effects on the liver and kidney, as well as on the nervous system. For at least six of the chemicals, no data was available regarding carcinogenic potential. He also testified that the exposure to multiple chemical substances posed additional hazards to plaintiffs because of the possibility of biological interaction among the chemicals that enhanced the risk to plaintiffs.

Dr. Highland testified that the Legler area residents, because of their exposure to toxic chemicals, had an increased risk of cancer; that unborn children and infants were more susceptible to the disease because of their immature biological defense systems; and that the extent of the risk was variable with the degree of exposure to the chemicals. Dr. Highland testified that he could not quantify the extent of the enhanced risk of cancer because of the lack of scientific information concerning the effect of the interaction of the various chemicals to which plaintiffs were exposed. However, the jury could reasonably have inferred from his testimony that the risk, although unquantified, was medically significant.

Dr. Highland also testified that a sample of twelve plaintiffs was studied to assess their increased susceptibility to liver and kidney disease. A table prepared by Dr. Highland and admitted in evidence described these twelve plaintiffs as having a moderate, high, or very high likelihood of contracting liver or renal disorders because of their exposure to chemical substances known as chlorinated aliphatic hydrocarbons (CAH's).[7] Dr. Highland also testified that the exposure to chemicals had already caused actual physical injury to plaintiffs through its adverse effects on the genetic material within their cells.[8] . . .

. . . The enhanced risk claim seeks a damage award, not because of any expenditure of funds, but because plaintiffs contend that the unquantified injury to their health and life expectancy should be presently compensable, even though no evidence of disease is manifest. Defendant does not dispute the causal relationship between the plaintiffs' exposure to toxic chemicals and the plaintiffs' increased risk of diseases, but contends that the probability that plaintiffs will actually become ill from their exposure to chemicals is too remote to warrant compensation under principles of tort law. . . .

3

The trial court declined to submit to the jury the issue of defendant's liability for the plaintiffs' increased risk of contracting cancer, kidney or liver damage, or other diseases associated with the chemicals that had migrated from the landfill to their wells. If the issue had not been withheld, the jury could have concluded from the evidence that most or all of the plaintiffs had a significantly but unquantifiably enhanced risk of the identified diseases, and that such enhanced risk was attributable to defendant's conduct.

---

[7] The chemicals found in plaintiffs' wells in this category were: methylene chloride, chloroform, 1,1,1-trichloroethane, dichlorofluoromethane, 1,1,2-trichloroethylene, and 1,1,2,2-tetrachloroethane.

[8] Dr. Highland explained the effect of exposure to carcinogenic materials in terms of a "switch" that, when turned on, affects the genetic material and may or may not result in cancer:

> We don't understand scientifically yet the real biological steps throughout the whole chain, how exposure today to some agent initiates or starts a process which in 20, 30 years from now ultimately manifests itself or is seen as a cancer in an individual. . . .
>
> What we do know is that there is a progression of steps that must be occurring. There is an injury or insult that occurs. I use the analogy to a switch being turned on upon exposures, that generally, usually, when a switch is turned on, it's not turned off.
>
> There are some cases where a switch can be turned off; but, in general, we believe that this is a process of throwing switches and that the series of switches need[s] to be thrown before the disease is ultimately seen. Therefore, if you picture one cell of thousands, of millions, in the body, which is being exposed, you may get a switch turned on. That's the biological damage, injury, insult, whatever term you wish to use, that occurs upon the exposure. It may be actually seen in terms of 20 years from now when a cancer becomes evident, or it may never be seen. That's why what we did was a risk assessment which deals with probabilities.
>
> We are saying the population is at risk, increased risk of disease, of cancer, not a certainty that everyone will get cancer. There's a[n] increased risk from the exposure. In some individuals where the switches are turned on, ultimately they may have wound up with a cancer, and in others where the switch is turned on, where there's biological insult, maybe other factors take place in life and that never becomes clearly manifested.
>
> By the kind of biological change, something that occurs, we believe, with the genetic material in the cell to start the process, and along the way other things affect that cell, flip more switches, make it ultimately become a cancer cell and ultimately manifest as a physical cancer.

A preliminary question is whether a significant exposure to toxic chemicals resulting in an enhanced risk of disease is an "injury" for the purposes of the Tort Claims Act. The Act defines injury to include "damage to or loss of property or any other injury that a person may suffer that would be actionable if inflicted by a private person." N.J.S.A. 59:1–3. We also note that the Restatement defines "injury" as "the invasion of any legally protected interest of another." Restatement (Second) of Torts § 7(1) (1965):

> The word "injury" is used . . . to denote the fact that there has been an invasion of a legally protected interest which, if it were the legal consequence of a tortious act, would entitle the person suffering the invasion to maintain an action of tort. . . . The most usual form of injury is the infliction of some harm, but there may be an injury although no harm is done. [Id. Comment a.]

In our view, an enhanced risk of disease caused by significant exposure to toxic chemicals is clearly an "injury" under the Act. In this case, neither the trial court nor the Appellate Division challenged the contention that the enhanced risk of disease was a tortiously-inflicted injury, but both concluded that the proof quantifying the likelihood of disease was insufficient to submit the issue to the jury. As the Appellate Division observed:

> While it is true that damages are recoverable for the prospective consequences of a tortious injury, it must be demonstrated that the apprehended consequences are reasonably probable. As we explained in connection with plaintiffs' claims for future medical surveillance, the degree of increased risk was in no way quantified. Indeed, that function was described by plaintiffs' expert witness as "impossible," and we therefore conclude that a reasonable probability of enhanced risk is not supported by the evidence. We discern no way to compensate one for enhanced risk without knowing in some way the degree of enhancement. Additionally, the recoverability of damages for enhanced risk in this state has not been decided.

Except for a handful of cases involving traumatic torts causing presently discernible injuries in addition to an enhanced risk of future injuries,[9] courts have generally been reluctant to recognize claims for potential but unrealized injury

---

[9] See, e.g., *Martin v. City of New Orleans*, 678 F.2d 1321, 1327 (5th Cir. 1982) (bullet lodged in neck; despite plaintiff's favorable prognosis, the fact that there would always be a risk of life-threatening future complications supported large damage award); *Starlings v. Ski Roundtop Corp.*, 493 F. Supp. 507, 510 (M.D. Pa. 1980) (knee injury; it was proper to submit to jury evidence regarding plaintiff's possible increased risk of arthritis, in view of existing injury to plaintiff's knee); *Davis v. Graviss*, 672 S.W.2d 928, 932 (Ky. 1984) (basal skull fracture causing leakage of cerebral spinal fluid; compensation for increased likelihood of future complications permitted if supported by substantial evidence); *Feist v. Sears, Roebuck & Co.*, 267 Or. 402, 412 (1973) (four-year-old child sustained basal skull fracture; based on expert testimony, trial court permitted jury to award damages for enhanced susceptibility to meningitis); *Schwegel v. Goldberg*, 209 Pa. Super. 280, 286–87 (Pa. Super. Ct. 1967) (four-year-old child sustained fractured skull, brain contusion, and traumatic hemorrhage, and had a five percent likelihood of experiencing epileptic seizures in the future; recovery for enhanced risk of future epilepsy allowed despite its low probability because there was "no speculation or guessing" regarding serious present injury).

unless the proof that the injury will occur is substantial. Our most recent encounter with the question of enhanced risk damages occurred in *Evers v. Dollinger*, 95 N.J. 399 (1984). There, plaintiff's doctor failed to diagnose breast cancer and plaintiff's claim for damages sought recovery for her enhanced risk of recurrent disease occasioned by the misdiagnosis. Plaintiff underwent an extended mastectomy after her cancer was properly diagnosed, but by the time the case was decided by this Court her cancer had recurred. In reversing the judgment for defendant entered at the close of plaintiff's case, we held that on retrial plaintiff was entitled to prove that defendant's negligence increased the risk of metastasis and that such increased risk was a substantial factor in producing the recurrence of disease. We declined to address the compensability of enhanced risk in the abstract:

> Whether "increased risk," standing alone, is an actionable element of damage in a malpractice case is a provocative question the determination of which we leave for an appeal that requires, as this case does not, the answer.

Among the recent toxic tort cases rejecting liability for damages based on enhanced risk is *Anderson v. W. R. Grace & Co.*, 628 F.Supp. 1219 (D. Mass. 1986). That case, recently settled for an undisclosed amount, see N.Y. Times, Sept. 23, 1986, at A16, col. 1, involved defendants' alleged chemical contamination of the groundwater in areas of Woburn, Massachusetts. See generally P. DiPerna, Cluster Mystery: Epidemic and the Children of Woburn, Mass. (1985) (containing background information on the Woburn case).* Plaintiffs alleged that two wells supplying water to the City of Woburn drew upon the contaminated water, and that exposure to the contaminated water caused five deaths and severe personal injuries among plaintiffs. Among the claims for personal injuries dismissed before trial were plaintiffs' claims for damages based on enhanced risk. Relying on the Massachusetts rule regarding prospective damages, the *Anderson* court reasoned that "recovery depends on establishing a 'reasonable probability' that the harm will occur." Id. at 1231 (citing Restatement (Second) of Torts § 912 comment e). However, the *Anderson* court held that the plaintiffs failed to satisfy this threshold standard. They had not quantified their alleged enhanced risk: "Nothing in the present record indicates the magnitude of the increased risk or the diseases which plaintiffs may suffer." Id.

The court in *Anderson* explained that its reluctance to recognize the enhanced risk claims was based on two policy considerations. Its first concern was that recognition of the cause of action would create a flood of speculative lawsuits. In addition, the court stated:

> A further reason for denying plaintiffs' damages for the increased risk of future harm in this action is the inevitable inequity which would result if recovery were allowed. "To award damages based on a mere mathematical probability would significantly undercompensate those who actually do develop cancer and would be a windfall to those who do not."

The majority of courts that have considered the enhanced risk issue have agreed with the disposition of the District Court in *Anderson*. See *Schweitzer v.*

---

* [Editors' Note: This case is the subject of the popular book and film *A Civil Action*.]

Consolidated Rail Corp., 758 F.2d 936, 942 (3rd Cir.1985) ("[S]ubclinical injury resulting from exposure to asbestos is insufficient to constitute the actual loss or damage to a plaintiff's interest required to sustain a cause of action. . . ."); *Laswell v. Brown*, 683 F.2d 261, 269 (8th Cir.1982) (alleged latent cellular or genetic defects associated with nuclear testing; "[A] lawsuit for personal injuries cannot be based upon the mere possibility of some future harm.") (1983); *Mink v. University of Chicago*, 460 F.Supp. 713, 719 (N.D. Ill.1978) (DES; "The mere fact of risk without any accompanying physical injury is insufficient to state a claim. . . ."); *Morrissy v. Eli Lilly & Co.*, 76 Ill. App.3d 753, 761 (1979) (DES; mere exposure and the possibility of developing future illness is insufficient to state a present injury).

Other courts have acknowledged the propriety of the enhanced risk cause of action, but have emphasized the requirement that proof of future injury be reasonably certain. See *Hagerty v. L & L Marine Servs.*, supra, 788 F.2d at 319 ("[A] plaintiff can recover [damages for enhanced risk] only where he can show that the toxic exposure more probably than not will lead to cancer."); *Wilson v. Johns-Manville Sales Corp.*, 684 F.2d 111, 116-19 (D.C. Cir.1982) (holding that in latent disease cases statute of limitations period does not begin until disease is manifest and observing that "recovery of damages based on future consequences may be had only if such consequences are 'reasonably certain.' ")]; *Sterling v. Velsicol Chemical Corp.*, supra, 647 F.Supp. at 321–22 (upholding cause of action for enhanced susceptibility to injury based on chemical contamination of plaintiffs' wells where "reasonable probability" standard is met); *Lorenc v. Chemirad Corp.*, 37 N.J. 56, 76 (1962) (holding that evidence was sufficient to raise jury question whether future onset of cancer was probable); *Devlin v. Johns-Manville Corp.*, supra, 202 N.J. Super. at 565 (rejecting enhanced risk claim except where there is proof that it is reasonably probable or as a basis for damages for emotional distress or medical surveillance).

Additionally, several courts have permitted recovery for increased risk of disease, but only where the plaintiff exhibited some present manifestation of disease. See *Jackson v. Johns-Manville Sales Corp.*, 781 F.2d 394, 412–13 (5th Cir. 1986) (allowing recovery for increased risk of cancer where evidence indicated that due to asbestos exposure, plaintiff had greater than fifty percent chance of contracting cancer; "[o]nce the injury becomes actionable—once some effect appears—then the plaintiff is permitted to recover for all probable future manifestations as well"); *Brafford v. Susquehanna Corp.*, 586 F.Supp. 14, 17–18 (D. Colo.1984) (acknowledging that cause of action for increased risk of cancer requires proof of present physical injury, but denying defendant's motion for summary judgment to permit plaintiff to offer proof of present genetic and chromosomal damage due to exposure to radiation); cf. *DePass v. United States*, supra, 721 F.2d at 210 (Posner, J., dissenting) ("Accidents that require the amputation of a limb . . . create a high risk of premature death from heart disease. . . . [T]he case should be remanded . . . for a determination of the amount of damages necessary to compensate DePass for an 11-year reduction in his life expectancy.").

We observe that the overwhelming weight of the scholarship on this issue favors a right of recovery for tortious conduct that causes a significantly enhanced risk of injury. For the most part, the commentators concede the inadequacy of common-law remedies for toxic-tort victims. Instead, they recommend statutory or administrative mechanisms that would permit compensation to be awarded on the basis of exposure and significant risk of disease, without the necessity of proving the existence of present injury.

Our disposition of this difficult and important issue requires that we choose between two alternatives, each having a potential for imposing unfair and undesirable consequences on the affected interests. A holding that recognizes a cause of action for unquantified enhanced risk claims exposes the tort system, and the public it serves, to the task of litigating vast numbers of claims for compensation based on threats of injuries that may never occur. It imposes on judges and juries the burden of assessing damages for the risk of potential disease, without clear guidelines to determine what level of compensation may be appropriate. It would undoubtedly increase already escalating insurance rates. It is clear that the recognition of an "enhanced risk" cause of action, particularly when the risk is unquantified, would generate substantial litigation that would be difficult to manage and resolve.

Our dissenting colleague, arguing in favor of recognizing a cause of action based on an unquantified claim of enhanced risk, points out that "courts have not allowed the difficulty of quantifying injury to prevent them from offering compensation for assault, trespass, emotional distress, invasion of privacy or damage to reputation." Although lawsuits grounded in one or more of these causes of action may involve claims for damages that are difficult to quantify, such damages are awarded on the basis of events that have occurred and can be proved at the time of trial. In contrast, the compensability of the enhanced risk claim depends upon the likelihood of an event that has not yet occurred and may never occur—the contracting of one or more diseases the risk of which has been enhanced by defendant's conduct. It is the highly contingent and speculative quality of an unquantified claim based on enhanced risk that renders it novel and difficult to manage and resolve. If such claims were to be litigated, juries would be asked to award damages for the enhanced risk of a disease that may never be contracted, without the benefit of expert testimony sufficient to establish the likelihood that the contingent event will ever occur.

On the other hand, denial of the enhanced-risk cause of action may mean that some of these plaintiffs will be unable to obtain compensation for their injury. Despite the collateral estoppel effect of the jury's finding that defendant's wrongful conduct caused the contamination of plaintiffs' wells, those who contract diseases in the future because of their exposure to chemicals in their well water may be unable to prove a causal relationship between such exposure and their disease. We have already adverted to the substantial difficulties encountered by plaintiffs in attempting to prove causation in toxic tort litigation. Dismissal of the enhanced risk claims may effectively preclude any recovery for injuries caused by exposure to chemicals in plaintiffs' wells because of the difficulty of proving that injuries manifested in the future were not the product of intervening events or causes.

It may be that this dilemma could be mitigated by a legislative remedy that eases the burden of proving causation in toxic-tort cases where there has been a statistically significant incidence of disease among the exposed population. Other proposals for legislative intervention contemplate a funded source of compensation for persons significantly endangered by exposure to toxic chemicals. We invite the legislature's attention to this perplexing and serious problem.

In deciding between recognition or nonrecognition of plaintiffs' enhanced-risk claim, we feel constrained to choose the alternative that most closely reflects the legislative purpose in enacting the Tort Claims Act. We are conscious of the admonition that in construing the Act courts should "exercise restraint in the acceptance of novel causes of action against public entities." Comment, N.J.S.A. 59:2-1. In our view, the speculative nature of an unquantified enhanced risk claim, the difficulties inherent in adjudicating such claims, and the policies underlying the Tort Claims Act argue persuasively against the recognition of this cause of action. Accordingly, we decline to recognize plaintiffs' cause of action for the unquantified enhanced risk of disease, and affirm the judgment of the Appellate Division dismissing such claims. We need not and do not decide whether a claim based on enhanced risk of disease that is supported by testimony demonstrating that the onset of the disease is reasonably probable could be maintained under the Tort Claims Act. . . .

Handler, J., concurring in part and dissenting in part:

This case involves a municipality that operated a landfill over a long period of time in a palpably unreasonable way, directly subjecting its own residents to carcinogenic and otherwise toxic chemicals. These chemicals caused medical injury in the residents, creating a significant risk that they would develop cancer and other diseases equally grave. The risk of disease to these residents is indisputably greater than the risk of disease experienced by the general population. Because of limitations in current scientific knowledge and because of the number and variety of toxic chemicals involved, the victims of this toxic exposure were unable to measure or quantify the enhancement of their risk of disease. The Court focuses on this inability to measure the risk, rather than on the fact of contamination, and rules that these residents cannot therefore recover any damages referable to that enhanced risk. Further, while the majority does recognize a claim for medical monitoring that is clearly referable to the enhanced risk of disease, it rules that in the future the award of this limited item of special damages is not to be treated as compensation paid directly to aggrieved plaintiffs, but will be used only to reimburse actual expenses through a court-supervised fund. In effect, the Court's holding leaves these grievously wronged persons uncompensated for the injuries caused by the defendant's palpably unreasonable conduct. The Court thus affords the victims of tortious toxic exposure significantly less protection than it would plaintiffs in other tort actions. While in some respects the Court is influenced by the provisions of the New Jersey Tort Claims Act, and the status of defendant as a governmental entity covered by the Act, these considerations do not require or justify the unfairness to plaintiffs. Accordingly, I dissent in part from the majority's reasoning and holding. . . .

II

The essence of the claim for damages here is the reality of the physical injury caused by the wrongful exposure to toxic chemicals and the increased peril of cancer and other serious diseases that the residents have incurred. The Court does not dispute the fact of toxic contamination, nor does it contest the characterization of a significantly enhanced risk of disease as a tortiously inflicted injury. The majority also admits that "[d]ismissal of the enhanced risk claims may effectively preclude any recovery for injuries caused by exposure to chemicals in plaintiffs' wells." Nonetheless, the majority effectively denies plaintiffs any meaningful recovery. It asserts that "the speculative nature of an unquantified enhanced risk claim, the difficulties inherent in adjudicating such claims, and the policies underlying the Tort Claims Act argue persuasively against the recognition of this cause of action." The Court exaggerates the difficulties in recognizing this cause of action and minimizes the imperative to provide fair compensation for seriously injurious wrongs.

The Court cannot, and does not, dispute or denigrate the expert testimony presented at trial "that the exposure to chemicals had already caused actual physical injury to plaintiffs through its adverse effects on the genetic material within their cells" and "that plaintiffs' exposure to chemicals had produced 'a reasonable likelihood that they have now and will develop health consequences from this exposure.'" Dr. Joseph Highland gave uncontested testimony that plaintiffs had already suffered physical injury from the damage to their cellular and genetic material caused by the chemicals to which they were exposed. These chemicals are mutagenic agents: they destroy parts of the genetic material of cells they contact. This destruction may affect only the function of a few cells or it may lead to the failure of major organs. It may make the cells likely starting points for cancer, and it may lead to mutations in the victims' children.

The majority recognizes that plaintiffs have suffered injury. It is self-evident that exposure to highly toxic chemicals is the "infliction of ... harm," "an invasion of a legally protected interest." See Restatement (Second) of Torts, § 7(1) and Comment a (1965) (defining "injury"). Nevertheless, the majority concludes that plaintiffs' injury cannot be redressed. Its reasons for treating their claims different from other injury claims are an unsupported fear of "vast numbers of claims" and a belief that no "clear guidelines [exist] to determine what level of compensation may be appropriate."

These reasons are an evasion of the challenge posed by tortious injury that carries with it an enhanced risk of even greater injury, and the need to provide fair compensation for innocent victims suffering this form of injury. The Court postponed a similar determination in *Evers v. Dollinger*, 95 N.J. 399 (1984). There a woman brought suit claiming that her doctor's negligent diagnosis and treatment enhanced the risk that her cancer would recur. While her appeal of the trial court's judgment was pending, she suffered a recurrence of the cancer. The majority decided that it need not decide whether enhanced risk, standing alone, is an actionable element. Nevertheless, the Court held that because the disease had recurred, plaintiff would be allowed to recover damages for enhanced risk.

Allowing recovery for enhanced risk in *Evers* where the plaintiff suffered subsequent harm cannot be reconciled with the denial of recovery for enhanced risk in the present case. The majority professes to deny compensation because it cannot "measure" or "quantify" the enhanced risk of future injury. The fact that the plaintiffs in the present case have not—yet—suffered extreme symptoms is no justification for denying recovery. As in *Evers v. Dollinger*, "[t]he Court is ... troubled by a seeming inability to quantify the risk of future cancer. But, adding the incurrence of future harm as a requirement for the recovery for such increased risk does not resolve the dilemma since the risk still remains unquantified." When the Court allowed recovery for enhanced risk in *Evers*, it did not in the slightest way insist that the risk be quantified.

The majority reasons that plaintiffs' claim is not cognizable in part because the risk of future disease does not rise to the level of "reasonable probability." Yet

the court concedes that the plaintiffs have proven that they have a "significantly...enhanced risk" of contracting serious diseases. It nowhere explains why a
risk that generates the "reasonable probability" of future injury can be compensated
while one that "significantly enhances" the likelihood of future injury cannot.

I do not criticize the Court for illogic or inconsistency. I stress only that if it is
just and fair, and it is, to compensate a victim in one case for an unquantified
enhanced risk of future disease, it cannot be right to deny recovery in a second case
also involving a claim of unquantified enhanced risk. "[T]o deny...redress
for...injuries merely because damages cannot be measured with precise exactitude
would constitute a perversion of fundamental principles of justice." *Berman v.
Allan*, 80 N.J. 421, 433 (1979) (Handler, J., concurring in part and dissenting in part).
"[E]ven where the pitfalls of measuring damages have been genuine, we have not
refused to grapple with the complexities in order to recognize the justness and
fairness of relief." *Schroeder v. Perkel*, 87 N.J. 53, 77 (1981) (Handler, J., concurring in
part, dissenting in part). It is the reality of injury presented by evidence, informed
by experts, and tested by common sense and ordinary experience, that is the
benchmark for damages. "Some of these losses...might be hard to sense, difficult
to define and puzzling to evaluate. They are, nonetheless, actual and constitute a
sound basis for a lawful claim for redress and compensation." *Berman v. Allan*,
supra, 80 N.J. at 446 (Handler, J., concurring in part and dissenting in part).

The courts have not allowed the difficulty of quantifying injury to prevent
them from offering compensation for assault, trespass, emotional distress, invasion
of privacy, or damage to reputation. The claim in this case involves a tortious
invasion, as much an invasion as the trespass of gas and microscopic deposits on
someone else's property, or as in surgery performed without the patient's consent.
Where new forms of injury have been put before the courts, the courts have developed procedures, standards, and formulas for determining appropriate compensation. This perception was expressed in Capron, "Tort Liability in Genetic
Counseling," 79 Colum. L. Rev. 618, 649 (1979):

> [T]he collective wisdom of the community on the proper redress for a particular
> harm, informed by experience, common sense, and a desire to be fair to the
> parties, seems an acceptable way of arriving at a damage verdict and probably
> one that is preferable to a more scientific (and sterile) process that excludes
> nonquantifiable elements to achieve an aura of objectivity and precision.

The plaintiffs' claim of an unquantified enhanced risk should not be characterized as "depend[ing] upon the likelihood of an event that has not yet occurred and
may never occur." The injury involved is an actual event: exposure to toxic chemicals. The tortious contamination, moreover, is an event that has surely occurred; it is
not a speculative or remote possible happening. Among the consequences of this
unconsented-to invasion are genetic damage and a tangible risk of a major disease, a
peril that is real even though it cannot be precisely measured or weighed. The peril,
moreover, is unquestionably greater than that experienced by persons not similarly
exposed to toxic chemicals. The toxic injury and claim for damages are not attributable only to some possible future event. Like claims based on the doctrines of
trespass, assault, invasion of privacy, or defamation, the damages suffered are not
solely actual consequential damages, but also the disvalue of being subjected to an
intrinsically harmful event. The risk of dreadful disease resulting from toxic expo-

sure and contamination is more frightening and palpable than any deficits we may feel or imagine from many other wrongful transgressions.

I am bothered by the unintended morbidity of the Court's attitude. My discomfort was similar with respect to the Court's refusal to recognize a claim for enhanced risk in *Evers*:

> The inadvertent effect of such a court rule is that those victims, who undeservedly have been put in greater peril in terms of their survival, are not permitted to be compensated for this peril unless they have suffered . . . cancer. [*Evers*, supra, 95 N.J. at 418 (Handler, J., concurring).]

In deciding whether to recognize plaintiffs' claims, the majority focuses on the problem of sovereign defendants in tort suits involving the unquantified nature of certain injuries. The majority, however, fails to note the long-term benefits lost when compensation is not allowed for injuries caused. Compensation serves to deter negligent behavior. See, e.g., R. Posner, Economic Analysis of Law 142–43 (2nd ed. 1977). We disserve this policy in this case, where the defendant municipality has engaged not simply in negligent conduct, but in "palpably unreasonable" conduct causing real and serious injury to its residents. This Court recently offered the following reply to an argument that a particular cause of action not be recognized:

> In addressing these arguments, we must keep in mind the central goals of the law of torts. As we said in [*People Exp. Airlines, Inc. v. Consolidated Rail*, 100 N.J. 246, 255 (1985)], the primary purpose of the tort law is "that wronged persons should be compensated for their injuries and that those responsible for the wrong should bear the cost of their tortious conduct." Moreover, forcing tortfeasors to pay for the harm they have wrought provides a proper incentive for reasonable conduct.

But not merely as a matter of deterrence and efficiency, also as a matter of justice, those who cause injuries should be required to pay for them. Recognizing a claim for enhanced risk

> is appropriate in order to prevent a tortfeasor from being insulated from the real but elusive consequences of his negligent conduct. A tortfeasor should not be allowed to escape responsibility for causing an increased risk that would not have existed but for his negligence simply because of the statistical uncertainty of the risk.

The assertion that recognition of plaintiffs' claims will open a flood gate of litigations seems insubstantial when compared to the actuality of plaintiffs' injury. Courts should not allow speculative fears or undifferentiated anxiety over a possible rush of litigation to defeat a sound and fair cause of action. The majority does not even make the effort to consider standards—e.g., burdens of proofs, presumptions, required minimal showings—that might make claims for enhanced risk more manageable and more limited. The proper course is not to leave the injured without a legal recourse. If social conditions and legal standards interact in such a way that litigating a certain kind of claim becomes burdensome, interested parties can then go to the legislature seeking reform. There is no reason to believe that, if circumstances warranted it, the legislature would not respond to problems in toxic tort litigation. I reject the majority's solution of avoiding complexities in litigation by excusing negligence and allowing injuries to go uncompensated.

The majority speaks of the speculative nature of compensating claims of enhanced risk as if such would be an anomaly in the logical and orderly work of tort law compensation. The truth is to the contrary. There are relatively few injuries that can be easily or logically quantified. It is not merely the relatively new tort claims like "pain and suffering" and "emotional distress" that are difficult to quantify. What is the logical method of evaluation for compensating a claim of trespass on land, the battery of unconsented-to surgery, a violation of personal privacy, or an insult to character? When a jury awards $50,000 for an accident that led to the loss of a limb, how is that $50,000 a logical quantification of that injury?[2]

The severe limitation of damages imposed by the Court in this case is inadequate and unfair. No person in her right mind would trade places with any one of these plaintiffs. Does this not suggest that a person would have to be paid a considerable sum of money, more than that permitted here by the Court, before tolerating the injuries suffered by these plaintiffs? Why should not a jury be permitted to make this determination?[3]

. . . .

The citizens of Jackson Township endured extended exposure to serious toxic chemicals because of the township's palpably unreasonable misconduct. Their injuries are substantial—as real and as readily measurable as other injuries for which the courts allow compensation. Plaintiffs' claims in this case should be recognized and fully compensated. The majority's decision to grant only a limited portion of full compensation disrespects what the plaintiffs have had to go through. . . .

■ DePass v. United States of America
721 F.2d 203 (7th Cir. 1983)

Flaum, Circuit Judge:

This appeal arises out of the denial of damages to plaintiff James DePass for alleged increased risk of cardiovascular disease and loss of life expectancy. The

---

[2] But cf. Posner, supra, at 144, 149:

> A victim who loses a finger sustains a cost that can be conceived of in various ways including the price he would have demanded from someone who made a credible offer to purchase the finger. . . .
>
> It is true that such losses, if they do not impair market earning capacity, have no pecuniary dimension. But this is not because they are not true economic losses; it is because of the absence of markets in mutilation.

If anything, it is more sensible to speak in terms of how much persons would have to be paid before they would consent to being exposed to toxic chemicals th[a]n it would to ask a similar question about a loss of a limb.

[3] I note that because the majority's rejection of the claim for enhanced risk relies so heavily on the Tort Claims Act, today's holding must be read narrowly as applying only to claims brought against public-entity defendants. I disagree with the Court's denial of compensation for such enhanced risk even as against a governmental defendant. Nevertheless, I consider the general question of whether a claim for enhanced risk can be brought in the New Jersey courts to still be an open question.

district court, in a bench trial, found that DePass had not proved the injury by a preponderance of the evidence. This appeal requires us to determine whether the district court was "clearly erroneous" in its finding. Fed. R. Civ. P. 52(a). For the reasons set out below, we affirm the district court.

I

On December 9, 1978, DePass was struck by a car driven by an employee of the defendant United States. DePass sustained severe injuries, including a traumatic amputation of his left leg below the knee. DePass brought suit under the Federal Tort Claims Act, 28 U.S.C. §§ 2671–2680. The United States admitted liability, and the case was tried as to damages only.

At trial, DePass introduced evidence as to the nature and extent of his injuries, and as to past and future pain and suffering. DePass's witnesses included Dr. Jerome D. Cohen, a medical doctor.[1] Dr. Cohen testified that he had examined DePass and found that DePass had had a traumatic amputation of the left leg just below the knee. Dr. Cohen then testified that he had read an article, "Traumatic Limb Amputation and the Subsequent Mortality from Cardiovascular Disease and Other Causes," published in volume 33 of the Journal of Chronic Diseases, by Zdenek Hrubec and Richard Ryder ("the Hrubec and Ryder study").[2] This article involved a study of 3,890 Americans who had suffered traumatic limb amputations during World War II. The study established a statistical connection between traumatic limb amputations and future cardiovascular problems and decreased life expectancy.

Dr. Cohen testified that DePass fits within the class of persons who had sustained a traumatic amputation of a limb. He testified that, based on his own experience, his examination of DePass, and his analysis of the Hrubec and Ryder study, because DePass is a traumatic amputee he has a greater risk of cardiovascular problems and decreased life expectancy. At the conclusion of Dr. Cohen's testimony, the trial court questioned him as follows:

THE COURT: Is it your testimony that based on your examination of this plaintiff, Mr. DePass, plus your knowledge in the field of cardiovascular disease and including your analysis and a reading of the article which is Exhibit 10, is your opinion that he, because he is the amputee that he is on the left leg below the knee, that he has a greater risk for developing cardiovascular disease in the future and also a greater risk for shorter mortality, shorter longevity? Is that what you're saying, that he is a risk for that?

[DR. COHEN]: Yes, that's correct.

THE COURT: And you're not saying that he will develop it or that he will live shorter, but he is a greater risk for both of those?

[DR. COHEN]: That's correct.

---

[1] The record reveals that Dr. Cohen is board certified in internal medicine. Dr. Cohen's testimony at trial, and his curriculum vitae, fail to establish whether he is certified in cardiology or in the subspecialty of cardiovascular diseases.

[2] The study was mandated by the United States Congress, Pub. L. 94-433 (1976), and it was carried out by the Medical Follow-up Agency of the National Research Council's Assembly of Life Sciences.

On cross-examination, Dr. Cohen testified to the existence of several other studies on the relationship between traumatic limb amputation and decreased life expectancy. In particular, he testified as to a 1954 English study of 27,000 amputees that showed no statistical connection between amputation and decreased life expectancy. Several studies conducted on a smaller scale also failed to show a connection. One study, done in Finland, found a statistical connection. He testified that he had not personally reviewed any of the other studies. Dr. Cohen testified that no one knows if in fact the Hrubec and Ryder study is correct. Dr. Cohen then read from the study, "The reasons for the statistically significant relationship demonstrated between limb amputation and cardiovascular disorders are not obvious. Stringent deadlines set by Congress for the completion of this work made impossible detailed studies of individuals."

The district court, in its order, awarded DePass $800,000 for the nature and extent of his injuries and for his past and future pain and suffering. In its findings of fact, the court found no evidence demonstrating by a preponderance that DePass had suffered a loss of life expectancy. The court found that Dr. Cohen's testimony dealt with "possibilities and speculation."[4]

On appeal, DePass argues that the district court was clearly erroneous in its findings of fact. He argues that his evidence was clear, convincing, and uncontradicted. He also argues that the United States is bound by the Hrubec and Ryder study as an admission against interest. The United States argues that the district court could reject Dr. Cohen's testimony and the Hrubec and Ryder study. The United States also argues that the evidence at best establishes only that DePass is, on the average, at an increased risk of injury, and that this increased risk is not compensable under Illinois law.

II

An appellate court will only set aside the findings of a district court when those findings are clearly erroneous. The standard of review is clear. The Supreme Court has stated that "[a] finding is 'clearly erroneous' when although there is evidence to support it, the reviewing court on the entire evidence is left with the definite and firm conviction that a mistake has been committed." *United States v. United States Gypsum Co.*, 333 U.S. 364, 395 (1948). The appellate court cannot reweigh the evidence. The inquiry is whether the record contains substantial evidence to support the findings.

---

[4] The court's Finding of Fact No. 14 reads as follows:

The Court finds that there is no evidence demonstrating by a preponderance a loss of life expectancy due to the traumatic limb amputation. The Court heard the testimony of Dr. Jerome D. Cohen of St. Louis, Missouri, who testified to an American study of 3,600 traumatic single limb amputations, in which the researchers found a thirty percent higher than normal incidence of cardiovascular disease in the amputees. However, the doctor admitted to the existence of an English study of 27,000 traumatic limb amputations in the earlier part of the century which reached an opposite conclusion. More fundamentally, the doctor never established that this individual plaintiff would suffer a loss of life expectancy, or even that it was more likely than not that he would suffer the loss. At best, his testimony dealt with possibilities and speculation and failed to establish the existence of such a loss in plaintiff.

Based on the record before us, we cannot say that the district court was clearly erroneous. The findings of fact demonstrate that the district court considered the Hrubec and Ryder study and Dr. Cohen's testimony. The court, however, declined to accept the study and the testimony as establishing the fact of injury by a preponderance. There is substantial evidence in the record to support this. Dr. Cohen testified that he based certain of his conclusions on the Hrubec and Ryder study. The study itself states, and Dr. Cohen testified, that other studies exist that reach a different conclusion. Dr. Cohen stated that no one knows if the Hrubec and Ryder study is correct. The study does not establish a reason for the statistical relationship between amputation and decreased life expectancy.

There was conflicting evidence in the record as to the conclusiveness of the Hrubec and Ryder study. It was for the district court to weigh the evidence; the court did not find the evidence strong enough to be a preponderance.

Moreover, even if there were no contradictory evidence on this point, the district court could still reject the conclusions of the Hrubec and Ryder study. The plaintiff had the burden of proving injury. The court could reject the evidence even when the defendant introduces no contradictory evidence.

Because we find that the district court could reject the Hrubec and Ryder study as inconclusive, we do not reach the issue of whether merely placing plaintiff in a class of persons subject, on the average, to an increased risk of injury is sufficient to establish a compensable injury under Illinois law. We note, however, that Illinois law is not settled as to whether increased risk of future injury is compensable. Compare *Lindsay v. Appleby*, 91 Ill. App. 3d 705 (1980) with *Morrissy v. Eli Lilly and Co.*, 76 Ill. App. 3d 753 (1979). . . .

Posner, Circuit Judge, dissenting:

Although this may seem like a routine personal-injury case, it raises important questions relating to the use of scientific evidence in federal trials. The plaintiff, a 37-year-old man named DePass, was hit by a car owned and operated by the government. He was seriously injured—one of his legs had to be amputated just below the knee, the other was crippled, and one eye was badly injured. He brought suit under the Federal Tort Claims Act and the district court held the government liable and awarded DePass $800,000 in damages. The entire award is for "pain and suffering," since DePass incurred no medical expenses (he received all medical treatment free of charge from the Veterans Administration) and proved no loss of earnings from the accident. . . .

. . . Although the additional loss inflicted by shortening what is now likely to be a rather miserable life may be slight in pecuniary terms, especially after being discounted to present value, if DePass proved that the accident probably shortened his life he was entitled to some additional damages and it should be no concern of ours whether the addition would be small or large or whether as an original matter we might think $800,000 adequate or even excessive to compensate him for all of his losses.

If the finding that the accident will not shorten DePass's life had been based in whole or part on the judge's opinion of the believability of a witness I would agree that we should affirm. But there are no "credibility" issues in this case. The government acknowledged at oral argument that DePass's medical expert witness, Dr. Cohen, a cardiovascular epidemiologist, was a candid and truthful witness. I do not understand the district judge to have disbelieved Cohen. I do not even think the judge rejected the finding in the National Institutes of Health study on which Cohen relied (Hrubec and Ryder, Traumatic Limb Amputations and Subsequent Mortality from Cardiovascular Disease and Other Causes, 33 J. Chronic Diseases 239 (1980)) that a person who has had a major amputation—knee or above, or elbow or above—is more likely to develop heart disease and therefore likely to die younger than a person who has not had a major amputation. The judge did remark that a British study apparently had found no association between amputation and longevity. (I say "apparently" because no one connected with this case has ever read the study, which was not published in a medical journal and may not even be available in the United States. All remarks about it are based on a couple of sentences in the NIH study.) Dr. Cohen explained why he thought the British study was probably less pertinent than the NIH study to estimating DePass's life expectancy. The British study was older (1954 versus 1979); and it was of a foreign population in a much earlier period (British veterans of World War I versus American veterans of World War II in the NIH study), a population moreover that has different health characteristics from ours (heart disease is less common in Britain than in the United States). Cohen's testimony was not shaken by cross-examination and the government did not introduce any medical testimony, live or documentary, of its own. It did not even place the British study in evidence. The district judge could have had no basis for rejecting Dr. Cohen's assessment of the relative weight of the two studies.

But as I have said, I do not think the judge rejected DePass's medical evidence because he thought it false (how could he have?) or outweighed by other evidence (there was no contrary evidence). He appears to have rejected the entire class of evidence—statistical evidence—illustrated by the medical evidence in this case. This is suggested by his finding that "the doctor never established that this individual plaintiff would suffer a loss of life expectancy, or even that it was more likely than not that he would suffer the loss. At best, his testimony dealt with possibilities and speculation and failed to establish the existence of such a loss in plaintiff." Another clue is found at the close of Dr. Cohen's testimony when the judge asked him: "Is it your testimony . . . that because [DePass] is the amputee that he is . . . he has a greater risk for developing cardiovascular disease in the future and also a greater risk for shorter mortality, shorter longevity? Is that what you're saying, that he is a risk for that?" When Dr. Cohen answered, "That's correct," the judge said: "And you're not saying that he will develop [cardiovascular disease] or that he will live shorter, but he is a greater risk for both of those?" When Dr. Cohen again said, "That's correct," the judge remarked: "I won't get into any statistics. I'll just drop it at that."

Maybe the judge just misunderstood the term "life expectancy." When he said that Dr. Cohen had "never established that this individual plaintiff would suffer a loss of life expectancy," he was stating a truism rather than, as he thought, throwing doubt on the cogency of the plaintiff's medical evidence. A man's life expectancy is not his actual life span, which cannot be known till he dies; it is a prediction founded on the average experience of many people having the same characteristics as he. When we say that a heavy smoker has a shorter life expectancy than a nonsmoker we do not mean that Jones who smokes heavily will in fact predecease Smith who does not smoke or that Jones will die sooner than he would have if he did not smoke; we just mean that, on the average, nonsmokers outlive smokers.

But it seems more likely from his remarks that the district judge thought that all probabilities are too uncertain to provide a basis for awarding damages. Yet most knowledge, and almost all legal evidence, is probabilistic. Even the proposition that DePass will die some day is merely empirical. It is of course highly probable that he will die but it is not certain in the way it is certain that 10^3 is 1000 or that I am my wife's husband—propositions that are true as a matter of definition rather than of observation. If Dr. Cohen had testified that DePass had heart disease and was therefore likely to die younger than most men in his age group, he would have been making a probabilistic statement; and the probabilities that are derived from statistical studies are no less reliable in general than the probabilities that are derived from direct observation, from intuition, or from case studies of a single person or event—all familiar sources of legal evidence.

All this has long been recognized in personal-injury cases, as it is throughout the law. If a tort victim is seriously injured and will require medical attention for the rest of his life, the court in deciding how much to award him for future medical expenses will have to estimate how long he can be expected to live and it will make this estimate by consulting a mortality table, which is to say by looking at a statistical summation of the experience of thousands or millions of people none of whom is a party or a witness in the case, rather than by studying the lifelines on the victim's palms. And if a study has been made of the mortality of people with the same kind of injury as the plaintiff, the court will consult that study in addition to or instead of standard mortality tables. That is what DePass asked the district judge to do here.

It makes no logical or even legal difference whether the question is how long a permanently injured person will require medical attention or how soon a delayed consequence of the accident (death in this case) will occur. The factual question is the same: when will he die? The Illinois courts (Illinois law governs the substantive questions in this Federal Tort Claims Act suit) recognize that the risk of a future consequence of an accident, even though not certain to materialize, is compensable. Although *Morrissy v. Eli Lilly & Co.*, 76 Ill. App. 3d 753, 761 (1979), cited by the majority opinion in the present case, recites the formula, "possible future damages in a personal injury action are not compensable unless reasonably certain to occur," *Morrissy* is distinguishable from this case. The plaintiff had not yet suffered any ascertainable injury as a result of her mother's having taken DES while pregnant; the complaint was that she might some day develop an illness as a delayed consequence of the DES. DePass was seriously injured; the only issue is the extent of his injury, an issue on which courts traditionally do not impose a heavy burden of proof on plaintiffs. . . .

Although few reported cases (none from Illinois) deal with the specific question whether a reduction in life expectancy is compensable, the trend is toward allowing recovery in such cases. As it should be. A tortfeasor should not get off scot-free because instead of killing his victim outright he inflicts an injury that is likely though not certain to shorten the victim's life.

In any event, the government conceded at oral argument that a reduction in life expectancy is compensable under Illinois tort law. So the only question is the reliability of the study on which Dr. Cohen relied. The study is of the 30-year medical history of 12,000 Americans injured in combat in World War II of whom almost 4,000 had major amputations as a result of their injuries. (The British study was larger, but we do not know how many of the persons studied were major amputees, or even whether the study distinguished between major and minor—though no one seriously believes that losing your pinky will significantly increase the risk of dying prematurely from heart disease.) Although the NIH study does not establish the exact causal linkage between major amputation and early death from heart disease, it suggests a linkage. Emotional stress and (more important) lack of exercise are believed to be among the causes of heart disease, and a major amputation is a source of stress (reflected for example in higher suicide and alcoholism rates among amputees) and makes exercise more difficult. Consistently with this hypothesis, the study found that the increased incidence of heart disease was greater for men who had lost two legs than for men who had lost one (functionally, DePass is closer to the former than to the latter category), and greater for those who had lost one leg than for those who had lost just an arm.

The NIH study does not pretend to be conclusive and its results are presented with appropriate scientific caution. Subsequent studies may overthrow them. But as I have already noted a tort plaintiff's burden of proving the extent of his injury is not a heavy one. Doubts are resolved against the tortfeasor. All of the medical evidence introduced in this case (the government, it will be recalled, presented none) points in one direction—that DePass will probably die younger because of the accident. On the basis of the study Dr. Cohen testified that DePass had a 44–58 percent higher than normal risk of dying from heart disease, resulting in a 30 percent reduction in DePass's life expectancy—from 37 to 26 years, a difference of 11 years. This reduction in life expectancy is just a convenient summation of the probabilistic results of the NIH study applied to a man of DePass's age. To illustrate very simply what is involved, imagine that before the accident DePass had a 10 percent chance of dying at age 60, a 50 percent chance of dying at age 65, and a 40 percent chance of dying at age 70. Multiply each age by the corresponding percentage, sum up the results, and you have his expected age at death: 66.5 years. Assume the accident changed these percentages as follows: he now has a 40 percent chance of dying at age 60 and a 60 percent chance of dying at age 65. His expected age of death is now 63, so the accident reduced his life expectancy by 3½ years. From the way I have set up this highly stylized example we know for a fact that DePass will not die at the age of 63. All we know is that he is likelier, by given percentages, to die at either 60 or 65 than he was before the accident. But if we want to summarize all of our information in a single figure, we can do so by means of the concept of life expectancy. It provides a perfectly objective basis for awarding damages.

If any corroboration of the applicability of the NIH study to DePass's personal situation was needed, it was supplied by Dr. Cohen's finding, in an examination of DePass, that DePass's cardiovascular function had fallen below normal for men of his age. This is not evidence of heart disease but it shows that DePass is, as one would expect given the nature of his injuries, perforce leading an extremely sedentary life—which according to the NIH study is probably the main cause of the much greater incidence of heart disease among major amputees.

It is of course unlikely that DePass will die exactly 11 years earlier because of the accident. He may never get heart disease. Or he may be cut down by it long before he is within 11 years of the expected end of his life. It was unlikely that the accident victim in *Abernathy v. Superior Hardwoods, Inc.*, 704 F.2d 963, 972–74 (7th Cir. 1983), to pick a recent personal-injury case almost [at] random, would die 40 years after the accident—a number plucked from a mortality table, reflecting as the NIH study reflects statistical experience. And yet Abernathy was awarded damages as if he would die in 40 years. That is how damages are calculated in personal-injury cases; and a judge is not free to say, in my court we do not allow statistical inference. Knowledge increasingly is statistical, and judges must not let themselves lag too far behind the progress of knowledge. As a matter of fact they have not lagged. The kind of evidence that the district judge rejected in this case, evidence of probability of survival, invariably based on studies of a group of people rather than of just the individual plaintiff, is an increasingly common basis for awarding damages.

The district judge's rejection of such evidence, if widely followed, would lead to systematically undercompensating the victims of serious accidents and thus to systematically underdeterring such accidents. Accidents that require the amputation of a limb, particularly a leg, are apparently even more catastrophic than one had thought. They do not just cause a lifetime of disfigurement and reduced mobility; they create a high risk of premature death from heart disease. The goal of awarding damages in tort law is to put the tort victim as nearly as possible in the position he would have occupied if the tort had not been committed. This goal cannot be attained or even approached if judges shut their eyes to consequences that scientists have found are likely to follow from particular types of accident, merely because the scientists' evidence is statistical. But unless I have mistaken the true grounds of the district judge's decision in this case that is what he did.

The finding that DePass failed to prove a reduction in life expectancy as a result of the accident should be vacated as clearly erroneous and the case should be remanded to the district court for a determination of the amount of damages necessary to compensate DePass for an 11-year reduction in his life expectancy.

COMMENTS AND QUESTIONS

1. Note that the plaintiffs in *Ayers* sought damages for a number of injuries. Make sure that you can identify the different types of injury alleged, and for which ones the court allowed recovery. What is the basis for denying recovery?

2. What is the court's response in *Ayers* to the claim for damages due to increased risk? Under what circumstances would the court have recognized a cause of action for such damages? What are Justice Handler's reasons for disagreeing?

   As with all questions about liability for exposure to risk alone, consider whether damages might be awarded not for physical injury (as yet unrealized and perhaps never to be realized) but for something else, such as the plaintiffs' loss of autonomy. Would damages for such a loss be "speculative"? The court emphasizes that the risk can't be quantified. In what sense is that so? Why isn't it enough to say that the plaintiffs face a moderate, high, or very high likelihood of future disease? Reconsider these questions after you read the excerpts written by Paul Slovic in section 3 of this chapter.

3. Suppose the plaintiffs in *Ayers* waited until they actually suffered from one of the diseases referred to in the opinion. What obstacles might they face in recovering? (a) How does the court address the statute of limitations problem? The "single controversy" rule? (The "single controversy" rule in effect in New

Jersey at the time was a particularly strong version of claim preclusion, but the problem the court addresses would arise even in jurisdictions with weaker preclusion rules.) (b) Does the court deal with—and how might you deal with—problems associated with establishing the defendants' misconduct (negligence or "palpably unreasonable" conduct) when disease manifests itself? Problems associated with establishing causation of disease in particular individuals? Consider whether focusing on individuals who become ill is inconsistent with the idea that the underlying problem is one of risk, not realized harm.

4. *Ayers* is a state court case in which the court is developing (or applying) New Jersey tort law. *DePass* is an action against the United States, brought under the Federal Tort Claims Act. That act directs the federal court to apply state tort law, there the tort law of Illinois. Why did the district court reject DePass's evidence as insufficient? Can you identify defects in the NIH study that would justify its rejection? Are there "confounding variables" that might explain what, other than traumatic injury, might produce the results reported in the study?

Note that the district court judge referred to the fact that the evidence involved "possibilities and speculation." Is this an evidentiary ruling, or one on the merits—rejecting the substantive claim that one can recover for exposure to risk alone?

5. What, precisely, is the injury for which Judge Posner would allow recovery? If the injury is diminished life expectancy, how are damages to be measured? With reference to income lost during what would have been the final eleven years of DePass's life? How could that be determined? Consider the possibility that DePass should be compensated for the increased risk of death occasioned by his injury. Again, how should that be measured? And, to return to the questions raised about *Ayers*, are courts well suited to developing standards for imposing and measuring such damages?

6. *DePass* raises questions about the capacity of courts to place a value on exposure to risk. The readings from Paul Slovic in section 3 pose some theoretical and empirical questions about how people value risk, and we ask you there to consider whether either opinion in *Ayers* demonstrates sensitivity to the concerns Slovic identifies. *Ayers* (and *Buckley*, which follows in section 2) raises questions about the capacity of courts to design remedies for exposure to risk. The reading from Lon Fuller in section 4 introduces you to some concepts that may be useful in evaluating the courts' discussions, and we ask you there to consider *Ayers* and *Buckley* in light of Fuller's analysis.

2 ■ Recovery for Fear Resulting from Mere Exposure to Risk

The case in this section deals with the negligent infliction of mental distress. The traditional common law rule was that a person could recover damages for *severe* mental harm that itself had *physical consequences* (such as a rash resulting from stress) caused by *physical impact* to the plaintiff. Today most states have eliminated the "impact" requirement, with some requiring that the plaintiff merely have been in a "zone of danger" of physical impact. Tort doctrine in this area has been rather fluid in recent years, as the following case illustrates.

■ Metro-North Commuter Railroad Company v. Buckley
521 U.S. 424 (1997)

Justice Breyer delivered the opinion of the Court:

The basic question in this case is whether a railroad worker negligently exposed to a carcinogen (here, asbestos) but without symptoms of any disease can recover under the Federal Employers' Liability Act (FELA) for negligently inflicted emotional distress. We conclude that the worker before us here cannot recover unless, and until, he manifests symptoms of a disease. We also consider a related claim for medical monitoring costs, and we hold, for reasons set out below, that the respondent in this case has not shown that he is legally entitled to recover those costs.

I

Respondent, Michael Buckley, works as a pipefitter for Metro-North, a railroad. For three years (1985–1988) his job exposed him to asbestos for about one hour per working day. During that time Buckley would remove insulation from pipes, often covering himself with insulation dust that contained asbestos. Since 1987, when he attended an "asbestos awareness" class, Buckley has feared that he would develop cancer—and with some cause, for his two expert witnesses testified that, even after taking account of his now-discarded 15-year habit of smoking up to a pack of cigarettes per day, the exposure created an added risk of death due to cancer, or to other asbestos-related diseases of either 1% to 5% (in the view of one of plaintiff's experts), or 1% to 3% (in the view of another). Since 1989, Buckley has received periodic medical check-ups for cancer and asbestosis. So far, those check-ups have not revealed any evidence of cancer or any other asbestos-related disease.

Buckley sued Metro-North under the FELA, a statute that permits a railroad worker to recover for an "injury . . . resulting . . . from" his employer's "negligence." He sought damages for his emotional distress and to cover the cost of future medical check-ups. His employer conceded negligence, but it did not concede that Buckley had actually suffered emotional distress, and it argued that the FELA did not permit a worker like Buckley, who had suffered no physical harm, to recover for injuries of either sort. After hearing Buckley's case, the District Court dismissed the action. The court found that Buckley did not "offer sufficient evidence to allow a jury to find that he suffered a real emotional injury." And, in any event, Buckley suffered no "physical impact"; hence any emotional injury fell outside the limited set of circumstances in which, according to this Court, the FELA permits recovery. *Consolidated Rail Corporation v. Gottshall*, 512 U.S. 532 (1994). The District Court did not discuss Buckley's further claim for the costs of medical monitoring.

Buckley appealed, and the Second Circuit reversed. Buckley's evidence, it said, showed that his contact with the insulation dust (containing asbestos) was "massive, lengthy, and tangible," and that the contact "would cause fear in a reasonable person." Under these circumstances, the court held, the contact was what this Court in *Gottshall* had called a "physical impact"—a "physical impact" that, when present, permits a FELA plaintiff to recover for accompanying emotional distress.

The Second Circuit also found in certain of Buckley's workplace statements sufficient expression of worry to permit sending his emotional distress claim to a jury. Finally, the court held that Buckley could recover for the costs of medical check-ups because the FELA permits recovery of all reasonably incurred extra medical monitoring costs whenever a "reasonable physician would prescribe . . . a monitoring regime different than the one that would have been prescribed in the absence of" a particular negligently caused exposure to a toxic substance.

We granted certiorari to review the Second Circuit's holdings in light of *Gottshall*.

II

The critical question before us in respect to Buckley's "emotional distress" claim is whether the physical contact with insulation dust that accompanied his emotional distress amounts to a "physical impact" as this Court used that term in *Gottshall*. In *Gottshall*, an emotional distress case, the Court interpreted the word "injury" in § 1, FELA a provision that makes "every common carrier by railroad . . . liable in damages to any person suffering injury while . . . employed" by the carrier if the "injury" results from carrier "negligence." In doing so, it initially set forth several general legal principles applicable here. *Gottshall* described FELA's purposes as basically "humanitarian." It pointed out that the Act expressly abolishes or modifies a host of common-law doctrines that previously had limited recovery. It added that this Court has interpreted the Act's language "liberally" in light of its humanitarian purposes. But, at the same time, the Court noted that liability under the Act rests upon "negligence" and that the Act does not make the railroad "the insurer" for all employee injuries. The Court stated that "common-law principles," where not rejected in the text of the statute, "are entitled to great weight" in interpreting the Act, and that those principles "play a significant role" in determining whether, or when, an employee can recover damages for "negligent infliction of emotional distress."

The Court also set forth several more specific legal propositions. It recognized that the common law of torts does not permit recovery for negligently inflicted emotional distress unless the distress falls within certain specific categories that amount to recovery-permitting exceptions. The law, for example, does permit recovery for emotional distress where that distress accompanies a physical injury, and it often permits recovery for distress suffered by a close relative who witnesses the physical injury of a negligence victim. The Court then held that FELA § 1, mirroring the law of many States, sometimes permitted recovery "for damages for negligent infliction of emotional distress," and, in particular, it does so where a plaintiff seeking such damages satisfies the common law's "zone of danger" test. It defined that test by stating that the law permits "recovery for emotional injury" by "those plaintiffs who sustain a *physical impact* as a result of a defendant's negligent conduct, or who are placed in immediate risk of physical harm by that conduct."

The case before us, as we have said, focuses on the italicized words "physical impact." The Second Circuit interpreted those words as including a simple physical contact with a substance that might cause a disease at a future time, so long as the contact was of a kind that would "cause fear in a reasonable person." In our view, however, the "physical impact" to which *Gottshall* referred does not include a simple physical contact with a substance that might cause a disease at a substantially later time—where that substance, or related circumstance, threatens no harm other than that disease-related risk.

First, *Gottshall* cited many state cases in support of its adoption of the "zone of danger" test quoted above. And in each case where recovery for emotional distress was permitted, the case involved a threatened physical contact that caused, or might have caused, immediate traumatic harm. *Keck v. Jackson*, 122 Ariz. 114, 593 P.2d 668 (1979) (car accident); *Towns v. Anderson*, 195 Colo. 517, 579 P.2d 1163 (1978) (gas explosion); *Robb v. Pennsylvania R. Co.*, 58 Del. 454, 210 A.2d 709 (1965) (train struck car); *Rickey v. Chicago Transit Authority*, 98 Ill. 2d 546, 457 N.E.2d 1, 75 Ill. Dec. 211 (1983) (clothing caught in escalator choked victim); *Shuamber v. Henderson*, 579 N.E.2d 452 (Ind. 1991) (car accident); *Watson v. Dilts*, 116 Iowa 249, 89 N.W. 1068 (1902) (intruder assaulted plaintiff's husband); *Stewart v. Arkansas Southern R. Co.*, 112 La. 764, 36 So. 676 (1904) (train accident); *Purcell v. St. Paul City R. Co.*, 48 Minn. 134, 50 N.W. 1034 (1892) (near streetcar collision); *Bovsun v. Sanperi*, 61 N.Y.2d 219, 461 N.E.2d 843, 473 N.Y.S.2d 357 (1984) (car accident); *Kimberly v. Howland*, 143 N.C. 398, 55 S.E. 778 (1906) (rock from blasting crashed through plaintiffs' residence); *Simone v. Rhode Island Co.*, 28 R.I. 186, 66 A. 202 (1907) (streetcar collision); *Mack v. South-Bound R. Co.*, 52 S.C. 323, 29 S.E. 905 (1898) (train narrowly missed plaintiff); *Gulf, C. & S. F. R. Co. v. Hayter*, 93 Tex. 239, 54 S.W. 944 (1900) (train collision); *Pankopf v. Hinkley*, 141 Wis. 146, 123 N.W. 625 (1909) (automobile struck carriage); *Garrett v. New Berlin*, 122 Wis. 2d 223, 362 N.W.2d 137 (1985) (car accident). Cf. *Deutsch v. Shein*, 597 S.W.2d 141 (Ky. 1980) (holding that exposure to x rays was "physical contact" supporting recovery for emotional suffering where immediate physical harm to fetus was suspected).

Second, *Gottshall*'s language, read in light of this precedent, seems similarly limited. . . .

Taken together, language and cited precedent indicate that the words "physical impact" do not encompass every form of "physical contact." And, in particular, they do not include a contact that amounts to no more than an exposure—an exposure, such as that before us, to a substance that poses some future risk of disease and which contact causes emotional distress only because the worker learns that he may become ill after a substantial period of time.

Third, common-law precedent does not favor the plaintiff. Common law courts do permit a plaintiff who suffers from a disease to recover for related negligently caused emotional distress, and some courts permit a plaintiff who exhibits a physical symptom of exposure to recover. But with only a few exceptions, common law courts have denied recovery to those who, like Buckley, are disease and symptom free.

Fourth, the general policy reasons to which *Gottshall* referred—in its explanation of why common law courts have restricted recovery for emotional harm to cases falling within rather narrowly defined categories—militate against an expansive definition of "physical impact" here. Those reasons include: (a) special "difficulty for judges and juries" in separating valid, important claims from those that are invalid or "trivial"; (b) a threat of "unlimited and unpredictable liability"; and (c) the "potential for a flood" of comparatively unimportant, or "trivial," claims.

To separate meritorious and important claims from invalid or trivial claims does not seem easier here than in other cases in which a plaintiff might seek recovery for typical negligently caused emotional distress. The facts before us illustrate the problem. The District Court, when concluding that Buckley had failed to present "sufficient evidence to allow a jury to find…a real emotional injury," pointed out that, apart from Buckley's own testimony, there was virtually no evidence of distress. Indeed, Buckley continued to work with insulating material "even though…he could have transferred" elsewhere, he "continued to smoke cigarettes" despite doctors' warnings, and his doctor did not refer him "either to a psychologist or to a social worker." The Court of Appeals reversed because it found certain objective corroborating evidence, namely "workers' complaints to supervisors and investigative bodies." Both kinds of "objective" evidence—the confirming and disconfirming evidence—seem only indirectly related to the question at issue, the existence and seriousness of Buckley's claimed emotional distress. Yet, given the difficulty of separating valid from invalid emotional injury claims, the evidence before us may typify the kind of evidence to which parties and the courts would have to look.

. . . .

More important, the physical contact at issue here—a simple (though extensive) contact with a carcinogenic substance—does not seem to offer much help in separating valid from invalid emotional distress claims. That is because contacts, even extensive contacts, with serious carcinogens are common. See e.g., Nicholson, Perkel and Selikoff, Occupational Exposure to Asbestos: Population at Risk and Projected Mortality—1980–2030, 3 Am. J. Indust. Med. 259 (1982) (estimating that 21 million Americans have been exposed to work-related asbestos); U.S. Dept. of Health and Human Services, 1 Seventh Annual Report on Carcinogens 71 (1994) (3 million workers exposed to benzene, a majority of Americans exposed outside the workplace); Pirkle, et al., Exposure of the U.S. Population to Environmental Tobacco Smoke, 275 JAMA 1233, 1237 (1996) (reporting that 43% of U.S. children lived in a home with at least one smoker, and 37% of adult nonsmokers lived in a home with at least one smoker or reported environmental tobacco smoke at work). They may occur without causing serious emotional distress, but sometimes they do cause distress, and reasonably so, for cancer is both an unusually threatening and unusually frightening disease. See Statistical Abstract of United States 94 (1996) (23.5 percent of Americans who died in 1994 died of cancer); American Cancer Society, Cancer Facts and Figures—1997, p. 1 (half of all men and one third of all women will develop cancer). The relevant problem, however, remains one of evaluating a claimed emotional reaction to an increased risk of dying. An external circumstance—exposure—makes some emotional distress more likely. But how can one determine from the external circumstance of exposure whether, or when, a claimed strong emotional reaction to an increased mortality risk (say from 23% to 28%) is reasonable and genuine, rather than overstated—particularly when the relevant statistics themselves are controversial and uncertain (as is usually the case), and particularly since neither those exposed nor judges or juries are experts in statistics? The evaluation problem seems a serious one.

The large number of those exposed and the uncertainties that may surround recovery also suggest what *Gottshall* called the problem of "unlimited and unpredictable liability." Does such liability mean, for example, that the costs associated with a rule of liability would become so great that, given the nature of the harm, it would seem unreasonable to require the public to pay the higher prices that may result? The same characteristics further suggest what *Gottshall* called the problem of a "flood" of cases that, if not "trivial," are comparatively less important. In a world of limited resources, would a rule permitting immediate large-scale recoveries for widespread emotional distress caused by fear of future disease diminish the likelihood of recovery by those who later suffer from the disease?

We do not raise these questions to answer them (for we do not have the answers), but rather to show that general policy concerns of a kind that have led common law courts to deny recovery for certain classes of negligently caused harms are present in this case as well. That being so, we cannot find in *Gottshall's* underlying rationale any basis for departing from *Gottshall's* language and precedent or from the current common-law consensus. That is to say, we cannot find in *Gottshall's* language, cited precedent, other common law-precedent, or related concerns of policy, a legal basis for adopting the emotional-distress recovery rule adopted by the Court of Appeals.

Buckley raises several important arguments in reply. He points out, for example, that common law courts do permit recovery for emotional distress where a plaintiff has physical symptoms; and he argues that his evidence of exposure and enhanced mortality risk is as strong a proof as an accompanying physical symptom that his emotional distress is genuine.

This argument, however, while important, overlooks the fact that the common law in this area does not examine the genuineness of emotional harm case by case. Rather, it has developed recovery-permitting categories the contours of which more distantly reflect this, and other, abstract general policy concerns. The point of such categorization is to deny courts the authority to undertake a case by case examination. The common law permits emotional-distress recovery for that category of plaintiffs who suffer from a disease (or exhibit a physical symptom), for example, thereby finding a special effort to evaluate emotional symptoms warranted in that category of cases—perhaps from a desire to make a physically injured victim whole or because the parties are likely to be in court in any event. In other cases, however, falling outside the special recovery-permitting categories, it has reached a different conclusion. The relevant question here concerns the validity of a rule that seeks to redefine such a category. It would not be easy to redefine "physical impact" in terms of a rule that turned on, say, the "massive, lengthy, [or] tangible" nature of a contact that amounted to an exposure, whether to contaminated water, or to germ-laden air, or to carcinogen-containing substances, such as insulation dust containing asbestos. But, in any event, for the reasons we have stated, we cannot find that the common law has done so.

Buckley also points to a series of common-law cases that he believes offer him support. Many of these cases, however, find that the plaintiff at issue fell within a category where the law already permitted recovery for emotional distress. We have found only three asbestos-related cases, all involving state law, that support Buckley directly. None of them was decided by the highest court of the relevant State. And we do not find that minority view a sufficient basis for reaching Buckley's proposed conclusion.

Finally, Buckley argues that the "humanitarian" nature of the FELA warrants a holding in his favor. We do not doubt that, the FELA's purpose militates in favor of recovery for a serious and negligently caused emotional harm. But just as courts must interpret that law to take proper account of the harms suffered by a sympathetic individual plaintiff, so they must consider the general impact, on workers as well as employers, of the general liability rules they would thereby create. Here the relevant question concerns not simply recovery in an individual case, but the consequences and effects of a rule of law that would permit that recovery. And if the common law concludes that a legal rule permitting recovery here, from a tort law perspective, and despite benefits in some individual cases, would on balance cause more harm than good, and if we find that judgment reasonable, we cannot find that conclusion inconsistent with the FELA's humanitarian purpose.

III

Buckley also sought recovery for a different kind of "injury," namely the economic cost of the extra medical check-ups that he expects to incur as a result of his exposure to asbestos-laden insulation dust. The District Court, when it dismissed the action, did not discuss this aspect of Buckley's case. But the Second Circuit, when reversing the District Court, held that "a reasonable jury could award" Buckley the "costs" of "medical monitoring" in this case. We agreed to decide whether the court correctly found that the FELA permitted a plaintiff without symptoms or disease to recover this economic loss.

The parties do not dispute—and we assume—that an exposed plaintiff can recover related reasonable medical monitoring costs if and when he develops symptoms. As the Second Circuit pointed out, a plaintiff injured through negligence can recover related reasonable medical expenses as an element of damages. No one has argued that any different principle would apply in the case of a plaintiff whose "injury" consists of a disease, a symptom, or those sorts of emotional distress that fall within the FELA's definition of "injury." Much of the Second Circuit's opinion suggests it intended only to apply this basic principle of the law of damages. Insofar as that is so, Part II of our opinion, holding that the emotional distress at issue here is not a compensable "injury," requires reversal on this point as well.

Other portions of the Second Circuit's opinion, however, indicate that it may have rested this portion of its decision upon a broader ground, namely that medical monitoring costs themselves represent a separate negligently caused economic "injury," 45 U.S.C. § 51, for which a negligently exposed FELA plaintiff (including a plaintiff without disease or symptoms) may recover to the extent that the medical monitoring costs that a reasonable physician would prescribe for the plaintiff exceed the medical monitoring costs that "would have been prescribed in the absence of [the] exposure." This portion of the opinion, when viewed in light of Buckley's straightforward claim for an "amount of money" sufficient to "compensate" him for "future medical monitoring expenses," Plaintiff's Proposed Charges to the Jury 25, Record, Doc. 33, suggests the existence of an ordinary, but separate, tort law cause of action permitting (as tort law ordinarily permits) the recovery of medical cost damages in the form of a lump sum, and irrespective of insurance. As so characterized, the Second Circuit's holding, in our view, went beyond the bounds of currently "evolving common law." *Gottshall*, supra, at 558 (Souter, J., concurring).

Guided by the parties' briefs, we have canvassed the state-law cases that have considered whether the negligent causation of this kind of harm (i.e., causing a plaintiff, through negligent exposure to a toxic substance, to incur medical monitoring costs) by itself constitutes a sufficient basis for a tort recovery. We have found no other FELA decisions. We have put to the side several cases that involve special recovery-permitting circumstances, such as the presence of a traumatic physical impact, or the presence of a physical symptom, which for reasons explained in Part II are important but beside the point here. We have noted that federal courts, interpreting state law, have come to different conclusions about the matter. And we have ended up focusing on several important State Supreme Court cases that have permitted recovery.

We find it sufficient to note, for present purposes, that the cases authorizing recovery for medical monitoring in the absence of physical injury do not endorse a full-blown, traditional tort law cause of action for lump-sum damages—of the sort that the Court of Appeals seems to have endorsed here. Rather, those courts, while recognizing that medical monitoring costs can amount to a harm that justifies a tort remedy, have suggested, or imposed, special limitations on that remedy.... We believe that the note of caution, the limitations, and the expressed uneasiness with a traditional lump-sum damages remedy are important, for they suggest a judicial recognition of some of the policy concerns that have been pointed out to us here—concerns of a sort that *Gottshall* identified.

Since, for example, the particular, say cancer-related, costs at issue are the extra monitoring costs, over and above those otherwise recommended, their identification will sometimes pose special "difficulties for judges and juries." *Gottshall*, 512 U.S. at 557. Those difficulties in part can reflect uncertainty among medical professionals about just which tests are most usefully administered and when. And in part those difficulties can reflect the fact that scientists will not always see a medical need to provide systematic scientific answers to the relevant legal question, namely whether an exposure calls for extra monitoring. Cf. App. 182 (testimony by Buckley's expert conceding that periodic colon cancer screening "is recommended by the American Cancer Society anyway"); id., at 164 (testimony by Buckley's expert declining to rule out that periodic chest x rays would likely benefit smokers such as Buckley, even in the absence of asbestos exposure). Buckley's sole expert, then, was equivocal about the need for extra monitoring, and the defense had not yet put on its case.

Moreover, tens of millions of individuals may have suffered exposure to substances that might justify some form of substance-exposure-related medical monitoring.... And that fact, along with uncertainty as to the amount of liability, could threaten both a "flood" of less important cases (potentially absorbing resources better left available to those more seriously harmed) and the systemic harms that can accompany "unlimited and unpredictable liability" (say, for example, vast testing liability adversely affecting the allocation of scarce medical resources). The dissent assumes that medical monitoring is not a "costly" remedy. But Buckley here sought damages worth $950 annually for 36 years; by comparison, of all claims settled by the Center for Claims Resolution, a group representing asbestos manufacturers, from 1988 until 1993, the average settlement for plaintiffs injured by asbestos was about $12,500, and the settlement for non-malignant plaintiffs among this group averaged $8,810.

Finally, a traditional, full-blown ordinary tort liability rule would ignore the presence of existing alternative sources of payment, thereby leaving a court uncertain about how much of the potentially large recoveries would pay for otherwise unavailable medical testing and how much would accrue to plaintiffs for whom employers or other sources (say, insurance now or in the future) might provide monitoring in any event. Cf. 29 C.F.R. § 1910.1001(l) (1996) (requiring employers to provide medical monitoring for workers exposed to asbestos). The Occupational Safety and Health Administration regulations (which the dissent cites) help to demonstrate why the Second Circuit erred: where state and federal regulations already provide the relief that a plaintiff seeks, creating a full-blown tort remedy could entail systemic costs without corresponding benefits. Nor could an employer necessarily protect itself by offering monitoring, for that is not part of the rule of law that the dissent would endorse—a rule that, if traditional, would, as we have noted, allow recovery irrespective of the presence of a "collateral source" of payment.

We do not deny important competing considerations—of a kind that may have led some courts to provide a form of liability. Buckley argues, for example, that it is inequitable to place the economic burden of such care on the negligently exposed plaintiff rather than on the negligent defendant. He points out that providing preventive care to individuals who would otherwise go without can help to mitigate potentially serious future health effects of diseases by detecting them in early stages; again, whether or not this is such a situation, we may assume that such situations occur. And he adds that, despite scientific uncertainties, the difficulty of separating justified from unjustified claims may be less serious than where emotional distress is the harm at issue.

We do not deny that the dissent paints a sympathetic picture of Buckley and his co-workers; this picture has force because Buckley is sympathetic and he has suffered wrong at the hands of a negligent employer. But we are more troubled than is the dissent by the potential systemic effects of creating a new, full-blown, tort law cause of action—for example, the effects upon interests of other potential plaintiffs who are not before the court and who depend on a tort system that can distinguish between reliable and serious claims on the one hand, and unreliable and relatively trivial claims on the other. The reality is that competing interests are at stake—and those interests sometimes can be reconciled in ways other than simply through the creation of a full-blown, traditional, tort law cause of action.

We have not tried to balance these, or other, competing considerations here. We point them out to help explain why we consider the limitations and cautions to be important—and integral—parts of the state-court decisions that permit asymptomatic plaintiffs a separate tort claim for medical monitoring costs. That being so, we do not find sufficient support in the common law for the unqualified rule of lump-sum damages recovery that is, at least arguably, before us here. And given the mix of competing general policy considerations, plaintiff's policy-based arguments do not convince us that the FELA contains a tort liability rule of that unqualified kind.

This limited conclusion disposes of the matter before us. We need not, and do not, express any view here about the extent to which the FELA might, or might not, accommodate medical cost recovery rules more finely tailored than the rule we have considered.

. . . .

Justice Ginsburg, joined by Justice Stevens, dissenting in part:

. . .

As a pipefitter for Metro-North, Michael Buckley repaired and maintained the labyrinth of pipes in the steam tunnels of Grand Central Terminal in New York City. The pipes were surrounded by a white insulation material that Buckley and his co-workers had to remove to perform their jobs. Without any protective gear, the pipefitters would hammer, slice, and pull the insulation material, which broke apart as it was removed, scattering dust particles into the air. Fans used to mitigate the intense heat of the steam tunnels spread further dust from insulation pieces that had accumulated on tunnel floors. The dust coated Buckley's skin and clothing; he testified that he could taste the gritty insulation material as it entered his mouth and nose. The pipefitters would emerge from their work in the tunnels covered from head to toe with white dust; for this appearance, they were dubbed "the snowmen of Grand Central."

The insulation material covering Grand Central's pipes was made of asbestos, widely recognized as a carcinogen since the mid-1970's. Metro-North did not tell the pipefitters of, or provide protection against, the danger to which the workers were exposed until 1987, two years after Buckley started working in the steam tunnels. At an asbestos awareness class on August 31, 1987, Buckley and his co-workers learned of the asbestos in the pipe insulation and of the diseases asbestos exposure could cause. Buckley was then given a respirator and some instruction on the "glove bag" method of removing asbestos. He testified that his efforts to use the respirator and glove bag method proved frustrating: the respirator fit poorly and slid down his face as he perspired in the intense heat of the steam tunnels; the plastic bags used to isolate the asbestos melted on the hot pipes, spilling out the material instead of containing it.

Buckley and as many as 140 other asbestos-exposed workers sought legal counsel after their complaints to Metro-North management went unresolved. In the FELA action now before us, Buckley is serving as test plaintiff for the claims of all the exposed employees. Metro-North stipulated in the District Court that it had "negligently exposed the plaintiff Michael Buckley to asbestos while he was working in Grand Central Terminal from June 1985 to the beginning of September 1987." "No later than 1986," Metro-North also conceded, "[it] obtained actual notice of the presence of asbestos in Grand Central Terminal and notice of the hazard that working with or around asbestos posed to the health and welfare of its employees." Metro-North further acknowledged that "it exposed the plaintiff to asbestos without warning him that he was being exposed to asbestos and without training him how to safely handle and remove asbestos." Prior to Metro-North's stipulation conceding negligence, the New York Attorney General's Office and the Office of the Inspector General of the Metropolitan Transportation Authority conducted a joint investigation, leading to these conclusions: Metro-North had "seriously disregarded the health and safety of its workers"; the railroad's failings were "particularly egregious" because Metro-North was on notice of the asbestos problem as a result of complaints by its workers, a report by its own consultant, and inspections by the New York State Department of Labor.

. . .

Buckley asserted two claims for relief in his FELA-based complaint: first, he charged Metro-North with negligent infliction of emotional distress; second, he sought compensation for the cost of future medical monitoring. The Court definitively rejects Buckley's first claim by holding that, under the FELA, a railworker may not recover damages for emotional distress unless, and until, he manifests symptoms of a disease. As to Buckley's second claim, however, the Court speaks tentatively. "The respondent in this case," we are told, "has not shown that he is legally entitled to recover [medical monitoring] costs." "Arguably," the Court explains, Buckley demands an "unqualified rule of lump-sum damages recovery," a rule for which the Court finds "insufficient support in the common law." The Court pointedly refrains, however, from "expressing any view…about the extent to which the FELA might, or might not, accommodate medical cost recovery rules more finely tailored than [a rule of the unqualified kind]."

It is not apparent why (or even whether) the Court reverses the Second Circuit's determination on Buckley's second claim. The Court of Appeals held that a medical monitoring claim is solidly grounded, and this Court does not hold otherwise. Hypothesizing that Buckley demands lump-sum damages and nothing else, the Court ruminates on the appropriate remedy without answering the anterior question: Does the plaintiff have a claim for relief? Buckley has shown that Metro-North negligently exposed him to "extremely high levels of asbestos," 79 F.3d at 1341, and that this exposure warrants "medical monitoring in order to detect and treat [asbestos-related] diseases as they may arise." Id., at 1346. Buckley's expert medical witness estimated the annual costs of proper monitoring at $950. We do not know from the Court's opinion what more a plaintiff must show to qualify for relief.

In my view, the Second Circuit rightly held that a railworker negligently exposed to asbestos states a claim for relief under the FELA; recovery in such cases, again as the Court of Appeals held, should reflect the difference in cost between the medical tests a reasonable physician would prescribe for unexposed persons and the monitoring regime a reasonable physician would advise for persons exposed in the way Michael Buckley and his co-workers were. . . .

COMMENTS AND QUESTIONS

1. *Buckley* is a case brought under the Federal Employers' Liability Act. The Supreme Court has interpreted that statute to authorize the federal courts to act as common law courts in developing principles of liability. Consider how the deliberations in a legislature on the issue of *creating* a system for compensating workers for their emotional distress in circumstances like Buckley's would differ from those in the courts. How much weight would a legislature give to the reasons the Court gives for denying compensation for emotional distress? Consider, for example, the problem the Court identifies with coordinating a tort action for medical monitoring costs with existing systems of medical insurance. Reconsider the question of the legislative creation of a remedy after you read the article by Lon Fuller in section 4.

2. Why doesn't the Court think that Buckley's intimate contact with particles of asbestos would be a "physical impact" under the common law? The Court denies recovery for emotional distress unaccompanied by existing illness. What are its reasons? Consider these alternative propositions and the reasons the Court has, or might have, for rejecting them: (a) It is traditionally a job for juries to distinguish between valid and invalid claims. (Reconsider this claim after you read excerpts from Slovic in the next section.) (b) Chronic harms are

worse than traumatic ones, or near misses. (c) The issue in the case is whether a person who suffers injury (emotional distress caused by exposure to asbestos) should bear the cost of that injury or whether the party who exposes the person to injury should bear that cost; the Court fails to explain why the *distribution* of costs its decision endorses is justified.

3. Why does the Court in *Buckley* deny recovery for (the incremental costs of) medical monitoring? How easy is it, according to the Court, to ascertain those costs?

3 ▪ Placing a Value on Exposure to Risk

We begin this section with a case dealing with the valuation of exposure to risk. What factors does the court take into account in determining whether the trial court's valuation was correct? Do all of them seem relevant to determining damages? Does the court fail to consider some factors that might be relevant? The readings that follow the case raise questions about how people perceive risks such as exposure to cancer-causing substances.

▪ Sterling v. Velsicol Chemical Corporation
855 F.2d 1188 (6th Cir. 1987)

Guy, Circuit Judge:
        A number of persons, including these plaintiffs, who either lived or owned property near defendant's landfill, brought a class action for personal injuries and property damage resulting from hazardous chemicals leaking from the landfill and contaminating the local water supply. The district court held the corporation liable upon legal theories of strict liability, common law negligence, trespass, and nuisance. The court awarded five representative members of the class compensatory damages for their personal injuries, as well as property damages, plus prejudgment interest on the entire award. The district court further held the corporation liable to the class as a whole for punitive damages.
        Upon a review of the lengthy record in this difficult case, we find that the district court properly held Velsicol liable to the five representative plaintiffs but erred in the nature and amount of the damage awards. Accordingly, we affirm in part, reverse in part, and remand with directions for recalculation of some of the damages.

Facts

In August, 1964, the defendant, Velsicol Chemical Corporation (Velsicol), acquired 242 acres of rural land in Hardeman County, Tennessee. The defendant used the site as a landfill for by-products from the production of chlorinated hydrocarbon pesticides at its Memphis, Tennessee, chemical manufacturing facility. Before Velsicol purchased the landfill site and commenced depositing any chemicals into the ground, it neither conducted hydrogeological studies to assess the soil composition underneath the site, the water flow direction, and the location of the local water aquifer, nor drilled a monitoring well to detect and record any ongoing contamination. From October, 1964, to June, 1973, the defendant deposited a total of 300,000 55-gallon steel drums containing ultrahazardous liquid chemical waste and hundreds of fiber board cartons containing ultrahazardous dry chemical waste in the landfill.[1]

Shortly after Velsicol began its disposal operations at the landfill site, local residents and county, state, and federal authorities became concerned about the environmental impact of the defendant's activities. As a result of this concern, the United States Geological Survey (USGS), in 1967, prepared the first of several reports on the potential contamination effects of the chemicals deposited into the landfill up to that time. The 1967 report indicated that chlorinated hydrocarbons had migrated down into the subsoil and had contaminated portions of the surface and subsurface environment adjacent to the disposal site. While the chemicals had not reached the local water aquifer, the USGS concluded that both the local and contiguous ground water were in danger of contamination.[2] Subsequent to publication of the 1967 USGS report, Velsicol expanded the size of the landfill disposal site from twenty to forty acres.

State authorities increasingly became concerned about the defendant's disposal of ultrahazardous chemicals at the site. In 1972, the state filed an administrative action to close the landfill because the chlorinated hydrocarbons buried at the site allegedly were contaminating irreparably the subsurface waters. The state ordered Velsicol to cease disposal of all toxic chemicals by August 21, 1972, and all other chemicals by June 1, 1973.

In 1976, three years after the state permanently closed the landfill disposal site, the USGS, in conjunction with state authorities, commenced updating the 1967 USGS report. One major concern, which gave rise to the new USGS study, was the possibility of the chemicals migrating toward wells utilized by local residents. In 1978, the USGS issued a written report detailing the 1976 update of the 1967 report. The 1978 report found that the water table of the local aquifer was highly contaminated. The 1978 USGS report also indicated that the local aquifer moved toward the northwest, north, and northeast, rather than just toward the east as earlier indicated in the 1967 USGS report. Consequently, residents' wells, which were previously presumed safe from contamination, were now potentially polluted. In

---

[1] The district court concluded that spent hydrocarbons buried at the landfill disposal site included not only chlorobenzene, hexachlorobutadiene, hexachloroethane, hexachloronerbornadiene, napthalene, tetrachloroethylene, toluene, hexachlorocyclopentadiene, and benzene, but also the known carcinogens carbon tetrachloride and chloroform. The drums and cartons containing these chemicals were deposited in trenches that were 15 feet deep and 12 to 15 feet wide and covered with approximately 3 feet of soil. Velsicol took no precautions to insure the drums from bursting and, invariably, some of the drums would leak their contents into the soil. Furthermore, the trenches were neither lined nor covered with any impermeable material to prevent the chemical waste from leaking into the soil. Velsicol eventually placed a clay cap over the landfill site in 1980 only after state authorities threatened a lawsuit over the imminent danger the landfill posed to the environment.

[2] However, the 1967 USGS report erroneously concluded that, even once the chemicals reached the local aquifer, there was no danger of contamination to any existing domestic wells because the local aquifer moved to the east while the limited residential development in the area was located west. In actuality, the water aquifer flowed in a northwesterly direction.

view of the continued complaints by numerous local residents, the Department of Health conducted further well water sampling tests in 1978. These tests revealed the presence of certain chlorinated hydrocarbons in numerous wells. Additionally, in 1978, the state, the USGS, the EPA, and Velsicol all commenced numerous extensive ground water surveys of the site and surrounding area. The surveys collectively identified twelve to fifteen drinking water wells, which were adjacent to the site, as contaminated with high levels of chlorinated hydrocarbons. Specifically, the surveys established that six of these wells were contaminated by carbon tetrachloride in excess of 100 parts per billion and high amounts of chloroform. The users of these wells, and all wells within 1,000 acres around the landfill site, were advised to stop using them for any purpose.

. . . [Plaintiffs'] complaint sought $1.5 billion in compensatory damages and $1 billion in punitive damages. . . . The complaint sought relief for involuntary exposure to certain chemical substances known to cause cancer, affect the central nervous system and permanently damage other organs of the human body, and for loss of value to their real property in the region affected by the chemicals. . . .

After a bench trial of the five claims, the district court found Velsicol liable to the plaintiffs on legal theories of strict liability, common law negligence, trespass, and nuisance. . . .

Compensatory Damages

Velsicol argues that, even assuming proof of a proximate causation, the district court improperly awarded the five representative plaintiffs compensatory damages for their respective injuries and disabilities. The five representative plaintiffs, their exposure to Velsicol's chemicals, and their respective injuries are as follows:

Steven Sterling: Plaintiff Sterling, who was born December 25, 1922, in Hardeman County, Tennessee, utilized a well adjacent to his residence (Sterling well) for drinking purposes until November, 1977, and for all other purposes until November, 1978. During that time, he claimed to have drunk between ten and twelve glasses of the well water each day. He observed that, beginning in 1975, the well water developed a distinct odor, a bad taste, and contained an oily substance. Sterling testified that after ingesting, and otherwise using, the well water for a prolonged period of time, he suffered from headaches, nervousness, stomach and chest pains, shortness of breath, ringing in his ears, fatigue, loss of appetite and weight, nausea, coughing, vomiting, and peripheral neuropathy. Sterling further testified that he suffered from an enlarged liver with abnormal hepatic function, and an eighty percent reduction in his kidney function. Additionally, he developed emphysema in early 1976. Sterling was a heavy smoker for over forty-five years and previously worked in a cotton mill.

James Wilbanks: Plaintiff Wilbanks, who was born in Walton, Mississippi, on June 15, 1931, lived in a mobile home with his family across from the Velsicol landfill from 1968 through 1971. During that time period, both Wilbanks and his family used water from a well adjacent to his property for drinking and bathing purposes (Tavern well). Beginning in 1971, Wilbanks commuted to work and used water at a tavern located across from the Velsicol landfill until it was closed and the well was capped in 1972. Thereafter, he used water obtained from two other wells for drinking and bathing purposes until 1978 (Sterling well and Rosetta Brooks well). Wilbanks testified that he suffered from headaches, dizziness, fatigue, nausea, vomiting, numbness, nervousness, ringing in his ears, shortness of breath, skin irritation, partial loss of eyesight including optic atrophy and neuritis, and peripheral neuropathy. Wilbanks lost his left kidney in 1981 due to cancer and suffers from emphysema.

Curry Ivy: Plaintiff Ivy, who was born on January 3, 1926, in Chester County, Tennessee, drank contaminated water from three wells (Rosetta Brooks well, Velsicol Farm well, and Tavern well). He moved from the area in 1972. Ivy also was exposed to the ultrahazardous liquid and dry chemicals from January, 1972, through June, 1973, while he was employed by Velsicol to transport chemicals from its plant in Memphis, Tennessee, to its landfill in Hardeman County, Tennessee. Ivy testified that he suffered from headaches, dizziness, nausea, vomiting, nervousness, shortness of breath, fatigue, partial loss of eyesight including optic nerve neuritis and nerve dysfunction, and peripheral neuropathy. Ivy further testified that he suffered from liver and kidney damage and severe emphysema. Ivy's medical history prior to drinking, or otherwise using, any contaminated well water included ulcers, stomach problems, severe emphysema, partial loss of vision, a heart attack, and various psychological problems. Ivy was a heavy smoker and previously worked in a cotton mill.

Daniel Johnson: Plaintiff Johnson, who was born May 18, 1938, in Algoma, Mississippi, lived in Hardeman County from 1976 through 1978. During that time, Johnson and his family used water from a well adjacent to his property (Johnson well) for drinking and bathing purposes. Johnson testified that he suffered from headaches, loss of balance, fatigue, nausea, vomiting, numbness, nervousness, skin irritation, coughing, and partial loss of eyesight including optic nerve dysfunction. Johnson further testified that he suffered liver and kidney damage. Additionally, the Missouri Department of Health certified that, as of 1980, he was totally disabled and unable to continue employment as a result of psychological injuries. Johnson's wife and daughter developed breast and uterus tumors. Mrs. Johnson previously suffered from fibrocystic disease.

James Maness, Jr.: Plaintiff Maness, who was born on September 1, 1976, drank and was bathed in water obtained from two wells (Sterling well and Mosier well) until approximately 1978. Additionally, while Maness' mother was pregnant, she drank water obtained from the same wells. Maness allegedly suffered from frequent headaches, dizziness, nose bleeds, sore throat, nausea, and frequent vomiting. Additionally, Maness suffered from severe allergies, epilepsy, diabetes, blood discrasias [*sic*], and an abnormally enlarged liver.

. . . .

Fear of Increased Risk of Cancer and Other Diseases

Velsicol next argues that the district court erroneously awarded the five representative plaintiffs compensatory damages or, in the alternative, excessive damages for fear of increased risk of contracting cancer and other diseases. Mental distress, which results from fear that an already existent injury will lead to the future onset of an as yet unrealized disease, constitutes an element of recovery only where such distress is either foreseeable or is a natural consequence of, or reasonably expected to flow from, the present injury. However, damages for mental distress generally are not recoverable where the connection between the anxiety and the existing injury is either too remote or tenuous. While there must be a reasonable connection between the injured plaintiff's mental anguish and the prediction of a future disease, the central focus of a court's inquiry in such a case is not on the underlying odds that the future disease will in fact materialize. To this extent, mental anguish resulting from the chance that an existing injury will lead to the materialization of a future disease may be an element of recovery even though the underlying future prospect for susceptibility to a future disease is not, in and of itself, compensable inasmuch as it is not sufficiently likely to occur. In the context of certain types of injuries and exposures to certain chemicals, cancerphobia has been one basis of claims for mental anguish damages.

In Tennessee, damages for fear arising from an increased risk of disease are recoverable. In *Laxton v. Orkin Exterminating Co.*, the plaintiffs' water supply was contaminated by the carcinogens chlordane and heptachlor when defendant serviceman sprayed the exterior of plaintiffs' house for termites. The Department of Water Quality Control told plaintiffs to cease using the water for any purpose and to obtain a new water source. As a result of ingesting the contaminated water for over a period of eight months, the plaintiffs worried about their health and the health of their children. The court awarded the plaintiffs $6,000 each for their mental suffering resulting from their reasonable apprehension of the harmful effects to their own and their children's health due to consuming or otherwise using the contaminated water. The *Laxton* court noted that the period of "mental anguish" deserving compensation was confined to the time between the discovery of ingestion of toxic substances and the determination that puts to rest the fear of future injury.

In the instant case, the plaintiffs' fear clearly constitutes a present injury. Each plaintiff produced evidence that they personally suffered from a reasonable fear of contracting cancer or some other disease in the future as a result of ingesting Velsicol's chemicals. Consistent with the extensive line of authority in both Tennessee and other jurisdictions, we cannot say that the district court erred in awarding the five representative plaintiffs damages for their reasonable fear of increased risk of cancer and other diseases.

In the alternative, Velsicol asserts that the district court awarded excessive damages to the plaintiffs. The amount of the damage award in a personal injury action is for the jury or, in a non-jury case, the trial judge who heard the evidence. Absent a showing of bias, passion, or corruption, excessiveness of a verdict is left to the trial court's discretion. The appellate court will only consider whether the trial court abused that discretion by granting awards so large as to shock the judicial conscience. When considering whether an award is so excessive, this court considers other awards in other cases, as well as the nature and extent of the injuries.

The evidence credited by the court shows that each of the plaintiffs suffered from, and should be compensated for, a reasonable fear of contracting cancer or some other diseases in the future. The only issue is the amount of reasonable compensation. In *Laxton*, the court limited the amounts of recovery to $6,000 for each plaintiff's reasonable fear of future disease from ingesting known carcinogens over an extended period of time. In the instant case, the district court awarded plaintiffs damages ranging from $50,000 to $250,000. We find these awards to be excessive, particularly where plaintiffs failed to prove at trial that they have a significant increased risk of contracting cancer and other diseases. Upon a review of the opinion and the adopted findings of fact, we are unable to find any basis upon which the district court differentiated its damage awards to each plaintiff for his or her fear of increased risk of cancer and other diseases. The *Laxton* court awarded each plaintiff $6,000 for his or her fear of increased susceptibility to cancer from consuming known carcinogens for a duration of eight months. Using *Laxton* as a guidepost, we, accordingly, vacate the district court's award and award each of the five representative plaintiffs damages based upon the duration of their exposure to the contaminated water. Plaintiff Johnson, who was exposed to the chemicals for a period of approximately two years, is awarded $18,000 versus the district court's award of $250,000; plaintiff Maness, who was exposed for approximately three years (two years during infancy and approximately one year while his mother was exposed to the chemicals during pregnancy), is awarded $27,000 versus the district court's award of $250,000; plaintiff Ivy, who was exposed for approximately four years, is awarded $36,000 versus the district court's award of $50,000; plaintiff Wilbanks, who was exposed for approximately six years, is awarded $54,000 versus the district court's award of $100,000; and plaintiff Sterling, who was exposed for approximately eight years, is awarded $72,000 versus the district court's award of $75,000.

. . .

COMMENTS AND QUESTIONS

The court awards each representative plaintiff $9,000 per year of exposure. Do you agree that a uniform measure of damages for fear of increased risk of cancer is appropriate? Note that some of the representative plaintiffs were smokers whereas others were not, that one was exposed as an infant, and that another had a family history of cancer. Should these factors be relevant to measuring the damages each plaintiff suffered? (Note that this was a class action and that the more factors one treats as relevant to determining damages, the more subclasses—and representative plaintiffs—one might have to create, with the attendant risk that the class action would become unmanageable.)

- ■ *Perception of Risk*
  PAUL SLOVIC
  236 Science 280 (1987). Reprinted with permission from *Science*. © AAAS

The ability to sense and avoid harmful environmental conditions is necessary for the survival of all living organisms. Survival is also aided by an ability to codify and learn from past experience. Humans have an additional capability that allows them to alter their environment as well as respond to it. This capacity both creates and reduces risk.

In recent decades, the profound development of chemical and nuclear technologies has been accompanied by the potential to cause catastrophic and long-lasting damage to the earth and the life forms that inhabit it. The mechanisms underlying these complex technologies are unfamiliar and incomprehensible to most citizens. Their most harmful consequences are rare and often delayed, hence difficult to assess by statistical analysis and not well suited to management by trial-and-error learning. The elusive and hard to manage qualities of today's hazards have forced the creation of a new intellectual discipline called risk assessment, designed to aid in identifying, characterizing, and quantifying risk.

Whereas technologically sophisticated analysts employ risk assessment to evaluate hazards, the majority of citizens rely on intuitive risk judgments, typically called "risk perceptions." For these people, experience with hazards tends to come from the news media, which rather thoroughly document mishaps and threats occurring throughout the world. The dominant perception for most Americans (and one that contrasts sharply with the views of professional risk assessors) is that they face more risk today than in the past and that future risks will be even greater than today's ["Risk in a complex society," report of a public opinion poll conducted by L. Harris for the Marsh and McClennan Company, New York (1980)]. Similar views appear to be held by citizens of many other industrialized nations. These perceptions and the opposition to technology that accompanies them have puzzled and frustrated industrialists and regulators and have led numerous observers to argue that the American public's apparent pursuit of a "zero-risk society" threatens the nation's political and economic stability. Wildavsky [A. Wildavsky, Am. Sci., 67 (1979), p. 32] commented as follows on this state of affairs.

> How extraordinary! The richest, longest lived, best protected, most resourceful civilization, with the highest degree of insight into its own technology, is on its way to becoming the most frightened.
>
> Is it our environment or ourselves that have changed? Would people like us have had this sort of concern in the past?...Today, there are risks from numerous small dams far exceeding those from nuclear reactors. Why is the one feared and not the other? Is it just that we are used to the old or are some of us looking differently at essentially the same sorts of experience?

During the past decade, a small number of researchers has been attempting to answer such questions by examining the opinions that people express when they are asked, in a variety of ways, to evaluate hazardous activities, substances, and technologies. This research has attempted to develop techniques for assessing the complex and subtle opinions that people have about risk. With these techniques, researchers have sought to discover what people mean when they say that something is (or is not) "risky," and to determine what factors underlie those perceptions. The basic assumption underlying these efforts is that those who promote and regulate health and safety need to understand the ways in which people think about and respond to risk.

If successful, this research should aid policy-makers by improving communication between them and the public, by directing educational efforts, and by predicting public responses to new technologies (for example, genetic engineering), events (for example, a good safety record or an accident), and new risk management strategies (for example, warning labels, regulations, substitute products).

Risk Perception Research

Important contributions to our current understanding of risk perception have come from geography, sociology, political science, anthropology, and psychology. Geographical research focused originally on understanding human behavior in the face of natural hazards, but it has since broadened to include technological hazards as well. Sociological and anthropological studies have shown that perception and acceptance of risk have their roots in social and cultural factors. Short [J. F. Short Jr., Am. Sociol. Rev. 49, 711 (1984)] argues that response to hazards is mediated by social influences transmitted by friends, family, fellow workers, and respected public officials. In many cases, risk perceptions may form afterwards, as part of the ex post facto rationale for one's own behavior. Douglas and Wildavsky [M. Douglas and A. Wildavsky, Risk and Culture (Univ. of California Press, Berkeley, 1982)] assert that people, acting within social groups, downplay certain risks and emphasize others as a means of maintaining and controlling the group.

Psychological research on risk perception, which shall be my focus, originated in empirical studies of probability assessment, utility assessment, and decision-making processes. A major development in this area has been the discovery of a set of mental strategies, or heuristics, that people employ in order to make sense out of an uncertain world. Although these rules are valid in some circumstances, in others they lead to large and persistent biases, with serious implications for risk assessment. In particular, laboratory research on basic perceptions and cognitions has shown that difficulties in understanding probabilistic processes, biased media coverage, misleading personal experiences, and the anxieties generated by life's gambles cause uncertainty to be denied, risks to be misjudged (sometimes overestimated and sometimes underestimated), and judgments of fact to be held with unwarranted confidence. Experts' judgments appear to be prone to many of the same biases as those of the general public, particularly when experts are forced to go beyond the limits of available data and rely on intuition.

Research further indicates that disagreements about risk shouldn't be expected to evaporate in the presence of evidence. Strong initial views are resistant to change because they influence the way that subsequent information is interpreted. New evidence appears reliable and informative if it is consistent with one's initial beliefs; contrary evidence tends to be dismissed as unreliable, erroneous, or unrepresentative. When people lack strong prior opinions, the opposite situation exists—they are at the mercy of the problem formulation. Presenting the same information about risk in different ways (for example, mortality rates as opposed to survival rates) alters people's perspectives and actions.

The Psychometric Paradigm

One broad strategy for studying perceived risk is to develop a taxonomy for hazards that can be used to understand and predict responses to their risks. A taxonomic scheme might explain, for example, people's extreme aversion to some hazards, their indifference to others, and the discrepancies between these reactions and opinions of experts. The most common approach to this goal has employed the psychometric paradigm, which uses psychophysical scaling and multivariate analysis techniques to produce quantitative representations or "cognitive maps" of risk attitudes and perceptions. Within the psychometric paradigm, people make quantitative judgments about the current and desired riskiness of diverse hazards and the desired level of regulation of each. These judgments are then related to judgments about other properties, such as (i) the hazard's status on characteristics that have been hypothesized to account for risk perceptions and attitudes (for example, voluntariness, dread, knowledge, controllability), (ii) the benefits that each hazard provides to society, (iii) the number of deaths caused by the hazard in an average year, and (iv) the number of deaths caused by the hazard in a disastrous year.

In the rest of this article, I shall briefly review some of the results obtained from psychometric studies of risk perception and outline some implications of these results for risk communication and risk management.

Revealed and Expressed Preferences

The original impetus for the psychometric paradigm came from the pioneering effort of Starr [C. Starr, Science 165, 1232 (1969)] to develop a method for weighing technological risks against benefits in order to answer the fundamental question, "How safe is safe enough?" His "revealed preference" approach assumed that, by trial and error, society has arrived at an "essentially optimum" balance between the risks and benefits associated with any activity. One may therefore use historical or current risk and benefit data to reveal patterns of "acceptable" risk-benefit trade-offs. Examining such data for several industries and activities, Starr concluded that (i) acceptability of risk from an activity is roughly proportional to the third power of the benefits for that activity, and (ii) the public will accept risks from voluntary activities (such as skiing) that are roughly 1000 times as great as it would tolerate from involuntary hazards (such as food preservatives) that provide the same level of benefits. . . .

[Later] studies have shown that perceived risk is quantifiable and predictable. Psychometric techniques seem well suited for identifying similarities and differences among groups with regard to risk perceptions and attitudes (Table 1). They have also shown that the concept "risk" means different things to different people. When experts judge risk, their responses correlate highly with technical estimates of annual fatalities. Lay people can assess annual fatalities if they are asked to (and produce estimates somewhat like the technical estimates). However, their judgments of "risk" are related more to other hazard characteristics (for example, catastrophic potential, threat to future generations) and, as a result, tend to differ from their own (and experts') estimates of annual fatalities.

Another consistent result from psychometric studies of expressed preferences is that people tend to view current risk levels as unacceptably high for most activities. The gap between perceived and desired risk levels suggests that people are not satisfied with the way that market and other regulatory mechanisms have balanced risks and benefits. Across the domain of hazards, there seems to be little systematic relationship between perceptions of current risks and benefits. However, studies of expressed preferences do seem to support Starr's argument that people are willing to tolerate higher risks from activities seen as highly beneficial. But, whereas Starr concluded that voluntariness of exposure was the key mediator of risk acceptance, expressed preference studies have shown that other (perceived) characteristics such as familiarity, control, catastrophic potential, equity, and level of knowledge also seem to influence the relation between perceived risk, perceived benefit, and risk acceptance. . . .

Factor-Analytic Representations

Many of the qualitative risk characteristics are correlated with each other, across a wide range of hazards. For example, hazards judged to be "voluntary" tend also to be judged as "controllable"; hazards whose adverse effects are delayed tend to be seen as posing risks that are not well known, and so on. Investigation of these relations by means of factor analysis has shown that the broader domain of

Table 1 Ordering of perceived risk for 30 activities and technologies. The ordering is based on the geometric mean risk ratings within each group. Rank 1 represents the most risky activity or technology.

Activity or Technology	League of Women Voters	College Students	Active Club Members	Experts
Nuclear power	1	1	8	20
Motor vehicles	2	5	3	1
Handguns	3	2	1	4
Smoking	4	3	4	2
Motorcycles	5	6	2	6
Alcoholic beverages	6	7	5	3
General (private) aviation	7	15	11	12
Police work	8	8	7	17
Pesticides	9	4	15	8
Surgery	10	11	9	5
Fire fighting	11	10	6	18
Large construction	12	14	13	13
Hunting	13	18	10	23
Spray cans	14	13	23	26
Mountain climbing	15	22	12	29
Bicycles	16	24	14	15
Commercial aviation	17	16	18	16
Electric power (non-nuclear)	18	19	19	9
Swimming	19	30	17	10
Contraceptives	20	9	22	11
Skiing	21	25	16	30
X-rays	22	17	24	7
High school and college football	23	26	21	27
Railroads	24	23	29	19
Food preservatives	25	12	28	14
Food coloring	26	20	30	21
Power mowers	27	28	25	28
Prescription antibiotics	28	21	26	24
Home appliances	29	27	27	22
Vaccinations	30	29	29	25

characteristics can be condensed to a small set of higher order characteristics or factors.

The factor space presented in Fig. 1 has been replicated across groups of lay people and experts judging large and diverse sets of hazards. Factor 1, labeled "dread risk," is defined at its high (right-hand) end by perceived lack of control, dread, catastrophic potential, fatal consequences, and the inequitable distribution of risks and benefits. Nuclear weapons and nuclear power score highest on the characteristics that make up this factor. Factor 2, labeled "unknown risk," is defined at its high end by hazards judged to be unobservable, unknown, new, and delayed in their manifestation of harm. Chemical technologies score particularly high on this factor. A third factor, reflecting the number of people exposed to the risk, has been obtained in several studies. Making the set of hazards more or less specific (for example, partitioning nuclear power into radioactive waste, uranium

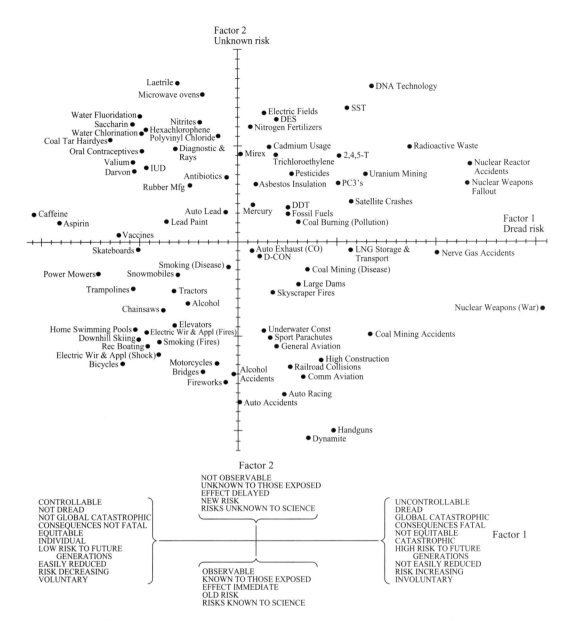

Figure 1 Location of 81 hazards on factors 1 and 2 derived from the relationships among 18 risk characteristics. Each factor is made up of a combination of characteristics, as indicated by the lower diagram.

mining, and nuclear reactor accidents) has had little effect on the factor structure or its relation to risk perceptions.

Research has shown that lay people's risk perceptions and attitudes are closely related to the position of a hazard within this type of factor space. Most important is the horizontal factor "dread risk." The higher a hazard's score on this factor (the

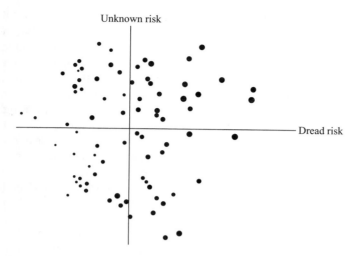

Figure 2 Attitudes toward regulation of the hazards in Fig. 1. The larger the point, the greater the desire for strict regulation to reduce risk.

. . . .

further to the right it appears in the space), the higher its perceived risk, the more people want to see its current risks reduced, and the more they want to see strict regulation employed to achieve the desired reduction in risk (Fig. 2). In contrast, experts' perceptions of risk are not closely related to any of the various risk characteristics or factors derived from these characteristics. Instead, as noted earlier, experts appear to see riskiness as synonymous with expected annual mortality. As a result, conflicts over "risk" may result from experts and lay people having different definitions of the concept.

. . . .

Accidents as Signals

Risk analyses typically model the impacts of an unfortunate event (such as an accident, a discovery of pollution, sabotage, product tampering) in terms of direct harm to victims—deaths, injuries, and damages. The impacts of such events, however, sometimes extend far beyond these direct harms and may include significant indirect costs (both monetary and nonmonetary) to the responsible government agency or private company that far exceed direct costs. In some cases, all companies in an industry are affected, regardless of which company was responsible for the mishap. In extreme cases, the indirect costs of a mishap may extend past industry boundaries, affecting companies, industries, and agencies whose business is minimally related to the initial event. Thus, an unfortunate event can be thought of as analogous to a stone dropped in a pond. The ripples spread outward, encompassing first the directly affected victims, then the responsible company or agency, and, in the extreme, reaching other companies, agencies, and industries.

Some events make only small ripples; others make larger ones. The challenge is to discover characteristics associated with an event and the way that it is managed that can predict the breadth and seriousness of those impacts. Early theories equated the magnitude of impact to the number of people killed or injured, or to the amount of property damaged. However, the accident at the Three Mile Island (TMI) nuclear reactor in 1979 provides a dramatic demonstration that factors besides injury, death, and property damage impose serious costs. Despite the fact that not a single person died, and few if any latent cancer fatalities are expected, no other accident in our history has produced such costly societal impacts. The accident at TMI devastated the utility that owned and operated the plant. It also imposed enormous costs on the nuclear industry and on society, through stricter regulation (resulting in increased construction and operation costs), reduced operation of reactors worldwide, greater public opposition to nuclear power, and reliance on more expensive energy sources. It may even have led to a more hostile view of other complex technologies, such as chemical manufacturing and genetic engineering. The point is that traditional economic and risk analyses tend to neglect these higher order impacts, hence they greatly underestimate the costs associated with certain kinds of events.

Although the TMI accident is extreme, it is by no means unique. Other recent events resulting in enormous higher order impacts include the chemical manufacturing accident at Bhopal, India, the pollution of Love Canal, New York, and Times Beach, Missouri, the disastrous launch of the space shuttle Challenger, and the meltdown of the nuclear reactor at Chernobyl. Following these extreme events are a myriad of mishaps varying in the breadth and size of their impacts.

An important concept that has emerged from psychometric research is that the seriousness and higher order impacts of an unfortunate event are determined, in part, by what that event signals or portends. The informativeness or "signal potential" of an event, and thus its potential social impact, appears to be systematically related to the characteristics of the hazard and the location of the event within the factor space described earlier. An accident that takes many lives may produce relatively little social disturbance (beyond that experienced by the victims' families and friends) if it occurs as part of a familiar and well-understood system (such as a train wreck). However, a small accident in an unfamiliar system (or one perceived as poorly understood), such as a nuclear reactor or a recombinant DNA laboratory, may have immense social consequences if it is perceived as a harbinger of further and possibly catastrophic mishaps.

The concept of accidents as signals was eloquently expressed in an editorial addressing the tragic accident at Bhopal.

> What truly grips us in these accounts is not so much the numbers as the spectacle of suddenly vanishing competence, of men utterly routed by technology, of fail-safe systems failing with a logic as inexorable as it was once—indeed, right up until that very moment—unforeseeable. And the spectacle haunts us because it seems to carry allegorical import, like the whispery omen of a hovering future.

One implication of the signal concept is that effort and expense beyond that indicated by a cost-benefit analysis might be warranted to reduce the possibility of "high-signal accidents." Unfortunate events involving hazards in the upper right quadrant of Fig. 1 appear particularly likely to have the potential to produce large ripples. As a result, risk analyses involving these hazards need to be made sensitive to these possible higher order impacts. Doing so would likely bring greater protection to potential victims as well as to companies and industries.

Analysis of Single Hazard Domains

Psychometric analyses have also been applied to judgments of diverse hazard scenarios within a single technological domain, such as railroad transport or automobiles. Kraus had people evaluate the riskiness of 49 railroad hazard scenarios that varied with respect to type of train, type of cargo, location of the accident, and the nature and cause of the accident (for example, a high-speed train carrying passengers through a mountain tunnel derails due to a mechanical system failure). The results showed that these railroad hazards were highly differentiated, much like the hazards in Fig. 1. The highest signal potential (and thus the highest potential for large ripple effects) was associated with accidents involving trains carrying hazardous chemicals.

A study by Slovic, MacGregor, and Kraus [P. Slovic, D. MacGregor, N. Kraus, Accident Anal. Prev., in press] examined perceptions of risk and signal value for 40 structural defects in automobiles. Multivariate analysis of these defects, rated in terms of various characteristics of risk, produced a two-factor space. As in earlier studies with diverse hazards, the position of a defect in this space predicted judgments of riskiness and signal value quite well. One defect stood out much as nuclear hazards do in Fig. 1. It was a fuel tank rupture upon impact, creating the possibility of fire and burn injuries. This, of course, is similar to the notorious design problem that plagued Ford Pinto and that Ford allegedly declined to correct because a cost-benefit analysis indicated that the correction costs greatly exceeded the expected benefits from increased safety. Had Ford done a psychometric study, the analysis might have highlighted this particular defect as one whose seriousness and higher order costs (lawsuits, damaged company reputation) were likely to be greatly underestimated by cost-benefit analysis.

Forecasting Public Acceptance

Results from studies of the perception of risk have been used to explain and forecast acceptance and opposition for specific technologies. Nuclear power has been a frequent topic of such analyses because of the dramatic opposition it has engendered in the face of experts' assurances of its safety. Research shows that people judge the benefits from nuclear power to be quite small and the risks to be unacceptably great. Nuclear power risks occupy extreme positions in psychometric factor spaces, reflecting people's views that these risks are unknown, dread, uncontrollable, inequitable, catastrophic, and likely to affect future generations (Fig. 1). Opponents of nuclear power recognize that few people have died thus far as a result of this technology. However, long before Chernobyl, they expressed great concern over the potential for catastrophic accidents.

These public perceptions have evoked harsh reactions from experts. One noted psychiatrist wrote that "the irrational fear of nuclear plants is based on a mistaken assessment of the risks" [R. L. Dupont, Bus. Week, 7 September 1981, pp. 8–9]. A nuclear physicist and leading advocate of nuclear power contended that ". . . the public has been driven insane over fear of radiation from nuclear power. I use the word 'insane' purposefully since one of its definitions is loss of contact with reality. The public's understanding of radiation dangers has virtually lost all contact with the actual dangers as understood by scientists" [B. L. Cohen, Before It's Too Late: A Scientist's Case for Nuclear Energy (Plenum, New York, 1983), p. 31].

Risk perception research paints a different picture, demonstrating that people's deep anxieties are linked to the reality of extensive unfavorable media coverage and to a strong association between nuclear power and the proliferation and use of nuclear weapons. Attempts to "educate" or reassure the public and bring their perceptions in line with those of industry experts appear unlikely to succeed because the low probability of serious reactor accidents makes empirical demonstrations of safety difficult to achieve. Because nuclear risks are perceived as unknown and potentially catastrophic, even small accidents will be highly publicized and may produce large ripple effects.

Psychometric research may be able to forecast the response to technologies that have yet to arouse strong and persistent public opposition. For example, DNA technologies seem to evoke several of the perceptions that make nuclear power so hard to manage. In the aftermath of an accident, this technology could face some of the same problems and opposition now confronting the nuclear industry.

Placing Risks in Perspective

A consequence of the public's concerns and its opposition to risky technologies has been an increase in attempts to inform and educate people about risk. Risk perception research has a number of implications for such educational efforts.

One frequently advocated approach to broadening people's perspectives is to present quantitative risk estimates for a variety of hazards, expressed in some unidimensional index of death or disability, such as risk per hour of exposure, annual probability of death, or reduction in life expectancy. Even though such comparisons have no logically necessary implications for acceptability of risk, one might still hope that they would help improve people's intuitions about the magnitude of risks. Risk perception research suggests, however, that these sorts of comparisons may not be very satisfactory even for this purpose. People's perceptions and attitudes are determined not only by the sort of unidimensional statistics used in such tables but also by the variety of quantitative and qualitative characteristics reflected in Fig. 1. To many people, statements such as, "the annual risk from living near a nuclear power plant is equivalent to the risk of riding an extra 3 miles in an automobile," give inadequate consideration to the important differences in the nature of the risks from these two technologies.

In short, "riskiness" means more to people than "expected number of fatalities." Attempts to characterize, compare, and regulate risks must be sensitive to this broader conception of risk. . . .

Whereas psychometric research implies that risk debates are not merely about risk statistics, some sociological and anthropological research implies that some of these debates may not even be about risk. Risk concerns may provide a rationale for actions taken on other grounds or they may be a surrogate for other social or ideological concerns. When this is the case, communication about risk is simply irrelevant to the discussion. Hidden agendas need to be brought to the surface for discussion.

Perhaps the most important message from this research is that there is wisdom as well as error in public attitudes and perceptions. Lay people sometimes lack certain information about hazards. However, their basic conceptualization of risk is much richer than that of the experts and reflects legitimate concerns that are typically omitted from expert risk assessments. As a result, risk communication and risk management efforts are destined to fail unless they are structured as a two-way process. Each side, expert and public, has something valid to contribute. Each side must respect the insights and intelligence of the other.

- *Trust, Emotion, Sex, Politics, and Science:*
  Surveying the Risk Assessment Battlefield
  PAUL SLOVIC
  1997 U. Chi. Legal F. 59. Reprinted with permission of University
  of Chicago Legal Forum

. . . .

[E]arly studies of risk perception demonstrated that the public's concerns could not simply be blamed on ignorance or irrationality. Instead, research has shown that many of the public's reactions to risk . . . can be attributed to a sensitivity to technical, social, and psychological qualities of hazards that are not well-modeled in technical risk assessments (for instance, qualities such as uncertainty in risk assessments, perceived inequity in the distribution of risks and benefits, and aversion to being exposed to risks that are involuntary, not under one's control, or dreaded).

More recently, another important aspect of the risk-perception problem has come to be recognized. This is the role of trust. In recent years there have been numerous articles and surveys pointing out the importance of trust in risk management and documenting the extreme distrust we now have in many of the individuals, industries, and institutions responsible for risk management. This pervasive distrust has also been shown to be strongly linked both to the perception that risks are unacceptably high and to political activism to reduce those risks.

A third insight pertains to the very nature of the concept "risk." Current approaches to risk assessment and risk management are based on the traditional view of risk as some objective function of probability (uncertainty) and adverse consequences. I shall argue for a conception of risk that is starkly different from this traditional view. This new approach highlights the subjective and value-laden nature of risk and conceptualizes risk as a game in which the rules must be socially negotiated within the context of a specific problem.

. . . .

Sex, Politics, and Emotion in Risk Judgments

Given the complex and subjective nature of risk, it should not surprise us that many interesting and provocative things occur when people judge risks. Recent studies have shown that factors such as gender, race, political worldviews, affiliation, emotional affect, and trust are strongly correlated with risk judgments. Equally important is that these factors influence the judgments of experts as well as judgments of laypersons.

Sex

Sex is strongly related to risk judgments and attitudes. Several dozen studies have documented the finding that men tend to judge risks as smaller and less problematic than do women. A number of hypotheses have been put forward to explain sex differences in risk perception. One approach has been to focus on biological and social factors. For example, women have been characterized as more concerned about human health and safety because they are socialized to nurture and maintain life. They have been characterized as physically more vulnerable to violence, such as rape, and this may sensitize them to other risks. The combination of biology and social experience has been put forward as the source of a "different voice" that is distinct to women.

A lack of knowledge and familiarity with science and technology has also been suggested as a basis for these differences, particularly with regard to nuclear and chemical hazards. Women are discouraged from studying science and there are relatively few women scientists and engineers. However, Barke, Jenkins Smith, and Slovic have found that female physical scientists judge risks from nuclear technologies to be higher than do male physical scientists. Similar results with scientists were obtained by Malmfors, Mertz, Neil, Slovic, and Purchase, who found that female members of the British Toxicological Society were far more likely than male toxicologists to judge societal risks as moderate or high. Certainly the female scientists in these studies cannot be accused of lacking knowledge and technological literacy. Something else must be going on.

Hints about the origin of these sex differences come from a study by Flynn, Slovic, and Mertz, in which 1512 Americans were asked, for each of 25 hazard items, to indicate whether the hazard posed (1) little or no risk, (2) slight risk, (3) moderate risk, or (4) high risk to society. . . . [T]he percentage of high-risk responses was greater for women on every item. . . . [T]he percentage of high-risk responses was greater among people of color than among white respondents for every item studied.

Perhaps the most striking result . . . [is that across] the 25 hazards, white males produced risk-perception ratings that were consistently much lower than the means of the other three groups.

Although perceived risk was inversely related to income and educational level, controlling for these differences statistically did not reduce much of the white-male effect on risk perception. . . . [W]hite males exhibited far lower perceived risk at each of three levels of income and educational status.

When the data . . . were examined more closely, Flynn, Slovic, and Mertz observed that not all white males perceived risks as low. The "white-male effect" appeared to be caused by about 30 percent of the white-male sample who judged risks to be extremely low. The remaining white males were not much different from the other subgroups with regard to perceived risk.

What differentiated these white males who were most responsible for the effect from the rest of the sample, including other white males who judged risks as relatively high? When compared to the remainder of the sample, the group of white males with the lowest risk-perception scores were better educated (42.7 percent college or postgraduate degree versus 26.3 percent in the other group), had higher household incomes (32.1 percent above $50,000 versus 21.0 percent in the other group), and were politically more conservative (48.0 percent conservative versus 33.2 percent more liberal).

Particularly noteworthy is the finding that the low risk-perception subgroup of white males also held very different attitudes than the other respondents. Specifically, they were more likely than the others to:

- Agree that future generations can take care of themselves when facing risks imposed on them from today's technologies (64.2 percent versus 46.9 percent).

- Agree that if a risk is very small it is okay for society to impose that risk on individuals without their consent (31.7 percent versus 20.8 percent).
- Agree that science can settle differences of opinion about the risks of nuclear power (61.8 percent versus 50.4 percent).
- Agree that government and industry can be trusted with making the proper decisions to manage the risks from technology (48.0 percent versus 31.1 percent).
- Agree that we can trust the experts and engineers who build, operate, and regulate nuclear power plants (62.6 percent versus 39.7 percent).
- Agree that we have gone too far in pushing equal rights in this country (42.7 percent versus 30.9 percent).
- Agree with the use of capital punishment (88.2 percent versus 70.5 percent).
- Disagree that technological development is destroying nature (56.9 percent versus 32.8 percent).
- Disagree that they have very little control over risks to their health (73.6 percent versus 63.1 percent).
- Disagree that the world needs a more equal distribution of wealth (42.7 percent versus 31.3 percent).
- Disagree that local residents should have the authority to close a nuclear power plant if they think it is not run properly (50.4 percent versus 25.1 percent).
- Disagree that the public should vote to decide on issues such as nuclear power (28.5 percent versus 16.7 percent).

In sum, the subgroup of white males who perceive risks to be quite low can be characterized by trust in institutions and authorities and by anti-egalitarian attitudes, including a disinclination toward giving decisionmaking power to citizens in areas of risk management.

The results of this study raise new questions. What does it mean for the explanations of gender differences when we see that the sizable differences between white males and white females do not exist for nonwhite males and nonwhite females? Why do a substantial percentage of white males see the world as so much less risky than everyone else sees it?

Obviously, the salience of biology is reduced by these data on risk perception and race. Biological factors should apply to nonwhite men and women as well as to white men and women. The present data thus move us away from biology and toward sociopolitical explanations. Perhaps white males see less risk in the world because they create, manage, control, and benefit from many of the major technologies and activities. Perhaps women and nonwhite men see the world as more dangerous because in many ways they are more vulnerable, because they benefit less from many of its technologies and institutions, and because they have less power and control over what happens in their communities and their lives. Although the survey conducted by Flynn, Slovic, and Mertz was not designed to test these alternative explanations, the race and gender differences in perceptions and attitudes point toward the role of power, status, alienation, trust, perceived government responsiveness, and other sociopolitical factors in determining perception and acceptance of risk.

To the extent that these sociopolitical factors shape public perception of risks, we can see why traditional attempts to make people see the world as white males do, by showing them statistics and risk assessments, are unlikely to succeed. The problem of risk conflict and controversy goes beyond science. It is deeply rooted in the social and political fabric of our society.

Risk Perception and Worldviews

The influence of social, psychological, and political factors also can be seen in studies examining the impact of worldviews on risk judgments.

Worldviews are general social, cultural, and political attitudes that appear to have an influence over people's judgments about complex issues. Dake has conceptualized worldviews as "orienting dispositions," because of their role in guiding people's responses. Some of the worldviews identified to date are listed below, along with representative attitude statements:

- Fatalism (for instance, "I feel I have very little control over risks to my health").
- Hierarchy (for instance, "Decisions about health risks should be left to the experts").
- Individualism (for instance, "In a fair system, people with more ability should earn more").
- Egalitarianism (for instance, "If people were treated more equally, we would have fewer problems").
- Technological enthusiasm (for instance, "A high-technology society is important for improving our health and social well-being").

People differ from one another in these views. Fatalists tend to think that what happens in life is pre-ordained. Hierarchists like a society organized such that commands flow down from authorities and obedience flows up the hierarchy. Egalitarians prefer a world in which power and wealth are more evenly distributed. Individualists like to do their own thing, unhindered by government or any other kind of constraints. . . .

. . . Egalitarians tended to be strongly anti-nuclear; persons endorsing fatalist, hierarchist, and individualistic views tended to be pro-nuclear. . . .

When scales measuring the various worldviews were combined into a regression equation they exhibited considerable ability to predict perceptions of risk from nuclear power and attitudes toward accepting a new nuclear power plant in one's community. . . .

Worldviews, Affect, and Toxicology

Affect and worldviews seem to influence the risk-related judgments of scientists, as well as laypersons. Evidence for this comes from studies of "intuitive toxicology" that Slovic, Malmfors, Neil, and Purchase have been conducting in the U.S., Canada, and the UK during the past eight years. These studies have surveyed both toxicologists and laypersons about a wide range of concepts relating to risks from chemicals. We have examined judgments about the effects of chemical concentration, dose, and exposure on risk. We have also questioned our respondents about the value of animal studies for predicting the effects of chemicals on humans. Before showing how worldviews and affect enter into toxicologists' judgments, a brief description of some basic results will be presented.

Consider two survey items that we have studied repeatedly. One is statement S1: "Would you agree or disagree that the way an animal reacts to a chemical is a reliable predictor of how a human would react to it?" The second statement, S2, is a little more specific: "If a scientific study produces evidence that a chemical causes cancer in animals, then we can be reasonably sure that the chemical will cause cancer in humans."

When members of the American and Canadian public responded to these items, they showed moderate agreement with S1; about half the people agreed and half disagreed that animal tests were reliable predictors of human reactions to chemicals. However, in response to S2, which stated that the animal study found evidence of cancer, there was a jump in agreement to about 70 percent among both male and female respondents. The important point about the pattern of response is that agreement was higher on the second item.

What happens if toxicologists are asked about these two state-ments? . . . [T]oxicologists in the U.S. and toxicologists in the UK responded simi-larly to the public on the first statement but differently on the second. They exhibited the same rather middling level of agreement with the general statement about animal studies as predictors of human health effects.[13] However, when these studies were said to find evidence of carcinogenicity in animals, then the toxicol-ogists were less likely to agree that the results could be extrapolated to humans. Thus, the same findings which lead toxicologists to be less willing to generalize to humans lead the public to see the chemical as more dangerous for humans.[14]

. . . [T]he responses for S1 and S2 among men and women toxicologists in the UK (208 men and 92 women) . . . [present] another interesting finding. The men agree less on the second statement than on the first, but the women agree more, just like the general public. Women toxicologists are more willing than men to say that one can generalize to humans from positive carcinogenicity findings in animals.

We created a change score between statements S1 and S2, with each individual getting a score of increasing agreement, decreasing agreement, or no change. . . .

A positive change score (meaning greater agreement with S2 than with S1) was associated with:

- higher mean perceptions of risk across 25 hazards (the risk-perception index);
- rating pesticides and industrial chemicals as "bad" on a task in which various items were rated on a scale ranging from good to bad;
- being female;
- being younger;
- agreeing that "I have little control over risks to my health";
- holding an academic position rather than a position in industry;
- disagreeing that "technology is important for social well-being"; and
- disagreeing that "economic growth is necessary for good quality of life."

These studies of intuitive toxicology have yielded a number of intriguing find-ings. One is the low percentage of agreement that animal studies can predict hu-man health effects. Another is that toxicologists show even less confidence in studies

---

[13] This is actually a very surprising result, given the heavy reliance on animal studies in toxicology.

[14] This pattern suggests that animal studies may be scaring the public without informing science.

that find cancer in animals resulting from chemical exposure. The public, on the other hand, has high confidence in animal studies that find cancer. Disagreements among toxicologists are systematically linked to gender, affiliation (academic versus other), worldviews, and affect. Thus, affective and sociopolitical factors appear to influence scientists' risk evaluations in much the same way as they influence the public's perceptions.

Trust

The Importance of Trust

The research described above has painted a portrait of risk perception influenced by the interplay of psychological, social, and political factors. Members of the public and experts can disagree about risk because they define risk differently, have different worldviews, different affective experiences and reactions, or different social status. Another reason why the public often rejects scientists' risk assessments is lack of trust. Trust in risk management, like risk perception, has been found to correlate with gender, race, worldviews, and affect.

Social relationships of all types, including risk management, rely heavily on trust. Indeed, much of the contentiousness that has been observed in the risk-management arena has been attributed to a climate of distrust that exists between the public, industry, and risk-management professionals. The limited effectiveness of risk-communication efforts can be attributed to the lack of trust. If you trust the risk manager, communication is relatively easy. If trust is lacking, no form or process of communication will be satisfactory.

How Trust Is Created and Destroyed

One of the most fundamental qualities of trust has been known for ages. Trust is fragile. It is typically created rather slowly, but it can be destroyed in an instant—by a single mishap or mistake. Thus, once trust is lost, it may take a long time to rebuild it to its former state. In some instances, lost trust may never be regained. Abraham Lincoln understood this quality. In a letter to Alexander McClure, he observed: "If you once forfeit the confidence of your fellow citizens, you can never regain their respect and esteem."

The fact that trust is easier to destroy than to create reflects certain fundamental mechanisms of human psychology, called here "the asymmetry principle." When it comes to winning trust, the playing field is not level. It is tilted toward distrust, for each of the following reasons:

1. Negative (trust-destroying) events are more visible or noticeable than positive (trust-building) events. Negative events often take the form of specific, well-defined incidents such as accidents, lies, discoveries of errors, or other mismanagement. Positive events, while sometimes visible, more often are fuzzy or indistinct. For example, how many positive events are represented by the safe operation of a nuclear power plant for one day? Is this one event? Dozens of events? Hundreds? There is no precise answer. When events are invisible or poorly defined, they carry little or no weight in shaping our attitudes and opinions.

2. When events are well-defined and do come to our attention, negative (trust-destroying) events carry much greater weight than positive events. This important psychological tendency is illustrated by a study in which 103 college students rated

the impact on trust of 45 hypothetical news events pertaining to the management of a large nuclear power plant in their community. Some of these events were designed to be trust increasing, such as:

- There have been no reported safety problems at the plant during the past year;
- There is careful selection and training of employees at the plant;
- Plant managers live near the plant; and
- The county medical examiner reports that the health of people living near the plant is better than the average for the region.

Other events were designed to be trust decreasing, such as:

- A potential safety problem was found to have been covered up by plant officials;
- Plant safety inspections are delayed to meet the electricity production quota for the month;
- A nuclear power plant in another state has a serious accident; and
- The county medical examiner reports that the health of people living near the plant is worse than the average for the region.

The respondents were asked to indicate, for each event, whether their trust in the management of the plant would be increased or decreased on learning of that event. After doing this, they rated how strongly their trust would be affected by the event on a scale ranging from 1 (very small impact on trust) to 7 (very powerful impact on trust).

The percentages of category 7 ratings . . . demonstrate that negative events are seen as far more likely to have a powerful effect on trust than are positive events. . . . The negative event, reporting plant neighbors' health as worse than average, was rated 6 or 7 on the impact scale by 50.0 percent of the respondents. A matched event, reporting neighbors' health to be better than average, was rated 6 or 7 by only 18.3 percent of the respondents.

There was only one event perceived to have any substantial impact on increasing trust. This event stated that: "An advisory board of local citizens and environmentalists is established to monitor the plant and is given legal authority to shut the plant down if they believe it to be unsafe."

This strong delegation of authority to the local public was rated 6 or 7 on the impact scale by 38.4 percent of the respondents. Although this was a far stronger showing than for any other positive event, it would have been a rather average performance in the distribution of impacts for negative events.

The importance of an event is at least in part related to its frequency (or rarity). An accident in a nuclear plant is more informative with regard to risk than is a day (or even a large number of days) without an accident. Thus, in systems where we are concerned about low-probability/high consequence events, adverse events will increase our perceptions of risk to a much greater degree than favorable events will decrease them.

3. Adding fuel to the fire of asymmetry is yet another idiosyncrasy of human psychology—sources of bad (trust-destroying) news tend to be seen as more credible than sources of good news. The findings regarding "intuitive toxicology" illustrate this point. In general, confidence in the validity of animal studies is not particularly high. However, when told that a study has found that a chemical is carcinogenic in animals, members of the public express considerable confidence in the validity of this study for predicting health effects in humans.

4. Another important psychological tendency is that distrust, once initiated, tends to reinforce and perpetuate distrust. This occurs in two ways. First, distrust tends to inhibit the kinds of personal contacts and experiences that are necessary to overcome distrust. By avoiding others whose motives or actions we distrust, we never get to see that these people are competent, well-meaning, and trustworthy. Second, initial trust or distrust colors our interpretation of events, thus reinforcing our prior beliefs. Persons who trusted the nuclear power industry saw the events at Three Mile Island as demonstrating the soundness of the "defense in depth" principle, noting that the multiple safety systems shut the plant down and contained most of its radiation. Persons who distrusted nuclear power prior to the accident took an entirely different message from the same events, perceiving that those in charge did not understand what was wrong or how to fix it and that catastrophe was averted only by sheer luck.

"The System Destroys Trust"

Thus far we have been discussing the psychological tendencies that create and reinforce distrust in situations of risk. Appreciation of those psychological principles leads us toward a new perspective on risk perception, trust, and conflict. Conflicts and controversies surrounding risk management are not due to public irrationality or ignorance but, instead, can be seen as expected side effects of these psychological tendencies, interacting with a highly participatory democratic system of government and amplified by certain powerful technological and social changes in society.

Technological change has given the electronic and print media the capability (effectively utilized) of informing us of news from all over the world—often right as it happens. Moreover, just as individuals give greater weight and attention to negative events, so do the news media. Much of what the media reports is bad (trust-destroying) news.

A second important change, a social phenomenon, is the rise of powerful special interest groups, well funded (by a fearful public) and sophisticated in using their own experts and the media to communicate their concerns and their distrust to the public to influence risk policy debates and decisions. The social problem is compounded by the fact that we tend to manage our risks within an adversarial legal system that pits expert against expert, contradicting each other's risk assessments and further destroying the public trust.

The young science of risk assessment is too fragile, too indirect, to prevail in such a hostile atmosphere. Scientific analysis of risks cannot allay our fears of low-probability catastrophes or delayed cancers unless we trust the system. In the absence of trust, science (and risk assessment) can only feed public concerns, by uncovering more bad news. A single study demonstrating an association between exposure to chemicals or radiation and some adverse health effect cannot easily be offset by numerous studies failing to find such an association. Thus, for example, the more studies that are conducted looking for effects of electric and magnetic fields or other difficult-to-evaluate hazards, the more likely it is that these studies will increase public concerns, even if the majority of these studies fail to find any association with ill health. In short, because evidence for lack of risk often carries little weight, risk-assessment studies tend to increase perceived risk. . . .

■ *Optimistic Biases about Personal Risks*

NEIL D. WEINSTEIN

246 Science 1232 (1989). Reprinted with permission of *Science*. © AAAS

The fact that the public overestimates the harm caused by some problems, such as toxic waste, yet underestimates the number of people harmed by other hazards, such as asthma, is now well recognized. Less familiar is the consistent, optimistic bias that exists concerning personal risks. When asked about their own chances, people claim that they are less likely to be affected than their peers.

This optimistic bias in "self-other" risk comparisons is easy to demonstrate. If these comparisons are not biased, claims of below-average risk will be balanced by admissions of above-average risk. In a representative sample, the mean response will be "average." Research shows, however, that the mean is usually shifted in the "below-average" direction. A random sample of New Jersey adults, for instance, yielded the following ratios of "below-average" to "above-average" responses: asthma, 9:1; drug addiction, 8:1; food poisoning, 7:1; influenza, 3:1; lung cancer, 2:1; and pneumonia, 5:1. A significant optimistic bias was found for 25 of 32 hazards in this study.

This bias in comparative risk judgments is robust and widespread. It appears with diverse hazards and samples and with different questions used to elicit the personal risk ratings. Optimistic biases also appear for positive events: people regard themselves as more likely than others to experience financial success, career advancement, and long life. Pessimistic biases are rare.

Some biases occur when people compare themselves with an incorrect norm. The risk of becoming addicted to drugs really is small for most of the population, but it seems that people conclude incorrectly that their risk is far below average by comparing themselves to drug users—a salient high-risk group—rather than to people like themselves who are far more numerous.

Optimism may also arise when ambiguous risk factors are interpreted in a biased manner. People who have not tested their homes for radon gas assert that they are less likely to have problems than their neighbors. Their most frequent explanation is that their houses are well ventilated. Although high air exchange rates do decrease radon levels, it is hard to consider these explanations unbiased when individuals claiming high ventilation rates outnumber those acknowledging low ventilation rates by a ratio of 26 to 1.

There are also times when people are clearly in high-risk groups but downplay the risk or refer to risk-countering practices of little value. When Bauman and Siegel asked gay men to rate the riskiness of their behavior for contracting AIDS, few who engaged in high-risk sex rated their own risk as high. They justified their beliefs by referring to their relatively low number of sex partners or to ineffective precautions, such as inspecting their partners for lesions or showering after sex.

In general, optimism is greatest for hazards with which subjects have little personal experience, for hazards rated low in probability, and for hazards judged to be controllable by personal action. Optimism is also strong if people think that signs of vulnerability appear early (as they think is true of diabetes, alcoholism, and asthma), so that an absence of present signs means they are exempt from future risk.

Predicting when optimism occurs does not tell us why it occurs. One idea is that optimistic biases represent attempts to shield ourselves from the fear of being harmed. Most data do not, however, support this view: life-threatening hazards elicit no greater optimism than minor illnesses.

A second proposal focuses on our desire to be better than other people. Admitting that peers are less susceptible to harm can threaten our feelings of competence and self-worth. Threats to self-esteem should be particularly strong for hazards like suicide and alcoholism that are thought to be controllable; victimization in such situations is often regarded as personal weakness. This reasoning is consistent with the strong optimism-controllability correlation that exists.

A third proposal is that optimistic biases are produced by simple cognitive errors. For example, if prevention campaigns create a stereotype of a high-risk individual, people may use this as a standard and conclude incorrectly that their own risk is below average. Excessive extrapolation from the present to the future can also be viewed as erroneous reasoning. Even the association with controllability could be cognitive in origin, because we are more likely to be aware of our own efforts to control risks than others' efforts.

Still, cognitive errors do not provide an adequate explanation for optimistic biases because they do not explain why pessimistic biases almost never appear. The notion that optimistic predictions are actively constructed, rather than arising from simple mental errors, is supported by instances where reasoning is distorted to yield self-serving predictions. For example, people who think they are particularly intelligent rate intelligence as very important to career success, whereas those who think they have a good sense of humor rate this attribute as more important.

Optimistic biases in personal risk perceptions are important because they may seriously hinder efforts to promote risk-reducing behaviors. If people believe they are not susceptible to AIDS, or less susceptible than others, it may be more difficult to convince them to adopt prudent precautions. There are many positive correlations in the literature between beliefs of personal vulnerability and protective behavior, but there are also situations where greater perceived susceptibility does not lead to greater action. There has been little research on these differences.

Although we usually think of biases as maladaptive, several authors have emphasized the benefits of illusions. Optimism about personal risks is associated with less depression. Optimism about successful performance leads people to try harder on difficult tasks, so that they really do succeed more often. A general tendency to be optimistic may even have positive consequences for physical health.

The benefits of illusions, though, surely depend on the nature of the illusion and the nature of the hazard. Overly optimistic expectations about the value of low-cholesterol diets and exercise may help a heart attack victim sustain these lifestyle changes and be happier and more productive. But a failure to admit that our smoking, driving while intoxicated, or unprotected sex puts us at risk may keep us from making changes, and this could prove disastrous.

COMMENTS AND QUESTIONS

1. We have presented the material on perceptions of risk because we think they might have some bearing on the resolution of the legal questions addressed in this chapter. Do they? Several questions arise: (a) To what extent should *legal* rules be justified by evidence from the social sciences? (b) How solid must the

social science evidence be for it to provide the basis for legal rules? (c) How solid is the evidence regarding risk perception?

2. What implications might the materials on risk perception have for the cases you have read? Note the difference between lay and experts' judgments on the magnitude of risks. The compensatory-wage-premium argument considered in chapter 1 argues that workers demand additional compensation for their exposure to risk. What can an employer do when an expert tells the employer that the workers' perceptions of risks are exaggerated? Consider the possibility that the employer could install risk-reducing equipment at a lower cost than the workers are demanding as compensation for exposure to risk. (What else must be true if this course of action is to make economic sense for the employer?) Consider the possibility that the demographic composition of the workforce might affect the size of the wage premiums workers demand and, in particular, that some workforces might underestimate the risk to which they are exposed. What is the proper policy response to that possibility? (You might want to speculate about the reasons why judgments about risk differ by gender and race.)

3. The existence of differences between lay and expert evaluations of risk also has institutional implications. Decisions made by democratically elected legislatures might be more responsive to lay perceptions than decisions made by administrative agencies staffed by experts in the fields that each agency regulates. (But, of course, democratically elected legislatures create the administrative agencies in the first place.) In *Ayers* and *Buckley*, consider whether the opinions might have been different had the authors expressly addressed the differences between lay and expert evaluations of risk.

4. Lay evaluators appear to be more concerned than experts with whether a risk is, in Slovic's terms, a "dread" risk and an "unknown" one. Can you describe the lay judgments as rational if laypeople are taking into account widely shared values other than those values that experts take into account? Note that being more concerned about exposure to risks (a) that are involuntary or not controllable might be responsive to concerns about infringements on autonomy, (b) that are irreversible and unfamiliar might be responsive to concerns about having an opportunity to learn via trial and error, and (c) that are catastrophic might be responsive to concerns about effects on communities rather than on individuals. Can you describe the lay judgments as other than rational if, for example, they result from mistrust of experts, difficulties in doing calculations, stubbornness in remaining attached to judgments even after additional information relevant to those beliefs is presented, and the like?

5. How might lawyers take the material on risk perception into account in their ordinary practice? Should it affect the decisions they make in accepting or challenging potential jurors in civil cases where one issue may be damages for exposure to risk?

6. Recall Easterbrook's discussion of the *ex ante* perspective in chapter 2. Easterbrook argues that policy making should be based on the expected value of alternative actions, determined by calculating the probability of harm and the

magnitude of harm. Consider two courses of action, one with a 0.01% chance that an entire population of 100,000 people will die and the other guaranteed to cause 10 deaths. The expected value of both actions is the same. Does the material you have read suggest that (and why) decision makers could reasonably treat the actions as not equivalent to each other?

7. We deal in more detail with laypeople's use of heuristics as a basis for policy making in chapters 5 and 10 in this book.

4 ▪ Courts and Legislatures as Policy-Making Institutions: An Introduction

In the following article, Lon Fuller attempts to distinguish between two types of disputes. Our excerpt discusses the "polycentric" dispute. Fuller contrasts such a dispute with what he calls "bipolar" disputes—the traditional two-party lawsuit that might arise out of an automobile accident or a dispute between a landlord and a tenant over whether the landlord should return the tenant's security deposit. As you read the article, pay attention to the ways in which he describes polycentric disputes, and consider whether some (or all?) bipolar disputes might have been described in similar terms. Fuller argues that polycentric disputes are best resolved by legislatures and that courts are best suited for dealing with bipolar disputes only. Do you agree? Which, if any, of the cases in this chapter involve bipolar disputes? Which involve polycentric ones?

▪ *The Forms and Limits of Adjudication*
LON L. FULLER
92 Harv. L. Rev. 353 (1978). Reprinted with permission of Lynn Fuller

. . .

Adjudication and Rationality

. . . Adjudication is . . . a device which gives formal and institutional expression to the influence of reasoned argument in human affairs. As such it assumes a burden of rationality not borne by any other form of social ordering. A decision which is the product of reasoned argument must be prepared itself to meet the rest of reason. We demand of an adjudicative decision a kind of rationality we do not expect of the results of contract or of voting. This higher responsibility toward rationality is at once the strength *and the weakness* of adjudication as a form of social ordering.

In entering contracts, men are of course, in some measure guided by rational considerations. The subsistence farmer who has a surfeit of potatoes and only a handful of onions acts reasonably when he trades potatoes for onions. But there is no test of rationality that can be applied to the result of the trade considered in abstraction from the interests of the parties. The trade of potatoes for onions, which is a rational act by one trader, might be considered irrational if indulged in by his opposite number, who has a storehouse full of onions and only a bushel of potatoes. If we asked one party to the contract, "Can you defend that contract?" he might answer, "Why, yes. It was good for me and it was good for him." If we then said, "But that is not what we meant. We meant, can you defend it on general grounds?" he might well reply that he did not know what we were talking about. Yet this is precisely the kind of question we normally direct toward the decision of a judge at arbitration. The results that emerge from adjudication are subject, then, to a standard of rationality that is different from that imposed on the results of an exchange.

. . .

Let me spell out rather painstakingly the steps of an argument. . . . (1) Adjudication is a process of decision that grants to the affected party a form of participation that consists in the opportunity to present proofs and reasoned arguments. (2) The litigant must therefore, if his participation is to be meaningful, assert some principle or principles by which his arguments are sound and his proofs relevant. (3) A naked demand is distinguished from a claim of right by the fact that the latter is a demand supported by a principle; likewise, a mere expression of displeasure or resentment is distinguished from an accusation by the fact that the latter rests upon some principle. Hence, (4) issues tried before an adjudicator tend to become claims of right or accusations of fault.

. . . [Consider] the case of an employee who desires an increase in pay. If he asks his boss for a raise, he may, of course, claim "a right" to the raise. He may argue the fairness of the principle of equal treatment and call attention to the fact that Joe, who is no better than he, recently got a raise. But, he does not have to rest his plea on any ground of this sort. He may merely beg for generosity, urging the needs of his family. Or he may propose an exchange, offering to take on extra duties if he gets the raise. If, however, he takes his case to an arbitrator he cannot, explicitly at least, support his case by an appeal to charity or by proposing a bargain. He will have to support his demand by a principle of some kind, and a demand supported by principle is the same thing as a claim of right. So, when he asks his boss for a raise, he may or may not make a claim of right; when he presents his demand to an arbitrator he must make a claim of right. . . .

If the analysis presented here is correct, three aspects of adjudication that seem to present distinct qualities are in fact all expressions of a single quality: (1) the peculiar mode by which the affected party participates in the decision; (2) the peculiarly urgent demand of rationality that the adjudicative process be prepared to meet; and (3) the fact that adjudication finds its normal and "natural" province in judging claims of right and accusations of fault. So, when we say that a party entering a contract, or voting in an election, has no "right" to any particular outcome, we are describing the same fundamental fact that we allude to when we say that adjudication has to meet a test of rationality or of "principle" that is applied to contracts and elections.

. . .

The Forms of Adjudication

. . . [The reader] should not . . . [be misled] into thinking that this paper condemns all departures of adjudication from a state of pristine purity. Certain mixed forms are valuable and almost indispensable, though their use is often attended by certain dangers.

In determining whether a deviant or mixed form impairs the integrity of adjudication the test throughout will be that already stressed repeatedly: Does it affect adversely the meaning of the affected party's participation in the decision by proofs and reasoned arguments?

. . .

May the Arbiter Act on His Own Motion in Initiating the Case?

. . . [I]n most of the practical manifestations of adjudication the arbiter's function has to be "promoted" by the litigant and is not initiated itself. But is this coy quality of waiting to be asked an essential part of adjudication?

It would seem that it is not. Suppose, for example, the collision of two ships under circumstances that suggest that one or both masters were at fault. Suppose a board is given authority to initiate hearings in such a case and to make a determination of fault. Such a board might conduct its hearings after the pattern of court proceedings. Both masters might be accorded counsel and a full opportunity for cross-examination. There would be no impairment of the affected parties' full participation by proofs and reasoned argument; the integrity of adjudication seems to be preserved.

Yet I think that most of us would consider such a case exceptional and would not be deterred by it from persisting in the belief that the adjudicative process should normally not be initiated by the tribunal itself. There are, I believe, sound reasons for adhering to that belief.

Certainly it is clear that the integrity of adjudication is impaired if the arbiter not only initiated the proceedings but also, in advance of the public hearing, forms theories about what happened and conducts his own factual inquiries. In such a case the arbiter cannot bring to the public hearing an uncommitted mind; the effectiveness of participation through proofs and reasoned arguments is accordingly reduced. Now it is probably true that under most circumstances the mere initiation of proceedings carries with it a certain commitment and often a theory of what occurred. The case of the collision at sea is exceptional because there the facts themselves speak eloquently for the need of some kind of inquiry, so that the initiation of the proceedings implies nothing more than a recognition of this need. In most situations the initiation of proceedings could not have the same neutral quality, as, for example, where the occasion consists simply in the fact that a corporation had gone two years without declaring a dividend.

. . . [To take a more central example, it] seems clear that a regime of contract (more broadly, a regime of reciprocity) implies that the determination whether to assert a claim must be left to the interested party.

. . .

. . . To enforce a contract for a party who is willing to leave it unenforced is just as absurd as making the contract for him in the first place. (I realize, of course, that there are contracts required by law, but this is obviously a derivative which would lose all meaning if every human relation were imposed by the state and were called a "contract.")

The belief that it is not normal for the arbiter himself to initiate the adjudicative process has, then, a twofold basis. *First*, it is generally impossible to keep even the bare initiation of proceedings untainted by preconceptions about what happened and what its consequences should be. In this sense, initiation of the proceedings by the arbiter impairs the integrity of the adjudication by reducing the effectiveness of the litigant's participation through proofs and arguments. Second, the great bulk

of claims submitted to adjudication are founded directly or indirectly on relationships of reciprocity. In this case, unless the affected party is deceived or ignorant of
his rights, the very foundations of the claim asserted dictate that the processes of
adjudication must be invoked by the claimant.

Must the Decision Be Accompanied by a Statement of the Reasons for It?

We tend to think of the judge or arbitrator as one who decides and who gives
reasons for his decision. Does the integrity of adjudication require that reasons be
given for the decision rendered? I think the answer is, not necessarily. In some
fields of labor arbitration (chiefly, I believe where arbitration is a facility made
available without charge by the state) it is the practice to render "blind" awards. The
reasons for this practice probably include a belief that reasoned awards are often
misinterpreted and "stir up trouble," as well as the circumstance that the arbitrator is
so busy he has no time to write opinions. Under the procedures of the American
Arbitration Association awards in commercial cases are rendered usually without
opinion. (Written opinions are, however, usual in *labor* cases.). . . .

By and large it seems clear that the fairness and effectiveness of adjudication
are promoted by reasoned opinions. Without such opinions the parties have to take
it on faith that their participation in the decision has been real, that the arbiter has
in fact understood and taken into account their proofs and arguments. A less
obvious point is that, where a decision enters into some continuing relationship, if
no reasons are given the parties will almost inevitably guess at reasons and act
accordingly. Here the effectiveness of adjudication is impaired, not only because
the results achieved may not be those intended by the arbiter, but also because his
freedom of decision in future cases may be curtailed by the growth of practices
based on a misinterpretation of decisions previously rendered.

May the Arbiter Rest His Decision on Grounds Not Argued by the Parties?

Obviously the bond of participation by the litigant is most secure when the arbiter
renders his decision wholly on the proofs and arguments actually presented to him
by the parties. In practice, however, it is not always possible to realize this ideal.
Even where all of the considerations on which the decision rests were touched on
by the parties' arguments, the emphasis may be very different. An issue dealt with
only in passing by one of the parties, or perhaps by both, may become the head-
stone of the arbiter's decision. This may mean not only that, had they foreseen this
outcome, the parties would have presented different arguments, but that they
might also have introduced evidence on very different factual issues.

If the ideal of a perfect congruence between the arbiter's view of the issues and
that of the parties is unattainable, this is no excuse for a failure to work toward an
achievement of the closest approximation of it. We need to remind ourselves that if
this congruence is utterly absent—if the grounds for the decision fall completely
outside the framework of the argument, making all that was discussed or proved at
the hearing irrelevant—then the adjudicative process has become a sham, for the
parties' participation in the decision has lost all meaning. We need to analyze what
factors influence the desired congruence and what measures may be taken to
promote it.

One circumstance of capital importance is the extent to which a particular process of adjudication takes place in a context of established rules. In branches of the law where the rules have become fairly settled and certain, it may be possible for lawyers to reach agreement easily in defining the crucial issues presented by a particular case. In such an area the risk is slight that the decision will fall outside the frame of reference set by the proofs and arguments. On the other hand, in areas of uncertainty, this risk is greatly increased. There are, to be sure, dangers in a premature crystallization of standards. On the other hand, one of the less obvious dangers of a too long delayed formulation of doctrine lies in the inevitable impairment of the integrity of adjudication that is entailed, for the reality of the parties' participation is reduced when it is impossible to foretell what issues will become relevant in the ultimate disposition of the case.

. . .

Qualifications and Disqualifications of the Arbiter

. . .

I shall merely suggest that the problem of securing a properly qualified and impartial arbiter be tried by the same touchstone that has been used throughout—what will preserve the efficacy and meaning of the affected parties' participation through proofs and arguments? Obviously, a strong emotional attachment by the arbiter to one of the interests involved in the dispute is destructive of that participation. In practice, however, a kind of "partiality" is much more dangerous. I refer to the situation where the arbiter's experience of life has not embraced the area of the dispute, or, worse still, where he has always viewed that area from some single vantage point. Here a blind spot of which he is quite unconscious may prevent him from getting the point of testimony or argument. By and large, I think the decisions of our courts in commercial cases do not represent adjudication at its highest level. The reason is a lack of judicial "feel" for the problems involved.

A sailor was once brought before a three-judge German court for violation of a provision of the criminal code which made it a serious offense to threaten another with bodily harm. Uncontradicted testimony proved that the prisoner had been heard to say, "I'll stick a knife in your guts and turn it around three times." Two judges, who had spent their lives in genteel surroundings far from the waterfront, were with great difficulty persuaded by the third to acquit.

. . .

The Limits of Adjudication

. . .

Attention is now directed to the question, What kinds of tasks are inherently unsuited to adjudication? The test here will be that used throughout. If a given task is assigned to adjudicative treatment, will it be possible to preserve the meaning of the affected party's proofs and arguments?

[For purposes of addressing the question of limits, this] section introduces a concept—that of the "polycentric" task—which has been derived from Michael Polanyi's book The Logic of Liberty [1951]. In approaching that concept it will be well to begin with a few examples.

Some months ago a wealthy lady by the name of Timken died in New York leaving a valuable, but somewhat miscellaneous, collection of paintings to the

Metropolitan Museum and the National Gallery "in equal shares," her will indicating no particular apportionment. When the will was probated the judge remarked something to the effect that the parties seemed to be confronted with a real problem. The attorney for one of the museums spoke up and said, "We are good friends. We will work it out somehow or other." What makes this problem of effecting an equal division of the paintings a polycentric task? It lies in the fact that the disposition of any single painting has implications for the proper disposition of every other painting. If it gets the Renoir, the Gallery may be less eager for the Cezanne but all the more eager for the Bellows, etc. If the proper apportionment were set for argument, there would be no clear issue to which either side could direct its proofs and contentions. Any judge assigned to hear such an argument would be tempted to play the role of mediator or to adopt the classical solution: Let the older brother (here the Metropolitan) divide the estate into what he regards as equal shares, let the younger brother (the National Gallery) take his pick.

As a second illustration suppose in a socialist regime it were decided to have all wages and prices set by courts which would proceed after the usual forms of adjudication. It is, I assume, obvious that here is a task that could not successfully be undertaken by the adjudicative method. The point that comes first to mind is that courts move too slowly to keep up with a rapidly changing economic scene. The more fundamental point is that the forms of adjudication cannot encompass and take into account the complex repercussions that may result from any change in prices or wages. A rise in the price of aluminum may affect in varying degrees the demand for, and therefore the proper price of, thirty kinds of steel, twenty kinds of plastics, an infinitude of woods, other metals, etc. Each of these separate effects may have its own complex repercussions in the economy. In such a case it is simply impossible to afford each affected party a meaningful participation through proofs and arguments. It is a matter of capital importance to note that it is not merely a question of the huge number of possibly affected parties, significant as that aspect of the thing may be. A more fundamental point is that, each of the various forms that award might take (say, a three-cent increase per pound, a four-cent increase, a five-cent increase, etc.) would have a different set of repercussions and might require in each instance a redefinition of the "parties affected."

We may visualize this kind of situation by thinking of a spider web. A pull on one strand will distribute tensions after a complicated pattern throughout the web as a whole. Doubling the original pull will, in all likelihood not simply double each of the resulting tensions but will rather create a different complicated pattern of tensions. This would certainly occur, for example, if the doubled pull caused one or more of the weaker strands to snap. This is a "polycentric" situation because it is "many centered"—each crossing of strands is a distinct center for distributing tensions.

. . .

It should be carefully noted that a multiplicity of affected persons is not an invariable characteristic of polycentric problems. This is sufficiently illustrated in the case of Mrs. Timken's will. That case also illustrated the fact that rapid changes with time are not an invariable characteristic of such problems. On the other hand, in practice polycentric problems of possible concern to adjudication will normally involve many affected parties and a somewhat fluid state of affairs. Indeed, the last characteristic follows from the simple fact that the more interacting centers there are, the more the likelihood that one of them will be affected by a change in circumstances, and, if the situation is polycentric, this change will communicate itself after a complex pattern to other centers. . . .

Now, if it is important to see clearly what a polycentric problem is, it is equally important to realize that the distinction involved is often a matter of degree. There are polycentric elements in almost all problems submitted to adjudication. A decision may act as a precedent, often an awkward one, in some situation not foreseen by the arbiter. Again, suppose a court in a suit between one litigant and a railway holds that it is an act of negligence for the railway not to construct an underpass at a particular crossing. There may be nothing to distinguish this crossing from other crossings on the line. As a matter of statistical probability it may be clear that constructing underpasses along the whole line would cost more lives (through accidents in blasting, for example) than would be lost if the only safety measure were the familiar "Stop, Look and Listen" sign. If so, then what seems to be a decision simply declaring the rights and duties of two parties is in fact an inept solution for a polycentric problem, some elements of which cannot be brought before the court in a simple suit by one injured party against a defendant railway. In lesser measure, concealed polycentric elements are probably present in almost all problems resolved by adjudication. It is not, then, a question of distinguishing black from white. It is a question of knowing when the polycentric elements have become so significant and predominant that the proper limits of adjudication have been reached.

. . .

The final question to be addressed is this: When an attempt is made to deal by adjudicative form with a problem that is essentially polycentric, what happens? As I see it, three things can happen, sometimes all at once. *First,* the adjudicative solution may fail. Unexpected repercussions make the decision unworkable; it is ignored, withdrawn, or modified, sometimes repeatedly. *Second,* the purported arbiter ignores judicial proprieties—he "tries out" various solutions in posthearing conferences, consults parties not represented at the hearings, guesses at facts not proved and not properly matters for anything like judicial notice. *Third,* instead of accommodating his procedures to the nature of the problem he confronts, he may reformulate the problem so as to make it amenable to solution through adjudicative procedures.

Only the last of these needs illustration. Suppose it is agreed that an employer's control over promotions shall be subject to review through arbitration. Now obviously an arbitrator cannot decide whether when Jones was made a Machinist Class A there was someone else more deserving in the plant, or whether in view of Jones' age, it would have been better to put him in another job with comparable pay. This is the kind of allocative problem for which adjudication is utterly unsuited. There are, however, two ways of obtaining a workable control over promotions through arbitration. One of these is through the posting of jobs; when a job is vacant, interested parties may apply for promotion into it. At the hearing, only those who have made application are entitled to be considered, and of course only the posted job is in issue. Here the problem is simplified in advance to the point where it can be arbitrated, though not without difficulty, particularly in the form of endless arguments as to whether there was in fact a vacancy that ought to have been posted, and whether a claimant filed his application on time and in the proper form, etc. The other way of accommodating the problem to arbitration is for the arbitrator to determine not who should be promoted but who *has* been promoted.

That is, the contract contains certain "job descriptions" with the appropriate rate for each; the claimant asserts that he is in fact doing the work of a Machinist A, though he is still assigned the pay and title of a Machinist B. The controversy has two parties—the company and the claimant as represented by the union—and a single factual issue, Is the claimant in fact doing the work of a Machinist A?

In practice the procedure of applying for appointment to posted jobs will normally be prescribed in the contract itself so that the terms of the agreement keep the arbitrator's function with respect to promotions within manageable limits. The other method of making feasible a control of promotions through arbitration will normally result from the arbitrator's own perception of the limitations of his role. The contract may simply contain a schedule of job rates and job classifications and a general clause stating that "discharges, promotions, and layoffs shall be subject to the grievance procedure." If the arbitrator were to construct such a contract to give him a small supervision over promotions, he would embark himself upon managerial tasks wholly unsuited by any arbitrative procedure. An instinct toward preserving the integrity of his role will move him, therefore, to construe the contract in the manner already indicated, so that he avoids any responsibility with respect to the assignment of duties and merely decides whether the duties actually assigned make appropriate the classification assigned by the company to the complaining employee.

. . .

In closing this discussion of polycentricity, it will be well to caution against two possible misunderstandings. The suggestion that polycentric problems are often solved by a kind of "managerial intuition" should not be taken to imply that it is an invariable characteristic of polycentric problems that they resist rational solution. There are rational principles for building bridges of structural steel. But there is no rational principle which states, for example, that the angle between girder A and girder B must always be 45 degrees. This depends on the bridge as a whole. One cannot construct a bridge by conducting successive separate arguments concerning the proper angle for every pair of intersecting girders. One must deal with the whole structure.

Finally, the fact that an adjudicative decision affects and enters into a polycentric relationship does not of itself mean that the adjudicative tribunal is moving out of its proper sphere. On the contrary, there is no better illustration of a polycentric relationship than an economic market, and yet the laying down of rules that will make a market function properly is one for which adjudication is generally well suited. The working out of our common law of contracts case by case has proceeded through adjudication, yet the basic principle underlying the rules thus developed is that they should promote the free exchange of goods in a polycentric market. The court gets into difficulty, not when it lays down rules about contracting, but when it attempts to write contracts. . . .

COMMENTS AND QUESTIONS

1. According to Fuller, what are the distinctions between adjudicative and legislative tasks? To what extent should the precedential effect of a decision in an individual case put it in the "polycentric/unsuitable for adjudication" category? In Fuller's terms, is *Ayers* a bipolar or a polycentric dispute? Do you

think that the New Jersey court's resolution of the questions presented shows that courts are suitable or unsuitable institutions for dealing with problems like those posed in *Ayers*?

2. At some points, Fuller appears to argue that the categories are distinguished by the fact that courts must act in a principled way, whereas legislatures need not do so. According to Fuller, why must courts be principled? When a legislature acts in a manner that is unprincipled, according to Fuller's definition, should we be satisfied with its performance? What are "principled" arguments? Consider the implications of Fuller's suggestion that an appeal predicated on "needs" is not principled. Why is the decision in *Buckley* principled in Fuller's sense? Would a legislature creating a cause of action for emotional distress for exposure to risk be acting in a principled manner? Why or why not?

3. At other points, Fuller appears to argue that the categories are distinguished by the procedures the different institutions use. Try to list aspects of legislative hearings that make them resemble judicial ones. What procedural revisions would make legislative hearings even more like judicial ones? Would it be a good idea to adopt such revisions? To eliminate the things that already make legislative hearings resemble judicial ones?

   Try to list aspects of judicial hearings that make them resemble legislative ones. Should they be eliminated?

4. In light of Fuller's analysis, consider whether the implications of Slovic's analysis support the positions taken by the majority or the dissent in *Ayers* on the question of whether there should be a judicially devised remedy for enhanced risk.

C An Introduction to Problems of Professional Ethics

What are the professional obligations of lawyers whose clients expose others to risk?

The Model Rules of the American Bar Association, which are the foundation of most state professional ethics requirements, provide:

RULE 1.6 CONFIDENTIALITY OF INFORMATION

(a) A lawyer shall not reveal information relating to the representation of a client unless the client gives informed consent, the disclosure is impliedly authorized in order to carry out the representation or the disclosure is permitted by paragraph (b).

(b) A lawyer may reveal information relating to the representation of a client to the extent the lawyer reasonably believes necessary:

  (1) to prevent reasonably certain death or substantial bodily harm;

  (2) to prevent the client from committing a crime or fraud that is reasonably certain to result in substantial injury to the financial interests or property of another and in furtherance of which the client has used or is using the lawyer's services;

(3) to prevent, mitigate or rectify substantial injury to the financial interests or property of another that is reasonably certain to result or has resulted from the client's commission of a crime or fraud in furtherance of which the client has used the lawyer's services;

(4) to secure legal advice about the lawyer's compliance with these Rules;

(5) to establish a claim or defense on behalf of the lawyer in a controversy between the lawyer and the client, to establish a defense to a criminal charge or civil claim against the lawyer based upon conduct in which the client was involved, or to respond to allegations in any proceeding concerning the lawyer's representation of the client; or

(6) to comply with other law or a court order.

Consider the obligations of the lawyer in the following hypothetical (but not unrealistic) story. What would you do in response to the inquiry?

- *A Fine Kettle of Fish (and Arsenic?)*

STEPHEN GILLERS

American Lawyer, March 1993, Supplement: In-House Ethics, p. 9. Reprinted and modified with permission from the March 1993 edition of the *American Lawyer*. © NLP IP Company. All rights reserved. Further duplication without permission is prohibited

Dear Counsel:

Thank you for taking the time to advise me in this urgent matter. As I told you on the telephone, you come highly recommended as an expert in legal ethics, including the responsibilities of lawyers for corporate entities. You asked me to put the facts in writing. Here they are.

My particular problem arises in the environmental law area, which you said is not one of your specialties. But the applicable [law] is simple and described below.

I am general counsel of Trover Electronics, which as you know has become the national leader in the design of special application software for the aeronautic and space industries. Trover is a closely held corporation.

Last year was very good for Trover. As a result, we began to consider a move to larger headquarters in a nearby county. The county was offering us a generous tax abatement package. We have been at our current main office nearly ten years, since we began operations with 32 employees. Now we have 400 employees in our crowded main office and four satellite offices.

The [clincher] on our decision to move was new business from American and foreign manufacturers of aircraft and aircraft components and from two major international carriers. We signed the agreement with the county, purchased land, and began building a state-of-the-art facility. A consortium of insurance companies is providing financing.

We also set about selling our main office. When Trover was founded, it rented its building from a soft drink bottler in financial trouble. Then we bought the building at foreclosure.

The broker we chose to sell the building was going to compile a portfolio of internal and external pictures of the building, pictures of the surrounding neighborhood, maps showing commercial areas and transportation hubs, residential and commercial tax and zoning information, and the like. That way prospective purchasers to whom she planned to send the portfolio could have all relevant data. This was information they'd want soon enough.

One section of the portfolio was supposed to give so-called technical information, like reports by architects and engineers on the building's age, condition, the integrity of its systems, and what needed repair.

The broker had contacts in each—from photographers to engineers—and we delegated the job to her to put it all together, which is customary.

One of the technical contributors to the portfolio was an environmental lab. Its job was to test the water, the quality of the air filtration and circulation systems, the paint (e.g., for lead), the insulation (e.g., for asbestos), and the water table and soil.

Before preparing final reports, the technical contributors submitted preliminary reports for review by our people. Those [came] in about two months ago. Two weeks later the company took the property off the market.

I'm not saying I detected a causal relationship at the time or do now. There could be a lot of reasons for taking it off the market—business reasons. We're still planning to move, of course; but someone decided that we weren't going to sell, at least not yet.

I probably wouldn't have given it much thought except that Al West, vice-president for operations, remarked at a budget meeting on how unfortunate it was that the environment report showed possible traces of benzene and arsenic in the groundwater and undersoil. The lab advised further tests to measure the precise quantities, if any, and whether it may have seeped into the local reservoir. I think Al thought, and still thinks, that I had already been told this information, which I hadn't. Al said the reservoir was filtered, but filtration systems vary in their effectiveness. Benzene and arsenic can be fatal even in small doses.

Trover doesn't use benzene or arsenic, so if they're there, it must be because the prior owner, the bottler, did. It went bankrupt years ago.

As I told you, before calling you I got advice from a lawyer who's active in the bar association and something of an armchair ethics person. I told him the problem and he said I should go to the company president and find out what was what.

Trover's president, Greta Holsom, came in a year ago from one of the mainframe makers. This was after the death of Teddy Trover, our founder and a lifelong friend, who had persuaded me to leave practice and join him in starting the company. I don't get along with Greta, the truth is. I figure she's let me stay because I hit mandatory retirement at the end of the year, which is also when my pension and stock options vest.

Following the advice I received, I asked Greta why we weren't going to sell. She told me that the board of directors had decided to take the property off the market for business reasons. When I pressed, she said the feeling was that the property would get more money when the economy turned around in a couple of years and that it was worth holding until then. Meanwhile, we'll rent it or use it as a storage facility.

I told Greta I was aware of the report from the environmental lab. (She pressed me to tell her how, but I avoided a direct answer.) She said that the report had nothing to do with the decision and that she and the board were sure it was wrong anyway. She said it had all been checked out eight years ago when Trover bought the property. She volunteered that even rumors about benzene and arsenic in the undersoil and groundwater could wreck Trover. It would jeopardize its new customers, the financing for the new office, and the deal with the county, not least of all because of the inevitable but baseless multimillion-dollar class action claims that plaintiffs' lawyers would solicit from users of the reservoir and former Trover employees.

We have a statute in this state, passed a little over a year ago, that says: "Anyone possessing information that [certain listed chemicals including benzene and arsenic] have been released to the environment shall report the information and its basis to the State Department of Environmental Affairs within 30 days."

The statute provides civil and criminal penalties and a private treble damage action. So far, it has not been used, and I could find no pertinent legislative history.

I don't know how many people here know of the lab's report or the statute. The lab is in a neighboring state and may not be aware of the statute. I mentioned the statute to Greta and she shrugged it off. She said Trover was beginning a major renovation of the entire property to increase its value when the economy turns around. This will include soil removal, water table purification, and other precautions. So even if there is excess benzene or arsenic or seepage into the reservoir, which she denied, it would end.

That's when I decided I really needed an expert. I called around and your name kept coming up.

I had my conversation with Al West two weeks ago, which means I have about two weeks before I must go to the state agency, if that's something I have to do. Or should I do something else? Or nothing? Perhaps I should just quit, but I'm not sure what that accomplishes. Also, it would look mighty suspicious for Trover's general counsel to quit a few months before retirement. And I'd lose my pension and stock options and my medical benefits. I need these to have any kind of modest retirement. I won't bother you with the kind of extraordinary expenses my family has.

Thank you for agreeing to help me. Please send me your opinion and your bill.
Sincerely,

Juliet Lowi

COMMENTS AND QUESTIONS

1. Which provisions of Rule 1.6 appear applicable to this problem? Who are those provisions designed to protect? In particular, which, if any, primarily protect clients, and which primarily protect the public generally? (Note that Rule 1.6 (b)(5) clearly is designed to protect lawyers themselves.) Are there any circumstances under which disclosure is required by the rule? What would the attorney's responsibilities be if a *federal* statute imposed a duty to disclose, in circumstances where the state's professional ethics rules prohibited disclosure?

2. Rule 2.1, Advisor, provides: "In representing a client, a lawyer shall exercise independent professional judgment and render candid advice. In rendering advice, a lawyer may refer not only to law but to other considerations such as moral, economic, social and political factors, that may be relevant to the client's situation." What guidance does this provide for the problem?

3. Suppose an attorney working for General Motors in the 1970s ran across the Ivey memo and realized that the Malibu was designed in a way that posed a

larger risk to the public than would an alternative design. Under the *present* Model Rule, could the attorney disclose the memo? Suppose an attorney working for Jackson Township in the *Ayers* case had documents showing that violations of applicable environmental regulations and orders were occurring at the landfill, and showing as well that contaminated groundwater was on its way to residents' drinking water wells. Could the attorney disclose the information? What would you do in that situation?

Institutional Strengths and Limits

5

In chapter 2, we considered the advantages and disadvantages of private markets in addressing the problem of risk. In chapter 4, through the work of Lon Fuller, we began to consider the strengths and limits of courts as decision-making institutions. We continue and expand on those discussions here. Most significantly, we add administrative agencies to the mix of institutions that can be called on to deal with risk. We also examine sociological and historical treatments of the transformation of social problems into legal problems. Running throughout our discussion in this chapter is a problem that plagues any attempt to deal with a social problem through the legal process: What if the people who are hurt don't invoke the legal process? What if we had a legal system and no one came?

A. Two General Accounts of Institutional Differences

The next two articles consider how successfully particular legal institutions are likely to respond to particular kinds of social problems. In the first article, Gillette and Krier consider the comparative advantages and disadvantages of courts and administrative agencies in addressing "public risks." Public risks may be characterized as those that tend to have a long latency period, are spread over a large population, and have a low probability of materializing in harm, yet have potentially catastrophic consequences if they do. Ultimately, Gillette and Krier defend the nonexpert perspectives on risk that Slovic and others have studied and conclude that courts are an indispensable part of the institutional structure for addressing public risks. In the second article, Komesar compares the institutional capabilities of the tort system, the criminal-regulatory system, and the market, in addressing several different kinds of social problems. Komesar draws distinctions between social problems based on the distributional consequences of the problems themselves and legal responses to them.

- ### Risk, Courts, and Agencies
  CLAYTON GILLETTE AND JAMES KRIER
  138 U. Pa. L. Rev. 1027 (1990). © 1990 University of Pennsylvania
  Law Review

Risk inheres in our condition. Whether brought on by nature in such forms as earthquakes and disease, or by humans with mundane machines like the automobile and high technologies like nuclear energy, hazard is ubiquitous and inevitable. Hence selective aversion to certain risks, most particularly to the manmade risks of advanced technologies, can prove to be counterproductive. Selective aversion might foreclose progressive new technologies that are, despite their dangers, on balance beneficial. A world with vaccines and nuclear power plants is not perfectly safe, for example, but might be safer than a world without. In other words, though risk by definition is costly, avoiding risk is costly as well. It entails the costs of controls and other risk-reduction measures, and at times the costs of forgone benefits (a risky new technology might guard against even more threatening natural hazards, such as disease; it might displace the greater risks of a technology already in place, or produce units of output at a lower cost than the existing technology, or both). So the objective of risk management must be not the elimination of risk, but rather the minimization of all risk-related costs.

All of this sounds platitudinous, yet it happens to be extraordinarily controversial—especially in the case of "public risks," a recently coined name for the distinctive hazards of high-tech times. Public risks have been defined as manmade "threats to human health or safety that are centrally or mass-produced, broadly distributed, and largely outside the individual risk bearer's direct understanding and control."[3] "Private risks," in contrast, are either of natural origin or, if manmade, produced in relatively discrete units, with local impacts more or less subject to personal control. In these terms, then, disease is a natural private risk; the hazards of commonplace artifacts like automobiles and wood stoves are manmade private risks. Public risks, on the other hand, originate in new or complex technologies like chemical additives, recombinant DNA, mass-produced vaccines, and nuclear power plants.

The public-private distinction is hardly perfect (consider the pollution pouring into the atmosphere from thousands of automobiles, or from thousands of wood stoves), but it is useful enough, especially for purposes of illuminating a currently important controversy that centers on the idea of cost minimization in the risk context. Public risks are precisely the risks that have recently captured the attention of the legal community and the world at large, in no small part because they give rise to such novel problems for lawyers and such grave apprehensions among lay people. Public risks have moved the legal system to relax doctrines—regarding, for example, standards of causation and culpability, burdens of proof, sharing of liability—that were designed to deal with the private risks that once dominated the landscape. And public risks have moved lay people to intensify their demands for risk control measures. These developments suggest that public risks are subject to especially harsh treatment, yet such treatment might often be contrary to minimizing the sum of all risk-related costs. If some public risks, whatever their dangers, are in fact safer or otherwise more beneficial than the risks they would displace, then cost minimization requires open-minded efforts to encourage many of the very technological threats that current legal and popular opinion would instead deter. As a consequence, the question of what to do about public risk has become a subject of considerable (and sometimes heated) debate.

---

[3] Peter Huber, *Safety and the Second Best: The Hazards of Public Risk Management in the Courts,* 85 Colum. L. Rev. 277, 277 (1985).

... [We give] particular attention to two important points of contention. The first of these has to do with attitudes. The general public, and to some degree the legal system as well, have a particular aversion to public risk. Is this justified? The second point of contention, intimately related to the first, has to do with institutions, and especially with judicial versus administrative rule. At present, the courts are playing an important part in shaping the legal response to public risk. Is this sensible?

According to one powerfully stated outlook—an outlook that runs directly against the grain of prevailing sentiments—the answer to each of the foregoing questions is a firm "no." Our actions increase, rather than minimize, risk costs. We worry too much about public risks and not enough about private ones. We control public risks with a haphazard mix of market, judicial, administrative, and legislative measures that too often proceed in the wrong direction, without coordination, and with too little reliance on agencies and too much on courts. The courts especially are said to pander to uninformed and irrational risk attitudes; their decisions show a myopic bias against new technology and in favor of its victims. New or complex technologies are subjected to a degree of scrutiny that riskier but established (often private) risk sources never underwent and could not survive. As a result, we have too much private risk and too little public risk, not more safety but less.

Some of the critics advancing this line call for a reduction of the judicial role in risk assessment and management, and for more reliance on administrative agencies. Agencies, they argue, have more expertise, are more objective and rational, can be more attentive to the net effects of technological advance. Courts, they conclude, should defer to them.

This is the set of views that we call into question here. . . .

II. Risk Production and Risk Reduction

... [C]ertain distinctive characteristics of public risks tend to dampen the incentives otherwise created by reputation and profit concerns. Many public risks are latent in their materialization. Adverse effects do not appear until long after exposure. In addition, public risks are often diffuse in their impact, spread over many victims, so the costs to any one victim might be small even though the aggregate cost to the total victim population is very large. Similarly, public risks are by definition probabilistic, and the likelihood that exposure will lead to adverse effects is often remote. The effects themselves might be of dramatic dimension, should they occur, but by virtue of low probabilities their expected costs are nevertheless negligible.

These characteristics skew the incentives of presumably self-interested producers and consumers of public risks. Even assuming some knowledge of risks, for example, consumers (including consumers of jobs—employees) and producers alike will generally discount the information because of long latency, low probability, or both. Where latency periods exceed ten to fifteen years, discounting effectively means ignoring the risk altogether.[33] Where probabilities are low, actors

---

[33] The standard formula for discounting a dollar amount to its present value is $x/(1+r)^n$ (where r = a stated interest rate and n = the number of periods during which the interest rate is earned). Assume a .01 probability that an event will occur in 10 years and that, if it does, there

commonly (if inappropriately) ignore potential consequences, notwithstanding their likely magnitude should they materialize. And diffuse effects are, on an individual basis, usually small to begin with, and thus of little interest. For any or all of these reasons, patterns of consumption are unlikely to be duly influenced by the presence of risk, so risk producers will receive misleadingly muted market signals.

The foregoing considerations are exacerbated where (as is likely) self-interested managers have incentives to make decisions that diverge from the actual interests of their firm. Even where managers of risk-producing firms are aware that possible calamity lies ahead, they still might not be sufficiently wary. The decision to discover and address possible long-term risks requires that costs be incurred in the short term, and managers with an interest in profits now will be disinclined to dedicate firm resources to programs the benefits of which will accrue to the firm, if at all, only in the distant future. Even managers who extend the time horizon by plotting the value of their remaining careers can be expected to discount, perhaps even disregard, risks with long latency periods. The lag between cause and effect shelters managers from the consequences of their decisions: evidence disappears, or the managers do.

The systematic tendency to resolve uncertainty in the direction of insufficient risk avoidance is especially acute in those instances where benefits consist of the nonappearance of a problem. Imagine, for example, a manager with sufficient resources to invest in either of two ventures, but not both. The first venture bears a .1 probability of increasing next year's profits by $10 million. The second is expected, with the same probability, to avoid distant losses from injuries by an amount presently valued at something more than $10 million. A desire for tangible and relatively quick indicia of success will incline the manager to pursue the former strategy, even if the latter has a higher expected value, simply because the manager can't demonstrate that she triggered a benefit by arranging that something bad won't eventually happen. This incentive to pursue tangible gains, rather than to avoid ethereal losses, may become greater as the relative certainty of the former increases, notwithstanding that the expected value of the two options is equal. Suppose that the first venture in our example is regarded as almost certain to increase profits by $1 million, while the second venture would avoid injury losses totaling $100 million were they to materialize, but the probability of materialization is only .01. The manager will now be even more tempted to pursue the first strategy, because certain and demonstrable gains are likely to enhance her standing in the firm more than would the tenuous avoidance of losses.

The distorting incentives arising from diffuseness, latency, and low probability, troublesome as they are, would be less so were effects reversible once they materialized. Yet one of the most sobering characteristics of modern-day public risks is the permanence of their effects. Irreversibility forecloses the benefits of learning by trial-and-error, and hence correction by that means; tremendously

---

will be a loss of $100,000,000. The expected value of the loss is $1,000,000 in 10 years. The present (discounted) value of that loss at an interest rate of 5 percent is $615,000; at 10 percent it is $385,000. If the event will materialize, if at all, only in 20 years, then the present value figures are $375,000 and $150,000 for 5 and 10 percent respectively.

important information, arising from events, is rendered virtually useless. It is most painfully useless in the case, again prevalent in public risks, of zero-infinity problems—those with a small probability (approaching zero) of ever eventuating, but with catastrophic consequences (approaching infinity) if they do.

The point of this discussion is that the risk market can fail even when risk transactions are possible. The market contains an ill-defined domain that calls for external control of some sort. The domain enlarges extraordinarily when we step outside the world of transactions, and hence out of ordinary markets. . . .

III. Risk, Courts, and Lawyers

. . . Process bias arises from the interplay of legal doctrine and adjudicative decision makers. It concerns the ways in which judges and juries interpret and apply the law that defines the rights and liabilities of the parties before them. Access bias, on the other hand, arises from the interplay of legal doctrine, the structure of litigation, and the nature of public risk. It concerns the ways in which victims decide whether (given prevailing doctrine, among other things) litigation is worthwhile, and the ability of victims to initiate claims. Access is anterior to process; only when obstacles to access are overcome, so that claims are actually filed and prosecuted, can process bias come into play. . . .

A. Access Bias

. . . Public risks, as we saw, are commonly latent in their manifestations, diffuse in their impacts, and of low probability. Moreover, as their name suggests, they share the characteristics of collective goods (or, here, collective bads). They tend to be nonrival: their adverse effects may have simultaneous consequences for a multitude of victims. Given the nature of modern technologies, these nonrival effects will commonly be dispersed over large geographic areas, so that victims—potential plaintiffs—are themselves broadly distributed. And as is always the case with collective goods and bads, public risks tend to be nonexclusive. This means that the benefits of abatement (should it occur) necessarily extend to all victims, and cannot be withheld on a piecemeal basis.

To see the significance of these characteristics, consider the general structure of litigation and how it relates, first, to private risks. Lawsuits are costly, and risky of themselves; prosecution entails the investment of time and money, and success is hardly assured. Only those among the injured who calculate expected judgments (judgments discounted by the probability of success) in excess of litigation costs will likely seek access to the adjudication process. In the case of private risks, where substantial injuries are typically discrete, immediate, and readily cognizable, the obstacles to recovery (identifying the responsible defendants, establishing their liability, showing causation, proving the dimensions of loss) may be relatively low. Thus, expected recoveries for victims of private risk are often sufficient to create incentives to sue, though even here collective goods effects can damp the rate of litigation. Potential plaintiffs who have been injured by a product or service identical or similar to the one at issue in an initial lawsuit can benefit from the information and the precedential value generated by that suit, even though they made no contribution to its prosecution. Thus potential plaintiffs find themselves in a strategic relationship— each wishing and waiting for others to file the initial suit—notwithstanding that all the plaintiffs want any lawsuit to succeed. This temptation to freeride on the efforts of others can induce even victims with current positive expected recoveries to hold back in hopes of enlarging their net recoveries later.

There are, however, considerations that combat the incentive to freeride in the case of private risk litigation. First, immediateness of injury reduces the difficulty of identifying the injuring party and showing cause and effect, and thus reduces the costs that contribute to the freeriding temptation. Second, injury is often sufficiently fact-specific to limit the expected gains of waiting for somebody else to proceed. Where the defendant's conduct placed a limited number of people at risk (as in slip-and-fall cases) or the plaintiff's conduct is a datum relevant to liability (as where a power lawnmower is alleged to expose users to unreasonable dangers of laceration), the chance of finding a significant number of others who suffered injuries under sufficiently similar circumstances to merit freeriding is remote. These and other features of private risk litigation suggest that injured parties (and their lawyers) will not generally figure their expected judgments to be increased by strategic delay.

Incentives to sue and disincentives to freeride usually diminish as risk moves from the private toward the public end of the spectrum. The characteristic diffuseness of public risks, for example, can mean small costs per victim notwithstanding large losses in the aggregate. From the individual litigant's perspective, a relatively small injury usually will not warrant the substantial costs associated with proving a case and recovering a judgment. The situation is aggravated by process concerns, legal doctrines that complicate the plaintiff's job and thus increase litigation costs. We have in mind, for example, the requirement of identifying a particular defendant who more probably than not caused the plaintiff's injury. Unlike the case of typical private risk litigation, where the party who caused the injury is usually readily identifiable, public risks often emanate from mysterious or multifarious sources. In either case, it may be that no one is sure who is responsible for what.

Victims might try, of course, to cope with relatively large litigation costs by forming a coalition, with each victim contributing a modest sum to what could be a substantial legal war chest. But the broad geographic dispersion of public risks means that victims too will be dispersed, and under these conditions coalition is cumbersome. Coalition can be difficult even when risks are concentrated, thanks to the strategic implications of nonexclusivity. Since public risk is borne in common, so too is its mitigation: abatement at the source benefits not only actual plaintiffs but potential ones as well. If P sues D successfully, I will win too. Why, then, should I agree to share a part of the burden of anybody else's lawsuit? Why not freeride instead, especially given the absence of the countervailing considerations—discussed above—that combat freeriding in the private risk context? Public risks tend to be involuntarily or passively borne, making each individual plaintiff's conduct largely irrelevant; the fact-specific inquiries that help defeat strategic behavior in the setting of private risk litigation play little part in public risk cases.

As the incentives to freeride tend to increase with public risk, so too do the costs of seeking individual (as opposed to collective) redress. The latency typical of public risks, for example, attenuates the connection between cause and effect. Statutes of limitations might foreclose recovery altogether; in any event, the difficulty of proving the necessary cause-effect relationship renders victim lawsuits more difficult (costly) and their conclusion less certain. Efforts to overcome these obstacles by suing now for exposure to risks the effects of which might materialize later run head on into a host of troubles arising from the probabilistic nature of public risk. Unable to show a matured injury, individuals at risk face expected recoveries discounted not only by the likelihood of losing but also by the uncertainty that the alleged risk will result, eventually, in actual injury.

In short, public risk litigation is structurally biased against victim access. Victims who might wish to seek redress in the courts confront significant obstacles that diminish the incentive to sue. Prosecution may well not be worthwhile from any individual victim's self-interested perspective, even if it would be socially desirable.

Might the potentially powerful triumvirate of entrepreneurial lawyer, class action, and contingent fee be a cure for at least some of these ills? The argument is that the lawyer—capable of building a portfolio of class suits seeking large recoveries, entitled to a percentage (say a quarter or more) of any recoveries obtained, and sufficiently skilled to win or favorably settle enough of the cases in the portfolio to make the enterprise profitable—will manage to surmount at least some of the structural obstacles that stand in the way of effective victim access. The lawyer can largely avoid freeriding and other strategic maneuvers. He typically needs relatively little money to initiate an action and rarely seeks active assistance from dispersed class members. Diffuse individual costs can be amalgamated into one large social cost and brought to bear on the responsible parties, the plaintiffs' lawyer(s) earning a nice fee in the process.

This picture looks sufficiently promising that one could imagine public risk lawsuits proceeding at a pace that actually exceeds the social optimum. Recent scholarship, however, suggests that the opposite is true, partly because class actions also induce strategy—on the part now of self-interested lawyers, not litigants.

Class attorneys are likely to select for their litigation portfolios only those cases that promise expected personal benefits in excess of personal costs (including opportunity costs). They will reject cases that fail this threshold test even if the cases would yield net social benefits. And while expected damages for a class (and thus the attorneys' expected personal benefits) might commonly be large in public risk cases, the costs of litigation can generally be expected to be large as well. Lawyers must first fight to get their class actions certified. If successful, they must then confront procedural and substantive difficulties dealing with proof of causation, standard of liability, identification of defendants, and (if there are multiple defendants) allocation of responsibility among them. Considerations such as these underlie concerns—voiced, for example, by Professor Rosenberg[67]—about the sheer, and costly, complexity of public risk litigation. Proceeding from the observation that the tort system delegates total discretion over public risk claim initiation to the plaintiff attorneys' bar, Rosenberg argues convincingly that lawyers tend to avoid new public risk lawsuits in favor of more rewarding alternatives ("sporadic accident" cases). They do so because public risk suits, rather than presenting overwhelmingly attractive entrepreneurial opportunities, actually offer relatively unprofitable investments. The suits can, to be sure, generate much larger

---

[67] *See e.g.* David Rosenberg, *The Causal Connection in Mass Exposure Cases: A "Public Law" Vision of the Tort System,* 97 Harv. L. Rev. 851, 855–9 (1984).

judgments than sporadic accident cases, but their complexity calls for a disproportionate amount of a lawyer's time and other resources. Exceptions like the ongoing asbestos litigation show that not every public risk case is regarded as unmarketable by plaintiffs' attorneys, but Rosenberg nevertheless considers it "clear that such attorneys . . . will systematically reject mass exposure claims." . . .

Even when class actions are taken into the entrepreneurial attorney's litigation portfolio, there remain opportunities for behavior that can end up understating the social costs of public risk. Since class members are unlikely to have the day-to-day contact and information that they need to monitor their attorneys' conduct, attorneys, in turn, face few disincentives to skew results in favor of their self-interest. They will be tempted to file claims merely in order to establish a stake, then neglect vigorous prosecution either because of rising opportunity costs or in the hope that damages will increase in the interim. They will also be tempted to settle on self-interested terms for an amount too small to vindicate victim interests but structured so as to include a handsome attorney's fee. Hence the filing and "successful" prosecution of class actions nevertheless leave reasons to suppose that the rate of recovery falls short of the optimum.

To summarize, public risk litigation is probably marked by too few claims and too little vigorous prosecution, with the likely consequence that too much public risk escapes the deterrent effects of liability. Those who think otherwise must believe that public risk claimants find an easy path into court and effective representation once there. If that conviction is founded on a denial of structural impediments, we can only respond that the point is neither clearly stated nor sufficiently examined, and that it flies in the face of current understanding. The same response is due those who might think that the trinity of entrepreneurial lawyer-class action-contingent fee can work litigation miracles. . . .

C. Bias on Balance

. . . The producers of public risks will be inclined to overindulge, absent signals that align their self-interest with the larger social interest. At times, market transactions can generate the necessary signals, in the form of price. Government intervention can generate price signals too, by way of the compliance costs of rules and regulations, by way of fines and other sanctions for violating those rules and regulations, and—most particularly here—by way of liability for court judgments. Risk producers make decisions not simply in reaction to but also in anticipation of any of these price signals, and in the latter event discount the signal (by the likelihood of its imposition) to an expected value. Our analysis suggests that access bias, viewed in isolation, may make the expected value of the signal generated by court judgments too low. When claims go unfiled, the social costs they represent are not brought to bear on producer decision making. Because the signal emanating from the courts is thus weakened, there is likely to be too much public risk. Those who conclude otherwise argue from process bias, again viewed in isolation; they contend that harsh doctrine makes the expected value of liability too high. Victim claims are treated too tenderly. Too many costs are internalized. Public risk producers are saddled with burdens that other risk producers avoid, and exit the market even though their activities are the less hazardous. There is likely too little public risk.

What this summary account makes apparent is that access bias and process bias have to be considered together, on balance, as elements of a larger system, rather than separately, each on its own. After all, only when obstacles to access are overcome, so that claims are actually filed and prosecuted, can any doctrinal bias come into full play. Litigation comprises two imperfect parts. Because each part is imperfect, isolated examination tends to reveal only flaws, and can inspire corrections that could actually make matters worse. Hence observers who focus mostly on problems of access should cautiously avoid advocating reforms that could accomplish too much. Similarly, so should those who fix their attention on process.

Taking bias on balance, the judicial system might simply be working to increase the expected value of producer liability for public risks to appropriate levels, with the overstatements induced by process offsetting (and offset by) the understatements caused by access. Liability judgments that look too harsh of themselves take on a different character when placed in this larger perspective. . . .

D. Judicial Competence

Even if the courts are balanced in their treatment of public risk, it does not automatically follow from this that the judiciary is a good risk management institution. The claim that the judicial system is "institutionally predisposed to favor regressive public risk choices" might fail for lack of proof, but the claim of judicial incompetence would still remain.

Imagine, for example, that the risk premium exacted by the courts proves to be worthwhile. Could it nevertheless be avoided or at least made significantly smaller? Are there alternative institutions that can achieve something like the optimal amount of public risk in a more adroit (less expensive) way? For critics of the courts, the answer is yes. Administrative agencies, however imperfect themselves, would be a very considerable improvement. For this reason, courts operating in the civil liability setting are implored to defer to the experts of administrative agencies that have undertaken "searching and complete . . . regulation." If an agency has determined (in the course of a licensing proceeding, for instance, or through regulatory hearings) that a particular public risk is progressive, liability on the producer's part should thereafter be foreclosed so long as it meets the terms of its license or complies with applicable regulations. . . .

The difficulty is that the argument on behalf of agency expertise fails to provide a satisfying systemic account. Suppose, for example, that courts *do* end up biased against public risk. Might agencies tend to be biased in the opposite direction? Barriers to access could, after all, result in agency bias if they limit the ability of potential public risk victims—but not public risk producers—to influence agency thinking. Similarly, agencies might process risk decisions in a biased way. Or suppose that courts are incapable of dealing with risk in a highly competent fashion. Might administrative agencies and the experts they employ be something less than competent themselves? A respectable comparative approach would consider questions like these. Whether in the setting of civil liability or in that of judicial review, a sensible assessment of the courts has to confront the skeptic's query: Compared to what? It is hardly enough to catalog judicial weaknesses and administrative strengths: the other side of each institution has to be considered too. Having done some of this with the courts, which the critics attack, we turn now to the agencies, which they defend as the less biased, more competent institution. Is their case a convincing one?

IV. Risk, Agencies, and Experts

. . . .

B. Access and the Problem of Capture

... As a way of beginning, recall the argument that in the litigation setting public risk victims (and their attorneys) are susceptible to incentives that work at cross purposes with actual victim interests and hold them back from the courts. As a result, and absent any corrective, one could expect too little by way of deterrence coming out of the courts because too little by way of claims goes in. The administrative setting looks at first to be different, because agencies are not formally dependent on outside initiative; they need not wait for victim claims in order to embark on "searching and complete" regulatory efforts. Hence it seems they can avoid the problem of access that burdens the judicial system.

Administrative power to seize the initiative is especially appealing to anyone who believes that when public agencies act, they act in the public interest. Just such a faith seems to be reflected in some of the views voiced by Mr. Huber, particularly the claim that public agencies can supply "a 'public' point of view on the problem" of risk assessment and management.[101] Less clear is the source of this public point of view, or the basis for believing that agency initiative would necessarily serve it. Assessment and management are, as we saw, heavily dependent on a wide range of information and values. How any particular risk decision comes out is likely to turn in part on what happened to go into an agency's deliberations. Hence an abiding faith that outcomes are in the public interest requires an underlying conviction that information and values filter into and out of agencies in some even-handed way. If, however, risk producers have a comparative advantage over risk consumers in getting the administrative ear, then agency decision making might be marred by access bias just as judicial decision making is.

The problem we have in mind is a variation on some central themes in the literature about agency "capture," a body of theory and evidence familiar enough to require only a brief account here. Capture theory proceeds from the notion that the motivations and behavior of private citizens and public officials in political markets are similar to those of producers and consumers in ordinary economic markets. Citizens (in this case, risk producers and risk consumers) and officials (here, those involved in the process of risk regulation) are assumed to be substantially self-interested and to want their private interests served by political and regulatory processes in ways that may have little in common with what would serve the larger public interest.

Self-interest is easy enough to picture in the case of risk producers and consumers, but its meaning regarding political officials, administrators in particular, is worth a few words. With respect to public actors, self-interest can mean something as obvious (and acceptable) as wanting to avoid embarrassing technical errors in the course of making decisions, as trivial as wanting to save time and effort during the day-to-day routine (in order to nurse the agency budget or enhance agency

---

[101] Peter Huber, *Safety and the Second Best: The Hazards of Public Risk Management in the Courts*, 85 Colum. L. Rev. 277, 331 (1985). . . .

leisure), or as substantial (and possibly tainted) as wanting to advance agency or personal power and resources. Agency and personal advancement, in turn, are likely to be a function of the reactions to agency decisions by the legislative and executive branches, by the electorate, by the presumed targets and supposed beneficiaries of agency action, and by potential employers of agency personnel, whether within the government, or without.

Just as public officials have the means to satisfy the interests of private citizens, citizens have the potential to serve the interests of officials. They can provide information and points of view. They can contribute money to political campaigns and administrators' pockets. They can assemble blocks [sic] of voters. They can offer employment opportunities. These examples mix sinister elements with benign ones, but the capture argument hardly depends on the former. There is nothing sinister in the fact that various citizens might cluster into interest groups for the purpose of contributing resources—data, perspectives, arguments—to administrative deliberations. Nor is it troubling that each such group might hold some sort of proxy for one or another popular attitude or value (whether the proxy is measured in the number of votes, or the number of dollars, that the group might be able to deliver to the political backers of administrators who make acceptable decisions). Information, points of view, voter attitudes, and dollars as a measure of intensity of voter attitudes are, after all, obviously relevant to making decisions in the public interest (unless the public interest means something utterly unrelated to what the public is interested in).

That interest groups express their views by these means, then, does not necessarily imply tawdry politics: to the contrary, there might be no other practical way to discern much of the meaning of "the public interest" in a democratic system. The model is interest group pluralism and its idea that agency output (self-interest notwithstanding) will approximate the social good as long as the output results from countervailing pressures brought to bear by any number of interested groups, each of which has roughly equal access to the decision making process. Capture theory shows how the pluralist model can go wrong. Almost by definition, interest group pluralism can endorse decisions as "in the public interest" only if all the various interest groups are indeed able to voice their wants effectively. If, instead, some groups enjoy a comparative advantage in catering to administrative needs and desires (that is, if the pluralist process is too singular, not sufficiently plural), there arises the danger that agency attention will be captivated by too narrow a range of interests and be diverted from an appropriately public perspective.

Whether, and how much, bias is likely to result from asymmetric access to the administrative process depends considerably on the nature of any particular item on the regulatory agenda. In the case of public risk generally, though, the problem appears to be a substantial one, as should be obvious from our discussion of access bias in the courts. We saw in that discussion how the typical characteristics of public risk—impacts that are latent, diffuse, widely dispersed, of low probability, and nonexclusive—limit the ability of potential and actual public risk victims to gain access to the courts. Our point here is that they can also frustrate the efforts of victims to mobilize for the purpose of influencing agency decisions about risk. Whatever the objective of the mobilization effort (it might be to prepare and provide a good research product for agency consideration, or to present a convincing brief for the victim point of view, or to gather a crowd to attend public hearings, or to organize an effective lobby), considerable amounts of time, effort, and money will be required. These resources will also, however, be hard to find. The diffuseness of public risks, coupled with the fact that materialization of any physical injury will usually be remote in time (latent) and in probability, reduces incentives to contribute much to the common cause. So does the nonexclusive nature of favorable agency action. Efforts to overcome some of these obstacles by appealing directly to potential group members for support confront the same obstacles. The appeals themselves require a force of personnel sufficiently large and energetic to address victims who will usually be dispersed over broad geographic areas. Hence the problem of mobilization remains.

Look now at the other side of the story, and consider the ability of public risk producers to muster effective interest groups. Their organizational burdens will generally be lighter for any number of well-known reasons: there are fewer potential group members; each member will usually know the identity of most others; each member is likely to have a relatively large, concentrated, and immediate stake in agency decisions, as compared to public risk victims; each has greater assets (wealth, information, personnel, facilities, and so forth) to tap than any one or several (or even many) victims; commonly all or many of the members will already be organized, say through a trade association. Taken together, these considerations facilitate effective communication, provide opportunities to monitor individual contributions and chastise noncontributors, increase the likelihood that the private benefits of group action will exceed private costs, and forestall freeriding behavior. In short, the costs of organizing collective efforts will generally be lower for the producers than for the victims of public risk, and this in turn means producers will generally enjoy a considerable comparative advantage in mobilizing interest groups and exercising influence, whether by benign or sinister means.

The foregoing analysis simply elaborates a familiar generalization. Large groups seeking agency decisions that would yield diffuse, remote, dispersed, and nonexclusive benefits are handicapped relative to small groups seeking decisions that would avoid (or fighting decisions that would impose) concentrated costs. The generalization applies to the case of risk regulation as much (if not more) as to any other, which is not to say that it is free of interesting exceptions. One can no doubt point to instances of risk regulation, and even to instances of risk-regulation agencies, that stand in contrast to our account. But we are concerned with tendencies, and especially with tendencies that would exist if there were broader deference to agency rule than at present. In this context, the problem of asymmetric access suggests that agency decisions would tend in the direction of producer interests, and thus toward too much public risk.

Before closing this section, let us briefly mention two points directly related to our earlier discussion of access bias in civil-claim litigation. First, note that just as class actions are not an easy answer to access barriers in the judicial setting, public interest organizations are not an easy answer in the agency setting (including within that setting judicial review of agency activity). Public interest organizations themselves require support—they are not a costless enterprise—and will, for just the reasons canvassed above, have difficulty getting it. Almost by definition, the organizations are likely to be in too short supply. Second, it is possible that agencies might present victims with more substantial access problems than do courts. Individual victims of public risk have at least some incentive to proceed on their own with claims in court for damages. In the agency setting, however, the notion of effective individual victim action seems virtually nonsensical: almost never would one or a few victims find it worthwhile (or possible) to deliver items of substantial interest to self-interested administrators. That public risk producers can initiate administrative but not (usually) judicial liability proceedings provokes further concern. This lets them anticipate problems and mobilize to influence an agency's agenda well in advance of focused public concern and pointed regulatory decision making, much in the manner of building bulwarks against an expected tide.

C. Process and the Meaning of Risk

The last section's story was a cautionary tale, warning that a deferential attitude toward agency decisions could lead to too much public risk. The story in this section ends with the same lesson, but it begins in a very different way. We worried above that asymmetric access might distort an egoistical agency's image of the public interest. Here we abandon the assumptions on which those concerns were based, happily grant every wish of public interest theorists, and hence suppose that agencies are invulnerable to undue outside influence and selflessly dedicated to a rational vision of the social good. Still, we think, the likely result of deference to such agencies would be too much public risk, at least so far as the public is concerned.

The key to this conclusion can be found by asking an important question that all the discussion thus far has simply begged: What does "risk" mean? To anticipate our argument, suppose that the concept signifies different things to different people—more particularly, one thing to agency experts and another to the lay public. Suppose, in addition, that while each of these meanings is sensible, the expert definition implies levels of public risk that are, by the lay definition, almost invariably too high. It then follows that a selfless agency, determined and free (because of expansive deference) to assess and manage public risk in accord with its own conception, will end up regulating less than called for from the public's point of view. The resulting contest is, at bottom, one of competing rationalities, and its resolution is a matter of ethics and politics, not technical expertise. Nothing in the training, credentials, or legitimacy of risk assessors or bureaucrats qualifies them to settle the issue. Hence deference to agencies would grant them ground they have no right to claim. Deference would beg a central question in the control of public risk. . . .

D. Bias on Balance Again

Our discussion of the courts introduced the idea that two kinds of bias (access and process) might affect judicial risk regulation, examined the likely operation of each, and concluded that critics of the courts have no reasonable basis for their confident charge that the current liability system diminishes safety by deterring public risk too much. Even if the courts process public risk claims in a very stringent fashion, to stop the analysis there neglects the fact that public risk victims have restricted access to this favorable judicial treatment. If access bias promotes public risk, then process bias is a kind of corrective that might help re-establish balance.

The agency picture is different. In the judicial setting, access and process bias almost surely cut in opposite directions. In the case of agencies, however, they probably tend in the same direction, and toward undue public risk (judged from the public's point of view). Without externally imposed discipline, either capture or body counting could, of itself, produce this result. Where the two work in concert the result seems all the more likely. One need only consider how neatly the expert definition of risk already fits the interests of public risk producers, then simply couple with that the producers' independent comparative advantage in bringing their views to agency attention. Conversely, public interest victims are burdened in their efforts to reach agencies, and should they manage to arrive it is usually to a hostile reception.

The confluence of bias in the agency setting complicates the institutional picture considerably. For example, suppose—contrary to our own views—that the courts do in fact end up regulating public risk too much. Evidence to that effect, even very convincing evidence would hardly be conclusive because agencies might well be regulating, on balance, too little. Hence, even if the critics' charges against the courts are justifiable, there remains the difficult problem of figuring out whether, and to what degree, judicial stringency, rather than representing overkill, serves instead to correct for administrative laxity. At present, after all, both institutions regulate risk, and there is some indication that risk producers are more responsive to the threat of judicially imposed liability than they are to agency regulation. What are the concrete grounds for altering the balance that presently exists in this larger judicial-administrative system?

Consider finally the possibility that agencies regulate public risk "too much"— in a sense very much like that developed in our account of the courts. Some students of the subject believe that although agencies fail to control many risks that should receive attention, they "overcontrol" the ones that do receive attention. If so, the administrative system too may have a kind of self-correcting mechanism, so long as the risk producers subjected to overcontrol are drawn into the regulatory web essentially at random. Is this, however, an argument for increased deference to agencies? The idea underlying the argument would have to be that because agencies end up sending out about the right signal and courts simultaneously send out an overstated one, the message emanating from the larger (judicial-administrative) system deters, on balance, too much public risk. But this is convincing only if courts do in fact overstate matters (because, for instance, process bias swamps access bias). Beyond this, one would have to establish that agencies would act in the same fashion even if the courts were to treat agency decisions more deferentially, and this is implausible. It is likely that agencies act as they do now only because their actions are subject to judicial scrutiny. After all, if expanded judicial deference to agencies would simply result in their behaving substantially as they do at present, then why would anyone bother to argue for more deference to agencies in the first place?

E. Administrative Competence

We saw earlier how critics of the courts have failed to carry their burden on the claim that the judiciary is biased against public risk. We can see now how they also fall short in making their case for administrative agencies: they fail to address too many of the considerations that might lead agencies to be biased in exactly the opposite direction. Still, though, we have to deal with comparative competence.

Recall the charge that courts lack the technical competence and institutional capacity thought to be essential to successful risk assessment and management, the assertion that expert administrative agencies are much better equipped in these respects, and the conclusion that, for these reasons, "courts should defer to the experts." Our discussion of judicial competence more or less conceded that the judiciary is not particularly adept at technical exercises, but wondered whether agencies might be less than entirely competent themselves. Let us now consider some of the grounds for our skepticism.

We saw earlier that risk assessment and management require a great deal of judgment particularly in the case of new or especially complex technology—the sort of technology that is most at issue in the public risk debate. Judgment and intuition are essential to the process simply because the risk sources are new and complex. Their novelty reduces the value of history and experience: their complexity demands something more than simplistic analysis, yet confounds efforts to be perfectly thoroughgoing. Practical lines must be drawn. So, addressing the particular case of nuclear reactor mishaps, Slovic, Fischhoff, and Lichtenstein observe that "[t]he technology is so new and the probabilities in question are so small that accurate risk estimates cannot be based on empirical observation. Instead, such assessments must be derived from complex mathematical models and subjective judgments." "Someone, relying on educated intuition, must determine the structure of the problem, the consequences to be considered, and the importance of the various branches of the fault tree."

How "educated" can intuition be in cases of the new and the complex—whether the problem is to determine the probabilities of events that have never happened, gauge their consequences if they do happen, or figure out how to build in safeguards against them? Here, intuition amounts to speculation, as even the champions of expertise seem ready enough to admit....

But even assuming, purely for the sake of argument, that not a single charlatan can find a place on the rolls of administrative personnel, there remains a second reason to be skeptical about agency expertise. Stated most briefly and generally, experts, however adroit, are merely human. They bear the burden of human limitations.... [A] growing literature...traces the implications of some of these limitations in the case of administrative and organizational behavior. We know from this literature that classical models of fully "rational" decision making do not describe how people actually behave. Even regulators who consciously and conscientiously aspire to comprehensive analysis of all possible alternatives will fall well short of what they strive to achieve. Their rationality is "bounded," such that optimal decisions are forgone in favor of satisfactory ones. The "best" is sacrificed for what is "good enough"—even though the point at which the process stops might lead to choices inferior to other, neglected options....

COMMENTS AND QUESTIONS

1. Gillette and Krier defend the view that courts can do a decent job as regulators. This contrasts with the classical legal process view, reflected in the work of Lon Fuller and others, which favors administrative agencies over courts. Gillette and Krier share common ground with the legal process theorists, however, insofar as they attend to the relative competencies of different government institutions.

2. What is the distinction between access bias and process bias? Try to identify examples of each type of bias in the context of risks to safety and health. What is the relationship between the characteristics of public risks and the questions of access and process bias? It may help you here to consider the relation between the distinction Gillette and Krier draw between public and private risks, and the three distributions discussed by Komesar in the next article (particularly with respect to the aspect involving the impact on victim and injurer).

3. What remedies might there be for access bias? For process bias?

4. Gillette and Krier write that "public risks are by definition probabilistic, and the likelihood that exposure will lead to adverse effects is often remote. The effects themselves might be of dramatic dimension, should they occur, but by virtue of low probabilities their expected costs are nevertheless negligible." Do you understand why companies might consider "adverse effects" of a "dramatic dimension" to be "negligible"?

   As one example of a danger that was essentially ignored because of its perceived unlikelihood, we can look at the "mad cow disease" outbreak in the United Kingdom in the 1980s. After the disease was discovered in 1982, the British Ministry of Agriculture refused to ban beef from "downer" cows (cows that exhibited symptoms of bovine spongiform encephalopathy, or BSE) and insisted that the illness could not make the jump to humans. In fact, by the mid-1990s, it became clear that this assertion was incorrect, and 150 people have died to date from a related illness that slowly destroyed their brains. The long latency period of the disease, as observed in cattle, means that it is possible that the disease will yet turn out to be more widespread. Do you agree with Gillette and Krier's suggestion that courts may be better at reducing a public risk like mad cow disease than an administrative agency like the Department of Agriculture? In a country where the meat from a single hamburger can come from as many as 200 different animals, how good do you think courts will be at addressing this problem?

5. Corporate short-termism: Most company executives' performance evaluations are based on quarterly earnings reports. As long as the numbers look good, they will be judged as having done a good job and be rewarded accordingly. Do you see how this can cause a tension with long-term decision making? The examples are practically innumerable; one recent example that may loom large on the horizon is energy companies' attitude to the issue of climate change.

   For more than a decade, the major industry players' reaction to the global warming crisis was consistent with a short-term perspective: question the science that said there was a crisis, and question the science of the proposed solutions; block implementation of treaties and other attempts to cap emissions. The primary problem was that, in the short term, the costs of addressing the problem were clear and the purely financial benefits were not. Eventually, pressure from national and local governments, expanding consumer interest in solar power and hybrid cars, and concern from the *insurance* industry about the effect on *their* bottom lines led some of the major players to stop blocking the search for a way to address this problem.

6. Many critics of administrative agencies do not agree with Gillette and Krier's conclusion that agencies are biased in favor of the "expert" view of risk. Perhaps most prominently, Justice Stephen Breyer has argued that agencies are part of a "vicious circle" in which the public clamors for regulation based on irrational fears of low-probability risks, Congress responds by enacting overly protective laws, and agencies—caught between political pressure and uncertain science—overregulate small risks and underregulate large ones. His solution is to lodge oversight authority of risk regulation in a small cadre of civil servants, trained in science, economics, and administration and insulated from the political process. See Stephen Breyer, Breaking the Vicious Circle: Toward Effective Risk Regulation (Harvard, 1993). What would Gillette and Krier think of Breyer's proposal? What do you think of it?

7. Gillette and Krier examine how the characteristics of different institutions fit (well or badly) some of the characteristics of different problems posed by risk. In the next reading, Komesar examines how the institutional characteristics fit the distribution of risks among "victims." The reading is more difficult than the preceding one, and you should pay particular attention to what Komesar means by "distribution" of risks.

- **Injuries and Institutions: Tort Reform, Tort Theory, and Beyond**
  NEIL K. KOMESAR
  65 N.Y.U. L. Rev. 23 (1990). Reprinted with permission of New York University Law Review

The first part of this Article presents a brief description of the competing institutions or systems lumped into three broad categories: the torts system, the criminal-regulatory system, and the market system. It traces the roles of the four primary groups of actors in such basic functions as prosecution, transacting, prevention, liability determination, and lawmaking. The second part of the Article examines three primary configurations of stakes for the four groups of actors, the behavioral responses of these actors, and the institutional implications that follow....

I

Institutional Description

This part will briefly describe the features of each of the institutional alternatives and the role of the four basic groups of actors in each system. These institutional alternatives are roughly categorized as the torts system, the criminal-regulatory system, and the market....

A. The Torts System

In the torts system, actual victims control the prosecution of legal actions. They decide on the targets of prosecution, investigate and prepare their actions, and present them to the liability determiner. They hire experts, most importantly lawyers, to help. Under the prevailing contingency-fee system, the lawyer and victim are, in effect, partners sharing both returns and costs. In the torts system, the behavior of victims and their lawyer-partners takes center stage. The system depends on these actors to bring and prosecute cases, and if they do not act, the system will not function. To an appreciable extent, the incentives for this action lie in the expected damage awards.

In the torts system, responsibility for the determination of liability varies with the form of liability and the functioning of a wide variety of rules within the forms of liability. But, in general, much of the responsibility in the classic torts case falls to the jury and the trial judge. These decision-makers take the information the parties (actual victims and actual injurers) supply and determine liability, and, therefore, distribute the impacts of the injuries.

If injury is to be prevented, the behavior of potential injurers must be altered. If their behavior is to be altered, they must be given incentives. In the torts system, these incentives take the form of potential damage awards and the other costs associated with tort liability (out-of-pocket expenses for lawyers, witnesses, and investigation, as well as time spent and aggravation). These incentives form a signal sent by the torts system to potential injurers. The characteristics of the signal—the size of the expected penalty and complexity of the signal—depend on the activities of the other actors in the torts system such as the propensity of the victims and their lawyers to bring and prosecute cases, and the abilities and capacities of the determiners of liability. But the potential injurer's actions also depend on the degree to which that injurer receives (perceives and understands) the signal sent.

B. Criminal Law and Administrative Regulation

Both classic criminal law and administrative regulation differ from the torts system at the prosecution stage. In criminal law and administrative regulation, the prosecution of a case is substantially in the hands of a public employee—a district attorney, U.S. attorney, or administrative prosecutor. These public employees are either elected or appointed to serve at the pleasure of some elected official. Here, the role of the actual victim is more tangential. Although the actual victim does not have to bear the expenses and uncertainties of prosecution, he or she no longer controls the prosecution. A prosecutor can bring an action even if there is little victim participation or interest and can refuse to bring suit even if the victim strongly desires it.

The determination of liability differs between criminal prosecution and administrative regulation. Criminal prosecutions are generally heard and decided by juries and trial judges. Although the rules of evidence and procedure differ between tort and criminal prosecution, the same determiners of liability—juries and trial judges—hear and decide both tort and criminal suits. The determiners of liability under administrative regulation usually are bureaucrats, appointed governmental employees of varying term and tenure. Unlike juries, they are not chosen randomly and serve for many cases or determinations.

As in the torts system, criminal law and administrative law achieve prevention by targeting the behavior of potential injurers. Again the size of the signal sent the potential injurer is dependent on such factors as the expected behavior of prosecutors and liability determiners. Also, injurer behavior is once again a product of the propensity to receive or understand the signal as well as the size of signal sent. The criminal law signal, however, differs from the tort signal in at least two ways.

First, criminal sanctions include incarceration as well as monetary payments. Second, unlike tort liability, both administrative regulation and the criminal law can target bad acts even if they are not accompanied by bad outcomes.

This second difference between the torts system and the criminal and regulatory systems has important implications both for the signal sent to the potential injurer and the administrative costs of the systems. Because the criminal and regulatory systems can target acts as well as outcomes, the number of prosecutable instances can be significantly greater in the administrative and criminal context than in the torts context. Thus, for example, the act of speeding or drunk driving is directly punishable and in fact punished in the criminal system even if it does not result in actual damage. To form the basis for a claim of negligence in the torts system, such activity would have to be accompanied by a bad outcome—compensable harm to some victim. More prosecutions can send more frequent and perhaps more direct signals but also can involve greater resources in sending the signal.

While it is clear that the possibility of recovering damages motivates private prosecutors—the actual victims and their contingency fee lawyers—to bring tort actions, it is not so apparent how public prosecutors and bureaucrats decide which cases to prosecute. What are the incentives of the public employee who does not pocket any profit, fines, or damage awards? How are these incentives related to the behavior of victims and injurers?

On the narrowest level, individual prosecutions might be brought or dropped according to the amount of political pressure applied to particular prosecutors by parties interested in these prosecutions, such as actual victims or injurers. On a broader level, interested parties may achieve more sweeping results by changing legislation or replacing prosecutors, through such strategies as lobbying, campaign contributions, and propaganda. Such activities focus on *prospective* prosecutions which means that potential injurers and victims rather than actual injurers and victims are more likely to be the interested parties in question.

The link between the efforts of these groups and public decisions does not require that public officials or even interest groups operate out of narrow self-interest. In a world of complexity and limited knowledge, even public servants honestly seeking the public good are dependent on others to provide information. In this context, lobbying and propaganda efforts by the various interests involved can be useful input into public decisionmaking. Serious distortions in public decisionmaking occur, however, when one position, because it is better able to organize such efforts, is overrepresented.

C. The Market (Voluntary Transactions)

In some settings, safety and prevention can be achieved without the existence of either tort liability or safety regulation. Potential victims can purchase safety or prevention from those whom, in the context of the torts system or criminal-regulatory system, we have called potential injurers. In the ideally functioning market, the signal is sent by consumer (potential victim) demand. Potential victims desire and are willing to pay for safety. Potential injurers are induced to supply this safety by the profit motive. Failure to provide safety, especially in the context of the sale of an associated product or service, would be disciplined by market forces; those who do not produce safer products and services would lose sales to those who do. In some injury settings, the prospect of such smoothly-working arrangements is preposterous. Where potential victims must make arrangements with a vast number of potential injurers (for example, pedestrians, who must deal with all drivers in the vicinity), it quickly becomes impossible to imagine such transactions because the transaction costs of identifying and bargaining with all potential injurers would be enormous. Where, however, the injury accompanies a transaction such as the provision of a good or service, it is not implausible to imagine that the transaction could also involve the purchase of sensible safety features. There is no need for separate one-on-one bargaining for this purchase of safety to be effectuated. To the extent that consumers demand safer products, producers have an incentive to consider this demand. The important issue here is the extent to which consumers of safety (potential victims) recognize the need for the safety, or even the extent to which they recognize the existence of the danger at all. The more complex or remote the danger, the more expensive it is to obtain this recognition; the smaller the potential injury, the less the incentive to expend resources to obtain this recognition.

II

Distributions of Impact and Institutional Performance

. . .

A. Distribution #1

	Potential	*Actual*
Victim	low impact	high impact
Injurer	low impact	high impact

This is the sort of injury for which there are many potential injurers and victims, each of whom has a low probability of injuring and being injured, respectively. The potential social (aggregate) impact can be very high, but it is distributed widely. On the other hand, although few people actually will injure or be injured, each occurrence of injury will be severe. An example of this distribution is forest fires started by carelessly thrown matches or cigarettes. Many matches and cigarettes are thrown without starting a fire, but, very infrequently, a match or cigarette may cause a major fire resulting in significant property damage and loss of life. The probability of being a victim of such carelessness is very low ex ante, but the impact, should the improbable occur, can be very great. A more common example of Distribution #1, although a more controversial one, is automobile accidents. The probability that a given driver will be a victim or injurer is low ex ante, but each injury ex post is substantial.

The setting described in Distribution #1 would produce active prosecution in the torts arena. High per capita actual victims (and their contingency fee lawyers) have the incentive to sue. However, the large number of cases (and the associated large administrative costs) that result may not produce much prevention because the low per capita impact on potential injurers (and potential victims) may mean that signals from the system will not be received.

Information on potential tort liability is hardly free. Potential injurers will have to expend resources to understand this tort liability signal. Whether, and to what extent, they are willing to expend these resources depends on the costs and benefits of receiving the signal. The benefits are related to the dangers of not receiving the signal—having to pay significant damage awards that the potential injurers could otherwise have avoided. The smaller the potential liability (per capita impact), the smaller the benefit of receiving the signal. The costs of understanding the signal depend on how complex and uncertain it is. The more complex and uncertain the signal, the more expensive it is to understand it and the less likely it will be received. This is especially important in the context of a vague standard like negligence, as opposed to a simple rule that proscribes specific conduct. A vague standard like negligence, which allows substantial variation in outcome case-by-case, makes the pattern of potential liability more complex and difficult to understand. . . .

The low deterrability potential in Distribution #1 can be exacerbated by the availability and pricing of liability insurance. If liability insurance is available to everyone at the same price without regard to his or her efforts to prevent and that price does not induce self-insurance, there is no incentive to prevent. If liability insurers were to differentiate among insureds based on their risk of causing injury, it would promote differential rates in a competitive insurance industry and provide the incentive for injurers to take safety steps. In Distribution #1, however, where potential liability is spread over so many potential injurers, this differential pricing based on individual predictions of the likelihood of tort liability (experience rating) is very unlikely. The culprit again is the balance between the cost of information and the incentives to acquire it. It would benefit insurance companies to 'experience rate'—to pick out only the low risks given the same premium. The information necessary to determine these differentiations, however, is not costless. Where there are a large number of potential injurers, identifying important differences among them and investigating to determine where and when those differences exist can be very expensive. At the same time, the low per capita liability means low average premiums and a lower return per capita for differentiation. Often it is not worthwhile to differentiate carefully among many low stakes (low premium) insureds.

Thus, in Distribution #1, low per capita stakes limit the possibility of injurer response to the deterrent signal both because the returns to understanding and responding to that signal are low and because the potential injurers' liability insurance rates are unlikely to respond to any preventative efforts that potential injurers might make. Under these circumstances, the torts system may produce many cases (and their associated costs) without much change in injurer behavior (the associated benefits). In other words, there is high potential for prosecution (the signal will be sent), but low deterrability (the signal will not be received).

At least at first blush, the shift from private to public prosecution does not promise any significant advantages. Deterring low stakes potential injurers is still a problem. The criminal law system and administrative regulation, however, do offer three potential advantages in connection with deterrability: the possibility of shifting the focus of prosecution to specified bad acts, rather than the bad act/bad outcome combination which characterizes tort liability; centralized decision-making, which allows for the rationing of prosecutorial resources; and the absence of liability insurance.

The fact that administrative regulation and criminal prosecution can target individual bad acts may increase prevention in two ways. First, by specifying particular acts for prohibition rather than using a vague standard like negligence, such a system makes the liability signal clearer and easier to understand (cheaper to acquire). Second, such a system defines a broader base for liability and, therefore, allows more frequent prosecutions. More frequent prosecution means that more people are likely to have direct, visible exposure to liability and, with it, easier (more accessible) awareness of the legal liability signal. In addition, the criminal and regulatory systems allow a centralized decision that can explicitly balance the costs of suits and the benefits of deterrability for society as a whole. In theory at least, public prosecutors can choose to decrease prosecution (thereby saving the administrative costs) where there is little chance for inducing preventative behavior. The torts process, with its decentralized, private prosecution decisions does not easily allow for this sort of societal calculation.

However, what the criminal and regulatory systems might do, in theory, can be quite different from what they will do in practice. We need to consider the behavioral incentives of the public officials who make these decisions and, in turn, the incentives and behavior of victims and injurers whose action as lobbyists, voters, or propagandists help determine the decisions of these public officials. Generally, individuals organize into a group to exert political influence when each of these individuals expects to be substantially affected by decisions the public officials will make (i.e., where per capita stakes are high). The low per capita stakes for both potential victims and potential injurers in Distribution #1 suggests the absence of much organized political activity by either group and, therefore the absence of the sort of overrepresentation of one group that we shall see in the next section. In Distribution #1, the image of an objective political process that even-handedly balances the costs and benefits of prosecution—impermissibly simplistic in other settings—may closely approximate reality. . . .

In Distribution #1, the prospects are remote that voluntary transactions and market forces will effectively increase prosecution. Low per capita stakes make it likely that neither victims nor injurers will recognize the risks or dangers involved and, therefore, appreciate the advantages of prevention. In addition, as the forest fire and automobile accident examples show, the prospect of many potential injurers and potential victims makes the costs of transactions very high. Each victim can affect his or her probability of injury in an appreciable way only by transacting with many potential injurers. It is also likely that precautions taken by any potential injurer will affect the safety of many potential victims in a way similar to how it affects the contracting potential victim. If a potential match tosser or driver acts more prudently, it will likely lower the chances of fire or traffic accidents for many potential victims. Such positive external effects will not be taken into account by the contracting victim. The result is the purchase of too little safety from a societal standpoint. This situation can be avoided only by organizing many victims in a cooperative effort to purchase the safety in question. Such an endeavor faces the problem that many potential victims would attempt to free ride, hoping that others would purchase safety from which they could benefit without paying. In turn, this free riding, when widespread, can lead to a failure to bargain for any safety. Free riding can be overcome, if at all, only with a further expenditure of resources in organizing and transacting.

B. Distribution #2

	Potential	*Actual*
Victim	low impact	high impact
Injurer	high impact	high impact

Distribution #2 changes only one element from Distribution #1—potential injurers now have high per capita impacts. This one change, however, makes this distribution the most analytically interesting and the most programmatically troubling. In this setting, the prospects of the torts system improve and those of the regulatory system decrease normatively but increase positively. This divergence produces the troubling prospect of perverse pressures for reform. In Distribution #2, market transactions are a more viable means of achieving optimal prevention than they were in Distribution #1, although the low per capita stakes of potential victims still cause difficulties. At least as a rough approximation, this distribution fits the common conception of products liability—numerous consumers as potential victims, relatively large-scale manufacturers as potential injurers, and low probability but serious injuries. The bursting pop bottle and the exploding gas tank are mishaps consistent with this distribution. This distribution also roughly fits at least some areas of service liability such as medical malpractice—numerous patients as potential victims, comparatively fewer doctors and hospitals as potential injurers and again, low probability but serious injuries.

In Distribution #2, the torts system is now a more robust prevention strategy because deterrability for injurers is now more feasible than was the case in Distribution #1. There are now greater incentives to expend the resources necessary to understand the signal sent. More complex signals associated with complex case-by-case liability rules can be sent because large-scale potential injurers have the incentive to decipher these complex signals.

High per capita stakes for potential injurers in Distribution #2 also will tend to dissipate the impediment to deterrence created by the presence of liability insurance. . . .

Although the torts system appears to handle Distribution #2 quite well, the other institutions may not fare as well due to the significant differential between ex ante stakes for injurers and those for victims. All the other institutions have significant ex ante features that cause serious distortions in their performance.

In Distribution #2, voluntary transactions (the market) can provide a viable institutional response to the extent that consumers (potential victims) appreciate the existing level of risk. This appreciation will vary with the size of the potential victims' per capita stakes. As was the case with Distribution #1, per capita stakes for Distribution #2 potential victims are low. The issue now becomes how low "low" is. Very low stakes can defeat serious recognition of the danger and willingness to purchase safety; the benefits gained from outlays to understand or even recognize the risk may be too low. On the other hand, as per capita stakes for consumers (potential victims) rise, the potential for market-produced prevention increases. The ability of potential victims to recognize the existence of the risk will also vary with the complexity of the risk—with how much it will cost to acquire the necessary information. A complex product may have risks that are remote and difficult to understand. This analysis suggests that at least those products and service injury settings where the technology is highly complex and the stakes for victims are very low ex ante are poor candidates for market provision of safety.

In Distribution #2, the significant difference in stakes between potential injurers and potential victims can cause serious distortions in the criminal and administrative systems, which are characterized by public, rather than private prosecution. To the extent that public prosecutors can be affected by the activities of persons outside the official process, there may be bias toward the injurer group. Potential injurers, because they have high per capita stakes, have more incentive to recognize the implications for themselves of active prosecution than do low-stakes potential victims. Consequently, potential injurers are more likely to organize the efforts necessary to influence prosecutors to decrease the frequency of prosecution. Such activities might take the form of graft, political contributions, political pressure on legislators or executives, or more subtle lobbying and propaganda aimed at influencing the attitude of the agency.

In administrative, as opposed to criminal, regulation, where both prosecution and liability determination are carried out by government employees (bureaucrats), these distortive tendencies are stronger. Now a board of bureaucrats has replaced the jury. Although, as a general matter, there are societal advantages in this shift, in the context of Distribution #2, this shift has troubling implications. Fixed decision-makers, like full-time bureaucrats, are better targets for graft, political pressure, and propaganda than are constantly changing juries. Fixed decision-makers are responsible for determining the outcome of many cases; a given jury is usually responsible for one. It is thus easier to identify the bureaucrats and to influence them over time than it is to influence jurors. More importantly, any investment in activities designed to influence bureaucrats covers more cases and, therefore, yields a higher return. Even public-minded and honest civil servants are capable of being influenced by propaganda and lobbying activities.

Lobbying and propaganda are necessary and socially valuable components of large-scale political systems that deal with complex societal issues. They provide information about the implications of these issues for various groups in the society. Problems arise, however, where there is a skewed representation of the views of one group. Such overrepresentation is inherent in the Distribution #2 setting because there is significant difference in ex ante stakes. In such a situation, political action is likely to reflect a bias toward the overrepresentation of high-stakes potential injurers. . . .

The preceding discussion has assumed that products liability is synonymous with Distribution #2 and that certain institutional implications for market and political response follow. The programmatic importance and analytical richness of Distribution #2 and products liability warrant further exploration of these implications. First, not all products liability injuries are characterized by Distribution #2. Products and services can be produced on a small scale with an accompanyingly smaller per capita stake per potential injurer. Furthermore, it is likely that there are at least some instances in which there are high per capita potential victims, or where there is some organized representation of victim interests. Unions, for example, may represent victims for some workplace product-related injuries. In addition, plaintiffs' lawyers and the plaintiffs' bar can and do exert organized political influence on behalf of potential tort victims.

Second, the institutional implications of Distribution #2 require further consideration of variations in the absolute per capita levels that characterize it—how low, how high? As we have seen as stakes rise for potential victims, the market becomes a more viable alternative. Variations in stakes can also change the character of the public response. Where the per capita stakes for potential victims are very low, the results of public decision-making will greatly favor potential injurers. At higher (but still low) per capita stakes for potential victims, the possibility of majoritarian reaction arises. This creates a counterforce to tort reform at the legislative level, although it is one that may be diminished in administrative implementation.

In the extreme, an increase in low per capita stakes, when accompanied by other factors, could cause a shift from overrepresentation of the concentrated, high-stakes minority to an overrepresentation of the dispersed, low stakes majority....

C. Distribution #3

	Potential	*Actual*
Victim	low impact	low impact
Injurer	high impact	high impact

Because Distribution #3 retains high stakes for potential injurers, the possibility remains that these injurers will have the incentives to understand any signal sent. However, because the stakes for actual victims are now low per capita, there may be problems obtaining the private prosecutions necessary to send the signal through the torts system.

If victims could be organized and pool their interests, then they might have the incentive necessary to expend resources for private prosecution. But organizing itself requires resources. At very low per capita stakes, there may not be sufficient incentives even to recognize injury. Even if the injury were recognized, there would exist a natural tendency to free ride, which could defeat any attempts to organize. In other words, low per capita impact actual victims face the same impediments to successful representation in the torts system that low per capita impact potential victims face in gaining representation in the political process.

The high stakes for potential injurers and low stakes for potential victims in Distribution #3 suggest the same problems with the political process, and, therefore with criminal and administrative regulation, as existed in Distribution #2. Because the tort system is likely to be less effective in Distribution #3 than in Distribution #2, there is greater need for a response from the political process. However, high-stakes potential injurers can be expected to be quite active in the political process, thereby inhibiting public or private prosecution.

Air and water pollution are injuries that fit Distribution #3. The victims are members of the general public, each of whom is injured to a small extent by each act of pollution. The injurers are frequently large-scale industrial polluters.

At first blush, political reality seems to contradict the picture of the political process previously suggested. There seems to be no absence of political response to pollution despite the presence of low per capita potential victims and high per capita potential injurers. Candidates for elective office seem to place protection of the environment high on their agenda. Generally, it would be political suicide for candidates to declare themselves to be against stopping pollution. Such a political response seems to indicate that potential victims' stakes are high enough so that they recognize the problem and threaten reaction at the ballot box. For pollution issues, low stakes become high enough to provoke an understanding of the issues and at least enough political activity to vote. This, in turn, causes office holders to express support for pollution regulation.

There may be reason, however, to doubt that these public expressions of support will translate into effective regulation. The political dynamics change when it comes time to implement the vague public expressions either at the stage of drafting the particulars in legislative committee or at the stage of implementing these regulations by administrative agencies. What a politician would never do on the soapbox, he or she can afford to do in the more complex, more hidden world of the legislative subcommittee or the administrative agency. A politician may public[ ]ly declare an abiding concern for the environment but then halt prosecution under the guise of a procedural or jurisdictional rationale, or by inhibiting particular prosecutions.

If pollution regulation were straightforward, such ploys would not be successful. But in a complex setting where reasonable people can differ on the proper strategy and approach, it is easy to hide from a low stakes constituency not willing and able to follow all the twists and turns of complicated procedures and issues, while, at the same time, serving a high stakes constituency able to understand the procedures and issues and reward efforts on their behalf. In such a world, polluters, the concentrated few, may prevail over the victims of pollution, the dispersed many. The majority may have sufficiently high stakes to induce political parties to include environmental planks in their platforms and even to induce legislators to pass general but vague legislation. The majority, however, may not have sufficiently high stakes to present a real threat in the complex world in which these broad policies are implemented.

Distribution #3 also does not bode well for market alternatives. Because market alternatives rely on the actions of potential injurers and potential victims, the analysis of market alternatives in Distribution #3 is the same as that in Distribution #2. The crucial issue is the extent to which low per capita stakes make potential victims unaware of the risks of injury and, therefore, poor purchasers of safety.

The problems of market alternatives in Distribution #3 can be shown to be greater than in Distribution #2 if we consider the primary examples of the two distributions—pollution and products injuries, respectively. In the pollution setting, there is a greater problem of overlapping benefits for pollution control and, therefore, higher transaction costs than in the products injury setting. If a given potential victim purchases a decrease in air or water pollution from a given potential injurer, that decrease will benefit more than the single potential victim. As shown in the case of auto accidents, these external benefits signal the need for collective action on the part of potential victims with all the problems of free riding and additional transaction costs.

All institutional alternatives present serious difficulties in Distribution #3. In a world of highly imperfect institutions, this outcome is not rare. Here the tough choice among imperfect institutions will depend on gradations in factors such as stakes and complexity, and likely will require further breakdowns of Distribution #3 injuries according to these gradations. . . . [L]ow per capita injuries for actual victims create serious problems for the torts system and force consideration of alternatives. Problems with private prosecution make Distribution #3 injuries the least likely of the three injuries represented in the three distributions to be present in the existing torts system and, therefore, least likely to be directly impacted by changes in the torts system. . . .

COMMENTS AND QUESTIONS

1. It is most important to understand Komesar's three "distributions" and how they relate to institutional choice. Start by identifying the basic characteristics of the three institutions. For example, the tort system is victim initiated after the event, provides a monetary signal after the event to injurers, and provides information to the jury or judge; what are the parallel points about the criminal-regulatory and market systems? Then determine the differences among the three distributions. Komesar's fundamental point is that the different distributions match up with the different characteristics of the institutions he has described.

2. Within the framework of Komesar's analysis, what is the best institution to use in responding to the problem of carpal tunnel syndrome associated with work? The best institution to use in responding to the problem of severe limb injuries due to malfunctioning presses in workplaces? The best institution to use in responding to climate change? Do you find Komesar's framework helpful in thinking about these questions, or do you believe that some other way of thinking about them would be more useful?

3. Komesar includes pollution within Distribution #3. Consider the fact that scientists believe that current levels of fine particulate matter—soot, in the vernacular—lead to tens of thousands of premature deaths in the United States every year. What kind of pollution problems do you think Komesar is talking about when he says that injuries to individual victims are small? Which distribution best fits the problem of particulate matter pollution?

B The Sociology of Claiming Legal Rights

Even if the legal regime is appropriately structured in the abstract, it may not create *effective* structures. People have to know that the problems they are experiencing have legal solutions, for example, and they have to be willing to use the law to resolve those problems. (Note how hard it is to avoid language of consent, choice, and voluntariness in discussing these questions.) The next reading raises questions about the social processes of claiming legal rights.

- ### The Emergence and Transformation of Disputes: Naming, Blaming, Claiming . . .
  WILLIAM L. F. FELSTINER, RICHARD ABEL, AND AUSTIN SARAT
  15 Law & Soc'y Rev. 531 (1980–81). Reprinted with permission of Blackwell Publishing

Disputes are not things: they are social constructs. Their shapes reflect whatever definition the observer gives to the concept. Moreover, a significant portion of any dispute exists only in the minds of the disputants.

These ideas, though certainly not novel, are important because they draw attention to a neglected topic in the sociology of law—the emergence and transformation of disputes—the way in which experiences become grievances, grievances become disputes, and disputes take various shapes, follow particular dispute processing paths, and lead to new forms of understanding. Studying the emergence and transformation of disputes means studying a social process as it occurs. It means studying the conditions under which injuries are perceived or go unnoticed and how people respond to the experience of injustice and conflict. . . .

Trouble, problems, personal and social dislocation are everyday occurrences. Yet, social scientists have rarely studied the capacity of people to tolerate substantial distress and injustice. . . . We do, however, know that such "tolerance" may represent a failure to perceive that one has been injured; such failures may be self-induced or externally manipulated. Assume a population living downwind from a nuclear test site. Some portion of that population has developed cancer as a result of the exposure and some has not. Some of those stricken know that they are sick and some do not. In order for disputes to emerge and remedial action to be taken, an unperceived injurious experience (unPIE, for short) must be transformed into a perceived injurious experience (PIE). The uninformed cancer victims must learn that they are sick. . . .

. . . [I]n many cases it will be difficult to identify and explain transformations from unPIE to PIE. This first transformation—saying to oneself that a particular experience has been injurious—we call *naming*. Though hard to study empirically, naming may be the critical transformation; the level and kind of disputing in a society may turn more on what is initially perceived as an injury than on any later decision. . . . For instance, asbestosis only became an acknowledged "disease" *and* the basis of a claim for compensation when shipyard workers stopped taking for granted that they would have trouble breathing after ten years of installing insulation and came to view their condition as a problem.

The next step is the transformation of a perceived injurious experience into a grievance. This occurs when a person attributes an injury to the fault of another individual or social entity. By including fault within the definition of grievance, we limit the concept to injuries viewed both as violations of norms and as remediable. The definition takes the grievant's perspective: the injured person must feel wronged and believe that something might be done in response to the injury, however politically or sociologically improbable such a response might be. A grievance must be distinguished from a complaint against no one in particular (about the weather, or perhaps inflation) and from a mere wish unaccompanied by a sense of injury for which another is held responsible (I might like to be more attractive). We call the transformation from perceived injurious experience to grievance *blaming*: our diseased shipyard worker makes this transformation when he holds his employer or the manufacturer of asbestos insulation responsible for his asbestosis.

The third transformation occurs when someone with a grievance voices it to the person or entity believed to be responsible and asks for some remedy. We call this communication *claiming*. A claim is transformed into a dispute when it is rejected in whole or in part. Rejection need not be expressed by words. Delay that the claimant construes as resistance is just as much a rejection as is a compromise offer (partial rejection) or an outright refusal.

The sociology of law should pay more attention to the early stages of disputes and to the factors that determine whether naming, blaming, and claiming will occur. Learning more about the existence, absence, or reversal of these basic transformations will increase our understanding of the disputing process and our ability to evaluate dispute processing institutions. We know that only a small fraction of injurious experiences ever mature into disputes. Furthermore, we know that most of the attrition occurs at the early stages: experiences are not perceived as injurious; perceptions do not ripen into grievances; grievances are voiced to intimates but not to the person deemed responsible.

. . . Transformations reflect social structural variables, as well as personality traits. People do—or do not—perceive an experience as an injury, blame someone else, claim redress, or get their claims accepted because of their *social position* as well as their individual characteristics. The transformation perspective points as much to the study of social stratification as to the exploration of social psychology.

Finally, attention to naming, blaming, and claiming permits a more critical look at . . . efforts to improve "access to justice." The public commitment to formal legal equality, required by the prevailing ideology of liberal legalism, has resulted in substantial efforts to equalize access at the later stages of disputing, where inequality becomes more visible and implicates official institutions; examples include the waiver of court costs, the creation of small claims courts, the movement toward informalism, and the provision of legal services. . . . Access to justice is supposed to reduce the unequal distribution of advantages in society; paradoxically it may amplify these inequalities. The ostensible goal of these reforms is to eliminate bias in the ultimate transformation: disputes into lawsuits. If, however, as we suspect, these very unequal distributions have skewed the earlier stages by which injurious experiences become disputes, then current access to justice efforts will only give additional advantages to those who have already transformed their experiences into disputes. That is, these efforts may accentuate the effects of inequality at the earlier, less visible stages, where it is harder to detect, diagnose, and correct. . . .

III. The Characteristics of Transformation

PIEs, grievances, and disputes have the following characteristics: they are subjective, unstable, reactive, complicated, and incomplete. They are *subjective* in the sense that transformations need not be accompanied by any observable behavior. A disputant discusses his problem with a lawyer and consequently reappraises the behavior of the opposing party. The disputant now believes that his opponent was not just mistaken but acted in bad faith. The content of the dispute has been transformed in the mind of the disputant, although neither the lawyer nor the opposing party necessarily knows about the shift.

Since transformations may be nothing more than changes in feelings, and feelings may change repeatedly, the process is *unstable*. This characteristic is notable only because it differs so markedly from the conventional understanding of legal controversies. In the conventional view of disputes, the sources of claims and rejections are objective events that happened in the past. It is accepted that it may be difficult to get the facts straight, but there is rarely an awareness that the events themselves may be transformed as they are processed. This view is psychologically naive: it is insensitive to the effect of feelings on the attribution of motive and to the consequences of such attributions for the subject's understanding of behavior.

A focus on transformations also expands, if it does not introduce, the notion of *reactivity*. Since a dispute is a claim and a rejection, disputes are reactive by definition—a characteristic that is readily visible when parties engage in bargaining or litigation. But attention to *transformations* also reveals reactivity at the earlier stages, as individuals define and redefine their perceptions of experience and the nature of their grievances in response to the communications, behavior, and expectations of a range of people, including opponents, agents, authority figures, companions, and intimates.

Even in ordinary understanding, disputing is a *complicated* process involving ambiguous behavior, faulty recall, uncertain norms, conflicting objectives, inconsistent values, and complex institutions. It is complicated still further by attention to changes in disputant feelings and objectives over time. Take the stereotypical case of personal injury arising out of an automobile accident. A conventional analysis (e.g., the one often borrowed from economics) assumes that the goals of the defendant driver are to minimize his responsibility and limit the complainant's recovery. A transformation view, on the other hand, suggests that the defendant's objectives may be both less clear and less stable. Depending on his insurance position, his own experience, his empathy for, relationship to, and interaction with the injured person, and the tenor of discussions he may have with others about the accident and its aftermath, the defendant may at various times wish to maximize rather than minimize both his own fault and the complainant's recovery or to take some intermediate position. . . .

IV. Subjects and Agents of Transformation

One way to organize the study of the transformations of PIES, grievances, and disputes is to identify what is being transformed (the subjects of transformation) and what does the transforming (the agents of transformation). Unfortunately, it is not possible to present subjects and agents in a simple matrix, since every factor can be construed as both.

Parties

Neither the identity nor the number of parties is fixed. New information about and redefinition of a conflict can lead a party to change his views about appropriate adversaries or desirable allies. Both may also be changed by officials of dispute processing agencies. The new parties, especially if they are groups like the NAACP, ACLU, or Sierra Club, may adopt a lawsuit as part of a campaign to use the courts as a mechanism of social change or to mobilize political activity, although social and political movements may also lose momentum as a collective struggle is translated into an individual lawsuit (e.g., school desegregation). Parties may be dropped as well as added. A grievance that was originally experienced collectively may be individualized, in the process of becoming a dispute; tort claims as a response to harm caused by unsafe conditions and disciplinary hearings as a response to labor disputes are examples.

Obviously, the parties to a conflict are central agents, as well as objects, in the transformation process. Their behavior will be a function of personality as it interacts with prior experience and current pressures. Experience includes involvement in other conflicts; contact with reference groups, representatives, and officials; and familiarity with various forms of dispute processing and remedies.... Personality variables that may affect transformations include risk preferences, contentiousness, and feelings about personal efficacy, privacy, independence, and attachment to justice (rule mindedness). Both experience and personality are in turn related to social structural variables: class, ethnicity, gender, age.

The relationship between the parties also has significance for transformations: the sphere of social life that brings them together (work, residence, politics, recreation)—which may affect the cost of exit—their relative status, and the history of prior conflict shape the way in which they will conduct their dispute. In addition, strategic interaction between the parties in the course of a conflict may have a major transformational role. An unusual example is the party who seeks proactively to elicit grievances against himself: the retail seller who asks purchasers about complaints, the employer who provides an anonymous suggestion box, even the neurotic spouse or lover who invites recriminations. But more common are the new elements disputes take on, the rise and fall in animosity and effort that occurs in response to or in anticipation of the "moves" of the opposition.

Attributions

Attribution theory asserts that the causes a person assigns for an injurious experience will be important determinants of the action he or she takes in response to it; those attributions will also presumably affect perception of the experience as injurious. People who blame themselves for an experience are less likely to see it as injurious, or, having so perceived it, to voice a grievance about it; they are more likely to do both if blame can be placed upon another, particularly when the responsible agent can be seen as intentionally causing or aggravating the problem. But attributions themselves are not fixed. As moral coloration is modified by new information, logic, insight, or experience, attributions are changed, and they alter the participants' understanding of their experience. Adversary response may be an important factor in this transformation, as may the nature of the dispute process. Some processes, such as counseling, may drain the dispute of moral content and diffuse responsibility for problems; others, like direct confrontation or litigation, may intensify the disputant's moral judgment and focus blame. Thus the degree and quality of blame, an important subject of transformations, also produces further transformations.

Scope

The scope of conflict—the extent of relevant discourse about grievances and claims—is affected both by the objectives and behavior of disputants and by the processual characteristics of dispute institutions. A hypothetical case frequently used in mediator training involves a man's wife and his lover. The wife has hit the lover with a rock, and the latter has complained to the police; at arraignment the judge has referred the women to mediation. The discussion there focuses initially on the rock incident and then expands to include the battle for the man's affections. The scope of this dispute is thus complicated by the confrontation between the women during the rock incident, narrowed to that incident alone as the dispute is handled by police and court, and then broadened to re-embrace the original conflict plus the rock incident through interaction between the disputants and the mediator.

Some types of dispute processing seek to narrow the disputes with which they deal in order to produce a construction of events that appears manageable. Others are alive to context and circumstance. They encourage a full rendering of events and exploration of the strands of interaction, no matter where they lead. The scope of conflict, in turn, affects the identity of the participants, the tactics used, and the outcomes that become feasible.

Choice of Mechanisms

The grievant's choice of an audience to whom to voice a complaint and the disputant's choice of an institution to which to take a controversy are primarily functions of the person's objectives and will change as objectives change.... Once a mechanism—court, administrative agency, mediator, arbitrator, or psychotherapist—is set in motion, it determines the rules of relevance, cast of actors, costs, delays, norms, and remedies.

Objectives Sought

A party may change his objectives in two ways: what he seeks or is willing to concede and how much. Stakes go up or down as new information becomes available, a party's needs change, rules are adjusted, and costs are incurred. Delay, frustration, and despair may produce a change in objectives: victims of job discrimination frequently want the job (or promotion) or nothing at the outset but later become willing to settle for money. As Aubert noted, the relationship between objectives and mechanisms is reciprocal: not only do objectives influence the choice of mechanisms, but mechanisms chosen may alter objectives. Because courts, for instance, often proceed by using a limited number of norms to evaluate an even more circumscribed universe of relevant facts, "the needs of the parties, their wishes for the future, cease to be relevant to the solution." Even where a legal remedy is anticipatory—alimony, worker's compensation, or tort damages for future loss—the legal system frequently prefers to award a lump sum rather than order periodic payments. Finally, the experience of disputing may stimulate a participant to take steps to avoid similar disputes in the future, or to structure his behavior so as to place him in a stronger position should a dispute occur.

Ideology

The individual's sense of entitlement to enjoy certain experiences and be free from others is a function of the prevailing ideology, of which law is simply a component. The consumer's dissatisfaction with a product or service may have been influenced by the campaigns of activists, like Ralph Nader, who assert that consumers have a right to expect high quality.[10] Legal change may sometimes be a highly effective way of transforming ideology to create a sense of entitlement. This is the sense in which, contrary to conventional wisdom, you *can* legislate morality. Although it would be foolish to maintain that after *Brown v. Board of Education* every minority

---

[10] This belief may explain why consumers from higher socioeconomic strata exhibit a higher level of dissatisfaction with their purchases—it is not the goods and services that are worse but the expectations that are more demanding, partly as a result of the consumer movement, which in its composition, is exclusively middle-class.

child had a sense of entitlement to integrated education, made a claim against segregation, and engaged in a dispute when that claim was rejected, surely this has happened more often *since* than before 1954. Following a recent television program in Chicago in which a woman subjected to a strip search during a routine traffic citation described her successful damage claim against the police department, *hundreds* of women telephoned the station with similar stories. In this instance, a legal victory transformed shame into outrage, encouraging the voicing of grievances, many of which may have become disputes. When the original victim chose a legal mechanism for her complaint, a collective grievance against police practices was individualized and depoliticized. When she broadcast her legal victory on television, the legal dispute was collectivized and repoliticized. Ideology—and law—can also instill a sense of disentitlement. The enactment of worker's compensation as the "solution" to the problem of industrial accidents early in this century may have helped convince workers to rely on employer paternalism to ensure their safety and relinquish claims to control the workplace.

Reference Groups

Disputes may be transformed through interaction with audiences or sponsors. A tenant's dispute with a landlord may be the cause around which a tenants' association is formed; a worker's grievance against a foreman may become the stimulus to a union organizing drive or a rank-and-file movement within an existing union. This transformation may not only make an individual dispute into a collective one: it also may lead to economic or political struggle displacing legal procedures. This is especially important in the remedy-seeking behavior of disadvantaged groups. The movement from law to politics, and the accompanying expansion of the scope of disputing, are prompted and guided by the reaction of a wide social network to individual instances of injustice. Absent the support of such a network, no such movement is likely to occur.

Representatives and Officials

Lawyers, psychotherapists, union officials, social workers, government functionaries, and other agents and public officials help people understand their grievances and what they can do about them. In rendering this service, they almost always produce a transformation: the essence of professional jobs is *to define the needs of the consumer* of professional services. Generally, this leads to a definition that calls for the professional to provide such services.

Of all of the agents of dispute transformation lawyers are probably the most important. This is, in part, the result of the lawyer's central role as gatekeeper to legal institutions and facilitator of a wide range of personal and economic transactions in American society. There is evidence that lawyers often shape disputes to fit their own interests rather than those of their clients. Sometimes they systematically "cool out" clients with legitimate grievances. In consumer cases lawyers may be reluctant to press claims for fear of offending potential business clients. In defending the accused criminal, lawyers may prefer negotiating a plea bargain to trying the case. In tort litigation they prefer to settle, and package deals to claims adjusters. In other cases they may amplify grievances: some divorce lawyers recommend litigation for which a substantial fee can be charged, rather than engage in difficult, problematic, and unprofitable negotiations about reconciliation.

Lawyers may affect transformations in another way—by rejecting requests for assistance or providing only minimal help and thereby arresting the further development of a dispute, at least through legal channels. Limited data suggest that lawyers respond differently to different categories of clients. This differential lawyer response contributes to variation in dispute behavior between poor and middle class, corporate entities and individuals, normal and deviant, members of ethnic majorities and minorities, and young and old.

Of course, lawyers also produce transformations about which we may be more enthusiastic. They furnish information about choices and consequences unknown to clients; offer a forum for testing the reality of the client's perspective; help clients identify, explore, organize, and negotiate their problems; and give emotional and social support to clients who are unsure of themselves or their objectives.

Enforcement personnel—police, prosecutors, regulatory agencies—may also produce transformations: seeking disputes in order to advance a public policy or generate a caseload that will justify increased budget demands; discouraging disputes because of personnel shortages; or selectively encouraging those disputes that enhance the prestige of the agency and discouraging those that diminish its significance or call for skills it lacks or are thought to be inappropriate.

Dispute Institutions

The transformation effects of dispute institutions have been analyzed at some length. Courts, which fall at one extreme along most of the dimensions useful for describing dispute institutions, may transform the content of disputes because the substantive norms they apply differ from rules of custom or ordinary morality, and their unique procedural norms may narrow issues and circumscribe evidence.

Courts may transform disputes by individualizing remedies.[13] Some of the victims of a defective product may want to force the manufacturer to alter the production process. But because courts award only money damages for unintentional torts, even those victims' concept of an acceptable outcome is transformed from a collective good (safety) into individual enrichment, a transformation greatly encouraged by the lawyer's interest in creating a fund out of which his fee can be paid.[14]

Because of the monopoly exercised by lawyers, the esoteric nature of court processes and discourse, and the burdens of pretrial procedure, the *attitude* of disputants may be altered by their minimal role in the courtroom and the way they are treated there. In effect, their "property" interest in the dispute is expropriated by lawyers and the state. The rediscovery of the victim in the criminal prosecution

---

[13] Even class actions are often merely collections of individual disputes, aggregated for reasons of convenience and efficiency, rather than a form of collective action aimed at achieving a group objective, such as a shift in control over production decisions.

[14] We acknowledge that in making money damages the quintessential remedy, courts are, in a sense, giving people what they "want." But what people "want" is powerfully structured by legal institutions and the media. Although it is difficult to document this process in action, we know that at the turn of the century, before money compensation for injuries was commonplace, workers demanded radical improvements in industrial safety, and only the intransigence of employers compelled them to accept the workers' compensation system instead.

is one recognition of this. Furthermore, delays caused by court overload or foot-dragging by an adversary may transform what disputants would otherwise consider a useful procedure into pointless frustration.

The nature and potential transformational effects of courts can be seen best if we contrast litigation with another technique for handling conflict—psychotherapy. Like law, therapy individualizes conflicts and remedies. In most other ways, however, it sharply contrasts with courts and lawyers. Disputants are encouraged to describe the conflict and express their feelings about it in whatever terms they find comfortable. Since mental health professionals are trained to use anger to reduce hostility, disputants will not need to deny their feelings. The nonjudgmental posture and reflective responses of the therapist should provide emotional support for disputants, who are urged to examine the pattern of their own responses to the behavior of others. They may find, for instance, that progress toward a solution may be obstructed not by the dilatory tactics or opposition of an adversary but rather by their own reluctance to act. One objective of the process is to increase the disputant's understanding of the motives, feelings, and behavior of others. Thus, where the outcome of successful litigation is usually an order directed to an adversary, the outcome of a successful psychotherapeutic intervention may be a change in the client.

In between courts and psychotherapy there are many other dispute institutions—arbitration, mediation, administrative hearings, and investigations—that use ingredients of each process in different combinations but always effect a transformation. . . . [T]ransformation studies render problematic one of the most fundamental political judgments about disputing—that there is too much of it, that Americans are an over-contentious people, far too ready to litigate. The transformation perspective suggests that there may be too *little* conflict in our society. Many studies are "court-centered." They assess conflict from the point of view of courts which perceive their resources to be limited. From this viewpoint, any level of conflict that exceeds the court's capacities is "too much." Things look very different, however, if we start with the *individual* who has suffered an injurious experience. That is what the transformations point of view makes us do. It encourages inquiry into why so few such individuals even get some redress. So the transformation perspective naturally prompts questions that have been largely ignored thus far: why are Americans so slow to perceive injury, so reluctant to make claims, and so fearful of disputing—especially of litigating? One hypothesis tentatively advanced in some early research is that the cult of competence, the individualism celebrated by American culture, inhibits people from acknowledging—to themselves, to others, and particularly to authority—that they have been injured, that they have been bettered by an adversary. . . .

COMMENTS AND QUESTIONS

1. Make sure that you understand the process of naming, blaming, and claiming. Devise a story about naming, blaming, and claiming in the contexts of sexual harassment at the workplace and exposure to secondhand smoke. Note the important role Felstiner, Abel, and Sarat give to "institutions" (broadly understood) in that process. What in particular are the roles of lawyers? How might lawyers affect the process with respect to workplace sexual harassment

and secondhand smoke? Compared with other institutions, how important are lawyers in the process?

2. Consider a man who tells his wife that he can't stop coughing after a day of work in a textile factory. Has he named a problem? Would you describe what happened as an unperceived injurious experience? Suppose he describes it to his wife as a workplace illness. Has he blamed anyone and, if so, who? How might he convert the situation into a claim? Against whom? According to what procedures?

3. A former student of one of us wrote the following (reprinted here in an edited form with her permission):

> I am *a potential* plaintiff in the Breast Implant Litigation Settlement. And "potential" is the key word here.
>
> In 1987, I was diagnosed, to no surprise to my mother and me, with "irregular breast development." One breast had no living cells and thus failed to grow. The other grew, but in a deformed shape. I underwent two surgeries, one in 1987 and the second in 1990. In 1987, I had a silicone implant inserted in the non-growth breast and reconstructive surgery (a reduction) on the other. In 1990, I had a small silicone implant inserted to complement what I considered to be only an adequate surgical performance for the reconstructed breast.
>
> Back in 1987, I perceived implants to be a medical divinity. It solved all of my problems. What if I were born a generation or two earlier, I thought? As a teenager, I would have undergone stigma enough to kill an otherwise pleasant childhood. Wow, I'm lucky, I thought. I had a problem, and a couple thousand dollars later, the problem was hidden.
>
> Today, I don't feel so lucky. Yesterday, I received in the mail a copy of the Proposed Settlement plan that I had requested. Through the media (not my doctor or health care providers), I heard about the lawsuit against Dow Corning Corp., etc. Then I saw an ad in the paper inviting potential plaintiffs to join the suit. And then I saw the ads on television.
>
> Why don't I feel lucky? Some may think that this suit is a huge gift: I've had no problems yet, and a successful settlement will assure me money. *"Yet,"* however, is as significant a word as *"potential."*
>
> If I knew that in the next thirty years (the limitation on the proposed settlement plan) I would have no troubles with my implants, I would enroll in the suit without hesitation. It sounds great; I do not have to go to a hearing, pay a lawyer, be bothered by litigation, publicize my surgery, or assert any energy beyond completing a form. And, for all that lack of energy, I am pretty much assured a monetary award.
>
> But this lawsuit has brought me nothing but anxiety. Why are all of these defendants willing to settle? Is this so obviously efficient for them? Is it that they fear litigation costs, or is it the damages juries would provide as a result of the devastating illnesses implant wearers may develop that drives them to settle? When I had my procedure, I was not aware of medical problems. I was told that my implants "may not take" and, if so, I could "do it again." I was not told of the slew of conditions I

was now vulnerable to, ranging from the uncomfortable to downright debilitating: systemic sclerosis, systemic lupus erythematosus, atypical neurological disease syndrome, mixed connective tissue disease, polymyositis, atypical connective tissue disease, primary Sjögren's syndrome, atypical rheumatic syndrome, nonspecific autoimmune condition, etc.

Do I really think I will develop one of these ailments? No, I don't. But who is to say that is not a result of a heuristic: before today I had not heard of more than one or two of these ailments. A lifetime resident of California, I am more threatened by an earthquake than by an implant-caused disease. Will I feel the same way after the media finishes with their new starring show? Who knows? But the descriptions of these ailments has got me stirred up enough to consider opting out of this lawsuit.

"Plaintiff autonomy" is not what would drive me away from a class action suit. An enemy of L&E, it is actually a cost-benefit analysis that has me worried. The only reason for me to opt out of this suit, as I see it, is if I think that I could receive more money in a suit of my own. But the only reason that I would ever engage in a suit of my own with the intent of receiving more money than this settlement may provide is if I were ill enough to motivate me to spend a lot of my own time and money so that I may pull on the hearts and purse strings of jurors. It is at this point in my own academic analysis that I am driven to stop thinking. First, if I am so sick one day, say twenty-five years from now, will I want to be in court? Second, why am I entertaining the notion of being so sick? I think I would rather avoid the turmoil and expense of litigation. There is something frightening and frustrating about choosing to opt out of a settlement plan because, maybe, one day I will be so sick that I can recover more money if I litigate on my own.

Note that the author says that there is a point at which she stops thinking, and that she finds the situation of choosing to opt out frightening and frustrating. Is she concerned about constructing her "self" as a victim?

4. Why do some people refrain from claiming or leaving an injurious situation? Can the law aggravate the situation rather than, as it purports to do, alleviate it? How does that happen in general? How does that happen in the student's situation described in the last question?

Consider whether the law sometimes aggravates the problem because legal institutions, including lawyers for the *claimant*, separate her or him from the grievance. In this connection, consider the following comment on how law firms ought to handle claims that partners sexually harassed secretaries:

"The very best attorneys who ever came before me saw to it that their clients apologized," [Joyce] Green [former deputy director of commerce for fair housing of Virginia] says. "They didn't make them say things like, 'I'm sorry we discriminated against you.' Instead, they approached the thing gently and approached the plaintiff with respect, saying, 'My client detests discrimination. We do not tolerate it in our organization, and to prove it to you, we are going to make our employee—the culprit—take courses on discrimination. We are sincerely sorry you had an unpleasant experience with our organization, and we want you to know that what you've described to us is intolerable.'

"Claimants rarely stayed angry after hearing this. When I was conciliating difficult cases—which means I'd already decided the defendants were probably guilty of discrimination—the claimants and their attorneys would whisper to me apologetically during breaks and say they would really like to be rid of the whole mess, and really didn't expect to get any money out of the case, but they just weren't going to let the defendants off the hook until they saw some sign that the defendants understood that what they had done was wrong. I wish I had gotten a dollar every time that was said to me—and every time a claimant settled for nominal damages after the apology was made. (John Morris, "Does Being a Lawyer Mean Never Having to Say You're Sorry?" *American Lawyer*, Oct. 1994, p. 6.)

Do you think the student in the last question would be satisfied with such an approach and outcome? Should she be? Some have argued that alternative dispute resolution techniques further disempower the already disadvantaged by "persuading" them to accept solutions that they should regard as less satisfactory than the ones available through the formal legal system.

5. Recall the question from the preceding article: "[W]hy are Americans so slow to perceive injury, so reluctant to make claims, and so fearful of disputing—especially of litigating?" No doubt this question struck many of you as counterintuitive—not to say absurd. Are Americans "fearful of litigating"? Aren't we in fact the most litigious society in the world? Views differ. Around the time that this article was written, Chief Justice Warren Burger lamented:

One reason our courts have become overburdened is that Americans are increasingly turning to the courts for relief from a range of personal distresses and anxieties. Remedies for personal wrongs that once were considered the responsibility of institutions other than the courts are now boldly asserted as legal "entitlements." The courts have been expected to fill the void created by the decline of church, family, and neighborhood unity.[a]

In response to such complaints about the "litigation explosion," Marc Galanter examined legal statistics for various countries and found evidence to call into question the critics' characterization of the "hyperlitigious" United States. Among his findings:

- In terms of numbers of civil cases filed per capita, the United States ranked fourth out of sixteen developed countries, after New Zealand, Canada, and Australia. The United States at the time saw 44 civil cases filed per 1,000 people; top-ranked Australia had 62 cases per 1,000.

[a] Burger, *Isn't There a Better Way?* 68 A.B.A. J. 274, 275 (1982) (quoted in Marc Galanter, *What We Know and Don't Know (and Think We Know) about Our Allegedly Contentious and Litigious Society*, 31 UCLA L. Rev. 4 (1983).

- Three other countries (Denmark, Sweden, and the United Kingdom) registered more than 35 lawsuits per 1,000 people.
- In one area, however, the United States was a clear leader: the number of lawyers in the United States, more than 2,300 per million people, was more than double that of second- and third-ranked New Zealand and Australia.[b]

  Galanter's statistics date from the 1970s. In the decades that followed, the calls for "tort reform" became significantly louder. See, for example, Philip K. Howard, *The Death of Common Sense* (New York, 1994). Of course, there are many—not all of them lawyers—who say that the sins of the civil courts have been greatly exaggerated. See, for example, Carl T. Bogus, *Why Lawsuits Are Good for America* (New York 2001).

6. Sarat was inspired to revisit this article nearly twenty years after first writing it, after watching the film *The Sweet Hereafter*.[c] The 1997 film by Canadian director Atom Egoyan is based on a 1992 novel by Russell Banks, itself inspired by a 1989 incident in a small Texas town where a school bus went off the road, killing twenty-one children. The lawsuits, countersuits, and slander suits that followed in the wake of the accident tore the small town apart.

   In the film and the book, a number of the town's residents express distaste at the idea of turning their tragedy into a lawsuit; they see what happened as a terrible accident and their grief as a personal thing that they must deal with as individuals and a community. The lawyer responds, "There's no such thing as an accident. The word doesn't mean anything to me." His task is to represent his clients "only in their anger, not in their grief." Do you see why this story provoked Sarat to reexamine the issue of "naming" injury, assigning "blame," and "claiming" for redress?

7. We next describe an empirical study of claiming behavior, in connection with medical malpractice: Frank A. Sloan and Chee-Ruey Hsieh, *Injury, Liability, and the Decision to File a Medical Malpractice Claim*, 29 Law & Soc'y Rev. 413 (1995). It uses the "naming, blaming, claiming" framework. What in your view is the most interesting empirical conclusion the authors arrive at?

   For the past several decades, there has been an ongoing debate in the United States over the issue of tort claims for medical malpractice. Critics of malpractice suits say that they are driving up the cost of malpractice insurance, which in turn drives up the cost of health care for everyone. They point to "frivolous" lawsuits and generally paint a picture of medical professionals afraid to do their jobs for fear of being sued if the outcome is "less than perfect," regardless of whether there is any actual fault. The proposed solution usually involves making it harder to sue for malpractice or placing a limit on the amount of damages an injured party can recover.

   Much of the case for tort reform is based on anecdotal evidence of outrageous claims or jury awards and on appeals to "common sense." However,

---

[b] Galanter, at 52.

[c] Austin Sarat, *Exploring the Hidden Domains of Civil Justice: "Naming, Blaming, and Claiming" in Popular Culture*, 50 DePaul L. Rev. 425 (2000).

one major study of birth-related injuries calls into question the basic assumptions of the tort reform movement.

In Florida in the early 1990s, Frank Sloan of the Center for Health Policy Research and Education and the Department of Economics at Duke University and Chee-Ruey Hsieh of the Academia Sinica in Taipei conducted a series of interviews with two groups: 127 families who had experienced birth-related injuries and filed medical malpractice claims in the late 1980s and 963 women who had given birth in 1987. Both groups were asked details of their pregnancies, medical treatment, and personal characteristics; those in the first group, as well as those in the latter group who had suffered some sort of adverse outcome (stillbirth, infant death, or permanent injury to child), also gave details of that. Out of 963 births in the latter group, 220 had suffered some sort of adverse birth outcome (the group deliberately oversampled probable bad outcomes for the study), but none had brought suit. The researchers also obtained permission from families to obtain medical charts for mother and child.

The charts from both groups were then presented to practicing obstetricians for evaluation of the standard of care. Two obstetricians were assigned to each case, and they were not told whether the case resulted in a claim. The study tested for the following variables in determining who had filed a claim:
(1) the degree of physician liability, as judged by the reviewing obstetricians;
(2) the extent of injury;
(3) the availability to the injured party of funds from sources other than tort claim (i.e., insurance);
(4) the degree of patient negligence (smoking, drinking during pregnancy, etc.);
(5) nonpecuniary motives for claiming (i.e., information-forcing, revenge);
(6) psychological and information costs to the injured party of obtaining compensation (measured in length of relationship to doctor, knowledge of legal resources in community, etc.); and
(7) demographic variables and family income.

The researchers found a clear correlation between peer evaluation of liability and the filing of malpractice claims. They also found that more serious injuries (the researchers' category of "minor permanent" injuries included loss of fingers and deafness) were more likely to have resulted in lawsuits. In particular, cases that involved a stay of five days or more in the neonatal intensive care unit were three times as likely to wind up in court. Uninsured injury victims were also at least three times as likely as insured patients to seek redress of their injuries through malpractice claims. Likewise, only one third as many families brought suit against physicians who had told them at some earlier stage in the pregnancy that there "might be a problem" as those who did not receive such a warning. The researchers suggested that this indicated many people bring lawsuits to force the discovery of more information or, alternately, to punish doctors who kept them in the dark. Patients who had changed doctors recently were more than twice as likely to sue as those who had long-standing relationships with their physicians. In one case, patient behavior was different from what was expected: women who said they drank alcohol during pregnancy were more, not less, likely to file claims.

The reviewing obstetricians found indications of negligent medical practice in every case of an adverse result in which the patients were Medicaid recipients, unmarried, or nonwhite, suggesting that socioeconomic factors played a significant role in the quality of medical care. In spite of this, nonwhites were much less likely to file claims than whites. Family income was not found to be a factor in the probability of claiming.

Overall, the results of Sloan and Hsieh's study contradict the claims that innocent doctors are just as likely to be sued as negligent ones. They found that, rather than just seeking money, people were also likely to use the courts as a means of gathering information to determine whether there is fault that should then be pursued in litigation.

Furthermore, the researchers pointed to the fact that, of the 220 families in the larger group who had experienced an adverse outcome, none filed a legal claim. Twenty-three had sought the services of a lawyer but were unable to obtain them. This, combined with the fact that Florida has one of the highest rates of medical malpractice claims in the country, indicated that patients were not just suing when they had a "less than perfect" result. It indicated that both lawyers and potential plaintiffs were filtering possible claims. The obstetricians' peer review of patient files also indicated that they were largely choosing the same claims that medical professionals would single out as examples of substandard care. Finally, the relative tendency of uninsured clients to take doctors to court when they have suffered a medical injury indicated that the implementation of a universal health care system would substantially reduce the number of malpractice lawsuits.

(a) Why might families fail to claim in the case of "minor permanent" injuries that were clearly associated with medical negligence?

(b) Why might families who had experienced an adverse outcome be unable to retain a lawyer?

(c) Why do you suppose the study authors "oversampled" bad outcomes? What effect does this have on interpretation of their results?

C. How Real-World Problems Become Social and Legal Problems

The next reading is a historical study of how one specific workplace illness—silicosis in mine workers—became recognized as a social and legal problem. As you read, note the different institutions that got involved and particularly note the points at which "transformations" occurred.

■ *"The Street of Walking Death": Silicosis, Health,*
   and Labor in the Tri-State Region, 1900–1950
   GERALD MARKOWITZ AND DAVID ROSNER
   77 J. Am. Hist. 525 (1990). © Organization of American Historians, http://www.oah.org. Reprinted with permission

Disease and disability have been endemic to the American workplace. Unguarded machinery and unregulated conditions produced so many accidents that the muckrakers compared the hazards at work with the risks of war. By the early twentieth century, the intensification of work and the introduction of new technologies produced extraordinary health hazards. Higher concentrations of toxic dust and new chemical poisons created serious chronic diseases for much of the industrial workforce despite an improvement in health statistics for the American population as a whole.

The study of occupational disease in the United States reveals the interlocking nature of the seemingly separate histories of labor, business, government, and public health. In the first half of the twentieth century, workers, management, government officials, and professional groups negotiated over fundamentally different approaches to the problem of occupationally related disease. In doing so, they not only reached compromises on legislative issues but also raised fundamental questions regarding health risks in an advanced industrial society: Can occupational disease be distinguished from disease of nonindustrial origin? Is occupational disease an acceptable and normal condition of modern industrial society? Is government, management, or the worker responsible for the risks of work? If government has some responsibility, how should it regulate the workplace?

Each party to the debates developed a characteristic explanation and definition of disease. Workers often saw disease as rooted in long hours, poor ventilation, exposure to dusts and other toxins, and low wages that eliminated the possibility of proper housing, clothing, and food. Unions sometimes responded to the new conditions of work by making safety and health central issues in organizing drives. Management and the insurance industry often downplayed the significance of working conditions, placing major responsibility for illness on the life-style and living conditions of the workers and their families. Government officials, physicians, and other professionals assumed differing positions depending on economic and social conditions and the pressures on them from labor and management. Together, collective bargaining, strikes, attempts at government regulation, and professional movements to set standards for exposure to toxic materials constituted an ongoing negotiation over occupational disease. Each group's changing perspective gained ascendancy and legitimacy at a different historical moment, under specific social and economic circumstances.

This study examines how the changing interests, definitions, and politics of occupational health interacted with a prolonged labor struggle in the country's most productive lead and zinc mining area: the Tri-State region of Missouri, Kansas, and Oklahoma. Changing conditions of work there led to widespread silicosis, an industrial lung disease that by the 1930s "typifie[d] the whole occupational disease problem." The story of silicosis in the Tri-State offers a case study illustrating the complex social negotiation over industrial disease. . . .

Lead and zinc—critical minerals used in products ranging from steel and brass alloys to batteries, munitions, and gasoline—were central to the emergence of the United States as the world's leading industrial power. These metals are often found in the same location and extracted from the same mine. In the mid-nineteenth century, lead and zinc ores were discovered in the sparsely populated agricultural countryside of southwestern Missouri. In the midst of open prairie and rolling hills, prospectors established small mines to extract high-grade ore from outcroppings of flint and quartz just below the surface. Mining communities flourished, and by the turn of the century, the area around Joplin, Missouri, became the world's major source of lead and zinc ores.

At first the industry was highly competitive, with hundreds of mines owned by scores of different producers. Before 1900, two-man teams worked the mines using picks and shovels and a horse or windlass to hoist the ore cans to the surface. One worker below ground broke rock and shoveled it into the can while another waited above to unload it. While these relatively primitive methods worked effectively in shallow mines with limited ore content, they were not adequate for the deeper and more extensive deposits. In the early twentieth century, larger and better capitalized companies began using more sophisticated machinery, dynamite, and power tools as the center of the industry shifted from Joplin to richer deposits around Picher, Oklahoma. Spurred by the skyrocketing demand for lead and zinc created by the outbreak of war in Europe, such new companies exploited mineral deposits in underground chambers hundreds of feet below the surface.

The deeper, more mechanized mines exacerbated safety and health problems for the workers. Drillers, blasters, haulers, powdermen, and others faced daily perils from mine collapses and explosions. But the shovelers who broke up rock and loaded it into cans were the vast bulk of the work force and in the greatest danger. The cans held between 1,000 and 1,630 pounds of rock and ore and each physically fit shoveler filled between sixty and ninety cans in an eight-hour shift. David Montgomery notes that for nearly three centuries common laborers had generally lifted between 32,000 and 38,000 pounds a day. A healthy shoveler in the Tri-State mines, however, loaded about two or three times that amount. Each worker would load between 75,000 and 100,000 pounds of rock a day, leading one federal public health official to comment that "one can hardly realize the severity of this work without seeing it." . . .

The growing use of power drills and high-intensity explosives also created new dangers with profound impact on the long-term health of the miners and their families. The new techniques created immense amounts of very fine dust composed largely of silica, an extraordinarily potent industrial poison. By 1915, soon after the introduction of power tools and dynamite blasting, miners and their families in the Tri-State and elsewhere were developing debilitating and life-threatening lung conditions. Miners in the Joplin area were at greater risk of dying from disease than from accidents, and their families had extraordinarily high death rates from tuberculosis. One owner told the United States Bureau of Mines that he had employed 750 men between 1907 and 1914. A year later, he reported, "only about 50 of these were still living, and all the others except not more than a dozen were said to have died" from tuberculosis.

Changing work conditions and the increasing prevalence of lung diseases spurred organizing drives in the Tri-State area. As ownership of the mines passed from entrepreneurs working in small teams to corporations such as the Eagle-Picher Lead Company, labor relations deteriorated. The Western Federation of Miners (WFM), then affiliated with the Industrial Workers of the World, organized a local in Joplin in 1906. By 1910, the union had achieved a membership of over six hundred, despite high labor turnover and out-migration of miners and their families. In that year, they struck to protest working conditions and poor pay. Although the strike was broken, five years later an independent, grass-roots union, the American Metal Miners Union, conducted another bitter strike over health and safety conditions. The union demanded the use of wet drilling to cut down on dust levels, the observance of existing state safety laws and standards, and the inclusion of occupational disease in workers' compensation statutes. Lacking external support and operating within a community that was totally controlled by the mine owners, the union lost the strike and soon collapsed. For the next decade and half, management dominated both the region and the definition of industrial disease that prevailed there. . . .

The Public Health Service Recognizes Silicosis

In 1914, the United States Public Health Service and the United States Bureau of Mines began the detailed study that identified silicosis as a separate and distinct lung condition. During the 1920s, public health professionals recognized it as the leading occupational illness of hard-rock miners, granite cutters, potters, buffers, glassworkers, sandblasters, and foundry and steelworkers. By the 1930s, it was generally considered the most important occupational disease in the country. Associated with the inhalation of finely ground silica dust, the disease was known by a variety of names: miners' asthma, stonecutters' phthisis, potters' rot, and pneumonoconiosis. The Public Health Service report, issued in 1917, laid out the clinical characteristics of the disease. "If we can imagine a man with his chest bound with transparent adhesive plaster, we can form a mental picture of how useless were the efforts at deep inhalation made by these patients.". . .

The disabilities and dependency caused by silicosis were a tremendous burden for families, but the community's plight was made worse by another scourge, tuberculosis. Since the 1880s, tuberculosis rates for the nation as a whole had been steadily declining. But in the Tri-State region, the trend was reversed. Rates of tuberculosis among its mining communities were high and actually on the rise. For the whole United States, the death rate from tuberculosis dropped from about 200 per 100,000 persons in 1900 to 160 per 100,000 in 1910 and 120 per 100,000 in 1920. In Jasper County (which included Joplin), in contrast, the death rate from tuberculosis stood at 200.8 per 100,000 in 1911. By 1913 the rate had increased to 229.7 per 100,000. Bureau of Mines officials suggested that the reported death rate understated the true prevalence of the disease.

Public health officials were aware of this terrible anomaly, which they explained in part in traditional terms—poor housing, inadequate or nonexistent sanitation, and the lack of heat and clothing. But they also posited a new explanation for the region's high rates of tuberculosis. They maintained that silicosis, an occupational disease, predisposed its victims to the double jeopardy of tuberculosis. Their argument overturned the common understanding of tuberculosis as a disease caused by poverty, poor living conditions, and unhygienic personal practices. The report emphasized the responsibility of the workplace in its creation. "While the cause of miners' consumption [silicosis] is found entirely in the underground work of the miners, yet the poor and often wretched conditions under which so many live, and the presence of tuberculosis foci all combined to reduce their vitality and resistance, on the one hand, and directly to increase their chances of tuberculosis infection on the other." Silicosis in the work force was the seedbed for tuberculosis in the community. Although silicosis was not communicable, it led to high rates of tuberculosis among the miners, placing their families at risk. The high rates of tuberculosis in the region therefore resulted from working conditions in the mines.

During the 1920s, in response to the report and the continuing labor agitation, industry and government took some measures to investigate and alleviate the threats to miners' health. Owners of some of the larger mines introduced "wet" drilling techniques in which water was constantly applied to the rock as it drilled. Industry officials predicted that "in two or three more years" silicosis would "be a thing of the past in the southwest Missouri district." Major industrial insurance companies such as Metropolitan Life Insurance Company and the Prudential Insurance Company of America had studied the effect of dust on workers' health. Their statisticians had concluded that mineral dust posed a substantial health hazard and, indirectly, a potential liability problem. If mineral dust caused disease and workers could show that employers knew of the hazard, workers could sue to recover damages for their illnesses. If industry and insurance companies could show that they had taken appropriate precautions to alleviate the dust hazard, they would prevail in such lawsuits. The interests of the Public Health Service and Bureau of Mines in evaluating the technological means of limiting exposure to dust and the industry's interest in "self-protection" led the federal government, the mining companies, and Metropolitan Life to organize a clinic to determine the extent of silicosis among Tri-State miners. The study evaluated 7,722 miners and prospective employees in the Picher area between July 1, 1927, and June 30, 1928. Contrary to the hopes of mine industry officials, however, researchers found that silicosis remained a major problem. . . .

Despite all the attention given to the Tri-State region, improvements in health status remained relatively limited. The stagnation resulted in part from mineowners' resistance to change in traditional practices. But another cause was that neither the Public Health Service nor the Bureau of Mines had statutory authority to enter the mines, much less to mandate reforms. To conduct their studies, officials of those agencies had to win the confidence of mineowners. Rather than publicly condemn the unhealthy conditions, the agencies sought privately to educate and cajole owners to make necessary reforms. They also allowed mineowners and the insurance company to administer and control the Picher Clinic for their own purposes. While management and government claimed that the clinic was part of a program "to improve the working conditions in the district," the workers claimed that the producers used the clinic to diagnose diseased miners and fire them. . . .

Labor Conflict over Silicosis

During the depression, conflict over deteriorating health conditions reached a climax as employment in the Tri-State mines plummeted from over 7,000 in 1929 to 1,331 in 1932. The International Union of Mine, Mill, and Smelter Workers began a concerted organizing effort that stressed the hazards of silicosis and tuberculosis as well as inadequate wages and speedups and other harsh working conditions. Inspired by Section 7(a) of the National Industrial Recovery Act, Mine-Mill representatives organized broadly, seeking to unionize "nearly everyone in the [Tri-State] district." In addition to organizing the miners, Mine-Mill set about developing a union of retail clerks, public relief workers, and smelter and lead plant workers in Galena and Joplin. While they made traditional demands for higher wages and shorter hours, the union organizers also called for "elimination of the examining bureau or clinic, so that physical examination would no longer be necessary and many unemployed men would be able to get jobs." The union charged that the decline in employment in the region and the use of the clinic to eliminate diseased workers masked the true prevalence of disease among workers and their families. Because most federal surveys only studied employed workers, they conveyed the misleading impression that conditions in the area's mines had improved. In a 1935 letter to Secretary of Labor Frances Perkins, James Robinson, the secretary-treasurer of the Mine-Mill International, noted that a census study that examined miners, working and unemployed, found 205 cases of silicosis in 544 homes in the city of Picher. He charged that "the mining companies in this district make no effort to alleviate this condition."

The international was well suited to organize the Tri-State because of its commitment to industrial unionism and mass organizing. Drawing on a radical and syndicalist heritage, Mine-Mill sought to organize the larger community to counteract mineowners' control of the economic and political life of the region. The problems of the work force transcended the workplace, inching into the home and community. The mines created dependence and disease. Silicosis and tuberculosis were part of a single problem that destroyed miners' health and their ability to earn a living and support their families. Writing to Eleanor Roosevelt, the secretary of one union local offered to send "plenty of factual and documentary evidence that men are dieing like flies and that 8 out of every 10 women in this district are widows, 75 percent of the children orphans." The union claimed that mineowners preferred to spend money "to buy tear gas, munitions, and to hire thugs and gunmen to terrorize union men and women" rather than to install "air cleaning devices" to combat silicosis.

While the union argued that it was impossible to separate the issues of work and community, the Tri-State Zinc and Lead Ore Producers Association maintained that those issues were unrelated and refused to bargain with a union that represented "a host of unemployed, and relief workers." Faced by the intransigence of the mineowners, the union called a strike in May 1935 against the producers, but union propaganda gave particular attention to the Eagle-Picher Lead Company, the area's largest producer. The company locked its workers out and established a company union that quickly negotiated a contract, which brought about two thousand of the forty-eight hundred workers back into the mines.

The owners' near total control over the region forced the international to seek national attention. After the National Labor Relations Act (NLRA) was passed in 1935, the international filed an unfair practices suit against Eagle-Picher with the National Labor Relations Board (NLRB) and also appealed for recognition as the bargaining agent for workers in the area. To prevent NLRB hearings, management obtained an injunction, which was in force until after the Supreme Court upheld the constitutionality of the NLRA in 1937. At the hearings, held in 1937 and 1938, scores of witnesses testified to the vicious union-busting tactics of the mineowners. In October 1939, the NLRB "confirmed most of the complaints of discrimination and denial of rights protected by the federal law."

Although the union was "fighting...in our strike to have pure air pumped down to the miners," union representatives did not raise the issue of health and disease in the hearings. The narrow requirements for determining unfair labor practices under the NLRA forced the international to ignore or deny the pervasiveness of disease and disability in the Tri-State. The union had to prove that the companies discriminated against union members, not that work conditions were horrendous. Management's strategy, however, was to show that a wide range of factors went into decisions to hire or fire workers. Disease or disability was, for management, one such factor. By showing that workers were diseased, the owners could claim that union busting was not their aim and that the union's suit was frivolous.

The union forged alliances both with the New Deal administration and with the political Left. During the 1936 election, the union attacked Roosevelt's Republican opponent, Alf Landon, then governor of Kansas, who had ordered the Kansas National Guard into the Tri-State area in June 1935. In a demonstration at a Landon rally in New York, union organizers carried a mock coffin with the inscription: "Here lies the body of one of the victims of the dreaded mine disease of Kansas-silicosis. This and thousands of other lives would have been saved if Landon had compelled the mine owners to take elementary safety measures to stop the spread of silicosis." The *New York Times* commented that this "Communist-arranged 'coffin act' stole the show."

The union's concern about silicosis paralleled and stimulated national consciousness of the issue. Just months before, in 1935, the nation had been rocked by the discovery of unmarked graves holding the bodies of hundreds of workers who had died of silicosis while drilling a tunnel for the Union Carbide Corporation in Gauley Bridge, West Virginia. In early 1936 a congressional investigation of the deaths at Gauley Bridge coupled with numerous lawsuits by industrial workers exposed to silica had widened awareness of silicosis. By 1936, the issue had become so explosive that the Department of Labor sponsored a National Silicosis Conference. The conference, dominated by business groups and public health professionals, recommended including silicosis in state workers' compensation laws, but it failed to quell growing public concern about the prevalence of the disease.

By the late 1930s, silicosis had transcended the domains of professionals, management, insurance, and labor. The groundwork had been laid for liberal and left-wing political groups to transform silicosis into a symbol. Just as the Scottsboro case represented lynch justice in the South, so silicosis in the Tri-State represented corporate greed that caused the slow death of working-class communities. The major propaganda effort on behalf of the workers was spearheaded by the National Committee for People's Rights, a left-wing organization based in New York whose leadership included such well-known Popular Front figures as Rockwell Kent. In fall 1939, the committee issued a report publicizing living, working, and health conditions of the Tri-State region. It charged that conditions in the area "represented a denial of the basic rights of decent living to a whole community, and therefore had to be considered as a matter of concern to the nation itself." It described the substandard housing, noting that living conditions had not improved since the Public Health Service first surveyed them twenty-five years earlier. It reminded readers that this poor housing contributed to the high tuberculosis rate in the area and that the poor sanitation exacerbated health problems in the area. While commending the owners of the mines for initiating efforts to control the dust hazard, the report pointed toward the inadequacy of those efforts. . . .

The national media picked up on the report. *Time* magazine, in an article titled "Zinc Stink," noted that silicosis was not only an occupational disease but also "a public health menace." The *New Republic*, in an article titled "American Plague Spot," suggested that the report should be "compulsory reading for all those who, under the pressure of news of wholesale misery abroad have forgotten that we have our share of it at home." Carrying out the report's recommendations required "educating the employers to their responsibility toward something besides profits.... Their best energies seem so far to have been aimed at crippling the miners' attempts to better their lot through organization." Even *Business Week* devoted a major article to what it called "a sizzling report detailing desperate living conditions among the miners." Walter Winchell announced on his radio program that the National Committee for People's Rights "would release a scandalous exposé of living and working conditions in the Tri-State mining district."...

The owners sought to counter this publicity in October 1939 by dispatching their secretary and spokesperson, Evan Just, to Washington to confer with Verne Zimmer, the director of the Department of Labor's Division of Labor Standards. The division had been organized in 1934 by Frances Perkins to develop national standards for hours, wages, and working conditions; one of its priorities was safety and health. In a summary of the meeting, Zimmer recorded that he initially believed Just wanted an investigation that would be "a white wash" of the producers' culpability for Tri-State problems. But Zimmer found that Just's true agenda was to keep the Department of Labor from intervening in any way. To the suggestion that the Department of Labor conduct a survey of the health and living conditions in the area, Just "rather hesitantly suggested that it would perhaps be more desirable if we did not come into the picture inasmuch as the employers in this section feel that the Labor Department is radical and definitely prejudiced." Just feared "that any investigation would be in the nature of a star chamber proceeding." The producers preferred that federal involvement come through the Public Health Service which had a long and sympathetic relationship with the mineowners. Zimmer, however, pointed out to Just "that Labor had more confidence in the Department of Labor... [because] the previous investigations [by the Public Health Service] resulted in no permanent improvements in the area from the standpoint of the worker."

Responding to pressure for recognition of health issues as a source of labor-management discord from local union representatives and the National Committee for People's Rights, the Department of Labor became involved in the Tri-State controversy. The department's entrance into the Tri-State highlighted two fundamentally different federal approaches to occupational safety and health issues. The Public Health Service and the Department of Labor's Division of Labor Standards, the federal agencies most directly involved in occupational safety and health issues, agreed that it was essential to identify the variety and types of industrial health hazards. But beyond this, there was little consensus. Because the Public Health Service had no statutory power to enter mines or to compel owners to remedy conditions unless they produced epidemic disease, the service relied on voluntary cooperation between the government and the industry. Its offices saw the issue of occupational safety and health as primarily a medical, not a labor, matter to be addressed by physicians and state public health officials. They believed that state departments of health and the Public Health Service should be neutral, objective, scientific agencies aloof from the political battles engulfing the labor movement in the 1930s. The service's primary role was to gather scientific information and distribute it to interested parties in the faith that knowledge itself would bring change. Under Secretary Perkins the Department of Labor took an activist and interventionist approach. Many of the administrators responsible for its safety and health activities believed that scientific study had to be part of a strong enforcement program with the right to inspect and issue corrective orders. It was not sufficient to study the medical problems that workers experienced; such study had to be linked to rebuilding, reorganizing, and reforming the workplace. Administrators in the Division of Labor Standards saw themselves as advocates, responsible for securing better conditions for their constituency. In the words of one of its top administrators, Clara Beyer, the division "should be a service agency for labor, just as the Department of Commerce is a service agency for business." They believed that the division could be more effective in securing change by aligning itself with labor than by maintaining neutrality. Division officials complained that the United States Public Health Service's neutrality usually reinforced the status quo and was tantamount to collaboration with industry.

By 1939 national publicity about the plight of Tri-State workers and their families had focused attention on the failure of the Public Health Service approach to industrial hygiene. Unlike other labor disputes that were wholly within one state, the problems of the Tri-State demanded federal coordination, at least. Further, the outbreak of war in Europe and the potential involvement of the United States made a settlement more urgent. In this context the Labor Department superseded the Public Health Service as the major federal agency in the region. Immediately after meeting with Just, Zimmer wrote to Perkins suggesting that the Labor Department call a conference of all the interested parties in the Tri-State. By doing so, the department would directly challenge the Public Health Service's longstanding cooperative and low-key approach to the problems of the area. Zimmer argued that the old Public Health Service approach, which involved owners, professionals, and government representatives but excluded workers and their representatives, had failed. Public health advocates and management viewed silicosis as a medical and public health problem, but it was also "a labor problem," he maintained, and that aspect had previously been neglected. It was also a federal rather than local issue because "the problem crosses state lines and . . . any remedial program involves unified effort by the states along with some help from the Federal Government." Predicting that silicosis in the area would get worse because of the "increasing activity due to war conditions," Zimmer saw a need to focus national attention on the Tri-State to stimulate action, rather than study.

In light of the new national significance of the Tri-State struggle, Zimmer hoped that federal power and publicity could be used to counter the enormous influence of mineowners at the state and local level. For years he had been frustrated by the Oklahoma Department of Labor's inability to act on behalf of the miners. The state labor commissioner acknowledged that "there always has been a serious condition in that section of our State," but, he confided to Zimmer, he was helpless to initiate action because of opposition from management. Another official confessed that he had avoided enforcing safety and health regulations in the Picher district for fear of destroying the mining economy of the area. Such confessions reinforced Zimmer's resolve to push Perkins to call a conference.

In April 1940, the two-day conference convened in Joplin, Missouri. It was the culmination of forty years of debate over silicosis, tuberculosis, and responsibility for disease in the Tri-State. Labor strife had forced government, management, union officials and others to attend, and the relationship of health and disease to the broader labor struggle dominated the conference. The debates among representatives of labor, managers, industrial hygienists, and government officials brought into high relief the question of who should bear the responsibility for risk.

The Conference

The position papers and proceedings of the conference revealed the intense politics that shaped the ostensibly objective and scientific debates over disease and public health. In the course of arguments over who should pay for the costs in life and limb of unsafe and unhealthy working conditions, a much more fundamental debate over the very notion of disease emerged. The mineowners promoted the view that industrialization had made the traditional dichotomy between the healthy and the diseased meaningless. The common understanding of medicine and public health had not kept pace with the revolutionary industrial changes that exposed millions of people to man-made dusts and chemicals. In modern societies dependent on coal, gasoline, and other new sources of energy, dust in the working and living environment was no longer exceptional. To inhale dust was a normal everyday occurrence for people living in industrial communities and cities. Under these modern conditions, health and disease were part of one continuum, not two dichotomous categories. The presence of dust in workers' lungs was not pathological; only "excessive" amounts that limited their activity could be considered pathological. Management argued that the boundaries between normal and abnormal, healthy and diseased, had to be redrawn to accommodate the new industrial realities.

Labor representatives and their advocates in the Department of Labor argued from a more traditional model of health and disease. The presence of dust and chemicals in the environment, however prevalent, could not be considered normal. In humans, they produced physiological changes that were part of a disease process. Such changes in working and living conditions indicated a fundamental imbalance between humans and their environment. Especially in the case of industrial disease, such imbalances were not natural but the product of choices made by the community. Disease was the result of conscious social decisions, and it was the role of social workers, public health and labor officials, and management to control and regulate the environment to protect the public.

Management and labor could have such radically different interpretations of the origins and nature of silicosis because chronic industrial disease posed a host of new problems for the medical and public health community. The cause and effect of such disease (unlike the causes and effects of accidents) were rarely clear-cut. Except in cases of acute poisoning or death, chronic disease might not show symptoms. Often, symptoms appeared years, even decades, after exposure to toxins. Some workers were affected by relatively limited exposures to toxic materials while others were far more tolerant. Some workers showed physiological changes without exhibiting behavioral symptoms. Others showed no physiological change yet found themselves losing strength. In the case of silicosis, diagnosis of the disease did not preclude conflicting opinions about its importance in the life of a worker. Some medical and public health experts believed that mild silicosis rarely interfered with the workers' ability to earn a living; hence the condition was of little significance.

Others believed that physical limitation, whether affecting work or not, was unacceptable and should be redressed. In the face of such medical uncertainty, the political agendas of management and labor became especially critical. . . .

Although the conference produced few concrete results, labor spokespeople were euphoric over the support they had gotten from Perkins and the Department of Labor. Reid Robinson, president of the Mine-Mill international, wrote Zimmer saying it was "one of the greatest things that has happened in the Tri-State area for many years." The publicity generated by the conference combined with the successful conclusion of the NLRB hearing to give new life to the union. An organizing drive undertaken in October 1941 made silicosis and health central issues once more: "During the past 20 or 30 years," one organizer declared, "thousands of miners, millmen and smeltermen have died from silicosis. . . . Many of these workers have been 'cliniced out' as soon as the company discovered the individual's health to be in a failing condition." The efforts reached fruition in 1946 with the successful organizing of all the Eagle-Picher plants and most of the other plants in the district. In mines throughout the area, joint union-management safety committees were formed, and ventilating equipment was installed in some of the worst. Silicosis was not eliminated as a hazard for drillers, haulers, and shovelers, but the union had established a mechanism for addressing health problems.

Temporary wartime changes in the area's economy contributed to the success of the union's efforts. As many of the healthy, younger men entered the armed forces, management turned to diseased or partially disabled and formerly blacklisted workers. By building defense plants, the federal government diversified the region's economy, thereby undermining the producers' control. In a memo to Perkins, Zimmer hailed the army's decision (which the Labor Department had strongly lobbied for) to build a nitrate plant in "our pet problem district in the country." He hoped that it would provide alternate employment for miners who had been fired or disabled by disease.

The Post-War Defeat of the Unions

However, the union victories were short-lived. The return of workers from the war gave management a new source of labor, and alternative employment once again became scarce. Furthermore, President Harry S. Truman's veto of wartime subsidies for lead and zinc undercut the union by forcing nearly all the mines to shut down or scale back production. Eagle-Picher closed twenty-four out of thirty-one mines immediately, and the smaller companies quickly followed suit as they were unable to compete with the more efficient western mines and cheaper foreign operations.

The crowning blow was the political attack on the left-wing International Union of Mine, Mill, and Smelter Workers. The passage of the Taft-Hartley Act of 1947 and, specifically, its requirement that unions seeking protection under the NLRA file affidavits affirming that their officers were not members of the Communist party tolled the death knell for the union in the Tri-State. More conservative unions began organizing in the area, including the United Cement, Lime, and Gypsum International Union, an American Federation of Labor union, and the Cherry Tri-State Association, a company union. In 1949, the NLRB authorized a new certification election that excluded Mine-Mill from the ballot because its officers had refused to sign the anticommunist affidavit. Mounting a last-ditch effort, the international emphasized safety and health, urging miners to "remember what it used to be like" before the union organized the region: "Hey, Joe Remember? When you didn't know what wet drilling was and you had to eat the dirt and die like flies with the con[sumption]?... When you had no say about the safety conditions?" In a futile attempt to remain the bargaining unit, the international urged miners to vote for "neither" of the other unions on the ballot. This campaign was the last serious attempt by Mine-Mill to maintain its position in the region.

In the 1950s and 1960s, the international continued to press the issue of silicosis on the national level, but in the Tri-State, with the union destroyed and the region in economic decline, the issue faded. With the passing of the New Deal, the resignation of Secretary Perkins, and the death of the Division of Labor Standards head Verne Zimmer, silicosis ceased to be a priority for an increasingly conservative Labor Department. Silicosis has continued to be a problem for miners, stonecutters, polishers, and others. In 1980, the United States Department of Labor estimated that over a million workers were exposed to silica dust and that nearly sixty thousand had contracted the disease nationwide....

What can we learn from the experience of the Tri-State struggle? How does work-linked disease become a part of the working-class experience? How does that experience shape the awareness of the scientific and medical communities? What have the experiences of the zinc and lead miners taught us about how occupational disease comes to be defined and ultimately controlled? Together, these questions tell us why historians should pay attention to this episode. To understand this prolonged conflict demands attention to the interrelationships among labor, business, political, and public health interests. As the process of production changed with the introduction of new tools and the intensification of work, workers were exposed to new and potentially more hazardous conditions. In the Tri-State, they organized and struggled to resist those changes. As larger companies employed pneumatic tools and introduced piecework into the mines, the conditions for labor unrest developed and focused attention of public health officials on the area. After the defeat of the union in 1915, management gained hegemony over the region and the issue of industrial disease was defined in purely medical and technical terms. It was not until the Great Depression, as the labor movement revitalized and thousands of workers were dismissed from their jobs, that health and disease were redefined as a social and labor issue as well. Ultimately, the definition of occupational disease depended on the social and economic context within which different groups vied for legitimacy and control. With the end of World War II, the issue was once again transformed into a medical and engineering problem. Without the pressures created by unemployment and labor strife, professionals could once again assert control over the issue.

Not until the 1960s, when coal miners, textile workers, asbestos workers, and others once again mobilized around the issues of industrial lung diseases, was occupational health placed back on the national agenda. The changing social environment again forced workers to struggle over the very definition of disease. The struggle involved public health workers, government, and industry in a public discourse over who was responsible for creating disease. That discourse ultimately led to the passage of national legislation, specifically the Federal Coal Mine Health and Safety Act of 1969 and the Occupational Safety and Health Act of 1970. These acts embodied the view of labor and its allies that the business community bore responsibility for the creation of occupational disease and that federal regulation was essential to protect workers from unhealthful conditions.

COMMENTS AND QUESTIONS

1. Recently, there have been assertions that long-term use of standard-design computer keyboards causes many cases of carpal tunnel syndrome (a painful condition affecting the use of one's hands). Suppose public health officials conclude that these assertions are correct and that alternative designs would not cause as many cases. What, if anything, makes this situation different from the one described in "The Street of Walking Death"? Who are the affected parties? How are they organized? What resources do they have?

2. Think about what kinds of legal responses might be appropriate to the carpal tunnel syndrome problem and how they might be brought about. One such response, as you've seen in connection with *Farwell* in chapter 1, is to leave it to keyboard operators, their employers, and keyboard manufacturers to work out a solution. On the one hand, this can be characterized as the "do nothing" solution, with the implication that the outcome will reproduce inequalities present in the status quo. On the other hand, it can be characterized as the "leave it to the market" solution, with the implication that the outcome will be satisfactory to all involved parties.

3. One setting in which courts have been called upon to decide whether a legally relevant injury has occurred—or to decide the merits of "claiming"—is in applying the Americans with Disabilities Act (ADA). The statute prohibits workplace discrimination on the basis of disability, and it defines disability as "a physical or mental impairment that substantially limits one or more of the major life activities." 42 U.S.C. § 12102(2)(A). In *Toyota Motor Mfg., Ky. v. Williams*, 534 U.S. 184 (2002), the Supreme Court held that the lower court had too hastily concluded that a woman who had carpal tunnel syndrome was disabled within the meaning of the ADA. The Court stated that the proper inquiry was to "ask whether respondent's impairments prevented or restricted her from performing tasks that are of central importance to most people's daily lives." Of the plaintiff's specific physical limitations, the Court had this to say:

   > [Plaintiff] admitted that she was able to do the manual tasks required by her original two jobs. . . . In addition, according to [plaintiff's] deposition testimony, even after her condition worsened, she could still brush her teeth, wash her face, bathe, tend her flower garden, fix breakfast, do laundry, and pick up around the house. The record also indicates that her medical conditions caused her to avoid sweeping, to quit dancing, to occasionally seek help dressing, and to reduce how often she plays with her children, gardens, and drives long distances. But these changes in her life did not amount to such severe restrictions in the activities that are of central importance to most people's daily lives that they establish a manual-task disability as a matter of law.

   Note that the Court did not hold that carpal tunnel syndrome could not be a disability under the ADA; it held that this question was to be decided on a case-by-case basis. Despite its apparent narrowness, might the Court's ruling have a significant effect on claiming behavior under the act? On what grounds could the Court decide that quitting dancing and playing less with one's children were not limits on "major life activities"?

4. The mining sites in the Tri-State region were contaminated with hazardous materials such as lead, zinc, iron, and cadmium. What had been regarded (eventually) as a problem of workplace health became recognized (eventually) as a problem of environmental health as well. In the 1980s, the mining sites were slated to be cleaned up under the federal Superfund law, which allowed the government to clean up abandoned hazardous waste sites and then sue the responsible parties for the costs of cleanup. Eagle-Picher filed for bankruptcy as a result of its environmental liabilities. The rise of environmental consciousness occurred later than the increased awareness of workplace risks, one instance of which was described by Markowitz and Rosner. Rachel Carson's *Silent Spring* is widely regarded as the opening act in the modern environmental era. As you read the following excerpt from this book, think about the similarities and differences between the "naming" and "blaming" that might be inspired by this book and the "naming" and "blaming" documented by Markowitz and Rosner.

■ *Silent Spring*
RACHEL L. CARSON
pp. 16–23 (Mariner Books, 1962). Reprinted with permission
of Houghton Mifflin Co.

The history of life on earth has been a history of interaction between living things and their surroundings. To the large extent, the physical form and the habits of the earth's vegetation and its animal life have been molded by the environment. Considering the whole span of earthly time, the opposite effect, in which life actually modifies its surroundings, has been relatively slight. Only within the moment of time represented by the present century has one species—man—acquired significant power to alter the nature of his world.

During the past quarter century this power has not only increased to one of disturbing magnitude but it has changed in character. The most alarming of all man's assaults upon the environment is the contamination of air, earth, rivers, and sea with dangerous and even lethal materials. This pollution is for the most part irrecoverable; the chain of evil it initiates not only in the world that must support life but in living tissues is for the most part irreversible. In this now universal contamination of the environment, chemicals are the sinister and little-recognized partners of radiation in changing the very nature of the world—the very nature of its life. Strontium 90, released through nuclear explosions into the air, comes to earth in rain or drifts down as fallout, lodges in soil, enters into the grass or corn or wheat grown there, and in time takes up its abode in the bones of a human being, there to remain until his death. Similarly, chemicals sprayed on croplands or forests or gardens lie long in soil, entering into living organisms, passing from one to another in a chain of poisoning and death. Or they pass mysteriously by underground streams until they emerge and, through the alchemy of air and sunlight, combine into new forms that kill vegetation, sicken cattle, and work unknown harm on those who drink from once-pure wells. As Albert Schweitzer has said, "Man can hardly even recognize the devils of his own creation."

It took hundreds of millions of years to produce the life that now inhabits the earth—eons of time in which that developing and evolving and diversifying life reached a state of adjustment and balance with its surroundings. The environment, rigorously shaping and directing the life it supported, contained elements that were hostile as well as supporting. Certain rocks gave out dangerous radiation; even within the light of the sun, from which all life draws its energy, there were short-wave radiations with power to injure. Given time—time not in years but in millennia—life adjusts, and a balance has been reached. For time is the essential ingredient; but in the modern world there is no time.

The rapidity of change and the speed with which new situations are created follow the impetuous and heedless pace of man rather than the deliberate pace of nature. Radiation is no longer merely the background radiation of rocks, the bombardment of cosmic rays, the ultraviolet of the sun that have existed before there was any life on earth; radiation is now the unnatural creation of man's tampering with the atom. The chemicals to which life is asked to make its adjustment are no longer merely the calcium and silica and copper and all the rest of the minerals washed out of the rocks and carried in rivers to the sea; they are the synthetic creations of man's inventive mind, brewed in his laboratories, and having no counterparts in nature.

To adjust to these chemicals would require time on the scale that is nature's; it would require not merely the years of a man's life but the life of generations. And even this, were it by some miracle possible, would be futile, for the new chemicals come from our laboratories in an endless stream; almost five hundred annually find their way into actual use in the United States alone. The figure is staggering and its implications are not easily grasped—500 new chemicals to which the bodies of men and animals are required somehow to adapt each year, chemicals totally outside the limits of biologic experience.

Among them are many that are used in man's war against nature. Since the mid-1940's over 200 basic chemicals have been created for use in killing insects, weeds, rodents, and other organisms described in the modern vernacular as "pests"; and they are sold under several thousand different brand names.

These sprays, dusts, and aerosols are now applied almost universally to farms, gardens, forests, and homes—nonselective chemicals that have the power to kill every insect, the "good" and the "bad," to still the song of birds and the leaping of fish in the streams, to coat the leaves with a deadly film, and to linger on in the soil—all this though the intended target may be only a few weeds or insects. Can anyone believe it is possible to lay down such a barrage of poisons on the surface of the earth without making it unfit for all life? They should not be called "insecticides," but "biocides."

The whole process of spraying seems caught up in an endless spiral. Since DDT was released for civilian use, a process of escalation has been going on in which ever more toxic materials must be found. This has happened because insects, in a triumphant vindication of Darwin's principle of the survival of the fittest, have evolved super races immune to the particular insecticide used, hence a deadlier one always has to be developed—and then a deadlier one than that. It has happened also because, for reasons to be described later, destructive insects often undergo a "flareback," or resurgence, after spraying, in numbers greater than before. Thus the chemical war is never won, and all life is caught in its violent crossfire.

Along with the possibility of the extinction of mankind by nuclear war, the central problem of our age has therefore become the contamination of man's total environment with such substances of incredible potential for harm—substances that accumulate in the tissues of plants and animals and even penetrate the germ cells to shatter or alter the very material of heredity upon which the shape of the future depends.

Some would-be architects of our future look toward a time when it will be possible to alter the human germ plasm by design. But we may easily be doing so now by inadvertence, for many chemicals, like radiation, bring about gene mutations. It is ironic to think that man might determine his own future by something so seemingly trivial as the choice of an insect spray.

All this has been risked—for what? Future historians may well be amazed by our distorted sense of proportion. How could intelligent beings seek to control a few unwanted species by a method that contaminated the entire environment and brought the threat of disease and death even to their own kind? Yet this is precisely what we have done. We have done it, moreover, for reasons that collapse the moment we examine them. We are told that the enormous and expanding use of pesticides is necessary to maintain farm production. Yet is our real problem not one of *overproduction*? Our farms, despite measures to remove acreages from production and to pay farmers *not* to produce, have yielded such a staggering excess of crops that the American taxpayer in 1962 is paying out more than one billion dollars a year as the total carrying cost of the surplus-food storage program. And is the situation helped when one branch of the Agriculture Department tries to reduce production while another states, as it did in 1958, "It is believed generally that reduction of crop acreages under provisions of the Soil Bank will stimulate interest in use of chemicals to obtain maximum production on the land retained in crops."

All this is not to say there is no insect problem and no need of control. I am saying, rather, that control must be geared to realities, not to mythical situations, and that the methods employed must be such that they do not destroy us along with the insects.

The problem whose attempted solution has brought such a train of disaster in its wake is an accompaniment of our modern way of life. Long before the age of man, insects inhabited the earth—a group of extraordinarily varied and adaptable beings. Over the course of time since man's advent, a small percentage of the more than half a million species of insects have come into conflict with human welfare in two principal ways: as competitors for the food supply and as carriers of human disease.

Disease-carrying insects become important where human beings are crowded together, especially under conditions where sanitation is poor, as in time of natural disaster or war or in situations of extreme poverty and deprivation. Then control of some sort becomes necessary. It is a sobering fact, however, as we shall presently see, that the method of massive chemical control has had only limited success, and also threatens to worsen the very conditions it is intended to curb.

Under primitive agricultural conditions the farmer had few insect problems. These arose with the intensification of agriculture—the devotion of immense acreages to a single crop. Such a system set the stage for explosive increases in specific insect populations. Single-crop farming does not take advantage of the principles by which nature works; it is agriculture as an engineer might conceive it to be. Nature has introduced great variety into the landscape, but man has displayed a passion for simplifying it. Thus he undoes the built-in checks and balances by which nature holds the species within bounds. One important natural check is a limit on the amount of suitable habitat for each species. Obviously then, an insect that lives on wheat can build up its population to much higher levels on a farm devoted to wheat than on one in which wheat is intermingled with other crops to which the insect is not adapted.

The same thing happens in other situations. A generation or more ago, the towns of large areas of the United States lined their streets with the noble elm tree. Now the beauty they hopefully created is threatened with complete destruction as disease sweeps through the elms, carried by a beetle that would have only limited chance to build up large populations and to spread from tree to tree if the elms were only occasional trees in a richly diversified planting.

Another factor in the modern insect problem is one that must be viewed against a background of geologic and human history: the spreading of thousands of different kinds of organisms from their native homes to invade new territories. This worldwide migration has been studied and graphically described by the British ecologist Charles Elton in his recent book *The Ecology of Invasions*. During the Cretaceous Period, some hundred million years ago, flooding seas cut many land bridges between continents and living things found themselves confined in what Elton calls "colossal separate nature reserves." There, isolated from others of their kind, they developed many new species. When some of the land masses were joined again, about 15 million years ago, these species began to move out into new territories—a movement that is not only still in progress but is now receiving considerable assistance from man.

The importation of plants is the primary agent in the modern spread of species, for animals have almost invariably gone along with the plants, quarantine being a comparatively recent and not completely effective innovation. The United States Office of Plant Introduction alone has introduced almost 200,000 species and varieties of plants from all over the world. Nearly half of the 180 or so major insect enemies of plants in the United States are accidental imports from abroad, and most of them have come as hitchhikers on plants.

In new territory, out of reach of the restraining hand of the natural enemies that kept down its numbers in its native land, an invading plant or animal is able to become enormously abundant. Thus it is no accident that our most troublesome insects are introduced species.

These invasions, both the naturally occurring and those dependent on human assistance, are likely to continue indefinitely. Quarantine and massive chemical campaigns are only extremely expensive ways of buying time. We are faced, according to Dr. Elton, "with a life-and-death need not just to find new technological means of suppressing this plant or that animal"; instead we need the basic knowledge of animal populations and their relations to their surroundings that will "promote an even balance and damp down the explosive power of outbreaks and new invasions."

Much of the necessary knowledge is now available but we do not use it. We train ecologists in our universities and even employ them in our governmental agencies but we seldom take their advice. We allow the chemical death rain to fall as though there were no alternative, whereas in fact there are many; and our ingenuity could soon discover many more if given opportunity.

Have we fallen into a mesmerized state that makes us accept as inevitable that which is inferior or detrimental, as though having lost the will or the vision to demand that which is good? Such thinking, in the words of the ecologist Paul Shepard, "idealizes life with only its head out of water, inches above the limits of toleration of the corruption of its own environment.... Why should we tolerate a diet of weak poisons, a home in insipid surroundings, a circle of acquaintances who are not quite our enemies, the noise of motors with just enough relief to prevent insanity? Who would want to live in a world which is just not quite fatal?"

Yet such a world is pressed upon us. The crusade to create a chemically sterile, insect-free world seems to have engendered a fanatic zeal on the part of many specialists and most of the so-called control agencies. On every hand there is evidence that those engaged in spraying operations exercise a ruthless power. "The regulatory entomologists . . . function as prosecutor, judge and jury, tax assessor and collector and sheriff to enforce their own orders," said Connecticut entomologist Neely Turner. The most flagrant abuses go unchecked in both state and federal agencies.

It is not my contention that chemical insecticides must never be used. I do contend that we have put poisonous and biologically potent chemicals indiscriminately into the hands of persons largely or wholly ignorant of their potentials for harm. We have subjected enormous numbers of people to contact with these poisons, without their consent and often without their knowledge. If the Bill of Rights contains no guarantee that a citizen shall be secure against lethal poisons distributed either by private individuals or by public officials, it is surely only because our forefathers, despite their considerable wisdom and foresight, could conceive of no such problem.

I contend, furthermore, that we have allowed these chemicals to be used with little or no advance investigation of their effect on soil, water, wildlife, and man himself. Future generations are unlikely to condone our lack of prudent concern for the integrity of the natural world that supports all life.

There is still very limited awareness of the nature of the threat. This is in an era of specialists, each of whom sees his own problem and is unaware of or intolerant of the larger frame into which it fit. It is also an era dominated by industry, in which the right to make a dollar at whatever cost is seldom challenged. When the public protests, confronted with some obvious evidence of damaging results of pesticide applications, it is fed little tranquilizing pills of half truth. We urgently need an end to these false assurances, to the sugar coating of unpalatable facts. It is the public that is being asked to assume the risks that the insect controllers calculate. The public must decide whether it wishes to continue on the present road, and it can do so only when in full possession of the facts. In the words of Jean Rostand, "The obligation to endure gives us the right to know."

COMMENTS AND QUESTIONS

1. What is the injury Carson is naming here? Why might that injury go un-detected? How is this injury different from the injuries described by Rosner and Markowitz?

2. Whom is Carson blaming? Pesticide manufacturers? Farmers? The govern-ment? All of us?

3. *Silent Spring* had an enormous influence in awakening Americans' conscious-ness about the environment and environmental problems. Within a few years of its publication, Congress began enacting the numerous laws that now provide the backbone for environmental law in this country. Within a single decade—1970 to 1980—all of the major federal environmental laws were passed. We will encounter several of these laws in the materials on the modern regu-latory state.

4. The primary target of Carson's book was the pesticide DDT. The use of DDT presents a classic "commons" problem: each DDT user reaps all the benefits of use but suffers only a fraction of the costs, but anyone who forgoes use of DDT incurs all of the costs but must share the benefits with everyone else. With DDT, moreover, the "commons" is the whole world: given its persistence and transportability, DDT ends up far removed from the place of application. When scientists studying DDT's health effects were looking for a "control group" (a group that had not been exposed to DDT), they went to the far Arctic regions, thinking that surely people there would not have been exposed to the pesticide. What they found was surprising: not only had Arctic inhab-itants been exposed to DDT that had been applied in distant places but also their fat tissue (and the breast milk of nursing mothers) contained *more* DDT than the tissue and milk of inhabitants of industrialized countries.

5. What is the nature of the risk posed by DDT? Can that risk be meaningfully described exclusively by reference to the numerical probability and magnitude of the physical harms the pesticide produces? Or is it also helpful, for regu-latory purposes, to consider as well the qualitative features of the risks posed by DDT? Think of the qualitative features of risk described by Slovic. Doesn't DDT fall on the "bad" side of each of these? Its persistence and transportability mean that it ends up in places far removed from where it was applied and thus, probably, far removed from the places where it produced benefits; the distance between the place of application and the place where DDT winds up makes it difficult to control exposures to DDT; the scientific uncertainty sur-rounding analysis of DDT's risks make those risks unknown; and so on.

When DDT was finally banned by the Environmental Protection Agency in the early 1970s, the expected substitutes for it were the organophosphates. These are acutely toxic pesticides, dangerous mainly to the farmworkers who work with the pesticides and the crops on which they are applied. Which of Slovic's categories are occupied by the organophosphates? Does their acutely toxic nature, and the fact that they are dangerous mostly to farmworkers and pesticide applicators, put them on the "good" side of Slovic's categories—the voluntary, controllable, equitable side? Do Slovic's risk categories sometimes permit most of us to foist risks off on a few of us by concluding that occupational hazards are voluntary, controllable, and equitably imposed in exchange for money?

6. As we have seen, the problem of access bias is particularly severe in the context of environmental harms. Courts reviewing agency actions relating to environmental issues have not necessarily helped to solve this problem; indeed, as the following case indicates, they have arguably exacerbated the problem by placing limits on the kinds of injuries that support "standing" to sue in the federal courts.

■ Lujan v. Defenders of Wildlife
504 U.S. 555 (1992)

Justice Scalia delivered the opinion of the Court with respect to Parts I, II, III-A, and IV, and an opinion with respect to Part III-B, in which the Chief Justice, Justice White, and Justice Thomas join.

This case involves a challenge to a rule promulgated by the Secretary of the Interior interpreting § 7 of the Endangered Species Act of 1973 (ESA), 16 U.S.C. § 1536, in such fashion as to render it applicable only to actions within the United States or on the high seas. The preliminary issue, and the only one we reach, is whether respondents here, plaintiffs below, have standing to seek judicial review of the rule.

I

The ESA seeks to protect species of animals against threats to their continuing existence caused by man. See generally *TVA v. Hill*, 437 U.S. 153 (1978). The ESA instructs the Secretary of the Interior to promulgate by regulation a list of those species which are either endangered or threatened under enumerated criteria, and to define the critical habitat of these species. 16 U.S.C. §§ 1533, 1536. Section 7(a)(2) of the Act then provides, in pertinent part:

> "Each Federal agency shall, in consultation with and with the assistance of the Secretary [of the Interior], insure that any action authorized, funded, or carried out by such agency . . . is not likely to jeopardize the continued existence of any endangered species or threatened species or result in the destruction or adverse modification of habitat of such species which is determined by the Secretary, after consultation as appropriate with affected States, to be critical." 16 U.S.C. § 1536(a)(2).

In 1978, the Fish and Wildlife Service (FWS) and the National Marine Fisheries Service (NMFS), on behalf of the Secretary of the Interior and the Secretary of Commerce respectively, promulgated a joint regulation stating that the obligations imposed by § 7(a)(2) extend to actions taken in foreign nations. 43 Fed. Reg. 874 (1978). The next year, however, the Interior Department began to reexamine its position. A revised joint regulation, reinterpreting § 7(a)(2) to require consultation only for actions taken in the United States or on the high seas, was proposed in 1983, and promulgated in 1986.

Shortly thereafter, respondents, organizations dedicated to wildlife conservation and other environmental causes, filed this action against the Secretary of the

Interior, seeking a declaratory judgment that the new regulation is in error as to the geographic scope of § 7(a)(2) and an injunction requiring the Secretary to promulgate a new regulation restoring the initial interpretation. The District Court granted the Secretary's motion to dismiss for lack of standing. The Court of Appeals for the Eighth Circuit reversed by a divided vote. On remand, the Secretary moved for summary judgment on the standing issue, and respondents moved for summary judgment on the merits. The District Court denied the Secretary's motion, on the ground that the Eighth Circuit had already determined the standing question in this case; it granted respondents' merits motion, and ordered the Secretary to publish a revised regulation. The Eighth Circuit affirmed. We granted certiorari.

II

While the Constitution of the United States divides all power conferred upon the Federal Government into "legislative Powers," Art. I, § 1, "the executive Power," Art. II, § 1, and "the judicial Power," Art. III, § 1, it does not attempt to define those terms. To be sure, it limits the jurisdiction of federal courts to "Cases" and "Controversies," but an executive inquiry can bear the name "case" (the Hoffa case) and a legislative dispute can bear the name "controversy" (the Smoot-Hawley controversy). Obviously, then, the Constitution's central mechanism of separation of powers depends largely upon common understanding of what activities are appropriate to legislatures, to executives, and to courts. In The Federalist No. 48, Madison expressed the view that "it is not infrequently a question of real nicety in legislative bodies whether the operation of a particular measure will, or will not, extend beyond the legislative sphere," whereas "the executive power [is] restrained within a narrower compass and . . . more simple in its nature," and "the judiciary [is] described by landmarks still less uncertain." The Federalist No. 48, p. 256 (Carey and McClellan eds. 1990). One of those landmarks, setting apart the "Cases" and "Controversies" that are of the justiciable sort referred to in Article III— "serving to identify those disputes which are appropriately resolved through the judicial process," *Whitmore v. Arkansas*, 495 U.S. 149, 155 (1990)—is the doctrine of standing. Though some of its elements express merely prudential considerations that are part of judicial self-government, the core component of standing is an essential and unchanging part of the case-or-controversy requirement of Article III.

Over the years, our cases have established that the irreducible constitutional minimum of standing contains three elements. First, the plaintiff must have suffered an "injury in fact"—an invasion of a legally protected interest which is (a) concrete and particularized, see id., at 756; *Warth v. Seldin*, 422 U.S. 490, 508 (1975); and (b) "actual or imminent, not 'conjectural' or 'hypothetical,'" Whitmore, supra, at 155 (quoting *Los Angeles v. Lyons*, 461 U.S. 95, 102 (1983)). Second, there must be a causal connection between the injury and the conduct complained of—the injury has to be "fairly . . . trace[able] to the challenged action of the defendant, and not . . . the result [of] the independent action of some third party not before the court." *Simon v. Eastern Ky. Welfare Rights Organization*, 426 U.S. 26, 41-42 (1976). Third, it must be "likely," as opposed to merely "speculative," that the injury will be "redressed by a favorable decision." Id., at 38, 43.

The party invoking federal jurisdiction bears the burden of establishing these elements. Since they are not mere pleading requirements but rather an indispensable part of the plaintiff's case, each element must be supported in the same way as any other matter on which the plaintiff bears the burden of proof, i.e., with the manner and degree of evidence required at the successive stages of the litigation. At the pleading stage, general factual allegations of injury resulting from the defendant's conduct may suffice, for on a motion to dismiss we "presume that general allegations embrace those specific facts that are necessary to support the claim." *National Wildlife Federation*, supra, at 889. In response to a summary judgment motion, however, the plaintiff can no longer rest on such "mere allegations," but must "set forth" by affidavit or other evidence "specific facts," Fed. Rule Civ. Proc. 56(e), which for purposes of the summary judgment motion will be taken to be true. And at the final stage, those facts (if controverted) must be "supported adequately by the evidence adduced at trial." *Gladstone*, supra, at 115, n. 31.

When the suit is one challenging the legality of government action or inaction, the nature and extent of facts that must be averred (at the summary judgment stage) or proved (at the trial stage) in order to establish standing depends considerably upon whether the plaintiff is himself an object of the action (or forgone action) at issue. If he is, there is ordinarily little question that the action or inaction has caused him injury, and that a judgment preventing or requiring the action will redress it. When, however, as in this case, a plaintiff's asserted injury arises from the government's allegedly unlawful regulation (or lack of regulation) of someone else, much more is needed. In that circumstance, causation and redressability ordinarily hinge on the response of the regulated (or regulable) third party to the government action or inaction—and perhaps on the response of others as well. The existence of one or more of the essential elements of standing "depends on the unfettered choices made by independent actors not before the courts and whose exercise of broad and legitimate discretion the courts cannot presume either to control or to predict," *ASARCO Inc. v. Kadish*, 490 U.S. 605, 615 (1989) (opinion of Kennedy, J.); and it becomes the burden of the plaintiff to adduce facts showing that those choices have been or will be made in such manner as to produce causation and permit redressability of injury. Thus, when the plaintiff is not himself the object of the government action or inaction he challenges, standing is not precluded, but it is ordinarily "substantially more difficult" to establish. *Allen*, supra, at 758.

III

We think the Court of Appeals failed to apply the foregoing principles in denying the Secretary's motion for summary judgment. Respondents had not made the requisite demonstration of (at least) injury. . . .

Respondents' claim to injury is that the lack of consultation with respect to certain funded activities abroad "increas[es] the rate of extinction of endangered and threatened species." Complaint P5, App. 13. Of course, the desire to use or observe an animal species, even for purely esthetic purposes, is undeniably a cognizable interest for purpose of standing. See, e.g., *Sierra Club v. Morton*, 405 U.S. at 734. "But the 'injury in fact' test requires more than an injury to a cognizable interest. It requires that the party seeking review be himself among the injured." Id., at 734-735. To survive the Secretary's summary judgment motion, respondents had to submit affidavits or other evidence showing, through specific facts, not only that listed species were in fact being threatened by funded activities abroad, but also that one or more of respondents' members would thereby be "directly" affected apart from their " 'special interest' in the subject." Id., at 735, 739.

With respect to this aspect of the case, the Court of Appeals focused on the affidavits of two Defenders' members—Joyce Kelly and Amy Skilbred. Ms. Kelly stated that she traveled to Egypt in 1986 and "observed the traditional habitat of the endangered nile crocodile there and intend[s] to do so again, and hope[s] to observe the crocodile directly," and that she "will suffer harm in fact as the result of [the] American . . . role . . . in overseeing the rehabilitation of the Aswan High Dam on the Nile . . . and [in] developing . . . Egypt's . . . Master Water Plan." App. 101. Ms. Skilbred averred that she traveled to Sri Lanka in 1981 and "observed the habitat" of "endangered species such as the Asian elephant and the leopard" at what is now the site of the Mahaweli project funded by the Agency for International Development (AID), although she "was unable to see any of the endangered species"; "this development project," she continued, "will seriously reduce endangered, threatened, and endemic species habitat including areas that I visited . . . [, which] may severely shorten the future of these species"; that threat, she concluded, harmed her because she "intend[s] to return to Sri Lanka in the future and hope[s] to be more fortunate in spotting at least the endangered elephant and leopard." Id., at 145-146. When Ms. Skilbred was asked at a subsequent deposition if and when she had any plans to return to Sri Lanka, she reiterated that "I intend to go back to Sri Lanka," but confessed that she had no current plans: "I don't know [when]. There is a civil war going on right now. I don't know. Not next year, I will say. In the future." Id., at 318.

We shall assume for the sake of argument that these affidavits contain facts showing that certain agency-funded projects threaten listed species—though that is questionable. They plainly contain no facts, however, showing how damage to the species will produce "imminent" injury to Mses. Kelly and Skilbred. That the women "had visited" the areas of the projects before the projects commenced proves nothing. As we have said in a related context, " 'Past exposure to illegal conduct does not in itself show a present case or controversy regarding injunctive relief . . . if unaccompanied by any continuing, present adverse effects.' " *Lyons*, 461 U.S. at 102 (quoting *O'Shea v. Littleton*, 414 U.S. 488, 495-496 (1974)). And the affiants' profession of an "intent" to return to the places they had visited before—where they will presumably, this time, be deprived of the opportunity to observe animals of the endangered species—is simply not enough. Such "some day" intentions—without any description of concrete plans, or indeed even any specification of when the some day will be—do not support a finding of the "actual or imminent" injury that our cases require.[2]

---

[2] The dissent acknowledges the settled requirement that the injury complained of be, if not actual, then at least imminent, but it contends that respondents could get past summary judgment because "a reasonable finder of fact could conclude . . . that . . . Kelly or Skilbred will soon return to the project sites." This analysis suffers either from a factual or from a legal defect, depending on what the "soon" is supposed to mean. If "soon" refers to the standard mandated by our precedents—that the injury be "imminent," *Whitmore v. Arkansas*, 495 U.S. 149, 155 (1990)—we are at a loss to see how, as a factual matter, the standard can be met by respondents' mere profession of an intent, someday, to return. But if, as we suspect, "soon" means nothing more than "in this lifetime," then the dissent has undertaken quite a departure from our precedents. Although "imminence" is concededly a somewhat elastic concept, it cannot be stretched

Besides relying upon the Kelly and Skilbred affidavits, respondents propose a series of novel standing theories. The first, inelegantly styled "ecosystem nexus," proposes that any person who uses any part of a "contiguous ecosystem" adversely affected by a funded activity has standing even if the activity is located a great distance away. This approach, as the Court of Appeals correctly observed, is inconsistent with our opinion in National Wildlife Federation, which held that a plaintiff claiming injury from environmental damage must use the area affected by the challenged activity and not an area roughly "in the vicinity" of it. 497 U.S. at 887–889. It makes no difference that the general-purpose section of the ESA states that the Act was intended in part "to provide a means whereby the ecosystems upon which endangered species and threatened species depend may be conserved," 16 U.S.C. 1531(b). To say that the Act protects ecosystems is not to say that the Act creates (if it were possible) rights of action in persons who have not been injured in fact, that is, persons who use portions of an ecosystem not perceptibly affected by the unlawful action in question.

Respondents' other theories are called, alas, the "animal nexus" approach, whereby anyone who has an interest in studying or seeing the endangered animals anywhere on the globe has standing; and the "vocational nexus" approach, under which anyone with a professional interest in such animals can sue. Under these theories, anyone who goes to see Asian elephants in the Bronx Zoo, and anyone who is a keeper of Asian elephants in the Bronx Zoo, has standing to sue because the Director of the Agency for International Development (AID) did not consult with the Secretary regarding the AID-funded project in Sri Lanka. This is beyond all reason. Standing is not "an ingenious academic exercise in the conceivable," *United States v. Students Challenging Regulatory Agency Procedures (SCRAP)*, 412 U.S. 669, 688 (1973), but as we have said requires, at the summary judgment stage, a factual showing of perceptible harm. It is clear that the person who observes or works with a particular animal threatened by a federal decision is

---

beyond its purpose, which is to ensure that the alleged injury is not too speculative for Article III purposes—that the injury is "'*certainly* impending,'" id., at 158 (emphasis added). It has been stretched beyond the breaking point when, as here, the plaintiff alleges only an injury at some indefinite future time, and the acts necessary to make the injury happen are at least partly within the plaintiff's own control. In such circumstances, we have insisted that the injury proceed with a high degree of immediacy, so as to reduce the possibility of deciding a case in which no injury would have occurred at all.

There is no substance to the dissent's suggestion that imminence is demanded only when the alleged harm depends upon "the affirmative actions of third parties beyond a plaintiff's control." Our cases mention third-party-caused contingency, naturally enough; but they also mention the plaintiff's failure to show that he will soon expose himself to the injury. And there is certainly no reason in principle to demand evidence that third persons will take the action exposing the plaintiff to harm, while *presuming* that the plaintiff himself will do so. Our insistence upon these established requirements of standing does not mean that we would, as the dissent contends, "demand . . . detailed descriptions" of damages, such as a "nightly schedule of attempted activities" from plaintiffs alleging loss of consortium. That case and the others posited by the dissent all involve *actual* harm; the existence of standing is clear, though the precise extent of harm remains to be determined at trial. Where there is no actual harm, however, its imminence (though not its precise extent) must be established.

facing perceptible harm, since the very subject of his interest will no longer exist. It is even plausible—though it goes to the outermost limit of plausibility—to think that a person who observes or works with animals of a particular species in the very area of the world where that species is threatened by a federal decision is facing such harm, since some animals that might have been the subject of his interest will no longer exist, see *Japan Whaling Assn. v. American Cetacean Society*, 478 U.S. 221, 231, n. 4 (1986). It goes beyond the limit, however, and into pure speculation and fantasy, to say that anyone who observes or works with an endangered species, anywhere in the world, is appreciably harmed by a single project affecting some portion of that species with which he has no more specific connection.[3] . . .

IV

The Court of Appeals found that respondents had standing for an additional reason: because they had suffered a "procedural injury." The so-called "citizen-suit" provision of the ESA provides, in pertinent part, that "any person may commence a civil suit on his own behalf (A) to enjoin any person, including the United States and any other governmental instrumentality or agency . . . who is alleged to be in violation of any provision of this chapter." 16 U. S. C. § 1540(g). The court held that, because § 7(a)(2) requires interagency consultation, the citizen-suit provision creates a "procedural right" to consultation in all "persons"—so that anyone can file suit in federal court to challenge the Secretary's (or presumably any other

---

[3] The dissent embraces each of respondents' "nexus" theories, rejecting this portion of our analysis because it is "unable to see how the distant location of the destruction necessarily (for purposes of ruling at summary judgment) mitigates the harm" to the plaintiff. But summary judgment must be entered "against a party who fails to make a showing sufficient to establish the existence of an element essential to that party's case, and on which that party will bear the burden of proof at trial." *Celotex Corp. v. Catrett*, 477 U.S. 317, 322 (1986). Respondents had to adduce facts, therefore, on the basis of which it could reasonably be found that concrete injury to their members was, as our cases require, "certainly impending." The dissent may be correct that the geographic remoteness of those members (here in the United States) from Sri Lanka and Aswan does not "*necessarily*" prevent such a finding—but it assuredly does so when no further facts have been brought forward (and respondents have produced none) showing that the impact upon animals in those distant places will in some fashion be reflected here. The dissent's position to the contrary reduces to the notion that distance never prevents harm, a proposition we categorically reject. It cannot be that a person with an interest in an animal automatically has standing to enjoin federal threats to that species of animal, anywhere in the world. Were that the case, the plaintiff in Sierra Club, for example, could have avoided the necessity of establishing anyone's use of Mineral King by merely identifying one of its members interested in an endangered species of flora or fauna at that location. Justice Blackmun's accusation that a special rule is being crafted for "environmental claims" is correct, but *he* is the craftsman.

Justice Stevens, by contrast, would allow standing on an apparent "animal nexus" theory to all plaintiffs whose interest in the animals is "genuine." Such plaintiffs, we are told, do not have to visit the animals because the animals are analogous to family members. We decline to join Justice Stevens in this Linnaean leap. It is unclear to us what constitutes a "genuine" interest, how it differs from a "nongenuine" interest (which nonetheless prompted a plaintiff to file suit), and why such an interest in animals should be different from such an interest in anything else that is the subject of a lawsuit.

official's) failure to follow the assertedly correct consultative procedure, notwith-standing his or her inability to allege any discrete injury flowing from that failure. To understand the remarkable nature of this holding one must be clear about what it does not rest upon: This is not a case where plaintiffs are seeking to enforce a procedural requirement the disregard of which could impair a separate concrete interest of theirs (e.g., the procedural requirement for a hearing prior to denial of their license application, or the procedural requirement for an environmental im-pact statement before a federal facility is constructed next door to them).[7] Nor is it simply a case where concrete injury has been suffered by many persons, as in mass fraud or mass tort situations. Nor, finally, is it the unusual case in which Congress has created a concrete private interest in the outcome of a suit against a private party for the Government's benefit, by providing a cash bounty for the victorious plaintiff. Rather, the court held that the injury-in-fact requirement had been satis-fied by congressional conferral upon all persons of an abstract, self-contained, noninstrumental "right" to have the Executive observe the procedures required by law. We reject this view.[8]

We have consistently held that a plaintiff raising only a generally available grievance about government—claiming only harm to his and every citizen's in-

---

[7] There is this much truth to the assertion that "procedural rights" are special: The person who has been accorded a procedural right to protect his concrete interests can assert that right without meeting all the normal standards for redressability and immediacy. Thus, under our case law, one living adjacent to the site for proposed construction of a federally licensed dam has standing to challenge the licensing agency's failure to prepare an environmental impact state-ment, even though he cannot establish with any certainty that the statement will cause the license to be withheld or altered, and even though the dam will not be completed for many years. (That is why we do not rely, in the present case, upon the Government's argument that, *even if* the other agencies were obliged to consult with the Secretary, they might not have followed his advice.) What respondents' "procedural rights" argument seeks, however, is quite different from this: standing for persons who have no concrete interests affected—persons who live (and propose to live) at the other end of the country from the dam.

[8] . . . We do *not* hold that an individual cannot enforce procedural rights; he assuredly can, so long as the procedures in question are designed to protect some threatened concrete interest of his that is the ultimate basis of his standing. The dissent, however, asserts that there exist "classes of procedural duties . . . so enmeshed with the prevention of a substantive, concrete harm that an individual plaintiff may be able to demonstrate a sufficient likelihood of injury just through the breach of that procedural duty." If we understand this correctly, it means that the Government's violation of a certain (undescribed) class of procedural duty satisfies the concrete-injury requirement by itself, without any showing that the procedural violation endangers a concrete interest of the plaintiff (apart from his interest in having the procedure observed). We cannot agree. The dissent is unable to cite a single case in which we actually found standing solely on the basis of a "procedural right" unconnected to the plaintiff's own concrete harm. Its suggestion that we did so in *Japan Whaling Assn. v. American Cetacean Soc.*, 478 U.S. 221 (1986), and *Robertson v. Methow Valley Citizens Council*, 490 U.S. 332 (1989), is not supported by the facts. In the former case, we found that the environmental organizations had standing because the "whale watching and studying of their members w[ould] be adversely affected by continued whale harvesting"; and in the latter we did not so much as mention standing, for the very good reason that the plaintiff was a citizens' council for the area in which the challenged construction was to occur, so that its members would obviously be concretely affected.

terest in proper application of the Constitution and laws, and seeking relief that no more directly and tangibly benefits him than it does the public at large—does not state an Article III case or controversy....

To be sure, our generalized-grievance cases have typically involved Government violation of procedures assertedly ordained by the Constitution rather than the Congress. But there is absolutely no basis for making the Article III inquiry turn on the source of the asserted right. Whether the courts were to act on their own, or at the invitation of Congress, in ignoring the concrete injury requirement described in our cases, they would be discarding a principle fundamental to the separate and distinct constitutional role of the Third Branch—one of the essential elements that identifies those "Cases" and "Controversies" that are the business of the courts rather than of the political branches. "The province of the court," as Chief Justice Marshall said in *Marbury v. Madison*, 5 U.S. 137 (1803), "is, solely, to decide on the rights of individuals." Vindicating the public interest (including the public interest in Government observance of the Constitution and laws) is the function of Congress and the Chief Executive. The question presented here is whether the public interest in proper administration of the laws (specifically, in agencies' observance of a particular, statutorily prescribed procedure) can be converted into an individual right by a statute that denominates it as such, and that permits all citizens (or, for that matter, a subclass of citizens who suffer no distinctive concrete harm) to sue. If the concrete injury requirement has the separation-of-powers significance we have always said, the answer must be obvious: To permit Congress to convert the undifferentiated public interest in executive officers' compliance with the law into an "individual right" vindicable in the courts is to permit Congress to transfer from the President to the courts the Chief Executive's most important constitutional duty, to "take Care that the Laws be faithfully executed," Art. II, § 3. It would enable the courts, with the permission of Congress, "to assume a position of authority over the governmental acts of another and co-equal department," *Massachusetts v. Mellon*, 262 U.S. at 489, and to become "'virtually continuing monitors of the wisdom and soundness of Executive action.'" *Allen*, supra, at 760 (quoting *Laird v. Tatum*, 408 U.S. 1, 15 (1972))....

Nothing in this contradicts the principle that "the ... injury required by Art. III may exist solely by virtue of 'statutes creating legal rights, the invasion of which creates standing.'" *Warth*, 422 U.S. at 500 (quoting *Linda R. S. v. Richard D.*, 410 U.S. 614, 617 (1973)). Both of the cases used by *Linda R. S.* as an illustration of that principle involved Congress' elevating to the status of legally cognizable injuries concrete, de facto injuries that were previously inadequate in law (namely, injury to an individual's personal interest in living in a racially integrated community, see *Trafficante v. Metropolitan Life Ins. Co.*, 409 U.S. 205, 208-212 (1972), and injury to a company's interest in marketing its product free from competition, see *Hardin v. Kentucky Utilities Co.*, 390 U.S. 1, 6 (1968)). As we said in *Sierra Club*, "[Statutory] broadening [of] the categories of injury that may be alleged in support of standing is a different matter from abandoning the requirement that the party seeking review must himself have suffered an injury." 405 U.S. at 738. Whether or not the principle set forth in *Warth* can be extended beyond that distinction, it is clear that in suits against the Government, at least, the concrete injury requirement must remain....

Justice Kennedy, with whom Justice Souter joins, concurring in part and concurring in the judgment.

Although I agree with the essential parts of the Court's analysis, I write separately to make several observations.

I agree with the Court's conclusion in Part III-A that, on the record before us, respondents have failed to demonstrate that they themselves are "among the injured." *Sierra Club v. Morton*, 405 U.S. 727, 735 (1972)....

While it may seem trivial to require that Mss. Kelly and Skilbred acquire airline tickets to the project sites or announce a date certain upon which they will return, see ante, at 564, this is not a case where it is reasonable to assume that the affiants will be using the sites on a regular basis, see *Sierra Club v. Morton*, supra, at 735, n. 8, nor do the affiants claim to have visited the sites since the projects commenced. With respect to the Court's discussion of respondents' "ecosystem nexus," "animal nexus," and "vocational nexus" theories, ante, at 565-567, I agree that on this record respondents' showing is insufficient to establish standing on any of these bases. I am not willing to foreclose the possibility, however, that in different circumstances a nexus theory similar to those proffered here might support a claim to standing. See *Japan Whaling Assn. v. American Cetacean Society*, 478 U.S. 221, 231, n. 4 (1986) ("Respondents... undoubtedly have alleged a sufficient 'injury in fact' in that the whale watching and studying of their members will be adversely affected by continued whale harvesting")....

I also join Part IV of the Court's opinion with the following observations. As Government programs and policies become more complex and far reaching, we must be sensitive to the articulation of new rights of action that do not have clear analogs in our common-law tradition. Modern litigation has progressed far from the paradigm of Marbury suing Madison to get his commission, *Marbury v. Madison*, 5 U.S. 137 (1803), or Ogden seeking an injunction to halt Gibbons' steamboat operations, *Gibbons v. Ogden*, 22 U.S. 1 (1824). In my view, Congress has the power to define injuries and articulate chains of causation that will give rise to a case or controversy where none existed before, and I do not read the Court's opinion to suggest a contrary view. See *Warth v. Seldin*, 422 U.S. 490, 500 (1975). In exercising this power, however, Congress must at the very least identify the injury it seeks to vindicate and relate the injury to the class of persons entitled to bring suit. The citizen-suit provision of the Endangered Species Act does not meet these minimal requirements, because while the statute purports to confer a right on "any person... to enjoin... the United States and any other governmental instrumentality or agency... who is alleged to be in violation of any provision of this chapter," it does not of its own force establish that there is an injury in "any person" by virtue of any "violation." 16 U. S. C. s. 1540(g)(1)(A)....

An independent judiciary is held to account through its open proceedings and its reasoned judgments. In this process it is essential for the public to know what persons or groups are invoking the judicial power, the reasons that they have brought suit, and whether their claims are vindicated or denied. The concrete injury requirement helps assure that there can be an answer to these questions; and, as the Court's opinion is careful to show, that is part of the constitutional design.

[Concurring opinion by Justice Stevens and dissent by Justice Blackmun omitted.]

COMMENTS AND QUESTIONS

1. The plaintiffs in this case alleged that the Department of the Interior had misinterpreted the Endangered Species Act in issuing a rule that held the act did not apply overseas. As we will see in chapters 7 and 8, courts commonly review claims that administrative agencies have misinterpreted the statutes they are charged with administering. Doesn't this suggest that this is the kind of claim that is "appropriately resolved through the judicial process"? Why does the Court think it is not? Will having Joyce Kelly and Amy Skilbred buy plane tickets to Egypt and Sri Lanka to demonstrate their interest in crocodiles and elephants make the case one that is more "appropriately resolved through the judicial process"?

2. Given the procedural posture of this case—it was decided at the summary judgment stage—one must assume that Kelly and Skilbred were telling the truth when they expressed concern about the endangered crocodiles and elephants. How can the Court then say that are not injured "in fact" by the threats to these species? Is injury "in fact" the correct term here? Or are some injuries that exist "in fact" simply not injuries the Court will recognize as legally significant? What in Article III tells us which injuries are legally cognizable and which are not?

3. In *Northeast Florida Chapter of the Associated General Contractors of America v. Jacksonville*, 508 U.S. 656 (1993), the Supreme Court held that an association of contractors had standing to challenge a contracting policy giving preference to minority-owned firms, even though the plaintiffs had not shown that they would have received contracts in the absence of the program. The Court stated that the injury was the denial of an opportunity to compete without regard to race, not "the ultimate inability to obtain the benefit." Why didn't this sort of argument work in *Lujan*? Wasn't the plaintiffs' injury really a threat to an opportunity—the opportunity to see crocodiles and elephants in the future?

4. Why does Justice Scalia think it is ordinarily more difficult for the beneficiary of regulation to establish standing than it is for the "object" of regulation to do so? Does this idea flow inevitably from Article III and its "cases or controversies" requirement?

5. How far does the Article II concern cited by Justice Scalia go? Suppose that the Department of the Interior had stated that agencies proposing projects overseas *must* consult with Interior before proceeding and that a private company wanted to build a power plant overseas that would jeopardize endangered species. Would the company have standing to challenge Interior's rule? If so, wouldn't the company's suit intrude on executive prerogatives just as much as the environmentalists' suit here did?

6. In *Friends of the Earth v. Laidlaw Environmental Services*, 528 U.S. 167 (2000), the Court held that plaintiffs had standing to sue a company for discharging mercury and other pollutants into a river in violation of its environmental permits. Even though the district court had held that the discharges did not

cause actual harm to the river, the Court stated that it was the harm to the plaintiffs—not to the river—that mattered for purposes of standing. Plaintiffs alleged that they did not use the river because of their concerns about pollution. The Court found that their "reasonable concerns" were enough to establish standing. Can *Laidlaw* be squared with *Lujan*?

Linking Common Law and Statutes

The Case of Workers' Compensation

6

So far we have examined the regulation of risk by the common law—and therefore by courts. Chapter 5 introduced the alternative of statutory regulation by identifying differences in the institutional capacities of courts and legislatures, as well as administrative agencies. That discussion also introduced some of the political dimensions of shifting from judicial to legislative and administrative regulation of risk, a topic we'll take up in more detail in part IV. In this chapter, we'll change our focus from the common law to legislative and administrative regulation and use the development of workers' compensation statutes as a case study of administrative efforts to regulate risk.

Section A describes how and why statutory and administrative regulation of workplace injury came to supplement common law regulation and examines some of the legal barriers that development initially faced. Sections B and C deal with problems associated with the provision of compensation for workplace risk. Section B introduces the general problem of "moral hazard," that is, behavioral adaptation in response to the possibility that compensation will be awarded if risks are realized, and section C uses the integration of workers' compensation systems with existing common law rules to illustrate some of the complexities associated with regulatory *systems* containing many "moving parts."

A ▐ Workers' Compensation Laws

The next group of materials examines the first great administrative response to the problem of workplace safety and health. Here we aim to (1) develop a deeper understanding of how legal regulation may change "in response to" social and legal developments and (2) examine in more detail the justifications, if any, for "compulsory terms," that is, regulation of the employer-employee relationship according to terms other than those chosen by the parties through individual or collective negotiations. (These terms result from choices made by third parties—the public. Think about when and why the public should be allowed to dictate terms to the parties.)

We begin by picking up the story of legal responses in the post-*Farwell* era. As you will recall, the fellow-servant rule in *Farwell* gave rise to—or at least allowed—numerous exceptions and qualifications, some of which were foreshadowed in *Farwell* itself. (For example, the court there rejected the "separate departments" rule, but courts in other jurisdictions accepted it.) Two other major restrictions on the ability of injured workers to recover also came into play—the doctrines of assumption of risk and of contributory negligence.[a]

In the late nineteenth century, a number of short-lived movements, such as those led by the Industrial Workers of the World (Wobblies), socialists like Eugene V. Debs, and later the Congress of Industrial Organizations (CIO), tried to mobilize unskilled industrial workers politically to secure from legislatures gains they were unable to get through collective bargaining. As you will see, the courts impeded the success of this strategy.[b] (Another distinct branch of organized labor organization during this period—usually called "voluntarist"—was associated with Samuel Gompers, the early American Federation of Labor, and workers in skilled crafts. It abjured politics and sought to achieve gains for labor solely through collective bargaining.)

The first stage in labor's political effort was relatively limited. Unions tried to get legislators to override the judicially developed common law defenses. Unfortunately, some of the first efforts were badly drafted. If a statute repealed the fellow-servant defense, for example, courts could invoke the very same considerations they had used in developing it but now under the heading "assumption of risk." And, obviously, repealing only the contributory negligence defense could have the same effect.

The following article by Friedman and Ladinsky is a classic exposition of what might be called a materialist account of post-*Farwell* developments (that is, one that attributes legal change to the financial and similar interests of participants in the political process) through the adoption of an administrative workers' compensation system. You should contrast it with what an ideological account (that is, one that attributes legal change to changes in values and ideas about how to implement them) might be.

■ *Social Change and the Law of Industrial Accidents*
LAWRENCE M. FRIEDMAN AND JACK LADINSKY
67 Colum. L. Rev. 50 (1967). Reprinted by permission

Development of the Law of Industrial Accidents

A. Background of the Fellow-Servant Rule

At the dawn of the industrial revolution, the common law of torts afforded a remedy, as it still does, for those who had suffered injuries at the hands of others. If

[a] You might well wonder how if at all a court could sensibly distinguish between those two doctrines; to the extent the distinction was coherent, the doctrines directed attention to two different periods of time: assumption of the risk directed attention to the risks of the job that the worker knew or should have known on taking the job or in continuing to work at it; contributory negligence directed attention to the worker's conduct in the moments just before the accident.

[b] One of the major current discussions among labor historians is an argument about the extent to which the distinctive U.S. system of judicial review obstructed the development of the kinds of labor movements characteristic of European industrial societies. For an introduction to the argument, see William Forbath, Law and the Shaping of the American Labor Movement (1991).

a man injured another by direct action—by striking him, or slandering him, or by trespassing on his property—the victim could sue for his damages. Similarly, the victim of certain kinds of negligent behavior had a remedy at law. But tort law was not highly developed. . . . The explosive growth of tort law was directly related to the rapidity of industrial development. The staple source of tort litigation was and is the impact of machines—railroad engines, then factory machines, then automobiles—on the human body. During the industrial revolution, the size of the factory labor force increased, the use of machinery in the production of goods became more widespread, and such accidents were inevitably more frequent. . . .

In theory, at least, recovery for industrial accidents might have been assimilated into the existing system of tort law. The fundamental principles were broad and simple. If a factory worker was injured through the negligence of another person—including his employer—an action for damages would lie. Although as a practical matter, servants did not usually sue their master nor workers their employers, in principle they had the right to do so.

In principle, too, a worker might have had an action against his employer for any injury caused by the negligence of any other employee. The doctrine of *respondeat superior* was familiar and fundamental law. A principal was liable for the negligent acts of his agent. . . . A definitive body of doctrine was slow to develop, however. When it did, it rejected the broad principle of *respondeat superior* and took instead the form of the so-called fellow-servant rule. Under this rule, a servant (employee) could not sue his master (employer) for injuries caused by the negligence of another employee. The consequences of this doctrine were far reaching. An employee retained the right to sue the employer for injuries, provided they were caused by the employer's personal misconduct. But the factory system and corporate ownership of industry made this right virtually meaningless. The factory owner was likely to be a "soulless" legal entity; even if the owner was an individual entrepreneur, he was unlikely to concern himself physically with factory operations. In work accidents, then, legal fault would be ascribed to fellow employees, if anyone. But fellow employees were men without wealth or insurance. The fellow-servant rule was an instrument capable of relieving employers from almost all the legal consequences of industrial injuries. Moreover, the doctrine left an injured worker without any effective recourse but an empty action against his co-worker. . . .

When labor developed a collective voice, it was bound to decry the rule as infamous, as a deliberate instrument of oppression—a sign that law served the interests of the rich and propertied, and denied the legitimate claims of the poor and the weak. The rule charged the "blood of the workingman" not to the state, the employer, or the consumer, but to the working man himself. Conventionally, then, the fellow-servant rule is explained as a deliberate or half-deliberate rejection of a well-settled principle of law in order to encourage enterprise by forcing workmen to bear the costs of industrial injury. And the overthrow of the rule is taken as a sign of a conquest by progressive forces. . . .

Shaw's opinion [in *Farwell*] makes extreme assumptions about behavior, justified only by a philosophy of economic individualism. Partly because of this, it has a certain heartlessness of tone. A disabled worker without resources was likely to be pauperized if he had no realistic right to damages. Unless his family could help him, he would have to fall back upon poor relief, the costs of which were borne by the public through taxation. The railroads and other industrial employers paid a share as taxpayers and, in addition, a kind of insurance cost as part of their wage rate—but no more. Additional damages had to be borne by the worker; if he could not bear them, society generally would pay the welfare costs. Thus the opinion expresses a preference for charging the welfare cost of industrial accidents to the public generally, rather than to the particular enterprise involved.

It is not surprising that such a preference was expressed. Shaw's generation placed an extremely high value on economic growth. As Willard Hurst has noted, that generation was thoroughly convinced it was "socially desirable that there be broad opportunity for the release of creative human energy," particularly in the "realm of the economy." The establishment of a functioning railroad net was an essential element in economic growth. Furthermore, Shaw's resolution of the *Farwell* case is cruel only insofar as society makes no other provision for the victims of accidents—that is, if social insurance and public assistance are inadequate, degrading, or unfair. In a society with a just and workable system of state medical insurance and disability pensions, the *Farwell* solution would be neither inhumane nor inappropriate, even today....

C. Weakening the Rule

A general pattern may be discerned which is common to the judicial history of many rules of law. The courts enunciate a rule, intending to "solve" a social problem—that is, they seek to lay down a stable and clear-cut principle by which men can govern their conduct or, alternatively, by which the legal system can govern men. If the rule comports with some kind of social consensus, it will in fact work a solution—that is, it will go unchallenged, or, if challenged, will prevail. Challenges will not usually continue, since the small chance of overturning the rule is not worth the cost of litigation. If, however, the rule is weakened—if courts engraft exceptions to it, for example—then fresh challenges probing new weaknesses will be encouraged. Even if the rule retains *some* support, it will no longer be efficient and clear-cut. Ultimately, the rule may no longer serve *anybody's* purposes. At this point, a fresh (perhaps wholly new) "solution" will be attempted.

The history of the fellow-servant rule neatly fits this scheme. Shaw wrote his *Farwell* opinion in 1842. During the latter part of the century, judges began to reject his reasoning. The "tendency in nearly all jurisdictions," said a Connecticut court in 1885, was to "limit rather than enlarge" the range of the fellow-servant rule. A Missouri judge in 1891 candidly expressed the change in attitude:

> In the progress of society, and the general substitution of ideal and invisible masters and employers for the actual and visible ones of former times, in the forms of corporations engaged in varied, detached and widespread operations ... it has been seen and felt that the universal application of the [fellow-servant] rule often resulted in hardship and injustice. Accordingly, the tendency of the more modern authorities appears to be in the direction of such a modification and limitation of the rule as shall eventually devolve upon the employer under these circumstances a due and just share of the responsibility for the lives and limbs of the persons in its employ.

The rule was strong medicine, and it depended for its efficacy upon continued, relatively certain, and unswerving legal loyalty. Ideally, if the rule were strong and commanded nearly total respect from the various agencies of law, it would eliminate much of the mass of litigation that might otherwise arise. Undoubtedly, it did prevent countless thousands of law suits; but it did not succeed in choking off industrial accident litigation. For example, industrial accident litigation dominated the docket of the Wisconsin Supreme Court at the beginning of the age of workmen's compensation; far more cases arose under that heading than under any other single field of law. Undoubtedly, this appellate case-load was merely the visible portion of a vast iceberg of litigation. Thus, the rule did not command the respect required for efficient operation and hence, in the long run, survival.

One reason for the continued litigation may have been simply the great number of accidents that occurred....

...Plaintiffs won many of their lawsuits; in so doing, they not only weakened the fellow-servant rule, but they encouraged still more plaintiffs to try their hand, still more attorneys to make a living from personal injury work. In trial courts, the pressure of particular cases—the "hard" cases in which the plight of the plaintiff was pitiful or dramatic—tempted judges and juries to find for the little man and against the corporate defendant. In Shaw's generation, many leading appellate judges shared his view of the role of the judge; they took it as their duty to lay down grand legal principles to govern whole segments of the economic order. Thus, individual hardship cases had to be ignored for the sake of higher duty. But this was not the exclusive judicial style, even in the appellate courts. And in personal injury cases, lower court judges and juries were especially prone to tailor justice to the case at hand....

Some weakening of the doctrine took place by means of the control exercised by trial court judge and jury over findings of fact. But sympathy for injured workers manifested itself also in changes in doctrine. On the appellate court level, a number of mitigations of the fellow-servant rule developed near the end of the nineteenth century. For example, it had always been conceded that the employer was liable if he was personally responsible (through his own negligence) for his worker's injury. Thus, in a Massachusetts case, a stable owner gave directions to his employee, who was driving a wagon, that caused an accident and injury to the driver (or so the jury found). The employer was held liable. Out of this simple proposition grew the so-called vice-principal rule, which allowed an employee to sue his employer where the negligent employee occupied a supervisory position such that he could more properly be said to be an alter ego of the principal than a mere fellow-servant. This was a substantial weakening of the fellow-servant doctrine. Yet some states never accepted the vice-principal rule; in those that did, it too spawned a bewildering multiplicity of decisions, sub-rules, and sub-sub-rules....

There were scores of other "exceptions" to the fellow-servant rule, enunciated in one or more states. Some of them were of great importance. In general, an employer was said to have certain duties that were not "delegable"; these he must do or have done, and a failure to perform them laid him open to liability for personal injuries. Among these was the duty to furnish a safe place to work, safe tools, and safe appliances. Litigation on these points was enormous, and here too the cases cannot readily be summed up or even explained. In *Wedgwood v. Chicago & Northwestern Railway Co.*, the plaintiff, a brakeman, was injured by a "large and long bolt, out of place, and which unnecessarily, carelessly and unskillfully projected beyond the frame, beam or brakehead, in the way of the brakeman going to couple the cars." The trial court threw the case out, but the Wisconsin Supreme Court reversed:

> It is true, the defendant . . . is a railroad corporation, and can only act through officers or agents. But this does not relieve it from responsibility for the negligence of its officers and agents whose duty it is to provide safe and suitable machinery for its road which its employees are to operate.

So phrased, of course, the exception comes close to swallowing the rule. Had the courts been so inclined, they might have eliminated the fellow-servant rule without admitting it, simply by expanding the safe place and safe tool rules. They were never quite willing to go that far, and the safe tool doctrine was itself subject to numerous exceptions. In some jurisdictions, for example, the so-called "simple tool" rule applied:

> Tools of ordinary and everyday use, which are simple in structure and requiring no skill in handling—such as hammers and axes—not obviously defective, do not impose a liability upon employers for injuries resulting from such defects.

Doctrinal complexity and vacillation in the upper courts, coupled with jury freedom in the lower courts, meant that by the end of the century the fellow-servant rule had lost much of its reason for existence: it was no longer an efficient cost-allocating doctrine. Even though the exceptions did not go the length of obliterating the rule, and even though many (perhaps most) injured workers who had a possible cause of action did not or could not recover, the instability and unpredictability of operation of the common law rule was a significant fact. . . .

D. Rising Pressures for Change

The common law doctrines were designed to preserve a certain economic balance in the community. When the courts and legislatures created numerous exceptions, the rules lost much of their efficiency as a limitation on the liability of businessmen. The rules prevented many plaintiffs from recovering, but not all; a few plaintiffs recovered large verdicts. There were costs of settlements, costs of liability insurance, costs of administration, legal fees and the salaries of staff lawyers. These costs rose steadily, at the very time when American business, especially big business, was striving to rationalize and bureaucratize its operations. It was desirable to be able to predict costs and insure against fluctuating, unpredictable risks. The costs of industrial accident liability were not easily predictable, partly because legal consequences of accidents were not predictable. Insurance, though available, was expensive.

In addition, industry faced a serious problem of labor unrest. Workers and their unions were dissatisfied with many aspects of factory life. The lack of compensation for industrial accidents was one obvious weakness. Relatively few injured workers received compensation. Under primitive state employers' liability statutes, the issue of liability and the amount awarded still depended upon court rulings and jury verdicts. Furthermore, the employer and the insurance carrier might contest a claim or otherwise delay settlement in hopes of bringing the employee to terms. The New York Employers' Liability Commission, in 1910, reported that delay ran from six months to six years . . . .

When an employee did recover, the amount was usually small. The New York Commission found that of forty-eight fatal cases studied in Manhattan, eighteen families received no compensation; only four received over $2,000; most received less than $500. The deceased workers had averaged $15.22 a week in wages; only eight families recovered as much as three times their average yearly earnings. The same inadequacies turned up in Wisconsin in 1907. Of fifty-one fatal injuries studied, thirty-four received settlements under $500; only eight received over $1,000.

Litigation costs consumed much of whatever was recovered. It was estimated that, in 1907, "of every $100 paid out by [employers in New York] on account of work accidents but $56 reached the injured workmen and their dependents." And even this figure was unrepresentative because it included voluntary payments by employers. "A fairer test of employers' liability is afforded by the $192,538 paid by these same employers as a result of law suits or to avoid law suits, whereof only $80,888, or forty-two percent, reached the beneficiaries." A large fraction of the disbursed payments, about one-third, went to attorneys who accepted the cases on a contingent basis.

These figures on the inadequacy of recoveries are usually cited to show how little the workers received for their pains. But what did these figures mean to employers? Assuming that employers, as rational men, were anxious to pay as little compensation as was necessary to preserve industrial peace and maintain a healthy workforce, the better course might be to pay a higher *net* amount direct to employees. Employers had little or nothing to gain from their big payments to insurance companies, lawyers, and court officials. Perhaps at some unmeasurable point of time, the existing tort system crossed an invisible line and thereafter, purely in economic terms, represented on balance a net loss to the industrial establishment. From that point on, the success of a movement for change in the system was certain, provided that businessmen could be convinced that indeed their self-interest lay in the direction of reform and that a change in compensation systems did not drag with it other unknowable and harmful consequences. . . .

When considerations of politics were added to those of business economics and industrial peace, it was not surprising to find that businessmen gradually withdrew their veto against workmen's compensation statutes. They began to say that a reformed system was inevitable—and even desirable. A guaranteed, insurable cost—one which could be computed in advance on the basis of accident experience—would, in the long run, cost business less than the existing system. In 1910, the president of the National Association of Manufacturers (NAM) appointed a committee to study the possibility of compensating injured workmen without time-consuming and expensive litigation, and the convention that year heard a speaker tell them that no one was satisfied with the present state of the law—that the employers' liability system was "antagonistic to harmonious relations between employers and wage workers." By 1911 the NAM appeared convinced that a compensation system was inevitable and that prudence dictated that business play a positive role in shaping the design of the law—otherwise the law would be "settled for us by the demagogue, and agitator and the socialist with a vengeance." Business would benefit economically and politically from a compensation system, but only if certain conditions were present. Business, therefore, had an interest in pressing for a specific kind of program, and turned its attention to the details of the new system. For example, it was imperative that the new system be in fact as actuarially predictable as business demanded; it was important that the costs of the program be fair and equal in their impact upon particular industries, so that no competitive advantage or disadvantage flowed from the scheme. Consequently the old tort actions had to be eliminated, along with the old defenses of the company. In exchange for certainty of recovery by the worker, the companies were prepared to demand certainty and predictability of loss—that is, limitation of recovery. The jury's caprice had to be dispensed with. In short, when workmen's compensation became law, as a solution to the industrial accident problem, it did so on terms acceptable to industry. Other pressures were there to be sure, but when workmen's compensation was enacted, businessmen had come to look on it as a positive benefit rather than as a threat to their sector of the economy.

E. The Emergence of Workmen's Compensation Statutes

The change of the businessman's, the judge's, and the general public's attitudes toward industrial injuries was accelerated by the availability of fresh information on the extent of accidents and their cost to both management and workers. By 1900, industrial accidents and the shortcomings of the fellow-servant rule were widely perceived as *problems* that had to be solved. After 1900, state legislatures began to look for a "solution" by setting up commissions to gather statistics, to investigate possible new systems, and to recommend legislation. The commissions held public hearings and called upon employers, labor, insurance companies, and lawyers to express their opinions and propose changes. A number of commissions collected statistics on industrial accidents, costs of insurance, and amounts disbursed to injured workmen. By 1916, many states and the federal government had received more-or-less extensive public reports from these investigating bodies. The reports included studies of industrial accident cases in the major industries, traced the legal history of the cases, and looked into the plight of the injured workmen and their families.

From the information collected, the commissions were able to calculate the costs of workmen's compensation systems and compare them with costs under employers' liability. Most of the commissions concluded that a compensation system would be no more expensive than the existing method, and most of them re-commended adoption, in one form or another, of workmen's compensation. In spite of wide variations in the systems proposed, there was agreement on one point: workmen's compensation must fix liability upon the employer regardless of fault.

Between 1910 and 1920 the method of compensating employees injured on the job was fundamentally altered in the United States. In brief, workmen's compensation statutes eliminated (or tried to eliminate) the process of fixing civil liability for industrial accidents through litigation in common law courts. Under the stat-utes, compensation was based on statutory schedules, and the responsibility for initial determination of employee claims was taken from the courts and given to an administrative agency. Finally, the statutes abolished the fellow-servant rule and the defenses of assumption of risk and contributory negligence. Wisconsin's law, passed in 1911, was the first general compensation act to survive a court test. Mississippi, the last state in the Union to adopt a compensation law, did so in 1948.

Compensation systems varied from state to state, but they had many features in common. The original Wisconsin law was representative of the earlier group of statutes. It set up a voluntary system—a response to the fact that New York's courts had held a compulsory scheme unconstitutional on due process grounds. Wisconsin abolished the fellow-servant rule and the defense of assumption of risk for employers of four or more employees. In turn, the compensation scheme, for employers who elected to come under it, was made the "exclusive remedy" for an employee injured accidentally on the job. The element of "fault" or "negligence" was eliminated, and the mere fact of injury at work "proximately caused by accident," and not the result of "wilful misconduct," made the employer liable to pay compensation but exempt from ordinary tort liability. The state aimed to make it expensive for employers to stay out of the system. Any employer who did so was liable to suit by injured employees and the employer was denied the common law defenses.

The compensation plans strictly limited the employee's amount of recovery. In Wisconsin, for example, if an accident caused "partial disability," the worker was to receive 65% of his weekly loss in wages during the period of disability, not to exceed four times his average annual earnings. The statutes, therefore, were compensatory, not punitive, and the measure of compensation was, subject to strict limitations, the loss of earning power of the worker. In the original Wisconsin act, death benefits were also payable to dependents of the worker. If the worker who died left "no person dependent upon him for support," the death benefit was limited to "the reasonable expense of his burial, not exceeding $100." Neither death nor injury as such gave rise to a right to compensation—only the fact of economic loss to someone, either the worker himself or his family. The Wisconsin act authorized employers to buy annuities from private insurance companies to cover projected losses. Most states later made insurance or self-insurance compulsory. Some states have socialized compensation insurance, but most allow the purchase of private policies.

In essence, then, workmen's compensation was designed to replace a highly unsatisfactory system with a rational, actuarial one. It should not be viewed as the replacement of a fault-oriented compensation system with one unconcerned with fault. It should not be viewed as a victory of employees over employers. In its initial stages, the fellow-servant rule was not concerned with fault, either, but with establishing a clear-cut, workable, and predictable rule, one which substantively placed much of the risk (if not all) on the worker. Industrial accidents were not seen as a social problem—at most as an economic problem. As value perceptions changed, the rule weakened; it developed exceptions and lost its efficiency. The exceptions and counter-exceptions can be looked at as a series of brief, ad hoc, and unstable compromises between the clashing interests of labor and management. When both sides became convinced that the game was mutually unprofitable, a compensation system became possible. But this system was itself a compromise: an attempt at a new, workable, and predictable mode of handling accident liability which neatly balanced the interests of labor and management. . . .

COMMENTS AND QUESTIONS

1. According to Friedman and Ladinsky, what positions did the major actors—organized labor, organized employers, and others—take with respect to the development of workers' compensation systems? Why, in particular, did

organized labor seek to preserve tort recovery? As you read the material about the contemporary state of workers' compensation, consider whether, at the time organized labor took that position, it made sense.

2. John Witt, *The Transformation of Work and the Law of Workplace Accidents, 1842–1910*, 107 Yale L.J. 1467 (1998), argues that the development of workers' compensation systems eroded worker control of the workplace. He argues that insurance already allowed employers to predict, stably, their outlays for compensating workplace injury. (But how can insurance premiums be calculated if the outcome of lawsuits seeking compensation is as unpredictable as Friedman and Ladinsky say it was?) According to Witt, liberalizing the tort rules in workplace injury cases "pushed employers to make their control of the workplace more effective. . . . By raising the price of work accidents, the workmen's compensation statutes pushed management to develop new modes of control over work. The increased managerial adoption of responsibility for safety in the workplace in the years after the enactment of workmen's compensation had the important effect of reducing accident rates in American workplaces. But it also entailed compromising the kinds of informal worker practices and discretionary authority that had undergirded the idea of work's intrinsic value." That latter idea "was wholly absent from the workmen's compensation debates."

3. We turn next to constitutional challenges that were mounted against workers' compensation systems. Those challenges drew on the jurisprudence growing out of *Lochner v. New York* (chapter 1) and especially on the proposition that the Constitution placed some limits on the power of legislatures to depart too substantially from the common law. The first case below, *Ives v. South Buffalo Ry. Co.*, 201 N.Y. 271 (1911), involved a challenge to the first workers' compensation law in the United States. As you read it, consider what theory of the proper role of government in regulating risk the court adopts.

■ Ives v. South Buffalo Railway Co.
201 N.Y. 271 (1911)

Werner, J.:

. . .

The statute, judged by our common-law standards, is plainly revolutionary. Its central and controlling feature is that every employer who is engaged in any of the classified industries shall be liable for any injury to a workman arising out of and in the course of the employment by "a necessary risk or danger of the employment or one inherent in the nature thereof, . . . provided that the employer shall not be liable in respect of any injury to the workman which is caused in whole or in part by the serious and willful misconduct of the workman." This rule of liability, stated in another form, is that the employer is responsible to the employee for every accident in the course of the employment, whether the employer is at fault or not, and whether the employee is at fault or not, except when the fault of the employee is so grave as to constitute serious and willful misconduct on his part. The radical character of this legislation is at once revealed by contrasting it with the rule of the common law, under which the employer is liable for injuries to his employee only when the employer is guilty of some act or acts of negligence which caused the occurrence out of which the injuries arise, and then only when the employee is shown to be free from any negligence which contributes to the occurrence....

...

...Process of law in its broad sense means law in its regular course of administration through courts of justice, and that is but another way of saying that every man's right to life, liberty and property is to be disposed of in accordance with those ancient and fundamental principles which were in existence when our Constitutions were adopted....One of the inalienable rights of every citizen is to hold and enjoy his property until it is taken from him by due process of law. When our Constitutions were adopted it was the law of the land that no man who was without fault or negligence could be held liable in damages for injuries sustained by another. That is still the law, except as to the employers enumerated in the new statute, and as to them it provides that they shall be liable to their employees for personal injury by accident to any workman arising out of and in the course of the employment which is caused in whole or in part, or is contributed to, by a necessary risk or danger of the employment or one inherent in the nature thereof, except that there shall be no liability in any case where the injury is caused in whole or in part by the serious and willful misconduct of the injured workman. It is conceded that this is a liability unknown to the common law and we think it plainly constitutes a deprivation of liberty and property under the Federal and State Constitutions, unless its imposition can be justified under the police power.... In arriving at this conclusion we do not overlook the cogent economic and sociological arguments which are urged in support of the statute. There can be no doubt as to the theory of this law. It is based upon the proposition that the inherent risks of an employment should in justice be placed upon the shoulders of the employer, who can protect himself against loss by insurance and by such an addition to the price of his wares as to cast the burden ultimately upon the consumer; that indemnity to an injured employee should be as much a charge upon the business as the cost of replacing or repairing disabled or defective machinery, appliances or tools; that, under our present system, the loss falls immediately upon the employee who is almost invariably unable to bear it, and ultimately upon the community which is taxed for the support of the indigent; and that our present system is uncertain, unscientific and wasteful, and fosters a spirit of antagonism between employer and employee which it is to the interests of the state to remove. We have already admitted the strength of this appeal to a recognized and widely prevalent sentiment, but we think it is an appeal which must be made to the people and not to the courts. The right of property rests not upon philosophical or scientific speculations nor upon the commendable impulses of benevolence or charity, nor yet upon the dictates of natural justice. The right has its foundation in the fundamental law. That can be changed by the people, but not by legislatures. In a government like ours theories of public good or necessity are often so plausible or sound as to command popular approval, but courts are not permitted to forget that the law is the only chart by which the ship of state is to be guided. Law as used in this sense means the basic law and not the very act of legislation which deprives the citizen of his rights, privileges or property. Any other view would lead to the absurdity that the Constitutions protect only those rights which the legislatures do not take away. If such economic and sociologic arguments as are here advanced in support of this statute can be allowed to subvert the fundamental idea of property, then there is not private right entirely safe, because there is no limitation upon the absolute discretion of legislatures, and the guarantees of the Constitution are a mere waste of words. . . . If the argument in support of the statute is sound we do not see why it cannot logically be carried much further. Poverty and misfortune from every cause are detrimental to the state. It would probably conduce to the welfare of all concerned if there could be a more equal distribution of wealth. Many persons have much more property than they can use to advantage and many more find it impossible to get the means for a comfortable existence. If the legislature can say to an employer, "you must compensate your employee for an injury not caused by you or by your fault," why can it not go further and say to the man of wealth, "you have more property than you need and your neighbor is so poor that he can barely subsist; in the interest of natural justice you must divide with your neighbor so that he and his dependents shall not become a charge upon the State?" The argument that the risk to an employee should be borne by the employer because it is inherent in the employment, may be economically sound, but it is at war with the legal principle that no employer can be compelled to assume a risk which is inseparable from the work of the employee, and which may exist in spite of a degree of care by the employer far greater than may be exacted by the most drastic law. If it is competent to impose upon an employer, who has omitted no legal duty and has committed no wrong, a liability based solely upon a legislative fiat that his business is inherently dangerous, it is equally competent to visit upon him a special tax for the support of hospitals and other charitable institutions, upon the theory that they are devoted largely to the alleviation of ills primarily due to his business. In its final and simple analysis that is taking the property of A and giving it to B, and that cannot be done under our Constitutions. . . .

COMMENTS AND QUESTIONS

1. What is the constitutional violation the court identifies? It appears to be that the common law as of 1868 (when the Fourteenth Amendment was adopted) allowed recovery for injury only on a showing of negligence and that that common law rule created a property right protected against legislative change by the Due Process Clause. Why is legislative alteration prohibited? In a portion of its opinion not excerpted in these materials, the court held that it was constitutionally permissible to abolish the common-law defenses such as assumption of risk. Can you reconcile that conclusion with the analysis we have excerpted? The court seems to suggest that the core negligence rule is unchangeable by the legislature but peripheral ones like assumption of risk are alterable. What is the basis for *that* distinction? Note the court's concern about the slippery slope leading to purely redistributive legislation. Recall Duncan Kennedy's discussion of the relation between the common law and redistribution in chapter 3.

2. When *Ives* was decided, the statutes regulating the jurisdiction of the Supreme Court did not give the Court jurisdiction over appeals from state court decisions invalidating state laws on the ground that such laws were inconsistent with the national constitution. (Why might Congress have decided not to

provide such jurisdiction?) After *Ives* was decided, two things occurred. First, Congress amended the jurisdictional statutes to allow review by the U.S. Supreme Court of decisions like *Ives*. Second, New York amended its constitution to authorize passage of a workers' compensation statute. These developments meant that those who challenged the New York workers' compensation statute could rely only on the federal Constitution and that the U.S. Supreme Court could review any decision striking down the statute. The following case upheld the new New York statute.

▪ New York Central Railroad Co. v. White
243 U.S. 188 (1916)

Mr. Justice Pitney delivered the opinion of the court:

A proceeding was commenced by defendant in error before the Workmen's Compensation Commission of the State of New York, established by the Workmen's Compensation Law of that state, to recover compensation from the New York Central & Hudson River Railroad Company for the death of her husband, Jacob White, who lost his life September 2, 1914, through an accidental injury arising out of and in the course of his employment under that company. The Commission awarded compensation in accordance with the terms of the law; its award was affirmed, without opinion, by the appellate division of the supreme court for the third judicial department, whose order was affirmed by the court of appeals, without opinion....

. . .

[The railroad claims that] to award compensation to [White] under the provisions of the Workmen's Compensation Law would deprive [the railroad] of its property without due process of law, and deny to it the equal protection of the laws, in contravention of the 14th Amendment....

. . .

...The Workmen's Compensation Law of New York establishes forty-two groups of hazardous employments, defines 'employee' as a person engaged in one of these employments upon the premises, or at the plant, or in the course of his employment away from the plant of his employer, but excluding farm laborers and domestic servants; defines 'employment' as including employment only in a trade, business, or occupation carried on by the employer for pecuniary gain, 'injury' and 'personal injury' as meaning only accidental injuries arising out of and in the course of employment, and such disease or infection as naturally and unavoidably may result therefrom; and requires every employer subject to its provisions to pay or provide compensation according to a prescribed schedule for the disability or death of his employee resulting from an accidental personal injury arising out of and in the course of the employment, without regard to fault as a cause, except where the injury is occasioned by the wilful intention of the injured employee to bring about the injury or death of himself or of another, or where it results solely from the intoxication of the injured employee while on duty, in which cases neither the injured employee nor any dependent shall receive compensation. By § 11 the prescribed liability is made exclusive, except that, if an employer fail to secure the payment of compensation as provided in § 50, an injured employee, or his legal representative, in case death results from the injury, may, at his option, elect to claim compensation under the act, or to maintain an action in the courts for damages, and in such an action it shall not be necessary to plead or prove freedom from contributory negligence, nor may the defendant plead as a defense that the injury was caused by the negligence of a fellow servant, that the employee assumed the risk of his employment, or that the injury was due to contributory negligence. Compensation under the act is not regulated by the measure of damages applied in negligence suits, but, in addition to providing surgical, or other like treatment, it is based solely on loss of earning power, being graduated according to the average weekly wages of the injured employee and the character and duration of the disability, whether partial or total, temporary or permanent; while in case the injury causes death, the compensation is known as a death benefit, and includes funeral expenses, not exceeding $100, payments to the surviving wife (or dependent husband) during widowhood (or dependent widowerhood) of a percentage of the average wages of the deceased, and if there be a surviving child or children under the age of eighteen years an additional percentage of such wages for each child until that age is reached. There are provisions invalidating agreements by employees to waive the right to compensation, prohibiting any assignment, release, or commutation of claims for compensation or benefits except as provided by the act, exempting them from the claims of creditors, and requiring that the compensation and benefits shall be paid only to employees or their dependents. Provision is made for the establishment of a Workmen's Compensation Commission with administrative and judicial functions, including authority to pass upon claims to compensation on notice to the parties interested. The award or decision of the Commission is made subject to an appeal, on questions of law only, to the appellate division of the supreme court for the third department, with an ultimate appeal to the court of appeals in cases where such an appeal would lie in civil actions. A fund is created, known as 'the state insurance fund,' for the purpose of insuring employers against liability under the law, and assuring to the persons entitled the compensation thereby provided. The fund is made up primarily of premiums received from employers, at rates fixed by the Commission in view of the hazards of the different classes of employment, and the premiums are to be based upon the total pay roll and number of employees in each class at the lowest rate consistent with the maintenance of a solvent state insurance fund and the creation of a reasonable surplus and reserve. Elaborate provisions are laid down for the administration of this fund. By § 50, each employer is required to secure compensation to his employees in one of the following ways: (1) By insuring and keeping insured the payment of such compensation in the state fund; or (2) through any stock corporation or mutual association authorized to transact the business of workmen's compensation insurance in the state; or (3) 'by furnishing satisfactory proof to the Commission of his financial ability to pay such compensation for himself, in which case the Commission may, in its discretion, require the deposit with the Commission of securities of the kind prescribed in § 13 of the Insurance Law, in an amount to be determined by the Commission, to secure his liability to pay the compensation provided in this chapter.' If an employer fails to comply with this section, he is made liable to a penalty in an amount equal to the pro rata premium that would have been payable for insurance in the state fund during the period of noncompliance; besides which, his injured employees or their dependents are at liberty to maintain an action for damages in the courts, as prescribed by § 11.

. . .

The scheme of the act is so wide a departure from common-law standards respecting the responsibility of employer to employee that doubts naturally have been raised respecting its constitutional validity. The adverse considerations urged or suggested in this case and in kindred cases submitted at the same time are: (a) That the employer's property is taken without due process of law, because he is subjected to a liability for compensation without regard to any neglect or default on his part or on the part of any other person for whom he is responsible, and in spite of the fact that the injury may be solely attributable to the fault of the employee; (b) that the employee's rights are interfered with, in that he is prevented from having compensation for injuries arising from the employer's fault commensurate with the damages actually sustained, and is limited to the measure of compensation prescribed by the act; and (c) that both employer and employee are deprived of their liberty to acquire property by being prevented from making such agreement as they choose respecting the terms of the employment.

In support of the legislation, it is said that the whole common-law doctrine of employer's liability for negligence, with its defenses of contributory negligence, fellow servant's negligence, and assumption of risk, is based upon fictions, and is inapplicable to modern conditions of employment; that in the highly organized and hazardous industries of the present day the causes of accident are often so obscure and complex that in a material proportion of cases it is impossible by any method correctly to ascertain the facts necessary to form an accurate judgment, and in a still larger proportion the expense and delay required for such ascertainment amount in effect to a defeat of justice; that, under the present system, the injured workman is left to bear the greater part of industrial accident loss, which, because of his limited income, he is unable to sustain, so that he and those dependent upon him are overcome by poverty and frequently become a burden upon public or private charity; and that litigation is unduly costly and tedious, encouraging corrupt practices and arousing antagonisms between employers and employees.

. . .

The close relation of the rules governing responsibility as between employer and employee to the fundamental rights of liberty and property is, of course, recognized. But those rules, as guides of conduct, are not beyond alteration by legislation in the public interest. No person has a vested interest in any rule of law, entitling him to insist that it shall remain unchanged for his benefit. The common law bases the employer's liability for injuries to the employee upon the ground of negligence; but negligence is merely the disregard of some duty imposed by law; and the nature and extent of the duty may be modified by legislation, with corresponding change in the test of negligence. Indeed, liability may be imposed for the consequences of a failure to comply with a statutory duty, irrespective of negligence in the ordinary sense; safety appliance acts being a familiar instance.

The fault may be that of the employer himself, or—most frequently—that of another for whose conduct he is made responsible according to the maxim respondeat superior. In the latter case the employer may be entirely blameless, may have exercised the utmost human foresight to safeguard the employee; yet, if the alter ego, while acting within the scope of his duties, be negligent,—in disobedience, it may be, of the employer's positive and specific command,—the employer is answerable for the consequences. It cannot be that the rule embodied in the maxim is unalterable by legislation.

The immunity of the employer from responsibility to an employee for the negligence of a fellow employee is of comparatively recent origin, it being the product of the judicial conception that the probability of a fellow workman's negligence is one of the natural and ordinary risks of the occupation, assumed by the employee and presumably taken into account in the fixing of his wages. The doctrine has prevailed generally throughout the United States, but with material differences in different jurisdictions respecting who should be deemed a fellow servant and who a vice principal or alter ego of the master, turning sometimes upon refined distinctions as to grades and departments in the employment. It needs no argument to show that such a rule is subject to modification or abrogation by a state upon proper occasion.

The same may be said with respect to the general doctrine of assumption of risk. By the common law the employee assumes the risks normally incident to the occupation in which he voluntarily engages; other and extraordinary risks and those due to the employer's negligence he does not assume until made aware of them, or until they become so obvious that an ordinarily prudent man would observe and appreciate them; in either of which cases he does assume them, if he continues in the employment without obtaining from the employer an assurance that the matter will be remedied; but if he receive such an assurance, then, pending performance of the promise, the employee does not, in ordinary cases, assume the special risk. Plainly, these rules, as guides of conduct and tests of liability, are subject to change in the exercise of the sovereign authority of the State.

So, also, with respect to contributory negligence. Aside from injuries intentionally self-inflicted, for which the statute under consideration affords no compensation, it is plain that the rules of law upon the subject, in their bearing upon the employer's responsibility, are subject to legislative change; for contributory negligence, again, involves a default in some duty resting on the employee, and his duties are subject to modification.

. . .

. . . [It is unnecessary], for the purposes of the present case, to say that a state might, without violence to the constitutional guaranty of 'due process of law,' suddenly set aside all common-law rules respecting liability as between employer and employee, without providing a reasonably just substitute. Considering the vast industrial organization of the state of New York, for instance, with hundreds of thousands of plants and millions of wage earners, each employer, on the one hand, having embarked his capital, and each employee, on the other, having taken up his particular mode of earning a livelihood, in reliance upon the probable permanence of an established body of law governing the relation, it perhaps may be doubted whether the state could abolish all rights of action, on the one hand, or all defenses, on the other, without setting up something adequate in their stead. No such question is here presented, and we intimate no opinion upon it. The statute under consideration sets aside one body of rules only to establish another system in its place. If the employee is no longer able to recover as much as before in case of being injured through the employer's negligence, he is entitled to moderate compensation in all cases of injury, and has a certain and speedy remedy without the difficulty and expense of establishing negligence or proving the amount of the damages. Instead of assuming the entire consequences of all ordinary risks of the occupation, he assumes the consequences, in excess of the scheduled compensation, of risks ordinary and extraordinary. On the other hand, if the employer is left without defense respecting the question of fault, he at the same time is assured that the recovery is limited, and that it goes directly to the relief of the designated beneficiary. And just as the employee's assumption of ordinary risks at common law presumably was taken into account in fixing the rate of wages, so the fixed responsibility of the employer, and the modified assumption of risk by the employee under the new system, presumably will be reflected in the wage scale. The act evidently is intended as a just settlement of a difficult problem, affecting one of the most important of social relations, and it is to be judged in its entirety. We have said enough to demonstrate that, in such an adjustment, the particular rules of the common law affecting the subject matter are not placed by the 14th Amendment beyond the reach of the lawmaking power of the state; and thus we are brought to the question whether the method of compensation that is established as a substitute transcends the limits of permissible state action.

We will consider, first, the scheme of compensation, deferring for the present the question of the manner in which the employer is required to secure payment.
. . .

Of course, we cannot ignore the question whether the new arrangement is arbitrary and unreasonable, from the standpoint of natural justice. Respecting this, it is important to be observed that the act applies only to disabling or fatal personal injuries received in the course of hazardous employment in gainful occupation. Reduced to its elements, the situation to be dealt with is this: Employer and employee, by mutual consent, engage in a common operation intended to be advantageous to both; the employee is to contribute his personal services, and for these is to receive wages, and, ordinarily, nothing more; the employer is to furnish plant, facilities, organization, capital, credit, is to control and manage the operation, paying the wages and other expenses, disposing of the product at such prices as he can obtain, taking all the profits, if any there be, and, of necessity, bearing the entire losses. In the nature of things, there is more or less of a probability that the employee may lose his life through some accidental injury arising out of the employment, leaving his widow or children deprived of their natural support; or that he may sustain an injury not mortal, but resulting in his total or partial disablement, temporary or permanent, with corresponding impairment of earning capacity. The physical suffering must be borne by the employee alone; the laws of nature prevent this from being evaded or shifted to another, and the statute makes no attempt to afford an equivalent in compensation. But, besides, there is the loss of earning power,—a loss of that which stands to the employee as his capital in trade. This is a loss arising out of the business, and, however it may be charged up, is an expense of the operation, as truly as the cost of repairing broken machinery or any other expense that ordinarily is paid by the employer. Who is to bear the charge? It is plain that, on grounds of natural justice, it is not unreasonable for the state, while relieving the employer from responsibility for damages measured by common-law standards and payable in cases where he or those for whose conduct he is answerable are found to be at fault, to require him to contribute a reasonable amount, and according to a reasonable and definite scale, by way of compensation for the loss of earning power incurred in the common enterprise, irrespective of the question of negligence, instead of leaving the entire loss to rest where it may chance to fall,—that is, upon the injured employee or his dependents. Nor can it be deemed arbitrary and unreasonable, from the standpoint of the employee's interest, to supplant a system under which he assumed the entire risk of injury in ordinary cases, and in others had a right to recover an amount more or less speculative upon proving facts of negligence that often were difficult to prove, and substitute a system under which, in all ordinary cases of accidental injury, he is sure of a definite and easily ascertained compensation, not being obliged to assume the entire loss in any case, but in all cases assuming any loss beyond the prescribed scale.

Much emphasis is laid upon the criticism that the act creates liability without fault. This is sufficiently answered by what has been said, but we may add that liability without fault is not a novelty in the law. The common-law liability of the carrier, of the innkeeper, or him who employed fire or other dangerous agency or harbored a mischievous animal, was not dependent altogether upon questions of fault or negligence. Statutes imposing liability without fault have been sustained.

. . .

. . . The provision for compulsory compensation, in the act under consideration cannot be deemed to be an arbitrary and unreasonable application of the principle, so as to amount to a deprivation of the employer's property without due process of law. The pecuniary loss resulting from the employee's death or disablement must fall somewhere. It results from something done in the course of an operation from which the employer expects to derive a profit. In excluding the question of fault as a cause of the injury, the act in effect disregards the proximate cause and looks to one more remote,—the primary cause, as it may be deemed,—and that is, the employment itself. For this, both parties are responsible, since they voluntarily engage in it as coadventurers, with personal injury to the employee as a probable and foreseen result. In ignoring any possible negligence of the employee producing or contributing to the injury, the lawmaker reasonably may have been influenced by the belief that, in modern industry, the utmost diligence in the employer's service is in some degree inconsistent with adequate care on the part of the employee for his own safety; that the more intently he devotes himself to the work, the less he can take precautions for his own security. And it is evident that the consequences of a disabling or fatal injury are precisely the same to the parties immediately affected, and to the community, whether the proximate cause be culpable or innocent. Viewing the entire matter, it cannot be pronounced arbitrary and unreasonable for the state to impose upon the employer the absolute duty of making a moderate and definite compensation in money to every disabled employee, or, in case of his death, to those who were entitled to look to him for support, in lieu of the common-law liability confined to cases of negligence.

This, of course, is not to say that any scale of compensation, however insignificant, on the one hand, or onerous, on the other, would be supportable. In this case, no criticism is made on the ground that the compensation prescribed by the statute in question is unreasonable in amount, either in general or in the particular case. Any question of that kind may be met when it arises.

But, it is said, the statute strikes at the fundamentals of constitutional freedom of contract; and we are referred to two recent declarations by this court. The first is this: "Included in the right of personal liberty and the right of private property—partaking of the nature of each—is the right to make contracts for the acquisition of property. Chief among such contracts is that of personal employment, by which labor and other services are exchanged for money or other forms of property. If this right be struck down or arbitrarily interfered with, there is a substantial impairment of liberty in the long-established constitutional sense." *Coppage v. Kansas*, 236 U.S. 1, 14. And this is the other: "It requires no argument to show that the right to work for a living in the common occupations of the community is of the very essence of the personal freedom and opportunity that it was the purpose of the [14th] Amendment to secure." *Truax v. Raich*, 239 U.S. 33, 41.

It is not our purpose to qualify or weaken either of these declarations in the least. And we recognize that the legislation under review does measurably limit the freedom of employer and employee to agree respecting the terms of employment, and that it cannot be supported except on the ground that it is a reasonable exercise of the police power of the state. In our opinion it is fairly supportable upon that ground. And for this reason: The subject matter in respect of which freedom of contract is restricted is the matter of compensation for human life or limb lost or disability incurred in the course of hazardous employment, and the public has a direct interest in this as affecting the common welfare. "The whole is no greater than the sum of all the parts, and when the individual health, safety, and welfare are sacrificed or neglected, the state must suffer." *Holden v. Hardy*, 169 U.S. 366, 397. It cannot be doubted that the state may prohibit and punish self-maiming and attempts at suicide; it may prohibit a man from bartering away his life or his personal security; indeed, the right to these is often declared, in bills of rights, to be "natural and inalienable;" and the authority to prohibit contracts made in derogation of a lawfully-established policy of the state respecting compensation for accidental death or disabling personal injury is equally clear.

We have not overlooked the criticism that the act imposes no rule of conduct upon the employer with respect to the conditions of labor in the various industries embraced within its terms, prescribes no duty with regard to where the workmen shall work, the character of the machinery, tools, or appliances, the rules or regulations to be established, or the safety devices to be maintained. This statute does not concern itself with measures of prevention, which presumably are embraced in other laws. But the interest of the public is not confined to these. One of the grounds of its concern with the continued life and earning power of the individual is its interest in the prevention of pauperism, with its concomitants of vice and crime. And, in our opinion, laws regulating the responsibility of employers for the injury or death of employees, arising out of the employment, bear so close a relation to the protection of the lives and safety of those concerned that they properly may be regarded as coming within the category of police regulations.

. . .

We conclude that the prescribed scheme of compulsory compensation is not repugnant to the provisions of the 14th Amendment and are brought to consider, next, the manner in which the employer is required to secure payment of the compensation. By § 50, this may be done in one of three ways: (a) State insurance; (b) insurance with an authorized insurance corporation or association; or (c) by a deposit of securities. The record shows that the predecessor of plaintiff in error chose the third method, and, with the sanction of the Commission, deposited securities to the amount of $300,000, under § 50, and $30,000 in cash as a deposit to secure prompt and convenient payment, under § 25, with an agreement to make a further deposit if required. This was accompanied with a reservation of all contentions as to the invalidity of the act, and had not the effect of preventing plaintiff in error from raising the questions we have discussed.

The system of compulsory compensation having been found to be within the power of the state, it is within the limits of permissible regulation, in aid of the system, to require the employer to furnish satisfactory proof of his financial ability to pay the compensation, and to deposit a reasonable amount of securities for that purpose. The third clause of § 50 has not been, and presumably will not be, construed so as to give an unbridled discretion to the Commission; nor is it to be presumed that solvent employers will be prevented from becoming self-insurers on reasonable terms. No question is made but that the terms imposed upon this railroad company were reasonable in view of the magnitude of its operations, the number of its employees, and the amount of its pay roll (about $50,000,000 annually); hence no criticism of the practical effect of the third clause is suggested.

This being so, it is obvious that this case presents no question as to whether the state might, consistently with the 14th Amendment, compel employers to effect insurance according to either of the plans mentioned in the first and second clauses. There is no such compulsion, since self-insurance under the third clause presumably is open to all employers on reasonable terms that it is within the power of the state to impose. Regarded as optional arrangements, for acceptance or rejection by employers unwilling to comply with that clause, the plans of insurance are unexceptionable from the constitutional standpoint. Manifestly, the employee is not injuriously affected in a constitutional sense by the provisions giving to the employer an option to secure payment of the compensation in either of the modes prescribed, for there is no presumption that either will prove inadequate to safeguard the employee's interests.

COMMENTS AND QUESTIONS

1. The Court holds that the abolition of fault-based liability is constitutionally permissible, at least when the legislature provides "a reasonably just substitute." What are the standards for determining the justice of a substitute? Consider the Court's discussion of the abolition of the three defenses, and then ask yourself whether that discussion indicates that it would be constitutionally permissible for a legislature to replace fault-based liability with absolute liability.

2. Is *White* consistent with *Lochner*? In both cases, the legislature intervened to displace the wage bargain struck by workers and employers. *White* appears to explain the difference in results on the ground that workers' compensation statutes addressed (real) issues of loss of life and limb, in seeming contrast to the *Lochner* Court's skepticism about the purported health justifications for limiting workers' hours.

3. In a case properly presenting the issue, could a court abolish the fellow-servant rule? Recall that the rule was *created* by the courts in the first place. In a case properly presenting the issue, could a court abolish the requirement that an

employer's liability for workplace injuries be based on fault? What system would replace fault-based liability? Would it (could it?) resemble a workers' compensation system? In regard to the last question, note that Fuller's idea of polycentricity appears to support legislative—as opposed to judicial— alteration of the common law.

4. Like workers in the heyday of the fellow-servant and other rules aimed at limiting common-law liability, smokers trying to recover from tobacco companies for smoking-related injuries in the late twentieth century faced common-law doctrines, like assumption of risk, that invariably blocked their claims. As with workers earlier, it was eventually argued that the limitations on liability to smokers went against the economic interests of powerful constituencies—here, governments, state and federal, that paid for smoking-related medical costs through programs like Medicare and Medicaid. A wave of litigation ensued, brought most prominently by state attorneys general against tobacco companies, seeking recovery for the states' expenditures on smoking-related illnesses. An omnibus settlement was reached in the late 1990s. For our purposes, the most interesting part of this episode was the enactment of state legislation designed to smooth the way for the state lawsuits. In Florida, for example, the legislature passed a law abrogating common-law defenses such as assumption of risk and contributory negligence in cases in which the state sought recovery from tortfeasors for the medical costs of injured parties. The Florida Supreme Court upheld this law against a constitutional challenge. See *Agency for Health Care Administration v. Associated Industries of Florida, Inc.,* 678 So. 2d 1239 (Fla. 1996). Do you see any potential for self-dealing in the Florida law? Does the principle of the tobacco litigation—that common-law liability can follow from causing injuries that lead to medical costs paid for by the government—have any stopping point? Could fast-food restaurants be targeted under this principle? Handgun dealers? Automobile manufacturers?

B Moral Hazard

Sometimes measures designed to increase health or safety do not do so—or at least not to the extent expected—because the measures encourage people to engage in riskier behavior than they would otherwise have engaged in. Child-safety caps on pill bottles might encourage parents to be less careful about putting the bottles out of reach of children; seatbelts might encourage drivers to drive faster; low-fat foods might encourage people to eat more. The actors making the decisions about health or safety measures—whether they are private companies or government agencies—might see their health and safety goals go unmet if they do not take into account the possibility that people will respond to these measures by acting in riskier ways. (In chapter 9, we will discuss in more detail the ways in which regulation can have a paradoxical effect— when, for example, safety regulation increases rather than decreases risk.)

One specific variant of this kind of offsetting behavior is moral hazard. The idea behind the concept of moral hazard is that people will change their behavior—including taking more risks—if they believe that they will be compensated in the (unlikely, to be sure) event that an accident occurs. The first article that follows shows that risky offsetting behavior is a real-world phenomenon. The second explains why insurers cannot completely eliminate the problem of moral hazard.

■ *As Cars Get Safer, Drivers Take Risks*
ROBERT S. CHIRINKO
New York Times, April 10, 1994. Reprinted with permission
of Robert S. Chirinko

People often type on word processors much more carelessly than they do on typewriters. The reason: it is much easier to correct a mistake on the former.

Hidden in this mundane fact is an important principle for corporations, insurers and regulatory authorities. The idea, which goes by the name "offsetting behavior," is simple. It holds that if the cost, or danger, of doing something goes down, people will do it more.

This tendency can help explain some puzzles about cars and their safety equipment. For example, a recent study showed that antilock braking systems, which help prevent uncontrollable skids, are not reducing the number or cost of accidents, as measured by insurance claims.

The study by the Highway Loss Data Institute, an insurers' research group, is naturally causing great consternation. Consumers pay more for cars with antilock brakes; insurers discount premiums to owners of cars so equipped, and government regulations encourage the devices. How can these brakes—which do control skidding—fail to reduce accidents?

The answer is offsetting behavior. When a new technology arrives, drivers—like typists—will alter their behavior. They will realize that cars with antilock brakes are safer, which means the cost of risky driving is lower. Many of them will drive more aggressively, or drive more often in dangerous, inclement weather. Thus, even if accidents are less serious because these brakes do control skidding, the number of potential accident situations will increase. The bottom line: using these brakes will not necessarily reduce accidents or insurance claims.

Air bags tell a similar story. After the Dodge Daytona was equipped with air bags beginning in 1989, for example, the injury rate rose even though injuries were less severe, according to data compiled by the Highway Loss Data Institute. Similar results have been found for other car models.

Of course, other forces may be at work in these situations. Motorist skills are one. Many drivers may not understand how to use antilock brakes, which require steady pressure in a skid and not the "pumping" approach drivers are traditionally taught. But, whatever these other forces may be, offsetting behavior is quantitatively important. In a recent study published in the Journal of Policy Analysis and Management [vol. 12, Spring 1993], for example, Edward P. Harper Jr. and I found that such behavior greatly weakens the ability of safety regulations to reduce traffic fatalities.

For business and government, offsetting behavior clearly carries broad implications. In calculating lower premiums for drivers of cars with antilock brakes, for instance, insurers now focus only on the brakes' ability to help people avoid mishaps. If insurers realized that the number of slippery situations also increased in these "safer" cars, their calculations would differ.

Drivers of the nation's 10 million cars with antilock brakes probably won't welcome this insurer realization. They should know, though, that offsetting behavior can have salutary effects, too.

For example, pollution laws will probably lead auto companies to make lighter cars. Some observers worry that these cars will cause more traffic fatalities. But the principle of offsetting behavior suggests that people will drive downsized autos less aggressively—thus tempering, perhaps greatly, adverse effects from the smaller vehicles.

As with antilock brakes, this offsetting behavior makes instinctive sense. It is just like a person walking more carefully on an icy sidewalk.

Offsetting behavior is neither good nor bad. It is neutral—but it is a force business and government should consider.

■ *An Introduction to Law and Economics*
A. MITCHELL POLINSKY

3d ed., pp. 53–55 (Aspen Publishers, 2003). Reprinted with permission
of Aspen Law & Business

One common way of eliminating risk is through insurance. For detrimental risks, the insured person pays some amount of money with certainty—the insurance premium—in return for which he is fully compensated if the undesirable risk materializes....

An insurance policy that completely eliminates the risk might, however, have an undesirable side effect.... For example, if personal items left in your car are completely insured against theft, you may be more likely to leave your camera on the back seat rather than to go to the trouble of putting it in the trunk. This ... illustrates a general problem—the provision of insurance may increase the probability of a loss or the size of the loss because the insured person has less of an incentive to take precautions. In the insurance literature this phenomenon is called the problem of *moral hazard*.

In principle, the moral hazard problem can be overcome by adjusting the insurance premium to reflect the increase in the expected loss resulting from the insured person's taking less care. For example, suppose your camera is worth $500 and that putting it in the trunk of your car eliminates the possibility of theft, whereas leaving it on the back seat leads to a one-in-a-hundred chance of having it stolen. In other words, leaving it on the back seat leads to an *expected* loss of $5. If your insurance premium were to increase by $5 if you regularly left your camera on the back seat of your car, then you would leave it there only if it is worth at least $5 to you to do so. It may or may not be worth this much to leave it there. For example, if you are a professional photographer specializing in outdoor photography, it probably would be worth paying $5 more for the extra convenience, whereas for most people the added convenience would not be worth this much. In either case, by being forced to pay more because of the increased expected loss, the insured person will have the appropriate incentive to take precautions. In other words, the moral hazard problem can be eliminated if the insurance premium is based on the care exercised by the insured person.

This solution to the moral hazard problem usually is not feasible in practice because the insurer cannot cheaply monitor the behavior of the person being insured. In the camera example, an ideal insurance policy would require that the insurance company determine whether the insured person regularly left his camera on the back seat of his car....

There are other alternatives in practice to monitoring the insured person's behavior and adjusting the premium accordingly. In general, these alternatives involve providing only partial insurance in order to induce the insured person to take some precautions. Sometimes this takes the form of a *deductible*, in which, for example, the insured person bears the first $100 of loss and the insurance company bears the rest. Other times it takes the form of *co-insurance*, in which, for example, the insured person bears 20 percent of all losses. In either case, this approach is obviously a compromise since it leaves some risk on a risk-averse person and, in general, it will not completely solve the problem of moral hazard. On balance, however, partial insurance may be preferable both to no insurance at all (which leaves the most risk on risk-averse persons) and to complete insurance (which provides little or no incentive to take precautions).

COMMENTS AND QUESTIONS

1. Make sure you understand the difference between the two kinds of moral hazard discussed in these articles. One involves offsetting behavior that increases risk. This behavior might occur in response to a variety of things—everything from consumer protection measures to health insurance. The other involves the specific context of insurance and the effect of insurance on the insured population's willingness to claim injury and seek compensation.

2. Workers' compensation has the potential to create both kinds of moral hazard: workers might be less careful about risks, knowing they will be compensated if they are injured, and they might file more claims against their employers due to the presence of insurance. In the next reading, Michael Moore and Kip Viscusi discuss both concepts in the context of workers' compensation. Their treatment is followed by Peter Dorman's observations about why one should not too quickly conclude that an increase in claims, following an increase in workers' compensation benefits, necessarily shows moral hazard at work. A third article in this series, by Malcolm Gladwell, disputes the relevance of moral hazard to a different insurance context, that relating to health care.

- ■ *Compensation Mechanisms for Job Risks: Wages, Workers' Compensation, and Product Liability*
  MICHAEL J. MOORE AND W. KIP VISCUSI
  pp. 28–29, 122, 135 (Princeton University Press, 1990). © 1990 Princeton University Press. Reprinted by permission of Princeton University Press

... Like any insurance program, workers' compensation does more than compensate insured workers for the pecuniary costs (lost earnings and medical expenses) of their injuries. In particular, economic models of rational firm and worker behavior predict that insurance benefits for on-the-job injuries alter risk-taking behavior in fundamentally opposed ways. The two primary forces are the safety incentive effects of workers' compensation premiums on firms and the moral hazard effects of benefits on workers.

To the extent that firms' safety records are reflected in their premiums, workers' compensation insurance will act as an injury tax on firms, providing financial incentives to increase workplace safety. Employer contributions to state funds are determined by an experience-rating procedure, so that premium levels potentially reflect a firm's safety record and, in effect, act as a tax on injuries. The importance of the injury tax role of workers' compensation is conditioned by the degree of this experience rating. In practice, larger firms are rated most closely in accordance with their actual experience. Such firms can also self-insure, if they have an approved means of doing so. Smaller firms are typically rated as a group and therefore do not pay the full cost of an accident in terms of increased premiums.

Since the financial losses to workers that result from workplace injuries are reduced by workers' compensation, increased benefits will at the same time result in reduced care by workers, which could offset the safety incentive effect. Of course, given the large implicit valuations that workers place on their health and safety, which are fundamentally irreplaceable, this particular form of moral hazard is probably not too important. Rather, moral hazard in the workers' compensation system takes the form of increases in the frequency of claims filed and in their duration.

. . . [A] broad sample of research on the effects of workers' compensation on measured job risks . . . indicate[s] that the moral hazard effects dominate the safety incentive effects. . . .

This general result—that benefit increases increase the incidence of less severe accidents, but decrease their severity—is examined in this chapter. The most severe accident—death—should reflect very little moral hazard. Deaths cannot be falsely claimed, of course, and the high values that workers implicitly attach to lives saved suggest that workers would not be willing to substitute fatality benefits for their own lives. Therefore, if workers' compensation provides any safety incentives to firms, these will be reflected most strongly in fatality rate data. . . .

[O]ur results indicate that workers' compensation generates truly dramatic reductions in workplace fatalities. This finding does not cast doubt on the moral hazard issue. It does, however, establish a function of workers' compensation that yields considerable benefits in the form of reduced workplace fatalities. . . .

The favorable evidence presented here with respect to the performance of workers' compensation is not intended to lead observers to dismiss as unimportant the difficult causality problems raised by health risks, litigation problems raised by permanent disabilities, and continuing moral hazard problems with respect to nonfatal injury claims and their duration. Nevertheless, our results do suggest that workers' compensation is more successful in promoting its intended objectives than previously believed.

- *Markets and Mortality: Economics, Dangerous Work, and the Value of Human Life*
PETER DORMAN
pp. 131–35, 198–99 (Cambridge University Press, 1996). Reprinted with permission of Cambridge University Press

Several studies have attempted to measure the incentive effect of [workers' compensation (WC)], mostly with an eye to assessing the importance of experience-rating. Since each state has its own WC program with its particular financing and benefit rules, the general strategy is to look for correlations between state-level WC features and safety records. The problem is complex, though: after all, higher benefits—and therefore higher premiums—might make firms more safety-conscious, but they might also change workers' incentives to report illnesses and injuries. This latter problem is almost universally described in the literature as "workers' moral hazard"; the assumption is that as benefit levels rise workers will try to cheat the system by filing spurious claims. As an example, consider the analysis of Dionne and St-Michel (1991). Workers, according to these economists, would like to make false WC claims, but face two costs—the difficulty of finding equally corrupt doctors to collude with and the risk that their scam will be revealed and benefits will be denied. So they "optimize" by equating the marginal benefits and costs of cheating, and in this formulation the effect of increasing benefits is to raise the equilibrium level of false claims. To test this model, they compare the recovery periods of different ailments for which WC has been filed. Since back ailments are more difficult to diagnose, and are therefore a potential bonanza for scam artists, they check to see whether increases in WC benefits have a differential effect on these claims. Their empirical results corroborate this hunch: when benefits rise workers claim a longer recovery period for back problems, but not for other, more easily diagnosed ailments. This is taken as evidence that worker moral hazard really exists.

What is wrong with this story? Behind the entire argument lies the unspoken assumption that, in a world of perfect information (no opportunity for cheating), workers would make all their legitimate claims and only their legitimate claims. Yet anyone with even a modest familiarity with working-class experience knows this is not true. WC pays only a portion of lost wages—generally about two-thirds. For someone living month-to-month, trying to make car and house payments, that may not be enough. More subtle, but perhaps even more important, is the pressure from the employer. Filing the extra claim or adding the extra week of recovery could jeopardize a promotion or even the job itself. Few supervisors will say openly that they penalize workers for filing under WC, but, all else being equal, a worker who simply sucks it in is more likely to be viewed as a "team player." Thus, when benefits rise and claims follow suit, it may well be that fewer legitimate claims are being suppressed. (Of course, with any increase in benefits claims will rise for both legitimate and illegitimate reasons; without additional information there is no way to know which effect predominates.) It is easy to see how this logic applies to Dionne and St-Michel: back pains are not only difficult for doctors and claims adjusters to diagnose; they are also difficult for workers to diagnose. It is all too easy to continue working, hoping that the pain will go away by itself. The incentive to tough it out will depend on the costs and benefits of filing. Increase the compensation, and stoicism becomes less attractive.

■ The Moral-Hazard Myth: The Bad Idea behind Our Failed Health-Care System

MALCOLM GLADWELL

The New Yorker (August 29, 2005). Reprinted with permission of the author

...One of the great mysteries of political life in the United States is why Americans are so devoted to their health-care system. Six times in the past century—during the First World War, during the Depression, during the Truman and Johnson Administrations, in the Senate in the nineteen-seventies, and during the Clinton years—efforts have been made to introduce some kind of universal health insurance, and each time the efforts have been rejected. Instead, the United States has opted for a makeshift system of increasing complexity and dysfunction. Americans spend $5,267 per capita on health care every year, almost two and [a] half times the industrialized world's median of $2,193; the extra spending comes to hundreds of billions of dollars a year. What does that extra spending buy us? Americans have fewer doctors per capita than most Western countries. We go to the doctor less than people in other Western countries. We get admitted to the hospital less frequently than people in other Western countries. We are less satisfied with our health care than our counterparts in other countries. American life expectancy is lower than the Western average. Childhood-immunization rates in the United States are lower than average. Infant-mortality rates are in the nineteenth percentile of industrialized nations. Doctors here perform more high-end medical procedures, such as coronary angioplasties, than in other countries, but most of the wealthier Western countries have more CT scanners than the United States does, and Switzerland, Japan, Austria, and Finland all have more MRI machines per capita. Nor is our system more efficient. The United States spends more than a thousand dollars per capita per year—or close to four hundred billion dollars—on health-care-related paperwork and administration, whereas Canada, for example, spends only about three hundred dollars per capita. And, of course, every other country in the industrialized world insures all its citizens; despite those extra hundreds of billions of dollars we spend each year, we leave forty-five million people without any insurance. A country that displays an almost ruthless commitment to efficiency and performance in every aspect of its economy—a country that switched to Japanese cars the moment they were more reliable, and to Chinese T-shirts the moment they were five cents cheaper—has loyally stuck with a health-care system that leaves its citizenry pulling out their teeth with pliers.

America's health-care mess is, in part, simply an accident of history. The fact that there have been six attempts at universal health coverage in the last century suggests that there has long been support for the idea. But politics has always got in the way. In both Europe and the United States, for example, the push for health insurance was led, in large part, by organized labor. But in Europe the unions worked through the political system, fighting for coverage for all citizens. From the start, health insurance in Europe was public and universal, and that created powerful political support for any attempt to expand benefits. In the United States, by contrast, the unions worked through the collective-bargaining system and, as a result, could win health benefits only for their own members. Health insurance here has always been private and selective, and every attempt to expand benefits has resulted in a paralyzing political battle over who would be added to insurance rolls and who ought to pay for those additions.

Policy is driven by more than politics, however. It is equally driven by ideas, and in the past few decades a particular idea has taken hold among prominent American economists which has also been a powerful impediment to the expansion of health insurance. The idea is known as "moral hazard." Health economists in other Western nations do not share this obsession. Nor do most Americans. But moral hazard has profoundly shaped the way think tanks formulate policy and the way experts argue and the way health insurers structure their plans and the way legislation and regulations have been written. The health-care mess isn't merely the unintentional result of political dysfunction, in other words. It is also the deliberate consequence of the way in which American policymakers have come to think about insurance.

"Moral hazard" is the term economists use to describe the fact that insurance can change the behavior of the person being insured. If your office gives you and your co-workers all the free Pepsi you want—if your employer, in effect, offers universal Pepsi insurance—you'll drink more Pepsi than you would have otherwise. If you have a no-deductible fire-insurance policy, you may be a little less diligent in clearing the brush away from your house. The savings-and-loan crisis of the nineteen-eighties was created, in large part, by the fact that the federal government insured savings deposits of up to a hundred thousand dollars, and so the newly deregulated S. & L.s made far riskier investments than they would have otherwise. Insurance can have the paradoxical effect of producing risky and wasteful behavior. Economists spend a great deal of time thinking about such moral hazard for good reason. Insurance is an attempt to make human life safer and more secure. But, if those efforts can backfire and produce riskier behavior, providing insurance becomes a much more complicated and problematic endeavor.

In 1968, the economist Mark Pauly argued that moral hazard played an enormous role in medicine, and, as John Nyman writes in his book "The Theory of the Demand for Health Insurance," Pauly's paper has become the "single most influential article in the health economics literature." Nyman, an economist at the University of Minnesota, says that the fear of moral hazard lies behind the thicket of co-payments and deductibles and utilization reviews which characterizes the American health-insurance system. Fear of moral hazard, Nyman writes, also explains "the general lack of enthusiasm by U.S. health economists for the expansion of health insurance coverage (for example, national health insurance or expanded Medicare benefits) in the U.S."

What Nyman is saying is that when your insurance company requires that you make a twenty-dollar co-payment for a visit to the doctor, or when your plan includes an annual five-hundred-dollar or thousand-dollar deductible, it's not simply an attempt to get you to pick up a larger share of your health costs. It is an attempt to make your use of the health-care system more efficient. Making you responsible for a share of the costs, the argument runs, will reduce moral hazard: you'll no longer grab one of those free Pepsis when you aren't really thirsty. That's also why Nyman says that the notion of moral hazard is behind the "lack of enthusiasm" for expansion of health insurance. If you think of insurance as producing wasteful consumption of medical services, then the fact that there are forty-five million Americans without health insurance is no longer an immediate cause for alarm. After all, it's not as if the uninsured never go to the doctor. They spend, on average, $934 a year on medical care. A moral-hazard theorist would say that they go to the doctor when they really have to. Those of us with private insurance, by contrast, consume $2,347 worth of health care a year. If a lot of that extra $1,413 is waste, then maybe the uninsured person is the truly efficient consumer of health care.

The moral-hazard argument makes sense, however, only if we consume health care in the same way that we consume other consumer goods, and to economists like Nyman this assumption is plainly absurd. We go to the doctor grudgingly, only because we're sick. "Moral hazard is overblown," the Princeton economist Uwe Reinhardt says. "You always hear that the demand for health care is unlimited. This is just not true. People who are very well insured, who are very rich, do you see them check into the hospital because it's free? Do people really like to go to the doctor? Do they check into the hospital instead of playing golf?"

For that matter, when you have to pay for your own health care, does your consumption really become more efficient? In the late nineteen-seventies, the RAND Corporation did an extensive study on the question, randomly assigning families to health plans with co-payment levels at zero per cent, twenty-five per cent, fifty per cent, or ninety-five per cent, up to six thousand dollars. As you might expect, the more that people were asked to chip in for their health care the less care they used. The problem was that they cut back equally on both frivolous care and useful care. Poor people in the high-deductible group with hypertension, for instance, didn't do nearly as good a job of controlling their blood pressure as those in other groups, resulting in a ten-per-cent increase in the likelihood of death. As a recent Commonwealth Fund study concluded, cost sharing is "a blunt instrument." Of course it is: how should the average consumer be expected to know beforehand what care is frivolous and what care is useful? I just went to the dermatologist to get moles checked for skin cancer. If I had had to pay a hundred per cent, or even fifty per cent, of the cost of the visit, I might not have gone. Would that have been a wise decision? I have no idea. But if one of those moles really is cancerous, that simple, inexpensive visit could save the health-care system tens of thousands of dollars (not to mention saving me a great deal of heartbreak). The focus on moral hazard suggests that the changes we make in our behavior when we have insurance are nearly always wasteful. Yet, when it comes to health care, many of the things we do only because we have insurance—like getting our moles checked, or getting our teeth cleaned regularly, or getting a mammogram or engaging in other routine preventive care—are anything but wasteful and inefficient. In fact, they are behaviors that could end up saving the health-care system a good deal of money.

Sered and Fernandopulle tell the story of Steve, a factory worker from northern Idaho, with a "grotesque[-]looking left hand—what looks like a bone sticks out the side." When he was younger, he broke his hand. "The doctor wanted to operate on it," he recalls. "And because I didn't have insurance, well, I was like 'I ain't gonna have it operated on.' The doctor said, 'Well, I can wrap it for you with an Ace bandage.' I said, 'Ahh, let's do that, then.'" Steve uses less health care than he would if he had insurance, but that's not because he has defeated the scourge of moral hazard. It's because instead of getting a broken bone fixed he put a bandage on it. . . .

COMMENTS AND QUESTIONS

1. According to Moore and Viscusi, what behavioral changes result from the existence of workers' compensation? What does Dorman add? Note Moore and Viscusi's distinction between workplace injuries and workplace fatalities. Why does workers' compensation increase the incidence of workplace injuries but decrease their severity?

2. Moore and Viscusi also find that the positive effects of workers' compensation on workplace safety dwarf the positive effects of OSHA, a system of directly prescribing workplace conditions. How could this happen?

3. As Dorman explains, it can be very difficult to determine whether an increase in workers' compensation claims, coincident with an increase in benefits, is the result of moral hazard. Sometimes compensation claims also increase when plants close. When a jeans manufacturer shut a factory in Oklahoma, for example, its workers' compensation claims increased from 6 the previous year to 400 in the year it closed. Peter Kerr, "As Plants Close, Injury Claims Rise," *New York Times* (Feb. 22, 1993). In these cases, too, it is hard to tell whether the increase in claims is due to workers' gaming the system or to the kinds of factors Dorman cites.

   Why might legitimate compensation claims be put off unless and until a plant closes? Several people who worked at the Oklahoma factory gave a simple but surprising explanation: they said they hadn't known about workers' compensation until the plant closed. One worker who said she hadn't known about workers' compensation said: "I'd been working at the plant for 17 years, and I had been hurting for 10 years. From doing the same thing every day, bending over the machines, the carts, I just hurt all over." If this employee had known about workers' compensation before the plant closed, would there be any reason for her to decline to file a claim?

4. Are you persuaded by Gladwell's suggestion that people do not consume health care in the same way they consume other goods and services? If so, does this eliminate the moral hazard problem associated with health insurance?

5. As the following report explains, moral hazard can operate on the employer's side as well. The incentives here depend on the structure for financing workers' compensation. Pay attention to the distinctions between different financing structures and to the incentives these structures create for employer-generated health and safety measures.

■ *Interim Report to Congress on Occupational Diseases*
U.S. DEPARTMENT OF LABOR
pp. 76–77 (1980)

In theory workers' compensation reflects a market approach to internalizing the costs of occupational diseases and injuries by altering the cost structure of firms through a system of taxes that enables private prices to reflect social costs. An additional objective, however, is to spread accident losses among a group of firms while providing minimum support for work-related disabilities.

As currently practiced, a three-tiered insurance system prevails—self-insurance, experience rating, and class rating. Self-insurance is a mechanism by which companies set aside a pool of funds to support workers' compensation payments. It necessitates financial strength to sustain the actuarial risk, the capability to disperse that risk, and the economies of scale to reduce administrative charges; therefore, it is restricted to large firms. Nationally, self-insurance plans encompass less than 1 percent of employers and between 10–15 percent of employees. At the opposite end of the spectrum, small firms operate under class manual rates with premium rates fixed as a payroll tax on the basis of industry injury/illness experience. Eighty-five percent of the employers and 15 percent of employees are covered under manual rate schemes. Medium sized firms are taxed under experience or retrospective rating schedules. The experience rating formulas are designed such that as a firm's injury frequency rate improves, more weight is given to the firm's experience and less to the industry class rate.

In practice, the potential accident deterrence role of the workers' compensation system has proved to be of little value. By definition, insurance spreads accident risks: premiums are transferred from those with below-average accident and illness costs to cover above-average contingencies. However, unless there exists sufficient distinction among risks, incentives to avoid losses are diluted. Consequently, the degree to which such insurance is rated by risk classes will positively influence-prevention incentives, but will concurrently weaken the loss spreading character of insurance.

Only self-insured firms avoid this insurance dilemma, since they assume all risks. Consequently, accident avoidance incentives are preserved. (In practice, many self insured firms re-insure catastrophic expenses.) On the other hand, manual rating systems do not discriminate between risk classes. Employers pay a fixed charge regardless of their records (although firms with excessively poor records may receive a surcharge). Consequently, individual incentives to invest in safety and health improvements and to avoid losses are diminished. In reality, the probabilities used to calculate the class rates are influenced by individual activity. Arrow (1963) has demonstrated that under this moral hazard situation, firms will underinvest in safety and health improvements. Experience rating represents the intermediate case. Risks are pooled but firms' premiums are subject to modification based on individual experience. However, Russell (1974) has shown that incentives to undertake safety and health investments, given current rate-making formulas, diminish rapidly as accident incidence rates are lowered.

Further, low levels of income replacement under workers' compensation may imply that regardless of the prevention incentive structure, the amount of accident costs internalized may prove insufficient to influence employers' behavior—i.e., only premiums exceeding a certain threshold may be marginally effectual in inducing investments. Indeed, there is no clear empirical evidence to support the hypothesis that the present pricing system reduces accident frequencies. This should carry over to the incidence of occupational diseases since relatively few occupational disease cases are compensated by the workers' compensation system. Further, those compensated receive relatively small lump-sum settlements awarded after long delays and extensive litigation. . . .

COMMENTS AND QUESTIONS

1. Why does moral hazard occur on the employer's part? Consider the following observation:

   > Suppose that a firm is thinking of spending $2,000 a year to maintain a device that will prevent injuries for which the annual compensable loss would total $2,500. If the firm were completely manual-rated, its premium savings attendant to this expenditure would be zero; that is, its premium reflects industry wide losses alone, and these losses are not

appreciably affected by the $2,500 reduction in one firm.... Only if the firm were fully self-rated (or very close to it) would firms have an unequivocal incentive to undertake the hypothesized safety expenditure. Chelius and Smith, "Experience-Rating and Injury Prevention," in Safety and the Work Force (J. Worrall ed., 1983)

2. How can moral hazard on the employer's part be reduced? Consider the following possibilities: increasing the use of experience rating (which entails high administrative costs); forcing workers to bear more of the costs of injury but allowing them to sue their employers for gross negligence; writing workers' compensation insurance with a deductible, in effect requiring employers to self-insure for the deductible amount.

3. The materials that follow describe other general problems with workers' compensation as an insurance system with effects on employers' incentives to provide a safe workplace. As you read them, keep in mind Moore and Viscusi's finding that workers' compensation has a much greater positive effect on workplace safety than OSHA. This perspective may help you appreciate that the evaluation of workers' compensation as a system for reducing workplace injury should be a comparative one; the question is whether, despite its failings, workers' compensation has advantages over other means of addressing workplace risks.

C Modern Workers' Compensation Systems

Given the continuing toll of work-related deaths, injuries, and illnesses, it remains important to evaluate the effect of regulatory systems such as workers' compensation on employers' incentives to improve workplace health and safety. The materials that follow give reasons to be critical of workers' compensation on this score. The first two articles describe how workers' compensation does not give adequate relief to workers who are killed, injured, or become ill on the job; the first deals with these issues in general, and the second specifically relates to why workers' compensation inadequately addresses the problem of occupational disease.

■ Crisis in the Workplace: Occupational Disease and Injury
NICHOLAS ASHFORD
p. 350 (MIT Press 1976). Reprinted with permission of MIT Press

[T]he bulk of the costs associated with occupational injury and illness do not presently befall the firm, directly or indirectly; and herein lies the primary explanation for the failure of the market mechanism to provide a socially tolerable level of workplace health and safety.[*] Most of the costs of occupational illness and injury are directly borne by working people and their families. Workers who become

---

[*] Many economists will disagree with this statement, on the grounds that "hazard pay" compensates workers for assuming differential job-related risk, and acts as an incentive for employers to reduce the risk to which their workforce is exposed.... I do not agree with this contention.

injured or ill as a result of their job, and their dependents, suffer a considerable loss of income and fringe benefits such as group medical and life insurance, and a general diminution of economic security and well-being. The removal of the right to sue in tort since establishment of the system of workmen's compensation has prevented disabled employees or their dependents from recovering money damages for pain and suffering, with the result that employers presently do not have to pay for the full consequences of their negligence.

Workmen's compensation payments do not reflect even the direct *wage* losses of disabled employees, much less such indirect economic losses as fringe benefits and the incalculable intangible costs of pain, suffering, and bereavement. Moreover, since most illness of occupational origin is not presently recognized as compensable, many disabled workers do not even enjoy the inadequate measure of income security which workmen's compensation provides.

Those victims of occupational injury and illness who are fortunate enough to receive workmen's compensation will typically find that benefits represent less than 50% of their prior earnings. Pay raises received for any reason by coworkers remaining on the job—such as promotion, cost-of-living adjustment, or union negotiation—are not reflected in the level of workmen's compensation benefits received by the previously disabled. The relevant factor in determining the impact of occupational illness and injury upon a victim's income is not his earnings prior to disability, but rather the level of income he would currently be earning had he not been disabled on the job.

Even if workmen's compensation payments fully restored the income losses sustained by the victims of occupational illness and injury and their families, the costs in terms of the value of human life and the pain and suffering inflicted would still not be fully internalized. As previously mentioned, industrial injury claims over 14,000 lives annually in this country, while industrial disease may claim as many as 100,000. Each year there are an estimated 390,000 new cases of occupational illness, and roughly one employee in eight suffers a disabling injury at work; 100,000 per year are disabled permanently as a result. The individual and social costs of this enormous amount of occupational illness and injury is in no sense limited to the attendant losses of income or production, though these are far from negligible. Though some economists equate the value of a human life with the person's income for purposes of cost-benefit analysis (as do many courts in assessing damages in civil suits), there is no justification in economic theory for employing such a procedure.

Furthermore, much of the cost of occupational illness and injury befalls, not the employer or worker, but society at large. The social cost of maintaining and rehabilitating victims and providing for their dependents is by no means entirely paid by the victims themselves, or by the firms which employ them. Victims of occupational illness and injury and their surviving dependents place an enormous burden on social-welfare services in terms of the costs of medical care, rehabilitation, retraining, and direct income maintenance. Family breakup sometimes ensues upon the death or disability of the primary breadwinner, with the result that surviving dependents may become wards of the state. Discouragement and disillusionment attendant upon the trauma experienced by the victim and members of his family may trigger or exacerbate emotional problems that require the publicly subsidized assistance of social workers, psychiatrists, or other costly professionals.

As victims of occupational illness and injury, large numbers of working people and their families are converted from economically self-sufficient taxpayers to economically dependent welfare recipients. The enormous social costs of this sad transition are not internalized by their employers, but are diffused more generally throughout society—ultimately, in large measure, in the form of higher taxes on those working people who remain healthy enough to work. Management, secure in the knowledge that it will probably not be held financially accountable for the costs of pain and suffering that accompany its decisions, may therefore not attach sufficient weight to maintaining the health and safety of the workforce. Thus, it could be said that the employer "free-rides" on the health and safety of his workers.

Furthermore, even if these measurable social costs could somehow be properly assigned to the responsible parties, there would still remain the problem of the intangible costs that befall individuals other than those directly involved in the decision-making process. People value the lives and well-being of their friends, relatives, and associates, and suffer intangible but nonetheless very real psychic loss if any of these people become victims of occupational illness or injury. Though workers may in principle receive compensation in the form of hazard pay or damage award commensurate with their personal assumption of job-related risk, there is no comparable mechanism through which potentially aggrieved friends and loved ones can receive adequate compensation.

■ *Responses to Occupational Disease: The Role of Markets, Regulation, and Information*
ELINOR P. SCHROEDER AND SIDNEY A. SHAPIRO
72 Geo. L.J. 1231 (1984). Reprinted with permission
of Georgetown Law Journal

[F]ew workers receive compensation for work-related illnesses. Studies estimate that only two to three percent of all workers' compensation payments compensate recipients for occupational disease. A 1980 U.S. Department of Labor report estimated that only about three percent of all workers severely disabled by occupational diseases received workers' compensation, and the payments they received replaced only about one-eighth of their lost wages. If these estimates are accurate, employers internalize little of the cost of occupational disease. The limited internalization occurs for six reasons.

First, there is little economic incentive for employers to spend money to prevent occupational disease. Decisions concerning how much to spend to prevent disease are not based on current workers' compensation expenses, which are the result of past actions, but on the likelihood that such efforts will prevent diseases in the future. Since future diseases may not occur until many years later, firms may heavily discount their consequences and spend little or nothing on prevention. Moreover, many firms are required to insure against the possibility of having to make workers' compensation payments. The structure of that insurance lessens their incentive to take preventive measures because premiums are based primarily on the experience of classes of employers rather than on the safety performance of individual employers.

Second, any employer liability for employee illness will be less than the social costs of the illness. workers' compensation payments are controlled by a statutorily prescribed formula which often limits compensation to less than the direct wage losses of disabled employees. Further, payments do not cover such items as lost fringe benefits and the intangible costs of pain and suffering and the spouse's loss of consortium.

Third, there is little internalization because many workers fail to recognize that they have a claim when their illnesses occur long after the hazardous exposure. Asbestos insulation workers studied by Dr. Selikoff, for example, filed workers' compensation claims for only thirty-three percent of their asbestos-related disabilities, and their families filed claims for only thirty-six percent of the asbestos-related deaths. In the first seven years that brown lung disease (byssinosis) was compensable in North and South Carolina, only 1,000 disabled workers filed claims out of an estimated population of 30,000 disabled workers.

Fourth, there is little internalization because those workers who do file claims often fail to establish their eligibility for benefits. Some workers fail because there is insufficient information available about their disease to establish that it is work related. The long latency period of many illnesses means that the employee may have had no recent contact with the hazard that caused the disease. In such a case, the worker is without persuasive evidence that the illness is work related. Epidemiological data can establish that all workers exposed to a certain hazard will have a greater probability of contracting a disease than other workers, but this research alone cannot prove that a given worker became ill from contact with the hazardous substance rather than from a non-work-related cause. Worker ignorance is sometimes caused by employers who have withheld information needed to establish claims.

Fifth, workers also fail to obtain compensation because many states have established eligibility requirements that are difficult or impossible to satisfy....

Sixth, employers, or their insurance companies, litigate most occupational disease claims because the difficulty of proving causation and the existence of restrictive standards for recovery make employer victories in disease cases more likely than in accident cases.

COMMENTS AND QUESTIONS

1. Recall the "deal" that helped to persuade the Court to uphold the workers' compensation scheme in *White*: the employer gave up fault-based liability in return for limited recovery on the part of the employee, and the employee gave up the more generous remedies of the common law in return for the more reliable relief afforded by workers' compensation. Given this "deal," why are scholars like Ashford, Schroeder, and Shapiro critical of workers' compensation on the ground that it affords incomplete compensation? Hasn't this feature been built into the system—deliberately—from the very beginning?

2. One problem with workers' compensation typified by the case of occupational disease is that of rigidity. Often, workers' compensation laws provide specific lists of the diseases they will cover (just as these laws also provide specific compensation schedules for injured workers). In thinking about the problem of rigidity, consider the following observations:

   These laws had the virtue of simplicity; where they applied they were a form of prima facie coverage, and workers faced minimal problems of proof. The theory promoting the adoption of schedules was that insurers would be inclined to pay benefits without contesting worker eligibility once a prima facie showing of injury had been made. Problems arose, however, when diseases not listed in the schedules afflicted workers. Only the legislatures could amend the schedules to include more diseases. A sufficient number of workers had to suffer from a condition before the medical profession deemed it an occupational disease, and then the legislatures had to be persuaded to add the disease to the schedules. Meanwhile workers suffered or died without compensation. Laurence Locke, *Adapting Worker's Compensation to the Special Problems of Occupational Disease*, 9 Harv. Envtl. L. Rev. 249, 255–68 (1985).

Would it be better if workers' compensation laws provided simply (as some do) that diseases "peculiar to" or "characteristic of" the relevant trade would be covered? What problems might arise in this setting?

3. Schroeder and Shapiro mention the difficulties associated with diseases that have a long latency period, that is, a long period between exposure to a harmful substance and manifestation of disease. One set of diseases particularly characterized by long latency periods are cancers. Here are the estimated latency periods for cancers resulting from particular hazardous substances:

Carcinogenic Substance	Range of Latent Period in Years	Average Limit Period in Years
Asbestos	15–21	18
Chromates	5–47	15
Nickel	6–30	22
Coal tar fumes	9–23	16
Ionizing radiations	7–50	15–35
Petroleum, Petroleum coke, Wax, Creosote, Anthracene, Paraffin, Shale, Mineral Oils	12–30	
Benzene	6–14	
Auramine, Benzidine, Alpha- and Beta-Naphthylamine, Magenta, 4-Aminodiphenyl, 4-Nitrodiphenyl	13–30	
Mustard Gas	10–25	
Isopropyl Oil	10	
Vinyl chloride	20–30	
Bis (chloromethyl) ether, Chloromythyl Methyl ether	5+	
Arsenic	10+	
Chromium	15–25	
Nickel	3–30	
Asbestos	4–50	
Wood	30–40	
Leather	40–50	
Ultraviolet rays	Varies with skin pigment and texture 10–25	
X-rays	10–25	
Uranium, Radon, Radium, Mesothorium	10–15	

P. S. Barth and H. A. Hunt, Workers' Compensation and Work-Related Illnesses and Diseases (MIT Press 1980).

Why might long latency periods pose problems for the workers' compensation system? Barth and Hunt offer the following explanation:

> Diseases with long latency cause two major types of problems for workers' compensation. First, because of the passage of time, the employee, the physician, and others may miss the link between the disease and a hazard encountered many years earlier. Even if the worker or the employer may have known that a particular substance was hazardous and the potential source of some disease, the employee may forget this contact occurred or that it might be responsible for an illness years later. Thus there is little reason to suppose that a worker—or his survivor—will even be aware that the disease is work-related, let alone compensable.
>
> The second major problem involving long latency periods is that of establishing sufficient proof to sustain a workers' compensation claim. The passage of time handicaps the employee and employer in their search for necessary evidence regarding the exposure to a hazard, the dose involved, the type of work being done, and so forth. Either side may face this difficulty; however, it is likely to be a far greater problem for the claimant because the burden of proof almost invariably fails on him or his survivor. . . .

4. Try to place the foregoing materials into the "naming, blaming, claiming" framework we encountered in chapter 3. Which aspects of the critiques of workers' compensation involve a failure to name? Failure to claim? Consider whether another common problem with workers' compensation—that of multiple causation, or the contribution of multiple employers to a single disease—might involve a failure to name, to blame, or both.

5. Many materials on continuing problems in the administration of workers' compensation systems, including the next article, illustrate a more general problem: Often when a social-legal problem is dealt with in some manner, the problem simply resurfaces elsewhere. In the present context, Friedman and Ladinsky argued that the inadequacies of the nineteenth-century tort system led to pressures to replace it with workers' compensation. But the new workers' compensation system is inadequate in different ways, which generates new pressures to again modify the system. Attorneys will seek out the pressure points within the new system and try to get for their clients a more adequate remedy.

   The workers' compensation system was designed to be an exclusive remedy against the employer with respect to injuries covered by the statute. This creates some obvious pressure points. If the employee can successfully claim that the injury is not covered by the workers' compensation statute, he will have traditional tort remedies available, and if the employee can identify a wrongdoer other than the employer, he will have traditional tort remedies against that party. And in some states, if the employer's conduct can be characterized as reckless, traditional tort remedies remain in place.

■ *Promoting Workplace Safety and Health in the Post-Regulatory Era: A Primer on Non-OSHA Legal Incentives That Influence Employer Decisions to Control Occupational Hazards*
WILLIAM J. MAAKESTAD AND CHARLES HELM
17 N. Ky. L. Rev. 9 (1989). Reprinted with permission
of Northern Kentucky Law Review

... The basic premise behind workers' compensation is the trade-off between employees getting prompt and certain compensation and their giving up the right to sue. In *New York Central R.R. Co. v. White*, which upheld the constitutionality of the workers' compensation system, the Supreme Court justified the abrogation of common law rights on both sides—the employees' right to sue vis-à-vis the employers' right to be held liable only for cause—by citing three factors: the special nature of the employment relationship, society's interest in its smooth operation, and the reciprocal advantages substituted for those rights.

The practical consequences of this *quid pro quo*, then, is that filing a workers' compensation claim is ordinarily the exclusive remedy available to employees or their survivors for injuries, illnesses or deaths arising out of and in the course of employment.... Nonetheless, the exclusivity rule is not absolute. Most states recognize four exceptions to the exclusivity rule, each of which would allow a worker to seek compensatory and possibly punitive damages from his or her employer: (1) the disability is not compensable under the workers' compensation statute; (2) federal law provides for dual recovery from workers' compensation and tort claims; (3) the employer occupies a "dual capacity" status; and (4) the employer has committed an intentional tort rather than negligence. The remainder of this section discusses the nature and extent of each exception in light of recent case and statutory law developments.

The first exception allows a tort action to lie when the disability is not compensable under the state statute, normally for one of two reasons: either (a) the injury occurred outside the scope of employment but resulted from the employer's negligence, as in a case where the employee is off-duty but injured by the employer's negligence, or (b) the injury or illness, as a matter of law, is considered not to have arisen out of employment, as in the case of an occupational disease not covered by the compensation statute. However, judicial decisions and statutory provisions which construe compensation acts liberally so as to favor coverage have generally led to narrow application of this exception.

The second exception exists when federal law specifically authorizes recovery under both workers' compensation statutes and tort law....

The third exception applies when an employer has a "dual capacity" relationship with the employee. For this exception to the exclusivity rule to apply, a second relationship, distinct from the employment relationship, must exist; the decisive test is whether the "non-employer" aspect of the employer's activity creates obligations different from those inherent in the employment relationship. Most dual capacity cases involve employers who manufacture the tools or equipment used by their employees, thus opening the door to suits grounded in product liability theory. In recent years, the dual capacity exception has also been applied where the employer offers medical care that is negligently administered. While potentially broader in scope than the two exceptions noted above, many courts have restricted dual capacity to exceptional cases in non-traditional industrial settings.

Historically there have been relatively few successful challenges to the limited scope of these first three exceptions, thus preserving employers' substantial insulation from tort liability. There have been some recent indications, however, that courts may be more willing to increase the interface between tort liability and the workplace by allowing plaintiffs' claims grounded in the fourth exception to exclusivity—intentional tort.

Until 1978, every state required proof that the employer actually intended to injure or kill the worker before the fourth exception—intentional tort—would allow a claim to be filed in civil court, where compensatory and even punitive damages could be sought. Such cases were extremely rare. But in *Mandolidis v. Elkins Industries, Inc.*, the West Virginia Supreme Court departed from settled doctrine by adopting a significantly broader definition of intentional tort—one that dimmed the bright line between reckless and intentional conduct and increased employers' exposure to civil liability.

The complaint alleged that Mandolidis was injured by an unguarded table saw and that (a) his employer knew it violated state and federal safety laws and had been cited previously by OSHA; (b) other workers had been injured by unguarded saws; (c) Mandolidis had complained about the condition and then was threatened with discharge; and (d) another employee has been sanctioned for refusing to use unguarded equipment. The majority allowed the common law suit to proceed, holding that "when death or injury results from willful, wanton, or reckless misconduct such death or injury is no longer accidental in any meaningful sense of the word, and must be taken as having been inflicted with deliberate intention for the purposes of the workmen's compensation act."

In explaining why the suit should be allowed, the court offered a plain public policy:

> The workmen's compensation system completely supplanted the common law tort system only with respect to negligently caused industrial accidents, and employers and employees gained certain advantages and lost certain rights they had heretofore enjoyed. Entrepreneurs were not given the right to carry on their enterprises without any regard to the life and limb of the participants in the endeavor and free from all common law liability....

As a result of the asbestos litigation that has been pervasive in their jurisdictions during the past decade, California and New Jersey have also reconsidered their exclusivity rules. The supreme court of each state has upheld the appropriateness of tort liability when employers fraudulently conceal medical records that show employees are suffering from asbestos poisoning. However, the 1980 California case, *Johns-Manville Products Corp. v. Superior Court*, and a 1989 New Jersey case, *Millison v. E.I. du Pont de Nemours & Co.*, drew an important distinction between causing and aggravating occupational diseases. Both decisions concluded that had the complaint alleged only that employees contracted the disease because the employer (a) concealed the hazardous condition, (b) failed to supply protective equipment, and (c) violated government regulations, workers' compensation would have remained the plaintiffs' exclusive remedy; however, if the allegation of concealment kept employees on the job unaware and prevented them from receiving treatment—thus aggravating the disease—that was sufficient to state a cause of action. In short, the courts reasoned that the fraudulent concealment which aggravated the disease was an unassumed risk, distinct from the job-related hazard that caused the disease, and thus provided sufficient cause to take the case out of workers' compensation.

Two basic questions are presented concerning the erosion—which has been driven primarily by state court decisions over the past decade—of the traditional exclusive remedy doctrine: (1) Will the erosion continue? and (2) Should it continue? While it is impossible to tell just how many other state appellate courts will decide the issue, the likelihood of a continuing stream of exclusivity challenges is high. Apart from the demands of distributive justice, plaintiffs' lawyers have two strong economic incentives to continue the assault. First, even the most generous workers' compensation benefits represent only a fraction of what might be recovered in tort damages; second, fees for representing a worker in workers' compensation are often prescribed by statute or by the courts at a percentage well below the standard tort contingency fee. Still, the likelihood of continued challenges reveals nothing about the likelihood of successful challenges.

As reflected in *Mandolidis* and its progeny, the argument favoring a more liberal interpretation of intentional tort liability has been simple and direct: denying common law suits in cases of wanton, willful or reckless employer misconduct is unjust and counterproductive to workplace safety. From both a moral and economic perspective, the law simply should not treat employers' reckless disregard for the health and/or safety of their workers the same as an accident. Unlike the possibility of punitive damages in tort, currently most workers' compensation schedules provide for no additional recovery for wanton or willful behavior, no matter how outrageous. As a result, workers' compensation provides employers with virtually no incentives of any kind to refrain from such conduct.

Yet the long overdue remedial steps taken by the courts in such states as West Virginia and Ohio since 1978 have been pruned back significantly by legislation. . . .

Reducing the scope of intentional tort in this way has profound implications for the law's reductive function as it would operate in the real world of business, which is populated not by malicious thugs but by cost-conscious managers:

> When employers provide unsafe working conditions in order to cut costs, their specific motive in doing so is to increase overall profits, not to injure their employees. Under the standard employed by the Ohio Supreme Court, employers so obsessed with cost-cutting that employee safety is jeopardized can be held accountable, but under the legislative definition no such accountability exists.

Such legislative reversals are likely due to political pressures engendered by the extreme sensitivity of business to increased tort liability exposure. While there are no studies indicating whether there was an actual increase in the costs to businesses, there is evidence that the number of tort suits filed in West Virginia rose dramatically after *Mandolidis*. With workers' compensation costs already a significant factor in many new or relocating companies' decisions about where to locate, businesses—and legislators—in states with *Mandolidis*-like policies may conclude that they are placed at a competitive disadvantage vis-à-vis states with the traditional exclusivity barriers to tort liability. As has been observed elsewhere, this political dilemma renders state-by-state reform impractical and thus necessitates either federal intervention and/or uniform model legislation. To date, however, neither has received serious attention.

The increase in workplace tort litigation has not been—and will never be—a panacea for the limitations of the workers' compensation system. But frequent litigation is often symptomatic of a dysfunctional system, and a growing number of state courts have determined that workers' access to the civil courts should be expanded—especially when it will serve the public interest by encouraging employers to be as sensitive to employee safety as they are to profits. While frequent litigation may create some problems and uncertainty in the short run, in the long run it may help to establish new boundaries leading to a more proactive workers' compensation system. . . .

COMMENTS AND QUESTIONS

1. If recklessness—which involves proceeding in the face of a known hazard—is enough to justify circumvention of the workers' compensation system, then will any recurring workplace injury or illness—which, by virtue of its continual recurrence, the employer will have reason to expect to occur—support resort to the traditional tort system? What if the employer tells the employees they can expect the recurring injuries or illnesses to strike again?

2. Recall the California appellate court's decision in *Gunnell v. Metrocolor Laboratories*, discussed in chapter 4. There, the court held that a worker injured by exposure to a hazardous substance in the workplace could not sue in tort because the employer's concealment of the hazard did not amount to a criminal battery. How do you suppose Maakestad and Helm would react to this decision?

3. This chapter has introduced you to one of the first major regulatory schemes for addressing health and safety risks. Next, in part III, we expand our focus to include other modern regulatory frameworks. Having moved from the common law to statute-based systems, we begin our consideration of modern regulatory frameworks with a discussion of the basic issue of how to interpret the statutes on which these frameworks are based.

The Modern Regulatory State

III

So far, we have examined the general justifications for state-imposed regulation in two contexts, environmental and workplace risk. In both contexts, we have examined how general common law principles such as coercion and fraud—themselves a form of regulation—limit both what an actor (an employer, for example) can do on its own and what actors (employers and workers) can agree to. However, as we have noted, the characteristic method of regulation in the modern state is by statute or administrative rules adopted pursuant to statutory authorization, not by means of the common law.

When statutory and administrative regulation becomes prominent, issues of interpretation arise. Statutes are enacted at one time, applied at another. They deal clearly with some problems, less clearly with others. They authorize administrative agencies to do some things, but it is not always clear what. In short, statutes must be "interpreted," not (merely) read—by courts and administrative agencies. This part provides an overview of the issues raised by statutory interpretation, each of which is the subject of an extensive scholarly literature. Chapter 7 addresses basic issues of statutory interpretation, including the role of statutory language and textual meaning and the role of legislative purposes and legislative history. Chapter 8 examines the procedures by which agencies translate the statutory directives governing their operation into more specific rules, as well as the standards courts use to review agency rules. Chapter 9 concludes our introduction to statutory interpretation in the modern regulatory state by exploring the ways in which regulation can fail, such as when legislative or agency action leads to an increase rather than a decrease of risk.

Statutory Interpretation

The Basic Issues

7

After reading some of the important scholarly writing on statutory interpretation, we turn to several cases of—and on—statutory interpretation. These cases, too, have been important in the literature on statutory interpretation. This chapter concludes with an examination of the role of administrative agencies in *interpreting* (not simply administering or applying) statutes.

◼ Statutory Interpretation: Theory

Courts and agencies rarely have trouble applying a "clear" statute. Difficulties arise when litigants—and judges—disagree over whether the statute is clear, or agree that it is unclear. In such cases, the statute's language must be "interpreted," raising questions such as: What does the statutory language mean, and how are courts to determine its meaning? Should they attempt to identify the underlying purpose of the statutory provision and then interpret it to promote (as best the judges can discern) that purpose? Do statutes *have* such a purpose? Should judges look to legislative history to give the provision meaning? What other resources might judges use? The readings that follow provide a preliminary examination of these and other questions. Be aware, however, that these materials, and our comments and questions, only scratch the surface of the rich recent discussions of statutory interpretation.[a]

- ◼ **Remarks on the Theory of Appellate Decision and the Rules or Canons about How Statutes Are to Be Construed**
  KARL LLEWELLYN
  3 Vand. L. Rev. 395 (1950). © 1950 Vanderbilt Law Review. Reprinted with permission

I

One does not progress far into legal life without learning that there is no single right and accurate way of reading one case, or of reading a bunch of cases. For

---

[a] For additional explorations of the general topic of statutory interpretation, see William N. Eskridge Jr., Philip P. Frickey, and Elizabeth Garrett, Cases and Materials on Legislation: Statutes and the Creation of Public Policy (3d ed., 2001); Kent Greenawalt, Legislation—Statutory Interpretation: 20 Questions (1999).

1. Impeccable and correct doctrine makes clear that a case "holds" with authority only so much of what the opinion says as is absolutely necessary to sustain the judgment. Anything else is unnecessary and "distinguishable" and noncontrolling for the future. Indeed, if the judgment rests on two, three or four rulings, any of them can be rightly and righteously knocked out, for the future, as being thus "unnecessary." Moreover, any distinction on the facts is rightly and righteously a reason for distinguishing and therefore disregarding the prior alleged holding. But

2. Doctrine equally impeccable and correct makes clear that a case "holds" with authority the rule on which the court there chose to rest the judgment; more, that that rule covers, with full authority, cases which are plainly distinguishable on their facts and their issue, whenever the reason for the rule extends to cover them. Indeed, it is unnecessary for a rule or principle to have led to the decision in the prior case, or even to have been phrased therein, in order to be seen as controlling in the new case: (a) "We there said . . ." (b) "That case necessarily decided . . ."

These divergent and indeed conflicting correct ways of handling or reading a single prior case as one "determines" what it authoritatively holds, have their counterparts in regard to the authority of a series or body of cases. Thus

1. It is correct to see that "That rule is too well settled in this jurisdiction to be disturbed"; and so to apply it to a wholly novel circumstance. But

2. It is no less correct to see that "The rule has never been extended to a case like the present"; and so to refuse to apply it: "We here limit the rule." Again,

3. It is no less correct to look over the prior "applications" of "the rule" and rework them into a wholly new formulation of "the true rule" or "true principle" which knocks out some of the prior cases as simply "misapplications" and then builds up the others.

In the work of a single opinion-day I have observed 26 different, describable ways in which one of our best state courts handled its own prior cases, repeatedly using three to six different ways within a single opinion.

What is important is that *all 26* ways (plus a dozen others which happened not to be in use that day) are correct. They represent not "evasion," but sound use, application and development of precedent. They represent not "departure from," but sound continuation of, our system of precedent as it has come down to us. The major defect in that system is a mistaken idea which many lawyers have about it— to wit, the idea that the cases themselves and in themselves, plus the correct rules on how to handle cases, provide one single correct answer to a disputed issue of law. In fact the available correct answers are two, three, or ten. The question is: *Which* of the available correct answers will the court select—and *why?* For since there is always more than one available correct answer, the court always has to select.

True, the selection is frequently almost automatic. The type of distinction or expansion which is always *technically* available may be psychologically or sociologically unavailable. This may be because of (a) the current tradition of the court or because of (b) the current temper of the court or because of (c) the sense of the situation as the court sees that sense. (There are other possible reasons a-plenty, but these three are the most frequent and commonly the most weighty.)

The *current tradition* of the court is a matter of period-style in the craft of judging. In 1820–1850 our courts felt in general a freedom and duty to move in the manner typified in our thought by Mansfield and Marshall. "Precedent" guided, but "principle" controlled; and nothing was good "Principle" which did not look like wisdom-in-result for the welfare of All-of-us. In 1880–1910, on the other hand, our courts felt in general a prime duty to order within the law and a duty to resist any "outside" influence. "Precedent" was to control, not merely to guide; "Principle" was to be tested by whether it made for order in the law, not by whether it made wisdom-in-result. "Legal" Principle could not be subjected to "political" tests; even legislation was resisted as disturbing. Since 1920 the earlier style (the "Grand Style") has been working its way back into general use by our courts, though the language of the opinions moves still dominantly (though waningly) in the style (the "Formal Style") of the late 19th Century. In any particular court what needs study is how far along the process has gotten. The best material for study is the latest volume of reports, read in sequence from page 1 through to the end: the current mine-run of the work.

The *current temper* of the court is reflected in the same material, and represents the court's tradition as modified by its personnel. For it is plain that the two earlier period-styles represent also two eternal types of human being. There is the man who loves creativeness, who can without loss of sleep combine risk-taking with responsibility, who sees and feels institutions as things built and to be built to serve functions, and who sees the functions as vital and law as a tool to be eternally reoriented to justice and to general welfare. There is the other man who loves order, who finds risk uncomfortable and has seen so much irresponsible or unwise innovation that responsibility to him means caution, who sees and feels institutions as the tested, slow-built ways which for all their faults are man's sole safeguard against relapse into barbarism, and who regards reorientation of the law in our polity as essentially committed to the legislature. Commonly a man of such temper has also a craftsman's pride in clean craftsman's work, and commonly he does not view with too much sympathy any ill-done legislative job of attempted reorientation. Judges, like other men, range up and down the scale between the extremes of either type of temper, and in this aspect (as in the aspect of intellectual power and acumen or of personal force or persuasiveness) the constellation of the personnel on a particular bench at a particular time plays its important part in urging the court toward a more literal or a more creative selection among the available accepted and correct "ways" of handling precedent.

More vital, if possible, than either of the above is *the sense of the situation as seen by the court*. Thus in the very heyday of the formal period our courts moved into tremendous creative expansion of precedent in regard to the labor injunction and the due process clause. What they saw as sense to be achieved, and desperately needed, there broke through all trammels of the current period-style. Whereas the most creative-minded court working in the most creative period-style will happily and literally apply a formula without discussion, and even with relief, if the formula makes sense and yields justice in the situation and the case. So strongly does the felt sense of the situation and the case affect the court's choice of techniques for reading or interpreting and then applying the authorities that one may fairly lay down certain generalizations:

A. In some six appealed cases out of ten the court feels this sense so clearly that lining up the authorities comes close to being an automatic job. *In the very process of reading an authority* a distinction leaps to the eye, and that is "all" that that case holds; or the language of another authority (whether or not "really" in point) shines forth as "clearly stating the true rule." Trouble comes when the cases do not line up this clearly and semi-automatically, when they therefore call for intellectual labor, even at times for a conclusion that the law as given will not allow the sensible result to be reached. Or trouble comes when the sense of the situation is not clear.

B. Technical leeways correctly available when the sense of the situation and the case call for their use cease to be correctly available *unless used in furtherance of what the court sees as such sense.* There is here in our system of precedent an element of uprightness, or conscience, of judicial responsibility; and motive becomes a factor in determining what techniques are correct and right. Today, in contrast with 1890, it may be fairly stated that even the literal application of a thoroughly established rule is not correct in a case or situation in which that application does not make sense unless the court in honest conscience feels forced by its office to make the application.

C. Collateral to B, but deserving of separate statement, is the proposition that *the greater the felt need, because of felt sense, the wider is the leeway, correctly and properly available in reshaping an authority or the authorities.* What is both proper and to be expected in an extreme case would become abuse and judicial usurpation if made daily practice in the mine-run of cases. All courts worthy of their office feel this in their bones, as being inherent in our system of precedent. They show the feeling in their work. Where differences appear is where they should appear: in divergent sizings up of what is sense, and of how great the need may be in any situation.

One last thing remains to be said about "sense."

There is a sense of *the type of situation* to be contrasted with the sense of *a particular controversy between particular litigants.* Which of these aspects of sense a court responds to more strongly makes a tremendous difference. Response primarily to the sense of the particular controversy is, in the first place, dangerous because a particular controversy may not be typical, and because it is hard to disentangle general sense from personalities and from "fireside" equities. Such response is dangerous in the second place because it leads readily to finding an out *for this case only*—and that leads to a complicating multiplicity of refinement and distinction, as also to repeated resort to analogies unthought through and unfortunate of extension. This is what the proverb seeks to say: "Hard cases make bad law."

If on the other hand the type of situation is in the forefront of attention, a solving rule comes in for much more thoughtful testing and study. Rules are thrust toward reasonable simplicity, and made with broader vision. Moreover, the idiosyncrasies of the particular case and its possible emotional deflections are set for judgment against a broader picture which gives a fair chance that accidental sympathy is not mistaken for long-range justice for all. And one runs a better chance of skirting the incidence of the other proverb: "Bad law makes hard cases."

On the case-law side, I repeat, we ought all thus to be familiar with the fact that the right doctrine and going practice of our highest courts leave them a very real leeway within which (a) to narrow or avoid what seem today to have been unfortunate prior phrasings or even rulings; or (b), on the other hand, to pick up, develop, expand what seem today to have been fortunate prior rulings or even phrasings.

It is silly, I repeat, to think of use of this leeway as involving "twisting" of precedent. The very phrase presupposes the thing which is not and which has never been. The phrase presupposes that there was in the precedent under consideration some one and single meaning. The whole experience of our case-law shows that that assumption is false. It is, instead, the business of the courts to use the precedents constantly to make the law always a *little* better, to correct old mistakes, to recorrect mistaken or ill-advised attempts at correction—but always within limits severely set not only by the precedents, but equally by the traditions of right conduct in judicial office.

What we need to see now is that all of this is paralleled, in regard to statutes, because of (1) the power of the legislature both to choose policy and to select measures; and (2) the necessity that the legislature shall, in so doing, use language—language fixed in particular words; and (3) the continuing duty of the courts to make sense, under and within the law.

For just as prior courts can have been skillful or unskillful, clear or unclear, wise or unwise, so can legislatures. And just as prior courts have been looking at only a single piece of our whole law at a time, so have legislatures.

But a court must strive to make sense *as a whole* out of our law *as a whole*. It must . . . take the music of any statute as written by the legislature; it must take the text of the play as written by the legislature. But there are many ways to play that music, to play that play, and a court's duty is to play it well, and, in harmony with the other music of the legal system.

Hence, in the field of statutory construction also, there are "correct," unchallengeable rules of "how to read" which lead in happily variant directions.

This must be so until courts recognize that here, as in case-law, the real guide is Sense-for-All-of-Us. It must be so, so long as we and the courts pretend that there has been only one single correct answer possible. Until we give up that foolish pretense there must be a set of mutually contradictory *correct* rules on How to Construe Statutes: either set available as duty and sense may require.

Until then, also, the problem will recur in statutory construction as in the handling of case-law: *Which* of the technically correct answers (a) *should* be given; (b) *will* be given—and Why?

And everything said above about the temper of the court, the temper of the court's tradition, the sense of the situation and the case, applies here as well.

Thus in the period of the Grand Style of case-law statutes were construed "freely" to implement their purpose, the court commonly accepting the legislature's choice of policy and setting to work to implement it. (Criminal statutes and, to some extent, statutes on procedure, were exceptions.) Whereas in the Formal Period statutes tended to be limited or even eviscerated by wooden and literal reading, in a sort of long-drawn battle between a balky, stiff-necked, wrong-headed court and a legislature which had only words with which to drive that court. Today the courts have regained, in the main, a cheerful acceptance of legislative choice of policy, but they are still hampered to some extent in carrying such policies forward by the Formal Period's insistence on precise language.

II

One last thing is to be noted:

If a statute is to make sense, it must be read in the light of some assumed purpose. A statute merely declaring a rule, with no purpose or objective, is nonsense.

If a statute is to be merged into a going system of law, moreover, the court must do the merging, and must in so doing take account of the policy of the statute—or else substitute its own version of such policy. Creative reshaping of the net result is thus inevitable.

But the policy of a statute is of two wholly different kinds—each kind somewhat limited in effect by the statute's choice of measures, and by the statute's choice of fixed language. On the one hand there are the ideas consciously before the draftsmen, the committee, the legislature: a known evil to be cured, a known goal to be attained, a deliberate choice of one line of approach rather than another. Here talk of "intent" is reasonably realistic; committee reports, legislative debate, historical knowledge of contemporary thinking or campaigning which points up the evil or the goal can have significance.

But on the other hand—and increasingly as a statute gains in age—its language is called upon to deal with circumstances utterly uncontemplated at the time of its passage. Here the quest is not properly for the sense originally intended by the statute, for the sense sought originally to be *put into it,* but rather for the sense which *can be quarried out of it* in the light of the new situation. Broad purposes can indeed reach far beyond details known or knowable at the time of drafting. A "dangerous weapon" statute of 1840 can include tommy guns, tear gas or atomic bombs. "Vehicle," in a statute of 1840, can properly be read, when sense so suggests, to include an automobile, or a hydroplane that lacks wheels. But for all that, the sound quest does not run primarily in terms of historical intent. It runs in terms of what the words can be made to bear, in making sense in the light of the unforeseen.

III

When it comes to presenting a proposed construction in court, there is an accepted conventional vocabulary. As in argument over points of case-law, the accepted convention still, unhappily requires discussion as if only one single correct meaning could exist. Hence there are two opposing canons on almost every point. An arranged selection is appended. Every lawyer must be familiar with them all: they are still needed tools of argument. At least as early as Fortescue the general picture was clear, on this, to any eye which would see.

Plainly, to make any canon take hold in a particular instance, the construction contended for must be sold, essentially, by means other than the use of the canon: The good sense of the situation and a *simple* construction of the available language to achieve that sense, *by tenable means, out of the statutory language.*

Table 1

Thrust	But	Parry
1. A statute cannot go beyond its text.		1. To effect its purpose a statute may be implemented beyond its text.
2. Statutes in derogation of the common law will not be extended by construction.		2. Such acts will be liberally construed if their nature is remedial.
3. Statutes are to be read in the light of the common law and a statute affirming a common law rule is to be construed in accordance with the common law.		3. The common law gives way to a statute which is inconsistent with it and when a statute is designed as a revision of a whole body of law applicable to a given subject it supersedes the common law.
4. Where a foreign statute which has received construction has been adopted, previous construction is adopted too.		4. It may be rejected where there is conflict with the obvious meaning of the statute or where the foreign decisions are unsatisfactory in reasoning or where the foreign interpretation is not in harmony with the spirit or policy of the laws of the adopting state.
5. Where various states have already adopted the statute, the parent state is followed.		5. Where interpretations of other states are inharmonious, there is no such restraint.
6. Statutes *in pari materia* must be construed together.		6. A statute is not *in pari materia* if its scope and aim are distinct or where a legislative design to depart from the general purpose or policy of previous enactments may be apparent.
7. A statute imposing a new penalty or forfeiture, or a new liability or disability, or creating a new right of action will not be construed as having a retroactive effect.		7. Remedial statutes are to be liberally construed and if a retroactive interpretation will promote the ends of justice, they should receive such construction.
8. Where design has been distinctly stated no place is left for construction.		8. Courts have the power to inquire into real—as distinct from ostensible—purpose.
9. Definitions and rules of construction contained in an interpretation clause are part of the law and binding.		9. Definitions and rules of construction in a statute will not be extended beyond their necessary import nor allowed to defeat intention otherwise manifested.
10. A statutory provision requiring liberal construction does not mean disregard of unequivocal requirements of the statute.		10. Where a rule of construction is provided within the statute itself the rule should be applied.
11. Titles do not control meaning; preambles do not expand scope; section headings do not change language.		11. The title may be consulted as a guide when there is doubt or obscurity in the body; preambles may be consulted to determine rationale, and thus the true construction of terms; section headings may be looked upon as part of the statute itself.

(*continued*)

Table 1 (*continued*)

Thrust	But	Parry
12. If language is plain and unambiguous it must be given effect.		12. Not when literal interpretation would lead to absurd or mischievous consequences or thwart manifest purpose.
13. Words and phrases which have received judicial construction before enactment are to be understood according to that construction.		13. Not if the statute clearly requires them to have a different meaning.
14. After enactment, judicial decision upon interpretation of particular terms and phrases controls.		14. Practice construction by executive officers is strong evidence of true meaning.
15. Words are to be taken in their ordinary meaning unless they are technical terms or words of art.		15. Popular words may bear a technical meaning and technical words may have a popular signification and they should be so construed as to agree with evident intention or to make the statute operative.
16. Every word and clause must be given effect.		16. If inadvertently inserted or if repugnant to the rest of the statute, they may be rejected as surplusage.
17. The same language used repeatedly in the same connection is presumed to bear the same meaning throughout the statute.		17. This presumption will be disregarded where it is necessary to assign different meanings to make the statute consistent.
18. Words are to be interpreted according to the proper grammatical effect of their arrangement within the statute.		18. Rules of grammar will be disregarded where strict adherence would defeat purpose.
19. Exceptions not made cannot be read.		19. The letter is only the "bark." Whatever is within the reason of the law is within the law itself.
20. Expression of one thing excludes another.		20. The language may fairly comprehend many different cases where some only are expressly mentioned by way of example.
21. General terms are to receive a general construction.		21. They may be limited by specific terms with which they are associated or by the scope and purpose of the statute.
22. It is a general rule of construction that where general words follow an enumeration they are to be held as applying only to persons and things of the same general kind or class specifically mentioned (*ejusdem generis*).		22. General words must operate on something. Further, *ejusdem generis* is only an aid in getting the meaning and does not warrant confining the operations of a statute within narrower limits than were intended.
23. Qualifying or limiting words or clauses are to be referred to the next preceding antecedent.		23. Not when evident sense and meaning require a different construction.

Thrust	But	Parry
24. Punctuation will govern when a statute is open to two constructions.		24. Punctuation marks will not control the plain and evident meaning of language.
25. It must be assumed that language has been chosen with due regard to grammatical propriety and is not interchangeable on mere conjecture.		25. "And" and "or" may be read interchangeably whenever the change is necessary to give the statute sense and effect.
26. There is a distinction between words of permission and mandatory words.		26. Words imparting permission may be read as mandatory and words imparting command may be read as permissive when such construction is made necessary by evident intention or by the rights of the public.
27. A proviso qualifies the provision immediately preceding.		27. It may clearly be intended to have a wider scope.
28. When the enacting clause is general, a proviso is construed strictly.		28. Not when it is necessary to ex-tend the proviso to persons or cases which come within its equity.

COMMENTS AND QUESTIONS

1. Llewellyn contends that the judicial role in statutory interpretation is the same as its role in developing the common law. If you think it should be different, consider the possibility that Llewellyn's argument rests on an analysis of judicial competence and capacity generally—with the implication that, whatever one's normative perspective on the possible differences between the judges' roles in statutory interpretation and common-law development, in practice we will be unable to observe differences.

2. What approach to statutory interpretation does Llewellyn recommend? Does the following offer an equivalent perspective? We should interpret statutes on the assumption that "the legislature was made up of reasonable persons pursuing reasonable purposes reasonably." The phrase is taken from Henry Hart and Albert Sacks, The Legal Process: Basic Problems in the Making and Application of Law 1378 (William N. Eskridge Jr. and Philip P. Frickey eds., 1994, originally distributed 1958). The literature on statutory interpretation now calls this approach *purposivist*. The article that follows raises questions about purposivist interpretation.

3. Given the availability of competing canons of interpretation, what use are they? Consider the possibility that not all of the canons are equally important or that the invocation of one rather than its counterpart might help us understand, not so much what the legislature was doing, but what the courts are doing. This possibility may be connected to the fact that Llewellyn (a) historicizes and (b) "psychologizes" approaches to statutory interpretation. What does Llewellyn's willingness to do so imply about his account of "law"?

4. In reading the materials and cases that follow, think about Llewellyn's distinction between the Grand Style and the Formal Style and his attribution of psychological characteristics to judges who adopt one or the other. Note as well that, although Llewellyn pretty clearly prefers the Grand Style, he does not suggest that the values he attributes to those who adopt the Formal Style are not worth advancing.

5. The next two readings provide introductions to the modern debates over statutory interpretation. In reading them, think about whether, or how, these approaches resemble the Grand and Formal Styles Llewellyn describes.

■ *Statutes' Domains*
FRANK H. EASTERBROOK
50 U. Chi. L. Rev. 533 (1983). Reprinted with permission
of University of Chicago Law Review

. . .

I

. . .

. . . The interesting questions in litigation involve statutes that are ambiguous when applied to a particular set of facts. The construction of an ambiguous document is a work of judicial creation or re-creation. Using the available hints and tools—the words and structure of the statute, the subject matter and general policy of the enactment, the legislative history, the lobbying positions of interest groups, and the temper of the times—judges try to determine how the Congress that enacted the statute either actually resolved or would have resolved a particular issue if it had faced and settled it explicitly at the time. Judges have substantial leeway in construction. Inferences almost always conflict, and the enacting Congress is unlikely to come back to life and "prove" the court's construction wrong. The older the statute the more the inferences will be in conflict, and the greater the judges' freedom.

If, however, the court finds a statute inapplicable to the subject of the litigation, it never begins this task of creative construction. Even if the judge knows how Congress would have handled the question presented, the court will do nothing. It will say to the litigant: "Too bad, but legislative intentions are not legal rules." Whoever relies on the statute loses. The court will tell the litigant to seek a statute embodying the never-expressed conclusions of the legislature.

. . .

II

A paper about the domain of statutes needs a preamble about its own domain. Throughout this paper I discuss the difference between "construing" and "not construing" a statute. The reader is entitled to object that there is no such distinction, that to declare a statute inapplicable to a dispute is an act of construction, and that I am therefore talking nonsense. There is certainly a sense in which every time a judge picks up and reads a statute, if only to put it down immediately, he has "construed" or "interpreted" it. Why else did he put it down? In distinguishing between construction and nonconstruction, I do not mean to deny the importance of finding the meaning of the enactment.[3] Finding the meaning is the aim of picking up the statute in the first instance. I address instead some of the considerations pertinent to deciding whether the statute indeed supplies an answer or whether it is to be put down and disregarded.

. . .

Consider, for example, whether a statute providing for the leashing of "dogs" also requires the leashing of cats (because the statute really covers the category "animals") or wolves (because the statute really covers the category "canines") or lions ("dangerous animals"). Most people would say that the statute does not go beyond dogs, because after all the verbal torturing of the words has been completed it is still too plain for argument what the statute means. Perhaps it is a quibble, but in my terminology this becomes a decision that the statute "applies" only to dogs. For rules about the rest of the animal kingdom we must look elsewhere.

The distinction between application and interpretation is a line worth drawing—however difficult to maintain—because of the malleability of words. To find the leash statute limited to dogs after a bout of interpretation inevitably has the air of arbitrariness. Why not treat it as a statute about "animals" or "dangerous animals" or "canines"? The invocation of "plain meaning" just sweeps under the rug the process by which meaning is divined. Too often the meaning of a statute is smuggled into the rules that determine when, and why, to cut off debate. The philosophy of language, and most particularly the work of Ludwig Wittgenstein, has established that sets of words do not possess intrinsic meanings and cannot be given them; to make matters worse, speakers do not even have determinative intents about the meanings of their own words. Thus when a speaker says "dogs" we cannot be certain that he did not mean "dangerous animals" unless that question was present to his mind and the structure of the utterance indicates his resolution of the problem. When Congress enacts a $10,000 jurisdictional amount, we cannot be certain whether it means $10,000 in nominal dollars or real (inflation-adjusted) ones. When the Constitution says that the President must be thirty-five years old, we cannot be certain whether it means thirty-five as the number of revolutions of the world around the sun, as a percentage of average life expectancy (so that the Constitution now has age fifty as a minimum), or as a minimum number of years after

---

[3] "Meaning of the enactment" and not the "intent of its framers." A statute has meaning apart from the drafters' personal intentions, and to speak of intent is to commit the "intentional fallacy" properly denounced in literary criticism. Thus Holmes had it right:

> [A statute] does not disclose one meaning conclusively according to the laws of language. Thereupon we ask, not what this man meant, but what those words would mean in the mouth of a normal speaker of English, using them in the circumstances in which they were used.... But the normal speaker of English is merely a special variety, a literary form, so to speak, of our old friend the prudent man. He is external to the particular writer, and a reference to him as a criterion is simply another instance of the externality of the law....
>
> ...We do not inquire what the legislature meant; we ask only what the statute means.

Holmes, The Theory of Legal Interpretation, 12 Harv. L. Rev. 417, 417–19 (1899), reprinted in O. W. Holmes, Collected Legal Papers 204, 207 (1920).

puberty (so the minimum now is thirty or so). Each of these treatments has some rational set of reasons, goals, values, and the like to recommend it. If the meaning of language depends on a community of understanding among readers, none is "right." But unless the community of readers is to engage in ceaseless (and thus pointless) babble—and unless, moreover, the community is willing to entrust almost boundless discretion to judges as oracles of the community's standards—there is a need for some broader set of rules about when to engage in the open-ended process of construction.

In a world of language skepticism, every attempt to "construe" a statute is a transfer of a substantial measure of decision-making authority from the speaker to the interpreter. To find that there is "law" on a given subject is to endow the courts with authority they lacked before. It is therefore worthwhile to demand that, before courts begin the process of "construction," they ascertain that the legislature has conferred the power of interpretation. Thus I ask for indulgence in referring to a first step, the step of determining the application or applicability of a statute.

III

I put to one side the possibility that determining the statute's applicability always is the same thing as determining whether the statute supports the party relying on it. The decision to construe the statute at all cannot be based on the legislature's actual decision, for if it made an ascertainable decision there is no difficult question of construction. Take, for example, the question whether the Federal Communications Commission, which under the Communications Act regulates the practices of radio and television broadcasters, also may regulate the practices of cable television operators. If the Communications Act said something like "the FCC may not regulate anything or anyone other than the practices and parties named in this Act," there would be nothing to discuss. One could invoke an actual decision of Congress concerning the domain of its enactment.

Statutes rarely contain anything like this, in part because Congress does not anticipate each problem that subsequently arises and in part because members of Congress know that zipper clauses in statutes just invite clear evasions. Thus the statute does not choose between the opposing lines of argument that, on the one hand, cable systems compete with over-the-air television and may, unless regulated, upset or undo the regulation of TV expressly created by the statute and that, on the other hand, the only reason for regulating over-the-air TV was the problem of many signals competing for few frequencies and interfering with one another, a problem that never arises for cable systems.

If the question of a statute's domain may not often be resolved by reference to actual design, it may never properly be resolved by reference to imputed design. To impute a design to Congress is to engage in an act of construction. There must be some reason, independent of the answer the court thinks Congress would give (or would have given) to the question under consideration, that justifies the court in supplying that answer in litigation.

The point may be clearest if we take a case in which the court can determine the legislators' design or meaning with certainty. Suppose that within a month after Congress passed the Communications Act a court declares the statute inapplicable to cable television. The FCC consequently lacks regulatory jurisdiction. Immediately thereafter, during the same session of Congress that passed the Communications Act, the pertinent committee in each house of Congress reports out a short amendment giving the FCC jurisdiction. The texts of the amendments are identical, and the unanimous committee reports state that the amendment is necessary to correct a terrible oversight. Each report states that the committee originally intended to confer on the FCC jurisdiction over cable systems, but that during the session the members of the staff charged with drafting the language to implement the design resigned, and their successors, unaware of the original plan, had not carried it out. As a result the legislation did not implement the agreed-on plan, and this technical amendment would perfect the statute.

Suppose further that the leaders of both parties endorse the amendment, and the President expresses willingness to sign it when it reaches his desk. Yet although the amendment encounters no opposition, it also does not pass. Perhaps it never is scheduled for time on the floor because other, more pressing legislation consumes the remainder of the session. Perhaps members who support the amendment hold it hostage in an effort to secure enactment of some other bill over which there is vigorous debate. Perhaps the bill is so popular that it becomes the vehicle for a school prayer amendment or some other factious legislation, in the hope that it will carry the disputed legislation with it, but the strategy succeeds only in killing both proposals. There are a hundred ways in which a bill can die even though there is no opposition to it.

What should a court do with this unambiguous evidence of legislative design or meaning? The conventional answer is that an abortive attempt to enact a bill has no effect. Despite the information it conveys about the meaning of Congress, it neither adds to nor detracts from the meaning of the legislation actually enacted. It is even conceivable, although on the facts of this hypothetical unlikely, that the failure to amend the statute will be taken as endorsement of the initial judicial treatment of it. And this rule works in both directions: if the initial Act had granted jurisdiction over cable systems, subsequent failed amendments could not have diminished that power.

The treatment of subsequent events as ineffective to alter the meaning of a statute is based on a realistic perception of the legislative process. Often proposals with wide support fail of enactment because the legislature lacks the time to enact them or because agreed-on bills become pawns in larger struggles. A court could not treat these widely-supported but never-enacted proposals as law without dishonoring the procedural aspects of the legislative process, in which lack of time is a vital ingredient. Under article I of the Constitution, not to mention the rules of the chambers of Congress, support is not enough for legislation. If the support cannot be transmuted into an enrolled bill, nothing happens. The world goes on as before.

If such powerful evidence of the intent of Congress about the domain of its statutes is not dispositive in matters of construction versus inapplicability, the usual kind of evidence is even less helpful. To delve into the structure, purpose, and legislative history of the original statute is to engage in a sort of creation. It is to fill in blanks. And without some warrant—other than the existence of the blank—for a court to fill it in, the court has no authority to decide in favor of the party invoking the blank-containing statute.

IV

. . .

At least some rules of statutory construction are useful for the same reason rules are useful in interpreting contracts. They spare legislators the need to decide and announce, law by law, the rules that will be used for interpreting the code of words they select. The general reduction in the costs of legislating makes up for the costs of reversing the background rule in the event it should be ill-adapted to some given statute. Rules are desirable not because legislators in fact know or use them in passing laws but because rules serve as off-the-rack provisions that spare legislators the costs of anticipating all possible interpretive problems and legislating solutions for them.

. . .

Almost all statutes are compromises, and the cornerstone of many a compromise is the decision, usually unexpressed, to leave certain issues unresolved. Whether these issues have been identified (so that the lack of their resolution might be called intentional) or overlooked (so that the lack of their resolution is of ambiguous portent) is unimportant. What matters to the compromisers is reducing the chance that their work will be invoked subsequently to achieve more, or less, than they intended, thereby upsetting the balance of the package.

This concern for balance is not confined to interest group (pieslicing) legislation, in which different people tug different ways on legislators for larger shares of a fixed pie, and the statute fixes the size of each slice. Balance is as important in public interest (pieenlarging) legislation, for the structure of the statute will determine how the public interest is to be achieved. Is it to be done strictly through governmental rules and regulation (in which case the statute supplies a rule of decision) or in part by the interactions and bargains of private parties (in which event the statute does not apply)? Legislators seeking only to further the public interest may conclude that the provision of public rules should reach so far and no farther, whether because of deliberate compromise, because of respect for private orderings, or because of uncertainty coupled with concern that to regulate in the face of the unknown is to risk loss for little gain. No matter how good the end in view, achievement of the end will have some cost, and at some point the cost will begin to exceed the benefits.

Thus it is exceptionally implausible to suppose that legislatures, faced explicitly with the task of selecting a background rule, would decide that all statutes invoked by litigants should be deemed to govern their disputes. Such a rule is the equivalent of charging courts with supplying, in cases of doubt, "more in the same vein" as the statute in question. In the case of interest group legislation it is most likely that the extent of the bargain—the pertinent "vein"—is exhausted by the subjects of the express compromises reflected in the statute. The legislature ordinarily would rebuff any suggestion that judges be authorized to fill in blanks in the "spirit" of the compromise. Most compromises lack "spirit," and in any event one part of the deal is to limit the number of blanks to be filled in. (Sometimes the compromise is on a principle to be applied later, and I suggest below that such statutes should be applied more readily than other compromises.)

In the case of public interest legislation it is more likely that the legislature would authorize blank filling, but the extent of this preference is far from certain. If the purpose of the public interest statute is to come as close to the line of over-regulation as possible—that is, to achieve the benefits of regulation right up to the point where the costs of further benefits exceed the value of those benefits—then to authorize blank filling defeats the purpose of the statute. If the court always responds to the invocation of this statute by attempting to read the minds of its framers and supply "more in the same vein," and makes its share of errors, every one of them will carry the statute to where costs exceed benefits. It will either do nothing or produce too much of a good thing.

An example may be helpful. Congress has regulated tender offers for corporate stock by establishing disclosure rules and minimum durations for such offers. The public interest justification advanced for the statute is that the time and information enable investors to make intelligent decisions and so perfect the market for corporate control. Another public interest justification, advanced more recently, is that the time enables auctions for targets to develop. The statute provides for enforcement by the SEC and the criminal law. It does not, however, address enforcement by means of suits filed by firms that are objects of offers. When a target files a suit, should the court fill in this blank by applying the statute and divining how Congress would have resolved the problem, or should it declare the statute inapplicable (and thus no support for the suit)? If the statute is a public interest statute that already has come right up to the line in offering protections for investors, and the court undertakes to construe this and similar laws, the process harms those the statute meant to protect. It overprotects investors by raising the costs to bidders, thus discouraging them without corresponding gains to the target's shareholders. A construction allowing the target to maintain the suit harms investors, and a construction disallowing the target's suit simply leaves the plan untouched (and thus offers no potential benefit to offset the potential harm of the inaccurate construction). A rule of no-application would avoid this risk.

This is not to argue that a uniform rule of no-construction in such cases best implements Congress's plan, or even that in the tender-offer case a decision permitting suits by targets would harm the group Congress wanted to help. The point, rather, is that a legislature rationally may conclude that the rule "apply all statutes" is undesirable even if all statutes are public interest statutes. The nature of the optimal meta-rule of construction depends not only on whether the statute at hand is private-interest or public-interest legislation but also on whether the legislation comes close to the line at which benefits begin to exceed costs. If the legislature regularly passes laws that, in its view, approach this line, then it may rationally prefer courts to tend to limit the domain of laws that do not speak directly to a subject. If, however, the legislature regularly passes public interest laws that still have some distance to go before they reach the point at which detriments begin to exceed benefits, it would be more sanguine about a rule of universal construction.

When enacting public interest laws legislators regularly attempt to approach that critical line—at least in light of the gains and losses they then perceive. A legislature that created a basket of laws containing many interest group statutes and many exhaustive public interest statutes would not be likely to adopt today's implicit judicial approach of universal construction. It would try to distinguish statutes to be applied (construed) from statutes to be declared inapplicable in the event of substantial ambiguity.

. . .

If a rule of universal construction is unsatisfactory, what of a rule of universal refusal to apply statutes whose domains do not clearly include the subject of the litigation? Here courts would encounter difficulties almost the mirror image of those produced by a rule of universal construction. A rule of universal refusal to extend a statute's domain would deny to the legislature the option of enacting public interest laws that, stopping well short of the point where they produce too much of a good thing, charge the judiciary with the task of creating remedies for whatever new problems show up later on. The statute books are full of laws, of which the Sherman Act is a good example, that effectively authorize courts to create new lines of common law.* These laws "apply" even though they do not always supply a rule of decision; the "state action exemption" to the antitrust laws is a good example of how a statute may apply to all combinations in restraint of trade but forbid only some. Unless such generative statutes are unconstitutional there is little warrant for refusing to implement them through the guise of adopting a meta-rule of statutory construction.

V

. . .

My suggestion is that unless the statute plainly hands courts the power to create and revise a form of common law, the domain of the statute should be restricted to cases anticipated by its framers and expressly resolved in the legislative process. Unless the party relying on the statute could establish either express resolution or creation of the common law power of revision, the court would hold the matter in question outside the statute's domain. The statute would become irrelevant, the parties (and court) remitted to whatever other sources of law might be applicable.

This approach overlaps the "clear statement" principle of construction that is often, but erratically, invoked by courts that deny the power to resolve the issue put to them. The court will say something like: "The legislature may well have supported the party relying on the statute, had it thought about this problem, but if the legislature expects us to reach such a result in so sensitive an area, it must state its conclusion clearly." The court then explains why it thinks the subject matter of the legislation counsels hesitation. Perhaps it affects state-federal relations, perhaps it creates startling remedies, perhaps it raises serious constitutional questions, perhaps it departs from the common law (and so from the judges' conception of the good).

As others have pointed out, the "clear statement" principle usually fails as a useful tool of construction because it cannot demonstrate why the legislature would have wanted the court to hesitate just because the subject matter of the law is "sensitive." Likely it thinks that making hard decisions in sensitive areas is what courts are for. The "clear statement" principle can be used by courts seeking to decide by indirection (the very thing they ask the legislature not to do) and to elide responsibilities given by statutes. Invocation of the "clear statement" rule thus has been taken by some as a sign of wilful misconstruction of the statute.

The "clear statement" approach nonetheless reflects the truth that some statutes support judicial gap filling more than others do. The problem in the "clear statement" approach lies not in the declaration that courts sometimes will demand explicit legislative resolution and will refuse to fill statutory gaps, but rather in the conditions giving rise to that demand. The meta-rule I have suggested above is a "clear statement" approach revised to turn on the method the legislature has

---

* [Editors' Note: For an argument that the Sherman Act does not confer general common-law lawmaking power on the courts, see Daniel A. Farber and Brett H. McDonnell, *"Is There a Text in This Class?": The Conflict between Textualism and Antitrust*, 14 J. Contemp. Legal Issues 619 (2005).]

adopted. If it enacts some sort of code of rules, the code will be taken as complete (until amended); gaps will go unfilled. If instead it charges the court with a common law function, the court will solve new problems as they arise, but using today's wisdom rather than conjuring up the solutions of a legislature long prorogued.

This is just a slightly different way of making the point that judicial pursuit of the "values" or aims of legislation is a sure way of defeating the original legislative plan. A legislature that seeks to achieve Goal X can do so in one of two ways. First, it can identify the goal and instruct courts or agencies to design rules to achieve the goal. In that event, the subsequent selection of rules implements the actual legislative decision, even if the rules are not what the legislature would have selected itself. The second approach is for the legislature to pick the rules. It pursues Goal X by Rule Y. The selection of Y is a measure of what Goal X was worth to the legislature, of how best to achieve X, and of where to stop in pursuit of X. Like any other rule, Y is bound to be imprecise, to be over- and under-inclusive. This is not a good reason for a court, observing the inevitable imprecision, to add to or subtract from Rule Y on the argument that, by doing so, it can get more of Goal X. The judicial selection of means to pursue X displaces and directly overrides the legislative selection of ways to obtain X. It denies to legislatures the choice of creating or withholding gapfilling authority. The way to preserve the initial choice is for judges to put the statute down once it becomes clear that the legislature has selected rules as well as identified goals.

This approach is faithful to the nature of compromise in private interest legislation. It also gives the legislature a low-cost method to signal its favored judicial approach to public interest legislation. A legislature that tries to approach the line where costs begin to exceed benefits is bound to leave a trail of detailed provisions, which on this approach would preclude judges from attempting to fill gaps. The approach also is supported by a number of other considerations. First, it recognizes that courts cannot reconstruct an original meaning because there is none to find. Second, it prevents legislatures from extending their lives beyond the terms of their members. Third, it takes a liberal view of the relation between the public and private spheres. Fourth, it takes a realistic view of judges' powers. I elaborate on these below.

1. *Original Meaning.* Because legislatures comprise many members, they do not have "intents" or "designs," hidden yet discoverable. Each member may or may not have a design. The body as a whole, however, has only outcomes. It is not only impossible to reason from one statute to another but also impossible to reason from one or more sections of a statute to a problem not resolved.

This follows from the discoveries of public choice theory. Although legislators have individual lists of desires, priorities, and preferences, it turns out to be difficult, sometimes impossible, to aggregate these lists into a coherent collective choice. Every system of voting has flaws. The one used by legislatures is particularly dependent on the order in which decisions are made. Legislatures customarily consider proposals one at a time and then vote them up or down. This method disregards third or fourth options and the intensity with which legislators prefer one option over another. Additional options can be considered only in sequence, and this makes the order of decision vital. It is fairly easy to show that someone with control of the agenda can manipulate the choice so that the legislature adopts proposals that only a minority support. The existence of agenda control makes it impossible for a court—even one that knows each legislator's complete table of preferences—to say what the whole body would have done with a proposal it did not consider in fact.

        . . .

        2. *Legislatures Expire.* Judicial interpolation of legislative gaps would be questionable even if judges could ascertain with certainty how the legislature would have acted. Every legislative body's power is limited by a number of checks, from the demands of its internal procedures to bicameralism to the need to obtain the executive's assent. The foremost of these checks is time. Each session of Congress, for example, lasts but two years, after which the whole House and one-third of the Senate stand for reelection. What each Congress does binds the future until another Congress acts, but what a Congress might have done, had it the time, is simply left unresolved. The unaddressed problem is handled by a new legislature with new instructions from the voters.

        If time is classified with the veto as a limit on the power of legislatures, then one customary argument for judicial gap filling—that legislatures lack the time and foresight to resolve every problem—is a reason why judges should not attempt to fill statutory gaps. The shortness of time and the want of foresight, like the fear of the veto and the fear of offending constituents, raise the costs of legislation. The cost of addressing one problem includes the inability, for want of time, to address others. If courts routinely construe statutory gaps as authorizing "more in the same vein," they reduce this cost.

        In a sense, gap-filling construction has the same effects as extending the term of the legislature and allowing that legislature to avoid submitting its plan to the executive for veto. Obviously no court would do this directly. If the members of the Ninety-third Congress reassembled next month and declared their legislative meaning, the declaration would have absolutely no force. This rump body would get no greater power by claiming that its new "laws" were intimately related to, and just filled gaps in, its old ones. Is there a better reason why the members of the Ninety-third Congress, the Eighty-third, and the Seventy-third, "sitting" in the minds of judges, should continue to be able to resolve new problems "presented" to them? The meta-rule I have suggested reduces the number of times judges must summon up the ghouls of legislatures past. In order to authorize judges (or agencies) to fill statutory gaps, the legislature must deny itself life after death and permit judges or agencies to supply their own conceptions of the public interest.

        3. *Liberal Principles.* A principle that statutes are inapplicable unless they either plainly supply a rule of decision or delegate the power to create such a rule is consistent with the liberal principles underlying our political order. Those who wrote and approved the Constitution thought that most social relations would be governed by private agreements, customs, and understandings, not resolved in the halls of government. There is still at least a presumption that people's arrangements prevail unless expressly displaced by legal doctrine. All things are permitted unless there is some contrary rule. It is easier for an agency to justify the revocation of rules (or simple nonregulation) than the creation of new rules. A rule declaring statutes inapplicable unless they plainly resolve or delegate the solution of the matter respects this position. It either preserves the private decisions or remits the questions to other statutes through which the legislature may have addressed the problem. A rule of universal construction, in contrast, assumes that statutes supply an answer to all questions.

Perhaps one day the "orgy of statute making"[27] will reach the point at which the preservation of private decisions is the exception, but that point is not yet here and, one hopes, will never arrive. Like nature, regulation abhors a vacuum, and the existence of one law may create problems requiring more laws. Until the legislature supplies the fix or authorizes someone else to do so, there is no reason for judges to rush in.

4. *Judicial Abilities.* Statutory construction is an art. Good statutory construction requires the rarest of skills. The judge must find clues in the structure of the statute, hints in the legislative history, and combine these with mastery of history, command of psychology, and sensitivity to nuance to divine how deceased legislators would have answered unasked questions.

It is all very well to say that a judge able to understand the temper of 1871 (and 1921), and able to learn the extent of a compromise in 1936, may do well when construing statutes. How many judges meet this description? How many know what clauses and provisos, capable of being enacted in 1923, would have been unthinkable in 1927 because of subtle changes in the composition of the dominant coalitions in Congress? It is hard enough to know this for the immediate past, yet who could deny that legislation that could have been passed in 1982 not only would fail but also could be repealed in 1983? The number of judges living at any time who can, with plausible claim to accuracy, "think [themselves]...into the minds of the enacting legislators and imagine how they would have wanted the statute applied to the case at bar," may be counted on one hand.

To deny that judges have the skills necessary to construe statutes well—at least when construction involves filling gaps in the statutes rather than settling the rare case that arises from conflicts in the rules actually laid down—is not to say that stupid and irresponsible judges can twist any rule. Doubtless the "judge's role should be limited, to protect against willful judges who lack humility and self-restraint." Yet there is a more general reason for limiting the scope of judicial discretion. Few of the best-intentioned, most humble, and most restrained among us have the skills necessary to learn the temper of time before our births, to assume the identity of people we have never met, and to know how 535 disparate characters from regions of great political and economic diversity would have answered questions that never occurred to them. Anyone of reasonable skill could tell that some answers would have been beyond belief in 1866. After putting the impossible to one side, though, a judge must choose from among the possible solutions, and here human ingenuity is bound to fail, often. When it fails, even the best intentioned will find that the imagined dialogues of departed legislators have much in common with their own conceptions of the good.

. . .

COMMENTS AND QUESTIONS

1. Easterbrook distinguishes between finding that a statute is inapplicable to the problem presented (lies outside the statute's domain) and construing the statute in a way that rejects the substantive interpretation proffered by the party

---

[27] G. Gilmore, The Ages of American Law 95 (1977).

seeking rights under the statute. Is this distinction coherent? Consider Easterbrook's example of the tender offer suit by a target company. Is there a difference between finding the statute inapplicable and construing it not to provide a cause of action for targets? (Does Easterbrook assume that construing the statute inevitably means "allowing the target to maintain the suit"?) What, if anything, in Easterbrook's argument would have to change, were one to find the distinction incoherent? (We think the answer is "nothing," so if you are puzzled by the distinction, the message is, "don't worry, nothing turns on accepting it.")

2. We use Easterbrook's article to present (a) a critique of purposivism and (b) a defense of what has come to be known as the new textualism. What are the elements of the critique? The affirmative arguments for textualism?

   (a) Do Easterbrook's arguments against the existence of "a" purpose behind a statute show that there is *never* a dominant purpose? For an argument that courts can identify such a purpose, see Kent Greenawalt, Legislation—Statutory Interpretation: 20 Questions 100–02 (1999). How, if at all, does the purposivist approach deal with what Easterbrook calls "the discoveries of public choice theory"?

   (b) A legislature, knowing that it lacked time to consider all the issues its enactment might raise, could deliberately authorize courts to fill in the gaps. Is such a legislature extending its power beyond the expiration of its term? Consider the possibility that Easterbrook's default rule, requiring some indication of delegation of law-making authority to the courts, is justified primarily by his libertarian (liberal, in his terms) preference that unconstrained private action prevails unless the legislature indicates otherwise. Should the modern regulatory state take such a preference as the basis for the default rule?

   (c) Delegation of law-making authority to the courts does give the courts power they would lack, absent the delegation. Putting aside special issues dealing with the power of the *federal* courts to develop the common law, is the power delegated pursuant to statutes with gaps greater than the power they would have to develop the common law?

   (d) In recent years, textualism has been associated with political conservatives, purposivism with political liberals. Is there some reason to think that the statutes characteristic of the modern regulatory state will do less to displace private ordering if they are construed textually than if they are construed purposively? Consider Easterbrook's discussion of the roles of compromise and of limited time on the development of such statutes. Consider also the possibility that legislators may find it in their interests to support far-reaching, aspirational legislation, which might then be thwarted by agencies unable or unwilling to put the law's broad mandates into effect. On this possibility, see Mark Tushnet and Larry Yackle, *Symbolic Statutes and Real Laws: The Pathologies of the Antiterrorism and Effective Death Penalty Act and the Prison Litigation Reform Act*, 47 Duke L. J. 1 (1997). What interpretive problems do symbolic statutes pose for courts?

3. The next reading presents an affirmative case for purposivism. How persuasive do you find it?

■ *On the Uses of Legislative History in Interpreting Statutes*
STEPHEN BREYER
65 S. Cal. L. Rev. 845 (1992). Reprinted with permission of the Southern California Law Review

I. Introduction

Until recently an appellate court trying to interpret unclear statutory language would have thought it natural, and often helpful, to refer to the statute's "legislative history." The judges might have examined congressional floor debates, committee reports, hearing testimony, and presidential messages in an effort to determine what Congress really "meant" by particular statutory language. Should courts refer to legislative history as they try to apply statutes correctly? Is this practice wise, helpful, or proper? Lawyers and judges, teachers and legislators, have begun to reexamine this venerable practice, often with a highly critical eye. Some have urged drastically curtailing, or even totally abandoning, its use. Some argue that courts use legislative history almost arbitrarily. Using legislative history, Judge Leventhal once said, is like "looking over a crowd and picking out your friends." Others maintain that it is constitutionally improper to look beyond a statute's language, or that searching for "congressional intent" is a semi-mystical exercise like hunting the snark.

. . .

Although I recognize the possible "rearguard" nature of my task, I should like to defend the classical practice and convince you that those who attack it ought to claim victory once they have made judges more sensitive to problems of the abuse of legislative history; they ought not to condemn its use altogether. They should confine their attack to the outskirts and leave the citadel at peace.

My defense focuses on the "law-declaring function" of federal appellate courts and considers only cases in which statutory language is unclear (for few other cases raise serious problems on appeal). First, I demonstrate that we need to use legislative history [by] providing examples of its usefulness. Second, I address the major arguments against its use in order to show that these arguments call, not for abandonment of the practice, but at most for its careful use. Finally, I offer some institutional reasons for why any significant change in the extent to which courts look to legislative history would likely prove harmful.

I concede at the outset that my arguments are more pragmatic than theoretical. They rest upon two important assumptions. First, I assume that appellate courts are in part administrative institutions that aim to help resolve disputes and, while doing so, interpret, and thereby clarify, the law. Second, I assume that law itself is a human institution, serving basic human or societal needs. It is therefore properly subject to praise, or to criticism, in terms of certain pragmatic values, including both formal values, such as coherence and workability, and widely shared substantive values, such as helping to achieve justice by interpreting the law in accordance with the "reasonable expectations" of those to whom it applies. If you do not accept these assumptions, then I am unlikely to convince you of the legitimate role of legislative history in the judicial process. If you do accept them and if, through example, I can suggest to you that legislative history helps appellate courts reach interpretations that tend to make the law itself more coherent, workable, or fair, then I may convince you that courts should not abandon the practice.

II. The Usefulness of Legislative History: Examples

Using legislative history to help interpret unclear statutory language seems natural. Legislative history helps a court understand the context and purpose of a statute. Outside the law we often turn to context and purpose to clarify ambiguity. Consider, for example, a sign that says "no animals in the park." The meaning of even so simple a sign depends heavily on context and purpose. Does "animal" include a squirrel, a dog, or an insect? If you think of an ordinary sign outside New York City's Central Park, you will arrive at one answer. But if I create an unusual context you may reach a different answer. Suppose the sign appears outside a parking lot in a city where much of the population rides donkeys or elephants. Does it then include dogs? Suppose the sign appears in a laboratory in England (where people call insects "animals") next to the rack where the microbiologists "park" their test tubes. The meaning of the sign, the scope of its rule, depends on context, on convention, and on purpose. Is this fact not true of words in statutes as well? Should one not look to the background of a statute, the terms of the debate over its enactment, the factual assumptions the legislators made, the conventions they thought applicable, and their expressed objectives in an effort to understand the statute's relevant context, conventions, and purposes?

Let me begin by providing examples of five circumstances in which courts reasonably use legislative history to help reach correct results in difficult cases. I start with the least controversial examples and end with the kind that most disturbs the critics.

A. Avoiding an Absurd Result

Blackstone himself, more than two hundred years ago, pointed out that a court need not follow the literal language of a statute where doing so would produce an absurd result. He said that if "collaterally . . . absurd consequences, manifestly contrary to common reason," arise out of statutes those statutes "are, with regard to those collateral consequences, void." Blackstone further explained:

> Where some collateral matter arises out of the general words [of a statute], and happens to be unreasonable; there the judges are in decency to conclude that this consequence was not foreseen by the parliament, and therefore they are at liberty to expound the statute by equity. . . .

Considering such problematic language in a case, should not a judge examine the history of the statute to see whether the language is, in fact, as absurd as it appears, or whether it may serve a reasonable purpose that did not occur to the parties or to the court?

Courts do just such checking. Consider, for example, the Supreme Court case *Green v. Bock Laundry Machine Co.*[9] A Federal Rule of Evidence, enacted into law as a statute, stated that evidence of a witness's prior convictions was admissible if the "court determines that the probative value of admitting this evidence outweighs its prejudicial effect to the defendant." Why does the Rule use the word "defendant?"

---

[9] 490 U.S. 504 (1989).

Should it not say either "accused," thus limiting the Rule's effect to criminal cases, or "other party?" Suppose the prejudicial effect is not "to the defendant" but to the civil plaintiff. Suppose, for example, that the plaintiff's star witness has a serious but almost irrelevant criminal record. Admission of that record would hurt the plaintiff and help the defendant. Why should anyone wish to distinguish between plaintiffs and defendants in this way in a civil case?

Before concluding that the distinction in a civil case was absurd, that no good reason supported it, and that the courts should read the Rule's instruction as applying only to criminal defendants, the Supreme Court checked the history of the Rule to see if the drafters had some special purpose in mind. Only after the Court found no evidence of any such purpose did it hold that the Rule, despite its language, did not apply to civil defendants. Justice Scalia, a vocal critic of the use of legislative history, wrote that this kind of use was proper. He said that a judge will, and presumably should, consult history "to verify that what seems ... an unthinkable disposition ... was indeed unthought-of, and thus to justify a departure from the ordinary meaning of the word[s]" in the statute. This kind of use of legislative history seems uncontroversial.

B. Drafting Error

Legislative history can also illuminate drafting errors. A statute's language might seem fairly clear. The language might produce a result that does not seem absurd. Yet, legislative history nonetheless might clearly show that the result is wrong because of a drafting error that courts should correct. Consider the following example:

A federal criminal statute says "whoever ... possesses any false, forged, or counterfeit coin, with intent to defraud any person" is guilty of a crime. The question in a case the First Circuit decided in 1982 was whether the statute covers a person who (with the requisite fraudulent intent) possesses, in the United States, false Krugerrands, gold coins used as currency in South Africa, but not in the United States.[14] Does this particular statutory provision protect against fraudulent use of South Africa's currency in the United States? The language indicates that it does. It refers to *"any ... counterfeit coin,"* and a false Krugerrand is a counterfeit coin.

The history of this statute, however, shows a narrower meaning. In 1965 Congress reorganized, and slightly rewrote, a set of anti-counterfeiting statutes, of which this particular provision was one. During the 150 years that preceded the reorganization, this provision constituted a small part of a statutory paragraph, most of which prohibited the making of counterfeit coins. This older paragraph contained an important qualifying phrase, indicating clearly that the provision applied to American coins and not to foreign coins. When Congress rewrote the statutes in 1965, it kept the qualifying phrase in the reorganized provision that governs the making of counterfeit coins. That provision now says that "whoever falsely makes ... any coin ... in resemblance of" any United States coin or any foreign gold or silver coin that is "current in the United States or in actual use and

---

[14] This example is drawn from *United States v. Falvey*, 676 F.2d 871 (1st Cir. 1982).

circulation as money within the United States" is guilty of a crime. But when Congress separated the "possession" provision from the larger paragraph, it did not include the qualifying provision that limited its application to coins "current" as money in the United States.

Now the question seems more difficult. Without this history, one might think that a false Krugerrand obviously falls within the scope of the statute's words "any . . . counterfeit coin." But does it? After all, the word "any" in a statute rarely means "any at all in the universe." It almost always has some context-implied limitation. Moreover, for 150 years this particular statute explicitly did not apply to ancient coins, Krugerrands, or counterfeits of any other coin not currently used as American currency. Should a court read the provision to continue this limitation, reading the word "any" as so limited, or should it assume that the "possession" statute, unlike its near cousin, the "making" statute, includes false Krugerrands? Either answer seems reasonable.

In answering this question, would you not want to know just what Congress had in mind in 1965 when it reorganized and rewrote the preexisting statutes? More specifically, would you not want to know why the human being who drafted the new "possession" language left out the qualifying phrase? Was it an accident? Did someone tell the drafter to leave it out? If so, did the legislator who told the drafter to omit the phrase have some policy change in mind? If so, what sort of change?

The 1965 House and Senate Reports on the counterfeiting legislation provide fairly clear answers. They specify that the congressional reenactment of the law, reorganizing it and rewriting some of it, was intended to serve purely organizational objectives. They say that Congress expected, after the changes, that the law would remain what it was before the changes. These reports reveal that the individual staff members who rewrote the law thought that the legislators wanted them to accomplish a purely technical, non-substantive drafting objective. The reports thereby indicate that no one in Congress intended to change substantive law or to rewrite federal counterfeiting law so that it helped protect the currency of all nations, including South Africa, or ancient Greece and Rome.

If a court has such good evidence that no one in Congress intended to change the law substantively, is that not grounds for saying, "Congress did not intend any substantive change?" And is this not grounds for reading the preexisting limitation back into the word "any?" The First Circuit used legislative history to uncover, and then to undo, a drafting error. This use seems to me perfectly appropriate and desirable.

C. Specialized Meanings

Even the strongest critics of the use of legislative history concede that a court should take full account of any special meaning that a statutory word may have. The word "standing," for example, means something quite different in a statute than on a subway poster because the word carries with it a host of technical meanings growing out of context, case law, and history more generally. Presumably the critics see nothing wrong with looking to history to help determine whether a particular word has a specialized meaning and, if so, what sort. But why should that history specifically exclude legislative history?

Consider *Pierce v. Underwood*,[17] a recent Supreme Court opinion authored by Justice Scalia. One of the legal questions in the case concerned the meaning of the phrase "substantially justified," as used in the Equal Access to Justice Act. A private party who wins a suit against the government is entitled to attorneys' fees unless the government's position was "substantially justified." The Court considered whether "substantially justified" means "better than reasonable," or even "less than reasonable."

The Court held that the word "substantial," in effect, means "reasonable." In reaching this conclusion, Justice Scalia made various comparisons with other areas of law, including the following:

> Judicial review of agency action, the field at issue here, regularly proceeds under the rubric of "substantial evidence" set forth in the Administrative Procedure Act, 5 U.S.C. § 706(2)(E). That phrase does not mean a large or considerable amount of evidence but rather "such relevant evidence as a reasonable mind might accept as adequate to support a conclusion."

For present purposes, the interesting part of this quotation is the date of the . . . case [which the opinion quotes], namely 1938. The reason it is interesting is that Justice Scalia uses that case to help explain the somewhat technical meaning of a word in the Administrative Procedure Act, which did not become law until 1946. It is worth asking how Justice Scalia knew that the meaning of the word in the 1946 statute was given in a case decided eight years earlier.

The well-known answer to this question is that the 1946 House and Senate Reports make clear that in the Administrative Procedure Act, Congress intended to enact into law recommendations contained in the Report of the Attorney General's Committee on Administrative Procedure. That report cites the . . . definition, as does a later report by the Attorney General, which focused specifically on the bill that Congress enacted into law in 1946. This later report appears as an appendix to the Senate Report on the bill, and in the Congressional Record, as an extension of remarks made during floor debate. That is how the administrative law community knows, and is very certain, that the APA's term "substantial evidence" means just what Justice Scalia says it means.

This example demonstrates a fairly common function of legislative history— explaining specialized meanings of terms or phrases in a statute which were previously understood by the community of specialists (or others) particularly interested in the statute's enactment. Justice Scalia's reliance on such materials in *Pierce*, widely accepted like most, represents a fairly noncontroversial use of legislative history.

D. Identifying a "Reasonable Purpose"

A court often needs to know the purpose a particular statutory word or phrase serves within the broader context of a statutory scheme in order to decide properly whether a particular circumstance falls within the scope of that word or phrase. Does the word "persons" in a welfare statute, for example, include a child, the

[17] 487 U.S. 552 (1988).

child's mother, a stepfather, or all of them? A clear understanding of the provision's purpose could lead a court to decide that exactly the same word, "persons," appearing three times in the same sentence refers to a different group each time.[24]

How does a court determine the purpose of a statutory phrase? Sometimes it can simply look to the surrounding language in the statute or to the entire statutory scheme and ask, "Given this statutory background, what would a reasonable human being intend this specific language to accomplish?" Often this question has only one good answer, but sometimes the surrounding statutory language and the "reasonable human purpose" test cannot answer the question. In such situations, legislative history may provide a clear and helpful resolution.

Consider, for example, Congress's 1984 revision of federal bankruptcy law. The statute contained a phrase, "core proceeding," not previously used in a federal statute. The statute authorized a federal Article I bankruptcy judge to hear and determine "core proceedings" without the consent of the parties. For non-core matters the bankruptcy judge could make binding decisions only with the parties' consent. What is a core proceeding? What is a non-core proceeding? The statute lists fifteen examples of core proceedings, but also says that "core proceedings include, but are not limited" to the fifteen enumerated examples. Why did Congress not set forth a complete list? Probably because those who drafted this provision feared they would not be able to imagine, in advance, every possible kind of proceeding that should be included. Such a reason is a common cause of generality, or lack of precision, in statutes. However, it is not a basis for criticizing the legislature. Were human vision not limited, if we could specify in advance all possible future circumstances, we would need to give courts only fact-finding power, not the power to interpret statutes.

The First Circuit found itself faced with a circumstance not on the fifteen-item list. We had to decide whether an Article I bankruptcy court could decide a debtor's post-petition state-law contract claim—a claim that arose after the debtor filed for bankruptcy—without the parties' consent.[27] Was such a post-petition state-law controversy a core or non-core proceeding?

The legislative history of the 1984 legislation provided the answer. First, it clearly stated that Congress passed the Act in response to the Supreme Court's decision in *Northern Pipeline Construction Co. v. Marathon Pipe Line Co.*,[28] which held that the Constitution's separation-of-powers principles did not permit Article I bankruptcy courts to adjudicate a debtor's pre-petition state-law contract claim— a claim that arose before the debtor filed its bankruptcy petition.

Second, floor statements made by the bill's sponsors, Democratic Representative Kastenmeier, and Republican Representative Kindness, clarified the relation

---

[24] See *Evans v. Commissioner*, 933 F.2d 1, 6–8 (1st Cir. 1991) (Statutory language permits, and legislative history, supported by agency interpretation, suggests that the use of the term "persons" in a section of the Aid to Families with Dependent Children statute, 42 U.S.C. §602(a)(8)(B)(ii) (1988), refers, variously, to all people living in the relevant family or assistance unit, and to only those members of the family or assistance unit who received aid in the previous four months and to whose income the agency considers applying a statutory "disregard.").

[27] See *In re Arnold Print Works, Inc.*, 815 F.2d 165 (1st Cir. 1987).

[28] 458 U.S. 50 (1982).

of the word "core" in the statute to the Marathon case. They explained in detail that they intended the words "core proceedings" (over which the bankruptcy courts would have full decision-making powers) to encompass as many different kinds of proceedings as the Constitution would permit. They referred to proceedings outside the "core" as "Marathon-type" cases, and explained that "jurisdiction in core bankruptcy proceedings is broader than the summary jurisdiction under pre-1978 law."

These two aspects of the statute's history led our court to consider the constitutional question first. Did the Constitution permit an Article I bankruptcy court to consider a "post-petition" contract claim? We concluded that "post-petition" and "pre-petition" claims differed significantly from a constitutional perspective and that the Constitution permitted the bankruptcy courts to determine the post-petition state-law claims. Did the "post-petition" claim fall within the statute's word "core"? The legislative history tying that word to the Marathon case suggested that it did. The reference to pre-1978 summary jurisdiction offered further support, for "summary jurisdiction under pre-1978 law" included jurisdiction over "post-petition" state-law contract claims. Consequently we concluded that the word "core" covered the circumstance before us.

Without the legislative history, without the floor statements, we might have reached a different result. After all, state-law contract claims, whether pre- or post-petition, look very much alike, and both sorts of claims are only peripherally related to bankruptcy itself. But the result suggested by any such "purpose-free" analogy would be pointless and wrong, for it would not comport with the legislators' basic statutory objectives.

More importantly, the incompatibility between the result we could have reached (but did not) and those congressional objectives, seen from a general institutional or governmental perspective, would be undesirable. The undesirability consists, not simply of the fact that Representatives Kastenmeier and Kindness were democratically elected, but also of the fact that the statute's general objectives (and the detailed provisions needed to implement the objectives) reflect far more than the work of the two Representatives themselves. The objectives, and the detailed provisions, reflect the work of all the representatives of the bankruptcy community involved in the legislative process that produced the bankruptcy bill, namely bankruptcy judges, practitioners, teachers, and many others who worked on the details of the law. Their knowledge and experience, likely communicated through staff, with or without compromises, is embodied both in particular statutory phrases and in reports and floor statement language. To take from the courts the power to refer to legislative history in a case such as this one is to cut an essential channel for communications with these informed communities of groups and individuals, a channel that runs from those affected by a law's implementation, through courts and legislators, to those involved in the law's creation. To reach a result inconsistent with their work denies the public a significant part of the benefit of their expertise—an important matter in so technical an area where the knowledge of informed groups is likely to produce a more workable, legally "better" statute. More significantly, reaching such an inconsistent result defeats the reasonable expectations of the many individuals and groups involved in the legislative process. As long as we believe that one important goal of a legal system is to maintain rules of law consistent with the reasonable expectations of those who live within it, this result is undesirable.

E. *Choosing among Reasonable Interpretations of a Politically Controversial Statute*

Consider as a final example a statute that evoked strong political support and opposition in Congress and was enacted with language that is unclear or silent about an important issue that faces a court. Judicial use of legislative history to determine meaning in this context seems to cause critics the greatest concern, for it is the kind of situation in which courts risk elevating the testimony to the level of a statute. Consider a 1981 case in our court that arose out of the Urban Mass Transportation Act of 1964.[30] That Act provided financial aid for urban mass transit systems, and it foresaw that the states receiving aid would likely acquire privately owned mass transit systems. The Act, in section 13(c), said that if a state received aid the federal Secretary of Labor had to certify that the state had made "fair and equitable arrangements...to protect the interests of employees affected" by the transit funding. The Secretary of Labor issued various regulations under section 13(c), the thrust of which was that the Secretary would consider an arrangement "fair and equitable" if the employees and the state employer agreed to them.

The case before us asked whether this provision of federal law, section 13(c), preempted a Massachusetts state statute that instructed its Transit Authority not to negotiate away its power to insist upon productivity-enhancing work-rule changes whenever it negotiated new contracts with the transit unions. The Authority previously had, in effect, given up this power to the unions and promised not to take it back, not even when the old contracts expired. The federal Secretary of Labor had approved the "arrangement" under which the Authority would never try to take the work-rule-change power back. Could Massachusetts, by statute, instruct its Authority to act contrary to this Secretary-approved arrangement? If section 13(c) and regulations promulgated pursuant to it preempted conflicting state law, the answer to this question was "no."

The text of the statute does not answer the preemption question. It simply says that the Secretary must certify that the "arrangements" between employer and employee are "fair and equitable." The legislative history of section 13(c), however, did suggest an answer.

First, the Secretary of Labor, Willard Wirtz, testified about the draft bill that became section 13(c) in the committee hearings that preceded its enactment into law. He said that when the Labor Department drafted the bill it had consulted the Amalgamated Transit Workers' Union and the AFL-CIO, and that section 13(c) would not supersede state law. Second, the preemptive effect of section 13(c) was discussed on the floor of Congress just prior to the bill's enactment. Senators hostile to the entire bill, such as Senator Barry Goldwater, asked whether or not it would preempt state law. Senators favoring the bill, such as Senator Pete Williams and Senator Jacob Javits, replied that section 13(c) would not preempt state law. Secretary Wirtz's testimony, and the floor debate, seemed clear and definite, and they helped our court decide that the provision did not preempt the Massachusetts law.

---

[30] See *Local Div. 589 v. Massachusetts*, 666 F.2d 618 (1st Cir. 1981), cert. denied, 457 U.S. 1117 (1982).

Were we right to rely upon legislative history in this way? The bill itself, and section 13(c) in particular, were controversial in Congress. But the legislative history with respect to preemption was fairly clear. Of course, the legislators themselves may not have written that history. But suppose that a civil servant actually wrote Secretary Wirtz's testimony after consulting with the unions. Suppose that legislative staff wrote the Goldwater/Williams floor colloquy after consulting with counsels for the Transit Workers' Union, employers groups, and the states. Indeed, suppose that union lawyers, or employer lawyers, wrote the debate word for word. Should that fact make the use of legislative history significantly less legitimate?

Before answering this question "yes," consider, for a moment, how Congress actually works. Congress is no longer (was it ever?) made up of part-time citizen-legislators, extemporaneous orators, who burn the midnight oil as they themselves draft the laws needed to resolve the social and political problems revealed during the day's interchange of spontaneous debate. Rather, Congress is a bureaucratic organization with twenty thousand employees, working full-time, generating legislation through complicated, but organized, processes of interaction with other institutions and groups, including executive branch departments, labor unions, business organizations, and public interest groups. These other institutions and groups (including interest groups) through their representatives (including lobbyists) often initiate legislation; they typically make clear to congressional staff just what they are trying to achieve, and why; they may suggest content and text, not only for statutes, but also for reports or floor statements; they review proposed changes; and they negotiate and compromise with staff, with legislators and with each other. The staff, working with these groups, the legislators, and other staff members, will do the same.

When this process works properly, staff members for each legislator carefully review statutory language, report language, and significant proposed language for floor statements (of the staff member's own, and of other legislators), checking for consistency with the legislator's own objectives and positions, suggesting changes, and negotiating compromises. The staff member flags matters of significant substantive or political controversy, brings them to the legislator's attention, discusses them with the legislator, and obtains instructions from the legislator about how to proceed. On important matters, staff members for legislators who are directly involved will examine with care each word and proposed change, often with representatives of affected interest groups or institutions not only in the language of the statute, but also in each committee report and the many floor statements. Significant matters will again be brought to the attention of the legislators for development of their individual positions, and for them to discuss and resolve with other legislators. The process involves continuous interaction among legislators, staff members, and representatives of those institutions or groups most likely to be affected by the proposed legislation. This process requires each legislator to rely upon staff, in the first instance, to separate the matters that are significant from those that are not; it requires each legislator to make decisions about, and to resolve with other legislators, each significant matter; and it requires each legislator further to rely upon drafters and negotiators to carry out the legislator's decisions.

The process I have just described is an institutional one, in which the legislator relies in part upon the work of staff. In this process, no legislator reads every word of every report or floor statement or proposed statute, which may consist of hundreds of pages of text. However, in this process those words are carefully reviewed by those whom they will likely affect and by the legislator's own employees. Moreover, in this process the legislator makes the significant decisions and takes responsibility for the outcome.

This institutional process, in which the legislator serves as a kind of manager, should seem familiar to those who manage other large institutions such as businesses, labor unions, and government departments. No one expects the top officials in such institutions to have read every document they generate. Yet those top officials typically are held responsible for those documents, and the outside world typically treats those documents as genuine reflections of the institution's position, whether or not the top officials actually read them. Many, if not most, institutions work through downward delegation, with responsibility flowing upward. Of course, the judicial branch, in principle, does not work this way. It is perhaps, then, understandable that law professors, judges and lawyers might hope that the legislative branch would function in a similarly centralized fashion. But, after a little reflection, this hope seems unachievable and perhaps undesirable. The judge's staff is smaller and the judge's involvement in the making of legal decisions is more direct and detailed. Why should the judicial ideal be the model for Congress? Why should the fairly public congressional legislative process, which involves checking with those whom the legislation will most likely affect, and then perhaps publicly adopting and explaining their related points of view, diminish the legitimacy of the resulting legislative history? I shall return to this question later, but, for the moment, emphasize that it is at least plausible to claim legitimacy for that history.

Consider the implications of a rule that forbids the court from examining a statute's history—say, the history of section 13(c) of the Urban Mass Transportation Act. First, how would our court have answered the interpretive question in the transit workers case without its history? Viewed from the perspective of those who worked on the law in 1964, might our answer not seem random? And would a different answer not have had at least one objectionable aspect, namely that it would frustrate the reasonable expectations of those (on both sides) who created the law in Congress?

Second, what would the effect on Congress be if it knew that courts would not consider legislative history? Suppose, in 1964, that the employers, unions, and states had thought that committee testimony, report language, floor statements, and the like could not influence a later judicial interpretation of the law's text. How would the states and employers have obtained the preemption assurance that they sought and that the unions were willing to give? They might have tried to write a statutory provision that embodied appropriate "preemption" language. But, one can easily imagine that time, the complexity and length of the overall bill, and the difficulty of foreseeing future circumstances (including how courts would interpret "anti-preemption" language) might have made it impossible for the groups to agree on statutory language. It was easier, however, for them to agree about floor statements or report language about an "intent." This language is more general in form, and would not bind courts in cases where it would make no sense to do so.

It is possible, then, that if the relevant groups, institutions, and individuals involved in the process did not believe courts would look to legislative history, they might not have agreed on the legislation. Without agreement, perhaps Congress would have enacted no "labor protection" at all, or perhaps it would have failed to pass the Urban Mass Transportation Act. An institutional device that facilitates compromise and helps develop the consensus needed to pass important legislation has at least that much to be said in its favor.

. . .

COMMENTS AND QUESTIONS

1. The debate over using legislative history in statutory interpretation was fueled by Justice Antonin Scalia's strong advocacy and the seeming success of his criticism in changing Supreme Court practice in the 1990s. By the early 2000s, though, the assault on the use of legislative history seemed to have failed, at least in the sense that there was no consistent Supreme Court majority committed to refraining from using legislative history. Legislative history has become—and perhaps always was—something of a tiebreaker when uncertainty about a statute's meaning remained even after careful analysis of statutory text and structure. Note that it might be easier to discern a legislature's (dominant) purposes from legislative history than from a statute's provisions alone—but also that the legislative history might be (deliberately?) misleading about the statute's dominant purposes.

2. Note the variety of materials that can be referred to as "legislative history." In discussing the Kruggerrand case, then-Judge Breyer refers to the provision's evolution from earlier statutory provisions and reports on the legislation by congressional committees. The category can also include statements made by a statute's sponsors and its opponents, statements made in formal documents like committee reports or statements made in debate on the legislature's floor, and even news accounts. Proponents of the use of legislative history do not contend that every item within the category receives equal weight; rather, they claim that the item should be used for whatever value it has in identifying the statute's dominant purposes. To that extent, then, the debate over the use of legislative history is one version of the apparently different debate over purposivism versus textualism.

3. In the cases Breyer discusses, legislative history—in the sense of committee reports and the like—appears to confirm conclusions reached by using other materials. At most, as Breyer says, the use serves to confirm those conclusions, or perhaps more broadly, to confirm that those conclusions are not undermined by other material. How much mileage can Breyer get for a general purposivist approach from the proposition that courts should refrain from interpreting statutes to reach absurd results? (For a discussion of the "absurdity" question, see John Manning, *The Absurdity Doctrine*, 116 Harv. L. Rev. 2387 [2003].) Ask yourself the same question with respect to his discussion of drafting errors and specialized meanings.

4. Using legislative materials to justify a departure from the apparent meaning of a provision is different from using it to confirm that meaning and even from using it to ensure that no purposes are served by the apparent meaning. In

addition, there are cases where the meaning is simply not apparent. In such cases, what should courts do? Easterbrook suggests a default rule that the statute is inapplicable in such cases, Breyer a rule that the provision should be given a meaning that serves the purposes that can be discovered by asking what a reasonable person might have been trying to accomplish by enacting the provision. Legislative history can inform Breyer's inquiry, but note that the inquiry remains hypothetical or objective and is not an effort to identify the subjective thoughts of individual legislators.

5. Note the resemblance between Breyer's approach and Llewellyn's: both seek to identify some "reasonable human purpose" for the provision at issue. Does that approach confer too much discretion on judges? Does it create too uncertainty about what a statute "means," such that persons may act in ways that give rise to litigation—litigation in which judges will determine what the statute means? Is purposivism in tension with some aspects of the ideal of the rule of law? But consider again the objection to textualism that it leaves some enacted provisions without legal effect and so is in tension with some (other) aspects of the rule of law.

6. How does (would) Breyer respond to Easterbrook's observation that many statutes are deals among interest groups? Easterbrook suggests that any interpretation going beyond the obvious meaning of a statutory provision will give one interest group more than it was able to achieve in the legislative process. Consider the proposition that Easterbrook's position divides statutory provisions into two groups, one with obvious meanings and the other having no legal effect whatsoever. Should a court treat language that has moved fully through the legislative process as having no legal effect? Consider the proposition that Breyer has a more optimistic, or less cynical, view of the legislative process. For additional discussion of the visions of public policymaking embodied in alternative views about statutory interpretation and regulation, see the excerpt from Shaviro in chapter 13.

B Cases

Statutory interpretation is often straightforward, with all indicators pointing in the same direction. Problems of interpretation arise when (a) statutory language is linguistically ambiguous, generating doubt about what rights are created or duties imposed by the statute, or (more often) (b) there seems (to whom?) to be tension between the apparent meaning of the words used in the statute and public goals that one (again, who?) could imagine a reasonable legislature attempting to advance. In cases involving the latter situation, typically litigants, and sometimes courts, will infer from the tension that the statutory language is unclear or ambiguous and then interpret the language, deploying whatever interpretive resources—textualism, purposivism, canons of interpretation, and the like—they believe appropriate. This section presents several important cases on statutory interpretation that provide a foundation for your examination in subsequent chapters of statutory interpretation in the area of risk.

■ **Church of the Holy Trinity v. United States**
143 U.S. 457 (1892)

Justice Brewer delivered the opinion of the Court.

Plaintiff in error is a corporation, duly organized and incorporated as a religious society under the laws of the State of New York. E. Walpole Warren was, prior to September, 1887, an alien residing in England. In that month the plaintiff in error made a contract with him, by which he was to remove to the city of New York and enter into its service as rector and pastor; and in pursuance of such contract, Warren did so remove and enter upon such service. It is claimed by the United States that this contract on the part of the plaintiff in error was forbidden by the act of February 26, 1885, 23 Stat. 332, c. 164, and an action was commenced to recover the penalty prescribed by that act. The Circuit Court held that the contract was within the prohibition of the statute, and rendered judgment accordingly, and the single question presented for our determination is whether it erred in that conclusion.

The first section describes the act forbidden, and is in these words:

"Be it enacted by the Senate and House of Representatives of the United States of America in Congress assembled, That from and after the passage of this act it shall be unlawful for any person, company, partnership, or corporation, in any manner whatsoever, to prepay the transportation, or in any way assist or encourage the importation or migration of any alien or aliens, any foreigner or foreigners, into the United States, its Territories, or the District of Columbia, under contract or agreement, parol or special, express or implied, made previous to the importation or migration of such alien or aliens, foreigner or foreigners, to perform labor or service of any kind in the United States, its Territories, or the District of Columbia."

It must be conceded that the act of the corporation is within the letter of this section, for the relation of rector to his church is one of service, and implies labor on the one side with compensation on the other. Not only are the general words labor and service both used, but also, as it were to guard against any narrow interpretation and emphasize a breadth of meaning, to them is added "of any kind;" and, further, . . . the fifth section, which makes specific exceptions, among them professional actors, artists, lecturers, singers and domestic servants, strengthens the idea that every other kind of labor and service was intended to be reached by the first section. While there is great force to this reasoning, we cannot think Congress intended to denounce with penalties a transaction like that in the present case. It is a familiar rule, that a thing may be within the letter of the statute and yet not within the statute, because not within its spirit, nor within the intention of its makers. . . . This is not the substitution of the will of the judge for that of the legislator, for frequently words of general meaning are used in a statute, words broad enough to include an act in question, and yet a consideration of the whole legislation, or of the circumstances surrounding its enactment, or of the absurd results which follow from giving such broad meaning to the words, makes it unreasonable to believe that the legislator intended to include the particular act. . . .

. . .

Among other things which may be considered in determining the intent of the legislature is the title of the act. We do not mean that it may be used to add to or take from the body of the statute, but it may help to interpret its meaning. In the case of *United States v. Fisher*, 2 Cranch, 358, 386, Chief Justice Marshall said: "On the influence which the title ought to have in construing the enacting clauses much has been said; and yet it is not easy to discern the point of difference between the opposing counsel in this respect. Neither party contends that the title of an act can control plain words in the body of the statute; and neither denies that, taken with other parts, it may assist in removing ambiguities. Where the intent is plain, nothing is left to construction. Where the mind labors to discover the design of the legislature, it seizes everything from which aid can be derived; and in such case the title claims of degree of notice, and will have is due share of consideration." And in the case of *United States v. Palmer*, 3 Wheat. 610, 631, the same judge applied the doctrine in this way: "The words of the section are in terms of unlimited extent. The words 'any person or persons' are broad enough to comprehend every human being. But general words must not only be limited to cases within the jurisdiction of the State, but also to those objects to which the legislature intended to apply them. Did the legislature intend to apply these words to the subjects of a foreign power, who in a foreign ship may commit murder or robbery on the high seas? The title of an act cannot control its words, but may furnish some aid in showing what was in the mind of the legislature. The title of this act is, 'An act for the punishment of certain crimes against the United States.' It would seem that offences against the United States, not offences against the human race, were the crimes which the legislature intended by this law to punish."

It will be seen that words as general as those used in the first section of this act were by that decision limited, and the intent of Congress with respect to the act was gathered partially, at least, from its title. Now, the title of this act is, "An act to prohibit the importation and migration of foreigners and aliens under contract or agreement to perform labor in the United States, its Territories and the District of Columbia." Obviously the thought expressed in this reaches only to the work of the manual laborer, as distinguished from that of the professional man. No one reading such a title would suppose that Congress had in its mind any purpose of staying the coming into this country of ministers of the gospel, or, indeed, of any class whose toil is that of the brain. The common understanding of the terms labor and laborers does not include preaching and preachers; and it is to be assumed that words and phrases are used in their ordinary meaning. So whatever of light is thrown upon the statute by the language of the title indicates an exclusion from its penal provisions of all contracts for the employment of ministers, rectors and pastors.

Again, another guide to the meaning of a statute is found in the evil which it is designed to remedy; and for this the court properly looks at contemporaneous events, the situation as it existed, and as it was pressed upon the attention of the legislative body. The situation which called for this statute was briefly but fully stated by Mr. Justice Brown when, as District Judge, he decided the case of *United States v. Craig*, 28 Fed. Rep. 795, 798: "The motives and history of the act are matters of common knowledge. It had become the practice for large capitalists in this country to contract with their agents abroad for the shipment of great numbers of an ignorant and servile class of foreign laborers, under contracts, by which the employer agreed, upon the one hand, to prepay their passage, while, upon the other hand, the laborers agreed to work after their arrival for a certain time at a low rate of wages. The effect of this was to break down the labor market, and to reduce other laborers engaged in like occupations to the level of the assisted immigrant. The evil finally became so flagrant that an appeal was made to Congress for relief by the passage of the act in question, the design of which was to raise the standard of foreign immigrants, and to discountenance the migration of those who had not sufficient means in their own hands, or those of their friends, to pay their passage."

It appears, also, from the petitions, and in the testimony presented before the committees of Congress, that it was this cheap unskilled labor which was making the trouble, and the influx of which Congress sought to prevent. It was never suggested that we had in this country a surplus of brain toilers, and, least of all, that the market for the services of Christian ministers was depressed by foreign competition. Those were matters to which the attention of Congress, or of the people, was not directed. So far, then, as the evil which was sought to be remedied interprets the statute, it also guides to an exclusion of this contract from the penalties of the act.

A singular circumstance, throwing light upon the intent of Congress, is found in this extract from the report of the Senate Committee on Education and Labor, recommending the passage of the bill: "The general facts and considerations which induce the committee to recommend the passage of this bill are set forth in the Report of the Committee of the House. The committee report the bill back without amendment, although there are certain features thereof which might well be changed or modified, in the hope that the bill may not fail of passage during the present session. Especially would the committee have otherwise recommended amendments, substituting for the expression 'labor and service,' whenever it occurs in the body of the bill, the words 'manual labor' or 'manual service,' as sufficiently broad to accomplish the purposes of the bill, and that such amendments would remove objections which a sharp and perhaps unfriendly criticism may urge to the proposed legislation. The committee, however, believing that the bill in its present form will be construed as including only those whose labor or service is manual in character, and being very desirous that the bill become a law before the adjournment, have reported the bill without change." And, referring back to the report of the Committee of the House, there appears this language: "It seeks to restrain and prohibit the immigration or importation of laborers who would have never seen our shores but for the inducements and allurements of men whose only object is to obtain labor at the lowest possible rate, regardless of the social and material well-being of our own citizens and regardless of the evil consequences which result to American laborers from such immigration. This class of immigrants care nothing about our institutions, and in many instances never even heard of them; they are men whose passage is paid by the importers; they come here under contract to labor for a certain number of years; they are ignorant of our social condition, and that they may remain so they are isolated and prevented from coming into contact with Americans. They are generally from the lowest social stratum, and live upon the coarsest food and in hovels of a character before unknown to American workmen. They, as a rule, do not become citizens, and are certainly not a desirable acquisition to the body politic. The inevitable tendency of their presence among us is to degrade American labor, and to reduce it to the level of the imported pauper labor."

We find, therefore, that the title of the act, the evil which was intended to be remedied, the circumstances surrounding the appeal to Congress, the reports of the committee of each house, all concur in affirming that the intent of Congress was simply to stay the influx of this cheap unskilled labor.

But beyond all these matters no purpose of action against religion can be imputed to any legislation, state or national, because this is a religious people. This is historically true. From the discovery of this continent to the present hour, there is a single voice making this affirmation. [The Court then discusses the historical importance of religion in American life.] . . .

Even the Constitution of the United States, which is supposed to have little touch upon the private life of the individual, contains in the First Amendment a declaration common to the constitutions of all the States, as follows: "Congress shall make no law respecting an establishment of religion, or prohibiting the free exercise thereof," etc. And also provides in Article 1, section 7, (a provision common to many constitutions,) that the Executive shall have ten days (Sundays excepted) within which to determine whether he will approve or veto a bill.

There is no dissonance in these declarations. There is a universal language pervading them all, having one meaning; they affirm and reaffirm that this is a religious nation. These are not individual sayings, declarations of private persons: they are organic utterances; they speak the voice of the entire people. While because of a general recognition of this truth the question has seldom been presented to the courts, yet we find that in *Updegraph v. The Commonwealth*, 11 S. & R. 394, 400, it was decided that, "Christianity, general Christianity, is, and always has been, a part of the common law of Pennsylvania; . . . not Christianity with an established church, and tithes, and spiritual courts; but Christianity with liberty of conscience to all men." . . .

If we pass beyond these matters to a view of American life as expressed by its laws, its business, its customs and its society, we find everywhere a clear recognition of the same truth. Among other matters note the following: The form of oath universally prevailing, concluding with an appeal to the Almighty; the custom of opening sessions of all deliberative bodies and most conventions with prayer; the prefatory words of all wills, "In the name of God, amen;" the laws respecting the observance of the Sabbath, with the general cessation of all secular business, and the closing of courts, legislatures, and other similar public assemblies on that day; the churches and church organizations which abound in every city, town and hamlet; the multitude of charitable organizations existing every where under Christian auspices; the gigantic missionary associations, with general support, and aiming to establish Christian missions in every quarter of the globe. These, and many other matters which might be noticed, add a volume of unofficial declarations to the mass of organic utterances that this is a Christian nation. In the face of all these, shall it be believed that a Congress of the United States intended to make it a misdemeanor for a church of this country to contract for the services of a Christian minister residing in another nation?

Suppose in the Congress that passed this act some member had offered a bill which in terms declared that, if any Roman Catholic church in this country should contract with Cardinal Manning to come to this country and enter into its service as pastor and priest; or any Episcopal church should enter into a like contract with Canon Farrar; or any Baptist church should make similar arrangements with Rev. Mr. Spurgeon; or any Jewish synagogue with some eminent Rabbi, such contract should be adjudged unlawful and void, and the church making it be subject to prosecution and punishment, can it be believed that it would have received a minute of approving thought or a single vote? Yet it is contended that such was in effect the meaning of this statute. The construction invoked cannot be accepted as correct. It is a case where there was presented a definite evil, in view of which the legislature used general terms with the purpose of reaching all phases of that evil, and thereafter, unexpectedly, it is developed that the general language thus employed is broad enough to reach cases and acts which the whole history and life of the country affirm could not have been intentionally legislated against. It is the duty of the courts, under those circumstances, to say that, however broad the language of the statute may be, the act, although within the letter, is not within the intention of the legislature, and therefore cannot be within the statute.

COMMENTS AND QUESTIONS

1. According to the Court, do the words used in the statute (reasonably) clearly include contracts of the sort involved in the case? Eskridge et al. report that the first definition of "labor" in the 1879 and 1886 editions of Webster's Dictionary was "Physical toil or bodily exertion...hard muscular effort..." and that the secondary definition was "Intellectual exertion, mental effort." How, if at all, does this information affect your evaluation of the Court's analysis? What arguments might be developed against its treatment of section 5? Of the statute's title? Of the committee reports? Recall Llewellyn's canon 11: titles do not control meaning, but titles may be consulted if there is doubt or obscurity. Does the title *create* doubt or obscurity?

2. According to the Court, what were the statute's *general* purposes? What materials does it rely on to identify those purposes? What is the argument that those purposes would in fact be served by applying the statute to this contract? According to the Court, did *Congress* reach the specific conclusion that contracts with ministers should be excluded from the statute's coverage? What materials does the opinion contain discussing that specific purpose? Consider the possibility that the church went abroad to hire a minister not because the minister was better at delivering sermons but because he delivered sermons of equal quality to those that a U.S. minister would deliver but at a lower price. Even if that is not so in the present case, might not applying the statute be consistent with the statute's purposes if there were *enough* cases of that sort to justify the application of a general rule against such contracts? For discussions of the statute's purposes as revealed in more extensive examinations of its background, see Adrian Vermeule, *Legislative History and the Limits of Judicial Competence: The Untold Story of* Holy Trinity Church, 50 Stan. L. Rev. 1833 (1998); Carol Chomsky, *Unlocking the Mysteries of* Holy Trinity: *Spirit, Letter, and History in Statutory Interpretation*, 100 Colum. L. Rev. 901 (2000).

3. Congress amended the statute, with prospective effect only, to exclude contracts for the employment of ministers. Does this action undermine—or confirm—the Court's decision? Congress might have amended the statute to correct the lower court's erroneous interpretation or to correct a mistake, identified by the lower court's interpretation, made in the statute itself.

4. Suppose a business corporation contracted with a mechanical engineer to come to the United States to design or invent a new elevator. According to the Court's interpretation, does the statute apply to such a contract? Does the discussion of the United States as a Christian nation limit the meaning to be given the statutory provision?

5. In light of the "Christian nation" discussion, is *Holy Trinity* simply a case in which the Court perceived absurdity in the statute's terms? Or does it articulate a purposive approach to statutory interpretation generally? Note the importance of the level of generality at which the statute's purposes are identified in generating the result. Consider the textualist proposition that the need to specify such a level of generality means that purposivist approaches confer too much discretion and power on judges and are to that extent in tension with some rule-of-law values.

■ United States of America v. Marshall
908 F.2d 1312 (7th Cir., 1990)

Easterbrook, Circuit Judge:

Two cases consolidated for decision in banc present three questions concerning the application and constitutionality of the statute and sentencing guidelines that govern sales of lysergic acid diethylamide (LSD). Stanley J. Marshall was convicted after a bench trial and sentenced to 20 years' imprisonment for conspiring to distribute, and distributing, more than ten grams of LSD, enough for 11,751 doses. Patrick Brumm, Richard L. Chapman, and John M. Schoenecker were convicted by a jury of selling ten sheets (1,000 doses) of paper containing LSD. Because the total weight of the paper and LSD was 5.7 grams, a five-year mandatory minimum applied. The district court sentenced Brumm to 60 months (the minimum), Schoenecker to 63 months, and Chapman to 96 months' imprisonment. All four defendants confine their arguments on appeal to questions concerning their sentences.

The [question] we must resolve [is this:] (1) Whether 21 U.S.C. § 841(b)(1)(A)(v) and (B)(v), which set mandatory minimum terms of imprisonment—five years for selling more than one gram of a "mixture or substance containing a detectable amount" of LSD, ten years for more than ten grams—exclude the weight of a carrier medium. . . .

I

According to the Sentencing Commission, the LSD in an average dose weighs 0.05 milligrams. Twenty thousand pure doses are a gram. But 0.05 mg is almost invisible, so LSD is distributed to retail customers in a carrier. Pure LSD is dissolved in a solvent such as alcohol and sprayed on paper or gelatin; alternatively the paper may be dipped in the solution. After the solvent evaporates, the paper or gel is cut into one-dose squares and sold by the square. Users swallow the squares or may drop them into a beverage, releasing the drug. Although the gelatin and paper are light, they weigh much more than the drug. Marshall's 11,751 doses weighed 113.32 grams; the LSD accounted for only 670.72 mg of this, not enough to activate the five-year mandatory minimum sentence, let alone the ten-year minimum. The ten sheets of blotter paper carrying the 1,000 doses Chapman and confederates sold weighed 5.7 grams; the LSD in the paper did not approach the one-gram threshold for a mandatory minimum sentence. This disparity between the weight of the pure LSD and the weight of LSD-plus-carrier underlies the defendants' arguments.

A

If the carrier counts in the weight of the "mixture or substance containing a detectable amount" of LSD, some odd things may happen. Weight in the hands of distributors may exceed that of manufacturers and wholesalers. Big fish then could receive paltry sentences or small fish draconian ones. Someone who sold 19,999 doses of pure LSD (at 0.05 mg per dose) would escape the five-year mandatory minimum of § 841(b)(1)(B)(v) and be covered by § 841(b)(1)(C), which lacks a minimum term and has a maximum of "only" 20 years. Someone who sold a single hit of LSD dissolved in a tumbler of orange juice could be exposed to a ten-year mandatory minimum. Retailers could fall in or out of the mandatory terms depending not on the number of doses but on the medium: sugar cubes weigh more than paper, which weighs more than gelatin. One way to eliminate the possibility of such consequences is to say that the carrier is not a "mixture or substance containing a detectable amount" of the drug. Defendants ask us to do this.

Defendants' submission starts from the premise that the interaction of the statutory phrase "mixture or substance" with the distribution of LSD by the dose in a carrier creates a unique probability of surprise results. The premise may be unwarranted. The paper used to distribute LSD is light stuff, not the kind used to absorb ink. Chapman's 1,000 doses weighed about 0.16 ounces. More than 6,000 doses, even in blotter paper, weigh less than an ounce. Because the LSD in one dose weighs about 0.05 milligrams, the combination of LSD-plus-paper is about 110 times the weight of the LSD. The impregnated paper could be described as "0.9% LSD".[1] Gelatin carrying LSD could be described as "2.5% LSD," if the weight for gelatin given in *United States v. McGeehan*, 824 F.2d 677, 680 (8th Cir. 1987), is accurate.

This is by no means an unusual dilution rate for illegal drugs. Heroin sold on the street is 2% to 3% opiate and the rest filler. Jerome J. Platt, Heroin Addiction: Theory, Research, and Treatment 48–50 (1986). Sometimes the mixture is even more dilute, approaching the dilution rate for LSD in blotter paper. E.g., *United States v. Buggs*, 904 F.2d 1070 (7th Cir. 1990) (conviction for sale of 9.95 grams of 1.2% heroin). Heroin and crack cocaine, like LSD, are sold on the streets by the dose, although they are sold by weight higher in the distributional chain. All of the "designer drugs" and many of the opiates are sold by the dose, often conveniently packaged in pills. The Sentencing Commission lists MDA, PCP, psilocin, psilocybin, methaqualone, phenmetrazine, and amphetamines (regular and meth-) along with LSD as drugs sold by the dose in very dilute form. 55 Fed.Reg. 19197 (May 8, 1990) (amending Application Note 11 to U.S.S.G. 2D1.1). Other drugs, such as dilaudid

---

[1] The 1,000 doses in *Chapman* weighed 5.7 grams, or 0.0057 grams per dose. The 11,751 doses in *Marshall* weighed 113.32 grams, or 0.00964 grams per dose. Marshall apparently sold premium LSD; the forensic chemist concluded that his 11,751 squares of blotter paper contained 670.72 milligrams of LSD, or 0.057 mg per dose—14% more per dose than the Sentencing Commission's norm of 0.05 mg. The substance Marshall sold was 0.59% LSD; the substance the other three sold was 0.877% LSD.

and dolaphine, are sold by the pill rather than weight, and it is safe to assume that all have far less than 100% active ingredients.

Just as it is hasty to assume that the carrier produces a unique dilution factor for LSD, so it is unwarranted to assume that LSD as it leaves the refinery is pure, and therefore weighs only 0.05 mg per dose. Solid LSD weighs that little, but is it shipped dry? Neither the record nor the sparse literature tells us. LSD is applied to a carrier in a solvent such as alcohol. How dilute is this solution? If we assume that one drop of liquid is applied to each square of blotter paper, then the liquid is only 0.1% LSD.[2] We do not know whether one drop per dose is right, but, if it is, the solution weighs 8.5 times as much per dose as blotter paper: a dose of LSD in alcohol weighs 0.0487 grams, while a dose of LSD in blotter paper weighs 0.0057 grams.[3] A manufacturer caught with wholesale quantities of LSD solution that had not been applied to blotter paper would face sentences higher than those who possess only the paper containing the drug.

So there may be nothing extraordinary about LSD, no reason to think that the statute operates differently for LSD than for heroin. Heroin comes into this country pure; it is sold diluted on the street, creating the possibility that § 841 will require higher sentences for retailers than for smugglers or refiners. The dilution factor for retail heroin is not significantly different from the factor for LSD on blotter paper. LSD in solution weighs more than LSD on blotter paper; pure heroin weighs (much) less per dose than the dilute heroin sold on the street. Heroin is sold in different cities at different dilution rates; that implies that the weight of a packet of heroin for a single administration weighs more in some cities than in others. The percentage difference exceeds the gap between paper and gelatin, the common carriers of LSD. Office of Intelligence, Drug Enforcement Administration, Domestic Monitor Program: Summary Report Fiscal Year 1989. So although § 841 creates the possibility of erratic application in LSD cases, it is important to recognize that the normal case involves neither extreme weight (LSD in orange juice) nor extreme purity (19,999 doses weighing less than a gram). With this understanding, we turn to the statute.

B

It is not possible to construe the words of § 841 to make the penalty turn on the net weight of the drug rather than the gross weight of carrier and drug. The statute speaks of "mixture or substance containing a detectable amount" of a drug. "Detectable amount" is the opposite of "pure"; the point of the statute is that the "mixture" is not to be converted to an equivalent amount of pure drug.

The structure of the statute reinforces this conclusion. The 10-year minimum applies to any person who possesses, with intent to distribute, "100 grams or more of phencyclidine (PCP) or 1 kilogram or more of a mixture or substance containing

---

[2] One drop is equivalent to one minim, or 0.06161 milliliters. That implies about 16,231 drops per liter. One liter of water weighs a kilogram. Ethyl alcohol has a specific gravity of 0.7893, so a liter of ethyl alcohol weighs 0.7893 kilograms. LSD weighs 0.05 mg per hit. So 16,231 doses of LSD weigh 0.811 grams. A liter of alcohol containing these doses weighs 790.11 grams (the 789.3 grams of alcohol plus the 0.811 grams of LSD). Thus the solution is 0.103% LSD.

[3] In *Chapman*, in which 1,000 doses weighed 5.7 grams. LSD dissolved in alcohol weighs only 5.05 times as much per dose as LSD in Marshall's heavier blotter paper (see note 1).

a detectable amount of phencyclidine (PCP)," § 841(b)(1)(A)(iv). Congress distinguished the pure drug from a "mixture or substance containing a detectable amount of" it. All drugs other than PCP are governed exclusively by the "mixture or substance" language. Even brute force cannot turn that language into a reference to pure LSD. Congress used the same "mixture or substance" language to describe heroin, cocaine, amphetamines, and many other drugs that are sold after being cut—sometimes as much as LSD. There is no sound basis on which to treat the words "substance or mixture containing a detectable amount of," repeated verbatim for every drug mentioned in § 841 except PCP, as different things for LSD and cocaine although the language is identical, while treating the "mixture or substance" language as meaning the same as the reference to pure PCP in 21 U.S.C. § 841(b)(1)(A)(iv) and (B)(iv).

Although the "mixture or substance" language shows that the statute cannot be limited to pure LSD, it does not necessarily follow that blotter paper is a "mixture or substance containing" LSD. That phrase cannot include all "carriers." One gram of crystalline LSD in a heavy glass bottle is still only one gram of "statutory LSD." So is a gram of LSD being "carried" in a Boeing 747. How much mingling of the drug with something else is essential to form a "mixture or substance"? The legislative history is silent, but ordinary usage is indicative.

"Substance" may well refer to a chemical compound, or perhaps to a drug in a solvent. LSD does not react chemically with sugar, blotter paper, or gelatin, and none of these is a solvent. "Mixture" is more inclusive. Cocaine often is mixed with mannitol, quinine, or lactose. These white powders do not react, but it is common ground that a cocaine-mannitol mixture is a statutory "mixture."

LSD and blotter paper are not commingled in the same way as cocaine and lactose. What is the nature of their association? The possibility most favorable to defendants is that LSD sits on blotter paper as oil floats on water. Immiscible substances may fall outside the statutory definition of "mixture." The possibility does not assist defendants—not on this record, anyway. LSD is applied to paper in a solvent; after the solvent evaporates, a tiny quantity of LSD remains. Because the fibers absorb the alcohol, the LSD solidifies inside the paper rather than on it. You cannot pick a grain of LSD off the surface of the paper. Ordinary parlance calls the paper containing tiny crystals of LSD a mixture.

United States v. Rose, 881 F.2d 386 (7th Cir. 1989), like every other appellate decision that has addressed the question, concludes that the carrier medium for LSD, like the "cut" for heroin and cocaine, is a "mixture or substance containing a detectable amount" of the drug. Although a chemist might be able to offer evidence bearing on the question whether LSD and blotter paper "mix" any more fully than do oil and water, the record contains no such evidence. Without knowing more of the chemistry than this record reveals, we adhere to the unanimous conclusion of the other courts of appeals that blotter paper treated with LSD is a "mixture or substance containing a detectable quantity of" LSD.

C

Two reasons have been advanced to support a contrary conclusion: that statutes should be construed to avoid constitutional problems, and that some members of the sitting Congress are dissatisfied with basing penalties on the combined weight of LSD and carrier. Neither is persuasive.

A preference for giving statutes a constitutional meaning is a reason to construe, not to rewrite or "improve." E.g., *United States v. Monsanto*, 491 U.S. 600 (1989); *United States v. Albertini*, 472 U.S. 675, 680 (1985). Canons are doubt-resolvers, useful when the language is ambiguous and "a construction of the statute is *fairly possible* by which the question may be avoided," *Crowell v. Benson*, 285 U.S. 22, 62 (1932) (emphasis added). "Substance or mixture containing a detectable quantity" is not ambiguous, avoidance not "fairly possible." Neither the rule of lenity nor the preference for avoiding constitutional adjudication justifies disregarding unambiguous language.

The canon about avoiding constitutional decisions, in particular, must be used with care, for it is a closer cousin to invalidation than to interpretation. It is a way to enforce the constitutional penumbra, and therefore an aspect of constitutional law proper. Constitutional decisions breed penumbras, which multiply questions. Treating each as justification to construe laws out of existence too greatly enlarges the judicial power. And heroic "construction" is unnecessary, given our conclusion in Part III that Congress possesses the constitutional power to set penalties on the basis of gross weight.

As for the pending legislation: subsequent debates are not a ground for avoiding the import of enactments. Although the views of a subsequent Congress are entitled to respect, ongoing debates do not represent the views of Congress. Judge Wilkins, Chairman of the Sentencing Commission, wrote a letter to Senator Biden, Chairman of the Judiciary Committee, remarking that "it is unclear whether Congress intended the carrier to be considered as a packaging material, or since it is commonly consumed along with the illicit drug, as a dilutent ingredient in the drug mixture." The Chairman of the Commission invited the Chairman of the Committee to introduce legislation choosing one or the other explicitly.

Senator Biden introduced an amendment to S. 1711, the Administration's omnibus drug bill, stating in materials read into the Congressional Record that the amendment changes the statute to omit the weight of the carrier. 135 Cong. Rec. S 12748 (daily ed. Oct. 5, 1989). So far as we can determine, the language he actually introduced did not contain the text to which his prepared statement referred. No language of this kind appears in the version the Senate passed. 135 Cong. Rec. S 13433 (daily ed. Oct. 16, 1989) (text of bill that Senate sent to House). The House is yet to act. Senator Kennedy has introduced an amendment to other legislation affecting the criminal code, which, like Senator Biden's, would exclude the carrier. Amendment No. 1716 to S. 1970, 136 Cong. Rec. S 7069 (daily ed. May 24, 1990). But this proposal, too, awaits enactment. Both Senator Kennedy's proposal and Senator Biden's statement are more naturally understood as suggestions for change than as evidence of today's meaning. At all events, the Senators were speaking for themselves, not for Congress as an institution.

Statements supporting proposals that have not been adopted do not inform our reading of the text an earlier Congress passed and the President signed, see *Firestone Tire & Rubber Co. v. Bruch*, 489 U.S. 101 (1989). We may not, in the name of faithful interpretation of what the political branches enacted, treat as authoritative the statements of legislators supporting change. Opinion polls of Senators are not law.

[The court upheld the statute as construed against constitutional challenges based on due process and equal protection.]

Posner, Circuit Judge, joined by Bauer, Chief Judge, and Cummings, Wood, Jr., and Cudahy, Circuit Judges, dissenting:

In each of these cases consolidated for decision en banc, the district court sentenced sellers of LSD in accordance with an interpretation of 21 U.S.C. § 841 that is plausible but that makes the punishment scheme for LSD irrational. It has been assumed that an irrational federal sentencing scheme denies the equal protection of the laws and therefore (*Bolling v. Sharpe,* 347 U.S. 497 (1954)) violates the due process clause of the Fifth Amendment. *Marshall v. United States,* 414 U.S. 417 (1974); *McGinnis v. Royster,* 410 U.S. 263, 270 (1973); *United States v. Cyrus,* 890 F.2d 1245, 1248 (D.C. Cir. 1989); *United States v. Pineda,* 847 F.2d 64 (2d Cir. 1988). The assumption is proper, and in order to avoid having to strike down the statute we are entitled to adopt a reasonable interpretation that cures the constitutional infirmity, even if that interpretation might not be our first choice were there no such infirmity.

The statute bases the range of permissible punishments on the weight of the "mixture or substance containing a detectable amount of" the illegal drug. The statute fixes the minimum and maximum punishments with respect to each drug. Examples are five years minimum and twenty years maximum for selling a hundred grams of a "mixture or substance containing a detectable amount of" heroin and ten years minimum and forty years maximum for selling a kilogram of such a mixture or substance. The corresponding weights for LSD are one gram and ten grams. The quoted words are critical. Drugs are usually consumed, and therefore often sold, in a diluted form, and the adoption by Congress of the "mixture or substance" method of grading punishment reflected a conscious decision to mete out heavy punishment to large retail dealers, who are likely to possess "substantial street quantities," which is to say quantities of the diluted drug ready for sale. H.R.Rep. No. 845, 99th Cong., 2d Sess. 11-12 (1986). That decision is well within Congress's constitutional authority even though it may sometimes result in less severe punishment for possessing a purer, and therefore a lighter, form of the illegal drug than a heavier but much less potent form.

The statute fixes only the minimum and maximum punishments and for the actual punishment in a particular case we must go to the Sentencing Guidelines. They proportion punishment to the weight of the mixture or substance, defined as in the statute. § 2D1.1, Application Note 1; § 2D.1, Drug Quantity Table, n. *. They permit an adjustment upward for sales of unusual purity, § 2D1.1, Application Note 9, but this takes care of the problem identified in the previous paragraph only in part; the statutory mandatory minimum sentences (which, like the Guidelines sentences themselves, are not subject to parole) truncate the effort of the Guidelines' framers to tie the severity of punishment in the particular case to the gravity of the defendant's misconduct.

Based as it is on weight, the system I have described works well for drugs that are sold by weight; and ordinarily the weight quoted to the buyer is the weight of the dilute form, although of course price will vary with purity. The dilute form is the product, and it is as natural to punish its purveyors according to the weight of the product as it is to punish moonshiners by the weight or volume of the moonshine they sell rather than by the weight of the alcohol contained in it. . . .

LSD, however, is sold to the consumer by the dose; it is not cut, diluted, or mixed with something else. Moreover, it is incredibly light. An average dose of LSD weighs .05 milligrams, which is less than two millionths of an ounce. To ingest something that small requires swallowing something much larger. Pure LSD in granular form is first diluted by being dissolved, usually in alcohol, and then a quantity of the solution containing one dose of LSD is sprayed or eyedropped on a sugar cube, or on a cube of gelatin, or, as in the cases before us, on an inch-square section of "blotter" paper. (LSD blotter paper, which is sold typically in sheets ten inches square containing a hundred sections each with one dose of LSD on it, is considerably thinner than the paper used to blot ink but much heavier than the LSD itself.) After the solution is applied to the carrier medium, the alcohol or other solvent evaporates, leaving an invisible (and undiluted) spot of pure LSD on the cube or blotter paper. The consumer drops the cube or the piece of paper into a glass of water, or orange juice, or some other beverage, causing the LSD to dissolve in the beverage, which is then drunk. This is not dilution. It is still one dose that is being imbibed. Two quarts of a 50-proof alcoholic beverage are more than one quart of a 100-proof beverage, though the total alcoholic content is the same. But a quart of orange juice containing one dose of LSD is not more, in any relevant sense, than a pint of juice containing the same one dose, and it would be loony to punish the purveyor of the quart more heavily than the purveyor of the pint. It would be like basing the punishment for selling cocaine on the combined weight of the cocaine and of the vehicle (plane, boat, automobile, or whatever) used to transport it or the syringe used to inject it or the pipe used to smoke it. The blotter paper, sugar cubes, etc. are the vehicles for conveying LSD to the consumer.

The weight of the carrier is vastly greater than that of the LSD, as well as irrelevant to its potency. There is no comparable disparity between the pure and the mixed form (if that is how we should regard LSD on blotter paper or other carrier medium) with respect to the other drugs in section 841, with the illuminating exception of PCP. There Congress specified alternative weights, for the drug itself and for the substance or mixture containing the drug. For example, the five-year minimum sentence for a seller of PCP requires the sale of either ten grams of the drug itself or one hundred grams of a substance or mixture containing the drug. 21 U.S.C. § 841(b)(1)(B)(iv).

Ten sheets of blotter paper, containing a thousand doses of LSD, weigh almost six grams. The LSD itself weighs less than a hundredth as much. If the thousand doses are on gelatin cubes instead of sheets of blotter paper, the total weight is less, but it is still more than two grams, which is forty times the weight of the LSD. In both cases, if the carrier plus the LSD constitutes the relevant "substance or mixture" (the crucial "if" in this case), the dealer is subject to the minimum mandatory sentence of five years. One of the defendants before us (Marshall) sold almost 12,000 doses of LSD on blotter paper. This subjected him to the ten-year minimum, and the Guidelines then took over and pushed him up to twenty years. Since it takes 20,000 doses of LSD to equal a gram, Marshall would not have been subject to even the five-year mandatory minimum had he sold the LSD in its pure form. And a dealer who sold fifteen times the number of doses as Marshall—180,000—would not be subject to the ten-year mandatory minimum sentence if he sold the drug in its pure form, because 180,000 doses is only nine grams.

At the other extreme, if Marshall were not a dealer at all but dropped a square of blotter paper containing a single dose of LSD into a glass of orange juice and sold it to a friend at cost (perhaps 35 cents), he would be subject to the ten-year minimum. The juice with LSD dissolved in it would be the statutory mixture or substance containing a detectable amount of the illegal drug and it would weigh more than ten grams (one ounce is about 35 grams, and the orange juice in a glass of orange juice weighs several ounces). So a person who sold one dose of LSD might be subject to the ten-year mandatory minimum sentence while a dealer who sold 199,999 doses in pure form would be subject only to the five-year minimum. Defendant Dean sold 198 doses, crowded onto one sheet of blotter paper: this subjected him to the five-year mandatory minimum, too, since the ensemble weighed slightly more than a gram.

There are no reported orange juice cases; for that matter there are no reported federal cases in which the carrier is a sugar cube rather than a gelatin cube, although sugar cubes are said to be a common LSD carrier, and in two state cases defendants have been prosecuted for unlawful possession of one and of six LSD-laced sugar cubes, respectively. A sugar cube weighs more than two grams, so a seller of a mere six sugar cubes laced with LSD—six doses—would, if prosecuted federally, have bought himself the mandatory minimum ten-year sentence.

All this seems crazy but we must consider whether Congress might have had a reason for wanting to key the severity of punishment for selling LSD to the weight of the carrier rather than to the number of doses or to some reasonable proxy for dosage (as weight is, for many drugs). The only one suggested is that it might be costly to determine the weight of the LSD in the blotter paper, sugar cube, etc., because it is so light! That merely underscores the irrationality of basing the punishment for selling this drug on weight rather than on dosage. But in fact the weight is reported in every case I have seen, so apparently it can be determined readily enough; it has to be determined in any event, to permit a purity adjustment under the Guidelines. If the weight of the LSD is difficult to determine, the difficulty is easily overcome by basing punishment on the number of doses, which makes much more sense in any event. To base punishment on the weight of the carrier medium makes about as much sense as basing punishment on the weight of the defendant.

A person who sells LSD on blotter paper is not a worse criminal than one who sells the same number of doses on gelatin cubes, but he is subject to a heavier punishment. A person who sells five doses of LSD on sugar cubes is not a worse person than a manufacturer of LSD who is caught with 19,999 doses in pure form, but the former is subject to a ten-year mandatory minimum no-parole sentence while the latter is not even subject to the five-year minimum. If defendant Chapman, who received five years for selling a thousand doses of LSD on blotter paper, had sold the same number of doses in pure form, his Guidelines sentence would have been fourteen months. And defendant Marshall's sentence for selling almost 12,000 doses would have been four years rather than twenty. The defendant in *United States v. Rose*, 881 F.2d 386, 387 (7th Cir. 1989), must have bought an unusually heavy blotter paper, for he sold only 472 doses, yet his blotter paper weighed 7.3 grams—more than Chapman's, although Chapman sold more than twice as many doses. Depending on the weight of the carrier medium (zero when the stuff is sold in pure form), and excluding the orange juice case, the Guidelines range for selling 198 doses (the amount in Dean) or 472 doses (the amount in Rose) stretches from ten months to 365 months; for selling a thousand doses (Chapman), from fifteen to 365 months; and for selling 11,751 doses (Marshall), from 33 months to life. In none of these computations, by the way, does the weight of the LSD itself make a difference—so slight is its weight relative to that of the carrier—except of course when it is sold in pure form. Congress might as well have said: if there is a carrier, weigh the carrier and forget the LSD.

This is a quilt the pattern whereof no one has been able to discern. The legislative history is silent, and since even the Justice Department cannot explain the why of the punishment scheme that it is defending, the most plausible inference is that Congress simply did not realize how LSD is sold.

. . .

Well, what if anything can we judges do about this mess? The answer lies in the shadow of a jurisprudential disagreement that is not less important by virtue of being unavowed by most judges. It is the disagreement between the severely positivistic view that the content of law is exhausted in clear, explicit, and definite enactments by or under express delegation from legislatures, and the natural lawyer's or legal pragmatist's view that the practice of interpretation and the general terms of the Constitution (such as "equal protection of the laws") authorize judges to enrich positive law with the moral values and practical concerns of civilized society. Judges who in other respects have seemed quite similar, such as Holmes and Cardozo, have taken opposite sides of this issue. Neither approach is entirely satisfactory. The first buys political neutrality and a type of objectivity at the price of substantive injustice, while the second buys justice in the individual case at the price of considerable uncertainty and, not infrequently, judicial willfulness. It is no wonder that our legal system oscillates between the approaches. The positivist view, applied unflinchingly to this case, commands the affirmance of prison sentences that are exceptionally harsh by the standards of the modern Western world, dictated by an accidental, unintended scheme of punishment nevertheless implied by the words (taken one by one) of the relevant enactments. The natural law or pragmatist view leads to a freer interpretation, one influenced by norms of equal treatment; and let us explore the interpretive possibilities here. One is to interpret "mixture or substance containing a detectable amount of [LSD]" to exclude the carrier medium—the blotter paper, sugar or gelatin cubes, and orange juice or other beverage. That is the course we rejected in *United States v. Rose*, 881 F.2d at 388, as have the other circuits. I wrote *Rose*, but I am no longer confident that its literal interpretation of the statute, under which the blotter paper, cubes, etc. are "substances" that "contain" LSD, is inevitable. The blotter paper, etc. are better viewed, I now think, as carriers, like the package in which a kilo of cocaine comes wrapped or the bottle in which a fifth of liquor is sold.

Interpreted to exclude the carrier, the punishment schedule for LSD would make perfectly good sense; it would not warp the statutory design. The comparison with heroin and cocaine is again illuminating. The statute imposes the five-year mandatory minimum sentence on anyone who sells a substance or mixture containing a hundred grams of heroin, equal to 10,000 to 20,000 doses. One gram of pure LSD, which also would trigger the five-year minimum, yields 20,000 doses. The comparable figures for cocaine are 3250 to 50,000 doses, placing LSD in about the middle. So Congress may have wanted to base punishment for the sale of LSD on the weight of the pure drug after all, using one and ten grams of the pure drug to trigger the five-year and ten-year minima (and corresponding maxima—twenty years and forty years). This interpretation leaves "substance or mixture containing" without a referent, so far as LSD is concerned. But we must remember that Congress used the identical term in each subsection that specifies the quantity of a drug that subjects the seller to the designated minimum and maximum punishments. In thus automatically including the same term in each subsection, Congress did not necessarily affirm that, for each and every drug covered by the statute, a substance or mixture containing the drug *must* be found.

The flexible interpretation that I am proposing is decisively strengthened by the constitutional objection to basing punishment of LSD offenders on the weight of the carrier medium rather than on the weight of the LSD. Courts often do interpretive handsprings to avoid having even to decide a constitutional question. *Gomez v. United States*, 490 U.S. 858 (1989). In doing so they expand, very questionably in my view, the effective scope of the Constitution, creating a constitutional penumbra in which statutes wither, shrink, are deformed. A better case for flexible interpretation is presented when the alternative is to nullify Congress's action: when in other words there is not merely a constitutional question about, but a constitutional barrier to, the statute when interpreted literally. *Hooper v. California*, 155 U.S. 648, 657 (1895). This is such a case.

. . .

[G]raduating punishment to the weight of the carrier medium produces, in the case of LSD, a systematically, unavoidably bizarre schedule of punishments that no one is able to justify. I would give respectful consideration to any rationale for the schedule advanced by the legislators, the framers of the Guidelines, or the Department of Justice. None has been advanced. And such give as there is in the Guidelines (the purity adjustment) is unavailing when defendants are subject to the mandatory minimum sentences in section 841, as all the defendants before us . . . are.

Granted, when the total system of federal criminal punishment is considered, including prosecutorial discretion and executive clemency, it becomes arguable that the grossest inequities enabled by reading section 841 to base punishment on the weight of the carrier rather than of the LSD are unlikely to occur. Maybe that is why we have seen no recent sugar-cube cases. But this argument is too powerful; it would eliminate or at least greatly curtail the judicial role in protecting criminal defendants from arbitrary statutes, by preventing the defendant from showing that the statute was arbitrary.

Our choice is between ruling that the provisions of section 841 regarding LSD are irrational, hence unconstitutional, and therefore there is no punishment for dealing in LSD—Congress must go back to the drawing boards, and all LSD cases in the pipeline must be dismissed—and ruling that, to preserve so much of the statute as can constitutionally be preserved, the statutory expression "substance or mixture containing a detectable amount of [LSD]" excludes the carrier medium. Given this choice, we can be reasonably certain that Congress would have preferred the second course; and this consideration carries the argument for a flexible interpretation over the top.

That interpretation would bring the statute into line with the punishment for other illegal drugs; but this is only an incidental benefit because, as ruled in *Rose* (correctly, as it seems to me and has seemed to the other courts that have considered the question), it is not a feasible judicial office to rationalize the thousands of different federal criminal prohibitions, passed at different times in different climates of opinion, that are scattered throughout the United States Code. The relevant irrationality—which was not presented as an issue in *Rose* and which has not received full consideration in any other case either—lies in making the punishment of LSD offenders vary by the adventitious and indeed perverse factor of the weight of the carrier. But it is reassuring that in removing this irrationality from section 841 we would create no new disparities between the punishment of sellers of LSD and the punishment of other drug offenders.

The literal interpretation adopted by the majority is not inevitable. All interpretation is contextual. The words of the statute—interpreted against a background that includes a constitutional norm of equal treatment, a (closely related) constitutional commitment to rationality, an evident failure by both Congress and the Sentencing Commission to consider how LSD is actually produced, distributed, and sold, and an equally evident failure by the same two bodies to consider the interaction between heavy mandatory minimum sentences and the Sentencing Guidelines—will bear an interpretation that distinguishes between the carrier vehicle of the illegal drug and the substance or mixture containing a detectable amount of the drug. The punishment of the crack dealer is not determined by the weight of the glass tube in which he sells the crack; we should not lightly attribute to Congress a purpose of punishing the dealer in LSD according to the weight of the LSD carrier. We should not make Congress's handiwork an embarrassment to the members of Congress and to us.

COMMENTS AND QUESTIONS

1. The outcome of this case turns on the meaning of the statutory term "mixture." Is there (serious) disagreement over what the term means? Put another way, does Judge Posner offer a reasonable interpretation of that term or does he, as Judge Easterbrook suggests, essentially read the term out of the statute? Are the judges divided over the question of whether it is absurd to interpret the term to include LSD-soaked paper?

2. Note the invocation—and rejection—of canons of interpretation in the two opinions. Judge Easterbrook offers two reasons for refusing to apply the canon cautioning against interpretations that might make the statute unconstitutional: (a) as interpreted, the statute is not unconstitutional, and (b) invoking the canon amounts to a concealed—and, as the majority concludes, erroneous—constitutional interpretation itself. Does the second reason imply that therefore the "unconstitutionality" canon should be abandoned altogether? For a suggestion to that effect, see Frederick Schauer, Ashwander *Revisited*, 1995 Sup. Ct. Rev. 71.

3. Judge Easterbrook finds irrelevant postenactment legislative discussions of the problem posed in the case. Should he?

4. What rule-of-law issues are raised by the dissent and its approach to statutory interpretation? By the majority opinion and its approach?

5. Judge Easterbrook's opinion is primarily (exclusively?) textualist, Judge Posner's primarily purposivist. Which opinion do you find more satisfying? Does your evaluation of the opinions indicate to you whether and why one or the other approach is preferable as a general matter?

- **Chisom v. Roemer**
   501 U.S. 380 (1991)

Justice Stevens delivered the opinion of the Court.

. . .

. . . In 1982, Congress amended § 2 of the Voting Rights Act to make clear that certain practices and procedures that *result* in the denial or abridgement of the right to vote are forbidden even though the absence of proof of discriminatory intent protects them from constitutional challenge. The question presented by this case is whether this "results test" protects the right to vote in state judicial elections. We hold that the coverage provided by the 1982 amendment is coextensive with the coverage provided by the Act prior to 1982 and that judicial elections are embraced within that coverage.

. . .

It is . . . undisputed that § 2 applied to judicial elections prior to the 1982 amendment. . . . The only matter in dispute is whether the test for determining the legality of such a practice, which was added to the statute in 1982, applies in judicial elections as well as in other elections.

. . .

Under the amended statute, proof of intent is no longer required to prove a § 2 violation. Now plaintiffs can prevail under § 2 by demonstrating that a challenged election practice has resulted in the denial or abridgement of the right to vote based on color or race. . . .

. . .

Respondents [Louisiana state officials charged with violating Voting Rights Act through the state's method for electing judges] contend . . . that Congress' choice of the word "representatives" in the phrase "have less opportunity than other members of the electorate to participate in the political process and to elect representatives of their choice" in subsection 2(b) is evidence of congressional intent to exclude vote dilution claims involving judicial elections from the coverage of § 2. We reject that construction because we are convinced that if Congress had such an intent, Congress would have made it explicit in the statute, or at least some of the Members would have identified or mentioned it at some point in the unusually extensive legislative history of the 1982 amendment. . . .

. . .

. . . [R]espondents . . . place their principal reliance on Congress' use of the word "representatives" instead of "legislators" in the phrase "to participate in the political process and to elect representatives of their choice." When Congress borrowed the phrase from [a Supreme Court decision], it replaced "legislators" with "representatives." This substitution indicates, at the very least, that Congress intended the amendment to cover more than legislative elections. Respondents argue, and the majority agreed, that the term "representatives" was used to extend § 2 coverage to executive officials, but not to judges. We think, however, that the better reading of the word "representatives" describes the winners of representative, popular elections. If executive officers, such as prosecutors, sheriffs, state attorneys general, and state treasurers, can be considered "representatives" simply because they are chosen by popular election, then the same reasoning should apply to elected judges.

Respondents suggest that if Congress had intended to have the statute's prohibition against vote dilution apply to the election of judges, it would have used the word "candidates" instead of "representatives." But that confuses the ordinary meaning of the words. The word "representative" refers to someone who has prevailed in a popular election, whereas the word "candidate" refers to someone who is seeking an office. Thus, a candidate is nominated, not elected. When Congress used "candidate" in other parts of the statute, it did so precisely because it was referring to people who were aspirants for an office....

. . .

Justice Scalia, with whom The Chief Justice and Justice Kennedy join, dissenting.

Section 2 of the Voting Rights Act of 1965 is not some all-purpose weapon for well-intentioned judges to wield as they please in the battle against discrimination. It is a statute. I thought we had adopted a regular method for interpreting the meaning of language in a statute: first, find the ordinary meaning of the language in its textual context; and second, using established canons of construction, ask whether there is any clear indication that some permissible meaning other than the ordinary one applies. If not—and especially if a good reason for the ordinary meaning appears plain—we apply that ordinary meaning. See, e.g., *West Virginia University Hospitals, Inc. v. Casey*, 499 U.S. 83, 98–99 (1991); *Demarest v. Manspeaker*, 498 U.S. 184, 190 (1991); *United States v. Ron Pair Enterprises, Inc.*, 489 U.S. 235, 241 (1989); *Pennsylvania Dept. of Public Welfare v. Davenport*, 495 U.S. 552, 557–558 (1990); *Caminetti v. United States*, 242 U.S. 470, 485 (1917); *Public Citizen v. Department of Justice*, 491 U.S. 440, 470 (1989) (Kennedy, J., concurring in judgment).

Today, however, the Court adopts a method quite out of accord with that usual practice. It begins not with what the statute says, but with an expectation about what the statute must mean absent particular phenomena ("[W]e are convinced that if Congress had . . . an intent [to exclude judges] Congress would have made it explicit in the statute, or at least some of the Members would have identified or mentioned it at some point in the unusually extensive legislative history"); and the Court then interprets the words of the statute to fulfill its expectation. Finding nothing in the legislative history affirming that judges were excluded from the coverage of § 2, the Court gives the phrase "to elect representatives" the quite extraordinary meaning that covers the election of judges.

As method, this is just backwards, and however much we may be attracted by the result it produces in a particular case, we should in every case resist it. Our job begins with a text that Congress has passed and the President has signed. We are to read the words of that text as any ordinary Member of Congress would have read them, see Holmes, The Theory of Legal Interpretation, 12 Harv. L. Rev. 417 (1899), and apply the meaning so determined. In my view, that reading reveals that § 2 extends to vote dilution claims for the elections of representatives only, and judges are not representatives.

. . .

As I said at the outset, these cases are about method. The Court transforms the meaning of § 2, not because the ordinary meaning is irrational, or inconsistent with other parts of the statute, see, e.g., *Green v. Bock Laundry Machine Co.*, 490 U.S. 504, 510–511 (1989); *Public Citizen v. Department of Justice*, 491 U.S., at 470 (Kennedy, J., concurring in judgment), but because it does not fit the Court's conception of what

Congress must have had in mind. When we adopt a method that psychoanalyzes Congress rather than reads its laws, when we employ a tinkerer's toolbox, we do great harm. Not only do we reach the wrong result with respect to the statute at hand, but we poison the well of future legislation, depriving legislators of the assurance that ordinary terms, used in an ordinary context, will be given a predictable meaning. Our highest responsibility in the field of statutory construction is to read the laws in a consistent way, giving Congress a sure means by which it may work the people's will. We have ignored that responsibility today....

COMMENTS AND QUESTIONS

1. Is the following a fair characterization of the disagreement in the case? Justice Scalia believes that the term "representatives" has a common meaning that excludes judges, and the majority believes that the term sometimes has a technical meaning, as it does in § 2. How does the majority go about establishing its position?

2. Do you think that Justice Scalia fairly describes the majority's approach to statutory interpretation? Why might he want to ensure that the term "representatives" be given what he contends is its common meaning?

■ **Chickasaw Nation v. United States**
534 U.S. 84 (2001)

Justice Breyer delivered the opinion of the Court.*

In these cases we must decide whether a particular subsection in the Indian Gaming Regulatory Act, 102 Stat. 2467–2486, 25 U.S.C. §§ 2701–2721, exempts tribes from paying the gambling-related taxes that chapter 35 of the Internal Revenue Code imposes—taxes that States need not pay. We hold that it does not create such an exemption.

I

The relevant Indian Gaming Regulatory Act (Gaming Act) subsection, as codified in 25 U.S.C. § 2719(d)(i), reads as follows:

> "The provisions of [the Internal Revenue Code of 1986] (including sections 1441, 3402(q), 6041, and 6050I, and chapter 35 of such Code) concerning the reporting and withholding of taxes with respect to the winnings from gaming or wagering operations shall apply to Indian gaming operations conducted pursuant to this chapter, or under a Tribal-State compact entered into under section 2710(d)(3) of this title that is in effect, in the same manner as such provisions apply to State gaming and wagering operations."

The subsection says that Internal Revenue Code provisions that "concern the reporting and withholding of taxes" with respect to gambling operations shall apply

---

*Justice Scalia and Justice Thomas join all but Part II-B of this opinion.

to Indian tribes in the same way as they apply to States. The subsection also says in its parenthetical that those provisions "include" Internal Revenue Code "chapter 35." Chapter 35, however, says nothing about the *reporting* or the *withholding* of taxes. Rather, that chapter simply *imposes* taxes—excise taxes and occupational taxes related to gambling—from which it exempts certain state-controlled gambling activities. See, *e.g.*, 26 U.S.C. § 4401(a) (1994 ed.) (imposing 0.25% excise tax on each wager); §4411 (imposing $50 occupational tax on each individual engaged in wagering business); § 4402(3) (exempting state-operated gambling operations, such as lotteries).

In this lawsuit two Native American Indian Tribes, the Choctaw and Chickasaw Nations, claim that the Gaming Act subsection exempts them from paying those chapter 35 taxes from which States are exempt. They rest their claim upon the subsection's explicit parenthetical reference to chapter 35. . . .

II

The Tribes' basic argument rests upon the subsection's explicit reference to "chapter 35"—contained in a parenthetical that refers to four other Internal Revenue Code provisions as well. The subsection's language outside the parenthetical says that the subsection applies to those Internal Revenue Code provisions that concern "reporting and withholding." The other four parenthetical references are to provisions that concern, or at least arguably concern, reporting and withholding. See 26 U.S.C. § 1441 (withholding of taxes for nonresident alien); § 3402(q) (withholding of taxes from certain gambling winnings); 26 U.S.C. § 6041 (reporting by businesses of payments, including payments of gambling winnings, to others); § 6050I (reporting by businesses of large cash receipts, arguably applicable to certain gambling winnings or receipts).

But what about chapter 35? The Tribes correctly point out that chapter 35 has nothing to do with "reporting and withholding." They add that the reference must serve some purpose, and the only purpose that the Tribes can find is that of expanding the scope of the Gaming Act's subsection beyond reporting and withholding provisions—to the tax-imposing provisions that chapter 35 does contain. The Gaming Act therefore must exempt them (like States) from those tax payment requirements. The Tribes add that at least the reference to chapter 35 makes the subsection ambiguous. And they ask us to resolve the ambiguity by applying a special Indian-related interpretative canon, namely, " 'statutes are to be construed liberally in favor of the Indians' with ambiguous provisions interpreted to their benefit." Brief for Petitioners 13 (quoting *Montana v. Blackfeet Tribe*, 471 U.S. 759, 766 (1985)).

We cannot accept the Tribes' claim. We agree with the Tribes that rejecting their argument reduces the phrase "(including . . . chapter 35) . . ." to surplusage. Nonetheless, we can find no other reasonable reading of the statute.

A

The language of the statute is too strong to bend as the Tribes would wish—*i.e.*, so that it gives the chapter 35 reference independent operative effect. For one thing, the language outside the parenthetical is unambiguous. It says without qualification that the subsection applies to "provisions . . . concerning the reporting and withholding of taxes." And the language inside the parenthetical, prefaced with the word "including," literally says the same. To "include" is to "contain" or "comprise as part of a whole." Webster's Ninth New Collegiate Dictionary 609 (1985). In this instance that which "contains" the parenthetical references—the "whole" of which the references are "parts"—is the phrase "provisions . . . concerning the reporting and withholding of taxes. . . ." The use of parentheses emphasizes the fact that that which is within is meant simply to be illustrative, hence redundant—a circumstance underscored by the lack of any suggestion that Congress intended the illustrative list to be complete. Cf. 26 U.S.C. § 3406 (backup withholding provision not mentioned in parenthetical).

Nor can one give the chapter 35 reference independent operative effect without seriously rewriting the language of the rest of the statute. One would have to read the word "including" to mean what it does not mean, namely, "including . . . and." One would have to read the statute as if, for example, it placed "chapter 35" outside the parenthetical and said "provisions of the . . . Code *including chapter 35 and also provisions* . . . concerning the reporting and withholding of taxes. . . ." Or, one would have to read the language as if it said "provisions of the . . . Code . . . concerning *the taxation and* the reporting and withholding of taxes. . . ." We mention this latter possibility because the congressional bill that became the law before us once did read that way. But when the bill left committee, it contained not the emphasized words ("the taxation and") but the cross-reference to chapter 35.

We recognize the Tribes' claim (made here for the first time) that one could avoid rewriting the statute by reading the language outside the parenthetical as if it referred to two kinds of "provisions of the . . . Code": first, those "concerning the reporting and withholding of taxes with respect to the winnings from gaming," and, second, those "concerning . . . wagering operations." The subsection's grammar literally permits this reading. But that reading, even if ultimately comprehensible, is far too convoluted to believe Congress intended it. Nor is there any reason to think Congress intended to sweep within the subsection's scope every Internal Revenue Code provision concerning wagering—a result that this unnatural reading would accomplish.

The subject matter at issue also counsels against accepting the Tribes' interpretation. That subject matter is tax exemption. When Congress enacts a tax exemption, it ordinarily does so explicitly. We can find no comparable instance in which Congress legislated an exemption through an inexplicit numerical cross-reference—especially a cross-reference that might easily escape notice.

As we have said, the more plausible role for the parenthetical to play in this subsection is that of providing an illustrative list of examples. So considered, "chapter 35" is simply a bad example—an example that Congress included inadvertently. The presence of a bad example in a statute does not warrant rewriting the remainder of the statute's language. Nor does it necessarily mean that the statute is ambiguous, *i.e.,* "capable of being understood in two or more possible senses or ways." Webster's Ninth New Collegiate Dictionary 77 (1985). Indeed, in ordinary life, we would understand an analogous instruction—say, "Test drive some cars, including Plymouth, Nissan, Chevrolet, Ford, and Kitchenaid"—not as creating ambiguity, but as reflecting a mistake. Here too, in context, common sense suggests that the cross-reference is simply a drafting mistake, a failure to delete an inappropriate cross-reference in the bill that Congress later enacted into law. Cf. *Little Six, Inc.* v. *United States,* 229 F.3d 1383, 1385 (CA Fed. 2000) (Dyk, J., dissenting from denial of rehearing en banc) ("The language of the provision has all the earmarks of a simple mistake in legislative drafting").

B

The Gaming Act's legislative history on balance supports our conclusion. The subsection as it appeared in the original Senate bill applied both to taxation and to reporting and withholding. It read as follows:

> "Provisions of the Internal Revenue Code . . . concerning *the taxation and* the reporting and withholding of taxes with respect to gambling or wagering operations shall apply to Indian gaming operations . . . the same as they apply to State operations," S. 555, 100th Cong., 1st Sess., 37 (1987).

With the "taxation" language present, it would have made sense to include chapter 35, which concerns taxation, in a parenthetical that included other provisions that concern reporting and withholding. But the Senate committee deleted the taxation language. Why did it permit the cross-reference to chapter 35 to remain? Committee documents do not say.

The Tribes argue that the committee intentionally left it in the statute in order to serve as a *substitute* for the word "taxation." An *amicus* tries to support this view by pointing to a tribal representative's testimony that certain Tribes were "opposed to any indication where Internal Revenue would be collecting taxes from the tribal bingo operations." Hearings on S. 555 and S. 1303 before the Senate Select Committee on Indian Affairs, 100th Cong., 1st Sess., 109 (1987) (statement of Lionel John, Executive Director of United South and Eastern Tribes). Other Tribes thought the "taxation" language too "vague," preferring a clear statement "that the Internal Revenue Service is not being granted authority to tax tribes." Id. at 433, 435 (statement of Charles W. Blackwell, Representative of the American Indian Tribal Government and Policy Consultants, Inc.).

Substitution of "chapter 35" for the word "taxation," however, could not have served the tribal witnesses['] purposes, for doing so took from the bill the very words that made clear the tribes would *not* be taxed and substituted language that made it more likely they would be taxed. Nor can we believe that anyone seeking to grant a tax exemption would intentionally substitute a confusion-generating numerical cross-reference, see Part A, *supra*, for pre-existing language that unambiguously carried out that objective. It is far easier to believe that the drafters, having included the entire parenthetical while the word "taxation" was still part of the bill, unintentionally failed to remove what had become a superfluous numerical cross-reference—particularly since the tax-knowledgeable Senate Finance Committee never received the opportunity to examine the bill. Cf. S. Doc. No. 100–1, Senate Manual, 30 (1987) (proposed legislation concerning revenue measures shall be referred to the Committee on Finance).

Finally, the Tribes point to a letter written by one of the Gaming Act's authors, stating that "by including reference to Chapter 35," Congress intended "that the tax treatment of wagers conducted by tribal governments be the same as that for wagers conducted by state governments under Chapter 35." App. to Pet. for Cert. 113a. This letter, however, was written after the event. It expresses the views of only one member of the committee. And it makes no effort to explain the critical legislative circumstance, namely, the elimination of the word "taxation" from the bill. The letter may express the Senator's interpretive preference, but that preference cannot overcome the language of the statute and the related considerations we have discussed. See *Heintz v. Jenkins*, 514 U.S. 291, 298 (1995) (A "statement [made] not during the legislative process, but *after* the statute became law ... is not a statement upon which other legislators might have relied in voting for or against the Act, but it simply represents the views of one informed person on an issue about which others may (or may not) have thought differently").

In sum, to adopt the Tribes' interpretation would read back into the Act the very word "taxation" that the Senate committee deleted. We ordinarily will not assume that Congress intended " 'to enact statutory language that it has earlier discarded in favor of other language.' " *INS v. Cardoza-Fonseca*, 480 U.S. 421, 443 (1987). There is no special reason for doing so here.

C

The Tribes point to canons of interpretation that favor their position. The Court has often said that " 'every clause and word of a statute' " should, " 'if possible,' " be given " 'effect.' " *United States v. Menasche*, 348 U.S. 528, 538–539 (1955) (quoting *Montclair v. Ramsdell*, 107 U.S. 147, 157 (1883)). The Tribes point out that our interpretation deprives the words "chapter 35" of any effect. The Court has also said that "statutes are to be construed liberally in favor of the Indians with ambiguous provisions interpreted to their benefit." *Montana v. Blackfeet Tribe*, 471 U.S. at 766; *South Carolina v. Catawba Tribe, Inc.*, 476 U.S. 498, 520 (1986) (Blackmun, J., dissenting). The Tribes point out that our interpretation is not to the Indians' benefit.

Nonetheless, these canons do not determine how to read this statute. For one thing, canons are not mandatory rules. They are guides that "need not be conclusive." *Circuit City Stores, Inc. v. Adams*, 532 U.S. 105, 115 (2001). They are designed to help judges determine the Legislature's intent as embodied in particular statutory language. And other circumstances evidencing congressional intent can overcome their force. In this instance, to accept as conclusive the canons on which the Tribes rely would produce an interpretation that we conclude would conflict with the intent embodied in the statute Congress wrote. Cf. *Choteau v. Burnet*, 283 U.S. 691 (1931) (upholding taxation where congressional intent reasonably clear). In light of the considerations discussed earlier, we cannot say that the statute is "fairly capable" of two interpretations, nor that the Tribes' interpretation is fairly "possible."

Specific canons "are often countered ... by some maxim pointing in a different direction." *Circuit City Stores, Inc. v. Adams, supra*, at 115. The canon requiring a court to give effect to each word "*if possible*" is sometimes offset by the canon that permits a court to reject words "as surplusage" if "inadvertently inserted or if repugnant to the rest of the statute. . . ." K. Llewellyn, The Common Law Tradition 525 (1960). And the latter canon has particular force here where the surplus words consist simply of a numerical cross-reference in a parenthetical. Cf. *Cabell Huntington Hospital, Inc. v. Shalala*, 101 F.3d 984, 990 (CA4 1996) ("A parenthetical is, after all, a parenthetical, and it cannot be used to overcome the operative terms of the statute").

Moreover, the canon that assumes Congress intends its statutes to benefit the tribes is offset by the canon that warns us against interpreting federal statutes as providing tax exemptions unless those exemptions are clearly expressed. See *United States v. Wells Fargo Bank*, 485 U.S. 351, 354 (1988) ("Exemptions from taxation . . . must be unambiguously proved"). Nor can one say that the pro-Indian canon is inevitably stronger—particularly where the interpretation of a congressional statute rather than an Indian treaty is at issue. This Court's earlier cases are too individualized, involving too many different kinds of legal circumstances, to warrant any such assessment about the two canons' relative strength. Compare, *e.g.*, *Choate v. Trapp*, 224 U.S. 665, 675–676 (1912) (interpreting statement in treaty-related Indian land patents that land is "nontaxable" as creating property right invalidating later congressional effort to tax); *Squire* [*v. Capoeman*, 351 U.S. 1, 3 (1956)] (Indian canon offsetting tax canon when related statutory provision and history make clear that language freeing Indian land " 'of all charge or incumbrance whatsoever' " includes tax); *McClanahan v. Arizona Tax Comm'n*, 411 U.S. 164, 174 (1973) (state tax violates principle of Indian sovereignty embodied in treaty), with *Mescalero* [*Apache Tribe v. Jones*, 411 U.S. 145 (1973)] (relying on tax canon to find Indians taxable); *Choteau, supra* (language makes clear no exemption); [*Superintendent of Five Civilized Tribes v. Commissioner*, 295 U.S. 418 (1935)] (same).

Consequently, the canons here cannot make the difference for which the Tribes argue. . . .

Justice O'Connor, with whom Justice Souter joins, dissenting.

The Court today holds that 25 U.S.C. § 2719(d) clearly and unambiguously fails to give Indian Nations (Nations) the exemption from federal wagering excise and related occupational taxes enjoyed by the States. Because I believe § 2719(d) is subject to more than one interpretation, and because "statutes are to be construed liberally in favor of the Indians, with ambiguous provisions interpreted to their benefit," *Montana v. Blackfeet Tribe*, 471 U.S. 759, 766 (1985), I respectfully dissent.

I

I agree with the Court that § 2719(d) incorporates an error in drafting. I disagree, however, that the section's reference to chapter 35 is necessarily that error.

As originally proposed in the Senate, the bill that became the Indian Gaming Regulatory Act (IGRA) would have applied all gambling and wagering-related sections of the Internal Revenue Code to the Nations in the same manner as the States:

> "Provisions of the Internal Revenue Code of 1986, concerning the taxation and the reporting and withholding of taxes with respect to gambling or wagering operations shall apply to Indian gaming operations conducted pursuant to this Act the same as they apply to State operations." S. 555, 100th Cong., 1st Sess., 37 (1987).

The Senate Indian Affairs Committee altered the language of this bill in two contradictory ways. It restricted the applicable Code sections to those relating to the "reporting and withholding of taxes with respect to the winnings" from gaming operations. 25 U.S.C. § 2719(d). It also added a parenthetical listing specific Code sections to be applied to the Nations in the same manner as the States, including chapter 35, a Code provision that relates to gambling operations generally, but not to the reporting and withholding of gambling winnings.

One of these two changes must have been made in error. There is no reason to assume, however, that it must have been the latter. It is equally likely that Congress intended § 2719(d) to apply chapter 35 to the Nations, but adopted too restrictive a general characterization of the applicable sections.

The Court can do no more than speculate that the bill's drafters included the parenthetical while the original restriction was in place and failed to remove it when that restriction was altered. Both the inclusion of the parenthetical and the alteration of the restriction occurred in the Senate committee, S. Rep. No. 100–446 (1988), and there is no way to determine the order in which they were adopted. If the parenthetical was added after the restriction, one could just as easily characterize the *restriction* as an unintentional holdover from a previous version of the bill.

True, reading the statute to grant the Nations the exemption requires the section's reference to the "reporting and withholding of taxes with respect to the winnings" from gaming operations to sustain a meaning the words themselves cannot bear. But the Court's reading of the statute fares no better: It requires excising from § 2719(d) Congress' explicit reference to chapter 35. This goes beyond treating statutory language as mere surplusage. See *Potter v. United States*, 155 U.S. 438, 446 (1894) (the presence of statutory language "cannot be regarded as mere surplusage; it means something"). Surplusage is redundant statutory language, *Babbitt v. Sweet Home Chapter, Communities for Great Ore.*, 515 U.S. 687, 697–698 (1995); W. Popkin, Materials on Legislation: Political Language and the Political Process 214 (3d ed. 2001)—the Court's reading negates language that undeniably bears separate meaning. This is not a step to be undertaken lightly.

Both approaches therefore require rewriting the statute. Neither of these re-writings is necessarily more "serious" than the other: At most, each involves doing no more than reversing a change made in committee.

The Court argues that, because the reference to chapter 35 occurs in a parenthetical, negating this language does less damage to the statute than concluding that the restrictive language outside the parenthetical is too narrowly drawn. I am aware of no generally accepted canon of statutory construction favoring language outside of parentheses to language within them, see, *e.g.*, W. Eskridge, P. Frickey, and E. Garrett, Legislation and Statutory Interpretation, App. C (2000) (listing canons), nor do I think it wise for the Court to adopt one today. The importance of statutory language depends not on its punctuation, but on its meaning.

The fact that the parenthetical is illustrative does not change the analysis: If Congress' illustration does not match its general description, there is as much reason to question the description as the illustration. Where another general description is possible—and was in fact part of the bill at an earlier stage—Congress' choice of an example that matches the earlier description is at least ambiguous. Moreover, as § 2719(d)'s parenthetical specifically lists statutory sections to be applied to the Nations, one might in fact conclude that the doctrine that the specific governs the general, *Crawford Fitting Co. v. J. T. Gibbons, Inc.*, 482 U.S. 437, 445 (1987), makes this specific parenthetical even more significant than the general restriction that follows.

Nor is negating Congress' clear reference to chapter 35 required by the policy behind the statute. If anything, congressional policy weighs in favor of the Nations. Congress' central purpose in enacting IGRA was "to provide a statutory basis for the operation of gaming by Indian tribes as a means of promoting tribal economic development, self-sufficiency, and strong tribal governments." § 2702(1). Exempting Nations from federal gaming taxation in the same manner as States preserves the Nations' sovereignty and avoids giving state gaming a competitive advantage that would interfere with the Nations' ability to raise revenue in this manner.

II

Because nothing in the text, legislative history, or underlying policies of § 2719(d) clearly resolves the contradiction inherent in the section, it is appropriate to turn to canons of statutory construction. The Nations urge the Court to rely upon the Indian canon, that "statutes are to be construed liberally in favor of the Indians, with ambiguous provisions interpreted to their benefit," *Montana v. Blackfeet Tribe*, 471 U.S. at 766, as a basis for deciding that the error in § 2719(d) lies in the restriction of the subclass, not in the specific listing of chapter 35. "Rooted in the unique trust relationship between the United States and the Indians," *County of Oneida v. Oneida Indian Nation of N. Y.*, 470 U.S. 226, 247 (1985), the Indian canon presumes congressional intent to assist its wards to overcome the disadvantages our country has placed upon them. Consistent with this purpose, the Indian canon applies to statutes as well as treaties: The form of the enactment does not change the presumption that Congress generally intends to benefit the Nations. In this case, because Congress has chosen gaming as a means of enabling the Nations to achieve self-sufficiency, the Indian canon rightly dictates that Congress should be presumed to have intended the Nations to receive more, rather than less, revenue from this enterprise.

Of course, the Indian canon is not the only canon with potential applicability in this case. Also relevant is the taxation principle, that exemptions from taxation must be clearly expressed. *United States Trust Co. v. Helvering*, 307 U.S. 57, 60 (1939). These canons pull in opposite directions, the former favoring the Nations' preferred reading, and the latter favoring the Government's.

This Court has repeatedly held that, when these two canons conflict, the Indian canon predominates. In *Choate v. Trapp*, 224 U.S. 665 (1912), a State attempted to rely on the taxation principle to argue that a treaty provision making land granted to Indians nontaxable was merely a bounty, capable of being withdrawn at any time. The Court acknowledged the taxation principle, responding:

> "But in the Government's dealings with the Indians, the rule is exactly the contrary. The construction, instead of being strict, is liberal; doubtful expressions, instead of being resolved in favor of the United States, are to be resolved in favor of [Indian nations.]" Id. at 674–675.

In *Squire v. Capoeman*, 351 U.S. 1, 3 (1956), the Federal Government had conveyed land to the Nations "free of all charge or encumbrance whatsoever." Although this phrase did not expressly mention nontaxability, the Court held that the language "might well be sufficient to include taxation." Invoking the Indian canon, we found the Nations exempt.

Likewise, in *McClanahan v. Arizona Tax Comm'n*, 411 U.S. 164 (1973), this Court inferred an exemption from state taxation of property inside reservations from a treaty reserving lands for the exclusive use and occupancy of the Nations. In doing so, the Court noted that: "It is true, of course, that exemptions from tax laws should, as a general rule, be clearly expressed. But we have in the past construed language far more ambiguous than this as providing a tax exemption for Indians."

As the purpose behind the Indian canon is the same regardless of the form of enactment, there is no reason to alter the Indian canon's relative strength where a statute rather than a treaty is involved. The primacy of the Indian canon over the taxation principle should not be surprising, as this Court has also held that the general presumption supporting the legality of executive action must yield to the Indian canon, a "counterpresumption specific" to Indians. *Minnesota v. Mille Lacs Band of Chippewa Indians,* 526 U.S. 172, 194, n. 5 (1999).

This Court has failed to apply the Indian canon to extend tax exemptions to the Nations only when nothing in the language of the underlying statute or treaty suggests the Nations should be exempted. *The Cherokee Tobacco,* 78 U.S. 616 (1871) (finding no exemption for the Nations from language imposing taxes on certain "'articles produced anywhere within the exterior boundaries of the United States'"); *Choteau v. Burnet,* 283 U.S. 691, 693–694 (1931) (finding no exemption in provisions "subjecting the income of 'every individual' to tax," including "income 'from any source whatever'"); *Mescalero Apache Tribe v. Jones,* 411 U.S. 145, 155, 36 L. Ed. 2d 114, 93 S. Ct. 1267 (1973) (refusing to exempt the Nations from taxes on land use income based on language that "on its face . . . exempts land and rights in land, not income derived from its use"). *Mescalero* also went further, suggesting that because of the taxation principle, the Court would refuse to find such an exemption absent "clear statutory guidance." *Mescalero*'s formulation is admittedly in tension with the Court's precedents giving the Indian canon primacy over the taxation principle where statutory language is ambiguous. As *Mescalero* was decided on the same day as one of those very precedents, the unanimous decision in *McClanahan v. Arizona Tax Comm'n, supra,* however, it cannot have intended to alter the Court's established practice.

Section 2719(d) provides an even more persuasive case for application of the Indian canon than any of our precedents. Here, the Court is not being asked to create out of vague language a tax exemption not specifically provided for in the statute. Instead, the Nations simply ask the Court to use the Indian canon as a tiebreaker between two equally plausible (or, in this case, equally implausible) constructions of a troubled statute, one which specifically makes chapter 35's tax exemption applicable to the Nations, and one which specifically does not. Breaking interpretive ties is one of the least controversial uses of any canon of statutory construction. See Eskridge, Frickey, and Garrett, Legislation and Statutory Interpretation, at 341 ("The weakest kind of substantive canon operates merely as a *tiebreaker* at the end of the interpretive analysis").

Faced with the unhappy choice of determining which part of a flawed statutory section is in error, I would thus rely upon the long-established Indian canon of construction and adopt the reading most favorable to the Nations.

COMMENTS AND QUESTIONS

1. The majority and the dissent agree that the statute contains a mistake, but they disagree about what the mistake was. On what basis does each author decide what the mistake was?

2. Do the opinions' uses of canons of construction confirm Llewellyn's observations? Recall the suggestion that the choices an author makes among the canons might help us understand the underlying policy judgments he or she makes. Is that true in *Chickasaw Nation*?

3. Justice Breyer's article, excerpted in section A of this chapter, argued that judges should seek to advance the "reasonable human purposes" disclosed by the statute in light of its language and history, including its legislative history. Where there is an obvious mistake in a statute, how can we determine what the purposes were? In these circumstances, what *result* would Easterbrook reach? What *method* would he use to reach that result?

4. Now that you have read several cases in which questions of interpretive method played an important role, which method of statutory interpretation seems better to you?

C Statutory Interpretation by Administrative Agencies

As we have seen, in the twentieth century, statutes displaced the common law as the major technique for regulating much private-sector activity imposing risk (and much else). The administration of these regulatory statutes might have been left in the hands of the courts, by means of civil enforcement actions brought by private parties or by means of criminal or civil enforcement actions brought by prosecutors and other traditional public employees. (Recall here Komesar's discussion of the institutional characteristics of these enforcement techniques in chapter 5.) However, the creators of the modern regulatory state made a different choice. They provided for enforcement in the first instance by administrative agencies, subject to judicial oversight. That fact raises important questions about the relationship between courts and agencies. You may later take a course in administrative law in which you will study many aspects of the relationship between courts and agencies in light of legislative choices. In the next chapter, you will examine the development of the modern regulatory state. The material there will enhance your understanding of the issues discussed here, but we believe it better to treat the modern approach to statutory interpretation in a single chapter.

Here we focus on one important aspect of that relationship: the degree to which courts should defer to agencies in their interpretation of the statute that created it, sometimes referred to as the agency's "organic" statute. This question of deference applies to the agency's interpretation of both the scope of its jurisdiction under the organic statute and the substantive provisions of the organic statute.

A range of views exists on this issue. For example, courts might give no deference to the agency's interpretation of the scope of its jurisdiction (on the theory, perhaps, that agencies will routinely seek to expand their power beyond the boundaries the legislature has placed on them). Or courts might take account of the agency's views, as coming from a body with expertise in the field, and treat the agency's interpretation in the manner it would a submission from an expert amicus curiae. Another view might be that the courts owe some degree of deference to the agency, depending on the circumstances, because the legislature created the agency in the first place. The strongest position in favor of agency interpretive authority is that the courts should defer to the agency's interpretation unless there are strong reasons not to do so. That position, in turn, raises questions about the place of agencies in a rule-of-law system where questions of law are (supposedly) to be determined by courts rather than by executive or other nonjudicial officials.

On what basis are courts to choose among these possible views and approaches? The Supreme Court has said that the choice should be made with reference to the agency's organic statute. Sometimes the organic statute is to be interpreted to direct the courts to interpret its substantive provisions on their own, sometimes to give the agency's interpretation the weight it rationally deserves, and sometimes to accept the agency's interpretation (unless there are strong indications otherwise with respect to particular substantive provisions). (But what degree of deference, if any, should be given to the agency's position on the question of what the legislature intended on this very question?) In *United States v. Mead Corp.*, 533 U.S. 218 (2001), the Court offered its most recent formulation: "It is fair to assume generally that Congress contemplates administrative action with the effect of law when it provides for a relatively formal administrative procedure tending to foster the fairness and deliberation that should underlie a pronouncement of such force," but Congress may sometimes intend that courts give substantial deference to agency interpretations even when such formalities are absent. The issue is whether Congress "meant to delegate authority...to issue...rulings with the force of law." The following case explains how courts are to act when Congress has delegated that authority to administrative agencies.

■ Chevron, U.S.A., Inc. v. Natural Resources Defense Council
467 U.S. 837 (1984)

Justice Stevens delivered the opinion of the Court.

In the Clean Air Act Amendments of 1977, Pub. L. 95–95, 91 Stat. 685, Congress enacted certain requirements applicable to States that had not achieved the national air quality standards established by the Environmental Protection Agency (EPA) pursuant to earlier legislation. The amended Clean Air Act required these "nonattainment" States to establish a permit program regulating "new or modified major stationary sources" of air pollution. Generally, a permit may not be issued for a new or modified major stationary source unless several stringent conditions are met. The EPA regulation promulgated to implement this permit requirement allows a State to adopt a plantwide definition of the term "stationary source." Under this definition, an existing plant that contains several pollution-emitting devices may install or modify one piece of equipment without meeting the permit conditions if the alteration will not increase the total emissions from the plant. The question presented by these cases is whether EPA's decision to allow States to treat all of the pollution-emitting devices within the same industrial grouping as though they were encased within a single "bubble" is based on a reasonable construction of the statutory term "stationary source."

I

The EPA regulations containing the plantwide definition of the term stationary source were promulgated on October 14, 1981. Respondents filed a timely petition for review in the United States Court of Appeals for the District of Columbia

Circuit pursuant to 42 U.S.C. § 7607(b)(1).[4] The Court of Appeals set aside the regulations.

The court observed that the relevant part of the amended Clean Air Act "does not explicitly define what Congress envisioned as a "stationary source, to which the permit program . . . should apply," and further stated that the precise issue was not "squarely addressed in the legislative history." In light of its conclusion that the legislative history bearing on the question was "at best contradictory," it reasoned that "the purposes of the non-attainment program should guide our decision here."[5] Based on two of its precedents concerning the applicability of the bubble concept to certain Clean Air Act programs, the court stated that the bubble concept was "mandatory" in programs designed merely to maintain existing air quality, but held that it was "inappropriate" in programs enacted to improve air quality. Since the purpose of the permit program—its "raison d'etre," in the court's view— was to improve air quality, the court held that the bubble concept was inapplicable in these cases under its prior precedents. It therefore set aside the regulations embodying the bubble concept as contrary to law. We granted certiorari to review that judgment, and we now reverse.

The basic legal error of the Court of Appeals was to adopt a static judicial definition of the term "stationary source" when it had decided that Congress itself had not commanded that definition. . . .

II

When a court reviews an agency's construction of the statute which it administers, it is confronted with two questions. First, always, is the question whether Congress has directly spoken to the precise question at issue. If the intent of Congress is clear, that is the end of the matter; for the court, as well as the agency, must give effect to the unambiguously expressed intent of Congress.[9] If, however, the court determines Congress has not directly addressed the precise question at issue, the court does not simply impose its own construction on the statute, as would be necessary in the absence of an administrative interpretation. Rather, if the statute is silent or ambiguous with respect to the specific issue, the question for the court

---

[4] Petitioners, Chevron U. S. A. Inc., American Iron and Steel Institute, American Petroleum Institute, Chemical Manufacturers Association, Inc., General Motors Corp., and Rubber Manufacturers Association, were granted leave to intervene and argue in support of the regulation.

[5] The court remarked in this regard:

"We regret, of course, that Congress did not advert specifically to the bubble concept's application to various Clean Air Act programs, and note that a further clarifying statutory directive would facilitate the work of the agency and of the court in their endeavors to serve the legislators' will."

[9] The judiciary is the final authority on issues of statutory construction and must reject administrative constructions that are contrary to clear congressional intent. See, e.g., *FEC v. Democratic Senatorial Campaign Committee*, 454 U.S. 27, 32 (1981). If a court, employing traditional tools of statutory construction, ascertains that Congress had an intention on the precise question at issue, that intention is the law and must be given effect.

is whether the agency's answer is based on a permissible construction of the statute.[11]

"The power of an administrative agency to administer a congressionally created ... program necessarily requires the formulation of policy and the making of rules to fill any gap left, implicitly or explicitly, by Congress." *Morton v. Ruiz*, 415 U.S. 199, 231 (1974). If Congress has explicitly left a gap for the agency to fill, there is an express delegation of authority to the agency to elucidate a specific provision of the statute by regulation. Such legislative regulations are given controlling weight unless they are arbitrary, capricious, or manifestly contrary to the statute. Sometimes the legislative delegation to an agency on a particular question is implicit rather than explicit. In such a case, a court may not substitute its own construction of a statutory provision for a reasonable interpretation made by the administrator of an agency.

We have long recognized that considerable weight should be accorded to an executive department's construction of a statutory scheme it is entrusted to administer, and the principle of deference to administrative interpretations

> has been consistently followed by this Court whenever decision as to the meaning or reach of a statute has involved reconciling conflicting policies, and a full understanding of the force of the statutory policy in the given situation has depended upon more than ordinary knowledge respecting the matters subjected to agency regulations.
>
> ... If this choice represents a reasonable accommodation of conflicting policies that were committed to the agency's care by the statute, we should not disturb it unless it appears from the statute or its legislative history that the accommodation is not one that Congress would have sanctioned." *United States v. Shimer*, 367 U.S. 374, 382, 383 (1961).

In light of these well-settled principles it is clear that the Court of Appeals misconceived the nature of its role in reviewing the regulations at issue. Once it determined, after its own examination of the legislation, that Congress did not actually have an intent regarding the applicability of the bubble concept to the permit program, the question before it was not whether in its view the concept is "inappropriate" in the general context of a program designed to improve air quality, but whether the Administrator's view that it is appropriate in the context of this particular program is a reasonable one. Based on the examination of the legislation and its history which follows, we agree with the Court of Appeals that Congress did not have a specific intention on the applicability of the bubble concept in these cases, and conclude that the EPA's use of that concept here is a reasonable policy choice for the agency to make.

III–V

[The Court reviewed the history and language of the Clean Air Act at length, noting that the question before it concerned "one phrase" of a "small portion" of

---

[11] The court need not conclude that the agency construction was the only one it permissibly could have adopted to uphold the construction or even the reading the court would have reached if the question initially had arisen in a judicial proceeding.

a "lengthy, detailed, technical, complex, and comprehensive response to a major social issue." The Court found that "[t]he legislative history of the portion of the [act] dealing with nonattainment areas does not contain any specific comment on the 'bubble concept' or the question whether a plantwide definition of a stationary source is permissible under the permit program. It does, however, plainly disclose that in the permit program Congress sought to accommodate the conflict between the economic interest in permitting capital improvements to continue and the environmental interest in improving air quality." In discussing EPA's history of implementing the Act, the Court noted that the agency had initially proposed interpretations like the one at issue here.]

VI

. . .

In August 1980, . . . the EPA adopted a regulation that, in essence, applied the basic reasoning of the Court of Appeals in these cases. The EPA took particular note of the two then-recent Court of Appeals decisions, which had created the bright-line rule that the "bubble concept" should be employed in a program designed to maintain air quality but not in one designed to enhance air quality. Relying heavily on those cases, EPA adopted a dual definition of "source" for nonattainment areas that required a permit whenever a change in either the entire plant, or one of its components, would result in a significant increase in emissions even if the increase was completely offset by reductions elsewhere in the plant. . . .

In 1981 a new administration took office and initiated a "Government-wide reexamination of regulatory burdens and complexities." 46 Fed. Reg. 16281. In the context of that review, the EPA reevaluated the various arguments that had been advanced in connection with the proper definition of the term "source" and concluded that the term should be given the same definition in both nonattainment areas and PSD areas.

In explaining its conclusion, the EPA first noted that the definitional issue was not squarely addressed in either the statute or its legislative history and therefore that the issue involved an agency "judgment as how to best carry out the Act." It then set forth several reasons for concluding that the plantwide definition was more appropriate. It pointed out that the dual definition "can act as a disincentive to new investment and modernization by discouraging modifications to existing facilities" and "can actually retard progress in air pollution control by discouraging replacement of older, dirtier processes or pieces of equipment with new, cleaner ones." Moreover, the new definition "would simplify EPA's rules by using the same definition of 'source' for PSD, nonattainment new source review and the construction moratorium. This reduces confusion and inconsistency." Finally, the agency explained that additional requirements that remained in place would accomplish the fundamental purposes of achieving attainment with NAAQS's as expeditiously as possible. These conclusions were expressed in a proposed rulemaking in August 1981 that was formally promulgated in October.

VII

In this Court respondents expressly reject the basic rationale of the Court of Appeals' decision. That court viewed the statutory definition of the term "source" as sufficiently flexible to cover either a plantwide definition, a narrower definition covering each unit within a plant, or a dual definition that could apply to both the entire "bubble" and its components. It interpreted the policies of the statute, however, to mandate the plantwide definition in programs designed to maintain clean air and to forbid it in programs designed to improve air quality. Respondents place a fundamentally different construction on the statute. They contend that the text of the Act requires the EPA to use a dual definition—if either a component of a plant, or the plant as a whole, emits over 100 tons of pollutant, it is a major stationary source. They thus contend that the EPA rules adopted in 1980, insofar as they apply to the maintenance of the quality of clean air, as well as the 1981 rules which apply to nonattainment areas, violate the statute.

Statutory Language

The definition of the term "stationary source" in § 111(a)(3) refers to "any building, structure, facility, or installation" which emits air pollution. This definition is applicable only to the NSPS program by the express terms of the statute; the text of the statute does not make this definition applicable to the permit program. Petitioners therefore maintain that there is no statutory language even relevant to ascertaining the meaning of stationary source in the permit program aside from § 302(j), which defines the term "major stationary source." We disagree with petitioners on this point.

The definition in § 302(j) tells us what the word "major" means—a source must emit at least 100 tons of pollution to qualify—but it sheds virtually no light on the meaning of the term "stationary source." It does equate a source with a facility—a "major emitting facility" and a "major stationary source" are synonymous under § 302(j). The ordinary meaning of the term "facility" is some collection of integrated elements which has been designed and constructed to achieve some purpose. Moreover, it is certainly no affront to common English usage to take a reference to a major facility or a major source to connote an entire plant as opposed to its constituent parts. Basically, however, the language of § 302(j) simply does not compel any given interpretation of the term "source."

Respondents recognize that, and hence point to § 111(a)(3). Although the definition in that section is not literally applicable to the permit program, it sheds as much light on the meaning of the word "source" as anything in the statute. As respondents point out, use of the words "building, structure, facility, or installation," as the definition of source, could be read to impose the permit conditions on an individual building that is a part of a plant. A "word may have a character of its own not to be submerged by its association." *Russell Motor Car Co. v. United States*, 261 U.S. 514, 519 (1923). On the other hand, the meaning of a word must be ascertained in the context of achieving particular objectives, and the words associated with it may indicate that the true meaning of the series is to convey a common idea. The language may reasonably be interpreted to impose the requirement on any discrete, but integrated, operation which pollutes. This gives meaning to all of the terms—a single building, not part of a larger operation, would be covered if it emits more than 100 tons of pollution, as would any facility, structure, or installation. Indeed, the language itself implies a "bubble concept" of sorts: each enumerated item would seem to be treated as if it were encased in a bubble. While respondents insist that each of these terms must be given a discrete meaning, they also argue that § 111(a)(3) defines "source" as that term is used in § 302(j). The latter section, however, equates a source with a facility, whereas the former defines "source" as a facility, among other items.

We are not persuaded that parsing of general terms in the text of the statute will reveal an actual intent of Congress. We know full well that this language is not dispositive; the terms are overlapping and the language is not precisely directed to the question of the applicability of a given term in the context of a larger operation. To the extent any congressional "intent" can be discerned from this language, it would appear that the listing of overlapping, illustrative terms was intended to enlarge, rather than to confine, the scope of the agency's power to regulate particular sources in order to effectuate the policies of the Act.

Legislative History

In addition, respondents argue that the legislative history and policies of the Act foreclose the plantwide definition, and that the EPA's interpretation is not entitled to deference because it represents a sharp break with prior interpretations of the Act.

Based on our examination of the legislative history, we agree with the Court of Appeals that it is unilluminating. The general remarks pointed to by respondents "were obviously not made with this narrow issue in mind and they cannot be said to demonstrate a Congressional desire. . . ." *Jewell Ridge Coal Corp. v. Mine Workers*, 325 U.S. 161, 168–169 (1945). . . . We find that the legislative history as a whole is silent on the precise issue before us. It is, however, consistent with the view that the EPA should have broad discretion in implementing the policies of the 1977 Amendments.

More importantly, that history plainly identifies the policy concerns that motivated the enactment; the plantwide definition is fully consistent with one of those concerns—the allowance of reasonable economic growth—and, whether or not we believe it most effectively implements the other, we must recognize that the EPA has advanced a reasonable explanation for its conclusion that the regulations serve the environmental objectives as well.[36] Indeed, its reasoning is supported by the public record developed in the rulemaking process, as well as by certain private studies.[37]

Our review of the EPA's varying interpretations of the word "source"—both before and after the 1977 Amendments—convinces us that the agency primarily responsible for administering this important legislation has consistently interpreted it flexibly—not in a sterile textual vacuum, but in the context of implementing

---

[36] See, for example, the statement of the New York State Department of Environmental Conservation, pointing out that denying a source owner flexibility in selecting options made it "simpler and cheaper to operate old, more polluting sources than to trade up. . . ."

[37] "Economists have proposed that economic incentives be substituted for the cumbersome administrative-legal framework. The objective is to make the profit and cost incentives that work so well in the marketplace work for pollution control. . . . [The 'bubble' or 'netting' concept] is a first attempt in this direction. By giving a plant manager flexibility to find the places and processes within a plant that control emissions most cheaply, pollution control can be achieved more quickly and cheaply." L. Lave and G. Omenn, Cleaning the Air: Reforming the Clean Air Act 28 (1981) (footnote omitted).

policy decisions in a technical and complex arena. The fact that the agency has from time to time changed its interpretation of the term "source" does not, as respondents argue, lead us to conclude that no deference should be accorded the agency's interpretation of the statute. An initial agency interpretation is not instantly carved in stone. On the contrary, the agency, to engage in informed rulemaking, must consider varying interpretations and the wisdom of its policy on a continuing basis. Moreover, the fact that the agency has adopted different definitions in different contexts adds force to the argument that the definition itself is flexible, particularly since Congress has never indicated any disapproval of a flexible reading of the statute.

Significantly, it was not the agency in 1980, but rather the Court of Appeals that read the statute inflexibly to command a plantwide definition for programs designed to maintain clean air and to forbid such a definition for programs designed to improve air quality. The distinction the court drew may well be a sensible one, but our labored review of the problem has surely disclosed that it is not a distinction that Congress ever articulated itself, or one that the EPA found in the statute before the courts began to review the legislative work product. We conclude that it was the Court of Appeals, rather than Congress or any of the decisionmakers who are authorized by Congress to administer this legislation, that was primarily responsible for the 1980 position taken by the agency.

Policy

The arguments over policy that are advanced in the parties' briefs create the impression that respondents are now waging in a judicial forum a specific policy battle which they ultimately lost in the agency and in the 32 jurisdictions opting for the "bubble concept," but one which was never waged in the Congress. Such policy arguments are more properly addressed to legislators or administrators, not to judges.[38]

In these cases the Administrator's interpretation represents a reasonable accommodation of manifestly competing interests and is entitled to deference: the regulatory scheme is technical and complex, the agency considered the matter in a detailed and reasoned fashion, and the decision involves reconciling conflicting policies. Congress intended to accommodate both interests, but did not do so itself on the level of specificity presented by these cases. Perhaps that body consciously desired the Administrator to strike the balance at this level, thinking that those with great expertise and charged with responsibility for administering the provision would be in a better position to do so; perhaps it simply did not consider the question at this level; and perhaps Congress was unable to forge a coalition on either side of the question, and those on each side decided to take their chances

---

[38] Respondents point out if a brand new factory that will emit over 100 tons of pollutants is constructed in a nonattainment area, that plant must obtain a permit pursuant to § 172(b)(6) and, in order to do so, it must satisfy the § 173 conditions, including the LAER requirement. Respondents argue if an old plant containing several large emitting units is to be modernized by the replacement of one or more units emitting over 100 tons of pollutant with a new unit emitting less—but still more than 100 tons—the result should be no different simply because "it happens to be built not at a new site, but within a *pre-existing plant*."

with the scheme devised by the agency. For judicial purposes, it matters not which of these things occurred.

Judges are not experts in the field, and are not part of either political branch of the Government. Courts must, in some cases, reconcile competing political interests, but not on the basis of the judges' personal policy preferences. In contrast, an agency to which Congress has delegated policymaking responsibilities may, within the limits of that delegation, properly rely upon the incumbent administration's views of wise policy to inform its judgments. While agencies are not directly accountable to the people, the Chief Executive is, and it is entirely appropriate for this political branch of the Government to make such policy choices—resolving the competing interests which Congress itself either inadvertently did not resolve, or intentionally left to be resolved by the agency charged with the administration of the statute in light of everyday realities. When a challenge to an agency construction of a statutory provision, fairly conceptualized, really centers on the wisdom of the agency's policy, rather than whether it is a reasonable choice within a gap left open by Congress, the challenge must fail. In such a case, federal judges—who have no constituency—have a duty to respect legitimate policy choices made by those who do. The responsibilities for assessing the wisdom of such policy choices and resolving the struggle between competing views of the public interest are not judicial ones: "Our Constitution vests such responsibilities in the political branches." *TVA v. Hill*, 437 U.S. 153, 195 (1978). We hold that the EPA's definition of the term "source" is a permissible construction of the statute which seeks to accommodate progress in reducing air pollution with economic growth. "The Regulations which the Administrator has adopted provide what the agency could allowably view as . . . [an] effective reconciliation of these twofold ends. . . ." *United States v. Shimer*, 367 U.S., at 383. The judgment of the Court of Appeals is reversed.

Justice Marshall and Justice Rehnquist took no part in the consideration or decision of these cases.

Justice O'Connor took no part in the decision of these cases.

COMMENTS AND QUESTIONS

1. *Chevron* is the foundational case dealing with the relationship between agency and judicial statutory interpretation. (It is also important for upholding a "market-based" approach to regulation, which we will examine in chapter 11.) The literature on the case's meaning and implications is enormous; here we provide only an introduction to the issues the case raises. Kent Greenawalt provides an overall description of the relationship at issue here: "[A]gencies are partners of the courts in the interpretation of statutory provisions that relate to their activities." Kent Greenawalt, Legislation—Statutory Interpretation: 20 Questions 242 (1999). On what basis does *Chevron* allocate responsibility between the partners?

2. Commentators distinguish between two stages of analysis in cases involving judicial review of agency interpretation. (The analysis might also be treated as having three steps by counting as "Step Zero" the preliminary determination of what degree of deference Congress intended the courts to give to agency interpretations.) In "Chevron Step One," the court asks whether Congress itself

resolved the substantive question in the organic statute. (In *Chevron*, the specific question confronting the court was: Did *Congress* preclude the agency from adopting the "bubble" rule?) If the answer to the Step One question is "Yes," the inquiry ends, and the court invalidates the regulation (or upholds it as mandated by Congress). If the answer is "No," the court proceeds to Step Two and asks whether the agency's interpretation of the organic statute is a reasonable one—even if not the interpretation the court would have adopted on its own. If the answer is "Yes," the court upholds the agency's regulation.

3. Justice Scalia has suggested that textualists will end the interpretive inquiry at Step One more frequently than purposivists and that textualism therefore preserves a larger role for the courts than purposivism (and so reduces the tension between *Chevron* and some rule-of-law assumptions about the role of courts as the primary institution for interpreting regulatory statutes). Antonin Scalia, *Judicial Deference to Administrative Interpretation of Law*, 1989 Duke L.J. 511. Do you agree with that assessment?

4. Justice Scalia dissented in *United States v. Mead Corp.*, 533 U.S. 218 (2001), which held that the courts should not give *Chevron* deference to agency interpretations when Congress did not delegate authority to "speak with the force of law." (Among the indications of whether Congress did so is whether the agency engaged in notice-and-comment rule making, a procedure you will examine in the next chapter.) Justice Scalia argued that the *Mead* decision replaced a clear rule of deference with a much less clear standard for determining when to defer. Note that the *Mead* decision increases the courts' power relative to agencies by reducing the number of occasions when Step Two deference is required.

   The *Mead* decision held that the courts should give so-called *Skidmore* deference to agency interpretations, established in *Skidmore v. Swift & Co.*, 323 U.S. 134 (1944), as "respect according to its persuasiveness." Is that different from giving "deference"—that is, taking into consideration—the arguments made in a government brief? Why give an agency interpretation *any* deference at all, when Congress has not delegated law-making authority to the agency? *Mead* quoted *Skidmore*:

   > The weight [accorded to an administrative] judgment in a particular case will depend upon the thoroughness evident in its consideration, the validity of its reasoning, its consistency with earlier and later pronouncements, and all those factors which give it power to persuade, if lacking power to control.

   Why should those considerations lead to any deference? Do agencies have any advantages over courts in "reasoning" and "consistency"? The *Mead* Court referred to *Skidmore's* recognition that agencies have available to them "specialized experience and broader investigations and information." In that case, why not give their decisions *Chevron* Step Two deference?

5. *Chevron's* final paragraph contains two themes:
   (a) *Agency expertise*. Note, though, that the issue in the case is one of statutory interpretation; are agencies experts at *that* task? Maybe so, if—on a roughly purposivist view—issues of statutory interpretation are also questions of policy implementation.

(b) *Democratic accountability*: One of the cornerstones of the modern regulatory state—democratic accountability—is represented in *Chevron*'s two steps. Step One embodies democratic accountability by means of congressional responsibility. The people elect members of Congress who can, if they choose, definitively resolve the substantive question. Step Two embodies democratic accountability by means of *executive* responsibility. The people elect a president who, in turn, selects agency administrators who will resolve the substantive question in line with the president's policies, themselves (implicitly) endorsed by the preceding election.

But note the possibility of "slippage" between the people and both Congress and the executive branch. Elections may endorse general lines of policy development ("deregulation" in the 1980 election of Ronald Reagan, for example), but rarely endorse the specifics of policy implementation. For a suggestive argument along these lines, though not focusing on *Chevron*, see Edward Rubin, *The Myth of Accountability and the Anti-Administrative Impulse*, 103 Mich. L. Rev. 2073 (2005). Consider the proposition that eliminating *Chevron* deference would imply that executive officials—who believe that their views on specific matters have been endorsed by the people—must obtain legislation from a Congress elected by the people as well, albeit not necessarily at the same time.

In light of this sort of slippage, would democratic accountability be improved by eliminating *Chevron* deference and replacing it with an approach that gives agency views the weight the courts believe they deserve? Is there reason to believe that courts will be *better* at implementing the public's views on specific policies than agencies (which themselves have to report to Congress and whose actions sometimes receive close media scrutiny)? Consider one possible implication of Llewellyn's historicized view of statutory interpretation: Courts will change their overall approach more slowly than legislatures, administrative agencies, and the executive branch. The courts that addressed the "bubble" issue were staffed largely by appointees of Democratic presidents, and yet the "bubble" concept was an expression of a deregulatory impulse that broke sharply with earlier approaches to regulation. It follows from this view that *Chevron* will be an important case during periods of transition or divided government but not otherwise. (Why?)

■ Food & Drug Administration v. Brown & Williamson Tobacco Corp.
529 U.S. 120 (2000)

Justice O'Connor delivered the opinion of the Court.

This case involves one of the most troubling public health problems facing our Nation today: the thousands of premature deaths that occur each year because of tobacco use. In 1996, the Food and Drug Administration (FDA), after having expressly disavowed any such authority since its inception, asserted jurisdiction to regulate tobacco products. The FDA concluded that nicotine is a "drug" within the meaning of the Food, Drug, and Cosmetic Act (FDCA or Act), and that cigarettes and smokeless tobacco are "combination products" that deliver nicotine to the body. Pursuant to this authority, it promulgated regulations intended to reduce tobacco consumption among children and adolescents. The agency believed that, because most tobacco consumers begin their use before reaching the age of 18, curbing tobacco use by minors could substantially reduce the prevalence of addiction in future generations and thus the incidence of tobacco-related death and disease.

Regardless of how serious the problem an administrative agency seeks to address, however, it may not exercise its authority "in a manner that is inconsistent with the administrative structure that Congress enacted into law." *ETSI Pipeline Project v. Missouri,* 484 U.S. 495, 517 (1988). And although agencies are generally entitled to deference in the interpretation of statutes that they administer, a reviewing "court, as well as the agency, must give effect to the unambiguously expressed intent of Congress." *Chevron U.S.A. Inc. v. Natural Resources Defense Council, Inc.,* 467 U.S. 837, 842–843 (1984). In this case, we believe that Congress has clearly precluded the FDA from asserting jurisdiction to regulate tobacco products. Such authority is inconsistent with the intent that Congress has expressed in the FDCA's overall regulatory scheme and in the tobacco-specific legislation that it has enacted subsequent to the FDCA. In light of this clear intent, the FDA's assertion of jurisdiction is impermissible.

I

The FDCA grants the FDA, as the designee of the Secretary of Health and Human Services, the authority to regulate, among other items, "drugs" and "devices." The Act defines "drug" to include "articles (other than food) intended to affect the structure or any function of the body." It defines "device," in part, as "an instrument, apparatus, implement, machine, contrivance,... or other similar or related article, including any component, part, or accessory, which is ... intended to affect the structure or any function of the body." The Act also grants the FDA the authority to regulate so-called "combination products," which "constitute a combination of a drug, device, or biologic product." § 353(g)(1). The FDA has construed this provision as giving it the discretion to regulate combination products as drugs, as devices, or as both.

On August 11, 1995, the FDA published a proposed rule concerning the sale of cigarettes and smokeless tobacco to children and adolescents. The rule, which included several restrictions on the sale, distribution, and advertisement of tobacco products, was designed to reduce the availability and attractiveness of tobacco products to young people. A public comment period followed, during which the FDA received over 700,000 submissions, more than "at any other time in its history on any other subject."

On August 28, 1996, the FDA issued a final rule entitled "Regulations Restricting the Sale and Distribution of Cigarettes and Smokeless Tobacco to Protect Children and Adolescents." The FDA determined that nicotine is a "drug" and that cigarettes and smokeless tobacco are "drug delivery devices," and therefore it had jurisdiction under the FDCA to regulate tobacco products as customarily marketed—that is, without manufacturer claims of therapeutic benefit. First, the FDA found that tobacco products " 'affect the structure or any function of the body' " because nicotine "has significant pharmacological effects." Specifically, nicotine "exerts psychoactive, or mood-altering, effects on the brain" that cause and sustain addiction, have both tranquilizing and stimulating effects, and control weight. Second, the FDA determined that these effects were "intended" under the FDCA because they "are so widely known and foreseeable that [they] may be deemed to have been intended by the manufacturers"; consumers use tobacco products "predominantly or nearly exclusively" to obtain these effects; and the statements, research, and actions of manufacturers revealed that they "have 'designed' cigarettes to provide pharmacologically active doses of nicotine to consumers." Finally, the agency concluded that cigarettes and smokeless tobacco are "combination products" because, in addition to containing nicotine, they include device components that deliver a controlled amount of nicotine to the body.

Having resolved the jurisdictional question, the FDA next explained the policy justifications for its regulations, detailing the deleterious health effects associated with tobacco use. It found that tobacco consumption was "the single leading cause of preventable death in the United States." According to the FDA, "[m]ore than 400,000 people die each year from tobacco-related illnesses, such as cancer, respiratory illnesses, and heart disease." The agency also determined that the only way to reduce the amount of tobacco-related illness and mortality was to reduce the level of addiction, a goal that could be accomplished only by preventing children and adolescents from starting to use tobacco. The FDA found that 82% of adult smokers had their first cigarette before the age of 18, and more than half had already become regular smokers by that age. It also found that children were beginning to smoke at a younger age, that the prevalence of youth smoking had recently increased, and that similar problems existed with respect to smokeless tobacco. The FDA accordingly concluded that if "the number of children and adolescents who begin tobacco use can be substantially diminished, tobacco-related illness can be correspondingly reduced because data suggest that anyone who does not begin smoking in childhood or adolescence is unlikely ever to begin."

Based on these findings, the FDA promulgated regulations concerning tobacco products' promotion, labeling, and accessibility to children and adolescents. The access regulations prohibit the sale of cigarettes or smokeless tobacco to persons younger than 18; require retailers to verify through photo identification the age of all purchasers younger than 27; prohibit the sale of cigarettes in quantities smaller than 20; prohibit the distribution of free samples; and prohibit sales through self-service displays and vending machines except in adult-only locations. The promotion regulations require that any print advertising appear in a black-and-white, text-only format unless the publication in which it appears is read almost exclusively by adults; prohibit outdoor advertising within 1,000 feet of any public playground or school; prohibit the distribution of any promotional items, such as T-shirts or hats, bearing the manufacturer's brand name; and prohibit a manufacturer from sponsoring any athletic, musical, artistic, or other social or cultural event using its brand name. The labeling regulation requires that the statement, "A Nicotine-Delivery Device for Persons 18 or Older," appear on all tobacco product packages.

The FDA promulgated these regulations pursuant to its authority to regulate "restricted devices." The FDA construed § 353(g)(1) as giving it the discretion to regulate "combination products" using the Act's drug authorities, device authorities, or both, depending on "how the public health goals of the act can be best accomplished." Given the greater flexibility in the FDCA for the regulation of devices, the FDA determined that "the device authorities provide the most appropriate basis for regulating cigarettes and smokeless tobacco." Under 21 U.S.C. § 360j(e), the agency may "require that a device be restricted to sale, distribution, or use ... upon such other conditions as [the FDA] may prescribe in such regulation, if, because of its potentiality for harmful effect or the collateral measures necessary to its use, [the FDA] determines that there cannot otherwise be reasonable assurance of its safety and effectiveness." The FDA reasoned that its regulations fell within the authority granted by § 360j(e) because they related to the sale or distribution of tobacco products and were necessary for providing a reasonable assurance of safety.

Respondents, a group of tobacco manufacturers, retailers, and advertisers, filed suit in United States District Court for the Middle District of North Carolina challenging the regulations.... [The district court held that the FDA had jurisdiction to regulate tobacco products, and the] Court of Appeals for the Fourth Circuit reversed, holding that Congress has not granted the FDA jurisdiction to regulate tobacco products....

We granted the Government's petition for certiorari, to determine whether the FDA has authority under the FDCA to regulate tobacco products as customarily marketed.

II

The FDA's assertion of jurisdiction to regulate tobacco products is founded on its conclusions that nicotine is a "drug" and that cigarettes and smokeless tobacco are "drug delivery devices." Again, the FDA found that tobacco products are "intended" to deliver the pharmacological effects of satisfying addiction, stimulation and tranquilization, and weight control because those effects are foreseeable to any reasonable manufacturer, consumers use tobacco products to obtain those effects, and tobacco manufacturers have designed their products to produce those effects....

A threshold issue is the appropriate framework for analyzing the FDA's assertion of authority to regulate tobacco products. Because this case involves an administrative agency's construction of a statute that it administers, our analysis is governed by *Chevron U.S.A. Inc. v. Natural Resources Defense Council, Inc.,* 467 U.S. 837 (1984). Under *Chevron,* a reviewing court must first ask "whether Congress has directly spoken to the precise question at issue." If Congress has done so, the inquiry is at an end; the court "must give effect to the unambiguously expressed intent of Congress." But if Congress has not specifically addressed the question, a reviewing court must respect the agency's construction of the statute so long as it is permissible. See *INS v. Aguirre-Aguirre,* 526 U.S. 415, 424 (1999). Such deference is justified because "[t]he responsibilities for assessing the wisdom of such policy choices and resolving the struggle between competing views of the public interest are not judicial ones," *Chevron, supra,* at 866, and because of the agency's greater familiarity with the ever-changing facts and circumstances surrounding the subjects regulated, see *Rust v. Sullivan,* 500 U.S. 173, 187 (1991).

In determining whether Congress has specifically addressed the question at issue, a reviewing court should not confine itself to examining a particular statutory provision in isolation. The meaning—or ambiguity—of certain words or phrases may only become evident when placed in context. See *Brown v. Gardner,* 513 U.S. 115, 118 (1994) ("Ambiguity is a creature not of definitional possibilities but of statutory context"). It is a "fundamental canon of statutory construction that the words of a statute must be read in their context and with a view to their place in the overall statutory scheme." *Davis v. Michigan Dept. of Treasury*, 489 U.S. 803, 809 (1989). A court must therefore interpret the statute "as a symmetrical and coherent regulatory scheme," *Gustafson v. Alloyd Co.*, 513 U.S. 561, 569 (1995), and "fit, if possible, all parts into an harmonious whole," *FTC v. Mandel Brothers, Inc.*, 359 U.S. 385, 389 (1959). Similarly, the meaning of one statute may be affected by other Acts, particularly where Congress has spoken subsequently and more specifically to the topic at hand. In addition, we must be guided to a degree by common sense as to the manner in which Congress is likely to delegate a policy decision of such economic and political magnitude to an administrative agency.

With these principles in mind, we find that Congress has directly spoken to the issue here and precluded the FDA's jurisdiction to regulate tobacco products.

A

Viewing the FDCA as a whole, it is evident that one of the Act's core objectives is to ensure that any product regulated by the FDA is "safe" and "effective" for its intended use. This essential purpose pervades the FDCA. For instance, 21 U.S.C. § 393(b)(2) defines the FDA's "mission" to include "protect[ing] the public health by ensuring that . . . drugs are safe and effective" and that "there is reasonable assurance of the safety and effectiveness of devices intended for human use." . . . Thus, the Act generally requires the FDA to prevent the marketing of any drug or device where the "potential for inflicting death or physical injury is not offset by the possibility of therapeutic benefit." *United States v. Rutherford*, 442 U.S. 544, 556 (1979).

In its rulemaking proceeding, the FDA quite exhaustively documented that "tobacco products are unsafe," "dangerous," and "cause great pain and suffering from illness." It found that the consumption of tobacco products "presents extraordinary health risks," and that "tobacco use is the single leading cause of preventable death in the United States." It stated that "[m]ore than 400,000 people die each year from tobacco-related illnesses, such as cancer, respiratory illnesses, and heart disease, often suffering long and painful deaths," and that "[t]obacco alone kills more people each year in the United States than acquired immunodeficiency syndrome (AIDS), car accidents, alcohol, homicides, illegal drugs, suicides, and fires, combined." Indeed, the FDA characterized smoking as "a pediatric disease," because "one out of every three young people who become regular smokers . . . will die prematurely as a result."

These findings logically imply that, if tobacco products were "devices" under the FDCA, the FDA would be required to remove them from the market. Consider, first, the FDCA's provisions concerning the misbranding of drugs or devices. The Act prohibits "[t]he introduction or delivery for introduction into interstate commerce of any food, drug, device, or cosmetic that is adulterated or misbranded." In light of the FDA's findings, two distinct FDCA provisions would render cigarettes and smokeless tobacco misbranded devices. First, § 352(j) deems a drug or device misbranded "[i]f it is dangerous to health when used in the dosage or manner, or with the frequency or duration prescribed, recommended, or suggested in the labeling thereof." The FDA's findings make clear that tobacco products are "dangerous to health" when used in the manner prescribed. Second, a drug or device is misbranded under the Act "[u]nless its labeling bears . . . adequate directions for use . . . in such manner and form, as are necessary for the protection of users," except where such directions are "not necessary for the protection of the public health." Given the FDA's conclusions concerning the health consequences of tobacco use, there are no directions that could adequately protect consumers. That is, there are no directions that could make tobacco products safe for obtaining their intended effects. Thus, were tobacco products within the FDA's jurisdiction, the Act would deem them misbranded devices that could not be introduced into interstate commerce. Contrary to the dissent's contention, the Act admits no remedial discretion once it is evident that the device is misbranded.

Second, the FDCA requires the FDA to place all devices that it regulates into one of three classifications. See § 360c(b)(1). The agency relies on a device's classification in determining the degree of control and regulation necessary to ensure that there is "a reasonable assurance of safety and effectiveness." The FDA has yet to classify tobacco products. . . . Given the FDA's findings regarding the health consequences of tobacco use, the agency would have to place cigarettes and smokeless tobacco in Class III because, even after the application of the Act's available controls, they would "presen[t] a potential unreasonable risk of illness or injury." As Class III devices, tobacco products would be subject to the FDCA's premarket approval process. Under these provisions, the FDA would be prohibited from approving an application for premarket approval without "a showing of reasonable assurance that such device is safe under the conditions of use prescribed, recommended, or suggested on the labeling thereof." In view of the FDA's conclusions regarding the health effects of tobacco use, the agency would have no basis for finding any such reasonable assurance of safety. Thus, once the FDA fulfilled its statutory obligation to classify tobacco products, it could not allow them to be marketed.

The FDCA's misbranding and device classification provisions therefore make evident that were the FDA to regulate cigarettes and smokeless tobacco, the Act would require the agency to ban them. . . .

Congress, however, has foreclosed the removal of tobacco products from the market. A provision of the United States Code currently in force states that "[t]he marketing of tobacco constitutes one of the greatest basic industries of the United States with ramifying activities which directly affect interstate and foreign commerce at every point, and stable conditions therein are necessary to the general welfare." More importantly, Congress has directly addressed the problem of tobacco and health through legislation on six occasions since 1965. When Congress enacted these statutes, the adverse health consequences of tobacco use were well known, as were nicotine's pharmacological effects. Nonetheless, Congress stopped well short of ordering a ban. Instead, it has generally regulated the labeling and advertisement of tobacco products, expressly providing that it is the policy of Congress that "commerce and the national economy may be . . . protected to the maximum extent consistent with" consumers "be[ing] adequately informed about any adverse health effects." Congress' decisions to regulate labeling and advertising and to adopt the express policy of protecting "commerce and the national economy . . . to the maximum extent" reveal its intent that tobacco products remain on the market. Indeed, the collective premise of these statutes is that cigarettes and smokeless tobacco will continue to be sold in the United States. A ban of tobacco products by the FDA would therefore plainly contradict congressional policy.

The FDA apparently recognized this dilemma and concluded, somewhat ironically, that tobacco products are actually "safe" within the meaning of the FDCA.

In promulgating its regulations, the agency conceded that "tobacco products are unsafe, as that term is conventionally understood." Nonetheless, the FDA reasoned that, in determining whether a device is safe under the Act, it must consider "not only the risks presented by a product but also any of the countervailing effects of use of that product, including the consequences of not permitting the product to be marketed." Applying this standard, the FDA found that, because of the high level of addiction among tobacco users, a ban would likely be "dangerous." In particular, current tobacco users could suffer from extreme withdrawal, the health care system and available pharmaceuticals might not be able to meet the treatment demands of those suffering from withdrawal, and a black market offering cigarettes even more dangerous than those currently sold legally would likely develop. The FDA therefore concluded that, "while taking cigarettes and smokeless tobacco off the market could prevent some people from becoming addicted and reduce death and disease for others, the record does not establish that such a ban is the appropriate public health response under the act."

It may well be, as the FDA asserts, that "these factors must be considered when developing a regulatory scheme that achieves the best public health result for these products." But the FDA's judgment that leaving tobacco products on the market "is more effective in achieving public health goals than a ban," is no substitute for the specific safety determinations required by the FDCA's various operative provisions. Several provisions in the Act require the FDA to determine that the *product itself* is safe as used by consumers. That is, the product's probable therapeutic benefits must outweigh its risk of harm. In contrast, the FDA's conception of safety would allow the agency, with respect to each provision of the FDCA that requires the agency to determine a product's "safety" or "dangerousness," to compare the aggregate health effects of alternative administrative actions. This is a qualitatively different inquiry. Thus, although the FDA has concluded that a ban would be "dangerous," it has *not* concluded that tobacco products are "safe" as that term is used throughout the Act.

. . . A straightforward reading of [the Act] dictates that the FDA must weigh the probable therapeutic benefits of [a] device to the consumer against the probable risk of injury. Applied to tobacco products, the inquiry is whether their purported benefits—satisfying addiction, stimulation and sedation, and weight control—outweigh the risks to health from their use. To accommodate the FDA's conception of safety, however, one must read "any probable benefit to health" to include the benefit to public health stemming from adult consumers' continued use of tobacco products, even though the *reduction* of tobacco use is the *raison d'etre* of the regulations. In other words, the FDA is forced to contend that the very evil it seeks to combat is a "benefit to health." This is implausible.

The FDA's conception of safety is also incompatible with the FDCA's misbranding provision. Again, § 352(j) provides that a product is "misbranded" if "it is dangerous to health when used in the dosage or manner, or with the frequency or duration prescribed, recommended, or suggested in the labeling thereof." According to the FDA's understanding, a product would be "dangerous to health," and therefore misbranded under § 352(j), when, in comparison to leaving the product on the market, a ban would not produce "adverse health consequences" in aggregate. Quite simply, these are different inquiries. Although banning a particular product might be detrimental to public health in aggregate, the product could still be "dangerous to health" when used as directed. Section 352(j) focuses on dangers to the consumer from use of the product, not those stemming from the agency's remedial measures.

Consequently, the analogy made by the FDA and the dissent to highly toxic drugs used in the treatment of various cancers is unpersuasive. Although "dangerous" in some sense, these drugs are safe within the meaning of the Act because, for certain patients, the therapeutic benefits outweigh the risk of harm. Accordingly, such drugs cannot properly be described as "dangerous to health" under 21 U.S.C. § 352(j). The same is not true for tobacco products. As the FDA has documented in great detail, cigarettes and smokeless tobacco are an unsafe means to obtaining *any* pharmacological effect.

The dissent contends that our conclusion means that "the FDCA requires the FDA to ban outright 'dangerous' drugs or devices," and that this is a "perverse" reading of the statute. This misunderstands our holding. The FDA, consistent with the FDCA, may clearly regulate many "dangerous" products without banning them. Indeed, virtually every drug or device poses dangers under certain conditions. What the FDA may not do is conclude that a drug or device cannot be used safely for any therapeutic purpose and yet, at the same time, allow that product to remain on the market. Such regulation is incompatible with the FDCA's core objective of ensuring that every drug or device is safe and effective.

Considering the FDCA as a whole, it is clear that Congress intended to exclude tobacco products from the FDA's jurisdiction. A fundamental precept of the FDCA is that any product regulated by the FDA—but not banned—must be safe for its intended use. Various provisions of the Act make clear that this refers to the safety of using the product to obtain its intended effects, not the public health ramifications of alternative administrative actions by the FDA. That is, the FDA must determine that there is a reasonable assurance that the product's therapeutic benefits outweigh the risk of harm to the consumer. According to this standard, the FDA has concluded that, although tobacco products might be effective in delivering certain pharmacological effects, they are "unsafe" and "dangerous" when used for these purposes. Consequently, if tobacco products were within the FDA's jurisdiction, the Act would require the FDA to remove them from the market entirely. But a ban would contradict Congress' clear intent as expressed in its more recent, tobacco-specific legislation. The inescapable conclusion is that there is no room for tobacco products within the FDCA's regulatory scheme. If they cannot be used safely for any therapeutic purpose, and yet they cannot be banned, they simply do not fit.

B

In determining whether Congress has spoken directly to the FDA's authority to regulate tobacco, we must also consider in greater detail the tobacco-specific legislation that Congress has enacted over the past 35 years. At the time a statute is enacted, it may have a range of plausible meanings. Over time, however, subsequent acts can shape or focus those meanings. The "classic judicial task of reconciling many laws enacted over time, and getting them to 'make sense' in combination, necessarily assumes that the implications of a statute may be altered by the implications of a later statute." *United States v. Fausto,* 484 U.S., at 453. This is particularly so where the scope of the earlier statute is broad but the subsequent statutes more specifically address the topic at hand. As we recognized recently in *United States v. Estate of Romani,* "a specific policy embodied in a later federal statute should control our construction of the [earlier] statute, even though it ha[s] not been expressly amended." 523 U.S., at 530–531.

Congress has enacted six separate pieces of legislation since 1965 addressing the problem of tobacco use and human health. Those statutes, among other things, require that health warnings appear on all packaging and in all print and outdoor advertisements; prohibit the advertisement of tobacco products through "any medium of electronic communication" subject to regulation by the Federal Communications Commission (FCC); require the Secretary of Health and Human Services (HHS) to report every three years to Congress on research findings concerning "the addictive property of tobacco"; and make States' receipt of certain federal block grants contingent on their making it unlawful "for any manufacturer, retailer, or distributor of tobacco products to sell or distribute any such product to any individual under the age of 18."

In adopting each statute, Congress has acted against the backdrop of the FDA's consistent and repeated statements that it lacked authority under the FDCA to regulate tobacco absent claims of therapeutic benefit by the manufacturer. In fact, on several occasions over this period, and after the health consequences of tobacco use and nicotine's pharmacological effects had become well known, Congress considered and rejected bills that would have granted the FDA such jurisdiction. Under these circumstances, it is evident that Congress' tobacco-specific statutes have effectively ratified the FDA's long-held position that it lacks jurisdiction under the FDCA to regulate tobacco products. Congress has created a distinct regulatory scheme to address the problem of tobacco and health, and that scheme, as presently constructed, precludes any role for the FDA.

. . .

The FDA's [previous] position [that it lacked jurisdiction to regulate tobacco] was . . . consistent with Congress' specific intent when it enacted the FDCA. Before the Act's adoption in 1938, the FDA's predecessor agency, the Bureau of Chemistry, announced that it lacked authority to regulate tobacco products under the Pure Food and Drug Act of 1906, unless they were marketed with therapeutic claims. In 1929, Congress considered and rejected a bill "[t]o amend the Food and Drugs Act of June 30, 1906, by extending its provisions to tobacco and tobacco products." And, as the FDA admits, there is no evidence in the text of the FDCA or its legislative history that Congress in 1938 even considered the applicability of the Act to tobacco products. Given the economic and political significance of the tobacco industry at the time, it is extremely unlikely that Congress could have intended to place tobacco within the ambit of the FDCA absent any discussion of the matter. Of course, whether the Congress that enacted the FDCA specifically intended the Act to cover tobacco products is not determinative; "it is ultimately the provisions of our laws rather than the principal concerns of our legislators by which we are governed." *Oncale v. Sundowner Offshore Services, Inc.*, 523 U.S. 75, 79 (1998). Nonetheless, this intent is certainly relevant to understanding the basis for the FDA's representations to Congress and the background against which Congress enacted subsequent tobacco-specific legislation.

Moreover, before enacting the FCLAA in 1965, Congress considered and rejected several proposals to give the FDA the authority to regulate tobacco. In April 1963, Representative Udall introduced a bill "[t]o amend the Federal Food, Drug, and Cosmetic Act so as to make that Act applicable to smoking products." Two months later, Senator Moss introduced an identical bill in the Senate. In discussing his proposal on the Senate floor, Senator Moss explained that "this amendment simply places smoking products under FDA jurisdiction, along with foods, drugs, and cosmetics." In December 1963, Representative Rhodes introduced another bill that would have amended the FDCA "by striking out 'food, drug, device, or cosmetic,' each place where it appears therein and inserting in lieu thereof 'food, drug, device, cosmetic, or smoking product.'" And in January 1965, five months before passage of the FCLAA, Representative Udall again introduced a bill to amend the FDCA "to make that Act applicable to smoking products." None of these proposals became law.

Congress ultimately decided in 1965 to subject tobacco products to the less extensive regulatory scheme of the FCLAA, which created a "comprehensive Federal program to deal with cigarette labeling and advertising with respect to any relationship between smoking and health." The FCLAA rejected any regulation of advertising, but it required the warning, "Caution: Cigarette Smoking May Be Hazardous to Your Health," to appear on all cigarette packages. In the Act's "Declaration of Policy," Congress stated that its objective was to balance the goals of ensuring that "the public may be adequately informed that cigarette smoking may be hazardous to health" and protecting "commerce and the national economy . . . to the maximum extent."

Not only did Congress reject the proposals to grant the FDA jurisdiction, but it explicitly preempted any other regulation of cigarette labeling: "No statement relating to smoking and health, other than the statement required by . . . this Act, shall be required on any cigarette package." The regulation of product labeling, however, is an integral aspect of the FDCA, both as it existed in 1965 and today. The labeling requirements currently imposed by the FDCA, which are essentially identical to those in force in 1965, require the FDA to regulate the labeling of drugs and devices to protect the safety of consumers. . . . In this sense, the FCLAA was—and remains—incompatible with FDA regulation of tobacco products. . . . Subsequent tobacco-specific legislation followed a similar pattern.

. . .

Under these circumstances, it is clear that Congress' tobacco-specific legislation has effectively ratified the FDA's previous position that it lacks jurisdiction to regulate tobacco. As in *Bob Jones Univ. v. United States,* 461 U.S. 574 (1983), "[i]t is hardly conceivable that Congress—and in this setting, any Member of Congress—was not abundantly aware of what was going on." Congress has affirmatively acted to address the issue of tobacco and health, relying on the representations of the FDA that it had no authority to regulate tobacco. It has created a distinct scheme to regulate the sale of tobacco products, focused on labeling and advertising, and premised on the belief that the FDA lacks such jurisdiction under the FDCA. As a result, Congress' tobacco-specific statutes preclude the FDA from regulating tobacco products as customarily marketed.

Although the dissent takes issue with our discussion of the FDA's change in position, our conclusion does not rely on the fact that the FDA's assertion of jurisdiction represents a sharp break with its prior interpretation of the FDCA. Certainly, an agency's initial interpretation of a statute that it is charged with administering is not "carved in stone." *Chevron,* 467 U.S., at 863. As we recognized in *Motor Vehicle Mfrs. Assn. of United States, Inc. v. State Farm Mut. Automobile Ins. Co.,* 463 U.S. 29

(1983), agencies "must be given ample latitude to 'adapt their rules and policies to the demands of changing circumstances.' " The consistency of the FDA's prior position is significant in this case for a different reason: it provides important context to Congress' enactment of its tobacco-specific legislation. When the FDA repeatedly informed Congress that the FDCA does not grant it the authority to regulate tobacco products, its statements were consistent with the agency's unwavering position since its inception, and with the position that its predecessor agency had first taken in 1914. Although not crucial, the consistency of the FDA's prior position bolsters the conclusion that when Congress created a distinct regulatory scheme addressing the subject of tobacco and health, it understood that the FDA is without jurisdiction to regulate tobacco products and ratified that position.

. . .

C

Finally, our inquiry into whether Congress has directly spoken to the precise question at issue is shaped, at least in some measure, by the nature of the question presented. Deference under *Chevron* to an agency's construction of a statute that it administers is premised on the theory that a statute's ambiguity constitutes an implicit delegation from Congress to the agency to fill in the statutory gaps. In extraordinary cases, however, there may be reason to hesitate before concluding that Congress has intended such an implicit delegation. Cf. Breyer, Judicial Review of Questions of Law and Policy, 38 Admin. L. Rev. 363, 370 (1986) ("A court may also ask whether the legal question is an important one. Congress is more likely to have focused upon, and answered, major questions, while leaving interstitial matters to answer themselves in the course of the statute's daily administration").

This is hardly an ordinary case. Contrary to its representations to Congress since 1914, the FDA has now asserted jurisdiction to regulate an industry constituting a significant portion of the American economy. In fact, the FDA contends that, were it to determine that tobacco products provide no "reasonable assurance of safety," it would have the authority to ban cigarettes and smokeless tobacco entirely. Owing to its unique place in American history and society, tobacco has its own unique political history. Congress, for better or for worse, has created a distinct regulatory scheme for tobacco products, squarely rejected proposals to give the FDA jurisdiction over tobacco, and repeatedly acted to preclude any agency from exercising significant policymaking authority in the area. Given this history and the breadth of the authority that the FDA has asserted, we are obliged to defer not to the agency's expansive construction of the statute, but to Congress' consistent judgment to deny the FDA this power.

. . .

. . . [W]e are confident that Congress could not have intended to delegate a decision of such economic and political significance to an agency in so cryptic a fashion. To find that the FDA has the authority to regulate tobacco products, one must not only adopt an extremely strained understanding of "safety" as it is used throughout the Act—a concept central to the FDCA's regulatory scheme—but also ignore the plain implication of Congress' subsequent tobacco-specific legislation. It is therefore clear, based on the FDCA's overall regulatory scheme and the subsequent tobacco legislation, that Congress has directly spoken to the question at issue and precluded the FDA from regulating tobacco products.

. . . .

By no means do we question the seriousness of the problem that the FDA has sought to address. The agency has amply demonstrated that tobacco use, particularly among children and adolescents, poses perhaps the single most significant threat to public health in the United States. Nonetheless, no matter how "important, conspicuous, and controversial" the issue, and regardless of how likely the public is to hold the Executive Branch politically accountable, an administrative agency's power to regulate in the public interest must always be grounded in a valid grant of authority from Congress. And " '[i]n our anxiety to effectuate the congressional purpose of protecting the public, we must take care not to extend the scope of the statute beyond the point where Congress indicated it would stop.' " *United States v. Article of Drug . . . Bacto-Unidisk,* 394 U.S. 784, 800 (1969) (quoting *62 Cases of Jam v. United States,* 340 U.S. 593, 600 (1951)). Reading the FDCA as a whole, as well as in conjunction with Congress' subsequent tobacco-specific legislation, it is plain that Congress has not given the FDA the authority that it seeks to exercise here. . . .

Justice Breyer, with whom Justice Stevens, Justice Souter, and Justice Ginsburg join, dissenting.

The Food and Drug Administration (FDA) has the authority to regulate "articles (other than food) intended to affect the structure or any function of the body. . . ." Federal Food, Drug and Cosmetic Act (FDCA), 21 U.S.C. § 321(g)(1)(C). Unlike the majority, I believe that tobacco products fit within this statutory language.

In its own interpretation, the majority nowhere denies the following two salient points. First, tobacco products (including cigarettes) fall within the scope of this statutory definition, read literally. Cigarettes achieve their mood-stabilizing effects through the interaction of the chemical nicotine and the cells of the central nervous system. Both cigarette manufacturers and smokers alike know of, and desire, that chemically induced result. Hence, cigarettes are "intended to affect" the body's "structure" and "function," in the literal sense of these words.

Second, the statute's basic purpose—the protection of public health—supports the inclusion of cigarettes within its scope. See *United States v. Article of Drug . . . Bacto-Unidisk,* 394 U.S. 784, 798 (1969) (FDCA "is to be given *a liberal construction consistent with [its] overriding purpose to protect the public health*" (emphasis added)). Unregulated tobacco use causes "[m]ore than 400,000 people [to] die each year from tobacco-related illnesses, such as cancer, respiratory illnesses, and heart disease." 61 Fed. Reg. 44398 (1996). Indeed, tobacco products kill more people in this country every year "than . . . AIDS, car accidents, alcohol, homicides, illegal drugs, suicides, and fires, *combined.*" *Ibid.* (emphasis added).

Despite the FDCA's literal language and general purpose (both of which support the FDA's finding that cigarettes come within its statutory authority), the majority nonetheless reads the statute as *excluding* tobacco products for two basic reasons:

1. the FDCA does not "fit" the case of tobacco because the statute requires the FDA to prohibit dangerous drugs or devices (like cigarettes) outright, and the agency concedes that simply banning the sale of cigarettes is not a proper remedy; and

2. Congress has enacted other statutes, which, when viewed in light of the FDA's long history of denying tobacco-related jurisdiction and considered together with Congress' failure explicitly to grant the agency tobacco-specific authority, demonstrate that Congress did not intend for the FDA to exercise jurisdiction over tobacco.

In my view, neither of these propositions is valid. Rather, the FDCA does not significantly limit the FDA's remedial alternatives. And the later statutes do not tell the FDA it cannot exercise jurisdiction, but simply leave FDA jurisdictional law where Congress found it. Cf. Food and Drug Administration Modernization Act of 1997, 111 Stat. 2380 (statute "shall" *not* "be construed to affect the question of whether" the FDA "has any authority to regulate any tobacco product").

The bulk of the opinion that follows will explain the basis for these latter conclusions. In short, I believe that the most important indicia of statutory meaning—language and purpose—along with the FDCA's legislative history . . . are sufficient to establish that the FDA has authority to regulate tobacco. The statute-specific arguments against jurisdiction that the tobacco companies and the majority rely upon . . . are based on erroneous assumptions and, thus, do not defeat the jurisdiction-supporting thrust of the FDCA's language and purpose. The inferences that the majority draws from later legislative history are not persuasive, since . . . one can just as easily infer from the later laws that Congress did not intend to affect the FDA's tobacco-related authority at all. And the fact that the FDA changed its mind about the scope of its own jurisdiction is legally insignificant because . . . the agency's reasons for changing course are fully justified. Finally, . . . the degree of accountability that likely will attach to the FDA's action in this case should alleviate any concern that Congress, rather than an administrative agency, ought to make this important regulatory decision.

I

Before 1938, the federal Pure Food and Drug Act contained only two jurisdictional definitions of "drug":

> "[1] medicines and preparations recognized in the United States Pharmacopoeia or National Formulary . . . and [2] any substance or mixture of substances intended to be used for the cure, mitigation, or prevention of disease."

In 1938, Congress added a third definition, relevant here:

> "(3) articles (other than food) intended to affect the structure or any function of the body. . . ."

It also added a similar definition in respect to a "device." As I have mentioned, the literal language of the third definition and the FDCA's general purpose both strongly support a projurisdiction reading of the statute.

The statute's history offers further support. The FDA drafted the new language, and it testified before Congress that the third definition would expand the FDCA's jurisdictional scope significantly. Indeed, "[t]he purpose" of the new definition was to "make possible the regulation of a great many products that have been found on the market that cannot be alleged to be treatments for diseased conditions." While the drafters focused specifically upon the need to give the FDA jurisdiction over "slenderizing" products such as "antifat remedies," they were aware that, in doing so, they had created what was "admittedly an inclusive, a wide definition." And that broad language was included *deliberately*, so that jurisdiction could be had over "*all* substances and preparations, other than food, and *all* devices intended to affect the structure or any function of the body...."

After studying the FDCA's history, experts have written that the statute "is a purposefully broad delegation of discretionary powers by Congress," J. O'Reilly, 1 Food and Drug Administration § 6.01, p. 6-1 (2d ed. 1995), and that, in a sense, the FDCA "must be regarded as a *constitution*" that "establish[es] general principles" and "permit[s] implementation within broad parameters" so that the FDA can "implement these objectives through the most effective and efficient controls that can be devised." Hutt, Philosophy of Regulation under the Federal Food, Drug and Cosmetic Act, 28 Food Drug Cosm. L.J. 177, 178–179 (1973) (emphasis added)....

That Congress would grant the FDA such broad jurisdictional authority should surprise no one. In 1938, the President and much of Congress believed that federal administrative agencies needed broad authority and would exercise that authority wisely—a view embodied in much Second New Deal legislation. Thus, at around the same time that it added the relevant language to the FDCA, Congress enacted laws granting other administrative agencies even broader powers to regulate much of the Nation's transportation and communication. Why would the 1938 New Deal Congress suddenly have hesitated to delegate to so well established an agency as the FDA all of the discretionary authority that a straightforward reading of the relevant statutory language implies?

Nor is it surprising that such a statutory delegation of power could lead after many years to an assertion of jurisdiction that the 1938 legislators might not have expected. Such a possibility is inherent in the very nature of a broad delegation.

. . .

II

A

The tobacco companies contend that the FDCA's words cannot possibly be read to mean what they literally say. The statute defines "device," for example, as "an instrument, apparatus, implement, machine, contrivance, implant, in vitro reagent, or other similar or related article . . . intended to affect the structure or any function of the body...." Taken literally, this definition might include everything from room air conditioners to thermal pajamas. The companies argue that, to avoid such a result, the meaning of "drug" or "device" should be confined to *medical* or *therapeutic* products, narrowly defined.

. . .

. . . [T]he statute's language itself supplies a . . . more suitable[] limitation: that a "drug" must be a *chemical* agent. The FDCA's "device" definition states that an article which affects the structure or function of the body is a "device" only if it "does *not* achieve its primary intended purposes through chemical action within . . . the body," and "is *not* dependent upon being metabolized for the achievement of its primary intended purposes." One can readily infer from this language that at least an article that *does* achieve its primary purpose through chemical action within the body and that *is* dependent upon being metabolized is a "drug," provided that it otherwise falls within the scope of the "drug" definition. And one need not hypothesize about air conditioners or thermal pajamas to recognize that the chemical nicotine, an important tobacco ingredient, meets this test.

Although I now oversimplify, the FDA has determined that once nicotine enters the body, the blood carries it almost immediately to the brain. Nicotine then binds to receptors on the surface of brain cells, setting off a series of chemical reactions that alter one's mood and produce feelings of sedation and stimulation. Nicotine also increases the number of nicotinic receptors on the brain's surface, and alters its normal electrical activity. And nicotine stimulates the transmission of a natural chemical that "rewards" the body with pleasurable sensations (dopamine), causing nicotine addiction. The upshot is that nicotine stabilizes mood, suppresses appetite, tranquilizes, and satisfies a physical craving that nicotine itself has helped to create—all through chemical action within the body after being metabolized.

This physiology—and not simply smoker psychology—helps to explain why as many as 75% of adult smokers believe that smoking "reduce[s] nervous irritation"; why 73% of young people (10- to 22-year-olds) who begin smoking say they do so for "relaxation"; and why less than 3% of the 70% of smokers who want to quit each year succeed. That chemistry also helps to explain the Surgeon General's findings that smokers believe "smoking [makes them] feel better" and smoke more "in situations involving negative mood." And, for present purposes, that chemistry demonstrates that nicotine affects the "structure" and "function" of the body in a manner that is quite similar to the effects of other regulated substances. Indeed, addiction, sedation, stimulation, and weight loss are *precisely* the kinds of product effects that the FDA typically reviews and controls. And, since the nicotine in cigarettes plainly is not a "food," its chemical effects suffice to establish that it is as a "drug" (and the cigarette that delivers it a drug-delivery "device") for the purpose of the FDCA.

B

The tobacco companies' principal definitional argument focuses upon the statutory word "intended." The companies say that "intended" in this context is a term of art. They assert that the statutory word "intended" means that the product's maker has made an *express claim* about the effect that its product will have on the body. Indeed, according to the companies, the FDA's inability to prove that cigarette manufacturers make such claims is precisely why that agency historically has said it lacked the statutory power to regulate tobacco.

The FDCA, however, does not use the word "claimed"; it uses the word "intended." And the FDA long ago issued regulations that say the relevant "intent" can be shown not only by a manufacturer's "expressions," *but also* "by the circumstances surrounding the distribution of the article." 41 Fed. Reg. 6896 (1976); see also 41 Fed. Reg. 6896 (1976) ("objective intent" shown if "article is, with the knowledge [of its makers], offered and used" for a particular purpose). Thus, even in the absence of express claims, the FDA has regulated products that affect the body if the manufacturer wants, and knows, that consumers so use the product.

Courts ordinarily reverse an agency interpretation of this kind only if Congress has clearly answered the interpretive question or if the agency's interpretation is unreasonable. *Chevron U.S.A. Inc. v. Natural Resources Defense Council, Inc.,* 467 U.S. 837, 842–843 (1984). The companies, in an effort to argue the former, point to language in the legislative history tying the word "intended" to a technical concept called "intended use." But nothing in Congress' discussion either of "intended" or "intended use" suggests that an express claim (which *often* shows intent) is *always* necessary. . . .

Nor is the FDA's "objective intent" interpretation unreasonable. It falls well within the established scope of the ordinary meaning of the word "intended." See *Agnew v. United States,* 165 U.S. 36, 53 (1897) (intent encompasses the known consequences of an act). . . .

The companies also cannot deny that the evidence of their intent is sufficient to satisfy the statutory word "intended" as the FDA long has interpreted it. In the first place, there was once a time when they actually *did* make express advertising claims regarding tobacco's mood-stabilizing and weight-reducing properties—and historical representations can portend present expectations. In the late 1920's, for example, the American Tobacco Company urged weight-conscious smokers to " 'Reach for a Lucky instead of a sweet.' " Kluger, Ashes to Ashes, at 77–78. The advertisements of R J Reynolds (RJR) emphasized mood stability by depicting a pilot remarking that " It Takes Steady Nerves to Fly the Mail at Night. . . . That's why I smoke Camels. And I smoke plenty!' " *Id.,* at 86. RJR also advertised the stimulating quality of cigarettes, stating in one instance that " 'You get a Lift with a Camel,' " and, in another, that Camels are " 'A Harmless Restoration of the Flow of Natural Body Energy.' " *Id.,* at 87. And claims of medical proof of mildness (and of other beneficial effects) once were commonplace. See, *e.g., id.,* at 93 (Brown & Williamson advertised Kool-brand mentholated cigarettes as "a tonic to hot, tired throats"); *id.,* at 101, 131 (Phillip Morris contended that "[r]ecognized laboratory tests have conclusively proven the advantage of Phillip Morris"); *id.,* at 88 (RJR proclaimed " 'For Digestion's sake, smoke Camels! . . . Camels make mealtime more pleasant—digestion is stimulated—alkalinity increased' "). Although in recent decades cigarette manufacturers have stopped making express health claims in their advertising, consumers have come to understand what the companies no longer need to express—that through chemical action cigarettes stabilize mood, sedate, stimulate, and help suppress appetite.

Second, even though the companies refused to acknowledge publicly (until only very recently) that the nicotine in cigarettes has chemically induced, and habit-forming, effects, see, *e.g.,* Regulation of Tobacco Products (Part 1): Hearings before the House Subcommittee on Health and the Environment, 103d Cong., 2d Sess., 628 (1994) (hereinafter 1994 Hearings) (heads of seven major tobacco companies testified under oath that they believed "nicotine is *not* addictive" (emphasis added)), the FDA recently has gained access to solid, documentary evidence proving that cigarette manufacturers have long *known* tobacco produces these effects within the body through the metabolizing of chemicals, and that they have long *wanted* their products to produce those effects in this way.

For example, in 1972, a tobacco-industry scientist explained that " '[s]moke is beyond question the most optimized vehicle of nicotine,' " and " 'the cigarette is the most optimized dispenser of smoke.' " That same scientist urged company executives to

> " '[t]hink of the cigarette pack as a storage container for a day's supply of nicotine. . . . Think of the cigarette as a dispenser for a dose unit of nicotine [and] [t]hink of a puff of smoke as a vehicle of nicotine.' " (Philip Morris). . . .

With such evidence, the FDA has more than sufficiently established that the companies "intend" their products to "affect" the body within the meaning of the FDCA.

C

The majority nonetheless reaches the "inescapable conclusion" that the language and structure of the FDCA as a whole "simply do not fit" the kind of public health problem that tobacco creates. That is because, in the majority's view, the FDCA requires the FDA to ban outright "dangerous" drugs or devices (such as cigarettes); yet, the FDA concedes that an immediate and total cigarette-sale ban is inappropriate.

This argument is curious because it leads with similarly "inescapable" force to precisely the opposite conclusion, namely, that the FDA *does* have jurisdiction but that it must ban cigarettes. More importantly, the argument fails to take into account the fact that a statute interpreted as requiring the FDA to pick a more dangerous over a less dangerous remedy would be a perverse statute, *causing*, rather than preventing, unnecessary harm whenever a total ban is likely the more dangerous response. And one can at least imagine such circumstances.

Suppose, for example, that a commonly used, mildly addictive sleeping pill (or, say, a kind of popular contact lens), plainly within the FDA's jurisdiction, turned out to pose serious health risks for certain consumers. Suppose further that many of those addicted consumers would ignore an immediate total ban, turning to a potentially more dangerous black-market substitute, while a less draconian remedy (say, adequate notice) would wean them gradually away to a safer product. Would the FDCA still *force* the FDA to impose the more dangerous remedy? For the following reasons, I think not.

First, the statute's language does not restrict the FDA's remedial powers in this way. The FDCA permits the FDA to regulate a "combination product"—*i.e.*, a "device" (such as a cigarette) that contains a "drug" (such as nicotine)—under its "device" provisions. And the FDCA's "device" provisions explicitly grant the FDA wide remedial discretion. For example, where the FDA cannot "otherwise" obtain "reasonable assurance" of a device's "safety and effectiveness," the agency may restrict by regulation a product's "sale, distribution, or use" upon *"such . . . conditions as the Secretary may prescribe"* (emphasis added). And the statutory section that most clearly addresses the FDA's power to ban (entitled "Banned devices") says that, where a device presents "an unreasonable and substantial risk of illness or injury," the Secretary *"may"*—not *must*—"initiate a proceeding . . . to make such device a banned device" (emphasis added).

The Court points to other statutory subsections which it believes require the FDA to ban a drug or device entirely, even where an outright ban risks more harm than other regulatory responses. But the cited provisions do no such thing. It is true, as the majority contends, that "the FDCA requires the FDA to place all devices" in "one of three classifications" and that Class III devices require "premarket approval." But it is not the case that the FDA *must* place cigarettes in Class III because tobacco itself "present[s] a potential unreasonable risk of illness or injury." In fact, Class III applies *only* where *regulation* cannot otherwise "provide reasonable assurance of . . . safety." §§ 360c(a)(1)(A), 360c(a)(1)(B) (placing a device in Class I or Class II when regulation can provide that assurance). Thus, the statute plainly allows the FDA to consider the relative, overall "safety" of a device in light of its regulatory alternatives, and where the FDA has chosen the least dangerous path, *i.e.*, the safest path, then it can—and does—provide a "reasonable assurance" of "safety" within the meaning of the statute. A good football helmet provides a reasonable assurance of safety for the player even if the sport itself is still dangerous. And the safest regulatory choice by definition offers a "reasonable" assurance of safety in a world where the other alternatives are yet more dangerous.

In any event, it is not entirely clear from the statute's text that a Class III categorization would require the FDA affirmatively to *withdraw* from the market dangerous devices, such as cigarettes, which are already widely distributed. See, *e.g.*, § 360f(a) (when a device presents an "unreasonable and substantial risk of illness or injury," the Secretary "may" make it "a banned device"); § 360h(a) (when a device "presents an unreasonable risk of substantial harm to the public health," the Secretary "may" require "notification"); § 360h(b) (when a defective device creates an "unreasonable risk" of harm, the Secretary "may" order "repair, replacement, or refund").

Noting that the FDCA requires banning a "misbranded" drug, the majority also points to 21 U.S.C. § 352(j), which deems a drug or device "misbranded" if "it is dangerous to health when used" as "prescribed, recommended, or suggested in the labeling." In addition, the majority mentions § 352(f)(1), which calls a drug or device "misbranded" unless "its labeling bears . . . adequate directions for use" as "are necessary for the protection of users." But this "misbranding" language is not determinative, for it permits the FDA to conclude that a drug or device is *not* "dangerous to health" and that it *does* have "adequate" directions *when regulated so as to render it as harmless as possible.* And surely the agency can determine that a substance is comparatively "safe" (*not* "dangerous") whenever it would be *less* dangerous to make the product available (subject to regulatory requirements) than suddenly to withdraw it from the market. Any other interpretation risks substantial harm of the sort that my sleeping pill example illustrates. And nothing in the statute prevents the agency from adopting a view of "safety" that would avoid such harm. Indeed, the FDA already seems to have taken this position when permitting distribution of toxic drugs, such as poisons used for chemotherapy, that are dangerous for the user but are not deemed "dangerous to health" in the relevant sense.

. . .

The statute's language, then, permits the agency to choose remedies consistent with its basic purpose—the overall protection of public health.

The second reason the FDCA does not require the FDA to select the more dangerous remedy is that, despite the majority's assertions to the contrary, the statute does not distinguish among the kinds of health effects that the agency may take into account when assessing safety. The Court insists that the statute only permits the agency to take into account the health risks and benefits of the "*product itself*" as used by individual consumers and, thus, that the FDA is prohibited from considering that a ban on smoking would lead many smokers to suffer severe withdrawal symptoms or to buy possibly stronger, more dangerous, black market cigarettes—considerations that the majority calls "the aggregate health effects of alternative administrative actions." But the FDCA expressly *permits* the FDA to take account of comparative safety in precisely this manner. See, *e.g.*, 21 U.S.C.

§ 360h(e)(2)(B)(i)(II) (no device recall if "risk of recall[l]" presents "a greater health risk than" no recall); § 360h(a) (notification "unless" notification "would present a greater danger" than "no such notification").

Moreover, one cannot distinguish in this context between a "specific" health risk incurred by an individual and an "aggregate" risk to a group. *All* relevant risk is, at bottom, risk to an individual; *all* relevant risk attaches to "the product itself"; and *all* relevant risk is "aggregate" in the sense that the agency aggregates health effects in order to determine risk to the individual consumer. If unregulated smoking will kill 4 individuals out of a typical group of 1,000 people, if regulated smoking will kill 1 out of 1,000, and if a smoking ban (because of the black market) will kill 2 out of 1,000; then these three possibilities mean that in each group four, one, and two individuals, on average, will die respectively. And the risk to each individual consumer is 4/1000, 1/1000, and 2/1000 respectively. A "specific" risk to an individual consumer and "aggregate" risks are two sides of the same coin; each calls attention to the same set of facts. While there may be a theoretical distinction between the risk of the product itself and the risk related to the presence or absence of an intervening voluntary act (*e.g.*, the search for a replacement on the black market), the majority does not rely upon any such distinction, and the FDA's history of regulating "replacement" drugs such as methadone shows that it has long taken likely actual alternative consumer behavior into account.

I concede that, as a matter of logic, one could consider the FDA's "safety" evaluation to be different from its choice of remedies. But to read the statute to forbid the agency from taking account of the realities of consumer behavior either in assessing safety or in choosing a remedy could increase the risks of harm—doubling the risk of death to each "individual user" in my example above. Why would Congress insist that the FDA ignore such realities, even if the consequent harm would occur only unusually, say, where the FDA evaluates a product (a sleeping pill; a cigarette; a contact lens) that is already on the market, potentially habit forming, or popular? I can find no satisfactory answer to this question. And that, I imagine, is why the statute itself says nothing about any of the distinctions that the Court has tried to draw. See 21 U.S.C. § 360c(a)(2) (instructing FDA to determine the safety and effectiveness of a "device" in part by weighing "*any* probable benefit to health . . . against *any* probable risk of injury or illness . . .") (emphasis added).

Third, experience counsels against an overly rigid interpretation of the FDCA that is divorced from the statute's overall health-protecting purposes. A different set of words, added to the FDCA in 1958 by the Delaney Amendment, provides that "no [food] additive shall be deemed to be safe if it is found [after appropriate tests] to induce cancer in man or animal." § 348(c)(3). The FDA once interpreted this language as requiring it to ban any food additive, no matter how small the amount, that appeared in any food product if that additive was ever found to induce cancer in any animal, no matter how large a dose needed to induce the appearance of a single carcinogenic cell. The FDA believed that the statute's ban mandate was absolute and prevented it from establishing a level of "safe use" or even to judge whether "the benefits of continued use outweigh the risks involved." This interpretation—which in principle could have required the ban of everything from herbal teas to mushrooms—actually led the FDA to ban saccharine, though this extremely controversial regulatory response never took effect because Congress enacted, and has continually renewed, a law postponing the ban.

The Court's interpretation of the statutory language before us risks Delaney-type consequences with even less linguistic reason. Even worse, the view the Court advances undermines the FDCA's overall health-protecting purpose by placing the FDA in the strange dilemma of either banning completely a potentially dangerous drug or device or doing nothing at all. Saying that I have misunderstood its conclusion, the majority maintains that the FDA "may clearly regulate many 'dangerous' products without banning them." But it then adds that the FDA *must* ban—rather than otherwise regulate—a drug or device that "cannot be used safely for any therapeutic purpose." If I misunderstand, it is only because this linchpin of the majority's conclusion remains unexplained. *Why* must a widely-used but unsafe device be withdrawn from the market when that particular remedy threatens the health of many and is thus more dangerous than another regulatory response? It is, indeed, a perverse interpretation that reads the FDCA to require the ban of a device that has no "safe" therapeutic purpose where a ban is the most dangerous remedial alternative.

In my view, where linguistically permissible, we should interpret the FDCA in light of Congress' overall desire to protect health. That purpose requires a flexible interpretation that both permits the FDA to take into account the realities of human behavior and allows it, in appropriate cases, to choose from its arsenal of statutory remedies. A statute so interpreted easily "fit[s]" this, and other, drug- and device-related health problems.

III

In the majority's view, laws enacted since 1965 require us to deny jurisdiction, whatever the FDCA might mean in their absence. But why? Do those laws contain language barring FDA jurisdiction? The majority must concede that they do not. Do they contain provisions that are inconsistent with the FDA's exercise of jurisdiction? With one exception, the majority points to no such provision. Do they somehow repeal the principles of law that otherwise would lead to the conclusion that the FDA has jurisdiction in this area? The companies themselves deny making any such claim. Perhaps the later laws "shape" and "focus" what the 1938 Congress meant a generation earlier. But this Court has warned against using the views of a later Congress to construe a statute enacted many years before. See *Pension Benefit Guaranty Corporation v. LTV Corp.*, 496 U.S. 633, 650 (1990) (later history is " 'a hazardous basis for inferring the intent of an earlier' Congress"). And, while the majority suggests that the subsequent history "control[s] our construction" of the FDCA, this Court expressly has held that such subsequent views are not "controlling." *Haynes v. United States*, 390 U.S. 85, 87–88, n. 4 (1968); accord, *Southwestern Cable Co.*, 392 U.S., at 170 (such views have " 'very little, if any, significance' "); see also *Sullivan v. Finkelstein*, 496 U.S. 617, 632 (1990) (Scalia, J., concurring) ("Arguments based on subsequent legislative history . . . should not be taken seriously, not even in a footnote.").

Regardless, the later statutes do not support the majority's conclusion. That is because, whatever individual Members of Congress after 1964 may have assumed about the FDA's jurisdiction, the laws they enacted did not embody any such "no jurisdiction" assumption. And one cannot automatically *infer* an antijurisdiction intent, as the majority does, for the later statutes are both (and similarly) consistent with quite a different congressional desire, namely, the intent to proceed without interfering with whatever authority the FDA otherwise may have possessed. See, *e.g.*, Cigarette Labeling and Advertising—1965: Hearings on H.R. 2248 et al. before the House Committee on Interstate and Foreign Commerce, 89th Cong., 1st Sess., 19 (1965) (hereinafter 1965 Hearings) (statement of Rep. Fino that the proposed legislation would *not* "erode" agency authority). . . . [T]he subsequent legislative history is critically ambivalent, for it can be read *either* as (a) "ratif[ying]" a no-jurisdiction assumption *or* as (b) leaving the jurisdictional question just where Congress found it. And the fact that both inferences are "equally tenable," *Pension Benefit Guaranty Corp.*, at 650, prevents the majority from drawing from the later statutes the firm, antijurisdiction implication that it needs.

Consider, for example, Congress' failure to provide the FDA with express authority to regulate tobacco—a circumstance that the majority finds significant. In fact, Congress *both* failed to grant express authority to the FDA when the FDA denied it had jurisdiction over tobacco *and* failed to take that authority expressly away when the agency later asserted jurisdiction. See, *e.g.*, S. 1262, 104th Cong., 1st Sess., § 906 (1995) (failed bill seeking to amend FDCA to say that "[n]othing in this Act or any other Act shall provide the [FDA] with any authority to regulate in any manner tobacco or tobacco products"); see also H.R. 516, 105th Cong., 1st Sess., § 2 (1997) (similar); H.R. Res. 980, reprinted in 142 Cong. Rec. 5018 (1996) (Georgia legislators unsuccessfully requested that Congress "rescind any action giving the FDA authority" over tobacco); H.R. 2283, 104th Cong., 1st Sess. (1995) (failed bill "[t]o prohibit the [FDA] regulation of the sale or use of tobacco"); H.R. 2414, 104th Cong., 1st Sess., § 2(a) (1995) (similar). Consequently, the defeat of various different proposed jurisdictional changes proves nothing. This history shows only that Congress could not muster the votes necessary either to grant or to deny the FDA the relevant authority. It neither favors nor disfavors the majority's position.

The majority also mentions the speed with which Congress acted to take jurisdiction away from other agencies once they tried to assert it. But such a congressional response again proves nothing. On the one hand, the speedy reply might suggest that Congress somehow resented agency assertions of jurisdiction in an area it desired to reserve for itself—a consideration that supports the majority. On the other hand, Congress' quick reaction with respect to *other* agencies' regulatory efforts contrasts dramatically with its failure to enact any responsive law (at any speed) after the FDA asserted jurisdiction over tobacco more than three years ago. And that contrast supports the opposite conclusion.

In addition, at least one post-1938 statute reveals quite a different congressional intent than the majority infers. See Note following 21 U.S.C. § 321 (FDA Modernization Act of 1997) (law "shall [*not*] be construed to affect the question of whether the [FDA] has any authority to regulate any tobacco product," and "[s]uch authority, if any, shall be exercised under the [FDCA] as in effect on the day before the date of [this] enactment"). Consequently, it appears that the only interpretation that can reconcile *all* of the subsequent statutes is the inference that Congress did not intend, either explicitly or implicitly, for its later laws to answer the question of the scope of the FDA's jurisdictional authority. See 143 Cong. Rec. S8860 (Sept. 5, 1997) (the Modernization Act will "not interfere or substantially negatively affect any of the FDA tobacco authority").

. . .

...Congress itself has addressed expressly the issue of the FDA's tobacco-related authority only once—and, as I have said, its statement was that the statute was *not* to "be construed to affect the question of whether the [FDA] has any authority to regulate any tobacco product." The proper inference to be drawn from *all* of the post-1965 statutes, then, is one that interprets Congress' general legislative silence consistently with this statement.

IV

I now turn to the final historical fact that the majority views as a factor in its interpretation of the subsequent legislative history: the FDA's former denials of its tobacco-related authority.

Until the early 1990's, the FDA expressly maintained that the 1938 statute did not give it the power that it now seeks to assert. It then changed its mind. The majority agrees with me that the FDA's change of positions does not make a significant legal difference. Nevertheless, it labels those denials "important context" for drawing an inference about Congress' intent. In my view, the FDA's change of policy, like the subsequent statutes themselves, does nothing to advance the majority's position.

When it denied jurisdiction to regulate cigarettes, the FDA consistently stated *why* that was so. In 1963, for example, FDA administrators wrote that cigarettes did not satisfy the relevant FDCA definitions—in particular, the "intent" requirement—because cigarette makers did not sell their product with accompanying "therapeutic claims." And subsequent FDA Commissioners made roughly the same assertion. One pointed to the fact that the manufacturers only "recommended" cigarettes "for smoking pleasure." Two others reiterated the evidentiary need for "health claims." Yet another stressed the importance of proving "intent," adding that "[w]e have not had sufficient evidence" of "intent with regard to nicotine." Tobacco company counsel also testified that the FDA lacked jurisdiction because jurisdiction "depends on . . . intended use," which in turn "depends, *in general*, on the claims and representations made by the manufacturer." Health Consequences of Smoking: Nicotine Addiction, Hearing before the Subcommittee on Health and the Environment of the House Committee on Energy and Commerce, 100th Cong., 2d Sess., 288 (1988) (testimony of Richard Cooper) (emphasis added).

Other agency statements occasionally referred to additional problems. Commissioner Kessler, for example, said that the "enormous social consequences" flowing from a decision to regulate tobacco counseled in favor of obtaining specific Congressional "guidance." 1994 Hearings 69. But a fair reading of the FDA's denials suggests that the overwhelming problem was one of proving the requisite manufacturer intent.

What changed? For one thing, the FDA obtained evidence sufficient to prove the necessary "intent" despite the absence of specific "claims." This evidence, which first became available in the early 1990's, permitted the agency to demonstrate that the tobacco companies *knew* nicotine achieved appetite-suppressing, mood-stabilizing, and habituating effects through chemical (not psychological) means, even at a time when the companies were publicly denying such knowledge.

Moreover, scientific evidence of adverse health effects mounted, until, in the late 1980's, a consensus on the seriousness of the matter became firm. That is not to say that concern about smoking's adverse health effects is a new phenomenon. See, *e.g.*, Higginson, A New Counterblast, in Out-door Papers 179, 194 (1863) (characterizing tobacco as "'a narcotic poison of the most active class'"). It is to say, however, that convincing epidemiological evidence began to appear mid-20th century; that the First Surgeon General's Report documenting the adverse health effects appeared in 1964; and that the Surgeon General's Report establishing nicotine's addictive effects appeared in 1988. At each stage, the health conclusions were the subject of controversy, diminishing somewhat over time, until recently—and only recently—has it become clear that there is a wide consensus about the health problem.

Finally, administration policy changed. Earlier administrations may have hesitated to assert jurisdiction for the reasons prior Commissioners expressed. Commissioners of the current administration simply took a different regulatory attitude.

Nothing in the law prevents the FDA from changing its policy for such reasons. By the mid-1990's, the evidence needed to prove objective intent—even without an express claim—had been found. The emerging scientific consensus about tobacco's adverse, chemically induced, health effects may have convinced the agency that it should spend its resources on this important regulatory effort. As for the change of administrations, I agree with then-Justice Rehnquist's statement in a different case, where he wrote:

> "The agency's changed view . . . seems to be related to the election of a new President of a different political party. It is readily apparent that the responsible members of one administration may consider public resistance and uncertainties to be more important than do their counterparts in a previous administration. A change in administration brought about by the people casting their votes is a perfectly reasonable basis for an executive agency's reappraisal of the costs and benefits of its programs and regulations. As long as the agency remains within the bounds established by Congress, it is entitled to assess administrative records and evaluate priorities in light of the philosophy of the administration." *Motor Vehicle Mfrs. Assn. of United States, Inc. v. State Farm Mut. Automobile Ins. Co.*, 463 U.S. 29, 59 (1983) (concurring in part and dissenting in part).

V

One might nonetheless claim that, even if my interpretation of the FDCA and later statutes gets the words right, it lacks a sense of their "music." See *Helvering v. Gregory*, 69 F.2d 809, 810–811 (C.A.2 1934) (L. Hand, J.) ("[T]he meaning of a [statute] may be more than that of the separate words, as a melody is more than the notes . . ."). Such a claim might rest on either of two grounds.

First, one might claim that, despite the FDA's legal right to change its mind, its original statements played a critical part in the enactment of the later statutes and now should play a critical part in their interpretation. But the FDA's traditional view was largely premised on a perceived inability to prove the necessary statutory "intent" requirement. The statement, "we cannot assert jurisdiction over substance X unless it is treated as a food" would not bar jurisdiction if the agency later establishes that substance X is, and is intended to be, eaten. The FDA's denials of tobacco-related authority sufficiently resemble this kind of statement that they should not make the critical interpretive difference.

Second, one might claim that courts, when interpreting statutes, should assume in close cases that a decision with "enormous social consequences," should be made by democratically elected Members of Congress rather than by unelected agency administrators. If there is such a background canon of interpretation, however, I do not believe it controls the outcome here.

Insofar as the decision to regulate tobacco reflects the policy of an administration, it is a decision for which that administration, and those politically elected officials who support it, must (and will) take responsibility. And the very importance of the decision taken here, as well as its attendant publicity, means that the public is likely to be aware of it and to hold those officials politically accountable. Presidents, just like Members of Congress, are elected by the public. Indeed, the President and Vice President are the *only* public officials whom the entire Nation elects. I do not believe that an administrative agency decision of this magnitude— one that is important, conspicuous, and controversial—can escape the kind of public scrutiny that is essential in any democracy. And such a review will take place whether it is the Congress or the Executive Branch that makes the relevant decision.

. . . .

According to the FDA, only 2.5% of smokers successfully stop smoking each year, even though 70% say they want to quit and 34% actually make an attempt to do so. The fact that only a handful of those who try to quit smoking actually succeed illustrates a certain reality—the reality that the nicotine in cigarettes creates a powerful physiological addiction flowing from chemically induced changes in the brain. The FDA has found that the makers of cigarettes "intend" these physical effects. Hence, nicotine is a "drug"; the cigarette that delivers nicotine to the body is a "device"; and the FDCA's language, read in light of its basic purpose, permits the FDA to assert the disease-preventing jurisdiction that the agency now claims.

The majority finds that cigarettes are so dangerous that the FDCA would require them to be banned (a result the majority believes Congress would not have desired); thus, it concludes that the FDA has no tobacco-related authority. I disagree that the statute would require a cigarette ban. But even if I am wrong about the ban, the statute would restrict only the agency's choice of remedies, not its jurisdiction.

The majority also believes that subsequently enacted statutes deprive the FDA of jurisdiction. But the later laws say next to nothing about the FDA's tobacco-related authority. Previous FDA disclaimers of jurisdiction may have helped to form the legislative atmosphere out of which Congress' own tobacco-specific statutes emerged. But a legislative atmosphere is not a law, unless it is embodied in a statutory word or phrase. And the relevant words and phrases here reveal nothing more than an intent not to change the jurisdictional status quo.

The upshot is that the Court today holds that a regulatory statute aimed at unsafe drugs and devices does not authorize regulation of a drug (nicotine) and a device (a cigarette) that the Court itself finds unsafe. Far more than most, this particular drug and device risks the life-threatening harms that administrative regulation seeks to rectify. The majority's conclusion is counter-intuitive. And, for the reasons set forth, I believe that the law does not require it.

Consequently, I dissent.

COMMENTS AND QUESTIONS

1. The statutory issue in *Brown and Williamson* is whether the FDA's organic statute gave it jurisdiction to regulate tobacco. The FDA's decision to regulate showed that *it* interpreted its organic statute to give it that jurisdiction. Does the Court's discussion of *Chevron* demonstrate that that case is indeed applicable to agency interpretations of the scope of jurisdiction conferred by their organic statutes?

2. Consider the proposition that nicotine contained in cigarettes is—plainly (that is, according to the plain meaning of the terms)—a "drug" delivered by a "device." What is the argument that it is *not* encompassed by the plain meaning of the statute's terms?

3. The Court treats the case as a *Chevron* Step One case, holding that a fair reading of the entire course of congressional legislation with respect to tobacco regulation demonstrates that Congress precluded the FDA from regulating tobacco. What materials does the majority rely on? The Court argues that the FDA's organic statute would *require* it to ban the distribution of cigarettes, given their danger, but that Congress had barred the FDA from doing so. The Court infers from these two propositions that the FDA had no authority to *regulate* the distribution of cigarettes, short of banning them. How does the dissent counter this syllogism? Is the Court's opinion better described as textualist or as purposivist?

4. FDA's earlier refusal to regulate tobacco might have been based on two factors:
   (a) *Expertise*: Evidence finally accumulated to the point that the agency concluded, on the basis of its expertise on matters of public health, that regulation was desirable. Note that evidence regarding the tobacco industry's adjustment of the nicotine content of cigarettes came to light relatively shortly before the FDA asserted jurisdiction over tobacco.
   (b) *Politics*: The tobacco industry had sufficient political power to block congressional enactment of strict regulatory requirements, as demonstrated by its ability to repeatedly water down regulatory initiatives. Federal agencies had failed to act because they believed that such action would be futile, anticipating that Congress would override regulatory initiatives (and the president would not veto such an override). By the mid-1990s, at least one important aspect of the political picture had changed. President Clinton made it clear to the FDA that he would veto legislation seeking to override the agency's regulatory initiatives. That freed the agency to pursue its vision of good public policy.

   Note that one could extend the political account one step further and see the tobacco industry's recourse to the courts as its effort to secure there what it could not secure from legislation. Eskridge et al., who suggest this point, write, "The five Justices in the majority are the most conservative Republican Justices. . . .The case can be viewed as a strong signal to the Clinton Administration, and subsequent ones, that the Court will slap down new regulatory initiatives that are too ambitious. (Congress has shown itself unwilling to enact them; now the President and agencies cannot adopt them under prior authorizing statutes.)" Eskridge et al., Legislation, at p. 799.

■ Concluding Note

This chapter and the next one provide a foundation for assessing specific questions of statutory interpretation that arise in later chapters. As those questions arise, you should ask yourself (1) whether the theoretical material—such as the descriptions of canons of interpretation, the analogy between common law and statutory interpretation, the concepts of textualism and purposivism—help you understand what the courts are doing in the cases you read, (2) whether cases involving real tensions between the apparent meaning of statutory language and the apparent purposes of the statutes help you understand the cases you read, and (3) what, if anything, is distinctive about the judicial role in the modern regulatory state.

From Statutes to Rules

8

A dministrative agencies operate pursuant to, and sometimes interpret, their organic statutes. Chapter 7 examined how administrative agencies interpret their organic statutes in the course of adjudicating claims arising under such statutes, including claims of statutory violations. It also presented the test for determining how much deference such agency interpretations should receive when the agency brings a civil enforcement action (as occurs with respect to some environmental regulations) or when an individual seeks some benefit administered by the agency (as occurs in most workers' compensation systems). In this chapter, we consider another purpose for which agencies interpret statutes—rule making—and examine the procedures by which agencies translate the substantive directives in their organic statutes into rules to govern conduct within the agency's orbit of responsibility. We begin by providing you with some background on the development of modern administrative law.

A. The Development of Administrative Law

Workers' compensation commissions were early administrative agencies. The Interstate Commerce Commission, created in 1887, is often described as the first modern administrative agency on the national level. (Early regulatory agencies at the state level dealt with rate setting for railroads and grain elevators.) Over the next decades, Congress created a number of additional agencies. Each operated under its own organic act, and those acts varied widely among themselves in specifying the procedures the agencies should use to decide cases and make rules.

Opponents of regulation—usually, of course, the regulated industries and the lawyers who represented them—began to mount a series of objections to the emerging regulatory state. They raised constitutional questions about the very existence of administrative agencies, one of which (the question of whether Congress impermissibly delegated lawmaking authority to agencies) we take up in chapter 12. They also objected to the blending of adjudicatory and rule-making functions and proposed that enforcement actions be brought before some entity other than the agency itself, meaning primarily the courts. And finally (for our purposes), they argued that the procedures used by agencies were unfair, in two ways: The procedures, they claimed, did not give their clients sufficient notice of what the agency proposed to do or an adequate opportunity to influence the agency's rules, and the wide variation among agency procedures subjected regulated industries to excessive costs.

Responding to these concerns, and to the weakened political position of the Roosevelt administration as New Deal innovations failed to alleviate the distress of the Great Depression, Congress passed the Walter-Logan bill in 1940. The bill purported to impose a uniform set of procedural requirements on federal administrative agencies—although in fact the bill picked and chose among favored and disfavored agencies in determining which would have to follow what rules. It also would have given the federal courts fairly wide authority to review and overturn agency regulations. President Roosevelt vetoed the bill.

Roosevelt was aware of the political need to respond to the pressures represented by the Walter-Logan bill and had already appointed the Attorney General's Committee on Administrative Procedure. That committee reported to Roosevelt in 1941. The majority report's primary proposal was to transfer final decision-making authority in adjudications from the agencies themselves to a corps of independent hearing examiners (now called administrative law judges or ALJs). The majority also favored a less well-defined program of standardized procedures across agencies. The commission's proposals went through several years of congressional consideration, which ultimately produced the Administrative Procedure Act (APA) of 1946. The APA offered a procedural solution to the perceived problems of accommodating agency expertise with constitutional accountability. Agencies had to base their decisions on a record compiled after the public had an opportunity to comment, and they also had to offer explanations for the rules they adopted. In the initial years of the APA, the primary participants in agency processes were the regulated industries themselves, which led some to question whether the agencies were acting as experts or, rather, as bodies "captured" by the industries they purported to regulate.

The following excerpt takes up the story from 1945 to the mid-1970s. It introduces you to some concepts—such as standing—that you will encounter in more detail in administrative and constitutional law courses. Its primary importance, for our purposes, is in the overall picture it draws of administrative law in the modern era.

■ *The Reformation of American Administrative Law*
RICHARD STEWART
88 Harv. L. Rev. 1669 (1975). Reprinted by permission of the Harvard Law Review Association and William S. Hein Company from the Harvard Law Review

. . . .

The traditional model of administrative law . . . conceives of the agency as a mere transmission belt for implementing legislative directives in particular cases. It legitimates intrusions into private liberties by agency officials not subject to electoral control by ensuring that such intrusions are commanded by a legitimate source of authority—the legislature. Requiring agencies to show that intrusions on private liberties have been directed by the legislature provides a rationale for judicial review and also serves to define the appropriate role of the courts vis-à-vis the agencies. The court's function is one of containment; review is directed toward keeping the agency within the directives which Congress has issued. On the other hand, this conception of the reviewing function implies that the court is to pass upon only those matters as to which the statute provides ascertainable direction; all other issues of choice, whether general or interstitial, are for the agency. By subjecting agency impositions of sanctions to judicial review in order to ensure compliance with legislative directives, the traditional model of administrative law also seeks to mediate the inconsistency between the doctrine of separation of government powers and the agencies' conspicuous combination of various lawmaking and law-enforcing functions. To the extent that the separation of powers doctrine is construed as demanding only that the exercise of power by one organ of government be subject to check by some other governmental body, the traditional model furnishes such a check through the judiciary....

Defenders flaunted the breadth of the discretion afforded the new agencies by Congress, maintaining that such discretion was necessary if the agencies were to discharge their planning and managerial functions successfully and restore health to the various sectors of the economy for which they were responsible. Given the assumption that the agencies' role was that of manager or planner with an ascertainable goal, "expertise" could plausibly be advocated as a solution to the problem of discretion if the agency's goal could be realized through the knowledge that comes from specialized experience. For in that case the discretion that the administrator enjoys is more apparent than real. The policy to be set is simply a function of the goal to be achieved and the state of the world. There may be a trial and error process in finding the best means of achieving the posited goal, but persons subject to the administrator's control are no more liable to his arbitrary will than are patients remitted to the care of a skilled doctor. This analysis underlay the notion that administrators were not political, but professional, and that public administration has an objective basis. It also supported arguments by New Deal defenders that it would be unwise for the Congress to lay down detailed prescriptions in advance, and intolerably inefficient to require administrators to follow rigid judicial procedures.

. . .

...[After 1945,] the courts, reacting in part to the Administrative Procedure Act and its history, turned to a number of alternative (and more enduring) techniques to control the exercise of administrative discretion.

First, by undertaking a more searching scrutiny of the substantiality of the evidence supporting agency factfinding and by insisting on a wider range of procedural safeguards, the courts have required agencies to adhere more scrupulously to the norms of the traditional model. This judicial stance has promoted more accurate application of legislative directives. Additionally, more rigorous enforcement of procedural requirements, such as hearings, may have influenced agencies' exercise of their discretion and may have served as a partial substitute for political safeguards by, for example, facilitating input from affected interests. These developments may also have reduced effective agency power by affording litigating tools to resistant private interests and by providing judges with an additional basis for setting aside decisions.

A second technique which was developed to control the broad discretion granted by New Deal legislation was the requirement of reasoned consistency in agency decisionmaking. Under this doctrine, an agency might be required to articulate the reasons for reaching a choice in a given case even though the loose texture of its legislative directive allowed a range of possible choices. Courts might also impose the further requirement that choices over time be consistent, or at least that departures from established policies be persuasively justified, particularly where significant individual expectation interests were involved. Again, these requirements were not directly addressed to the substance of agency policy. Their aim was . . . simply to ensure that the agency's action is rationally related to the achievement of some permissible societal goal, and to promote formal justice in order to protect private autonomy. Yet these requirements may also have an impact on the substance of agency policy. A requirement of reasoned consistency may hobble the agency in adapting to new contingencies or in dealing with an individual case of abuse whose basis is not easily susceptible to generalized statements, and such a requirement may provide additional tools for litigants resisting agency sanctions and for judges seeking procedural grounds for setting aside dubious decisions.

Third, courts began to demand a clear statement of legislative purpose as a means of restraining the range of agency choice when fundamental individual liberties were at risk.

. . .

. . . [One] theme of contemporary criticism of agency discretion has been the agencies' asserted failure affirmatively to carry out legislative mandates and to protect the collective interests that administrative regimes are designed to serve. The possibility of such failure was no concern of the traditional model, which was directed at protecting private autonomy by curbing agency power. It was simply assumed that agency zeal in advancing the "unalloyed, nonpolitical, long-run economic interest of the general public" would be assured by the professionalism of administrators or by political mechanisms through which the administrative branch would "eternally [refresh] its vigor from the stream of democratic desires."

Experience has withered this faith. To the extent that belief in an objective "public interest" remains, the agencies are accused of subverting it in favor of the private interests of regulated and client firms. Such a "devil" theory at least holds out the possibility of redemption. However, we have come not only to question the agencies' ability to protect the "public interest," but to doubt the very existence of an ascertainable "national welfare" as a meaningful guide to administrative decision. Exposure on the one hand to the complexities of a managed economy in a welfare state, and on the other to the corrosive seduction of welfare economics and pluralist political analysis, has sapped faith in the existence of an objective basis for social choice.

Today, the exercise of agency discretion is inevitably seen as the essentially legislative process of adjusting the competing claims of various private interests affected by agency policy. The unravelling of the notion of an objective goal for administration is reflected in statements by judges and legal commentators that the "public interest is a texture of multiple strands," that it "is not a monolith," and "involves a balance of many interests." Courts have asserted that agencies must consider all of the various interests affected by their decisions as an essential predicate to "balancing all elements essential to a just determination of the public interest."

Once the function of agencies is conceptualized as adjusting competing private interests in light of their configuration in a given factual situation and the policies reflected in relevant statutes, it is not possible to legitimate agency action by either the "transmission belt" theory of the traditional model, or the "expertise" model of the New Deal period. The "transmission belt" fails because broad legislative directives will rarely dispose of particular cases once the relevant facts have been accurately ascertained. More frequently, the application of legislative directives requires the agency to reweigh and reconcile the often nebulous or conflicting policies behind the directives in the context of a particular factual situation with a particular constellation of affected interests. The required balancing of policies is an inherently discretionary, ultimately political procedure. . . .

The sense of uneasiness aroused by this resurgence of discretion is heightened by perceived biases in the results of the agency balancing process as it is currently carried on. Critics have repeatedly asserted . . . that in carrying out broad legislative directives, agencies unduly favor organized interests, especially the interests of regulated or client business firms and other organized groups at the expense of diffuse, comparatively unorganized interests such as consumers, environmentalists, and the poor. In the midst of a "growing sense of disillusion with the role which regulatory agencies play," many legislators, judges, and legal and economic commentators have accepted the thesis of persistent bias in agency policies. At its crudest, this thesis is based on the "capture" scenario, in which administrations are systematically controlled, sometimes corruptly, by the business firms within their orbit of responsibility, whether regulatory or promotional. But there are more subtle explanations of industry orientation, which include the following:

First.—The division of responsibility between the regulated firms, which retain primary control over their own affairs, and the administrator, whose power is essentially negative and who is dependent on industry cooperation in order to achieve his objectives, places the administrator in an inherently weak position. The administrator will, nonetheless, be held responsible if the industry suffers serious economic dislocation. For both of these reasons, he may pursue conservative policies.

Second.—The regulatory bureaucracy becomes "regulation minded." It seeks to elaborate and perfect the controls it exercises over the regulated industry. . . .

Third.—The resources—in terms of money, personnel, and political influence—of the regulatory agency are limited in comparison to those of regulated firms. Unremitting maintenance of an adversary posture would quickly dissipate agency resources. Hence, the agency must compromise with the regulated industry if it is to accomplish anything of significance.

Fourth.—Limited agency resources imply that agencies must depend on outside sources of information, policy development, and political support. This outside input comes primarily from organized interests, such as regulated firms, that have a substantial stake in the substance of agency policy and the resources to provide such input. By contrast, the personal stake in agency policy of an individual member of an unorganized interest, such as a consumer, is normally too small to justify such representation. Effective representation of unorganized interests might be possible if a means of pooling resources to share the costs of underwriting collective representation were available. But this seems unlikely since the transaction costs of creating an organization of interest group members increase disproportionately as the size of the group increases. Moreover, if membership in such an organization is voluntary, individuals will not have a strong incentive to join, since if others represent the interests involved, the benefits will accrue not only to those participating in the representation, but to nonparticipants as well, who can, therefore, enjoy the benefits without incurring any of the costs (the free rider effect). As a somewhat disillusioned James Landis wrote in 1960, the result is industry dominance in representation, which has a "daily machine-gun like impact on both [an] agency and its staff" that tends to create an industry bias in the agency's outlook.

. . .

With the breakdown of both the "transmission belt" and "expertise" conceptualizations of the administrative process, administrative law theories that treat agencies as mere executors of legislative directives are no longer convincing. . . . Faced with the seemingly intractable problem of agency discretion, courts have changed the focus of judicial review (in the process expanding and transforming traditional procedural devices) so that its dominant purpose is no longer the prevention of unauthorized intrusions on private autonomy, but the assurance of fair representation for all affected interests in the exercise of the legislative power delegated to agencies.

Implicit in this development is the assumption that there is no ascertainable, transcendent "public interest," but only the distinct interests of various individuals and groups in society. Under this assumption, legislation represents no more than compromises struck between competing interest groups. This analysis suggests that if agencies were to function as a forum for all interests affected by agency decisionmaking, bargaining leading to compromises generally acceptable to all might result, thus replicating the process of legislation. Agency decisions made after adequate consideration of all affected interests would have, in microcosm, legitimacy based on the same principle as legislation and therefore the fact that statutes cannot control agency discretion would become largely irrelevant.

. . .

The transformation of the traditional model into a model of interest representation has in large degree been achieved through an expansion of the class of interests entitled to seek judicial review of agency action. . . .

. . .

. . . Restraining governmental power within statutory bounds and securing a minimum of formal justice no longer suffice as tests of validity in agency conduct. The pluralist diagnosis of bias in discretionary agency policy choices requires that administrators also take into account each of the wide variety of relevant interests differentially affected by possible policy alternatives.

Under this diagnosis, the problem of administrative procedure is to provide representation for all affected interests; the problem of substantive policy is to reach equitable accommodations among these interests in varying circumstances; and the problem of judicial review is to ensure that agencies provide fair procedures for representation and reach fair accommodations. These difficulties are ultimately attributable to the disintegration of any fixed and simple boundary between private ordering and collective authority. The extension of government administration into so many areas formerly left to private determination has outstripped the capacities of traditional political and judicial machinery to control and legitimate its exercise. In the absence of authoritative directives from the legislature, decisional processes have become decentralized and agency policy has become in large degree a function of bargaining and exchange with and among the competing private interests whom the agency is supposed to rule. Private ordering has been swallowed up by government, while government has become in part a species of private ordering. Where the governmental and private spheres are thus melded, administrative law must devise a process, distinct from either traditional political or judicial models, that both reconciles the competing private interests at stake and justifies the ultimately coercive exercise of governmental authority. The notion of adequate consideration of all affected interests is one ideal of such a process. Whether judicial resources and machinery can realize that ideal is the question that must next be addressed.

. . .

[T]he expansion of participation rights at the agency level is unlikely to resolve the fundamental problem of asserted bias in agency choice under broad legislative delegations. By multiplying the range of interests that must be considered, by underscoring the complexity of the issues involved, and by developing a more complete record of alternatives and competing considerations, expanded participation rights may reduce the extent to which procedures will effectively control agency discretion in decisionmaking. Indeed, by emphasizing the polycentric character of controversies, expanded representation may decrease their tractability to general rules and exacerbate the ad hoc, discretionary character of their resolution.

. . .

The ideal of rational decision [making] assertedly consists in the best resolution and harmonization of conflicting interests, but since there is generally no agreed-upon criterion of what constitutes a "best solution," decisionmaking will normally be a question of preferring some interests to others. After even the most attentive consideration of the contending affected interests, there is still the inescapable question of the weight to be accorded to each interest and the values invoked in its support. Statutory directives will generally be of little assistance in assigning weights to the various affected interests, since the problem of broad agency discretion generally grows out of a legislative inability or unwillingness to strike a definitive balance among competing values and interest groups.

. . .

It is perhaps surprising that any different outcome should have been expected. As long as agency discretion to set substantive policy is unconstrained by legislative directives or any other exogenous limits, formal procedures may serve to delineate conflicting claims, but procedures alone cannot resolve them. Although broad statutory delegations have eroded the justifications for the procedural requirements of the traditional model and impaired their effectiveness in controlling outcomes, the contemporary enthusiasm for public interest representation suggests that formal procedures maintain great symbolic power as guarantors of just results. However, where agencies exercise considerable d[i]scretion over policy choices, there is no a priori reason to believe that a "more equitable policy" will necessarily "evolve out of an adversary proceeding in which all affected interests [are] effectively represented."

. . .

. . . Because it is so directly concerned with reconciling government power and private interests, administrative law is peculiarly vulnerable to the intellectual and social pressures resulting from the juxtaposition of frayed ideals and current realities. In response to such pressures, stemming from the expansion of governmental influence over personal welfare and the contemporary perception that agencies enjoy discretion and that they have misused it to favor organized and regulated interests, judges have expanded formal participation rights in a fashion that points toward the development of an interest representation theory of administrative law to replace the traditional model. Whether a fully-articulated model of interest representation will emerge from these efforts, or whether interest representation is simply an interim stage in the emergence of some totally new conception of the relation between administrative institutions, legal controls, private groups, and social and individual values, is as yet unclear.... On the other hand, it is quite possible that no new encompassing theory of administrative law will emerge. The instinct for satisfying integration may remain a vain shuttlecock between no longer tenable conceptions of administrative legitimacy and the exigent difficulties of the present which have so far eluded a consistent general theory. Given "the undefined foreboding of something unknown," we can know only that we must spurn superficial analysis and simplistic remedies, girding ourselves to shoulder, for the indefinite future, the intellectual and social burdens of a dense complexity.

COMMENTS AND QUESTIONS

1. *Developments since the mid-1970s.* The basic contours of the processes Stewart described remained in place through the twentieth century. There were, of course, some modifications. As you will see in part IV, successive presidents have required federal regulatory agencies to engage in some form of cost-benefit analysis prior to issuing regulations. Presidents have sought to capture some of the political benefits that accrue from issuing popular regulations while distancing themselves from less popular ones. (For the classic analysis, see Elena Kagan, *Presidential Administration*, 114 Harv. L. Rev. 2245 (2001).) There has been some ratcheting down of the ability of "outside" groups, such as those described by Stewart as "public interest" groups, to participate in and secure review of agency rule making. But Stewart's account remains generally accurate.

For a summary a decade after Stewart wrote, consider these comments, from Robert Rabin, *Federal Regulation in Historical Perspective*, 38 Stan. L. Rev. 1189 (1986):

. . .

By the late 1970s, . . . the expansionist period of the Public Interest era had, in turn, run its course. For the first time in a century, a discernible political movement sought to reassess the need for regulatory programs that administered markets as a means of promoting the health of particular industries. This movement was exceedingly widespread: The regulatory system came under close scrutiny by policy institutes and journals, academic disciplines, and politically influential public officials who all came to focus on a clear and dominant emerging theme—deregulation.

. . .

. . . The increased focus on deregulation was not principally a reaction to the latest wave of regulatory reform—the social regulation of the Public Interest era. No serious effort was mounted to revoke the recent congressional initiatives in the areas of health, safety, and environmental protection—let alone to reassess the need for earlier Progressive era efforts to establish policing controls on the market. . . .

...

... [T]he rising storm of criticism over excessive regulation extended far beyond the field of legislative activity. Traditional administrative rulemaking—so-called command and control rulemaking—came under general attack for its economic inefficiency in failing to discriminate between low-cost and high-cost compliance activity. Critics excoriated administrative adjudication for its expense and delay. They further challenged agency priorities in establishing policy as failing to give precise consideration to the costs and benefits of various regulatory options—including the possibility of taking no action at all.

Lending a sympathetic ear, the Carter and Reagan administrations successively sought to sustain further the deregulatory mood through economic efficiency measures at the agency implementation stage—such as allowing the offsetting and trading of air pollution emissions credits under the Clean Air Act, and requiring cost-benefit justification from the agencies for "major" regulatory initiatives prior to administrative action. Indeed, the Reagan administration appeared to pursue a broader-based de facto deregulation policy by appointing unsympathetic agency administrators and proposing drastic budget cuts in regulatory programs untainted by congressional disapproval.

These latter efforts raised a serious question whether the development of the federal regulatory system had reached a major crossroad....

... [R]ecent efforts to place major ongoing regulatory programs in the hands of fundamentally unsympathetic administrators might suggest a far more ambitious ideological aim, namely, to reassess the need for regulatory institutions as a mechanism for policing the market. Whether such a phenomenon—which would place principal reliance on tort law, as in the nineteenth century, for regulating competitive practices—is imminent remains to be seen. Since Congress has shown no disposition to dismantle the plenary policing system it has established over the last century, the lines of tension caused by the new shift in regulatory politics, though faint, have been sufficiently evident to cause reverberations in the courts.

...

Under close scrutiny, the Court's tendency to oscillate between rejection and acceptance when encountering regulatory reform reveals a pattern of sustained concerns about the nature of administrative government. Through the New Deal, the principal concern was *legitimacy*. ...

After the New Deal, the Court became preoccupied with the nature of agency *discretion*, as distinguished from its legitimacy. Concerns about process replaced those related to substantive reach. For a time in the post–New Deal era, this emerging set of new concerns yielded a quiescent period of grace. But then in the early 1970s the regulatory system was exposed to a new set of shock-waves as the courts—including the Supreme Court, for a brief moment—proclaimed the dawning of a new era of relations between the judiciary and the administrative system.

This new and dramatically assertive judicial mood was marked from the outset by expressions of doubt. Since the New Deal, deference to the agencies had been rationalized in terms of expertise. Now, in an era marked by burgeoning claims on behalf of the environment, public health, and consumer safety, agency expertise had to be given new meaning. As the agencies took seriously the mandate to engage in long-term planning the courts were confronted with fundamental questions of process. Were the agencies required to adopt a comprehensive approach to decisionmaking in which no stone was left unturned? Were the regulators mandated to provide purely technocratic resolutions to issues of policy, or were they free to respond to "political" considerations in implementing statutory commands? Were administrative officials hybrid decisionmakers—operating somewhere in the netherland among the roles of legislator, policy expert, and judge—and, if so, how might a reasonable measure of control be exercised over their activities?

These intractable questions accounted for the judicial oscillation between a search for the Right Answer and tolerance of a Best Effort during the 1970s. . . .

. . .

Thus, a half-century after the New Deal—a century after the birth of the federal regulatory system—the world-wise French aphorism seems not entirely out of place, "*plus ca change, plus c'est la meme chose.*" The system has grown by leaps and bounds, yet it remains devoid of any coherent ideological framework. In the political sphere, while a broad-ranging commitment to government intervention seems a continuing legacy of the New Deal, no consensus exists on the appropriate scope of federal regulatory activities. The long-standing tension between a regulatory system dedicated to effective policing of the market and one which would stimulate cooperation among private interests—a tension as venerable as the federal regulatory presence itself—has never been conclusively resolved. . . .

. . . The courts have not developed a consistent approach to controlling agency discretion. Such an approach would have to draw on a theory of administrative expertise that dealt coherently with the technical and political dimensions of the regulatory process. Lacking an intelligible theoretical framework, the Supreme Court has oscillated between activism and restraint in reviewing agency decisions. Like Congress, the judicial system gets higher marks for pragmatism and flexibility in dealing with each successive wave of regulatory reform than it does for intellectual coherence and certainty of approach.

2. Note Stewart's invocation of the idea of polycentricity and his argument that committing polycentric decisions to administrative agencies may be an inadequate method of dealing with polycentricity. For Fuller, the alternative would then be to commit the decisions to legislatures. But in the modern regulatory state, is that possible? Stewart describes several adaptations designed to alleviate the problems associated with administrative discretion in the regulatory state. If those are inadequate, as he suggests they might be, what else might be

done? We take up some ideas about larger innovations in regulatory techniques in chapter 15.

3. Administrative agencies have been justified as vehicles for the deployment of the knowledge held by experts in particular fields. Stewart describes efforts to increase the accountability of agencies to democratic majorities, a theme in the *Chevron* doctrine as well. Recall the Slovic articles in chapter 4, which suggest that there may be an inevitable tension between expertise and democratic accountability. If so, is there any ultimately satisfactory solution to the problems Stewart describes?

B Rule Making under the Administrative Procedure Act

Federal administrative agencies must translate the substantive standards of their organic statutes into agency-developed rules. Administrative lawyers refer to rule making as "formal" and "informal." Our focus here is on informal or "notice-and-comment" rule making, which is the predominant form. Agencies use formal rule making only when their organic statutes require them to do so, using the "code words" for formal rule making: "rule making on the record after opportunity for an agency hearing."

In notice-and-comment rule making, the agency gives a "notice of proposed rule making," basically making a proposal for a new rule, backed up by the agency's reasons for the rule. The public is given an opportunity to comment on the proposed rule, after which the agency issues a final rule, sometimes modified in response to the comments. Judicial review typically ensues, requested either by regulated industries that believe the rule too stringent or by public interest groups that believe it too lax.

The notice-and-comment rule-making process is a hybrid of expertise and democratic accountability. The agency relies on its expertise to identify a problem to target and to develop a proposal. The public's comments largely reflect a concern for public accountability but also reflect a concern for expertise—both the possibility that the agency's experts will have some sort of bias (recall the article by Gillette and Krier in chapter 5) and the availability of different expertise outside the agency. And it can be argued that the reasoned elaboration with which the agency defends its rule following public comments itself serves as an accountability device (see the excerpt from Fuller in chapter 4).

It is questionable, however, whether expertise and accountability exist in judicial review of agency rules. Federal judges are generalists, not experts, and they are only indirectly accountable (at the point when they take their jobs with presidential nomination and Senate confirmation). Thus we might ask: Are judges particularly good at identifying whether agency processes have been fair? At identifying whether agencies have provided an adequately reasoned elaboration in defense of their rules?

Read carefully the following provisions of the Administrative Procedure Act (APA). The provisions are followed by a case that deals with rule making under the APA, which is one of the early reactions against some of the developments Stewart describes.

5 U.S.C. § 553. RULE MAKING

(a) This section applies, according to the provisions thereof, except to the extent that there is involved—

    (1) a military or foreign affairs function of the United States; or

    (2) a matter relating to agency management or personnel or to public property, loans, grants, benefits, or contracts.

(b) General notice of proposed rule making shall be published in the Federal Register, unless persons subject thereto are named and either personally served or otherwise have actual notice thereof in accordance with law. The notice shall include—

    (1) a statement of the time, place, and nature of public rulemaking proceedings;

    (2) reference to the legal authority under which the rule is proposed; and

    (3) either the terms or substance of the proposed rule or a description of the subjects and issues involved. Except when notice or hearing is required by statute, this subsection does not apply—

        (A) to interpretative rules, general statements of policy, or rules of agency organization, procedure, or practice; or

        (B) when the agency for good cause finds (and incorporates the finding and a brief statement of reasons therefor in the rules issued) that notice and public procedure thereon are impracticable, unnecessary, or contrary to the public interest.

(c) After notice required by this section, the agency shall give interested persons an opportunity to participate in the rule making through submission of written data, views, or arguments with or without opportunity for oral presentation. After consideration of the relevant matter presented, the agency shall incorporate in the rules adopted a concise general statement of their basis and purpose. When rules are required by statute to be made on the record after opportunity for an agency hearing, sections 556 and 557 of this title apply instead of this subsection.

(d) The required publication or service of a substantive rule shall be made not less than 30 days before its effective date, except—

    (1) a substantive rule which grants or recognizes an exemption or relieves a restriction;

    (2) interpretative rules and statements of policy; or

    (3) as otherwise provided by the agency for good cause found and published with the rule.

(e) Each agency shall give an interested person the right to petition for the issuance, amendment, or repeal of a rule.

5 U.S.C. § 706. SCOPE OF REVIEW

To the extent necessary to decision and when presented, the reviewing court shall decide all relevant questions of law, interpret constitutional and statutory provisions, and determine the meaning or applicability of the terms of an agency action. The reviewing court shall—

    (1) compel agency action unlawfully withheld or unreasonably delayed; and

(2) hold unlawful and set aside agency action, findings, and conclusions found to be—

    (A) arbitrary, capricious, an abuse of discretion, or otherwise not in accordance with law;

    (B) contrary to constitutional right, power, privilege, or immunity;

    (C) in excess of statutory jurisdiction, authority, or limitations, or short of statutory right;

    (D) without observance of procedure required by law;

    (E) unsupported by substantial evidence in a case subject to sections 556 and 557 of this title or otherwise reviewed on the record of an agency hearing provided by statute; or

    (F) unwarranted by the facts to the extent that the facts are subject to trial de novo by the reviewing court. In making the foregoing determinations, the court shall review the whole record or those parts of it cited by a party, and due account shall be taken of the rule of prejudicial error.

■ Vermont Yankee Nuclear Power Corp. v. Natural Resources Defense Council

435 U.S. 519 (1978)

Justice Rehnquist delivered the opinion of the Court, in which all other Members joined except Justices Blackmun and Powell, who took no part in the consideration or decision of the cases.

In 1946, Congress enacted the Administrative Procedure Act, which as we have noted elsewhere was not only "a new, basic and comprehensive regulation of procedures in many agencies," *Wong Yang Sung v. McGrath*, 339 U.S. 33 (1950), but was also a legislative enactment which settled "long-continued and hard-fought contentions, and enacts a formula upon which opposing social and political forces have come to rest." Id., at 40. Section 4 of the Act, 5 U.S.C. § 553, dealing with rulemaking, requires in subsection (b) that "notice of proposed rule making shall be published in the Federal Register...," describes the contents of that notice, and goes on to require in subsection (c) that after the notice the agency "shall give interested persons an opportunity to participate in the rule making through submission of written data, views, or arguments with or without opportunity for oral presentation. After consideration of the relevant matter presented, the agency shall incorporate in the rules adopted a concise general statement of their basis and purpose." Interpreting this provision of the Act in *United States v. Allegheny-Ludlum Steel Corp.*, 406 U.S. 742 (1972), and *United States v. Florida East Coast R. Co.*, 410 U.S. 224 (1973), we held that generally speaking this section of the Act established the maximum procedural requirements which Congress was willing to have the courts impose upon agencies in conducting rulemaking procedures. Agencies are free to grant additional procedural rights in the exercise of their discretion, but reviewing courts are generally not free to impose them if the agencies have not chosen to grant them. This is not to say necessarily that there are no circumstances which would ever justify a court in overturning agency action because of a failure to employ procedures beyond those required by the statute. But such circumstances, if they exist, are extremely rare.

Even apart from the Administrative Procedure Act this Court has for more than four decades emphasized that the formulation of procedures was basically to be left within the discretion of the agencies to which Congress had confided the responsibility for substantive judgments. In *FCC v. Schreiber*, 381 U.S. 279, 290 (1965), the Court explicated this principle, describing it as "an outgrowth of the congressional determination that administrative agencies and administrators will be familiar with the industries which they regulate and will be in a better position than federal courts or Congress itself to design procedural rules adapted to the peculiarities of the industry and the tasks of the agency involved." . . .

It is in the light of this background of statutory and decisional law that we granted certiorari to review two judgments of the Court of Appeals for the District of Columbia Circuit because of our concern that they had seriously misread or misapplied this statutory and decisional law cautioning reviewing courts against engrafting their own notions of proper procedures upon agencies entrusted with substantive functions by Congress. We conclude that the Court of Appeals has done just that in these cases, and we therefore remand them to it for further proceedings. . . .

I

A

Under the Atomic Energy Act of 1954, 68 Stat. 919, as amended, 42 U.S.C. § 2011 et seq., the Atomic Energy Commission[2] was given broad regulatory authority over the development of nuclear energy. Under the terms of the Act, a utility seeking to construct and operate a nuclear power plant must obtain a separate permit or license at both the construction and the operation stage of the project. In order to obtain the construction permit, the utility must file a preliminary safety analysis report, an environmental report, and certain information regarding the antitrust implications of the proposed project. This application then undergoes exhaustive review by the Commission's staff and by the Advisory Committee on Reactor Safeguards (ACRS), a group of distinguished experts in the field of atomic energy. Both groups submit to the Commission their own evaluations, which then become part of the record of the utility's application. The Commission staff also undertakes the review required by the National Environmental Policy Act of 1969 (NEPA), 42 U.S.C. § 4321 et seq., and prepares a draft environmental impact statement, which, after being circulated for comment, is revised and becomes a final environmental impact statement. Thereupon a three-member Atomic Safety and Licensing Board conducts a public adjudicatory hearing, and reaches a decision[4] which can be appealed to the Atomic Safety and Licensing Appeal Board, and currently, in the Commission's discretion, to the Commission itself. The final agency decision may

---

[2] The licensing and regulatory functions of the Atomic Energy Commission (AEC) were transferred to the Nuclear Regulatory Commission (NRC) by the Energy Reorganization Act of 1974. Hereinafter both the AEC and NRC will be referred to as the Commission.

[4] The Licensing Board issues a permit if it concludes that there is reasonable assurance that the proposed plant can be constructed and operated without undue risk, and that the environmental cost-benefit balance favors the issuance of a permit.

be appealed to the courts of appeals. The same sort of process occurs when the utility applies for a license to operate the plant, except that a hearing need only be held in contested cases and may be limited to the matters in controversy....

B

In December 1967, after the mandatory adjudicatory hearing and necessary review, the Commission granted petitioner Vermont Yankee a permit to build a nuclear power plant in Vernon, Vt. Thereafter, Vermont Yankee applied for an operating license. Respondent Natural Resources Defense Council (NRDC) objected to the granting of a license, however, and therefore a hearing on the application commenced on August 10, 1971. Excluded from consideration at the hearings, over NRDC's objection, was the issue of the environmental effects of operations to reprocess fuel or dispose of wastes resulting from the reprocessing operations.[6] This ruling was affirmed by the Appeal Board in June 1972.

In November 1972, however, the Commission, making specific reference to the Appeal Board's decision with respect to the Vermont Yankee license, instituted rulemaking proceedings "that would specifically deal with the question of consideration of environmental effects associated with the uranium fuel cycle in the individual cost-benefit analyses for light water cooled nuclear power reactors." The notice of proposed rulemaking offered two alternatives, both predicated on a report prepared by the Commission's staff entitled Environmental Survey of the Nuclear Fuel Cycle. The first would have required no quantitative evaluation of the environmental hazards of fuel reprocessing or disposal because the Environmental Survey had found them to be slight. The second would have specified numerical values for the environmental impact of this part of the fuel cycle, which values would then be incorporated into a table, along with the other relevant factors, to determine the overall cost-benefit balance for each operating license.

Much of the controversy in this case revolves around the procedures used in the rulemaking hearing which commenced in February 1973. In a supplemental notice of hearing the Commission indicated that while discovery or cross-examination would not be utilized, the Environmental Survey would be available to the public before the hearing along with the extensive background documents cited therein. All participants would be given a reasonable opportunity to present their position and could be represented by counsel if they so desired. Written and, time permitting, oral statements would be received and incorporated into the record. All persons giving oral statements would be subject to questioning by the Commission. At the conclusion of the hearing, a transcript would be made available to the public and the record would remain open for 30 days to allow the filing of supplemental

---

[6] The nuclear fission which takes place in light-water nuclear reactors apparently converts its principal fuel, uranium, into plutonium, which is itself highly radioactive but can be used as reactor fuel if separated from the remaining uranium and radioactive waste products. Fuel reprocessing refers to the process necessary to recapture usable plutonium. Waste disposal, at the present stage of technological development, refers to the storage of the very long lived and highly radioactive waste products until they detoxify sufficiently that they no longer present an environmental hazard. There are presently no physical or chemical steps which render this waste less toxic, other than simply the passage of time.

written statements. More than 40 individuals and organizations representing a wide variety of interests submitted written comments. On January 17, 1973, the Licensing Board held a planning session to schedule the appearance of witnesses and to discuss methods for compiling a record. The hearing was held on February 1 and 2, with participation by a number of groups, including the Commission's staff, the United States Environmental Protection Agency, a manufacturer of reactor equipment, a trade association from the nuclear industry, a group of electric utility companies, and a group called Consolidated National Intervenors which represented 79 groups and individuals including respondent NRDC.

After the hearing, the Commission's staff filed a supplemental document for the purpose of clarifying and revising the Environmental Survey. Then the Licensing Board forwarded its report to the Commission without rendering any decision. The Licensing Board identified as the principal procedural question the propriety of declining to use full formal adjudicatory procedures. The major substantive issue was the technical adequacy of the Environmental Survey.

In April 1974, the Commission issued a rule which adopted the second of the two proposed alternatives described above. The Commission also approved the procedures used at the hearing,[7] and indicated that the record, including the Environmental Survey, provided an "adequate data base for the regulation adopted." Finally, the Commission ruled that to the extent the rule differed from the Appeal Board decisions in Vermont Yankee "those decisions have no further precedential significance," but that since "the environmental effects of the uranium fuel cycle have been shown to be relatively insignificant, . . . it is unnecessary to apply the amendment to applicant's environmental reports submitted prior to its effective date or to Final Environmental Statements for which Draft Environmental Statements have been circulated for comment prior to the effective date."

Respondents appealed from both the Commission's adoption of the rule and its decision to grant Vermont Yankee's license to the Court of Appeals for the District of Columbia Circuit.

. . .

D

With respect to the challenge of Vermont Yankee's license, the court first ruled that in the absence of effective rulemaking proceedings, the Commission must deal with the environmental impact of fuel reprocessing and disposal in individual licensing

---

[7] The Commission stated:

"In our view, the procedures adopted provide a more than adequate basis for formulation of the rule we adopted. All parties were fully heard. Nothing offered was excluded. The record does not indicate that any evidentiary material would have been received under different procedures. Nor did the proponent of the strict 'adjudicatory' approach make an offer of proof—or even remotely suggest—what substantive matters it would develop under different procedures. In addition, we note that 11 documents including the Survey were available to the parties several weeks before the hearing, and the Regulatory staff, though not requested to do so, made available various drafts and handwritten notes. Under all of the circumstances, we conclude that adjudicatory type procedures were not warranted here."

proceedings. The court then examined the rulemaking proceedings and, despite the fact that it appeared that the agency employed all the procedures required by 5 U.S.C. § 553 and more, the court determined the proceedings to be inadequate and overturned the rule. Accordingly, the Commission's determination with respect to Vermont Yankee's license was also remanded for further proceedings. . . .

II

A

. . . [A]t this stage of the proceedings the only question presented for review in this regard is whether the Commission may consider the environmental impact of the fuel processes when licensing nuclear reactors. In addition to the weight which normally attaches to the agency's determination of such a question, other reasons support the Commission's conclusion.

Vermont Yankee will produce annually well over 100 pounds of radioactive wastes, some of which will be highly toxic. The Commission itself, in a pamphlet published by its information office, clearly recognizes that these wastes "pose the most severe potential health hazard. . . ." Many of these substances must be isolated for anywhere from 600 to hundreds of thousands of years. It is hard to argue that these wastes do not constitute "adverse environmental effects which cannot be avoided should the proposal be implemented," or that by operating nuclear power plants we are not making "irreversible and irretrievable commitments of resources." . . . For these reasons we hold that the Commission acted well within its statutory authority when it considered the back end of the fuel cycle in individual licensing proceedings.

B

We next turn to the invalidation of the fuel cycle rule. . . .

. . . [T]he majority of the Court of Appeals struck down the rule because of the perceived inadequacies of the procedures employed in the rulemaking proceedings. The court first determined the intervenors' primary argument to be "that the decision to preclude 'discovery or cross-examination' denied them a meaningful opportunity to participate in the proceedings as guaranteed by due process." The court then went on to frame the issue for decision thus:

> "Thus, we are called upon to decide whether the procedures provided by the agency were sufficient to ventilate the issues."

The court conceded that absent extraordinary circumstances it is improper for a reviewing court to prescribe the procedural format an agency must follow, but it likewise clearly thought it entirely appropriate to "scrutinize the record as a whole to insure that genuine opportunities to participate in a meaningful way were provided. . . ." The court also refrained from actually ordering the agency to follow any specific procedures, but there is little doubt in our minds that the ineluctable mandate of the court's decision is that the procedures afforded during the hearings were inadequate. This conclusion is particularly buttressed by the fact that after the court examined the record, particularly the testimony of Dr. Pittman, and declared it insufficient, the court proceeded to discuss at some length the necessity for further procedural devices or a more "sensitive" application of those devices employed during the proceedings....

In prior opinions we have intimated that even in a rule-making proceeding when an agency is making a " 'quasi-judicial' " determination by which a very small number of persons are " 'exceptionally affected, in each case upon individual grounds,' " in some circumstances additional procedures may be required in order to afford the aggrieved individuals due process.[16] *United States v. Florida East Coast R. Co.*, 410 U.S., at 242, 245, quoting from *Bi-Metallic Investment Co. v. State Board of Equalization*, 239 U.S. 441, 446 (1915). It might also be true, although we do not think the issue is presented in this case and accordingly do not decide it, that a totally unjustified departure from well-settled agency procedures of long standing might require judicial correction.

But this much is absolutely clear. Absent constitutional constraints or extremely compelling circumstances the "administrative agencies 'should be free to fashion their own rules of procedure and to pursue methods of inquiry capable of permitting them to discharge their multitudinous duties.' " *FCC v. Schreiber*, 381 U.S., at 290, quoting from *FCC v. Pottsville Broadcasting Co.*, 309 U.S., at 143....

. . .

Respondent NRDC argues that § 4 of the Administrative Procedure Act, 5 U.S.C. § 553, merely establishes lower procedural bounds and that a court may routinely require more than the minimum when an agency's proposed rule addresses complex or technical factual issues or "Issues of Great Public Import." We have, however, previously shown that our decisions reject this view. We also think the legislative history, even the part which it cites, does not bear out its contention. The Senate Report explains what eventually became § 4 thus:

> "This subsection states . . . the minimum requirements of public rule making procedure short of statutory hearing. Under it agencies might in addition confer with industry advisory committees, consult organizations, hold informal 'hearings,' and the like. Considerations of practicality, necessity, and public interest . . . will naturally govern the agency's determination of the extent to which public proceedings should go. Matters of great import, or those where the public submission of facts will be either useful to the agency or a protection to the public, should naturally be accorded more elaborate public procedures." S. Rep. No. 752, 79th Cong., 1st Sess., 14–15 (1945).

The House Report is in complete accord.... And the Attorney General's Manual on the Administrative Procedure Act 31, 35 (1947), a contemporaneous interpretation previously given some deference by this Court because of the role played by the Department of Justice in drafting the legislation, further confirms that view. In short, all of this leaves little doubt that Congress intended that the discretion of the agencies and not that of the courts be exercised in determining when extra procedural devices should be employed.

---

[16] Respondent NRDC does not now argue that additional procedural devices were required under the Constitution. Since this was clearly a rulemaking proceeding in its purest form, we see nothing to support such a view.

There are compelling reasons for construing § 4 in this manner. In the first place, if courts continually review agency proceedings to determine whether the agency employed procedures which were, in the court's opinion, perfectly tailored to reach what the court perceives to be the "best" or "correct" result, judicial review would be totally unpredictable. And the agencies, operating under this vague injunction to employ the "best" procedures and facing the threat of reversal if they did not, would undoubtedly adopt full adjudicatory procedures in every instance. Not only would this totally disrupt the statutory scheme, through which Congress enacted "a formula upon which opposing social and political forces have come to rest," *Wong Yang Sung v. McGrath*, 339 U.S., at 40, but all the inherent advantages of informal rulemaking would be totally lost.

Secondly, it is obvious that the court in these cases reviewed the agency's choice of procedures on the basis of the record actually produced at the hearing, and not on the basis of the information available to the agency when it made the decision to structure the proceedings in a certain way. This sort of Monday morning quarter-backing not only encourages but almost compels the agency to conduct all rulemaking proceedings with the full panoply of procedural devices normally associated only with adjudicatory hearings.

Finally, and perhaps most importantly, this sort of review fundamentally misconceives the nature of the standard for judicial review of an agency rule. The court below uncritically assumed that additional procedures will automatically result in a more adequate record because it will give interested parties more of an opportunity to participate in and contribute to the proceedings. But informal rulemaking need not be based solely on the transcript of a hearing held before an agency. Indeed, the agency need not even hold a formal hearing. See 5 U.S.C. § 553 (c). Thus, the adequacy of the "record" in this type of proceeding is not correlated directly to the type of procedural devices employed, but rather turns on whether the agency has followed the statutory mandate of the Administrative Procedure Act or other relevant statutes. If the agency is compelled to support the rule which it ultimately adopts with the type of record produced only after a full adjudicatory hearing, it simply will have no choice but to conduct a full adjudicatory hearing prior to promulgating every rule. In sum, this sort of unwarranted judicial examination of perceived procedural shortcomings of a rulemaking proceeding can do nothing but seriously interfere with that process prescribed by Congress....

In short, nothing in the APA, NEPA, the circumstances of this case, the nature of the issues being considered, past agency practice, or the statutory mandate under which the Commission operates permitted the court to review and overturn the rulemaking proceeding on the basis of the procedural devices employed (or not employed) by the Commission so long as the Commission employed at least the statutory minima, a matter about which there is no doubt in this case.

There remains, of course, the question of whether the challenged rule finds sufficient justification in the administrative proceedings that it should be upheld by the reviewing court. Judge Tamm, concurring in the result reached by the majority of the Court of Appeals, thought that it did not. There are also intimations in the majority opinion which suggest that the judges who joined it likewise may have thought the administrative proceedings an insufficient basis upon which to predicate the rule in question. We accordingly remand so that the Court of Appeals may review the rule as the Administrative Procedure Act provides. We have made it abundantly clear before that when there is a contemporaneous explanation of the agency decision, the validity of that action must "stand or fall on the propriety of that finding, judged, of course, by the appropriate standard of review. If that finding is not sustainable on the administrative record made, then the Comptroller's decision must be vacated and the matter remanded to him for further consideration." *Camp v. Pitts*, 411 U.S. 138, 143 (1973). See also *SEC v. Chenery Corp.*, 318 U.S. 80 (1943). The court should engage in this kind of review and not stray beyond the judicial province to explore the procedural format or to impose upon the agency its own notion of which procedures are "best" or most likely to further some vague, undefined public good.

. . . .

All this leads us to make one further observation of some relevance to this case. To say that the Court of Appeals' final reason for remanding is insubstantial at best is a gross understatement. Consumers Power first applied in 1969 for a construction permit—not even an operating license, just a construction permit. The proposed plant underwent an incredibly extensive review. The reports filed and reviewed literally fill books. The proceedings took years, and the actual hearings themselves over two weeks. To then nullify that effort seven years later because one report refers to other problems, which problems admittedly have been discussed at length in other reports available to the public, borders on the Kafkaesque. Nuclear energy may some day be a cheap, safe source of power or it may not. But Congress has made a choice to at least try nuclear energy, establishing a reasonable review process in which courts are to play only a limited role. The fundamental policy questions appropriately resolved in Congress and in the state legislatures are not subject to reexamination in the federal courts under the guise of judicial review of agency action. Time may prove wrong the decision to develop nuclear energy, but it is Congress or the States within their appropriate agencies which must eventually make that judgment. In the meantime courts should perform their appointed function. . . . Administrative decisions should be set aside in this context, as in every other, only for substantial procedural or substantive reasons as mandated by statute, not simply because the court is unhappy with the result reached. . . .

COMMENTS AND QUESTIONS

1. The (unanimous) Supreme Court gives short shrift to the position taken by the court of appeals that the record failed to show that the objectors had been given "genuine opportunities to participate in a meaningful way" and whether the agency had taken a "hard look" at the questions before it. The court of appeals held that, to ensure that participants did indeed have such opportunities, additional procedures, beyond those clearly mandated by the APA, had to be provided, using discovery and cross-examination as examples. The statute says that the agency "shall give interested persons an opportunity to participate." Does that imply that the opportunity must be "meaningful"? (How would Llewellyn answer that question?) Would the opportunity lack meaning in the absence of discovery and the like? Consider the proposition that adding those procedures converts notice-and-comment rule making into formal, on-the-record rule making.

2. The Supreme Court allows the agency to determine the procedures it will use to decide the substantive questions presented. Is this an appropriate allocation of responsibility? Why aren't *courts* the place to decide what procedures should be used? Agencies are experts in the substantive matters they deal with (nuclear power and its effects in *Vermont Yankee*), but do they have any advantage over courts in determining what procedures are the right ones to use to determine the answers to substantive questions? Note that judicially mandated procedures impose costs on the agencies, which could impede their ability to carry out as much of their substantive mandate as they could under procedures chosen by the agencies themselves.

3. Would it be constitutional for a legislature to eliminate discovery and cross-examination in a typical tort action? The case would be decided (by a jury?) based on written submissions and responses. Would such a procedure provide the fundamental fairness that the Due Process Clauses attempt to ensure? Note that the Supreme Court says that nothing in *Vermont Yankee* would support the argument that the Constitution required the agency to use the procedures the court of appeals required. What differences might there be between the kinds of factual determinations the agency makes in *Vermont Yankee* and those made by juries in tort cases? Administrative lawyers distinguish between *adjudicative* facts—those that deal with the particulars of specific incidents—and *legislative* facts, which involve larger numbers of facts and strongly implicate policy questions. They acknowledge that this distinction breaks down around the edges, as a case like *Farwell* indicates. (Ask yourself why we refer to *Farwell* here.) Nevertheless, they contend there is a difference between ordinary tort cases and *Vermont Yankee*. Do you agree?

4. The Supreme Court in *Vermont Yankee* remands the case and directs the court of appeals to review the rule based on the record the agency compiled. On remand, how might the court of appeals have accomplished the result it initially sought? The court might have found that the record did not provide a sufficient basis for the rule. One catalogue of techniques suggests that the court tell the agency to "explore more alternatives, give a more detailed explanation, disclose considerations and staff information, [and] demonstrate adequate consideration of statutory factors." Christopher Edley Jr., Administrative Law: Rethinking Judicial Control of Bureaucracy 228 (1990). We revisit the *Vermont Yankee* rule making in section C.

   A finding of insufficient basis to support the rule would have required the agency to determine how to supplement the record, which might have led to the adoption of the procedures the court of appeals initially mandated—procedures that would enhance the record on which the agency acted. In light of such a judicial response, how much does *Vermont Yankee* actually accomplish? (In practice, quite a bit: Not surprisingly, the courts of appeals heeded the case's signal to back off from aggressive review of agency notice-and-comment rule making.)

5. *Vermont Yankee* was decided by interpreting the APA and does not foreclose Congress from requiring additional procedures beyond those the agencies choose. (Indeed, the APA itself contains provisions dealing with formal,

on-the-record rule making that are more stringent than those used in notice-and-comment rule making.) *Vermont Yankee*'s effect, thus, is to shift from the courts to Congress the power to innovate procedurally, with respect to particular problems.

Consider these observations by then-professor Antonin Scalia:

> [O]ne of the functions of procedure is to limit power—not just the power to be unfair, but the power to act in a political mode, or the power to act at all. Such limitation is sometimes an incidental result of pursuing other functions, such as efficiency and fairness; but it may be an end in itself.... Congress can ... refrain from making use of the connection between procedure and power, but it cannot make that connection itself disappear. Thus, to the extent that the choice of procedures is left to the agencies themselves, to that same extent the agencies are left to determine a substantial aspect of their own power....
>
> Scalia, Vermont Yankee: *The APA, the D.C. Circuit*
> *and the Supreme Court*, 1978 Sup. Ct. Rev. 345

Does the system that results from *Vermont Yankee* sensibly allocate responsibility among Congress, courts, and agencies? Why—or when—would Congress focus on the procedures agencies use? Do members of Congress have greater incentives than judges to deliberate about appropriate procedures? More expertise? Note again, though, that procedure is inevitably bound up with substance: The more elaborate the procedures mandated, the harder it is to develop a rule (that will survive judicial review). Is the choice of the substance-procedure package itself a polycentric problem?

6. The news account that follows describes some aspects of contemporary notice-and-comment rule making. In light of the developments it describes, does that procedure today promote a desirable combination of expertise and accountability?

■ *Flooded with Comments, Officials Plug Their Ears*
KATHARINE Q. SEELYE
New York Times (Nov. 17, 2002). Reprinted with permission
of the *New York Times*

Over the last several years, the Interior Department has proposed a number of controversial ideas, like reintroducing wolves in Yellowstone, that have generated lots of mail during a public comment period. But few proposals have flooded the department with more mail—paper and electronic—than the one by the Bush administration to keep snowmobiles in Yellowstone and Grand Teton National Parks.

Last week, Interior Department officials said they had received 360,000 comments on the matter, the most ever on any question related to the national parks. The verdict? Ban the machines. Fully 80 percent of the writers wanted snowmobiles barred from the parks, just as the Clinton administration had proposed.

Yet even as officials of the National Park Service acknowledged the results of the comment period, they proposed to do just the opposite. They not only would allow the use of snowmobiles to continue in Yellowstone and Grand Teton and on a part of the John D. Rockefeller Jr. Memorial Parkway that connects them, but they would also allow for a 35 percent increase in the numbers, up to 1,100 a day from an average of 840 a day.

How did such overwhelming opposition to snowmobiles result in such a snowmobile-friendly decision? Officials said that there would be more snowmobiles, but that they would be newer, cleaner and quieter and that therefore any environmental damage would be reduced.

Beyond that, officials say the sheer volume of public comment is not a determining factor. "It was not a vote," said Steve Iobst, assistant superintendent of Grand Teton. The point of the comment period, he said, is to yield substantive, informed letters that alert park officials to something they might have missed in reaching their conclusion.

In fact, the public comment period has become a widely discredited measure of public sentiment because it has been susceptible to what critics call AstroTurf campaigns, the opposite of real grass-roots efforts, in which advocacy groups encourage their members to sign their names on form letters.

This is especially true since the emergence of e-mail. Mr. Iobst said that over the three-day Memorial Day weekend alone, the Park Service received 45,000 e-mail messages on snowmobiles. He said the agency considered those comments in its decision, "but not at face value."

A court decision in 1987 gave officials clearance to ignore mass mailings. The United States Court of Appeals for the District of Columbia, in a ruling written by then Judge Kenneth W. Starr, said that a determination of a clean-water issue should not be based on the number of comments, most urging the Environmental Protection Agency to allow them to discharge pollutants into the water.

"The substantial-evidence standard has never been taken to mean that an agency rule-making is a democratic process by which the majority of commenters prevail by sheer weight of numbers," Judge Starr wrote.

Has a comment period ever truly influenced a decision? Chris Wood, a senior adviser to the Forest Service chief in the Clinton administration, said that typical agency behavior is to "develop the plan you want, announce a public comment period and then do what you want to do."

But, he said, the Forest Service actually relied on public comment when it developed its "roadless rule," intended to protect 58 million acres of undeveloped national forest from most commercial logging and road building. It drew 1.6 million comments, the most ever in the history of federal rule-making. Almost all the comments—95 percent—supported the protections but wanted the plan to go even further, which it eventually did.

But the Bush administration delayed putting the rule into effect and sought more comments, receiving 726,000. Of those, it said that only 52,000, or 7 percent, were "original," meaning that the administration discounted 93 percent of the comments. The rule is now being challenged in court.

Bush administration officials still say they value public opinion. In a speech in July, John Graham, head of the office of regulatory affairs in the Office of Management and Budget, said he was actively seeking public comment on various regulations and making an electronic comment form available.

Although the snowmobilers won their battle, the groups representing them say that the public comment period should be abolished. "What this outcome shows is that these huge hate-mail campaigns are not effective now and won't be in the future," said Clark Collins, executive director of the Blue Ribbon Coalition, an industry-backed lobbying group based in Idaho.

If the public comment periods ceased, he said, both sides could save a lot of time.

c Judicial Review of Agency Rules on the Merits: The "Arbitrary and Capricious" Standard

Vermont Yankee can be said to confine the judicial role to reviewing the merits of the agency's rules. The next cases examine the standard the courts use in that inquiry. In reading them, you should remember that the agency can defend its rules by referring only to the materials assembled in the record produced during rule making.

■ Motor Vehicle Manufacturers Assoc. v. State Farm Mutual Automobile Insurance Co.
463 U.S. 29 (1983)

Justice White delivered the opinion of the Court.

The development of the automobile gave Americans unprecedented freedom to travel, but exacted a high price for enhanced mobility. Since 1929, motor vehicles have been the leading cause of accidental deaths and injuries in the United States. In 1982, 46,300 Americans died in motor vehicle accidents and hundreds of thousands more were maimed and injured. While a consensus exists that the current loss of life on our highways is unacceptably high, improving safety does not admit to easy solution. In 1966, Congress decided that at least part of the answer lies in improving the design and safety features of the vehicle itself. But much of the technology for building safer cars was undeveloped or untested. Before changes in automobile design could be mandated, the effectiveness of these changes had to be studied, their costs examined, and public acceptance considered. This task called for considerable expertise and Congress responded by enacting the National Traffic and Motor Vehicle Safety Act of 1966 (Act). The Act, created for the purpose of "[reducing] traffic accidents and deaths and injuries to persons resulting from traffic accidents," directs the Secretary of Transportation or his delegate to issue motor vehicle safety standards that "shall be practicable, shall meet the need for motor vehicle safety, and shall be stated in objective terms." In issuing these standards, the Secretary is directed to consider "relevant available motor vehicle safety data," whether the proposed standard "is reasonable, practicable and appropriate" for the particular type of motor vehicle, and the "extent to which such standards will contribute to carrying out the purposes" of the Act.[3]

---

[3] The Secretary's general authority to promulgate safety standards under the Act has been delegated to the Administrator of the National Highway Traffic Safety Administration (NHTSA). This opinion will use the terms NHTSA and agency interchangeably when referring to the National Highway Traffic Safety Administration, the Department of Transportation, and the Secretary of Transportation.

The Act also authorizes judicial review under the provisions of the Administrative Procedure Act (APA), 5 U.S.C. § 706, of all "orders establishing, amending, or revoking a Federal motor vehicle safety standard." Under this authority, we review today whether NHTSA acted arbitrarily and capriciously in revoking the requirement in Motor Vehicle Safety Standard 208 that new motor vehicles produced after September 1982 be equipped with passive restraints to protect the safety of the occupants of the vehicle in the event of a collision. Briefly summarized, we hold that the agency failed to present an adequate basis and explanation for rescinding the passive restraint requirement and that the agency must either consider the matter further or adhere to or amend Standard 208 along lines which its analysis supports.

I

The regulation whose rescission is at issue bears a complex and convoluted history. Over the course of approximately 60 rulemaking notices, the requirement has been imposed, amended, rescinded, reimposed, and now rescinded again.

As originally issued by the Department of Transportation in 1967, Standard 208 simply required the installation of seatbelts in all automobiles. It soon became apparent that the level of seatbelt use was too low to reduce traffic injuries to an acceptable level. The Department therefore began consideration of "passive occupant restraint systems"—devices that do not depend for their effectiveness upon any action taken by the occupant except that necessary to operate the vehicle. Two types of automatic crash protection emerged: automatic seatbelts and airbags. The automatic seatbelt is a traditional safety belt, which when fastened to the interior of the door remains attached without impeding entry or exit from the vehicle, and deploys automatically without any action on the part of the passenger. The airbag is an inflatable device concealed in the dashboard and steering column. It automatically inflates when a sensor indicates that deceleration forces from an accident have exceeded a preset minimum, then rapidly deflates to dissipate those forces. The lifesaving potential of these devices was immediately recognized, and in 1977, after substantial on-the-road experience with both devices, it was estimated by NHTSA that passive restraints could prevent approximately 12,000 deaths and over 100,000 serious injuries annually.

In 1969, the Department formally proposed a standard requiring the installation of passive restraints, thereby commencing a lengthy series of proceedings. In 1970, the agency revised Standard 208 to include passive protection requirements, and in 1972, the agency amended the Standard to require full passive protection for all front seat occupants of vehicles manufactured after August 15, 1975. In the interim, vehicles built between August 1973 and August 1975 were to carry either passive restraints or lap and shoulder belts coupled with an "ignition interlock" that would prevent starting the vehicle if the belts were not connected. On review, the agency's decision to require passive restraints was found to be supported by "substantial evidence" and upheld.

In preparing for the upcoming model year, most car makers chose the "ignition interlock" option, a decision which was highly unpopular, and led Congress to amend the Act to prohibit a motor vehicle safety standard from requiring or permitting compliance by means of an ignition interlock or a continuous buzzer designed to indicate that safety belts were not in use. The 1974 Amendments also provided that any safety standard that could be satisfied by a system other than seatbelts would have to be submitted to Congress where it could be vetoed by concurrent resolution of both Houses.

The effective date for mandatory passive restraint systems was extended for a year until August 31, 1976. But in June 1976, Secretary of Transportation William T. Coleman, Jr., initiated a new rulemaking on the issue. After hearing testimony and reviewing written comments, Coleman extended the optional alternatives indefinitely and suspended the passive restraint requirement. Although he found passive restraints technologically and economically feasible, the Secretary based his decision on the expectation that there would be widespread public resistance to the new systems. He instead proposed a demonstration project involving up to 500,000 cars installed with passive restraints, in order to smooth the way for public acceptance of mandatory passive restraints at a later date.

Coleman's successor as Secretary of Transportation disagreed. Within months of assuming office, Secretary Brock Adams decided that the demonstration project was unnecessary. He issued a new mandatory passive restraint regulation, known as Modified Standard 208. The Modified Standard mandated the phasing in of passive restraints beginning with large cars in model year 1982 and extending to all cars by model year 1984. The two principal systems that would satisfy the Standard were airbags and passive belts; the choice of which system to install was left to the manufacturers. In *Pacific Legal Foundation v. Department of Transportation*, 593 F.2d 1338 (1979), the Court of Appeals upheld Modified Standard 208 as a rational, nonarbitrary regulation consistent with the agency's mandate under the Act. The Standard also survived scrutiny by Congress, which did not exercise its authority under the legislative veto provision of the 1974 Amendments.

Over the next several years, the automobile industry geared up to comply with Modified Standard 208. As late as July 1980, NHTSA reported:

> "On the road experience in thousands of vehicles equipped with air bags and automatic safety belts has confirmed agency estimates of the life-saving and injury-preventing benefits of such systems. When all cars are equipped with automatic crash protection systems, each year an estimated 9,000 more lives will be saved, and tens of thousands of serious injuries will be prevented."

In February 1981, however, Secretary of Transportation Andrew Lewis reopened the rulemaking due to changed economic circumstances and, in particular, the difficulties of the automobile industry. Two months later, the agency ordered a one-year delay in the application of the Standard to large cars, extending the deadline to September 1982, and at the same time, proposed the possible rescission of the entire Standard. After receiving written comments and holding public hearings, NHTSA issued a final rule (Notice 25) that rescinded the passive restraint requirement contained in Modified Standard 208.

II

In a statement explaining the rescission, NHTSA maintained that it was no longer able to find, as it had in 1977, that the automatic restraint requirement would produce significant safety benefits. This judgment reflected not a change of opinion on the effectiveness of the technology, but a change in plans by the automobile industry. In 1977, the agency had assumed that airbags would be installed in 60%

of all new cars and automatic seatbelts in 40%. By 1981 it became apparent that automobile manufacturers planned to install the automatic seatbelts in approximately 99% of the new cars. For this reason, the lifesaving potential of airbags would not be realized. Moreover, it now appeared that the overwhelming majority of passive belts planned to be installed by manufacturers could be detached easily and left that way permanently. Passive belts, once detached, then required "the same type of affirmative action that is the stumbling block to obtaining high usage levels of manual belts." For this reason, the agency concluded that there was no longer a basis for reliably predicting that the Standard would lead to any significant increased usage of restraints at all.

In view of the possibly minimal safety benefits, the automatic restraint requirement no longer was reasonable or practicable in the agency's view. The requirement would require approximately $1 billion to implement and the agency did not believe it would be reasonable to impose such substantial costs on manufacturers and consumers without more adequate assurance that sufficient safety benefits would accrue. In addition, NHTSA concluded that automatic restraints might have an adverse effect on the public's attitude toward safety. Given the high expense and limited benefits of detachable belts, NHTSA feared that many consumers would regard the Standard as an instance of ineffective regulation, adversely affecting the public's view of safety regulation and, in particular, "poisoning . . . popular sentiment toward efforts to improve occupant restraint systems in the future."

State Farm Mutual Automobile Insurance Co. and the National Association of Independent Insurers filed petitions for review of NHTSA's rescission of the passive restraint Standard. The United States Court of Appeals for the District of Columbia Circuit held that the agency's rescission of the passive restraint requirement was arbitrary and capricious.

. . .

III

Unlike the Court of Appeals, we do not find the appropriate scope of judicial review to be the "most troublesome question" in these cases. Both the Act and the 1974 Amendments concerning occupant crash protection standards indicate that motor vehicle safety standards are to be promulgated under the informal rulemaking procedures of the Administrative Procedure Act. 5 U.S.C. § 553. The agency's action in promulgating such standards therefore may be set aside if found to be "arbitrary, capricious, an abuse of discretion, or otherwise not in accordance with law." 5 U.S.C. § 706(2)(A); *Citizens to Preserve Overton Park v. Volpe*, 401 U.S. 402, 414 (1971). We believe that the rescission or modification of an occupant-protection standard is subject to the same test. . . .

Petitioner Motor Vehicle Manufacturers Association (MVMA) disagrees, contending that the rescission of an agency rule should be judged by the same standard a court would use to judge an agency's refusal to promulgate a rule in the first place—a standard petitioner believes considerably narrower than the traditional arbitrary-and-capricious test. We reject this view. The Act expressly equates orders "revoking" and "establishing" safety standards; neither that Act nor the APA suggests that revocations are to be treated as refusals to promulgate standards. Petitioner's view would render meaningless Congress' authorization for judicial review of orders revoking safety rules. Moreover, the revocation of an extant regulation is substantially different than a failure to act. Revocation constitutes a reversal of the agency's former views as to the proper course. A "settled course of behavior embodies the agency's informed judgment that, by pursuing that course, it will carry out the policies committed to it by Congress. There is, then, at least a presumption that those policies will be carried out best if the settled rule is adhered to." *Atchison, T. & S. F. R. Co. v. Wichita Bd. of Trade*, 412 U.S. 800, 807–808 (1973). Accordingly, an agency changing its course by rescinding a rule is obligated to supply a reasoned analysis for the change beyond that which may be required when an agency does not act in the first instance.

In so holding, we fully recognize that "[regulatory] agencies do not establish rules of conduct to last forever," *American Trucking Assns., Inc. v. Atchison, T. & S. F. R. Co.*, 387 U.S. 397, 416 (1967), and that an agency must be given ample latitude to "adapt their rules and policies to the demands of changing circumstances." *Permian Basin Area Rate Cases*, 390 U.S. 747, 784 (1968). But the forces of change do not always or necessarily point in the direction of deregulation. In the abstract, there is no more reason to presume that changing circumstances require the rescission of prior action, instead of a revision in or even the extension of current regulation. If Congress established a presumption from which judicial review should start, that presumption—contrary to petitioners' views—is not against safety regulation, but against changes in current policy that are not justified by the rulemaking record. While the removal of a regulation may not entail the monetary expenditures and other costs of enacting a new standard, and, accordingly, it may be easier for an agency to justify a deregulatory action, the direction in which an agency chooses to move does not alter the standard of judicial review established by law.

The Department of Transportation accepts the applicability of the "arbitrary and capricious" standard. It argues that under this standard, a reviewing court may not set aside an agency rule that is rational, based on consideration of the relevant factors, and within the scope of the authority delegated to the agency by the statute. We do not disagree with this formulation.[9] The scope of review under the "arbitrary and capricious" standard is narrow and a court is not to substitute its judgment for that of the agency. Nevertheless, the agency must examine the relevant data and articulate a satisfactory explanation for its action including a "rational connection between the facts found and the choice made." *Burlington Truck Lines, Inc. v. United States*, 371 U.S. 156, 168 (1962).... The reviewing court should not attempt itself to make up for such deficiencies; we may not supply a reasoned basis for the agency's action that the agency itself has not given. *SEC v. Chenery Corp.*, 332 U.S. 194, 196 (1947).... For purposes of these cases, it is also relevant that Congress required a record of the rulemaking proceedings to be compiled and submitted to a reviewing court, 15 U.S.C. § 1394, and intended that agency findings under the Act would be supported by "substantial evidence on the record

---

[9] The Department of Transportation suggests that the arbitrary-and-capricious standard requires no more than the minimum rationality a statute must bear in order to withstand analysis under the Due Process Clause. We do not view as equivalent the presumption of constitutionality afforded legislation drafted by Congress and the presumption of regularity afforded an agency in fulfilling its statutory mandate.

considered as a whole." S. Rep. No. 1301, 89th Cong., 2d Sess., 8 (1966); H. R. Rep. No. 1776, 89th Cong., 2d Sess., 21 (1966).

IV

The Court of Appeals correctly found that the arbitrary-and-capricious test applied to rescissions of prior agency regulations, but then erred in intensifying the scope of its review based upon its reading of legislative events. It held that congressional reaction to various versions of Standard 208 "[raised] doubts" that NHTSA's rescission "necessarily demonstrates an effort to fulfill its statutory mandate," and therefore the agency was obligated to provide "increasingly clear and convincing reasons" for its action. Specifically, the Court of Appeals found significance in three legislative occurrences:

> "In 1974, Congress banned the ignition interlock but did not foreclose NHTSA's pursuit of a passive restraint standard. In 1977, Congress allowed the standard to take effect when neither of the concurrent resolutions needed for disapproval was passed. In 1980, a majority of each house indicated support for the concept of mandatory passive restraints and a majority of each house supported the unprecedented attempt to require some installation of airbags."

From these legislative acts and nonacts the Court of Appeals derived a "congressional commitment to the concept of automatic crash protection devices for vehicle occupants."

This path of analysis was misguided and the inferences it produced are questionable. It is noteworthy that in this Court respondent State Farm expressly agrees that the postenactment legislative history of the Act does not heighten the standard of review of NHTSA's actions. State Farm's concession is well taken for this Court has never suggested that the standard of review is enlarged or diminished by subsequent congressional action. While an agency's interpretation of a statute may be confirmed or ratified by subsequent congressional failure to change that interpretation, in the cases before us, even an unequivocal ratification—short of statutory incorporation—of the passive restraint standard would not connote approval or disapproval of an agency's later decision to rescind the regulation. That decision remains subject to the arbitrary-and-capricious standard.

That we should not be so quick to infer a congressional mandate for passive restraints is confirmed by examining the postenactment legislative events cited by the Court of Appeals. Even were we inclined to rely on inchoate legislative action, the inferences to be drawn fail to suggest that NHTSA acted improperly in rescinding Standard 208. First, in 1974 a mandatory passive restraint standard was technically not in effect; Congress had no reason to foreclose that course. Moreover, one can hardly infer support for a mandatory standard from Congress' decision to provide that such a regulation would be subject to disapproval by resolutions of disapproval in both Houses. Similarly, no mandate can be divined from the tabling of resolutions of disapproval which were introduced in 1977. The failure of Congress to exercise its veto might reflect legislative deference to the agency's expertise and does not indicate that Congress would disapprove of the agency's action in 1981. And even if Congress favored the Standard in 1977, it—like NHTSA—may well reach a different judgment, given changed circumstances four years later. Finally, the Court of Appeals read too much into floor action on the 1980 authorization bill, a bill which was not enacted into law. Other contemporaneous events could be read as showing equal congressional hostility to passive restraints.

V

The ultimate question before us is whether NHTSA's rescission of the passive restraint requirement of Standard 208 was arbitrary and capricious. We conclude, as did the Court of Appeals, that it was. We also conclude, but for somewhat different reasons, that further consideration of the issue by the agency is therefore required. We deal separately with the rescission as it applies to airbags and as it applies to seatbelts.

A

The first and most obvious reason for finding the rescission arbitrary and capricious is that NHTSA apparently gave no consideration whatever to modifying the Standard to require that airbag technology be utilized. Standard 208 sought to achieve automatic crash protection by requiring automobile manufacturers to install either of two passive restraint devices: airbags or automatic seatbelts. There was no suggestion in the long rulemaking process that led to Standard 208 that if only one of these options were feasible, no passive restraint standard should be promulgated. Indeed, the agency's original proposed Standard contemplated the installation of inflatable restraints in all cars. Automatic belts were added as a means of complying with the Standard because they were believed to be as effective as airbags in achieving the goal of occupant crash protection. At that time, the passive belt approved by the agency could not be detached. Only later, at a manufacturer's behest, did the agency approve of the detachability feature—and only after assurances that the feature would not compromise the safety benefits of the restraint. Although it was then foreseen that 60% of the new cars would contain airbags and 40% would have automatic seatbelts, the ratio between the two was not significant as long as the passive belt would also assure greater passenger safety.

The agency has now determined that the detachable automatic belts will not attain anticipated safety benefits because so many individuals will detach the mechanism. Even if this conclusion were acceptable in its entirety, standing alone it would not justify any more than an amendment of Standard 208 to disallow compliance by means of the one technology which will not provide effective passenger protection. It does not cast doubt on the need for a passive restraint standard or upon the efficacy of airbag technology. In its most recent rulemaking, the agency again acknowledged the lifesaving potential of the airbag:

> The agency has no basis at this time for changing its earlier conclusions in 1976 and 1977 that basic air bag technology is sound and has been sufficiently demonstrated to be effective in those vehicles in current use....

Given the effectiveness ascribed to airbag technology by the agency, the mandate of the Act to achieve traffic safety would suggest that the logical response to the faults of detachable seatbelts would be to require the installation of airbags. At the very least this alternative way of achieving the objectives of the Act should have been addressed and adequate reasons given for its abandonment. But the agency not only did not require compliance through airbags, it also did not even consider the possibility in its 1981 rulemaking. Not one sentence of its rulemaking statement discusses the airbags-only option. Because, as the Court of Appeals stated, "NHTSA's . . . analysis of airbags was nonexistent," what we said in *Burlington Truck Lines, Inc. v. United States*, 371 U.S., at 167, is apropos here:

> There are no findings and no analysis here to justify the choice made, no indication of the basis on which the [agency] exercised its expert discretion. We are not prepared to and the Administrative Procedure Act will not permit us to accept such . . . practice. . . . Expert discretion is the lifeblood of the administrative process, but 'unless we make the requirements for administrative action strict and demanding, expertise, the strength of modern government, can become a monster which rules with no practical limits on its discretion.' *New York v. United States*, 342 U.S. 882, 884 (dissenting opinion) (footnote omitted).

We have frequently reiterated that an agency must cogently explain why it has exercised its discretion in a given manner; and we reaffirm this principle again today.

The automobile industry has opted for the passive belt over the airbag, but surely it is not enough that the regulated industry has eschewed a given safety device. For nearly a decade, the automobile industry waged the regulatory equivalent of war against the airbag and lost—the inflatable restraint was proved sufficiently effective. Now the automobile industry has decided to employ a seatbelt system which will not meet the safety objectives of Standard 208. This hardly constitutes cause to revoke the Standard itself. Indeed, the Act was necessary because the industry was not sufficiently responsive to safety concerns. The Act intended that safety standards not depend on current technology and could be "technology-forcing" in the sense of inducing the development of superior safety design. If, under the statute, the agency should not defer to the industry's failure to develop safer cars, which it surely should not do, a fortiori it may not revoke a safety standard which can be satisfied by current technology simply because the industry has opted for an ineffective seatbelt design.

Although the agency did not address the mandatory airbag option and the Court of Appeals noted that "airbags seem to have none of the problems that NHTSA identified in passive seatbelts," petitioners recite a number of difficulties that they believe would be posed by a mandatory airbag standard. These range from questions concerning the installation of airbags in small cars to that of adverse public reaction. But these are not the agency's reasons for rejecting a mandatory airbag standard. Not having discussed the possibility, the agency submitted no reasons at all. The short—and sufficient—answer to petitioners' submission is that the courts may not accept appellate counsel's post hoc rationalizations for agency action. It is well established that an agency's action must be upheld, if at all, on the basis articulated by the agency itself. *SEC v. Chenery Corp.*, 332 U.S., at 196.

Petitioners also invoke our decision in *Vermont Yankee Nuclear Power Corp. v. Natural Resources Defense Council, Inc.*, 435 U.S. 519 (1978), as though it were a talisman under which any agency decision is by definition unimpeachable. Specifically, it is submitted that to require an agency to consider an airbags-only alternative is, in essence, to dictate to the agency the procedures it is to follow. Petitioners both misread *Vermont Yankee* and misconstrue the nature of the remand that is in order. In *Vermont Yankee*, we held that a court may not impose additional procedural requirements upon an agency. We do not require today any specific procedures which NHTSA must follow. Nor do we broadly require an agency to consider all policy alternatives in reaching [a] decision. It is true that rulemaking "cannot be found wanting simply because the agency failed to include every alternative device and thought conceivable by the mind of man . . . regardless of how uncommon or unknown that alternative may have been. . . ." *Id.*, at 551. But the airbag is more than a policy alternative to the passive restraint Standard; it is a technological alternative within the ambit of the existing Standard. We hold only that given the judgment made in 1977 that airbags are an effective and cost-beneficial life-saving technology, the mandatory passive restraint rule may not be abandoned without any consideration whatsoever of an airbags-only requirement.

B

Although the issue is closer, we also find that the agency was too quick to dismiss the safety benefits of automatic seatbelts. NHTSA's critical finding was that, in light of the industry's plans to install readily detachable passive belts, it could not reliably predict "even a 5 percentage point increase as the minimum level of expected usage increase." The Court of Appeals rejected this finding because there is "not one iota" of evidence that Modified Standard 208 will fail to increase nationwide seatbelt use by at least 13 percentage points, the level of increased usage necessary for the Standard to justify its cost. Given the lack of probative evidence, the court held that "only a well justified refusal to seek more evidence could render rescission non-arbitrary."

Petitioners object to this conclusion. In their view, "substantial uncertainty" that a regulation will accomplish its intended purpose is sufficient reason, without more, to rescind a regulation. We agree with petitioners that just as an agency reasonably may decline to issue a safety standard if it is uncertain about its efficacy, an agency may also revoke a standard on the basis of serious uncertainties if supported by the record and reasonably explained. Rescission of the passive restraint requirement would not be arbitrary and capricious simply because there was no evidence in direct support of the agency's conclusion. It is not infrequent that the available data do not settle a regulatory issue, and the agency must then exercise its judgment in moving from the facts and probabilities on the record to a policy conclusion. Recognizing that policymaking in a complex society must account for uncertainty, however, does not imply that it is sufficient for an agency to merely recite the terms "substantial uncertainty" as a justification for its actions. As previously noted, the agency must explain the evidence which is available, and must offer a "rational connection between the facts found and the choice made." *Burlington Truck Lines, Inc. v. United States, supra*, at 168. Generally, one aspect of that explanation would be a justification for rescinding the regulation before engaging in a search for further evidence.

. . . We start with the accepted ground that if used, seatbelts unquestionably would save many thousands of lives and would prevent tens of thousands of crippling injuries. Unlike recent regulatory decisions we have reviewed, *Industrial Union Dept. v. American Petroleum Institute*, 448 U.S. 607 (1980), the safety benefits of wearing seatbelts are not in doubt, and it is not challenged that were those benefits to accrue, the monetary costs of implementing the Standard would be easily justified. We move next to the fact that there is no direct evidence in support of the agency's finding that detachable automatic belts cannot be predicted to yield a substantial increase in usage. The empirical evidence on the record, consisting of surveys of drivers of automobiles equipped with passive belts, reveals more than a doubling of the usage rate experienced with manual belts. Much of the agency's rulemaking statement—and much of the controversy in these cases—centers on the conclusions that should be drawn from these studies. The agency maintained that the doubling of seatbelt usage in these studies could not be extrapolated to an across-the-board mandatory standard because the passive seatbelts were guarded by ignition interlocks and purchasers of the tested cars are somewhat atypical. Respondents insist these studies demonstrate that Modified Standard 208 will substantially increase seatbelt usage. We believe that it is within the agency's discretion to pass upon the generalizability of these field studies. This is precisely the type of issue which rests within the expertise of NHTSA, and upon which a reviewing court must be most hesitant to intrude.

But accepting the agency's view of the field tests on passive restraints indicates only that there is no reliable real-world experience that usage rates will substantially increase. To be sure, NHTSA opines that "it cannot reliably predict even a 5 percentage point increase as the minimum level of expected usage." But this and other statements that passive belts will not yield substantial increases in seatbelt usage apparently take no account of the critical difference between detachable automatic belts and current manual belts. A detached passive belt does require an affirmative act to reconnect it, but—unlike a manual seatbelt—the passive belt, once reattached, will continue to function automatically unless again disconnected. Thus, inertia—a factor which the agency's own studies have found significant in explaining the current low usage rates for seatbelts—works in favor of, not against, use of the protective device. Since 20% to 50% of motorists currently wear seatbelts on some occasions, there would seem to be grounds to believe that seatbelt use by occasional users will be substantially increased by the detachable passive belts. Whether this is in fact the case is a matter for the agency to decide, but it must bring its expertise to bear on the question.

The agency is correct to look at the costs as well as the benefits of Standard 208. The agency's conclusion that the incremental costs of the requirements were no longer reasonable was predicated on its prediction that the safety benefits of the regulation might be minimal. Specifically, the agency's fears that the public may resent paying more for the automatic belt systems is expressly dependent on the assumption that detachable automatic belts will not produce more than "negligible safety benefits." When the agency reexamines its findings as to the likely increase in seatbelt usage, it must also reconsider its judgment of the reasonableness of the monetary and other costs associated with the Standard. In reaching its judgment, NHTSA should bear in mind that Congress intended safety to be the pre-eminent factor under the Act....

The agency also failed to articulate a basis for not requiring nondetachable belts under Standard 208. It is argued that the concern of the agency with the easy detachability of the currently favored design would be readily solved by a continuous passive belt, which allows the occupant to "spool out" the belt and create the necessary slack for easy extrication from the vehicle. The agency did not separately consider the continuous belt option, but treated it together with the ignition interlock device in a category it titled "Option of Adopting Use-Compelling Features." The agency was concerned that use-compelling devices would "complicate the extrication of [an] occupant from his or her car." "[To] require that passive belts contain use-compelling features," the agency observed, "could be counterproductive[, given] . . . widespread, latent and irrational fear in many members of the public that they could be trapped by the seat belt after a crash." In addition, based on the experience with the ignition interlock, the agency feared that use-compelling features might trigger adverse public reaction.

By failing to analyze the continuous seatbelts option in its own right, the agency has failed to offer the rational connection between facts and judgment required to pass muster under the arbitrary-and-capricious standard. We agree with the Court of Appeals that NHTSA did not suggest that the emergency release mechanisms used in nondetachable belts are any less effective for emergency egress than the buckle release system used in detachable belts. In 1978, when General Motors obtained the agency's approval to install a continuous passive belt, it assured the agency that nondetachable belts with spool releases were as safe as detachable belts with buckle releases. NHTSA was satisfied that this belt design assured easy extricability: "[the] agency does not believe that the use of [such] release mechanisms will cause serious occupant egress problems. . . ." While the agency is entitled to change its view on the acceptability of continuous passive belts, it is obligated to explain its reasons for doing so.

The agency also failed to offer any explanation why a continuous passive belt would engender the same adverse public reaction as the ignition interlock, and, as the Court of Appeals concluded, "every indication in the record points the other way." We see no basis for equating the two devices: the continuous belt, unlike the ignition interlock, does not interfere with the operation of the vehicle. More importantly, it is the agency's responsibility, not this Court's, to explain its decision.

VI

"An agency's view of what is in the public interest may change, either with or without a change in circumstances. But an agency changing its course must supply a reasoned analysis. . . ." *Greater Boston Television Corp. v. FCC*, 444 F.2d 841, 852 (1970). We do not accept all of the reasoning of the Court of Appeals but we do conclude that the agency has failed to supply the requisite "reasoned analysis" in this case. Accordingly, we vacate the judgment of the Court of Appeals and remand the cases to that court with directions to remand the matter to the NHTSA for further consideration consistent with this opinion.

Justice Rehnquist, with whom The Chief Justice, Justice Powell, and Justice O'Connor join, concurring in part and dissenting in part.

I join Parts I, II, III, IV, and V-A of the Court's opinion. In particular, I agree that, since the airbag and continuous spool automatic seatbelt were explicitly approved in the Standard the agency was rescinding, the agency should explain why it declined to leave those requirements intact. In this case, the agency gave no explanation at all. . . .

. . .

[T]he agency's explanation [with respect to automatic seatbelts], while by no means a model, is adequate. The agency acknowledged that there would probably be some increase in belt usage, but concluded that the increase would be small and not worth the cost of mandatory detachable automatic belts. The agency's obligation is to articulate a " 'rational connection between the facts found and the choice made.' " . . .

. . .

The agency's changed view of the standard seems to be related to the election of a new President of a different political party. It is readily apparent that the responsible members of one administration may consider public resistance and uncertainties to be more important than do their counterparts in a previous administration. A change in administration brought about by the people casting their votes is a perfectly reasonable basis for an executive agency's reappraisal of the costs and benefits of its programs and regulations. As long as the agency remains within the bounds established by Congress,* it is entitled to assess administrative records and evaluate priorities in light of the philosophy of the administration.

COMMENTS AND QUESTIONS

1. Is there a (substantial) difference between the majority's interpretation of the "arbitrary and capricious" standard of review and Justice Rehnquist's "rational connection" standard? The application of the former standard in *State Farm* is often referred to as (a version of) giving the agency's rationale a "hard look." (Originally, the term "hard look" referred to the inquiry the agency was supposed to give to the evidence, but it soon came to refer to the courts' approach to reviewing agency actions.) What are the advantages and disadvantages of the "hard look" approach as compared with the "rational connection" approach?

   Why was the failure to consider rescinding only the seatbelt part of the rule, leaving the airbag part untouched, arbitrary and capricious? Is the reason only that the agency paid no attention to the airbags-only alternative? Why was such an alternative a reasonable one, in light of the fact that the agency had always assumed that safety improvements would be achieved by some mix of airbags and seatbelts?

2. Does "hard look" review give agencies incentives to stick with the status quo? In *State Farm*, the status quo was a regulatory proposal. Note, though, that the Court assumes that an agency's failure to begin a rule-making proceeding— that is, a failure to develop regulations to address problems arising under the common law—will be subject to less stringent review than even a decision to rescind a proposed rule (and that regulatory interventions, once adopted, will also be given a "hard look," this time at the insistence of those who would prefer less stringent regulation).

   Justice Breyer has suggested that the combination of *Chevron* and the "hard look" doctrine is exactly backward: *Chevron* gives the agencies deference in statutory interpretation where they have no special advantages over the courts, and the "hard look" doctrine leads the courts to examine with some care agency decisions that rest on the expertise that distinguishes them from courts. Stephen Breyer, *Judicial Review of Questions of Law and Policy*, 38 Admin. L. Rev. 363 (1986). This argument focuses on the relative positions of courts

---

* Of course, a new administration may not refuse to enforce laws of which it does not approve, or to ignore statutory standards in carrying out its regulatory functions. But in this case, as the Court correctly concludes, Congress has not required the agency to require passive restraints.

and agencies with respect to expertise. Does the concern for political accountability reinforce or undermine Justice Breyer's argument?

3. Justice Rehnquist's dissent makes the political context of the decision clear: The rescission was adopted by a new administration that had been elected on a platform promoting deregulation. (Note, however, that the agency's position shifted as the Ford administration was replaced by the Carter administration and again when the Reagan administration took office. Jerry L. Mashaw and David L. Harfst, *The Struggle for Auto Safety* (Harvard University Press, 1990), provide a good account of the political environment in which the airbag requirement was developed.) Should *State Farm* be understood as (a) a rebuke to deregulators, (b) an effort to moderate the pace of deregulation by stressing the expertise rationale for agencies and deemphasizing the political accountability dimensions of agency actions, or (c) something else? Note that the stated reason for reconsidering the rule was "the difficulties of the automobile industry." Car makers chose passive seatbelts over airbags because the latter would increase the price of cars by a substantially larger amount than the former (or, some have suggested, as a strategy to undermine the rationale for regulation entirely by ensuring that the method they chose would be ineffective). Could the agency have given the cost differential as a reason for rescinding the rule insofar as it dealt with airbags?

After the *State Farm* decision, NHTSA adopted a rule requiring new cars to have automatic passive restraints of some sort, unless states with two thirds of the U.S. population adopted statutes requiring drivers and passengers to "buckle up" with active safety belts. Not enough states adopted such mandatory use laws in a form that satisfied NHTSA's requirements, and the passive restraint rule went into effect in 1989, leading to the installation of airbags. (Note, though, that mandatory use laws of some sort are now nearly universal.)

Should *Congress* have taken responsibility for resolving the obviously controversial question of what system car makers should be required to adopt?

4. The Court criticizes NHTSA's reliance on congressional developments—or, in one aspect, lack of developments—after the act's enactment. Do you agree that those developments fail to cast light on the statute's meaning? Do the arguments the Court uses against relying on this sort of postenactment legislative "history" undermine or strengthen the use of preenactment legislative history?

5. The next case involves what happened in *Vermont Yankee* on remand, when the court of appeals considered the agency's rule making on the merits. It also involves the "arbitrary and capricious" standard. The decision in this case was handed down a couple of weeks before the decision in *State Farm*. Do you think the Court scrutinized the agency's rule as much as it did in *State Farm*?

■ **Baltimore Gas & Electric Co. v. Natural Resources Defense Council, Inc.**
462 U.S. 87 (1983)

Justice O'Connor delivered the opinion of the Court, in which all other Members joined, except Justice Powell, who took no part in the consideration or decision of the cases.

Section 102(2)(C) of the National Environmental Policy Act of 1969, 83 Stat. 853, 42 U.S.C. § 4332(2)(C) (NEPA), requires federal agencies to consider the environmental impact of any major federal action. As part of its generic rulemaking proceedings to evaluate the environmental effects of the nuclear fuel cycle for nuclear powerplants, the Nuclear Regulatory Commission (Commission) decided that licensing boards should assume, for purposes of NEPA, that the permanent storage of certain nuclear wastes would have no significant environmental impact and thus should not affect the decision whether to license a particular nuclear powerplant. We conclude that the Commission complied with NEPA and that its decision is not arbitrary or capricious within the meaning of § 10(e) of the Administrative Procedure Act (APA), 5 U.S.C. § 706.

I

The environmental impact of operating a light-water nuclear powerplant[4] includes the effects of offsite activities necessary to provide fuel for the plant ("front end" activities), and of offsite activities necessary to dispose of the highly toxic and long-lived nuclear wastes generated by the plant ("back end" activities). The dispute in these cases concerns the Commission's adoption of a series of generic rules to evaluate the environmental effects of a nuclear powerplant's fuel cycle. At the heart of each rule is Table S-3, a numerical compilation of the estimated resources used and effluents released by fuel cycle activities supporting a year's operation of a typical light-water reactor.[5] The three versions of Table S-3 contained similar numerical values, although the supporting documentation has been amplified during the course of the proceedings.

The Commission first adopted Table S-3 in 1974, after extensive informal rulemaking proceedings. This "original" rule, as it later came to be described, declared that in environmental reports and impact statements for individual licensing proceedings the environmental costs of the fuel cycle "shall be as set forth" in Table S-3 and that "[no] further discussion of such environmental effects shall be required."[6] The original Table S-3 contained no numerical entry for the long-term

---

[4] A light-water nuclear powerplant is one that uses ordinary water (H_2O), as opposed to heavy water (D_2O), to remove the heat generated in the nuclear core. The bulk of the reactors in the United States are light-water nuclear reactors.

[5] For example, the tabulated impacts include the acres of land committed to fuel cycle activities, the amount of water discharged by such activities, fossil fuel consumption, and chemical and radiological effluents (measured in curies), all normalized to the annual fuel requirement for a model 1,000 megawatt light-water reactor.

[6] Under the Atomic Energy Act of 1954, 68 Stat. 919, a utility seeking to construct and operate a nuclear powerplant must obtain a separate permit or license at both the construction and the operation stage of the project. After the Commission's staff has examined the application for a construction license, which includes a review of possible environmental effects as required by NEPA, a three-member Atomic Safety and Licensing Board conducts a public adjudicatory hearing and reaches a decision which can be appealed to the Atomic Safety and Licensing Appeal Board and, in the Commission's discretion, to the Commission itself. The final agency decision may be appealed to the courts of appeals. A similar procedure occurs when the utility applies for an operating license, except that a hearing need be held only in contested cases.

environmental effects of storing solidified transuranic and high-level wastes,[7] because the Commission staff believed that technology would be developed to isolate the wastes from the environment. The Commission and the parties have later termed this assumption of complete repository integrity as the "zero-release" assumption: the reasonableness of this assumption is at the core of the present controversy.

The Natural Resources Defense Council (NRDC), a respondent in the present cases, challenged the original rule and a license issued under the rule to the Vermont Yankee Nuclear Power Corp. The Court of Appeals for the District of Columbia Circuit affirmed Table S-3's treatment of the "front end" of the fuel cycle, but vacated and remanded the portion of the rule relating to the "back end" because of perceived inadequacies in the rulemaking procedures. Judge Tamm disagreed that the procedures were inadequate, but concurred on the ground that the record on waste storage was inadequate to support the zero-release assumption.

In *Vermont Yankee Nuclear Power Corp. v. Natural Resources Defense Council, Inc.*, 435 U.S. 519 (1978), this Court unanimously reversed the Court of Appeals' decision that the Commission had used inadequate procedures, finding that the Commission had done all that was required by NEPA and the APA and determining that courts generally lack the authority to impose "hybrid" procedures greater than those contemplated by the governing statutes. We remanded for review of whether the original rule was adequately supported by the administrative record, specifically stating that the court was free to agree or disagree with Judge Tamm's conclusion that the rule pertaining to the "back end" of the fuel cycle was arbitrary and capricious within the meaning of § 10(e) of the APA, 5 U.S.C. § 706.

While *Vermont Yankee* was pending in this Court, the Commission proposed a new "interim" rulemaking proceeding to determine whether to adopt a revised Table S-3. The proposal explicitly acknowledged that the risks from long-term repository failure were uncertain, but suggested that research should resolve most of those uncertainties in the near future. After further proceedings, the Commission promulgated the interim rule in March 1977. Table S-3 now explicitly stated that solidified high-level and transuranic wastes would remain buried in a federal repository and therefore would have no effect on the environment. Like its predecessor, the interim rule stated that "[no] further discussion of such environmental effects shall be required." The NRDC petitioned for review of the interim rule, challenging the zero-release assumption and faulting the Table S-3 rule for failing to consider the health, cumulative, and socioeconomic effects of the fuel cycle activities. The Court of Appeals stayed proceedings while awaiting this Court's decision in *Vermont Yankee*. In April 1978, the Commission amended the interim rule to clarify that health effects were not covered by Table S-3 and could be litigated in individual licensing proceedings.

In 1979, following further hearings, the Commission adopted the "final" Table S-3 rule. Like the amended interim rule, the final rule expressly stated that Table S-3 should be supplemented in individual proceedings by evidence about the

---

[7] High-level wastes, which are highly radioactive, are produced in liquid form when spent fuel is reprocessed. Transuranic wastes, which are also highly toxic, are nuclides heavier than uranium that are produced in the reactor fuel.

health, socioeconomic, and cumulative aspects of fuel cycle activities. The Commission also continued to adhere to the zero-release assumption that the solidified waste would not escape and harm the environment once the repository was sealed. It acknowledged that this assumption was uncertain because of the remote possibility that water might enter the repository, dissolve the radioactive materials, and transport them to the biosphere. Nevertheless, the Commission predicted that a bedded-salt repository would maintain its integrity, and found the evidence "tentative but favorable" that an appropriate site would be found. The Commission ultimately determined that any undue optimism in the assumption of appropriate selection and perfect performance of the repository is offset by the cautious assumption, reflected in other parts of the Table, that all radioactive gases in the spent fuel would escape during the initial 6- to 20-year period that the repository remained open, and thus did not significantly reduce the overall conservatism of Table S-3.

The Commission rejected the option of expressing the uncertainties in Table S-3 or permitting licensing boards, in performing the NEPA analysis for individual nuclear plants, to consider those uncertainties. It saw no advantage in reassessing the significance of the uncertainties in individual licensing proceedings:

"In view of the uncertainties noted regarding waste disposal, the question then arises whether these uncertainties can or should be reflected explicitly in the fuel cycle rule. The Commission has concluded that the rule should not be so modified. On the individual reactor licensing level, where the proceedings deal with fuel cycle issues only peripherally, the Commission sees no advantage in having licensing boards repeatedly weigh for themselves the effect of uncertainties on the selection of fuel cycle impacts for use in cost-benefit balancing. This is a generic question properly dealt with in the rule-making as part of choosing what impact values should go into the fuel cycle rule. The Commission concludes, having noted that uncertainties exist, that for the limited purpose of the fuel cycle rule it is reasonable to base impacts on the assumption which the Commission believes the probabilities favor, i.e., that bedded-salt repository sites can be found which will provide effective isolation of radioactive waste from the biosphere."

The NRDC and respondent State of New York petitioned for review of the final rule. The Court of Appeals consolidated these petitions for all purposes with the pending challenges to the initial and interim rules. By a divided panel, the court concluded that the Table S-3 rules were arbitrary and capricious and inconsistent with NEPA because the Commission had not factored the consideration of uncertainties surrounding the zero-release assumption into the licensing process in such a manner that the uncertainties could potentially affect the outcome of any decision to license a particular plant. The court first reasoned that NEPA requires an agency to consider all significant environmental risks from its proposed action. If the zero-release assumption is taken as a finding that long-term storage poses no significant environmental risk, which the court acknowledged may not have been the Commission's intent, it found that the assumption represents a self-evident error in judgment and is thus arbitrary and capricious. As the evidence in the record reveals and the Commission itself acknowledged, the zero-release assumption is surrounded with uncertainty.

. . .

We granted certiorari. We reverse.

II

We are acutely aware that the extent to which this Nation should rely on nuclear power as a source of energy is an important and sensitive issue. Much of the debate focuses on whether development of nuclear generation facilities should proceed in the face of uncertainties about their long-term effects on the environment. Resolution of these fundamental policy questions lies, however, with Congress and the agencies to which Congress has delegated authority, as well as with state legislatures and, ultimately, the populace as a whole. Congress has assigned the courts only the limited, albeit important, task of reviewing agency action to determine whether the agency conformed with controlling statutes. As we emphasized in our earlier encounter with these very proceedings, "[administrative] decisions should be set aside in this context, as in every other, only for substantial procedural or substantive reasons as mandated by statute . . . , not simply because the court is unhappy with the result reached." *Vermont Yankee*, 435 U.S., at 558.

. . .

In its Table S-3 rule here, the Commission has determined that the probabilities favor the zero-release assumption, because the Nation is likely to develop methods to store the wastes with no leakage to the environment. The NRDC did not challenge and the Court of Appeals did not decide the reasonableness of this determination, and no party seriously challenges it here. The Commission recognized, however, that the geological, chemical, physical, and other data it relied on in making this prediction were based, in part, on assumptions which involve substantial uncertainties. Again, no one suggests that the uncertainties are trivial or the potential effects insignificant if time proves the zero-release assumption to have been seriously wrong. After confronting the issue, though, the Commission has determined that the uncertainties concerning the development of nuclear waste storage facilities are not sufficient to affect the outcome of any individual licensing decision.

. . .

. . . The sheer volume of proceedings before the Commission is impressive.[11] Of far greater importance, the Commission's Statement of Consideration announcing the final Table S-3 rule shows that it has digested this mass of material and disclosed all substantial risks. The Statement summarizes the major uncertainty of long-term storage in bedded-salt repositories, which is that water could infiltrate the repository as a result of such diverse factors as geologic faulting, a meteor strike, or accidental or deliberate intrusion by man. The Commission noted that the probability of intrusion was small, and that the plasticity of salt would tend to heal some types of intrusions. The Commission also found the evidence "tentative but favorable" that an

---

[11] The record includes more than 1,100 pages of prepared direct testimony, two rounds of questions by participants and several hundred pages of responses, 1,200 pages of oral hearings, participants' rebuttal testimony, concluding statements, the 137-page report of the hearing board, further written statements from participants, and oral argument before the Commission. The Commission staff has prepared three studies of the environmental effects of the fuel cycle.

appropriate site could be found. Table S-3 refers interested persons to staff studies that discuss the uncertainties in greater detail. Given this record and the Commission's statement, it simply cannot be said that the Commission ignored or failed to disclose the uncertainties surrounding its zero-release assumption.

. . .

. . . In assessing whether the Commission's decision is arbitrary and capricious, it is crucial to place the zero-release assumption in context. Three factors are particularly important. First is the Commission's repeated emphasis that the zero-release assumption—and, indeed, all of the Table S-3 rule—was made for a limited purpose. The Commission expressly noted its intention to supplement the rule with an explanatory narrative. It also emphasized that the purpose of the rule was not to evaluate or select the most effective long-term waste disposal technology or develop site selection criteria. A separate and comprehensive series of programs has been undertaken to serve these broader purposes. In the proceedings before us, the Commission's staff did not attempt to evaluate the environmental effects of all possible methods of disposing of waste. Rather, it chose to analyze intensively the most probable long-term waste disposal method—burial in a bedded-salt repository several hundred meters below ground—and then "estimate its impacts conservatively, based on the best available information and analysis." The zero-release assumption cannot be evaluated in isolation. Rather, it must be assessed in relation to the limited purpose for which the Commission made the assumption.

Second, the Commission emphasized that the zero-release assumption is but a single figure in an entire Table, which the Commission expressly designed as a risk-averse estimate of the environmental impact of the fuel cycle. It noted that Table S-3 assumed that the fuel storage canisters and the fuel rod cladding would be corroded before a repository is closed and that all volatile materials in the fuel would escape to the environment.[16] Given that assumption, and the improbability that materials would escape after sealing, the Commission determined that the overall Table represented a conservative (i.e., inflated) statement of environmental impacts. It is not unreasonable for the Commission to counteract the uncertainties in postsealing releases by balancing them with an overestimate of presealing releases. A reviewing court should not magnify a single line item beyond its significance as only part of a larger Table.

Third, a reviewing court must remember that the Commission is making predictions, within its area of special expertise, at the frontiers of science. When examining this kind of scientific determination, as opposed to simple findings of fact, a reviewing court must generally be at its most deferential. See, e.g., *Industrial Union Dept. v. American Petroleum Institute*, 448 U.S. 607, 656 (1980) (plurality opinion); id., at 705–706 (Marshall, J., dissenting).

With these three guides in mind, we find the Commission's zero-release assumption to be within the bounds of reasoned decisionmaking required by the

---

[16] The Commission also increased the overall conservatism of the Table by overestimating the amount of fuel consumed by a reactor, underestimating the amount of electricity produced, and then underestimating the efficiency of filters and other protective devices. Additionally, Table S-3, which analyzes both a uranium-recycle and no-recycle system, conservatively lists, for each effluent, the highest of the two releases that would be expected under each cycle.

APA. We have already noted that the Commission's Statement of Consideration detailed several areas of uncertainty and discussed why they were insubstantial for purposes of an individual licensing decision. The Table S-3 rule also refers to the staff reports, public documents that contain a more expanded discussion of the uncertainties involved in concluding that long-term storage will have no environmental effects. These staff reports recognize that rigorous verification of long-term risks for waste repositories is not possible, but suggest that data and extrapolation of past experience allow the Commission to identify events that could produce repository failure, estimate the probability of those events, and calculate the resulting consequences.[18] The Commission staff also modeled the consequences of repository failure by tracing the flow of contaminated water, and found them to be insignificant. Ultimately, the staff concluded that

> [the] radiotoxic hazard index analyses and the modeling studies that have been done indicate that consequences of all but the most improbable events will be small. Risks (probabilities times consequences) inherent in the long term for geological disposal will therefore also be small.

We also find significant the separate views of Commissioners Bradford and Gilinsky. These Commissioners expressed dissatisfaction with the zero-release assumption and yet emphasized the limited purpose of the assumption and the overall conservatism of Table S-3. Commissioner Bradford characterized the bedded-salt repository as a responsible working assumption for NEPA purposes and concurred in the zero-release figure because it does not appear to affect Table S-3's overall conservatism. Commissioner Gilinsky was more critical of the entire Table, stating that the Commission should confront directly whether it should license any nuclear reactors in light of the problems of waste disposal, rather than hide an affirmative conclusion to this issue behind a table of numbers. . . . For the limited purpose of individual licensing proceedings, however, Commissioner Gilinsky found it "virtually inconceivable" that the Table should affect the decision whether to license, and characterized as "naive" the notion that the fuel cycle effluents could tip the balance in some cases and not in others.

In sum, we think that the zero-release assumption—a policy judgment concerning one line in a conservative Table designed for the limited purpose of individual licensing decisions—is within the bounds of reasoned decisionmaking. It is not our task to determine what decision we, as Commissioners, would have reached. Our only task is to determine whether the Commission has considered the

---

[18] For example, using this approach the staff estimated that a meteor the size necessary to damage a repository would hit a given square kilometer of the earth's surface only once every 50 trillion years, and that geologic faulting through the Delaware Basin in southeast New Mexico (assuming that were the site of the repository) would occur once in 25 billion years. The staff determined that a surface burst of a 50 megaton nuclear weapon, far larger than any currently deployed, would not breach the repository. The staff also recognized the possibility that heat generated by the waste would damage the repository, but suggested this problem could be alleviated by decreasing the density of the stored waste. In recognition that this suggestion would increase the size of the repository, the Commission amended Table S-3 to reflect the greater acreage required under these assumptions.

relevant factors and articulated a rational connection between the facts found and the choice made. Under this standard, we think the Commission's zero-release assumption, within the context of Table S-3 as a whole, was not arbitrary and capricious.

   ...

COMMENTS AND QUESTIONS

1. One of the principal issues in *BG & E* is the proper regulatory response to uncertainty (and the degree of deference courts should give agency decisions regarding uncertainty). Why did the agency assume that there would be no releases of solid radioactive waste from storage facilities? Everyone agrees that uncertainties surround the question. Why wouldn't a "hard look" at the agency's action lead a court to require that the agency place *some* value on the uncertainties?

2. Why did *State Farm* give the rule there a harder look than *BG & E* gave the rule in that case? Perhaps because the former involved cars and car safety, a subject matter about which generalist judges can claim some familiarity, whereas the subject matter in *BG & E* was considerably more technical. Note the Court's reference in *BG & E* to the fact that the issue lay "at the frontiers of science." Or perhaps because the agency in *BG & E* appeared to the Court to be acting in evident good faith in dealing with a difficult policy problem, whereas the agency in *State Farm* appeared to be driven too much by political concerns, too little by ones deriving from the agency's expertise.

3. As of 2005, there was no permanent disposal site for nuclear waste from power plants. The Department of Energy has settled on Yucca Mountain in Nevada as the location for disposal and spent $6 billion to study the site. But a final decision had not been made, largely for political reasons. Utility companies that operate nuclear power plants have sued the department for the costs of temporarily storing wastes and to force the department to take custody of the waste from decommissioned plants. The Court of Appeals for the District of Columbia Circuit has ruled that the agency's choice of a 10,000-year period for measuring risks of discharges from the Yucca Mountain site was not based on and consistent with recommendations by the National Academy of Sciences, as Congress had required. *Nuclear Energy Institute v. Environmental Protection Agency*, 373 F.3d 1251 (D.C. Cir. 2004).

   In the fall of 2005, the Nuclear Regulatory Commission granted a license to the Skull Valley Goshute tribe in Utah for the "temporary" storage of up to 44,000 tons of highly radioactive waste. The tribe agreed to accept the waste in return for an undisclosed sum of money from a consortium of electric utilities. Is this private agreement a better way of resolving the nuclear waste issue than the government-dictated choice of Yucca Mountain? Do you think it likely that the tribe received adequate compensation in the deal? What does adequate compensation in this context mean? Recall the debates over such issues from chapters 2 and 3.

4. Is it possible to engage in reasoned deliberation about events that will occur more than 10,000 years from now? At some point, does uncertainty simply

outstrip our analytical capacity? Consider the following observations from sociologist Kai Erickson:

> ...What will happen if something goes wrong not in the *operational life of the repository* but in the *radioactive life of the wastes*? What if there is a leak into the biosphere at any moment in the ten millennia the repository is required by law to remain secure? In posing a question like that one is asking something very special of the social science imagination. . . . [T]he period of years we are being asked to think about stretches from 1998 to 11,998; . . . [or] from 2010 until 12,010. Now if one were to write the numbers 11,998 and 12,010 on every blackboard in America, how many people would guess that they referred to dates? Figures like those lie outside our normal reckonings of time. They lie outside the span we usually count as human history. And they are certainly outside the reach of even the most hysterical efforts at prediction.
>
> So what can contemporary researchers, adept in the ways of the social sciences but anchored to their own time and place, do about all that? Nothing, perhaps, except to allow over and over again that it is mighty hard to see ten thousand years into the future. The summary reports issuing from Nevada sound that warning as often as one could ask. Indeed, some form of the word "uncertainty" appears thirty-two times in the first several pages of one of them, along with a reference to "future conditions that will be very difficult to fully anticipate" and a grave acknowledgment that "these hazards are not at all knowable." The report speaks of "external perturbations and surprises" and "unanticipated events"; it concedes that "the range of uncertainty is great" and that "any methodology that claims precision in the anticipation of repository consequences must be viewed with appropriate caution."
>
> Comments like these accent such reports from beginning to end. But they are like the warnings found on packs of cigarettes. They are cautionary notes, parenthetic remarks, annotations. They are not worked into the flow of the argument at all. And in the end the effect of all that talk about "uncertainties" and "perturbations" and "surprises" is oddly comforting, as if the empirical territories covered by the report were broad and secure, even if the outer edges were a bit soft and tinged with ambiguity.
>
> . . .
>
> ...[W]hat is the logic of choosing a term like "surprise" to refer to events that may take place five or ten thousand years from now? The expression may have an established meaning in technical conversations, but to use it carelessly in a context like this has telling implications. "Surprise" seems to speak of something out of the ordinary, something that bolts from the blue and imposes itself upon a pattern of life events that one would otherwise have expected to have remained fixed and immutable. As if absence of change were nature's way. As if absence of change were the way of human history.
>
> . . .
>
> The most mature and accurate scientific report we can issue, it seems to me, would conclude: We do not know, we cannot know, and we dare

not act as though we do know. To speak thus is not to introduce a note of drama into what can otherwise seem a dry and technical business but to assess the matter in as rational and unemotional a way as language permits. Things will change drastically over the next few hundred years—never mind the next few thousand—and in ways that we cannot, by definition, foresee. To think otherwise is unrealistic, unscientific, and more than a little crazy.

A New Species of Trouble: The Human Experience
of Modern Disasters (Norton, 1994)

What do you suppose the Supreme Court would have said if the agency had offered a report along the lines Erickson suggests? Is it arbitrary or capricious to admit profound uncertainty—or not to?

5. *Concluding Observations*: What do you conclude from the saga of nuclear waste disposal as recounted in *Vermont Yankee, BG & E,* and thereafter? Is it a tale of the pathologies of the modern regulatory state? Of the failures of the courts to develop appropriate mechanisms for supervising modern regulatory agencies? Of the difficulties inherent in the problem of nuclear power and therefore without larger implications?

Assessing Regulation

9

You now should understand *why* we sometimes think that regulation is desirable and *how* agencies go about translating regulatory statutes into regulations. The next question, taken up in this chapter and those that follow, is: How effective are agencies (and legislatures) at the job of translation? We begin by examining some forms of regulatory failure. Section A describes some general forms of regulatory failure, and section B examines problems in which claims of regulatory failure might be made. As you will see, often the definition of "failure" turns on the author's view that the regulation being examined fails to provide benefits sufficient to justify the costs of administering and complying with the regulation. Section C therefore presents a more systematic explication of cost-benefit (and a related method, "cost-effectiveness") analysis. Finally, section D provides a normative examination of cost-benefit analysis by presenting defenses and critiques.

A How Regulation Can Fail: Theory

We begin with an excerpt from a political scientist's analysis of administrative risk regulation. John Mendeloff describes some of the mechanisms that can lead to the adoption and enforcement of regulations that may accomplish less, in terms of reducing risk (for example), than other regulatory approaches. These mechanisms should be your primary focus as you read the excerpt. Mendeloff's analysis also introduces you to the role of cost-benefit analysis in designing and evaluating regulatory instruments, a topic dealt with later in the chapter. Mendeloff also looks at why, as a practical political matter, less-than-optimal regulations get adopted and enforced, and this serves as a prelude to a more extended examination of the politics of regulation in chapter 13.

- *The Dilemma of Toxic Substance Regulation*
  JOHN MENDELOFF
  pp. 1–17 (MIT Press, 1988). © 1988 MIT Press. Reprinted with permission

  ### Overregulation, Underregulation, and the Rule-Making Dilemma

The 1960s and 1970s witnessed the enactment of a new wave of federal regulatory programs designed to protect citizens from hazards ranging from automobile accidents and unsafe products to toxic substances in the workplace and in the ambient air. Proponents of these programs believed that existing regulatory agencies, whether at the state or federal level, lacked the political will and the capability to force firms to behave in a socially responsible manner. Underlying this critique of regulatory programs was a body of scholarship that argued that regulatory agencies frequently cater to the interests of the regulated rather than to a broader notion of the public interest. These outcomes were attributed to the domination of the policymaking process by the "iron triangle" of regulated industry, regulatory agency, and the legislative committees that oversee the agency.

Transmitted to a generation of professionals in virtually every college and law school, this critique of regulation was reinforced by increased questioning of business legitimacy and by heightened concern with environmental deterioration and toxic chemicals. Legislators discovered that these popular concerns could be used to their own political advantage. Mistrustful of administrative discretion, reformers tried to write statutory language that precluded sacrificing safety to other objectives. They also sought to mandate procedures allowing outside parties to request action, requiring agencies to respond to them in a timely fashion and requiring agency decisions to be well documented.

To a considerable extent, these statutes, aided by popular support for protective regulation, have prevented the pro-business backsliding that their architects sought to avoid. (Even the Reagan administration, despite some attempts, was largely unable to dismantle the underpinnings of these programs.) However, this accomplishment should be balanced against two other features of our recent regulatory experience.

First, many of the programs have been sharply criticized for their inefficiency. Although this criticism includes complaints that the goals have been pursued through unnecessarily costly methods, it often goes on to argue that the goals themselves have been set too high, beyond the point at which the benefits of reducing hazards justify the costs. For example, staff on the Council of Economic Advisers have complained that the Environmental Protection Agency (EPA) set too low an exposure limit for smog-producing ozone, requiring over $12 billion in annual costs, more than could be justified by the benefits from the resulting drop in smog levels. Economists on the Council on Wage-Price Stability have lambasted the Occupational Safety and Health Administration (OSHA) for promulgating rules on such chemicals as benzene, arsenic, and vinyl chloride that may cost tens of millions of dollars per fatal cancer prevented.

Although many economists and business leaders have protested that regulations have required large outlays for trivial benefits, advocates of strict protection have been disappointed with the slow pace of standard setting. They feel that many serious hazards have simply not been addressed, causing deaths and diseases that we should be preventing (although others question whether the magnitude of the threat from these hazards is significant).

. . .

After fifteen years, OSHA ha[d] established new workplace exposure limits for only ten health hazards. During the same period, the private standard-setting organization, which OSHA was designed to supplant, has recommended lower exposure limits for hundreds of chemicals.

. . .

...I present and examine two arguments drawn from this experience. The first is normative, concerned with what our policy *should* be; the second is positive, attempting to explain *why* policy has developed as it has.

1. For many protective regulatory programs we would be better off setting standards less strictly but more extensively. This prescription departs both from economists who have focused only on "overregulation" and from the environmental and health lobbies who have focused only on "underregulation." Many defenders of regulation dispute the claim that existing standards have been set too strictly, and many economists tend to be skeptical of claims that there are hazards "out there" worth regulating.

2. Setting standards (for example, exposure or emission limits) strictly is a significant cause of the slow pace of the standard-setting process. Although the strictness of standards is not the only influence on the pace of standard setting, a program with stricter standards will, holding all other things constant, tend to have a slower pace.

. . .

The prescription that we should set standards less strictly but more frequently provides one motivation for examining what the relationship between the strictness and frequency of standard setting actually is. If strict regulation is one cause of the lack of extensiveness, then looser regulation will speed the pace. This argument is also controversial. Based on his study of regulation in the United States and Britain, David Vogel concurs that "the American experience demonstrates that overregulation can readily lead to underregulation," and Lester Lave argues that "if Congress writes . . . rigid frameworks into law, inevitably a few substances will arbitrarily be selected for special treatment, while the rest will languish until some real or imagined disaster elevates them to the spotlight." Yet many proponents of strict regulation argue that the pace of rule making would not speed up in response to laxer rules. Even if it is correct, the relevance of my argument for policymaking would still depend on whether a policy of less strict but more extensive regulation is politically feasible. Answering these questions presents a real test for our understanding of the politics of regulation.

. . .

A Concise Statement of the Normative Argument

Judgments about whether a particular regulation is justified depend on assessments of the value of reducing risks. Valuing the benefits of reducing mortality and morbidity is ethically, politically, and analytically controversial. A major argument in favor of explicit valuation of these benefits is that they will be valued implicitly even if they are not valued explicitly. Thus, for example, a decision to spend $2 million to prevent an estimated two deaths indicates that the policymaker places a value on preventing each of those deaths of at least $1 million. Refusal to acknowledge this valuation explicitly may have several consequences; policy-makers may not clarify confusion in their own minds, and valuations across programs are less likely to reflect consistent judgments, with a consequent sacrifice of efficiency. Of course, . . . public distaste for explicit evaluations of human lifesaving indicates that explicitness imposes costs as well as benefits.

. . .

Although many risk reduction programs have low or moderate costs per fatality prevented, others, especially those dealing with toxic substances, have high costs. For example, one major review found relatively low costs (that is, under $1 million and often much lower) for auto safety standards and relatively high costs ($3 million and up) for most efforts to regulate toxic substances. An estimate of the cost of meeting the EPA's 1980 benzene standard was $6.5 million per death prevented. Looking at standards at OSHA, a team of analysts estimated that the average costs per cancer death averted were $20.2 million for the arsenic standard, $18.9 million for benzene, $4.5 million for coke oven emissions, and $3.5 million for acrylonitrile. For the asbestos standard, however, which accounts for almost 90 percent of the estimated fatal cancers averted by these five standards, the estimated costs were below $200,000.

It is important to keep in mind that these are *average* costs. In the case of acrylonitrile, for example, it is the average cost of moving from the preexisting exposure level of 20 ppm (parts per million) to 2 ppm. With acrylonitrile and probably with most toxic substances, it becomes increasingly expensive to achieve added reductions in exposure. Thus the extra cost per death averted in moving from 3 ppm to 2 ppm was undoubtedly much higher than $3.5 million, probably at least twice as much. It is this higher figure that is the valuation implicit in a decision to adopt a 2-ppm standard. Thus, even if preventing cancer deaths is valued at $3.5 million each, a 2-ppm standard should not be supported unless the only choices are 20 ppm and 2 ppm, with no options in between. Because the same point applies to the standards on arsenic and the others, the overall numbers are clearly high. Although these numbers are subject to major uncertainties, it should be apparent why the overregulation argument has merit.

The finding that overly strict health and safety standards have frequently been set does not preclude the possibility that some more moderate regulatory action is justifiable. The high costs of these standards typically resulted from exposure reductions of 90 to 99.8 percent. But because the cost per death averted is strongly affected by the degree to which exposures are reduced, reductions of 50 percent might have been easily justifiable. By the same token, the finding that past standards have been set too strictly does not preclude the possibility that additional standards are needed. In addition, of course, new hazards may be identified that have not been addressed at all.

The Reagan administration campaigned in 1980 against overregulation and made regulatory relief a major component of its initial economic package (along with budget cuts and tax cuts). It tried, with mixed success, to require agencies to use benefit-cost analyses to guide their decisions. The other leg of the regulatory relief effort was to encourage a slowdown in the generation of new regulations, reflecting a strongly held view of many of its leaders that most rules were, on net, undesirable.

The casual lumping together of the charges that regulation has been both too strict and too extensive is particularly unfortunate because it obscures some important relationships between the two issues and, in so doing, some possible remedies. It is generally agreed that, where markets "fail" (because of inadequate information or externalities), regulation of hazards can *potentially* be beneficial. Yet, if we expect that the regulatory response will be improper—that standards will not reflect the most efficient approach or will be set far too strictly—we may prefer inaction on the grounds that it is the lesser of two evils. In this manner overregulation may cause underregulation. Ironically, the costs of overregulation would include not only the excessive costs of strict regulation but also the potential benefits forgone when we decide that no standard is better than an overly strict one.

An important implication of this view is that, if standards are set more sensibly, with more attention to weighing costs and benefits, we should be willing to regulate more extensively than we would otherwise. For example, suppose that an agency, instead of issuing one new standard a year with a reduction in exposure of 95 percent, issued five new standards with reductions of 50 percent each. It is highly likely that the second approach of regulating more hazards less strictly would be more cost-effective—would lower the average cost for each fatality averted. (As noted, however, critics might still claim that even these less strict standards impose net costs and thus that more extensive regulation should be shunned.) The Reagan administration's regulatory policy comes down hard on the side of weighing costs and benefits but ignores altogether the implications for extensiveness.

The lesson of this book is that a comprehensive plan for regulatory reform of standard-setting programs should simultaneously consider the pace and extent of regulation as well as the strictness of individual standards.

My emphasis on standard-setting programs is deliberate, for there are important differences between regulatory programs that rely on "screening" new products or processes before they are marketed or used and programs that rely on setting standards to address the hazards of products that are already on the market. Examples of standard-setting programs include the EPA's program for hazardous air pollutants (for example, asbestos), the Food and Drug Administration's (FDA's) regulation of "old" food additives (for example, saccharin), the National Highway Traffic Safety Administration's (NHTSA's) auto safety measures, and OSHA's standards for workplace safety and health. Examples of screening programs include the FDA's approval of new drugs and new food additives, the Nuclear Regulatory Commission's licensing of nuclear power plants, and the EPA's review of premanufacture notices for new chemicals under the Toxic Substances Control Act (TSCA).

The screening programs place the burden of showing that products are "safe" on the firms that produce them. Thus the firms are hurt by delays. In contrast, standard-setting programs place the burden of proof on the regulatory agencies. Until agencies can meet it, products can stay on the market. Thus firms benefit from delays.

Regulators in both types of programs should seek to minimize the sum of the costs imposed by hazards and the costs imposed by hazard prevention. But the "lesson" stated for guiding the reform of standard-setting programs does not fit screening programs because the policy problems that regulators face with screening programs are different. In screening programs there is only one key policy issue: how high to set the standard of proof that firms have to meet to show that their products are not too risky. If the standard of proof is set too high, many worthwhile products (some of which might even reduce risks) will be stillborn. If it is set too low, too many hazardous products will be approved. In standard-setting programs, as we have seen, there are several key policy issues in addition to the proper burden of proof that the agencies should bear: the choice of hazards to address, the number of hazards to address, and the strictness of individual standards.

One great paradox found in many standard-setting agencies is the disparity between their activist rhetoric and their cautious actions. The statutes and regulations emphasize their preventive goals: they should not wait until "the bodies are counted" before taking action. The agencies have adopted rules for interpreting evidence, especially animal bioassay data, that clearly take more pains to avoid false negatives (that is, identifying hazardous chemicals as innocuous) than false positives (identifying innocuous chemicals as hazardous). Yet, if we look at programs with highly protective mandates and potentially broad scope, such as OSHA's health program and the EPA's hazardous air pollutant program, we find that not only have they addressed a paltry number of hazards but also in almost every case they have chosen hazards from the small category for which evidence of disease in humans (as opposed to animals) is available. In these programs regulations based solely on animal evidence have not been attempted, even though they are the quintessential preventive measure.

Several factors help to explain this apparent anomaly, but I need mention only one here. The statutory requirement to set standards stringently makes it more difficult to justify them as sensible public policy. Of course, courts are not supposed to assess regulations in these terms. Yet, faced with standards that they perceive as constituting overregulation, judges sometimes reject them on procedural grounds, arguing that the agency has not amassed enough evidence to show that they are necessary or feasible.

. . .

The Positive Argument

The argument that overregulation causes underregulation implies that the initial direction of any policy change—for example, toward less or greater protection—will be at least partially offset by its impact on the pace of that activity. For example, the Supreme Court's 1981 cotton dust decision forbidding the use of cost-benefit analysis in OSHA health standards was hailed as a union victory, but one effect was to strengthen the Reagan administration's resolve to avoid setting new standards. The most obvious alternative model of standard setting views strictness and extensiveness as unrelated. The implication of this alternative view would be that Reagan officials would not have issued rules at a faster pace even if they had been allowed to set less stringent standards.

. . .

The actual mechanisms by which stricter standards generate delays include the following.

1. Court appeals by industry become more likely and better funded. Of course, less strict standards increase the threat of appeals by pro-regulatory groups. This threat is probably not fully offsetting. Defenders of strict regulation have smaller resources than industry groups. More important, their objective is to reduce delay, which will sometimes preclude challenging rules that they view as too lax.
2. Strict standards face a higher probability of failing judicial scrutiny. Again, lax standards also face a higher probability of being overturned. Thus the relationship between strictness and reversals is U-shaped. My assumption is that we are usually operating on the upward-sloping side of the U so that increases in strictness increase the probability of reversal.

3. The information that an agency needs to justify a standard is more likely to be withheld by industry groups if they believe that the agency will behave unreasonably.

4. Both White House economists and political operatives are more likely to try to delay rules that they (or industry) perceive as particularly inefficient or burdensome.

5. In the larger ideological arena it also seems likely that there are long-run trade-offs between strictness and pace. Industry complaints about overregulation are less likely to elicit sympathy from the attentive public when there are only a few highly protective standards to complain about. But the political and symbolic attractions of strict regulation may wear thin when it becomes more extensive. Thus many who would accept a decision to require a major industry to spend $1 billion a year to prevent a hundred fatal cancers a year—or $10 million each—would probably balk at proposals to spend $100 billion to prevent ten thousand—also $10 million each.

We should also note that similar processes are at work in the area of enforcement. A stricter standard will elicit more opposition from firms in the enforcement stage. Specifically, we would expect firms to make greater efforts to avoid having noncompliance detected; and, once their noncompliance is detected, to litigate more frequently to delay or avoid compliance measures. In addition, with a stricter standard, fewer firms will voluntarily comply; at least this is true if we assume (as is usually the case) that penalties are a fixed sum, not related to the magnitude of the violation. The reason is that the stricter standard raises the costs of compliance but not the costs of noncompliance. Although these responses will probably not prevent actual exposures from decreasing when a stricter standard is adopted, the decrease will be less than a model of perfect compliance would predict. How much less is an empirical question.

Similarly, the model presented here does not, as I will emphasize, say *how much* the pace of standard setting declines for a given increase in stringency. There is certainly no reason to assume that the size of the relationship will be the same in all situations.

Is the relationship between strictness and extensiveness unidirectional, or do the causal arrows run both ways? Does extensiveness also affect strictness? If so, how? One analysis has noted that "faced with such a high fixed cost of regulatory analysis per regulatory decision, the agencies have had a strong incentive to concentrate on a few, really big decisions, often where there is a constituency that will defend the massive effort." Although I will show that agencies do not always concentrate on the "really big decisions," this observation does capture an important truth. To see *why*, consider the following argument.

What analysis underlies the argument that strictness does reduce extensiveness? When regulation of business is involved, a plausible model of profit-maximizing firms suggests that, when the net costs imposed on them by a government program or activity increase, the firms will have a stronger incentive to try to prevent the activity from occurring. Cross-nationally, there is some evidence that industry is more cooperative when regulators show more concern with costs.

. . .

Although it may be obvious that the degree of opposition by a firm to a regulation will increase as the net cost imposed on the firm grows, it is less clear that the same can be said of an industry. In part, the problem is one of defining the "industry" involved. If one chemical is banned, the manufacturers of substitute chemicals will benefit from the ban. More generally, firms within an industry are not homogeneous. Some firms may benefit from a regulation and others will incur differing net costs. With such differential effects, predicting the "industry's" response to a proposed regulation becomes problematic.... Suffice it to say here that, although these differentials can influence regulatory outcomes, stricter standards still tend to generate stronger overall business opposition than laxer ones. Thus it is difficult to find cases, especially in the area of toxic substances, where firms have sued agencies for issuing standards that were too lax.

Now we can return to the question of the impact of the institutional setting in which regulation takes place.

Although conflict among industry and other interest groups determines the broad patterns of regulatory politics, regulatory policies are less fully determined by interest group pressures than are legislative policies. With regulation, political conflict must be filtered through an unusually large number of analytical and procedural requirements. The American regulatory process requires that decisions be "based upon substantial evidence, affected parties be given the right to participate in the process by submitting evidence and argument in support of their interests, decisions of an agency must be logically derived from its legislative mandate, and decisions are subject to judicial review should any affected party believe that these requirements have not been satisfied."

The slow pace of standard setting has four interrelated causes: (1) Political conflict between health or environmental lobbies and industry groups will generally lead standards to be appealed to the courts; (2) the effects of the standards are complex and uncertain; (3) the burden of proof to demonstrate that standards are needed is on the agencies; and (4) agency resources are quite limited. These four causes interact in the following manner. Because of the political conflict, agencies must assume that rules will be reviewed in court. Because they bear the burden of proof and because the evidence is rarely clear-cut, agencies face a time-consuming task; often the evidence is suggestive of a hazard but far from clear-cut, and agencies will be uncertain about whether or not courts will uphold the rule. Because agency resources are limited, it is difficult to carry on many standard-setting activities at the same time. In turn, their limited resources are due in part to the impact of the political conflict on the appropriations process. Similarly, the legislative choice of the standard of proof was influenced by the relative power of the interests when the statute was enacted.

Although there are obvious exceptions, I will assume that agency leaders typically try to maximize the protective impact of their programs, subject to the constraints of not jeopardizing either their own jobs or the agency's autonomy. Agencies vary, however, in the extent to which they can control their agenda and determine which hazards they address. Moreover, they are all constrained in their ability to regulate more extensively. For example, suppose that an OSHA leader wanted to follow the prescription offered and proposed to reduce exposures by 50 percent for a group of chemicals for which the suspicion of greater hazard was only suggestive. Under the current interpretation of the Occupational Safety and Health (OSH) Act, that leader would fail because the courts would rule both that he was not reducing exposures to the "lowest feasible level" and (very likely) that he had not demonstrated that exposure to the chemicals presented a "significant risk." Given the impossibility of pursuing protective goals through an "extensive" strategy, the protective regulator could indeed become more likely to set stringent standards.

Nevertheless, I suggest that, although strictness plays an important role in explaining lack of extensiveness, lack of extensiveness plays only a small role in explaining strictness. More important for strictness . . . are the terms of the statutes themselves, the interpretations judges place on them, the media's role in rewarding protective efforts by politicians, and the protective values of those charged with administering the programs.

    . . .

COMMENTS AND QUESTIONS

1. What does it mean to regulate "less strictly but more extensively"? How does overregulation cause underregulation?

2. One of the regulatory programs many critics would cite as an example of "overregulation" is the Superfund program, under which private parties responsible for hazardous waste contamination must pay the costs of cleanup. Consider these observations comparing this system with European systems:

> At the risk of oversimplification, we can characterize the American system, with its "big stick" liability system and substantial administrative powers, as producing expensive cleanups, financed by private parties, and achieved at the price of substantial transaction costs. And because the public frequently benefits without paying directly, the value they assign to high levels of cleanup may overstate what they would be willing to provide for themselves on a voluntary basis. European systems produce a different constellation of results. The "little stick" liability systems of the Netherlands and Denmark and the more substantial, though clumsy, police powers in Germany, force greater reliance on negotiation with a smaller set of private parties than in the United States. And the claims that governments can make on these parties are more modest. The results, not surprisingly, are lower levels of cleanup and a large portion of the bill being picked up by the public. While less is achieved on the ground by way of remediation, and the public pays more, transaction costs are almost certainly lower.
>
> Is this, then, a matter of picking which set of mistakes to make: the American system, offering acrimony, transaction costs and delays, but cleaner sites and a low public price tag; while the Europeans produce amity accompanied by amelioration rather than remediation of pollution, and a higher public price tag?
>
> Thomas W. Church and Robert Nakamura, *Beyond Superfund: Hazardous Waste Cleanup in Europe and the United States,* 7 Geo. Int'l. Envtl. L. Rev. 15, 56–57 (1994)

3. Note that Mendeloff includes a "positive" argument about why the political process has produced the situation he describes. If his positive analysis is

accurate, why should we—or he—believe that the political process is likely or even able to adopt his policy prescription?

4. In the next reading, Cass Sunstein examines several regulatory paradoxes, including Mendeloff's "overregulation produces underregulation." Consider how the mechanisms Sunstein identifies as being at work with respect to that paradox differ from the ones Mendeloff identifies, and consider to what extent the mechanisms that produce the other paradoxes are similar to the ones that produce Mendeloff's. (The answer to the latter question may have some bearing on what kinds of reforms are politically feasible.)

■ *Paradoxes of the Regulatory State*
CASS R. SUNSTEIN
57 U. Chi. L. Rev. 407 (1990). Reprinted with permission
of University of Chicago Law Review

By "paradoxes of the regulatory state," I mean self-defeating regulatory strategies— strategies that achieve an end precisely opposite to the one intended, or to the only public-regarding justification that can be brought forward in their support. . . . An example of a regulatory paradox would be a Clean Air Act that actually made the air dirtier, or a civil rights law that increased the incidence of racial discrimination.

. . . I do not conclude . . . that the appropriate response to regulatory paradoxes is to abandon regulation altogether and rest content with the operation of private markets. In many cases the market itself produces harmful or even disastrous results, measured in terms of efficiency or justice.[5] The appropriate response to the paradoxes of regulation is not to return to a system of "laissez faire,"[6] but to learn from past failures. To this end, I outline the lessons, for legislators, judges, and administrators, that are to be drawn from the omnipresence of regulatory paradoxes. My most general goal is to describe some reforms by which we might restructure regulatory institutions so as to achieve their often salutary purposes, while at the same time incorporating the flexibility, respect for individual autonomy and initiative, and productive potential of economic markets.

---

[5] Much of the relevant literature focuses on the evils of "rent-seeking"—the expenditure of resources on the transfer of wealth through law rather than on the production of wealth through markets. Insofar as this is a normative critique, it is an ideological one, and a peculiar one at that. All laws have redistributive functions, and some such laws have powerful arguments in their support. Consider measures preventing environmental degradation or race and sex discrimination. Moreover, the expenditure of resources on laws is part and parcel of the practice of citizenship, and it would be wrong to devalue that practice because of the admittedly frequent phenomenon of self-interested political behavior on behalf of causes lacking public-regarding justifications.

[6] The term is of course misleading insofar as it suggests an absence of governmental controls. Even a system of laissez faire is pervaded by legal duties and disabilities that arise from contract, tort, and property law.

I. The Performance of the Regulatory State: A Prefatory Note

In even the most prominent evaluations of the performance of the regulatory state, explorations of the real world consequences of regulatory intervention are strikingly infrequent. Work in administrative law, throughout the long history of that subject, has been conspicuously silent on the question. That silence is unfortunate, for evaluation of regulatory controls and legal doctrines must depend in large part on their effects in the world. The purpose of the Environmental Protection Agency (EPA), the Occupational Safety and Health Administration (OSHA), and the Federal Communications Commission (FCC) is to alter the conduct of private actors in certain ways. Evaluations that refer to "checks and balances" or "legitimacy," or that deal in general or speculative terms with the effects of bureaucratic incentives or well-organized private groups, are of limited use if unaccompanied by a solid understanding of the actual consequences of regulatory programs. Attention to those consequences, and their implications for legislative and administrative policy, is perhaps the principal task for administrative law in the next generation.

Unfortunately, empirical assessments of the consequences of regulation remain in a primitive state; but it is possible to draw several general conclusions. I outline some of them here.[9] Though fashionable in many circles, the view that regulation has generally proved unsuccessful is far too crude. For example, efforts to reduce air pollution have in many respects been quite successful. Regulatory controls have helped to produce substantial decreases in both the levels and emissions of major pollutants, including sulfur dioxide, carbon monoxide, lead, and nitrogen dioxide. Ambient concentrations of lead have decreased especially dramatically, declining eighty-five percent between 1975 and 1988; transportation emissions of lead decreased from 122.6 million metric tons in 1975 to 3.5 in 1986. Most important, the vast majority of counties in the United States are now in compliance with air quality goals.

Water pollution control has shown significant successes as well. The Great Lakes are substantially cleaner than they were in 1965. A number of harmful nutrients have been reduced by nearly fifty percent in national rivers. Governmentally-required lead and nitrate reductions have produced significant improvements in water quality. All in all, both air and water are substantially cleaner than they would have been without regulatory controls, and despite a wide range of errors, the American experience serves in some respects as a model for the rest of the world.

Similarly, automobile safety regulation has significantly reduced deaths and serious injuries. Automobiles are much safer for occupants. For example, highway fatalities would have been about forty percent higher in 1981 if not for governmental controls. Between 1966 and 1974, the lives of about 34,000 passenger car occupants were saved as a result of occupant safety standards. The annual benefits from regulation exceed ten billion dollars. Moreover, for automobile regulation the ratio of benefits to costs is extremely high. Indeed, some of the regulations pay for

---

[9] Two disclaimers are necessary. First, the methodological problems are severe, partly because of the difficulty of valuing costs and (especially) benefits, and partly because of the difficulty of holding everything else constant in measuring regulatory effects. For this reason the numbers and assessments in the text are contestable. Second, any evaluation must have a significant normative dimension; it cannot depend on the facts alone.

themselves in terms of health and related savings, and the large number of deaths actually prevented is of course a bonus.

More generally, studies of the costs and benefits of regulatory initiatives show that a number of other measures have produced health and other benefits at especially low costs. OSHA's regulation of asbestos prevents an estimated 396 deaths per year, and it does so at relatively low expense. EPA's regulation of trihalomethanes saves a life at only $300,000 per year; the National Highway Traffic Safety Administration's (NHTSA) fuel system integrity controls, also $300,000; the Consumer Product Safety Commission's (CPSC) mandatory smoke detector rule, between $0 and $85,000; NHTSA's roadside hazard removal rule, $0.[20]

Finally, regulatory successes are not limited to the areas of safety and health. The Civil Rights Act of 1964 has led to a decrease in racial discrimination in employment. There have been gains in the area of sex discrimination as well. And the Endangered Species Act has saved a number of species from extinction and endangerment.

On the other hand, regulation has frequently failed. Sometimes it has imposed enormously high costs for speculative benefits; sometimes it has accomplished little or nothing; and sometimes it has aggravated the very problem it was designed to solve. For example, the United States spent no less than $632 billion for pollution control between 1972 and 1985, and some studies suggest that alternative strategies could have achieved the same gains at less than one-fifth the cost. The fuel economy standards for new cars appear to have produced no substantial independent gains in fuel economy, given consumer demands for fuel efficient cars in response to gas shortages and high gas prices. Worse, they have led manufacturers to produce smaller, more dangerous cars; an estimated 2,200–3,900 mortalities are expected over the next ten years as a result of regulatory changes in 1989 alone. There is little question that the administration of the Natural Gas Act helped produce the energy crisis of the late 1970s—with huge attendant costs to investment and employment—by artificially restraining the price of gas. Some of OSHA's carcinogen regulations impose enormous costs for uncertain gains. Indeed, the pattern of OSHA regulation of carcinogens is a crazy quilt; regulations costing up to $40 million per life saved exist in some areas, with no regulations at all in others. The EPA has promulgated only seven regulations controlling toxic substances, so that a huge number of such substances remain uncontrolled. By delaying the entry of beneficial drugs into the market, the Food and Drug Administration has, in many settings, dramatically increased risks to life and health.

The general task of regulatory reform raises issues far beyond the scope of this discussion. Ironically, a large source of regulatory failure in the United States is the use of Soviet-style command and control regulation, which dictates, at the national level, technologies and control strategies for hundreds, thousands, or millions of companies and individuals in a nation that is exceptionally diverse in terms of geography, costs and benefits of regulatory controls, attitudes, and mores. A valuable perspective on this problem can be obtained by examining the paradoxes of regulation, which pose a particular dilemma for the administrative state. A govern-

[20] . . . These studies also show a bizarre pattern of controls, with some programs saving lives at exceptionally high costs. Thus the FDA ban on DES in cattlefeed saves a life at $132 million each year, while much regulation of automobiles costs $400,000 or less per life.

ment that eliminated self-defeating regulatory strategies would eliminate a significant source of regulatory failure. . . .

II. The Paradoxes

I have defined a regulatory paradox as a self-defeating regulatory strategy; but
whether a strategy is self-defeating depends on how its purposes are described. Any
statute that fails to produce a net benefit to society can be described as self-defeating
if its purpose is described as the improvement of the world. But if the statute's
purpose is to benefit a particular group or segment of society, and that purpose
is achieved, then the statute is not self-defeating at all. For example, a statute
benefiting the agricultural industry at the expense of the public will not be self-
defeating if its purpose is described as helping farmers. Throughout this discussion I
describe the relevant statutory purposes at an intermediate level of generality and as
public-regarding rather than as benefiting special interest groups. Under this approach, a statute whose costs outweigh its benefits, or that produces irrationality of
various sorts, is not necessarily paradoxical.

Moreover, I mean to assess whether a statute is self-defeating by comparing
the result it has produced to the likely state of affairs had Congress enacted a
different and better statute or no statute at all. Measured against these benchmarks,
regulation has produced a wide range of paradoxes.

Importantly, nearly all of the paradoxes are a product of the government's
failure to understand how the relevant actors—administrators and regulated
entities—will adapt to regulatory programs. The world simply cannot be held constant after regulations have been issued. Strategic responses, the creation of perverse incentives for administrators and regulated entities, unanticipated changes in
product mix and private choice—these are the hallmarks of the paradoxes of the
regulatory state. The adoption of strategies that take account of these phenomena
would produce enormous savings in both compliance costs and safety and health
gains. In this sense, a response to the regulatory paradoxes would produce no
losers, or at least no losers who have a legitimate basis for complaint.

A. Paradox 1: Overregulation Produces Underregulation

The first paradox is that especially aggressive statutory controls frequently produce
too little regulation of the private market. This surprising outcome arises when
Congress mandates overly stringent controls, so that administrators will not issue
regulations at all, or will refuse to enforce whatever regulations they or Congress
have issued.

. . .

Statutes containing stringent regulatory requirements have . . . yielded no protection at all in many settings. What is responsible for this astonishing outcome?
One is tempted to find answers in the power of regulated industries or in the
intransigence and deregulatory zeal of government officials. But the pattern of
underregulation can be found in the Carter Administration as well as the Reagan
Administration, even though President Carter's appointees, drawn in large number
from the consumer and environmental movements, were hardly eager to prevent
the government from curbing the proliferation of toxic substances. Elaborate and
costly procedural requirements for the promulgation of federal regulations undoubtedly provide some explanation, since the process, including judicial review,

has built into it enormous delays and perverse incentives.[45] These requirements surely slow down and deter rulemaking. Industry has every opportunity and every incentive to fend off regulation by making plausible claims that additional information is necessary before regulation can be undertaken. This explanation is not in itself adequate, however, because organized interests have not prevented agencies from being far more aggressive in other settings.

A large part of the explanation lies in the stringency of the regulatory standard itself. A stringent standard—one that forbids balancing or calls for regulation to or beyond the point of "feasibility"—makes regulators reluctant to act. If, as is customary, regulators have discretion not to promulgate regulations at all, a stringent standard will provide them with a powerful incentive for inaction. Their inaction is not caused by venality or confusion. Instead, it reflects their quite plausible belief that the statute often requires them to regulate to an absurd point. If regulators were to issue controls under the statute, government and private resources would be unavailable to control other toxic substances; domestic industry costs would increase; and ultimately industries competing in world markets would face a serious risk of shutdown. Under these circumstances, a stringent standard will mobilize political opposition to regulation from within and without government. It will also increase the likelihood of judicial invalidation. Finally, it will require agencies to obtain greater supporting information to survive political and judicial scrutiny, while at the same time making it less likely that such information will be forthcoming from regulated class members. All the incentives are therefore in the direction of issuing fewer regulations.

It is thus unsurprising that a draconian standard produces underregulation as well as overregulation. A crazy quilt pattern of severe controls in some areas and none in others is the predictable consequence of a statute that forbids balancing and tradeoffs.

The problem goes deeper still. Even if the resistance of the agency has been overcome, and some or many regulations have been issued under a statute calling for stringent regulatory controls, the risk of underregulation does not disappear. Levels of enforcement—inspections and fines—will reflect the agency's reluctance. This has in fact been the pattern with OSHA's safety and health regulations, some of which have been effectively unenforced by Democratic as well as Republican administrations. This, then, is the first paradox of the regulatory state: stringent regulatory standards produce underregulation.[49]

---

[45] . . . For an intriguing solution to this problem, see the discussion of California's Proposition 65 in David Roe, *An Incentive-Conscious Approach to Toxic Chemical Controls*, 3 Econ. Dev. Q. 179 (1979). Proposition 65 requires businesses to warn people exposed to any one of a list of specified chemicals, unless there has been a governmental finding that the chemical in question poses no significant risk. By putting the burden of inertia on regulated industry, Proposition 65 creates incentives rather than disincentives for the issuance of regulations distinguishing safe from unsafe levels.

[49] At least in theory, it is possible that this effect will not occur—if the agency has no enforcement discretion, or if it is determined (for example) to eliminate all risk-creating substances from the atmosphere. But the absence of enforcement discretion is rare, and an agency determined to eliminate all risks will create paradoxes of its own—causing ancillary social harms, or producing greater risks of different sorts.

B. Paradox 2: Stringent Regulation of New Risks
   ## Can Increase Aggregate Risk Levels

Frequently Congress is presented with a risk or problem that can be found both in existing entities and in potential entrants. For example, automobiles produce carbon monoxide; modern electricity plants emit sulfur dioxide; many existing buildings are inaccessible to the handicapped; and drugs currently on the market pose health hazards to consumers. In such situations, a common strategy has been to impose especially severe limitations on new sources but to exempt old ones. Indeed, such exemptions might be a political prerequisite for enactment of the regulation. Congress might require that new automobiles be equipped with pollution control devices, that new plants emitting pollution meet stringent regulatory controls, that new buildings be accessible to the handicapped, and that new drugs survive special safety requirements.

This strategy is a pervasive one in current regulatory law, and it has obvious advantages. Retroactive application of regulatory requirements can be extremely costly; the expense of altering existing practices is often high. Requiring the specified approach only prospectively can achieve significant savings. In addition, it may be unfair to impose costs on people who would have ordered their affairs quite differently had they been informed beforehand of the regulatory regime.

As a control technique, however, the strategy of imposing costs exclusively on new sources or entrants can be self-defeating. Most important, it will discourage the addition of new sources and encourage the perpetuation of old ones. The problem is not merely that old risks will continue, but that, precisely because of regulatory programs, those risks will become more common and last longer than they otherwise would.

Two different phenomena underlie the old risk–new risk paradox. First, those who plan regulatory programs often assume that the programs will not influence private choices. Private choices are, however, a function of current supply and demand. If the program raises the price of new products it will shift choices in the direction of old risks. Second, a focus on new risks reduces the entry of potentially superior sources or technologies and thus perpetuates old ones. Regulatory controls eliminate possibilities that might have turned out to be substantially safer than currently available options. The result is to increase the life of those options.

Examples are not difficult to find. The EPA's program requiring the installation of anti-pollution technology in new automobiles belongs in the first category. This program has prolonged the use of old, dirty vehicles, retarding the ordinary, salutary retirement of major sources of environmental degradation. Command and control regulation of new pollution sources creates incentives to use existing facilities longer, with harmful consequences for the environment. Prescription requirements probably discourage people from purchasing beneficial drugs and to that extent impair health. Imposition of high, safety-related costs on new airplanes may well encourage airlines to retain (and repair) old, risky planes.

One might put the EPA's requirement of costly "scrubbing" strategies for new sources of sulfur dioxide in the second category. This rule has perpetuated the existence of old sources of sulfur dioxide, thus aggravating in many parts of the country the very problem it was designed to solve. So too, the imposition of stringent barriers to nuclear power plants has perpetuated the risks produced by coal, a significantly more dangerous power source. And perhaps worst of all, the FDA's stringent regulatory standards for approving new drugs have forced consumers to resort to old drugs, which are frequently more dangerous or less beneficial than the new drugs being kept off the market.

A final example of the old risk/new risk paradox is the Delaney Clause, which prohibits manufacturers from using food additives containing carcinogens. Ironically, this provision has probably increased safety and health risks. The Clause forces manufacturers to use noncarcinogenic, but sometimes more dangerous, substances. In addition, it makes consumers resort to substances already on the market that often pose greater risks than new entrants would. Since the newest and best detection equipment is used on proposed new additives, the statutorily prohibited additive may well pose fewer risks to consumers than substances already on the market that were tested with cruder technology. Thus the Delaney Clause defeats its own purpose.[60]

The phenomenon of careful regulation of new risks and lenient or no regulation of old ones may not simply reflect legislative myopia or confusion. Public choice theory provides a plausible explanation for the phenomenon. A system of regulation that imposes controls solely on new products or facilities should have considerable appeal for those in possession of old ones. If new sources will face regulatory costs, the system of government controls will immunize existing producers from fresh competition. Indeed, the regulatory statute will create a partial cartel, establishing a common interest among current producers and giving them a significant competitive advantage over potential new entrants. The victims of the old-new division, however, often do not yet exist. They are usually hard to identify, do not perceive themselves as victims, and are not politically organized.

It may be for this reason that the careful regulation of new risks is such a popular strategy. It is apt to be favored both by existing industry and by many of those who seek to impose controls in the first instance. The potential victims—consumers and new entrants—often have insufficient political strength to counter the proposals. When this phenomenon is combined with the apparently sensible but sometimes self-defeating idea that a phase-in strategy is better than one that requires conversions of existing producers, it is no surprise that the old risk–new risk division remains so popular.

C. Paradox 3: To Require the Best Available Technology Is to Retard Technological Development

Industry frequently fails to adopt the best technology for controlling environmental or other harms. The technology exists or can be developed relatively cheaply, but

---

[60] . . . A qualification is necessary here. It is possible that people are especially fearful of cancer and not so fearful of other, equally dangerous health risks, and that this configuration of fears underlay the Delaney Clause. In that case, the Clause would serve its specific purpose of keeping carcinogens off the market, irrespective of the relative health risks of various products. Although the Clause might in fact increase overall health risks, it would not be a regulatory paradox, since it successfully implements its primary goal.

polluters simply refuse to use it. Congress and the EPA have often responded by requiring that all industries use the best available technology (BAT). The BAT strategy is pervasive in federal environmental law, and may indeed be its most distinctive characteristic.

The BAT strategy is motivated by a desire to produce technological innovation, and here it has a surface plausibility. As discussed above, recent years have witnessed large decreases in air and water pollution, and these decreases are partly attributable to the use of emission control technologies. Requiring the adoption of the best available control technology seems a sensible way to ensure that all industries are doing their utmost to prevent pollution. This strategy also appears inexpensive to enforce. The government simply decides on the best technology and then requires all industries to comply.

The BAT approach, however, can defeat its own purposes and thus produce a regulatory paradox. It is an extremely clumsy strategy for protecting the environment. To be sure, the approach is a plausible one if the goal is to ensure that all firms use currently established technology. But a large goal of regulation should be to promote technological innovation in pollution control. Regulation should increase rather than decrease incentives to innovate. Government is rarely in a good position to know what sorts of innovations are likely to be forthcoming; industry will have a huge comparative advantage here. Perversely, requiring adoption of the BAT eliminates the incentive to innovate at all, and indeed creates disincentives for innovation by imposing an economic punishment on innovators. Under the BAT approach, polluting industries have no financial interest in the development of better pollution control technology that imposes higher production costs. Indeed, the opposite is true. The BAT approach encourages industry to seek any means to delay and deter new regulation. Industry will have the information as well as the incentive to persuade administrators, courts, and other authorities that a suggested technology is not "feasible" and should not be required.

If government requires whatever technology is available, then, industry has no economic reason to develop new mechanisms for decreasing safety and health risks. Moreover, the BAT approach, applicable as it is only to new sources, raises the cost of retiring old facilities, which delays capital turnover and in that way aggravates environmental degradation. The paradox, in a nutshell, is this: designed to promote good control technology, the BAT strategy actually discourages innovation. It is therefore self-defeating.

One might respond to this hypothesis by arguing that under the BAT approach outsiders should have an incentive to innovate, precisely because government will force industry to adopt the resulting technology. But no well-functioning market in pollution control technology exists for those outside of the regulated industries, and for good reasons. First, outsiders often lack the relevant information, which is unusually expensive because it turns on facts that are highly technical and known best to participants in the industry. In practice, outsiders must depend on cooperation from regulated class members, which is unlikely to be forthcoming. The start-up costs are therefore exceptionally high for third parties. Second, regulation often changes dramatically over time, a phenomenon that discourages a stable market in control technology. The result is that innovations by outsiders have not come about under BAT approaches. . . .

E. Paradox 5: Disclosure Requirements May Make People Less Informed

Sometimes markets fail because people are deceived or lack information. Regulatory agencies commonly respond by requiring correction or full disclosure. Congress and agencies have imposed disclosure regulations in many areas, ranging from occupational and environmental risks to potentially deceptive advertising. Here the rationale is straightforward. Whether or not ignorance is bliss, it is an obstacle to informed consumer choice. Surely, it might be asked, regulation cannot be condemned for increasing information?

Disclosure strategies are indeed valuable in many circumstances. But for two reasons, they can be self-defeating. The first is that people sometimes process information poorly. After being given certain data, they actually "know" less than they did beforehand. In particular, when people receive information about probabilities, especially low ones, they frequently rely on heuristics that lead to systematic errors. Thus, for example, people assess probabilities by asking if the event was a recent one and by misunderstanding the phenomenon of regression to the mean. In addition, disclosure or corrective language can help straighten out one form of false belief but at the same time increase the level of other kinds of false beliefs. Finally, there is a risk of information overload, causing consumers to treat a large amount of information as equivalent to no information at all. All this suggests that with respect to information, less may be more. Additional information can breed confusion and a weaker understanding of the situation at hand.

The second problem is that a requirement of disclosure or perfect accuracy will sometimes lead producers or other regulated entities to furnish no information whatsoever. For example, if producers are prohibited from advertising unless they eliminate all potential deception or offer strong substantiation for their claims, they might not advertise at all. The result will be the removal from the market of information that is useful overall. If advertisers must conduct extensive tests before they are permitted to make claims, they will be given a strong incentive to avoid making claims at all. More generally, almost all substantive advertisements will deceive at least some people in light of the exceptional heterogeneity of listeners and viewers. If this is so, efforts to eliminate deception will significantly reduce advertising with substantive content.

These various difficulties suggest that the recent enthusiasm for disclosure requirements is in at least some settings a mistake, for the simple reason that it defeats its own purpose. Disclosure requirements sometimes ensure that people are less informed.

. . .

COMMENTS AND QUESTIONS

1. How avoidable are the paradoxes Sunstein identifies? Do they arise from errors by those who design regulatory programs, from political constraints on those designers, or both?

2. Consider whether the paradoxes reinforce each other or might (sometimes) offset each other's deficiencies. For example, a designer of the regulatory program, who is aware of the possibility that requiring industries to use the best available

technology can discourage innovation, might impose a "technology-forcing" regulation, in the form of a specific target that the industry *must* reach. That target, though, might be a form of overregulation. How might a designer respond to this difficulty? One possibility might be to set gradually increasing targets and at each stage require industries to adopt "best practices," that is, techniques that some within the industry have *already* used to reach the prior stage target.

3. A similar question might be asked about the paradox of "excessive" information provision. Consider that, for example, disclosure of risks associated with the use of a product might result in consumers demanding a "risk reduction" in the price, or that disclosure of risks associated with a chemical used in the workplace might encourage workers to demand a compensatory wage premium. One regulatory response to that paradox would be the imposition of substantive regulatory requirements, that is, issuing a ban on the harmful product rather than requiring disclosure of the harm to the potentially affected persons. Reconsider here Kennedy's arguments supporting mandatory terms.

4. A narrower question: Sunstein addresses, and discounts, the possibility that new entrants will compete to provide better technology. With respect to information provision, what might a "new entrant" (or an existing producer seeking to carve out a market niche) do when confronted with a regulatory requirement that claims be substantiated?

5. Finally, note that the paradoxes might exist, but their scope needs to be identified empirically. (Sunstein says that they are a "pervasive source" of problems in the regulatory state.) Their impact might be small relative to the political constraints Mendeloff and Sunstein identify—or they might be large. Again, recall Kennedy's observation that policy choices are (often?) made on the basis of undefended empirical assessments, which (he argues) are preferred in U.S. policy discourse to direct normative judgments.

■ *Richer Is Safer*
AARON WILDAVSKY
60 *The Public Interest* 23 (1980). Reprinted with permission
of *The Public Interest*

The proverbial man from Mars, observing our safety efforts in the past decade, could not help but conclude that the youth of America were dropping like flies in the streets. Why else would the United States federal government be engaged in a desperate, multi-billion-dollar effort to increase life expectancy? But the Martian historian of earthly safety would note that in the hundred years from 1870 to 1970 every increase in industrialization and wealth, except possibly at the highest levels, was accompanied by a corresponding increase in safety from accident and disease. Thus he would surely wonder: Since personal safety and economic growth advanced together, why is present policy based precisely on severing that link by deliberately decreasing wealth in order to remove risk?

. . .

The issue should be confronted head on: how much reduction of risk by direct expenditure on that very purpose versus how much increase in safety by expanding the national product? Existing public policy is based on the belief that the way to reduce risk is to do so directly for each and every group of people adversely affected. What are believed to be excessive risks are identified and policies are proposed to reduce them by direct action of government. This view may be mistaken. Though efforts to reduce risk in individual instances may be successful, the very same actions may increase risk for more people. To the current conventional wisdom that the way to reduce risk is deliberately to make the nation poorer than it would have been, I counterpose the perception of our parents that, having tried the alternative, "richer is better" and, I would add, safer too.

Health and Wealth

Consider the condition of poor countries. Death rates go up as income goes down. Though death rates show considerable improvement after inexpensive public-health measures are introduced, poor countries not only lag behind richer countries, but among themselves have higher or lower death rates according to their relative incomes. The same is true within the United States; health and income remain highly related. Increasing the income of nations and classes is evidently one way of improving safety.

A study by Irma Adelman in *The American Economic Review* of some five countries in 1953 showed the usual "negative long run association between death rates and economic conditions." She goes on to state what everyone then took for granted:

> For it stands to reason that such factors as better nutrition, improved housing, healthier and more humane working conditions, and a some what more secure and less careworn mode of life, all of which accompany economic growth, must contribute to improvements in life expectancy. In addition, as pointed out by Spiegelman, "Fundamentally, health progress depends upon economic progress. By the rapid advance in their economies in the postwar period the highly developed countries have produced wealth for the development of health programs. Also, more efficient technologies in industry are releasing the manpower needed for an extension of medical care and public health services. The intangible contribution of economic progress to lower mortality is derived from the advantage of a high standard of living—abundant, better and more time for healthful recreation."

The classic study of England and Wales in the 1920's by Jean Daric led him to conclude that social class was a more powerful predictor of mortality rates than risk of work.

Within the United States, the same conclusion about "a strong inverse association between mortality and income" was reached by Evelyn Kitagawa and Philip Hauser in their *Trends and Differentials in Mortality* (Harvard University Press, 1973):

> Over the years mortality has declined by reason of a number of factors, including increased productivity, higher standards of living, decreased internecine warfare, environmental sanitation, personal hygiene, public health measures, and modern medicine climaxed by the advent of the pesticides and chemotherapy. Programs aimed at the reduction of death rates have been primarily based on biomedical epidemiology and biomedical ameliorative

programs. This analysis of socioeconomic differentials in mortality may be viewed as documentation of the need for increasing attention to socioeconomic epidemiology. The evidence indicates that further reductions in death rates in the United States may be achieved more readily through programs designed to improve the socioeconomic conditions of the disadvantaged elements of the population than through further advances in biomedical knowledge.

The data on life expectancy and economic level for more recent times all point in the same direction: the lower the income, the higher the death rate at earlier ages.... As Ernest Siddall puts it: "It appears that the creation of wealth leads to the saving of lives in very large numbers at a net long-term cost which is zero or negative." Improving countries' or classes' incomes increases their safety more than new efforts to reduce risk.

. . .

The conclusion stares us in the face: If health and wealth are positively related, sacrificing one for the other may not only lead to less wealth but also to less health.
. . .

COMMENTS AND QUESTIONS

1. Starting from Wildavsky's thesis that wealth breeds health, several economists have attempted to identify the precise level at which governmental regulation begins to harm health—indeed, to kill people—because of its sheer costliness. These estimates vary substantially in both magnitude and methodology. One early study, by Ralph Keeney, concluded that regulations costing more than approximately $7.5 million per life saved would lead to one death through their effect on individual wealth. Ralph L. Keeney, *Mortality Risks Induced by Economic Expenditures*, 10 Risk Analysis 147, 155 (1990). One key assumption of Keeney's study was that wealth leads to health. Critics of his study have argued that it is just as likely that health leads to wealth. Is it even more likely that the truth lies in between, that is, that the wealth-health relationship works in both causal directions?

2. Kip Viscusi has offered at least two different estimates of the point at which regulation designed to save lives will become self-defeating because of the relationship between health and wealth. In one study, described in *Regulating the Regulators*, 63 U. Chi. L. Rev. 1423 (1996), Viscusi concluded that regulations costing more than approximately $50 million will lead to one death because of the relationship between income and mortality. He based this estimate on two important subsidiary estimates: (1) the value of life is $5 million, and (2) the marginal propensity to spend on health-improving goods and services is 0.1, or in other words, for every $10 individuals spend, they spend $1, on average, on health-improving goods and services. Put simply, Viscusi's claim is that, given $50 million to spend absent a regulation costing that much, society would spend $5 million of this on risk-reducing activities; if $50 million is spent instead on regulation, this private risk-reducing activity is lost.

3. Viscusi and coauthors later offered a substantially lower estimate of the point at which regulation becomes self-defeating. Randall Lutter, John F. Morrall, III,

and W. Kip Viscusi, *The Cost-per-Life-Saved Cutoff for Safety-Enhancing Regulations*, 37 Econ. Inquiry 599 (1999). There Viscusi estimates that regulation will lead to one death when it costs more than $15 million per life saved. Viscusi's later estimate is based on a methodology similar to the one described in note 2, except that this study also takes account of consumption activities that tend to increase risk. Note that even the lowered estimate of the tipping point in this study is twice that in Keeney's study. How useful is an approach that must rely on such a wide range of valuations?

4. Should agencies be required to consider the wealth-health relationship in setting health and safety standards? What if a regulation costs $50 million per life saved, but the cost of the regulation is borne by Bill Gates alone? Will his health be affected by such a regulation? What if the cost of the regulation is $50 million, but it is borne by 50 million different people? Will their health be affected by the extra $1 expenditure? What if a regulation also creates jobs?

5. One judicial opinion has suggested that agencies should consider the indirect health effects of regulation that purportedly occur because of the economic impact of regulation. In *International Union, United Automobile, Aerospace & Agricultural Implement Workers of America, UAW v. Occupational Safety & Health Administration ("Lockout/Tagout I")*, 938 F.2d 1310 (D.C. Cir. 1991), Judge Williams concurred in his own majority opinion remanding a workplace safety rule, observing as follows:

> ...More regulation means some combination of reduced value of firms, higher product prices, fewer jobs in the regulated industry, and lower cash wages. All the latter three stretch workers' budgets tighter (as does the first to the extent that the firms' stock is held in workers' pension trusts). And larger incomes enable people to lead safer lives. One study finds a 1 percent increase in income associated with a mortality reduction of about 0.05 percent. Jack Hadley and Anthony Osei, "Does Income Affect Mortality?" 20 Medical Care 901, 913 (September 1982). Another suggests that each $7.5 million of costs generated by regulation may, under certain assumptions, induce one fatality. Ralph L. Keeney, "Mortality Risks Induced by Economic Expenditures," 10 Risk Analysis 147, 155 (1990) (relying on E. M. Kitagawa and P. M. Hauser, Differential Mortality in the United States of America: A Study of Socioeconomic Epidemiology (1973)). Larger incomes can produce health by enlarging a person's access to better diet, preventive medical care, safer cars, greater leisure, etc. See Aaron Wildavsky, Searching for Safety 59–71 (1988).
>
> Of course, other causal relations may be at work too. Healthier people may be able to earn higher income, and characteristics and advantages that facilitate high earnings (e.g., work ethic, education) may also lead to better health. Compare C. P. Wen, et al., "Anatomy of the Healthy Worker Effect: A Critical Review," 25 J. of Occupation Medicine 283 (1983). Nonetheless, higher income can secure better health, and there is no basis for a casual assumption that more stringent regulation will always save lives.
>
> It follows that while officials involved in health or safety regulation may naturally be hesitant to set any kind of numerical value on human

life, undue squeamishness may be deadly. Incremental safety regulation reduces incomes and thus may exact a cost in human lives. For example, if analysis showed that "an individual life was lost for every $12 million taken from individuals [as a result of the regulation], this would be a guide to a reasonable value trade-off for many programs designed to save lives." Keeney, "Mortality Risks Induced by Economic Expenditures," 10 Risk Analysis at 158. Such a figure could serve as a ceiling for value-of-life calculated by other means, since regulation causing greater expenditures per life expected to be saved would, everything else being equal, result in a net loss of life.

B How Regulation Can Fail: Practice

Competitive Enterprise Institute v. National Highway Traffic Safety Admin.
956 F.2d 321 (D.C. Cir. 1992)

Stephen Williams, Circuit Judge (joined by Judge Clarence Thomas):

Choice means giving something up. In deciding whether to relax the previously established "corporate average fuel economy" ("CAFE") standard for model year 1990, the National Highway Traffic Safety Administration ("NHTSA") confronted a record suggesting that refusal to do so would exact some penalty in auto safety. Rather than affirmatively choosing extra energy savings over extra safety, however, NHTSA obscured the safety problem, and thus its need to choose. Because NHTSA failed to reason through to its decision, we remand the case for further consideration.

. . .

The Energy Policy and Conservation Act requires every major carmaker to keep the average fuel economy of its fleet, in each model year, at or above a prescribed level. The Act holds manufacturers to a standard of 27.5 miles per gallon for model year 1985 and each model year thereafter, but authorizes NHTSA to modify the standard, up or down. Where the agency chooses to modify, it must set the replacement standard at the "maximum feasible average fuel economy level." In determining "feasibility," NHTSA has always taken passenger safety into account, and the agency maintains that safety concerns are relevant to whether the agency should adopt one CAFE standard over another.

In August 1988, at the behest of various parties, including several major carmakers and petitioner Competitive Enterprise Institute ("CEI"), NHTSA initiated a rulemaking proceeding on whether to reduce the CAFE standards for model years 1989 and 1990. The agency quickly lowered the standard for model year 1989 to 26.5 mpg, but it continued to hear public comment on whether to reduce the 1990 standard as well. Then, in May 1989, NHTSA terminated its proceedings on that issue and left the statutory standard in place.

While the agency rejected a variety of attacks on that standard, we are concerned with only one of the defeated arguments: the contention that the standard will force carmakers to produce smaller, less safe cars, thus making it more difficult and expensive for consumers to buy larger, safer cars. We find that the agency has not coherently addressed this concern.

. . .

. . . [W]e must determine whether NHTSA has offered a reasoned explanation for terminating its inquiry into whether to relax the 27.5 standard. The statute does not specify criteria for when NHTSA must persevere in a rulemaking it has already initiated, but the agency does not dispute that there is "law to apply." The parties do disagree on the appropriate degree of deference owed to an agency's decision to terminate a rulemaking proceeding. But the exact degree is unimportant. Petitioners' essential claim is an attack not on NHTSA's judgment call, but on NHTSA's attempt to paper over the need to make a call. We cannot defer to mere decisional evasion.

When the automaking firms petitioned for a reduction in the model year 1990 standard down to 26.5 mpg, and petitioners pressed the argument that failure to reduce the standard would cost lives, NHTSA had three basic choices. First, it might have concluded that the statute does not require it to consider safety effects when deciding whether to embark on a modification proceeding. It could then have dismissed petitioners' claims without further ado. While a court might have reversed, the statutory framework is so loose and deference under *Chevron U.S.A. v. NRDC*, 467 U.S. 837 (1984), so broad that the agency would have had a fair shot at being upheld.

Second, NHTSA might have seriously examined the record data. On its face this suggested (as we shall see) the overwhelming likelihood that a 27.5 mpg standard reduces the supply of safe cars available to American consumers. Conceivably, of course, a sophisticated analysis might have overcome the record's apparent implications, but even if it did not, all NHTSA would have had to do was face the trade-off. It could have said that while the 27.5 standard might cost, say, 200-to-500 American lives a year for ten years, it would also reduce American oil imports by, say, 50,000-to-400,000 barrels a year, and that in its judgment the trade-off was worth it. And it could have expressed any such trade-off in less numerical terms.

Finally, NHTSA could have fudged the analysis, held the standard at 27.5, and, with the help of statistical legerdemain, made conclusory assertions that its decision had no safety cost at all. That is what it chose. The people petitioners represent, consumers who do not want to be priced out of the market for larger, safer cars, deserve better from their government.

We must remand this case to NHTSA if the agency has not adequately explained why one of the following is false: (1) adopting a 27.5 standard (as opposed to a lower standard) will have some constraining effect on carmakers; (2) carmakers will, as one consequence of the standard, decrease the average size of their cars below what it would have been absent the standard; (3) this decrease will make it more difficult for consumers to drive large cars; and (4) all other things being equal, a large car is safer than a small car. The agency actually admits the truth of the fourth proposition, and we can find no passage in the record where the agency has coherently explained the falsehood of any of the others.

Constraining Automakers

As the agency conceded at oral argument, the 27.5 mpg standard obviously affects carmakers' behavior—if not in model year 1990, at least in subsequent years. Under the statute, if a carmaker exceeds the applicable CAFE standard in one year, it earns credits that it may use to offset CAFE deficiencies over the next three years. At the very least, keeping the 1990 standard at 27.5 mpg reduces the number of carryover credits that GM can use to blunt the effect of the CAFE standards for model years 1991–93. Accordingly, NHTSA expressed its quite reasonable belief that "the potential actual [*sic*] impacts on energy conservation [from retention of the 27.5 mpg standard for model year 1990] are largely related to multi-year considerations." In fact, NHTSA recently declared that it would be unlawful for it to set "CAFE standards deliberately low enough to be 'nonconstraining.'" It seems obvious, then, that the 27.5 mpg standard is constraining in one way or another.

Automakers' Likely Choice to Downsize

Second, the agency insisted at oral argument that even if the 27.5 standard constrains the behavior of carmakers, it will not lead to smaller cars. Yet nowhere has the agency actually justified this claim or even purported to make such a finding. It came closest in the following passage:

> There are still a number of fuel-efficiency enhancing methods that [GM and Ford have] not fully utilized throughout their fleets. . . . NHTSA believes that the domestic manufacturers should be able to improve their fuel economy in the future by these and/or other technological means, without outsourcing their larger cars, without further downsizing or mix shifts toward smaller cars, and without sacrificing acceleration or performance.

Why the agency expressed itself in the normative ("should be") is anybody's guess. At any rate, it has never claimed that domestic manufacturers will in fact meet the standard without downsizing their fleets, or even that there is a substantial probability that they will do so, or even that there is a substantial likelihood that they will use methods other than downsizing for the lion's share of the work. Presumably NHTSA does not assert such facts because it could not ground them in the record.

Moreover, to the extent that carmakers choose technological innovation over downsizing (and further assuming that such innovation would not itself compromise aspects of auto safety), that choice would involve significant costs in implementation, even if we assume that research and development are complete. That cost would translate into higher prices for large cars (as well as small), thereby pressuring consumers to retain their old cars and make the associated sacrifice in safety. The result would be effectively the same harm that concerns petitioners and that the agency fails to negate or justify.

The historical fact is, however, that carmakers respond to CAFE standards by reducing the size of their fleets. NHTSA itself has explicitly acknowledged as much in the past, and we ourselves have insisted that "the evidence shows that manufacturers are likely to respond to lower CAFE standards by continuing or expanding production of larger, heavier vehicles." Even in the decision below the agency acknowledged this link, explaining that "Chrysler's CAFE has been higher than that of GM or Ford in recent years primarily because it does not compete, or compete as heavily, in all the market segments in which GM and Ford sell cars, particularly the large car market."

The agency now tries to obscure this reality by pointing out that "the average fuel economy of the new car fleet has improved steadily from 26.6 mpg in model year 1982 to 28.2 mpg in model year 1987, while the average weight of a new car increased two pounds during the same period." This argument misses the point. The appropriate comparison, which NHTSA must but did not address, is between the world with more stringent CAFE standards and the world with less stringent standards. The fact that weight has remained constant over time despite mileage improvements shows the effect of technological improvements, to be sure, but in no way undermines the natural inference that weight is lower than it would be absent CAFE regulation. Here we can be quite sure that it is lower, since, as NHTSA observed in this decision, economic recovery and declining gasoline prices sharply raised consumer demand for large cars over the relevant period. If consumers demanded substantially bigger cars, carmakers—absent regulation—would have produced substantially bigger cars, not cars that remained, on average, within two pounds of the cars made when consumers favored smaller cars. Moreover, NHTSA has given us no reason to think that whatever technological innovations permitted automakers to meet CAFE requirements while keeping weight constant did not also cost consumers more, again pricing some consumers out of the market for new large cars.

Effect on Consumer Access to Large Cars

NHTSA also argues that even if the 27.5 mpg standard will deplete the supply of large GM or Ford cars, a consumer looking for a big car "will buy a large car from another manufacturer, or will buy a minivan, or will keep his or her older, large car.... Any one of those alternative consumer outcomes is far more likely than the possibility that the consumer will buy a smaller car than he or she wanted to buy." Nothing in the record suggests that any of these will give consumers large-car safety at the prices that would have prevailed if NHTSA had made a less stringent choice.

The reference to buying large cars from "another manufacturer" is somewhat in the spirit of Marie Antoinette's suggestion to "let them eat cake." By NHTSA's own hypothesis, the "other manufacturers" are Chrysler, which has essentially removed itself from the large car market, and foreign manufacturers, which are subject to CAFE standards on their U.S. sales. To the limited extent that foreign firms produce truly large cars at all, they are expensive ones.

In suggesting minivans (which are exempt from the 27.5 standard), the agency disingenuously obscures their dangers by citing safety figures only for vans in general. As NHTSA itself has amply documented, however, minivans are considerably less safe than vans generally, with a fatality rate per registered vehicle about 25–33% higher than that of large cars. Finally, NHTSA's notion that the consumer should "keep his or her older, large car" ignores both its own finding that new cars "appear to experience fewer accidents per mile traveled," and the plight of consumers seeking to buy a large car for the first time.

Impact on Safety

By making it harder for consumers to buy large cars, the 27.5 mpg standard will increase traffic fatalities if, as a general matter, small cars are less safe than big ones. They are, as NHTSA itself acknowledges. The agency explains:

> Occupants of the smaller cars generally are at greater risk because: (a) the occupant's survival space is generally less in small cars (survival space, in simple terms, means enough room for the occupant to be held by the vehicle's occupant restraint system without being smashed into injurious surfaces, and

enough room to prevent being crushed or hit by a collapsing surface); (b) smaller and lighter vehicles generally have less physical structure available to absorb and manage crash energy and forces; and (c) in most collisions between vehicles of different weight, the forces imposed on occupants of lighter cars are proportionately greater than the forces felt by occupants of heavier vehicles.[2]

The agency tries to skirt the obvious conclusion with two specious arguments. First, it essentially argues that the 27.5 mpg standard will have no effect on the availability of large cars (i.e., will accomplish nothing at all). This, we have seen, is simply untrue. Second, the agency observes that new cars now come with a variety of mandatory and optional safety features (airbags, anti-lock brakes, etc.) that will presumably compensate for a decline in size.

There are two things wrong with this latter argument. First, so far as we can tell, the agency nowhere claims that these safety innovations fully or even mostly compensate for the safety dangers associated with downsizing. More critically, as in the relation between fuel economy and downsizing, the relevant inquiry is whether stringent CAFE standards reduce auto safety below what it would be absent such standards. That new safety devices may be coming on the market is all well and good, but it is immaterial to our inquiry unless the implementation of those devices somehow depends on or is caused by more stringent CAFE standards; no one even hints at such a link. Whatever extra safety devices may contribute to either type, small cars remain more dangerous than large ones, *all other things being equal*.

. . .

Nothing in the record or in NHTSA's analysis appears to undermine the inference that the 27.5 mpg standard kills people, although, as we observed before, we cannot rule out the possibility that NHTSA might support a contrary finding. Assuming it cannot, the number of people sacrificed is uncertain. Forced to confront the issue, the agency might arrive at an estimate lower than that of two independent analysts who came up with an annual death rate running into the thousands (for the cars produced in any one model year). See Robert W. Crandall and John D. Graham, *The Effect of Fuel Economy Standards on Automobile Safety*, 32 J. Law & Econ. 97 (April 1989). Yet the actual number is irrelevant for our purposes. Even if the 27.5 mpg standard for model year 1990 kills "only" several dozen people a year, NHTSA must exercise its discretion; that means conducting a serious analysis of the data and deciding whether the associated fuel savings are worth the lives lost.

When the government regulates in a way that prices many of its citizens out of access to large-car safety, it owes them reasonable candor. If it provides that, the

---

[2] One might argue that the third factor indicates that if all cars were small, there would be fewer traffic fatalities. Any such inference appears quite doubtful. Cars can hit a variety of objects, including trucks, trees, and other cars; fatalities in car-to-car crashes do not account for even a majority of passenger-car occupant fatalities. Unless NHTSA outlaws trucks and trees, smaller cars will probably always mean higher fatality rates, as NHTSA recognizes. Moreover, while the record is not clear on the matter, it appears that the chance of fatality in crashes involving two big cars is substantially lower than the chance of fatality in crashes involving two small ones.

affected citizens at least know that the government has faced up to the meaning of its choice. The requirement of reasoned decisionmaking ensures this result and prevents officials from cowering behind bureaucratic mumbo-jumbo. Accordingly, we order NHTSA to reconsider the matter and provide a genuine explanation for whatever choice it ultimately makes.

[Judge Mikva dissented.]

COMMENTS AND QUESTIONS

1. *A brief review of administrative law*: Can you construct an argument that the Court of Appeals in *CEI* improperly imposed additional procedural requirements on the agency, in conflict with *Vermont Yankee*? How would you analyze this case under *Chevron* had NHTSA concluded that the statutory standard "maximum feasible average fuel economy level" (a) did not permit it to consider safety effects of increasing the CAFE level or (b) allowed it to ignore such safety effects?

2. NHTSA argued that there was no real trade-off between increased fuel efficiency and safety. What (if anything) was the factual basis for that argument? The Court of Appeals holds that the agency's conclusion on this question was arbitrary and capricious, because the agency had failed to "face up to" the real trade-off.

3. The Court of Appeals requires that the agency make explicit the fuel efficiency versus safety risk trade-off. Is that a good idea as a matter of policy? Doing so increases the transparency of the agency's decision-making process. It also might bring to the public's attention the fact, which the public might find troubling, that such trade-offs are inevitable. Should the fact that the public finds it troubling to acknowledge such trade-offs be part of the policy analysis? Recall the Ford Pinto litigation you examined in chapter 4, and consider whether making the trade-off explicit would discredit the regulatory enterprise entirely. For a subtle and classic analysis of the pervasiveness of processes that conceal the existence of real trade-offs, see Guido Calabresi and Philip Bobbitt, *Tragic Choices* (1978).

4. One problem with evaluating trade-offs is that it may be difficult to compare increases in fuel efficiency with increases in risks to life. One at least interim solution might be to confine our attention to one category at a time. This process is sometimes called "risk-risk" evaluation. The idea is to see whether, for example, a regulatory intervention that has some beneficial effects on health might have offsetting and larger adverse effects *on health*. (But is "health" a single category? Consider that some effects on health might be on the incidence of pulmonary disease while others might be on the incidence of cancer—or, in the context of workplace safety and health, some effects might be on the risk of loss of limbs while others might be on the risk of loss of life.)

5. The following regulatory decision serves as a summary and a transition. It involves the cancellation of the registration of DDT, that is, the effective imposition of a ban on DDT's use in nearly all settings where it had been common. As you read the decision, note which parties opposed cancellation,

and pay attention to their arguments. What regulatory paradox did they identify?

■ *Consolidated DDT Hearings: Opinion and Order of the Administrator*
WILLIAM D. RUCKELSHAUS
37 Fed. Reg. 13369 (June 14, 1972)

This hearing represents the culmination of approximately 3 years of intensive administrative inquiry into the uses of DDT. . . . I am persuaded for reasons set forth in Part III of this opinion that the long-range risks of continued use of DDT for use on cotton and most other crops is unacceptable and outweighs any benefits. . . .

DDT is the familiar abbreviation for the chemical (1,1,1, trichlorophenyl ethane), which was for many years the most widely used chemical pesticide in this country. DDT's insecticidal properties were originally discovered, apparently by accident, in 1930, and during World War II it was used extensively for typhus control. Since 1945, DDT has been used for general control of mosquitoes, boll weevil infestation in cotton-growing areas, and a variety of other uses. Peak use of DDT occurred at the end of the 1950s and present domestic use of DDT in various formulations has been estimated at 6,000 tons per year. According to Admission 7 of the record, approximately 86 percent of 10,277,258 pounds of domestically used DDT is applied to cotton crops. The same admission indicates that 603,053 pounds and 937,901 pounds, or approximately 5 percent and 9 percent of the total formulated by 27 of the petitioners in these hearings are used respectively on soybean and peanut crops. All other uses of the 11,966,196 pounds amount to 158,833 of the total, or little over 1 percent.

. . .

Public concern over the widespread use of pesticides was stirred by Rachel Carson's book, *Silent Spring*, and a natural outgrowth was the investigation of this popular and widely sprayed chemical. DDT, which for many years had been used with apparent safety, was, the critics alleged, a highly dangerous substance which killed beneficial insects, upset the natural ecological balance, and collected in the food chain, thus posing a hazard to man, and other forms of advanced aquatic and avian life. . . .

. . .

The testimony and exhibits cover in exhaustive fashion all aspects of DDT's chemical and toxicological properties. The evidence of record, however, is not so extensive concerning the benefits from using DDT, and most of it has been directed to the major use, which is on cotton crops.

The Pesticides Office and Environmental Defense Fund (EDF), in presenting their cases against continued registration for DDT, lean most heavily on evidence which, they contend, establishes: (1) That DDT and its metabolites are toxicants which persist in soil and the aquasphere; (2) that once unleashed, DDT is an uncontrollable chemical which can be transported by leaching, erosion, runoff, and volatilization; (3) that DDT is not water soluble and collects in fat tissue; (4) that organisms tend to collect and concentrate DDT; (5) that these qualities result in accumulations of DDT in wildlife and humans; (6) that once stored or consumed,

DDT can be toxic to both animals and humans, and in the case of fish and wildlife inhibit regeneration of species; and (7) that the benefits accruing from DDT usage are marginal, given the availability of alternative insecticides and pest management programs, and also the fact that crops produced with DDT are in ample supply. The testimony and exhibits include numerous reports of expert scientists who have described observed effects of DDT in the environment and the laboratory.

. . .

The Federal Insecticide, Fungicide and Rodenticide Act establishes a strict standard for the registration of pesticides. Any "economic poison" which cannot be used without injury to "man or other vertebrate animals, vegetation, and useful invertebrate animals" is "misbranded," and is therefore subject to cancellation.

While the language of the statute, taken literally, requires only a finding of injury to nontarget species, the inquiry cannot, however, end with a simplistic application of this plain statutory language. Both judicial and administrative precedent recognize that Congress intended the application of a balancing test, that would measure the risks of using a particular chemical against its benefits. . . .

. . .

I am convinced by a preponderance of the evidence that, once dispersed, DDT is an uncontrollable, durable chemical that persists in the aquatic and terrestrial environments. Given its insolubility in water and its propensity to be stored in tissues, it collects in the food chain and is passed up to higher forms of aquatic and terrestrial life. There is ample evidence to show that under certain conditions DDT or its metabolites can persist in soil for many years, that it will volatilize or move along with eroding soil. While the degree of transportability is unknown, evidence of record shows that it is occasionally found in remote areas or in ocean species, such as whales, far from any known area of application.

Persistence and biomagnification in the food chain are, of themselves, a cause for concern, given the unknown and possibly forever undeterminable long-range effects of DDT in man, and the environment.[19] Laboratory tests have, however, produced tumorigenic effects on mice when DDT was fed to them at high levels. Most of the cancer research experts who testified at this hearing indicated that it was their opinion that the tumorigenic results of tests thus far conducted are an indicator of carcinogenicity and that DDT should be considered a potential carcinogen. . . .

The case against DDT involves more, however, than a long-range hazard to man's health. The evidence presented by the Agency's Pesticides Office and the Intervenors, EDF, compellingly demonstrates the adverse impact of DDT on fish and bird life. Several witnesses testified to first-hand observed effects of DDT on fish and bird life, reporting lethal or sub-acute effects on aquatic and avian life exposed in DDT-treated areas. Laboratory evidence is also impressively abundant

---

[19] It is particularly difficult to anticipate the long-range effects of exposure to a low dose of a chemical. It may take many years before adverse effects would take place. Diseases like cancer have an extended latency period. Mutagenic effects will be apparent only in future generations. Lastly, it may be impossible to relate observed pathology in man to a particular chemical because of the inability to isolate control groups which are not exposed in the same degree as the rest of the population.

to show the acute and chronic effects of DDT on avian animal species and suggest that DDT impairs their reproductive capabilities.[22] . . .

Finally, I am persuaded that a preponderance of the evidence shows that DDT causes thinning of eggshells in certain bird species. The evidence presented included both laboratory data and observational data. Thus, results of feeding experiments were introduced to show that birds in the laboratory, when fed DDT, produced abnormally thin eggshells. In addition, researchers have also correlated thinning of shells by comparing the thickness of eggs found in nature with that of eggs taken from museums. The museum eggs show little thinning, whereas eggs taken from the wild after DDT use had become extensive reveal reduced thickness.

. . .

I am convinced by the evidence that continued use of DDT is not necessary to insure an adequate supply of cotton at a reasonable cost. . . . The record contains testimony by witnesses called by registrants and USDA attesting to the efficacy of organophosphate chemicals as substitutes for DDT and, long-range, the viability of pest management methods, such as the diapause program. . . .

There is evidence that organophosphates would not raise costs to the farmer and might, indeed, be cheaper. Any suggestion that the organophosphates are not economically viable cannot be maintained in face of the undisputed evidence that cotton continues to be [a] tenable crop in Arkansas and Texas where DDT use has declined. There is also testimony in the record to the effect that methyl parathion costs less per application than the DDT-toxaphene formula. Nor are the testimony and exhibits that show cotton insects develop resistance to organophosphate chemicals to the point. The very same exhibits make clear that DDT is also subject to resistance.

Group Petitioners and USDA, while not disputing the lesser persistence of organophosphates, have stressed their demonstrated acute toxicity. While they are toxic to beneficial soil insects and non-target species, particularly birds alighting on treated fields, these organophosphates break down more readily than DDT. They apparently are not transported in their toxic state to remote areas, unlike DDT which has been found far from treated areas, and consequently do not pose the same magnitude of risk to the aquasphere. Both testimony and exhibits also demonstrate that organophosphates are less acutely toxic to aquatic life, although different compounds have different toxicities. The effect of organophosphates on non-target terrestrial life can, unlike the effects of DDT, also be minimized by prudent use. Application in known nesting areas for rare or extinct [sic] birds can be avoided.

. . .

The application of the risk-benefit test to the facts of record is, by no means, simple. . . . [T]he variables are numerous. It should also be borne in mind that the variables are not static in point of time. As buildup of a chemical occurs or is detected in the environment, risk increases. Indeed, it may be that the same

[22] . . . While the Examiner erroneously excluded testimony as to economic losses caused by DDT's contamination of the aquatic environment—losses to commercial fishermen caused by inability to market contaminated fish—that risk is significant, even if it could not be economically quantified. Not all risks can be translated into dollars and cents, nor can all benefits be assessed in cash terms.

tendency of a chemical to persist or build up in the food chain is present but not known about substitute chemicals. It may also be that circumspect application of a chemical in limited quantities for those uses most necessary changes the benefit-risk coefficients so as to tilt the scales differently than when we weight aggregate use for all purposes against aggregate benefits.

. . .

The Agency and EDF have established that DDT is toxic to nontarget insects and animals, persistent, mobile, and transferable and that it builds up in the food chain. No label directions for use can completely prevent these hazards. In short, they have established at the very least the risk of the unknown. That risk is compounded where, as is the case with DDT, man and animals tend to accumulate and store the chemical.[34] These facts alone constitute risks that are unjustified where apparently safer alternatives exist to achieve the same benefit. Where, however, there is a demonstrated laboratory relationship between the chemical and toxic effects in man or animals, this risk is, generally speaking, rendered even more unacceptable, if alternatives exist. In the case before us the risk to human health from using DDT cannot be discounted. While these risks might be acceptable were we forced to use DDT, they are not so trivial that we can be indifferent to assuming them unnecessarily.

The evidence of record showing storage in man and magnification in the food chain is a warning to the prudent that man may be exposing himself to a substance that may ultimately have a serious effect on his health.

As Judge Leventhal recently pointed out, cancer is a "sensitive and fright-laden" matter and noted earlier in his opinion that carcinogenic effects are "generally cumulative and irreversible when discovered." The possibility that DDT is a carcinogen is at present remote and unquantifiable; but if it is not a siren to panic, it is a semaphore which suggests that an identifiable public benefit is required to justify continued use of DDT. Where one chemical tests tumorigenic in a laboratory and one does not, and both accomplish the same task, the latter is to be preferred, absent some extenuating circumstances.

The risks to the environment from continued use of DDT are more clearly established. There is no doubt that DDT runoff can cause contamination of waters and given its propensity to volatilize and disperse during application, there is no assurance that curtailed usage on the order of 12 million pounds per year will not continue to affect widespread areas beyond the location of application. The Agency staff established, as well, the existence of acceptable substitutes for all crop uses of DDT except on onions and sweet potatoes in storage and green peppers.

Registrants attempted but failed to surmount the evidence of established risks and the existence of substitutes by arguing that the buildup of DDT in the environment and its migration to remote areas has resulted from past uses and misuses. There is, however, no persuasive evidence of record to show that the aggregate volume of use of DDT for all uses in question, given the method of application, will not result in continuing dispersal and buildup in the environment and thus add to or maintain the stress on the environment resulting from past use. The Department

---

[34] In enacting the present law one of the greatest concerns expressed to Congress was the risk of the unknown.

of Agriculture has, for its part, emphasized DDT's low acute toxicity in comparison to that of alternative chemicals and thus tried to make the risk and benefit equation balance out favorably for the continued use of DDT. While the acute toxicity of methyl parathion must, in the short run, be taken into account, it does not justify continued use of DDT on a long-term basis. Where a chemical can be safely used if label directions are followed, a producer cannot avoid the risk of his own negligence by exposing third parties and the environment to a long-term hazard.

. . .

The record before me leaves no doubt that the chief substitute for most uses of DDT, methyl parathion, is a highly toxic chemical and, if misused, is dangerous to applicators. This was the virtually unanimous opinion of all the witnesses. The introduction into use of organophosphates has, in the past, caused deaths among users who are untrained in their application and the testimony and exhibits of record point of the unhappy experience of several years ago where four deaths occurred at the time methyl parathion began to be used on tobacco crops. Other testimony noted the increase in non-fatal accidents and attributed almost one-half [of] reported pesticide poisonings to the organophosphate group. A survey conducted after the organophosphates began to replace chlorinated hydrocarbons in Texas suggests a significantly increased incidence of poisonings.

That the skilled and trained user may apply organophosphates with complete safety is of comfort only if there is an orderly transition from DDT to methyl parathion so as to train workers now untutored in the ways of proper use.

I am accordingly marking this order effective as of December 31, 1972, insofar as the cancellations of any particular use is predicated on the availability of methyl parathion as a substitute. In the months that follow the Department of Agriculture and State extension services and representatives of EPA will have time to begin educating those workers who will have to use methyl parathion in future growing seasons. Such a program can also introduce farmers to the less acutely toxic organophosphates, like carbaryl, which may be satisfactory for many uses.

. . .

COMMENTS AND QUESTIONS

1. How does the decision deal with the argument that canceling DDT's registration will lead to increased use of methyl parathion? Is this a case of "risk-risk" trade-off, or is it something else? Who (or what) is endangered by DDT? By methyl parathion? The administrator addresses the risks posed by methyl parathion by delaying cancellation for a period, during which those who handle methyl parathion can obtain training in its safe use. Do you think that sufficient? Consider the proposition that the decision maker here, the administrator of the Environmental Protection Agency, might overvalue risks to the environment and undervalue risks to human life and health. (What if OSHA was the agency confronted with the cancellation decision?) Where a problem poses different types of risks, how might we deal with the fact that one agency may be differentially sensitive to one *type* of risk and insensitive to another and that other agencies might have exactly the opposite sensitivities? Should "risk-risk" problems that implicate risks to different categories or populations, or different types of risk, be resolved solely by legislatures? Consider the possibility that

such an approach would lead to "underregulation" from the perspective of those equally concerned with both types of risk.

2. The agency assesses costs and benefits but in a generally unquantified way. Do you find the administrator's analysis satisfactory? After you read the materials in the next sections on cost-benefit analysis, particularly the materials dealing with quantified risk-benefit analysis, reconsider the DDT decision.

C What Is Cost-Benefit Analysis?

Critics of regulation often point to cost-benefit analysis as the solution to regulatory failure. Indeed, as we have already seen, regulatory "failure" is often identified by looking at whether the costs of a regulation exceed its benefits. Thus, understanding cost-benefit analysis—how it works and the arguments in favor of and against it—is crucial to understanding current debates over regulatory performance.

The first readings in this section describe basic features of cost-benefit analysis. They also introduce a similar form of analysis called cost-effectiveness analysis. In studying these materials, think about how the form cost-benefit analysis takes might affect one's normative assessment of the methodology, and consider why a decision maker might prefer cost-effectiveness analysis to cost-benefit analysis.

■ *Pricing the Priceless: Cost-Benefit Analysis of Environmental Protection*
FRANK ACKERMAN AND LISA HEINZERLING
150 U. Pa. L. Rev. 1553 (2002). © 2002 University
of Pennsylvania Law Review

...Cost-benefit analysis tries to mimic a basic function of markets by setting an economic standard for measuring the success of the government's projects and programs. That is, cost-benefit analysis seeks to perform, for public policy, a calculation that happens routinely in the private sector. In evaluating a proposed new initiative, how do we know if it is worth doing or not? The answer is much simpler in business than in government.

Private businesses, striving to make money, only produce things that they believe someone is willing to pay for. That is, firms only produce things for which the benefits to consumers, measured by consumers' willingness to pay for them, are expected to be greater than the costs of production. It is technologically possible to produce men's business suits in brightly colored polka dots. Successful producers suspect that no one is willing to pay for such products, and usually stick to at most minor variations on suits in somber, traditional hues. If some firm *did* happen to produce a polka-dotted business suit, no one would be forced to buy it; the producer would bear the entire loss resulting from the mistaken decision.

Government, in the view of many critics, is in constant danger of drifting toward producing polka dot suits—and making people pay for them. Policies, regulations, and public spending do not face the test of the marketplace; there are no consumers who can withhold their dollars from the government until it produces the regulatory equivalent of navy blue and charcoal gray. There is no single quantitative objective for the public sector comparable to profit maximization for businesses. Even with the best of intentions, critics suggest, government programs can easily go astray for lack of an objective standard by which to judge whether or not they are meeting citizens' needs.

Cost-benefit analysis sets out to do for government what the market does for business: add up the benefits of a public policy and compare them to the costs. The two sides of the ledger raise very different issues.

Estimating Costs

The first step in a cost-benefit analysis is to calculate the costs of a public policy. For example, the government may require a certain kind of pollution control equipment, which businesses must pay for. Even if a regulation only sets a ceiling on emissions, it results in costs that can be at least roughly estimated through research into available technologies and business strategies for compliance.

The costs of protecting human health and the environment through the use of pollution control devices and other approaches are, by their very nature, measured in dollars. Thus, at least in theory, the cost side of cost-benefit analysis is relatively straightforward. In practice, as we shall see, it is not quite that simple.

The consideration of the costs of environmental protection is not unique to cost-benefit analysis. Development of environmental regulations has almost always involved consideration of economic costs, with or without formal cost-benefit techniques. What is unique to cost-benefit analysis, and far more problematic, is the other side of the balance, the monetary valuation of the benefits of life, health, and nature itself.

Monetizing Benefits

Since there are no natural prices for a healthy environment, cost-benefit analysis requires the creation of artificial ones. This is the hardest part of the process. Economists create artificial prices for health and environmental benefits by studying what people would be willing to pay for them. One popular method, called "contingent valuation," is essentially a form of opinion poll. Researchers ask a cross-section of the affected population how much they would be willing to pay to preserve or protect something that can't be bought in a store.

Many surveys of this sort have been done, producing prices for things that appear to be priceless. For example, the average American household is supposedly willing to pay $257 to prevent the extinction of bald eagles, $208 to protect humpback whales, and $80 to protect gray wolves. These numbers are quite large: since there are about 100 million households in the country, the nation's total willingness to pay for the preservation of bald eagles alone is ostensibly more than $25 billion.

An alternative method of attaching prices to unpriced things infers what people are willing to pay from observation of their behavior in other markets. To assign a dollar value to risks to human life, for example, economists usually calculate the extra wage—or "wage premium"—that is paid to workers who accept more risky jobs. Suppose that two jobs are comparable, except that one is more dangerous and better paid. If workers understand the risk and voluntarily accept the more dangerous job, then they are implicitly setting a price on risk by accepting the increased risk of death in exchange for increased wages.

What does this indirect inference about wages say about the value of a life? A common estimate in recent cost-benefit analyses is that avoiding a risk that would lead, on average, to one death is worth roughly $6.3 million. This number, in particular, is of great importance in cost-benefit analyses because avoided deaths are the most thoroughly studied benefits of environmental regulations.

Discounting the Future

One more step requires explanation to complete this quick sketch of cost-benefit analysis. Costs and benefits of a policy frequently occur at different times. Often, costs are incurred today, or in the near future, to prevent harm in the more remote future. When the analysis spans a number of years, future costs and benefits are *discounted*, or treated as equivalent to smaller amounts of money in today's dollars.

Discounting is a procedure developed by economists in order to evaluate investments that produce future income. The case for discounting begins with the observation that $100, say, received today is worth more than $100 received next year, even in the absence of inflation. For one thing, you could put your money in the bank today and earn a little interest by next year. Suppose that your bank account earns 3 percent interest. In that case, if you received the $100 today rather than next year, you would earn $3 in interest, giving you a total of $103 next year. Likewise, in order to get $100 next year you only need to deposit $97 today. So, at a 3% *discount rate*, economists would say that $100 next year has a *present value* of $97 in today's dollars.

For longer periods of time, the effect is magnified: at a 3% discount rate, $100 twenty years from now has a present value of only $55. The larger the discount rate, and the longer the time intervals involved, the smaller the present value: at a 5% discount rate, for example, $100 twenty years from now has a present value of only $38.

Cost-benefit analysis routinely uses the present value of future benefits. That is, it compares current costs, not to the actual dollar value of future benefits, but to the smaller amount you would have to put into a hypothetical savings account today to obtain those benefits in the future. This application of discounting is essential, and indeed commonplace, for many practical financial decisions. If offered a choice of investment opportunities with payoffs at different times in the future, you can (and should) discount the future payoffs to the present in order to compare them to each other. The important issue for environmental policy, as we shall see, is whether this logic also applies to outcomes far in the future, and to opportunities—like long life and good health—that are not naturally stated in dollar terms. . . .

■ *Benefit-Cost Analysis: Do the Benefits Exceed the Costs?*
LESTER B. LAVE
From *Risks, Costs, and Lives Saved: Getting Better Results from Regulation,*
Robert W. Hahn, ed., pp. 105–6 (American Enterprise Institute for Public
Policy Research, 1996). © The American Enterprise Institute for Public Policy
Research, Washington, DC. Used by permission of Oxford University
Press

Texts praise cost-benefit analysis for a number of reasons. Some textbook authors think of benefit-cost analysis as an "accounting framework" for exploring social decisions. Theorists tend to see it as an optimizing tool that maximizes social welfare. I order the following thirteen descriptions from those needed for an accounting framework to those needed for the tool to optimize social welfare. Benefit-cost analysis encourages a systematic statement of the goals to be accomplished (attribute 1) and encourages analysts to identify and evaluate a wide range of options for accomplishing the stated goals (attribute 2). In addition, it is a systematic, analytic approach that attempts to explore the implications of each option (attribute 3). Benefit-cost analysis requires the analyst to confront the trade-offs among options, both at the detailed level of each individual dimension and at the aggregate level in terms of total expenditures (attribute 4). Moreover, the approach encourages a search for externalities and an evaluation of those that have been identified (attribute 5). Benefit-cost analysis focuses on the allocation of benefits and costs over time and translates them to a single time period (attribute 6). The approach seeks to accomplish the stated goals at the least cost (attribute 7). The tool can be used to identify the data and analyses of importance (attribute 8) and to specify a research and development agenda to provide important data not currently available (attribute 9). Benefit-cost analysis seeks to isolate and quantify social interest, not self-interest (attribute 10). The approach recognizes that there are desirable and undesirable aspects of each situation and characterizes them as "benefits" and "costs" (attribute 11). Benefit-cost analysis encourages objective, value-free analysis (attribute 12). Finally, benefit-cost analysis identifies the option with the greatest net benefit, which is described as the one that is best for society (attribute 13).

The first six descriptions characterize an accounting framework that can be extremely helpful in examining social decisions. Attribute 7 sharpens the economic focus by introducing a goal that might not be stated in attribute 1: cost-effectiveness. Attribute 10 adds a further goal, the social interest. With a social goal defined, "benefits" and "costs" can be defined. Attribute 12 is a myth widely believed among benefit-cost analysts; unfortunately, the analysis cannot be value-free. . . . Attribute 13 is true . . . only under stringent assumptions.

■ *Crisis in the Workplace*

NICHOLAS ASHFORD

pp. 328–29, 350–51 (MIT Press, 1976). Reprinted with permission of MIT Press

Cost-benefit analysis is a methodology for evaluating and comparing the consequences of different policy alternatives. Even though cost-benefit analysis is sometimes thought of as a single "technique," there are, in fact, a variety of approaches to using it. For the purposes of clarifying the decision-making process, cost-benefit analysis can be of value to individuals, private corporations, labor unions, public institutions, and government.

A user of cost-benefit analysis is obliged to specify his goals (or alternative sets of goals) as precisely as possible. He must understand the alternatives open to him in meeting his goals, as well as their consequences. He can then use the results of this understanding to find the "best" way of achieving his objectives. The "best" method is often taken to be the one that is most economically efficient.

Suppose that a decision-maker had as his only goal the reduction of occupational injury and disease. He could employ one of the three modes of calculation to efficiently meet this goal. First, given a fixed budget, he could choose actions that would minimize injury and disease subject to the constraint of this fixed expenditure. Second, he could set a predetermined target level of injury and disease incidence and seek a way to achieve this goal at minimum cost.

These two methods of evaluation are limited by somewhat arbitrary (although often very real) constraints. A third method would be to attempt to find the "best" combination of expenditure and incidence of harm. . . .

The first two methods are the ones most likely to be used by decision-makers concerned with occupational health and safety, since no direct attempt need be made to quantify in economic terms the value of reduced injury or disease. To be sure, the value of human life and suffering is established *implicitly* when one decides upon the constraints facing the decision-maker, i.e., the amount of money to be spent (Case 1) or the maximum tolerable incidence rate (Case 2). For many decision-makers the third method is too theoretical, in that it requires a difficult-to-arrive-at *explicit* monetary equivalent of human life or suffering. One caveat, however, is necessary. If the decision-maker limits the value of reduced accidents and disease to the more readily quantifiable benefits such as reduced insurance premiums, absenteeism, and measurable production losses, then a determination by the third method can be readily made. However, such an approach overlooks a broad range of difficult-to-quantify benefits to the worker, his family, and society. Hence, the "optimal" point level is a fiction (i.e., will in fact be suboptimal) as far as the employee and society are concerned. . . .

COMMENTS AND QUESTIONS

1. Are the two distinctive features of cost-benefit analysis as described by Ackerman and Heinzerling—monetization and discounting—necessary to the "accounting framework" described by Lave?

2. What is the difference between cost-benefit analysis and cost-effectiveness analysis? Why might a politically sensitive actor—such as the head of an agency—prefer cost-effectiveness analysis?

3. Is Ashford correct that, even in his Cases 1 and 2, the decision maker *implicitly* establishes the value of human life and suffering? If so, why is explicit valuation of life and suffering so contentious? Even if one can impute a dollar value to the lives saved by a given rule (by dividing economic costs by the number of lives saved), does this mean that regulators had this dollar value in mind when they came to their decision? What else might they have been thinking about?

4. Not surprisingly, one of the most controversial issues relating to cost-benefit analysis is the translation of human lives into dollar terms. The next reading returns to Kip Viscusi's work on compensating wage differentials for risky work, a topic we first encountered in chapter 2. Here, we see that compensating wage differentials are used as inputs to cost-benefit analysis; they form the basis for most estimates of the value of saving lives through regulation.

■ *Fatal Tradeoffs*

W. KIP VISCUSI

pp. 17–22, 28–29 (Oxford University Press, 1992). Reprinted
with permission of Oxford University Press

Valuation Methodology

Traditionally, issues pertaining to the valuation of human life had been treated as
strictly moral concepts, not matters to be degraded through economic analysis of
choices and tradeoffs. However, as [Thomas] Schelling observed, substantial insight can be obtained by assessing the benefits of risk reduction in the same manner
as we value other economic effects. In general, the appropriate benefit measure for
risk reductions is the willingness to pay to produce the particular outcome. Similarly, the selling price for changes in risk establishes the value for risk increases.

In the usual risk policy decision—for example, determining what safety characteristics to provide in automobiles—the policy result to be assessed is an incremental risk reduction rather than a shift involving the certainty of life or death. This
need to think in terms of statistical lives as opposed to certain lives defines the main
character of our choice problem. In particular, the matter of interest is individuals'
valuation of lotteries involving life and death.

Addressing value-of-life issues by focusing on our attitudes toward lotteries
involving small risks of death provides a methodology for formulating these issues
in a sound economic manner. This approach also avoids the more difficult task of
confronting the valuation of lives at risk of certain death, which understandably
raises a different class of ethical issues. Nevertheless, even when only small risks
are involved, the concerns involved remain inherently sensitive, and we should not
be cavalier in making these judgments.

Because of the central role of individual preferences, individual values of life
may differ considerably, just as do other tastes. A central concern is who is valuing
the life and for what reason. A particular life may have one value to the individual,
another to his or her family, and still another to society at large.

As the willingness-to-pay methodology has become better understood, the
controversy surrounding the entire line of research on the value of life has diminished. Much of the early opposition to the economic valuation of life stemmed
from the reliance on value-of-life concepts that had been developed to inform
decisions on compensating survivors rather than on reducing risks to life. Initial
efforts consequently sought to value life using the human capital approach. In
particular, analysts . . . estimated values of life based on various measures of earnings. This technique, which continues to be used throughout the United States
court system to assess damages for personal injury, addresses only the financial
losses involved. The death of a family member, for example, would impose a
financial loss on survivors, which would be measured as the present value of the
income the deceased would have earned net of taxes and his or her consumption.
Similarly, the present value of taxes the deceased would have paid represents the
financial loss to the rest of society.

Value-of-life issues raise a series of questions for research. The first is how we
should think about these issues methodologically. The second class of issues involves estimating the risk-dollar tradeoffs that, in effect, represent the value of life.

Third, how can individuals make sound decisions regarding the risks they face? Finally, what approach should guide choices when society is making protective decisions?

Although the role of altruism complicates all policy valuations, the final class of questions becomes most problematic when we depart substantially from the private market analogy. When the government is providing risk reductions to a group with similar preferences and similar risks, then matters are relatively straightforward. However, if preferences differ because of wealth, if individuals cannot make fully rational decisions with respect to a risk, or if the parties affected are not currently alive, the choice process involves a greater leap because we become less confident of how hypothetical markets would function if they were perfect. . . .

The Value of Statistical Lives

The ultimate purpose of the value-of-life literature is to provide some basis for sensitive social decisions. Before investigating how society should make decisions involving the saving of lives, we will first assess whether we can establish an empirical reference point for making tradeoffs involving life and health. In the absence of such empirical information, there will be few operational contexts in which economic analysis of value-of-life decisions is instructive. Some sense of the order of magnitude of the value-of-life estimates will also assuage many of the concerns expressed about the morality of this line of work. If the appropriate economic value of life is over $1 million, resistance to this methodology will probably be much less than if the estimate is, say, $200,000. . . .

The basic approach to establishing a value of risk reduction parallels the technique for benefit assessment for other contexts. If, for example, one were attempting to assign benefits to the building of a new public parking garage, the appropriate benefit measure would be the sum of the willingness to pay of all the residents for this new facility. In a similar manner, when assessing the benefits of risk reduction, the pertinent value is the willingness to pay for the risk reduction. What we are purchasing with our tax dollars is not the certainty of survival. Rather, it is the incremental reduction in the probability of an adverse outcome that might otherwise have affected some random member of our community. What is at stake is consequently statistical lives, not certain identified lives.

In the case of risks that we must bear, the concern shifts from our willingness to pay for added safety to the amount that we require to bear the risk, which is usually termed our willingness-to-accept amount. For sufficiently small changes in risk, the willingness-to-pay and willingness-to-accept amounts should be approximately equal, but in practice they are not. . . . [T]here is often an alarmist reaction to increases in risk above the accustomed level so that willingness-to-accept amounts may dwarf the willingness-to-pay amounts if we respond irrationally to the risks.

In each case, the underlying concern is with a lottery involving a small probability of an adverse outcome. Our attitude toward this lottery defines the terms of trade that we believe are appropriate, where these terms of trade represent our risk-dollar tradeoff.

[The philosopher John Broome] suggests, however, that if lives have an infinite value, then use of value-of-life lotteries cannot provide us with a solution to this intractable problem. This observation does not indicate a flaw in our methodology.

An infinite value of life would be mirrored in an infinite value for a lottery in- *awesome economics knowe* volving a risk of death. The fact that we make a myriad of decisions involving life *assume limited* and death—including choosing the animal fats we ingest and the risky but fuel- *resources* efficient cars that we drive—indicates that we are willing to trade off small risks of death for other valued objectives. The approach I will take here will adopt the value-of-life lottery methodology recognizing that this formulation structures the difficult choices but does not eliminate them.

Consider a specific example. Suppose that our municipality could relocate its landfill to decrease the fatality risk from our drinking water by 1/100,000. Suppose that you were willing to pay $20 for a risk reduction of this magnitude. The summary manner in which economists have characterized the terms of trade re- *move from* flected in this tradeoff is the following. Suppose that there are 100,000 people at *lottery to* risk. On average, one expected life will be saved by the relocation of the landfill. As *individual* a group, the 100,000 residents are willing to pay $2 million ($20 × 100,000) for the one expected life that is saved. The economic value of this one expected life saved is consequently $2 million. This result is frequently termed the "value of life," even though this terminology implies in a somewhat misleading manner that what we are valuing is certain lives rather than statistical lives involving very small probabilities.

Another way of conceptualizing this calculation is to view it as simply as-certaining the value we are willing to pay per unit risk. Viewed in this manner, one estimates the value of a statistical life by dividing our willingness to pay for added safety ($20) by the risk increment that is involved (1/100,000), with the result being the same—$2 million.

It is important to recognize exactly what these tradeoffs mean. They only reflect attitudes toward small probabilities. They do not imply that we would accept certain death in return for $2 million, or even that we would accept a .5 probability of death for $1 million. Nor should we confuse these amounts with the appropriate level of compensation to our survivors should we die, as these amounts will generally be quite different. . . .

The pertinence of risk-dollar tradeoffs to valuing small changes in risk is not a substantial limitation. Most of the risks we face involve relatively small chances of death and other severe outcomes. Moreover, if we are faced with much greater risks, then we would still adopt the same willingness-to-pay approach except that the rate of tradeoff that was present for a very small risk reduction may not be what we would select if the risk change were quite different.

The relative orders of magnitude reflected in the estimates of the value of life are considerable. The empirical evidence on the value of life . . . suggests that the value of life of workers who have selected themselves into very high-risk jobs is on *into costs)* the order of $1 million, whereas workers in more representative jobs have esti-mated values of life in the range of $3 to $7 million. These numbers greatly exceed the workers' lifetime earnings—roughly by an order of magnitude. The economic value of life clearly extends well beyond the financial stakes involved. Moreover, there is no attempt by any external observer to limit the magnitude of these as-sessments. All we are asking is how much the individuals themselves value a particular risk reduction, and we will respect these values when designing social policies to protect them.

Valuing Life for Policy Decisions

Adopting the willingness-to-pay approach and establishing empirical estimates considerably simplify the task of addressing value-of-life issues in policy contexts. For private decisions the dominant concern will be the private willingness-to-pay amount. For public choices it will be society's overall willingness to pay for the risk reduction. One would expect that the greatest benefit from a life-extension policy will be that received by the individual whose life is directly affected, so private valuations provide a good starting point for assessing the value of life. The extent and implications of altruistic concerns have yet to be estimated precisely.

Identified versus Statistical Lives

Consider the situation of identified lives that are highly publicized as being at risk. Society is willing to spend a considerable sum to rescue a child who falls down a well or a man who is trapped under a collapsed freeway after an earthquake. The valuation of identified lives involving 0–1 probabilities of life or death will, of course, be quite different from the valuation of statistical lives. On an economic basis, the willingness to pay per unit risk reduction should be lower for large risks than for small risks. In practice, we often observe the opposite. Society exhibits greater life valuations when saving identified lives than for policies with small effects on statistical lives.

Which reaction better reflects our true underlying risk valuations? From an economic standpoint, the statistical life valuation is the more correct approach to valuing statistical lives, but if our individual decision processes cannot deal effectively with probabilistic events, then the valuation of identified lives might be a more meaningful index of our preferences. Because value-of-life questions involve a complex mixture of morality, economics, and decision making under uncertainty, ascertaining the true underlying preference structure that should be used for policy purposes will often be difficult.

The dilemma in ascertaining our true preferences can be illustrated by the following example. Suppose that improved water treatment facilities will reduce the rate of a fatal form of cancer by 1/10,000 for a municipality of 20,000, so that on average two lives will be saved. Suppose that we knew in fact that exactly two lives would be saved, but we did not know whose they would be. Should our benefit value remain the same as when there were two statistical lives to be saved, as opposed to two lives saved with certainty? If we are applying a standard Bayesian decision theory approach, there should be no change.

Now suppose that the lives saved are known in advance to be Kira and Michael. Should our answer change? Strict application of willingness-to-pay principles suggests that the collective valuation of a 1/10,000 risk reduction by 20,000 people will exceed the value to 2 people of a risk reduction from 1.0 to 0. The value we are willing to pay per unit risk reduction is greater for small increments than larger changes since our resources become depleted when we must purchase a large decrease in risk. The role of altruism may, however, alter this relationship. In practice, the societal value for saving Kira's and Michael's lives may be greater since these are identified lives. Should society's valuation of these lives be allowed to reflect the identified aspect? A more appropriate and consistent basis for decision would result if we were to value two certain lives to be saved at random. However, it may be that the reality of dealing with probabilistic events may not be understood until there is more tangible evidence of the risk-reduction benefits. How, for example, would we modify our thinking if we placed the same value on the lives of Richard and Sally or any other pair of identified residents as we would on the lives of Kira and Michael? The reality that lives will actually be lost and that we are not dealing with abstract events may not be apparent until the prospective victims are identified. . . .

Income Distribution at a Point in Time

. . . [D]istributional issues arise with all government programs, which inevitably benefit some parties more than others. Benefit assessment procedures are generally based on the willingness to pay of project beneficiaries, rather than on some systematic inflation of benefit values for the poor and compression of those for the wealthy. This approach does not mean that society has no concern for the poor, only that redistribution can be handled more efficiently through focused income transfer programs.

This kind of division of labor is consistent with the well-known Kaldor-Hicks compensation principle. If the policy is based on willingness-to-pay guidelines, then the parties that benefit can potentially compensate the losers from the policy. To override the willingness-to-pay values and tilt the policy mix toward risk reduction and environmental preservation, when the poor want education and housing, does not seem to be in anyone's best interests.

Most policies do not better the lot of some individuals at the expense of others but benefit one segment of the population disproportionately. Should we place a higher value on promoting airline safety, because of the relative affluence of the passengers, as compared with improved highway safety, which provides more broadly based benefits for the U.S. population? Reliance on willingness to pay would generate more stringent standards for airline safety, which in turn would raise the price that the (more affluent) airline passengers pay for their tickets. Somewhat paradoxically, however, the Federal Aviation Administration (FAA) sets the least stringent safety regulations of any federal agency, because FAA regulations were long based on the present value of victims' lost earnings, as opposed to willingness-to-pay estimates of the value of life. Rather than raise its standards in areas where the private valuation of the publicly provided benefits is high, the government has for the most part ignored these concerns.

In some situations, of course, it would be difficult or undesirable to make distinctions along income lines. The Titanic had enough lifeboats for the first-class passengers, but the other passengers apparently were expected to swim ashore. One could imagine an economic argument for making such distinctions, if the wealthier passengers were willing to pay the extra fare needed to support the purchase of lifeboats, whereas the less affluent passengers were not. Of course, there is no evidence that such a rational market process drove the Titanic lifeboat decision. In any case, such bargains will not hold up in practice, since once the catastrophe happens it is impossible to deny access to the lifeboats to those who did not pay. In situations that lead directly to a certainty of life or death rather than a small probability of death, denial of lifesaving alternatives based on income is highly controversial and understandably objectionable. For similar reasons, if medical support measures can preserve a life that would otherwise be lost, society spares little expense in doing so, whatever the patient's income.

Differences in safety protection are less troublesome when death is not an inevitable prospect but remains a more remote probability. Because of the heterogeneity in the value of life, market pressures have led to the introduction of air bags and antilock braking systems for the luxury car segment of the market. Cars such as the Mercedes-Benz and the Acura have introduced such safety-enhancing measures because their more affluent customers value them, whereas the Ford Escort and the Toyota Tercel have avoided such devices, which would lead to a dramatic relative price increase. There has been no public outcry that all cars should be equipped with the thousands of dollars worth of extra safety equipment as in the luxury class. It is highly unlikely that less affluent drivers would favor requirements that all cars meet the highest possible safety standards.

More observant airline passengers might notice the difference in buoyancy of the foam seat cushions provided to coach passengers and the inflatable life vests provided to those who ride in first class. Similarly, corporate jet fleets have invested in smoke hoods to better enable their executive passengers to escape a crash, whereas commercial airlines have not.

Recognizing the heterogeneity of the value of life could have substantial implications for the design and targeting of risk policies. . . . [F]or the range of risks now faced by American workers, risk valuations seem to be highly responsive to income (income elasticity is on the order of 1.0). The role of individual income in assessing the value of life has long been accepted in legal contexts, where the basis for compensation is the present value of earnings or some other linear function of income, consumption, and taxes. As our estimates of the value of life become increasingly refined, policies will probably be designed to reflect these differences, thus replicating the outcomes that would be expected if individuals could express their attitudes toward risk in a market for safety. . . .

COMMENTS AND QUESTIONS

1. If individuals in private markets do indeed bargain for risks, with some individuals accepting money for taking on increased risks, what is the appropriate role of the government in addressing risks? The answer might depend on whether bargaining is possible in the relevant situation. If, for example, the context is one in which parties already have a contractual relationship—perhaps they are employer and employee, or producer and consumer—then, in Viscusi's view, it would make sense for government to limit its role to the enforcement of the private bargain struck by the parties. (See chapter 2.) If, on the other hand, bargaining is not possible—such as when, for example, hundreds or thousands of people are exposed to the same harmful pollution—then Viscusi would use the valuations observed in private market settings to limit the interventions of government in the nonmarket setting. If, for example, the value of a statistical life discerned in market settings were $5 million, then Viscusi would limit required lifesaving expenditures in nonmarket settings to approximately this amount.

2. Consider again Nicholas Ashford's claim that a decision maker selecting a cutoff point for life-saving regulation *implicitly* establishes the value of human

life and suffering. Is this claim true for individual decision making? One much-discussed study attempted to estimate the value of "statistical" children's lives by examining mothers' practices in fastening car seats. The researchers calculated the difference between the time required to fasten the seats correctly and the time mothers actually spent fastening their children into their seats. They then assigned a monetary value to this difference of time based on the mothers' hourly wage rate (or, in the case of nonworking moms, based on a guess at the wages they might have earned). When mothers saved time—and, by hypothesis, money—by fastening their children's car seats incorrectly, they were, according to the researchers, implicitly placing a finite monetary value on the life-threatening risks to their children posed by car accidents. See Paul S. Carlin and Robert Sandy, *Estimating the Implicit Value of a Young Child's Life*, 58 So. Econ. J. 186 (1991). Do you agree? Is there something else that might have been going on when the mothers incorrectly fastened their children's car seats? Suppose the mothers were hurrying to get their children to school, were distracted by other children in the car, or just didn't realize they were fastening the seats incorrectly. Would these kinds of circumstances be relevant or irrelevant to estimates of the mothers' valuation of risks to their children?

3. What is the value of a statistical life? Kip Viscusi and Joseph Aldy recently conducted a meta-analysis of dozens of studies, done worldwide, trying to ascertain the value of a statistical life (VSL) through willingness to pay. They found that U.S. labor market data studies currently support a VSL of between $4 million and $9 million. They also found that the VSL tends to be lower in other countries, though it is within the same order of magnitude. They acknowledged that the VSL also varies with income, age, and other characteristics, such as union membership. W. Kip Viscusi and Joseph E. Aldy, *The Value of a Statistical Life: A Critical Review of Market Estimates throughout the World*, Nat'l Bureau of Econ. Res., Working Paper No. 9487 (2003), available at http://www.nber.org/papers/w9487.

4. Are all lives (risks) equally valuable? No, Cass Sunstein argues (in line with Viscusi's recognition of the heterogeneity of the value of life). For example, because cancer risks are more feared than other risks, Sunstein thinks that the VSL for cancer should be higher than the VSL for, say, workplace accidents. Another result of this approach is the explicit realization that because poor people have less money, they will, by definition, be willing to pay less to avoid risk. And because the VSL is based on willingness to pay, the VSL for the poor will be smaller. Sunstein goes on to argue, however, that this could actually be in the interests of the poor; for instance, China will be able to set appropriate levels of regulation by using a China-specific VSL rather than a U.S.-specific VSL. See Cass R. Sunstein, *Valuing Life: A Plea for Disaggregation*, 54 Duke L.J. 385 (2004).

5. A further extension of this argument is the recognition of different VSLs for the old and young. Because, as Sunstein and others have put it, lives are never saved but only extended, it is appropriate to disaggregate VSLs based on age. See Cass Sunstein, *Lives, Life-Years, and Willingness to Pay*, 104 Colum. L. Rev. 205 (2004). This can cut both ways, in terms of the ultimate value; although the old have fewer years left to live than the young, implying a lower VSL for

them, they also tend to be wealthier, implying a higher VSL. In any event, the very idea of using different VSLs for the old and young has sparked a strong public outcry. When the federal Environmental Protection Agency offered an economic analysis of an air pollution program that used different values for the old and the young ($3.7 million for those under 70, $2.3 million for those over), senior citizens reacted with outrage and forced the agency to retract the analysis.

The logical extension of the argument for disaggregation, as Sunstein admits, would be an individualized VSL for each individual and every risk. Quite apart from the difficulty of gathering so much information, this approach creates a paradox that Sunstein fails to discuss. It creates individualized values for a supposedly statistical construct. Once individualized, each VSL would match a unique human being, who would no longer be purely statistical but actually realized. Then, according to Viscusi and other economists, economic valuation would become impossible.

6. Does it make sense to identify an acontextual value for human life? Consider the following observations from Lester Lave:

> [V]alues and judgments are often situation-specific; they change radically from one setting to another. For example, my willingness to pay to reduce the chance of immediate death by one in 100,000 is different depending on whether the risk comes from a hazardous waste site that I opposed or a ski trip that I welcomed. What is the dollar value associated with not having to shoot someone? Is that value different for shooting a burglar in your home at night from what it is for shooting your child? Our actions have subtle implications that make valuing an item or action dependent on the precise setting. Thus, the dollar values that Viscusi estimates for lowering the chance of premature death in an occupational setting may have little relationship to the dollar value that people would put on lowering the chance of cancer from tolerating carcinogens in their drinking water.
>
> Lester B. Lave, Benefit-Cost Analysis: Do the Benefits Exceed the Costs? in Risks, Costs, and Lives Saved: Getting Better Results from Regulation, Robert W. Hahn, ed. (Oxford University Press and AEI Press, 1996), pp. 113–14

7. What is a statistical life, anyway? Consider the following discussion, from Lisa Heinzerling, *The Rights of Statistical People*, 24 Harv. Envtl. L. Rev. 189 (2000).

> The use of cost-benefit analysis to evaluate the wisdom of life-saving regulatory programs presents a puzzle. Deciding to allow one person to harm, even to kill, another person on the basis of how much it costs the person doing the harm to refrain from doing it denies the person harmed a right against harm. It makes a person's freedom from harm, indeed her life, contingent upon the financial profile of the life-threatening activity.
>
> The puzzle is that we do not allow this kind of cost-benefit balancing in all life-threatening contexts. We do not, for example, believe that so long as it is worth $10 million to one person to see another person dead,

and so long as current estimates of the value of human life are lower than $10 million, it is acceptable for the first person to shoot and kill the second. Indeed, in this setting we refrain entirely from placing a monetary value on life. Yet when it comes to regulatory programs that prevent deaths—deaths also due to the actions of other people—it has become commonplace to argue that the people doing the harm should be allowed to act so long as it would cost more for them to stop doing the harm than the harm is worth in monetary terms. Why are these two situations coming to be viewed so differently?

. . . [T]he use of cost-benefit analysis to evaluate life-saving regulatory programs has, in a society that eschews reliance on cost-benefit analysis in other life-saving situations, been justified by the creation of a new kind of entity—the statistical person. A primary feature of the statistical person . . . is that she is unidentified; she is no one's sister, or daughter, or mother. Indeed, in one conception, the statistical person is not a person at all, but rather only a collection of risks. By distinguishing statistical lives from the lives of those we know, economic analysts have attempted to sidestep the uncomfortable fact that most of us profess ourselves quite incapable of identifying the monetary equivalent of the lives of our sisters, daughters, mothers, and friends.

The framing of life in statistical terms has generated, for statistical people, two disadvantages not suffered by those whose lives are not so framed. First, the people whose lives are framed in statistical terms are explicitly priced in advance of their deaths. Second, this pricing has come to vary depending on the age, health, disability status, and wealth of the people who might be harmed. Thus the most basic kind of right—the right to be protected from physical harm caused by other people, [ ] on equal terms with other people—is denied to those whose lives are framed in statistical terms.

Despite the increasing importance of the concept of statistical life in informing regulatory policy, regulatory scholars to date have not provided a standard definition of the statistical life. There are two possible conceptions of statistical life. According to the first conception, a statistical life is a life expected to be lost as a function of probabilities of death applied to a population of persons. On this understanding, the salient features of the statistical life are unidentifiability and uncertainty: the person who is expected to die is not identifiable before (or perhaps even after) death, and the probabilistic estimates are uncertain. The second conception of statistical life is that it is not a life at all, but only an aggregation of relatively small risks of harm to the individuals in a population. These risks can be summed, together with the size of the population, to estimate how many lives are likely to be lost as a result of the risk. But, under this conception, "statistical life" refers to the collective risk, not to life itself.

Neither of these two conceptions of the statistical life justifies the differential treatment that regulatory policy has begun to afford statistical and nonstatistical life. Identifiability does not explain our differing responses to situations that threaten the lives of others; our varying reactions likely have more to do with identifying with the victim of the threat. Moreover, any person in a situation of risk can be framed in statistical or nonstatistical terms. Making regulatory policy turn on this framing threatens to ratify the apathy or prejudice society may exhibit toward certain kinds of people or certain kinds of risks. As for uncertainty, the analytical devices that have sprung up around statistical lives—monetization according to willingness-to-pay and according to age, health, and disability—simply have nothing to do with the uncertainty of estimates of physical risk. Using monetary valuations, and discriminatory ones at that, to adjust for scientific uncertainty cloaks scientific uncertainty in the garb of moral choice. It is, among other things, a strange commentary on our times that it has proven easier to persuade regulatory agencies to abandon their longstanding commitment to the equal worth of human lives than it has proven to persuade them that their scientific analysis is unsound. . . .

Regulatory analysts have predicated their pricing of, and discriminations among, human lives on the idea that the lives protected by regulation are statistical. By this, they either mean that no lives will be lost or that only risk, not life itself, is at stake. In either case, the notion is that statistical people do not die. But this is true only if our scientific estimates of risk are so unreliable that they commonly predict deaths will occur where, in fact, none will. I believe this is an inaccurate, even hysterical, account of scientific uncertainty. In any event, if the problem were scientific uncertainty, the solution would not be to monetize the lives subject to an uncertain risk, nor to discriminate among them based on characteristics such as age, health, and wealth. The solution would be to develop better scientific estimates of risk.

In defending the monetization of, and discrimination among, human lives based on the statistical nature of those lives, economic analysts have dehumanized the suffering and death that scientific risk assessments tell us will occur due to particular hazards. It is hard to understand, much less empathize with, statistical pain and loss. It is easier to assume that statistical suffering and death are things that do not happen to us—real people—but only to others—statistical people—and then to assume that the other people—statistical people—do not exist. Describing pain and loss in statistical terms allows us to think coolly about them; it strips life-threatening risks of the moral and emotional texture they derive from their association with real humans with real bodies and real loved ones. Describing human lives in statistical terms thus creates the conditions under which human suffering and loss can be conceived of in economic terms, and under which this suffering and loss can be allowed to continue simply because the monetary value we have attached to them is lower than the costs of avoiding them. In inventing the statistical life, economic analysis has contrived the very entity it seeks to value.

Isn't it a good thing to construct a model that "creates the conditions under which human suffering and loss can be conceived of in economic terms," insofar as this means that the resources that go to avoiding suffering and loss are limited like any other resource and we should think rationally about how best to allocate these resources? Isn't that what the "statistical life" idea helps us do?

D. The Case for, and against, Cost-Benefit Analysis

The next two readings argue in favor of cost-benefit (and cost-effectiveness) analysis as a framework for making regulatory decisions. The first claims that cost-benefit analysis is a good way of organizing information, making sensible decisions, and achieving transparent decision making. The second grounds its endorsement of cost-benefit (or cost-effectiveness) analysis in an examination of agencies' performance under non-cost-benefit regimes.

■ American Trucking Associations v. Whitman

Brief Amici Curiae of AEI-Brookings Joint Center for Regulatory
Studies, et al., in support of American Trucking Associations, et al.,
1999 U.S. Briefs 1426

The concern of [amici] is how analytical methods, such as benefit-cost analysis, should be used in regulatory decisionmaking. These methods can help promote the design of better regulations by providing a sensible framework for comparing the alternatives involved in any regulatory choice. Such analysis improves the chances that regulations will be designed to achieve a particular social goal specified by legislators at a lower cost. In addition, they can make the regulatory process more transparent by providing an analytical basis for a decision. Greater transparency in the process, in turn, will help hold regulators and lawmakers more accountable for their decisions.

These analytical methods are neither anti- nor proregulation; they can suggest reasons why it would be desirable to have tighter or more lenient standards depending on the results of an analysis. . . .

Over the past two decades, support has been growing for the proposition that weighing of benefits and costs should play a more central role in regulatory decisionmaking. All three branches of government have recognized the importance of considering benefits and costs in designing regulation.

To address the increase in regulatory activity over the past three decades, the past five presidents and President Clinton have introduced different analytical requirements and oversight mechanisms with varying degrees of success. A central component of later oversight mechanisms was formal economic analysis, which included benefit-cost analysis and cost-effectiveness analysis. Since 1981, presidents have required the preparation of RIAs for a predefined class of significant regulations. President Reagan's Executive Order 12291 required an RIA for each significant regulation whose annual impact on the economy was estimated to exceed $100 million. President Bush used the same executive order. President Clinton's and President Reagan's executive orders require a benefit-cost analysis for significant regulations as well as an assessment of reasonably feasible alternatives to the planned regulation.

Congress has also shown increasing interest in emphasizing the balancing of benefits and costs in regulatory decisions. The Small Business Regulatory

Enforcement Fairness Act of 1996 requires agencies to submit final regulations to Congress for review. The regulatory accountability provisions of 1996, 1997, and 1998 require the Office of Management and Budget to assess the benefits and costs of existing federal regulatory programs and to recommend programs or specific regulations to reform or eliminate. The Unfunded Mandates Reform Act of 1995 requires agencies, unless prohibited by law, to choose the most cost-effective regulatory approach or otherwise explain why they have not chosen this alternative.

The courts have also been receptive to the use of benefit-cost analysis in decisionmaking. Indeed, the D.C. Circuit recently held in *State of Michigan v. EPA*, 213 F.3d 663 (2000), that "[i]t is only where there is 'clear congressional intent to preclude consideration of cost' that we find agencies barred from considering costs." The court went on to cite various cases and legal authorities for the "general view that preclusion of cost consideration requires a rather specific congressional direction." Id. This case and others led Professors Robert H. Frank and Cass R. Sunstein to conclude that "[f]ederal law now reflects a kind of default principle: Agencies will consider costs, and thus undertake cost-benefit analysis, if Congress has not unambiguously said that they cannot.". . .

. . . Without delving into the legal aspects of the case, we present below why we think the Court should allow the EPA to consider costs in setting standards. In particular, we believe that, as a general principle, regulators should be allowed to consider explicitly the full consequences of their regulatory decisions. These consequences include the regulation's benefits, costs, and any other relevant factors. . . .

Benefit-cost analysis is simply a tool that can aid in making decisions. Most people do a kind of informal benefit-cost analysis when considering the personal pros and cons of their actions in everyday life—more for big decisions, like choosing a college or job or house, than for little ones, like driving to the grocery store. Where decisions, such as federal environmental regulations, are by their nature public rather than private, the government, as a faithful agent of its citizens, should do something similar.

Carefully considering the social benefits and social costs of a course of action makes good sense. Economists and other students of government policy have developed ways of making those comparisons systematic. Those techniques fall under the label benefit-cost analysis. Benefit-cost analysis does not provide the policy answer, but rather defines a useful framework for debate, either by a legislature or, where the legislature has delegated to a specialized agency the responsibility of pursuing a general good, by that agency.

Economists, other policy experts, and the regulatory agencies themselves have produced a large literature on the methods and applications of benefit-cost analysis. There are, and always will be, many uncertainties and disagreements about those methods and their application in particular cases. Nevertheless, a wide consensus exists on certain fundamental matters. In 1996, a group of distinguished economists, including Nobel laureate Kenneth Arrow, were assembled to develop principles for benefit-cost analysis in environmental, health, and safety regulation. Here, we summarize and paraphrase for the Court a number of principles that we think could be helpful in this case, which involves the review of the EPA's NAAQS standard-setting decisions.

A benefit-cost analysis is a useful way of organizing a comparison of the favorable and unfavorable effects of proposed policies. Benefit-cost analysis can help the decision-maker better understand the implications of a decision. It should be used to inform decisionmakers. Benefit-cost analysis can provide useful estimates of the overall benefits and costs of proposed policies. It can also assess the impacts of proposed policies on consumers, workers, and owners of firms and can identify potential winners and losers.

In many cases, benefit-cost analysis cannot be used to prove that the economic benefits of a decision will exceed or fall short of the costs. Yet benefit-cost analysis should play an important role in informing the decisionmaking process, even when the information on benefits, costs, or both is highly uncertain, as is often the case with regulations involving the environment, health, and safety.

Economic analysis can be useful in designing regulatory strategies that achieve a desired goal at the lowest possible cost. Too frequently, environmental, health, and safety regulation has used a one-size-fits-all or command-and-control approach. Economic analysis can highlight the extent to which cost savings can be achieved by using alternative, more flexible approaches that reward performance.

Benefit-cost analysis should be required for all major regulatory decisions. The scale of a benefit-cost analysis should depend on both the stakes involved and the likelihood that the resulting information will affect the ultimate decision.

Agencies should not be bound by a strict benefit-cost test, but should be required to consider available benefit-cost analyses. There may be factors other than economic benefits and costs that agencies will want to weigh in decisions, such as equity within and across generations.

Not all impacts of a decision can be quantified or expressed in dollar terms. Care should be taken to ensure that quantitative factors do not dominate important qualitative factors in decisionmaking. A common critique of benefit-cost analysis is that it does not emphasize factors that are not easily quantified or monetized. That critique has merit. There are two principal ways to address it: first, quantify as many factors as are reasonable and quantify or characterize the relevant uncertainties; and second, give due consideration to factors that defy quantification but are thought to be important. . . .

We believe all of the available information should be considered in making any important decision. If costs or other types of data are deliberately left out, the quality of decisionmaking is likely to suffer. . . .

■ *A Review of the Record*
JOHN F. MORRALL III
Regulation, Nov.–Dec. 1986, pp. 25–34. Reprinted with permission
of Cato Institute

Reducing health and safety risks has been a top priority of federal regulation for almost two decades, yet there is little systematic information describing the kinds of risks the government has chosen to regulate or the effectiveness of these interventions. This article is a modest attempt to fill the gap—I hope no more than a first step. I collected data on the best documented federal health and safety regulations and, for the 44 rules for which fairly complete information was available, examined the kinds of risks addressed and the benefits and costs of the regulations. . . .

Table 4 lists the 44 regulations along with their year of issuance, issuing agency, and present legal status (proposed, final, or rejected). The important analytic data

Table 4 The Cost of Various Risk-Reducing Regulations per Life Saved

Regulation	Year	Agency	Status*	Initial Annual Risk**	Annual Lives Saved	Cost per Life Saved (Thousands of 1984 $)
Steering Column Protection	1967	NHTSA	F	7.7 in 10^5	1,300.000	$100
Unvented Space Heaters	1980	CPSC	F	2.7 in 10^5	63.000	100
Oil & Gas Well Service	1983	OSHA-S	P	1.1 in 10^3	50.000	100
Cabin Fire Protection	1985	FAA	F	6.5 in 10^5	15.000	200
Passive Restraints/Belts	1984	NHTSA	F	9.1 in 10^5	1,850.000	300
Fuel System Integrity	1975	NHTSA	F	4.9 in 10^6	400.000	300
Trihalomethanes	1979	EPA	F	6.0 in 10^6	322.000	300
Underground Construction	1983	OSHA-S	P	1.6 in 10^3	8.100	300
Alcohol and Drug Control	1985	FRA	F	1.8 in 10^6	4.200	500
Servicing Wheel Rims	1984	OSHA-S	F	1.4 in 10^5	2.300	500
Seat Cushion Flammability	1984	FAA	F	1.6 in 10^7	37.000	600
Floor Emergency Lighting	1984	FAA	F	2.2 in 10^4	5.000	700
Crane Suspended Personnel Platform	1984	OSHA-S	P	1.8 in 10^3	5.000	900
Children's Sleepware Flammability	1973	CPSC	F	2.4 in 10^6	106.000	1,300
Side Doors	1970	NHTSA	F	3.6 in 10^5	480.000	1,300
Concrete and Masonry Construction	1985	OSHA-S	P	1.4 in 10^5	6.500	1,400
Hazard Communication	1983	OSHA-S	F	4.0 in 10^5	200.000	1,800
Grain Dust	1984	OSHA-S	P	2.1 in 10^4	4.000	2,800
Benzene/Fugitive Emissions	1984	EPA	F	2.1 in 10^5	0.310	2,800
Radionuclides/Uranium Mines	1984	EPA	F	1.4 in 10^4	1.100	6,900
Asbestos	1972	OSHA-H	F	3.9 in 10^4	396.000	7,400
Benzene	1985	OSHA-S	P	8.8 in 10^4	3.800	17,100

Substance	Year	Agency	Status*	Risk	Annual deaths**	
Arsenic/Glass Plant	1986	EPA	F	8.0 in 10^4	0.110	19,200
Ethylene Oxide	1984	OSHA-H	F	4.4 in 10^5	2,800	25,600
Arsenic/Copper Smelter	1986	EPA	F	9.0 in 10^4	0.060	26,500
Uranium Mill Tailings/Inactive	1983	EPA	F	4.3 in 10^4	2,100	27,600
Acrylonitrile	1978	OSHA-H	F	9.4 in 10^4	6,900	37,600
Uranium Mill Tailings/Active	1983	EPA	F	4.3 in 10^4	2,100	53,000
Coke Ovens	1976	OSHA-H	F	1.6 in 10^4	31,000	61,800
Asbestos	1986	OSHA-H	F	6.7 in 10^5	74.700	89,300
Arsenic	1978	OSHA-H	F	1.8 in 10^3	11.700	92,500
Asbestos	1986	EPA	P	2.9 in 10^5	10.000	104,200
DES (Cattlefeed)	1979	FDA	F	3.1 in 10^7	68.000	132,000
Arsenic/Glass Manufacturing	1986	EPA	R	3.8 in 10^5	0.250	142,000
Benzene/Storage	1984	EPA	R	6.0 in 10^7	0.043	202,000
Radionuclides/DOE Facilities	1984	EPA	R	4.3 in 10^5	0.001	210,000
Radionuclides/Elemental Phosphorus	1984	EPA	R	1.4 in 10^4	0.046	270,000
Acrylonitrile	1978	OSHA-H	R	9.4 in 10^4	0.600	308,000
Benzene/Ethylobenzene Styrene	1984	EPA	R	2.0 in 10^6	0.006	483,000
Arsenic/Low-Arsenic Copper	1986	EPA	R	2.6 in 10^4	0.090	764,000
Benzene/Maleic Anhydride	1984	EPA	R	1.1 in 10^6	0.029	820,000
Land Disposal	1986	EPA	P	2.3 in 10^8	2.520	3,500,000
EDB	1983	OSHA-H	P	2.5 in 10^4	0.002	15,600,000
Formaldehyde	1985	OSHA-H	P	6.8 in 10^7	0.010	72,000,000

*P, Proposed; R, Rejected; F, Final rule.
**Annual deaths per exposed person. An exposed population of 10^3, 1,000, 10^4, 10,000, etc.

appear in the last three columns. The initial risk of those exposed to the thing or activity regulated, the number of lives saved by the regulation, and the cost-effectiveness of the regulation measured by cost per life saved. The rules are ranked in order of decreasing cost-effectiveness.

There are several important qualifications to the data in Table 4. First and foremost, the benefits (lives saved) and costs (dollars per life saved) of the rules are not actual benefits and costs of the rules in action—obviously they could not be in the case of proposed and rejected rules. Rather, they are generally based on agencies' estimates at the time of the decision, estimates which I sometimes revised for reasons described in a moment. Second, many regulations were projected to yield benefits in addition to saving lives, such as reducing non-fatal injuries and property damage. I accounted for these additional benefits by subtracting monetary benefits from costs and converting non-lifesaving health benefits into an index equivalent to additional lives saved. The conversions were based on leading economic studies of individuals' willingness to pay to avoid risks of death, disease, and injury; 50 non-fatal hospitalizations avoided, or two permanent disabilities avoided, were assumed to be equivalent to one death avoided. Third and finally, the benefits and costs of regulations are typically uneven, both for individual rules and across rules—one rule may impose costs long before it averts fatalities, and one may avert fatalities long before another rule does. For the sake of consistency, I adjusted these temporal variations using a uniform 10-percent discount rate for both benefits and costs.

The use of agency benefit and cost data also merits elaboration. Regulatory agencies, like other organizations public and private, tend to overstate the effectiveness of their actions. Where such biases were evident and easily corrected, I made the corrections. For example, where an agency presented a range of risk estimates but relied on the highest estimate, I used either the intermediate estimate or the one that appeared to be the most reliable. In 12 instances I used estimates from published studies that appeared to reflect prevailing scientific views more accurately than the agency estimate. For example, in the case of OSHA's ethylene oxide rule, I used a risk estimate from another agency, the EPA, because it was based on epidemiologic evidence rather than on an extrapolation from an animal experiment. For safety regulations, I often deflated agency assumptions concerning accident reduction from 100-percent effectiveness to a more reasonable figure such as 50 percent.

I should mention that agency procedures for estimating risk and effectiveness typically contain numerous, and subtle inflationary factors . . . ; I attempted to correct only for the most obvious. As a result, many of the risk and cost-effectiveness figures in Table 4 surely remain overstated, especially those for cancer-reducing rules. I doubt, however, that any resulting arbitrariness in the ranking of the regulations is large enough to affect the general conclusions set forth below.

I generally accepted agency cost estimates without adjustment. In part, this is because agencies do not follow any explicit policy of underestimating costs. In addition, this is in recognition of the fact that while agencies have incentives to underestimate costs, and often focus on "compliance costs" rather than true economic costs or welfare losses, regulated firms and consumers often discover new—and unanticipated—ways to minimize compliance costs.

What the Record Shows

The regulations in this sample address a very wide range of risks, five orders of magnitude to be exact, which is greater than the difference in the risks of dying from heavy cigarette smoking and playing basketball. At one extreme are several OSHA rules which address occupation risks of 1 or 2 in 1,000; at the other extreme are two FAA aircraft safety rules which address risks of 2 and 7 in 100 million. The EPA and OSHA each have a proposal which would address similarly tiny risks. (Numerous FDA and EPA bans in recent years—not in this sample because of lack of cost information—have addressed even slighter risks; the FDA's proposed ban of the cosmetic coloring Orange No. 17, for example, would have averted a calculated risk of death of 1 in 10 billion and was projected to save one life [in] 2,000 years.) On average, however, the rules listed in Table 4 address risks that are not insignificant. At about 3 in 10,000, the average annual risk is greater than that of dying in a motor vehicle accident.

The 26 final rules were estimated to save a total of 5,381 lives annually, which is the equivalent of about three-tenths of 1 percent of annual U.S. deaths. The 10 proposed rules (currently in rulemaking) are projected to save a total of only 89 additional lives per year, the eight rejected rules were projected to save a total of only one life per year. A very large share of the regulatory benefits of the rules that were issued—4,030 lives saved annually, or 75 percent of the benefits of all final rules—was due to just four regulations, all dealing with motor vehicle design. These were the NHTSA's collapsible steering column requirement, its passive restraint rule requiring air bags or automatic seat belts, and its standards for fuel system integrity and side-door strength. In contrast, the EPA has issued just one rule estimated to save a large number of lives, which is its ban of trihalomethanes (chloroform and other organics in drinking water), estimated to save 322 lives annually. The other six final rules issued by the EPA save an estimated five lives per year *in total*. OSHA's eight final rules save an estimated 725 lives annually, mostly from the initial (1972) asbestos standard and the recent (1984) hazard communication (chemical labeling) requirements. The other seven final rules, issued by the CPSC, FAA, FDA, and FRA, save a total of 298 lives annually.

Cost-Effectiveness

Initial risk is not a very good measure of the desirability of a government rule, since small risks may affect large populations and vice versa. Number-of-lives-saved is not much better, since a rule with large lifesavings may be disproportionately more costly than a rule which saves relatively few lives. It may be perfectly appropriate, for example, to regulate bee stings rather than heart attacks if bee sting risks can be reduced cheaply and heart attack risks can be reduced only at great cost. In principle, the best measure of desirability is net social benefits: the value in dollars of the number of deaths averted by a regulation minus the cost of the regulation. Given a ranking of regulations by net social benefits, one would conclude that all those with positive net benefits are worthwhile policies and all those with negative net benefits are not (assuming, of course, one has confidence in the underlying data and the value-of-life figures).

To elide the controversies and uncertainties of choosing a single dollar figure for the value of saving a life, I have chosen a second-best measure of desirability, cost-effectiveness, measured by cost per life saved. . . .

The most obvious implication of these figures is that the range of cost-effectiveness among rules is enormous. . . . Even excluding all proposed rules and the least cost-effective final rule, issued by the FDA, the range is still three orders of magnitude: OSHA's arsenic standard costs nearly 1,000 times as much per life saved as NHTSA's steering column standard. Notwithstanding the data limitations mentioned above, it is reasonable to conclude that large improvements in welfare—many more lives saved for the same investment or the same number of lives saved for a much smaller investment—are likely to be achieved by reallocating resources within these 25 final rules.

There are also some striking variations in cost-effectiveness between and within regulatory agencies. Taken as a group, the final rules issued by the three Department of Transportation agencies (the FAA, FRA, and NHTSA) are about 83 times more cost-effective than those of OSHA and 40 times more cost-effective than those of the EPA. But there are even greater variations within the EPA and OSHA. The EPA's 1979 trihalomethanes rule is 177 times more cost-effective than its 1983 standards for mill tailings at active uranium mines. OSHA's 1978 arsenic rule is 185 times less cost-effective than its 1984 servicing-of-wheel-rims rule. . . .

Health vs. Safety

While it is tempting to attribute the differences in cost-effectiveness among regulatory agencies to differences in management or political pressures, there seems to be a more fundamental difference: *safety regulation appears to be far more cost-effective than health regulation.*

. . . The median of cost-per-life-saved estimates for the cancer regulations (which largely eliminates the effect of the few highly ineffective proposals at the bottom of the list) is 75 times higher than for the safety regulations—$37.0 million compared to $500,000. For OSHA, the one agency that issues both safety and health (in practice, cancer) regulations, the median of cost-per-life-saved estimates for the seven safety rules is 123 times lower than the median for the six cancer rules. In fact, even OSHA's most costly safety regulation costs less per life saved than its least costly cancer regulation. On the basis of this data, it can be concluded that with $1 billion in resources available for risk reduction, we could save 2,000 lives through safety regulation or 27 lives through cancer regulation. (This assumes that additional opportunities exist for promoting safety and health similar to those addressed by the rules in this sample.)

These differences between health and safety regulations really should not be surprising; in large part, they are dictated by statute. The safety statutes, such as those authorizing the NHTSA, the CPSA, and OSHA, almost invariably speak in terms of regulations that are "reasonable," "practicable," "appropriate," and so forth. In contrast, the health statutes, including not only the much-discussed FDA Delaney clause but also the relevant portions of the Clean Air Act and the OSHA statute, speak in terms of absolute or near absolute protection.

While these differences in cost-effectiveness may appear extraordinarily large, they are probably understated by a large margin. For one thing, . . . the risks of cancer, and thus the likely effectiveness of cancer rules, are routinely overestimated by federal agencies; safety risks, by contrast, are less likely to be over-estimated because of the greater availability of hard data. I was unable to correct fully for the bias in cancer risk estimates. Also, cancer is primarily a disease of old age, while accidents, especially occupational accidents, strike a younger group. A more re-fined measure of regulatory benefits, such as cost *per year of life* saved, would likely show an even greater difference in cost-effectiveness.

This finding stands in sharp contrast to the conventional view of the effec-tiveness of health and safety regulation. Students of OSHA regulation such as Robert S. Smith, W. Kip Viscusi, Zeckhauser, Nichols, and John Mendeloff have all recommended that OSHA shift its focus from safety to health risks. Their essential argument is that private incentives are stronger for safe conduct than for health-improving conduct, meaning that OSHA—and by extension other regulatory agencies—has more to contribute, in the way of cost-effective lifesaving, to health than to safety. The assumption is that safety risks are more obvious than health risks to potential victims, and that causation and hence private liability is usually clearer for accidents than for diseases.

Based on this data, we may speculate that the received wisdom on health and safety regulation is incorrect. Perhaps, as some have suggested, workers' com-pensation programs (which limit liability for accidents) have seriously dulled pri-vate incentives for occupational safety—although this would leave unexplained the relatively high cost-effectiveness of transportation regulations. Perhaps the same "fear of cancer" which has led to such extreme regulatory efforts and political histrionics has also led to careful private behavior (for example in factories where asbestos, arsenic, and other known carcinogens are in use), leaving little for gov-ernment standards to contribute. Certainly our lack of definite knowledge about the etiology of cancer, which is a major reason private incentives for cancer pro-tection are said to be inadequate, is a problem afflicting government as well as private decisionmaking. It may simply be easier for government officials to commit resources in the face of ignorance. In any event, these data suggest that regulatory reformers should attend not only to reducing the overregulation of cancer risks, but also to the possibility of increasing safety regulation.

COMMENTS AND QUESTIONS

1. The economists' brief in *American Trucking* was filed by a distinguished group that included several Nobel laureates. The brief focused entirely on the policy issues raised by cost-benefit analysis, leaving the relevant legal issues to be discussed by others. As we will see in chapter 11, the Court ultimately sided with the Environmental Protection Agency's long-standing view that air quality standards are to be set without considering costs.

2. If, as the economists recommend, cost-benefit analysis is to be used as one input into regulatory decision making, rather than as a decision rule, how useful is it? What considerations, beyond monetizable costs and benefits, should be rele-vant to regulatory decisions about risk?

3. Consider Morrall's article as a piece of advocacy. What is the evidentiary basis for his conclusions? How would a stronger supporter of regulation than Morrall go about criticizing Morrall's argument? One critic of Morrall's work points out

that many of the highest cost regulations in Morrall's table were only proposed but never adopted. See Lisa Heinzerling, *Regulatory Costs of Mythic Proportions*, 107 Yale L.J. 1981 (1998). Does the fact that the regulations were proposed show a regulatory failure? That they were not adopted a regulatory success? Heinzerling also argues that Morrall's results are highly sensitive to the discount rates he adopts and to some of the adjustments he makes to the agencies' assessments of risk. In addition, Heinzerling observes that Morrall's table includes only one benefit from most of the costliest regulations—the prevention of deaths due to cancer—even though the agencies described many other, unquantified benefits that their rules would produce (such as prevention of illnesses other than cancer and prevention of ecological harm). Discounting and the limits of quantification are discussed at some length in the next reading, which offers an argument against the use of cost-benefit analysis in setting risk-related policies. Note that many of the arguments that can be deployed against the cost-effectiveness analysis used by Morrall also apply to cost-benefit analysis.

For another set of articles making the same kinds of competing claims, compare Tammy O. Tengs et al., *Five-Hundred Life-Saving Interventions and Their Cost-Effectiveness*, 15 Risk Analysis 369 (1995), and Tammy O. Tengs and John D. Graham, "The Opportunity Costs of Haphazard Social Investments in Life-Saving," in *Risks, Costs, and Lives Saved: Getting Better Results from Regulation* (Robert W. Hahn ed., AEI and Oxford University Press, 1996) (making Morrall-like claims), with Lisa Heinzerling, *Five-Hundred Life-Saving Regulations and Their Misuse in the Debate over Regulatory Reform*, 13 Risk: Health, Safety & Env't 151 (2002), and Richard W. Parker, *Grading the Government*, 70 U. Chi. L. Rev. 1345 (2003) (criticizing the Tengs and Graham studies).

■ *Pricing the Priceless: Cost-Benefit Analysis of Environmental Protection*
FRANK ACKERMAN AND LISA HEINZERLING
150 U. Pa. L. Rev. 1553 (2002). © 2002 University
of Pennsylvania Law Review

. . . [C]ost-benefit analysis involves the creation of artificial markets for things—like good health, long life, and clean air—that are not bought and sold. It also involves the devaluation of future events through discounting.

So described, the mindset of the cost-benefit analyst is likely to seem quite foreign. The translation of all good things into dollars and the devaluation of the future are inconsistent with the way many people view the world. Most of us believe that money doesn't buy happiness. Most religions tell us that every human life is sacred; it is obviously illegal, as well as immoral, to buy and sell human lives. Most parents tell their children to eat their vegetables and do their homework, even though the rewards of these onerous activities lie far in the future. Monetizing human lives and discounting future benefits seem at odds with these common perspectives.

The cost-benefit approach also is inconsistent with the way many of us make daily decisions. Imagine performing a new cost-benefit analysis to decide whether to get up and go to work every morning, whether to exercise or eat right on any given day, whether to wash the dishes or leave them in the sink, and so on. Inaction would win far too often—and an absurd amount of effort would be spent on analysis. Most people have long-run goals, commitments, and habits that make such daily balancing exercises either redundant or counterproductive. The same might be true of society as a whole undertaking individual steps in the pursuit of any goal, set for the long haul, that cannot be reached overnight—including, for example, the achievement of a clean environment.

Moving beyond these intuitive responses, we offer in this Section a detailed explanation of why cost-benefit analysis of environmental protection fails to live up to the hopes and claims of its advocates. There is no quick fix, because these failures are intrinsic to the methodology, appearing whenever it is applied to any complex environmental problem. In our view, cost-benefit analysis suffers from four fundamental flaws, addressed in the next four Sections:

- the standard economic approaches to valuation are inaccurate and implausible;
- the use of discounting improperly trivializes future harms and the irreversibility of some environmental problems;
- the reliance on aggregate, monetized benefits excludes questions of fairness and morality; and
- the value-laden and complex cost-benefit process is neither objective nor transparent.

A. Dollars without Sense

Recall that cost-benefit analysis requires the creation of artificial prices for all relevant health and environmental impacts. To weigh the benefits of regulation against the costs, we need to know the monetary value of preventing the extinction of species, preserving many different ecosystems, avoiding all manner of serious health impacts, and even saving human lives. Without such numbers, cost-benefit analysis cannot be conducted.

Artificial prices have been estimated for many, though by no means all, benefits of regulation. As discussed, preventing the extinction of bald eagles reportedly goes for somewhat more than $250 per household. Preventing retardation due to childhood lead poisoning comes in at about $9000 per lost IQ point in the standard view, or as low as $1100 per point in Lutter's alternative. Saving a life is ostensibly worth $6.3 million.

This quantitative precision, achieved through a variety of indirect techniques for valuation, comes at the expense of accuracy and sometimes, common sense. Though problems arise in many areas of valuation, we will focus primarily on the efforts to attach a monetary value to human life, both because of its importance in cost-benefit analysis and because of its glaring contradictions.

We note, however, that the same kind of problems we are about to discuss affect other valuation issues raised by cost-benefit analysis, such as estimating the value of clean water, biodiversity, or entire ecosystems. The upshot is that cost-benefit analysis is fundamentally incapable of delivering on its promise of more economically efficient decisions about protecting human life, health, and the environment. Absent a credible monetary metric for calculating the benefits of regulation, cost-benefit analysis is inherently unreliable.

1. There Are No "Statistical" People

What can it mean to say that saving one life is worth $6.3 million? Human life is the ultimate example of a value that is not a commodity and does not have a price. You cannot buy the right to kill someone for $6.3 million, nor for any other price. Most systems of ethical and religious belief maintain that every life is sacred. If analysts calculated the value of life itself by asking people what it is worth to them (the most common method of valuation of other environmental benefits), the answer would be infinite, as "no finite amount of money could compensate a person for the loss of his life, simply because money is no good to him when he is dead."

The standard response is that a value like $6.3 million is not actually a price on an individual's life or death. Rather, it is a way of expressing the value of small risks of death; for example, it is one million times the value of a one in a million risk. If people are willing to pay $6.30 to avoid a one in a million increase in the risk of death, then the "value of a statistical life" is $6.3 million.

Unfortunately, this explanation fails to resolve the dilemma. It is true that risk (or "statistical life") and life itself are distinct concepts. In practice, however, analysts often ignore the distinction between valuing risk and valuing life. Many regulations reduce risk for a large number of people and avoid actual death for a much smaller number. A complete cost-benefit analysis should, therefore, include valuation of both of these benefits. However, the standard practice is to calculate a value only for "statistical" life and to ignore life itself.

The confusion between the valuation of risk and the valuation of life itself is embedded in current regulatory practice in another way as well. The Office of Management and Budget, which reviews cost-benefit analyses prepared by federal agencies pursuant to executive order, instructs agencies to discount the benefits of life-saving regulations from the moment of avoided death, rather than from the time when the risk of death is reduced. This approach to discounting is plainly inconsistent with the claim that cost-benefit analysis seeks to evaluate risk. When a life-threatening disease, such as cancer, has a long latency period, many years may pass between the time when a risk is imposed and the time of death. If monetary valuations of statistical life represented risk, instead of life, then the value of statistical life would be discounted from the date of a change in risk (typically, when a new regulation is enforced) rather than from the much later date of avoided actual death.

In acknowledging the monetary value of reducing risk, economic analysts have contributed to our growing awareness that life-threatening risk itself—and not just the end result of such risk, death—is an injury. But they have blurred the line between risks and actual deaths, by calculating the value of reduced risk while pretending that they have produced a valuation of life itself. The paradox of monetizing the infinite or immeasurable value of human life has not been resolved; it only has been glossed over.

2. People Care about Other People

Another large problem with the standard approach to valuation of life is that it asks individuals (either directly through surveys or indirectly through observing wage and job choices) only about their attitudes toward risks to themselves.

A recurring theme in literature suggests that our deepest and noblest sentiments involve valuing someone else's life more highly than our own: think of parents' devotion to their children, soldiers' commitment to those whom they are protecting, lovers' concern for each other. Most spiritual beliefs call on us to value the lives of others—not only those closest to us, but also those whom we have never met.

This point echoes a procedure that has become familiar in other areas of environmental valuation. Economists often ask about existence values: how much is the existence of a wilderness area or an endangered species worth to you, even if you never will experience it personally? If this question makes sense for bald eagles and national parks, it must be at least as important when applied to safe drinking water and working conditions for people we don't know.

What is the existence value of a person you will never meet? How much is it worth to you to prevent a death far away? The answer cannot be deduced solely from your attitudes toward risks to yourself. We are not aware of any attempts to quantify the existence value of the life of a stranger, let alone a relative or a friend, but we are sure that most belief systems affirm that this value is substantial (assuming, of course, that the value of life is a number in the first place).

3. Voting Is Different from Buying

Cost-benefit analysis, which relies on estimates of individuals' preferences as consumers, also fails to address the collective choice presented to society by most public health and environmental problems.

Valuation of environmental benefits is based on individuals' private decisions as consumers or workers, not on their public values as citizens. However, policies that protect the environment are often public goods and are not available for purchase in individual portions. In a classic example of this distinction, the philosopher Mark Sagoff found that his students, in their role as citizens, opposed commercial ski development in a nearby wilderness area, but, in their role as consumers, would plan to go skiing there if the development were built. There is no contradiction between these two views: as individual consumers, the students would have no way to express their collective preference for wilderness preservation. Their individual willingness to pay for skiing would send a misleading signal about their views as citizens.

It is often impossible to arrive at a meaningful social valuation by adding up the willingness to pay expressed by individuals. What could it mean to ask how much you are personally willing to pay to clean up a major oil spill? If no one else contributes, the clean-up will not happen regardless of your decision. As the Nobel Prize–winning economist Amartya Sen has pointed out, if your willingness to pay for a large-scale public initiative is independent of what others are paying, then you probably have not understood the nature of the problem. Instead, a collective decision about collective resources is required.

In a similar vein, the philosopher Henry Richardson argues that reliance on the cost-benefit standard forecloses the process of democratic deliberation that is necessary for intelligent decision making. In his view, attempts to make decisions based on monetary valuation of benefits freeze preferences in advance, leaving no room for the changes in response to new information, rethinking of the issues, and negotiated compromises that lie at the heart of the deliberative process.

Cost-benefit analysis turns public citizens into selfish consumers and interconnected communities into atomized individuals. In this way, it distorts the question it sets out to answer—how much do we, as a society, value health and the environment?

4. Numbers Don't Tell Us Everything

A few simple examples illustrate that numerically equal risks are not always equally deserving of regulatory response. The death rate is roughly the same (somewhat less than one in a million) from a day of downhill skiing, from a day of working in the construction industry, or from drinking about twenty liters of water containing fifty parts per billion of arsenic—the old regulatory limit that was recently revised by the EPA. This does not mean that society's responsibility to reduce risks is the same in each case.

Most people view risks imposed by others, without an individual's consent, as more worthy of government intervention than risks that an individual knowingly accepts. On that basis, the highest priority among our three examples is to reduce drinking water contamination—a hazard to which no one has consented. The acceptance of a risky occupation such as construction is at best quasi-voluntary; it involves somewhat more individual discretion than the "choice" of public drinking water supplies even though many people go to work under great economic pressure and with little information about occupational hazards. In contrast, the choice of risky recreational pursuits such as skiing is entirely discretionary; obviously, no one is forced to ski. Safety regulation in construction work is thus more urgent than regulation of skiing, despite the equality of numerical risk.

In short, even for ultimate values such as life and death, the social context is decisive in our evaluation of risks. Cost-benefit analysis assumes the existence of generic, acontextual risk and thereby ignores the contextual information that determines the manner in which many people, in practice, think about real risks to real people.

5. Artificial Prices Are Expensive

Finally, the economic valuation called for by cost-benefit analysis is fundamentally flawed because it demands an enormous volume of consistently updated information, which is beyond the practical capacity of our society to generate.

All attempts at valuation of the environment begin with a problem: the goal is to assign monetary prices to things that have no prices because they are not for sale. One of the great strengths of the market is that it provides so much information about real prices. For any commodity that actually is bought and sold, prices are communicated automatically almost costlessly, and with constant updates as needed. To create artificial prices for environmental values, economists have to find some way to mimic the operation of the market. Unfortunately, the process is far from automatic, certainly not costless, and has to be repeated every time an updated price is needed.

As a result, there is constant pressure to use outdated or inappropriate valuations. Indeed, there are sound economic reasons for doing so: no one can afford constant updates, and significant savings can be achieved by using valuations created for other cases. In the EPA's original cost-benefit analysis of a revised standard for arsenic in drinking water, a valuation estimated for a case of chronic bronchitis, taken from a study performed ten years earlier, was used to represent the value of a case of nonfatal bladder cancer.

This is not, we hope and believe, because anyone thinks that bronchitis and bladder cancer are the same disease. The reason is more mundane: no one has performed an analysis of the cost of bladder cancer, and even the extensive analysis of arsenic regulations did not include enough time and money to do so. Therefore, the investigators used an estimated value for a very different disease. The only explanation offered for this procedure was that it had been done before, and the investigators thought nothing better was available.

Use of the bronchitis valuation to represent bladder cancer can charitably be described as "grasping at straws." Lacking the time and money to fill in the blank carefully, the economists simply picked a number. This is not remotely close to the level of rigor that is seen throughout the natural science, engineering, and public health portions of the arsenic analysis, yet it will happen again for exactly the same reason. It is not a failure of will or intellect, but rather the inescapable limitations of time and budget that lead to reliance on dated, inappropriate, and incomplete information to fill in the gaps on the benefit side of a cost-benefit analysis.

B. Trivializing the Future

One of the great triumphs of environmental law is its focus on the future: it seeks to avert harms to people and to natural resources in the future, not only within this generation, but within future generations as well. Indeed, one of the primary objectives of the National Environmental Policy Act, which has been called our basic charter of environmental protection, is to nudge the nation into "fulfilling the responsibilities of each generation as trustee of the environment for succeeding generations."

Protection of endangered species and ecosystems, reduction of pollution from persistent chemicals such as dioxin and DDT, prevention of long-latency diseases such as cancer, protection of the unborn against the health hazards from exposure to toxins in the womb—all of these protections are afforded by environmental law, and all of them look to the future as well as to the present. Environmental law seeks, moreover, to avoid the unpleasant surprises that come with discontinuities and irreversibility—the kinds of events that outstrip our powers of quantitative prediction. Here too, environmental law tries to protect the future in addition to the present.

Cost-benefit analysis systematically downgrades the importance of the future in two ways: through the technique of discounting and through predictive methodologies that take inadequate account of the possibility of catastrophic and irreversible events.

The most common, and commonsense, argument in favor of discounting future human lives saved, illnesses averted, and ecological disasters prevented, is that it is better to suffer a harm later rather than sooner. What's wrong with this argument? A lot, as it turns out.

1. Do Future Generations Count?

The first problem with the later-is-better argument for discounting is that it assumes that one person is deciding between dying or falling ill now, or dying or falling ill later. In that case, virtually everyone would prefer later. But many environmental programs protect the far future, beyond the lifetime of today's decision makers. Thus, the choice implicit in discounting is between preventing harms

Revise only

to the current generation and preventing similar harms to future generations. Seen in this way, discounting looks like a fancy justification for foisting our problems off onto the people who come after us.

The time periods involved in protecting the environment are often enormous—many decades for a wide range of problems, and even many centuries, in the case of climate change, radioactive waste, and other persistent toxins. With time spans this long, discounting at any positive rate will make even global catastrophes seem trivial. At a discount rate of five percent, for example, the death of a billion people 500 years from now becomes less serious than the death of one person today.

2. Does Haste Prevent Waste?

The justification for discounting often assumes that environmental problems will not get any worse if we wait to address them. In the market paradigm, buying environmental protection is just like buying any other commodity. You can buy a new computer now or later, and if you don't need it this year, you should probably wait. The technology will undoubtedly keep improving, so next year's models will do more yet cost less. An exactly parallel argument has been made about climate change (and other environmental problems) by some economists: if we wait for further technological progress, we will get more for our climate change mitigation dollars in the future.

If environmental protection were mass produced by the computer industry, and if environmental problems would agree to stand still indefinitely and wait for us to respond, this might be a reasonable approach. In the real world, however, it is a ludicrous and dangerous strategy.

Too many years of delay might mean that the polar ice cap melts, the spent uranium leaks out of the containment ponds, the hazardous waste seeps into groundwater and basements and backyards—at which point we cannot put the genie back in the bottle at any reasonable cost (or perhaps not at all).

Environmentalists often talk of potential "crises"—threats that problems will become suddenly and irreversibly worse. In response to such threats, environmentalists and some governments advocate the so-called "precautionary principle," which calls upon regulators to err on the side of caution and protection when risks are uncertain. Cost-benefit analysts, for the most part, do not assume the possibility of crisis. Their world view assumes stable problems, with control costs that are stable or declining over time, and thus finds precautionary investment in environmental protection to be a needless expense. Discounting is part of this noncrisis perspective. By implying that the present cost of future environmental harms declines, lockstep, with every year that we look ahead, discounting ignores the possibility of catastrophic and irreversible harms.

For this very reason, some prominent economists have rejected the discounting of intangibles. As William Baumol wrote in an important early article on discounting the benefits of public projects:

> There are important externalities and investments of the public goods variety which cry for special attention. Irreversibilities constitute a prime example. If we poison our soil so that never again will it be the same, if we destroy the Grand Canyon and turn it into a hydroelectric plant, we give up assets which like Goldsmith's bold peasantry, "...their country's pride, when once

destroy'd can never be supplied." All the wealth and resources of future generations will not suffice to restore them.

Most cost-benefit analysts do not exhibit this kind of humility about what the future might hold in store for us.

3. Begging the Question

Extensive discounting of future environmental problems lies at the heart of many recent reviews of regulatory costs and benefits that charge "statistical murder." When the costs and benefits of environmental protection are compared to those of safety rules (like requiring fire extinguishers for airplanes) or medical procedures (like vaccinating children against disease), environmental protection almost always comes out the loser. Why is this so?

These studies all discount future environmental benefits by at least five percent per year. This has little effect on the evaluation of programs—like auto safety rules requiring seat belts and fire safety rules requiring smoke alarms—that could start saving lives right away. However, for environmental programs like hazardous waste cleanups and control of persistent toxins that save lives in the future, discounting matters a great deal. Especially since, as explained above, the benefits are assumed to occur in the future when deaths are avoided, rather than in the near term when risks are reduced.

By using discounting, analysts assume the answer to the question they purport to address. That is, which programs are most worthwhile? The researchers begin with premises that guarantee that programs designed for the long haul (like environmental protection) are not as important as programs that look to the shorter term. When repeated without discounting (or with benefits assumed to occur when risks are reduced), these studies support many more environmental programs, and the cry of "statistical murder" rings hollow.

4. Citizens and Consumers—Reprise

The issue of discounting illustrates once again the failure of cost-benefit analysis to take into account the difference between citizens and consumers. Many people advocate discounting on the ground that it reflects people's preferences, as expressed in market decisions concerning risk. But again, this omits the possibility that people will have different preferences when they take on a different role. The future seems to matter much more to American citizens than to American consumers, even though they are of course the same people.

For example, Americans are notoriously bad at saving money on their own, apparently expressing a disinterest in the future. Still, Social Security is arguably the most popular entitlement program in the United States. The tension between Americans' personal saving habits and their enthusiasm for Social Security implies a sharp divergence between the temporal preferences of people as consumers and as citizens. Thus, private preferences for current over future consumption should not be used to subvert public judgments that future harms are as important as immediate ones.

C. *Exacerbating Inequality*

The third fundamental defect of cost-benefit analysis is that it tends to ignore, and therefore has the effect of reinforcing, patterns of economic and social inequality.

Cost-benefit analysis consists of adding up all the costs of a policy, adding up all the benefits, and comparing the totals. Implicit in this innocuous-sounding procedure is the controversial assumption that it does not matter who gets the benefits and who pays the costs. Both benefits and costs are measured simply as dollar totals; those totals are silent on questions of equity and distribution of resources.

In our society, concerns about equity frequently do, and should, enter into debates over public policy. There is an important difference between spending state tax revenues to improve the parks in rich communities and spending the same revenues to clean up pollution in poor communities. The value of these two initiatives, measured using cost-benefit analysis, might be the same in both cases, but this does not mean that the two policies are equally urgent or desirable.

The problem of equity runs even deeper. Benefits are typically measured by willingness to pay for environmental improvement, and the rich are able and willing to pay for more than the poor. Imagine a cost-benefit analysis of siting an undesirable facility, such as a landfill or incinerator. Wealthy communities are willing to pay more for the benefit of not having the facility in their backyards; thus, the net benefits to society as a whole will be maximized by putting the facility in a low-income area. (Note that wealthy communities do not actually have to pay for the benefit of avoiding the facility; the analysis depends only on the fact that they are willing to pay.) . . .

If decisions are based strictly on cost-benefit analysis and willingness to pay, most environmental burdens will end up being imposed on the countries, communities, and individuals with the least resources. This theoretical pattern bears an uncomfortably close resemblance to reality. Cost-benefit methods should not be blamed for existing patterns of environmental injustice; we suspect that pollution is typically dumped on the poor without waiting for formal analysis. Still, cost-benefit analysis rationalizes and reinforces the problem, allowing environmental burdens to flow downhill along the income gradients of an unequal world. It is hard to see this as part of an economically optimal or politically objective method of decision making.

In short, equity is an important criterion for evaluation of public policy, but it does not fit into the cost-benefit framework. The same is true of questions of rights and morality principles that are not reducible to monetary terms. Calculations that are acceptable, even commonsense, for financial matters can prove absurd or objectionable when applied to moral issues, as shown by the following example.

A financial investment with benefits worth five times its costs would seem like an obviously attractive bargain. Compare this to the estimates that front airbags on the passenger side of automobiles may cause one death, usually of a child, for every five lives saved. If we really believed that lives—even statistical lives—were worth $6 million, or any other finite dollar amount, then endorsing the airbags should be no more complicated than accepting the financial investment. However, many people do find the airbag tradeoff troubling or unacceptable, implying that there is a different, nonquantitative value of a life that is at stake here. If a public policy brought some people five dollars of benefits for every one dollar it cost to others, the winners could in theory compensate the losers. No such compensation is possible if winning and losing are measured in deaths rather than dollars.

In comparing the deaths of adults prevented by airbags with the deaths of children caused by airbags, or in exploring countless other harms that might be mitigated through regulation, the real debate is not between rival cost-benefit analyses. Rather, it is between environmental advocates who frame the issue as a matter of rights and ethics, and others who see it as an acceptable area for economic calculation. That debate is inescapable, and it logically comes before the details of evaluating costs and benefits.

D. Less Objectivity and Transparency

A fourth fundamental flaw of cost-benefit analysis is that it is unable to deliver on the promise of more objective and more transparent decision making. In fact, in most cases the use of cost-benefit analysis is likely to deliver less objectivity and less transparency.

For the reasons we have discussed, there is nothing objective about the basic premises of cost-benefit analysis. Treating individuals solely as consumers, rather than as citizens with a sense of moral responsibility to the larger society, represents a distinct and highly contestable world view. Likewise, the use of discounting reflects judgments about the nature of environmental risks and citizens' responsibilities toward future generations that are, at a minimum, debatable. Because value-laden premises permeate cost-benefit analysis, the claim that cost-benefit analysis offers an "objective" way to make government decisions is simply bogus.

Furthermore, as we have seen, cost-benefit analysis relies on a byzantine array of approximations, simplifications, and counterfactual hypotheses. Thus, the actual use of cost-benefit analysis inevitably involves countless judgment calls. People with strong, and clashing, partisan positions naturally will advocate that discretion in the application of this methodology be exercised in favor of their positions, further undermining the claim that cost-benefit analysis is objective.

Perhaps the best way to illustrate how little economic analysis has to contribute, objectively, to the fundamental question of how clean and safe we want our environment to be is to refer again to the controversy over cost-benefit analysis of the EPA's regulation of arsenic in drinking water. As Cass Sunstein has recently argued, the available information on the benefits of arsenic reduction supports estimates of net benefits from regulation ranging from less than zero up to $560 million or more. The number of deaths avoided annually by regulation is, according to Sunstein, between zero and 112. A procedure that allows such an enormous range of different evaluations of a single rule is certainly not the objective, transparent decision rule that its advocates have advertised.

These uncertainties arise from the limited knowledge of the epidemiology and toxicology of exposure to arsenic as well as the controversial series of assumptions required for valuation and discounting of costs and (particularly) benefits. As Sunstein explains, a number of different positions, including most of those heard in the recent controversy over arsenic regulation, could be supported by one or another reading of the evidence.

Some analysts might respond that this enormous range of outcomes is not possible if the proper economic assumptions are used—if, for example, human lives are valued at $6 million apiece and discounted at a five percent yearly rate (or, depending on the analyst, other favorite numbers). But these assumptions beg fundamental questions about ethics and equity, and one cannot decide whether to embrace them without thinking through the whole range of moral issues they raise. Yet once one has thought through these issues, there is no need then to collapse the complex moral inquiry into a series of numbers. Pricing the priceless merely translates our inquiry into a different, and foreign, language—one with a painfully impoverished vocabulary.

For many of the same reasons, cost-benefit analysis also generally fails to achieve the goal of transparency. Cost-benefit analysis is a complex, resource-intensive, and expert-driven process. It requires a great deal of time and effort to attempt to unpack even the simplest cost-benefit analysis. Few community groups, for example, have access to the kind of scientific and technical expertise that would allow them to evaluate whether, intentionally or unintentionally, the authors of a cost-benefit analysis have unfairly slighted the interests of the community or some of its members. Few members of the public can participate meaningfully in the debates about the use of particular regression analyses or discount rates which are central to the cost-benefit method.

The translation of lives, health, and nature into dollars also renders decision making about the underlying social values less rather than more transparent. As we have discussed, all of the various steps required to reduce a human life to a dollar value are open to debate and subject to uncertainty. However, the specific dollar values kicked out by cost-benefit analysis tend to obscure these underlying issues rather than encourage full public debate about them.

IV. Practical Problems

The last Part showed that there are deep, inherent problems with cost-benefit analysis. In practice, these problems only get worse; leading examples of cost-benefit analysis fall far short of the theoretical ideal. The continuing existence of these practical problems further undercuts the utility and wisdom of using cost-benefit analysis to evaluate environmental policy.

A. The Limits of Quantification

Cost-benefit studies of regulations focus on quantified benefits of the proposed action and generally ignore other, nonquantified, health and environmental benefits. This raises a serious problem because many benefits of environmental programs—including the prevention of many nonfatal diseases and harms to the ecosystem—either have not been quantified or are not capable of being quantified at this time. Indeed, for many environmental regulations, the only benefit that can be quantified is the prevention of cancer deaths. On the other hand, one can virtually always come up with some number for the costs of environmental regulations. Thus, in practice, cost-benefit analysis tends to skew decision making against protecting public health and the environment.

For example, regulation of workers' exposure to formaldehyde is often presented as the extreme of inefficiency, supposedly costing $72 billion per life saved. This figure is based on the finding that the regulation prevents cancers that occur only in small numbers, but which have been thoroughly evaluated in numerical terms. But the formaldehyde regulation also prevents many painful but nonfatal illnesses excluded from the $72 billion figure. If described solely as a means of reducing cancer, the regulation indeed would be very expensive. But if described as a means of reducing cancer and other diseases, the regulation would make a good deal of sense. Workplace regulation of formaldehyde is not a bad answer, but it does happen to be an answer to a different question.

The formaldehyde case is by no means unique. Often, the only regulatory benefit that can be quantified is the prevention of cancer, yet cancer has a latency period of between five and forty years. When discounted at five percent, a cancer death forty years from now has a "present value" of only one-seventh of a death today. Thus, one of the benefits that most often can be quantified—allowing it to be folded into cost-benefit analysis—is also one that is heavily discounted, making the benefits of preventive regulation seem trivial.

B. Ignoring What Cannot Be Counted

A related practical problem is that even when the existence of unquantified or unquantifiable benefits is recognized, their importance is frequently ignored. Many advocates of cost-benefit analysis concede that the decision-making process must make some room for non-quantitative considerations. Some environmental benefits never have been subjected to rigorous economic evaluation. Other important considerations in environmental protection (such as the fairness of the distribution of environmental risks) cannot be quantified and priced.

In practice, however, this kind of judgment is often forgotten, or even denigrated, once all the numbers have been crunched. No matter how many times the EPA, for example, says that one of its rules will produce many benefits—like the prevention of illness or the protection of ecosystems—that cannot be quantified, the non-quantitative aspects of its analyses are almost invariably ignored in public discussions of its policies.

When the Clinton administration's EPA proposed, for example, strengthening the standard for arsenic in drinking water, it cited many human illnesses that would be prevented by the new standard but that could not be expressed in numerical terms. Subsequent public discussion of the EPA's cost-benefit analysis of this standard, however, inevitably referred only to the EPA's numerical analysis and forgot about the cases of avoided illness that could not be quantified.

C. Overstated Costs

There is also a tendency, as a matter of practice, to overestimate the costs of regulations in advance of their implementation. This happens in part because regulations often encourage new technologies and more efficient ways of doing business; these innovations reduce the cost of compliance. It is also important to keep in mind, when reviewing cost estimates, that they are usually provided by the regulated industry itself, which has an obvious incentive to offer high estimates of costs as a way of warding off new regulatory requirements.

One study found that costs estimated in advance of regulation were more than twice the actual costs in eleven out of twelve cases. Another study found that advance total cost estimates were more than 25% higher than actual costs for fourteen out of twenty-eight regulations; advance estimates were more than 25% too low in only three of the twenty-eight cases. Before the 1990 Clean Air Act Amendments took effect, industry anticipated that the cost of sulfur reduction under the amendments would be $1500 per ton. In 2000, the actual cost was under $150 per ton. Of course, not all cost-benefit analyses overstate the actual costs of regulation, but given the technology-forcing character of environmental regulations, it is not surprising to find a marked propensity to overestimate the costs of such rules.

In a related vein, many companies have begun to discover that environmental protection actually can be good for business in some respects. Increased energy efficiency, profitable products made from waste, and decreased use of raw materials are just a few of the cost-saving or even profit-making results of turning more corporate attention to environmentally protective business practices. Cost-benefit analyses typically do not take such money-saving possibilities into account in evaluating the costs of regulation.

V. The Many Alternatives to Cost-Benefit Analysis

A common response to the criticisms of cost-benefit analysis is a simple question: what is the alternative? The implication is that despite its flaws, cost-benefit analysis is really the only tool we have for figuring out how much environmental protection to provide.

This is just not true. Indeed, for thirty years, the federal government has been protecting human health and the environment without relying on cost-benefit analysis. The menu of regulatory options that has emerged from this experience is large and varied. Choosing among these possibilities depends on a variety of case-specific circumstances, such as the nature of the pollution involved, the degree of scientific knowledge about it, and the conditions under which people are exposed to it. As the following brief sketch of alternatives reveals, cost-benefit analysis—a "one-size-fits-all" approach to regulation—cannot be squared with the multiplicity of circumstances surrounding different environmental problems.

For the most part, environmental programs rely on a form of "technology-based" regulation, the essence of which is to require the best available methods for controlling pollution. This avoids the massive research effort needed to quantify and monetize the precise harms caused by specific amounts of pollution, which is required by cost-benefit analysis. In contrast, the technology-based approach allows regulators to proceed directly to controlling emissions. Simply put, the idea is that we should do the best we can to mitigate pollution we believe to be harmful.

Over the years, the EPA has learned that flexibility is a good idea when it comes to technology-based regulation and thus has tended to avoid specifying particular technologies or processes for use by regulated firms; instead, the agency increasingly has relied on "performance-based" regulation, which tells firms to clean up to a certain, specified extent, but does not tell them precisely how to do it. Technology-based regulation generally takes costs into account in determining the required level of pollution control but does not demand the kind of precisely quantified and monetized balancing process that is needed for cost-benefit analysis.

Another regulatory strategy that has gained a large following in recent years is the use of "pollution trading," as in the sulfur dioxide emissions trading program created for power plants under the 1990 Clean Air Act Amendments. That program grants firms a limited number of permits for pollution, but allows them to buy permits from other firms. Thus, firms with high pollution control costs can save money by buying permits, while those with low control costs can save money by controlling emissions and selling their permits. The fixed supply of permits, created by law, sets the cap on total emissions; the trading process allows industry to decide where and how it is most economical to reduce emissions to fit under the cap. Trading programs have become an important part of the federal program for controlling pollution. These programs, too, have not used cost-benefit analysis in their implementation. Congress, the EPA, or other officials set the emissions cap, and the market does the rest.

It is theoretically possible that cost-benefit analysis could be used to choose the overall limit on pollution that guides both performance-based and market-based regulatory programs. However, this has not been standard practice in the past; the limit on sulfur emissions in the 1990 Clean Air Act Amendments, for example, was set by a process of political compromise; given the problems with cost-benefit analysis, political compromise cannot be viewed as an inferior way to set a cap on emissions. Many regulatory programs have been a terrific success without using cost-benefit analysis to set pollution limits.

One last example (a desire for reasonable brevity prevents us from listing more) is informational regulation, which requires disclosures to the public and/or to consumers about risks they face from exposures to chemicals. These "right-to-know" regimes allow citizens and consumers not only to know about the risks they face, but also empower them to do something about those risks. The Toxic Release Inventory created by the Emergency Planning and Community Right-to-Know Act, the product warning labels required by California's "Proposition 65," and the consumer notices now required regarding drinking water that contains hazardous chemicals, are all variants of this type of information-based regulation. Not one of these popular and effective programs relies on cost-benefit analysis.

The arguments for flexible technology-based regulation and for incentive-based programs like pollution trading and disclosure requirements are sometimes confused with the arguments for cost-benefit analysis. But both technology-based and incentive-based regulation take their goals from elected representatives rather than from economic analysts, even though the means adopted by these regulatory strategies are strongly influenced by attention to costs. The current style of cost-benefit analysis, however, purports to set the ends, not just the means, of environmental policy, and that is where its aspirations amount to arrogance.

Economic analysis has had its successes and made its contributions; it has taught us a great deal over the years about how we can most efficiently and cheaply reach a given environmental goal. It has taught us relatively little, however, about what our environmental goals should be. Indeed, while economists have spent three decades wrangling about how much a human life, or a bald eagle, or a beautiful stretch of river is worth in dollars, ecologists, engineers, and other specialists have gone about the business of saving lives and eagles and rivers without waiting for formal, quantitative analysis proving that saving these things is worthwhile.

Conclusion

Two features of cost-benefit analysis distinguish it from other approaches to evaluating the advantages and disadvantages of environmentally protective regulations: the translation of lives, health, and the natural environment into monetary terms, and the discounting of harms to human health and the environment that are expected to occur in the future. These features of cost-benefit analysis make it a terrible way to make decisions about environmental protection, for both intrinsic and practical reasons.

Nor is it useful to keep cost-benefit analysis around as a kind of regulatory tag-along, providing information that regulators may find "interesting" even if not decisive. Cost-benefit analysis is exceedingly time- and resource-intensive, and its flaws are so deep and so large that this time and these resources are wasted on it. Once a cost-benefit analysis is performed, its bottom line number offers an irresistible sound bite that inevitably drowns out more reasoned deliberation. Moreover, given the intrinsic conflict between cost-benefit analysis and the principles of fairness that animate, or should animate, our national policy toward protecting people from being hurt by other people, the results of cost-benefit analysis cannot simply be "given some weight" along with other factors, without undermining the fundamental equality of all citizens—rich and poor, young and old, healthy and sick.

Cost-benefit analysis cannot overcome its fatal flaw: it is completely reliant on the impossible attempt to price the priceless values of life, health, nature, and the future. Better public policy decisions can be made without cost-benefit analysis, by combining the successes of traditional regulation with the best of the innovative and flexible approaches that have gained ground in recent years.

COMMENTS AND QUESTIONS

1. Are Ackerman and Heinzerling opposed to cost-benefit analysis in principle or merely to the way it has operated in practice?

2. Even if one granted that cost-benefit analysis has the flaws Ackerman and Heinzerling identify, couldn't one still endorse it as the "least bad" regulatory framework? Keep in mind that we must evaluate these frameworks comparatively and at the margin.

3. Can we avoid cost-benefit analysis? Don't we—if we are acting rationally—compare costs and benefits all the time? In the "Lockout/Tagout" case cited in part B of this chapter, Judge Stephen Williams observed:

> [W]e make implicit life and safety valuations each day when we decide, for example, whether to travel by train or car, the former being more costly (at least if several family members are traveling together) but safer per passenger-mile. Where government makes decisions for others, it may reasonably be expected to make the trade-offs somewhat more explicitly than individuals choosing for themselves. The difficulty of securing agreement even on a range of values hardly justifies making decisions on the basis of a pretense that resources are not scarce. . . .

> Thus, cost-benefit analysis entails only a systematic weighing of pros and cons, or what Benjamin Franklin referred to as a "moral or prudential algebra." Writing to a friend who was perplexed by a difficult decision, he explained his own approach:

>> When those difficult cases occur, they are difficult, chiefly because while we have them under consideration, all the reasons pro and con are not present to the mind at the same time. . . . To get over this, my way is to divide half a sheet of paper by a line into two columns; writing over the one Pro, and over the other Con. Then, during three or four days consideration, I put down under the different heads short hints of the different motives, that at different times occur to me,

for or against the measure. When I have thus got them all together in one view, I endeavor to estimate their respective weights.... And, though the weight of reasons cannot be taken with the precision of algebraic quantities, yet when each is thus considered, separately and comparatively, and the whole lies before me, I think I can judge better, and am less liable to make a rash step, and in fact I have found great advantage from this kind of equation, in what may be called moral or prudential algebra.

> 938 F.2d 1310, 1320–21, quoting Franklin as reprinted in
> Edward M. Gramlich, *Benefit-Cost Analysis of*
> *Government Programs* 1–2 (1981)

Is the cost-benefit analysis described in this chapter the kind of "moral or prudential algebra" Ben Franklin endorsed? If so, how could anyone oppose it?

4. Ackerman and Heinzerling argue against discounting regulatory benefits such as lives saved in the future. If we do not discount future benefits, however, doesn't this mean that we must be willing to spend all of our resources today to benefit the billions of people who will one day inhabit the planet? If we're not willing to do this, aren't we in fact applying some discount rate to these future lives, just without specifying what it is? In that case, isn't cost-benefit analysis—in which the discount rate is transparent—a better approach?

5. Are the alternatives to cost-benefit analysis offered by Ackerman and Heinzerling satisfactory? Is it fair to say Ackerman and Heinzerling describe various tools for regulating, once we decide regulation is appropriate, but fail to tell us how to decide when regulation is a good idea?

6. The following reading attempts to reconcile cost-benefit analysis with respectful attention to citizens' (arguably irrational) perceptions of risk. How successful is it?

■ *Reinventing the Regulatory State*
RICHARD H. PILDES AND CASS R. SUNSTEIN
62 U. Chi. L. Rev. 1 (1995). Reprinted with permission
of University of Chicago Law Review

...Laypeople assess risk through different value frameworks from those implicitly embedded in expert approaches. Laypeople do not look only or even primarily to expected annual mortality; they look as well at a number of factors determining the acceptability of different risks in different contexts. These factors cannot be said to generate a "hard" model of risk assessment, but they do represent an articulable framework for making judgments about risk levels....

These different systems of value mean that judgment about risk is frequently context-dependent. Decision-analytic techniques traditionally used by experts are concerned with aggregate annual mortality or morbidity rates. However, for laypeople, the most salient contextual features include: (1) the catastrophic nature of the risk; (2) whether the risk is uncontrollable; (3) whether the risk involves irretrievable or permanent losses; (4) the social conditions under which a particular risk is generated and managed, a point that connects to issues of consent, voluntariness, and democratic control; (5) how equitably distributed the danger is or how concentrated on identifiable, innocent, or traditionally disadvantaged victims, which ties to both notions of community and moral ideals; (6) how well understood the risk process in question is, a point that bears on the psychological disturbance produced by different risks; (7) whether the risk would be faced by future generations; and (8) how familiar the risk is. Different formulations for these and similar distinctions include how "dreaded" and how "observable" particular risks are. In particular, "[c]itizens' responses to technological risks . . . are far more likely to be dictated by their perceptions of whether they can exercise personal control in the event of an accident than by the careful weighing of the worths of uncertain outcomes."

People systematically assign a high valuation to risks that are perceived to be involuntarily run—compare public reactions to risks from smoking to public reactions to risks from nuclear power accidents. About 150,000 people die each year from smoking-related causes, as compared with no apparent deaths from nuclear power accidents; yet enormous resources are invested in preventing the latter, and until recently almost no resources were invested in preventing the former. (It is notable that recent regulatory efforts with respect to smoking have followed and produced important changes in social norms, a point that we take up below.) Qualitative differences of this kind are not included within ordinary cost-benefit techniques to the extent that the latter concentrate only on end states.

The important point is that it can be fully rational to attend to contextual differences of this sort. Indeed, approaches that attend to such differences are, in many contexts, more rational than approaches that concentrate only on end states. It is fully plausible to believe that expenditures per life saved ought to vary in accordance with (for example) the voluntariness of the risk or its catastrophic quality. Such beliefs appear widespread. Interviews with workers, for example, reveal that their valuations of workplace risks depend upon such contextual features as the overall structure of workplace relations, how much say workers have in how the risks are managed, and the nature of the particular jobs performed.

Consider also the fact that the quantitatively identical level of exposure to certain chemicals is viewed as more acceptable by research scientists, exposed during the course of carrying out basic research, than by laboratory assistants, who clean the hazards up after an experiment is finished. To aggregate these different perspectives and assume that one common value is at stake in reducing mercury exposure is therefore wrong. For the scientist, the meaning of the risk, and the appropriate level of social resources to be spent to eliminate it, depend on the fact that it is tied up with professional work that is highly valued socially, personally rewarding, voluntarily assumed, and associated with traditions of scientific inquiry. If people do value risks differently depending on these sorts of contextual features, and if these valuations are reasonable, then democratic policy should recognize the relevant contextual differences. . . .

Attention to context, and particularly to the social conditions under which risks are produced and managed, returns us to the crucial role of public trust in effective regulatory policy. Among the features that determine lay attitudes toward risk are people's judgments about the "acceptability of [the] social processes for making decisions about risk." This point has at least three consequences for the morality and strategy of government risk regulation. First, risk policy cannot reasonably focus on end states alone. If institutions are restructured to bring about more (apparently) consistent outcomes, but through processes that are less publicly acceptable, public institutions will be correspondingly less effective. Second, it is doubtful whether such institutions will be able, in fact, to bring about these more consistent results, at least if consistency is defined as uniform expenditures per life saved. In the absence of public support, policies recommended by decision theory are not likely to be effectively implemented. Third, in evaluating policies, we should be quite cautious about comparisons that involve only end states. In moral or democratic terms, greater expenditures may be justifiably demanded for quantitatively similar risks precisely because people consider the values at stake to differ in the various contexts in which these risks are imposed.

All this is no reason to be complacent about the dramatic disparitie[s]. Divergences in regulatory policies that are so extreme might well reflect little more than interest-group pressures, confusion, lack of appreciation for trade-offs, or reflexive responses to sensationalist anecdotes. Moreover, we do not mean to suggest that policymakers should blindly defer to citizen assessments of risks in all circumstances. Ours is a republic, not a pure democracy, and a high premium is placed on deliberation rather than on snapshots of public opinion. It therefore makes sense to ensure that citizens' judgments result from an appropriately structured deliberative process. . . .

The question of how policy should respond in situations of conflict between expert and lay assessments of risk is thus complex and not resolvable through any general rule. Nonetheless, we can offer some initial distinctions.

At one pole, lay assessments of risk sometimes rest on certain heuristics, or rules of thumb for processing information, that may make sense in the contexts in which they are adopted, but that are inappropriate bases for making public policy. These heuristics include psychological devices that lead to risk assessments that policymakers should treat as factually erroneous. For example, cognitive psychologists have uncovered the central role of the "availability" heuristic in ordinary decision making. "Availability" means that people's assessment of one risk depends, at times, on how readily similar events come to their minds. When this effect is at work, people will overestimate the probability that an event will occur if the occurrence of similar events comes easily to mind, but will underestimate the probability otherwise.

Whether similar events do come to mind can depend on how recently they occurred or how dramatically they were presented when they did occur. The "facts" about a certain risk do not differ when someone happens to remember a particularly salient recent event, but people's assessments of those facts can be greatly affected. Lay estimates of how high the risk is from hazardous landfills, for example, may depend on how readily people recall Love Canal or similar episodes. The gap here between objective and perceived levels of risk is not a function of different values, but of what can properly be viewed as cognitive errors based on misinformed understandings of the actual probabilities of certain events.

At the other pole are the cases we seek to emphasize: those in which experts and laypeople value differently the same "objective" risk (understood in terms, say, of aggregate lives at stake) as a result of features of the context that expert decision-theoretic or cost-benefit techniques obscure. These are the contexts in which people might demand, for example, that fewer social resources be devoted to "the same level" of risk reduction when the risks are viewed as voluntarily assumed rather than when they are viewed as involuntarily imposed, or when the risks occur in social conditions viewed as illegitimate rather than legitimate.

Between these poles are situations in which it is unclear whether expert and lay differences stem from factual errors or alternative values. For example, experts are often troubled by the public's refusal to view risks in linear terms; laypeople sometimes express greater concern over a low-probability event with large potential tragic costs than probability theory would consider rational. This difference might reflect the well-known cognitive difficulties people manifest in dealing with low- and high-probability events. Alternatively, it might reflect the view that catastrophic events entail costs considerably beyond deaths, injuries, and other material costs—such as the destruction of social stability.

For example, the "Buffalo Creek Syndrome" has been documented several times in the aftermath of major disasters. Nearly two years after the collapse of a dam that left 120 dead and 4,000 homeless, psychiatric researchers continued to find significant psychological and sociological changes; survivors were "characterized by a loss of direction and energy," other "disabling character changes," and a "loss of communality." One evaluator attributed this loss of direction specifically to "the loss of traditional bonds of kinship and neighborliness." The nonlinearity of lay evaluations of risk in the context of potential disasters may thus reflect a high premium on avoiding the distinctive kinds of losses associated with disasters. If so, differences between lay and expert assessments rest on genuine value differences (four times as many deaths may be much more than four times as bad) rather than on factual errors in cognitive processes of ordinary people.

The proper response to conflicts between lay and expert assessments of risk should therefore depend on an understanding of the reasons for these differences in different contexts. Where differences stem from cognitive errors, such as the availability heuristic, policymakers can properly exert leadership and not defer to lay assessments. Indeed, policymakers would do well to seek to educate the public about the factual fallacies underlying popular assessments. . . . Policymakers might also "strike when the iron is cold" by postponing policy-making until some time after a triggering event has occurred—thus reducing the distorting effects of availability. Because regulatory overkill is a frequent short-term response to sensationalist triggering events, it may well make sense to wait until the crisis period has ended, notwithstanding the difficulty of doing so.

The matter should be analyzed differently when the differences arise from clashes between the value frameworks of experts and laypeople. In such cases there is no reason to defer to experts; democracies should be responsive to the informed values of their citizens. . . .

Our final point is that often there is no way to know, a priori, whether expert and lay differences turn on facts or values (putting to one side the complex relation between the two). Yet another reason for promoting participation in regulatory processes (to the extent that it is feasible) is therefore that public participation is required to elicit the reasons that lay assessments of risk might differ from expert ones. This participation should take the form of informed deliberation about regulatory means and goals. Only after policymakers understand the reasons behind these differences can they know whether the reasons rest on factual errors or value conflicts; only with such information can policymakers know how best to respond to the systematic problem of conflicts between expert and lay evaluations of risk....

... [A] reinvented regulatory state that appreciates this principle might seek to (1) adapt analytic models so that they better incorporate appropriately informed lay evaluations; (2) design, to the extent feasible, more effective mechanisms for citizen participation and education to enable articulation of informed perspectives; (3) emphasize contextual features of risk-exposure and process concerns as well as those of end states; and (4) focus on the importance of building public trust in risk-producing and risk-managing institutions.

D. Incommensurability and Disaggregating Costs and Benefits

Thus far, our principal suggestion has been that CBA is inadequate to the extent that it is solely concerned with end states. A generalization of this criticism is that traditional CBA is obtuse—in the sense of insufficiently fine grained—insofar as it tries to measure diverse social goods along the same metric. Suppose, for example, that we are told that the cost of a certain occupational safety regulation is $1 million, and that the benefit is $1.2 million. To make a sensible evaluation, we need to know a great deal more. What do these numbers mean? To which groups do they refer, with what histories and claims? Are the cost-bearing groups those that are appropriately faced with this burden, because (for example) they are imposing nonvoluntary risks on others? Or consider the decision whether to fund more AIDS research rather than research exploring the risks posed by destruction of the ozone layer. What is the relevance of the fact that AIDS often comes from voluntary activity, in which the associated risk may be known? That gay men are disproportionately at risk? That AIDS strikes young people with many productive years ahead of them? That the risks posed by destruction of the ozone layer might be faced mostly by future generations and very broadly shared throughout the population? How would we know if we are devoting too much of our limited regulatory resources to AIDS or ozone layer research? Or consider the problem of distributional effects of regulatory problems and solutions. Does it matter if a certain environmental hazard is concentrated in low-income or minority neighborhoods? Does it matter if the costs of disposing of hazardous waste, for example, are borne disproportionately by minority group members? ...

We do not do well if we see such diverse goods as greater employment, protection of endangered species, lower prices, distributional effects, and cleaner air along a single metric, one that erases the qualitative differences among these goods. At least in principle, it would be better to have a disaggregated system for assessing the qualitatively different effects of regulatory impositions. Not all benefits are fungible, nor are all costs. This is a separate problem from the more familiar difficulty of comparing costs and benefits against each other once they have been aggregated.

Through considerations of this sort, we might be able to make some progress toward reform of existing cost-benefit analyses. Through regulatory-impact analyses, people should be allowed to see the diverse effects of regulations for themselves, and to make judgments based on an understanding of the qualitative differences. If all of the relevant goods are aligned along a single metric, they become less visible, or perhaps invisible. In addition to conventional cost-benefit analysis, what is necessary is a full accounting of the various social consequences of regulation. Those consequences should be described in a way that allows a detailed view of what the costs and benefits specifically are. Once greater specificity is added, we will not be thinking in terms of simple costs and benefits at all. There is no algorithm to say what ought to be done once the more specific accounting is before us. Judgments involving controversial political and moral values will necessarily be made through ordinary administrative and democratic processes.

Disaggregating costs and benefits, identifying qualitatively different effects, and taking account of effects on diverse groups makes sense on several grounds. First, it is a way of taking into account certain features of ordinary evaluations of risk. Second, this approach enables regulators to focus on distributional issues—on issues of who gains and who loses. Third, judgments about the relevant moral context of risks can be made more intelligently once we have a more specific understanding of the interests that bear the costs and benefits.

Public deliberation will be enhanced when analytic tools are used to generate information calibrated to the kinds of considerations that appropriately informed citizens consider relevant. It should be unnecessary to emphasize that regulatory choices typically have effects along multiple dimensions. Rather than reducing these to a single metric of "costs" or "benefits," it is better to enable decision makers to assess the different kinds of effects on different interests. To be sure, there are advantages in simplicity, and on this count conventional CBA has virtues in spite of its crudeness. But for those who want aggregate data on costs and benefits, nothing precludes arguing that the disaggregated data should be used in a simpler way.

E. Expressive Dimensions of Regulatory Policies

A third problem with CBA approaches is that they necessarily focus on the quantitative or material effects of policies. They cannot take into account what we will call *the expressive dimensions of legal and political choices*. By expressive dimensions—what might be understood as cultural consequences of choice—we mean the values that a particular policy choice, in the specific context in which it is taken, will be generally understood to endorse. Policy choices do not just bring about certain immediate material consequences; they also will be understood, at times, to be important for what they reflect about various value commitments—about which values take priority over others, or how various values are best understood. Both the material consequences and the expressive consequences of policy choices are appropriate concerns for policymakers.

The expressive dimensions of policy choices can become relevant in several ways. Let us take a contentious and somewhat stylized example. Trade issues often involve difficult trade-offs between the interests of current workers and those of current and future consumers (and perhaps future workers as well). Lowering protective tariffs might displace current workers who might or might not be able to find substitute employment, while enhancing consumer welfare by making the same goods available more cheaply. An aggregate cost-benefit analysis would require that all these effects be treated as qualitatively the same. We might reject that approach, however, on the view that the interests of various workers and various consumers are qualitatively distinct. In that case, we could not resolve this conflict simply by determining which choice maximized net benefits. Instead, we would face a political and moral choice about how to assess the interests of the workers affected as against those of the consumers benefited. Of course, we would still want to know as much as possible about the precise quantifiable effects on workers and consumers of the proposed policy. But we would ultimately have to decide how to value the various interests affected. That valuation might in turn affect remedial measures, including efforts to facilitate alternative employment for displaced workers.

These conflicts arise regularly in the trade area. Now suppose policymakers repeatedly prefer consumer interests in these conflicts. This sequence might leave affected workers with the sense that, in every case, the political community is subordinating their interests to those of others. When officials are next faced with a similar conflict, it could well be rational to opt for a policy that valued the interests of workers (at least if they are in the same affected sectors) over those of consumers. That might be so even if, in aggregate cost-benefit terms, consumer benefits would "outweigh" the harms to adversely affected workers.

Such a choice would be important precisely because it would express the social conviction that the interests of workers are seriously valued. This is a highly stylized example, of course, and the right choice in any particular context will depend on many factors, including the precise magnitude of the relevant costs and benefits (at some point, the sacrifice in material benefits might become too great to justify the expressive or social gains). The important point is that a concern for the values being expressed through policy choices—the expressive dimensions of political decisions—is itself an appropriate matter for policymakers.

Many other legal issues, such as protection of endangered species, recycling requirements, affirmative action, "hate speech" codes, and others similarly implicate concerns for the expressive dimensions of legal judgments. Often legal debates are partly about the appropriate attitude to express via legal norms, and many people urge that a certain measure is desirable because it expresses the appropriate attitude toward the interests at stake.

When evaluating a legal norm, then, we might ask whether the norm expresses an appropriate valuation of an event, person, group, or practice. The point matters for two reasons. The first is, broadly speaking, based on a prediction about the facts: an inappropriate valuation via law may influence social norms and experiences, and push them in the wrong direction. If the law wrongly treats something solely as a commodity, for example, the social understanding of what that good is may be adversely affected. That is, the good might come to be treated more generally as a commodity. It is appropriate to criticize the law on this ground.

This objection is based on an empirical claim that the kinds of valuation reflected in law will affect social valuations in general. Sometimes this is right, but sometimes it is not. Society is filled, for example, with market exchange of goods (like pets, which are not valued in the same way as money) that are valued for reasons other than use. The question therefore remains whether the asserted effect on social norms actually occurs. It is fully plausible, for example, to say that although a law that permits prostitution reflects an inappropriate valuation of sexuality, the speculative effect of the law on social norms is an implausible basis for objection.

But there is a second ground for endorsing the expressive function of law, and this ground is not about social effects in the same sense. To understand this idea, it is helpful to start with the personal interest in integrity. Following the suggestive discussion by Bernard Williams, we might say that individual behavior is not concerned solely with states of affairs, and that if it were, we would have a hard time making sense of important aspects of our lives. Personal integrity, commitment, and the narrative continuity of a life matter enormously as well. In Williams's example, someone might refuse to kill an innocent person at the request of a terrorist, even if the consequence of the refusal is that many more people will be killed. Our responses to this case are not adequately captured in purely consequentialist terms.

At the social and legal level, there may be an analogue. A society might identify the kind of valuation to which it is committed, and insist on that kind, even if the consequences of the insistence are obscure or unknown. A society might (for example) insist on an antidiscrimination law for expressive reasons even if it is unclear whether the law actually helps members of minority groups. A society might protect endangered species partly because it believes that the protection makes best sense of its self-understanding, by expressing an appropriate valuation of what it means for one species to eliminate another.

These expressive or symbolic dimensions of policy are central in many regulatory contexts. They are just as real and significant as other dimensions of policy. Part of what policy-making does is to define, interpret, and create collective understandings and values. Moreover, current decisions can structure the ways future problems will be characterized and can help determine what counts as a problem at all. Decisions today crystallize collective understandings in ways that shape the perceived meaning and appropriate resolution of future choices. Understandably, people often evaluate present choices with these considerations in mind.

CBA approaches cannot adequately capture all the expressive dimensions of policy choices. They are designed to address other dimensions. CBA deals with the material or quantitative dimensions, not the interpretive and expressive ones. CBA examines alternative end states; it compares, for example, how much it would cost to reach a state in which health was protected to a certain degree against a particular risk. It cannot take account of the meaning of the transition—the values the transition will be socially understood to express—from one end state to another. The meaning of the policy depends on interpretation of the background against which it is enacted. This process of interpretation must take place in ways other than through CBA.

Perhaps in theory, some types of expressive concerns could be incorporated into CBA. This is perhaps most conspicuously true when the concern is the way law shapes social attitudes and the resulting effects of social attitudes on the allocation of resources. For example, mandatory recycling policies might be justified, in part, as a means of shifting attitudes about consumption and the environment in general; the resulting changes in social norms might change consumption patterns themselves. In theory, the predicted shifts in attitudes, and hence in actual consumption, could be quantitatively modeled. In practice, of course, incorporating the way legal policies might shape attitudes, and the effect on material goods of such attitudinal changes, is likely to be extremely difficult, not least because of the highly speculative empirical questions involved.

Other ways in which expressive concerns are relevant to policy are even more difficult to capture through CBA. Consider the fact that policies express values that maintain the integrity of important national commitments; this concern cannot be addressed through CBA unless it could somehow be based on highly refined

measures that reflect (a distinctive form of) public judgments about those commitments. Where policies are relevant intrinsically for the importance of the values
they express, CBA cannot incorporate this concern, unless measures of willingness
to pay could somehow be designed to capture public judgments about intrinsic
value. Sometimes what is at stake is ensuring various groups that their interests are
valued in the political process, rather than consistently subordinated to other interests. The values of political legitimacy, stability, and fairness are not taken into
account via CBA....

COMMENTS AND QUESTIONS

1. How do Pildes and Sunstein respond to critics of laypeople's judgments about
   risk? To critics of cost-benefit analysis? In light of their analysis, can you design
   policy modifications—either substantive or procedural—that would address
   the difficulties they describe? Because of their emphasis on contextual factors,
   you might have to think about specific problems: carpal tunnel syndrome, the
   use of a specific hazardous chemical in consumer products and the workplace,
   and the like.

2. Pildes and Sunstein appear to argue that policy makers properly take public
   misunderstandings into account in formulating policy. Is this a correct interpretation of their work? Are you persuaded?

3. The following decision is one of the few judicial responses to an agency-
   conducted cost-benefit analysis. The rule under review here involves the EPA's
   ban of most uses of asbestos in the United States, under the authority of the
   Toxic Substances Control Act. Note that the cost-benefit analysis conducted by
   EPA in developing its ban on asbestos was more rough-hewn than the more
   formal cost-benefit analysis we have so far been discussing; EPA did not, for
   example, attempt to set a dollar value for the human lives saved by its regulation.

■ **Corrosion Proof Fittings v. EPA**
  947 F.2d 1201 (5th Cir. 1991)

Smith, J.:...First, we note that there was some dispute in the record regarding
the appropriateness of discounting the perceived benefits of the EPA's rule. In
choosing between the calculated costs and benefits, the EPA presented variations in
which it discounted only the costs, and counter-variations in which it discounted
both the costs and the benefits, measured in both monetary and human injury
terms. As between these two variations, we choose to evaluate the EPA's work
using its discounted benefits calculations.

  Although various commentators dispute whether it ever is appropriate to discount benefits when they are measured in human lives, we note that it would skew
the results to discount only costs without according similar treatment to the benefits
side of the equation. Adopting the position of the commentators who advocate not
discounting benefits would force the EPA similarly not to calculate costs in present
discounted real terms, making comparisons difficult. Furthermore, in evaluating
situations in which different options incur costs at varying time intervals, the EPA

would not be able to take into account that soon-to-be-incurred costs are more harmful than postponable costs. Because the EPA must discount costs to perform its evaluations properly, the EPA also should discount benefits to preserve an apples-to-apples comparison, even if this entails discounting benefits of a non-monetary nature. See *What Price Posterity?*, The Economist, March 23, 1991, at 73 (explaining use of discount rates for non-monetary goods).

When the EPA does discount costs or benefits, however, it cannot choose an unreasonable time upon which to base its discount calculation. Instead of using the time of injury as the appropriate time from which to discount, as one might expect, the EPA instead used the time of exposure.

The difficulties inherent in the EPA's approach can be illustrated by an example. Suppose two workers will be exposed to asbestos in 1995, with worker X subjected to a tiny amount of asbestos that will have no adverse health effects, and worker Y exposed to massive amounts of asbestos that quickly will lead to an asbestos-related disease. Under the EPA's approach, which takes into account only the time of exposure rather than the time at which any injury manifests itself, both examples would be treated the same. The EPA's approach implicitly assumes that the day on which the risk of injury occurs is the same day the injury actually occurs. Such an approach might be proper when the exposure and injury are one and the same, such as when a person is exposed to an immediately fatal poison, but is inappropriate for discounting toxins in which exposure often is followed by a substantial lag time before manifestation of injuries.[19]

Of more concern to us is the failure of the EPA to compute the costs and benefits of its proposed rule past the year 2000, and its double-counting of the costs of asbestos use. In performing its calculus, the EPA only included the number of lives saved over the next thirteen years, and counted any additional lives saved as simply "unquantified benefits." The EPA and intervenors now seek to use these unquantified lives saved to justify calculations as to which the benefits seem far outweighed by the astronomical costs. For example, the EPA plans to save about three lives with its ban of asbestos pipe, at a cost of $128–227 million (i.e., approximately $43–76 million per life saved). Although the EPA admits that the price tag is high, it claims that the lives saved past the year 2000 justify the price.

Such calculations not only lessen the value of the EPA's cost analysis, but also make any meaningful judicial review impossible. While TSCA contemplates a useful place for unquantified benefits beyond the EPA's calculation, unquantified benefits never were intended as a trump card allowing the EPA to justify any cost calculus, no matter how high.

The concept of unquantified benefits, rather, is intended to allow the EPA to provide a rightful place for any remaining benefits that are impossible to quantify after the EPA's best attempt, but which still are of some concern. But the allowance for unquantified costs is not intended to allow the EPA to perform its calculations over an arbitrarily short period so as to preserve a large unquantified portion.

Unquantified benefits can, at times, permissibly tip the balance in close cases. They cannot, however, be used to effect a wholesale shift on the balance beam.

---

[19] We also note that the EPA chose to use a real discount rate of 3%. Because historically the real rate of interest has tended to vary between 2% and 4%, this figure was not inaccurate.

Such a use makes a mockery of the requirements of TSCA that the EPA weigh the costs of its actions before it chooses the least burdensome alternative.[20]

We do not today determine what an appropriate period for the EPA's calculations would be, as this is a matter better left for agency discretion. We do note, however, that the choice of a thirteen-year period is so short as to make the unquantified period so unreasonably large that any EPA reliance upon it must be displaced.

Under the EPA's calculations, a twenty-year-old worker entering employment today still would be at risk from workplace dangers for more than thirty years after the EPA's analysis period had ended. The true benefits of regulating asbestos under such calculations remain unknown. The EPA cannot choose to leave these benefits high and then use the high unknown benefits as a major factor justifying EPA action. . . .

The final requirement the EPA must satisfy before engaging in any TSCA rulemaking is that it only take steps designed to prevent "unreasonable" risks. In evaluating what is "unreasonable," the EPA is required to consider the costs of any proposed actions and to "carry out this chapter in a reasonable and prudent manner [after considering] the environmental, economic, and social impact of any action." 15 U.S.C. §2601(c).

As the District of Columbia Circuit stated when evaluating similar language governing the Federal Hazardous Substances Act, "[t]he requirement that the risk be 'unreasonable' necessarily involves a balancing test like that familiar in tort law: The regulation may issue if the severity of the injury that may result from the product, factored by the likelihood of the injury, offsets the harm the regulation itself imposes upon manufacturers and consumers." *Forester v. CPSC*, 559 F.2d 774, 789 (D.C. Cir. 1977). We have quoted this language approvingly when evaluating other statutes using similar language.

That the EPA must balance the costs of its regulations against their benefits further is reinforced by the requirement that it seek the least burdensome regulation. While Congress did not dictate that the EPA engage in an exhaustive, full-scale cost-benefit analysis, it did require the EPA to consider both sides of the regulatory equation, and it rejected the notion that the EPA should pursue the reduction of workplace risk at any cost. See *American Textile Mfrs. Inst.*, 452 U.S. at 510 n. 30 ("unreasonable risk" statutes require "a generalized balancing of costs and benefits"

---

[20] We thus reject the arguments made by the Natural Resources Defense Council, Inc., and the Environmental Defense Fund, Inc., that the EPA's decision can be justified because the EPA "relied on many serious risks that were understated or not quantified in the final rule," presented figures in which the "benefits are calculated only for a limited time period," and undercounted the risks to the general population from low-level asbestos exposure. In addition, the intervenors argue that the EPA rejected using upper estimates, and that this court now should use the rejected limits as evidence to support the EPA. They thus would have us reject the upper limit concerns when they are not needed, but use them if necessary.

We agree that these all are valid concerns that the EPA legitimately should take into account when considering regulatory action. What we disagree with, however, is the manner in which the EPA incorporated these concerns. By not using such concerns in its quantitative analysis, even where doing so was not difficult, and reserving them as additional factors to buttress the ban, the EPA improperly transformed permissible considerations into determinative factors.

(citing *Aqua Slide*, 569 F.2d at 839)). Thus, "Congress also plainly intended the EPA to consider the economic impact of any actions taken by it under . . . TSCA." *Chemical Mfrs. Ass'n*, 899 F.2d at 348.

Even taking all of the EPA's figures as true, and evaluating them in the light most favorable to the agency's decision (non-discounted benefits, discounted costs, analogous exposure estimates included), the agency's analysis results in figures as high as $74 million per life saved. For example, the EPA states that its ban of asbestos pipe will save three lives over the next thirteen years, at a cost of $128–227 million ($43–76 million per life saved), depending upon the price of substitutes; that its ban of asbestos shingles will cost $23–34 million to save 0.32 statistical lives ($72–106 million per life saved); that its ban of asbestos coatings will cost $46–181 million to save 3.33 lives ($14–54 million per life saved); and that its ban of asbestos paper products will save 0.60 lives at a cost of $4–5 million ($7–8 million per life saved). See 54 Fed. Reg. at 29,484–85. Were the analogous exposure estimates not included, the cancer risks from substitutes such as ductile iron pipe factored in, and the benefits of the ban appropriately discounted from the time of the manifestation of an injury rather than the time of exposure, the costs would shift even more sharply against the EPA's position.

While we do not sit as a regulatory agency that must make the difficult decision as to what an appropriate expenditure is to prevent someone from incurring the risk of an asbestos-related death, we do note that the EPA, in its zeal to ban any and all asbestos products, basically ignored the cost side of the TSCA equation. The EPA would have this court believe that Congress, when it enacted its requirement that the EPA consider the economic impacts of its regulations, thought that spending $200–300 million to save approximately seven lives (approximately $30–40 million per life) over thirteen years is reasonable. . . .

The EPA's willingness to argue that spending $23.7 million to save less than one-third of a life reveals that its economic review of its regulations, as required by TSCA, was meaningless. As the petitioners' brief and our review of EPA caselaw reveals, such high costs are rarely, if ever, used to support a safety regulation. If we were to allow such cavalier treatment of the EPA's duty to consider the economic effects of its decisions, we would have to excise entire sections and phrases from the language of TSCA. Because we are judges, not surgeons, we decline to do so.[23]

COMMENTS AND QUESTIONS

1. How did the court determine how much was appropriate to spend to save a human life? Would $10 million per life have been too much to spend? $1 million? What standard is the court using to evaluate EPA's rule?

---

[23] As the petitioners point out, the EPA regularly rejects, as unjustified, regulations that would save more lives at less cost. For example, over the next 13 years, we can expect more than a dozen deaths from ingested toothpicks—a death toll more than twice what the EPA predicts will flow from the quarter-billion-dollar bans of asbestos pipe, shingles, and roof coatings. See L. Budnick, Toothpick-Related Injuries in the United States, 1979 through 1982, 252 J. Am. Med. Ass'n, Aug. 10, 1984, at 796 (study showing that toothpick-related deaths average approximately one per year).

2. The court requires EPA to treat the avoidance of future cancers like an economic benefit that must be discounted to present value. What would Ackerman and Heinzerling have to say about this approach?

3. EPA discussed substantial unquantified benefits in support of its rule, including benefits extending beyond its (thirteen-year) analytical horizon and the avoidance of asbestosis and other harmful effects of asbestos. The court says unquantified benefits can play a role in close cases but cannot be used to "effect a wholesale shift on the balance beam." Does the court's position make sense? If important benefits are unquantified, how can we tell whether it is a close case or not? But if there was no constraint on the ability of unquantified benefits to trump quantified costs, would there be any meaningful limits on the agency's discretion?

Information Provision

10

We've already seen how disclosure (or nondisclosure) of information about risks to human health and life affects the regulation of risk. The economic theory of compensating wage differentials for risky jobs, which we explored in chapter 2, depends on workers knowing what the risks of their jobs are. If workers—or others exposed to risks—are unaware of the risks they face, it is much harder to argue that contractual arrangements should dictate whether the risk should be reduced. In such situations, the government might be justified in requiring disclosure of risks so that contracting parties can decide what actions, if any, to take, based on the information. Information also played a central role in our discussion of institutional limits in chapter 5. There, we saw that gaps in information might lead to a failure to name, blame, or claim—in other words, to identify and to act on one's legal rights.

So far, however, we have not discussed in detail the incentives (and disincentives) that might encourage (or discourage) private parties to disclose risk-related information. Nor have we explored the collective mechanisms short of government action, such as bargaining by labor unions, that might promote information disclosure. We take up these matters in the first two sections of this chapter, after which we consider information provision pursuant to government regulation. Then, we consider the efficacy of information provision as a risk management strategy in light of research relating to how humans process risk-related information. The chapter concludes with an examination of possible First Amendment limitations on information-provision requirements, returning briefly to some themes developed in chapter 1.

More generally, in this chapter and the next, we will be considering the advantages and disadvantages of several different regulatory instruments for addressing risk. Regulatory instruments, including information provision and—as discussed in chapter 11—health-based standards, technology-based standards, and trading regimes, comprise the modern regulator's toolkit, potentially applicable to a wide range of social problems. We begin with disclosure requirements, because most students of regulation appear to agree—in theory, at least—that good information is essential even if one generally wants to rely on private market arrangements to allocate risk.

A General Considerations

It is so often observed that good information is a precondition of competitive markets that one can easily forget that information is itself a marketable commodity. The readings in this section explore the implications of this fact for private incentives to produce information.

■ *Regulation and Its Reform*
STEPHEN BREYER
pp. 26–28 (Harvard University Press, 1982). Reprinted with permission of Harvard University Press

For a competitive market to function well, buyers must have sufficient information to evaluate competing products. They must identify the range of buying alternatives and understand the characteristics of the buying choices they confront. At the same time, information is a commodity that society must spend resources to produce. The buyer, looking for alternative suppliers, spends time, effort, and money in his search. The seller spends money on research, labeling, and advertising to make his identity and his product's qualities known. In well-functioning markets, one would expect to find as much information available as consumers are willing to pay for in order to lower the cost or to improve the quality of their choices. . . .

Markets for information may on occasion not function well for several reasons. First, the incentives to produce and to disseminate information may be skewed. . . . [S]ome information (particularly that requiring detailed research) is expensive to produce initially but very cheap to make available once produced. Since it can be repeated by word of mouth, televised, or printed and reprinted at low cost, it may easily benefit many recipients who never pay its original producer. Thus, those in the best position to produce the information may not do so, or they may hesitate to disseminate it, for fear that the benefits will go not to themselves but only to others.

The importance of this problem varies considerably depending upon the type of information and its use. A firm that manufactures breakfast foods, for example, would have every incentive to produce information showing that its cereal was more nutritious than that of its competitors and to disseminate that information widely. Moreover, the production, use, and dissemination of much information is protected by copyright and patent laws. Further, the inadequate incentive to produce information typically leads to a demand not for regulation but for governmental support of production and dissemination.

Nonetheless, occasionally the problem may lead to a demand for regulation. Drug manufacturers, for example, are required to print the generic (general scientific) name of their product, as well as the brand name, on the label. Thus, the buyer sees that a host of competitors in fact offer to sell the same product. This labeling requirement can be seen as lowering the cost to buyers of searching for competing sellers, by quickly making them aware of the competitors' existence. And it does so by requiring those with the information most readily at hand to make it available.

Second, one of the parties to a transaction may seek deliberately to mislead the other, by conveying false information or by omitting key facts. A seller of securities may lie about the assets of the company; a seller of a used car may turn back the mileage indicator. Of course, false statements or active misrepresentations may be grounds for rescinding a contract or suing for damages. Yet the cost of court action is often high enough to weaken it or give it minimal effect as a deterrent. Nor can one necessarily rely upon fear of declining reputation to act as a deterrent. The importance of reputation in securing sales depends upon the particular product, the particular seller, and a host of other circumstances. The rationale for governmental action to prevent false or misleading information rests upon the assumption that court remedies and competitive pressures are not adequate to provide the consumer with the true information he would willingly pay for. Thus, the Securities and Exchange Commission (SEC) regulates the issuances of securities, while the buyer of used cars is typically left to his basic judicial remedies.

Third, even after locating potentially competing sellers, the buyer may not be able to evaluate the characteristics of the products or services they offer. The layman cannot readily evaluate the competence of a doctor or lawyer. Nor can he, unaided, evaluate the potential effectiveness or dangers of a drug. And he is unlikely at the time of purchase to know if a car is a lemon. Formal or informal understandings among those on the supply side—whether doctors, lawyers, or drug producers—may make difficult or impossible the creation of objectively applied labels that aid evaluation. Governmental intervention may be desired to prescribe the type of information that must be provided, as well as to help buyers evaluate the information that is being supplied. . . .

Criticisms of the rationale for regulating the provision of information usually focus on whether the rationale applies to the particular case at issue. Critics may claim, for example, that in a particular case the market is functioning competitively, consumers are sufficiently capable of evaluating a product's qualities, or there is little deliberate deception. They may argue that a particular agency's efforts to provide information are too expensive, that the information is unnecessary, that disclosure itself may mislead consumers, or that it may interfere with the competitive workings of the marketplace.

■ *Progressive Law and Economics and the New Administrative Law*
SUSAN ROSE-ACKERMAN
98 Yale L.J. 341 (1988). Reprinted with permission
of Yale Law Journal

The analysis of occupational health and safety begins with three familiar points. First, most people voluntarily take many risks in their daily lives because of the accompanying benefits. No one lives as if his or her main goal were maximizing the number of breaths taken. Second, people tend to be poorly informed about actual levels of risk. Many studies have documented these misperceptions and the general tendency to overestimate the probability of events that are beyond one's control while underestimating other risky possibilities. Third, it is often difficult to present risk assessments in ways that can be easily used by ordinary people in their daily lives.

These observations about individual behavior form a familiar starting point for an analysis of health and safety risks in the workplace. The simple economic story told by Chicagoans posits a labor market with many competing employers. If workers are informed about risks, they will demand higher wages for high risk jobs. They will also sort themselves over the available jobs depending upon their preferences toward risk.

Even in this simple competitive world, one complication must be introduced immediately. Knowing that they must compensate workers to take risks, employers would like to keep job hazards secret. Therefore, the market will then only work efficiently if potential new employees can observe the riskiness of jobs. One way such information might be provided is through a learning process. The first round of employees are uninformed, but after they are injured, other members of the labor force observe their injuries and illnesses and demand that the company pay a wage premium or reduce workplace hazards.

There are many reasons why this learning process will work poorly in the real world. First, many hazards take a long time to produce injuries. Second, even if they happen quickly, participants in a large labor market will not observe many of the injured. Third, the level of hazard depends on workers as well as workplaces. Some workers are more susceptible to hazards because of their genetic characteristics or their life style—for example, whether they smoke. Therefore, it may be difficult for job applicants correctly to infer their own risk by observing the harm suffered by others. Fourth, workplace conditions change with technology—so the past may be a poor guide to the future. For all these reasons, regulations that require employers to inform employees of hazards are easy to justify. The information must, however, be provided in a form that employees can understand and use to compare job market options.

But the mere provision of information may not be sufficient for two different reasons. The first turns on the limited information-processing capacities of people, especially regarding probabilistic information. Rather than engage in a massive educational campaign, it may be more efficient to regulate workplace health and safety directly through administrative orders or incentive schemes. This justification will be especially strong when the employer's action affects all employees, the plant employs a large number of people, and most people, if informed, would assert that the benefits of added safety outweigh the costs.

A second reason why an information strategy may be inadequate concerns the production function for health and safety. Many actions employers take are "local public goods." If dust collectors are installed, they will benefit all employees on a shop floor, and if a harmless chemical is substituted for a toxic, everyone who comes in contact with the material will benefit. However, if the employees are not organized into a union, individual workers may be unwilling to modify their wage demands enough to make the health and safety investment worthwhile. If employers do not know the value workers place on safety, they may be unwilling to experiment with costly changes that may not pay off in lower wage increases or improved productivity. Established employers are especially unlikely to act if money wages are sticky downward and thus cannot be reduced in the face of an acknowledged improvement in working conditions. . . .

- ■ *OSHA after a Decade: A Time for Reason*
  ALBERT NICHOLS AND RICHARD ZECKHAUSER
  From *Case Studies in Regulation: Revolution and Reform*,
  Leonard W. Weiss and Michael W. Klass eds., pp. 206, 208–8 (Little, Brown,
  1981). Reprinted with permission of Aspen Law & Business

Levels of occupational safety and health are determined by the decisions of both
workers and employers. . . . The perfectly competitive model assumes that both
workers and management know the magnitude of risks and the costs of reducing
those risks. This information must be available, transmitted to the affected parties,
and understood.

Problems arise at each of these three stages. Not surprisingly, the data relating
workplace conditions to health and safety outcomes are poor. Although such information would be valuable across a wide range of workplaces, no individual or firm
has sufficient incentive to produce the optimum amount. After all, he would have
to bear the full cost while reaping only a small fraction of the benefits. Here is a
clear potential role for government—to collect and disseminate information on the
causes of occupational injuries and illnesses and on mechanisms for reducing them.

To be useful, information must also be disseminated in a form that is understandable to workers and firms. Experimental and empirical evidence suggests that
individuals have a great deal of difficulty processing information about small
probabilities, which characterize most occupational safety and health problems.
Firms are unlikely to provide accurate information on risk levels to their workers, if
indeed they have it themselves. Information problems are likely to be particularly
severe with regard to health (as distinct from safety) threats. Even with large-scale,
long-term studies using relatively sophisticated statistical techniques, epidemiolo-
gists find it difficult to identify occupational carcinogens unless the increased risk is
substantial. The chance[] that an individual worker will notice that working with a
particular chemical even doubles his long-term risk of lung cancer is almost nil. By
contrast, safety problems are likely to result in much more immediate effects that
workers or their representatives can detect.

It seems quite possible that workers are reasonably well informed about the
relative riskiness of different occupations and industries but cannot tell, for example, whether one metal-stamping plant is safer than another. If so, wage premiums will still be observed between industries but not between firms within an
industry. The impact of such premiums on company behavior will be limited, since,
continuing the example above, improvements in health or safety at one metal-
stamping plant will not lower wage premiums at that plant, except indirectly
through a minor lowering of the overall industry risk level. The critical element for
effective market behavior is that each firm receive full recognition, and hence full
credit, for improvements in its safety performance. . . .

- ■ *Risk by Choice: Regulating Health and Safety in the Workplace*
  W. KIP VISCUSI
  pp. 59–78 (Harvard University Press, 1983). Reprinted with permission
  of Harvard University Press

The principal limitation of the compensating differential process is that appropriate
risk premiums and efficient matchups of jobs and workers may not result if

workers are not fully aware of the risks they face. Some job risks are widely known and should generate risk premiums. In the usual situation, however, the exact probabilities of being killed or injured are not known by anyone. Owing to the retarded state of occupational medicine, even the underlying medical ramifications of different exposures to hazards of the workplace such as radiation, noise, high temperatures, and chemical vapors are not well understood. This uncertainty is often compounded by lack of knowledge about characteristics of the work situation—for example, the concentration of asbestos fibers in the air. Adverse health effects that occur very infrequently and are not apparent for decades create especially severe difficulties, since it is often not possible to ascertain the cause of the ailment. . . .

. . . Workers are aware of many job risks, and for these the risk premium mechanism is relatively effective in promoting efficient levels of safety. Workers who are not fully cognizant of the risks associated with a job often can learn more about these risks once they begin work on it. If this information is sufficiently unfavorable, given the wage they are paid, they will quit. . . . The quitting response reduces the problems associated with workers having inadequate information about the job risks they face, but it may not eliminate the fundamental difficulties. . . .

The fundamental issue involved in any assessment of the classic model of compensating differentials for risk is whether or not workers are aware of the risks they face. Most workers have many sources of information for making some judgment about these risks. Before working on the job, they can use information about the firm's reputation, the nature of the job, or the experiences of friends who have worked there. Some risks, particularly newly discovered carcinogenic hazards or the black lung problems of coal miners, have been highly publicized and are familiar to the general public as well as to the workers themselves. Once he is on the job, the worker can observe the workplace conditions and the effects of the job on his well-being and that of his coworkers.

These diverse sources of information about job risks are reflected in workers' risk perceptions. Over half of all blue-collar workers surveyed believe that their jobs expose them to dangerous or unhealthy conditions. Although this result contradicts the widespread belief that workers are ignorant of the risks they face, it in no way implies that they accurately perceive the risks cited or that they are aware of all of the hazards posed by their jobs. . . . The hazards mentioned most often were those posed by inherently dangerous materials (chemicals, gases, smoke, and fumes), inherently hazardous equipment, inherently hazardous procedures, placement hazards, and dangerous exposures to dust and other materials. Detailed examination of these hazards reveals that the risks are broadly consistent with the particular job. Temperature and humidity extremes were cited by a truck driver for a canning company, inadequate shoring was listed by a construction worker, and slippery floors and footing was cited by a manufacturing worker in the plastic products industry. . . .

It is standard to characterize workers as being aware of safety hazards but ignorant of health risks. But such sweeping statements are not borne out by the responses of workers, since two-fifths of the hazards cited are health risks. Although many health risks, such as those posed by the bewildering array of toxic substances, are difficult to assess precisely, nevertheless workers appear to be aware of many important health-related concerns.

Ideally, one might like to compare workers' job risk perceptions with an objective index of the hazard actually faced to ascertain the extent to which these judgments are accurate. Such a comparison is well beyond the capacity of existing data and in some cases beyond our limited understanding of the determinants of the "true" risk levels of a job. However, one can compare the risk perceptions of workers in various industries of different overall risk levels. The principal drawback of this procedure is that the overall industry record may not accurately characterize the risk of each job within the industry. Despite this limitation, the evidence is quite striking. . . . [T]he fraction of workers in each risk group who consider their job hazardous increases fairly steadily with the industry injury rate. Indeed, all workers in the most hazardous industry group consider their jobs hazardous.

Although there is no way of ascertaining whether the workers' beliefs coincide with actual risk levels, there does appear to be widespread worker perception of both health and safety risks. Moreover, these perceptions appear to be reasonably well founded, since they closely parallel objective job risk measures. . . .

These risk perception data do not indicate when a worker begins to perceive his job as hazardous. In the idealized compensating differential model, workers' risk perceptions are always accurate—and consequently do not change after beginning work on the job. In the usual situation, work experience enables the worker to reassess the risk he faces and to quit if he finds the risk unattractive. This potential for learning gives rise to a job hazard-quit relationship, which is the focus of this section.

In the typical learning process, the worker uses different sources of information to continually update his assessment of the job risk. Many workplace characteristics that generate risks or are correlated with job hazards can be readily observed—safety training procedures, noise level, the presence of noxious fumes, and the degree of care taken by coworkers. Injuries to himself and others also may be instructive in forming a worker's risk assessments.

The impact of this learning on worker decisions hinges on being able to acquire some information about the risk and to use this information when facing similar risks in the future. Learning of this type is widespread. The highly publicized problems at the Three Mile Island nuclear reactor, for example, clearly led to a major change in the public's perception of nuclear safety. If we exclude the role of anxiety about risks, this change in perceptions is only relevant to our welfare insofar as future decisions will be affected by it. Since individual decisions to live near nuclear plants, as well as future nuclear safety policies, undoubtedly will be altered by the shift in risk perceptions induced by this accident, learning about nuclear risks has an economic value. The high incidence of lung cancer among shipyard workers with previous exposure to asbestos has had a similarly dramatic effect on our risk perceptions, but this information primarily benefits new workers rather than those who have suffered irreversible damage from exposure over the past few decades.

For many chronic diseases, it may be difficult for a worker to make any reliable causal inferences that would improve future job decisions. One cannot be confident of the efficiency of this learning process until one first ascertains whether learning will occur and, if it does, whether it will enable those now incurring the hazards to make sounder job decisions. It is possible, however, to make some overall judgments, using the information we have on worker perceptions. Statistical analyses of the determinants of risk perceptions cannot be conclusive, but they are consistent with the relationships that would hold if workers formed their risk assessments before working on the job and then revised these assessments based on subsequent information. . . .

[W]orkers in more hazardous industries are more likely to view their jobs as hazardous, as one would expect if the general reputation of the industry influenced their initial risk perceptions. Characteristics of the job, such as the physical effort required, the regularity of work, and the pleasantness of the physical conditions, are also instrumental in affecting workers' assessment of risks.

The most powerful determinant of a worker's risk perception is his own injury experience. Seventy-one percent of all workers who have experienced a job-related injury or illness view their job as hazardous. . . . Taking into account other determinants of risk perceptions, including the overall riskiness of the industry, a worker's being injured increases the probability that he will view his job as hazardous by 0.2.

It is particularly striking that almost one-third of all workers who had experienced injuries did not view their jobs as hazardous. This aberrational result appears to be due mainly to illnesses and injuries that occurred on the job but were not an intrinsic part of it. The injuries least likely to be associated with risk perceptions were: muscle or joint inflammation, poisoning, dermatitis, and other job-aggravated ailments. Since these injuries are principally due to the worker's own limitations (job-aggravated ailments) or unusual acts of carelessness (poisoning), it is not surprising that many injured workers do not view their jobs as the source of the hazard.

Overall, workers' risk perceptions accord with what one would expect if learning about risks occurred on the job. A more conclusive test for this learning effect would be possible if we had evidence on the evolution of workers' risk perceptions and the information that influenced these beliefs. The data we do have enable us to conclude only that those who work in unpleasant environments or who have been injured are more likely to view their jobs as risky.

The empirical implications of this learning process are more clear-cut. I will view workers as being engaged in the following adaptive process. A worker's decision to accept a potentially hazardous job is based on his assessment of the risk, the wage rate paid, and his expectations regarding the implications of the job for his future well-being. Risk premiums are still relevant since increases in the assessed probabilities of injury boost the wage that the worker will require to take the job. If the worker's on-the-job experience generates sufficiently adverse risk information, given this wage rate, he will quit.

We would observe no job hazard-quit relationship if workers fully understood the risks before starting the job. Similarly, if workers never learned about the risks they face, they would remain with the position until they retired, became disabled, or switched jobs because of other economic factors. In either case there would be no relationship between hazardous and quitting.

This adaptive behavior is economically important partly because of the somewhat surprising aspects of the relationship, most notably workers' predilection for jobs posing risks that are not well understood. Before exploring these properties, it is useful to obtain some perspective on the empirical significance of this phenomenon. If few workers do quit their jobs after learning about the risk, the more subtle aspects of the analysis might best be regarded as theoretical curiosities.

Using the blue-collar worker data discussed earlier, I found that workers' risk perceptions had a powerful influence on their intentions to quit. The chance that the worker claimed that he was very likely to look for a new job with another employer in the next year was increased from 0.10 to 0.21—more than double—if the worker viewed his job as hazardous in some respect. Hazard perceptions had an identical effect on more moderate quit intentions (whether it was somewhat likely that the worker would search for an alternative job). Industry-injury rates have a similar impact on job satisfaction and job search activity in other sets of survey data.

The job risk-quit phenomenon takes on an additional dimension when viewed over a longer term. The average total length of employment at a hazardous firm tends to be less if workers quit more often, so more hazardous enterprises tend to have less experienced workforces. Inexperienced workers will tend to have more injuries because there will be greater concentrations of these employees in high-risk situations. Even if workers are not more accident-prone when they start the job, we would observe a strong relationship between job risks and the number of years of workers' experience at the firm.

This pattern is reinforced by firms' assignments of workers to different jobs. Since firms have a substantial investment in the training of experienced workers, they attempt to hold down these costs by assigning inexperienced workers to hazardous positions, as in the case of the B. F. Goodrich Company, where the polyvinyl chloride exposures were greatest for those in entry-level positions.

The oft-cited statistics on the high accident rates of inexperienced workers consequently overstate the extent to which workers are responsible for the accidents. Less experienced workers tend to be more accident-prone because the employer assigns them to high-risk jobs and because the high rate of quitting from these positions further reduces the average experience of the group. The conventional attribution of accidents to irresponsible behavior of inexperienced workers may be in large part misplaced.

The most fundamental implication of the job hazard-quit process pertains to the nature of workers' job choices. In particular, when choosing among jobs posing comparable initial risks, should the worker select the job posing a precisely known risk or a job posing a risk about which little is known? He will tend to prefer the more uncertain job since it affords the opportunity for on-the-job learning about the risk. If the worker finds out that the job is very risky he can quit, and if he learns that it is safe he can remain on the job. . . .

In most firms worker turnover is costly because of the hiring and training costs involved whenever a worker is replaced. The firm could reduce these costs by decreasing its training investment through job assignment and training practices. Alternatively, it could reduce costs by eliminating the job risk-quit relationship, which the firm can do in a variety of ways. First, it can attempt to attract only these employees who will not quit. Second, it can adopt a technology whose level of risk is well known. Finally, it can provide complete job risk information to workers to eliminate any subsequent learning. I will consider whether it is in the employer's interest to take these actions and, if so, whether learning-induced quits will be eliminated.

If workers knew before accepting the job that they would quit because of the risks, the employer could eliminate these turnover costs quite readily without having to identify the quit-prone workers. In particular, it could pay employees a very low salary during their initial years with the firm and guarantee a very high wage if they remain for a substantial period. Workers who expect to quit will not find this wage structure attractive since they do not expect to remain with the firm long enough to reap the high wage. Tilting the wage structure in this fashion will lead the workers themselves to choose whether they will work at the firm, thus screening out the quit-prone employees.

In the case of learning-induced quits, this wage policy cannot be fully effective since the workers do not know whether they will quit until after some period of work on the job. Furthermore, if turnover costs are small, it will be in the employer's financial interest to attract imperfectly informed workers to the firm. Workers' preference for jobs with less well-known risks enables firms to offer a lower wage than they would otherwise. Since the wage bill increases as workers' probabilistic beliefs become more precise, employers have a financial interest in hiring workers who are not cognizant of the risks they will face.

Very high turnover costs might make it desirable for a firm to prevent quitting by raising the wage rate. However, the level of turnover costs is not predetermined but is typically subject to the discretion of the firm. If the job risks in a firm generate quit behavior, the firm will reduce its hiring and training expenditures, since worker turnover diminishes the value of this investment. Actual training patterns reflect this influence, as workers in high-risk industries are less likely to receive any formal job training. Only in a highly unusual situation would we expect to see a firm sacrifice the wage reductions that are possible if it does not attempt to eliminate learning-induced quits.

Similarly, there is little financial incentive for a firm to reduce hazard-related quits by adopting a technology whose risks are well known. From the standpoint of the wages it must pay, the firm will find the uncertain technology preferable. Under the relatively neutral assumption that workers' initial risk judgments are unbiased, the firm will adopt a technology that is not well understood and that poses a higher risk than would be optimal if workers fully understood the risk....

Since it is typically not in the firm's self-interest to provide job risk information to resolve worker uncertainties, job choices will be made on the basis of imperfect information. Incomplete knowledge of the risks does not simply erode the efficacy of the compensating differential process. In many instances, workers have the opportunity to learn about these risks, and if they choose not to incur them, they will quit. The resulting job hazard-quit relationship is borne out quite strongly in available data. Although the relative importance of risk premiums and learning-induced quits cannot be meaningfully compared, each of these mechanisms should be viewed as major parts of an interrelated process by which workers attempt to match themselves to appropriate jobs. These market processes do not, however, ensure that outcomes will be fully efficient. With imperfect information, workers facing risks on a continuing basis will display a systematic preference for risks that are not precisely known.

Even if workers do not make biased risk judgments initially, they will systematically prefer jobs whose risks are not fully understood. While on-the-job learning about risks and subsequent quit behavior serves as a beneficial market response, the quit mechanism does not guarantee efficient outcomes. In the extreme case in which a worker learns that he has contracted a fatal disease, for example, his welfare has been affected irreversibly, so quitting will do him no good. Under a broad set of circumstances, the imprecision in workers' job risk beliefs will lead to too high a level of risk, a bias toward technologies that are not fully understood, and too little insurance coverage for workers in hazardous jobs. . . .

COMMENTS AND QUESTIONS

1. The preceding readings give us reasons to doubt that private markets will produce the "right" level of information about risk. But how do we know what the right level is?

2. Are you persuaded by Viscusi's explanation of the "aberrational" result—the finding that some injured workers do not perceive their jobs as risky?

3. The following is a standard risk-disclosure on asbestos packages used in the 1950s. What, if anything, is wrong with it, and what might be done to improve it? (Thinking about this question anticipates some of the issues about cognitive processes you will consider later in this chapter.)

> Caution, this product contains asbestos fibre.
> Inhalation of asbestos in excessive quantities over long periods of time may be harmful.
> If dust is created when this product is inhaled, avoid breathing the dust.
> If adequate ventilation control is not possible, wear respirators approved by the U.S. Bureau of Mines for pneumoconiosis-producing dust.

B Generating Information Collectively

The preceding readings describe why employers might not voluntarily provide full job-risk information and why employees might not acquire it through on-the-job experience. One way to overcome the "public goods" problem is to force information disclosure through collective action, such as bargaining by labor unions. As the next reading describes, labor unions sometimes seek to bargain over information about on-the-job risk.

- *Markets and Mortality: Economics, Dangerous Work, and the Value of Human Life*
  PETER DORMAN
  pp. 131–135 (Cambridge University Press, 1996). Reprinted with permission of Cambridge University Press

[U]nions often assign a high priority to safety issues. Most union contracts contain language pertaining to health and safety concerns . . . and the trend has been for a greater percentage of strikes to involve safety disputes. [Researchers] present survey evidence indicating that, while few union officials regard health and safety issues as more important than competing concerns, a majority give them overall parity. Moreover, there is at least some evidence that, when unions fail to give sufficient attention to health and safety, rank-and-file pressure for change increases. . . . [T]he movement which ultimately swept away the corrupt leadership of the United Mine Workers was spearheaded by health and safety activists, and

Noble (1986) adds the Teamsters (whose reformers have since taken power) to that list as well. Thus a fair generalization may be that union officials are torn between their personal and political interest in advancing safety issues on the one hand, and the structural limits to this type of union activity on the other.

If unions are committed to addressing the safety concerns of their members, there are three general ways they can go about this. First, they can address working conditions directly by including contract language which mandates specific policies and standards to be followed by management. Second, they can follow the indirect path of setting up special committees or other structures through which workers can influence company policy on the shop floor. Finally, they can accept dangerous conditions in return for hazard pay—that is, explicitly bargain over compensating differentials. In each case the use of collective bargaining to achieve these goals is supported by existing labor law; Gersuny (1981) cites an NLRB ruling that "safety provisions constitute an essential part of the employees' terms and conditions of employment, and, as such, are a mandatory subject of bargaining." Table 4.1 clearly shows that there has been an increasing tendency for unions to pursue safety in one manner or another.

Increasingly, contracts are incorporating a "right-to-know" clause: the firm is obligated to inform workers of all relevant safety hazards, including the potential effects of chemicals used in the workplace. This trend has been furthered by state laws mandating employer disclosure and a federal regulation promulgated under OSHA requiring that workers be informed of the presence of substances known to cause cancer. How well these stipulations are adhered to in practice, of course, is another matter. Nonetheless, access to information, especially when combined with adequate technical expertise, can be a powerful weapon in the hands of a union that is genuinely committed to promoting health and safety....

The next level of protection is provided when unions move from the right to know to the right to say "no"—the right to refuse hazardous work. An ambiguous formulation of this right already appeared in US labor law as early as 1947; section 502 of the Taft-Hartley Act states: "Nothing in this Act shall be construed to require an individual employee to render labor or service without his consent... nor shall the quitting of labor by any employee or employees in good faith because of abnormally dangerous conditions for work at the place of employment... be deemed a strike under this Act." But subsequent court decisions have greatly restricted the

Table 4.1 Percentage of Contracts Containing Selected Health and Safety Clauses, 1954–1981

Year	Any Clause	Firm to Take Measures	Firm to Provide Safety Equipment	Health and Safety Committees
1954	60%	38%	27%	18%
1961	65	34	32	28
1966	62	35	28	29
1971	65	42	32	31
1976	82	50	36	39
1981	82	50	42	43

Source: OTA (1985, p. 315).

scope of this provision, and workers who refuse hazardous work outside the scope of specific contract provisions do so at their own risk. Union negotiators have attempted to provide protection for the right-to-refuse, and one study found 371 agreements covering nearly two million workers in which this right was stipulated under certain conditions. In an additional 42 agreements the union was authorized to refuse work on behalf of its members in the face of an excessive level of risk (BLS, 1976). In practice, however, the right to refuse is exercised only in extreme circumstances and therefore currently represents a targeted response to acute problems, rather than a general health and safety strategy....

Grievance mechanisms, as indicated earlier in this section, are not employed as frequently over health and safety issues as worker interest would appear to require. Possible explanations could include the unwillingness of unions to pursue grievances of this sort..., the time lag in grievance resolution compared to the highly transient nature of many workplace hazards, and the personal risk of being written up, transferred, or discharged borne by workers who initiate grievances, particularly without union support.

Finally, many unionized firms have instituted joint labor-management safety committees. An extensive study of committees of this type was undertaken by Kochan, Dyer, and Lipsky (1977), who found them to be most effective when addressing areas of common interest. Although there are many potential safety improvements that both labor and management would welcome, and there is therefore much to be accomplished by committees based on a cooperative model, there remain other issues in which conflicts of interest are irreconcilable. These cases... cannot be resolved administratively on the side of greater safety without overcoming management opposition. It is a central conclusion of Kochan et al. that using joint safety committees to address this second type of issue is not only ineffective, it also undermines the voluntary cooperation necessary to bring about improvement in the areas of common interest. In their view, joint safety committees are an alternative to collective bargaining, not an extension of it:

> the parties must be concerned about buffering the joint committee process from the polemical pressures that surround contract negotiations. The union must guard carefully against allowing the committee to be used as a political stepping-stone for aspirants to higher union office. It must also guard against using safety and health committees as another forum for extending the collective-bargaining process. Although only a few examples of this were found in the cases studied in the sample, such behavior is usually fatal to the committees because of management's fear that the safety committees could simply turn out to be a forum for union harassment, with no benefits accruing to management, and that some encroachment on management prerogatives might occur.

The conclusion would appear to be that labor-management safety committees have useful functions to perform, but determining the provision of costly health and safety conditions is not one of them.

These, then, are the mechanisms through which collective bargaining can sometimes influence working conditions directly: embedding detailed standards in the contract, the right to know about hazards, the right to refuse dangerous work, the opportunity to grieve poor working conditions, and the empaneling of health and safety committees. Although each has its limitations, together they can have an impact, provided the union has sufficient bargaining power—an increasingly unlikely circumstance. Of course, workers may eschew any direct attempt to alter conditions and negotiate hazard pay instead; what evidence indicates that they do this?

Two surveys of collective bargaining agreements come to similar conclusions: hazard pay is negotiated by unions but appears far less often than the other mechanisms described above. Each year the Bureau of National Affairs publishes their own study of collective bargaining; their 1992 report, based on a sample of 400 contracts, found these results: 88 percent of the contracts had some form of safety or health language, 60 percent called on firms to take general measures to bring about safe conditions, 50 percent established joint safety committees, 43 percent specified safety equipment to be furnished, but only 13 percent provided hazard pay for *any* workers in the bargaining unit (BNA, 1992). The findings of a second group, led by Mark Erenburg of the Industrial Relations Center at Cleveland State University, were similar: in a sample of 500 contracts, 63 percent had safety language, 24 percent established joint committees, 22 percent enabled workers to grieve unsafe conditions, 15 percent created a right to refuse unsafe work, and only 12 percent created hazard pay (Erenburg, 1989). In both studies, hazard pay was the least common form of collective bargaining over safety; moreover, given the relative frequency of different contract mechanisms, there are probably few if any workers for whom compensating pay differentials are the only recourse.

These results, which accord well with the popular view of the role of safety in labor relations, are in striking contrast to the views held by most economists. Recall, for instance, the discussion of union preferences . . . during the theoretical analysis of compensating wage differentials. The economists surveyed disagreed over which workers' preferences will be represented when unions negotiate over wages and working conditions—young or old, marginal or average—but they all proceeded on the assumption that unions make this tradeoff in some fashion. Yet, as we have already noted, collective bargaining is public and can be studied directly, so we can see whether unions really do this. Many volumes have been written on union strategies for health and safety, contract clauses have been tabulated, and major agreements have been analyzed for their strengths and weaknesses, and here is the verdict: compensating wage differentials play at most a minor role in union objectives; bargaining over safety takes the form of seeking a reduction in risk, not more money for assuming it. Where explicit compensation does exist, as in street-level versus upper-story building construction, it is seen as the exception rather than the rule. Of course, a stubborn believer in economic orthodoxy can always reply that wage compensation might be detected in a properly conducted wage regression using a unionized sample, but then we are back once more in the world of invisible rabbits, from which the observation of collective bargaining agreements was intended to set us free.

COMMENTS AND QUESTIONS

1. The proportion of workers in private sector jobs who are members of unions has been declining since the mid-1950s and is now not much more than ten percent. (What's called the "union density" of public sector jobs is higher.)

2. Dorman discusses the reasons unions bargain (or do not bargain) for various safety-related items. What reasons might Viscusi offer to explain bargaining behavior?

3. Another way to generate information collectively is through government disclosure requirements. The next reading describes some of the most prominent regulatory regimes governing information disclosure, along with their advantages and disadvantages.

- *Informing America: Risk, Disclosure, and the First Amendment*
  CASS R. SUNSTEIN
  20 Fla. St. U. L. Rev. 653 (1993). Originally published by Florida
  State University Law Review. © 1994 Florida State
  University Law Review

I. The Case for Informational Remedies

Many Americans are unaware of the risks they face in day-to-day life. Workers often do not know about toxic substances in the workplaces or about the risks that these substances cause. Consumers of ordinary foods are unable to evaluate the dangers posed by fats, calcium, sugar, and salt. People in small communities do not know that toxic waste dumping has occurred. If they know the facts, they do not know the risks. . . .

II. Empirical Evidence: What We've Done, What We Know . . .

A. *What We've Done*

The national government has started a series of steps in the direction of information disclosure. Mandatory messages about risks from cigarette smoking, first set out in 1965 and modified in 1969 and 1984, are, of course, the most familiar example. The FDA has long maintained a policy of requiring risk labels for pharmaceutical products. The EPA has done the same for pesticides and asbestos. Congress requires warnings on products with saccharin. There are numerous other illustrations. Indeed, the effort to provide information counts as one of the most striking, if still incipient, developments in modern regulatory law. Three recent initiatives are especially notable.

In 1983 the Occupational Safety and Health Administration issued a Hazard Communication Standard (HCS) that applied to the manufacturing sector. In 1986 the HCS was made generally applicable. Under the HCS, chemical producers and importers must evaluate the hazards of the chemicals they produce or import; develop technical hazard information for materials safety data sheets and for hazardous substances labels; and, most importantly, transmit this information to users of the relevant substances. All employers must adopt a hazard communication program—including individual training—and inform workers of the relevant risks.

In 1986 Congress enacted an ambitious new statute, the Emergency Planning and Community Right to Know Act (EPCRA). Under this statute, firms and individuals must report to state and local government the quantities of potentially hazardous chemicals that have been stored or released into the environment. Users of such chemicals must report to their local fire departments about the location, types, and quantities of stored chemicals. They must also give information about potential adverse health effects. A detailed report suggests that EPCRA has had important beneficial effects, spurring innovative, cost-effective programs from the EPA and from state and local government.[19] ...

B. What We Know

We now have some empirical information about disclosure of risks. In general, the information suggests that disclosure can be a helpful and cost-effective strategy.[21] Workers appear to respond to new information about risks by quitting or demanding higher salaries. Consumers often react well to the disclosure about danger levels. There is every reason to think that governmentally-mandated disclosure, if suitably designed, is an effective mechanism for promoting economic efficiency and other regulatory goals.

Let me add some specifics. The Superfund statute, EPCRA, requires a "toxic release inventory" requiring reports on toxic emissions. A 1991 government report shows that the statute has had substantial good effects.[23] The inventory played a large informational role in the 1990 Clean Air Act Amendments. It has also contributed to legislative efforts in many states, including Oregon and Massachusetts. It has greatly assisted the EPA in its pollution prevention strategy, a leading new weapon in risk regulation, and it has also contributed to the development of cross-environmental media approaches. Environmental groups and the media have made good use of the inventory, listing the highest polluting companies. Best of all, the inventory has led major companies to reduce pollution even without legislation. It appears that more than half of all reporting facilities have made changes as a result of the inventory requirement.

Evidence of this sort is highly suggestive, but it does not show whether consumers and citizens react rationally to new information. We know disclosure has had some political consequences. It is important also to know how such information is received by ordinary people. Here too, however, we are beginning to accumulate valuable data. ...

A ... study attempted to test workers' responses to labels of potentially hazardous chemicals.[32] There was evidence—suggestive by itself—that workers in dangerous occupations received risk premiums for the dangers they faced. Workers who perceived their jobs as quite dangerous received an annual risk premium of $700 to $800, while workers who thought their jobs were only somewhat risky received a premium of about $100 less. I say that this evidence is suggestive by itself

---

[19] See G.A.O., *Toxic Chemicals: EPA's Toxic Release Inventory Is Useful but Can Be Improved*, Rep. to Congress (June 1991).

[21] See W. Kip Viscusi and Wesley A. Magat, *Learning about Risk* (1987); W. Kip Viscusi et al., *Informational Regulation of Consumer Health Risks: An Empirical Evaluation of Hazard Warnings*, 17 Rand J. Econ. 351 (1986); W. Kip Viscusi and Charles J. O'Connor, *Adaptive Responses to Chemical Labeling: Are Workers Bayesian Decision Makers?* 74 Am. Econ. Rev. 942 (1984). The empirical work also shows the need for care in designing disclosure requirements.

[23] G.A.O., *Toxic Chemicals*, Rep. to Congress (1991).

[32] Viscusi and O'Connor, *Adaptive Responses to Chemical Labeling*, at 942.

because it shows that workers will demand a higher salary or other compensating benefits when they know that they face workplace dangers.

The study presented each worker with a hazard warning label for a chemical that was not a current part of his job. When presented with the labels, workers generally adjusted their perception of the risk assessment in their jobs. Thus the adjustment shows a rational learning process. Moreover, and crucially, the workers indicated they would require a higher salary, calibrated to the degree of risk that was disclosed. Many workers also indicated they would refuse to continue to work in the now-riskier job. The greater the information, the better the reaction.

There is also a valuable study of the effects of warning labels on diet soft drinks containing saccharin.[33] The data show that after the warning labels were required, there were significant adverse effects on sales. The initial effects were produced primarily by well-educated and high-income households. Soon thereafter there were similar effects on households with young children. Interestingly, there was no such effect on the soft drink purchase habits of the elderly.

Consumer behavior was also significantly modified by a Stanford study designed to promote heart disease education.[34] Three California communities were selected; two of them were saturated with information about lifestyle changes that would reduce heart disease. A "control town" was not affected. Knowledge increases were significant in the two saturated communities; there were no real changes in the control town. Intriguingly, there were large gains in knowledge in the less-advantaged Spanish-speaking community. Behavioral changes were also shown with respect to reported changes in diets, exercise, and smoking, and also with weight and plasma cholesterol levels. Plasma cholesterol levels changed significantly during the course of the campaign.

Less encouraging is the evidence from educational campaigns designed to increase seat belt use. It seems clear that if everyone used seat belts, motor vehicle deaths could be halved, and billions of dollars could be saved. But efforts to promote seat belt use have produced little results, at least in the United States. (Campaigns in Great Britain and Sweden produced increased usage rates of twenty percent to thirty-five percent.) In its most recent, more sophisticated efforts, the government's campaign showed a negligible 2.6% increase, ranging from 11.3% to 13.9%.

California's Proposition 65, requiring cancer warnings, appears to have been only a mixed success. One study shows that it has actually decreased information by making people think certain products are much more dangerous than they are in fact.[37] Similarly, one study shows that widely used chemical labels had minimal effects because the relevant information was not provided in an effective manner.[38]

---

[33] George W. Schucker et al., *The Impact of the Saccharin Warning Label on Sales of Diet Soft Drinks in Supermarkets*, 2 J. Pub. Pol'y & Mktg. 46 (1983).

[34] See Robert S. Adler and R. David Pittle, *Cajolery or Command: Are Education Campaigns an Adequate Substitute for Regulation*, 1 Yale J. on Reg. 159, 184 (1984).

[37] See W. Kip Viscusi, *Predicting the Effects of Food Cancer Risk Warnings on Consumers*, 43 Food Drug Cosm. L.J. 283 (1988).

[38] Viscusi et al., *Informational Regulation of Consumer Health Risks*, at 365.

On balance, the existing evidence gives reason for cautious optimism at the very least. Certainly much more research is necessary; here the obligatory call for further empirical work is especially important. But what we know is sufficient to suggest that it is fully appropriate to continue to work with information strategies and that such strategies can accomplish their intended purposes in many settings. I discuss possible lessons for reform in Part III.

III. The Limits of Information

The picture thus far has been quite optimistic, and I do believe that optimism is on the whole quite warranted. But the case for informational remedies is not unqualified. There are three major problems with such strategies. First, the provision of information can be expensive. Second, the provision of information is sometimes ineffectual or even counterproductive. Third, informational strategies deal inadequately with some external effects of risk.

A. Expense

. . . OSHA's hazard communication policy is estimated to save 200 lives per year—a lot—but at an annual cost of $360 million.[40] The expenditure per life saved is therefore $1.8 million. This is far better than a large number of regulations, and probably an amount well worth spending, but it is more than many agencies spend for life-saving regulations. It is therefore not the case that the OSHA rule stands out as a means of saving lives especially cheaply. There are many life-saving programs that achieve the same goal—saved lives—at lower cost. . . .

B. Little, No, or Bad Effects

1. How Information Can Go Wrong: An Outline

Even when informational strategies are not prohibitively expensive, they may be ineffectual and thus have low benefits. There are many possible problems here. . . .

(d) Overload

There is also a pervasive risk of information overload, causing consumers to treat a large amount of information as equivalent to no information at all. If employers are forced to list all risks and to explain them in detail, people may absorb little or nothing. If advertisers are required to have detailed disclosure labels, consumers may obtain relatively little information.

(e) Disclosure Requirements That Deter Disclosure

Yet another problem is that companies may respond to disclosure requirements by refusing to provide information at all (if this is an available option). If industry responds to a requirement of evidentiary support for scientific claims with mere "puffing," consumers may have less information than they did to begin with. If advertisers must conduct extensive tests before they are permitted to make claims, they will be given a strong incentive to avoid making claims at all. The result will be the removal from the market of information that is useful overall.

---

[40] The figures come from John F. Morrall, III, *A Review of the Record*, 10 Regulation 25 (1986).

(f) Disclosure and the Disadvantaged

Disclosure strategies may also have disproportionately little effect on people who are undereducated, elderly, or poor. This is to be expected, for information remedies require an ability to read and process. This ability is most pronounced among the well-educated and the wealthy.

(g) Public Good Issues

Finally, information may be an inadequate strategy when greater safety is a public good. Imagine, for example, that the replacement of carcinogen X with safe product Y would benefit all workers simultaneously because all of them would simultaneously be exposed to Y rather than X. Imagine too that each worker is bargaining separately with the employer. In that case, no individual employee may have a sufficient incentive to decrease his demand for wages and other benefits to obtain increased safety. Because the benefits of the new substance are provided to everyone, no individual employee will "pay" enough to obtain them, preferring instead to take a free ride on others. The result will be too little safety on conventional economic criteria. Here a regulatory response is appropriate. . . .

D. Responding to Limitations

All this suggests that there are real limitations to informational strategies. The limitations should, however, be taken merely as qualifications of the broader point, or as providing helpful guidance to those seeking to design effective information requirements. They do not argue fundamentally against reform efforts. While informational strategies are no panacea, they would accomplish considerable good, at least if the possible obstacles are kept firmly in mind.

The first and most important point is that some of these very limitations can be overcome through more and better information. An awareness of the distorting effects of current heuristics can help overcome those effects. General publicity about those effects might therefore supply a corrective. The "availability" heuristic in particular would be overcome through making public and private sector changes in what risks come readily to mind.

Existing studies also suggest that some disclosure remedies will work better than others. Well-tailored programs would minimize the relevant risks by putting the information in its most understandable form. Instead of labeling a substance a "carcinogen," a uniform system of risk regulation could give better awareness of risk levels. Excessive detail should be avoided; the relevant information should be crisp and simple. Any disclosure requirements should attend to difficulties in processing information.

In this light, the current initiatives are simply a beginning. Broader and more ambitious programs, coordinating the general communication of social risks, are very much in order. It has been suggested that government might eventually develop a "national warnings system" containing a systematized terminology for warnings. Such a system could apply to all contexts and risks and give a uniform sense of risk levels. The existence of a uniform language would make it possible to assess risks across a wide range of social spheres. This step would introduce a healthy degree of coordination and priority-setting in regulation.

Most important of all, such a system would perform a vital educative function, one that could complement the functioning of markets and provide a necessary precondition for democratic choice. . . .

COMMENTS AND QUESTIONS

1. Like information provided voluntarily, information provided as a result of government mandates can promote worker and consumer autonomy, by letting people know what risks they are taking, and can reduce risks, as consumers and workers adjust their behavior in light of the information.

   Why might information provision fail? Perhaps the potential recipients do not read the disclosures because they cannot (consider here disclosures with respect to goods consumed primarily by children, as well as the extent of functional illiteracy). Might there be intermediaries who can transmit the information from the discloser to the intended recipient (again, consider the role of parents—and the limitations *they* face—in shaping their children's choices)?

2. Sunstein observes that strategies that rely on information provision are unsuitable for situations in which there are negative externalities of the activity subject to the disclosure: "If a company is emitting carbon dioxide into the atmosphere, it is not enough for everyone to know about this fact. Instead the government should impose a tax or emissions fee designed to require the company to 'internalize' the cost of its activity."

   Consider in this connection the EPCRA to which Sunstein refers, which sometimes is described as requiring companies to compile and disclose a "toxic release inventory." What functions does such an inventory serve? (a) For those in contractual relations with the discloser, the inventory may provide them the information they need to determine the price they will charge (e.g., the wages they will demand). (b) The larger impact of such inventories, though, seems to be, as Sunstein suggests, on the surrounding communities. Information disclosure can spur political activities aimed at the adoption of direct regulatory strategies. This suggests that information-provision strategies should not be sharply distinguished from other regulatory strategies.

3. Following a case study in information disclosure, we present readings that explore issues of human cognition that might limit the effectiveness of information disclosure strategies.

C California's Proposition 65: A Case Study in Information Provision

In 1998, California's voters adopted Proposition 65, the Safe Drinking Water and Toxic Enforcement Act. The act provides, "[N]o person in the course of doing business shall knowingly and intentionally expose any individual to a chemical known to the state to cause cancer or reproductive toxicity without first giving clear and reasonable warning to such individual." The disclosure requirement does not apply if the person exposing others to the chemical can establish that "the exposure poses no significant risk assuming lifetime exposure at the level in question for substances known to the state to cause cancer, and that the exposure will have no observable effect assuming exposure at one thousand (1000) times the level in question for substances known to the state to cause reproductive toxicity." The case that follows deals with a challenge to a regulation dealing with disclosure requirements for chemicals that are present in food in its "natural," unprocessed state.

- **Nicolle-Wagner v. Deukmejian**
  230 Cal. App. 3d 652 (1991)

Opinion by Grignon, J., with Turner, P. J., and Boren, J., concurring.

. . .

Section 12501 [the regulation in question] provides that, "[h]uman consumption of a food shall not constitute an 'exposure' for purposes of Health and Safety Code section 25249.6 to a listed chemical in the food to the extent that the person responsible for the contact can show that the chemical is naturally occurring in the food." A chemical is considered "naturally occurring" if "it is a natural constituent of a food, or if it is present in a food solely as a result of absorption or accumulation of the chemical which is naturally present in the environment in which the food is raised, or grown, or obtained. . . ." The chemical is not naturally occurring to the extent that it is the result of any human activity or failure to observe "good agricultural or good manufacturing practices," such as the "addition of chemicals to irrigation water applied to soil or crops." Even where the chemical is a naturally occurring one, the regulations require that the producer, manufacturer, distributor, or holder of the food at all times utilize measures to reduce that chemical to the lowest level currently feasible.

Following the adoption of section 12501, plaintiff filed, on October 6, 1989, a first amended complaint for declaratory and injunctive relief against the Governor of the State of California, the Secretary of the Agency, and his Deputy Secretary (defendants), seeking a determination that the regulation is unlawful. Plaintiff contends that Proposition 65 created no categorical exemption for naturally occurring carcinogens or naturally occurring reproductive toxins, which are as threatening to health as man-made toxins. Plaintiff maintains that there is no scientific basis for distinguishing between manmade and naturally occurring substances, and that Proposition 65 did not sanction such distinctions.

. . .

The only issue contested in the court below was whether section 12501 was in conflict with Health and Safety Code section 25249.5 et seq., or was not reasonably necessary to effectuate the statutory purpose of those sections. . . .

. . .

The sole issue on appeal is whether section 12501 is in conflict with or is not reasonably necessary to effectuate the statutory purpose of Health and Safety Code section 25249.5 et seq. . . .

We find that the regulation is not in conflict with the statute. . . .

. . .

Our determination rests on whether the Agency's definition of exposure conflicts with the statute or its purposes. Proposition 65, and the corresponding sections of the Health and Safety Code, are silent on the subject of naturally occurring carcinogens and reproductive toxins. We must search then, for whatever more subtle expressions of the electorate's intent may exist in the language of the statute, as well as the ballot arguments both for and against the proposition. Those sources indicate that Proposition 65 sought to regulate toxic substances which are deliberately added or put into the environment by human activity. The controlling language of the Proposition, now Health and Safety Code section 25249.6, provides that "no person in the course of doing business shall *knowingly and intentionally expose* any individual" (italics added), thereby suggesting that some degree of human activity which results in toxins being added to the environment is required.

Of course, one could argue that furnishing foods to consumers which are known to contain naturally occurring carcinogens or reproductive toxins might constitute a "knowing and intentional" exposure of individuals to the chemicals. However, the ballot argument in favor of Proposition 65 explains that "[Proposition 65] will not take anyone by surprise. [It] applies only to businesses that *know* they are putting one of the chemicals out into the environment...." (Italics in original.) A chemical is not "put" into the environment if it is naturally occurring in, for example, fruits and vegetables.

The ballot argument against Proposition 65 also includes strong language indicating that naturally occurring substances are not intended to be controlled by the proposed statute: "The simple scientific fact of the matter is that manmade carcinogens represent only a tiny fraction of the total carcinogens we are exposed to, most of which are natural substances such as tobacco, alcohol, and chemicals in green plants. Significant amounts of manmade carcinogens are highly regulated in California under the most stringent laws in the United States. This initiative will result in chasing after trivial amounts of manmade carcinogens at *enormous cost* with minimal benefit to our health."

To be sure, one could find some support for plaintiff's position that no exemption for naturally occurring chemicals was intended, based on the absence of such distinctions in both the general language of the proposition and in the specific definition of the substances proposed to be controlled. The ballot proposition itself stated, by way of introduction, that:

> "[t]he people of California find that hazardous chemicals pose a serious threat to their health and well-being, that state government agencies have failed to provide them with adequate protection and that these failures have been serious enough to lead to investigations by federal agencies of the administration of California's toxic protection programs. The people therefore declare their rights:...(b) To be informed about exposures to chemicals that cause cancer, birth defects, or other reproductive harm."

Similarly, the list of chemicals to be controlled is defined in the proposition as "those chemicals known to the state to cause cancer or reproductive toxicity" and makes no distinction between man-made and naturally occurring substances.

Thus, although some language may be found in the proposition and ballot arguments which both supports and refutes plaintiff's position that naturally occurring toxins are subject to the initiative statute, we are persuaded, on balance, that the better view is that the electorate did not intend naturally occurring substances to be controlled by Proposition 65. Use of terms such as "knowingly and intentionally" and "putting" implies that human conduct which results in toxins being added to the environment is the activity to be controlled. The opponents of the initiative expressly indicated that only "man-made" substances would be regulated. We find that section 12501 is consistent with the governing statutes.[3]

. . .

We also find that substantial evidence was presented that the regulation reasonably effectuates the statutory purpose. Evidence was presented at the public hearings on this regulation, and was made part of the original petition for the proposed regulation, that most food products contain at least trace amounts of carcinogens and reproductive toxins which appear on the Governor's list. The administrative record also includes commentary regarding the paucity of scientific data regarding the risks posed by exposure to such naturally occurring substances.

We all presume, to some extent, that foods that have been eaten for thousands of years are healthful, despite the presence of small amounts of naturally occurring toxins. Were these substances not exempted from Health and Safety Code section 25249.6's warning requirements, the manufacturer or seller of such products would bear the burden of proving, under subdivision (c) of Health and Safety Code section 25249.10, that the exposure poses no "significant risk" to individuals. The administrative record in this matter indicates that such evidence largely does not exist. Thus, grocers and others would be required, in order to avoid liability under these statutes, to post a warning label on most, if not all, food products. The Agency's final statement of reasons for section 12501 includes the observation that the "[a]bsence of such an exemption could unnecessarily reduce the availability of certain foods or could lead to unnecessary warnings, which could distract the public from other important warnings on consumer products." Since one of the principal purposes of the statutes in question is to provide "clear and reasonable warning" of exposure to carcinogens and reproductive toxins, such warnings would be diluted to the point of meaninglessness if they were to be found on most or all food products.

The final statement of reasons also provides that the rationale for this special treatment for foodstuffs is the historical desire to preserve naturally occurring foods in the American food supply, despite the presence in those foods of small amounts of potentially deleterious substances, as well as to recognize the general safety of unprocessed foods as a matter of consumer experience. This exemption, therefore, will further the statutory purpose in safeguarding the effectiveness of warnings which are given, and in removing from regulatory scrutiny those substances which pose only an "insignificant risk" of cancer or birth defects, within the meaning of the statute.

The regulation is also narrowly drawn. It is applicable only to naturally occurring chemicals in foodstuffs and not other products, such as pharmaceuticals and cosmetics. It takes pains to define "naturally occurring" in such a fashion so as to preclude chemicals which are in whole or in part the product of human activity. Thus, a chemical is "naturally occurring" only if it is a natural constituent of food or if it is present solely as a result of the absorption or accumulation of

---

[3] Proposition 65 also created exemptions from the warning requirement for exposures [that pose no significant risk]. . . . Since the proposition plainly provided for a categorical exemption for exposures which pose no "significant risk," it would not be inconsistent for the Agency to enact regulations defining more specifically those exposures which pose an insignificant risk to individuals.

chemicals which are naturally present in the environment. Even if a chemical occurs naturally in a food, it is not deemed to be "naturally occurring," under the regulation, to the extent it is avoidable by good agricultural or manufacturing techniques. Natural chemical contaminants must be reduced to the "lowest level currently feasible."

. . .

COMMENTS AND QUESTIONS

1. Under the regulations currently implementing Proposition 65, warnings must be provided for exposures that occur through ambient air, indoor air, water, and soil. The warning must be in the "most appropriate" form, including signs, newspaper or other media communications every three months, or mailings to "each occupant in the affected area." Do you think such warnings are likely to be effective? Consider what a person living in an area exposed by ambient air could do in response to a warning. Consider what such a person's response to the first, second, third, . . . mailed warnings might be.

2. W. Kip Viscusi, *Predicting the Effects of Food Cancer Risk Warnings on Consumers*, 43 Food, Drug, & Cosmetics L.J. 283 (1988), provides the following critique of the implementation of Proposition 65. Which, if any, of his criticisms seem cogent?

    . . .What risk is significant is essentially a policy question that depends on how people will respond to this risk. . . .

    The state of California is currently interpreting significant risk in terms of a lifetime cancer risk of 1 in 100,000. Even if this were the actual policy threshold, it would be at too low a risk level to pose truly significant risks for individual decisions. If individuals with typical attitudes towards risk-dollar tradeoffs fully understood the risks involved and could act upon them, they would alter their purchase decisions by under a penny for a product they purchased weekly and which posed a lifetime risk of 1 chance in 100,000. . . .

    Unfortunately, California has adopted a variety of risk assessment assumptions that are intended to be "conservative." . . . Use of the animal studies that display the most sensitivity to a chemical exposure will overstate the average animal response and may be a misleading guide to the likely human response. . . . The significant risk level should be based on the mean risk assessment . . . not the upper bound of what this risk conceivably could be. Such a procedure necessarily distorts the impled risk level and leads to greatly overstated risk levels in situations where scientific evidence is most uncertain. . . .

    . . .

    . . . In the case of food products, the warning states first the human hazard signal word WARNING, which will be followed by a succinct fourteen word sentence that indicates that the product includes a chemical known to cause cancer. . . .

    The basic standard [I propose] is that a warning will be most successful if it conveys to consumers risk information in an accurate and effective manner. Thus, it is desired that individuals read the information, process it, and form accurate assessments of the risk based upon the warning message. . . .

. . .

In the case of the food warning that has been suggested under Proposition 65, the content of the warning is wholly inappropriate for the modest levels of risk involved. . . . [T]he California risk warning threshold requires that consumers be warned of risks that should alter their willingness to buy particular products by as little as a penny. . . . Ideally, the content of the warning should reflect the low levels of risks involved.

Instead, the legislation requires a warning that begins with a very strong human hazard signal [intermediate between "Danger" and "Caution"]. . . . The use of the "warning" terminology conveys the impression of a high level of risk. . . .

The verbal description of the risk following the signal word is also quite strong. Essentially, the claim is that the product contains a chemical known to cause cancer. The use of the cancer terminology evokes a strong response among readers in terms of the risk that is perceived to be presented. In addition, the warning does not indicate that our knowledge of the risk may be highly uncertain, or that the level of risk may be very low. . . .

. . .

Viscusi reports the results of a survey he conducted: "In response to a survey question regarding whether they would purchase a $2.50 box of cereal bearing such a warning, 34% said that they would not do so at any price, and the remaining 61% wanted an average price discount of $1.60. These are substantial responses indeed for a warning intended to convey low risk of carcinogeneity." In postsurvey debriefings of participants, "the dominant response was two-fold. First, if the products really are risky enough to warrant these labels, the government should have banned them. Second, if such labeling will affect a wide class of products, many will dismiss it as a ridiculous regulation." Viscusi concluded that "the content of the Proposition 65 approach greatly exaggerates the actual risks, creating the twin dangers of excessive alarm and possible dismissal of the warning program."

Viscusi contrasts the California warning with that appearing on food products containing saccharin, which, according to Viscusi, poses "a risk believed to be forty times greater" than the California risk threshold. The saccharin warning is this: "USE OF THIS PRODUCT MAY BE HAZARDOUS TO YOUR HEALTH. THIS PRODUCT CONTAINS SACCHARIN WHICH HAS BEEN DETERMINED TO CAUSE CANCER IN LABORATORY ANIMALS."

Viscusi proposes a "two-tier warning system," distinguishing between low-risk and higher-risk goods. For the lower tier, "[c]onsumers could consult a reference binder at stores"; for the higher one, there would be "a more visible warning such as on-product labeling or a point-of-purchase display."

Consider these aspects of Viscusi's argument:

(a) *Risk assessment*: The regulatory agency's rule-making procedures identify the assumptions it makes in setting the threshold. Should those assumptions be made known to the consumers who receive the warnings? How?

(b) *Animal versus human studies*: The saccharin warning's information about laboratory animals is accurate. Is it informative?

(c) *Reference to cancer risk*: Recall that people ordinarily respond to the term *cancer* with high levels of concern. Can you draft an information disclosure that reduces the "exaggeration" due to the use of the term? Given that people actually do place a high value on knowing about cancer risks, even when experts believe that the risk is taken to be higher than it actually is, should you?

(d) *Terminology*: How finely tuned should the hierarchy of warnings be? Why should a government choose anything other than "For Your Information"?

3. Do you think that warning labels are generally a failure because people do not understand the real risks and either ignore the information or take it too seriously or that they are a success because people change their behavior in response to what they perceive to be the risks (even if they did so because they thought that the risks were higher than experts believe them to be)?

4. So far we have been using relatively informal and intuitive ideas to raise questions about the way consumers and workers process information. We now turn to a more systematic examination of what psychologists have learned about how people process information.

D Understanding Information: What Psychologists Might Tell Us

As an introduction, consider the results of the following study: Applicants for marriage licenses were asked what proportion of marriages formed that year would end in divorce. The median answer—50% for the relevant period—was the correct one. They were asked a second question: What's the chance that your marriage will end in divorce? Here the median answer was zero. Lynn Baker and Robert Emery, *When Every Relationship Is Above Average: Perceptions and Expectations of Divorce at the Time of Marriage*, 17 Law & Human Behavior 439 (1993). Were they "blinded by love"? (What does that mean?) Did they know so much more about themselves and their relationship that they were properly confident that they would not divorce?

■ *Taking Behavioralism Seriously: The Problem of Market Manipulation*
JON D. HANSON AND DOUGLAS A. KYSAR
74 N.Y.U. L. Rev. 630 (1999). Reprinted with permission
of New York University Law Review

. . . .

B. A Review of the Behavioral Literature

In a well known experiment, Amos Tversky and Daniel Kahneman asked subjects to imagine that they must select between alternative vaccine programs to combat an unusual disease that will kill 600 people if nothing is done. The first group of subjects was presented with these choices:

> If program A is adopted, 200 people will be saved.
> If program B is adopted, there is a ⅓ probability that 600 people will be saved, and a ⅔ probability that none of the 600 people will be saved.

The second group was asked to select from these choices:

> If program C is adopted, 400 people will die.
> If program D is adopted, there is a ⅓ probability that nobody will die, and a 2⅔ probability that 600 people will die.

Under von Neumann and Morgenstern's expected utility theory, one might predict that the subjects would be indifferent between all four programs because each presented the same expected result: 200 people will live and 400 will die.... The way Kahneman and Tversky's subjects actually responded, however, could not have been predicted with expected utility theory, at least not without violating its most basic axioms. In the first scenario, seventy-two percent of subjects chose program A; in the second scenario, seventy-eight percent chose program D. Yet, programs A and C are logically identical, as are programs B and D; they both present the same consequences but inspire vastly different reactions. Put differently, the options offered to each group of subjects were identical, yet the subjects' choice between the two options appears to depend largely on how the options were described. Such inconsistency calls into question the central principle of expected utility theory—that individuals seek to maximize their expected utility. If individuals behave differently when presented with identical possible consequences, then they must be operating under some other influence.

Kahneman and Tversky's study provides an example of what cognitive psychologists call *framing effects*. People prefer program A because it is framed in terms of guaranteed lives saved; people reject program C because it is framed in terms of guaranteed lives lost. Framing effects are representative of the type of phenomena that behavioral researchers encountered when they began testing the veracity of economic predictions about human behavior. Similar nonrational mental processes and representations have steadily been identified over the past two decades such that recent commentators can now cite "a whole range of systematic errors and biases." Largely because of the nature of the biases, the discoveries have been slow in coming and subject to considerable challenge. At this point, however, as two of the pioneers in the field of cognitive biases have concluded, "the deviations of actual behavior from the normative model are too widespread to be ignored, too systematic to be dismissed as random error, and too fundamental to be accommodated by relaxing the normative system." These discoveries have not only found their way into the law review literature, they have given rise to a cascade of articles and to what might well turn out to be the most significant conceptual development in legal theory since the emergence of law and economics.

This Section will review those deviations and cognitive illusions, dividing them into two rough categories: those affecting the way in which individuals attempt to make "scientific" and probabilistic judgments and those affecting the way in which individuals determine and exhibit their preferences. We will discuss some important examples of both, bearing in mind that "[behavioral] research is moving rapidly, and it is a daunting task to comprehend its scope."

1. *Manipulability of Scientific and Probabilistic Judgments*

In this subsection, we will review a series of cognitive biases that impact the way in which individuals make scientific and probabilistic judgments. As will be shown, these biases do not merely represent erroneous or imprecise applications of reasoning—they do not represent reasoning in the classical sense at all. Instead, these biases reveal a deep misunderstanding of the nature of scientific judgment and a series of mental crutches awkwardly constructed to take up the slack. Their cumulative effect is to impair our appreciation of risk and uncertainty so severely that one commentator has termed the condition probability blindness. Whether blind or just impaired, people's sense of scientific and probabilistic judgment is inarguably of doubtful acuity.

a. The Formation and Influence of Personal Hypotheses

Considerable research indicates that individuals act, in effect, as lay scientists, adopting and testing hypotheses, or explanations for understanding the world. People have a strong tendency to construct "theories" to account for events or relationships that they find salient. Such theories enable individuals to organize and, perhaps, understand the world around them. Unfortunately, however, lay scientists, much like professionals, often fail to practice "good science." Put differently, people's constructed theories often can be a source of confusion and misestimation rather than clarification and understanding.

i. Belief Perseverance

One of our most basic flaws as lay scientists, for example, is that after constructing a hypothesis or explanation, we tend to disregard evidence that contradicts that hypothesis and exaggerate evidence that confirms it. There is, in other words, strong support for the common-sense view that first impressions carry disproportionate weight. One of the better known experiments demonstrating this tendency was a 1964 study in which subjects were shown blurred pictures that were gradually brought into focus. Different subjects were introduced to the photos at different stages of sharpened focus, but the pace of the sharpening process and the final degree of focus was identical for all subjects. Interestingly, the more of the sharpening process that subjects viewed, the less likely they were to be able to identify the object in the photograph. That is, if a subject began looking at the photo when it was severely blurred, that subject had a more difficult time identifying the object than a subject who began viewing the photo when it was less severely blurred. As the researchers concluded, "Interference may be accounted for partly by the difficulty of rejecting incorrect hypotheses based on substandard cues." Put differently, if individuals construct their initial hypothesis at a time when their basis for, or ability to, make such a judgment is particularly weak, they may be unable to interpret correctly subsequent better information that is inconsistent with that hypothesis.

ii. Confirmatory Bias

Our inadequacies as scientists run deeper than mere cognitive stubbornness. As Matthew Rabin recently expressed the point, "psychological evidence reveals a stronger and more provocative phenomenon: People tend to misread evidence as additional support for initial hypotheses." Numerous experiments have demonstrated, for example, that the same ambiguous information can further polarize people who already hold differing beliefs on certain topics. In one such experiment, researchers asked forty-eight undergraduate students to review evidence on the deterrent effect of capital punishment. Half of those students had indicated in an earlier questionnaire that they supported capital punishment and believed that it had a deterrent effect and that research supported their view; half indicated that they opposed capital punishment and believed that it had little or no deterrent effect and that research supported their view. The subjects were then exposed to randomly selected studies on the deterrent effect of capital punishment and asked to assess both whether a given study supported or discredited their views and whether the study had affected their views in any way. The researchers found that the subjects' attitudes were polarized at high confidence levels; that is, proponents of capital punishment became more in favor of it and believed more in its deterrent effect, while opponents of capital punishment became less in favor of it and believed less in its deterrent effect.

Research of this sort also suggests that the strength of the confirmatory bias may depend in part on the type of evidence an individual views. The more ambiguous and complex the evidence, the more that evidence seems to be susceptible to the confirmatory bias. As the authors of the experiment regarding capital punishment put it: "With confirming evidence, we suspect that both lay and professional scientists rapidly reduce the complexity of the information and remember only a few well-chosen supportive impressions." With disconfirming evidence, they continue to reflect upon any information that suggests less damaging "alternative interpretations." Indeed, lay scientists may even view ambiguities or conceptual weaknesses in data opposing their theory as somehow supporting their theory's fundamental veracity (rather than simply serving to discredit any other theories that would have relied on the flawed data).

In a slightly different study of the effects of confirming and disconfirming data, Nancy Pennington and Reid Hastie found that mock jurors remember different facts depending upon the stories that they construct to decide their verdicts. Not only do they forget facts that are incongruent with their stories, they "remember" facts that were not in evidence. This type of "self-serving bias" may be just as pronounced among the litigants themselves. Consider, for example, several studies involving an actual Texas tort case in which subjects were randomly allocated the role of plaintiff or defendant in settlement negotiations. The subjects received a case summary along with twenty-seven pages of materials from the trial and were told that a judge had awarded an amount between $0 and $100,000. Prior to the settlement exercise, the subjects were asked to guess the amount that the judge awarded and to state what they believed was a "fair" amount for the plaintiff to receive in settlement. For the judge's award, plaintiffs guessed an average $14,527 higher than defendants; for the fair settlement amount, plaintiffs stated an average $17,709 higher than defendants. Thus, not only do individuals selectively recall evidence to suit a particular story that they have constructed, but they weigh the merits of an entire body of evidence wildly differently depending on something as simple as which side they have been assigned in a role-playing exercise.

Finally, according to behavioralists, one of the most significant effects of the confirmatory bias is the tendency to exaggerate a correlation when doing so confirms one's hypothesis or to underestimate a correlation when one does not subscribe to a hypothesis or theory that might explain the correlation. As an initial matter, Loren J. Chapman and Jean P. Chapman's seminal work on illusory correlations demonstrated that clinicians and laypersons often perceive correlations between variables based on their preconceived notions of the relationship that "should" exist, rather than any actual correlations between the variables. Later researchers extended this concept to cases in which the individual has no preconceived notion or "theory" to explain observed data, and in which the individual does have a theory but the data itself is imprecise or nonexistent. These researchers found that individuals underestimate correlation when they have no theory to explain it, and imagine or exaggerate correlation when they do have a preconceived theory to explain it. In short, the lay scientist appears to be driven by theory rather than data when making judgments and decisions—an approach dramatically at odds with the classical scientific model.

iii. Hypothesis-Based Filtering

There is a related type of confirmatory bias, which Matthew Rabin has dubbed "hypothesis-based filtering." As Rabin explains, although it may be "sensible to interpret ambiguous data according to current hypotheses, people tend to use the consequent 'filtered' evidence as further evidence for these hypotheses." Put differently, the confirmatory bias seems to have a self-reinforcing and escalating quality: An individual interprets ambiguous evidence as consistent with her initial hypothesis and then views that evidence, as interpreted, as further confirmation of her hypothesis. That confirmation in turn strengthens her faith in the initial hypothesis and makes her even more willing to interpret future ambiguous evidence as consistent with it. This process continues in circular fashion, further solidifying the initial "theories" or beliefs of the lay scientist.

iv. Entity Effect

Finally, perhaps the most striking finding is that people's hypotheses often take on a life of their own—that is, they persevere even when the evidence that initially gave rise to them is thoroughly and completely discredited. For example, it seems that people's impressions of their own abilities (or the abilities of their peers) often survive even after the evidence upon which the initial impression is based is invalidated. In one study, subjects, who had been told that their social sensitivity and empathetic ability were being assessed, received fabricated feedback indicating their ability to distinguish authentic from inauthentic suicide notes. Subjects were then thoroughly "debriefed" in a way that made very clear that the feedback they had received had been bogus. Subjects' subsequent predictions of future task success and ratings of their own abilities were nevertheless heavily influenced by the earlier (but discredited) feedback. The same sort of perseverance effects were observable in the predictions of observers who witnessed the subjects' original feedback and debriefings.

More recent studies have continued to demonstrate the same phenomenon and, furthermore, have begun to shed light on the way in which individuals' causal theories can take on their own momentum. In one pair of experiments, for instance, subjects were provided a small amount of evidence to suggest that either a positive or negative empirical relationship existed between a trainee's preference for risk—as measured by a paper and pencil test—and his or her subsequent success as a firefighter. The fictitious evidence consisted of background information, such as age, marital status, and hobbies, of one successful firefighter and one unsuccessful firefighter along with each firefighter's scores on the risk-preference test. Some of the subjects were asked to provide an explanation for any relationship that they discovered when reviewing that evidence. Then, as with the previous study, some subjects were "debriefed"—that is, they were informed that the evidence they were shown suggesting a relationship between risk preferences and success as a firefighter was fictitious and of absolutely no probative value. The researchers then examined whether the subjects would continue after the debriefings to be influenced by the theories they constructed before the debriefings. The results were striking:

> Although the "data" to which subjects had been initially exposed were objectively quite weak (consisting of only two cases) and in a domain of little personal relevance, this initial ostensible evidence clearly exerted a strong effect on subjects' theories about the true relationship between the two variables. Thus, in the no-debriefing conditions, subjects exposed to a positive relationship saw risky responses as highly diagnostic of later success, whereas subjects exposed to an apparent negative relationship believed the opposite to be true.... The total discrediting of the evidence on which subjects' initial theories had been based had only a minimal impact on subjects' beliefs concerning the relationship between risk preference and firefighting ability. Within the debriefing conditions, subjects initially exposed to data indicative of a positive relationship continued to believe that a positive relationship existed, whereas subjects in the negative relationship condition continued to believe in a negative relationship.... In fact, the slight decrease in the strength of subjects' beliefs following debriefing...was not statistically significant....

The authors concluded that the studies provide support for three general conclusions. First, the studies provide further evidence for the basic hypothesis that individuals persist in their beliefs even when such persistence is neither normatively nor logically warranted. Second, the studies illustrate that earlier research may have underestimated the tenacity of belief perseverance: "Initial beliefs may persevere in the face of a subsequent invalidation of the evidence on which they are based, *even when this initial evidence is itself as weak and inconclusive as a single pair of dubiously representative cases.*" Finally, the studies provide support for the hypothesis that belief perseverance is exacerbated when an individual generates her own causal explanations or scenarios to imply the correctness of her initial beliefs, even if the original data underlying those beliefs is later discredited.

It bears noting that the subjects in this experiment seemed to understand the debriefing procedure that thoroughly discredited the original evidence. Nevertheless, subjects also seemed to believe that their hypotheses were independent of the invalidated evidence and were worthy of independent deference. As the authors of the study explained, subjects "simply felt that the relationship they had examined—whether positive or negative—appeared to be the correct one and that the discrediting of the evidential value of the initial cases was largely irrelevant to their personal beliefs concerning the 'true' relationship existing between these variables." If these studies provide an accurate indicator, then clearly the perseverance bias is powerful and pervasive; attitudes and beliefs do not change easily. New data or the refutation of old data does not necessarily influence our beliefs because the hypotheses that we begin with are "largely autonomous" and they "remain available and continue to imply the existence of particular relationships or outcomes even if the data on which they were initially based subsequently prove to be completely devoid of evidential value."

v. Motivated Reasoning

Belief perseverance, the confirmatory bias, hypothesis-based filtering, and the entity effect may all be understood as examples of a more general phenomenon known as motivated reasoning. This refers to the tendency for individuals to utilize a variety of cognitive mechanisms to arrive, through a process of apparently unbiased reasoning, at the conclusion they privately desired to arrive at all along. As Ziva Kunda has noted, "when one wants to draw a particular conclusion, one feels obligated to construct a justification for that conclusion that would be plausible to a dispassionate observer." In order to ensure that those justifications still reach the desired conclusion, "one accesses only a biased subset of the relevant beliefs and rules." Thus, not only does the lay scientist perceive and interpret evidence in a manner designed to confirm initial hypotheses, but she constructs the initial hypotheses themselves through biased cognitive processes designed to "reason" toward a desired conclusion.

This selective belief construction can have unfortunate consequences. As Kunda points out:

> People who play down the seriousness of early symptoms of severe diseases such as skin cancer and people who see only weaknesses in research pointing to the dangers of drugs such as caffeine or of behaviors such as drunken driving may literally pay with their lives for their motivated reasoning.

Despite the possibility for such regrettable consequences, the practice of motivated reasoning appears to be a universal and, perhaps, immutable characteristic of human nature.

b. False Self-Confidence

The next set of biases, which involve individuals' own self-assessments, are often treated by scholars as independent from the biases described above. Whether or not they are in fact independent, they can be usefully understood simply as manifestations of the motivated reasoning biases. To see how, imagine that individuals begin with the following hypotheses about themselves: "I'm more talented, intelligent, and agile than most; I'm a more competent lay scientist than most; and I'm less likely to be injured than most." With that sort of self-confidence or theory of the self, the following can be viewed as the perseverance and confirmatory biases, among others, at work in those people's assessment of the risks that they themselves face. This section will summarize evidence that people are indeed overoptimistic or overconfident regarding their own susceptibility to risks.

i. Optimistic Bias

An old saying defines a pessimist as "an informed optimist." Behavioral researchers might change that definition to "a debiased optimist," for there is growing evidence that we are naively and stubbornly optimistic at heart, regardless of how well informed we are. For instance, respondents in one study, although correctly estimating that fifty percent of American couples end up in divorce, estimated their own chance of divorce at zero. Similarly, college students are six times more likely to think they will have above average job satisfaction than below average. They are also about six times more likely to think they will own their own homes, two times more likely to think they will have a mentally gifted child, seven times less likely to think they will have drinking problems, and nine and one-half times less likely to think they will divorce soon after marriage. Overoptimism such as this is present not just among freshman and honeymooners; it exists even in the world of professionals. More generally, it is not limited to any particular age, sex, education level, or occupational group. In short, it appears that most people are overconfident with regard to future life events, even when they understand the actuarial probabilities of such events.

One particular manifestation of this bias is the tendency of people to underestimate their own chance of suffering some adverse outcome even when they accurately state or even overstate everyone else's chance of suffering that same outcome. In other words, we tend to exhibit the "it can't happen to me" syndrome or, more properly, the "it's less likely to happen to me than the average person" syndrome. As a result, ninety percent of drivers consider themselves to be above-average drivers, and ninety-seven percent of consumers believe that they are average or above average in their ability to avoid bicycle or power-mower accidents. Similarly, more people than is logically possible perceive themselves to be less likely than average to suffer negative experiences such as disease, divorce, criminal victimization, or unemployment.

Overoptimism stems from a general tendency to use past experience to estimate future susceptibility. As a result, the risks most likely to cause naive optimism are those in which the individual believes that if the problem has not happened yet, it will not happen at all. Other factors strongly correlated with the operation of the optimistic bias include the perception that a risk is preventable by individual action, the perception that a risk is of low frequency, and the lack of personal experience with a risk. For policymakers, a final important feature of the optimistic bias is that it is largely resistant to "debiasing interventions." In a study of the effects of the provision of risk-factor information, Neil Weinstein and William Klein concluded that "four studies testing a variety of approaches and using a variety of health hazards were unsuccessful in reducing optimistic biases about familiar health hazards." In short, it seems that the optimistic bias is an indiscriminate and indefatigable cognitive feature, causing individuals to underestimate the extent to which a threat applies to them even when they can recognize the severity it poses to others.

ii. Cognitive Dissonance

In addition to identifying countless manifestations of overconfidence such as those discussed above, behavioralists have attempted to explain the phenomenon using the concept of *cognitive dissonance*. One aspect of this concept is the tendency to reject or downplay information that contradicts other, more favorable views about oneself. In light of this tendency, it is perhaps easy to understand the basic source of people's optimistic bias: People prefer to believe that they are intelligent and are not subjecting themselves to a substantial risk. In the face of a known risk, therefore, individuals come readily to the opinion that they themselves—unlike the average person—are relatively immune, and they hold onto these optimistic assessments tenaciously.

iii. The Illusion of Control

Scholars have also identified a bias known as the *illusion of control*, referring to the human tendency to "treat chance events as if they involve skill and hence are controllable." A simple example of this tendency can be seen as gamblers throw dice harder when they need high numbers and softer when they need low numbers. The tendency was even more evident in a series of experiments conducted by Ellen Langer to test the subjective values people placed on lottery tickets. The experiment involved a lottery in which each participant was given a card containing the name and picture of a National Football League player; an identical card was placed in a bag and the person whose card was chosen from the bag won the lottery. In one trial, cards were randomly allocated while in another subjects were allowed to select their cards. Prior to the drawing, subjects were offered a chance to sell their cards to an experimental collaborator. Subjects who had selected their own player cards demanded *more than four times* as much money to sell their cards as did those with randomly allocated cards.

In another experiment, Yale undergraduates were convinced that they were better or worse than the average person at predicting the outcome of coin tosses. By giving subjects feedback on their predictions that was rigged to show either much greater or much less than 50% accuracy, researchers led subjects to view themselves, not as lucky or unlucky coin-toss predictors, but as good or bad predictors. Indeed, a significant portion of the subjects reported that their performance would be hampered by distraction and that they would improve with practice! Finally, Amos Tversky and Ward Edwards uncovered a similar overconfidence in subjects' tactics for predicting the results of random selections from a bag in which 70% of chips were blue and 30% were red. The maximizing strategy is to predict blue every time, leading to an eventual success rate of 70%. Tversky and Edwards' subjects, however, attempted to match probabilities—they predicted blue only 70% of the time in hopes of hitting 100% of the results. That strategy, however, only leads to a 58% success rate $((.70 \times .70) + (.30 \times .30) = .58)$. Despite being paid for the accuracy of their predictions and despite receiving feedback through thousands of trials, most subjects refused to adopt the maximizing strategy of always predicting blue—the strategy which, of course, admits that skill and control are irrelevant to the task.

iv. Hindsight Bias

In circumstances in which individuals are confronted with unambiguous evidence of a past outcome, they often construct a hypothesis from which they claim that they could have and would have predicted (and perhaps did predict) that outcome. In essence, most of us believe ourselves to be better than average at predicting outcomes and we use known outcomes as our means of confirming our own "scientific" acumen. This widely recognized and researched cognitive tendency is known as the *hindsight bias*. In 1975, one of the founders of the cognitive-bias literature, Baruch Fischhoff, observed that "reporting an outcome's occurrence increases its perceived probability of occurrence; and . . . people who have received outcome knowledge are largely unaware of its having changed their perceptions. . . ." Apparently, the mere fact that a probabilistic outcome eventuates alters our perception of how probabilistic it was. Indeed, subjects even tend to overestimate the accuracy of their own estimations. That is, not only do subjects overestimate the likelihood of an event after learning of its occurrence, but they also incorrectly recall their own earlier predictions as being more accurate than they actually turned out to be. This tendency to exaggerate the extent to which our beliefs before an event would have been our beliefs (and that others' beliefs before the event should have been their beliefs) is widely acknowledged even outside of the scholarly literature; hence, the expressions "20/20 hindsight" and "Monday-morning quarterbacking." That we may be aware of the bias seems not to eliminate it.

v. The Surprising Effect of Reasoning

It is sometimes suggested that individuals become more realistic when they have experience with a certain risk. To be sure, it is generally the case that some experts have a reasonably correct sense of the accuracy of their own predictions. But that tends to be the case primarily in the limited circumstances in which "feedback takes the form of unambiguous statistical evidence." In contrast, when the pertinent events are not easily predictable and the feedback is not unambiguous, experts tend to be even more overconfident than laypersons. The explanation sometimes offered for that finding is closely related to the "entity effect" of causal theories described above. Specifically, because experts tend to develop elaborate causal theories with which to generate predictions, the independent weight of those theories can yield especially robust overconfidence. As Griffin and Tversky explain,

> If the future state of a mental patient, the Russian economy, or the stock market cannot be predicted from present data, then experts who have rich models of the system in question are more likely to exhibit overconfidence than lay people who have a very limited understanding of these systems. Studies of clinical psychologists ... and stock market analysts ... are consistent with this hypothesis.

The counterintuitive lesson is this: Elaborate theories and careful reasoning may foster, rather than mitigate, overconfidence.

It should be noted that this phenomenon, although most pronounced in experts, is not limited to them. Several studies of laypersons have demonstrated that the quality of decisionmaking sometimes declines when individuals are prompted to deliberate and offer reasons for their decision. Because the individuals' confidence levels do not similarly decline, the result is an overconfidence fostered by deliberation.

Timothy Wilson and Suzanne LaFleur recently conducted an experiment that illustrates this false-confidence-building effect of reasoning. In this experiment, members of six sororities at the University of Virginia were asked to predict whether they would engage in each of six different behaviors toward fellow sorority members during the upcoming semester. Randomly, some subjects were asked to list reasons why they might or might not perform each of the behaviors. At the end of the semester, subjects were asked whether they had performed each of the six behaviors. While both groups of subjects—those who reasoned about their predictions and those who did not—had stated roughly the same confidence level in their predictions at the beginning of the semester, those who reasoned were in fact significantly less accurate than the control group in their predictions. Thus, both laypeople and experts exhibit a heightened degree of overconfidence when their predictions and decisions are characterized by a process of reasoning.

c. Bad Statisticians

Special attention must be given to the subject of probabilistic judgment, for this is an area where researchers have uncovered a veritable fool's gold mine of nonrational cognitive anomalies.

The seminal work in the field remains Tversky and Kahneman's *Judgment under Uncertainty: Heuristics and Biases*. In it, they describe the way in which individuals rely on heuristics, or mental rules of thumb, to "reduce the complex tasks of assessing probabilities and predicting values to simpler judgmental operations." These heuristics provide a rough and ready means for approximating the results of complex computational tasks; however, they can lead to biases, or "severe and systematic errors" in probabilistic judgment.

i. Availability

In making decisions about uncertain future events, people tend to ignore statistical data in favor of evidence that is particularly salient, vivid, or easily "available" to them. That is, their probability judgment is driven by the ease with which they can recall previous occurrences of the event or the ease with which they can imagine the event occurring in the future. Much of the time a person's experience or available memories can provide a fairly sound sample on which to base a judgment. At other times, however, the *availability heuristic* biases an individual's estimate.

For instance, in one experiment Tversky and Kahneman asked subjects to state whether words that begin with "r" are more or less common in the English language than those that have an "r" as the third letter. A significant majority of the subjects said that words that begin with an "r" are more likely. The statistical fact is the reverse, but words that begin with "r" are easier to recall or generate than words that have an "r" in the third place. In another of their experiments, subjects listened to recorded lists of the names of thirty-nine people, some of whom could be described only as well known, the remainder of whom could be described as famous. Some lists included nineteen women and more famous women than men, some included nineteen men and more famous men than famous women. When asked whether men or women predominated on the list they had heard, eighty of ninety-nine subjects chose the sex that involved the larger number of famous individuals.

The availability heuristic can be quite powerful in our everyday decisions. In making risk assessments, individuals will often allow "available" evidence to trump much more probative statistical information of which they are aware. As Matthew Rabin describes:

> Our assessment of a given city's crime rate is likely to be too influenced by whether we personally know somebody who has been assaulted, even if we are familiar with much more relevant general statistics. Likewise, dramatic stories by people we know about difficulties with a brand of car are likely to be overly influential even if we are familiar, via *Consumer Reports*, with general statistics of the reliability of different brands.

That is, we use availability as a substitute for rigorous scientific or probabilistic analysis not only when we lack information on a given subject, but also when we have information but lack the cognitive willpower to utilize it properly.

ii. Representativeness

There is another well-known mental rule of thumb, which scholars have dubbed the *representativeness heuristic*. This refers to the tendency of individuals to judge the frequency or likelihood of something by the degree to which the individual believes it resembles something else (i.e., its class). One consequence of representativeness is that people often pay too much attention to specific details (which may or may not contain relevant information), while ignoring or paying too little attention to background information that is relevant. To understand this heuristic, consider a famous experiment conducted by Tversky and Kahneman. Subjects were given the following information and asked to respond to a set of questions in an anonymous survey:

> A panel of psychologists have interviewed and administered personality tests to 30 engineers and 70 lawyers, all successful in their respective fields. On the basis of this information, thumbnail descriptions of the 30 engineers and 70 lawyers have been written.... For each description, please indicate your probability that the person described is an engineer, on a scale from 0 to 100....
>
> Jack is a 45-year-old man. He is married and has four children. He is generally conservative, careful, and ambitious. He shows no interest in political and social issues and spends most of his free time on his many hobbies which include home carpentry, sailing, and mathematical puzzles.
>
> The probability that Jack is one of the 30 engineers in the sample of 100 is ___%.
>
> Dick is a 30-year-old man. He is married with no children. A man of high ability and high motivation, he promises to be quite successful in his field. He is well liked by his colleagues.
>
> The probability that Dick is one of the 30 engineers in the sample of 100 is ___%.
>
> Suppose now that you are given no information whatsoever about an individual chosen at random from the sample. The probability that this man is one of the 30 engineers in the sample of 100 is ___%.

Tversky and Kahneman found that responses to the first two questions were often based on how much the described person was judged to sound like an engineer or lawyer without regard to the 30:70 ratio. For example, the description of Jack was judged with very high probability to involve an engineer. Of course, only three in ten will be engineers. But that fact seems to have been forgotten by many. The description of Bill was intended to provide no information. Tversky and Kahneman found that Bill was judged at 50:50, not 30:70. As they explained, most subjects recognized that the description said nothing relevant about a lawyer-engineer distinction, but apparently forgot the base rate information. If subjects believed that the description did not help them determine the occupation of the person, then they should have gone back to base rates and estimated thirty percent. Finally, with respect to the third question, Tversky and Kahneman found that subjects correctly gave 30:70 odds, indicating that they did know how to use the base rate information.

From their many studies of this sort, Tversky and Kahneman conclude that "evidently, people respond differently when given no evidence and when given worthless evidence. When no specific evidence is given, prior probabilities are properly utilized; when worthless evidence is given, prior probabilities are ignored." Worthless information trumps more relevant evidence, resulting in a *failure to honor base rates*.

Tversky and Kahneman observed a related misconception in a study of experienced research psychologists who honored the fallacious *law of small numbers*. This is the belief that "even small samples are highly representative of the populations from which they are drawn." As a result of this bias, the psychologists in the experiments, who were asked to make predictions from a limited set of evidence and assess their confidence levels in the predictions, afforded too much credence to results from small samples and "grossly overestimated the replicability of such results."

In another demonstration of this effect, Tversky and Kahneman asked undergraduate students the following question:

> A certain town is served by two hospitals. In the larger hospital about 45 babies are born each day, and in the smaller hospital about 15 babies are born each day. As you know, about 50 percent of all babies are boys. However, the exact percentage varies from day to day. Sometimes it may be higher than 50 percent, sometimes lower.
>
> For a period of 1 year, each hospital recorded the days on which more than 60 percent of the babies born were boys. Which hospital do you think recorded more such days?

The same percentage—twenty-two—of respondents estimated that either the large or the small hospital recorded more. The rest—fifty-six percent—estimated that it was about the same for both hospitals. Only the twenty-two percent that responded that the small hospital recorded more were correct; that is, seventy-eight percent were wrong. The law of large numbers—which, unlike the law of small numbers, is not fallacious—tells us that the larger hospital with more births per day on average would be more likely to replicate the overall distribution. Subjects obviously did not understand that, nor did they understand that the small hospital would be less likely to replicate the overall distribution.

Individuals experience an inverse bias to the law of small numbers whenever they honor the *gambler's fallacy*, the belief that the roulette wheel is "due" to hit red after a long streak of black. "Chance is commonly viewed as a self-correcting process in which a deviation in one direction induces a deviation in the opposite direction to restore the equilibrium." Thus, just as Tversky and Kahneman's psychologist subjects believed that a global pattern could be predicted from a local sample, gamblers believe that a local sample must replicate the global pattern. In truth, neither supposition is valid, for probabilities only become meaningful over sufficiently large sample sizes.

A final manifestation of the law of small numbers is that people expect too few lengthy streaks in sequences of random events. In the face of such a streak, people tend to invent spurious explanations for the seeming deviation from randomness, when, in fact, there has been no such deviation. For example, basketball coaches, players, and spectators have long believed in something called a "hot hand"—when a basketball player has made a series of shots and when that streak seems too long to be random. Psychologists have shown, however, that a seemingly hot-handed player is in fact no more likely to make his or her next shot than at other times. Put differently, there appears to be no such thing as a truly "hot hand," only random streaks of success that appear to us too long to be truly random.

The danger in using representativeness as shorthand for proper probabilistic decisionmaking is significant. The erroneous belief or desire to see patterns in random events causes decisionmakers to have unrealistic expectations about the stability of observed patterns and the replicability of prior beneficial experiences. Likewise, the failure to honor base rates when making predictions can lead to estimates bearing little or no relationship to actual probabilities. In either case, decisionmakers may also tend to have undue confidence in their assessments, believing that the world is much more ordered and deterministic than it actually is.

iii. Anchoring and Adjustment

In yet another series of their famous experiments, Tversky and Kahneman identified the heuristics of *anchoring* and *adjustment*. For reasons that should become clear, this heuristic can be understood as a combination of framing and perseverance. When people are asked to generate an estimate, they frequently anchor on an obvious or convenient number (e.g., the mean or the mode) and then adjust upward or downward from that anchor if there is reason to believe that the correct number should be moved in either direction. This procedure naturally leads to estimations which are skewed toward the initial value.

For instance, in one of Tversky and Kahneman's experiments, subjects were asked to estimate the number of African countries in the United Nations as a percentage of total membership. Before the subjects responded, however, a large wheel of chance was spun in the subjects' presence. Though the wheel contained numbers from one to one hundred, it was rigged to land either on ten or sixty-five. When the wheel landed on ten, subjects estimated that African countries comprised twenty-five percent of the United Nations; when the wheel landed on sixty-five, the estimation rose to forty-five percent. What is striking about this demonstration is that *the anchor provided to the subjects was overtly random and irrelevant, yet still it had a significant impact on the subjects' intuitive judgments.*

. . .

d. Experiential Thinking, Affect, and the Perception of Risk

There is wide consensus among psychologists that individuals process information through two parallel mechanisms: a rational system and an emotionally driven experiential system. The former is logical, deliberate, and abstract. As a consequence, it is also inefficient and ill-suited for the majority of everyday judgments and decisions. Instead, individuals typically rely on experiential thinking that is largely automatic and removed from consciousness. This type of information processing is associated with intuitive judgments, emotional responses, and other subtle, nonconscious reactions to external stimuli. These reactions are referred to collectively in the literature as *affect*.

Significantly, "because [experiential thinking] is generally associated with affect, it is apt to be experienced as more compelling than is dispassionate logical thinking." That is, individuals often will be swayed by the force of their affective responses to events and decisions, regardless of whether their rational, sequential, analytical system would opt for a different course. Moreover, "because the influence is usually outside of awareness, the rational system fails to control it because the person does not know there is anything to control."

Reliance on experiential thinking has important consequences for individual perceptions of risk. In contrast to the expected utility maximizer of the economist's model—who would assess all risks based solely on a probabilistic analysis of costs and benefits—the experiential thinker can be expected to view risks as multidimensional concepts entailing a range of beliefs, prejudices, and predispositions. Because most information processing occurs automatically and effortlessly "outside of awareness," the individual's perception of a given risk is likely to be heavily influenced, if not determined, by the affect associated with that risk. To give just one example of how this type of processing might work, assume that individuals are empirically more likely to associate a feeling of dread with technologically imposed risks such as nuclear power than naturally imposed risks such as earthquakes. If that were the case, individuals could be expected to perceive the magnitude of a technologically imposed risk to be greater than a probabilistically equal natural risk, solely because of the individual's negative affective response to the idea of technological hazards.

In an early and influential series of articles, Paul Slovic, Baruch Fischhoff, and Sarah Lichtenstein began to explore seriously this potential for qualitative, affective responses to bias individual risk perceptions. Utilizing a psychometric study of the determinants of risk perception, these researchers were able to identify a range of characteristics that heavily influence the way in which individuals perceive a given risk. For instance, as described above, a feeling of "dread" can have powerful influences over the risk that individuals associate with a given activity or technology: "The higher a hazard's score [on a 'dread' impression scale] the more people want to see its current risks reduced, and the more they want to see strict regulation employed to achieve the desired reduction in risk." Conversely, the more hazards are viewed as "controllable," "voluntary," and "well-known," the less likely individuals will view the hazard as excessive or undesirable. Other relevant attributes include whether the hazard is observable, whether its effect is immediate or delayed, whether it is a "new" risk, whether its consequences are fatal, whether it is globally catastrophic, and whether it poses high risks to future generations. What is significant is that none of these attributes are relevant under a strict probabilistic assessment of expected costs and benefits. Thus, the principal determinants of risk perception are affective and experiential, not deliberate and rational.

While early researchers focused on the risk characteristics that tend to lead toward positive or negative evaluative feelings about certain risks, more recent studies have focused on the actual mechanism whereby affective responses influence and bias risk perceptions. The most robust finding from the literature is that perceptions of the costs and benefits posed by risks are inversely related. That is, where a risk is perceived as posing high costs, it tends also to be perceived as posing low benefits, and vice versa. In a series of experiments designed to explore this relationship, Ali Siddiq Alhakami and Paul Slovic found that affect significantly influences the degree and direction of individual risk perceptions:

When the attitude [about an activity or technology] is favorable, the activity or technology being judged may be seen as having high benefit and low risk. On the other hand, when the item being evaluated is viewed unfavorably, with negative affect, it may be seen as having low benefit and high risk. Our general attitudes or affective states may thus "confound" the risk/benefit judgment.

Thus, individuals consistently fail to assess costs and benefits separately, as an analytic approach to decisionmaking would require, and instead seem to allow their overall impression of the risk to bias both judgments. In that manner, and consistent with the early findings of Slovic, Fischoff, and Lichtenstein, affect becomes a crucial determinant of individual risk perceptions.

As one can see, the manner in which individuals actually perceive and understand uncertainty departs significantly from the actuarial assessments of the scientist or the expected utility functions of the economist. We wish to emphasize that this does not necessarily mean that human understanding of risk is misguided or naive simply because it does not comport with the probabilistic understanding of risk. As Paul Slovic has eloquently put it, "risk does not exist 'out there,' independent of our minds and cultures, waiting to be measured. Human beings have invented the concept 'risk' to help them understand and cope with the dangers and uncertainties of life. There is no such thing as 'real risk' or 'objective risk.'" Instead, "real risk" and "objective risk" merely represent the central concepts of an alternative theory of how to perceive and comprehend uncertainty in the world, a theory that is necessarily laden with the subjective values and beliefs of the individuals who constructed and perpetuate it. Our point is simply that there is no reason, standing alone, to give primacy to probabilistic judgments of risk, especially when the overwhelming experience of individuals bears little or no relationship to strict probabilistic assessments.

2. Manipulability of Preferences

The preceding discussion should underscore the fact that we are far from flawless assessors of scientific and probabilistic judgments. Unlike the classical economic actor who "can perfectly process available information about alternative courses of action, and can rank possible outcomes in order of expected utility," human individuals display a startling ineptitude for comprehending causality and probability. We mistake familiarity with numerosity, we allow our predictions to be skewed by something as arbitrary and irrelevant as the spinning of a wheel, and we report that with a little more practice and concentration, we might do a better job at predicting coin tosses.

Apart from these biases, however, behavioralists have also identified numerous ways in which preferences—holding probability estimates constant—can vary by context. We offer descriptions of these biases to emphasize that the way in which humans think about and exert their preferences is complicated. Von Neumann and Morgenstern's elegantly simple conception of expected utility was just that: simple. Behavioral researchers have shown that we do not order our preferences according to simple maximization axioms, but rather our preferences are shaped at least in part by the manner in which they are elicited: "Alternative descriptions of the same choice problems lead to systematically different preferences; strategically equivalent elicitation procedures give rise to different choices; and the preference between x and y often depends on the choice set in which they are embedded." In this manner, for the past three decades, behavioral researchers have been offering a compelling criticism of expected utility theory; the time now has come to incorporate their findings into legal analysis so that we may have a fuller, more textured model of human decisionmaking.

a. The Status Quo Bias and Endowment Effect

There is what one economist has called "overwhelming evidence showing that humans are often more sensitive to how their current situation differs from some reference level than to the absolute characteristics of the situation." Put differently, individuals have a tendency to prefer the state of affairs which they perceive as the status quo rather than switching to an alternative state, other things being equal. That tendency is sometimes referred to as the *status quo bias*.

Russell Korobkin has demonstrated the status quo bias in an experiment involving the reaction of first year law students to a hypothetical contractual setting in which they were asked to advise a shipping company during negotiations with a commercial customer. By changing the applicable contract default rule between subjects, Korobkin found that "subjects exhibited *a large and statistically significant bias in favor of the term embedded in the default rule—the status quo term*." Thus, for example, subjects in one group were asked to recommend a per-package dollar amount (on a scale of one dollar to ten dollars) that the shipping company should pay to contract around a default rule of full consequential damages liability; subjects in a second group were asked to recommend an amount that the company should demand in order to accept full liability beyond a statutory default of limited liability. Subjects in the first group recommended paying a *maximum* of $4.46 to limit consequential damages liability, while subjects in the second group recommended a *minimum* asking price of $6.96 to accept full liability. Similarly, when faced with a choice between "pay your own fees" or "loser pays" attorney fee provisions, subjects overwhelmingly preferred whichever provision was designated as the state default rule, despite a clear admonition that, "if the parties wish to specify [otherwise] by contract . . . such a provision would be fully enforceable." These two findings, along with others provided by Korobkin, vividly demonstrate for legal scholars the manner in which the status quo bias affects how individuals register their preferences.

Many behavioral tendencies related to the status quo bias have been identified. For instance, when it comes to choosing between options that represent deviations from the status quo, people are substantially more averse to losses from some given reference point than they are attracted to same-sized gains. In addition to this *loss aversion*, behavioralists have also identified an *endowment effect*. Once an individual comes to possess an item, she instantaneously (or nearly so) values that item more than she did prior to possessing it. In one well-known study, for example, several scholars randomly allocated to subjects either a coffee mug or six dollars. Mug holders were then asked to state the minimum amount they would be willing to accept to sell their mugs, while cash holders were asked to state the maximum amount they would be willing to pay for a mug. Despite the fact that mugs were distributed randomly, mug holders as a group turned out to value mugs at approximately twice the amount that cash holders did. Scholars now attribute this peculiar behavior, which has been replicated in many studies, to the endowment effect: The initial allocation of mug ownership affected the value which subjects attached to mugs.

In a recent study by George Loewenstein and Daniel Adler, subjects were asked to "imagine that we gave you a mug exactly like the one you can see, and that we gave you the opportunity to keep it or trade it for some money." Minimal selling prices were then elicited from subjects both before and after they actually received mugs. This formulation of the now familiar mug study allowed Loewenstein and Adler to test the ability of subjects to predict the operation of the endowment effect. Prior to receiving the mugs, subjects on average predicted that their minimal selling price would be $3.73. Once they actually received the mugs, however, their minimal selling price averaged $5.40. Thus, subjects significantly and systematically underestimated the impact that the endowment effect would have on their valuations. As with so many of these biasing or preference-altering phenomena, even when people appreciate their effect, they underestimate their magnitude.

b. Context Effects and the Effect of Irrelevant Options

Behavioralists have identified a variety of ways in which the context of a choice influences the choice itself. For example, researchers have discovered that the addition of a new option to a set of options may increase the proportion of individuals who choose one of the initial options. This anomaly, an example of context effects, has been demonstrated by student subjects asked to train rats with electric shocks. In one trial, subjects could only select between "mild" and "slightly painful" shocks; in other trials, a third option was present, labeled either "moderately painful" or "extremely painful." Subjects were told not to use the more extreme option and none did; thus, the researchers were able to observe whether an individual's preference between A and B would change in the presence of an irrelevant alternative C. While the "slightly painful" option was selected only twenty-four percent of the time in the first trial, it was chosen twenty-eight percent of the time when "moderately painful" was also present and thirty-nine percent of the time when "extremely painful" was present. In another experiment designed to test this phenomenon, subjects were offered a choice of either six dollars or an attractive Cross pen, and only thirty-six percent chose the pen. However, when subjects were offered a three-way choice among the cash, the Cross pen, and an inferior pen, forty-six percent chose the Cross pen.

It is likely that context effects such as these originate from our view of ourselves as "lay scientists." As "lay scientists," we want "reasons" (or "theories" or "hypotheses") for our decisions or conduct. The reasons need not actually be good; they just need to be good enough. As Loewenstein writes:

> Most people experience their own actions as resulting from decisions . . . or at least as deliberate. However, it is questionable whether these introspections represent veridical reports of underlying decision processes, or ex post rationalizations of behavior. The limitation of verbal reports is well established. . . . Trained to view behavior as the result of attribute-based decisions . . . most people in Western culture will almost inevitably interpret their own behavior accordingly.

The point is that the addition of a new option can provide a "reason" that otherwise was not available for choosing one of the initial options. As such, the findings "suggest[] that a simple axiom of conventional economic theory—involving the irrelevance of added, unchosen alternatives—is wrong."

c. Elastic Justification

Christopher Hsee has recently uncovered another way in which people's preferences can be altered through decision-irrelevant factors. By focusing on differences in individuals' decisions when expected outcomes are expressed as an uncertain range of estimates (a condition that Hsee refers to as "elasticity") rather than a fixed point estimate, Hsee has found that individuals construct "reasons" to justify conclusions that they are already privately motivated to reach. Specifically, this process, which Hsee has termed elastic justification, refers to the tendency for individuals to use the fact that an option presents a range of outcomes as a justification for choosing among options in a way that, in the absence of elasticity, the individual would not find justifiable.

This bias may be best understood through an example:

> A salesman is asked by his company to take a trip to find as many buyers for a certain product as possible. He has a choice of two destination cities: He can find 60 buyers in one city and 40 in the other but the city with fewer buyers is more enjoyable.

As formulated, the decision should be clear: The salesman should travel to the first city because the number of buyers (the A factor) is a factor relevant to his task, while the enjoyability of the city (the B factor) is not. Hsee theorizes, and supports through empirical experiments, that if the decision is reformulated such that the first city will produce somewhere between thirty and ninety buyers, the salesman will be more likely to select the second, more enjoyable city. This is so regardless of the fact that the first city still presents an expected number of buyers equal to the first formulation of the decision, sixty.

The mental process at work in preference reversals such as these is simple:

> [E]lasticity in the A factor allows the decision maker to bias his or her view of the A values of the options in such a way that the B-superior option may seem not as inferior on the A factor as it originally is, and this biased view makes it more justifiable for the decision maker to choose the B-superior option.

In other words, the salesman will view the expected number of buyers in the less enjoyable city as being toward the low end of the range (say, thirty), thereby making it seem more justifiable to travel to the more enjoyable city. Conversely, if the first city still presented a fixed sixty buyers, but the second city presented a range of between ten and seventy buyers, the salesman would view the expected number of buyers in the second city as being toward the high end of the range (say, seventy). In that manner, regardless of which option is reformulated to have an elastic number of buyers, the salesman will find a way to "justify" selecting the option that is less attractive from the perspective of the only relevant criterion: the expected number of buyers.

This bias of decisionmaking parallels the mechanisms described earlier in connection with motivated reasoning. Both elastic justification and motivated reasoning capture ways in which individuals purport to "justify" or "reason through" their beliefs and decisions, when in actuality their initial impulses have biased the process all along.

d. Time-Variant Preferences

There is a great deal of evidence that, other things being equal, individuals will choose an activity that will deliver immediate benefits and delay any perceived costs. We prefer, in other words, immediate gratification and delayed dissatisfaction. But as this evidence suggests, there is a problem with that pair of preferences. Specifically, people's short-term willingness to delay rewards in exchange for higher returns in the future is often less than people's long-term willingness to delay those same rewards. For instance, most people say they would rather have a prize of a $100 check available immediately rather than a $200 certified check that could not be cashed for two years, but do not prefer a $100 check that could be cashed in six years to a $200 certified check that could be cashed in eight years, even though this is the same choice seen at six years greater delay.

In a recent experiment, Kris Kirby and Richard Herrnstein asked subjects to choose among a series of pairs of smaller, earlier rewards and larger, later rewards. In two experiments offering subjects actual monetary rewards, twenty-three of twenty-four subjects "consistently reversed their choices from the [smaller, earlier reward] to the [larger, later reward] as the delay to both rewards increased." When the moment of choice is relatively far away, we tend to give proper weight to the later consequence; however, when the moment of choice arrives, the smaller but earlier consequence overshadows the later one, causing an "impulsive" reversal of the original preference. In short, our willingness to delay gratification (or encounter risks) varies over time. Today we believe that we should stop smoking or diet tomorrow, but tomorrow we feel we should continue smoking or overeating, at least for another day.

In part because of that sort of intertemporal variation, economists have begun to model individuals as a collection of selves—"multiple selves"—each self with its own set of preferences. Scholars have employed the multiple-selves model to explain many sorts of common behavior that otherwise seem inexplicable within the conventional, single-self, rational-actor model. Greek mythology teaches us of Ulysses, who had himself tied to the mast in order to hear but withstand the song of the Sirens. Researchers today have identified many analogous self-commitment (sometimes called "pre-commitment" or "hands-tying") strategies that many of us employ in our daily lives, such as setting up automatic monthly transfers to investment accounts, entering alcohol treatment programs or diet clinics that restrict exit, or devising internal rules of conduct such as "only smoke outdoors." As with many of the other cognitive-biasing, preference-changing phenomena, individuals seem, at some level, to understand this source of preference shifting. Nevertheless they do not always fully appreciate the extent of deviation between the preference sets, and, in any case, cannot always manage to locate or create successful self-commitment (or pre-commitment) strategies.

e. Reciprocity and Attribution

Most economic models assume that preferences are defined solely over outcomes. But that assumption is clearly inaccurate. As reviewed above, for instance, choices are often determined in significant part by the extent or direction of deviation of the options from some reference point or by the presence or absence of certain options. In addition, there is considerable evidence indicating that preferences are also a function of an actor's perceived conduct or intentions to which a particular outcome is attributed. "The same people who are altruistic toward deserving people are often indifferent to the plight of undeserving people, and motivated to hurt those whom they believe to have misbehaved."

Put differently, there is considerable evidence to suggest that preferences are "reciprocal." Reciprocity norms manifest themselves in numerous ways, most of which seem relevant to the market context. For example, individuals are often more willing to cooperate with those actors they feel are behaving cooperatively or fairly. On the other hand, individuals will often refuse to cooperate with others who are being uncooperative. Moreover, individuals are often willing to sacrifice to hurt others who are being unfair. A consumer may refuse to buy a product sold by a monopolist at an "unfair" price, even if she hurts herself by foregoing the product.

These sorts of phenomena have been repeatedly demonstrated in experiments employing one or another version of what game theorists call "the ultimatum game." In the most basic version of the game (or experiment), two players are given a sum of money to split. One of the two players, known as the Proposer, decides how the sum should be split and announces that decision to the Responder, who is left with the option of either accepting or rejecting that split. If the Responder rejects the offer, neither of the two players gets any of the money, and the game is over. For most economic or game-theoretic models, which assume self-interest on the part of all actors, the outcome was extremely easy to predict: Proposers would split the sum (e.g., ten dollars) disproportionately such that the Responder would get a nominal amount (e.g., one penny) and the Proposer would get the rest. That is the prediction, but "instead, offers typically average about thirty to forty percent of the total, with a fifty-fifty split often the mode. Offers of less than twenty percent frequently are rejected." Self-interest clearly does not capture the complete psychological picture of findings such as these.

In a related manner, people tend to care about whether an injurer's act was intentional or volitional or whether, instead, the injury was, in some sense, unpreventable. Thus, where the injurer's act is *volitional*, the victim is far more likely to reciprocate or retaliate with negative actions. To get some sense of how this sort of reaction might play a role in bargaining or market relationships, consider a recent ultimatum-game experiment conducted by Sally Blount, in which she asked three groups of subjects to state their willingness to accept take-it-or-leave-it offers made by anonymous parties regarding how to split ten dollars. The first group was told that the offer was coming from anonymous students and that their response would affect the division between them and the anonymous students. The second group was told that a third party would determine the offer and that the third party would not be affected by their response. The final group was told that the offer would be produced randomly by computer. In one study, subjects accepted average minimal offers of $2.91, $2.08, and $1.20, respectively. Thus, subjects were more willing to accept low offers when those offers were not perceived as the result of volition by the person who would be hurt by rejecting the offer.

f. Preference-Trumping Effect of Visceral Factors

While many of the cognitive biases discussed in the behavioral literature address ways in which people incorrectly perceive their self-interest, George Loewenstein has recently offered a compelling theory which seeks to account for cases in which people correctly perceive their self-interest, yet still behave in contradiction to that interest. He argues that disjunctions between behavior and perceived self-interest result from visceral factors such as the feelings associated with drug addiction, drive states like hunger, thirst and sexual desire, moods and emotions, and physical pain. "At sufficient levels of intensity, these, and most other visceral factors, cause people to behave contrary to their own long-term self-interest, often with full awareness that they are doing so."

The most obvious example of such self-destructive behavior can be seen in the actions of drug addicts, who often consume drugs to the exclusion of nourishment, sleep, and even the desire to survive. The visceral factor—drug addiction—causes the impacted individual to narrow her focus almost exclusively to the object of that factor, drugs. In a similar manner, visceral factors can cause the individual to experience "a good-specific collapsing of one's time-perspective toward the present." Thus, a hungry person is likely to make short-sighted tradeoffs between food now and food delayed, even if that person knows that tomorrow's hunger will be equally intense. Loewenstein explains such behavior by identifying two central premises of the visceral factor theory. First, visceral factors that are experienced now tend to dominate one's attention, crowding out all goals other than satiating the drive behind the visceral factor. Second, visceral factors that will be experienced in the future, have been experienced in the past, or are experienced by other people tend to be discounted by individuals; that is, individuals fail to predict, recall, or perceive in others the force of visceral factors correctly.

Together, these two factors form the basis for a new account of *impulsivity*. Rather than simply being prone to hyperbolic discount functions, as some commentators have argued, individuals might be suffering the "effect of visceral factors on the desirability of immediate consumption." That is, the impact of visceral factors such as hunger might cause individuals both to overestimate the desirability of immediate consumption and underestimate the desirability of delayed consumption. As a result, they will behave impulsively. The advantage of this account of impulsivity is that it predicts for which goods and in which situations individuals will be most likely to behave impulsively (i.e., when visceral factors such as hunger, thirst, physical pain, or emotions are strong).

Additionally, the visceral factors theory is able to account for "one of the most difficult patterns of behavior to subsume under a conventional rational choice framework[:] . . . the phenomenon of intrapersonal conflict and self-control." While other theorists have attempted to account for such human behavior according to the "multiple selves" models described above, Loewenstein describes the behavior in terms of visceral factors. The experience of being "out of control" is attributable to the effect of visceral factors. Because those factors overwhelm an individual's self-interest, of which that individual is fully aware, one experiences the event as if another self were in control of the behavior. For Loewenstein, this represents a more plausible account of the widely recognized sense of intrapersonal conflict that individuals often feel: "The fact that impulsive selves never promote one-another's behavior is not surprising if these selves are not, in fact, coherent entities with consciousness and personal motives, but instead represent the motivational impact of visceral factors."

Loewenstein's account of visceral factors provides an important insight heretofore absent from the behavioral account of human behavior: "Much behavior is nonvolitional or only partly volitional—*even in situations characterized by substantial deliberation.*" Moreover, individuals may experience irrationality, not just in the sense of violating axioms of rational decisionmaking, but also in the sense of engaging in "impulsive and self-destructive behavior and . . . actions that violate generally accepted norms about the relative importance of different goals."

g. Framing Effects

We have already introduced the concept of framing effects through Kahneman and Tversky's famous vaccine example at the outset of this Section. We revisit it briefly here, however, to emphasize that framing effects are somewhat different from the other cognitive anomalies that have been identified by behavioral researchers. They are perhaps the most obviously exploitable of the biases, capable, for instance, of causing dramatic preference reversals based on an entirely nonsubstantive shift in terminology. And that is true inasmuch as they trigger or reflect the operation of other cognitive biases. For instance, Kahneman and Tversky's vaccine example relies not only on the operation of framing effects, but also on loss aversion in order to elicit its contradictory results. Whether something is coded as a loss, thus raising the possibility of loss aversion, depends on how it is framed. In this respect, one may usefully conceive of framing effects as a mechanism for eliciting other cognitive biases—in other words, a mechanism for manipulating individual perceptions and decisions.

Consider, for instance, a recent study of how framing affects the allocation decisions of university staff employees between two retirement savings funds with different risk-return attributes: bonds (the safe fund) and stocks (the risky fund). Although the employees were shown actual historical data on the returns of the two funds, the data were framed in two different ways: One group of employees was shown the distribution of one-year rates of return, while the second was shown a simulated distribution of thirty-year rates of return. Employees shown the thirty-year returns chose to invest almost all of their savings in stocks, while those shown the one-year returns invested a majority of their funds in bonds. As Jolls, Sunstein, and Thaler explain, this result highlights the fact that "the way firms decide to describe and display information . . . will have a powerful influence on the choices" of those who receive the information. In other words, because firms are in a position to frame the choice, they can alter the decision.

The cognitive influence of framing effects has been demonstrated in numerous other studies, including at least one in which both sets of options were given to the same group of subjects (rather than to separate groups of subjects). Not only did the subjects continue to demonstrate the inconsistency, many persisted in their beliefs even after the logical incompatibility of their selections was pointed out to them. Throughout these studies, subjects have shown a remarkable proclivity to exhibit different preferences based solely on the manner in which the options are presented. As Kahneman and Tversky have commented, the significance of framing "is both pervasive and robust . . . [and] as common among sophisticated respondents as among naive ones. . . . In their stubborn appeal, framing effects resemble perceptual illusions more than computational errors." We believe that framing effects provide particularly strong evidence in support of the basic thesis of this Article—that the numerous biases to which people are subject can be tapped into by those who set the frame. This follows from our "tendency to accept problem formulations as they are given . . . [to] remain, so to speak, mental prisoners of the frame provided to us by the experimentalist, or by the 'expert,' or by a certain situation."

   . . .

COMMENTS AND QUESTIONS

1. Can you now explain the results of the marriage-license applicant study described in the introduction to this article?

2. What implications, if any, does the evidence presented in the preceding article have for regulatory strategies that rely on information provision? Consider these skeptical responses: (a) Regulators must work with people as they are. "Imperfections" in information processing are inevitable, but well-designed information-provision strategies can take those imperfections into account. (Or, even more skeptically, because the imperfections are inevitable, those designing information-provision strategies need not worry much about them.) (b) At least where large numbers of people experience the same underlying events (including receipt of information) repeatedly, the imperfections "wash out," and the overall social result—the amount of risk produced—will match the experts' judgments about what outcomes are socially optimal.

3. Howard Latin, *"Good" Warnings, Bad Products, and Cognitive Limitations*, 41 UCLA L. Rev. 1193 (1994), discusses possible tensions between explicit information provision and the information consumers and workers can gain from experience with products and on the job. He argues that the relative effectiveness of experience and mandated disclosures is a function of specific contexts, and that in many contexts collectively mandated disclosures are ineffective.

> Most product uses entail small probabilities of harm, which means the great majority of experiences will be safe ones. People who generalize from their own experiences may treat this limited sample as "representative" of overall product risks and therefore anticipate continued safety. . . .
>
>   . . . When consumers use particular products without injury, the "input" in their assessment of product safety—these safe experiences—will lead to an expected "outcome" of continued safety. Because safe use is the norm and harm the rare exception, the "input" will appear very consistent in most product-use contexts and consumers may therefore be unduly confident that products will continue to perform safely.
>
>   Even if consumers do not generalize from their limited experiences, they may treat advertising and promotional claims as representative of a product's virtues without recognizing the doubtful reliability of the manufacturer's assertions. Manufacturers are much more likely to advertise goods as safe than to emphasize their dangers, which suggests that people who take product ads as representative of actual product attributes may underestimate the risks. . . .

. . .

. . . [E]ven for relatively risky products, harm will be an unusual occurrence. Consumers may overvalue the harm when it does happen, but safe usage will be far more typical and hence more available in most product-use contexts. It is true that people may overestimate the risks of airplane travel in the aftermath of a plane crash and may exaggerate the danger posed by activities such as nuclear energy and toxic waste dumping that are often the subjects of unfavorable publicity. Yet, the vast majority of common product risks—adverse reactions to cosmetics and drugs, falls from ladders, injuries from power tools and lawn-mowers, electrocution from hair dryers or other common appliances—are seldom publicized nor intrinsically vivid. Most uncommon hazards are even less likely to be available because by definition they rarely produce notable injuries. When a product-related injury occurs and is widely publicized, people may temporarily overestimate the particular hazard; yet, the salience of that product risk will recede as other types of accidents and other issues attract public attention. Vivid risks seldom remain immutably vivid and available because newly publicized hazards gradually supplant old ones.

No balanced discussion of the availability heuristic should omit recognition that availability is limited and usually transitory, nor that safe experiences with virtually all products are far more frequent than injuries. Once these facts are acknowledged, it should be clear that the great majority of product risks cannot be available to product users. Because people seldom think about unavailable risks, the effect is precisely the same as if they were unduly optimistic about those product hazards. . . .

. . .

Cognitive dissonance leads people to reject or underemphasize information inconsistent with their beliefs and actions. Consumers must evaluate many products with both positive and negative attributes: A Corvette, for example, may be fast and stylish but also dangerous and costly. If people are attracted by attributes such as style or power, dissonance may lead them to undervalue safety considerations. If someone has enjoyed ownership of a particular sports car in the past, he may suppress information that current models are dangerous. If a home buyer finds one neighborhood attractive or has lived there peacefully in the past, she may discount a statistically high crime rate. People seldom make decisions as *tabulae rasae* and any prior beliefs or conflicting impulses may lead to cognitive dissonance affecting their selections of products.

Cognitive dissonance may be a particularly serious problem in the context of user responses to product warnings. In many instances, such as when package inserts and instruction manuals accompany products, people cannot read warnings and directions until *after* they have purchased the good. At this point, careful attention to material warnings may render the product less useful than the buyer anticipated. Cognitive dissonance can lead users to minimize the significance of product hazards discovered after purchase.

When consumers have positive views of their own abilities, cognitive dissonance may induce them to discount the possibility of unintentional mistakes. Many accidents are caused by momentary inattention, improper reactions under stress, or inadvertent carelessness; yet, consumers may seldom acknowledge that they are just as prone to these forms of imperfect behavior as other people would be. To do so would be to impugn their own sense of personal competence. Thus, dissonance leads to underestimation of the risks associated with inattention and carelessness. This problem arises when consumers initially search for product attributes and also in their subsequent decisions on whether to comply with warnings that decrease the product's perceived utility.

. . .

. . . Kahneman and Tversky noted that "people greatly undervalue a reduction in the probability of a hazard in comparison to the complete elimination of that hazard." Because warnings and instructions can seldom eliminate all product risks and because most people are risk seeking in the domain of losses, users may underestimate the utility of complying with partial risk-reduction measures recommended in warnings. . . .

An important conclusion of prospect theory is that consumer responses to risk information can be deliberately or unintentionally manipulated by the ways in which manufacturers and other actors with superior information frame their disclosures. The distortions associated with framing effects, as when choices are expressed as "lives saved" or "lives lost," may be compounded by attitudes of risk aversion or risk seeking in response to the frame presented in the warning. Yet, . . . virtually any probabilistic outcome can be expressed as either a potential gain or a potential loss.

. . .

Can these observations—if accurate—be translated into the context of workplace risks? Risks of environmental harm?

4. Can cognitive imperfections be overcome by educating people about them? There is a substantial body of psychological research on this question. The answer, in short, appears to be: Some, but not a lot.

Russell Korobkin and Chris Guthrie, *Psychology, Economics, and Settlement: A New Look at the Role of the Lawyer*, 76 Tex. L. Rev. 77 (1997), report an experiment of this sort focused on the legal system. They gave their subjects—college students—various litigation-related scenarios and examined "settlement" rates. The subjects were told that their lawyers provided some additional information beyond that contained in the scenarios. This additional information was of four types:

(a) "The Psychology Lesson": The subjects were told that "your attorney has advised you to be aware of a psychological tendency that many people exhibit when making settlement decisions. When choosing between options that appear to represent a financial loss, people are much more likely to gamble than they are in other circumstances." An example was given.

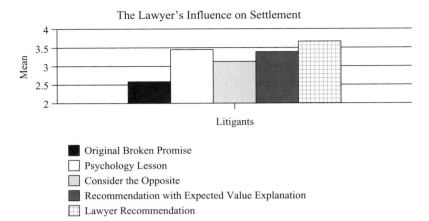

The Lawyer's Influence on Settlement

Mean

Litigants

- ■ Original Broken Promise
- □ Psychology Lesson
- ▢ Consider the Opposite
- ■ Recommendation with Expected Value Explanation
- ▦ Lawyer Recommendation

Figure 4. The broken heater.

(b) "Consider the Opposite": Here the subjects were told that "your attorney has advised you to think carefully about your decision, pointing out both the negative and positive aspects of the settlement offer." These aspects were specifically identified.

(c) "Recommendation with Expected Value Explanation": The subjects were told that the lawyer recommended accepting the settlement with an explanation that the expected value of going to trial, taking the risk of losing into account, was less than the settlement offer.

(d) "Lawyer Recommendation": The subjects were told only that the lawyer "has recommended that you accept the offer."

As the table above indicates, all the interventions increased the likelihood of settlement. The fourth had the largest effect; the psychology lesson and the expected value explanation had effects of roughly equal size.

5. Government-mandated information disclosure has, in recent years, confronted constitutional challenges based on the First Amendment's guarantee of freedom of expression. The next section examines those challenges.

◾ The First Amendment and Information-Based Regulation

Because of the confluence of two recent doctrinal streams, government-mandated disclosures today raise First Amendment problems. First, the Supreme Court has held that the First Amendment guarantees not only the right to speak but also a right *not* to speak.[a] Second, rejecting earlier holdings that

---

[a] *See, e.g., West Virginia State Board of Education v. Barnette*, 319 U.S. 624 (1943) (holding unconstitutional a state law requiring all children in public schools to salute and pledge allegiance to the United States flag); *Wooley v. Maynard*, 430 U.S. 705 (1977) (holding unconstitutional a state statute requiring that all motorists leave unobstructed the state motto, "Live Free or Die," on their cars' license plates).

commercial speech was wholly unprotected by the First Amendment, see, for example, *Valentine v. Chrestensen*, 316 U.S. 52 (1942), the Supreme Court has held that commercial speech is entitled to some degree of constitutional protection. As of 2005, the Court had uneasily settled on a standard generally regarded as a form of "intermediate scrutiny," articulated first in *Central Hudson Gas Co. v. Public Service Comm'n*, 447 U.S. 557 (1980). The standard has four parts: the commercial speech "must concern lawful activity and not be misleading"; the regulation must serve a "substantial" government interest; the regulation must do so "directly"; and "if the government interest could be served as well by a more limited restriction on commercial speech, the excessive restrictions cannot survive."

Several justices have argued for a stricter test for permitting government regulation of commercial speech. These justices have raised concern that government regulation of speech typically rests on paternalistic judgments to the effect that consumers cannot be trusted to adequately process information (typically, advertising). See, for example, *Virginia State Board of Pharmacy v. Virginia Citizens Consumer Council*, 425 U.S. 748, 769 (1976) ("There is, of course, an alternative to this highly paternalistic approach. That alternative is to assume that this information is not in itself harmful, that people will perceive their own best interests if only they are well enough informed, and that the best means to that end is to open the channels of communication rather than to close them."). Consider whether this concern is applicable as well to government-mandated information disclosures, which might be said to rest on the paternalistic judgment that individuals do not know what information they need to make the decisions that are best for them.

In reading the case that follows, consider as well whether the First Amendment has replaced the Due Process Clause as the constitutional basis for objections to government regulation—that is, whether the First Amendment claims in these cases should be understood as revivals of the theory underlying *Lochner v. New York* (chapter 1).

■ International Dairy Foods Association v. Amestoy
92 F.3d 67 (2d Cir. 1996)

Altimari, Circuit Judge:

... The [appellant] dairy manufacturers challenged the constitutionality of Vt. Stat. Ann. tit. 6, § 2754(c), which requires dairy manufacturers to identify products which were, or might have been, derived from dairy cows treated with a synthetic growth hormone used to increase milk production. The dairy manufacturers alleged that the statute violated the United States Constitution's First Amendment. ...

Because we find that the district court abused its discretion in failing to grant preliminary injunctive relief to the dairy manufacturers on First Amendment grounds, we reverse and remand.

...

In 1993, the federal Food and Drug Administration ("FDA") approved the use of recombinant Bovine Somatotropin ("rBST") (also known as recombinant Bovine Growth Hormone ("rGBH")), a synthetic growth hormone that increases milk production by cows. It is undisputed that the dairy products derived from herds treated with rBST are indistinguishable from products derived from untreated herds; consequently, the FDA declined to require the labeling of products derived from cows receiving the supplemental hormone.

In April 1994, defendant-appellee the State of Vermont ("Vermont") enacted a statute requiring that "if rBST has been used in the production of milk or a milk product for retail sale in this state, the retail milk or milk product shall be labeled as such." Vt. Stat. Ann. tit. 6, § 2754(c). The State of Vermont's Commissioner of Agriculture ("Commissioner") subsequently promulgated regulations giving those dairy manufacturers who use rBST four labeling options, among them the posting of a sign to the following effect in any store selling dairy products:

> rBST INFORMATION: THE PRODUCTS IN THIS CASE THAT CONTAIN OR MAY CONTAIN MILK FROM rBST-TREATED COWS EITHER (1) STATE ON THE PACKAGE THAT rBST HAS BEEN OR MAY HAVE BEEN USED, OR (2) ARE IDENTIFIED BY A BLUE SHELF LABEL LIKE THIS [BLUE RECTANGLE] OR (3) A BLUE STICKER ON THE PACKAGE LIKE THIS. [BLUE DOT]
>
> The United States Food and Drug Administration has determined that there is no significant difference between milk from treated and untreated cows. It is the law of Vermont that products made from the milk of rBST-treated cows be labeled to help consumers make informed shopping decisions.

> . . .

Generally, preliminary injunctive relief is appropriate when the movant shows "(a) irreparable harm and (b) either (1) likelihood of success on the merits or (2) sufficiently serious questions going to the merits to make them a fair ground for litigation and a balance of hardships tipping decidedly toward the party requesting the preliminary relief." However, because the injunction at issue stays "government action taken in the public interest pursuant to a statutory . . . scheme," this Court has determined that the movant must satisfy the more rigorous "likelihood of success prong."

. . .

1. Irreparable Harm

Focusing principally on the economic impact of the labeling regulation, the district court found that appellants had not demonstrated irreparable harm to any right protected by the First Amendment. We disagree.

Irreparable harm is "injury for which a monetary award cannot be adequate compensation." See *Jackson Dairy, Inc.*, 596 F.2d at 72. It is established that "the loss of First Amendment freedoms, for even minimal periods of time, unquestionably constitutes irreparable injury." *Elrod v. Burns*, 427 U.S. 347, 373 (1976). . . . Because the statute at issue requires appellants to make an involuntary statement whenever they offer their products for sale, we find that the statute causes the dairy manufacturers irreparable harm.

. . .

. . . The wrong done by the labeling law to the dairy manufacturers' constitutional right not to speak is a serious one that was not given proper weight by the district court. See *Wooley v. Maynard*, 430 U.S. 705, 714 (1977) ("We begin with the proposition that the right of freedom of thought protected by the First Amendment against state action includes both the right to speak freely and the right to refrain from speaking at all."); *West Virginia State Bd. of Ed. v. Barnette,* 319 U.S. 624, 633 (1943) ("involuntary affirmation could be commanded only on even more immediate and urgent grounds than silence").

The right not to speak inheres in political and commercial speech alike, see *Zauderer v. Office of Disciplinary Counsel,* 471 U.S. 626, 651 (1985), and extends to statements of fact as well as statements of opinion, see *Riley v. National Federation of the Blind,* 487 U.S. 781, 797-98 (1988). If, however, as Vermont maintains, its labeling law compels appellants to engage in purely commercial speech, the statute must meet a less rigorous test. See *Central Hudson Gas & Elec. Corp. v. Public Serv. Comm'r,* 447 U.S. 557, 562-63 (1980) ("The Constitution . . . accords a lesser protection to commercial speech than to other constitutionally guaranteed expression."). The dairy manufacturers insist that the speech is not purely commercial because it compels them "to convey a message regarding the significance of rBST use that is 'expressly contrary to' their views." . . .

. . . [E]ven assuming that the compelled disclosure is purely commercial speech, appellants have amply demonstrated that the First Amendment is sufficiently implicated to cause irreparable harm. The dairy manufacturers have clearly done more than simply "assert" their First Amendment rights: The statute in question indisputably requires them to speak when they would rather not. Because compelled speech "contravenes core First Amendment values," appellants have "satisfied the initial requirement for securing injunctive relief."

. . .

2. Likelihood of Success on the Merits

. . .

In *Central Hudson*, the Supreme Court articulated a four-part analysis for determining whether a government restriction on commercial speech is permissible. We need not address the controversy concerning the nature of the speech in question—commercial or political—because we find that Vermont fails to meet the less stringent constitutional requirements applicable to compelled commercial speech.

. . .

In our view, Vermont has failed to establish the second prong of the *Central Hudson* test, namely that its interest is substantial. . . . Vermont "does not claim that health or safety concerns prompted the passage of the Vermont Labeling Law," but instead defends the statute on the basis of "strong consumer interest and the public's 'right to know'. . . ." These interests are insufficient to justify compromising protected constitutional rights.[1]

---

[1] Although the dissent suggests several interests that if adopted by the state of Vermont may have been substantial, the district court opinion makes clear that Vermont adopted no such rationales for its statute. Rather, Vermont's sole expressed interest was, indeed, "consumer curiosity." The district court plainly stated that, "Vermont takes no position on whether rBST is beneficial or detrimental. However," the district court explained, "Vermont has determined that its consumers want to know whether rBST has been used in the production of their milk and milk products." It is clear from the opinion below that the state itself has not adopted the concerns of the consumers; it has only adopted that the consumers are concerned. Unfortunately, mere consumer concern is not, in itself, a substantial interest.

Vermont's failure to defend its constitutional intrusion on the ground that it negatively impacts public health is easily understood. After exhaustive studies, the FDA has "concluded that rBST has no appreciable effect on the composition of milk produced by treated cows, and that there are no human safety or health concerns associated with food products derived from cows treated with rBST." Because bovine somatotropin ("BST") appears naturally in cows, and because there are no BST receptors in a cow's mammary glands, only trace amounts of BST can be detected in milk, whether or not the cows received the supplement. Moreover, it is undisputed that neither consumers nor scientists can distinguish rBST-derived milk from milk produced by an untreated cow. Indeed, the already extensive record in this case contains no scientific evidence from which an objective observer could conclude that rBST has any impact at all on dairy products. It is thus plain that Vermont could not justify the statute on the basis of "real" harms.

We do not doubt that Vermont's asserted interest, the demand of its citizenry for such information, is genuine; reluctantly, however, we conclude that it is inadequate. We are aware of no case in which consumer interest alone was sufficient to justify requiring a product's manufacturers to publish the functional equivalent of a warning about a production method that has no discernable impact on a final product. See, e.g., *Ibanez [v. Florida Dep't of Business and Professional Regulation*, 512 U.S. 136, 146 (1994)]* (invalidating state requirement that Certified Financial Planner ("CFP") disclose in advertisement that CFP status was conferred by unofficial private organization despite unsubstantiated claim that public might otherwise be misled by CFP's advertisement).

Although the Court is sympathetic to the Vermont consumers who wish to know which products may derive from rBST-treated herds, their desire is insufficient to permit the State of Vermont to compel the dairy manufacturers to speak against their will. Were consumer interest alone sufficient, there is no end to the information that states could require manufacturers to disclose about their production methods. For instance, with respect to cattle, consumers might reasonably evince an interest in knowing which grains herds were fed, with which medicines they were treated, or the age at which they were slaughtered. Absent, however, some indication that this information bears on a reasonable concern for human health or safety or some other sufficiently substantial governmental concern, the manufacturers cannot be compelled to disclose it. Instead, those consumers interested in such information should exercise the power of their purses by buying products from manufacturers who voluntarily reveal it.

Accordingly, we hold that consumer curiosity alone is not a strong enough state interest to sustain the compulsion of even an accurate, factual statement, in a commercial context. See, e.g., *United States v. Sullivan*, 332 U.S. 689, 693 (1948) (upholding federal law requiring warning labels on "harmful foods, drugs and cosmetics"); see also *Zauderer*, 471 U.S. at 651 (disclosure requirements are permissible "as long as [they] are reasonably related to the State's interest in preventing deception of consumers."); *In re R.M.J.*, 455 U.S. 191, 201 (1982) ("warnings or disclaimers might be appropriately required . . . in order to dissipate the possibility of consumer confusion or deception."); *Bates v. State Bar of Arizona*, 433 U.S. 350, 384 (1977) (state bar association could not ban advertising that was neither misleading nor deceptive); *Virginia State Bd. of Pharmacy v. Virginia Citizens Consumer Council, Inc.*, 425 U.S. 748, 771-72 (1975) (regulation aimed at preventing deceptive or misleading commercial speech would be permissible). Because Vermont has demonstrated no cognizable harms, its statute is likely to be held unconstitutional.

Conclusion

Because appellants have demonstrated both irreparable harm and a likelihood of success on the merits, the judgment of the district court is reversed, and the case is remanded for entry of an appropriate injunction.

Leval, Circuit Judge, dissenting:

I respectfully dissent. Vermont's regulation requiring disclosure of use of rBST in milk production was based on substantial state interests, including worries about rBST's impact on human and cow health, fears for the survival of small dairy farms, and concerns about the manipulation of nature through biotechnology. The objective of the plaintiff milk producers is to conceal their use of rBST from consumers. The policy of the First Amendment, in its application to commercial speech, is to favor the flow of accurate, relevant information. The majority's invocation of the First Amendment to invalidate a state law requiring disclosure of information consumers reasonably desire stands the Amendment on its ear. In my view, the district court correctly found that plaintiffs were unlikely to succeed in proving Vermont's law unconstitutional.

. . .

Recent advances in genetic technologies led to the development of a synthetically isolated metabolic protein hormone known as recombinant bovine somatotropin (rBST), which, when injected into cows, increases their milk production. Monsanto Company, an amicus in this action on the side of the plaintiff milk producers, has developed the only commercially approved form of rBST and markets it under the brand name "Posilac." This is, of course, at the frontiers of bioscience. A 1994 federal government study of rBST describes it as "one of the first major commercial biotechnology products to be used in the U.S. food and agricultural sector and the first to attract significant attention." Executive Branch of the Federal Government, Use of Bovine Somatotropin (BST) in the United States: Its Potential Effects (January 1994) [hereafter "Federal Study"], at 58.

The United States Food and Drug Administration ("FDA") and others have studied rBST extensively. Based on its study, the FDA authorized commercial use of rBST on November 5, 1993, concluding that "milk and meat from [rBST-treated] cows is safe" for human consumption.

The impending use of rBST caused substantial controversy throughout the country. The Federal Study reports, based on numerous surveys, that consumers favor the labeling of milk produced by use of rBST. In Vermont, a state highly attuned to issues affecting the dairy industry, use of rBST was the subject of frequent press commentary and debate, and provoked considerable opposition. In response to public pressure, the state of Vermont enacted a law requiring that "if rBST has been used in the production of milk or a milk product for retail sale in this state, the retail milk or milk product shall be labeled as such." 6 V.S.A. § 2754(c). . . .

The interests which Vermont sought to advance by its statute and regulations were explained in the Agriculture Department's Economic Impact Statement accompanying its regulations. The Statement reported that consumer interest in disclosure of use of rBST was based on "concerns about FDA determinations about the product as regards health and safety or about recombinant gene technology"; concerns "about the effect of the product on bovine health"; and "concerns about the effect of the product on the existing surplus of milk and in the dairy farm industry's economic status and well-being." This finding was based on "consumer comments to Vermont legislative committees" and to the Department, as well as published reports and letters to the editors published in the press.

The state offered survey evidence which demonstrated similar public concern. Comments by Vermont citizens who had heard or read about rBST were overwhelmingly negative. The most prevalent responses to rBST use included: "Not natural," "More research needs to be done/Long-term effects not clear," "Against additives added to my milk," "Worried about adverse health effects," "Unhealthy for the cow," "Don't need more chemicals," "It's a hormone/Against hormones added to my milk," "Hurts the small dairy farmer," "Producing enough milk already."

On the basis of this evidence the district court found that a majority of Vermonters "do not want to purchase milk products derived from rBST-treated cows," *International Dairy Farmers Ass'n v. Amestoy*, 898 F. Supp. 246, 250 (D. Vt. 1995) (hereafter "IDFA"), and that the reasons included:

(1) They consider the use of a genetically-engineered hormone in the production unnatural; (2) they believe that use of the hormone will result in increased milk production and lower milk prices, thereby hurting small dairy farmers; (3) they believe that the use of rBST is harmful to cows and potentially harmful to humans; and, (4) they feel that there is a lack of knowledge regarding the long-term effects of rBST.

The court thus understandably concluded that "Vermont has a substantial interest in informing consumers of the use of rBST in the production of milk and dairy products sold in the state."

. . .

In the face of this evidence and these explicit findings by the district court, the majority oddly concludes that Vermont's sole interest in requiring disclosure of rBST use is to gratify "consumer curiosity," and that this alone "is not a strong enough state interest to sustain the compulsion of even an accurate factual statement." The majority seeks to justify its conclusion in three ways.

First, it simply disregards the evidence of Vermont's true interests and the district court's findings recognizing those interests. Nowhere does the majority opinion discuss or even mention the evidence or findings regarding the people of Vermont's concerns about human health, cow health, biotechnology, and the survival of small dairy farms.

Second, the majority distorts the meaning of the district court opinion. It relies substantially on Judge Murtha's statement that Vermont "does not claim that health or safety concerns prompted the passage of the Vermont Labeling Law," but "bases its justification...on strong consumer interest and the public's 'right to know.'" The majority takes this passage out of context. The district court's opinion went on, as quoted above, to explain the concerns that underlie the interest of Vermont's citizenry. Unquestionably the district court found, and the evidence showed, that the interests of the citizenry that led to the passage of the law include health and safety concerns, among others. In the light of the district judge's further explicit findings, it is clear that his statement could not mean what the majority concludes.[2] More likely, what Judge Murtha meant was that Vermont does not claim to know whether rBST is harmful. And when he asserted that Vermont's rule was passed to vindicate "strong consumer interest and the public's right to know," this could not mean that the public's interest was based on nothing but "curiosity," because the judge expressly found that the consumer interest was based on health, economic, and ethical concerns.

Third, the majority suggests that, because the FDA has not found health risks in this new procedure, health worries could not be considered "real" or "cognizable."

I find this proposition alarming and dangerous; at the very least, it is extraordinarily unrealistic. Genetic and biotechnological manipulation of basic food products is new and controversial. Although I have no reason to doubt that the FDA's studies of rBST have been thorough, they could not cover long-term effects of rBST on humans.[3] Furthermore, there are many possible reasons why a government agency might fail to find real health risks, including inadequate time and budget for testing, insufficient advancement of scientific techniques, insufficiently large sampling populations, pressures from industry, and simple human error. To suggest that a government agency's failure to find a health risk in a short-term study of a new genetic technology should bar a state from requiring simple disclosure of the use of that technology where its citizens are concerned about such health risks would be unreasonable and dangerous. Although the FDA's conclusions may be reassuring, they do not guarantee the safety of rBST.

Forty years ago, when I (and nearly everyone) smoked, no one told us that we might be endangering our health. Tobacco is but one of many consumer products once considered safe, which were subsequently found to cause health hazards. The limitations of scientific information about new consumer products were well illustrated in a 1990 study produced at the request of Congress by the General

------

[2] Indeed had the judge really intended such a finding, it would be unsupportable in view of the evidence that the concerns of the citizenry were communicated to the legislature. When the citizens of a state express concerns to the legislature and the state's lawmaking bodies then pass disclosure requirements in response to those expressed concerns, it seems clear (without need for a statutory declaration of purpose) that the state is acting to vindicate the concerns expressed by its citizens, and not merely to gratify their "curiosity." Vermont need not, furthermore, take the position that rBST is harmful to require its disclosure because of potential health risks. The mere fact that it does not know whether rBST poses hazards is sufficient reason to justify disclosure by reason of the unknown potential for harm.

[3] One of Vermont's experts, a specialist in medical information and the review of scientific literature, stated in an affidavit:

> It is not reasonable to conclude that there is uniform agreement that milk from rBST treated cows is 100% safe for human consumption. . . . Longitudinal studies have been called for to establish the long-term health effects of the use of rBST on cows, and until the results of these studies are published, disagreement on the effects of rBST will likely continue. . . . Milk from rBST treated cows is generally considered safe by the Food and Drug Administration and some scientists, while the General Accounting Office and other scientists feel that more research is needed before a universal agreement can be reached.

> Affidavit of Dr. Julie McGowan, at 26–27

Accounting Office. Looking at various prescription drugs available on the market, the study examined the risks associated with the drugs that became known only after they were approved by the FDA, and concluded:

> Even after approval, many additional risks may surface when the general population is exposed to a drug. These risks, which range from relatively minor (such as nausea and headache) to serious (such as hospitalization and death) arise from the fact that preapproval drug testing is inherently limited. . . .
>
> In studying the frequency and seriousness of risks identified after approval, GAO found that of the 198 drugs approved by FDA between 1976 and 1985 for which data were available, 102 (or 51.5 percent) had serious postapproval risks, as evidenced by labeling changes or withdrawal from the market. All but six of these drugs . . . are deemed by FDA to have benefits that outweigh their risks. The serious postapproval risks are adverse reactions that could lead to hospitalization . . . severe or permanent disability, or death.
>
> GAO Report, "FDA Drug Review: Postapproval
Risks, 1976–85," April 1990, at 2–3

As startling as its results may seem, this study merely confirms a common sense proposition: namely, that a government agency's conclusion regarding a product's safety, reached after limited study, is not a guarantee and does not invalidate public concern for unknown side effects.

In short, the majority has no valid basis for its conclusion that Vermont's regulation advances no interest other than the gratification of consumer curiosity, and involves neither health concerns nor other substantial interests. . . .

Freedom of speech is not an absolute right, particularly in the commercial context. . . . [G]overnment's power to regulate commercial speech includes the power to compel such speech. *Zauderer v. Office of Disciplinary Counsel*, 471 U.S. 626, 651 (1985) (upholding state law requiring attorneys who advertised contingent fee services to disclose specific details about how contingent fee would be calculated and to state that certain costs might be borne by the client even in the event of loss).

Except for its conclusion that Vermont had no substantial interest to support its labeling law, the majority finds no fault with the district court's application of these governing standards. Nor do I. Accordingly, the sole issue is whether Vermont had a substantial interest in compelling the disclosure of use of rBST in milk production.

In my view, Vermont's multifaceted interest, outlined above, is altogether substantial. Consumer worries about possible adverse health effects from consumption of rBST, especially over a long term, is unquestionably a substantial interest. As to health risks to cows, the concern is supported by the warning label on Posilac, which states that cows injected with the product are at an increased risk for: various reproductive disorders, "clinical mastitis [udder infections] (visibly abnormal milk)," "digestive disorders such as indigestion, bloat, and diarrhea," "enlarged hocks and lesions," and "swellings" that may be permanent. As to the economic impact of increased milk production, caused by injection of rBST, upon small dairy farmers, the evidence included a U.S. Department of Agriculture economist's written claim that, "if rBST is heavily adopted and milk prices are reduced, at least some of the smaller farmers that do not use rBST might be forced out of the dairy business, because they would not be producing economically sufficient volumes of milk." Public philosophical objection to biotechnological mutation is familiar and widespread.

Any one of these concerns may well suffice to make Vermont's interest substantial; all four, taken together, undoubtedly constitute a substantial governmental justification for Vermont's labeling law.

Indeed, the majority does not contend otherwise. Nowhere does the majority assert that these interests are not substantial. As noted above, the majority justifies its conclusion of absence of a substantial interest by its assertion that Vermont advanced no interest other than consumer curiosity, a conclusion that is contradicted by both the record and the district court's findings.

. . .

The milk producers argue that because the sign which Vermont's law requires retailers to post goes beyond disclosure of rBST use and makes statements about it, they . . . are entitled to the full protection of the First Amendment, rather than the more limited protection afforded to commercial speech. They contend that the disclosure required of them is "inextricably intertwined" with fully protected speech. Because the blue dot they affix to their milk containers is linked to the sign retailers post in the stores, they also contend they are forced to subscribe to a message on that sign with which they do not agree.

This argument is merely a contrivance. In the first place, apart from disclosing use of rBST, Vermont's law imposes no speech requirements on the plaintiff milk producers. It is the retailers who are obligated to post signs containing text that relates to the rBST process. No reasonable consumer would understand the signs as constituting any statement by the milk producers.

Second, the text posted by retailers under Vermont's law is innocuous. Apart from enabling the consumer to tell which products derive from rBST-treated cows, the only additional required text states:

> The United States Food and Drug Administration has determined that there is no significant difference between milk from treated and untreated cows. It is the law of Vermont that products made from the milk of rBSt-treated cows be labeled to help consumers make informed shopping decisions.

The producers cannot contend they disagree with the first sentence, whose only function is to reassure consumers that the FDA found no health hazard in rBST products.[5] They focus rather on the second sentence, asserting that they disagree with the proposition that "informed shopping decisions" are advanced by disclosure of rBST treatment because they contend it is irrelevant to any legitimate consumer concern. Their argument has no force. The "informed shopping decisions" statement is clearly identified as made by the state of Vermont, not by the milk producers. Furthermore, the statement is virtually meaningless and harmless,

---

[5] Indeed, a statistical sampling shows that this labeling makes milk from rBST-treated cows more acceptable to Vermont consumers. Before reading this sign, 86% of respondents preferred milk from untreated cows; after reading the sign, preference for milk from untreated cows fell to 73%.

especially following the sentence stating that the FDA found no significant difference between milk from treated and untreated cows. The producers cannot even contend that they are obligated by Vermont's regulation to enter into debate.

It is quite clear that the producers' real objection is to the mandatory revelation of the use of rBST, which many Vermonters disfavor, and not to the bland sentence announcing that products are labeled "to help consumers make informed shopping decisions."

. . .

Notwithstanding their self-righteous references to free expression, the true objective of the milk producers is concealment. They do not wish consumers to know that their milk products were produced by use of rBST because there are consumers who, for various reasons, prefer to avoid rBST. Vermont, on the other hand, has established a labeling requirement whose sole objective (and whose sole effect) is to inform Vermont consumers whether milk products offered for sale were produced with rBST.[6] The dispute under the First Amendment is over whether the milk producers' interest in concealing their use of rBST from consumers will prevail over a state law designed to give consumers the information they desire. The question is simply whether the First Amendment prohibits government from requiring disclosure of truthful relevant information to consumers.

In my view, the interest of the milk producers has little entitlement to protection under the First Amendment. The caselaw that has developed under the doctrine of commercial speech has repeatedly emphasized that the primary function of the First Amendment in its application to commercial speech is to advance truthful disclosure—the very interest that the milk producers seek to undermine.

In *Virginia State Bd. of Pharmacy v. Virginia Citizens Consumer Council, Inc.*, 425 U.S. 748 (1976), the Court struck down a provision of the Virginia Code that essentially barred pharmacists, on the grounds of professional ethics, from advertising their prices. The Court noted society's "strong interest in the free flow of commercial information." Against Virginia's argument that advertisements of low-cost pharmaceutical products would blind consumers to the likelihood that low prices would be accompanied by low-quality pharmaceutical service, the Court said, "It is precisely this kind of choice, between the dangers of suppressing information, and the dangers of its misuse if it is freely available, that the First Amendment makes for us. Virginia is free to require whatever professional standards it wishes of its pharmacists. . . . But it may not do so by keeping the public in ignorance. . . ."

. . .

---

[6] I disagree with the majority's contention, that voluntary labeling by producers who do not use rBST can be relied on to effectuate Vermont's purpose. There is evidence that, notwithstanding the FDA's determination to permit such voluntary labeling, certain states, no doubt influenced by the rBST lobby, will "not allow any labeling concerning rBST." Affidavit of Ben Cohen, at 3–4. This effectively prevents multistate distributors from including such labeling on their packaging. Producers complying with Vermont's law do not face the same problem. The blue dot has meaning only in conjunction with the signs posted in Vermont retail establishments. Thus producers can inexpensively affix the blue dot without violating the laws of states that forbid all rBST labeling.

The application of these principles to the case at bar yields a clear message. The benefit the First Amendment confers in the area of commercial speech is the provision of accurate, non-misleading, relevant information to consumers. Thus, regulations designed to prevent the flow of such information are disfavored; regulations designed to provide such information are not.

The milk producers' invocation of the First Amendment for the purpose of concealing their use of rBST in milk production is entitled to scant recognition. They invoke the Amendment's protection to accomplish exactly what the Amendment opposes. And the majority's ruling deprives Vermont of the right to protect its consumers by requiring truthful disclosure on a subject of legitimate public concern.

. . .

COMMENTS AND QUESTIONS

1. *Competing "paternalisms"?* Judge Leval suggests that the Vermont statute is aimed at overcoming the manufacturers' "concealment" of their use of rBGH and invokes the antipaternalist concerns articulated in *Virginia Board of Pharmacy*. Is he right to do so? Note the majority's response: that consumers who want to know whether the milk products they buy came from rBGH-fed cows can simply purchase goods only from manufacturers who disclose what their practices are. Suppose there is a significant market for non-rBGH-treated products, and that one manufacturer responds to that market by disclosing that it does not use such products. What would interested consumers infer from the fact that a manufacturer did *not* make such a disclosure?

   For its part, the FDA has issued guidance on the voluntary disclosure of information concerning whether food has been developed using bioengineering, and this guidance quite obviously is meant to discourage makers of products made without use of modern bioengineering techniques from advising consumers of this fact. The agency states, for example, that it would likely be "misleading"—and thus a violation of the federal Food, Drug, and Cosmetic Act—to state that a food product is "GMO free" or even to state that it was made without use of bioengineering unless the producer has developed tests to verify that fact. (In this regard, note that one reason for opposition to bioengineered foods is that it is very difficult to avoid contaminating non-bioengineered crops and food supplies, hence the term "genetic pollution," used by some opponents of the technology.)

2. *The Ben and Jerry's story*: Ben & Jerry's, the ice cream manufacturer founded in Vermont, wanted to include a statement on its ice cream packages to the effect that its products were made from milk from cows that had not been fed rBGH-treated feed. Illinois informed Ben & Jerry's that including such a statement on its packages would violate a state consumer protection law that required all statements on food labels be "proven," because there is no test for determining whether a cow's milk is rBGH-free. Ben & Jerry's filed an action claiming that the Illinois statute violated *its* First Amendment rights. The case was settled with an agreement that Ben & Jerry's could make a more extended statement about its use of rBGH-free products. The current statement on Ben & Jerry's packages is:

We Oppose Recombinant Bovine Growth Hormone. The family farmers who supply our milk and cream pledge not to treat their cows with rBGH. The FDA has said no significant difference has been shown and no test can now distinguish between milk from rBGH treated and untreated cows.

3. The majority in *Amestoy* distinguishes between "real" harms and mere consumer curiosity. Why are these different for First Amendment purposes? Is the same remedy for failure to disclose "real" harms—voluntary disclosure to appeal to consumers particularly interested in information about such harms—available? Consider the possibility that an entire class of goods might pose a "real" harm, so that no manufacturer *could* truthfully disclose that its product did not pose a risk of inflicting such a harm. But consider also the possibility that producers of goods that compete with that class could make relevant truthful disclosures.

Some students find this entire line of argument strained. If so, does that undermine the majority's distinction between mere curiosity and real harms? And, why is it an insubstantial government interest to satisfy consumer curiosity when that curiosity is widespread enough to generate legislation and regulations?

4. The Court of Appeals for the Second Circuit elaborated on the distinction between curiosity and real harms in *National Electrical Manufacturers Ass'n v. Sorrell*, 272 F.3d 104 (2d Cir. 2001). The case involved a Vermont statute requiring that manufacturers of some products containing mercury (including thermometers, switches, and batteries) place a label to that effect on their products, which label would also advise that the product, when disposed of, should be recycled or disposed of as hazardous waste. The Court of Appeals held that the state could prevail if it showed "a rational connection between the purpose of a commercial disclosure requirement and the means employed to realize that purpose." Here the purpose was "protecting human health and the environment from mercury poisoning." (The court distinguished *Amestoy* on the ground that there the only state interest asserted was satisfying consumer curiosity.) A "reasonable relationship is plain," the Court of Appeals wrote:

> The prescribed labeling would likely contribute directly to the reduction of mercury pollution, whether or not it makes the greatest possible contribution. It is probable that some mercury lamp purchasers, newly informed by the Vermont label, will properly dispose of them and thereby reduce mercury pollution. By encouraging such changes in consumer behavior, the labeling requirement is rationally related to the state's goal of reducing mercury contamination.

This was true even though "the statute may ultimately fail to eliminate all or even most mercury pollution in the state," because most of the mercury in the environment does not come from the regulated products.

5. Another take on these constitutional issues comes from the D.C. Circuit's opinion in *Pearson v. Shalala*, 164 F.3d 650 (1999). There, the court held that the FDA could not prohibit a marketer of dietary supplements from claiming that folic acid helps to prevent certain diseases and adverse health conditions. Even

though the FDA had decided that the scientific evidence did not support the relevant claims, the court stated that the agency could not therefore simply ban the claims outright but must ordinarily allow the claim, accompanied by a disclaimer from the agency. The decision has led to a whole new category of health claims under the federal Food, Drug, and Cosmetic Act—known as "qualified health claims"—which take the following general form: "Substance A cures cancer. The FDA does not approve this claim. The FDA does not believe there is scientific evidence supporting this claim."

In light of everything you now know about how people process information, how well do you suppose consumers understand these qualified health claims?

Concluding Note

Regulation in the form of required information provision is sometimes defended as different in kind from other forms of regulation, including bans on the sale of certain products, because it is said to be more respectful of individual liberty and more consistent with consumer sovereignty. In light of the material in this chapter, do you agree? (What are the implications if the asserted distinction does *not* hold up upon examination—that all forms of regulation are justified, or that none are?)

Standard Setting

Feasibility, Health, Technology, and Trading

11

The preceding chapter introduced a "market-based" regulatory technique—information provision—designed to increase the likelihood that consumers and other affected persons will know enough to demand a "price" for being subjected to risk that maximizes their self-designated welfare. This chapter turns to another regulatory technique—mandatory performance standards that require risk producers to stay below specified levels. It examines several different performance measures that are found in contemporary law and their respective advantages and disadvantages. The chapter concludes with a discussion of how regulated entities can implement and achieve performance standards.

Standard setting is often criticized as a "command and control" technique that experience has shown frequently fails even to reduce risk, much less to achieve the levels of risk sought by regulators. (Section D shows that standard setting need not go hand in hand with command-and-control techniques.) In thinking about the adequacy of standard setting, remember that the question is always comparative and about margins: How well does this technique do when compared with the common-law techniques we examined earlier (the compensatory wage premium, for example, or nuisance law) or compared with market-based techniques such as information provision or insurance against the realization of risk? How much, if at all, does adding this technique reduce risk levels below those achieved by common-law and market-based techniques? Note the tensions concerning the role of cost-benefit analysis in standard setting.

A Zero or De Minimis Risk

■ Les v. Reilly
968 F.2d 985 (9th Cir. 1992)

Schroeder, Circuit Judge:

Petitioners seek review of a final order of the Environmental Protection Agency permitting the use of four pesticides as food additives although they have been found to induce cancer. Petitioners challenge the final order on the ground that it violates the provisions of the Delaney clause, 21 U.S.C. § 348(c)(3), which prohibits the use of any food additive that is found to induce cancer.

Prior to 1988, EPA regulations promulgated in the absence of evidence of carcinogenicity permitted use of the four pesticides at issue here as food additives. In 1988, however, the EPA found these pesticides to be carcinogens. Notwithstanding the Delaney clause, the EPA refused to revoke the earlier regulations, reasoning that, although the chemicals posed a measurable risk of causing cancer, that risk was "de minimis."

We set aside the EPA's order because we agree with the petitioners that the language of the Delaney clause, its history and purpose all reflect that Congress intended the EPA to prohibit all additives that are carcinogens, regardless of the degree of risk involved.

Background

The Federal Food, Drug, and Cosmetic Act (FFDCA) is designed to ensure the safety of the food we eat by prohibiting the sale of food that is "adulterated." 21 U.S.C. § 331(a). Adulterated food is in turn defined as food containing any unsafe food "additive." 21 U.S.C. § 342(a)(2)(C). A food "additive" is defined broadly as "any substance the intended use of which results or may reasonably be expected to result...in its becoming a component...of any food." 21 U.S.C. § 321(s). A food additive is considered unsafe unless there is a specific exemption for the substance or a regulation prescribing the conditions under which it may be used safely. 21 U.S.C. § 348(a).

Before 1988, the four pesticide chemicals with which we are here concerned—benomyl, mancozeb, phosmet and trifluralin—were all the subject of regulations issued by the EPA permitting their use. In October 1988, however, the EPA published a list of substances, including the pesticides at issue here, that had been found to induce cancer. *Regulation of Pesticides in Food: Addressing the Delaney Paradox Policy Statement*, 53 Fed. Reg. 41,104, 41,119 (Oct. 19, 1988). As known carcinogens, the four pesticides ran afoul of a special provision of the FFDCA known as the Delaney clause, which prescribes that additives found to induce cancer can never be deemed "safe" for purposes of the FFDCA. The Delaney clause is found in FFDCA section 409, 21 U.S.C. § 348. That section limits the conditions under which the Secretary may issue regulations allowing a substance to be used as a food additive:

> No such regulation shall issue if a fair evaluation of the data before the Secretary—(A) fails to establish that the proposed use of the food additive, under the conditions of use to be specified in the regulation, will be safe: Provided, That no additive shall be deemed to be safe if it is found to induce cancer when ingested by man or animal, or if it is found, after tests which are appropriate for the evaluation of the safety of food additives, to induce cancer in man or animal.... 21 U.S.C. § 348(c)(3).

The FFDCA also contains special provisions which regulate the occurrence of pesticide residues on raw agricultural commodities. Section 402 of the FFDCA provides that a raw food containing a pesticide residue is deemed adulterated unless the residue is authorized under section 408 of the FFDCA, which allows tolerance regulations setting maximum permissible levels and also provides for exemption from tolerances under certain circumstances. When a tolerance or an exemption has been established for use of a pesticide on a raw agricultural commodity, then the FFDCA allows for the "flow-through" of such pesticide residue to processed foods, even when the pesticide may be a carcinogen. This flow-through is allowed, however, only to the extent that the concentration of the pesticide in the processed food does not exceed the concentration allowed in the raw food. The flow-through provisions are contained in section 402 which provides:

> That where a pesticide chemical has been used in or on a raw agricultural commodity in conformity with an exemption granted or a tolerance prescribed under section 346a of this title [FFDCA section 408] and such raw agricultural commodity has been subjected to processing such as canning, cooking, freezing, dehydrating, or milling, the residue of such pesticide chemical remaining in or on such processed food shall, notwithstanding the provisions of sections 346 and 348 of this title [FFDCA sections 406 and 409], not be deemed unsafe if such residue in or on the raw agricultural commodity has been removed to the extent possible in good manufacturing practice and the concentration of such residue in the processed food when ready to eat is not greater than the tolerance prescribed for the raw agricultural commodity.

21 U.S.C. § 342(a)(2)(C). It is undisputed that the EPA regulations at issue in this case allow for the concentration of cancer-causing pesticides during processing to levels in excess of those permitted in the raw foods.

The proceedings in this case had their genesis in October 1988 when the EPA published a list of substances, including these pesticides, that were found to induce cancer. Simultaneously, the EPA announced a new interpretation of the Delaney clause: the EPA proposed to permit concentrations of cancer-causing pesticide residues greater than that tolerated for raw foods so long as the particular substances posed only a "de minimis" risk of actually causing cancer. Finding that benomyl, mancozeb, phosmet and trifluralin (among others) posed only such a de minimis risk, the Agency announced that it would not immediately revoke its previous regulations authorizing use of these substances as food additives.

. . .

Discussion

The issue before us is whether the EPA has violated section 409 of the FFDCA, the Delaney clause, by permitting the use of carcinogenic food additives which it finds to present only a de minimis or negligible risk of causing cancer. The Agency acknowledges that its interpretation of the law is a new and changed one. From the initial enactment of the Delaney clause in 1958 to the time of the rulings here in issue, the statute had been strictly and literally enforced. The EPA also acknowledges that the language of the statute itself appears, at first glance, to be clear on its face. ("Section 409 mandates a zero risk standard for carcinogenic pesticides in processed foods in those instances where the pesticide concentrates during processing or is applied during or after processing.").

The language is clear and mandatory. The Delaney clause provides that no additive shall be deemed safe if it induces cancer. 21 U.S.C. § 348(c)(3). The EPA states in its final order that appropriate tests have established that the pesticides at issue here induce cancer in humans or animals. The statute provides that once the finding of carcinogenicity is made, the EPA has no discretion. As a leading work on food and drug regulation notes:

> The Delaney Clause leaves the FDA room for scientific judgment in deciding whether its conditions are met by a food additive. But the clause affords no

flexibility once FDA scientists determine that these conditions are satisfied. A food additive that has been found in an appropriate test to induce cancer in laboratory animals may not be approved for use in food for any purpose, at any level, regardless of any "benefits" that it might provide.

Richard A. Merrill and Peter B. Hutt, *Food and Drug Law* 78 (1980)

This issue was litigated before the D.C. Circuit in connection with the virtually identical "color additive" prohibition of 21 U.S.C. § 376(b)(5)(B). The D.C. Circuit concluded that "the natural—almost inescapable—reading of this language is that if the Secretary finds the additive to 'induce' cancer in animals, he must deny listing." *Public Citizen v. Young*, 831 F.2d 1108, 1112 (D.C. Cir. 1987). The court concluded that the EPA's de minimis interpretation of the Delaney clause in 21 U.S.C. § 376 was "contrary to law." The *Public Citizen* decision reserved comment on whether the result would be the same under the food additive provisions as it was under the food color provisions, but its reasoning with respect to the language of the statute is equally applicable to both.

The Agency asks us to look behind the language of the Delaney clause to the overall statutory scheme governing pesticides, which permits the use of carcinogenic pesticides on raw food without regard to the Delaney clause. Yet section 402 of the FFDCA expressly harmonizes that scheme with the Delaney clause by providing that residues on processed foods may not exceed the tolerance level established for the raw food. The statute unambiguously provides that pesticides which concentrate in processed food are to be treated as food additives, and these are governed by the Delaney food additive provision contained in section 409. If pesticides which concentrate in processed foods induce cancer in humans or animals, they render the food adulterated and must be prohibited.

The legislative history, too, reflects that Congress intended the very rigidity that the language it chose commands. The food additive Delaney clause was enacted in response to increasing public concern about cancer. It was initially part of a bill, introduced in the House of Representatives in 1958 by Congressman Delaney, to amend the FFDCA. The bill, intended to ensure that no carcinogens, no matter how small the amount, would be introduced into food, was at least in part a response to a decision by the FDA to allow a known carcinogen, the pesticide Aramite, as an approved food additive. Of the FDA's approval for sale of foods containing small quantities of Aramite, Congressman Delaney stated:

> The part that chemical additives play in the cancer picture may not yet be completely understood, but enough is known to put us on our guard. The safety of the public health demands that chemical additives should be specifically pretested for carcinogenicity, and this should be spelled out in the law. The precedent established by the Aramite decision has opened the door, even if only a little, to the use of carcinogens in our foods. That door should be slammed shut and locked. That is the purpose of my anticarcinogen provision.

The scientific witnesses who testified before Congress stressed that because current scientific techniques could not determine a safe level for carcinogens, all carcinogens should be prohibited. While Congressman Delaney's bill was not ultimately passed, the crucial anticancer language from the bill was incorporated into the Food Additives Amendment of 1958 which enacted section 409 of the FFDCA into law. Thus, the legislative history supports the conclusion that Congress intended to ban all carcinogenic food additives, regardless of amount or significance of risk, as the only safe alternative.

Throughout its 30-year history, the Delaney clause has been interpreted as an absolute bar to all carcinogenic food additives. In 1958, the Department of Health, Education, and Welfare (which would be charged with administering the food additive provisions of the newly enacted Delaney clause) interpreted the clause as removing all agency discretion regarding carcinogens. As a contemporaneous agency construction of the statute, this interpretation is entitled to great weight. Further, Congress has repeatedly ratified a strict interpretation of the Delaney clause by reenacting all three FFDCA provisions which contain Delaney clauses without changing the Agency's interpretation. . . .

The EPA contends that the legislative history shows that Congress never intended to regulate pesticides, as opposed to other additives, with extraordinary rigidity under the food additives provision. The Agency is indeed correct that the legislative history of the food additive provision does not focus on pesticides, and that pesticides are regulated more comprehensively under the Federal Insecticide, Fungicide, and Rodenticide Act (FIFRA). Nevertheless, the EPA's contention that Congress never intended the food additive provision to encompass pesticide residues is belied by the events prompting passage of the provision into law: FDA approval of Aramite was the principal impetus for the food additive Delaney clause and Aramite was itself a regulated pesticide. Thus, Congress intended to regulate pesticides as food additives under section 409 of the FFDCA, at least to the extent that pesticide residues concentrate in processed foods and exceed the tolerances for raw foods.

Finally, the EPA argues that a de minimis exception to the Delaney clause is necessary in order to bring about a more sensible application of the regulatory scheme. It relies particularly on a recent study suggesting that the criterion of concentration level in processed foods may bear little or no relation to actual risk of cancer, and that some pesticides might be barred by rigid enforcement of the Delaney clause while others, with greater cancer-causing risk, may be permitted through the flow-through provisions because they do not concentrate in processed foods. The EPA in effect asks us to approve what it deems to be a more enlightened system than that which Congress established. The EPA is not alone in criticizing the scheme established by the Delaney clause. See, e.g., Richard A. Merrill, *FDA's Implementation of the Delaney Clause: Repudiation of Congressional Choice or Reasoned Adaptation to Scientific Progress*, 5 Yale J. on Reg. 1, 87 (1988) (concluding that the Delaney clause is both unambiguous and unwise: "at once an explicit and imprudent expression of legislative will"). Revising the existing statutory scheme, however, is neither our function nor the function of the EPA. There are currently bills pending before the House and the Senate which would amend the food additive provision to allow the Secretary to establish tolerance levels for carcinogens, including pesticide residues in processed foods, which impose a negligible risk. If there is to be a change, it is for Congress to direct.

The EPA's refusal to revoke regulations permitting the use of benomyl, mancozeb, phosmet and trifluralin as food additives on the ground the cancer risk they pose is de minimis is contrary to the provisions of the Delaney clause prohibiting food additives that induce cancer. The EPA's final order is set aside.

COMMENTS AND QUESTIONS

1. Consider *Les v. Reilly* as a case study in statutory interpretation. The court finds the statute clear. How did the agency attempt to introduce uncertainty about the statute's meaning? What would the consequences have been, had the court agreed that the statute was ambiguous?

2. In August 1996, Congress passed the Food Quality Protection Act, which repeals the Delaney clause with respect to pesticides and replaces it with a standard of "reasonable certainty of no harm" for all foods treated with pesticides. This standard is defined in part as no more than a one-in-a-million chance of getting cancer from a lifetime of exposure to the pesticide in question. (Are these truly equivalent formulations? Note that the "one-in-a-million chance" definition implies that there may be 250 deaths in a population of 250 million people. Why "one-in-a-million"? Probably because it is a culturally significant way of saying "really, really small.") Does this action refute (because it shows that Congress—eventually—agreed that the zero-risk policy of the Delaney clause was unwise) or confirm (because it was *Congress*, not the agency, that came to that conclusion) the policy wisdom of the court's decision in *Les v. Reilly*?

3. The court of appeals notes the FDA's reasons for its change in regulatory position: the concentration level of carcinogens in processed foods may have nothing to do with actual cancer risk, and other pesticides, substituted for those that are concentrated in such foods, might pose higher cancer risks. What basis in policy might there be for adopting a zero-risk principle? "Zero" is an easy figure to work with; alternatives—like "significant risk"—require judgments that are themselves likely to be controversial. Note that the technical ability to identify carcinogens increased dramatically between 1958, when the Delaney clause was adopted, and 1992, when *Les v. Reilly* was decided.

4. Does the Delaney clause create a regulatory paradox? Removing carcinogens from the market might lead to the substitution of other pesticides, which might have a higher risk of causing diseases other than cancer. This might be particularly true because of the increased technical ability to identify carcinogens, which might result in the removal from the market of pesticides that posed an extremely small risk of cancer. But recall the studies reported in chapter 4 indicating that people fear cancer substantially more than they fear other diseases. How, if at all, should that fact affect the determination of whether the Delaney clause creates a regulatory paradox?

B. Significant Risk and Feasibility

■ Industrial Union Department, AFL-CIO v. American Petroleum Institute (the Benzene Case)
448 U.S. 607 (1980)

Justice Stevens announced the judgment of the Court and delivered an opinion, in which the Chief Justice and Justice Stewart joined and in Parts I, II, III-A, III-B, III-C, and III-E of which Justice Powell joined:

The Occupational Safety and Health Act of 1970 (Act) was enacted for the purpose of ensuring safe and healthful working conditions for every working man and woman in the Nation. This litigation concerns a standard promulgated by the Secretary of Labor to regulate occupational exposure to benzene, a substance which has been shown to cause cancer at high exposure levels. The principal question is whether such a showing is a sufficient basis for a standard that places the most stringent limitation on exposure to benzene that is technologically and economically possible.

The Act delegates broad authority to the Secretary to promulgate different kinds of standards. The basic definition of an "occupational safety and health standard" is found in § 3(8), which provides:

> "The term 'occupational safety and health standard' means a standard which requires conditions, or the adoption or use of one or more practices, means, methods, operations, or processes, reasonably necessary or appropriate to provide safe or healthful employment and places of employment." 29 U.S.C. § 652 (8).

Where toxic materials or harmful physical agents are concerned, a standard must also comply with § 6(b)(5), which provides:

> "The Secretary, in promulgating standards dealing with toxic materials or harmful physical agents under this subsection, shall set the standard which most adequately assures, to the extent feasible, on the basis of the best available evidence, that no employee will suffer material impairment of health or functional capacity even if such employee has regular exposure to the hazard dealt with by such standard for the period of his working life. Development of standards under this subsection shall be based upon research, demonstrations, experiments, and such other information as may be appropriate. In addition to the attainment of the highest degree of health and safety protection for the employee, other considerations shall be the latest available scientific data in the field, the feasibility of the standards, and experience gained under this and other health and safety laws." 29 U.S.C. § 655 (b)(5).

Wherever the toxic material to be regulated is a carcinogen, the Secretary has taken the position that no safe exposure level can be determined and that § 6 (b)(5) requires him to set an exposure limit at the lowest technologically feasible level that will not impair the viability of the industries regulated. In this case, after having determined that there is a causal connection between benzene and leukemia (a cancer of the white blood cells), the Secretary set an exposure limit on airborne concentrations of benzene of one part benzene per million parts of air (1 ppm), regulated dermal and eye contact with solutions containing benzene, and imposed complex monitoring and medical testing requirements on employers whose workplaces contain 0.5 ppm or more of benzene.

. . . .

I

Benzene is a familiar and important commodity. It is a colorless, aromatic liquid that evaporates rapidly under ordinary atmospheric conditions. Approximately 11 billion pounds of benzene were produced in the United States in 1976. Ninety-four percent of that total was produced by the petroleum and petrochemical industries, with the remainder produced by the steel industry as a byproduct of coking operations. Benzene is used in manufacturing a variety of products including motor fuels (which may contain as much as 2% benzene), solvents, detergents, pesticides, and other organic chemicals.

The entire population of the United States is exposed to small quantities of benzene, ranging from a few parts per billion to 0.5 ppm, in the ambient air. Over one million workers are subject to additional low-level exposures as a consequence of their employment. The majority of these employees work in gasoline service stations, benzene production (petroleum refineries and coking operations), chemical processing, benzene transportation, rubber manufacturing, and laboratory operations.[6]

Benzene is a toxic substance. Although it could conceivably cause harm to a person who swallowed or touched it, the principal risk of harm comes from inhalation of benzene vapors. When these vapors are inhaled, the benzene diffuses through the lungs and is quickly absorbed into the blood. Exposure to high concentrations produces an almost immediate effect on the central nervous system. Inhalation of concentrations of 20,000 ppm can be fatal within minutes; exposures in the range of 250 to 500 ppm can cause vertigo, nausea, and other symptoms of mild poisoning. Persistent exposures at levels above 25–40 ppm may lead to blood deficiencies and diseases of the blood-forming organs, including aplastic anemia, which is generally fatal.

Industrial health experts have long been aware that exposure to benzene may lead to various types of nonmalignant diseases. By 1948 the evidence connecting high levels of benzene to serious blood disorders had become so strong that the Commonwealth of Massachusetts imposed a 35 ppm limitation on workplaces within its jurisdiction. In 1969 the American National Standards Institute (ANSI) adopted a national consensus standard of 10 ppm averaged over an 8-hour period with a ceiling concentration of 25 ppm for 10-minute periods or a maximum peak concentration of 50 ppm. In 1971, after the Occupational Safety and Health Act was passed, the Secretary adopted this consensus standard as the federal standard, pursuant to 29 U.S.C. § 655(a).[7]

---

[6] OSHA's figures indicate that 795,000 service station employees have some heightened exposure to benzene as a result of their employment. These employees are specifically excluded from the regulation at issue in this case. OSHA states that another 629,000 employees, who are covered by the regulation, work in the other industries described.

[7] Section 6 (a) of the Act, as set forth in 29 U.S.C. § 655 (a), provides:

"Without regard to chapter 5 of Title 5 or to the other subsections of this section, the Secretary shall, as soon as practicable during the period beginning with the effective date of this chapter and ending two years after such date, by rule promulgate as an occupational safety or health standard any national consensus standard, and any established Federal standard, unless he determines that the promulgation of such a standard would not result in improved safety or health for specifically designated employees. In the event of conflict among any such standards, the Secretary shall promulgate the standard which assures the greatest protection of the safety or health of the affected employees."

In this case the Secretary complied with the directive to choose the most protective standard by selecting the ANSI standard of 10 ppm, rather than the 25 ppm standard adopted by the American Conference of Government Industrial Hygienists.

As early as 1928, some health experts theorized that there might also be a connection between benzene in the workplace and leukemia. In the late 1960's and early 1970's a number of epidemiological studies were published indicating that workers exposed to high concentrations of benzene were subject to a significantly increased risk of leukemia. In a 1974 report recommending a permanent standard for benzene, the National Institute for Occupational Safety and Health (NIOSH), OSHA's research arm, noted that these studies raised the "distinct possibility" that benzene caused leukemia. But, in light of the fact that all known cases had occurred at very high exposure levels, NIOSH declined to recommend a change in the 10 ppm standard, which it considered sufficient to protect against nonmalignant diseases. . . .
. . . .

In its published statement giving notice of the proposed permanent standard, OSHA did not ask for comments as to whether or not benzene presented a significant health risk at exposures of 10 ppm or less. Rather, it asked for comments as to whether 1 ppm was the minimum feasible exposure limit. As OSHA's Deputy Director of Health Standards, Grover Wrenn, testified at the hearing, this formulation of the issue to be considered by the Agency was consistent with OSHA's general policy with respect to carcinogens. Whenever a carcinogen is involved, OSHA will presume that no safe level of exposure exists in the absence of clear proof establishing such a level and will accordingly set the exposure limit at the lowest level feasible. The proposed 1 ppm exposure limit in this case thus was established not on the basis of a proven hazard at 10 ppm, but rather on the basis of "OSHA's best judgment at the time of the proposal of the feasibility of compliance with the proposed standard by the [affected] industries." Given OSHA's cancer policy, it was in fact irrelevant whether there was any evidence at all of a leukemia risk at 10 ppm. The important point was that there was no evidence that there was not some risk, however small, at that level. The fact that OSHA did not ask for comments on whether there was a safe level of exposure for benzene was indicative of its further view that a demonstration of such absolute safety simply could not be made.

. . . In its final form, the benzene standard is designed to protect workers from whatever hazards are associated with low-level benzene exposures by requiring employers to monitor workplaces to determine the level of exposure, to provide medical examinations when the level rises above 0.5 ppm, and to institute whatever engineering or other controls are necessary to keep exposures at or below 1 ppm.
. . . .

Whenever initial monitoring indicates that employees are subject to airborne concentrations of benzene above 1 ppm averaged over an 8-hour workday, with a ceiling of 5 ppm for any 15-minute period, employers are required to modify their plants or institute work practice controls to reduce exposures within permissible limits. Consistent with OSHA's general policy, the regulation does not allow respirators to be used if engineering modifications are technologically feasible.[24] Employers in this category are also required to perform monthly monitoring so

---

[24] Indeed, in its explanation of the standard OSHA states that an employer is required to institute engineering controls (for example, installing new ventilation hoods) even if those controls are insufficient, by themselves, to achieve compliance and respirators must therefore be used as well.

long as their workplaces remain above 1 ppm, provide semiannual medical examinations to exposed workers, post signs in and restrict access to "regulated areas" where the permissible exposure limit is exceeded, and conduct employee training programs where necessary.

. . . .

The permanent standard is expressly inapplicable to the storage, transportation, distribution, sale, or use of gasoline or other fuels subsequent to discharge from bulk terminals. This exception is particularly significant in light of the fact that over 795,000 gas station employees, who are exposed to an average of 102,700 gallons of gasoline (containing up to 2% benzene) annually, are thus excluded from the protection of the standard.

As presently formulated, the benzene standard is an expensive way of providing some additional protection for a relatively small number of employees. According to OSHA's figures, the standard will require capital investments in engineering controls of approximately $266 million, first-year operating costs (for monitoring, medical testing, employee training, and respirators) of $187 million to $205 million and recurring annual costs of approximately $34 million. The figures outlined in OSHA's explanation of the costs of compliance to various industries indicate that only 35,000 employees would gain any benefit from the regulation in terms of a reduction in their exposure to benzene. Over two-thirds of these workers (24,450) are employed in the rubber-manufacturing industry. Compliance costs in that industry are estimated to be rather low with no capital costs and initial operating expenses estimated at only $34 million ($1,390 per employee); recurring annual costs would also be rather low, totaling less than $1 million. By contrast, the segment of the petroleum refining industry that produces benzene would be required to incur $24 million in capital costs and $600,000 in first-year operating expenses to provide additional protection for 300 workers ($82,000 per employee), while the petrochemical industry would be required to incur $20.9 million in capital costs and $1 million in initial operating expenses for the benefit of 552 employees ($39,675 per employee).

Although OSHA did not quantify the benefits to each category of worker in terms of decreased exposure to benzene, it appears from the economic impact study done at OSHA's direction that those benefits may be relatively small. Thus, although the current exposure limit is 10 ppm, the actual exposures outlined in that study are often considerably lower. For example, for the period 1970–1975 the petrochemical industry reported that, out of a total of 496 employees exposed to benzene, only 53 were exposed to levels between 1 and 5 ppm and only 7 (all at the same plant) were exposed to between 5 and 10 ppm.

II

The critical issue at this point in the litigation is whether the Court of Appeals was correct in refusing to enforce the 1 ppm exposure limit on the ground that it was not supported by appropriate findings.

Any discussion of the 1 ppm exposure limit must, of course, begin with the Agency's rationale for imposing that limit. The written explanation of the standard fills 184 pages of the printed appendix. Much of it is devoted to a discussion of the voluminous evidence of the adverse effects of exposure to benzene at levels of concentration well above 10 ppm. This discussion demonstrates that there is ample justification for regulating occupational exposure to benzene and that the prior limit of 10 ppm, with a ceiling of 25 ppm (or a peak of 50 ppm) was reasonable. It does not, however, provide direct support for the Agency's conclusion that the limit should be reduced from 10 ppm to 1 ppm.

The evidence in the administrative record of adverse effects of benzene exposure at 10 ppm is sketchy at best. OSHA noted that there was "no dispute" that certain nonmalignant blood disorders, evidenced by a reduction in the level of red or white cells or platelets in the blood, could result from exposures of 25–40 ppm. It then stated that several studies had indicated that relatively slight changes in normal blood values could result from exposures below 25 ppm and perhaps below 10 ppm. OSHA did not attempt to make any estimate based on these studies of how significant the risk of nonmalignant disease would be at exposures of 10 ppm or less. Rather, it stated that because of the lack of data concerning the linkage between low-level exposures and blood abnormalities, it was impossible to construct a dose-response curve at this time.[33] OSHA did conclude, however, that the studies demonstrated that the current 10 ppm exposure limit was inadequate to ensure that no single worker would suffer a nonmalignant blood disorder as a result of benzene exposure. Noting that it is "customary" to set a permissible exposure limit by applying a safety factor of 10–100 to the lowest level at which adverse effects had been observed, the Agency stated that the evidence supported the conclusion that the limit should be set at a point "substantially less than 10 ppm" even if benzene's leukemic effects were not considered. OSHA did not state, however, that the nonmalignant effects of benzene exposure justified a reduction in the permissible exposure limit to 1 ppm.[34]

OSHA also noted some studies indicating an increase in chromosomal aberrations in workers chronically exposed to concentrations of benzene "probably less than 25 ppm." However, the Agency took no definitive position as to what these aberrations meant in terms of demonstrable health effects and stated that no quantitative dose-response relationship had yet been established. Under these circumstances, chromosomal effects were categorized by OSHA as an "adverse biological event of serious concern which may pose or reflect a potential health risk and as such, must be considered in the larger purview of adverse health effects associated with benzene."

---

[33] . . . OSHA's comments with respect to the insufficiency of the data were addressed primarily to the lack of data at low exposure levels. OSHA did not discuss whether it was possible to make a rough estimate, based on the more complete epidemiological and animal studies done at higher exposure levels, of the significance of the risks attributable to those levels, nor did it discuss whether it was possible to extrapolate from such estimates to derive a risk estimate for low-level exposures.

[34] OSHA did not invoke the automatic rule of reducing exposures to the lowest limit feasible that it applies to cancer risks. Instead, the Secretary reasoned that prudent health policy merely required that the permissible exposure limit be set "sufficiently below the levels at which adverse effects have been observed to assure adequate protection for all exposed employees." While OSHA concluded that application of this rule would lead to an exposure limit "substantially less than 10 ppm," it did not state either what exposure level it considered to present a significant risk of harm or what safety factor should be applied to that level to establish a permissible exposure limit.

With respect to leukemia, evidence of an increased risk (i.e., a risk greater than that borne by the general population) due to benzene exposures at or below 10 ppm was even sketchier. Once OSHA acknowledged that the NIOSH study it had relied upon in promulgating the emergency standard did not support its earlier view that benzene had been shown to cause leukemia at concentrations below 25 ppm, there was only one study that provided any evidence of such an increased risk. That study, conducted by the Dow Chemical Co., uncovered three leukemia deaths, versus 0.2 expected deaths, out of a population of 594 workers; it appeared that the three workers had never been exposed to more than 2 to 9 ppm of benzene. The authors of the study, however, concluded that it could not be viewed as proof of a relationship between low-level benzene exposure and leukemia because all three workers had probably been occupationally exposed to a number of other potentially carcinogenic chemicals at other points in their careers and because no leukemia deaths had been uncovered among workers who had been exposed to much higher levels of benzene. In its explanation of the permanent standard, OSHA stated that the possibility that these three leukemias had been caused by benzene exposure could not be ruled out and that the study, although not evidence of an increased risk of leukemia at 10 ppm, was therefore "consistent with the findings of many studies that there is an excess leukemia risk among benzene exposed employees." The Agency made no finding that the Dow study, any other empirical evidence, or any opinion testimony demonstrated that exposure to benzene at or below the 10 ppm level had ever in fact caused leukemia. . . .

In the end OSHA's rationale for lowering the permissible exposure limit to 1 ppm was based, not on any finding that leukemia has ever been caused by exposure to 10 ppm of benzene and that it will not be caused by exposure to 1 ppm, but rather on a series of assumptions indicating that some leukemias might result from exposure to 10 ppm and that the number of cases might be reduced by reducing the exposure level to 1 ppm. In reaching that result, the Agency first unequivocally concluded that benzene is a human carcinogen. Second, it concluded that industry had failed to prove that there is a safe threshold level of exposure to benzene below which no excess leukemia cases would occur. In reaching this conclusion OSHA rejected industry contentions that certain epidemiological studies indicating no excess risk of leukemia among workers exposed at levels below 10 ppm were sufficient to establish that the threshold level of safe exposure was at or above 10 ppm. It also rejected an industry witness'[s] testimony that a dose-response curve could be constructed on the basis of the reported epidemiological studies and that this curve indicated that reducing the permissible exposure limit from 10 to 1 ppm would prevent at most one leukemia and one other cancer death every six years.

Third, the Agency applied its standard policy with respect to carcinogens, concluding that, in the absence of definitive proof of a safe level, it must be assumed that any level above zero presents some increased risk of cancer. As the federal parties point out in their brief, there are a number of scientists and public health specialists who subscribe to this view, theorizing that a susceptible person may contract cancer from the absorption of even one molecule of a carcinogen like benzene.[41]

---

[41] The so-called "one hit" theory is based on laboratory studies indicating that one molecule of a carcinogen may react in the test tube with one molecule of DNA to produce a mutation. The

Fourth, the Agency reiterated its view of the Act, stating that it was required by § 6(b)(5) to set the standard either at the level that has been demonstrated to be safe or at the lowest level feasible, whichever is higher. If no safe level is established, as in this case, the Secretary's interpretation of the statute automatically leads to the selection of an exposure limit that is the lowest feasible. Because of benzene's importance to the economy, no one has ever suggested that it would be feasible to eliminate its use entirely, or to try to limit exposures to the small amounts that are omnipresent. Rather, the Agency selected 1 ppm as a workable exposure level, and then determined that compliance with that level was technologically feasible and that "the economic impact of . . . [compliance] will not be such as to threaten the financial welfare of the affected firms or the general economy." It therefore held that 1 ppm was the minimum feasible exposure level within the meaning of § 6 (b)(5) of the Act.

Finally, although the Agency did not refer in its discussion of the pertinent legal authority to any duty to identify the anticipated benefits of the new standard, it did conclude that some benefits were likely to result from reducing the exposure limit from 10 ppm to 1 ppm. This conclusion was based, again, not on evidence, but rather on the assumption that the risk of leukemia will decrease as exposure levels decrease. Although the Agency had found it impossible to construct a dose-response curve that would predict with any accuracy the number of leukemias that could be expected to result from exposures at 10 ppm, at 1 ppm, or at any intermediate level, it nevertheless "determined that the benefits of the proposed standard are likely to be appreciable."[43] In light of the Agency's disavowal of any

---

theory is that, if this occurred in the human body, the mutated molecule could replicate over a period of years and eventually develop into a cancerous tumor. Industry witnesses challenged this theory, arguing that the presence of several different defense mechanisms in the human body make it unlikely that a person would actually contract cancer as a result of absorbing one carcinogenic molecule. Thus, the molecule might be detoxified before reaching a critical site, damage to a DNA molecule might be repaired, or a mutated DNA molecule might be destroyed by the body's immunological defenses before it could develop into a cancer. In light of the improbability of a person's contracting cancer as a result of a single hit, a number of the scientists testifying on both sides of the issue agreed that every individual probably does have a threshold exposure limit below which he or she will not contract cancer. The problem, however, is that individual susceptibility appears to vary greatly and there is at present no way to calculate each and every person's threshold. Thus, even industry witnesses agreed that if the standard must ensure with absolute certainty that every single worker is protected from any risk of leukemia, only a zero exposure limit would suffice.

[43] At an earlier point in its explanation, OSHA stated:

"There is general agreement that benzene exposure causes leukemia as well as other fatal diseases of the bloodforming organs. In spite of the certainty of this conclusion, there does not exist an adequate scientific basis for establishing the quantitative dose response relationship between exposure to benzene and the induction of leukemia and other blood diseases. The uncertainty in both the actual magnitude of expected deaths and in the theory of extrapolation from existing data to the OSHA exposure levels places the estimation of benefits on 'the frontiers of scientific knowledge.' While the actual estimation of the number of cancers to be prevented is highly uncertain, the evidence indicates that the number may be appreciable. There is general agreement

ability to determine the numbers of employees likely to be adversely affected by exposures of 10 ppm, the Court of Appeals held this finding to be unsupported by the record.

It is noteworthy that at no point in its lengthy explanation did the Agency quote or even cite § 3(8) of the Act. It made no finding that any of the provisions of the new standard were "reasonably necessary or appropriate to provide safe or healthful employment and places of employment." Nor did it allude to the possibility that any such finding might have been appropriate.

III

Our resolution of the issues in these cases turns, to a large extent, on the meaning of and the relationship between § 3(8), which defines a health and safety standard as a standard that is "reasonably necessary and appropriate to provide safe or healthful employment," and § 6(b)(5), which directs the Secretary in promulgating a health and safety standard for toxic materials to "set the standard which most adequately assures, to the extent feasible, on the basis of the best available evidence, that no employee will suffer material impairment of health or functional capacity. . . ."

In the Government's view, § 3(8)'s definition of the term "standard" has no legal significance or at best merely requires that a standard not be totally irrational. It takes the position that § 6(b)(5) is controlling and that it requires OSHA to promulgate a standard that either gives an absolute assurance of safety for each and every worker or reduces exposures to the lowest level feasible. The Government interprets "feasible" as meaning technologically achievable at a cost that would not impair the viability of the industries subject to the regulation. The respondent industry representatives, on the other hand, argue that the Court of Appeals was correct in holding that the "reasonably necessary and appropriate" language of § 3(8), along with the feasibility requirement of § 6(b)(5), requires the Agency to quantify both the costs and the benefits of a proposed rule and to conclude that they are roughly commensurate.

In our view, it is not necessary to decide whether either the Government or industry is entirely correct. For we think it is clear that § 3(8) does apply to all permanent standards promulgated under the Act and that it requires the Secretary, before issuing any standard, to determine that it is reasonably necessary and appropriate to remedy a significant risk of material health impairment. Only after the Secretary has made the threshold determination that such a risk exists with respect to a toxic substance, would it be necessary to decide whether § 6 (b)(5) requires him to select the most protective standard he can consistent with economic and technological feasibility, or whether, as respondents argue, the benefits of the regulation must be commensurate with the costs of its implementation. Because the Secretary did not make the required threshold finding in these cases, we have no

---

that even in the absence of the ability to establish a 'threshold' or 'safe' level for benzene and other carcinogens, a dose response relationship is likely to exist; that is, exposure to higher doses carries with it a higher risk of cancer, and conversely, exposure to lower levels is accompanied by a reduced risk, even though a precise quantitative relationship cannot be established."

occasion to determine whether costs must be weighed against benefits in an appropriate case.

A

Under the Government's view, § 3(8), if it has any substantive content at all, merely requires OSHA to issue standards that are reasonably calculated to produce a safer or more healthy work environment. Apart from this minimal requirement of rationality, the Government argues that § 3(8) imposes no limits on the Agency's power, and thus would not prevent it from requiring employers to do whatever would be "reasonably necessary" to eliminate all risks of any harm from their workplaces. With respect to toxic substances and harmful physical agents, the Government takes an even more extreme position. Relying on § 6(b)(5)'s direction to set a standard "which most adequately assures . . . that no employee will suffer material impairment of health or functional capacity," the Government contends that the Secretary is required to impose standards that either guarantee workplaces that are free from any risk of material health impairment, however small, or that come as close as possible to doing so without ruining entire industries.

If the purpose of the statute were to eliminate completely and with absolute certainty any risk of serious harm, we would agree that it would be proper for the Secretary to interpret §§ 3(8) and 6(b)(5) in this fashion. But we think it is clear that the statute was not designed to require employers to provide absolutely risk-free workplaces whenever it is technologically feasible to do so, so long as the cost is not great enough to destroy an entire industry. Rather, both the language and structure of the Act, as well as its legislative history, indicate that it was intended to require the elimination, as far as feasible, of significant risks of harm.

B

By empowering the Secretary to promulgate standards that are "reasonably necessary or appropriate to provide safe or healthful employment and places of employment," the Act implies that, before promulgating any standard, the Secretary must make a finding that the workplaces in question are not safe. But "safe" is not the equivalent of "risk-free." There are many activities that we engage in every day—such as driving a car or even breathing city air—that entail some risk of accident or material health impairment; nevertheless, few people would consider these activities "unsafe." Similarly, a workplace can hardly be considered "unsafe" unless it threatens the workers with a significant risk of harm.

Therefore, before he can promulgate any permanent health or safety standard, the Secretary is required to make a threshold finding that a place of employment is unsafe—in the sense that significant risks are present and can be eliminated or lessened by a change in practices. This requirement applies to permanent standards promulgated pursuant to § 6(b)(5), as well as to other types of permanent standards. For there is no reason why § 3(8)'s definition of a standard should not be deemed incorporated by reference into § 6(b)(5). The standards promulgated pursuant to § 6(b)(5) are just one species of the genus of standards governed by the basic requirement. That section repeatedly uses the term "standard" without suggesting any exception from, or qualification of, the general definition; on the contrary, it directs the Secretary to select "the standard"—that is to say, one of various possible alternatives that satisfy the basic definition in § 3(8)—that is most protective. Moreover, requiring the Secretary to make a threshold finding of significant risk is consistent with the scope of the regulatory power granted to him by § 6(b)(5), which empowers the Secretary to promulgate standards, not for chemicals and physical agents generally, but for "toxic materials" and "harmful physical agents."

This interpretation of §§ 3(8) and 6(b)(5) is supported by the other provisions of the Act. Thus, for example, § 6(g) provides in part that

> [in] determining the priority for establishing standards under this section, the Secretary shall give due regard to the urgency of the need for mandatory safety and health standards for particular industries, trades, crafts, occupations, businesses, workplaces or work environments.

The Government has expressly acknowledged that this section requires the Secretary to undertake some cost-benefit analysis before he promulgates any standard, requiring the elimination of the most serious hazards first. If such an analysis must precede the promulgation of any standard, it seems manifest that Congress intended, at a bare minimum, that the Secretary find a significant risk of harm and therefore a probability of significant benefits before establishing a new standard.

Section 6 (b)(8) lends additional support to this analysis. That subsection requires that, when the Secretary substantially alters an existing consensus standard, he must explain how the new rule will "better effectuate" the purposes of the Act. If this requirement was intended to be more than a meaningless formality, it must be read to impose upon the Secretary the duty to find that an existing national consensus standard is not adequate to protect workers from a continuing and significant risk of harm. Thus, in this case, the Secretary was required to find that exposures at the current permissible exposure level of 10 ppm present a significant risk of harm in the workplace.

In the absence of a clear mandate in the Act, it is unreasonable to assume that Congress intended to give the Secretary the unprecedented power over American industry that would result from the Government's view of §§ 3(8) and 6(b)(5), coupled with OSHA's cancer policy. Expert testimony that a substance is probably a human carcinogen—either because it has caused cancer in animals or because individuals have contracted cancer following extremely high exposures—would justify the conclusion that the substance poses some risk of serious harm no matter how minute the exposure and no matter how many experts testified that they regarded the risk as insignificant. That conclusion would in turn justify pervasive regulation limited only by the constraint of feasibility. In light of the fact that there are literally thousands of substances used in the workplace that have been identified as carcinogens or suspect[ed] carcinogens, the Government's theory would give OSHA power to impose enormous costs that might produce little, if any, discernible benefit.

If the Government were correct in arguing that neither § 3(8) nor § 6(b)(5) requires that the risk from a toxic substance be quantified sufficiently to enable the Secretary to characterize it as significant in an understandable way, the statute would make such a "sweeping delegation of legislative power" that it might be unconstitutional under the Court's reasoning in *A. L. A. Schechter Poultry Corp. v. United States*, 295 U.S. 495, 539, and *Panama Refining Co. v. Ryan*, 293 U.S. 388. A construction of the statute that avoids this kind of open-ended grant should certainly be favored.

C

. . .

Finally, with respect to the legislative history, it is important to note that Congress repeatedly expressed its concern about allowing the Secretary to have too much power over American industry. Thus, Congress refused to give the Secretary the power to shut down plants unilaterally because of an imminent danger, and narrowly circumscribed the Secretary's power to issue temporary emergency standards. This effort by Congress to limit the Secretary's power is not consistent with a view that the mere possibility that some employee somewhere in the country may confront some risk of cancer is a sufficient basis for the exercise of the Secretary's power to require the expenditure of hundreds of millions of dollars to minimize that risk.

D

Given the conclusion that the Act empowers the Secretary to promulgate health and safety standards only where a significant risk of harm exists, the critical issue becomes how to define and allocate the burden of proving the significance of the risk in a case such as this, where scientific knowledge is imperfect and the precise quantification of risks is therefore impossible. The Agency's position is that there is substantial evidence in the record to support its conclusion that there is no absolutely safe level for a carcinogen and that, therefore, the burden is properly on industry to prove, apparently beyond a shadow of a doubt, that there is a safe level for benzene exposure. The Agency argues that, because of the uncertainties in this area, any other approach would render it helpless, forcing it to wait for the leukemia deaths that it believes are likely to occur[60] before taking any regulatory action.

We disagree. As we read the statute, the burden was on the Agency to show, on the basis of substantial evidence, that it is at least more likely than not that long-term exposure to 10 ppm of benzene presents a significant risk of material health impairment. Ordinarily, it is the proponent of a rule or order who has the burden of proof in administrative proceedings. In some cases involving toxic substances, Congress has shifted the burden of proving that a particular substance is safe onto the party opposing the proposed rule. The fact that Congress did not follow this course in enacting the Occupational Safety and Health Act indicates that it intended the Agency to bear the normal burden of establishing the need for a proposed standard.

In this case OSHA did not even attempt to carry its burden of proof. The closest it came to making a finding that benzene presented a significant risk of harm in the workplace was its statement that the benefits to be derived from lowering the permissible exposure level from 10 to 1 ppm were "likely" to be "appreciable." The Court of Appeals held that this finding was not supported by

---

[60] As noted above, OSHA acknowledged that there was no empirical evidence to support the conclusion that there was any risk whatsoever of deaths due to exposures at 10 ppm. What OSHA relied upon was a theory that, because leukemia deaths had occurred at much higher exposures, some (although fewer) were also likely to occur at relatively low exposures. The Court of Appeals specifically held that its conclusion that the number was "likely" to be appreciable was unsupported by the record.

substantial evidence. Of greater importance, even if it were supported by substantial evidence, such a finding would not be sufficient to satisfy the Agency's obligations under the Act.

The inadequacy of the Agency's findings can perhaps be illustrated best by its rejection of industry testimony that a dose-response curve can be formulated on the basis of current epidemiological evidence and that, even under the most conservative extrapolation theory, current exposure levels would cause at most two deaths out of a population of about 30,000 workers every six years. In rejecting this testimony, OSHA made the following statement:

"In the face of the record evidence of numerous actual deaths attributable to benzene-induced leukemia and other fatal blood diseases, OSHA is unwilling to rely on the hypothesis that at most two cancers every six years would be prevented by the proposed standard. By way of example, the Infante study disclosed seven excess leukemia deaths in a population of about 600 people over a 25-year period. While the Infante study involved higher exposures th[a]n those currently encountered, the incidence rates found by Infante, together with the numerous other cases reported in the literature of benzene leukemia and other fatal blood diseases, make it difficult for OSHA to rely on the [witness's] hypothesis to assure the statutorily mandated protection of employees. In any event, due to the fact that there is no safe level of exposure to benzene and that it is impossible to precisely quantify the anticipated benefits, OSHA must select the level of exposure which is most protective of exposed employees."

There are three possible interpretations of OSHA's stated reason for rejecting the witness'[s] testimony: (1) OSHA considered it probable that a greater number of lives would be saved by lowering the standard from 10 ppm; (2) OSHA thought that saving two lives every six years in a work force of 30,000 persons is a significant savings that makes it reasonable and appropriate to adopt a new standard; or (3) even if the small number is not significant and even if the savings may be even smaller, the Agency nevertheless believed it had a statutory duty to select the level of exposure that is most protective of the exposed employees if it is economically and technologically feasible to do so. Even if the Secretary did not intend to rely entirely on this third theory, his construction of the statute would make it proper for him to do so. Moreover, he made no express findings of fact that would support his 1 ppm standard on any less drastic theory. Under these circumstances, we can hardly agree with the Government that OSHA discharged its duty under the Act.

Contrary to the Government's contentions, imposing a burden on the Agency of demonstrating a significant risk of harm will not strip it of its ability to regulate carcinogens, nor will it require the Agency to wait for deaths to occur before taking any action. First, the requirement that a "significant" risk be identified is not a mathematical straitjacket. It is the Agency's responsibility to determine, in the first instance, what it considers to be a "significant" risk. Some risks are plainly acceptable and others are plainly unacceptable. If, for example, the odds are one in a billion that a person will die from cancer by taking a drink of chlorinated water, the risk clearly could not be considered significant. On the other hand, if the odds are one in a thousand that regular inhalation of gasoline vapors that are 2% benzene will be fatal, a reasonable person might well consider the risk significant and take appropriate steps to decrease or eliminate it. Although the Agency has no duty to calculate the exact probability of harm, it does have an obligation to find that a significant risk is present before it can characterize a place of employment as "unsafe."[62]

Second, OSHA is not required to support its finding that a significant risk exists with anything approaching scientific certainty. Although the Agency's findings must be supported by substantial evidence, § 6(b)(5) specifically allows the Secretary to regulate on the basis of the "best available evidence." As several Courts of Appeals have held, this provision requires a reviewing court to give OSHA some leeway where its findings must be made on the frontiers of scientific knowledge. Thus, so long as they are supported by a body of reputable scientific thought, the Agency is free to use conservative assumptions in interpreting the data with respect to carcinogens, risking error on the side of overprotection rather than underprotection.[63]

Finally, the record in this case and OSHA's own rulings on other carcinogens indicate that there are a number of ways in which the Agency can make a rational judgment about the relative significance of the risks associated with exposure to a particular carcinogen.[64]

[62] In his dissenting opinion, Mr. Justice Marshall states: "[When] the question involves determination of the acceptable level of risk, the ultimate decision must necessarily be based on considerations of policy as well as empirically verifiable facts. Factual determinations can at most define the risk in some statistical way; the judgment whether that risk is tolerable cannot be based solely on a resolution of the facts." We agree. Thus, while the Agency must support its finding that a certain level of risk exists by substantial evidence, we recognize that its determination that a particular level of risk is "significant" will be based largely on policy considerations. At this point we have no need to reach the issue of what level of scrutiny a reviewing court should apply to the latter type of determination.

[63] Mr. Justice Marshall states that, under our approach, the Agency must either wait for deaths to occur or must "deceive the public" by making a basically meaningless determination of significance based on totally inadequate evidence. Mr. Justice Marshall's view, however, rests on the erroneous premise that the only reason OSHA did not attempt to quantify benefits in this case was because it could not do so in any reasonable manner. As the discussion of the Agency's rejection of an industry attempt at formulating a dose-response curve demonstrates, however, the Agency's rejection of methods such as dose-response curves was based at least in part on its view that nothing less than absolute safety would suffice.

[64] For example, in the coke-oven emissions standard, OSHA had calculated that 21,000 exposed coke-oven workers had an annual excess mortality of over 200 and that the proposed standard might well eliminate the risk entirely. In hearings on the coke-oven emissions standard, the Council on Wage and Price Stability estimated that 8 to 35 lives would be saved each year, out of an estimated population of 14,000 workers, as a result of the proposed standard. Although noting that the range of benefits would vary depending on the assumptions used, OSHA did not make a finding as to whether its own staff estimate or CWPS's was correct, on the ground that it was not required to quantify the expected benefits of the standard or to weigh those benefits against the projected costs.

In other proceedings, the Agency has had a good deal of data from animal experiments on which it could base a conclusion on the significance of the risk. For example, the record on the vinyl chloride standard indicated that a significant number of animals had developed tumors of the liver, lung, and skin when they were exposed to 50 ppm of vinyl chloride over a period

It should also be noted that, in setting a permissible exposure level in reliance on less-than-perfect methods, OSHA would have the benefit of a backstop in the form of monitoring and medical testing. Thus, if OSHA properly determined that the permissible exposure limit should be set at 5 ppm, it could still require monitoring and medical testing for employees exposed to lower levels. By doing so, it could keep a constant check on the validity of the assumptions made in developing the permissible exposure limit, giving it a sound evidentiary basis for decreasing the limit if it was initially set too high. Moreover, in this way it could ensure that workers who were unusually susceptible to benzene could be removed from exposure before they had suffered any permanent damage.

E

Because our review of these cases has involved a more detailed examination of the record than is customary, it must be emphasized that we have neither made any factual determinations of our own, nor have we rejected any factual findings made by the Secretary. We express no opinion on what factual findings this record might support, either on the basis of empirical evidence or on the basis of expert testimony; nor do we express any opinion on the more difficult question of what factual determinations would warrant a conclusion that significant risks are present which make promulgation of a new standard reasonably necessary or appropriate. The standard must, of course, be supported by the findings actually made by the Secretary, not merely by findings that we believe he might have made.

In this case the record makes it perfectly clear that the Secretary relied squarely on a special policy for carcinogens that imposed the burden on industry of proving the existence of a safe level of exposure, thereby avoiding the Secretary's threshold responsibility of establishing the need for more stringent standards. In so interpreting his statutory authority, the Secretary exceeded his power.

. . .

[The opinions by Chief Justice Burger, concurring, and by Justice Powell, concurring in the judgment, are omitted.]

Justice Rehnquist, concurring in the judgment. [We omit this opinion, which deals with the nondelegation doctrine and is discussed in chapter 12.]

Justice Marshall, with whom Justices Brennan, White, and Blackmun join, dissenting:

---

of 11 months. One hundred out of 200 animals died during that period. Similarly, in a 1974 standard regulating 14 carcinogens, OSHA found that one of the substances had caused lung cancer in mice or rats at 1 ppm and even 0.1 ppm, while another had caused tumors in 80% of the animals subjected to high doses.

In this case the Agency did not have the benefit of animal studies, because scientists have been unable as yet to induce leukemia in experimental animals as a result of benzene exposure. It did, however, have a fair amount of epidemiological evidence, including both positive and negative studies. Although the Agency stated that this evidence was insufficient to construct a precise correlation between exposure levels and cancer risks, it would at least be helpful in determining whether it is more likely than not that there is a significant risk at 10 ppm.

. . .

In this case the Secretary found that exposure to benzene at levels above 1 ppm posed a definite albeit unquantifiable risk of chromosomal damage, nonmalignant blood disorders, and leukemia. The existing evidence was sufficient to justify the conclusion that such a risk was presented, but it did not permit even rough quantification of that risk. Discounting for the various scientific uncertainties, the Secretary gave "careful consideration to the question of whether [the] substantial costs" of the standard "are justified in light of the hazards of exposure to benzene," and concluded that "these costs are necessary in order to effectuate the statutory purpose . . . and to adequately protect employees from the hazards of exposure to benzene."

In these circumstances it seems clear that the Secretary found a risk that is "significant" in the sense that the word is normally used. There was some direct evidence of chromosomal damage, nonmalignant blood disorders, and leukemia at exposures at or near 10 ppm and below. In addition, expert after expert testified that the recorded effects of benzene exposure at higher levels justified an inference that an exposure level above 1 ppm was dangerous. The plurality's extraordinarily searching scrutiny of this factual record reveals no basis for a conclusion that quantification is, on the basis of "the best available evidence," possible at the present time. If the Secretary decided to wait until definitive information was available, American workers would be subjected for the indefinite future to a possibly substantial risk of benzene-induced leukemia and other illnesses. It is unsurprising, at least to me, that he concluded that the statute authorized him to take regulatory action now.

Under these circumstances, the plurality's requirement of identification of a "significant" risk will have one of two consequences. If the plurality means to require the Secretary realistically to "quantify" the risk in order to satisfy a court that it is "significant," the record shows that the plurality means to require him to do the impossible. But regulatory inaction has very significant costs of its own. The adoption of such a test would subject American workers to a continuing risk of cancer and other serious diseases; it would disable the Secretary from regulating a wide variety of carcinogens for which quantification simply cannot be undertaken at the present time.

. . .

. . . [T]he record amply demonstrates that in light of existing scientific knowledge, no purpose would be served by requiring the Secretary to take steps to quantify the risk of exposure to benzene at low levels. Any such quantification would be based not on scientific "knowledge" as that term is normally understood, but on considerations of policy. For carcinogens like benzene, the assumptions on which a dose-response curve must be based are necessarily arbitrary. To require a quantitative showing of a "significant" risk, therefore, would either paralyze the Secretary into inaction or force him to deceive the public by acting on the basis of assumptions that must be considered too speculative to support any realistic assessment of the relevant risk. It is encouraging that the Court appears willing not to require quantification when it is not fairly possible.

. . .

COMMENTS AND QUESTIONS

1. The plurality requires that the agency make a "threshold" determination that the risk posed by benzene is "significant." What *is* a "significant" risk? The

plurality asserts that it is not requiring that the agency develop some quantitative measure of significance (why not?), but doesn't the term itself suggest some degree of quantitative assessment, even if within broad limits? If so, why did the plurality find that the agency had *not* made a determination that the risk was significant? Stephen Breyer et al., *Administrative Law and Regulatory Policy* (5th ed. Aspen Law & Business, 2002), at 71, ask, "Suppose that a lifetime cancer risk from a certain substance is 1/1000, faced by 10,000 workers. Is that risk 'significant'? Would the answer be different if the same lifetime cancer risk was faced by 10 million workers?" They report that OSHA has said that "a lifetime risk of over 1.64/1000 is 'significant,' but that a risk of 0.6/100,000 'may be approaching a level that can be viewed as safe.'"

2. Consider the proposition that the issue in the Benzene Case was framed—and perhaps badly framed—by the agency's prior policy decision that *any* cancer risk required a standard requiring that all feasible actions be taken, and that an alternative policy decision, allowing *some* exposure to cancer risk to go unaddressed or to trade off some exposure to cancer risk against the costs of reducing overall cancer risk, might have produced a record that the plurality might have found acceptable. For a discussion of the background against which the agency's "Generic Carcinogen Policy" was developed, see Thomas O. McGarity, "The Story of the Benzene Case: Judicially Imposed Regulatory Reform through Risk Assessment," in *Environmental Law Stories* (Richard A. Lazarus and Oliver A. Houck eds., Foundation Press, 2005).

3. What should the agency do on remand, in light of its position that there are no relevant studies at the relevant levels of exposure? Do more studies? Extrapolate from existing data by using the dose-response model the agency criticized? Note that any course will take time, during which workers are exposed to risks that may be "significant," both in the statute's terms and in everyday terms. The plurality's position clearly places the burden of inertia—that is, the burden of bearing risk until the agency comes up with an acceptable policy—on workers. On what basis should that burden be allocated? (Can it be allocated one way or the other without engaging in some sort of cost-benefit analysis?)

4. The plurality supports its conclusion that the statutory term "safe" does not mean "risk-free" by pointing out that everyday activities such as driving a car entail risk but are not commonly regarded as unsafe. Do you agree? (The alternative is that people regard such activities as unsafe but worth it anyway—a sort of commonsense cost-benefit analysis.)

5. Does the "significant risk" requirement make judicial review easier or harder? The agency's position in the Benzene Case was that once *some* risk existed, it could require all feasible measures, meaning those that would not drive the regulated industry out of business. In your view, how difficult would it be to determine whether the agency's conclusions on the existence of risk and on feasibility were not arbitrary and capricious? How difficult would it be to determine whether the agency's conclusion that a risk was significant was not arbitrary and capricious?

6. A decade later the agency issued the same standard—1 ppm—after additional studies showed risks of 95/1,000 at 10 ppm and 5–16/1,000 at 1 ppm. The

record supporting that standard was much more extensive than the one available in 1980, and there had been ten years of worker exposure to the higher level of risk. OSHA also shifted its regulatory focus—in part because of changes in the political environment—from the development of health standards to efforts to reduce workplace accidents. We will discuss some of those efforts in chapter 15.

The Benzene Case resulted in a large increase in the use of quantitative risk assessment throughout government. Prior to the decision, regulatory agencies had been divided over the value of engaging in such assessments, with the Environmental Protection Agency relatively enthusiastic and OSHA relatively unenthusiastic. The Benzene decision reduced resistance to the use of quantitative risk assessment.

7. The Court in the Benzene Case avoided addressing the agency's claim that the statutory requirement of feasibility barred it from using cost-benefit analysis. That issue returned to the Court a year later, in *American Textile Manufacturers Institute, Inc. v. Donovan, Secretary of Labor ("Cotton Dust")*, 452 U.S. 490 (1981). Justice Brennan's opinion for the Court rejected the proposition that "OSHA must demonstrate that the reduction in risk of material health impairment is significant in light of the costs of attaining that reduction":

> The plain meaning of the word "feasible" supports [OSHA's] interpretation of the statute. According to *Webster's Third New International Dictionary of the English Language* 831 (1976), "feasible" means "capable of being done, executed, or effected." Accord, the *Oxford English Dictionary* 116 (1933) ("Capable of being done, accomplished or carried out"); *Funk & Wagnalls New "Standard" Dictionary of the English Language* 903 (1957) ("That may be done, performed or effected"). Thus, § 6(b)(5) directs the Secretary to issue the standard that "most adequately assures...that no employee will suffer material impairment of health," limited only by the extent to which this is "capable of being done." In effect then,...Congress itself defined the basic relationship between costs and benefits, by placing the "benefit" of worker health above all other considerations save those making attainment of this "benefit" unachievable. Any standard based on a balancing of costs and benefits by the Secretary that strikes a different balance than that struck by Congress would be inconsistent with the command set forth in § 6(b)(5). Thus, cost-benefit analysis by OSHA is not required by the statute because feasibility analysis is.

Justice Brennan's opinion referred to numerous statutes expressly requiring cost-benefit analysis (at least when read in light of their legislative histories), including the Consumer Product Safety Act of 1972.

Addressing the argument that "reasonably necessary or appropriate" "might be construed to contemplate some balancing of the costs and benefits of a standard," Justice Brennan wrote:

> ...We need not decide whether § 3(8), standing alone, would contemplate some form of cost-benefit analysis. For even if it does, Congress specifically chose in § 6(b)(5) to impose separate and additional

requirements for issuance of a subcategory of occupational safety and health standards dealing with toxic materials and harmful physical agents: it required that those standards be issued to prevent material impairment of health to the extent feasible. Congress could reasonably have concluded that health standards should be subject to different criteria than safety standards because of the special problems presented in regulating them.

Agreement with petitioners' argument that § 3(8) imposes an additional and overriding requirement of cost-benefit analysis on the issuance of § 6(b)(5) standards would eviscerate the "to the extent feasible" requirement. Standards would inevitably be set at the level indicated by cost-benefit analysis, and not at the level specified by § 6(b)(5). For example, if cost-benefit analysis indicated a protective standard of 1,000 $\mu g/m^3$ PEL, while feasibility analysis indicated a 500 $\mu g/m^3$ PEL, the agency would be forced by the cost-benefit requirement to choose the less stringent point. We cannot believe that Congress intended the general terms of § 3(8) to countermand the specific feasibility requirement of § 6(b)(5). Adoption of petitioners' interpretation would effectively write § 6(b)(5) out of the Act. We decline to render Congress' decision to include a feasibility requirement nugatory, thereby offending the well-settled rule that all parts of a statute, if possible, are to be given effect. Congress did not contemplate any further balancing by the agency for toxic material and harmful physical agents standards, and we should not " 'impute to Congress a purpose to paralyze with one hand what it sought to promote with the other.' " *Weinberger v. Hynson, Westcott and Dunning, Inc.* [412 U.S. 609, 631 (1973)], quoting *Clark v. Uebersee Finanz-Korporation*, 332 U.S. 480, 489 (1947).

Justice Brennan also wrote:

Not only does the legislative history confirm that Congress meant "feasible" rather than "cost-benefit" when it used the former term, but it also shows that Congress understood that the Act would create substantial costs for employers, yet intended to impose such costs when necessary to create a safe and healthful working environment. Congress viewed the costs of health and safety as a cost of doing business. Senator Yarborough, a cosponsor of the Williams bill, stated: "We know the costs would be put into consumer goods but that is the price we should pay for the 80 million workers in America." He asked:

"One may well ask too expensive for whom? Is it too expensive for the company who for lack of proper safety equipment loses the services of its skilled employees? Is it too expensive for the employee who loses his hand or leg or eyesight? Is it too expensive for the widow trying to raise her children on [a] meager allowance under workmen's compensation and social security? And what about the man—a good hardworking man—tied to a wheel chair or hospital bed for the rest of his life? That is what we are dealing with when we talk about industrial safety. . . .

"We are talking about people's lives, not the indifference of some cost accountants."

Senator Eagleton commented that "[the] costs that will be incurred by employers in meeting the standards of health and safety to be established under this bill are, in my view, *reasonable and necessary costs of doing business.*"

Other Members of Congress voiced similar views. Nowhere is there any indication that Congress contemplated a different balancing by OSHA of the benefits of worker health and safety against the costs of achieving them. Indeed Congress thought that the financial costs of health and safety problems in the workplace were as large as or larger than the financial costs of eliminating these problems. In its statement of findings and declaration of purpose encompassed in the Act itself, Congress announced that "personal injuries and illnesses arising out of work situations impose a substantial burden upon, and are a hindrance to, interstate commerce in terms of lost production, wage loss, medical expenses, and disability compensation payments." The Senate was well aware of the magnitude of these costs:

> [The] economic impact of industrial deaths and disability is staggering. Over $1.5 billion is wasted in lost wages, and the annual loss to the Gross National Product is estimated to be over $8 billion. Vast resources that could be available for productive use are siphoned off to pay workmen's compensation benefits and medical expenses.

Senator Eagleton summarized: "Whether we, as individuals, are motivated by simple humanity or by simple economics, we can no longer permit profits to be dependent upon an unsafe or unhealthy worksite."

8. Is a rule requiring the agency to find a significant risk but barring it from doing cost-benefit analysis good public policy? The uncertainties associated with the idea of "significant risk" suggest that improvements in health may be quite uncertain, and the absence of cost-benefit analysis suggests that whatever improvements occur might be excessive. Recall Mendeloff's argument that overregulation produces underregulation by increasing the stakes for regulated entities, thereby inducing them to fight extremely hard against the adoption of "strong" regulations. Would allowing OSHA to engage in cost-benefit analysis eliminate (or reduce substantially) this effect, or would regulated entities still fight quite hard against the imposition of regulatory standards that meet a cost-benefit test? (How would you go about answering that question?)

9. *Concluding comment*: The Benzene Case and *Cotton Dust* deal with the interaction between regulatory goals and regulatory means. This chapter deals with *standards* as means, that is, targets that industries are required to reach. But even within the standard-based approach, there can be variations: Industries could be given targets and told how to meet them (typically, by using the "best available technology"), or be given targets and allowed the choice of means to reach them, for example. Other more market-based variants are discussed in chapter 15.

Ⓒ Public Health Standards

■ Whitman v. American Trucking Associations, Inc.
531 U.S. 457 (2001)

Justice Scalia delivered the opinion of the Court.

. . . .

Section 109(a) of the [Clean Air Act (CAA)] requires the Administrator of the [Environmental Protection Agency (EPA)] to promulgate [National Ambient Air Quality Standards (NAAQS)] for each air pollutant for which "air quality criteria" have been issued under § 108. Once a NAAQS has been promulgated, the Administrator must review the standard (and the criteria on which it is based) "at five-year intervals" and make "such revisions . . . as may be appropriate." CAA § 109(d)(1). These cases arose when, on July 18, 1997, the Administrator revised the NAAQS for particulate matter (PM) and ozone. American Trucking Associations, Inc., and its co-respondents . . . —which include, in addition to other private companies, the States of Michigan, Ohio, and West Virginia—challenged the new standards in the Court of Appeals for the District of Columbia Circuit.

. . .

The District of Columbia Circuit . . . rejected respondents' argument that the court should depart from the rule of *Lead Industries Assn., Inc. v. EPA*, 647 F.2d 1130, 1148 (CADC 1980), that the EPA may not consider the cost of implementing a NAAQS in setting the initial standard. . . .

. . .

Section 109(b)(1) instructs the EPA to set primary ambient air quality standards "the attainment and maintenance of which . . . are requisite to protect the public health" with "an adequate margin of safety." 42 U.S.C. § 7409(b)(1). Were it not for the hundreds of pages of briefing respondents have submitted on the issue, one would have thought it fairly clear that this text does not permit the EPA to consider costs in setting the standards. The language, as one scholar has noted, "is absolute." D. Currie, Air Pollution: Federal Law and Analysis 4–15 (1981). The EPA, "based on" the information about health effects contained in the technical "criteria" documents compiled under § 108(a)(2), 42 U.S.C. § 7408(a)(2), is to identify the maximum airborne concentration of a pollutant that the public health can tolerate, decrease the concentration to provide an "adequate" margin of safety, and set the standard at that level. Nowhere are the costs of achieving such a standard made part of that initial calculation.

Against this most natural of readings, respondents make a lengthy, spirited, but ultimately unsuccessful attack. They begin with the object of § 109(b)(1)'s focus, the "public health." When the term first appeared in federal clean air legislation— in the Act of July 14, 1955 (1955 Act), 69 Stat. 322, which expressed "recognition of the dangers to the public health" from air pollution—its ordinary meaning was "the health of the community." Webster's New International Dictionary 2005 (2d ed. 1950). Respondents argue, however, that § 109(b)(1), as added by the Clean Air Amendments of 1970 (1970 Act), meant to use the term's secondary meaning: "the ways and means of conserving the health of the members of a community, as by preventive medicine, organized care of the sick, etc." Words that can have more than one meaning are given content, however, by their surroundings, *FDA v. Brown & Williamson Tobacco Corp.*, 529 U.S. 120, 132–133 (2000), and in the context of § 109(b)(1) this second definition makes no sense. Congress could not have meant to instruct the Administrator to set NAAQS at a level "requisite to protect" "the art and science dealing with the protection and improvement of community health." *Webster's Third New International Dictionary* 1836 (1981). We therefore revert to the primary definition of the term: the health of the public.

Even so, respondents argue, many more factors than air pollution affect public health. In particular, the economic cost of implementing a very stringent standard might produce health losses sufficient to offset the health gains achieved in cleaning the air—for example, by closing down whole industries and thereby impoverishing the workers and consumers dependent upon those industries. That is unquestionably true, and Congress was unquestionably aware of it. Thus, Congress had commissioned in the Air Quality Act of 1967 (1967 Act) "a detailed estimate of the cost of carrying out the provisions of this Act; a comprehensive study of the cost of program implementation by affected units of government; and a comprehensive study of the economic impact of air quality standards on the Nation's industries, communities, and other contributing sources of pollution." § 2, 81 Stat. 505. The 1970 Congress, armed with the results of this study, see The Cost of Clean Air, S. Doc. No. 91-40 (1969) (publishing the results of the study), not only anticipated that compliance costs could injure the public health, but provided for that precise exigency. Section 110(f)(1) of the CAA permitted the Administrator to waive the compliance deadline for stationary sources if, *inter alia*, sufficient control measures were simply unavailable and "the continued operation of such sources is *essential . . . to the public health* or welfare." 84 Stat. 1683 (emphasis added). Other provisions explicitly permitted or required economic costs to be taken into account in implementing the air quality standards. Section 111(b)(1)(B), for example, commanded the Administrator to set "standards of performance" for certain new sources of emissions that as specified in § 111(a)(1) were to "reflect the degree of emission limitation achievable through the application of the best system of emission reduction which (taking into account the cost of achieving such reduction) the Administrator determines has been adequately demonstrated." Section 202(a)(2) prescribed that emissions standards for automobiles could take effect only "after such period as the Administrator finds necessary to permit the development and application of the requisite technology, giving appropriate consideration to the cost of compliance within such period." 84 Stat. 1690. See also § 202(b)(5)(C) (similar limitation for interim standards); § 211(c)(2) (similar limitation for fuel additives); § 231(b) (similar limitation for implementation of aircraft emission standards). Subsequent amendments to the CAA have added many more provisions directing, in explicit language, that the Administrator consider costs in performing various duties. See, e.g., 42 U.S.C. § 7545(k)(1) (reformulate gasoline to "require the greatest reduction in emissions . . . taking into consideration the cost of achieving such emissions reductions"); § 7547(a)(3) (emission reduction for nonroad vehicles to be set "giving appropriate consideration to the cost" of the standards). We have therefore refused to find implicit in ambiguous sections of the CAA an authorization to consider costs that has elsewhere, and so often, been expressly granted.

Accordingly, to prevail in their present challenge, respondents must show a textual commitment of authority to the EPA to consider costs in setting NAAQS under § 109(b)(1). And because § 109(b)(1) and the NAAQS for which it provides are the engine that drives nearly all of Title I of the CAA, 42 U.S.C. §§ 7401–7515, that textual commitment must be a clear one. Congress, we have held, does not alter the fundamental details of a regulatory scheme in vague terms or ancillary provisions—it does not, one might say, hide elephants in mouseholes. See *MCI Telecommunications Corp. v. American Telephone & Telegraph Co.*, 512 U.S. 218, 231 (1994); *FDA v. Brown & Williamson Tobacco Corp.*, at 159–160. Respondents' textual arguments ultimately founder upon this principle.

Their first claim is that § 109(b)(1)'s terms "adequate margin" and "requisite" leave room to pad health effects with cost concerns. Just as we found it "highly unlikely that Congress would leave the determination of whether an industry will be entirely, or even substantially, rate-regulated to agency discretion—and even more unlikely that it would achieve that through such a subtle device as permission to 'modify' rate-filing requirements," *MCI Telecommunications Corp. v. American Telephone & Telegraph Co.*, at 231, so also we find it implausible that Congress would give to the EPA through these modest words the power to determine whether implementation costs should moderate national air quality standards.

The same defect inheres in respondents' next two arguments: that while the Administrator's judgment about what is requisite to protect the public health must be "based on [the] criteria" documents developed under § 108(a)(2), see § 109(b)(1), it need not be based *solely* on those criteria; and that those criteria themselves, while they must include "effects on public health or welfare which may be expected from the presence of such pollutant in the ambient air," are not necessarily *limited* to those effects. Even if we were to concede those premises, we still would not conclude that one of the unenumerated factors that the agency can consider in developing and applying the criteria is cost of implementation. That factor is *both* so indirectly related to public health *and* so full of potential for canceling the conclusions drawn from direct health effects that it would surely have been expressly mentioned in §§ 108 and 109 had Congress meant it to be considered. Yet while those provisions describe in detail how the health effects of pollutants in the ambient air are to be calculated and given effect, see § 108(a)(2), they say not a word about costs.

Respondents point, finally, to a number of provisions in the CAA that *do* require attainment cost data to be generated. Section 108(b)(1), for example, instructs the Administrator to "issue to the States," simultaneously with the criteria documents, "information on air pollution control techniques, which information shall include data relating to the cost of installation and operation." 42 U.S.C. § 7408(b)(l). And § 109(d)(2)(C)(iv) requires the Clean Air Scientific Advisory Committee to "advise the Administrator of any adverse public health, welfare, social, economic, or energy effects which may result from various strategies for attainment and maintenance" of NAAQS. 42 U.S.C. § 7409(d)(2)(C)(iv). Respondents argue that these provisions make no sense unless costs are to be considered in setting the NAAQS. That is not so. These provisions enable the Administrator to assist the States in carrying out their statutory role as primary *implementers* of the NAAQS. It is to the States that the Act assigns initial and primary responsibility for deciding what emissions reductions will be required from which sources. See 42 U.S.C. §§ 7407 (a), 7410 (giving States the duty of developing implementation plans). It would be impossible to perform that task intelligently without considering which abatement technologies are most efficient, and most economically feasible—which is why we have said that "the most important forum for consideration of claims of economic and technological infeasibility is before the state agency formulating the implementation plan," *Union Elec. Co. v. EPA*, 427 U.S. at 266. Thus, federal clean air legislation has, from the very beginning, directed federal agencies to develop and transmit implementation data, including cost data, to the States. That Congress chose to carry forward this research program to assist States in choosing the means through which they would implement the standards is perfectly sensible, and has no bearing upon whether cost considerations are to be taken into account in formulating the standards.

. . . The text of § 109(b), interpreted in its statutory and historical context and with appreciation for its importance to the CAA as a whole, unambiguously bars cost considerations from the NAAQS-setting process, and thus ends the matter for us as well as the EPA.[4] We therefore affirm the judgment of the Court of Appeals on this point.

. . .

Justice Breyer, concurring in part and concurring in the judgment.

. . .

. . . [C]ontrary to the suggestion of the Court of Appeals and of some parties, [our] interpretation of § 109 does not require the EPA to eliminate every health risk, however slight, at any economic cost, however great, to the point of "hurtling" industry over "the brink of ruin," or even forcing "deindustrialization." *American Trucking Assns., Inc. v. EPA*, 175 F.3d 1027, 1037, 1038, n. 4 (C.A.D.C. 1999). The statute, by its express terms, does not compel the elimination of *all* risk; and it grants the Administrator sufficient flexibility to avoid setting ambient air quality standards ruinous to industry.

Section 109(b)(1) directs the Administrator to set standards that are "requisite to protect the public health" with "an adequate margin of safety." But these words do not describe a world that is free of all risk—an impossible and undesirable objective. See *Industrial Union Dept., AFL-CIO v. American Petroleum Institute.* Nor are the words "requisite" and "public health" to be understood independent of context. We consider football equipment "safe" even if its use entails a level of risk that would make drinking water "unsafe" for consumption. And what counts as "requisite" to protecting the public health will similarly vary with background circumstances, such as the public's ordinary tolerance of the particular health risk in the particular context at issue. The Administrator can consider such background circumstances when "decid[ing] what risks are acceptable in the world in which we live." *Natural Resources Defense Council, Inc. v. EPA*, 824 F.2d 1146, 1165 (C.A.D.C. 1987).

The statute also permits the Administrator to take account of comparative health risks. That is to say, she may consider whether a proposed rule promotes

---

[4] Respondents' speculation that the EPA is secretly considering the costs of attainment without telling anyone is irrelevant to our interpretive inquiry. If such an allegation could be proved, it would be grounds for vacating the NAAQS, because the Administrator had not followed the law. See, e.g., *Chevron U.S.A. Inc. v. Natural Resources Defense Council, Inc.*, 467 U.S. 837, 842–843 (1984). It would not, however, be grounds for this Court's changing the law.

safety overall. A rule likely to cause more harm to health than it prevents is not a rule that is "requisite to protect the public health." For example, as the Court of Appeals held and the parties do not contest, the Administrator has the authority to determine to what extent possible health risks stemming from reductions in tropospheric ozone (which, it is claimed, helps prevent cataracts and skin cancer) should be taken into account in setting the ambient air quality standard for ozone.

The statute ultimately specifies that the standard set must be "requisite to protect the public health" *"in the judgment of the Administrator,"* § 109(b)(1), 84 Stat. 1680 (emphasis added), a phrase that grants the Administrator considerable discretionary standard-setting authority.

The statute's words, then, authorize the Administrator to consider the severity of a pollutant's potential adverse health effects, the number of those likely to be affected, the distribution of the adverse effects, and the uncertainties surrounding each estimate. They permit the Administrator to take account of comparative health consequences. They allow her to take account of context when determining the acceptability of small risks to health. And they give her considerable discretion when she does so.

This discretion would seem sufficient to avoid the extreme results that some of the industry parties fear. After all, the EPA, in setting standards that "protect the public health" with "an adequate margin of safety," retains discretionary authority to avoid regulating risks that it reasonably concludes are trivial in context. Nor need regulation lead to deindustrialization. Preindustrial society was not a very healthy society; hence a standard demanding the return of the Stone Age would not prove "requisite to protect the public health."

. . .

COMMENTS AND QUESTIONS

1. The Court relies on the statute's plain language and its references to specific circumstances under which costs of implementation can be taken into account in setting air quality standards as the basis for its holding that, in general, the agency cannot engage in cost-benefit analysis in setting standards. How can the agency determine what an acceptable "margin of safety" is without engaging in cost-benefit analysis? Consider the possibility that the challenge to the air quality standards was simply misframed: Instead of asserting that the agency acted arbitrarily in failing to engage in cost-benefit analysis, the challengers should have asserted that the agency acted arbitrarily in failing to explain in cost-benefit terms the margin of safety it selected. (How can there be a margin of safety in exposure to "non-threshold" pollutants, that is, those that have adverse health effects at every level of exposure?)

2. On the Court's analysis, is considering costs in circumstances other than those specified prohibited by the statute? Justice Breyer emphasizes that the agency has discretion in evaluating comparative health risks. In exercising that discretion, may the agency take implementation costs into account? Can it avoid doing so?

   How widely may the agency look for comparative health effects? Recall Wildavsky's argument that richer is safer (chapter 9). So, too, richer may be healthier. Can the agency consider the adverse health effects of unemployment produced by a proposed standard? See *Natural Resources Defense Council, Inc. v. Administrator, United States Environmental Protection Agency*, 902 F.2d 962 (D.C. Cir. 1990) (concluding that the agency may not do so). What justification might there be for precluding the agency from doing so?

3. As a matter of policy, should costs be irrelevant in setting standards?

   (a) *Against taking costs into account*: Industries have differential access to cost information and are likely to overstate the costs of implementation (and remedies for differential access, such as agency discovery or mandatory reporting requirements, are themselves costly). Industries (and others?) may be unduly pessimistic about implementation costs and fail to recognize that there are unexploited technological opportunities for implementation at lower cost than they sincerely believe. (Sometimes this is referred to as one aspect of the "technology-forcing" argument for setting high standards.) Finally, clean air should not be commodified to the degree that cost-benefit analysis commodifies it. Even if agencies are likely to take costs into account implicitly, it may be better in the U.S. culture that the partial commodification of clean air (and of risk more generally) be concealed.

   (b) *For taking costs into account*: How can we know how much we want to protect health unless we know what we are sacrificing in setting standards at some specific level? Cost-benefit analysis gives us that information. In addition, the pressures to take costs into account are so great that they are very likely to figure into the agency's decision-making process (for example, in the analysis of comparative health risks or in setting the margin of safety), and it is better that the process be transparent about what matters to the agency. Finally, the regulatory paradox: Perhaps one reason for industry resistance to standard setting is the absence of consideration of implementation costs. (As of 2005, standards had been set for six pollutants in the thirty years since the adoption of the Clean Air Act.)

Note that taking costs into account might *support* the adoption of stringent standards. A study conducted by the Environmental Protection Agency (as mandated by Congress), concluded in 1997:

> When the human health, human welfare, and environmental effects which could be expressed in dollar terms were added up for the entire 20-year period [from 1970 to 1990], the total benefits of Clean Air Act programs were estimated to range from about $6 trillion to about $50 trillion, with a mean estimate of about $22 trillion. These estimated benefits represent the estimated value Americans place on avoiding the dire air quality conditions and dramatic increases in illness and premature death which would have prevailed without the 1970 and 1977 Clean Air Act and its associated state and local programs. By comparison, the actual costs of achieving the pollution reductions observed over the 20 year period were $523 billion, a small fraction of the estimated monetary benefits.
>
> While the estimated net benefits may seem large, they reflect the huge differences between actual historical air quality achieved in the U.S. and a model-predicted world without the Clean Air Act in which seven

metropolitan areas in the U.S. would have had higher concentrations of particulate matter (a critical pollutant responsible for much of the adverse human health consequences) than Bangkok, Thailand. Six metropolitan areas would have been worse than Bombay, India; two would have been worse than Manila, Philippines; and one U.S. metropolitan area would even have been worse than Delhi, India (one of the most polluted cities in the world).

The full report is available at http://www.epa.gov/air/sect812/copy.html.

■ American Lung Association v. Environmental Protection Agency
134 F.3d 388 (D.C. Cir. 1998)

Tatel, Circuit Judge:

On behalf of the nation's nearly nine million asthmatics, the American Lung Association and the Environmental Defense Fund challenge the Environmental Protection Agency's refusal to revise the primary national ambient air quality standards for sulfur dioxide (SO_2). Declining to promulgate a more stringent national standard, the EPA Administrator concluded that the substantial physical effects experienced by some asthmatics from exposure to short-term, high-level SO_2 bursts do not amount to a public health problem. Because the Administrator failed adequately to explain this conclusion, we remand for further elucidation.

I

Driven by its "deep concern for protection of the health of the American people," Sen. Rep. No. 91-1196, at 1 (1970) ("Senate Report"), Congress enacted the Clean Air Act Amendments of 1970, Pub. L. No. 91-604, 84 Stat. 1676 (1970) (codified as amended at 42 U.S.C. §§ 7401–7671q (1994)), mandating a "massive attack on air pollution," Senate Report at 1. As amended, the Clean Air Act erects a comprehensive system of national ambient air quality standards ("NAAQS") to regulate health-threatening air pollutants. The statute defines primary NAAQS as "ambient air quality standards the attainment and maintenance of which in the judgment of the Administrator, based on such criteria and allowing an adequate margin of safety, are requisite to protect the public health." 42 U.S.C. § 7409(b)(1).

Once the EPA Administrator concludes that a pollutant "may reasonably be anticipated to endanger public health or welfare" and that it comes from "numerous or diverse mobile or stationary sources," id. § 7408(a)(1)(A)–(B), the Act requires the Administrator to produce "criteria," defined as the latest scientific data on "all identifiable effects on public health" caused by that pollutant. Id. § 7408(a)(2). Based on these comprehensive criteria and taking account of the "preventative" and "precautionary" nature of the act, *Lead Industries Ass'n, Inc. v. EPA*, 647 F.2d 1130, 1155 (D.C. Cir. 1980), the Administrator must then decide what margin of safety will protect the public health from the pollutant's adverse effects—not just known adverse effects, but those of scientific uncertainty or that "research has not yet uncovered." Then, and without reference to cost or technological feasibility, the Administrator must promulgate national standards that limit emissions sufficiently to establish that margin of safety. States bear primary responsibility for attaining, maintaining, and enforcing these standards.

In its effort to reduce air pollution, Congress defined public health broadly. NAAQS must protect not only average healthy individuals, but also "sensitive citizens"—children, for example, or people with asthma, emphysema, or other conditions rendering them particularly vulnerable to air pollution. If a pollutant adversely affects the health of these sensitive individuals, EPA must strengthen the entire national standard. *Lead Industries*, 647 F.2d at 1153 (NAAQS "must be set at a level at which there is 'an absence of adverse effect' on these sensitive individuals").

Sulfur Dioxide and Asthmatics

A highly reactive colorless gas smelling like rotten eggs, sulfur dioxide derives primarily from fossil fuel combustion. Best known for causing "acid rain," at elevated concentrations in the ambient air, SO_2 also directly impairs human health. As the Administrator explains in the Final Decision on review here, at concentrations above 2.0 parts per million ("ppm"), SO_2 can affect healthy nonasthmatic individuals; below 2.0 ppm, it primarily affects people with asthma.

Following the passage of the Clean Air Act, EPA promulgated the SO_2 NAAQS in effect today. The primary standards consist of a 24-hour standard (0.14 ppm averaged over 24 hours not to be exceeded more than once a year) and an annual standard (0.03 ppm annual arithmetic mean). EPA also established a "secondary" three-hour standard (0.50 ppm averaged over three hours not to be exceeded more than once a year), designed to protect the "public welfare" against non-health-related effects such as visibility impairment or environmental degradation. Petitioners do not challenge these existing standards.

Approximately four percent of the nation's population suffers from asthma. Characterized by bronchoconstriction—shortness of breath, coughing, wheezing, chest tightness, and sputum production—asthma is triggered by many different stimuli, including cold or dry air, exercise or pollen as well as airborne pollutants. The effects of bronchoconstriction can vary from short-term discomfort, such as an hour-long reaction with no lasting after-effects, to asthma attacks requiring medication or hospitalization. Although rare, death can result.

Sulfur dioxide induces bronchoconstriction in asthmatics, but only under certain conditions. To experience adverse effects from SO_2 concentrations below 1.0 ppm, asthmatics must be exposed for five minutes or longer while breathing quickly and heavily through both nose and mouth, the sort of breathing induced by light exercise, shoveling snow, climbing several flights of stairs, or jogging to catch a bus. At concentrations above 2.0 ppm, SO_2 causes adverse effects even if the exposure lasts less than five minutes or the asthmatic breathes regularly.

The Challenged Final Decision

This case concerns the effect on asthmatics of what are known as high-level SO_2 bursts, defined as emissions of 0.50 ppm or more lasting at least five minutes. Occurring sporadically and from specific sources, SO_2 bursts come primarily from power utilities; the rest come from nonutility sources such as industrial boilers, petroleum refineries, pulp and paper mills, sulfuric acid plants, and aluminum smelters.

Citing the health concerns of asthmatics and relying on a 1977 amendment to the Clean Air Act, in which Congress ordered the Agency to review and revise all criteria and NAAQS by 1980 and at five-year intervals thereafter, petitioners urged

EPA to issue a new NAAQS limiting short-term SO_2 bursts. Not until 1996, after petitioners sued twice to compel a decision, and after two rounds of public notice and comment, did EPA issue its final decision regarding SO_2 NAAQS. Rejecting petitioners' arguments, EPA concluded not only that the annual and 24-hour primary standards needed no revision, but also that an additional five-minute standard was unnecessary to protect asthmatics.

In arriving at her final decision, the Administrator reviewed a decade of data on the extent of high-level short-term SO_2 bursts and their effects on public health. Based on clinical studies of mild to moderate asthmatics, she found that when such individuals breathe rapidly while exposed to SO_2 concentrations of 0.60 ppm for five minutes, "substantial percentages (≥ 25 percent)" experience effects "distinctly exceeding . . . [the] typical daily variation in lung function" that asthmatics routinely experience. The severity of these atypical effects, she found, "is likely to be of sufficient concern to cause disruption of ongoing activities, use of bronchodilator medication, and/or possible seeking of medical attention."

The scientific community disagreed about the medical significance of these effects and whether they should be considered "adverse." Some experts took the position that such symptoms usually have no lasting impact, amounting at worst to a brief period of reversible discomfort; others argued that even a one-hour disruption of activity can amount to a worrisome adverse health effect. The Administrator left this dispute unresolved. Instead, she discerned in the medical debate a consensus, which she adopted, that "repeated occurrences of such effects should be regarded as significant from a public health standpoint."

The Administrator then discussed the three exposure analyses on which the 1994 version of the proposed rule rested. These studies estimated that from 180,000 to 395,000 "exposure events"—defined as a heavily breathing asthmatic exposed to an SO_2 burst—occur annually, affecting from 68,000 to 166,000 asthmatic individuals. In view of the Administrator's previous finding, reiterated by agency counsel at oral argument, that at least 25 percent of asthmatics experience atypical effects from exposure events, these data suggest that as many as 41,500 (≥ 25 percent of 166,000) asthmatics experience atypical effects from repeated SO_2 bursts each year. At the same time, the Administrator acknowledged that subsequent industry studies of four nonutility sources suggest that the 1994 studies may have overestimated exposure for certain SO_2 sources, id., meaning that the number of affected asthmatics could be lower. The Administrator did not resolve the conflict between the studies.

Armed with all these data, the Administrator concluded that "the likelihood that asthmatic individuals will be exposed . . . is very low when viewed from a national perspective," that "5-minute peak SO_2 levels do not pose a broad public health problem when viewed from a national perspective," and that "short-term peak concentrations of SO_2 do not constitute the type of ubiquitous public health problem for which establishing a NAAQS would be appropriate." Describing SO_2 bursts as "localized, infrequent and site-specific," she concluded that a new national standard was unnecessary. The Administrator nevertheless decided to encourage individual states to address short-term high-level SO_2 emissions, initiating a rulemaking to provide appropriate guidance.

Petitioners now challenge the Administrator's decision declining to promulgate a new NAAQS. They assert that by failing to establish a five-minute NAAQS capping SO$_2$ emissions at 0.60 ppm, EPA has violated its statutory responsibility to protect the public health. We review the Administrator's decision pursuant to 42 U.S.C. § 7607(d)(9)(A)–(C) ("Court may reverse any such [agency] action found to be . . . arbitrary, capricious, an abuse of discretion, or otherwise not in accordance with law; . . . [or] in excess of statutory . . . authority, or limitations. . . .").

II

Petitioners challenge much of the data the Administrator relied on, as well as the conclusions she drew. Generally speaking, we will not second-guess EPA in its area of special expertise. Applying this deferential standard of review, we accept the Administrator's analysis of the exposure studies in the record, as well as the implication of her analysis—that thousands of asthmatics can be expected to react atypically to SO$_2$ bursts each year.

Petitioners contend that the Administrator's analysis amounts to a conclusive finding that SO$_2$ bursts adversely affect asthmatics' health, thus triggering her duty to promulgate a new NAAQS. At oral argument, counsel for EPA vigorously disputed petitioners' contention that the Administrator "found" an adverse health effect. As we read the record, agency counsel appears to be correct: The Administrator did not decide whether asthmatic reaction to SO$_2$ bursts—"disruption of ongoing activities, use of bronchodilator medication, and/or possible seeking of medical attention"—amounts to an adverse health effect or merely, as some medical experts argued, run-of-the-mill asthma symptoms indistinguishable from bronchodilation due to cold air or exercise. Skipping this disputed question, the Administrator concluded that, regardless of the impact of single occurrences, "repeated occurrences of such effects should be regarded as significant from a public health standpoint."

Disagreeing with this approach, petitioners argue that the Administrator had to answer the subsidiary "adverse effects" question, pointing to her warning to all states in the subsequent rulemaking that "although these episodes are few, it is clear that 5-minute SO$_2$ ambient concentration peaks pose a health threat to sensitive exposed populations." We need not decide that issue at this time, however, because we think the Administrator has failed to explain the answer she did give, i.e., that SO$_2$ bursts do not amount to a "public health" problem within the meaning of the Act. The link between this conclusion and the factual record as interpreted by EPA—that "repeated" exposure is "significant" and that thousands of asthmatics are exposed more than once a year—is missing. Why is the fact that thousands of asthmatics can be expected to suffer atypical physical effects from repeated five-minute bursts of high-level sulfur dioxide not a public health problem? Why are from 180,000 to 395,000 annual "exposure events" (the range indicated by the 1994 studies) or some fewer number (as suggested by the industry studies) so "infrequent" as to warrant no regulatory action? Why are disruptions of ongoing activities, use of medication, and hospitalization not "adverse health effects" for asthmatics? Answers to these questions appear nowhere in the administrative record.

In her only statement resembling an explanation for her conclusion that peak SO$_2$ bursts present no public health hazard, the Administrator characterizes the bursts as "localized, infrequent and site-specific." But nothing in the Final Decision explains away the possibility that "localized," "site-specific" or even "infrequent" events might nevertheless create a public health problem, particularly since, in some sense, all pollution is local and site-specific, whether spewing from the tailpipes of millions of cars or a few offending smoke stacks. From the record, we know that at least six communities experience "repeated high 5-minute peaks greater than 0.60 ppm SO_2," and agency counsel told us at oral argument that these so-called "hot spots" are not the only places where repeated exposure occurs. Nowhere, however, does the Administrator explain why these data amount to no more than a "local" problem.

Without answers to these questions, the Administrator cannot fulfill her responsibility under the Clean Air Act to establish NAAQS "requisite to protect the public health," 42 U.S.C. § 7409(b)(1), nor can we review her decision. Judicial deference to decisions of administrative agencies like EPA rests on the fundamental premise that agencies engage in reasoned decision-making. See *Vermont Yankee Nuclear Power Corp. v. Natural Resources Defense Council*, 435 U.S. 519, 524–25, 544–45, 558 (1978); *SEC v. Chenery Corp.*, 332 U.S. 194, 209 (1947) (agency's experience, appreciation of complexities and policies, and responsible treatment of the facts "justifies the use of the administrative process"). With its delicate balance of thorough record scrutiny and deference to agency expertise, judicial review can occur only when agencies explain their decisions with precision, for "it will not do for a court to be compelled to guess at the theory underlying the agency's action...." *SEC v. Chenery Corp.*, 332 U.S. at 196–97. Where, as here, Congress has delegated to an administrative agency the critical task of assessing the public health and the power to make decisions of national import in which individuals' lives and welfare hang in the balance, that agency has the heaviest of obligations to explain and expose every step of its reasoning. For these compelling reasons, we have always required the Administrator to "cogently explain why [she] has exercised [her] discretion in a given manner." *Motor Vehicle Mfrs. Ass'n v. State Farm Mut. Auto. Ins.*, 463 U.S. 29, 48 (1983).

In this case, the Administrator may well be within her authority to decide that 41,500 or some smaller number of exposed asthmatics do not amount to a public health problem warranting national protective regulation, or that three or six or twelve annual exposures present no cause for medical concern. But unless she describes the standard under which she has arrived at this conclusion, supported by a "plausible" explanation, id. at 43, we have no basis for exercising our responsibility to determine whether her decision is "arbitrary, capricious, an abuse of discretion, or otherwise not in accordance with law; . . . [or] in excess of statutory . . . authority, or limitations. . . ." 42 U.S.C. § 7607(d)(9)(A)–(C).

Given the gaps in the Final Decision's reasoning, we must remand this case to permit the Administrator to explain her conclusions more fully. We therefore need not resolve the debate between the parties over whether the Clean Air Act authorizes the Administrator to decline to protect an identifiable group of asthmatics from a known adverse health effect. Although our cases make clear that the Administrator has broad discretion to establish an "adequate margin of safety" above and beyond what scientific certainty prescribes and to craft regulations that protect against unknown harms, see *Lead Industries*, 647 F.2d at 1153–55 (Administrator must "err on the side of caution" when establishing the margin of safety, even where the "medical significance [of the effects] is a matter of disagreement"), they do not necessarily establish the converse proposition—that the Administrator may decline to establish a margin of safety in the face of documented adverse health effects. Since in this case the Administrator has failed adequately to explain her conclusion that no public health threat exists, we can leave the issue of the scope of her authority for another day.

We remand this case to the agency for further proceedings consistent with this opinion.

COMMENTS AND QUESTIONS

1. This case demonstrates that risk is relative to populations. You have already considered whether the *size* of a population is relevant to determining whether a risk is significant. This case shows that the *composition* of the population matters, too, because it affects the way risk is distributed among sectors of the population. Note that Congress identified "sensitive individuals" to whom the agency was required to pay special attention. How would you go about identifying "sensitive individuals," obviously on a classwide basis? What subpopulations, other than asthmatics and children, might have been added (but were not)?

   The court leaves open the question of whether the agency could decline to protect an identifiable group of asthmatics from a known adverse health effect. The *Lead Industries* case, discussed in *American Trucking Ass'n*, involved a regulatory standard that was set to protect 99.5% of children between one and five years of age from exposures to lead that had adverse health effects—that is, a standard that left 0.5% of the target population unprotected. Is the only justification for such an approach that protecting the group would be excessively costly? If so, is that consistent with the statutory scheme as you understand it?

2. Could the agency on remand say that the adverse health effects of "bursts" on sensitive individuals were not significant? Could it support that conclusion by observing that sensitive individuals could avoid or reduce the adverse health impacts by taking actions on their own—staying indoors or wearing masks (as is common in Japan)? What if the individual avoidance activities were difficult or intrusive (avoiding exercise, wearing gas masks rather than paper masks)?

3. In 1999, the agency proposed, and the American Lung Association agreed, that the agency would have until January 15, 2000, to propose a response to the remand. As of 2005, the agency had not developed a substantive response and was still gathering information on SO_2's short-term effects on asthmatics. The last document available discussed the "status" of the agency's "ongoing activities" in response to the remand. 66 Fed. Reg. 1665 (Jan. 9, 2001).

D. Implementing Standards: Technology and Market-Based Systems

Once a standard is set, industries must develop methods of ensuring that their operations are in compliance with that standard. A common approach is to require that industries use the "best available technology" to achieve the required level of risk reduction. Such an approach has two variants. The first collapses the standard-setting decision into the implementation decision by directing industries to employ the best available technology to achieve the level of risk reduction that technology can achieve. The second, and more common, variant uses the term "best available technology" to capture the idea that the agency probably has set a standard at a level that can readily (or can best) be achieved by employing the best available technology—but allows the regulated entities to employ other means as well to meet the standard. Think about how each variant affects industry incentives to develop risk-reduction techniques.

The next reading proposes a different technique, "tradable permits." A company would receive a permit to discharge some amount of pollution (or, more generally, to impose some degree of risk) but could sell some portion of what it is allowed to discharge (and therefore discharge even less pollution) to someone who finds it more expensive to reduce pollution from *its* facility. Recall the "bubble" concept described in the *Chevron* case (chapter 7), which allowed "trades" within a single facility owned by a single polluter; a tradable permit system can be seen as expanding the bubble to cover a wider geographic range, perhaps even the entire country.

As you read the proposal, think about (a) difficulties that might arise in developing a tradable permit system, (b) the possible extension of such a system beyond environmental law to other areas, such as workplace safety, and (c) the normative premises of such a system as compared with the "best available technology" approach.

■ *Reforming Environmental Law*

BRUCE A. ACKERMAN AND RICHARD B. STEWART
37 Stan. L. Rev. 1333 (1985). Stanford Law Review, by Bruce Ackerman/
Richard Stewart/Tony West. © 1985 by Stanford Law Review. Reproduced
with permission of Stanford Law Review in the format Textbook via
Copyright Clearance Center

. . .

. . . The present regulatory system wastes tens of billions of dollars every year, misdirects resources, stifles innovation, and spawns massive and often counter-productive litigation. There is a variety of fundamental but practical changes that could be made to improve its environmental and economic performance. Why have such changes not been adopted? Powerful organized interests have a vested stake in the status quo. The congressional committees, government bureaucracies, and industry and environmental groups that have helped to shape the present system want to see it perpetuated. But the current system is also bolstered by an often inarticulate sense that, however cumbersome, it "works," and that complexity and limited information make major improvements infeasible.

. . .

. . . The current system does not in fact "work" and its malfunctions, like those of Soviet-style central planning, will become progressively more serious as the economy grows and changes and our knowledge of environmental problems develops.

. . .

I. The Existing System

The existing system of pollution regulation . . . is primarily based on a Best Available Technology (BAT) strategy. If an industrial process or product generates some nontrivial risk, the responsible plant or industry must install whatever technology is available to reduce or eliminate this risk, so long as the costs of doing so will not cause a shutdown of the plant or industry. BAT requirements are largely determined through uniform federal regulations. Under the Clean Water Act's BAT strategy, the EPA [adopts] nationally uniform effluent limitations for some 500 different industries. A similar BAT strategy is deployed under the Clean Air Act for new industrial sources of air pollution, new automobiles, and industrial sources of toxic air pollutants. BAT strategies are also widely used in many fields of environmental regulation other than air and water pollution. . . .[5]

BAT was embraced by Congress and administrators in the early 1970s in order to impose immediate, readily enforceable federal controls on a relatively few widespread pollutants, while avoiding widespread industrial shutdowns. Subsequent experience and analysis has demonstrated:

1. Uniform BAT requirements waste many billions of dollars annually by ignoring variations among plants and industries in the cost of reducing pollution and by ignoring geographic variations in pollution effects. A more cost-effective strategy of risk reduction could free enormous resources for additional pollution reduction or other purposes.

2. BAT controls, and the litigation they provoke, impose disproportionate penalties on new products and processes. A BAT strategy typically imposes far more stringent controls on new sources because there is no risk of shutdown. . . . By contrast, existing sources can use the delays and costs of the legal process to burden regulators and postpone or "water-down" compliance. BAT strategies also impose disproportionate burdens on more productive and profitable industries because these industries can "afford" more stringent controls. This "soak the rich" approach penalizes growth and international competitiveness.

3. BAT controls can ensure that established control technologies are installed. They do not, however, provide strong incentives for the development of new, environmentally superior strategies, and may actually discourage their development. Such innovations are essential for maintaining long-term economic growth without simultaneously increasing pollution and other forms of environmental degradation.

4. BAT involves the centralized determination of complex scientific, engineering, and economic issues regarding the feasibility of controls on hundreds of thousands of pollution sources. Such determinations impose massive information-gathering burdens on administrators, and provide a fertile ground for complex litigation in the form of massive adversary rulemaking proceedings and protracted judicial review. Given the high costs of regulatory compliance and

---

[5] Examples include control of low-level radioactive emissions from normal operation of nuclear power plants and standards for treatment and disposal of toxic substances under the Resource Conservation and Recovery Act. . . .

the potential gains from litigation brought to defeat or delay regulatory requirements, it is often more cost-effective for industry to "invest" in such litigation rather than to comply.

5. A BAT strategy is inconsistent with intelligent priority setting. Simply regulating to the hilt whatever pollutants happen to get on the regulatory agenda may preclude an agency from dealing adequately with more serious problems that come to scientific attention later. BAT also tends to reinforce regulatory inertia. Foreseeing that "all or nothing" regulation of a given substance under BAT will involve large administrative and compliance costs, and recognizing that resources are limited, agencies often seek to limit sharply the number of substances on the agenda for regulatory action.

This indictment is not idle speculation, but the product of years of patient study by lawyers, economists, and political scientists. There are, for example, no fewer than 15 careful efforts to estimate the extra cost burden generated by a wide range of traditional legalistic BAT systems used to control a variety of air and water pollutants in different parts of the country. Of the twelve studies of different air pollutants—ranging from particulates to chlorofluorocarbons—seven indicated that traditional forms of regulation were more than 400% more expensive than the least-cost solution; four revealed that they were about 75% more expensive; one suggested a modest cost-overrun of 7%. Three studies of water pollution control in five different watersheds also indicate the serious inefficiency of traditional forms of command-and-control regulation. These careful studies of selected problems cannot be used to estimate precisely the total amount traditional forms of regulation are annually costing the American people. Nonetheless, very large magnitudes are at stake. Even if a reformed system could cut costs by "only" one-third, it could save more than $15 billion a year from the nation's annual expenditure of $50 billion on air and water pollution control alone.

. . .

II. Implementation

A BAT system has an implicit environmental goal: achievement of the environmental quality level that would result if all sources installed BAT controls on their discharges. The usual means for implementing this goal are centralized, industry-uniform regulations that command specific amounts of cleanup from specific polluters. When a polluter receives an air or water permit under existing law, the piece of paper does not content itself, in the manner of Polonius, with the vague advice that he "use the best available technology." Instead, the permit tries to be as quantitatively precise as possible, telling each discharger how much of the regulated pollutants he may discharge.[18]

---

[18] While the text describes the existing system's implicit regulatory objective, in fact the process of writing, monitoring, and enforcing permits is the Achilles heel of the BAT strategy. While officials in Washington promulgate regulations that are supposed to govern the operation of every plant in an industry, such regulations must be adapted to the specific and varying conditions of different plants throughout the nation. Thus, the actual writing of permits is often accomplished by low-level state or federal field personnel. These permits are often vague and obsolescent. Moreover, enforcement of permit conditions is often ineffective.

...[W]e have [one]...objection...to the existing permit mechanism.... [Permits] are non-transferable. This is bad because polluter A is obliged to cut back his own wastes even if it is cheaper for him to pay his neighbor B to undertake the extra cleanup instead.

Our basic reform would respond...by allowing polluters to buy and sell each other's permits—thereby creating a powerful financial incentive for those who can clean up most cheaply to sell their permits to those whose treatment costs are highest. This reform will, at one stroke, cure many of the basic flaws of the existing command-and-control regulatory systems discussed earlier.

A system of tradeable rights will tend to bring about a leastcost allocation of control burdens, saving many billions of dollars annually. It will eliminate the disproportionate burdens that BAT imposes on new and more productive industries by treating all sources of the same pollutant on the same basis.[20] It will provide positive economic rewards for polluters who develop environmentally superior products and processes. It will...reduce the incentives for litigation, simplify the issues in controversy, and facilitate more intelligent setting of priorities.

...

First, marketability would immediately eliminate most of the information-processing tasks that are presently overwhelming the federal and state bureau-cracies. No longer would the EPA be required to conduct endless adversary proceedings to determine the best available control technologies in each major industry of the United States, and to defend its determinations before the courts; nor would federal and state officials be required to spend vast amounts of time and energy in adapting these changing national guidelines to the particular conditions of every important pollution source in the United States. Instead of giving the job of economic and technological assessment to bureaucrats, the marketable rights mechanism would put the information-processing burden precisely where it belongs: upon business managers and engineers who are in the best position to figure out how to cut back on their plants' pollution costs. If the managers operating plant A think they can clean up a pollutant more cheaply than those in charge of plant B, they should be expected to sell some of their pollution rights to B at a mutually advantageous price; cleanup will occur at the least cost without the need for constant bureaucratic decisions about the best available technology....

---

[20] Equal treatment of old and new sources will not necessarily lead...to shutdowns of old plants. It is true, of course, that old plants may evade cleanup under BAT if their profits are too low to bear the expense. Because of concern over shutdown, they are often allowed to discharge large wasteloads that could otherwise be treated at low cost. The tradeable permits strategy, however, can provide the needed financing for cleanup by enabling the old plant to sell its pollution rights to others. Thus, a marketable rights system may allow old plants to stay in business and clean up. If shutdown does occur, it may be more readily accepted as the product of market forces rather than as a deliberate, isolated government decision.

If the unemployment and dislocation caused by plant shutdowns due to pollution control programs are judged unacceptable, the appropriate response is not...to weaken the program or impose disproportionate controls on new sources so as to throttle investment and productivity gains. The appropriate response is remedial: Compensation programs should be designed to deal with unemployment and dislocation.

Auction

Second, marketable permits would open up enormous financial resources for effective and informed regulation. While polluters would have the right to trade their permits among themselves during the n years they are valid, they would be obliged to buy new ones when their permits expired at an auction held by the EPA in each watershed and air-quality control region. These auctions would raise substantial sums of money for the government on a continuing basis. While no study has yet attempted to make global estimates for the United States as a whole, existing work suggests that auction revenues could well equal the amount polluters would spend in cost-minimizing control activities. Even if revenues turned out to be a third of this amount, the government would still be collecting more than $6–10 billion a year. Moreover, it seems reasonable to suppose that Congress would allow the EPA (and associated state agencies) to retain a substantial share of these revenues. Since the current EPA operating budget is $1.3 billion, using even a fraction of the auction fund to improve regulatory analyses, research, and monitoring would allow a great leap forward in the sophistication of the regulatory effort. . . . Given its revenue-raising potential, environmental reform is hardly a politically unrealistic pipe dream. To the contrary, it is only a matter of time before the enormous federal deficit forces Congress and the President to consider the revenue-raising potential of an auction scheme.[27]

Third, the auction system would help correct one of the worst weaknesses of the present system: the egregious failure of the EPA and associated state agencies to enforce the laws on the books in a timely and effective way. Part of the problem stems from the ability of existing polluters to delay regulatory implementation by using legal proceedings to challenge the economic and engineering bases of BAT regulations and permit conditions. But agencies also invest so little in monitoring that they must rely on polluters for the bulk of their data on discharges. Since polluters are predictably reluctant to report their own violations, the current system perpetuates a Panglossian view of regulatory reality. For example, a General Accounting Office investigation of 921 major air polluters officially considered to be in compliance revealed 200, or 22%, to be violating their permits; in one region, the number not complying was 52%. Even when illegal polluters are identified, they are not effectively sanctioned: The EPA's Inspector General in 1984 found that it was a common practice for water pollution officials to respond to violations by issuing administrative orders that effectively legitimized excess discharges. Thus, while the system may, after protracted litigation, eventually "work" to force the

---

[27] Not that the political fight for an auction will be an easy one. . . . [O]ur market reform will be opposed by businesses who (despite their promarket rhetoric) will predictably resist the prospect of buying pollution rights after all these years of polluting for free. Nonetheless, we believe that the reformist claim that the air and water of America belong to the people, and that polluters should pay if they wish to use it for limited periods, has enormous popular appeal. While it is possible to design efficient auction systems that ameliorate, or eliminate entirely, the financial burdens imposed upon polluters, we would oppose these schemes on principle. We believe that just as firms are obliged to pay for other raw materials they require for their production process, they should be obliged to pay for the air and water they degrade. (Unlike current proposals to impose new taxes on all industries to finance toxic cleanup, tradeable permits would make sources pay in proportion to their contribution to pollution.) . . .

slow installation of expensive control machinery, there is no reason to think this machinery will run well when eventually installed. Although there are many reasons for this appalling weakness in enforcement, one stands out above all others: The present system does not put pressure on agency policymakers to make the large investments in monitoring and personnel that are required to make the tedious and unending work of credible enforcement a bureaucratic reality.

The auction system would change existing compliance incentives dramatically. It would reduce the opportunity and incentive of polluters to use the legal system for delay and obstruction by finessing the complex BAT issues, and it would limit dispute to the question of whether a source's discharges exceeded its permits. It would also eliminate the possibility of using the legal system to postpone implementation of regulatory requirements by requiring the polluter that lost its legal challenge to pay for the permits it would have been obliged to buy during the entire intervening period of noncompliance (plus interest).

The marketable permit system would also provide much stronger incentives for effective monitoring and enforcement. If polluters did not expect rigorous enforcement during the term of their permits, this fact would show up at the auction in dramatically lower bids: Why pay a lot for the right to pollute legally when one can pollute illegally without serious risk of detection? Under a marketable permit approach, this problem would be at the center of bureaucratic attention. For if, as we envisage, the size of the budget available to the EPA and state agencies would depend on total auction revenues, the bureaucracy's failure to invest adequately in enforcement would soon show up in a potentially dramatic drop in auction income available for the next budgetary period. This is not a prospect that top EPA administrators will take lightly. Monitoring and enforcement will become agency priorities of the first importance. Moreover, permit holders may themselves support strong enforcement in order to ensure that cheating by others does not depreciate the value of the permit holders' investments.

. . .

The reformed system we have described involves the execution of four bureaucratic tasks. First, the agency must estimate how much pollution presently is permitted by law in each watershed and air quality region. Second, it must run a system of fair and efficient auctions in which polluters can regularly buy rights for limited terms. Third, it must run an efficient title registry in each region that will allow buyers and sellers to transfer rights in a legally effective way. Fourth, it must consistently penalize polluters who discharge more than their permitted amounts.

And that's that. So far as the fourth bureaucratic task is concerned, we have already given reasons to believe that the EPA would enforce the law far more effectively under the new regime than it does at present. So far as the first three management functions are concerned, we think that they are, in the aggregate, far less demanding than those they displace under the BAT system.

Taking the three functions in reverse order, . . . [certainly] a system of title registration is within the range of bureaucratic possibility. In contrast, the second task—running fair and efficient auctions—is a complicated affair, and it is easy to imagine such a system run incompetently or corruptly. Nonetheless, other agencies seem to have done similar jobs in satisfactory fashions: If the Department of Interior can auction off oil and gas leases competently, we see no reason the EPA could not do the same for pollution rights. Finally, there remains the task of estimating the total allowable wasteload permitted under existing law in each watershed and air control region. If the BAT system functioned properly, these numbers would be easy to obtain. EPA's regional administrators would simply have to add up the allowed amounts appearing in the permits that are in their filing cabinets. We have no illusions, however, about present realities: So much bureaucratic time and energy has been diverted into the counterproductive factfinding tasks generated by the BAT system, and so little attention has been paid to actual discharges, that even the data needed for these simple arithmetic operations may well be incomplete and inadequate. Nonetheless, total permitted emissions in a region can be approximated in order to get a system of permits and auctions started. Surely this start-up effort would be less complex than the unending inquiries into available technologies required by the existing system.

. . . While it is true that the three new tasks involved in running the reformed system are novel, they seem, in the aggregate, a good deal easier to discharge than the bureaucratic functions they displace. Moreover, what little experience the EPA has had with market approaches supports this conclusion. . . . [T]he fact is that the EPA has effectively discharged the bureaucratic tasks necessary to develop its market-based "bubble" and "tradeoff" control strategies under the Clean Air Act. These strategies create limited markets in pollution rights by: 1) allowing a new source to offset its new emissions by inducing an existing source to reduce its discharges (this is the so-called "tradeoff" policy); 2) allowing an existing source that is expanding to reallocate control burdens among its existing and new units (new source bubble); and 3) allowing existing sources in the same region to reallocate control burdens (state implementation plan bubble). The use of these innovations was for many years clouded by legal uncertainties until the Supreme Court recently rejected challenges from some environmental groups. Despite this uncertainty, the Clean Air Act bubble policy alone, in limited use for only a few years, has achieved compliance cost savings of over $700 million without any reduction (and in some cases an increase) in pollution control.

. . .

. . . The time is ripe for a market reform of the kind we have just described. Rather than using tradeable emission rights as a limited modification of BAT strategies, the bubble and tradeoff approaches should be generalized to permit regional trading of all air and water pollution permits. Moreover, the tradeable permit strategy should be used to deal with pollution problems—such as acid rain— that are currently unregulated and could be handled efficiently and effectively through economic incentives.[39]

Would a system of marketable rights preclude improvement of environmental quality? By no means. The initial stock of rights can be amortized on a fixed

---

[39] Nor do we see any reason to limit the use of tradeable permits to air and water pollution problems. . . . [H]azards from toxic chemicals might appropriately be controlled through a system of "risk rights." Under this system, producers of new pesticides or other chemicals would purchase rights from existing producers or compete successfully for rights at one of the regular EPA auctions. Either way, the entry of new producers would force existing producers to reduce existing risk, thereby ensuring that the new product would not increase the total risk from chemicals faced by society.

schedule in order to reach a targeted goal, or the government may decide not to reissue existing rights after they expire. Any such reductions will increase the price of rights by reducing supply. Prices will also automatically tend to rise over time as the economy grows and the demand for rights increases. Under a BAT approach, by contrast, regulators must consistently undertake new, difficult, and unpopular initiatives to impose ever more stringent BAT controls on existing sources in order to accommodate economic growth without increased pollution. The prospect of steady increases in the price of rights will be a powerful incentive—far more powerful than the patchwork efforts at "technology forcing" under the BAT system—for businesses to develop cleaner products and processes.

. . .

. . . [However, a] reformed implementation system would not easily solve all foreseeable regulatory problems. In particular, the market system we have described could allow the creation of relatively high concentrations of particular pollutants in small areas within the larger pollution control region. In tolerating "hot spots," of course, our reform proposal shares the defects of the existing BAT system, which also generates risk of "hot spots" by imposing the same controls on sources regardless of their location, the size of the human population affected by their discharges, and the nature and vulnerability of affected ecosystems. Nonetheless, the blindness of both systems to intraregional variation is a serious source of concern. The extensive literature on marketable permits . . . points to a variety of feasible means for dealing with the hot spot problem.[44] We believe that a long-run strategy for institutional reform should strive to take advantage of these more sophisticated market solutions to the problem of intraregional variation. For the present, it will be enough to emphasize our agreement . . . that administrative feasibility is an important constraint on the degree of sophistication that we may reasonably expect.

. . .

III. Goals

We now address reforms that have more to do with the way existing policy goals are established than with the way they are implemented. . . .

. . .

. . . Rather than imagining reform as one extravagant "great leap forward," we envision a series of steps in an ongoing process of piecemeal improvement. Each element in the reform program can be implemented at a different time and should be evaluated on its own merits. Thus, the market implementation mechanism described in the preceding section was a piecemeal reform based on the allowable pollution loads *prevailing under existing law*. . . . Similarly, we regard the policymak-

---

[44] Existing federal laws contain some provisions to prevent excessive local environmental damage from sources that already comply with BAT standards. But . . . these provisions have not been effectively implemented. We believe that an important reason for this failure is the diversion of bureaucratic energies into BAT determinations. Thus, even in our first-generation proposals for reform, it may be possible to design crude, but useful, mechanisms by which the EPA can realistically respond to "hot spots" once it has been liberated from its BAT routines. All we can do here, however, is to flag this problem of statutory design as deserving high priority on the reform agenda.

ing proposals we make in this section as a series of discrete steps toward a more democratic, and more enlightened, dialogue on the nature of America's evolving environmental objectives. While some immediate reforms will lay the foundation for further advances, we hope that doubts about the institutional feasibility of some of our long-run proposals will not deflect attention from feasible short-term reforms that promise immediate and substantial improvements.

A. A Short-Term Strategy: Redesigning Statutory Variables

... At present, the BAT system focuses congressional debate, as well as administrative and judicial proceedings, upon arcane technological and definitional questions which rapidly outstrip the time and energy that most politicians and citizens are willing to spend on environmental matters. In contrast, the marketable permit system will allow the policymaking debate to take a far more intelligible shape. Rather than debating the difference between the "best available control technology" and "lowest achievable emission rate," citizens will be encouraged to focus on a different question when the environmental acts come up for revision: During the next n years, should we instruct the EPA gradually to decrease (or increase) the number of pollution rights by x percent? Environmentalists will, of course, argue for big reductions; others, who are more impressed with the costs of control, will argue for smaller reductions or even selective increases. But at least the congressional debate would be encouraged to focus upon the fundamental question: Speaking broadly, do the American people believe existing environmental objectives are too ambitious (in which case Congress should increase the number of rights), or do they think that Congress should cut back further on pollution by cutting back on the number of rights?

Return to politics *

Rather than supposing ... that such a question should be answered by a cost-benefit analysis, we believe that it is the quintessentially political question that should be answered by the legislative process. The great virtue of the marketable permit program is that it puts the question in an operational form accessible to the general public. ...

To put the point more broadly, we propose the use of a new statutory control variable in the design of our environmental statutes. Rather than speaking in technology-based terms, the key statutory variables would be pollution-based. More precisely, they would specify the rate of change in existing levels of pollution that Congress wishes to achieve during the period until the Clean Air Act once more comes up for congressional reconsideration. Under the revised system, Congress would no longer content itself with mouthing pieties about the need to achieve "reasonable further progress" in environmental protection. It would instead specify, in quantitative terms, how much change is "reasonable" by voting for an n percent reduction (or increase) in the number of aggregate permits that the EPA would be allowed to auction off annually to the nation's polluters. This single change, we believe, would vastly increase the degree to which the critical questions of environmental policy can be framed in a way that is more transparent to the general public.

This single change, however, can only serve as a first step toward more transparent decisionmaking. Because it is limited to upward or downward adjustment of the aggregate pollution levels permitted under federal standards, it does not allow for more discriminating regulation of particular pollution problems. We see no reason, though, for Congress to content itself with the crude uniformity that Latin commends. For example, within the general context of a 20% rights reduction, Congress might target certain pollutants for a 40% reduction, while allowing others to be reduced by only 5%. Similarly, Congress may announce principles concerning the way in which the reductions should be allocated across the nation: For example, should stricter cutbacks be scheduled in areas violating primary or secondary health standards? In ecologically sensitive areas? If so, by how much?

... [S]uch decisions would [surely] require Congress to guess about countless contestable matters involving both facts and values.... The fact is, however, that these uncertainties already exist, and it is precisely because they cannot be resolved technocratically that they should be framed in a way that invites self-conscious political decision by the Congress. In contrast, the BAT system fails to focus attention on the overall rate at which America should clean up the environment, leaving it to unguided and disjointed bureaucratic and judicial decision[s] in an endless series of BAT inquiries into the "availability" of one or another cleanup technology.

B. Long-Term Strategies: Toward Decentralization and Constrained Cost-Effectiveness Analysis

While the piecemeal "first-generation" change described in the previous subsection stands on its own merits, it also lays the foundation for a "second-generation" reform in setting environmental goals: Congress would create a statutory foundation for legally constrained cost-effectiveness analysis. Like the first-generation approach, this second-generation statute would express itself in terms of a change-oriented, pollution-based command. Imagine, for example, that the reformed statute mandated a 20% reduction in allowable pollution levels over the next ten years. In contrast to our first-generation approach, however, the statute would not insist that the 20% cutback be obtained in each and every part of the country, or in those areas specified by Congress. Instead, the EPA, in conjunction with state and regional authorities, would be given discretion to allocate the cleanup effort. So long as an average 20% cutback was achieved, the statute would enable administrators to force some areas to cut back up to 30% while allowing others to cut back only 10%—provided that they could support these judgments [with] a thoughtful cost-effectiveness analysis indicating that such variations would lead to cutbacks where they would do the most good in reducing health risks and harm to the environment.

In allowing for limited regional variation, we would be making a final break with the BAT insistence upon nationwide uniformity. We believe that completely uniform goals are seriously dysfunctional, producing too much control in some regions, too little in others, and completely missing special problems in still other regions. A notorious example of mindless uniformity is the effluent limitations imposed by the present Clean Water Act, which have required the same level of cleanup by all plants in a given industry, regardless of whether a plant discharges into an ocean or large lake, where the discharges will have little or no effect, or into a pristine river. This blindness to environmental reality—which is replicated in many other areas—is a parody of the ecological consciousness that should motivate sound policymaking.

... Our own study of particular problems ... has convinced us that it is possible to conduct an intelligent debate about whether, for example, it makes more sense to clean up the Delaware River in the vicinity of Philadelphia or whether greater percentage cutbacks are warranted in the ecologically threatened regions of the Delaware Bay. We fully agree that a narrow economic analysis can only serve as part of an answer to such questions; nonetheless, it is also wrong to imagine that these questions can be responsibly answered without taking costs, as well as benefits, into account. In the end, of course, there will be no escaping the inherently controversial nature of the particular administrative judgments in which cost-effectiveness analysis plays some role. So long as particular agency decisions are made within a larger framework of Congressional policy, however, we believe that they will generate an ongoing public discussion that will, over time, greatly enhance the insight with which the nation confronts its environmental dilemmas.

. . .

. . . In our view, such analyses only serve to guide, and not displace, intelligent guesswork. The question is whether we operate under a system, like BAT, which tries to ignore or suppress uncertainty, or whether we operate in a world in which decisionmakers are encouraged to make their guesses as openly and intelligently as they can. The goal for a second-generation statute is to create a system in which decisionmakers can make limited variations in national priorities in the light of their best guesses about the regional realities they confront.

. . .

C. Priority-Setting

Our final set of proposals seeks to correct serious deficiencies in the process by which the current BAT system sets priorities in the light of changing information about environmental realities. BAT discourages intelligent priority-setting for two related reasons. First, the EPA is so overwhelmed by factfinding tasks required to implement a technology-based approach that it has relatively few resources left for exploration of risks posed by new pollutants. Second, BAT imposes heavy bureaucratic costs on the EPA every time it recognizes a new threat to the environment. Once a new pollutant has been identified, BAT requires the agency to exhaust itself with yet another series of never-ending inquiries into the state of control technology in each of the industries that have been discharging the "newly discovered" pollutant and to establish an elaborate set of new industry-by-industry standards. Finally, once a pollutant has been targeted for regulation, BAT automatically requires the imposition of controls to the full extent of available technology—a potentially enormous commitment of compliance resources that may not be justified by the benefits achieved and that is likely to be strongly opposed by industry through protracted litigation. It should be no surprise, then, that the EPA has, in fact, been reluctant to expand the number of its pollution targets.[61]

---

[61] Courts have empowered environmental plaintiffs to force agency action upon presentation of a prima facie case that a currently unregulated pollutant presents a substantial hazard, and Congress has codified these rulings in "action-forcing" statutory "citizen-suit" provisions. While agency inaction is, as we have noted, a serious problem under a BAT regime, the reliance on "action-forcing" through litigation may well be a cure worse than the disease. Such a strategy invites a "pollutant of the month" approach to priority-setting. There is no assurance that the initiatives selected by different environmental groups will result in a sensible allocation of limited administrative and compliance resources. . . .

The administrative inertia generated by BAT was, perhaps, of secondary concern so long as one could believe that environmental degradation was the product of a few widespread pollutants, each of which should be controlled to the greatest extent feasible within a period of years. After a decade's practical experience with environmental regulation, however, it should be clear that there are thousands of substances that pose at least some risk and that we cannot deal with all of them simultaneously or impose BAT on all of them within the near future. The defect of the BAT system is that it tends to select, more or less arbitrarily, a relatively few pollutants and devotes enormous administrative and control resources to regulating them to the hilt.

The reforms we have already advocated will create new incentives for the innovative priority-setting that is needed in today's world. First, a statute whose control variables were pollution-based, rather than technology-based, would encourage a more focused discussion of whether the goals set for different pollutants reflect sensible priorities. Indeed, it is not fanciful to suppose that a risk portfolio strategy eventually might emerge that would explicitly attempt to rank the comparative risks confronted by an EPA or an OSHA and then use cost-effectiveness analysis to determine how available administrative and control resources might best be devoted to minimizing overall risk in a given time period.[62] Such a strategy need not be limited to conventional air and water pollutants. It could also be used, for example, to manage the risks posed by pesticides, chemicals, or hazardous wastes.

. . .

Our proposed shift in bureaucratic incentives . . . does reinforce the need for a regulatory structure that endorses thoughtful cost-effectiveness analysis in the priority-setting process. Up to the present time, legislators have been able to indulge in apparently absolute statutory prohibitions of all harmful pollutants. This was possible because legislators could count on regulatory lethargy and covert consideration of costs by administrators in defining BAT to blunt statutory calls for an all-out war on pollution. Once a reformed statute has changed the balance of incentives for bureaucratic innovation, we should insist on thoughtful cost-effectiveness analysis before a new pollutant is made the subject of a marketable permit auction. The critical question, in each case, should be whether available administrative and compliance resources will achieve more reduction in environmental risks if they are used to control the new pollutant rather than being used to deal with other pollutants. (For these purposes, costs—like benefits—should not be measured in any mechanical way, and will inevitably involve major social judgments.) If so, the "new" pollutant should be regulated on the basis of the same pollution-based principles that we have elaborated previously; if not, it should not be regulated. Of course, even if an agency refused to list a new pollutant, Congress would be free to force the agency to change its mind the next time the governing

---

[62] In order to reduce some of the administrative and other problems involved in establishing separate permits and markets for many different pollutants, a "mutual fund" variant of the portfolio approach might be used, where appropriate, to control related pollutants through permits based on a weighted average of volume and risk.

statute is reappraised. Once again, cost-benefit analysis would be subordinated to democratic decision.

. . .

Conclusion

In urging the fundamental reform of environmental law, we do not mean to disparage the very great accomplishments of the generation that enacted sweeping federal legislation in the late 1960s and early 1970s. Apart from the many unambiguous achievements of this statutory revolution, even the embrace of a BAT approach made some sense as a crude first-generation strategy. During the early days of federal environmental concern, perhaps it was plausible for politicians and other policymakers to suppose that only a few pollution problems were out of hand and that these problems could be "solved" in a short time by an all-out war against "pollution." From this perspective, it could seem reasonable to try to force everyone to adopt the best available technology everywhere.

Our complaint is not with the statutory draftsmen of the early 1970s, but with lawyers of the 1980s who fail to put these early statutes in historical perspective. Experience with more than a decade of intensive regulation emphasizes that the environmental risks we confront are numerous and vary widely in seriousness. Our strategies for managing these risks must set intelligent priorities, make maximum use of the resources devoted to improving environmental quality, encourage environmentally superior technologies, and avoid unneeded penalties on innovation and investment. Rather than wringing our hands helplessly before these complexities, the challenge is to incorporate maturing perceptions about regulatory problems into the evolving legal structure—and help our fellow Americans build a system that will not only save many billions of dollars a year, but make environmental law more democratically accountable and bureaucratically effective. It is time for environmental lawyers to stop celebrating the statutory revolution of the 1970s and to start building a statutory structure worthy of the year 2000.

COMMENTS AND QUESTIONS

1. The primary argument for the tradable permit system is that it is a more efficient method of achieving reductions in pollution than the "best available technology" approach. Ackerman and Stewart describe the efficiency arguments against the BAT approach and the efficiency arguments for a market-based approach.

Ackerman and Stewart note some objections to a tradable permit system: distributional concerns (the "hot spots" problem) and a rights-based objection to the (partial) commodification of exposure to pollution. To focus your thinking, try to design a tradable permit system for workplace safety (or for the safety of food products), and consider why tradable permit systems seem to have much more support in connection with environmental law than in connection with workplace and food product safety. Recall here Kennedy's argument about the ideological attractiveness of efficiency arguments compared to distributive and paternalist arguments. Is paternalism easier to accept (in general or in U.S. culture) with respect to workplace and food product safety than with respect to environmental pollution?

2. A tradable permit system requires the agency to set a "global" level of acceptable pollution, that is, the amount of pollution allowed in the area covered by the permit system. Ackerman and Stewart observe that the BAT approach implicitly sets such a level, when they note that the agency could simply add up the amount of pollution allowed under plant-by-plant permits. (Note that this implicit determination is another way of describing the aggregate effects of the standards the agency sets, according to whatever approach—of the sort examined earlier in this chapter—it uses or is required by statute to use.) What are the advantages and disadvantages of making that global determination explicit?

   In addition, a tradable permit system requires that permits be allocated initially and then—perhaps—periodically thereafter. Ackerman and Stewart propose an auction of permits with specific expiration dates. Why might utility managers oppose the adoption of an auction system? Consider the uncertainty such a mechanism introduces for any individual utility company. What other options are there? The government might allocate initial permits based on some criteria, for example, past fuel usage and employment of particular technologies. Consider the opportunities that such an approach provides for special-interest deals. Another possibility is a lottery. Again, what are the advantages and disadvantages of that mechanism?

   A tradable permit system also requires a choice about the *scope* of the system. Why should a tradable permit system be confined to trades dealing with permits to emit one specific pollutant? Why shouldn't the system allow trades *across* pollutants? One difficulty is that it may be difficult to compare improvements in performance across pollutants. Suppose a trade results in a one-ton reduction of sulfur dioxide emissions in place of a 300-pound reduction of nitrogen oxide emissions. How can we measure whether the trade improves the environment? Consider the possibility that quantitative risk assessments, of the sort examined in the first sections of this chapter, allow such measurements.

3. Acting under a provision of the Clean Air Act adopted in 1990, the government established a trading program for sulfur dioxide (SO_2), aimed at reducing acid rain. The program sets a national cap on SO_2 emissions, approximately 8.9 million tons. Initial permits are awarded only to existing utilities, for no fee, with the amount each utility is permitted to discharge determined by historic emission rates. New entrants must buy permits from existing utilities. (Note that this program differs from the one proposed by Ackerman and Stewart and retains the bias against new sources that they say is found in the BAT approach.) Permits can be traded on the Chicago Board of Trade, and any citizen (not just utilities) can buy and sell them. Despite initially low levels of trading, analysts concluded that the program is generating large cost savings and a great deal of innovation. For a discussion of the program, see Jeffrey M. Hirsch, *Emissions Allowance Trading under the Clean Air Act: A Model for Future Environmental Regulations?*, 7 N.Y.U. Envtl. L.J. 352 (1999).

4. Something akin to a tradable permit system, or at least a bubble concept, has been used to achieve desired levels of fuel efficiency in automobile production. Congress sets a "corporate average fuel efficiency" (CAFE) standard, a measure of the fuel efficiency of the total output of each automobile producer. Each producer can decide for itself how to achieve that standard, by deciding on the mix of low-efficiency and high-efficiency cars and by engineering different cars with different fuel efficiencies. Problems have arisen in administering the CAFE system because the fuel efficiency of some motor vehicles (including sports utility vehicles and minivans) is weighted less heavily in the measurement of the corporate average; making engineering modifications that push a vehicle from just outside the category into it allows the manufacturer to achieve the CAFE standard without actually improving overall fuel efficiency. Paul E. Godek, *The Regulation of Fuel Economy and the Demand for "Light Trucks,"* 40 J. Law & Econ. 495, 506 (1997), argues that the CAFE system produced a regulatory paradox, as carmakers initially produced lighter and less safe cars, until consumers shifted to purchasing SUVs and minivans. For a discussion and a critique of the argument that the CAFE system is a regulatory "backfire," see Robert A. Hillman, *The Rhetoric of Legal Backfire*, 43 B.C. L. Rev. 819 (2002).

5. Concluding question: You have now examined cost-benefit analysis, associated critiques, and alternatives to cost-benefit analysis as methods of designing regulatory standards. In your judgment, which is the best (or least bad) method?

The Nondelegation Problem

12

A s you have now seen, administrative agencies play a large role in the modern regulatory state in both applying statutes to specific factual circumstances and interpreting the statutes they administer. Indeed, these roles are so large that you might wonder why *agencies* are playing them rather than legislatures themselves. You have seen that one justification for agency authority is their relevant expertise—and implicitly, the lack of equivalent expertise by legislatures. But, of course, legislatures inherently possess democratic accountability that administrative law seeks to achieve through procedures like notice-and-comment rule making and judicial review based on the "arbitrary and capricious" standard.

Does the combination of expertise and mechanisms for ensuring some degree of democratic accountability alleviate all concerns about the role agencies play? Would it be wise for a legislature to enact a statute that creates an agency to improve safety and health conditions in the workplace, and give it the following charge: "Develop and enforce rules that reduce safety and health risks in the workplace to an acceptable level"?

Some observers would be troubled by such a vague directive. The Supreme Court has suggested that there is a constitutional problem associated with similar directives, at least for federal agencies. (As you will see, the nondelegation doctrine as such does not impose federal constitutional limitations on state legislatures, but some courts have used the Due Process and other clauses to address the concerns that the nondelegation doctrine deals with on the national level.)

According to the nondelegation doctrine, Article I of the Constitution forbids Congress from delegating the legislative power there conferred. At the same time, the Court has acknowledged that government (and not merely the modern regulatory state) could not function if *all* decisions that might be described as "legislative" had to be made by Congress through statutes adopted by both houses and signed by the president. From early in the nation's constitutional history, Congress has delegated authority to make rules to other bodies, which we can call for convenience "agencies." And the Supreme Court has upheld such delegations where the statutes doing so give the agencies an "intelligible principle" by which to guide their action. So, the question about the statute described above would be "Does 'reduce risks to an acceptable level' provide an intelligible principle?"

We begin this chapter with a single case, *American Trucking*, and its treatment by two courts, the Court of Appeals for the District of Columbia Circuit and the Supreme Court. The court of appeals decision, though reversed by the Supreme Court, is instructive on the meaning and application of the "intelligible principle" standard. In reading the cases, keep in mind the tension between expertise and democratic accountability. In your judgment, which decision provides the better accommodation of that tension? Then we turn to the application of nondelegation-like ideas to lawmaking processes in the states. One way of approaching the full set of cases is to consider whether this is an accurate description: The federal nondelegation doctrine places a great deal of weight on the importance of expertise and relatively little on the importance of democratic accountability; in the state-level case, the court objects to processes that involve "too much" democratic accountability, and so the case is similar to the federal nondelegation cases.

A brief bit of historical background: The earliest decision usually cited in nondelegation cases is *The Brig Aurora*, 11 U.S. (7 Cranch) 382 (1813), which found no constitutional objection to a statute that authorized the president to withdraw restrictions on imports from France or Great Britain if he found that either nation had "ceased to violate the neutral commerce" of the United States. *Field v. Clark*, 143 U.S. 649 (1892), upheld a statute that authorized the president to impose retaliatory tariffs if he found that another nation had placed tariffs on U.S. products that were "reciprocally unequal and unreasonable." The Court characterized that determination as one of "fact." In 1928, the Court upheld a statute giving the president the power to change tariffs whenever he determined that a revision was necessary to "equalize the costs of production in the United States and the principal competing country." *J. W. Hampton, Jr. & Co. v. United States*, 276 U.S. 394 (1928). *J. W. Hampton* is the origin of the phrase "intelligible principle." The Court held that "equalize the costs of production" provided such a standard.

Prior to 1935, the Court's decisions suggested that there might be some limits on Congress's ability to delegate "legislative" authority and had come to formulate those limits as a requirement of an intelligible principle. But the Court had never found that Congress had in fact gone beyond the bounds of a permissible delegation. Then in 1935—as part of what contemporaries saw as the Court's reaction (or opposition) to President Franklin Roosevelt's New Deal—came two decisions striking down statutes as impermissible delegations. *Panama Refining Co. v. Ryan*, 293 U.S. 388 (1935), invalidated a statute granting the president authority to ban the interstate shipment of what was known as "hot oil," that is, oil produced in violation of state-imposed production limits. The Court held, with only one dissent, that the delegation was impermissible because Congress had not indicated the circumstances under which the president was to impose such a ban on "hot oil." It had not said that he should do so for all shipments of "hot oil," nor provided any criteria providing any guidance on which shipments he should ban. *A.L.A. Schechter Poultry Corp. v. United States*, 295 U.S. 495 (1935) (which you are likely to encounter when you discuss Congress's power to regulate interstate commerce in your constitutional law course), invalidated a statute on nondelegation grounds, as well as Commerce Clause grounds. The problem, according to a Court that was unanimous on this point, was that the president, acting through the National Relief Administration, was authorized to adopt and enforce codes of "fair competition," but Congress had given no content to the idea of fairness.

Panama Refining and *Schechter* remain the only Supreme Court cases finding a federal statute unconstitutional because Congress delegated its legislative power to an administrative agency. Note that all the cases described here involved delegations either to the president or to an agency under the president's control. To the extent that the issue is one of democratic accountability, it is one dealing with the *relative* accountability of Congress as against either the president or the agency—or, perhaps, with some kind of accountability that arises from the distinctive capacities of Congress. Consider the possibility that the procedures Congress and the courts have required of agencies are designed to reproduce those capacities in the agencies—or at least to reduce the differences between congressional and agency capacity to a level at which serious concerns about accountability should not arise.

Although the nondelegation doctrine has not been used to *invalidate* statutes, it has sometimes been invoked as a reason to *construe* statutes "creatively," that is, to find in them an intelligible principle that the text, read in ordinary ways, would not suggest. The leading case is *Industrial Union Dept., AFL-CIO v. American Petroleum Institute*, 448 U.S. 607 (1980), the Benzene Case discussed in chapter 11. Recall that the Court there suggested that if it had not adopted the "significant risk" principle as a way of narrowing OSHA's authority to issue rules on workplace toxics, the statute "would make such a 'sweeping delegation of legislative power' that it might be unconstitutional" under *Schechter Poultry*, and then observed that "[a] construction of the statute that avoids this kind of open-ended grant should certainly be favored." Does the "significant risk" requirement provide an intelligible principle?

We begin with the opinion of the court of appeals in *American Trucking*, despite its reversal by the Supreme Court, because it provides a good basis for exploring what the "intelligible principle" standard *might* mean. Do not be distracted by the court of appeals' novel, and quickly rejected, holding that an administrative agency's interpretation of its organic statute might supply an intelligible principle that the statute itself lacks. Focus instead on the opinion's suggestion of various intelligible principles.

- ### American Trucking Associations, Inc. v. Environmental Protection Agency
  175 F.3d 1027 (D.C. Cir. 1999)

PER CURIAM [Circuit Judge Williams wrote the portions of the opinion set out below]:

The Clean Air Act requires EPA to promulgate and periodically revise national ambient air quality standards ("NAAQS") for each air pollutant identified by the agency as meeting certain statutory criteria. See Clean Air Act §§ 108–09, 42 U.S.C. §§ 7408–09. For each pollutant, EPA sets a "primary standard"—a concentration level "requisite to protect the public health" with an "adequate margin of safety"—and a "secondary standard"—a level "requisite to protect the public welfare." Id. § 7409(b).

In July 1997 EPA issued final rules revising the primary and secondary NAAQS for particulate matter ("PM") and ozone. . . .

. . . [W]e find that the construction of the Clean Air Act on which EPA relied in promulgating the NAAQS at issue here effects an unconstitutional delegation of legislative power. See U.S. Const. art. I, § 1 ("All legislative powers herein granted shall be vested in a Congress of the United States."). We remand the cases for EPA to develop a construction of the act that satisfies this constitutional requirement.

. . .

Certain "Small Business Petitioners" argue in each case that EPA has construed §§ 108 & 109 of the Clean Air Act so loosely as to render them unconstitutional delegations of legislative power. We agree. Although the factors EPA uses in determining the degree of public health concern associated with different levels of ozone and PM are reasonable, EPA appears to have articulated no "intelligible principle" to channel its application of these factors; nor is one apparent from the statute. The nondelegation doctrine requires such a principle. See *J. W. Hampton, Jr. & Co. v. United States*, 276 U.S. 394, 409 (1928). Here it is as though Congress commanded EPA to select "big guys," and EPA announced that it would evaluate candidates based on height and weight, but revealed no cut-off point. The announcement, though sensible in what it does say, is fatally incomplete. The reasonable person responds, "How tall? How heavy?"

EPA regards ozone definitely, and PM likely, as nonthreshold pollutants, i.e., ones that have some possibility of some adverse health impact (however slight) at any exposure level above zero. See Ozone Final Rule, 62 Fed. Reg. at 38,863/3 ("Nor does it seem possible, in the Administrator's judgment, to identify [an ozone concentration] level at which it can be concluded with confidence that no 'adverse' effects are likely to occur."); National Ambient Air Quality Standards for Ozone and Particulate Matter, 61 Fed. Reg. 65,637, 65,651/3 (1996) (proposed rule) ("The single most important factor influencing the uncertainty associated with the risk estimates is whether or not a threshold concentration exists below which PM-associated health risks are not likely to occur."). For convenience, we refer to both as non-threshold pollutants; the indeterminacy of PM's status does not affect EPA's analysis, or ours.

Thus the only concentration for ozone and PM that is utterly risk-free, in the sense of direct health impacts, is zero. Section 109(b)(1) says that EPA must set each standard at the level "requisite to protect the public health" with an "adequate margin of safety." 42 U.S.C. § 7409(b)(1). These are also the criteria by which EPA must determine whether a revision to existing NAAQS is appropriate. See 42 U.S.C. § 7409(d)(1) (EPA shall "promulgate such new standards as may be appropriate in accordance with . . . [§ 7409(b)]"). For EPA to pick any non-zero level it must explain the degree of imperfection permitted. The factors that EPA has elected to examine for this purpose in themselves pose no inherent nondelegation problem. But what EPA lacks is any determinate criterion for drawing lines. It has failed to state intelligibly how much is too much.

We begin with the criteria EPA has announced for assessing health effects in setting the NAAQS for non-threshold pollutants.[1] They are "the nature and se-

---

[1] Technically, EPA describes the criteria as used only for setting the "adequate margin of safety." There might be thought to be a separate step in which EPA determines what standard would protect public health without any margin of safety, and that step might be governed by different criteria. But EPA did not use such a process, and it need not. See *NRDC v. EPA*, 902 F.2d 963, 973 (D.C. Cir. 1990). Thus, the criteria mentioned in the text govern the whole standard-setting process.

verity of the health effects involved, the size of the sensitive population(s) at risk, the types of health information available, and the kind and degree of uncertainties that must be addressed." Ozone Final Rule, 62 Fed. Reg. at 38,883/2. Although these criteria, so stated, are a bit vague, they do focus the inquiry on pollution's effects on public health. And most of the vagueness in the abstract formulation melts away as EPA applies the criteria: EPA basically considers severity of effect, certainty of effect, and size of population affected. These criteria, long ago approved by the judiciary, see *Lead Industries Ass'n v. EPA*, 647 F.2d 1130, 1161 (D.C. Cir. 1980) (*"Lead Industries"*), do not themselves speak to the issue of degree.

Read in light of these factors, EPA's explanations for its decisions amount to assertions that a less stringent standard would allow the relevant pollutant to inflict a greater quantum of harm on public health, and that a more stringent standard would result in less harm. Such arguments only support the intuitive proposition that more pollution will not benefit public health, not that keeping pollution at or below any particular level is "requisite" or not requisite to "protect the public health" with an "adequate margin of safety," the formula set out by § 109(b)(1).

Consider EPA's defense of the 0.08 ppm level of the ozone NAAQS. EPA explains that its choice is superior to retaining the existing level, 0.09 ppm, because more people are exposed to more serious effects at 0.09 than at 0.08. In defending the decision not to go down to 0.07, EPA never contradicts the intuitive proposition, confirmed by data . . . , that reducing the standard to that level would bring about comparable changes. Instead, it gives three other reasons. The principal substantive one is based on the criteria just discussed:

> The most certain O_3-related effects, while judged to be adverse, are transient and reversible (particularly at O_3 exposures below 0.08 ppm), and the more serious effects with greater immediate and potential long-term impacts on health are less certain, both as to the percentage of individuals exposed to various concentrations who are likely to experience such effects and as to the long-term medical significance of these effects. Ozone Final Rule, 62 Fed. Reg. at 38,868/2.

In other words, effects are less certain and less severe at lower levels of exposure. This seems to be nothing more than a statement that lower exposure levels are associated with lower risk to public health. The dissent argues that in setting the standard at 0.08, EPA relied on evidence that health effects occurring below that level are "transient and reversible," evidently assuming that those at higher levels are not. But the EPA language quoted above does not make the categorical distinction the dissent says it does, and it is far from apparent that any health effects existing above the level are permanent or irreversible.

In addition to the assertion quoted above, EPA cited the consensus of the Clean Air Scientific Advisory Committee ("CASAC") that the standard should not be set below 0.08. That body gave no specific reasons for its recommendations, so the appeal to its authority . . . adds no enlightenment. The dissent stresses the undisputed eminence of CASAC's members, but the question whether EPA acted pursuant to lawfully delegated authority is not a scientific one. Nothing in what CASAC says helps us discern an intelligible principle derived by EPA from the Clean Air Act.

Finally, EPA argued that a 0.07 standard would be "closer to peak background levels that infrequently occur in some areas due to nonanthropogenic sources of O_3 precursors, and thus more likely to be inappropriately targeted in some areas on such sources." But a 0.08 level, of course, is also closer to these peak levels than 0.09. The dissent notes that a single background observation fell between 0.07 and 0.08, and says that EPA's decision "ensured that if a region surpasses the ozone standard, it will do so because of controllable human activity, not uncontrollable natural levels of ozone." EPA's language, coupled with the data on background ozone levels, may add up to a backhanded way of saying that, given the national character of the NAAQS, it is inappropriate to set a standard below a level that can be achieved throughout the country without action affirmatively extracting chemicals from nature. That may well be a sound reading of the statute, but EPA has not explicitly adopted it.

EPA frequently defends a decision not to set a standard at a lower level on the basis that there is greater uncertainty that health effects exist at lower levels than the level of the standard....But the increasing-uncertainty argument is helpful only if some principle reveals how much uncertainty is too much. None does.

The arguments EPA offers here show only that EPA is applying the stated factors and that larger public health harms (including increased probability of such harms) are, as expected, associated with higher pollutant concentrations. The principle EPA invokes for each increment in stringency (such as for adopting the annual coarse particulate matter standard that it chose here)—that it is "possible, but not certain" that health effects exist at that level[2]—could as easily, for any non-threshold pollutant, justify a standard of zero. The same indeterminacy prevails in EPA's decisions not to pick a still more stringent level. For example, EPA's reasons for not lowering the ozone standard from 0.08 to 0.07 ppm—that "the more serious effects . . . are less certain" at the lower levels and that the lower levels are "closer to peak background levels,"—could also be employed to justify a refusal to reduce levels below those associated with London's "Killer Fog" of 1952. In that calamity, very high PM levels (up to 2,500 Sg/m^3) are believed to have led to 4,000 excess deaths in a week. Thus, the agency rightly recognizes that the question is one of degree, but offers no intelligible principle by which to identify a stopping point.

The latitude EPA claims here seems even broader than that OSHA asserted in *International Union, UAW v. OSHA ("Lockout/Tagout I")*, 938 F.2d 1310, 1317 (D.C. Cir. 1991), which was to set a standard that would reduce a substantial risk and that was not infeasible. In that case, OSHA thought itself free either to "do nothing at all" or to "require precautions that take the industry to the brink of ruin," with "all positions in between . . . evidently equally valid." Here, EPA's freedom of movement between the poles is equally unconstrained, but the poles are even

---

[2] EPA did cite qualitative evidence for further support for its annual standard, and argued that the evidence "does not provide evidence of effects below the range of 40–50 Sg/m^3," the standard level. PM Final Rule, 62 Fed. Reg. at 38,678/3. The referenced document, however, bears no indication that the qualitative evidence demonstrates effects at the level of the standard, either. See EPA, "Air Quality Criteria for Particulate Matter," at 13–79 (April 1996).

farther apart—the maximum stringency would send industry not just to the brink of ruin but hurtling over it, while the minimum stringency may be close to doing nothing at all.

. . . The standards in question affect the whole economy, requiring a "more precise" delegation than would otherwise be the case, see *A.L.A. Schechter Poultry Corp. v. United States*, 295 U.S. 495, 553 (1935). No "special theories" justifying vague delegation such as the war powers of the President or the sovereign attributes of the delegatee have been or could be asserted. Nor is there some inherent characteristic of the field that bars development of a far more determinate basis for decision. (This is not to deny that there are difficulties; we consider some below.)

EPA cites prior decisions of this Court holding that when there is uncertainty about the health effects of concentrations of a particular pollutant within a particular range, EPA may use its discretion to make the "policy judgment" to set the standards at one point within the relevant range rather than another. [E.g.,] *Lead Industries*, 647 F.2d at 1161 (D.C. Cir. 1980). We agree. But none of those panels addressed the claim of undue delegation that we face here, and accordingly had no occasion to ask EPA for coherence (for a "principle," to use the classic term) in making its "policy judgment." The latter phrase is not, after all, a self-sufficient justification for every refusal to define limits.

. . .

Where (as here) statutory language and an existing agency interpretation involve an unconstitutional delegation of power, but an interpretation without the constitutional weakness is or may be available, our response is not to strike down the statute but to give the agency an opportunity to extract a determinate standard on its own. Doing so serves at least two of three basic rationales for the nondelegation doctrine. If the agency develops determinate, binding standards for itself, it is less likely to exercise the delegated authority arbitrarily. See *Amalgamated Meat Cutters v. Connally*, 337 F. Supp. 737, 758–59 (D.D.C. 1971) (Leventhal, J., for three-judge panel). And such standards enhance the likelihood that meaningful judicial review will prove feasible. A remand of this sort of course does not serve the third key function of non-delegation doctrine, to "ensure[] to the extent consistent with orderly governmental administration that important choices of social policy are made by Congress, the branch of our Government most responsive to the popular will," *Industrial Union Dep't, AFL-CIO v. American Petroleum Inst.*, 448 U.S. 607, 685 (1980) ("Benzene") (Rehnquist, J., concurring). The agency will make the fundamental policy choices. But the remand does ensure that the courts not hold unconstitutional a statute that an agency, with the application of its special expertise, could salvage. In any event, we do not read current Supreme Court cases as applying the strong form of the nondelegation doctrine voiced in Justice Rehnquist's concurrence. See *Mistretta v. United States*, 488 U.S. 361, 377–79 (1989).

What sorts of "intelligible principles" might EPA adopt? Cost-benefit analysis, mentioned as a possibility in *Lockout/Tagout I*, 938 F.2d at 1319–21, is not available under decisions of this court. Our cases read § 109(b)(1) as barring EPA from considering any factor other than "health effects relating to pollutants in the air."

In theory, EPA could make its criterion the eradication of any hint of direct health risk. This approach is certainly determinate enough, but it appears that it would require the agency to set the permissible levels of both pollutants here at zero. No party here appears to advocate this solution, and EPA appears to show no inclination to adopt it.[4]

EPA's past behavior suggests some readiness to adopt standards that leave non-zero residual risk. For example, it has employed commonly used clinical criteria to determine what qualifies as an adverse health effect. On the issue of likelihood, for some purposes it might be appropriate to use standards drawn from other areas of the law, such as the familiar "more probable than not" criterion.

Of course a one-size-fits-all criterion of probability would make little sense. There is no reason why the same probability should govern assessments of a risk of thousands of deaths as against risks of a handful of people suffering momentary shortness of breath. More generally, all the relevant variables seem to range continuously from high to low: the possible effects of pollutants vary from death to trivialities, and the size of the affected population, the probability of an effect, and the associated uncertainty range from "large" numbers of persons with point estimates of high probability, to small numbers and vague ranges of probability. This does not seem insurmountable. Everyday life compels us all to make decisions balancing remote but severe harms against a probability distribution of benefits; people decide whether to proceed with an operation that carries a 1/1000 possibility of death, and (simplifying) a 90% chance of cure and a 10% chance of no effect, and a certainty of some short-term pain and nuisance. To be sure, all that requires is a go/no-go decision, while a serious effort at coherence under § 109(b)(1) would need to be more comprehensive. For example, a range of ailments short of death might need to be assigned weights. Nonetheless, an agency wielding the power over American life possessed by EPA should be capable of developing the rough equivalent of a generic unit of harm that takes into account population affected, severity and probability. Possible building blocks for such a principled structure might be found in the approach Oregon used in devising its health plan for the poor. In determining what conditions would be eligible for treatment under its version of Medicaid, Oregon ranked treatments by the amount of improvement in "Quality-Adjusted Life Years" provided by each treatment, divided by the cost of the treatment.[5] Here, of course, EPA may not consider cost, and indeed may well

---

[4] A zero-risk policy might seem to imply deindustrialization, but in fact even that seems inadequate to the task (and even if the calculus is confined to direct risks from pollutants, as opposed to risks from the concomitant poverty). First, PM (at least) results from almost all combustion, so only total prohibition of fire or universal application of some heretofore unknown control technology would reduce manmade emissions to zero. Second, the combustion associated with pastoral life appears to be rather deadly. See World Bank, *World Development Report 1992: Development and the Environment* 52 (1992) (noting that "biomass" fuels (i.e., wood, straw, or dung) are often the only fuels that "poor households, mostly in rural areas" can obtain or afford, and that indoor smoke from biomass burning "contributes to acute respiratory infections that cause an estimated 4 million deaths annually among infants and children").

[5] The "quality" of various health states was determined by poll, and medical professionals determined the probabilities and durations of various health states with and without the treatment in question. Oregon was twice forced to revise its system because the United States Department of Health and Human Services determined that the original proposal and a revision violated the Americans with Disabilities Act, 42 U.S.C. §§ 12101–12213. The reason given for this

find a completely different method for securing reasonable coherence. Alternatively, if EPA concludes that there is no principle available, it can so report to the Congress, along with such rationales as it has for the levels it chose, and seek legislation ratifying its choice.

   . . .

[Judge Tatel dissented from this portion of the panel's opinion.]

COMMENTS AND QUESTIONS

Assume that the statute does *not* provide an intelligible standard and that you have to rewrite it to provide a standard that will reduce the amount of "nonthreshold pollutants" in the air, without bankrupting industries or the overall national economy. (The latter consideration rules out setting the standard at zero.) What standards might you devise that would allow the agency to set a standard to keep the air from getting "too" polluted? Remember that the argument of the court of appeals is that the agency does not have any principle to determine how much is too much. Consider some possibilities (some suggested in the preceding case, others not).

(1) *Cost-benefit analysis*: The agency should set the standard at a level where the benefits to health from the reduction are greater than (or just equal to) the costs of accomplishing the reduction. The *Lead Industries* decision precluded the agency from using cost-benefit analysis in standard setting.

---

determination was that both versions undervalued the lives of persons with disabilities: The original plan measured quality of life according to the attitudes of the general population rather than the attitudes of persons with disabilities. See HHS, "Analysis under the Americans with Disabilities Act ('ADA') of the Oregon Reform Demonstration" (Aug. 3, 1992), reprinted in 9 Issues in L. & Med. 397, 410, 410 (1994). The revised plan ranked treatments leaving the patient in a "symptomatic" state lower than those leaving the patient asymptomatic, and certain disabling conditions were considered "symptoms." See Letter from Timothy B. Flanagan, Assistant Attorney General, to Susan K. Zagame, Acting General Counsel, HHS (Jan. 19, 1993), reprinted in 9 Issues in L. & Med. 397, 418, 421 (1994). The Department's determination was extensively criticized when issued. See Maxwell J. Mehlman et al., "When Do Health Care Decisions Discriminate against Persons with Disabilities?" 22 J. Health Politics, Policy & L. 1385, 1390 (1997) (HHS's "decision provoked a storm of disbelief and denunciation").

We take no position on whether HHS's view was correct, or if the underlying norm also governs EPA's decisions under § 109(b)(1). An affirmative answer, however, would not seem to preclude use of some of Oregon's approach. The first step would be giving appropriate weight to the views of persons with disabilities. The second might be measuring the seriousness of a pollution-induced health effect by the absolute level of well-being that the effect brings about, not by the decrease in level that the effect causes. In other words, if the maximum well-being level is 100 and the average asthmatic whose asthma constitutes a disability has a well-being of 80 in the absence of air pollution (according to a measure that appropriately considers asthmatics' own assessments of their condition), then a response to air pollution that reduces the asthmatics' well-being to 70 could be counted as an effect of magnitude 30 (the difference from full health), rather than 10 (the difference from the level without the pollution). That approach would ensure that effects on persons with disabilities were not underestimated, even in the broad sense of that term apparently adopted by HHS.

Think about the discussion of cost-benefit analysis in chapter 9 and consider why Congress might want to avoid cost-benefit analysis in this context. When the Supreme Court reversed the court of appeals, it observed that Justice Rehnquist thought that the statute in the Benzene Case was an unconstitutional delegation of legislative authority *because* it authorized the agency to use cost-benefit analysis.

(2) *Avoiding irreversible effects, or reducing levels to those occasionally occurring naturally*: The court of appeals rejects these on the ground that the agency did not actually rely on them. Do they provide intelligible principles? Reconsider this question after you read the Supreme Court's opinion in the same case.

(3) *Quality-adjusted life years (QALYs)*: This is one version of what the court of appeals refers to as a "generic unit of harm." It attempts to measure how people (in various populations) rank choices involving the conditions under which they might live, taking into account the probability that they would actually experience those conditions. The court of appeals refers to the Oregon experience in attempting to use QALYs to determine how to allocate scarce resources for medical care for the poor. As the opinion notes, the list Oregon came up with was found to violate the Americans with Disabilities Act. Apart from that, the list had some apparent anomalies: It ranked having crooked teeth as producing a lower quality of life than having an ectopic pregnancy (a life-threatening condition in some pregnancies). Why might an effort to identify QALYs produce that result?

Why would recourse to QALYs provide an intelligible standard? The court of appeals seems to suggest that QALYs would allow the agency to determine when a standard was more likely than not to—do what? Increase the number of QALYs the American people "live"?

▪ Whitman v. American Trucking Associations, Inc.
531 U.S. 457 (2001)

Justice Scalia delivered the opinion of the Court.

. . .

Section 109(b)(1) of the CAA instructs the EPA to set "ambient air quality standards the attainment and maintenance of which in the judgment of the Administrator, based on [the] criteria [set out in the Ozone Final Rule, based on § 108] and allowing an adequate margin of safety, are requisite to protect the public health." 42 U.S.C. § 7409(b)(1). The Court of Appeals held that this section as interpreted by the Administrator did not provide an "intelligible principle" to guide the EPA's exercise of authority in setting NAAQS. "[The] EPA," it said, "lack[ed] any determinate criteria for drawing lines. It has failed to state intelligibly how much is too much." The court hence found that the EPA's interpretation (but not the statute itself) violated the nondelegation doctrine. We disagree.

In a delegation challenge, the constitutional question is whether the statute has delegated legislative power to the agency. Article I, § 1, of the Constitution vests "[a]ll legislative Powers herein granted . . . in a Congress of the United States." This text permits no delegation of those powers, *Loving v. United States*, 517 U.S. 748, 771 (1996); see *id.*, at 776–777 (Scalia, J., concurring in part and concurring in judgment), and so we repeatedly have said that when Congress confers decisionmaking authority upon agencies *Congress* must "lay down by legislative act an intelligible principle to which the person or body authorized to [act] is directed to conform." *J. W. Hampton, Jr., & Co. v. United States*, 276 U.S. 394, 409 (1928). We have never suggested that an agency can cure an unlawful delegation of legislative power by adopting in its discretion a limiting construction of the statute. . . . The idea that an agency can cure an unconstitutionally standardless delegation of power by declining to exercise some of that power seems to us internally contradictory. The very choice of which portion of the power to exercise—that is to say, the prescription of the standard that Congress had omitted—would *itself* be an exercise of the forbidden legislative authority. Whether the statute delegates legislative power is a question for the courts, and an agency's voluntary self-denial has no bearing upon the answer.

We agree with the Solicitor General that the text of § 109(b)(1) of the CAA at a minimum requires that "[f]or a discrete set of pollutants and based on published air quality criteria that reflect the latest scientific knowledge, [the] EPA must establish uniform national standards at a level that is requisite to protect public health from the adverse effects of the pollutant in the ambient air." Requisite, in turn, "mean[s] sufficient, but not more than necessary." These limits on the EPA's discretion are strikingly similar to the ones we approved in *Touby v. United States*, 500 U.S. 160 (1991), which permitted the Attorney General to designate a drug as a controlled substance for purposes of criminal drug enforcement if doing so was " 'necessary to avoid an imminent hazard to the public safety.' " They also resemble the Occupational Safety and Health Act provision requiring the agency to " 'set the standard which most adequately assures, to the extent feasible, on the basis of the best available evidence, that no employee will suffer any impairment of health' "— which the Court upheld in *Industrial Union Dept., AFL-CIO v. American Petroleum Institute*, 448 U.S. 607, 646 (1980), and which even then-Justice Rehnquist, who alone in that case thought the statute violated the nondelegation doctrine, see id., at 671 (opinion concurring in judgment), would have upheld if, like the statute here, it did not permit economic costs to be considered. See *American Textile Mfrs. Institute, Inc. v. Donovan*, 452 U.S. 490, 545 (1981) (Rehnquist, J., dissenting).

The scope of discretion § 109(b)(1) allows is in fact well within the outer limits of our nondelegation precedents. In the history of the Court we have found the requisite "intelligible principle" lacking in only two statutes, one of which provided literally no guidance for the exercise of discretion, and the other of which conferred authority to regulate the entire economy on the basis of no more precise a standard than stimulating the economy by assuring "fair competition." See *Panama Refining Co. v. Ryan*, 293 U.S. 388 (1935); *A.L.A. Schechter Poultry Corp. v. United States*, 295 U.S. 495 (1935). We have, on the other hand, upheld the validity of § 11(b)(2) of the Public Utility Holding Company Act of 1935, 49 Stat. 821, which gave the Securities and Exchange Commission authority to modify the structure of holding company systems so as to ensure that they are not "unduly or unnecessarily complicate[d]" and do not "unfairly or inequitably distribute voting power among security holders." *American Power & Light Co. v. SEC*, 329 U.S. 90 (1946). We have approved the wartime conferral of agency power to fix the prices of commodities at a level that " 'will be generally fair and equitable and will effectuate the [in some respects conflicting] purposes of th[e] Act.' " *Yakus v. United States*, 321 U.S. 414, 420, 423–426 (1944). And we have found an "intelligible principle" in various statutes authorizing regulation in the "public interest." See, e.g., *National Broadcasting Co. v. United States*, 319 U.S. 190, 225–226 (1943) (FCC's power to regulate airwaves); *New York Central Securities Corp. v. United States*, 287 U.S. 12, 24–25 (1932) (ICC's power to approve railroad consolidations). In short, we have "almost never felt qualified to second-guess Congress regarding the permissible degree of policy judgment that can be left to those executing or applying the law." *Mistretta v. United States, 488* U.S. 361, 416 (1989) (Scalia, J., dissenting); see id., at 373 (majority opinion).

It is true enough that the degree of agency discretion that is acceptable varies according to the scope of the power congressionally conferred. While Congress need not provide any direction to the EPA regarding the manner in which it is to define "country elevators," which are to be exempt from new-stationary-source regulations governing grain elevators, see § 7411(i), it must provide substantial guidance on setting air standards that affect the entire national economy. But even in sweeping regulatory schemes we have never demanded, as the Court of Appeals did here, that statutes provide a "determinate criterion" for saying "how much [of the regulated harm] is too much." In *Touby*, for example, we did not require the statute to decree how "imminent" was too imminent, or how "necessary" was necessary enough, or even—most relevant here—how "hazardous" was too hazardous. 500 U.S., at 165–167. . . . It is therefore not conclusive for delegation purposes that, as respondents argue, ozone and particulate matter are "nonthreshold" pollutants that inflict a continuum of adverse health effects at any airborne concentration greater than zero, and hence require the EPA to make judgments of degree. "[A] certain degree of discretion, and thus of lawmaking, inheres in most executive or judicial action." *Mistretta v. United States, supra,* at 417 (Scalia, J., dissenting) (emphasis deleted); see 488 U.S., at 378–379 (majority opinion). Section 109(b)(1) of the CAA, which to repeat we interpret as requiring the EPA to set air quality standards at the level that is "requisite"—that is, not lower or higher than is necessary—to protect the public health with an adequate margin of safety, fits comfortably within the scope of discretion permitted by our precedent.

. . .

[Concurring opinions of Justices Thomas, Stevens, and Breyer are omitted.]

COMMENTS AND QUESTIONS

1. The Supreme Court rejects the appeals court holding that the agency can eliminate the lack of an intelligible principle by supplying one by means of statutory interpretation. The Court says that determining whether a statute has an intelligible principle is a question for the courts, not the agency. What is the relationship between this holding and *Chevron*? Consider the proposition that the court of appeals relied on an agency's action at *Chevron* Step Two as the basis for saving the constitutionality of a statute that should never have been considered ambiguous under *Chevron* Step One (and note that Justice Scalia takes the position that he will find statutes clear—that is, will find it unnecessary to reach Step Two—more often than purposivist judges).

2. Does the Administrative Procedure Act have something of the nondelegation doctrine in it? Consider *Pearson v. Shalala*, described in chapter 10, in which the D.C. Circuit held that the FDA could not, consistent with the First Amendment,

completely prohibit certain health claims relating to dietary supplements. The court also stated that the Administrative Procedure Act required the FDA to explain a key standard underlying FDA's regulation of health claims. The Food, Drug, and Cosmetic Act itself makes approval of health claims for foods contingent on "significant scientific agreement," and the FDA had by regulation applied the same standard to health claims for dietary supplements. In *Pearson*, the court required the FDA to explain its understanding of this criterion. The court rested its holding on the arbitrary and capricious standard and observed that "[t]o refuse to define the criteria [the agency] is applying is equivalent to simply saying no without explanation." 164 F.3d 650, 660 (D. C. Cir. 1999). Does this holding look like the nondelegation doctrine, relocated to the APA? What would an explanation of "significant scientific agreement" look like? Would it help to resolve the underlying concern with agency arbitrariness?

3. According to the Court, what is the statute's intelligible principle? Can you explain why that standard is sufficient to overcome Judge Williams's "big guys" or "London fog" objections?

4. The next case involves federal constitutional limitations on *state* delegations of lawmaking authority. As you have seen, the nondelegation doctrine itself arises from principles embedded in Articles I and II of the national Constitution, and those principles are not applicable to state legislatures and executive agencies.

   In reading this case, keep in mind the tension that pervades the modern regulatory state between democratic accountability and technocratic expertise. Consider the proposition that the case relies on the view that the federal Constitution *requires* that the regulatory state utilize some degree of expertise and cannot rely exclusively on democratic decision making. One way of posing the question raised by the case is this: Would it be constitutionally permissible for a state legislature to make the specific decision challenged here?

■ **Geo-Tech Reclamation Industries, Inc. v. Hamrick**
  886 F.2d 662 (4th Cir. 1989)

Ervin, Chief Judge:

In this consolidated appeal, several West Virginia state environmental officials (collectively "West Virginia") and an organization known as "Citizens to Fight North Mountain Waste Site" appeal from determinations on summary judgment that a provision of West Virginia's Solid Waste Management Act, W. Va. Code § 20-5F-4(b), is facially unconstitutional. Because we find that the statutory language in question bears no rational relation "to the public health, safety, morals or general welfare," we must affirm the decision below.

West Virginia, like many other states, has enacted a statutory scheme governing solid waste disposal. In accordance with the provisions of the state's Solid Waste Management Act ("the Act"), landfills are regulated by the Department of Natural Resources ("the Department"). The Act flatly prohibits the operation of open dumps and requires landfill operators to obtain a permit from the Department before constructing, operating, or abandoning any solid waste disposal facility.

Permits may be issued by the Department's Director, after notice and opportunity for a public hearing, and may contain reasonable terms and conditions for the operation of a proposed waste facility. Among the various reasons for which a permit may be denied,

> the director may deny the issuance of a permit on the basis of information in the application or from other sources including public comment, if the solid waste facility may cause adverse impacts on the natural resources and environmental concerns under the director's purview in chapter twenty of the Code, destruction of aesthetic values, destruction or endangerment of the property of others or is significantly adverse to the public sentiment of the area where the solid waste facility is or will be located.

It is the final clause of this section—giving the Director authority to deny a permit solely because it is "significantly adverse to the public sentiment"—which is at issue in this case.

The facts relevant to this consolidated appeal are undisputed and straightforward. Geo-Tech Reclamation Industries, Inc. ("GRI") and LCS Services, Inc. ("LCS"), desire to operate a landfill on a site in West Virginia's panhandle country near the North Mountain community. GRI obtained an option to purchase the 331 acre site in 1986 and subsequently filed an application for a landfill operating permit. Its application was denied by the Director of the Department of Natural Resources on the ground that the proposed landfill had engendered "adverse public sentiment." The Director's letter terminating the permit application process stated:

> [T]he Department has received approximately 250 letters representing individual citizens, businesses, and groups in the Hedgesville area. All are vehemently opposed to the project. We have also received a petition in which similar feelings were expressed by many more hundreds of local citizens. . . . Due to the significant concern voiced by the residents of the area, I believe it is inappropriate to continue further technical review and am denying the permit application on the basis of adverse public sentiment, as prescribed in § 20-5F-4(b). The staff review of the Part I application has not revealed any insurmountable technical problems with the site.

Subsequently, LCS acquired an option to purchase the site in 1987. Its application to operate a solid waste disposal facility was also rejected because of adverse public sentiment. In his letter denying LCS' permit application, however, the Director added "destruction of aesthetic values, and the destruction and endangerment of the property of others" as further reasons for the denial. LCS appealed the decision to the West Virginia Water Resources Board pursuant to W. Va. Code § 20-5F-7. During hearings before the Board, Robert D. Seip, a former Department employee who supervised the technical review of LCS' application, testified that LCS' site was particularly well suited to serve as a landfill and that LCS' plan had no significant technical failings. Based in part on this testimony, the Board ruled that neither aesthetic or property value related concerns would justify the denial of LCS' application. It affirmed, though, the Director's decision on the basis of adverse public sentiment.

After the State Water Resources Board upheld the Director's decision, LCS and GRI brought declaratory judgment actions challenging § 20-5F-4(b)'s constitutionality. LCS and GRI argued that § 20-5F-4(b) violated due process by impermissibly delegating legislative authority to local citizens. They also argued that the statute exceeded the state's police power. On cross motions for summary judgment, the district court found § 20-5F-4(b) to be unconstitutional. Relying on decisions by the Supreme Court in *Eubank v. City of Richmond*, 226 U.S. 137 (1912) and *Washington ex rel. Seattle Title Trust Co. v. Roberge*, 278 U.S. 116 (1928), the court accepted the plaintiffs' argument that "this provision is on its face violative of due process rights guaranteed under the United States Constitution insofar as it allows a few citizens to deny an individual the use of his property." ...

 . . .

West Virginia now appeals from the district court's determination that the "significantly adverse to the public sentiment" clause of § 20-5F-4(b) violates the Constitution. . . .

In *Eubank* the Court confronted a Richmond ordinance that required the city's Building Committee to establish set-back lines for a given piece of property whenever requested to do so by two-thirds of the adjacent property owners. The Court ruled that this ordinance violated due process, stating:

> One set of owners determines not only the extent of use, but the kind of use which another set of owners may make of their property. . . . The statute and ordinance, while conferring the power on some property holders to virtually control and dispose of the property rights of others, creates no standard by which the power thus given is to be exercised. . . . The only discretion which exists in the street committee, or in the committee of public safety, is in the location of the line, between 5 and 30 feet.

Eubank, 226 U.S., at 143–44. The *Roberge* Court threw out a Seattle ordinance, on similar grounds, that conditioned a building permit for a charitable home on obtaining the consent of two-thirds of the owners located within four hundred feet of the proposed building. In his opinion for a unanimous court, Justice Butler wrote:

> The [ordinance] purports to give the owners of less than one-half the land within 400 feet of the proposed building authority—uncontrolled by any standard or rule prescribed by legislative action—to prevent the trustee from using its land for the proposed home. The superintendent is bound by the decision or inaction of such owners. There is no provision for review under the ordinance; their failure to give consent is final. [Local residents] are not bound by any official duty, but are free to withhold consent for selfish reasons or arbitrarily, and may subject the trustee to their will or caprice. The delegation of power so attempted is repugnant to the due process clause of the 14th Amendment. *Roberge*, 278 U.S., at 121–122 (citations omitted).

West Virginia's response to this argument is straight-forward. The state contends that the statute does not impermissibly delegate legislative authority to private citizens because § 20-5F-4(b) does not give local residents any legal power to block the approval of an otherwise qualified permit application. The state points to the fact that the statute does not require the Director's decision to conform to local public sentiment but merely states that he "may" reject an application on the ground that it has engendered adverse local opinion. Thus § 20-5F-4(b) merely gives the Director the authority to consult local public sentiment as one of many factors to be considered in the exercise of his discretion. This fact, according to West Virginia, distinguishes § 20-5F-4(b) from the laws invalidated in *Eubank* and *Roberge*.

We see no reason, however, to decide whether § 20-5F-4(b) works an impermissible delegation of power to local residents because the statute suffers from a more profound constitutional infirmity. It is well settled that land-use regulations "must find their justification in some aspect of the police power, asserted for the public welfare." *Euclid v. Ambler Realty Co.*, 272 U.S. 365, 387 (1926). West Virginia strenuously argues that it acts well within the broad confines of its police power in regulating the development of solid waste disposal facilities. With this we certainly agree. No one would question the state's power to impose a broad array of restrictions on an activity, such as the operation of a landfill, which was recognized as a nuisance even by the early common law.

West Virginia also argues that within this broad array of restrictions, the state may legislate to protect its communities against not only such tangible effects as increased traffic, noise, odors, and health concerns, but also against the possibility of decreased community pride and fracturing of community spirit that may accompany large waste disposal operations. Here again, we do not quarrel with the state's position. "The concept of the public welfare is broad and inclusive. The values it represents are spiritual as well as physical, aesthetic as well as monetary." *Berman v. Parker*, 348 U.S. 26, 33 (1954) (citations omitted). *Accord Village of Belle Terre v. Boraas*, 416 U.S. 1 (1974). West Virginia may undoubtedly regulate the siting and operation of solid waste disposal facilities so as to eliminate or at least alleviate the deleterious effects of such facilities on more inchoate community values.

The question raised in this case, however, is whether § 20-5F-4(b) does in fact further this laudable purpose or whether it is instead "arbitrary and capricious, having no substantial relation" to its purported goal. See *Euclid*, 272 U.S., at 395. The state argues that the statute's adverse public sentiment clause promotes its stated purpose by allowing citizens to comment upon a proposed landfill's impact on community pride, spirit, and quality of life. But, with commendable candor, the state also recognizes that many who may speak out against a landfill will do so because of self-interest, bias, or ignorance. These are but a few of the less than noble motivations commonly referred to as the "Not-in-My-Backyard" syndrome.

West Virginia argues that § 20-5F-4(b) nonetheless protects the administrative permit process from such base criteria for decision-making by vesting final authority in the Director who must exercise his or her discretion in determining whether adverse public sentiment is "significant." We are unable, however, to discern within the language of § 20-5F-4(b) any meaningful standard by which the Director is to measure adverse sentiment.[2] Indeed, the facts of these consolidated

---

[2] We do not suggest that federal law places any general restraints on the delegation of state power to state administrators or generally requires state power to be delegated according to well defined standards. See *United Beverage Co. v. Indiana Alcoholic Beverage Commission*, 760 F.2d 155 (7th Cir. 1985) (listing a few limited areas where constitutional interests require state regulatory power to be exercised according to clearly articulated standards). We merely note that the absence of any standard by which the Director must evaluate adverse public sentiment, in part, deprives § 20-5F-4(b) of any rational relation to the goal of protecting civic pride and general communal welfare.

cases plainly show that the Director made no effort to cull out the wheat from the chaff of public opposition to these permits.[3] And in the absence of any such effort, whether it be mandated by the statute or attempted as a matter of administrative policy, we can find no substantial or rational relationship between the statute's goals and its means. "Where property interests are adversely affected by zoning, the courts generally have emphasized the breadth of municipal power to control land use and have sustained the regulation if it is rationally related to legitimate state concerns. . . . But an ordinance may fail even under that limited standard of review." *Schad v. Mt. Ephraim*, 452 U.S. 61, 68 (1981) (citations omitted). Nothing in the record suggests, nor can we conceive, how unreflective and unreasoned public sentiment that "a dump is still a dump" is in any way rationally related to the otherwise legitimate goal of protecting community spirit and pride.

While we need express no opinion as to whether § 20-5F-4(b) works an impermissible delegation of legislative authority of the sort condemned in *Eubank* and *Roberge*, we find it instructive to note that the evil there denounced is equally present here. In both cases, the Court noted that administrative decision-making was made potentially subservient to selfish or arbitrary motivations or the whims of local taste. *Eubank*, 226 U.S., at 144, *Roberge*, 278 U.S., at 122. Cf. *Silverman v. Barry*, 851 F.2d 434 (DC Cir. 1988) (Silberman J., concurring in the denial of rehearing en banc, suggesting that delegation of authority to private citizens was not the Supreme Court's real concern in *Eubank* and *Roberge*). The same potential is present here. The Director has been commanded, without the benefit of any legislated standard by which to separate public sentiment grounded upon reasoned considerations substantially related to civic spirit from irrational public sentiment or whim, to act upon adverse public sentiment in issuing waste facility operating permits. The potential that, by virtue of § 20-5F-4(b), sensitive administrative decisions regarding waste disposal will be made by mob rule is too great to ignore.

Accordingly, we find that § 20-5F-4(b)'s clause authorizing the Director to reject permits that are "significantly adverse to the public sentiment" bears no substantial or rational relationship to the state's interest in promoting the general public welfare.

COMMENTS AND QUESTIONS

1. Why is it unconstitutional for a legislature to direct an agency to deny a permit if there is "public sentiment in the area" against allowing the waste facility? Why do people oppose locating a facility in their neighborhoods? Suppose the opposition rests on concerns that the facility is badly designed, will emit excessive noise and odors, will adversely affect property values, or will destroy the sense people in the neighborhood have that they form a valuable and valued

---

[3] The Director, in his testimony before the West Virginia Water Resources Board, suggested that the statute's use of the term "significant" merely required adverse sentiment be expressed by a sufficient number of local residents and that opposition from just a handful of residents would not suffice. This total emphasis on the quantity rather than the quality or content of public comment helps to illustrate the lack of any rational relation between the statute and its purported goal.

community. Would it be unconstitutional to deny a permit if public sentiment rested on those grounds? (Put another way, would it be unconstitutional to authorize an agency to deny a permit on any or all of those grounds?) Is the problem with the statute that it does not eliminate the possibility that public sentiment rests on some other grounds that could *not* be the basis for a permit denial? The obvious example is public opposition based on the fact that the facility's owners are members of a racial group against which the people in the area harbor animus. Is dislike of operators of solid waste facilities in itself an impermissible ground? If the problem is that the statute does not eliminate the risk that adverse public sentiment rests on impermissible grounds, should the court try to figure out how likely it is that impermissible reasons are at work in the range of cases where the "adverse public sentiment" criteria is invoked?

2. Take the agency out of the picture. Could a state legislature retain in its own hands the power to award licenses for solid waste facilities? Would a statute providing exactly that—and identifying no criteria whatever for awarding or denying licenses—be unconstitutional, given the court's analysis in *Geo-Tech*? Direct legislative awards of licenses were common in the nineteenth century but are rare these days, eliminated in large measure because of (a) the corruption that accompanied such awards and (b) the burdens placed on legislatures of awarding licenses. Consider, though, whether it would be constitutional for a legislature to hold in its own hands the power to award licenses to build laboratories in which embryonic stem-cell research was to be conducted.

3. The *Geo-Tech* court says that the statute is unconstitutional because taking adverse public sentiment into account has no rational relationship to a permissible public goal. Does this amount to saying that there is (too great?) a risk that public sentiment will not have a rational relationship to a permissible public goal? Is this the same as saying that the Constitution places some obligation on the public to be rational when it acts in a *legislative* capacity?

4. Which of the following statements more closely matches your views: (a) "*Geo-Tech* places far too much weight on the importance of expertise and technical rationality in agency decision making and seriously undervalues the importance of ensuring that agencies be accountable to the public" or (b) "The statute in *Geo-Tech* does indeed inject a high degree of public accountability into agency decision making, and that is why it is a bad statute; we should *want* agencies to temper what the public wants with the knowledge that comes with expertise."

■ Concluding Note

So far this part has dealt with the *legal* and *policy* questions that arise when legislatures—and their delegees, administrative agencies—choose particular methods of regulating risk. Legislative and agency choices are affected by more than law and considerations of what constitutes good public policy. They are affected as well by *politics*. The following chapter therefore concludes this part's treatment of choices among regulatory instruments by presenting some analyses of the political processes that affect such choices.

13

Political Approaches to Choices among Regulatory Institutions

In chapter 5, we considered the question of how to choose among regulatory institutions. There, we framed our discussion from the perspective of a disinterested social scientist, attempting to determine what choices among institutions would best serve the public interest. We saw that the problems of access bias and process bias, described by Gillette and Krier, and the distributional alignments, discussed by Komesar, may have implications for one's choice of institutional arrangements. In the discussion of Mendeloff's "positive" argument in chapter 9, we saw that large firms, threatened with concentrated regulatory costs, are likely to challenge strict regulation, thus contributing to the "over-regulation produces underregulation" paradox Mendeloff identifies.

In this chapter, we view the choice of regulatory institutions from the perspective of politicians, as understood by (disinterested?) social scientists. Politicians—the people who actually make those choices—are not disinterested social scientists. They may try to serve the public interest and may seek the best available advice, but they also have interests in securing reelection, in satisfying campaign contributors, in doing what is best for their individual constituency even if that might not be best for the society as a whole, and the like. In predicting how political struggles will turn out in light of politicians' manifold aims, the insights from chapter 5 will again prove useful.

The idea that the "public interest" might be different from a politician's aims is a central insight of so-called public choice theory, our primary subject in this chapter. Simply stated, public choice theory tries to apply the lessons of microeconomics to political decisions and institutions; the premise is that the kind of self-interested behavior one sees in markets can also be seen in the political realm. In section A, this chapter introduces you to the core concepts in public choice theory and offers several critiques. In Section B, the chapter turns to potential implications of the theory for regulatory priority setting.

A The Politics of Institutional Choice

Most theories get their start by rejecting some other theory, and public choice theory is no exception. Its foil is the public interest theory of legislation, which holds that legislators are motivated by public-spirited aspirations. Before examining the politics of institutional choice, we offer an introduction that lays out the public interest theory of legislation and explains why economists and political scientists have become skeptical about its accuracy. The article identifies precisely what might be wrong with the public interest theory of legislation; it turns out that the defects are quite subtle.

■ *Beyond Public Choice and Public Interest: A Study of the Legislative Process as Illustrated by Tax Legislation in the 1980s*
DANIEL SHAVIRO
139 U. Pa. L. Rev. 1 (1990). Reprinted with permission of University of Pennsylvania Law Review

. . .

III. The Public Interest Theory of Legislation

A. *The Various Strands of Public Interest Theory*

In contemporary law and economics literature, the public interest theory of legislation is little more than a strawman. Writers describe it as an old-fashioned and now universally rejected school of economic thought, discuss it very briefly, and then move on to the real (public choice-based) discussion. The term is nonetheless useful because it describes a basic attitude, involving optimism about the legislative process, that in sympathetic hands often has specific content. I will mention three varieties of what I (but not necessarily the exponents) call public interest theory: the traditional economic view, the pluralist view from political science, and the ideological view.

1. Public Interest Theory in Economics

Market economists since Adam Smith have recognized that government could play a wealth-enhancing role in the economy by responding to instances of market failure. Smith identified the problem of public goods noting that there were "certain public works and certain public institutions, which it can never be for the interest of any individual, or small number of individuals, to erect and maintain." Later economists discussed using government to correct externalities, or costs and benefits associated with consumption or production that are not reflected in market prices. By the middle of the twentieth century, welfare economists such as Arthur Pigou and William Baumol had recognized that these theoretical justifications for government action could reach quite far. Moreover, John Maynard Keynes had pioneered the view that the government should take responsibility for economic stability and prosperity through macroeconomic budgetary policy.

Economic literature about the government was almost entirely normative, rather than descriptive. The question of whether actual government behavior might vary sharply from ideal behavior tended to be ignored, under the assumption (often merely implicit) that government could be trusted to pursue the public interest. Pigou argued that recent increases in public education and affluence would permit sufficient monitoring of government to ensure its probity and unselfishness. Keynes assumed control of government by a small and enlightened intellectual elite.

A cynic might say that economists had reason to favor expansion of the government's role, since this promised to enhance their power, prestige, and employment. Legislation of which they disapproved "typically elicited laments about the ignorance of politicians and recommendations for the hiring of more economists in key governmental positions." There are other explanations for their optimism, however. They may have shared the widespread faith in government that dominated public perceptions for several decades after the New Deal. They may have thought—as Ronald Coase apparently did—that perceived moral differences between private and public action might make the latter relatively altruistic. Or, as Pigou's views suggest, they may have believed that democracy naturally produces public interest outcomes. If the public interest is the sum of everyone's private interests, there is universal suffrage, and people accurately perceive and act in their interests, it may seem logical to expect "good" legislation: legislators must supply it in order to be reelected. This rosy view of politics was well in keeping with a contemporaneous school of thought in the political science literature.

2. The Pluralist School in Political Science

One of the dominant themes in American political history, reflected in the study of political science, is the relationship between "special interests" and the public or general interest. Concern about interest groups dates back to James Madison, who in the famous Federalist No. 10 discusses "faction," or the tendency of particular groups (principally, but not exclusively, economic groups such as the rich, poor, debtors, creditors, farmers, and manufacturers) to seek legislation injurious to members of other groups. While the terms "special interest" and "interest group" tend to be pejorative, the role that such groups play has not always been viewed negatively. Madison argued that the evils of faction could largely be controlled, through means including the creation of a polity too large and diverse for any one interest group to command a ready majority. Alexis de Tocqueville later described the American passion for participating in political and social groups of all kinds as an essential and largely beneficial aspect of American democracy.

Among certain political scientists, principally in the 1950s, the vision of political power shared among a wide array of interest groups took on a distinctly laudatory cast. Exponents of pluralism argued that the consequent dispersal of governmental power yields numerous benefits for society, including political stability, widely distributed political satisfaction, and a process of negotiation and compromise between interests that promotes political moderation and acceptance of others' reasonable claims.

The above claims focus on by-products of political activity, more than on the desirability of specific political outcomes. Yet pluralists were similarly optimistic about such outcomes. While mostly denying the existence of a public or general interest, apart from the aggregation of particular interests, pluralists shared an, at least implicit, notion of equity, under which each interest should be weighed accurately (based on numbers and intensity) in the political balance. To demonstrate that the existing balance of power was reasonably equitable, pluralists argued that each person is represented by numerous interest groups, including "potential" groups, that, while as yet unorganized, stand ready to protect their members if necessary. With groups' power generally proportionate to size and intensity of interest, legislative outcomes tend to aggregate accurately the underlying interests of all individuals and thus of society. Moreover, since everyone's interests are heard and weighed, decisions that were not abstractly correct in advance may be legitimated ex post by universal, process-based consent.

This pluralist defense of the legislative process differs significantly in emphasis from the public interest view of the economists. It emphasizes wealth distribution and value choices concerning the nature of the good that are not objectively reducible to wealth. Economists, by contrast, often emphasize maximizing aggregate social wealth. In addition to having different concerns, the pluralists and public interest economists were not conscious allies; indeed, they appear to have been largely unaware of each other. Their respective views nonetheless can be amalgamated as part of a single broader view. The pluralist account of politics strongly suggests that wealth-maximizing policies generally will be adopted. Moreover, it provides an attractive account of how decisions apart from wealth maximization are made.

3. Ideological Views of the Public Interest

We have thus far defined public interest theory objectively, or as holding that legislation actually tends to be "good" in the economic or pluralistic sense. The theory can also be defined subjectively, or as describing people's motives without regard to what is actually good. In this sense, it holds only that legislators or those who influence them pursue altruistic or ideological goals as ends in themselves, and seek to do good (as they conceive of the good) rather than solely to pursue self-interest in the narrow sense. . . .

B. Criticisms of Public Interest Theory

One could not sensibly assert that the public interest view of American politics is wholly false. Surely the government does many things that increase social well-being, such as maintaining public roads, enforcing contracts, and deterring violent crime and foreign invasion. Moreover, the political system reflects and responds to the public's wishes, at least in the extreme sense that no one proposing the policies of a Pol Pot or a Nicolae Ceausescu would have good prospects of sustained electoral success. Disagreements with the public interest view are in part a matter of degree (the pluralists were not unrelievedly sanguine), as well as of emotional predilection regarding whether to focus on the system's elements of success or failure.

Nonetheless, the public interest view has been criticized on theoretical and empirical grounds for misapprehending both the balance between good and bad and its underlying causation. In keeping with academic fashions, the attack by economists has been largely theoretical and that by political scientists largely empirical.

1. (Largely Theoretical) Criticisms by Economists

By the early 1960s, many economists had come to realize that Congress often has little interest in deferring to their wisdom. For example, Congress had never attempted to tailor excise taxes to correlate with professionally estimated externalities. Moreover, economists' empirical investigations of government activity failed to confirm their belief that government acts to correct market failure. Finally, the fashion that Mark Kelman calls "economic imperialism," or extending economic analysis "to all spheres of human activity," suggested viewing legislators through the conventional prism of rational self-interest. Economists began to believe that politicians would reduce social welfare deliberately if this happened to benefit them. Economists almost simultaneously became aware of public interest theory as a contestable way of thinking and by consensus rejected it. We can divide the elements of economists' rejection of public interest theory into two categories.

a. When Everyone "Wins," Everyone May Lose

The pluralists applaud a system where power is decentralized and everyone occasionally wins—for example, where each interest group constituency receives a share of government largesse. To many economists, however, this pleasant distributional dream is instead an efficiency nightmare that threatens to reduce social wealth and leave everyone worse off than if there were no largesse at all. They identify two principal reasons for the inefficiency of a system that gives everyone the benefit of an occasional wealth transfer. First, the means of transferring wealth may involve using resources inefficiently. For example, assume that each of the country's 435 congressional districts pays $1 billion dollars of Federal taxes and is the site of $1 billion dollars of wasteful Federal pork barrel spending (such as building army bases that serve no military purpose). Each district benefits greatly from its own pork barrel project (since it receives the entire benefit and bears only 1/435th of the cost), yet loses overall because, given its share of the costs of all projects, it is exchanging $1 billion dollars cash for a worthless asset.

The second reason advanced by economists for the inefficiency of governmental wealth transfers is that, when they are available, people sometimes expend substantial resources seeking them. For example, imagine that each military base depends politically on the efforts of lobbyists who must churn out favorable propaganda and make campaign contributions to members of Congress. Many of the resources used in seeking all the reciprocal transfers will be consumed, not just transferred, and thus are essentially wasted.

If everyone loses in the aggregate from transfers of government largesse, one might think that all could simply agree to dispense with the transfers. This solution is impeded, however, by a collective action problem, or "prisoner's dilemma." Recall, for example, that each congressional district benefits from its own pork barrel project, whether or not any other district has a project. No district benefits from [forgoing] its own transfer unless its decision influences significant numbers of others to [forgo] seeking transfers as well. In the vast and decentralized political arena celebrated by the pluralists, any such coordination between different groups' decisions about whether to seek transfers may be impossible.

b. Wealth-Reducing Transfers and the Theory of Groups

A question still remains as to why the transfers obtained by districts or interest groups should be inefficient (costs of seeking them aside). This premise was explicit in the economists' analysis described above. Yet one might expect efficient transfers (such as militarily useful bases) to be the norm even if the persons seeking a transfer are utterly indifferent to its efficiency. As an example, anyone who seeks an army base presumably must claim that it will be militarily useful. Those outside the locality have self-interested reasons for opposing the base unless this claim is persuasive. In political competition, the stronger arguments for transfers seemingly should defeat the weaker ones.

The problem, economists argue, is that this asks too much of people outside the area where the useless army base would be located. Information and political action—such as determining that a base is useless and punishing politicians who support it—are costly to voters unless they happen to enjoy politics as a hobby.

Therefore, most voters choose to become well-informed about only a small number of issues, principally those in which they have a substantial direct stake—such as a military base in one's own district. On all other issues, voters engage in "efficient shirking": they make no effort even to understand, because the cost of one's efforts would exceed the expected benefit. In particular, voters shirk with regard to widely shared public goods (including the avoidance of "public bads" such as inefficient expenditures). Shirking is individually efficient not only because each person's share of the benefit (or avoided detriment) is small, but because of a collective action problem. If all affected voters cooperated to learn and implement their interests, they all might benefit on balance despite the costs of information and political action. Yet each individual voter, having only a trivial capacity to affect political outcomes, is tempted to free ride on others' efforts and is aware that others may free ride on hers. From each voter's perspective, "everyone else" will determine the outcome. One is therefore better off not incurring the costs of diligence, regardless of whether or not others assume this burden.

Accordingly, economists expect voters to function for most purposes as virtual ciphers who ignore the legislative process for rationally self-interested reasons, and who in turn are ignored by participants in the process. This view, however, fails to describe the behavior of voters who belong to small interest groups that seek transfers from the rest of the public. One example of such an interest group is the group of members of a congressional district who seek a useless military base. The benefits expected by members of an interest group may be sufficiently great to justify seeking information and engaging in political action. Moreover, while the free rider problem still exists, it is less acute than for the rest of the public. Small groups find it cheaper than do large groups to coordinate their members' efforts and monitor shirking.

The result is a "systematic tendency for 'exploitation' of the great [in number] by the small." Contrary to the expectations of the pluralists, "potential groups" of great numbers remain unorganized and ineffective even in the face of exploitation. Consumers, for example, often lose to business interests. The former are a vast and undifferentiated group while the latter are divided into industries, each containing only a small number of firms that can solve the free rider problem fairly well.

This explanation still does not account for why interest group transfers should be inefficient, the costs of obtaining and administering them aside. In the military base example, assuming that the government would spend $1 billion dollars in a particular district, residents in that district would benefit even more if the cash were paid to them directly instead of being spent on the base. If, as we have posited, the residents have the power to direct a $1 billion dollar expenditure, one would expect them to have it paid directly to themselves. This result would be efficiency-neutral, the costs of seeking the transfer aside. To the economist, $1 billion dollars in the hands of one group is no better or worse than one billion dollars in the hands of another group.

As Gordon Tullock explains, however, a direct transfer of this sort would simply be too "raw." Rent-seekers, those who pursue transfers artificially contrived by the political process, are constrained to advocate inefficient means of transferring wealth because only then can they conceal from the public at large what is really going on. The public, despite its general indifference to politics, seems to enjoy following obvious scandals.

In short, the public is not quite the cipher economists otherwise assume. This explains the need for a fig leaf that reduces the value of a transfer to its recipients. Yet it still does not fully explain why the transfer should be inefficient. For example, those who seek a local army base should be at most indifferent to questions of military need: they have no reason to prefer that the base be useless. More generally, people can conceal rent-seeking motives behind valid as well as spurious rationales.

The economists' probable response to this problem is twofold. First, economists who already believe in the chronic inefficiency of entire areas of government activity (such as economic regulation) find it reasonable to assume that in each particular case their general belief will be validated. Second, if rent seekers are indifferent to anything beyond their private gain and all other voters are sufficiently ignorant, then rationales need not have much plausibility—for one to be correct would be wildly coincidental. Indeed, if the public is highly cynical, the rationale for a transfer may need to reduce significantly the percentage of value that is transferred (or the directness of the transfer), even if the rationale need not otherwise be plausible. . . .

2. (Largely Empirical) Criticisms by Political Scientists

In recent years many political scientists, like economists, have become skeptical of the pluralist/public interest view of legislation. This skepticism arises principally from empirical studies of who interest groups represent and how interest groups participate in the legislative process. The pluralists' optimism about the balance and universality of group representation in Washington is contradicted by substantial evidence. For example, registered interest groups disproportionately represent corporate business interests (as expected under the economic theory of groups), despite recent growth among citizen, civil rights, and social welfare groups. The extent to which one's interests are represented also tends to vary positively with wealth. Even without explicit reference to the economic theory of groups, political scientists have come to recognize that "potential groups" cannot redress the balance. Thus, Elmer Schattschneider distinguished organized and unorganized groups, noting the implausibility of assuming that "a few workmen who habitually stop at a corner saloon for a glass of beer are essentially the same [in political influence] as the United States Army. . . ."

Schattschneider's work suggested that influence upon legislation was as highly skewed as one would expect from the interests' uneven representation in Washington. His classic study of interest group lobbying on the Smoot-Hawley Tariff demonstrated that business groups seeking high tariffs were virtually unopposed by those (such as consumers) who would have benefitted from low tariffs. Instead of pluralist competition, he found a pattern of pervasive logrolling, whereby business lobbyists agreed to "reciprocal non-interference" or support for each other's high tariff demands. If one group sought a tariff on items that a second group needed to purchase, the second group would settle for a "compensatory duty" on its own products. Thus, the legislative process was a positive sum game for its participants, and probably a highly negative sum game for the country as a whole. . . .

. . . Interest groups may not always dictate to the extent they did in the enactment of Smoot-Hawley, but today they are often well-financed and influential, and usually are found only, or at least disproportionately, on one side of an issue. . . .

... Theodore Lowi pioneered the notion that the role played by interest groups depends upon the nature of the issue at any given time. Lowi posited three principal categories of public policy: distribution, regulation, and redistribution. Distribution involves pork barrel issues, the quest by narrow interest groups for subsidies, chiefly at the expense of the rarely represented general public. The contestants, as reported by Schattschneider, accommodate each other through logrolling and reciprocal noninterference. Regulation involves direct choices between the interests of well-organized competing groups (such as one industry against another). It thus fits the pluralist model of negotiation and compromise and also manifests instability as the winning alliances change. Finally, redistribution again involves direct choices between competing groups, but here the groups are large social classes, such as rich versus poor or big business versus organized labor. While redistribution resembles regulation in having opposite sides represented, redistribution is more conflictive and ideological in style, and more stable in outcome. The classes are long-term antagonists but given the scale and duration of conflict, a balance of power develops and persists.

Lowi's typology suggests that the pluralists are clearly wrong about distributional issues, and possibly wrong about redistributional ones as well, given the wealth bias of interest group representation. Even issues that superficially look like pure (pluralist) regulation might also be distributional if some interested parties are unrepresented. For example, several groups that have cooperated to win a transfer from the general public might then more visibly compete regarding its allocation among themselves.

C. Public Interest Theory and the Problem of Cognitive Bias

... [W]e have [heretofore] assumed both that people seek wealth (defined narrowly, although taking account of the psychic cost of time and effort), and that they are rational in deciding how to seek it. Failures by the political system to maximize and distribute equitably social wealth have been attributed to poorly aligned incentives (as when free rider problems distort responses due to information costs) and to unequal political access and power.

The one hint that people may be more idiosyncratic than the rational-pursuit-of-wealth model recognizes came when I noted that a district seeking a wealth transfer may need to conceal this objective (and reduce the value transferred) by using the fig leaf of a militarily useless Army base. This example is not necessarily inconsistent with the model: it can be seen as showing the need to raise information costs for those outside the district so that they will not find it worth their while to question the expenditure. Yet the example raises some interesting problems with the model. Might people be unusually susceptible to spurious claims about the need for military spending? If so, does this show a lack of rationality? Alternatively, might it suggest that people prefer high military spending without regard to effectiveness? Such a preference, while seemingly perverse, cannot be called irrational if "rationality" implies only the selection of appropriate means to advance one's objectives.

I have in mind two related issues with different implications for public interest theory. The first is whether people's cognitive biases and illusions shape political choices in such a way as to provide further grounds for skepticism about the theory. The second is whether we can properly say that people are cognitively biased. If they want something and the political system gives it to them, how can they be wrong and the "true" public interest different from what they want?

1. Cognitive Biases and Illusions as Favoring Bad Legislation and Interest Group Transfers

We have been thinking of people as making rationally self-interested decisions based on limited knowledge. They process with reasonable accuracy the information that has come to their attention, and seek more information if the expected benefit of doing so exceeds the expected cost. While this assumption does not lead inevitably to public interest legislation (instead, it makes certain types of political "market failure" predictable), it appears at least moderately helpful. Interest group transfers must be sufficiently small or well-concealed to avoid arousing the public from its rational ignorance. Note also that politicians may have every incentive to alert the public to inefficient transfers supported by their opponents.

Unfortunately, the above view of human behavior is to a certain extent false. Instead of seeking information, people often shun it lest it prove unpleasant, for example, by contradicting their cherished beliefs. As Gordon Tullock has commented, "[t]he liberals who read *The National Review* or the conservatives who read *The Nation*, are few. Neither group really wants information which might lead it to change its mind." For similar reasons political rhetoric often is designed to soothe rather than inform, and so mollifies by confirming stereotyped views even if world events must be ignored or misinterpreted.

To the extent people receive new information, they tend to process it in systematically inaccurate ways. Empirically demonstrated examples include the "constancy principle" (interpreting information in such a way as to make it consistent with one's predispositions), "consistency bias" (agreeing with people one likes and disagreeing with those one dislikes), "positivity bias" (the common though not universal tendency to interpret ambiguous information in a positive rather than a negative light), and "agreement bias" (tending to agree with what one hears). In addition, people often mistakenly consider visual information more trustworthy than verbal information: as a Reagan Administration official once put it, "What are you going to believe, the facts or your eyes?" These biases can be exploited by politicians or interest groups to benefit themselves at the expense of the general public. Examples include the "big lie" technique of constant repetition and the calculated crafting of a likeable personal image.... These methods affect principally the public's factual beliefs, but some have suggested that self-interested politicians can also shape the public's preferences. John Kenneth Galbraith's claim that businesses, through advertising, can first create and then satisfy new consumer desires may apply to politicians and legislation.

Perhaps the most far-reaching study of how people's irrationality (from a narrow self-interest perspective) can further interest group dominance is Murray Edelman's *The Symbolic Uses of Politics*. Edelman argues that, in a mass society where government is enormously powerful but remote from everyday life, politics becomes a "passing parade of abstract symbols ... [onto which most people project] private emotions, especially strong anxieties and hopes." They ignore substance because they feel powerless, lack information, cannot accurately assess the effects of a politician or a policy, and are seduced by the emotional content of verbal abstractions. Instead of demanding tangible benefit from government policy, they settle for easily provided symbolic reassurance, such as speeches blaming scapegoats for their problems and anxieties, or regulatory legislation that supposedly protects the "little man" but actually enriches narrow elites. . . .

2. Can People Really Be "Biased" about What They Want?

The previous section suggested that people's cognitive biases and taste for deceptive symbolic reassurance help to show why the public interest theory of legislation is wrong. One could argue, however, that if people are getting what they want, as Edelman's and even Galbraith's views suggest, then by definition the public interest is being served. For example, assume that consumers support existing safety regulation of the automobile industry but that an economist could show that the regulation has no effect on safety and enriches the industry at the consumers' expense. The economist's view is of no relevance if definitionally people's interest is whatever they think it is.

In this simple case, it may be easy to show that the public interest is not being served. If people support the safety regulation because they want to save lives, and the regulation, contrary to their belief, fails to do so, then they are not really getting what they want. Yet what if people, in addition to wanting increased safety, if possible, want to be comforted and reassured by a show of government concern? (This desire may be responsible for their clinging to the false belief that the regulation saves lives.) They may implicitly regard the cost of the regulation as a price worth paying for psychic reassurance in a world where automobiles are unavoidably dangerous.

Making the problem even harder is the fact that not all legislation that economists scorn as wealth-reducing is based on falsifiable factual claims. Consider farm subsidies that lower the gross national product (by supporting an "inefficiently" large farm sector), but cater to a popular sentiment that farmers and rural life are admirable. If one assigns sufficient value to increasing the size of the farm sector, the subsidy is by definition "wealth-maximizing." It provides a public good (more farms) that private individuals might not be able to provide through voluntary contributions, even if everyone wanted a society with more farms, due to collective action problems. Thus, while an economist can demonstrate that the subsidy has costs (since it lowers the gross national product), she cannot show that it is bad without specifying the appropriate value choice about farms.

The underlying danger is clear. To insist that publicly supported policies are bad, and thus that people do not know their own interests, is to risk engaging in the insidious elitism of ascribing "false consciousness" to anyone whose values differ from one's own. Even granted that people often misperceive their interests, it is wise to be skeptical of anyone who claims to know better. Economists are only human, and may suffer like the rest of us from ideological bias and egocentrism.

Nonetheless, strong grounds exist for resisting the view that transfers to small interest groups must serve the public interest if they are popularly supported. Public support may be founded on misapprehension of causal relationships or on the failure to understand costs. The psychic reassurance provided by legislation may even correlate positively with the likelihood that it will be ineffective. One also may question whether the public benefits from being deceived, or truly wants to be deceived, even if its embrace of false factual claims suggests some such (at least subconscious) inclination.

A further problem is suggested by Edelman's account of government as systematically creating public anxiety through the manipulation of supposed crises (as with McCarthyism or the drug war) and then easing this anxiety through symbolic responses. Despite the sense of relief created by the symbolic response, government may have lessened public well-being, just as, though one may be better off paying blackmail than not, it may be better still if the blackmailers could not make their threats. . . .

COMMENTS AND QUESTIONS

1. The most complex parts of Shaviro's analysis put aside what is usually called the "rent-seeking" objection to legislation—in his terms, the costs of seeking transfers. He asks why the transfers that occur would be inefficient. Note that, as Shaviro works the analysis out, cognitive imperfections and ideology appear to play a significant role. It is not that voters are mere economic automatons, seeking to advance their self-interests, narrowly defined. Rather, they are people with complex values and limited information-processing ability. Consider the ways in which Shaviro's analysis converges with and diverges from Duncan Kennedy's arguments in favor of paternalism (chapter 3). How did Kennedy get around the refutation of public interest theory?

2. To introduce you to public choice analysis, here is a problem of the sort that gave rise to the field.

   Suppose a legislature is considering three policy proposals: (1) increase subsidies to farmers by $100 million; (2) increase aid to inner cities by $100 million; (3) increase spending on prisons by $100 million. There are three equal groups in the legislature: (a) *urban* legislators (whose constituents want urban aid most and new prisons least); (b) *rural* legislators (whose constituents want farm subsidies most, new prisons next, and urban aid least); and (c) *suburban* legislators (whose constituents want new prisons most, urban aid next, and farm subsidies the least).

   Suppose the legislature operates under these quite standard rules. First, one proposal is put on the table. A motion to substitute another proposal is in order. If the *first* motion to substitute fails, the alternative proposal may never be reintroduced, but a *second* motion to substitute—and thus bring forward a third proposal—is in order. The winner on this vote becomes the law. If the first motion to substitute succeeds, the first proposal may never be reintroduced. However, a *second* motion to substitute the third proposal is in order. Again, the winner on this motion becomes the law.

   What happens if the first proposal is to increase aid to the cities, and a motion to substitute the proposal to increase farm subsidies is made? The motion to substitute is defeated, because the urban and the suburban legislators combine to defeat the farm legislators. Now a motion to substitute the proposal to build more prisons is made. The motion succeeds, because the suburban and farm legislators combine in support. Thus, the "new prisons" proposal becomes law.

   Suppose, though, that the first proposal is to build more prisons, and a motion to substitute increased farm subsidies is made. This time the motion wins, as urban and farm legislators combine. The next vote will pit increased farm subsidies against increased urban aid, and here increased urban aid will win, as urban and suburban legislators combine. The result is that "increased urban aid" becomes law.

If you could decide which proposal to introduce first, what would you think about? Public choice literature analyzes this under the heading of "agenda control."

3. The phenomenon here—known as the paradox of voting—illuminates a more general problem arising from the use of voting mechanisms to aggregate preferences. (The particular example results from the assumed distribution of preferences in the legislature, but other paradoxes can be generated on other assumptions about preferences and procedures.) The economist Kenneth Arrow proved that *every* mechanism of aggregating preferences produces contradictions like the paradox of voting. Arrow's so-called Impossibility Theorem established that such paradoxes arise if we make only a few, seemingly quite reasonable assumptions. As summarized by a mathematician, these are the assumptions:

(1) *The decision-making procedure must yield a unique preference order.* Whatever the preferences of society's members, the procedure should come up with one and only one preference order for society.

(2) *Society should be responsive to its members.* The more the individuals in a society like an alternative, the more the society should like it, too. Suppose a decision-making procedure yields a preference order for society on the basis of its members' preferences in which alternative X is preferred to Y. If the individual preference orders were changed so that some liked X even better but Y just the same, then in the new preference order, society should still prefer X to Y.

(3) *Society's choice between two alternatives is based on its members' choices between two alternatives (and not any others).* Suppose society prefers X to Y and people change their minds about other alternatives but not about X and Y. Then X should still be preferred to Y. Society's decision about whether X is better than Y shouldn't depend on its decision about whether U is better than V.

(4) *The decision-making procedure should not prejudge.* For any two alternatives X and Y, there must be some possible individual preferences that would allow society to prefer X to Y. Otherwise, Y is automatically preferred to X, and the group preferences are unresponsive to those of its members.

(5) *There is no prejudgment by an individual.* Arrow assumes there is no dictator; that is, society's choices are not identical to the choices of any single individual. If this condition didn't have to be satisfied, it would be easy enough to find a voting mechanism, but Arrow wouldn't consider it representative of the individuals in the whole group.

Morton Davis, *Mathematically Speaking* (1980).

Arrow's Impossibility Theorem shows that voting systems in which the majority's choice always prevails must violate one of the conditions.

Still, you might wonder, How often do these problems actually arise? Perhaps agenda control and strategic voting do occur, but we seem to go along in our public lives without much sense that we are daily living in a paradoxical situation. Although that may well be true, the reasons the paradox doesn't arise that often are themselves quite interesting. Consider the following, from Bernard Grofman, *Public Choice, Civic Republicanism, and American Politics*, 71 Tex. L. Rev. 1541, 1553–66 (1993):

> Why has the likelihood of cyclic preferences in real-world situations been so overstated . . ? . . . [T]he Social Choice models often wrongly assume that democracies are impartial cultures in which all preference orderings are equally likely. In fact the shared values within a given culture reduce the likelihood of shifting preferences. Additionally, informal norms may bias a given culture toward a particular outcome.
>
> Second, Social Choice models neglect the impact of a two-party system on preference orderings. A two-party system creates a largely single-dimensional competition within the legislature. Single-dimensional competition stabilizes the preferences of the majority and thereby decreases the frequency of cycling. . . .
>
> [I]f some relatively small subset of voters sees the world in single-peaked ideological terms while the rest of the electorate is a veritable cloud of random choice, the views of the ideological minority become the signal that emerges from the noise. Alternatively, elites and news media may provide the ideological orientation by portraying the world in left-right terms. Even if most citizens do consistently see the world in those terms, the media impact may be sufficient to make the left-right ordering the most probable way that voters *in the aggregate* see the world. . . .
>
> Cyclic preferences will be less likely to occur in a two-party system, because a two-party system inevitably creates a single-dimensional competition along the ideological spectrum. . . .
>
> [Finally,] the existence of certain norms and institutional structures has been shown to inhibit the tendency of cycles to lead to instability.
>
> Norms such as "benefit of the doubt" and "no-quibbling" turn instability into stability. Special rules, such as one requiring a super-majority for the adoption of new policies, create further resistance to change and thereby enhance stability. Other political institutions force choices into one-issue-at-a-time or take-it-or-leave-it decisionmaking, constrain the number of options among which choice is to be made, or create complex and multi-tiered decision processes that are the analogue of supermajoritarian decisionmaking. [These processes include "bicameralism with an executive veto and a legislative override."] . . .
>
> The idea of *benefit of the doubt* is quite simple: voters will choose to shift from the status quo to some other alternative only when that other alternative is "clearly" superior, thus giving the status quo some benefit of the doubt. . . . Voters are motivated to give the benefit of the doubt as a risk-avoidance mechanism in the presence of uncertainty as to the true location—or the true consequences—of any proposed replacement for the status quo. The status quo, in contrast, is a known commodity.

The idea of a *no-quibbling norm* is equally straightforward: voters will not bother to consider alternatives that are only "trivially" different from one another. Voters gravitate towards such a no-quibbling norm because there are costs to considering alternatives; because there is uncertainty as to the true location of alternatives; and because they tend to engage in behaviors that lead to satisfactory results.

Should we as citizens be pleased with or troubled by the fact that ideology, institutional structures, and norms eliminate from practical consideration some options that might be adopted by a democratic process?

4. The next reading presents a "supply-demand" model of legislation. How would you apply it to the problem of workplace safety and health or environmental protection?

■ *Cases and Materials on Legislation: Statutes and the Creation of Public Policy*
WILLIAM N. ESKRIDGE, JR., AND PHILIP P. FRICKEY
pp. 51–56 (West Publishing, 1988)

. . . .

Heavily indebted to the work of Elmer E. Schattschneider, Theodore Lowi, James Q. Wilson, and others, Michael Hayes in *Lobbyists and Legislators: A Theory of the Political Process* (1981) posits a transactional theory to explain how the interest group system works. Consistent with public choice theory that political markets are analogous to economic markets, Hayes outlines demand and supply patterns for political issues.

In defining the demand patterns (the groups and their lobbyists), he notes that legislators are often faced with a myriad of interest groups on any given issue and these groups may either agree (consensual pattern) or disagree (conflictual pattern) with each other. A consensual demand pattern is similar to a non-zero-sum situation, while a conflictual demand pattern is basically zero sum. That is, if an issue is consensual, then everyone who is aware and actively interested in the issue can come out a winner, while if it is conflictual, then the resolution of the conflict will necessarily result in winners and losers. . . .

a. Demand Patterns in Political Markets. Hayes views demand for legislation largely within the interest group framework. The extent to which an interest group is formally organized is a key to its lobbying effectiveness. Organized groups provide useful information for the political system and tend to frame the issues more clearly and precisely for legislators, thus helping to effectuate legislative reform. Murray Edelman argues that formal organization adds to interest group proficiency by contending that organized groups will almost invariably dominate at the expense of unorganized groups. He divides interest groups into two categories: Pattern A—highly organized, relatively few in number, and an interest in tangible resources—and Pattern B—disorganized, inadequate information, large membership, and susceptibility to symbolic reassurances. Edelman argues that Pattern A groups will monopolize the available tangible benefits through the manipulation of the distribution of symbolic reassurances to Pattern B groups.

This situation is exacerbated by the fact that Pattern B voters are woefully misinformed due to the perceived costs of obtaining information exceeding the expected benefits. Moreover, Pattern A groups are very attentive to the consequences of their legislators' positions on various issues and will be less forgiving when they vote, participate, and make contributions in the next election. Hayes qualifies this theory, noting that the same reasoning that keeps Pattern B groups misinformed on many issues may also contribute to their ignorance of the intended effect of symbolic reassurances and that Pattern A groups are not necessarily rational and monolithic, because their first concern is organizational survival and maintenance.

When will organized interest groups form? Hayes borrows heavily from Professor James Q. Wilson, who posited that the degree and nature of interest group organization is determined by the perceived incidence of costs and benefits. Costs related to a policy or issue may be broadly distributed, such as a sales tax, or densely concentrated, such as a license fee. Similarly, benefits may be widely distributed, such as national security, or narrowly concentrated, such as the oil depletion allowance. Following [Mancur] Olson's theory [as elaborated in *The Logic of Collective Action* (1965)], Hayes argues that concentrated costs or benefits will be more likely to affect small and/or privileged groups and thereby to stimulate organizational activity. Distributed costs or benefits will not tend to produce organized activity, because each individual's incentive to join will be small, and Olson's free rider problem will be present....

b. Supply Patterns in Legislative Markets. In developing his supply configurations, Hayes rejects the premise that politicians will vote for the optimum "public good." He instead adopts the view expressed in M. Fiorina, *Congress: Keystone of the Washington Establishment* (1977), and D. Mayhew, *Congress: The Electoral Connection* (1974), that legislative behavior can best be explained by a rational choice theory based on the assumption that the primary goal of legislators is to be reelected....

It is apparent that the conflictual demand pattern presents major problems for legislators, though it is equally apparent that legislators deal with those problems, for the large majority of them are re-elected time after time. Fiorina has suggested that abstention (when the legislator just doesn't vote) or casework (the legislator dollops out individual favors to the groups voted against) are viable solutions to ameliorating the harmful effects of conflicting constituents. Because neither of these options can really effectively shift the blame from an individual representative, Hayes argues that the most efficacious response is for the legislator to act so that each of the conflicting groups will believe it has won. Due to the poor quality of information available to constituents and the various disincentives to acquire any information at all, political deception becomes a powerful tool for legislators. Hayes thus suggests that passing an ambiguous bill which delegates policy responsibility to an administrative agency is the ideal way for a legislator to avoid making a choice and thereby to enhance the prospects for reelection.

Hayes borrows again from Wilson's typology in his theory of supply configuration. Hence, Hayes suggests that wherever there are concentrated costs, legislators will not want to allocate in the public interest, but rather to avoid policy choices and delegate them to a regulatory agency, such as the NLRB (concentrated benefits, concentrated costs) or the EPA (distributed benefits, concentrated costs).

In cases of concentrated benefits and distributed costs, however, legislators can often reward friendly interest groups with self-regulation or distributive benefits, because the cost-bearers will typically not know they are bearing the costs or can be deceived by public-regarding half-truths about the statutory purposes. Since there is neither great pressure one way or another in connection with distributed benefits, distributed costs measures, legislators are free to ignore them or to favor symbolic laws. . . .

c. The Implications of Hayes' Model. The Hayes model leaves us with considerable pessimism regarding the results of imperfect political markets, such as the size of the public sector and the distribution of income. Two antithetical views of the size and composition of the public sector have been posited—that the degree of government intervention is too large and that the degree of government intervention is too small.

Proponents of the theory that the public sector is too large point to the obvious tendency to logroll in a specific benefit-general taxation scheme such as ours. After the 1964 tax cut, for example, politicians were not compelled by public opinion to balance the budget. This gave Congress a virtual blank check to provide benefits without raising taxes. However, in order to raise the money, the government was forced to print more currency and borrow more heavily, thus limiting the supply of funds to the private sector and causing high interest rates and inflation. Moreover, the incremental nature of the budgetary process is a major contributor to the oversized public sector. Discussion in Congress centers not around whether spending should be cut, but how much or little it should be *increased*. This practice results in a steady increase in government spending which is not tied in any way to the growth rate of the economy. Ironically, if the economy slows down, then Congress must spend more because cutting back would be political suicide.

Other scholars argue that the public sector is inherently too small. Olson contends that because benefits are spread so expansively, there is no real guarantee that every individual will receive any of the benefits. In addition, since the free rider problem precludes many large masses from formally organizing, it is possible that in many cases Congress will be unaware of the demand. Downs has suggested that imperfect information explains the constrained public sector. He notes that in contrast to the quid pro quo exchange of costs and benefits in the private sector, the public sphere does not have such a relationship. That is, taxes are not assessed for prescribed benefits, but usually on a basis of ability to pay. Since most of the citizenry is uninformed or misinformed about the benefits of the public policies but are acutely aware of the taxes paid, many people support eliminating certain programs from the budget because they receive no concrete benefit from them. Therefore, because Congress will be vote-maximizing and cater to the desires of the voters and not the public interest, legislators will spend only to the extent the return will be more votes.

Hayes agrees with *both* camps: there will be too much distributive and self-regulatory and too little appropriate redistributive policy in our government. As to the latter problem, it is simply difficult to enact laws redistributing advantages to people who need them, because the "haves" will be opposed. Hayes notes that when faced with such a highly conflictual demand pattern, Congress will tend to bail out through delegation or nondecision to avoid adverse electoral consequences.

Previously excluded groups thus have an especially difficult time in changing the status quo.

Ostensibly redistributive legislation often turns out to be distributive or even self-regulative. For example, public assistance—allegedly a redistributive policy—is essentially regulatory in that it delegates broad discretion to welfare administrators. Public housing and urban renewal are, according to Hayes, blatantly distributive in that they benefit builders and lending groups at the expense of the unaware and unorganized poor. Finally, Medicare is actually only slightly redistributive, since it applies primarily to the aged, is based on a regressive financing system, and delegates authority to administrators who exhibit perhaps untempered bias to the medical profession. Income redistribution can also occur in policies outside the redistributive arena. For instance, in the distributive arena, a consensual demand pattern results in the direct allocation of benefits at the expense of the inattentive through logrolling. In the regulatory and self-regulatory arenas, the redistribution *effects* are more indirect. In the upper income groups, redistribution occurs when regulated industries are in effect sanctioned as government cartels. In the lower income groups, redistribution is achieved when large groups are forced into concessions by smaller groups. . . .

COMMENTS AND QUESTIONS

1. What is the difference between consensual and conflictual patterns? How, if at all, is that distinction related to the different supply and demand patterns Hayes describes?

2. Consider these observations, from Donald Wittman, *The Myth of Democratic Failure: Why Political Institutions Are Efficient* 78 (1995):

   [Q]uite plausible arguments can be made that concentrated interests are at a great disadvantage in majority rule systems. Consider the case in which a candidate's policy would result in taking a dollar from a million voters and distributing the proceeds to one thousand members of a pressure group. Obviously, the probability that each of the thousand members of the pressure group votes for the candidate is a lot greater than the probability that each of the one million voters (most of whom may not even be aware of the policy) votes against the candidate. But even if this policy reduces the probability of each of the million voters voting for the candidate by only .005, such a redistribution will not take place, for it involves a loss of five thousand votes from the diffuse majority in return for a thousand more from the pressure group. And even if the pressure group donates $500,000 and the resulting advertising reduces the probability loss from .005 to only .002, the candidate would lose undertaking such a policy. Indeed, given these stylized facts, we would observe the diffuse majority taxing the concentrated minority.

   Wittman argues in addition that competition among pressure groups also limits their ability to prevail over diffuse majorities.

3. Is there any relation between the patterns Hayes describes and the normative recommendations made by Komesar and Gillette and Krier?

4. The next readings flesh out the public-choice analysis of legislation. Again, as you read them, keep the problem of risk in mind. In particular, consider whether public-choice analysis should (could?) inform the interpretation of statutes addressing risk.

■ *Congress: The Electoral Connection*
DAVID MAYHEW
pp. 49–50, 52–55, 60–62, 130–36 (Yale University Press, 1975). Reprinted with permission of Yale University Press

Whether they are safe or marginal, cautious or audacious, congressmen must constantly engage in activities related to reelection. There will be differences in emphasis, but all members share the root need to do things—indeed, to do things day in and day out during their terms. The next step here is to present a typology, a short list of the *kinds* of activities congressmen find it electorally useful to engage in. . . .

One activity is *advertising*, defined here as any effort to disseminate one's name among constituents in such a fashion as to create a favorable image but in messages having little or no issue content. A successful congressman builds what amounts to a brand name, which may have a generalized electoral value for other politicians in the same family. The personal qualities to emphasize are experience, knowledge, responsiveness, concern, sincerity, independence, and the like. Just getting one's name across is difficult enough; only about half the electorate, if asked, can supply their House members' names. It helps a congressman to be known. "In the main, recognition carries a positive valence; to be perceived at all is to be perceived favorably." A vital advantage enjoyed by House incumbents is that they are much better known among voters than their November challengers. They are better known because they spend a great deal of time, energy, and money trying to make themselves better known. There are standard routines—frequent visits to the constituency, nonpolitical speeches to home audiences, the sending out of infant care booklets and letters of condolence and congratulation. . . .

A second activity may be called *credit claiming*, defined here as acting so as to generate a belief in a relevant political actor (or actors) that one is personally responsible for causing the government, or some unit thereof, to do something that the actor (or actors) considers desirable. The political logic of this, from the congressman's point of view, is that an actor who believes that a member can make pleasing things happen will no doubt wish to keep him in office so that he can make pleasing things happen in the future. The emphasis here is on individual accomplishment (rather than, say, party or governmental accomplishment) and on the congressman as doer (rather than as, say, expounder of constituency views). Credit claiming is highly important to congressmen, with the consequence that much of congressional life is a relentless search for opportunities to engage in it.

Where can credit be found? If there were only one congressman rather than 535, the answer would in principle be simple enough. Credit (or blame) would attach . . . to the doings of the government as a whole. But there are 535. Hence it becomes necessary for each congressman to try to peel off pieces of governmental accomplishment for which he can believably generate a sense of responsibility. For the average congressman the staple way of doing this is to traffic in what may be called "particularized benefits." Particularized governmental benefits, as the term will be used here, have two properties: (1) Each benefit is given out to a specific individual group, or geographical constituency, the recipient unit being of a scale that allows a single congressman to be recognized (by relevant political actors and other congressmen) as the claimant for the benefit (other congressmen being perceived as indifferent or hostile). (2) Each benefit is given out in apparently ad hoc fashion (unlike, say, social security checks) with a congressman apparently having a hand in the allocation. A particularized benefit can normally be regarded as a member of a class. That is, a benefit given out to an individual, group, or constituency can normally be looked upon by congressmen as one of a class of similar benefits given out to sizable numbers of individuals, groups, or constituencies. Hence the impression can arise that a congressman is getting "his share" of whatever it is the government is offering. (The classes may be vaguely defined. Some state legislatures deal in what their members call "local legislation.")

In sheer volume the bulk of particularized benefits come under the heading of "casework"—the thousands of favors congressional offices perform for supplicants in ways that normally do not require legislative action. High school students ask for essay materials, soldiers for emergency leaves, pensioners for location of missing checks, local governments for grant information, and on and on. Each office has skilled professionals who can play the bureaucracy like an organ— pushing the right pedals to produce the desired effects. But many benefits require new legislation, or at least they require important allocative decisions on matters covered by existent legislation. Here the congressman fills the traditional role of supplier of goods to the home district. It is a believable role: when a member claims credit for a benefit on the order of a dam, he may well receive it. Shiny construction projects seem especially useful. . . .

The third activity congressmen engage in may be called *position taking*, defined here as the public enunciation of a judgmental statement on anything likely to be of interest to political actors. The statement may take the form of a roll call vote. The most important classes of judgmental statements are those prescribing American governmental ends (a vote cast against the war; a statement that "the war should be ended immediately") or governmental means (a statement that "the way to end the war is to take it to the United Nations"). The judgments may be implicit rather than explicit, as in: "I will support the president on this matter." But judgments may range far beyond these classes to take in implicit or explicit statements on what almost anybody should do or how he should do it: "The great Polish scientist Copernicus has been unjustly neglected"; "The way for Israel to achieve peace is to give up the Sinai." The congressman as position taker is a speaker rather than a doer. The electoral requirement is not that he make pleasing things happen but that he make pleasing judgmental statements. The position itself is the political commodity. Especially on matters where governmental responsibility is widely diffused it is not surprising that political actors should fall back on positions as tests of incumbent virtue. For voters ignorant of congressional processes the recourse is an easy one. . . .

[A] purely symbolic congressional act is one expressing an attitude but prescribing no policy effects. An example would be a resolution deploring communism or poverty. But the term *symbolic* can also usefully be applied where Congress prescribes policy effects but does not act (in legislating or overseeing or both) so as to achieve them. No doubt the main cause of prescription-achievement gaps is the intractability of human affairs. But there is a special reason why a legislative body arranged like the United States Congress can be expected to engage in symbolic action by this second, impure construction of the term. The reason, of course, is that in a large class of legislative undertakings the electoral payment is for positions rather than for effects.

An interesting subclass consists of enactments that are "charitable" in nature. That is, they are designed to benefit people other than the ones whose gratification is the payment for passage. If the gratified receive muddled feedback on programmatic accomplishment, the actual supplying of the prescribed benefits becomes a distinctly secondary congressional concern. Thus the civil rights acts of 1957 and 1960 were passed to benefit nonvoting southern blacks but to please northern audiences. No one should be surprised that they had little impact in the South. Title I of the Elementary and Secondary Education Act of 1965 allocated money to aid the poor. The audience for the enactment was middle class. In the implementation the money went elsewhere. Laws regulating private conduct have a "charitable" flavor to them. Thus Prohibition—its audience teetotalers and its beneficiaries others who were given the pleasure of having their liquor taken away. That the enforcement was indifferent should cause no surprise.

In the more general case there is reason to expect Congress to act "symbolically" whether audiences and beneficiaries are separate, overlapping, or identical. Position-taking politics may produce statutes that are long on goals but short on means to achieve them. Or bureaucrats may sense that there is little congressional interest in enforcement. Or efforts to achieve proclaimed goals may run up against congressional particularism or clientelism. Or all these things may happen at once. Thus when water pollution became an issue, it was more or less predictable that Congress would pass a law characterized as an antipollution act, that the law would take the form of a grant program for localities, and that it would not achieve its proclaimed end. Probably the best examples of congressional symbolism are those arising out of efforts to regulate business. Regulatory statutes are the by-products of congressional position taking at times of public dissatisfaction. They tend to be vaguely drawn. What happens in enforcement is largely a result of congressional credit-claiming activities on behalf of the regulated: there is every reason to believe that the regulatory agencies do what Congress wants them to do. The ambitious "public interest" aims of the statutes are seldom accomplished. Another place where symbolism occurs is in housing programs: there exists no close analysis of housing politics in Congress, but it is fair to say that the programs offer members a complex mix of opportunities for position taking and credit claiming. To point to congressional symbolism is not, of course, to denounce it. The Constitution does not require, nor does political theory decisively insist that legislative processes enshrine high standards of instrumental rationality. By some defensible criteria it is perfectly proper to put laws on the books and then not to enforce them. Among other things doing so may offer a murky way of maximizing governmental satisfaction of popular preferences; Prohibition is a case in point.

- *Congress—Keystone of the Washington Establishment*
MORRIS P. FIORINA
pp. 71–81 (Yale University Press, 1977). Reprinted with permission
of Yale University Press

... Traditionally, constituents appeal to their Congressman for myriad favors and services. Sometimes only information is needed, but often constituents request that their congressman intervene in the internal workings of federal agencies to affect a decision in a favorable way, to reverse an adverse decision, or simply to speed up the glacial bureaucratic process....

Actually congressmen are in an almost unique position in system, a position shared only with high-level members of the executive branch. Congressmen possess the power to expedite and influence bureaucratic decisions. This capability flows directly from congressional control over what bureaucrats value most: higher budgets and new program authorizations. In a very real sense each congressman is a monopoly supplier of bureaucratic unsticking services for his district....

From the standpoint of capturing voters, the congressman's law-making activities differ in two important respects from his pork-barrel and casework activities. First, programmatic actions are inherently controversial. Unless his district is homogeneous, a congressman will find his district divided on many major issues. Thus whenever he casts a vote, introduces a piece of nontrivial legislation, or makes a speech with policy content he will displease some elements of his district.... On such policy matters the congressman can expect to make friends as well as enemies. Presumably he will behave so as to maximize the excess of the former over the latter, but nevertheless a policy stand will generally make some enemies.

In contrast, the pork barrel and casework are relatively less controversial....

In sum, when considering the benefits of his programmatic activities, the congressman must tote up gains and losses to arrive at a net profit. Pork barreling and casework, however, are basically pure profit.

A second way in which programmatic activities differ from casework and the pork barrel is the difficulty of assigning responsibility to the former as compared with the latter. No congressman can seriously claim that he is responsible for the 1964 Civil Rights Act, the ABM, or the 1972 Revenue Sharing Act.... [But, in] dealing with the bureaucracy, the congressman is not merely one vote of 435. Rather, he is a nonpartisan power, someone whose phone calls snap an office to attention.... The constituent who receives aid believes that his congressman and his congressman alone got results. Similarly, congressmen find it easy to claim credit for federal projects awarded their districts....

Overall then, programmatic activities are dangerous (controversial), on the one hand, and programmatic accomplishments are difficult to claim credit for, on the other. While less exciting, casework and pork barreling are both safe and profitable. For a reelection-oriented congressman the choice is obvious.

The key to the rise of the Washington establishment ... is the following observation: *the growth of an activist federal government has stimulated a change in the mix of congressional activities*. Specifically, a lesser proportion of congressional effort is now going into programmatic activities and a greater proportion into pork-barrel and casework activities. As a result, today's congressmen make relatively fewer enemies and relatively more friends among the people of their districts....

What should we think of such a system, beyond the trace of disillusionment we always feel upon finding that childhood ideals are not reflected in political reality? There are three recognizably distinct reactions to my description of the Washington system: (1) the cynical reaction that runs through the pages of this book, (2) a more optimistic reaction that looks at the bright side of the system, (3) an alarmist reaction that holds that the Washington system will evolve into something worse. Let us take these in order.

The Cynical View

Congressmen actively exploit the bureaucracy and the citizenry. The bureaucracy passively exploits Congress and the people. And the people? They are put in a position of attempting futilely to exploit each other. There is a difference between exchange and exploitation. People do receive services from their congressmen, and in return they provide votes. But when grateful constituents reelect their congressmen, they fail to realize that they are helping to perpetuate a system which subordinates the content of public policy to the desires of congressmen to obtain special credits with which to impress their districts. . . .

. . . Public policy emerges from the system almost as an afterthought. The shape of policy is a by-product of the way the system operates, rather than a consciously directed effort to deal with social and economic problems. Congressmen know that the specific impact of broad national policies on their districts is difficult to see, that effects are hidden, so to speak. They know too that individual congressmen are not held responsible for the collective outcome produced by 535 members of Congress. Thus, in order to attain reelection, congressmen focus on things that are both more recognizable in their impact and more credible indicators of the individual congressman's power—federal projects and individual favors for constituents. In order to purchase a steady flow of the latter, congressmen trade away less valuable currency—their views on public policy. The typical public law is simply the outcome of enough individual bargains to build a majority. Maybe that's just politics, but we don't have to like it, and political scientists need not construct silly defenses for it.

The existence of the Washington system locks us into the New Deal way of doing things: pass a law, appropriate a lot of money, and establish a new federal bureaucracy. . . .

The Optimistic View

. . . Basically the optimistic view differs from the cynical view in two respects. First, it treats incumbent congressm[e]n as much more innocent than the cynical view. Incumbents are just public-spirited good old boys protecting their constituents from the ravages of the bureaucracy. Certainly they are not compounding the problem. Second, the optimistic view holds ombudsman activities in sufficiently high regard that it accepts the decline of the programmatic role of congressmen and Congress as a fair exchange or else considers that decline a reflection of an inevitable growth of executive dominance. . . .

The Alarmist View

. . . What began as harmless or even beneficial dabbling in bureaucratic affairs has become (or threatens to become) congressional addiction to the bureaucratic "fix." Each of the preceding two views presumes that congressmen have the upper hand in dealing with the bureaucracy. Do they? Will they always? As the federal role grows larger and larger, as more and more citizens are directly affected by bureaucratic decisions, will the bureaucracy come to dominate the Congress-bureaucracy relationship, at least on significant decisions? Will we reach a state in which the Congress becomes so dependent on the constituency service function that the bureaucracy has make-or-break power over congressmen or at least the ability to inflict great political pain and suffering? . . .

This, then, is the basis of the cynical view of the Washington system. The incentives of incumbent congressmen lead them to protect and encourage the structure and operation of a centralized bureaucratic state almost irrespective of the kind of public policy that constrains our present and shapes our future. . . .

COMMENTS AND QUESTIONS

1. Why might a member of Congress sponsor occupational safety and health or environmental legislation? What sort of legislation will a member be interested in sponsoring? Do you see Mayhew's predictions at work in any of the regulatory programs we have studied? Might the National Ambient Air Quality Standards (NAAQS) program of the Clean Air Act, which we encountered in chapters 11 and 12, be viewed as the kind of symbolic legislation Mayhew describes?

2. Do you think that Mayhew identifies real problems in the legislative process? Can you come up with solutions? Note the dates of publication of Mayhew's and Fiorina's work. Do you think that Congress today operates in the same way? Consider whether the recent practice of including highly focused provisions in appropriations bill to benefit specific constituents and donors to campaigns might be seen as a new form of "casework," using the legislative process to get around bureaucratic rigidity. Note, though, that such casework requires the cooperation of other legislators. Which of Fiorina's perspectives—cynical, optimistic, or alarmist—do you share, and why?

3. So far we have seen public choice theory applied to legislators and administrators. May it also be applied to the courts? In an opinion concerning judicially created federal damage remedies for constitutional violations, Judge Laurence Silberman concluded that the best solution would be for the Supreme Court to overrule the cases creating the remedies. However, Judge Silberman observed,

    [S]ince the Supreme Court, in accordance with public choice theory, *see generally* J. Buchanan & G. Tulloch, The Calculus of Consent (1962) (arguing that all rational actors, including those in government, pursue power), follows its own version of the Breznev Doctrine—no significant retreat from extensions of federal constitutional power (unless perhaps, if confronted by Congress)—that is a vain hope.[8]

    Crawford-El v. Britton, 93 F.3d 813, 832
    (D.C. Cir. 1996) (concurring opinion)

---

[8] It could be argued that the Supreme Court's withdrawal from *Lochner* is an exception, but of course substantive due process grew back anew in "politically correct" gardens.

4. The next readings provide broader critiques of public choice theories of legislation. The first suggests that such theories are unrealistic, the second that they are oversimplified. Note the important role that ideology plays, according to the authors of both articles. The third reading takes issue with the empirical claims of public choice theory.

■ *Beyond Public Choice and Public Interest: A Study of the Legislative Process as Illustrated by Tax Legislation in the 1980s*
DANIEL SHAVIRO
139 U. Pa. L. Rev. 1 (1990). Reprinted with permission of University of Pennsylvania Law Review

. . .

IV. The Public Choice Theory of Legislation

A. *Overview of Public Choice Theory*

In the law and economics literature, the perennially favored alternative to public interest theory is public choice theory. In its broadest sense, public choice theory is simply the economic study of nonmarket (i.e., political) decision-making. At this level of generality, it requires no stronger assumption than that people act rationally in light of their objectives, whatever these may happen to be. Following common usage, however, I will use the term "public choice theory" to describe what is actually a sub-genre, sometimes called the economic theory of regulation. As we will see, this sub-genre makes considerably stronger and more questionable assumptions.

In the words of Fred McChesney, "[t]he essential insight of the economic model is that, like any other good or service, regulation [i.e., legislation] will be provided to the highest bidder." The sellers are legislators, and they are paid in votes, campaign contributions, and personal benefits such as honoraria and free vacations. The buyers, drawing on the economic theory of groups, are organized interest groups seeking wealth transfers.

McChesney's "essential insight" has a certain rhetorical force. If we assume that everthing else in life works a certain way, why should politics be any different? As other public choice writers have put it:

> The point is that there is no bifurcation of personality as between our "political" and "private" selves. We do not seek to satisfy the "public interest" when we vote and the "private interest" when we buy groceries. We seek our "self-interests" in both cases. While the story of Dr. Jekyll and Mr. Hyde may make for good cinema, it is a poor basis on which to analyze political behavior.

Unfortunately, this argument is somewhat misleading. Public choice theory does not automatically follow from accepting the continuity between our public and private selves. Take the basic analogy to a market where people buy and sell items such as groceries. This market has two important attributes: specific goods to be bought and sold, and the use of money as a uniform medium of exchange. Standard economic analysis, such as the drawing of supply and demand curves, does not require making theoretical assumptions about what goods people want (i.e., what nonmonetary preferences they bring to market). It assumes only that, once in the market, they generally try to do as well as possible in monetary terms. All else being equal, buyers try to pay as little, and sellers to receive as much, as possible. This assumption seems eminently reasonable. Nonmonetary preferences are not being denied; they merely have little effect at this stage of the process. Thus, the economic model of a market does not (to quote a standard criticism of economists) "posit . . . [a] shallow and incomplete . . . caricature" of human nature as concerned only with narrow material gain.

Now consider politics. Here we have a "market" where the goods are unspecified unless we make assumptions about people's preferences. Voters, for example, may care about ideological or symbolic issues that have no direct bearing on their monetary interests. In voting, they are deciding what to buy, not how much to pay, since each voter has but one vote and cash sales of votes are discouraged. Politicians similarly may care about ideological or symbolic issues that have no direct bearing on their monetary or professional interests. Although public choice classifies them as "sellers" of legislation, there is no theoretical reason why they may not want at times to "buy" particular outcomes. Even treating politicians purely as "sellers" who seek to maximize professional self-interest, we encounter a further difference between politics and the standard private market. In politics, despite the importance of money, there is no uniform medium of exchange, unless we simply assume that money is all that politicians want, as opposed to, say, power, prestige, and flattering press coverage (either as ends in themselves or as useful for reelection).

Public choice theory ignores these problems with the analogy to a private market, and treats monetary exchange between interest groups and politicians as all that matters. The public is not only ignorant but irrelevant. Interest groups are all-powerful and concerned purely with monetary wealth. Politicians are not only self-interested but narrowly so; they are literally for sale. By viewing politics so reductively, public choice theory begins to look like the "shallow and incomplete" caricature of human nature expected by critics of economists. Good economic analysis takes people's preferences as a given and asks what consequences will follow from them, assuming only means-ends rationality. Public choice theory instead makes crudely reductive assumptions about the preferences that people actually have. It is as if one predicted that people will buy only healthful and nutritious groceries, or will not pay anything extra for Cadillacs with tail fins.

. . . As we will see, it thereby falsifies not only human nature, but observable facts about the legislative process. Flattening and minimizing the roles of politicians and unorganized voters, and overlooking empirical evidence that could be found through a simple library search, it resurrects a pure interest group view of politics that political science research has long since discredited. In the remainder of this section, I will discuss some representative examples from the legal literature [and] explore the broader theoretical and empirical problems with public choice theory. . . .

B. Public Choice Theory as Practiced in the Law Schools

1. Style and Its Ad Hominem Significance

Public choice articles emanating from the law schools are so distinctive in tone and style as to reveal something about their substance. They tend to be slyly knowing, based on the premise that the author has seen through some set of hollow illusions that political insiders use to conceal from the naive and gullible what is really going on. Consider this opening from a recent piece by Jonathan Macey:

> The concept of federalism... is one of the most revered sacred cows on the American political scene. Conservatives and liberals alike extol the virtues of state autonomy whenever deference to the states happens to serve their political needs at a particular moment. Yet both groups are also quick to wield the power of the supremacy clause, while citing vague platitudes about the need for uniformity among the states, whenever a single national rule... furthers their political interests.

Macey continues that the relationship between state autonomy and federal supremacy is "one of the most convenient of political expedients," whose real meaning public choice theory reveals....

While the legal public choice writers are unrelentingly hostile towards politics, they are contented to the point of complacency towards the academy. They repeatedly remind us that their discipline is making great strides and that increasingly everyone realizes they are correct. Academic critics of public choice theory not only go unanswered, but are misleadingly cited in footnotes as supporters. This complacency harms the public choice writers' work by encouraging them to inhabit an airless realm of self-congratulatory preoccupation with their abstract models at the expense of empirical analysis beyond supportive anecdotes....

C. What Public Choice Theory Omits

... [P]ublic choice theory can be [wide of the mark] when interpreted narrowly and applied universally. Yet, one should not conclude from the theory's failure here that it lacks significant explanatory power. It needs to be supplemented, not abandoned. To improve public choice theory, we need a more systematic account of how and why it fails to explain legislative politics. This section will discuss the theory's shortcomings and the principal factors that it omits. Though only a complex and multi-faceted approach can achieve reasonable descriptive accuracy, two factors are particularly important: voters' taste for symbolic legislation and politicians' taste for power and prestige. Under circumstances of high publicity, these factors can easily outweigh interest group politics.

1. Voters

Public choice theory treats voters as narrow profit-maximizers who, due to information costs and collective action problems, remain rationally ignorant and thus politically irrelevant to the extent they are not organized into interest groups. The view, however, runs into an immediate logical problem. The rational voter that public choice theory posits would find the act of voting to be irrational, even assuming full knowledge about the candidates and issues. Given the arithmetical unimportance of any one vote, even if the election's outcome is very important, the expected monetary gain from voting in one's interest is almost infinitesimal and the costs of voting (such as the expenditure of time) seem clearly greater. In view of the adverse cost-benefit tradeoff, the fact that millions of people vote is paradoxical to many public choice writers, as is the fact that better-educated voters, whom one would think more likely to be aware that voting is "irrational," vote more than others.

As the best public choice writers have come to recognize, the paradox suggests that voting is based, not on narrow self-interest, but on consumption motives, typically involving symbolic or expressive behavior. Voters "buy" ideological, emotional, or moral satisfaction in the course of satisfying what they may regard as a civic duty, at an individually low cost even if voting conflicts directly against their narrow interests. The satisfaction is derived from the vote itself, as distinct from the electoral outcome, and thus is a strict private good unaffected by its arithmetical unimportance or by collective action problems.

The low value of a single vote provides only one reason for questioning the rational voter model. Consider as well the significance, described by Murray Edelman, of politics' status as a "spectator sport" that most people observe only from a great distance and as a confusing abstraction. . . .

Thus, in economic terms, voters' political consumption functions often embrace considerably more (and less) than the rational calculation of narrow self-interest. Emotional involvement is facilitated by the fact that, even if one's interest in politics remains low, much information (both true and false) may come one's way casually, as when one watches the local news during dinner or glances at newspaper headlines.

Voters' consumption motives and emotional involvement, along with their capacity to absorb some information passively, suggest fertile opportunities for manipulation by political actors. If voters were perfectly manipulable and only interest groups did the manipulating, political outcomes might be roughly the same as under the standard public choice account of voters as ignorant profit-maximizers. Both of these premises, however, are false. On the public's complete manipulability, consider . . . the failure of the advertising campaign for the Edsel. Voters may be strongly inclined to "buy" some things and not others. On who manipulates, consider the possible role of political actors apart from interest groups.

Given both the arithmetical unimportance of a single vote and voters' emotional involvement, politics evokes behavior far less centered on narrow wealth maximization than does a private market, even though voters, presumably without schizophrenic personalities, participate in both. Some critics of public choice theory see politics as a realm of greater altruism, where people sacrifice their own interests in order to act properly towards others. This conclusion does not necessarily follow, however, from the lesser importance of monetary self-interest. It depends on what preferences people substitute for wealth maximization. Gary Orren, a believer in political altruism, regards "the human desire for solidarity, for belonging, for attachment, for approval" as a fundamental motivation for people's political beliefs. Yet this desire can lead to self-interested behavior on a group basis, overcoming collective action problems, as well as to gratuitous hostility to rival social, ethnic, or geographic groups. Orren also argues that political beliefs reflect people's desire to find "larger purposes that transcend their own immediate situation." Yet selfishness, at least in the broad sense of a taste for self-justifying and self-flattering beliefs, may play a role. Consider the childishly egoistic "ethical imperialism" that some think underlies much of American foreign policy.

A further aspect of voter behavior apart from altruism arises from the pervasive role of television in bringing prominent national and local politicians into people's living rooms on a regular basis. The false intimacy created can lead voters to identify with and support a politician on much the same basis as the star of a dramatic television series. . . . Here, the motive for voting may simply be affection for the politician who seems to be a "regular person" and to understand and share one's values (or to have attractive values of her own). Gary Orren thinks politics has "more in common with religion than with economics." In an age of weak party allegiances and high focus on personality, with frequent ticket-splitting, numerous independent voters, and an increasingly fickle electorate, a better analogy may be to the entertainment industry.

In summary, the public choice model of voters as narrowly self-interested profit-maximizers seems inaccurate. It confuses low information with no information and ignores important motivations apart from narrow self-interest. To understand more fully the systematic implications of these inaccuracies, it is necessary to examine some of the other descriptive shortcomings of public choice theory.

2. *Politicians*

. . .

a. Politicians' Varied Motives

To the extent that one can generalize, what sort of people are politicians? . . .

. . . [P]oliticians generally are motivated to an unusual degree by what is variously described as a "desire for attention and adulation," "intense and ungratified craving for deference," "ache for applause and recognition," and an "urge for that warm feeling of importance." Thus, self-interest is agreed to be extremely important to politicians, but not primarily the narrow monetary self-interest emphasized by economists. (It is of course likely that some politicians fit the public choice model, and one would expect to find broad variation among individuals' motives.)

. . . [Richard] Fenno found that three goals espoused by House members are "the most widely held and the most consequential for committee activity." They are (in no particular order of priority): (1) reelection, (2) "influence" within the House, meaning power and prestige, and (3) good public policy. . . .

Of the three goals cited by Fenno, reelection, while obviously a prerequisite to all else, is not a serious problem for everyone. Incumbents win reelection well over 90 percent of the time (at least in the House), and some incumbents, being stronger than others, are particularly safe. While incumbents' success results in part from their doing what they have to do, the high success rate does suggest some freedom to pursue goals other than reelection. . . .

Beginning with power and prestige, its implications obviously depend on the context. For a leader, such as the Speaker of the House or a committee chairman, it often depends on winning legislative victories. . . .

For members not in leadership positions, the routes to power and prestige are more varied. A member can gain status by introducing ideas that become widely discussed, whether or not the ideas are enacted. . . . In addition, even a junior member can gain influence by emerging as a compromise broker and coalition builder. One can gain stature from involvement in the drudgery of committee work and development of legislation. With the . . . popularity of TV talk shows such as "Nightline" and "20/20," along with C-SPAN's full-time coverage, one can pursue a career as a television celebrity, although at the risk of gaining an inside reputation as a "show horse" who is all talk and no action.

In the struggle for power and prestige, interest groups can help a member. They can provide the political support that is crucial to winning a legislative contest.... They can be a source of politically salient ideas.... It seems clear, however, that interest groups are relatively less important in the quest for power and prestige than they are with regard to fund-raising. Ideas, for example, emanate far more from government insiders and academics than from interest groups. The political salience of an idea, as with tax reform, often varies positively with it being hostile to what the media perceives as the "special interests." Thus, interest groups are far less powerful and important in a world where members compete for power and prestige than in a world of McChesneyian money monsters.

Now consider the goal of making good policy or furthering one's ideology. This goal is so important, according to some studies, that ideology is a better predictor of legislative voting behavior than economic interest variables. Moreover, there is anecdotal evidence that members often derive great pleasure from putting ideas into action and having an effect on society. Again, while interest groups can help a member (for example, by exploiting an ideology that serves their purposes, or suggesting workable legislative proposals), their dominance is far less than in fund-raising.

Perhaps the most serious problem that results from members' goals apart from reelection has little to do with interest groups. In today's Congress, seemingly everyone wants to be an influential policy-maker. As one member put it, "Congress exists to do things. There isn't much mileage in doing nothing." Members often want to participate in making policy to a far greater extent than they know what they want to do. Moreover, those who favor activism in a particular area tend to be the ones who seek and get the committee assignments in that area. What results is a bias in favor of action over inaction, a reluctance to consider carefully the merits of legislation (which become subordinate to one's own or one's colleagues' personal investment in it), and a tendency to legislate for legislation's sake....

b. Politicians' Means of Pursuing Reelection

An important factor in support of the public choice writers' claim that Congress cares only about money is the vital link between campaign financing and reelection....

Yet the implications of campaign financing for interest group politics can easily be overstated. Only a small fraction of the money spent on lobbying takes the form of contributions to candidates—suggesting surprising inefficiency or irrationality on the part of interest groups if campaign financing is the unique engine of legislative success....

Even more significantly, campaign financing is only one factor among many that affects reelection and other factors may dilute or even counter interest groups' influence. Perhaps the most thorough study of how members pursue reelection is David Mayhew's *Congress: The Electoral Connection*. Mayhew finds that members engage principally in three kinds of activities in pursuit of reelection. The first is advertising.... The second is position taking.... Finally, members engage in credit claiming.... A variation of credit claiming is blame avoidance, or deflecting perceived responsibility for unpopular government action.

Each of these activities lends importance to factors apart from interest group influence. Consider first advertising. While paid advertising requires campaign funds, it is generally considered inferior to favorable free media, such as television news coverage. Not only is free media cheaper (an especial advantage between elections, when members need to retain high visibility), it also tends to have greater credibility and to attract a larger and more attentive audience. Members' success with both free and paid media depends in large part on personality (whether actual or apparent), and perhaps even more on sheer repetitive exposure, since in general "to be perceived at all is to be perceived favorably." . . .

Advertising, other than the use of paid media, dilutes interest group influence in two respects. First, the need for constant exposure suggests finding ways to be continually newsworthy, and this may involve calling for legislation that is unrelated or even hostile to interest group demands. Second, while advertising can complement making interest group deals, it also, as a separate source of electoral support, lowers the political cost of opposing interest groups.

Now consider position-taking, or making people feel good by saying things that they like. In common with advertising, position-taking can increase a member's political support while having no relation to substance, as when she praises abstractions (such as patriotism or competitiveness) or endorses goals that she does not actually intend to advance through any substantive action. At times, it does involve substance, however, as when a legislator publicly proposes or votes on significant legislation. Position-taking, like advertising, can lower the cost of opposing interest groups, and can even make such opposition politically beneficial—in effect, a purchase of goodwill that exceeds in value the future campaign contributions [forgone].

Finally, consider credit-claiming. Mayhew argues that it encourages pork barrel legislation favoring local interests, because such legislation usually is more plausibly attributed to the local representative than is major national legislation. While this may be true on balance, there are countervailing influences. David Stockman, for example, found while in Congress that he could oppose pork barrel legislation and then claim credit for it anyway by attending the ribbon-cutting ceremonies. Moreover, a member who, like Stockman, has ideological views about national issues may find that her lack of perceived personal responsibility for legislation on such issues facilitates blame avoidance. In some cases credit-claiming and blame avoidance become the basis for competition between the Democratic and Republican parties regarding national issues. In such circumstances, interest groups can be either helped or hurt. Thus, during consideration of the 1981 tax bill, the parties bid against each other for interest group backing because each wanted the credit for cutting taxes. By contrast, in 1986, concern for credit-claiming (in the early stages) and blame avoidance (later on) encouraged the parties to sacrifice the concerns of many interest groups. Given the vast number of legislative issues, most of which receive little public attention, members may only infrequently benefit politically from opposing transfers to interest groups from the general public. Yet the public need not feel strongly about an issue, or even remember it beyond the brief period when it appears on television, in order for a pro-interest group position (if portrayed unfavorably) to prove costly. The negative goodwill may outlive the public's memory of the specific story. The political importance of this type of thinking is suggested by evidence that members are obsessed with surveying public opinion and keeping their positions consistent with it.

Thus, while interest groups may have undue influence, they are not the only important force affecting the legislative process. Public choice writers, driven by the misleading analogy between legislation and goods sold in the marketplace, have missed a far more promising analogy: that between politicians and mass-marketed commercial products. Note how Mayhew's reelection activities fit this analogy. Advertising is the creation of a brand name; position-taking (as an end in itself) and the subjects of credit-claiming are what the "product" is actually supposed to do. The problem with this market is poor information. Voters cannot closely monitor how even Congress as a whole affects them, much less the effects of an individual legislator. Thus, politicians gain approval without the same level of feedback that may result from using commercial products.

The factors leading to public approval may be unrelated or even adverse to good policy. As an example, position-taking encourages Congress to enact regulatory statutes that provide "fatuous, self-contradictory wish-lists" instead of specific mandates. This tendency creates uncertainty and complexity, which a regulatory agency, subject to "capture" by the groups that it is supposed to regulate, must try to resolve. Complaints about the agency are relayed to Congress, allowing members to gain further public approval through casework on behalf of complainants without being blamed for the vague legislation.

c. Policy Entrepreneurship

As we have seen, both reelection and members' other goals (such as serving ideology and enhancing prestige) encourage both public posturing and substantive legislative activity that may be unrelated or even hostile to interest group influence. The phenomenon is commonly called "policy entrepreneurship," or the investment of personal resources in promoting a particular policy, with the anticipated "return" often depending on the enactment of legislation....

I have thus far been critical of policy entrepreneurship, because members' demand for it is high while the discipline of seriously considering a proposal's effects seems low. Augmenting the problems caused by voters' lack of information, prestige within the Washington establishment attaches to power and political importance as an end in itself. The goal is to be an effective "player," almost regardless of the consequences of one's "playing." Yet policy entrepreneurship also has a positive side: it produces much good legislation that might not emerge from a less wide-open system. Tax reform is only one example. Consider as well the successes of regulatory legislation, promoted by policy entrepreneurs, that addressed air and water pollution, automobile safety, consumer product safety, and racial discrimination. Or consider recent (and arguably beneficial) examples of deregulation, as of the trucking industry, undertaken despite interest group opposition.

Without the incentives and opportunities for policy entrepreneurship that our political system provides, much of this legislation might not have been enacted. Policy entrepreneurship, for all its faults, is the principal alternative to interest group politics, making possible legislation that pits widely dispersed benefits against narrowly concentrated costs. Yet public choice theory fails to account for it.

3. Organized Interest Groups

The public choice view of organized interest groups is as narrow and stereotyped as the public choice views of voters and politicians. An interest group ostensibly consists of rational profit-maximizers, cooperating to seek transfers from the rest of society because for each participating individual the expected marginal benefit of cooperating exceeds the expected marginal cost. . . . [T]his begs the question of why free riding does not prove as fatal to interest group activity as it does to purposive activity by the *public*. . . .

The answer to the "paradox" of interest group formation, as several empirical studies have revealed, is that, like so much else in politics, the groups respond to more than narrow monetary motives. Interest group rank and file members are in some ways like voters. They join for a variety of reasons, including not only narrow self-interest (i.e., expected economic benefit from successful lobbying and demand for goods like trade magazines), but also what James Q. Wilson calls solidarity and purposive incentives: the social and status pleasures of belonging to a cohesive group, and emotional attachment to a group's political goals. They do not closely monitor their leaders' activities, and can be kept in line through symbolic behavior such as position-taking. Interest group leaders exploit their own resulting freedom to pursue a combination of goals resembling those held by members of Congress, i.e., institutional survival (the equivalent of reelection), ideological goals that their members may not share, and the desire for power and prestige within the Washington political community. This observation suggests once again that legislation reflects considerably more than the narrowly economic goals emphasized by public choice theory.

4. The Media . . .

5. Ideas and Ideology

The critical importance of ideas and ideology is one of the most difficult aspects of politics for most public choice writers to appreciate. A mechanical view of wealth maximization has the appeal of a pseudo-science, purporting to unmask underlying realities and ostensibly leading to testable theorems and predictions. Yet the truth, of course, is that people often like ideas, find them interesting, and believe in them, with the result that ideas matter a great deal. Individual politicians pursue ideological ends, whether it is Ronald Reagan's anti-Communism or Bill Bradley's tax reform. An idea can sway people en masse as well as individually, whether it is Keynes's rationalization of budget deficits or deregulation of the trucking industry. . . .

Again, the problem with thinking about the role of ideas is that they cannot readily be modeled or predicted, whereas public choice writers, influenced by a perhaps outdated notion of science, crave "usable" theories with predictive power. . . . Yet even if understanding of ideas' causation and effect remains elusive, one can posit some broad generalizations. First, in a political environment like Washington—perhaps in any environment (including, say, academia) where people hope to gain from their association with novel ideas—there is a tendency towards faddishness. As an interviewee told one researcher:

> In Washington the world of ideas is like the world of fashion. Ideas don't last for more than four or five years. They catch on, they become very popular, and because of that, they burn themselves out in a burst of growth, and others take their place. It's like a hula hoop craze.

Second, ideas often appeal to people for reasons of emotional convenience that resemble but are not quite identical to conventional self-interest. Farmers and oil company executives easily convince themselves that they should receive subsidies for the good of America. Economists and social scientists naturally believe that their rational analysis leads to policies superior to those resulting from messy and venal politics. Third, intellectual and academic elites can powerfully influence political agendas, although perhaps not quite so powerfully as the members of these elites would prefer. Fourth, when intellectual ideas are "sold" to a mass public, they tend to get simplified and distorted in the translation. . . .

6. Political Rules and Structures

Public choice theory often is too grandly abstract to pay close attention to the role played by legal rules or the structure of political institutions. If one believes that the theory is an inevitable application of the iron laws of markets and human nature, these may seem to be mere minutiae. Yet legal rules and political institutions can have an enormous effect on the role played by and success of interest groups. Campaign financing laws are an obvious example. Unless they are a nullity, they must be relevant to the claim that legislation is for sale to the highest bidder. Political science literature has identified two additional factors that enormously affect interest group politics: the power of congressional leaders and the power of political parties. . . .

7. Implications of the Factors Apart from Interest Group Influence

For the reasons described above, members of Congress in enacting legislation both have considerable leeway and are subject to significant constraints apart from interest group influence. Specifically, members of Congress seek reelection, power, prestige, and ideological goals in a world where ill-informed voters are subject to symbolic responses and where the media can exercise great and often populist influence. Beyond these broad generalizations, the details of legislative behavior are inherently unpredictable. In particular, the incentives for policy entrepreneurship can stimulate any number of responses. An example is taxation, in which one may gain either by being a reformer who opposes interest groups or by championing tax instrumentalism.

The choice of how to seek success as a policy entrepreneur is controlled by the individual legislator. Members of Congress may seek the approbation of their colleagues, the media, the Washington political establishment, or the voters in any number of ways. No abstract model, whether narrowly economic or otherwise, can predict in detail either what proposals will be made at any time or which ones will succeed. Fortuity and the choices made by a small number of idiosyncratic individuals simply play too large a role here.

The choices made by policy entrepreneurs are heavily influenced by and responsive to the media, but this link does not necessarily increase predictability. In tax, for example, the media can choose to emphasize any of a wide range of stories, since all can probably be found anecdotally at any time. . . . How the media will choose is hard to say, but presumably its choices will reflect some combination of what reporters think is important or representative at the time and what they think their audience wants to hear.

An interesting analogy can be made between the political-legislative world of Washington and the movie-making world of Hollywood. Decision-makers in the two worlds have a similar range of motives. In Hollywood, one may seek money (the equivalent of reelection), intra-Hollywood (or broader public) power and prestige, or commitment to an artistic ideal (the equivalent of ideology). Self-evidently, economic theory cannot predict in specific detail what movies people will make or which movies will become popular. (It may, however, tell us something about what types of movies and publicity campaigns will generally be made and succeed.) Commercially successful movie-making, like electorally successful politics, is an art as well as a science, and cannot be modeled in a crudely deterministic fashion.

■ *Self-Interest in Political Life*
JANE MANSBRIDGE
18 Political Theory 132 (1990). Reprinted with permission
of Sage Publications

In political science, a theory of "adversary" democracy based on conflict and self-interest has been evolving since the seventeenth century. When the rational choice school in the second half of the twentieth century made explicit some of the underlying assumptions of adversary democracy, the ensuing clarity had a dual effect. It inspired some to work out, in provocative detail, the implications for actual politics of the logic of self-interested action. It provoked others to challenge the factual accuracy of the theory....

Preparing the Ground

Self-interest has perennially tempted thinkers in the Western politics tradition by seeming to offer a firmer fundament for political life than tradition or diffuse social sentiments. Since the Sophists of the fourth and fifth centuries B.C., contract theorists have argued that human beings come together in political association for the self-interested reason of mutual defense. Before Thomas Hobbes, contract theorists conceived of conflict in the state of nature as involving the crimes of some against other, not as "war of all against all." Hobbes derived from self-interest a state of universal conflict. Although some individuals might be content with sufficiency, he reasoned, self-preservation required that even these seek infinitely more power in order to protect themselves against the predations of the insatiable. The universal structural position of vulnerability combined with self-interest to produce a war of all against all, which Hobbes proposed could end only with the decision to submit to a superordinate authority, the sovereign.

Today's rational choice theorists have pointed out that Hobbes's theory of third-party control is a crude but effective solution to the prisoners' dilemma in which a strategy that is rational in the short run for each individual ("collect as much power as possible for yourself") produces collective outcomes that are not in any individual's interest. Self-interest by itself can lead one to submit to a sovereign, and thus provide the basis for political legitimacy....

The Dawn of Adversary Democracy

The mid-seventeenth century saw self-interest advanced as a weapon against a monarch who used the language of public interest to promote foreign adventure. It also saw the beginning of a democratic theory that incorporated a legitimate role for self-interest. Colonel Rainborough argued in the Putney debates that if the poor did not have the vote, the rich would "crush" them. This is a new argument, justifying the vote as a means of protecting one's interests. Departing from the medieval understanding of majority vote as the best way without endless discussion to ascertain the good of the whole, it was the first step toward the claim in full-fledged adversary theory of moral neutrality between one set of interests and another.

If individuals pursue endless power after power, they are likely to clash when they make contact. Self-interest and conflict, two analytically distinct ideas, thus have a logical connection once one posits an asocial self. Historically as well, the legitimation of self-interest began to evolve at the same time as the legitimation of conflict. In the mid-seventeenth century, the English Parliament, which had previously made almost all its decisions by consensus, began making most decisions by majority vote. Representatives to Parliament, who had previously been selected in various ways without explicit contest, began to compete for office through elections. . . .

Thus several currents in the seventeenth century led writers to recommend recognizing and adapting to, rather than trying to fight, the two unshakable facts of self-interest and opposing interests in the polity. . . .

The framers of the American Constitution mixed the growing reliance on self-interest that had developed both in England and on the Continent with other strands from Scotland and the Continent that stressed virtue among citizens and representative, and the constant danger of corruption.

Establishing the Disciplinary Paradigm on Self-Interest

. . . .

In the . . . theory of "adversary democracy" there is no common good or public interest. Voters pursue their individual interests by making demands on the political system in proportion to the intensity of their feelings. Politicians, also pursuing their own interests, adopt policies that buy them votes, thus ensuring accountability. In order to stay in office, politicians act like entrepreneurs and brokers, looking for formulas that satisfy as many and alienate as few interests as possible. From the interchange between self-interested voters and self-interested brokers emerge decisions that come as close as possible to a balanced aggregation of individual interests. Normatively, the balance is legitimated when each individual's interests are weighted equally. Equal weighting is legitimated both by the equal moral worth of each individual's interests and by the absence of accepted standards for arguing that some interests deserve greater [weight] than others.

The evolution of adversary democracy from the seventeenth century to the present made possible democracy on the level of the nation state. Transforming the conception of majority rule from a substitutive measure of the good of the whole to a procedure that merely summed competing individual preferences made it possible to generate democratically, rather than through monarchy or elite consensus, a single will that could speak for the nation as a whole. As the theory evolved, this transformation also legitimated private self-interest in the motivation of citizens.

While the procedures of adversary democracy make decisions possible in large polities and under conflict, they do not meet the deliberative, integrative, and transformative needs of citizens who must not only aggregate self-interests but choose among politics in the name of a common good—at least among the representatives and sometimes among the citizens themselves. For these reasons, adversary democracy in its pure form—the battle of interest against interest decided by the procedure of majority rule—may not even meet the criteria for democracy implicit in the decisions of the United States Supreme Court....

The postwar determination to make political science a genuine science contributed to the "hard-nosed" approach of a politics based on self-interest. But as important as the attraction of science was the attraction of scientific elegance....

Some extremists in the rational choice enterprise have concluded, "as a result of empirical research . . . that the average human being is about 95 percent selfish in the narrow sense of the term." But most others . . . slide from modeling the world according to self-interest into assuming that self-interest, often in its narrowest form, is "usually" the end toward which political actors strive.

In the heyday of this version of rational choice, which insisted on the self-interest assumption, two books on the United States Congress seemed to argue that members of Congress were solely interested in reelection [citing works by Mayhew and Fiorina]. Because the United States Congress is the most studied democratic assembly in the world, their claims had important consequences for understanding democracy more generally. Although neither researcher actually claimed that representatives cared only about reelection, they did argue either that one could reinterpret all professed concern with public policy as in some way self-interested or, more narrowly, that because of the great uncertainty surrounding the circumstances of reelection, including the possibility that a challenger might raise even the most obscure vote into issue, enough representatives acted as if they were primarily concerned with reelection enough of the time to make predictions on that basis valuable....

. . . As rational choice modelers made clearer the self-interested premises and implications of the larger theory of adversary democracy, that larger theory came under attack.

Partial Anticipations

Empirical political science after World War II saw both partial anticipations of the coming crisis in adversary theory and holdovers from an earlier tradition. In several empirical studies from 1961, James Q. Wilson contended that wanting solidarity with a group ("solidarity" incentives) and wanting to promote a cause ("purposive" incentives) account in some contexts for a large fraction of political motivation. Edward Banfield and he also suggested that some cultural groups in the United States tended to vote for "public-regarding" reasons, others more according to self-interest. While the "public-regarding" studies faded after provoking a decade or so of research in the urban politics field, Wilson's categories of motivation became quasi-canonical, coexisting uneasily with the increasing emphasis in the profession on self-interest.

While Wilson actively opposed the prevailing emphasis on self-interest, Richard Fenno's classic 1973 study, *Congressmen in Committees*, which pointed out that members of certain congressional committees tried to join those committees because they wanted to help make good public policy, found little opposition in the profession, perhaps because it was based so firmly in believable fieldwork. Subsequent researchers confirmed the existence of a "policy orientation" among members of Congress, although younger scholars might have made their reputations by showing that it had declined or had never existed....

The Awareness of Anomaly

Some political scientists stumbled on anomalies in adversary theory in the course of field research. . . .

In the study of social movements during the 1970s and 1980s, the evidence for the importance of nonself-interested motivation became incontrovertible. No one could understand the decisions that either proponents or opponents saw made in the political struggle for the Equal Rights Amendment, for example, without plumbing motivations only remotely related to self-interest.

But of all the anomalies that perplexed researchers, "the paradox of the rational voter" had the most classic Kuhnian form. As Morris Fiorina succinctly put it, this was "the paradox that ate rational choice theory." In Downs's original formulation, the value of a single citizen's vote (its likelihood of having a decisive impact) is "tiny; hence it is outweighed by a very small cost of voting," for example, the time it takes to vote. Looking only at returns to self-interest, it is not rational to vote. Yet many people do vote. The obvious conclusion is that voters are acting for "irrational," that is, non-self-interested, reasons. They may vote because they are calculating incorrectly. But they also may vote because they feel solidarity with a group, because they have never thought of voting in cost-benefit terms, or because they believe in a principle that prompts their actions. . . .

By the late 1970s, the paradox of the rational voter had begun to take on the characteristics of a paradigm-challenging anomaly. In 1974 and 1975, the *American Political Science Review* devoted eight articles to Morris Fiorina and John Ferejohn's thesis that it was rational to vote if, in the extremely improbable case that your favored candidate lost the election by one vote, you would feel a regret so extreme as to make the small cost of voting a reasonable price to pay for not taking that gamble. This explanation met with immediate opposition and did not win many converts. . . .

. . . By 1980, political scientists were attending to Brian Barry's 1970 conclusions from Riker and Ordeshook's data, which showed that believing in the importance of voting (sometimes called "citizen duty") has a greater effect on whether or not one votes than does thinking an election will be close or caring who won. Since believing in the importance of voting is the strongest determinant of voting among these measures, and since, in Barry's words, voting does not therefore seem to be "undertaken with any expectation of changing the state of the world, it fails to fit the minimum requirements of the means-end model of rational behavior." Nor did it fit the requirements of a model based on self-interest.

Crisis

. . . [A]t the same time that economists were advancing rational choice models based on self-interest to explain phenomena as varied as industry regulation, marital stability, and suicide, social science disciplines other than political science were preparing the theoretical and empirical ground for a massive revision both of the larger adversary paradigm and of the rational choice strands within it.

In economics, Amartya Sen fired the first major theoretical salvo at the self-interest assumptions of economists and rational-choice theorists with his classic 1977 paper, "Rational Fools." Sen argued that sympathy for other people and commitment to a principle produce two key departures from self-interest, and that commitment, which involves counterpreferential choice, "drives a wedge between personal choice and personal welfare" while "much of traditional economic theory relies on the identity of the two." He suggested the now highly influential concept of a "meta-ranking" of preferences to explain how one might place commitment above a subjective preference. . . .

. . . In two empirical studies, James Kau and Paul Rubin argued that beliefs about the structure of the world and ways of improving it explain congressional votes on regulatory legislation better than do the economic interests of constituents or campaign contributors, and Joseph Kalt and Mark Zupan argued that "ideological shirking" (ignoring reelection concerns for the sake of "individuals['] altruistic, publicly interested goals") is an important political phenomenon in certain congressional contexts.

Cognitive psychologists joined these renegade economists. Daniel Kahneman, a psychologist, teaming up with economists Jack Knetch and Richard Thaler to investigate the kinds of economic behavior that people think are fair, found that behavior that the public thinks "unfair" often violates the implicit commitments of an ongoing relationship or "deliberately exploits the special dependence of a particular individual."

In departments of psychology, management, and economics, scores of recent experiments with prisoners' dilemma and other games that reward self-interested behavior at the expense of the group indicate a stubborn refusal on the part of a significant fraction (usually 25% to 35%) to take rational self-interested action, even under conditions of complete anonymity with no possibility of group punishment. Those who instantly take the cooperative stance usually say that their motive was to "do the right thing." Experiments like these can raise the level of cooperative behavior to 85% by allowing discussion and other procedures that increase feelings of group identity. On the other hand, they can raise the level of self-interested behavior by raising the payoff (indicating that morality can be extinguished), or by using economics students (indicating that self-interested people chose to study economics, or that socialization into the profession generates a self-interested outlook, or both.)

In political psychology, survey research by David Sears and others shows that political principles often have more effect than self-interest on political attitudes. Thinking of oneself as a "liberal" or a "conservative" explains opposition to busing more than having a child in a school liable to be integrated through busing, views on Vietnam more than having relatives or friends fighting there, views on national health insurance more than being privately insured or not, and, among corporate executives views on foreign policy more than whether or not one's company has defense contracts, or investments overseas. Tom Tyler showed that citizens evaluate courts, police, and political figures more positively if they conclude that these institutions and individuals acted fairly than if they personally benefited from the decisions. Even among convicted criminals, attitudes towards legal authorities, law, and government are affected more by assessments of the fairness of the procedure in one's case than by the severity of one's sentence. . . .

The Near-Irrelevance of Philosophy

In 1990, we see a mini-revolt in political science against the self-interested model of the way a democratic polity actually works. The surprise is how tangentially this revolt is related to the strands in normative democratic theory that since World War II have come to focus on this issue.

Deliberation was the essence of democracy in the empirical description as well as the normative prescriptions of major 19th- and early 20th-century writers like Bagehot and Baker. After World War II, as empirical description focused more and more on self-interest, the concern for a politics that transcended self-interest was preserved in several almost independent philosophical traditions—the anti-modernist tradition associated with Leo Strauss, the republican virtue tradition associated with the historical work of J. G. A. Pocock, the communal tradition associated with Sheldon Wolin, and the Frankfurt tradition associated with Jurgen Habermas. Many contemporary democratic theorists, most notably Benjamin Barber in *Strong Democracy*, but also Hanna Pitkin and others, have stressed transformation of self and polity through communal deliberations. Recent influential "communitarian" theorists, such as Michael Sandel and Charles Taylor, put collective attributes at the core of individual identity, pointing out that the self must always be "situated" and "encumbered," and that many goods, like language, are "irreducibly social." Feminist theorists have turned political thinking toward relationships and mutuality from rights and individuality, suggesting, for example, that mothering is a model of human behavior as applicable to political life as contract. Yet, while the insights of rational choice have informed political philosophy, the concerns of philosophers for deliberation and the translation of interests through political discourse have had relatively little effect on either the subfield of rational choice or empirical political science more generally.

What Now? . . .

Rational choice models need now to expand the range of motives they take into account and the contexts in which they are deployed, asking, specifically in what contexts a model premised on one kind of motivation best predicts the behavior of certain actors, and in what contexts it fails. Many rational choice modelers, like William Riker, insist only on maximization and consistency, not on the assumption of self-interest. Many economists who turn their skills to the political world would now also lean in that direction. James Buchanan, who in 1986 won the Nobel Prize in economics for applying to politics a rational choice model based on self-interest, has repudiated the single assumption of self-interest. In the same year that he won the prize, he suggested that both those who imagine a world of benevolent public servants following only the public interest and those who "have modelled politicians and bureaucrats as self-interested maximizers" share the "fatal flaw" of assuming their images to be descriptions of a total reality of politics, when, in fact, both images are partial. "The whole point of constitutional inquiry," he concluded, "is the proposition that the constraints, rules, and institutions within which persons make choices politically can and do influence the relative importance of the separate motivational elements."

Buchanan's recognition, like Hamilton and Madison before him, that motivation can be both public and self-interested, and that institutions can influence motivation, suggests a new direction for empirical political science. It invites empirical political scientists to engage with the contemporary political philosophers who analyze the political transformation of both preferences and perhaps even deep seated interests. Among many other things, we would want to know what political forms encourage individuals to replace self-interest with a concern for the collective good, to what extent elections in a representative system can transform the electorate's preferences, what is the potential for good and ill in such transformations, how ritual, symbols, schema, and scripts work in the transformative process, and how people take on political identity, how the different arenas for deliberation—courts, legislatures, staffs, the executive branch and its agencies, interest groups, universities, grant-making foundations, the media, the citizenry, and the interaction among these—contribute to and detract from political life, and how we can distinguish usefully among the three major components of deliberation—bargaining according to self-interest under different constraints on power, negotiation that appeals both to principled standards and to what the other parties actually want, and arguments, with evidence, on questions of the common good.

After three centuries of evolution, we may be now at a point again where democratic theory and the study of democratic practice can give both self-interest and concern for the common good a significant role in the analysis of political action.

COMMENTS AND QUESTIONS

1. At points Shaviro appears to treat as identical "the goal[s] of making good policy or furthering one's ideology." Can these be distinguished (in a nonideological way)?

2. Assume for the moment that the critiques of public choice theories of legislation are correct. What, then, can you—as citizens or as lawyers engaged in the legislative process—say about it? What standards might we have for claiming that a particular form of workplace safety and health regulation or environmental regulation was good public policy and ought to be adopted for that reason alone?

3. What are the possible solutions to the problems identified by public choice theorists? Shaviro suggests several, including campaign finance reform; increasing the power of congressional leadership and political parties, moving ultimately in the direction of parliamentary government; and interpreting statutes from the perspective of a (hypothetical?) "reasonable legislator." Notably, Shaviro dismisses the idea, championed by many reformers, of moving away *generally* from government and toward markets, as he recognizes that markets, too, have "a range of predictable problems, such as failing to account for externalities or sufficiently providing public goods." Given the public choice difficulties Shaviro identifies, how likely is it that the kinds of reforms he mentions will be adopted? This basic question will arise again in chapter 15, when we consider other possible regulatory reforms.

4. Stephen Croley, *Incorporating the Administrative Process*, 98 Colum. L. Rev. 1 (1998), argues that you can test the accuracy of competing theories of the modern administrative process by examining whether their predictions for how the administrative process will be structured are matched by the actual processes. A few terminological points relate to the two tables that follow: Croley's "neopluralist theory" is roughly the one we have described as interest-group pluralism. His "public interest theory" is a more elaborate version of the

"disinterested policy maker" approach; the primary elaboration is the observation that administrators can act as disinterested policy makers only if they have some space in which to operate free of overt political control. The "civic republican theory" was touched on in the conclusion of Mansbridge's article.

Table 1 sets out Croley's predictions, and table 6 presents his results. Croley finds that public choice theory doesn't do a very good job of predicting how the administrative process will be structured, nor does civic republican theory. (The problems are identified in parentheses in each entry; the more parentheses, the more problems.) Pluralist theory and the public interest theory both do reasonably well, with neither having a clear advantage over the other.

Croley's conclusions appear to undermine the "cynical" view outlined in the readings and support the idea that some sort of moderate, blended theory is likely to be most accurate. Do you agree with these conclusions?

5. With this background in public choice theory and some critiques of that theory, we examine priority setting by legislatures, the president, and administrative agencies. As you read the materials, think about what aspects of public choice theory and the critiques help you understand them.

B Applying the Analysis: Setting Regulatory Priorities

You now have seen, in general terms, both normative and descriptive accounts of why the institutions of the modern regulatory state, including legislatures and administrative agencies, might choose one or another regulatory technique. You will now be presented with descriptive accounts of regulatory choice regarding specifically the regulation of environmental and workplace risks. In reading these materials, think about which elements in the descriptive accounts provide the best understanding of specific (which ones?) aspects of the narratives. In each reading, consider which parts of the story seem to fit Croley's public choice, neopluralist, public interest, and civic republican theories.

- *Industrial Resistance to Occupational Safety and Health Legislation: 1971–1981*
  ANDREW SZASZ
  32 Social Problems 103 (1984). © 1984 by University of California Press (J).
  Reproduced with permission of University of California Press (J)
  in the format Textbook via Copyright Clearance Center

...[I]ndustry strategies played a critical role in the evolution of OSHA in the 1970s.... I show how industry changed from defensive action in the first half of the 1970s to offensive action in the second half of the decade.... I show how the election of President Reagan in 1980 signalled a victory for industry in the long battle against OSHA. I conclude by discussing differences in the evolution of social and economic regulation and the necessary antagonism between industry and the goals of social regulation.

...

Table 1 The Theories' Administrative-Process Expectations: Predicted Features of the Administrative Process

	Legal Process Rules	Information Generated	Agency Oversight	Patterns of Participation
Public Choice Theory	Closed process rules; wide participation not procedurally encouraged; rules facilitate rent-seeking	Information about interest groups' regulatory demands flows to agency; information about consequences of regulatory decision especially about social costs, not widely disseminated	Reinforces agency supply of regulatory goods; not critically scrutinizing; deferential toward rent-supplying agencies	Relatively few parties participate; overrepresentation of regulatory beneficiaries, in particular business-oriented special-interest groups; participation by parties with opposing interests not typical
Neopluralist Theory	Open process rules which promote participation; procedures formally accommodating to many parties with competing interests	Information about many groups' regulatory goals; two-way, reiterated information flow, including information about potential regulatory compromises	"Interest representation" model of oversight: oversight protects many types of groups' access to agencies	Fairly widespread participation in many agency decisions; many participants, including parties with conflicting goals and interests
Public Interest Theory	Spectrum of process rules; some process rules shroud agency decisionmakers; others expose the consequences of agency decisions	Information about regulatory consequences often shrouded; on important occasions information starkly revealed	Day-to-day oversight deferential; on important occasions oversight raises salience of regulatory stakes	Many or most decisions involve few parties; others involve many parties mobilized around particular high-salience regulatory issues
Civic Republican Theory	Open process rules which promote participation; participation open also to those without direct material stake in a given decision	Information facilitating "give-and-take" among participants; information about competing regulatory values, information above evaluative standards for assessing outcomes; information flows among groups, not only between group and agency	Promotes deliberation, not simply access by all parties; encourages agency decision-makers to identify emergent collective judgments about desirable regulatory outcomes	Many parties participate; participation by at least some public-spirited parties whose direct material interests not implicated in a decision

Table 6 Administrative-Process Findings: Easily (and Uneasily) Reconciled Features of the Administrative Process

	Legal Process Rules	Information Generated	Agency Oversight	Patterns of Participation
Public Choice Theory	Off-record informational decision-making; restricted access in formal adjudication process; (open nature of decision-making); (adjudication based on record); (bar on ex parte communication in adjudication)	Bases of informal decision-making not publicized; (notice-and-comment generation of public information); (agency promulgation of decisions and maintenance of records)	Little publicity surrounding most regulatory decision (FOIA & Sunshine Act); (judicial review); (somewhat great judicial scrutiny of agency adjudication)	Overrepresentation of business and trade groups access; many decision-making fora; high cost of participation; (agency perceptions of participation in rulemaking); (agency perceptions of group influence in rulemaking); (groups' success estimates); (presence of broad-based groups on advisory committees and in OIRA meetings)
Neopluralist Theory	Rulemaking's openness; FACA's representation requirements; negotiated rulemaking; public-participation initiatives of executive branch	Notice-and-comment requirements mandating agency disclosure of pertinent data; promulgation of bases of adjudication decision; (agency ability to consider information from any source in rulemaking)	Fairly inclusive judicial standing doctrine; encouraging ex ante participations by diverse groups; FOIA & Sunshine Act	Presence of public interest groups; pluralist membership of many advisory committees; comparable group influence scores; success estimates; (high costs of participation); (low percentage of participation by broad-based groups)
Public Interest Theory	Rulemaking & adjudication mix, with possible spectrum of silence	Promulgation of adjudication; Fed. Reg. notice requirements, (infrequent publicity of consequences of agency decisions)	Slack-reducing quality of judicial review; FOIA & Sunshine Act; (deferential judicial review of rulemaking)	(consistent presence of general interest group representatives across many decisionmaking fora); (significant underrepresentation of environmental groups in RCRA rulemaking); (group success estimates)
Civic Republican Theory	Negotiated rulemaking; FACA; successive rounds of notice-and-comment; (adjudication process); (off-record nature of informal adjudication); (ex parte rulemaking communication)	(information about group preferences more common than information about parties' values); (final agency decisions not explained in terms clearly communicating underlying regulatory values)	FOIA & Sunshine Act (judicial oversight generally deferential; ensuring at most that relevant factors justify agency decision, but not that agency balanced competing values)	Presence of public interest groups; composition of advisory committees; (relatively infrequent participation by public-spirited groups); (over-representation of business groups); (missed opportunities for dialogue at OIRA meetings)

To a large degree, federal inaction in the United States was due to the mobilization of a variety of industrial strategies aimed at keeping the issue of worker safety and health off the policy agenda and out of the public eye. Industry restricted knowledge of the scope of the problem by controlling information: records were poorly kept and little research was done on the potential hazards of industrial processes. Information showing the hazards of certain substances was actively suppressed, as in the cases of asbestos, beryllium, cotton dust, PCBs, and Kepone. Industrial management supported the ideology of accident proneness which blamed workers for their injuries.

Management also created and funded a network of organizations through which they sought to control how society dealt with and thought about occupational safety and health. They influenced workmen's compensation through the National Council for Compensation Insurance (created in 1923); research and standard-setting through the American National Standards Institute (1926) and the Industrial Health Foundation (1935); company doctors and other industrial health professionals through the American Occupational Medical Association (1915), the American Industrial Hygiene Association (1939), and the American Conference of Government Industrial Hygienists (1938); and general public debate through the National Safety Council (1913). When directly challenged, industry asserted that working conditions were solely the prerogative of management. Industrial inactivity on the health and safety issue was compounded by the ineffectiveness of state regulatory laws and the absence of adequate action by labor unions.

In the late 1960s, a number of conditions and events coincided to stimulate federal regulatory activity. The U.S. economy was healthy, inflation was modest, and unemployment was low.... Favorable economic conditions allowed workers to become concerned with noneconomic issues at a time when injury rates were rising: the rate of industrial accidents rose 29 percent between 1961 and 1970. Meanwhile, researchers and some unions began to produce solid evidence about the causes of occupational illnesses.... Rank-and-file movements in several industrial unions brought in new leaders ... who were also conscious of the health and safety issue and aware of its potential as a focal point for rank-and-file discontent. These new union officials later led the labor movement in lobbying for federal intervention. These conditions within the labor movement helped stimulate policy formation, but they were insufficient in themselves. When President Lyndon Johnson and Congressional Democrats first proposed new health and safety legislation in 1968, organized labor was tepid in its support and the effort died when Johnson declined to seek re-election.

However, when the Democrats reintroduced the legislation in 1969, chances for passage of an OSHA Act had improved. On November 20, 1968, an explosion at the Consolidated Coal Company's mine at Farmington, West Virginia, killed 78 miners. This disaster triggered both union and Congressional action, the former by strengthening a rank-and-file movement within the United Mine Workers which had arisen earlier in opposition to the union's leader, Tony Boyle. Miners responded to the accident with widespread wildcat strikes in West Virginia and thousands of miners marched on the West Virginia statehouse to demand protection. The reaction impressed the leaders of other unions with the potential of the health and safety issue for rank-and-file disaffection and contributed to their growing interest in federal action. Meanwhile, Congress responded to the

Farmington disaster with hearings into the mining industry and the Coal Mine Health and Safety Act, which it quickly passed. The hearings "served as a constant reminder of the larger, unsolved problem of job safety and health conditions" and helped generate "Congressional momentum" for the passage of the OSHA act.

The final step came in August, 1969, when newly-elected President Richard Nixon and the Republicans in Congress introduced their own version of an occupational safety and health bill. This was Nixon's way of attempting to limit the extent of federal intervention in the face of near-certain action from Congress, while giving the impression that the Republicans were willing to do something for workers. Both parties had bills pending in Congress. Labor leaders, motivated by the Farmington disaster and aghast at the possibility of the weak Republican version passing and thus preempting federal action for years, made passage of a strong occupational safety bill their top legislative priority. The strategies that industry had historically employed to keep the issue of safety and health off the policy agenda had failed. And, once they failed, industrial lobbyists could not force the genie back into the bottle. Sufficient political momentum finally existed to ensure passage of some kind of regulatory law.

As Congress debated the various versions of the legislation, industry's strategic options narrowed, leaving it with only two feasible goals: (1) to try to work with the Republicans to limit the future regulatory agency's powers; and (2) to lobby for the creation of procedures in the legislation which would allow industry to contain the agency's impact later. In support of the first goal, industry supported Republican efforts to create an agency which would not do its own research and set its own standards but which would, instead, depend on research by the American National Standards Institute, the Industrial Health Foundation, and other industry-funded organizations. Industry also supported wording of the legislation which would have split enforcement authority between the Secretary of Labor and two independent commissions, thereby weakening OSHA's enforcement powers. And it lobbied against "worker rights" language in the legislation. In support of the second goal, industry fought for procedures which would force OSHA to go through many drafts, hearings, and discussions before establishing a safety or health standard. Industry also fought for procedural safeguards in the enforcement process, so that violations of standards could be appealed both to an independent board and to the federal courts.

The OSHA Act passed by Congress on December 16, 1970, was closer in language to the Democratic version supported by organized labor than to Nixon's version which was preferred by industry. However, Congress compromised on some issues and met some industrial demands. Although the Department of Labor would eventually write its own standards based on its own research, OSHA would start off by borrowing existing, "consensus" standards written by industry. The Labor Department would do all the inspecting and fining, but an independent review commission would hear appeals against OSHA citations. Industry was successful in its strategy to introduce procedural safeguards, but it won relatively little on substantive policy during the Congressional struggle. Despite these modest accomplishments, all was not lost. The new OSHA Act would be implemented by a president who was hostile, or at best indifferent, to its goals. The stage was set for a decade of serious social struggles on the issue of occupational safety and health.

. . .

Industrial reaction to the passage of OSHA can be divided into three stages, the first one very short and the last two roughly equal in length. First, just after the passage of the OSHA act, industrial actors tried to affect the Nixon Administration's initial implementation. Second, from mid-1971 to about 1974, industrial strategies were mainly defensive and aimed at containing the agency's effects. Third, from roughly 1975 to 1981, industry went on the offensive with an aggressive deregulatory campaign.

1971: Initial Strategies

After Congress passes a bill, considerable latitude remains in how the new law will actually function. The OSHA Act gave the Executive Branch four months to establish a new agency. . . . During the implementation period, industrial lobbying aimed at limiting OSHA's powers and establishing procedures which would allow future resistance. Industry focused on advising the Nixon Administration on ways to limit OSHA's enforcement powers. Large firms and business trade associations sent their lobbyists to advise that management be given advance notice of inspections, that management be allowed to refuse entry to OSHA inspectors, that management be allowed to limit inspections in the name of protecting trade secrets, and that inspection results be kept secret by OSHA. Industry asked for rules limiting the access of OSHA inspectors to company health data and establishing the right of management to legal counsel during inspections. Lobbyists also demanded that enforcement be applied to employees as well as management, so that employees would be equally liable for health practices and would be penalized for false complaints to OSHA. And industry continued to emphasize due process safeguards in both enforcement and standard-setting.

The Nixon Administration agreed to protect trade secrets, but rejected other suggestions that would have overtly gutted OSHA's enforcement capability. Nonetheless, the Administration was openly sympathetic to industry concerns and found other ways to accommodate them. Nixon proposed an OSHA start-up budget of $25 million for fiscal year 1972, its first full year of operation—a meager amount considering OSHA's mandate and its need for data, equipment, and trained personnel. George C. Guenther, appointed to head the new agency, stressed fairness to business during his Senate confirmation hearings. His actions in office reflected this orientation. Under Guenther's leadership (from 1971 to late 1972), OSHA stressed minor safety violations and imposed modest fines, a policy that his successor, John Stender, continued until 1974. OSHA under Guenther adopted only one new health standard, for asbestos, and the worker rights clause in the OSHA Act was not implemented in any serious way. Guenther's attitude toward OSHA came to light later during the 1973 Watergate investigation which eventually led to Nixon's resignation. Investigators found a secret memo from Guenther to Nixon's re-election committee proposing that non-implementation of OSHA standards be promised to industry in exchange for corporate campaign contributions.

1971–1974: Defense and Containment Strategies

Despite all efforts to blunt the new regulatory program, the OSHA machinery began to function in May, 1971. OSHA inspectors began visiting worksites to enforce a massive number of "consensus" standards that had been adopted *en masse.*

The number of inspections grew rapidly. In its second year, for example, OSHA made 48,400 inspections and cited 155,800 violations. Though most of the violations were "minor" and resulted in an average fine of less than $30, the enforcement and inspection affected thousands of angry factory owners and managers. Although OSHA adopted only three new health standards in its first three years—for asbestos, vinyl chloride, and a package standard for 14 carcinogens—work started on a number of health standards with a potentially great impact.[4] Industrial actors began to develop strategies to cope with the threat.

Given the political conditions of the early 1970s, industrial actors could do no more than react defensively to contain the effects of the agency. There was widespread support in the United States for environmental regulation. Organized labor and its Congressional allies were on the offensive as they sought fuller implementation of the OSHA Act. Industrial actors had no coherent ideological position, no single rallying cry or policy slogan around which to unite. They professed to support the goals of safety and health, but their actions showed that they had begun to work to contain the potential effects of the new regulatory agency. In reacting to OSHA, industry divided into two distinct sectors. One sector consisted of large firms and corporations at the heart of the U.S. economy—auto, steel, chemicals, plastics, textiles, oil, and rubber. The other was the self-defined "small business" sector. These two sectors had different fears about OSHA's potential impact, vastly different political resources, and, as a result, different strategic responses to OSHA.

Small Businesses

The majority of the four million workplaces covered by the OSHA Act are small firms. Over 90 percent of them employ 25 or fewer workers. Small firms typically had no safety program of any kind and, unlike the large corporations, they had no part in writing the consensus standards initially adopted by OSHA. Most small businesses first confronted OSHA when an inspector arrived unannounced at the door, armed with a thick book of regulations and the power to enter, inspect, and fine. OSHA, in fact, focused much of its enforcement apparatus in this period on firms with less than 50 employees.[5] Not surprisingly, small businesses wanted relief from enforcement. They sought total exemption for all firms with fewer than a certain number of employees. Failing that, they wanted penalty-free consultation in place of "punitive" enforcement, or advance notice of inspection, or no fines on first inspection.

This sector of industry had limited organizational resources and capacities. They lacked the large managerial structures, powerful Washington law firms, and wealthy trade associations which large corporations use to lobby the federal government. Thus, small businesses concentrated on lobbying their Congressional representatives. Members of the Congress reported being flooded by mail soon after OSHA inspections began in 1971. There was a "tremendous outcry of objection by the nation's small businessmen," according to Representative William

---

[4] Work commenced on over 50 standards, including such potentially serious ones as coke oven emissions, noise, heat stress, cotton dust, lead, pesticides, benzene, and arsenic.

[5] OSHA enforcement statistics show that during fiscal year 1973, 52.6 percent of inspections were carried out at firms with fewer than 50 workers; during 1974, 63.3 percent; during 1975, 70.3 percent.

Hungate (D-MO). In response to the pressure the House Subcommittee on Environmental Problems Affecting Small Business scheduled hearings in June, 1972, so that small owners and their organizations (the National Federation of Independent Business, the National Association of Home Builders, and the American Retail Federation) could vent their rage. Small business and its allies also testified at hearings held by both House and Senate Labor Subcommittees, where they declared that OSHA inspectors were running "roughshod over thousands of struggling small enterprises . . . in the name of safety," according to Senator Carl Curtis (R-NE). A second round of these hearings were held in 1974, by both Labor Subcommittees and the Oversight Subcommittee on Government Regulations of the Senate Select Committee on Small Business. Members of Congress amplified the pressure brought to bear through such hearings by proposing numerous amendments to the OSHA Act. By June 1974, 82 amendments had been introduced in Congress, 66 of them calling for various forms of enforcement relief for small businesses. However, OSHA's Congressional friends on the Labor Subcommittees managed to bottle up all such amendments during this period.

Elements of the small business community also pursued enforcement relief through the federal court system. Several firms challenged the constitutionality of OSHA's power to inspect and fine firms. They lost their cases in the lower courts but pursued some all the way to the Supreme Court. The Supreme Court refused a blanket condemnation of OSHA's enforcement powers in these cases, but subsequently ruled in favor of significant limits to these powers (*Marshall v. Barlow's*, 1978).

Large Corporations

Most large corporations had at least some safety program in place and were at least familiar with the consensus standards initially adopted by OSHA. Moreover, OSHA inspectors were concentrating their efforts on small businesses. So, while individual large corporations resisted enforcement and appealed citations and fines, as a sector they were generally unconcerned with enforcement. Instead, they focused on the implications of the OSHA Act for labor relations and the prospect that OSHA might someday adopt more stringent health standards.

The corporations worried that certain OSHA rules would give new power to workers: a worker's right to accompany OSHA inspectors might permit union organizers into unorganized shops; a worker's right to request inspection might be used to shut down plants during a strike; a worker's right to abandon imminently hazardous sites might be used to legitimize wildcat walkouts. . . . However, the threat was only a potential one in this period, as neither Guenther nor Stender showed much enthusiasm for using the Act to extend worker rights. Thus, the corporations could deal with this threat by simply codifying a low level of worker rights through the collective bargaining process. Before OSHA, management had refused to negotiate health and safety issues with their unions; by 1973, 65 percent of all new contracts contained health and safety clauses, though the wording of these clauses was vague and gave workers few specific rights. When, in the next period, OSHA intensified its efforts to implement worker rights, corporations switched to a more aggressive strategy of litigation in the federal courts.

Guenther and Stender did not aggressively promulgate strict health standards, either. Nonetheless, work was slowly progressing on issues such as coke oven emissions, noise, heat stress, cotton dust, lead, pesticides, and arsenic, which, if ever regulated, would have a major impact on the relevant industries. Faced with the prospect of eventually having to comply with stricter health standards, the corporations mobilized a combination of strategies: information control, delay, organizational cooptation, and legal action.

Resistance began with the withholding of vital information. The first step in developing a new standard is the collection of data on the exposure levels of workers to potentially hazardous substances and the analysis of employee health records. Most of this data, if it existed at all, was held by the corporations themselves. Both OSHA and its adjunct, the National Institute of Occupational Safety and Health (NIOSH) reported that industrial groups and individual firms consistently failed to cooperate with requests for basic data on toxicity and exposure. (When, in the subsequent period, OSHA aggressively asserted its right to industry data, major firms vigorously, but unsuccessfully, challenged this claim in the courts....)

Withholding data created delay and made work on new standards difficult, but OSHA still moved forward on a number of health hazards. Whenever OSHA announced that it was beginning work on a new health standard, corporate representatives moved to control and coopt the process, under the name of "participation." In actual practice, "participation" meant a variety of actions, depending on the particular stage of the standard-setting process. At the first stage, when OSHA formed an advisory committee to gather scientific data and to formulate a proposal, industrial representatives on the advisory committee spoke consistently for delay, caution, and weak standards. Firms from the relevant industry also "participated" by suddenly funding research into the substance to be regulated and requesting that OSHA wait for their findings. This created delays of several years and industry-funded research inevitably supported standards weaker than those recommended by NIOSH, independent scientists, or organized labor.

When OSHA determined that a standard was warranted—based on the work of the advisory committee, NIOSH, or in response to pressure from unions—it published the proposed standard in the *Federal Register*, a daily publication of the federal government listing all agency rulings, announcements of hearings, and notices from the executive branch. Included with the published proposal was a call for comments from interested parties. "Participation" at this stage meant making full use of these discussion periods to mobilize economic, scientific, technical, and managerial experts to argue that the proposals were too stringent, were based on inadequate data, were economically harmful, and were technologically infeasible. Industry consistently supported higher levels of worker exposure to hazardous substances and compliance through the use of personal protective equipment—face masks, ear plugs—rather than through engineering controls.

"Participation" reduced the number of standards created by OSHA and weakened those that were adopted. For the few standards which OSHA actually adopted, industry had a final recourse—legal challenge in the federal courts. These strategies were all developed from 1971 to 1974, although they were used more intensively later in the decade....

The United Steelworkers (USW) first requested a standard for coke oven emissions in September, 1971. NIOSH sent its recommendation to OSHA in March, 1973. After intense pressure from the USW, OSHA formed an advisory committee in

October, 1974. Industry representatives on the committee claimed repeatedly that there was insufficient data for a standard and that compliance was technologically feasible only through face masks, not changes in factory equipment. The advisory committee forwarded its recommendation to OSHA in May, 1975. OSHA published a proposal in July. Industry officials repeatedly attacked it during the discussion period, arguing that the standard was economically and technologically infeasible. This argument was repeated until 1980 when the American Iron and Steel Institute and six steel companies withdrew their legal challenges to the standard and admitted that, in the intervening years, most of the industry had come into compliance with the standard.

     . . .

1975–1981: Offensive Strategies

While industry appeared to use the same strategies in the second half of the decade as it had during the first, a real, qualitative change had occurred. Reaction to OSHA changed from containment to counterattack. In part, this shift was made necessary by the fact that OSHA was intensifying its activities. More critically, it was made possible by the growing economic crisis of the 1970s, which altered the political balance among the parties interested in health and safety policies, and compromised general public support for regulation. This shift in the balance of forces allowed industry to unite its disparate strategies into a coherent and offensive campaign.

    OSHA intensified its work under Dr. Morton Corn, head of OSHA during Gerald Ford's presidency, and Dr. Eula Bingham under Jimmy Carter's administration. Enforcement increasingly targeted larger firms and more serious health hazards; average fines were also increased. But progress was especially notable in the areas of worker rights and health standards. OSHA promoted the right of workers to be paid to accompany OSHA inspectors, to abandon a hazardous site without penalty, to know the substances they handle, and to have access to company medical records. OSHA also issued health standards at a faster rate. Bingham issued standards for cotton dust, lead, hearing conservation, arsenic, benzene, acrylonitrile (AN), and DBCP, and promoted the so-called "generic carcinogen standard," a mechanism for accelerating the standard-setting process. Industrial actors responded with litigation in the federal courts. The right to abandon hazardous worksites was challenged both by the construction industry and other corporations. The right to be paid for accompanying OSHA inspectors was challenged by large and small firms. . . . Virtually all of the new health standards were challenged in court, but the central issue at stake in these cases—the role of economic factors and cost/benefit analysis in standard-setting—was decided in the chemical industry's challenge to the benzene standard. Thus, industry responded to improvements in OSHA implementation by intensifying its resistance, but this only partially and inadequately describes the nature of the period. Traditional resist[a]nce strategies were transformed by an altered political and ideological context.

Economic Downturn Alters the Political Configuration

The recession of 1974–75 cast a pall over the latter half of the decade and altered the political balance of forces in the debate over occupational safety and health. The gross national product fell in 1974 and 1975; the unemployment rate rose to 8.5 percent in 1975, up from 4.9 percent in 1973; and the rate of inflation reached 9.1

percent in 1975. The recession and the growing national economic crisis weakened organized labor and compromised public concern over environmental issues. Workers were weakened both economically and politically.... Organizational weakness followed economic weakness. Unions lost members.... Organized labor's political influence with the federal government waned. Organized labor continued to support full implementation of OSHA, but it lost the power to effectively resist industry's counterattack. The economic crisis also undermined public support for regulations by inducing fear of economic turmoil.... The economic crisis thus weakened the political power and resolve of OSHA supporters. It also provided fertile ground for an ideological campaign to build public support for deregulation.

The Ideological Campaign

Industry's diverse strategies were given coherence by the ideology of deregulation. The theoretical basis for this campaign had been developed previously by economists with close ties to conservative foundations, but it only became a national movement when an ailing economy provided a fearful, receptive audience. The ideology of deregulation asserted that overregulation was a cause of rising prices, stagnating productivity, plant closings, and other economic problems. It proposed that national economic well-being could only be restored by giving the business world significant relief from regulation. And it called for the application of economic, cost/benefit criteria to regulatory decision-making.

Deregulatory ideology was introduced into public discourse through many channels. Books were written for the educated audience. The argument was tirelessly repeated by corporate leaders and economists in speeches and articles. Some of the largest corporations spread the word in privately produced glossy magazines and in advertising. By the late 1970s, variants of the message could also be heard from both Republican President Ford and Democratic President Carter, their economic advisors, and from candidates seeking office. The message pervaded public debate. As a result, polls conducted between 1975 and 1980 by the Advertising Council, Cambridge Reports, Louis Harris, and CBS/New York Times showed that the U.S. public was increasingly likely to agree that overregulation had been harming the economy.

Politically on the Offensive and Increasingly Victorious

Deregulatory theory gave new unity to previous strategies of containment: it also gave them a new coherence and transformed them into virtuous efforts to save the economy from irrational and harmful government intervention. As a result, both small firms and large corporations began to win on their traditional issues.

The desire of small firms for relief from enforcement had met with failure in the early 1970s, but between 1975 and 1981 all three branches of government gave relief to small business. In *Marshall v. Barlow's* (1978), the Supreme Court ruled that management could refuse entry to OSHA inspectors and demand that they obtain a search warrant. OSHA under both Morton Corn and Eula Bingham eased up on the smaller firms. Finally, a succession of Department of Labor appropriations bills in Congress increasingly limited OSHA's enforcement powers over small business. In fiscal year 1977, enforcement over small farmers was banned and first fines for nonserious violations were banned for firms with fewer than 11 workers. In fiscal 1980,

OSHA inspections of small firms were prohibited if a state agency had inspected the firm in the previous six months, and fines were prohibited if a firm had used OSHA consultation services.

The corporate sector used deregulatory theory to link economic criteria to OSHA's standard-setting process. Here, too, gains were made in all branches of government. In 1974, Ford had required inflation impact statements to be written for each proposed standard. In 1977, the newly elected Carter was advised by his economic aides to intensify the White House's supervision of standards and to integrate "economic analysis into the early stages of the decision-making process." In 1978, Carter created the Regulatory Analysis and Review Group and empowered it to analyze the economic impact of proposed regulations. The application of economic criteria to standards was promoted in hearings by the House Banking Subcommittee on Economic Stabilization and the Senate Government Affairs Committee. By 1980, both the Democratic and Republican parties had regulatory reform bills pending in Congress. These bills would, if passed, have formalized the policies already in effect in the executive branch. Finally, a landmark Supreme Court decision in the case of the benzene standard declared that OSHA had to take economic factors into consideration when adopting standards and that there had to be a "reasonable relationship" between costs and benefits. Taken as a whole, the corporate campaign against standards was the fullest expression of deregulatory strategy, an attempt to get all branches of the federal government to accept the dominant importance of economic factors in any effort to protect workers from the effects of industrial production.

. . .

The November, 1980, election of Ronald Reagan as president signaled victory for industry in its decade-long battle against OSHA. Industrial lobbyists handed their policy shopping lists to the incoming Republican president and he moved quickly and dramatically after taking office in 1981 to meet their demands. Reagan appointed Thorne Auchter, a Republican activist and construction company official, to replace Eula Bingham, a trained occupational epidemiologist, as head of OSHA. Auchter declared that enforcement would no longer aim at "punishing" industry, but at seeking its cooperation instead. He declared that strict cost/benefit analyses would be applied to all new and existing standards, and that worker rights promoted by past OSHA heads would be re-examined. By 1984, all of industry's traditional demands had been satisfied. . . . [W]ork on new standards had come to a halt as OSHA devoted its energies to reviewing existing standards. Such reviews led to attempts to weaken the standards already in effect. Enforcement had been systematically weakened, as well. One third of the field offices had been closed and there were 20 percent fewer OSHA inspectors. On every significant measure—total number of inspections, number of workers covered by inspections, average time spent per inspection, fines levied, inspections due to worker complaints, reinspections following findings of violations—OSHA enforcement had suffered. Finally, there had been an unrelenting attack on the worker rights that OSHA had attempted to promulgate in the late 1970s. Worker education funds were severely cut and films, slide shows, and pamphlets designed by Bingham's OSHA for worker education were withdrawn. The right to be paid to accompany OSHA inspectors was withdrawn. The labeling standard, giving workers the right to know what chemicals they work with, was withdrawn. Thus, the Reagan administration completed the strategic offensive initiated by industrial actors and undid much of the environmental concessions that had been forced on industry during the previous decade.

. . .

Analysts of economic regulation have used the military metaphor of "capture" to conceptualize the relationship between regulatory agencies and industry. My investigation of industry's role in the evolution of OSHA suggests that the military metaphor may also be appropriate for understanding the relationship between agencies and industry in cases of social regulation as well. When OSHA's supporters were strong and united, industry used defensive tactics; when conditions changed and the balance of power shifted in industry's favor after 1975, it went on the offensive. Industry finally "captured" OSHA in 1980 through the election of President Ronald Reagan.

However, the "capture" of OSHA differs from the notion of agency capture described in the literature. . . . [E]conomic agencies have not been directly, physically captured by industry. . . . [I]ndustrial influence is exerted without actual capture: control of information, litigation, and manipulation of regulators through rewards such as friendship and promises of future employment. Through such actions industry can make an economic agency do for them what they find difficult or illegal to do for themselves, namely fix prices, block the entry of new firms into the sector, and reduce competition. In contrast, . . . agencies such as OSHA and the Environmental Protection Agency (EPA) have been directly captured by anti-regulatory businessmen and their allies under the Reagan Administration; yet, despite such direct capture, industries have been unable to make these agencies serve their interests in any *positive* sense. The most that industries have been able to achieve is to muzzle the agency; Reagan's OSHA only serves them in the negative sense of relieving them from the burden of complying with its mandate.

. . .

COMMENTS AND QUESTIONS

1. Note the importance Szasz gives to the macroeconomic context within which political maneuvering over occupational safety and health regulation occurred. Which of the perspectives developed earlier in this chapter most easily accommodates that context?

2. Which perspective provides the best account of why the "capture" Szasz describes was merely negative?

3. Throughout Szasz's account, you can see elements that fit more readily into one perspective than another. For example, the differential access of businesses generally, as compared with labor unions, and the different roles of large and small businesses fit reasonably well into a public choice framework, whereas the role of deregulatory ideology fits better into a public interest account. (Note, though, Szasz's account of the material support business provided to those who articulated and promulgated the deregulatory ideology.) Is it possible to come up with a judgment about which perspective, on balance, yields more insight? Or is the lesson that each perspective offers something valuable as you try to understand how the regulatory process operates?

4. Szasz is obviously skeptical about the value of participation in decisions regarding the enforcement of OSHA. As a normative matter, could participation be restructured to reduce the problems Szasz believes it entailed (without making the process unfair)? Descriptively, how could such a restructuring occur? You will consider this sort of question in more detail in chapter 15, in connection with proposals to reform regulation in the twenty-first century.

5. Szasz describes how the OSHA statute provided opportunities for members of Congress to do casework on behalf of their small business constituents and to take positions by holding hearings. The arguments about congressional motivation offered by Mayhew and Fiorina suggest that it is unlikely that the statute was enacted in order to provide these opportunities. (Why?) How important are the ideas that legislators profit from casework and position taking, if those practices are collateral effects of legislation adopted for other reasons?

6. The next reading moves the story up by a decade. What *new* developments occurred during that period?

■ *Overcoming Barriers to Better Regulation*
JOHN MENDELOFF
18 Law & Social Inquiry 711, 722–29 (1993). Reprinted with permission of Blackwell Publishers

We might ask the following questions about OSHA's enforcement policies:
1. What should they be?
2. What are they? Are they changing? If so, are they changing in the right direction?
3. What has been learned about "what works"?
4. Why hasn't more been learned? What would be necessary to learn more?

The answer to the first question is easy: No one knows. To answer it, we would first have to decide what the objectives of the enforcement policy should be and how to weight them. Political disagreements make that very difficult. However, even if we could agree on the objectives, we would still face the problems that we don't know the effects of particular policies and we don't know their effects at the margin and in combination with each other. In other words, there is a difficult analytical problem, as well as a political problem.

Part of the answer to the second problem is presented below. We see that OSHA's enforcement policies have often changed. Some of the changes occurred primarily due to pressures from Congress, the White House, or the courts. In other cases, internal developments predominated as agency leaders tried to figure out how to manage their resources more effectively. It does seem clear, at least to me, that OSHA's policies are superior to those of 20 years ago. Even if we cannot design the optimal set of policies, it is still sometimes possible to appraise whether marginal changes are in the right direction.

Before tackling the last questions, let us review what some of the major changes at OSHA have been. In OSHA's first few years, staff and inspections shot up sharply. During this period, the agency issued a large number of "other than serious" violations, which often carried small penalties.

In 1977 the Democrats took over and implemented a policy that cosmetically redefined violations so that more would be labeled as "serious" and tried modestly to focus the agency on the more serious ones. Total inspections fell 30% as a new emphasis was placed on more thorough inspections of large manufacturers. In 1976, following a scandal caused by OSHA's failure to respond to a worker's complaint about what later turned out to be a major hazard, OSHA loosened its criteria for responding to complaints, no longer requiring that they be written. Complaint inspections jumped from just over 10% to almost 35% of the total. Total penalties increased significantly and so did the percentage of inspections triggering employers' appeals.

With Reagan, OSHA's inspection resources dropped, but the total number of inspections increased, largely because of a major shift from manufacturing to small construction contractors. From less than 30% of safety inspections, construction rose to account for almost 60%. Complaint inspections also continued the slide they had begun in the late 1970s, when OSHA, its flexibility hobbled by the huge number of complaints, had developed a new policy of responding by letter to requests that were not in writing.

The Reagan administration's early deregulatory thrust resulted in dramatically fewer violations and smaller average penalties. From 1980 to 1982 proposed penalties fell by 70% and employer contests declined by 80%. In 1982, OSHA initiated a "record-check" policy in manufacturing that called for inspectors to first determine whether an establishment's injury rate exceeded the average rate in manufacturing. If it did not, the inspector would leave. The intent here was to focus on the "bad apples." Criticized for providing employers an incentive to underreport injuries, the policy was phased out during the late 1980s. Complaint inspections made a resurgence.

The next major change was the development of an "egregious" case policy in 1986. For willful, repeated, high-gravity serious, and failure-to-abate violations, OSHA began to assess penalties for each instance of a violation rather than grouping them. OSHA's proposed penalties rose from under $10 million in 1986 to over $60 million in 1990. Case-hours per inspection increased as inspectors devoted more time to establishing evidence to support the citations. Employer contests rose as the penalties increased, although the contest rate did not reach the levels of 1980.

Can one draw any normative conclusions about these changes? In some cases, yes, although they are not always unambiguous. The reduction in follow-up inspections was clearly warranted. Given the significant penalties for failing to correct violations that had been cited and the high probability that workers would detect those failures, scheduling follow-up inspections so often was clearly unnecessary to achieve deterrence. Second, the efforts to curb complaint inspections seemed warranted because in many regions, OSHA no longer had any ability to target its inspections. However, we should note that the evidence bearing on the relative efficacy of different inspection types in either detecting violations or preventing injuries was skimpy. Finally, it seems plausible that OSHA will be more effective in preventing injuries now that it is willing to levy much larger penalties. With its occasional seven figure penalties, it now has a big gun; and flea bites have declined. However, note that the accompanying increase in the resources required to conduct an inspection means that fewer workplaces can be inspected.

. . .

What has OSHA learned in over 20 years about "what works" and what works best in enforcement policy? I would suggest that the answer is "not too much." This is, of course, a common finding of such inquiries in many policy areas. Many of the reasons are similar for OSHA as for other domains, but it is worth trying to think them through. . . .

There are many different mechanisms through which OSHA's enforcement program might lead to a reduction in injuries. The first is *detection*. Compliance officers can prevent injuries by inspecting workplaces, detecting injury-causing violations of standards, and compelling firms to abate them. The second mechanism is *deterrence*. Firms correct violations (and thus prevent injuries) because they want to avoid the penalties that OSHA can impose for noncompliance. A third mechanism is *providing* information to employers to help them prioritize their problems and find better ways of addressing them. Ayres and Braithwaite would also emphasize that contacts with OSHA personnel inform firm officials of what their legal obligations are. A fourth mechanism is the *attention-grabbing* impact on managers who, as a result of the inspection or the penalties that are issued, beef up their safety programs. Scholz and Gray have argued that the impact of inspections depends less on what inspectors actually detect than on whether their penalties alert management that more needs to be done. A fifth mechanism is *providing information to workers* both in the course of inspections and by regulations requiring the provision of information about safety and health risks. That information may help the market for occupational risk work more efficiently.

Different inspection strategies rely on different mixes of these mechanisms. On theoretical grounds, we can draw some conclusions about what types of mechanisms might work best for dealing with certain types of problems. However, theory takes us only so far. For example, would a program of enforced self-regulation for large firms—exempting them from regular inspections—reduce injuries to a greater extent than a program of inspecting high-hazard establishments in the same group of firms? Would injuries be prevented by switching 5,000 inspections from manufacturing to construction? Or vice versa? If a further doubling of penalties led to greater compliance, what would the costs of compliance be and how many injuries would be prevented?

. . .

The data needed to answer these questions have rarely been available and are often not of the quality needed. . . .

However, to discover what works in a systematic fashion, there is no substitute for conducting experiments in the field and evaluating the results. Unfortunately, the track record at OSHA is not a very good one in this respect. It is worth reviewing some of the problems.

First, the agency's top priorities are to be responsive to the pressures exerted on it by unions and firms, acting through Congress and the White House. Unions have two main concerns: that OSHA respond to their members' requests for action in a timely and sensitive manner and that OSHA keep the pressure on nonunion workplaces so that they do not gain a competitive advantage from laxer enforcement. Firms prefer a weak OSHA presence but also want consistent and predictable enforcement. Neither group places a very high priority on making OSHA enforcement more effective or efficient. Consequently, neither does Congress. If the agency does, it will be due either to strong White House pressure or because of the professional norms of the agency chief.

Second, it requires a very strong commitment by top management to make experiments work. The chief mission of the agency is to enforce compliance with standards. Detailed field operation manuals try to structure the discretion of the compliance officers, the "street-level bureaucrats" who do the inspections that comprise the basic work of the agency. Establishing planned variations for subsets of the agency requires designing new manuals and monitoring compliance with their protocols across a number of offices. These new protocols are often viewed as burdensome and disruptive by the local staff who must carry them out.

Third, OSHA's analytical staff is small and has little authority within the agency. When OSHA was established, the research component (the National Institute of Occupational Safety and Health) was placed in the Department of Health and Human Services. Data gathering activities were placed in the Bureau of Labor Statistics. Cut off from important sources of organizational intelligence, OSHA was clearly designated as a law enforcement agency. Outside of the sciences, the agency has less than a handful of persons with Ph.D.'s, a measure of the weakness of the internal lobby for a more analytical approach to policymaking. When new ideas are broached and receive initial support from top management, they are often severely compromised in order to make them acceptable to the enforcement officials who must implement them.

Fourth, the injury data needed to evaluate the experiments are often unavailable. Federal OSHA does not have ready access to establishment level injury data. No one has a data base linking inspection results to causal information about the types of injuries that are occurring. These shortcomings have several roots. Federalism has created widely disparate state data systems (generated by worker compensation programs) and created barriers to federal access to them. At the federal level, the Bureau of Labor Statistics fears that making data available to OSHA would jeopardize the voluntary reporting on which it relies for all of its other business statistics. Again, although these problems could be successfully addressed, the task would require considerable political commitment and clout.

Despite these gloomy considerations, OSHA has always shown some interest in exploring new ideas. Recently, OSHA's office in Maine has launched an enforced self-regulation program for the largest 200 employers in that state. In Florida, OSHA is trying to use data from past inspections to identify and target for inspection those contractors who had been previously cited for serious violations. Nevertheless, the factors cited above do not augur very well for the prospects for organizational learning at OSHA.

Given the absence of hard data to support policy choices, it is not surprising that we fall back on approaches consistent with our ideological predispositions and theoretical tastes.

. . .

The record of American safety and environmental regulation is neither a smashing success story nor a litany of unrelieved failure. In general, the programs have achieved some gains in protection although the process has been contentious and unnecessarily costly.

To a large extent, effectiveness has been a product of tough laws. The efficiency of these laws—a much dicier issue—depends not only on how stringently the standards are set, but also on whether the laws allow flexibility both in allocating the burdens of compliance among firms and in allowing them choices about the methods of compliance. Finally, effectiveness and efficiency may depend on how the laws are enforced.

I argue that many of the most worthwhile regulatory measures—those that have achieved significant protection at reasonable cost—were adopted when agency leaders were relatively insulated from strong ideological pressures and therefore better able to respond to professional judgments about what makes sense. This claim is consistent with . . . a long line of reformist complaints that if the "politicians" would respect bureaucratic autonomy and expertise, we would get better policies. It is naive to rest too much hope for regulatory reform on insulating policymaking from the White House, Congress, and the courts.

Nevertheless, it is noteworthy that the decade following 1983 represented a period of greater autonomy at some agencies. In that year, the Reagan administration lost a major public relations battle when congressional Democrats convinced the media and the public that the deregulatory policies at EPA represented concessions to industry that threatened public safety. At both EPA and OSHA, the leaders shifted gears and stiffened their enforcement efforts. They saw not only that deregulation in those areas was politically unpopular but also that the administration would not necessarily protect them from congressional attack.

The Supreme Court had dealt the deregulatory program significant setbacks in 1981—in upholding OSHA's cotton dust standard against the claim that it must pass a benefit-cost test—and in 1983—in overturning the re[s]cission of the National Highway Traffic Safety Administration's (NHTSA) passive restraint standard. Yet the very next year in its *Chevron* decision, the Court supported EPA's discretion to interpret statutes as long as its interpretation was a reasonable construction; appeals courts were no longer to overturn agencies on the grounds that a *more* reasonable interpretation might exist.

The combination of less ideological direction from the White House and more deferential courts helped to create more maneuverability for some regulators. EPA benefited least, as Congress stepped in to narrow that discretion sharply with new legislation dealing with toxic waste generation, drinking water standards, superfund sites, and air pollution.

During the mid-1980s, Congress did not play as active a role with OSHA because organized labor continued to resist any efforts to open up the OSH Act for amendments. Despite the absence of strong congressional pressure, in 1986 OSHA's new leaders authorized the "egregious citation" policy, which allowed the agency to increase penalties dramatically. In 1987 they also began work to remedy a longtime professional embarrassment; the new health standards that OSHA had adopted over 16 years were usually very strict, but there had been only a handful. As a result, for the vast majority of hazards, the exposure limits that OSHA enforced were much less protective than those adopted by industry-dominated groups. OSHA promulgated a rule adopting, en masse, these industry-recommended exposure levels. Although not as strict and costly as OSHA's usual standards, this regulation was projected to prevent more deaths than all of the other OSHA health standards put together at a fraction of the cost per death prevented.

At NHTSA, the Supreme Court's rebuke on passive restraints and the White House's growing disinterest gave Transportation Secretary Elizabeth Dole the opportunity to invent a more creative solution to the long-running stalemate between advocates and opponents of air bags. She resurrected the long dormant issue of seatbelt-use laws (which could, if effective, promise cheap and immediate protection) by making the imposition of a new passive restraint standard contingent on the failure of states with two-thirds of the nation's population to adopt such laws. With one step, she put the focus back on injury prevention rather than on the techniques of passive restraints. Her proposal pushed the auto industry into a strong, often successful, lobbying campaign for seatbelt-use laws. The uncertainty about whether passive restraints would be required undermined auto industry opposition and compelled the firms to begin introducing models with air bags and passive belts in order to be ready in case the two-thirds requirement was not met.

At the Food and Drug Administration, the pattern of policy changes differed in timing and process. In the late 1980s AIDS activists helped to neutralize the liberal congressional committee heads who had been the severest critics of looser approval standards for new drugs. However, in this case, the agency's career staff was not anxious to change their approval policies in a fundamental way. From 1987 through 1992, the White House maintained strong pressure on FDA leaders to incorporate these changes into the organization's standard operating procedures.

I would argue that the changes at OSHA, NHTSA, and the FDA were desirable because they offered a better balance of the costs and benefits of regulation. . . .

. . .

COMMENTS AND QUESTIONS

1. Mendeloff describes several changes in enforcement priorities. Are they better explained by a public choice, neopluralist, public interest, or civic republican account?

2. Mendeloff describes political circumstances that gave the managers at several agencies more room to develop their own policies without substantial congressional—or presidential—checks. Stewart's history of the development of the modern regulatory state (chapter 8) suggests that these circumstances represent a (cyclical?) return to the Progressive era's view that expert agencies insulated from politics advance the public interest. Do you think that the political circumstances Mendeloff describes are common enough to provide a general defense of the Progressive era view in the twenty-first century?

3. For thirty years (since President Nixon), the White House has reviewed major rules issued (or proposed) by federal agencies. This review has long included some balancing of costs against benefits. It has also often reflected the White House's views as to what the agencies' priorities should be. In the first five years of the administration of George W. Bush, John D. Graham headed the Office of Information and Regulatory Affairs (OIRA), the White House office that reviews agency rules. In the memo that follows, Graham announced OIRA's intentions with respect to White House review of agency rules. What are the likely patterns of participation in the consultations the memorandum requires?

■ *Memo from John D. Graham to Agency Heads (Sept. 2001)*

Memorandum for the President's Management Council

From: John D. Graham [Administrator, Office of Information and Regulatory Affairs (OIRA)]

Subject: Presidential Review of Agency Rulemaking by OIRA

Federal regulations can provide cost-effective solutions to many problems. If not properly developed, regulations can lead to an enormous burden on the economy.

In this context, I call your attention to Executive Order No. 12866, "Regulatory Planning and Review." Under this Executive Order, the Administrator of the Office of Information and Regulatory Affairs (OIRA) carries out a regulatory review process on behalf of the President. The President's Chief of Staff, Andrew H. Card, Jr., has directed me to work with the agencies to implement vigorously the principles and procedures in E.O. 12866 until a modified or new Executive Order is issued.

I want to stress that it is my goal to work with you to carry out OIRA's regulatory reviews thoroughly and cooperatively. To help us work together more effectively, I have attached a detailed description of how OIRA carries out this regulatory review, summarizing the principles we follow and the procedures we use. I request that you send this attachment to the appropriate officials in your agency that are responsible for regulatory development.

Working together to apply the regulatory principles in E.O. 12866, I believe we will strengthen the country's regulatory structure. I look forward to working with all of you and your staff.

[The following attachment was distributed with the foregoing memorandum.]

OMB Regulatory Review: Principles and Procedures

This attachment describes the general principles and procedures that will be applied by OMB in the implementation of E.O. 12866 and related statutory and executive authority.

OIRA Review of Significant Regulations

E.O. 12866, "Regulatory Planning and Review," governs OIRA's oversight of agency rulemaking, requiring OIRA review of "significant" agency regulatory actions before they are proposed for public comment, and again before they are issued in final form. The Order defines "regulatory action" broadly to include all substantive action by an agency that is expected to lead to the issuance of a final rule. Over the past several years, OIRA staff have worked with agencies to develop a common understanding of what is meant by a "significant" regulatory action (see section 3(f)). While OIRA does not formally review non-significant regulatory actions, agencies are expected to ensure that they are consistent with the Order's regulatory principles.

Following agency transmittal to OIRA of a draft rule, OIRA reviews the draft rule for consistency with the regulatory principles stated in the Order, and with the President's policies and priorities. The review determines whether the agency has, in deciding whether and how to regulate, assessed the costs and benefits of available regulatory alternatives (including the alternative of not regulating).

Specifically, E.O. 12866 states that, "in choosing among alternative regulatory approaches, agencies should select those approaches that maximize net benefits...." E.O. 12866 further states that, "Each agency shall assess both the costs and the benefits of the intended regulation and, recognizing that some costs and benefits are difficult to quantify, propose or adopt a regulation only upon a reasoned determination that the benefits of the intended regulation justify its costs."

Regulatory Impact Analysis

Agencies must prepare a Regulatory Impact Analysis (RIA) for each regulation that OIRA or the agency designates as "economically significant." Section 3(f)(1) of the Order defines an "economically significant" rule as one likely to "have an annual effect on the economy of $100 million or more or adversely affect in a material way the economy, a sector of the economy, productivity, competition, jobs, the environment, public health or safety, or State, local, or tribal governments or communities."

This definition is functionally equivalent to the definition of a "major" rule as that term is used in the Congressional Review Act.

The RIA must provide an assessment of benefits, costs, and potentially effective and reasonably feasible alternatives to the planned regulatory action (see section 6(a)(3)(C)). This is submitted to OIRA along with the applicable draft regulatory action. Preparing RIAs helps agencies evaluate the need for and consequences of possible Federal action. By analyzing alternate ways to structure a rule, agencies can select the best option while providing OIRA and the public a broader understanding of the ranges of issues that may be involved. Accordingly, it is important that a draft RIA be reviewed by agency economists, engineers, and scientists, as well as by agency attorneys, prior to submission to OIRA.

OIRA also relies on RIAs to meet its obligations (1) under the Congressional Review Act, which directs the OIRA Administrator to determine if final rules are "major" and (2) under another law, which requires the OMB Director to submit an annual report to Congress on the costs and benefits of Federal regulation. As a result, agency submissions to OIRA of economically significant rules shall include RIAs, regardless of the extent to which an agency is permitted by law to consider risks, costs, or benefits in issuing a regulation. RIAs should be prepared in a way consistent with OMB Memorandum M-00–08....

Peer Review

For economically significant and major rulemakings, OMB recommends that agencies subject RIAs and supporting technical documents to independent, external peer review by qualified specialists. Given the growing public interest in peer review at agencies, OMB recommends that (a) peer reviewers be selected primarily on the basis of necessary technical expertise, (b) peer reviewers be expected to disclose to agencies prior technical/policy positions they may have taken on the issues at hand, (c) peer reviewers be expected to disclose to agencies their sources of personal and institutional funding (private or public sector), and (d) peer reviews be conducted in an open and rigorous manner. OIRA will be giving a measure of deference to agency analysis that has been developed in conjunction with such peer review procedures....

Public Disclosure of OIRA Communications with Outside Parties

On occasion, parties outside the Executive branch will meet with the OIRA Administrator or his or her designee regarding a rule under review. OIRA will invite representatives of relevant agencies to such meetings and OIRA appreciates having agencies make senior regulatory policy officials available to attend such meetings. In addition, written materials received from those outside the Executive branch are retained for public inspection in OIRA's public docket room and forwarded to the rulemaking agency. It is the responsibility of each agency to place these in the rulemaking docket. These communications are disclosed to the public as described in E.O. 12866, section 6(b)(4).

The "Return" Letter

During the course of OIRA's review of a draft regulation, the Administrator may decide to send a letter to the agency that returns the rule for reconsideration. Such a return may occur if the quality of the agency's analyses is inadequate, if the regulatory standards adopted are not justified by the analyses, if the rule is not consistent with the regulatory principles stated in the Order or with the President's policies and priorities, or if the rule is not compatible with other Executive orders or statutes. As Director Daniels stated in an earlier memorandum, "if OMB determines that more substantial work is needed, OMB will return the draft rule to the agency for improved analysis." Since that memo was issued, OIRA has returned two agency draft rules, in both cases due to analytical problems.

It is important to understand that such a return does not necessarily imply that either OIRA or OMB is opposed to the draft rule. Rather, the return letter will explain why OIRA believes that the rulemaking would benefit from further consideration by the agency.

The "Prompt" Letter

The agencies prepare semi-annual regulatory agendas under E.O. 12866, section 4(b), outlining the agencies foreseeable regulatory priorities. OIRA plans to send, as occasion arises, what will be referred to as "prompt" letters. The purpose of a prompt letter is to suggest an issue that OMB believes is worthy of agency priority. Rather than being sent in response to the agency's submission of a draft rule for OIRA review, a "prompt" letter will be sent on OMB's initiative and will contain a suggestion for how the agency could improve its regulations. For example, the suggestion might be that an agency explore a promising regulatory issue for agency action, accelerate its efforts on an ongoing regulatory matter, or consider rescinding or modifying an existing rule. We will request prompt agency response to "prompt" letters, normally within 30 days. . . .

We are looking forward to working cooperatively with you and your staff to meet our respective statutory obligations and to move the President's programs forward.

COMMENTS AND QUESTIONS

1. What would the public choice, neopluralist, public interest, and civic republican perspectives lead you to expect about the way in which OIRA's review process will operate?

2. Compare the Graham memorandum with a proposal offered by then-Judge Stephen Breyer, in *Breaking the Vicious Circle: Toward Effective Risk Regulation* (1993). Breyer severely criticizes modern health and safety regulation and opines that too much money is spent on small problems and too little money on big problems. He proposes that a new agency be created, housed in the White House and staffed with an elite corps of civil servants trained in science, economics, and law. Breyer recommends that this new group be given the authority to transfer resources from one lifesaving program (e.g., hazardous waste cleanup) to another (e.g., vaccinations) to save the largest possible number of lives with the money we now spend. He envisions that the agency would be insulated from politics and from judicial review of its decisions. Does this seem like a good idea? What are the political circumstances that would allow such an agency to be created?

3. To what extent may the courts review agency decisions about enforcement priorities? Of course, they may review decisions to enforce their regulations (when the target appeals, for example), decisions to adopt regulations, and decisions to rescind existing regulations. What about decisions *not* to enforce existing regulations or decisions not to adopt regulations?

   Heckler v. Chaney, which follows, addresses the first of those questions. In reading it, keep in mind these provisions of the Administrative Procedure Act:

   5 U.S.C. § 701. Application; definitions

   (a) This chapter applies, according to the provisions thereof, except to the extent that
      (1) statutes preclude judicial review; or
      (2) agency action is committed to agency discretion by law.

   5 U.S.C. § 706. Scope of review
   To the extent necessary to decision and when presented, the reviewing court shall decide all relevant questions of law, interpret constitutional and statutory provisions, and determine the meaning or applicability of the terms of an agency action. The reviewing court shall—
      (1) compel agency action unlawfully withheld or unreasonably delayed. . . .
   5 U.S.C. § 551 Definitions . . .
      (13) "agency action" includes the whole or a part of an agency rule, order, license, sanction, relief, or the equivalent or denial thereof, or failure to act. . . .

■ Heckler v. Chaney
470 U.S. 821 (1985)

[Respondents were prisoners under sentence of death, to be administered by lethal injection of drugs. They initially petitioned the Food and Drug Administration, claiming that the drugs to be used had not been tested for the intended use, and that their use would be an "unapproved use of an approved drug," in violation of the Food and Drug Act's prohibition on "misbranding." They argued that the FDA was required to approve the drugs as "safe and effective" for human execution—which, they argued, the drugs were not, because they were likely to be administered by poorly trained technicians. The Commissioner of the FDA refused, saying that he disagreed with the prisoners' claims about misbranding and that, "Were the FDA clearly to have jurisdiction in the area, . . . we believe we would be authorized to decline to exercise it under our inherent discretion to decline to pursue certain enforcement matters. The unapproved use of approved drugs is an area in which the case law is far from uniform. Generally, enforcement proceedings in this area are initiated only when there is a serious danger to the public health or a blatant scheme to defraud." On appeal, the court of appeals held that the FDA did have to take action, invoking a presumption that "all agency action is subject to judicial review" and finding "law to apply" in an FDA policy statement asserting that the agency was "obligated" to investigate the unapproved use of an approved drug when such use became "widespread" or "[endangered] the public health." Refusing to investigate the use in this instance was arbitrary and capricious, the court of appeals held, in light of the FDA's investigation of drugs used to "put animals to sleep" and of the unapproved use of drugs on prisoners in clinical trials.]

Justice Rehnquist delivered the opinion of the Court. . . .

. . . Petitioner urges that the decision of the FDA to refuse enforcement is an action "committed to agency discretion by law" under § 701(a)(2).

This Court has not had occasion to interpret this second exception in § 701(a) in any great detail. On its face, the section does not obviously lend itself to any particular construction; indeed, one might wonder what difference exists between § (a)(1) and § (a)(2). The former section seems easy in application; it requires construction of the substantive statute involved to determine whether Congress intended to preclude judicial review of certain decisions. . . . But one could read the language "committed to agency discretion by law" in § (a)(2) to require a similar inquiry. . . . How is it, [commentators] ask, that an action committed to agency discretion can be unreviewable and yet courts still can review agency actions for abuse of that discretion? . . .

This Court first discussed § (a)(2) in *Citizens to Preserve Overton Park v. Volpe*, 401 U.S. 402 (1971). That case dealt with the Secretary of Transportation's approval of the building of an interstate highway through a park in Memphis, Tennessee. The relevant federal statute provided that the Secretary "shall not approve" any program or project using public parkland unless the Secretary first determined that no feasible alternatives were available. Interested citizens challenged the Secretary's approval under the APA, arguing that he had not satisfied the substantive statute's requirements. This Court first addressed the "threshold question" of whether the agency's action was at all reviewable. After setting out the language of § 701(a), the Court stated:

> "In this case, there is no indication that Congress sought to prohibit judicial review and there is most certainly no 'showing of "clear and convincing evidence" of a . . . legislative intent' to restrict access to judicial review. *Abbott Laboratories v. Gardner*, 387 U.S. 136, 141 (1967). . . . Similarly, the Secretary's decision here does not fall within the exception for action 'committed to agency discretion.' This is a very narrow exception. . . . The legislative history of the Administrative Procedure Act indicates that it is applicable in those rare instances where 'statutes are drawn in such broad terms that in a given case there is no law to apply.' S. Rep. No. 752, 79th Cong., 1st Sess., 26 (1945)."

Overton Park, supra, at 410. The above quote answers several of the questions raised by the language of § 701(a), although it raises others. First, it clearly separates the exception provided by § (a)(1) from the § (a)(2) exception. The former applies when Congress has expressed an intent to preclude judicial review. The latter applies in different circumstances; even where Congress has not affirmatively precluded review, review is not to be had if the statute is drawn so that a court would have no meaningful standard against which to judge the agency's exercise of discretion. In such a case, the statute ("law") can be taken to have "committed" the decisionmaking to the agency's judgment absolutely. This construction avoids conflict with the "abuse of discretion" standard of review in § 706—if no judicially manageable standards are available for judging how and when an agency should exercise its discretion, then it is impossible to evaluate agency action for "abuse of discretion." . . .

Overton Park did not involve an agency's refusal to take requested enforcement action. It involved an affirmative act of approval under a statute that set clear guidelines for determining when such approval should be given. Refusals to take enforcement steps generally involve precisely the opposite situation, and in that situation we think the presumption is that judicial review is not available. This Court has recognized on several occasions over many years that an agency's decision not to prosecute or enforce, whether through civil or criminal process, is a decision generally committed to an agency's absolute discretion. This recognition of the existence of discretion is attributable in no small part to the general unsuitability for judicial review of agency decisions to refuse enforcement.

The reasons for this general unsuitability are many. First, an agency decision not to enforce often involves a complicated balancing of a number of factors which are peculiarly within its expertise. Thus, the agency must not only assess whether a violation has occurred, but whether agency resources are best spent on this violation or another, whether the agency is likely to succeed if it acts, whether the particular enforcement action requested best fits the agency's overall policies, and, indeed, whether the agency has enough resources to undertake the action at all. An agency generally cannot act against each technical violation of the statute it is charged with enforcing. The agency is far better equipped than the courts to deal with the many variables involved in the proper ordering of its priorities. Similar concerns animate the principles of administrative law that courts generally will defer to an agency's construction of the statute it is charged with implementing, and to the procedures it adopts for implementing that statute.

In addition to these administrative concerns, we note that when an agency refuses to act it generally does not exercise its coercive power over an individual's liberty or property rights, and thus does not infringe upon areas that courts often are called upon to protect. Similarly, when an agency does act to enforce, that action itself provides a focus for judicial review, inasmuch as the agency must have exercised its power in some manner. The action at least can be reviewed to determine whether the agency exceeded its statutory powers. Finally, we recognize that an agency's refusal to institute proceedings shares to some extent the characteristics of the decision of a prosecutor in the Executive Branch not to indict—a decision which has long been regarded as the special province of the Executive Branch, inasmuch as it is the Executive who is charged by the Constitution to "take Care that the Laws be faithfully executed." U.S. Const., Art. II, § 3. We of course only list the above concerns to facilitate understanding of our conclusion that an agency's decision not to take enforcement action should be presumed immune from judicial review under § 701(a)(2). For good reasons, such a decision has traditionally been "committed to agency discretion," and we believe that the Congress enacting the APA did not intend to alter that tradition. In so stating, we emphasize that the decision is only presumptively unreviewable; the presumption may be rebutted where the substantive statute has provided guidelines for the agency to follow in exercising its enforcement powers.[4] Thus, in establishing this presumption in the APA, Congress did not set agencies free to disregard legislative direction in the statutory scheme that the agency administers. Congress may limit an agency's exercise of enforcement power if it wishes, either by setting substantive priorities, or by otherwise circumscribing an agency's power to discriminate among issues or cases it will pursue. How to determine when Congress has done so is the question left open by *Overton Park*.

. . . The danger that agencies may not carry out their delegated powers with sufficient vigor does not necessarily lead to the conclusion that courts are the most appropriate body to police this aspect of their performance. That decision is in the first instance for Congress, and we therefore turn to the FDCA to determine whether in this case Congress has provided us with "law to apply." If it has indicated an intent to circumscribe agency enforcement discretion, and has provided meaningful standards for defining the limits of that discretion, there is "law to apply" under § 701(a)(2), and courts may require that the agency follow that law; if it has not, then an agency refusal to institute proceedings is a decision "committed to agency discretion by law" within the meaning of that section.

[The Court then examined several provisions of the Food and Drug Act, and concluded that none of the Act's enforcement provisions provided the required "law to apply." The policy statement on which the court of appeals relied "was attached to a rule that was never adopted. Whatever force such a statement might have, . . . we do not think the language of the agency's "policy statement" can plausibly be read to override the agency's express assertion of unreviewable discretion. . . ."]

[Justice Brennan concurred, and Justice Marshall concurred in the judgment.]

COMMENTS AND QUESTIONS

1. How far does *Heckler v. Chaney* reach? Suppose the administrator of the Environmental Protection Agency announces that she believes that the technology-based requirements of the Clean Air Act are inefficient, and as a result she will no longer institute enforcement actions against violators of these requirements. Is that decision reviewable?

---

[4] We do not have in this case a refusal by the agency to institute proceedings based solely on the belief that it lacks jurisdiction. Nor do we have a situation where it could justifiably be found that the agency has "consciously and expressly adopted a general policy" that is so extreme as to amount to an abdication of its statutory responsibilities. See, e.g., *Adams v. Richardson*, 480 F.2d 1159 (1973) (en banc). Although we express no opinion on whether such decisions would be unreviewable under § 701(a)(2), we note that in those situations the statute conferring authority on the agency might indicate that such decisions were not "committed to agency discretion."

The Clean Air Act requires the administrator of the Environmental Protection Agency to set National Ambient Air Quality Standards (NAAQS) for a limited subset of air pollutants. At present, NAAQS exist for six air pollutants. Section 109(d)(1) of the Clean Air Act, 42 U.S.C. § 7409(d)(1), provides:

> Not later than December 31, 1980, and at five-year intervals thereafter, the Administrator shall complete a thorough review of the criteria published under section 7408 of this title and the national ambient air quality standards promulgated under this section and shall make such revisions in such criteria and standards and promulgate such new standards as may be appropriate in accordance with section 7408 of this title and subsection (b) of this section.

Suppose that the administrator fails to undertake the five-year review required by section 109(d)(1). Is this (in)action judicially reviewable after *Heckler v. Chaney*?

2. How might a failure to institute rule-making proceedings be distinguished from a failure to enforce a statute? Lower courts have held that a failure to institute rule-making proceedings is not entitled to the presumption of unreviewability that *Heckler v. Chaney* confers on a failure to enforce a statute. They have reasoned that decisions not to institute rule making are likely to be subject to less frequent legal challenges, are more likely to turn on questions of law than fact, and that the Administrative Procedure Act itself gives interested persons a right to petition for rulemaking and requires the agency to state the grounds for denying such a petition. Administrative Procedure Act §§ 553(e), 555(e).

3. The Clean Water Act, section 309(a)(3), provides:

> Whenever on the basis of any information available to him the Administrator finds that any person is in violation of [conditions of permits for discharge of pollutants into surface waters], he shall issue an order requiring such person to comply with such section or requirement, or he shall bring a civil action in accordance with subsection (b) of this section.

Subsection (b), referred to in this passage, states that the administrator "is authorized to commence a civil action for appropriate relief . . . for any violation for which he is authorized to issue a compliance order under subsection (a)." Suppose that a citizen group brings a lawsuit against EPA to claim that a polluter has violated the conditions of its discharge permit, and suppose that the group's claims are factually accurate. May a court, after *Heckler v. Chaney*, force the EPA to bring an enforcement action against the violator? For one of several cases answering "no," see *Sierra Club, Grand Canyon Chapter v. Whitman*, 268 F.3d 898 (9th Cir. 2001).

◼ Concluding Note

The following reaction to *Heckler v. Chaney* returns us to some of the themes developed in earlier chapters:

Judicial review of agency inaction raises a number of distinctive problems. Perhaps agency inaction is like a prosecutor's failure to act, which is, as the *Heckler* Court said, traditionally unreviewable. It is possible that Article II of the Constitution [which vests the executive power in the President] gives the executive branch immunity from judicial supervision of prosecutorial discretion. Moreover, the private law model of administrative law makes a distinction, as did the *Heckler* Court, between "coercive" intrusion on common law interests and "noncoercive" failure to act.

On the other hand, the [Administrative Procedure Act] does allow judicial review for agency action "unlawfully withheld or unreasonably delayed," § 706(1), and it defines *action* to include "failure to act," § 551(13). Moreover, it is possible to question whether a sharp distinction between *action* and *inaction* can be sustained in a regulatory-welfare state. In some sense, the government is always acting (at least through the common law of property, contract, and tort), even if the particular agency at issue appears to be sitting on its hands. . . . Mightn't the distinction between action and inaction depend on a form of private law thinking that the rise of that state has repudiated? In this view, the belief that "action" is especially troublesome, or coercive, and that "inaction" is not a proper source of legal concern, depends on pre–New Deal assumptions, to the effect that common law rights are "real" and that new statutory rights are less important or in some sense privileges or gratuities. Perhaps these assumptions have generally been repudiated by the legal culture and should no longer form the basis for judge-made law.

Stephen G. Breyer, et al., *Administrative Law and Regulatory Policy: Problems, Text, and Cases* 861 (1999)

The modern regulatory state seems to break decisively from the earlier system in which the government's role consisted of enforcing the rights, duties, and liabilities imposed by the common law. The common law nevertheless continues to play an important role in the modern regulatory state. Consider, for example, the extent to which the political dynamics described throughout this chapter arise from the fact that citizens, corporations, labor unions, and other groups have their resources as a result of the common law. Yet, is it possible to escape entirely from the legacy of the common law? Desirable? Or, indeed, would it be more desirable to return to a system in which common law rights, duties, and liabilities played a larger role than they do in the modern regulatory state?

The Regulatory and Administrative State in the Twenty-First Century: New Perspectives

IV

B ecause there is no reason to think that the regulatory and administrative state reached its final form in the twentieth century, we conclude this book with materials designed to help you think about what might come next. We have included materials on regulatory techniques and styles more common outside the United States (though not absent within it, as you will see), in part because you should think about the possibility that innovations in regulation flow across borders. You should be in a position to evaluate the alternative regulatory techniques described in this part both normatively (how well do they respond to the underlying rationales for regulation?) and descriptively (what are the practical constraints on their adoption and implementation?).

Comparative Approaches

14

This chapter introduces you to some comparative perspectives on the problem of regulating risk. The materials are drawn from studies of environmental regulation in Great Britain and Japan. As with all study of comparative law, there are gains and risks from reading these materials.

The main advantage, for our purposes, is that the materials can open our minds to alternative ways of doing things that might not be apparent if we simply looked at the United States. The main risk is that we might end up thinking that the comparative materials provide "models" for alternative approaches that could simply be transplanted to the United States. However, the ways a legal system approaches a problem are deeply embedded in the nation's general culture. At the very least, transplants must be adapted to the legal culture into which they are imported.

A Great Britain

This section begins with a classic comparative look at the "policy styles" of Great Britain and the United States. Although much has changed in the twenty years since Vogel wrote this book, Vogel's basic account of the adversarialism of the United States, in contrast to the corporatism of Great Britain, remains well taken.

> ■ *National Styles of Regulation: Environmental Policy*
> *in Great Britain and the United States*
> DAVID VOGEL
> pp. 21–28 (Cornell University Press, 1986). Reprinted
> with permission of David Vogel

. . . .

On balance, the American approach to environmental regulation is the most rigid and rule-oriented to be found in any industrial society; the British, the most flexible and informal. The United States makes more extensive use of uniform standards for emissions and environmental quality than does any other nation; the British, with a handful of exceptions, employ neither. The United States requires the preparation of elaborate environmental impact statements; their use remains optional in Britain. The United States makes virtually no use of industry self-regulation to improve environmental quality; the British rely on it extensively. Regulatory authorities in America take companies to court more frequently than those of any other country; prosecution in Great Britain is extremely rare. The thrust of American environmental regulation has been to restrict administrative discretion as much as possible; in Britain regulatory officials remain relatively insulated from both parliamentary and judicial scrutiny. While environmental regulation in Great Britain has exhibited remarkable continuity over the last three decades, only in Japan has the direction of environmental policy changed as rapidly over the last twenty years as it has in the United States. And while the saliency of environmental issues in different countries has varied over time, over the last fifteen years in no nation has environmental policy been the focus of so much political conflict as it has in the United States.

The most striking difference between the environmental policies of Great Britain and the United States has to do with the relationship between business and government. While in every industrial nation businesses have had to confront an increase in environmental regulation since the late 1960s, no other business community is so dissatisfied with its nation's system of environmental controls as the American business community. In Great Britain, by contrast, the relations between the two sectors have been relatively cooperative. Not only do regulatory officials tend to believe that virtually all companies are making a good-faith effort to comply with environmental regulations, but in the scores of interviews that I conducted with corporate executives in Great Britain, including several with the subsidiaries of American-based multinationals, not one could cite an occasion when his firm had been required to do anything it regarded as unreasonable. In fact, the British business community has been among the most consistent defenders of its nation's system of environmental controls in the face of efforts by the European Economic Community to "harmonize" Britain's regulatory policies with those of other European nations.

In America, environmental regulation has seriously exacerbated tension between business and government: each tends to accuse the other of acting in bad faith. Many American executives and students of regulation blame environmental regulation for many of the difficulties that have confronted the American economy in recent years. It has been accused of reducing productivity, increasing inflation and unemployment, impairing the rate of new capital formation, needlessly delaying important new investments—particularly in the area of energy—creating additional paperwork, and diverting corporate research and development expenditures from productive to nonproductive uses. But while there is no shortage of explanations for the poor performance of British industry in the postwar period, environmental regulation is not among them. Significantly, while both the Thatcher government and the Reagan administration have sought to reduce the burdens of government on industry, only the latter has attempted to make any substantial changes in environmental policy.

Is the relative lack of tension between government officials and industrial managers in Britain due to the latter's "capture" of the former? How do the two countries compare in regard to the effectiveness of environmental regulation? While American rules and regulations enacted since 1969 do demand more from industry, environmental quality has not improved more rapidly in the United States. Instead policy implementation in the United States has become more contentious. While it is difficult to make cross-national comparisons of policy effectiveness, on balance the two nations appear to have made comparable progress in controlling industrial emissions, safeguarding public health, and balancing conservation values with industrial growth. . . .

My argument is *not* that either nation's environmental controls have been effective, but that Britain's emphasis on voluntary compliance has not proved any more—or less—effective in achieving its objectives than the more adversarial and legislative approach adopted by policy makers in the United States. American regulatory policy has been more ambitious, but as a result it has produced greater resistance from business. British regulatory authorities demand less, but because their demands are perceived as reasonable, industry is more likely to comply with them.

Is environmental regulation less contentious in Britain because compliance has been less costly? Over the last decade, both nations have devoted approximately the same share of their gross national product to pollution control. While particular American industries have incurred heavier compliance costs than their British counterparts, they have also been more able to afford them. On balance, business opposition to environmental regulation in the United States has less to do with economics than with politics. It is not that the American system of regulation is an adversarial one because the costs of compliance are so high; rather it is the adversarial nature of American environmental regulation that makes both the direct and indirect costs of compliance appear excessive. It is the way in which environmental policy is made and implemented—not the direct cost of complying with it—that accounts for the resentment it has aroused within the American business community and the relative lack of such resentment on the part of the British business community.

Administrators in Britain enjoy substantially more discretion than their counterparts in the United States. Less bound by fixed standards, they are able to tailor regulations to the particular circumstances of individual firms and industries. Moreover, the rules they issue tend to be based on a consensus among engineers and scientists. . . . This is particularly true in the highly controversial area of risk assessment. In America, on the other hand, regulatory officials have often found themselves pressured by the courts and the Congress to make and enforce rules that are perceived as both unreasonable and arbitrary by the firms that have to comply with them. American environmental regulations have tended to be technology-forcing, while British regulatory requirements have been tied to both the technological and financial capacity of industry to comply with them. The British system also imposes fewer administrative and legal costs on industry. Because the pace of policy innovation is more gradual, moreover, the British system creates less uncertainty on the part of corporate planners. In sum, environmental regulation may have similar environmental and economic impacts in the two countries, but its political consequences differ substantially. . . .

What is the origin of these national differences in regulatory style? The approaches of the British and American governments to the regulation of corporate social conduct were not always so dissimilar. Government-business relations were highly adversarial during the period of rapid industrial growth in both societies: modest initial efforts to temper some of the worst abuses associated with industrial development met with strong and effective resistance from each nation's industrial community. To read the novels of Charles Dickens or Upton Sinclair is scarcely to be impressed by any substantial differences in the politics or cultures of government regulation in the two societies during their industrial revolutions. The patterns of business-government relations subsequently underwent substantial change in both nations. There are important similarities between the pattern of government regulation of industry established during the 1860s and 1870s in Great Britain—the period of mid-Victorian reform—and that of the Progressive Era in the United States. Both nations established systems of regulation that substituted statutory controls for the common law, provided officials with substantial discretion, made minimal use of prosecution, placed a high value on technical expertise, and encouraged regulatory authorities to act as educators rather than as policemen.

In many respects, the contemporary British approach to regulation resembles the pattern of government regulation adopted in the United States at both the state and federal levels during the Progressive Era. In America, however, the politics and administration of social regulation changed substantially in the late 1960s and early 1970s, becoming more centralized, more legalistic, more visible, and more contentious. This shift can be seen not only in environmental regulation but also in consumer protection and occupational health and safety. Why did one nation respond to its citizenry's increased concern with the externalities associated with industrial growth during the 1960s by making only marginal modifications in the approach to regulation that it had developed a century earlier, while the other chose fundamentally to transform its strategy for controlling the social dimensions of corporate conduct?

In brief, the mid-Victorian style of regulation proved resilient because it rested on three elements: a highly respected civil service, a business community that was prepared to defer to public authority, and a public that was not unduly suspicious of either the motives or the power of industry. Together these three elements make possible a system of regulation based on a high degree of cooperation and trust between industry and government. The legacy of Progressivism, by contrast, proved ephemeral in large measure because America remained very much a "business civilization"—a society in which civil servants continue to enjoy relatively low status, in which business has remained highly mistrustful of government intervention, in which much of the public tends to mistrust both institutions. As a result, while the consultation of industry by regulatory officials continued to be regarded as legitimate in Britain, in America cooperation between industry and government became identified with a betrayal of the public trust. . . .

Students of American politics have invariably viewed the United States as the most conservative of capitalist polities: its government plays a marginal role in the allocation of capital, it has relatively little public ownership, and its citizens appear to be uniquely committed to the values of capitalism and private enterprise. Yet this portrait of American "exceptionalism" is incapable of accounting for the fact that on balance the United States has attempted to adopt a more coercive approach to the regulation of corporate social conduct than any other industrial society. The United States remains exceptional, but, at least with respect to this dimension of business-government relations, this exceptionalism is precisely the opposite of what much of the literature on American politics would have led one to expect. . . .

COMMENTS AND QUESTIONS

1. What are the differences between the "policy styles" of the United States and Great Britain? What are the risks associated with the British style?

2. The British style is one example of what some scholars call *corporatism*. In this system, organized interest groups participate *directly* in the development and implementation of regulations. In its longest-established form, the leadership of national labor unions meets with the leadership of some organization of which all manufacturers in an industry are members. Perhaps under the supervision of government representatives, these leaders hammer out a regulatory policy acceptable to both sides, and that policy becomes law—sometimes because the leadership group has been delegated lawmaking authority, sometimes because the legislature routinely ratifies the agreement. Corporatism occurs at the level of implementation as well, with representatives of labor unions at each plant working with the manufacturer's managers to implement regulatory policies. (Note the contrast between corporatism and interest-group pluralism, where interest groups influence regulatory policy and implementation indirectly, by lobbying legislatures and regulatory agencies.)

    Historically, corporatism has been used most often in developing workplace policies. Corporatism is possible where there are appropriate organizations—in the example we've used, national-level labor unions and national organizations of employers in the relevant industries. Even with respect to workplace policy, such organizations might not exist. Corporatism structures are even harder to develop in other policy areas. How can you decide which organizations, if they exist, should participate in developing and implementing environmental policy? In the next chapter, you will examine some reform proposals that have a corporatist tinge.

3. In light of the apparent convergence in outcomes between the two countries, does it matter which approach to regulation one takes?

4. Not everyone paints as rosy a picture of the British system as Vogel does. Discussing the British approach to workplace safety, sociologist Steve Tombs has observed that a formal system of safety committees in which workers participated arose at approximately the same time that trade unions in general were becoming marginalized. Thus the formal appearance of worker control gave way to the reality of what Tombs called a "cycle of regulatory non-enforcement." Tombs also notes that workplace death and injury rates increased during this same period. Steve Tombs, *Law, Resistance and Reform: "Regulating" Safety Crimes in the UK*, 4 Social & Legal Studies 343 (1995).

5. In addition, according to one study that examined forty British enterprises "varying in size, risk and unionization of the workforce," "self-regulation was shown to operate only under a very narrow range of conditions. . . . It is most successful in companies that have a 'natural interest' in safety . . . matters, due to the high risk of the production process or the social 'visibility' of the company. The management of companies other than these large and hazardous sites [is] not highly motivated and therefore less likely to comply (proactively) with regulations or invest capital in safety projects." The author argues that "in certain situations more vigorous enforcement is required in order to obtain a significant and enduring change in the approach of employers to compliance with health and safety regulation." The study is described in Ton Wilthagen, "Reflexive Rationality in the Regulation of Occupational Safety and Health," in

Reflexive Labor Law: Studies in Industrial Relations and Employment Regulation (Ralf Rogowski and Ton Wilthagen eds., 1994).

6. In recent work, Vogel has recognized that much has changed since he compared the policy styles of the United States and Great Britain. In fact, Vogel has observed, the United States and Europe (including Great Britain) have to some extent "switched places" in terms of regulatory approaches. The European Union is now widely regarded as taking a more "precautionary" approach to environmental risks than the United States has embraced. Vogel attributes the changing regulatory style in Europe to increased public support for environmentally protective regulation, the growing influence of the European Union as a regulatory body, and several large regulatory failures (including Great Britain's bungled response to the outbreak of mad cow disease). He believes these developments have begun to put pressure on the consultative regulatory style described in his earlier book. See David Vogel, *The Hare and the Tortoise Revisited: The New Politics of Consumer and Environmental Regulation in Europe*, 33 Brit. J. Pol. Sci. 557 (2003). (For a skeptical perspective on the claim that Europe has embraced precaution more enthusiastically than the United States has, see Jonathan B. Wiener, *Whose Precaution After All? A Comment on the Comparison and Evolution of Risk Regulatory Systems*, 13 Duke J. Comp. & Int'l L. 207 (2003).)

B Japan

This section takes us to Japan and introduces us to a more collectivist vision of justice than we have seen in our studies of the U.S. regulatory system. As you read the material by Sanders, think about how the problem of mercury pollution would have been addressed by the U.S. system.

■ *Courts and Law in Japan*
JOSEPH SANDERS
In *Courts, Law, and Politics in Comparative Perspective* (Herbert Jacob et al. eds., Yale University Press, 1996). Reprinted with permission of Yale University Press

Air and water pollution created one of the most serious postwar problems faced by the Japanese government. Japan's recovery from the war was built on a foundation of rapid industrial growth. Inevitably the goal of rapid economic development came in conflict with the ideal of a clean and safe environment. Pollution problems first surfaced in the mid-1950s. Not until the mid-1960s, however, did they dominate the national political agenda, culminating in a body of new legislation in 1970 that made Japan a leader in pollution control. The history of the fight against pollution reveals how citizens can use the courts to receive redress, but also how regimes can discourage litigation as a method of dispute resolution.

Japanese pollution disputes are forever linked with Minamata, a small city in a fishing and agricultural region in the far south of Japan. The town was the home of the Chisso Corporation, which made chemical fertilizers and, later, plastics. In the early fifties birds and cats in the area began to act strangely, which local fishermen called the "disease of the dancing cats." Within a year or so the humans also began to exhibit symptoms, including trembling, numbness in limbs, and vision and speech problems. Eventually many victims became bedridden, and 40 percent died. Initially some thought the disease was the result of hygienic deficiencies, and victims felt a sense of shame for their illness. However, by 1956 it was discovered that the probable cause of the illness was the consumption of local fish. By 1958 it was clear to the victims that the source of the illness was pollution by the Chisso Corporation. Victims formed a mutual assistance society to negotiate with Chisso, and their claim strengthened when researchers discovered in 1959 that the illness was the result of people eating fish poisoned with mercury. The victims and the local fishermen's union sought compensation and were rebuffed by Chisso, who claimed the cause of their disease was "scientifically ambiguous." The fishermen's response was to storm the factory and take the plant manager hostage overnight. Finally Chisso agreed to mediation and settled with the local union but offered no compensation to the victims or unions in adjacent communities. A sit-in at the factory gates followed and the mediation committee recommended a ¥74 million ($200,000) payment to the victims collectively. When the victims refused, the mayor and other officials in the town threatened to dissolve the committee, leaving them with nothing. Faced with this threat, the mutual assistance society settled for very small sums of money: ¥300,000 ($830) per person for deaths, ¥100,000 ($280) annual payment for the disabled, and ¥20,000 ($55) for funeral expenses. More important, the company included a clause in the agreement saying this was a full settlement of present and future claims.

After the 1959 agreement there was a hiatus in the Minamata dispute for several years, and had there been no other pollution problems it might have stood as an example of informal dispute settlement accomplished without the use of the courts or litigation. Chisso continued to deny that there was clear proof that mercury caused the problem and found a powerful ally in the government, which actively covered up existing evidence that Chisso's effluents poisoned the fish and thwarted further research into the problem. Most telling, perhaps, was the government's decision to remove the question of the cause of Minamata disease from the Ministry of Health and Welfare and give it to the Ministry of International Trade and Industry (MITI).

The effort to evade the issue began to unravel when, in 1964, another strange disease of unknown cause arose in Niigata Prefecture. The symptoms were similar to Minamata disease, and the victims' diet consisted of fish from a local river. Not surprisingly, upstream a factory owned by Showa Denko used the same process Chisso used in Minamata. A new study by the Niigata University Medical School was again suppressed by MITI and government funding for the research was halted. This time, however, the report was made public and the victims, with the help of leftist lawyers, sued Showa Denko in 1967. Within two years suits followed in the Yokkaichi air pollution case, the Toyama cadmium poisoning case, and the Minamata case. Collectively these became known as the Big Four pollution cases.

Upham* notes that many of the victims at Minamata were reluctant to join in a lawsuit against Chisso. Doing so brought attention to the fact that one was sick and

---

*[Editors' Note: Frank Upham, *Law and Social Change in Postwar Japan* (Harvard University Press, 1987).]

Community perspective

might threaten the economic well being of an organization that paid 45 percent of the Minamata city taxes. Eventually the victim group split into three factions: one group brought suit, one entered into direct negotiation with Chisso, and a third agreed again to mediation organized by the Ministry of Health and Welfare. The mediation group reached a new agreement with Chisso in 1970, providing for maximum awards of ¥2 million ($5,500) and annuities of ¥50,000 ($140) per person.

Those who did sue in the Minamata case and the other pollution cases were called selfish for pursuing their own ends ahead of the good of the community and other victims. When the litigation began, few thought the plaintiffs stood much of a chance. As the cases progressed, however, victory became possible. The trial courts substantially liberalized the standard of proof for negligence. An opinion in the Yokkaichi case emphasized the high degree of care required in selecting an industrial site and declared that the defendant had a duty to use the best available technology regardless of economic feasibility. Such rules cause a negligence rule to approximate strict liability rules, where proof of a lack of care is unnecessary. The courts also relaxed the proof of causation by allowing the plaintiffs to prevail without showing a "precise medical cause" of their injury. Eventually, the Minamata plaintiffs who pursued a litigation strategy received up to nine times the 1970 mediation awards, with the largest individual awards approaching ¥18 million ($60,000).

Surprisingly, the court award was a starting point for still further negotiations. The plaintiffs demanded and received a promise that all victims, including those who had not been a party to the suit, would receive equal treatment. Equally important, the president of Chisso knelt before the victims and apologized. Later the Chisso Corporation issued the following public apology.

> Chisso deeply apologizes to those patients and their families already in great poverty, who experienced further suffering from contracting Minamata disease, who suffered as a result of Chisso's attitudes, and who experienced various types of humiliation and, as a result, suffered from discrimination by local society.
> Furthermore, Chisso deeply apologizes to all of society ... for its regrettable attitude of evading its responsibility and for delaying a solution, as this caused much inconvenience to society.

Eventually, some Chisso executives were convicted of manslaughter.

It was not only Chisso and its victims, however, who lost a good deal in the pollution controversy. The government lost as well. Upham argues that the threat to the government was significant. First, of course, was the lack of faith and trust that inevitably followed disclosure of the government's role in the cover-up. Even more important, according to Upham, was the fact that the Big Four cases "challenged the ... self-image of the Japanese as preferring harmony to conflict. In addition to exposing underlying social conflict, the pollution experience had also demonstrated that rights assertion and litigation could be valuable tools in achieving social justice."

The pollution suits had a direct effect on the political agenda in Japan. They threatened to undermine the mediation and conciliation based approaches to disputing that had been developed before and after World War II and that had been attempted in the 1959 and 1970 Minamata mediation agreements. As Upham notes, "the very posing of fundamental social questions as legal issues meant that...informal, closed, particularistic decision-making process...would be subject to public and judicial scrutiny, if not actual judicial usurpation." To avoid this the government...passed a series of strict pollution control statutes...[and] created a new system to identify and mediate pollution disputes.

Pollution control was in some ways the easiest goal to achieve. Within a decade Japan had moved from being one of the most polluted developed countries to having a relatively clean environment. Much of this was done with legal devices once again borrowed from the West, this time ideas from environmental statutes in the United States. This was an essential first step to diffuse citizens' movements....

The centerpiece of the government's legal response to the pollution crisis is the Law for the Resolution of Pollution Disputes. This law creates a three-tiered system to identify, investigate, and resolve disputes. At the local level, complaint counselors consult with residents, investigate reports of pollution, and advise people as to steps they might take following a pollution incident. Pollution review boards at the prefect level are designed to settle complaints that have become disputes. The members of the board tend to be law professors, retired judges, and attorneys. They can mediate, conciliate, and arbitrate disputes between private parties and between citizens and the government. At the national level, the Central Pollution Dispute Coordination Committee also can mediate, conciliate, and arbitrate disputes, either at the request of a complainant or on its own initiative. In addition, it has wide ranging fact-finding powers.

The dispute law attempts to investigate and resolve disputes while they are still small and is similar to mediation systems in other areas.

> The stated purpose was to provide relief to pollution victims that would be cheaper, faster, and more effective than litigation, but the drafter's goals were clearly more ambitious than simple dispute processing. Third-party intervention, in particular governmental intervention, was also touted as consistent with Japanese tradition and responsive to the Japanese preference for informal, noncontentious modes of conflict resolution.

The statute has had the desired effect. Throughout the 1970s complaint counselors processed hundreds of thousands of complaints, and the mediation system handled hundreds of disputes. By the 1980s environmental litigation was greatly reduced, and plaintiffs usually lost as the litigation has moved from questions of public health to the more ambiguous agenda of quality-of-life issues. Much of what a claimant might wish to achieve could be achieved through the mechanisms established under the dispute law, the compensation law, and environmental impact hearings. The Supreme Court also helped to minimize the benefits to bring suits...by denying them the right to injunctive relief against the government. It remains to be seen if the 1993 Fundamental Act for the Environment, along with proposed changes in Japanese civil procedure laws, will cause the courts to become more open to litigation in the future....

The Japanese civil justice system offers another window into Japanese society, albeit one that has often been misunderstood. Some have argued that the civil justice legal structure reflects a set of cultural values which dictate that one should [forgo] redress of injury in the name of the common good. Indeed, the interwar conciliation statutes were sometimes justified by an appeal to the cultural value of harmony. It was said that the statutes ensured that social disputes would be re-solved according to Japanese morals, and at the center of "moral" resolution was an emphasis on harmony that made a demand for recognition of one's rights itself an unworthy act. As we can see from the pollution cases, this belief has remained a central part of Japanese ideology. It is reflected in "a tendency to regard lawsuits as a kind of vice." For example, in a 1976 survey more than 1,000 respondents in the Tokyo area were asked whether it was preferable to sue, use court-appointed me-diation, or work out disputes through private discussion. Only 8 percent thought it was better to sue, 43 percent favored mediation, and 41 percent thought it best to settle privately (8 percent did not know or had no answer).

These beliefs have created what Haley has called the "myth" of the reluctant litigant. The myth, in its most extreme form, suggests that a Japanese disputant not only would prefer to settle disputes in some forum other than formal adjudication but also would altruistically [forgo] or compromise an entitlement or a benefit to avoid formal litigation. The Minamata case indicates there is some truth to the myth, in the sense that many prefer an alternative to formal litigation when it is available.

Use of the courts has not grown enormously during the post–World War II period. In fact, the per-capita rate of cases filed for formal trial proceedings was higher during the 1920s than at any time during the post–World War II period. Since 1945 the Japanese civil litigation rate has risen slightly, from fewer than one case per thousand to approximately three cases per thousand in 1993. By way of comparison, the civil litigation rate in Arizona, a typical American state, stood at approximately sixty-four per thousand in 1992. However, one does not have to adopt a theory of universal, individual, altruistic self-denial to explain this fact.

When given the opportunity, many Japanese will behave in a legalistic fashion. As Upham notes when discussing the one-sided terms of settlement of the 1959 Minamata mediation, "One searches in vain for the paternalism, communal sense of responsibility, and preference for legal ambiguity that stereotypes about Japa-nese law would lead one to expect." The Big Four pollution cases also indicate that a substantial number of claimants will litigate when other alternatives are unavailable or inferior to litigation.

The causes of low rates of litigation are to be found elsewhere. The courts remain congested, imposing substantial delays on those who choose to litigate. More important, confronted with a legal structure such as exists . . . in the pollution dispute area, a disputant's failure to litigate is an economically rational choice. . . . In pollution cases, mediation structures and statutory compensation schemes provide a surer route to recovery than litigation.

From a sociological perspective, however, the pollution control statutes of the 1970s . . . tell us a good deal about Japanese legal consciousness. Like the criminal justice system, they are among a large number of other legal structures that min-imize formal litigation. Rosch reports how the Japanese Civil Liberties Bureau was, over time, transformed from an organization created to enforce individual rights into an organization that mediates disputes between private parties. Two formal alternatives to "ordinary litigation"—pre-commencement compromise (*wakai*) and civil conciliation (*minji chotei*)—comprise a significant part of the caseload of the summary courts. Reminiscent of interwar policy, when confronted with ris-ing litigation in various areas the government has passed statutes designed to deflect disputes from the formal tort system. The pollution statutes are the most noteworthy example, but similar statutes have been enacted to deal with drugs, vaccines, and other products. The general pattern is the same: Events generate a substantial number of suits, and the government responds with a statutory scheme that rejects the judicial system as an appropriate institution for allocating loss, deprives the legal profession of a central role, and "significantly reduces the role of individuals as an instrument of law enforcement or law reform through the enforcement, reinforcement, or assertion of individual rights."

The last point is key. This unwillingness to allow individual actors to be the primary agency of law enforcement once again reflects a societal perception of persons as contextual actors whose identity is defined by social relationships, not as individual actors whose identity is separate from the community.

This perception is due in part to the distribution of social relationships. Both within specific types of relationships and across different relationships, ties between actors in Japan are more complex and more enduring than those of Americans....

Historically, one way the legal consciousness has reflected this perception is by leaving most "law" in the hands of local communities. As Smith notes with respect to Tokugawa society: "By and large the system did allocate to representatives of groups both complete authority and total responsibility for the performance and conduct of group members, based squarely on the principles of vicarious liability and collective responsibility.... Domain [i.e., national] law was never intended to deal with civil disputes in the village, which was expected to see to it that its residents behaved according to local custom and were properly cared for if in need."... Similarly, throughout the interwar period the movement toward mandatory conciliation was justified as a way to ensure that outcomes would reflect the morality of the specific circumstances surrounding a dispute, not the formal legal rights of the parties. For example, the government report accompanying the Land Lease and House Lease statute stated, "Conciliation means resolution [of disputes] not by adjudication of the rights between the parties but rather in terms of their own morality and their particular circumstances."

The postwar solutions to pollution injuries... are a part of this long tradition. They, too, are an effort to avoid the routine legal assertion of individual, universal legal rights and are perceived by many in Japan as a reflection of Japanese cultural values. As Ramseyer notes, "Japanese barbers, taxi-drivers, and bureaucrats still lose no time in telling American law professors that the Japanese, being Japanese, think suing is un-Japanese." By restricting the ability and the incentive of individuals to litigate, the Japanese legal structure reinforces cultural norms about the relationship of people and society.

The postwar pollution controversies reveal the limits of this set of arrangements. At the beginning of the Minamata controversy, the traditional mechanisms of resolving disputes in a consensual manner clearly broke down. Even more important, so did the social contract between the government and the citizenry. The government failed in its essential obligation to provide citizens with social stability and a safe environment within which to live. This breakdown could not be remedied by consensual institutions.... [T]he pollution cases... led to widespread collective action and mass demonstrations. Litigation is a very useful companion to such actions, and those who litigated the Big Four cases often worked closely with others engaged in mass protest and direct negotiation with defendants.

The court rulings in the pollution cases reflect these extraordinary circumstances. The judiciary recognized that these were not simply private disputes. Perhaps most revealing was the criminal trial of the leader of the direct-negotiation faction of the Minamata victims, Teruo Kawamoto. He was indicted in 1972 on five counts of assault and battery. Because Kawamoto admitted to the acts with which he was charged, the trial court found him guilty, although it allowed him to turn the trial into a trial of the government's complicity in years of cover-up. On appeal the Tokyo High Court went even further, going beyond the facts surrounding the assault charges to write in a wide-ranging opinion recounting the years of negligence and worse on the part of Chisso and the government and the victims' widespread suffering and loss of dignity. The ruling compared the government's vigorous prosecution of people harmed by the pollution with its lenience toward Chisso. The concluding part of the opinion inquired into the nature of justice and cited the Anglo-American maxim that when necessary a good judge will base a decision on equity rather than the strict dictates of the common law. In the end the court concluded that the defendant's behavior was a minor infraction when compared to the government's misconduct and that the government's indictment was unjust.

The Japanese Supreme Court was not willing to affirm on the ground that there had been prosecutorial abuse in this case. It did, however, uphold the Tokyo High Court opinion, reviewed the history of the Minamata case, and concluded, "Considering all these factors, it cannot be said that the failure to reverse the High Court would be manifestly unjust."

In the pollution cases the courts played the invaluable role of an institution one could turn to when ordinary governmental institutions fail. This role was played by the Star Chamber in England before that court was corrupted by Henry VIII, and by the United States Supreme Court on occasion, perhaps most notably in *Brown v. Board of Education* when it struck down the legal structures that maintained a segregated South. In Japan, as in other societies, mediative structures cannot work without a substantial degree of trust and good faith on the part of the parties. When these break down, litigation provides a valuable alternative.

The pollution cases reveal a second point about the success of governmental efforts to restrict the use of formal litigation. Such suppression is most successful when there are effective alternatives. In the Big Four cases, the plaintiffs were presented with an unsatisfactory set of alternatives. The Minamata victims who litigated received awards many times larger than the victims who mediated. Only when nonlitigation alternatives offer results equal to or better than litigation will efforts to suppress litigation meet with substantial success. It is not an accident that after the enactment of the pollution Dispute Law, pollution litigation dropped dramatically....

COMMENTS AND QUESTIONS

1. Recall Markowitz and Rosner's description (chapter 5) of the social and legal responses to silicosis and the account of the rise of workers' compensation laws offered by Friedman and Ladinsky (chapter 6). Consider whether a purely "economic" account of such responses is supported by Sanders's description of the Japanese events.

2. Note the recurrent pattern of violence and negotiation in Sanders' account. (His source, *Law and Social Change in Postwar Japan* (1987), by Frank Upham,

provides additional detail on this recurrent pattern.) Should we make something of the apparent fact that the more rigid, legalistic U.S. approach to addressing similar problems (as described for example by Mendeloff, chapter 9) has not been accompanied by similar recurrent episodes of violence?

3. The claimants in Japan were not primarily interested in monetary compensation for the harm inflicted on them. How culturally specific do you think that is? In particular, are there any aspects of the problem of risk in the United States such that people harmed might be satisfied with some response other than compensation?

4. In other work, Sanders contrasts the Japanese legal system to that of the United States and expresses doubts that the U.S. "policy style" of "adversarial legalism" will change markedly anytime soon:

> Those who hope for a sharp turn away from adversarial legalism in the United States will be...disappointed. Living within the buffeting winds of controversy and change that are part of everyday life, it is easy to lose sight of the fact that the United States is a stable society. The fundamental sociological reason this is so is because the nation's social structure and its culture are in rough correspondence. Adversarial legalism as a set of structural arrangements reflects deep-seated cultural values that in turn help to create and maintain the structural arrangements that give them expression. Absent a fundamental change at other levels of the social order, a much stronger state or a turn from individualism, adversarial legalism will remain a defining characteristic of American civil law and particularly of American tort law.
>
> Joseph Sanders, *Adversarial Legalism and Civil Litigation: Prospects for Change*, 28 Law & Soc. Inquiry 719, 730–38 (2003)

5. You should keep in mind that the less legalistic and less adversarial style of the Japanese regulatory system does not necessarily translate into a smaller range for government intervention of some type. Political scientist Joel Rosch begins an article describing the activities of the Japanese Civil Liberties Bureau with the following observation: "A Japanese colleague...once told me that when he was living in New York he always wondered which agency of government someone went to if nobody in their apartment building would talk to them." Joel Rosch, *Institutionalizing Mediation: The Evolution of the Civil Liberties Bureau in Japan*, 24 Law & Soc'y Rev. 461 (1987).

6. An important—perhaps the most important—distinction between the U.S. and Japanese responses to pollution is reflected in the apology described by Sanders; imagine the president of W. R. Grace kneeling before the residents of Woburn, Massachusetts, and apologizing for the contamination of the residents' drinking water. (If you have seen the movie *A Civil Action* or read the book on which it is based, you know that this didn't happen.) The next series of articles deals with the role of apology in resolving legal disputes. The first article describes an experiment designed to test whether a defendant's apology affects a plaintiff's willingness to settle. What conclusion do the authors draw? Do you think the evidence supports their conclusion? If you were a defense attorney, how might you use the information provided by this experiment?

The two other articles raise questions about the moral value of apologies and their efficacy in the U.S. context. Should U.S. law move in the direction of encouraging apologies in the context of risk-creating activities? In other areas? (What criteria might there be for determining whether an area was appropriate for the expanded use of apology as a "remedy"? Consider whether Komesar's analysis (chapter 5) might suggest some guidelines.)

■ *Psychological Barriers to Litigation Settlement:*
An Experimental Approach
RUSSELL KOROBKIN AND CHRIS GUTHRIE
93 Mich. L. Rev. 107 (1994). Originally published by Michigan Law Review.
Reprinted with permission of Russell Korobkin and Chris Guthrie

. . . .

We provided subjects with a simple landlord-tenant dispute. Subjects were told that they signed a six-month lease to live in an off-campus apartment beginning September 1. After two months the heater broke down. Although they immediately notified the landlord and requested repair, the landlord failed to fix the heater. As a result, according to the scenario, the subjects spent four winter months in a cold apartment attempting to keep warm with a space heater before moving out at the end of the lease period. Throughout this time period, the subjects had continued to pay $1,000 per month in rent. After moving out, they learned from a student legal service lawyer that "there was a good chance" of recovering a portion of the $4,000 in rent paid over that four-month period of time. The lawyer gave neither a specific prediction of the likelihood of success nor any estimate of the exact magnitude of a judgment. Subjects learned that, with the assistance of their attorney, they had filed an action in small claims court against the landlord. Prior to the court date, the landlord offered to settle the case out of court for $900.

The variable tested in this scenario was the landlord's reason for failing to repair the heater in spite of the tenant's prompt request that he do so. Group A subjects learned that they had made a number of calls to the landlord, to no avail. "The landlord promised to fix your heater, but he never did. A week later, you called him again. Again, he promised to fix it, but he never did. Over the next several weeks, you called him a half-dozen times, but he did not return your calls." Group B participants received a different explanation: After the second call to the landlord, "[y]ou learned that he had left the country unexpectedly due to a family emergency and that he was expected to be gone for several months." Both Group A and Group B subjects chose one of the five usual answer choices to indicate their likelihood of accepting the $900 settlement offer.

The given explanation had a significant impact on how likely subjects were to accept the settlement offer and forgo their day in court. Knowing that the landlord did not fix the heater because he was out of the country due to a family emergency, most Group B (Family Emergency) subjects were willing to accept the landlord's offer and let the matter rest. Their mean response was 3.41 (n = 58). Group A subjects (Broken Promise), in contrast, were more likely to reject the $900 offer and risk a less favorable decision in small claims court than to accept the offer. Their average score was 2.60 (n = 60). The difference between the two groups is highly significant. Fifty-nine percent of the Family Emergency subjects said they would "definitely" or "probably" accept the settlement offer, while only 35% of the Broken Promise subjects provided those same responses. Thirty percent of the Broken Promise subjects said they would "definitely reject" the $900 settlement offer in favor of small claims court, while only 9% of the Family Emergency subjects would "definitely reject" the offer. . . .

We tested the value of the apology, empirically and in the litigation context, by adding a third group to our landlord-tenant dispute experiment. Group C (Apology) subjects received the same explanation for the landlord's failure to repair the heater as the Broken Promise subjects: the landlord repeatedly promised, but never followed through. But Apology subjects were given one additional piece of information prior to the landlord making the $900 settlement offer: "Prior to the small claims court trial, you agreed to meet with the landlord. At the meeting, the landlord apologized to you for his behavior. 'I know this is not an acceptable excuse,' he told you, 'but I have been under a great deal of pressure lately.'"

Apology subjects were more inclined to accept the settlement offer than Broken Promise subjects. Apology subjects gave a mean response of 2.93 (n = 59) compared to the 2.60 score given by the Broken Promise group. Although the difference between these means falls short of statistical significance, we find the distribution of the responses along the five-point scale enlightening nonetheless: whereas 30% of the Broken Promise subjects said they would "definitely reject" the settlement offer, only 12% of the Apology group similarly rejected the landlord's offer out of hand. Apparently, while the apology we tested did not mitigate all of the subjects' bad feelings, it provided enough vindication of the tenant[s'] moral position and sense of equity to prevent subjects from definitively rejecting the offer. Whereas the modal response from the Broken Promise group was to "definitely reject" the offer, subjects in the Apology group were more likely to select any of the other choices than the "definitely reject" option.

Moreover, we believe our experiment understates the efficacy of apology for at least two reasons. First, the apology in the scenario, as written, was not particularly forceful. Although the narration referred to it as an apology, the landlord never used the phrase I'm sorry, or any similar expression. Second, it is likely that the force of an apology resonates more when it is expressed face-to-face than when it is simply written down on paper. Given these limitations, it is surprising that our results are as strong as they are. . . .

■ *Apology Subverted: The Commodification of Apology*
LEE TAFT
109 Yale L.J. 1135 (2000). Reprinted with permission of Yale Law Journal

. . . .

Carole Coe, a criminal defense lawyer in Missouri, was trying a protracted conspiracy case in federal district court. During the course of the trial, Coe was held in contempt four times, and on the fourth finding was ordered into custody. After she apologized, the district judge vacated the contempt decree. Coe was later charged with violations of the Missouri rules of professional conduct, and, finding her guilty of professional misconduct, the Missouri Supreme Court suspended her from practice for six months. Two members of the court filed opinions "that suggested that if [Coe] would issue a public apology, they would consider changing their votes to impose only a public reprimand." Not surprisingly, Coe apologized. True to their word, the judges changed their votes and Coe was given only a public reprimand.

Some members of the court observed that Coe's apology failed to meet the markers of authentic apology. . . . One judge noted that Coe's apology was not prompted by remorse, but rather by the incentive offered by the court to reduce the penalty imposed: "Given that incentive, [Coe] apologized. Who wouldn't?" The dissent found the majority's acceptance of Coe's "post-opinion apology" an affront to precedent, her insincerity compounding "the injury to the process." While they did not use Radin's words, these judges described the process of commodification, where everything has a price, where a moral process becomes a market trade. Coe helps us see how the moral dimension of apology is easily lost when it is injected into the legal arena, even when it occurs under the scrutiny of an en banc court. When apology occurs in civil mediation, it is even more prone to commodification, more likely to be subverted. . . .

. . . If apology is to be authentic, the offender must clearly admit his wrongdoing; he must truly repent if the apology is to be considered a moral act. When an offender says, "I'm sorry," he must be willing to accept all of the consequences—legal and otherwise—that flow from his violation. If a person is truly repentant, he will not seek to distance himself from the consequences that attach to his action; rather, he will accept them as a part of the performance of a moral act and the authentic expression of contrition.

If the apology is made at the insistence of a mediator or encouraged by a lawyer as a strategic choice during a mediated proceeding, the moral process is potentially corrupted, the moral dialectic challenged. At the very least, it is proper to question the legitimacy of an apology in such a context. Such an apology occurs in an environment that values and encourages bargained-for exchange, and such an apology may be prompted more by a desire to expedite settlement than to respond to a call to repent. When the apology is shrouded with legal protection, when it cannot be considered an admission, when no legal consequence can attach to the party through the apology, apologetic discourse moves from potential to actual corruption. The moral process of apology in such a protected environment is now subverted.

This protected apology is the kind that causes me to shudder. It becomes "merely a pawn or gambit in a power game," full of words but devoid of meaning. This is the kind of apology that should be rejected and discouraged. This is not the time for an offended party to accept such an "apology"; rather, it is the time for the offended or the offended's lawyer to maintain focus on the offender's actions, not his words. This is a time to hold on to one's self-respect, not a time to trade resentment for air.

What becomes apparent from this argument is that it is not the law that corrupts the moral dimension of apology; it is the disregard of the law's reason. The law recognizes that an apology, when authentically and freely made, is an admission; it is an unequivocal statement of wrongdoing. The law permits such an acknowledgment to enter the legal process as a way to allow the performer of apology to experience the full consequences of the wrongful act. An apology made in this context, with full knowledge of the legal ramifications, is much more freighted than an apology made in a purely social context. Now the offender must confront not only shame, fear, and humiliation, but financial risk as well. This calls on the offender to exercise great courage, one of the markers of a truly moral act.

When lawyers, legislators, judges, and mediators disrupt this process by viewing apology in utilitarian terms, they subvert the moral potential of apology in the legal arena. When the performer of apology is protected from the consequences of the performance through carefully crafted statements and legislative directives, the moral thrust of apology is lost. The potential for meaningful healing through apologetic discourse is lost when the moral component of the syllogistic process in which apology is situated is erased for strategic reasons. This is why I write: to remind all of those involved in mediation that apology is a moral process, that moral meaning attaches to the purpose for which the performative utterance of apology is employed. . . .

- *Does Law Mean Never Having to Say You're Sorry?*
  Going to Trial over a Case Is Costly, Frustrating—
  and Can Perhaps Be Avoided with a Simple Apology
  STEVEN KEEVA
  85 A.B.A. Journal 64 (Dec. 1999). © 1999 A.B.A. Journal. Reprinted
  by permission

In his 49 years as a plaintiffs lawyer, Chicago's Philip H. Corboy has represented thousands of clients in hundreds of civil cases, many of them highly celebrated. During that time, he says, he has seen exactly two defendants express regret over injuries sustained by his clients.

The first came from an airline executive who wrote to convey his company's sorrow over the loss of family members in a DC-10 crash. (The executive also took the opportunity to express—futilely—his considered opinion that the families should avoid making contact with a contingency-fee attorney.)

The second contrite missive came in October after a woman was killed by a falling pane of glass while walking with her 4-year-old daughter on a street in Chicago's Loop. In a handwritten letter to the victim's husband, the CEO of the company that owns the building expressed his deep sadness over the loss, adding that the family had been in his prayers.

Corboy found the letter deeply moving, its eloquence heartfelt, and he called the chairman to thank him.

Yet Corboy doesn't characterize either letter as an apology. To him, they simply were expressions of empathy. Nor has he ever asked for an apology. "We're in the redress business, the business of seeking justice under the justice system," he points out. "The role of the tort system is compensation, not apology."

Yet, say many observers, apology is underrated and underused as a tool in legal settings. It is too often overlooked as a means for helping to resolve disputes, for serving as a lubricant to advance settlement talks, and for contributing to a solution that looks to the client's needs.

And, say proponents, becoming sensitive to the role of apology in one's practice can provide a lens through which the human side of a case—the side that is often over-looked in the hurly-burly of litigation—can be gauged.

For the lawyer who tries to cultivate the legal version of a good bedside manner, a sense of when and where an apology might prove salutary is vital.

In fact, humans have found apologies so valuable for so long as a way of mending damaged relationships that it's a wonder they are not generally seen among the many devices lawyers can employ to help resolve disputes.

Hardly a New Concept

History shows that in many societies apologies were used regularly by community leaders to resolve disputes that threatened the peace. David Link, dean emeritus of Notre Dame law school, has done extensive research into the role of these earliest lawyers, who, he says, functioned primarily as healers.

"What has happened in recent years," he says, "is that legal ethics have become almost exclusively adversarial ethics." Link prefers a healing ethic, under which apology would be a part of the picture, rather than being thwarted, as it so often is now.

However, there are reasons for lawyers to be apprehensive when clients express a desire to apologize to the other side. Despite the distinctly human need to convey and receive expressions of regret and contrition, there are legal considerations, including the concern that an apology may be tantamount to an admission of guilt or liability.

Stories abound of physicians who clam up after an unfortunate medical outcome. And yet, many patients would insist they would never have become plaintiffs if only the doctor had apologized, or at least expressed concern for their well-being.

"When you think that in the medical malpractice context somewhere around 30 percent of plaintiffs claim they wouldn't have sued if only there had been an apology, well, the costs of the system are very high," says Jonathan Cohen, an assistant professor at the University of Florida College of Law.

"You often have a vicious cycle," says Cohen, who has studied the ins and outs of advising clients to apologize. "You have a doctor who wants to offer an apology and a client who wants to get it, but the doctor says nothing out of fear of liability. So it is precisely the absence of the apology that is triggering the lawsuit."

Says Cohen, "If you're looking at how to reduce lawsuits and push settlements, the legal system should foster apology." Besides, say Cohen and others who have studied the issue, the common knee-jerk fear of apology is overblown.

Feel the Pain

"There is certainly a shyness about it," says Deborah Levi, author of an influential 1997 *NYU Law Review* article on the role of apology in mediation. "And you do have to be careful about how you make an apology. But you can get a lot of the beneficial impact with little or no risk, and often avert having things blow up."

Now a litigator at Boston's Ropes & Gray, Levi says she has learned how alternative dispute resolution, particularly mediation, can hasten the resolution of a conflict before it falls into the never-never land of litigation.

"There are ways to move things forward and thereby save time, which saves the client money," she says. A recent case of hers, for example, was settled in mediation after the plaintiff made clear to her client that, as she puts it, "He wanted blood. He wanted to inflict some pain on the defendant.

"An expression from our client that he felt pain went a long way toward solving things," she adds. Such an expression rarely is sufficient on its own to resolve a case that has already made it to mediation. But it is often part of a package that goes down more easily because it includes the element of contrition.

Even if a civil case involving an apology does go to court, it may be difficult to establish liability based on the apology alone.

In Vermont, for example, the state supreme court ruled in two medical malpractice cases that an apology by a physician for an "inadequate" operation is not an admission of liability. The court also held that an apology for a serious mistake made during surgery does not establish an element of a malpractice claim.

In addition, at least two states have statutes that encourage what they term as "benevolent gestures."

Massachusetts describes them as "actions which convey a sense of compassion or commiseration emanating from humane impulses," and excludes them as evidence of admission of liability in civil cases. Georgia also excludes actions "made on the impulse of benevolence or sympathy."

Juries, too, may look kindly on evidence of contrition. "We ought to encourage apology for those individuals for whom it's therapeutic, and we ought to allow juries to consider this," says Daniel Shuman, a law professor at Southern Methodist University in Dallas and author of an upcoming article in *Judicature* magazine on apology and tort law.

"Even though compensatory damage awards aren't supposed to take into consideration the magnitude of the wrong, . . . almost all the research shows that that's exactly what juries do. . . . If the defendant says, 'I was just not there, I wasn't thinking and I feel awful about it,' the jury may conclude that he's not as culpable as someone who is not repentant."

For a Therapeutic Result

The work of William Schma, a circuit judge in Kalamazoo, Mich., is, like Shuman's, informed by a school of thought known as Therapeutic Jurisprudence. TJ, as it is commonly called, asks judges and lawyers to consider, at each juncture in a legal process, whether the course of action they are considering is likely to lead to a result that is therapeutic—that is, contributing to the psychological health and well-being of the people involved.

For Schma, the issue of apology is one that highlights the defects in a system that, he says, overemphasizes adversarial relationships. For example, he says, insurance companies include provisions in policies that prohibit parties from apologizing after an auto accident.

"It's a perfect example of where it's at work in a very destructive way. We don't allow people to apologize," Schma says.

"Unfortunately, in the law we have tolerated the breakdown of communication so readily that we have structured it into our system. We end up separating people and making them fight with each other."

Hurt feelings, often at the heart of a plaintiff's motivation to sue, may never claim a lawyer's attention to the degree that the facts of the case do. But proponents urge giving those emotions some consideration in the calculus that determines the best approach to fostering resolution.

Positive Outcomes

Teresa J. Ayling, a litigator and mediator in Minneapolis, offers examples of cases in which expressions of remorse made all the difference.

In one, a minority student threatened to sue a Twin Cities newspaper that made him the subject of an unflattering caricature in connection with an article on activism. The newspaper provided a written apology and conducted a course in sensitivity training for its staff, thus averting a lawsuit.

In another case, a dissident member of a professional organization in St. Paul sued when she was suspended from the group and threatened with expulsion for disrupting meetings. She was restored to full membership when she agreed to apologize to the group, says Ayling. She dropped the lawsuit.

Ayling, an employment lawyer who has represented both employees and management, says the lack of an apology is frequently the crucial factor leading to legal action. "I have dealt with many employees who have experienced difficulties in the workplace—harassment or other types of bad behavior—and they will say, 'If only they said they were sorry and wouldn't do it again, it would have been just fine.'"

Lawyers who would advise clients on the effectiveness of apologies should first consider the nature of the injury. There must be more than a physical or tangible injury; there also must be a feeling of having been wronged—either willfully or through neglect or disregard. This, says Shuman of SMU, is the intangible hurt.

"It is fair to be compensated for the physical hurt. There's no way that words can make that go away. They can't pay the rent or the hospital bills. But words can often help with the intangible pains."

Cohen of the University of Florida law school sees this as a matter of "taking the insult out of the injury," leading to a decoupling of apology from liability, which he favors. When viewed that way, many lawyers say, apologizing has little if anything to do with admitting fault.

"It's about empathy and compassion. It has nothing to do with admitting fault," says David Erickson, senior counsel for Intermountain Health Care, a Salt Lake City–based company that owns two dozen hospitals in Utah, Wyoming and Idaho. For example, just after an incident, "People aren't in command of all the facts. They're not going to say, 'We committed negligence.' Usually, you don't even know that, anyway. The thing to do is express your concern and empathy, then let the patient participate in what would make things right for him or her. If you refuse to acknowledge the suffering, you don't allow people to heal."

A former plaintiffs lawyer, Erickson says that in nearly 20 years of law practice he has never seen a case in which someone is sued because he or she apologized.

Reversing the Equation

The reverse—suing because no apology was forthcoming—is commonplace, he says. Erickson is particularly sensitive to the issue: He counsels physicians to express their feelings to patients who have suffered when something has gone awry.

According to Dr. Aaron Lazare, chancellor of the University of Massachusetts Medical Center and a recognized authority on apology, both sides gain by a simple expression of sympathy and concern for the injured person in a heartfelt way. "'I'm awfully sorry you've had so much pain,' or 'I can see what you're going through' are empathic statements, not admissions of guilt, and I think they can help a lot," he says.

Rules Do Matter

As important as what to say are where and when to say it. Immediately after the damage is done is the most natural occasion, where the urge to apologize is strongest. However, such statements are not covered by Federal Rule of Evidence 408, or its state spin-offs, which protect most apologies when they are made during settlement talks, but not in the immediate aftermath of the event that gave rise to legal action.

So it is a good idea to limit full-dressed apologies—the kind in which responsibility is acknowledged—to settlement talks or mediation. But be advised: Although mediation is the forum most widely assumed to be appropriate and safe to apologize in, there are exceptions to confidentiality protections in a number of states.

An effort is under way by the National Conference of Commissioners on Uniform State Laws and the American Bar Association to draft a uniform mediation act, the centerpiece of which is very strong confidentiality protection.

"This would include within its scope an apology," says Richard Reuben, a fellow at Harvard Law School's Negotiation Project and the reporter for the ABA committee working on the act. "The idea is that if an apology is stated during the mediation, it would fall within the scope of the act and could not be used for purposes of discovery or anything else."

Until then, caution is advised, but not to the point of refusing to consider the possible value of apologizing. On one level it can be particularly valuable.

"In torts, the whole thing is about something in the past, some harm that was done," says Levi of Ropes & Gray. "It's not something you're going to patch up. But it can really help to have a good settlement feeling going forward, a sense that it may even be possible for the same players to come together again.

"Sometimes, if you listen to your client, you can hear that she feels it's going to be a real loss, say, to not be able to do business with the person on the other side anymore. But we grow through conflict—at least that's possible in everyday life—and business is made up of personal relationships, so it should be able to happen there, too.

"Apology can really help; it's one tool for a lawyer who wants to do a real good service for the client in order to possibly get a good resolution going into the future."

COMMENTS AND QUESTIONS

1. What would Lee Taft have to say about the apologies discussed in the preceding article? Would he even call them "apologies"?

2. Recall Ward Farnsworth's study of old-fashioned nuisance cases, in which he found that parties did not bargain around the results they obtained in the legal system (chapter 2). Among other things, he found that animosity between the parties prevented bargaining. Might an apology have made room for bargaining in these cases?

▣ Adversarial Legalism

The preceding materials have identified what Robert Kagan treats as a distinctive American style of regulation, which he calls adversarial legalism. This concept is discussed in greater detail in the excerpt that follows. As you read it, keep the following questions in mind: Are there any ways in which the U.S. legal and regulatory systems could benefit from looking at systems used in other countries? If so, what adjustments would need to be made to the systems described here to work in an American context? If you think that these systems would not work in the United States, why not? Can you think of any reasons not to try similar systems even if they *would* better achieve the systems' stated goals? These questions will pave the way for our work in the next chapter, which offers proposals for reform of the U.S. regulatory system.

■ *Adversarial Legalism: The American Way of Law*
ROBERT A. KAGAN
pp. 182–87, 190–206 (Harvard University Press 2001). Reprinted
with permission of Harvard University Press

. . . .

Adversarial Legalism in Action: PREMCO's Regulatory Experience

Between 1995 and 1998 I directed a research program that conducted ten detailed case studies of multinational corporations that have similar business operations in the United States and in Europe, Canada, or Japan. Each company studied interacts repeatedly with different national regulatory regimes with respect to the same technologies and regulatory issues. By "holding the regulated entity constant" (or as close as one might expect to come to that condition), the research highlighted the differences in national legal regimes as they actually operate. For example, Kazumasu Aoki and John Cioffi, authors of one of the case studies, compared the Japanese and American regulatory regimes for industrial wastes by studying the experience of "PREMCO" (a pseudonym), a leading multinational manufacturer of precision metal parts. PREMCO operates similar factories in both countries, generating virtually identical manufacturing wastes—solvents, oily water, and contaminated metal particles.

It appears that PREMCO is an environmentally responsible corporation. The company won EPA recognition for developing a method to phase out the use of chlorofluorocarbons and trichloroethylene two years before the deadline established by the Montreal Protocol (designed to protect the earth's ozone layer). PREMCO also has instituted an aggressive corporate environmental auditing and waste reduction program, certified under the International Standards Organization's important ISO 14000 series. Aoki and Cioffi found that in both its U.S. and Japanese factories, PREMCO had instituted similar shopfloor controls on the collection and storage of wastes, as well as controls on their shipment and disposal. The two *regulatory regimes* differed sharply, however. According to Aoki and Cioffi:

> Viewed through the lenses of PREMCO's comparative experience, American
> environmental regulations are more detailed and prescriptive, and American

enforcement processes, in contrast with Japan's, emphasize the legalistic interpretation of formal regulations and the imposition of sanctions to modify economic behavior. In contrast to Japanese waste management regulation, the complex American regulatory scheme poses more difficulties in compliance, imposes substantial additional economic costs on regulated entities, and engenders antagonism and defensiveness on the part of firm personnel.

The Japanese mode of environmental regulation is far more cooperative and non-adversarial. "Administrative guidance" (*gyōsei shidō*) reduces the Japanese regulatory system's reliance on formal legal rules, sanction-based enforcement, and litigious relations. In addition, the Japanese regulatory framework tends to emphasize (1) "performance standards," rather than specific, mandatory methods of waste control, and (2) informal regulatory initiatives formulated and implemented jointly by industry associations and government ministries and agencies. In comparison with the United States, corporate antagonism towards regulators in Japan is extremely low, as the system appears to facilitate corporate acceptance of regulatory norms. Shopfloor environmental practices in PREMCO's Japanese plant are equal or superior to those imposed on the U.S. factories by prescriptive American regulations.

To illustrate this contrast Aoki and Cioffi recount the experience of AMERCO—PREMCO's subsidiary in the United States—with the environmental regulatory agency in the American state in which three AMERCO factories are located. The federal Resource Conservation and Recovery Act (RCRA) authorized the U.S. Environmental Protection Agency (EPA) to turn over the administration of the mandated waste control program to state governments, so long as the state adopts each provision of RCRA, along with implementing regulations and procedures that are at least as stringent as the federal program. The federal statute and rules, moreover, are extraordinarily detailed and prescriptive, and the regional EPA office monitors state RCRA enforcement regarding the number of violations found and penalties imposed.

Comprehension as well as compliance is a primary challenge under RCRA. The facilities managers at two AMERCO plants estimated that they spend approximately 15 to 20 percent of their time on RCRA issues. One prescriptive provision, for example, is "the twelve-hour rule," which provides that hazardous wastes must be moved from shopfloor collection containers to a satellite or a main storage area once every shift or every twelve hours. The state agency has classified waste oil as a hazardous waste under RCRA, which brings most of AMERCO's production processes within the ambit of RCRA regulations, including the twelve-hour rule.

In October 1992 state RCRA inspectors visited AMERCO Plant A, a facility that was scheduled to close two weeks later. The inspectors issued a citation to the plant manager for a number of violations, including failures to properly collect, label, and store waste oil under the twelve-hour rule and other state RCRA provisions. AMERCO's current management officials insisted to Aoki and Cioffi that these violations did not result in any environmental contamination, or even in any significant environmental risks, and none was alleged by the regulators.

In April 1993 state regulatory officials launched simultaneous inspections of AMERCO Plants B and C (located in different cities) and cited them for numerous violations similar to those found in the 1992 inspection at Plant A. Once again, according to company officials and AMERCO's outside counsel (a former state environmental agency attorney), the vast majority of these violations posed no significant risk to the environment and none had caused any environmental contamination.

At that time, each of the three AMERCO factories regarded itself as autonomous in production, management, and regulatory affairs. But to the regulators, the failure of Plants B and C to respond to the warning provided by the first inspection was symptomatic either of persistently disorganized, haphazard waste management practices or of outright defiance. Consequently, for each violation of the twelve-hour rule, regulators cited the company not merely for violating the rule but for violating labeling, sealing, and storage requirements for hazardous wastes. Thus a single violation immediately mushroomed into four or five violations; two-thirds of the approximately 150 citations issued following the 1993 inspections were derived from violations of the twelve-hour rule. Subsequently, AMERCO submitted two status reports and additional correspondence confirming rectification of all violations, and in March 1994 the agency issued a notice of compliance to both plants. Nevertheless, two months later the agency sent AMERCO a legal notice demanding $495,000 in fines for violations found during *both* inspections at *all three* plants.

The company and its attorneys, outraged by the punitive response to its efforts to remedy the violations, argued that the regulators had grossly inflated the environmental risk factor and thus the size of the fine. Aoki and Cioffi's review of the litigation file convinced them that the company managers' position was justified. Negotiations between AMERCO and the government took six months and cost the company over $50,000 in attorneys' fees—far more than the cost of remedying the original violations themselves. The government ultimately settled for approximately $200,000—$100,000 in fines, a $10,000 donation to a local environmental group, and a credit of $92,500 in return for $185,000 in capital expenditures for new pollution controls, which addressed issues that had not constituted violations and required the company to undertake waste reduction measures not mandated by RCRA.

AMERCO also hired a new environmental manager with responsibility for coordinating environmental compliance across all plants. But the bitterness between AMERCO and the agency reportedly persists, and shopfloor supervisors regard any possible agency RCRA inspection with trepidation. Moreover, a statewide political backlash, Aoki and Cioffi note, led in the late 1990s to the total repeal of the regulation that classified machine-lubricating waste oil as a hazardous waste under RCRA, reducing the risk of overregulation but increasing the risk of underregulation.

PREMCO-JAPAN's regulatory experience could hardly be more different. Rather than employing detailed, prescriptive legal rules, Japanese environmental statutes articulate broad regulatory goals. They are implemented through informal "administrative guidance" and custom-tailored agreements between individual firms and the prefects or municipal governments that enforce the national laws. Regulators view extensive consultation with regulated industry trade associations and with individual facilities as the most important means of formulating and achieving policy goals. Japanese law and administrative guidance, rather than prescribing the *means* of achieving regulatory goals—such as the U.S. twelve-hour rule—simply require industries, in Aoki and Cioffi's paraphrased translation, "to employ any necessary measures to prevent [hazardous wastes and ordinary wastes] from scattering, flowing away, seeping into the ground, or emitting an offensive odor." The sole prescriptive rule requires factories to enclose waste storage areas, post signs identifying them as such, and store wastes in sealed containers to prevent evaporation or exposure to high temperatures.

When violations of these waste storage provisions are found, Japanese law requires regulators to issue an "improvement order" containing no financial penalties. Only if an improvement order is ignored or if harm to human health occurs are officials authorized to seek legal sanctions—in this case, criminal penalties. But resort to formal enforcement mechanisms is discouraged and extremely rare. Thus, in the municipality in which PREMCO's Japanese plant is located, regulators told Aoki and Cioffi that formal sanctions have never been imposed for violation of storage standards and, in contrast with AMERCO's experience, regulators inspecting the Japanese plant have never formally found a violation of waste management regulations. Japanese regulators instead focus on monitoring the firm's waste manifests and on waste reduction as their primary regulatory goal.

Japanese environmental law requires companies and individual facilities to appoint a senior plant official as the factory's "pollution control supervisor" and in addition to appoint a "pollution control manager." These officials are then legally responsible for compliance with, and violations of, environmental regulations and orders. Here too the emphasis is on institutionalizing responsibility for overall environmental outcomes rather than for complying with specific legal rules. According to Aoki and Cioffi:

> In contrast with AMERCO, PREMCO has taken advantage of the opportunities afforded by the performance-based character of the Japanese waste storage standards to diffuse environmental knowledge, training, and responsibility throughout the firm, including to shopfloor workers and supervisors. Performance-based regulation also allows greater flexibility in compliance efforts. Perhaps as a consequence, PREMCO's Japanese managers display none of the negative attitudes towards environmental regulation and regulators detected among AMERCO's managers.

The American Regulatory Style

The PREMCO case ... replicates the findings of a substantial body of comparative sociolegal studies, covering different regulatory programs, concerning the distinctiveness of the American style of social regulation. Of course, there are a great number of regulatory programs in the United States at all levels of government. While some regulatory statutes and implementing rule books are highly prescriptive, setting out regulatory obligations in excruciating detail, others grant implementing agencies considerable discretion to balance regulatory goals and economic considerations, depending on the particular circumstances. Some American regulatory agencies have employed a legalistic enforcement style, automatically imposing fines on all detected rule violations, even those that pose no significant risk of harm, but most agencies employ a more flexible enforcement style, and some a decidedly accommodative, cooperation-seeking style. Different regional or state offices charged with implementing the same law have been found to employ different enforcement styles. Repeatedly, politicians and agency chiefs announce plans for making regulation more cooperative.

Nevertheless, as in the Aoki and Cioffi study, whenever researchers have carefully compared specific regulatory regimes in the United States with their counterparts in other economically advanced democracies, the American regulatory regime has been found to entail a number of distinctive features. First, American regulatory law almost invariably is more legalistic—that is, more detailed, prescriptive, and complex (yet confusing and difficult to comply with). Second, American regulatory regimes more often enforce the law legalistically: they are more likely to issue formal legal sanctions when they encounter rule violations, and their legal penalties tend to be much more severe. Third, relationships between regulators and regulated entities in the United States are much more often *adversarial*; legal contestation of regulatory rules and decisions, in administrative appeal boards or in courts, is far more common, both by regulated entities and by citizen advocates of stricter regulation. Fourth, regulatory rules and methods in the United States usually are more often enmeshed in political controversy and conflict, as rival interests and politicians battle over regulatory appointments and strive to lock their policy preferences into law. . . .

Implementation and Enforcement

The large, punitive fine imposed on PREMCO for only moderately serious, quickly remedied regulatory violations is far from unusual, and it contrasts sharply with the regulatory enforcement styles of other economically advanced democracies. On the other hand, it is not entirely representative of American regulatory enforcement. Some American agencies, as noted earlier, pursue a flexible or even an accommodative enforcement style, emphasizing remedial orders more than punishment. Some American agencies are too lenient, or perhaps simply understaffed and overwhelmed: reports regularly surface concerning cases in which regulatory officials declined or failed to punish obvious and significant regulatory violations. Regulated industries sometimes beat back legalistic enforcement in the political arena: in the late 1990s the meat and poultry industry managed to ward off legislation calling for larger and automatically imposed fines for regulatory violations.

Nevertheless, American regulatory officials are constantly subject to political pressures to employ legalistic methods and to prosecute regulatory violations. In response, agencies often measure their progress in terms of prosecutions brought and fines recovered. As noted in the PREMCO case, the federal EPA systematically audits state environmental agencies' records with respect to failure to seek legal sanctions against violators; periodic EPA reports criticizing failures to prosecute are sure to make newspaper headlines. When President Reagan appointed pro-business administrators to federal regulatory agencies in the early 1980s and the number of formal enforcement actions dropped, the political backlash was so intense that virtually every agency reversed course; within two or three years the number of enforcement actions in those agencies had bounced back and then surpassed levels during the preceding Democratic administration. These political pressures for legalistic regulation are manifested both in day-to-day enforcement practices by regulatory bureaucracies and in the comparative harshness of American legal sanctions for regulatory violations. Notwithstanding variation among American agencies, numerous cross-national studies in various fields of social regulation have found regulatory implementation in the United States to be far more legalistic and deterrence-oriented than in other economically advanced democracies, where enforcement officials who encounter shortcomings more consistently employ a problem-solving, cooperation-seeking style.

When John Braithwaite and colleagues compared nursing home regulation in the United States, England, Japan, and Australia, they found that enforcement in the United States was more legalistic and punishment oriented. For most violations American state nursing home regulators accept the filing of a satisfactory plan of correction, but formal legal enforcement—administrative fines, suspensions of new admissions, and license revocations—is far from infrequent, and far more common than in the other countries. Each journalistic report of substandard care triggers demands for harsher penalties. Thus nursing home regulation in the United States, Braithwaite concludes, is "tougher than nursing home regulation in the rest of the world, and much tougher than most other domains of business regulation." Moreover, Braithwaite was struck by the "culture of distrust" generated by the legalistic approach to regulation. At least until 1990, Braithwaite notes, federal training of state inspectors "emphasized the need for inspectors to be in control during [end-of-inspection] exit conferences, not to be distracted by questions raised by nursing home staff, [and] to stick to the facts of the deficiencies that require a written plan of correction"—a posture that would be shocking to nursing home regulators in Australia or England. In consequence, Braithwaite points out:

> Inspectors in the United States spend most of their time alone in a room poring over resident charts, whereas English and Australian inspectors spend most of their time out in the nursing home observing care and talking to staff, residents, and visitors about care. The theory of the recent [1990 federal statutory] reforms was that the inspection process would become more resident-centered and less document-centered. But our research team's observation is of no significant change because the new element of resident interviews has been balanced by extra documents for inspectors to check and extra pieces of paper for them to fill out.

The greater impersonality of American regulatory implementation—its often formalistic, "by the book" character—is commented on by numerous sociolegal studies.

Perhaps the most striking feature of American regulatory enforcement is the severity of its legal sanctions, both "on the books" and in practice. No other nation authorizes or imposes such weighty criminal penalties for violations of regulatory laws. In 1988 Congress increased criminal fines for insider trading to $1,000,000 for individuals and $2,500,000 for entities, and doubled the maximum prison term for violations of any securities law provision from five to ten years. In the late 1980s and early 1990s Congress upgraded most criminal offenses in environmental laws from misdemeanors to felonies, thereby increasing the maximum potential prison sentences. Under both federal and California law, courts can impose a criminal fine of up to $1,000,000 on a corporation for violations of water pollution law that "knowingly endanger another person"; for such violations individuals can be fined up to $250,000 and sentenced to prison for up to fifteen years. Congress also funded large increases in the number of EPA investigators assigned to the task of building criminal prosecutions against environmental offenders. In the 1995–1997 period, EPA sought criminal penalties against more than 250 offenders per year, as compared to an average of 40 per year a decade earlier. Increasingly, prosecutions for environmental violations have been brought against individual corporate officers, rather than corporate entities, and more than a third of those convicted are sentenced to prison.

American law also provides for much heavier civil penalties for regulatory offenses than does the law of other countries. The federal Clean Air Act and the Toxic Substances Control Act authorize civil penalties of up to $25,000 per day for ongoing violations. The EPA can impose administrative penalties equal to the financial "benefit" the violator gained by not making the required abatement. Several federal environmental statutes require violators to pay for the damages to natural resources caused by unauthorized pollution, a provision that encourages enforcement officials to act like trial lawyers seeking the largest possible damage calculations. In 1989 the Exxon *Valdez* . . . went aground in Prince William Sound, Alaska, spilling eleven million gallons of oil in the wildlife-rich waters. Exxon Corporation, after spending $2 billion on cleanup efforts, pled guilty to criminal charges and was fined $125 million, based on damages to the environment. In addition, the state of Alaska and the federal government each brought civil actions against Exxon for natural resource damages, and Exxon settled those suits for almost $1 billion. Exxon also was sued for damages by scores of plaintiffs' lawyers who signed up thousands of fishermen, Indian tribes, and other private parties allegedly injured by the spill, and a federal court jury handed down a $5 billion punitive damages award.

Exxon's simultaneous exposure to criminal prosecution, governmental civil penalties, and private lawsuits for damages for the same accident highlights another distinctive feature of American regulatory law: the unique extent to which it encourages *private* enforcement of *public* law. Congress repeatedly has provided incentives for entrepreneurial lawyers to act as "private attorneys general." Thus the federal antitrust law holds out the prospect of "treble damage" awards to plaintiffs who can prove a violation in court. The federal Truth-in-Lending Act gave debtors a cause of action against lenders who fall afoul of the statute's complex disclosure rules. To encourage suits Congress provided that prevailing plaintiffs would receive a $100 minimum award, regardless of actual losses, plus their attorneys' fees. The act further enabled enterprising attorneys to bundle thousands of bank customers together in a class action, "raising the specter of enormous damages suits for minor violations of the statute." As is typical for such one-way fee-shifting statutes, plaintiffs who lose do not have to reimburse the prevailing defendant's lawyers' fees.

One-way fee-shifting, together with the remarkable volume of reports that American corporations must file (disclosing financial data, industrial emissions, product complaints, chemical inventories, bank lending patterns, and more), has made class actions by entrepreneurial lawyers a prominent means of enforcing American regulatory law in many spheres, from securities laws to the Clean Water Act. Neither the private class action nor special incentives for private enforcement actions are prominent features of regulatory law in other countries.

The combination of criminal, civil, and private enforcement results in regulatory penalties in the United States that dwarf those in other countries. Karpoff, Lott, and Rankine, after studying legal responses to 283 environmental violations by publicly traded companies in the 1980–1991 period, wrote:

> We find that legal penalties frequently are substantial. The mean fine or damage award in our sample is $9.43 million (the median is $600,000), and the average forced compliance or remediation cost is $59.97 million (the median is $8 million). There is no robust evidence that the legal penalties are related to firm size, or, for that matter, the characteristics of the violation, the party bringing the action, or the type of action brought. These results are consistent with arguments that legal penalties are idiosyncratic and difficult to predict.

The adverse publicity that accompanies formal legal penalties adds another element to the deterrence equation. Karpoff and colleagues found that initial press announcements containing allegations of a violation are associated with losses in the defendant corporation's share value on the stock exchange (an average of 1.5 percent, and almost 2 percent if the announcement includes mention of a formal legal charge). Not surprisingly therefore, multinational corporations view American regulatory regimes as more unpredictable and more threatening than those of any other economically advanced democracy.

The Consequences of Legalistic Regulation

With its detailed and demanding rules, its potential to impose very tough penalties for deviations, its often legalistic enforcement style, and its openness to prodding by citizen advocacy organizations, social regulation in the United States is generally quite effective. U.S. securities regulation has helped make American financial markets more attractive for investors from around the world. American environmental regulation has been quite effective in reducing pollution from major industrial sources, municipal waste treatment plants, and motor vehicles. Thanks in part to regulation, supplies of food, water, and pharmaceuticals in the United States are remarkably safe, its motor vehicles have state-of-the-art safety features, and its workplaces have reduced employee exposure to harmful chemicals. Major federal and state social regulatory agencies, tightly controlled by law, are generally regarded as honest and evenhanded; stories of corruption or of favoritism for some firms over others are rare.

But would these successes persist if American regulation were less adversarial and legalistic? Even if adversarial legalism does increase the deterrent power of American regulation, do its social benefits outweigh its social and economic costs, which, as we will see, include high levels of legal uncertainty, large expenditures on legal services and proof of compliance, delays in issuing new rules and making industrial changes, and a sometimes divisive relationship between government and regulated businesses? These are not easy questions to answer but seem well worth discussing.

Is Adversarial Legalism Necessary?

Lyle Scruggs used national reports to the Organization for Economic Cooperation and Development (OECD) to analyze *rates of progress* by seventeen economically advanced democracies in reducing pollution during the 1970s and 1980s. Notwithstanding the greater prescriptiveness and deterrent threat of American environmental regulation, Scruggs found that the United States ranked thirteenth of the seventeen nations in reducing air pollution (sulphur dioxide, nitrous oxide), solid wastes (measured by reductions in municipal wastes and proportion of paper and glass recycled), and water pollution (measured by percent of population served by waste water treatment plants, and by reduction in pesticide use per acre of arable land). In terms of rates of progress, the United States trailed Germany (which ranked first) and several countries with decidedly nonlegalistic enforcement styles—the Netherlands (second), Sweden (third), Japan (fourth), and the United Kingdom (eleventh). The most important correlate of rapid environmental improvement, Scruggs found, was whether the nation had "neo-corporatist" institutions that fostered a more consensual mode of regulation—that is, whether well-organized, comprehensive industry associations were incorporated into the regulatory policymaking and enforcement process. "Pluralist" systems, in which political and economic power is more fragmented, ranked lower—and the United States is surely the most "hyper-pluralistic" of all the OECD countries.

Brickman, Jasanoff, and Ilgen compared the U.S. rulemaking process with the corporatist, more closed and informal, methods used by Great Britain, Germany, and France in setting regulatory standards for carcinogenic substances. They concluded:

> Germany has set the lowest [i.e., most stringent] standards for asbestos, nitrates, and benzene, and the United States the lowest for vinyl chloride. The United States has been the first to take significant restrictive action on many of the fourteen substances . . . but in several instances, particularly for pesticides, the Europeans have adopted final controls before the United States. After promulgation by an administrative agency, American regulations are more often amended, altered, or suspended than comparable policy measures in Europe. At least for carcinogens, then, the overall impression is of roughly comparable regulatory outputs among the four governments. Notwithstanding discrepancies in the handling of particular substances, no country appears notably more or less aggressive than another when regulatory records are compared over a period of years.

With respect to the effectiveness with which regulations are implemented, the social science evidence is limited. According to Allen, from the mid-1970s to the mid-1980s German chemical companies invested twice as much money as their American counterparts in complying with environmental protection measures. A comparative study found that Swiss, German, and French regulatory regimes reduced toxic effluents in the Rhine River more completely than did the comparable American regime for the Great Lakes. Some useful insights are also provided by the previously mentioned case studies of multinational corporations. Like the PREMCO study, they indicate that while the American regulatory processes entailed more adversarial legalism, regulatory *outcomes* in Germany, Japan, the Netherlands, and the United Kingdom, viewed in terms of the level of protection that the beneficiaries of regulation actually were accorded, were substantially similar to those achieved in the United States, at least when the targets of regulation are large corporations.

Overall, then, the existing evidence suggests that American adversarial legalism does not necessarily yield better regulatory outcomes than are achieved by economically advanced democracies in which there are relatively strong political pressures for effective regulation. Yet that does not quite settle the issue. While some other countries achieve comparable regulatory outcomes with less legalistic, more cooperative regulatory methods, it might be argued that such methods would not work in the United States. American businesses, some observers have contended, are less deferential to governmental authority than are Japanese and European firms. Perhaps, then, American regulation must be more adversarial, legalistic, and deterrence-oriented. There may be some merit to this argument, but it is worth noting that subsidiaries of American corporations in Japan or Western Europe do not have a reputation for being less compliant with those countries' regulations than are domestic companies.

Moreover, a regulation-disparaging American business culture may be just as much a *response* to the U.S. regulatory style as it is a cause of it. In a comparative study of innovation in reducing environmental harms, David Wallace observed:

> [F]irms are more comfortable innovating when risks are reduced, and risks are lower when environmental policy is stable and credible over the long term, and when regulatory processes are based on open, informed dialogue and executed by competent, knowledgeable regulators....
>
> When policy making has strong political independence from industry (e.g. due to the influence of environmental pressure groups), but dialogue is poor, environmental regulations are associated with high compliance costs. This can create a vicious circle, in which political polarization of environmental issues leads to less dialogue, resulting in poor and costly regulations and hence further polarization. However, political independence combined with good dialogue allows policy-makers to develop flexible regulatory mechanisms and schedules which accommodate innovation.

Wallace's prime example of poor industry-government dialogue and an inflexible regulatory structure is the United States. Legalistic enforcement in the United States, with its implicit distrust of the business community, also sometimes stimulates a business subculture of legalistic resistance. A Swedish occupational safety inspector told Steven Kelman, "Anytime [I'm] forced to use orders or prohibitions to achieve compliance with the regulations... it implies I've failed. I'm supposed to try to persuade; if I come in with a hammer, it makes the employer negative." If PREMCO's American managers, as noted earlier, are more antagonistic toward government regulation and regulators than their counterparts in Japan, the primary reason has been their unhappy experience with U.S. regulatory officials who wielded a legalistic, adversarial, and punitive hammer. Overall, therefore, the existing research suggests that even if American adversarial legalism adds *something* to the deterrence equation, it is not clear quite how much it adds or whether that added deterrence outweighs adversarial legalism's substantial social costs.

The Social and Economic Costs of Legalistic Regulation

Comparative research indicates that, when contrasted with cooperative modes of regulation, American adversarial legalism generates much more legal uncertainty, much higher litigation and lawyering expenses, higher compliance and opportunity costs, and more defensiveness and alienation among regulated enterprises. These troublesome costs are borne by the society at large, not merely by regulated firms.

Unpredictability

In theory, a regulatory regime that emphasizes detailed, strictly enforced legal rules should be more stable and predictable than regimes that emphasize discretionary adjustment of policies to particular circumstances. Paradoxically, however, regulatory compliance officials in multinational enterprises characterize American regulation as more legally uncertain than regulation in Western Europe or Japan. The uncertainty stems from several features of American regulatory systems. Institutional fragmentation results in overlapping imperfectly coordinated regulation by numerous local, state, and federal agencies, which may be dominated by different political parties with different regulatory policy preferences. Due to the political and legal openness of American government, business groups and advocacy organizations frequently battle for regulatory changes in agencies, courts, and legislatures, rendering American regulatory law particularly malleable. The ever-present prospect of legal and political challenge means that regulatory officials in the United States, compared to their counterparts in other countries, typically demand more scientific evidence to support permit applications, requests for variances, and new regulations, so that it is often unclear when a decision can be made and whether the studies and certifications provided will be regarded as legally sufficient.

"Q Corp." is a multinational electronic-parts maker with similar factories in California and Japan, subject to parallel water pollution regulations. Aoki, Kagan, and Axelrad found that

> Q USA environmental managers spend much more time than their Q Japan counterparts striving to assimilate and reconcile regulatory requirements that are promulgated—separately and not always consistently—by federal agencies, state agencies, municipal agencies, and courts. Q USA officials spend much more time attending meetings, communicating with regulatory enforcement officials, and going to private workshops aimed at clarifying the law and ascertaining how it applies to particular industrial operations. Q USA officials spend more time communicating with environmental lawyers retained by the company, from whom they seek a second opinion in an effort to reduce the legal uncertainty that they regularly experience.

Even so, legal uncertainty remains, because U.S. regulatory law is often in flux. To mention one example that affected Q USA, in 1987 Congress directed the states to adopt by 1990 numerical ambient water quality objectives for certain toxic pollutants. States were slow to do so, however, partly because of concern that their decisions would be challenged in the courts, either by industry or by environmentalists, for lack of an adequate scientific basis. In 1991 California promulgated the Inland Surface Water Plan (ISWP), but it omitted objectives for some bodies of water and some pollutants. The EPA then disapproved California's regulations as incomplete. Meanwhile, local California governments sued the state on the ground that the ISWP rules were too stringent and would compel them to build or renovate water treatment plants at great expense. A California court invalidated the ISWP rules for violating certain procedural requirements in the promulgation process. Back at the federal level, an environmental organization sued the EPA for failing to meet the

1987 law's deadline, and a federal court ordered EPA itself to issue regulations setting standards for the pollutants, which the agency did in 1992. The impact of the ongoing federal-state jousting on the local water treatment plant to which Q USA's effluents flow, and hence on Q USA's in-house treatment obligations, thus took years to figure out.

Lawyering Costs

Officials of PREMCO . . . assert that the corporation has spent more money on legal services for its U.S. subsidiary than for its corporate headquarters plus all its other manufacturing plants in Asia and Europe. A similar claim was made by several other multinational enterprises in the same research project. Their U.S. subsidiaries consult lawyers more often and longer on a wider range of matters, company officials say, because American law is generally more complex, changeable, and difficult to master; the legal sanctions for being wrong are generally much higher; litigation is more common; and litigation in the United States is vastly more expensive than in other economically advanced democracies.

Welles and Engel found that "Waste Corp.," a multinational builder and operator of waste disposal facilities, spent a staggering $15 million on legal services in the course of its efforts to obtain approval for a municipal solid waste landfill in California; for over ten years the company had approximately seven lawyers on retainer, busy addressing numerous regulatory agencies, two major administrative appeals, and three extended lawsuits. In Pennsylvania the same company retained seven lawyers (but only part-time) for the five years it took to get a landfill permit there, a process that entailed two administrative appeals but no lawsuits and "only" $1.45 million in lawyering costs. When Waste Corp. sought to develop a similar landfill in England, by contrast, the company retained two lawyers, part-time, for an eight-year process that also included at least one administrative appeal; its legal costs there were about $137,000. And in the Netherlands, despite having undergone two administrative appeals, the company did not have to retain lawyers at all (since lawyers are not required in administrative appeals) and spent "less than $50,000" on legal services.

Accountability Costs

Viewed in cross-national perspective, American regulatory regimes generally impose more extensive and specific requirements concerning reporting, record-keeping, testing, employee education, certifications, and so on. In addition to the costs of complying with substantive regulatory standards, therefore, regulated firms generally must spend more in the United States than they do overseas to prove that they are complying. In the early 1990s "B Corp." notified regulatory authorities in the United States, England, and the Netherlands that it had discovered that solvents had leaked from deteriorating underground tanks and pipes in its factories in those countries. The American regulators, Lee Axelrad found, demanded far more comprehensive analysis, more voluminous documentation, and more costly reports than did the European authorities. The documents submitted to American regulators for contaminated sites, B Corp. regulatory compliance officials said, would fill a four-drawer filing cabinet, compared to the less than half of a single file drawer of documentation submitted to regulators in the other countries. And behind each additional ten pages of documentation lay scores of hours that company officers devoted to research, testing, measurement, analysis, and preparation and checking of draft reports.

All in all, B Corp. officials estimated that "extra" studies, submissions, and negotiations with U.S. regulators added $8 to $10 million to the costs of designing the cleanup plan for the two sites in the United States (out of total costs per site of an estimated $22 million), whereas the "extra" regulatory accountability costs for comparable site investigations and cleanup planning in the United Kingdom and the Netherlands were negligible. Moreover, as of the time Axelrad interviewed B Corp. officials, actual remediation efforts in England and the Netherlands were well under way, but at the American sites action remained on hold while the firm still waited to learn if officials considered the company's analysis sufficient. In this case, therefore, the additional demands of the U.S. regulatory regime confirmed the maxim that when pushed too far, *accountability* (proving one has done the right thing) can displace *responsibility* (doing the right thing).

Opportunity Costs

Regulatory permitting systems are designed to slow the headlong rush of development and technological change, forcing business firms to look more carefully at potential adverse side effects before they leap. But prior regulatory review may also impose opportunity costs on society. Each month's further scrutiny of a new, perhaps more benign, pesticide means another month's delay in supplanting a more harmful pesticide. The European Union regulatory systems for prior review of genetically engineered products and new chemical substances are slower and impose longer delays on useful new products than the comparable U.S. regimes. For most products and processes, however, American regulatory regimes impose *longer* delays and *larger* opportunity costs than comparable national regimes in Western Europe. American opponents of new projects generally have more opportunities to challenge regulatory approvals in court than their counterparts in other countries, and litigation, crawling at a deliberate pace, typically results in substantial opportunity costs. The greater prospect of judicial review, moreover, often seems to make American regulatory officials more cautious and legalistic in reviewing proposals than their counterparts abroad. When Ford applied for air pollution permits for its two German plants, the time from application to approval in Germany took five months and seventeen months, respectively; the same permit applications for Ford's plants in Minnesota and New Jersey took over four years.

Adversarial legalism's combination of higher lawyering costs, accountability costs, and opportunity costs probably reaches its apotheosis in the Superfund program, launched by Congress in 1980 to clean up nonoperative hazardous waste disposal sites and abandoned dumps. In contrast to parallel European regulatory programs, the Superfund program operates as if it were designed by a plaintiffs' personal injury lawyer. Thanks in part to expansive judicial rulings, it imposed absolute, joint and several, and retroactive liability for cleanup costs on any enterprise whose wastes found their way into the disposal site—regardless of the disposer's *share* of the wastes, regardless of whether it acted lawfully under the legal rules and containment practices prevailing at the time of disposal, and regardless of any demonstrated current harm to human health. EPA enforcement officials bring lawsuits against a few large corporate waste disposers, who then sue other "potentially responsible parties" (PRPs). As Landy and Hague describe the result, "the shovels often remain in the tool shed while the EPA pursues PRPs along the slow and tortuous path of litigation." According to research in the late 1980s, Superfund litigation, studies, and related transaction costs, governmental and private, added up to at least one-third of the funds actually expended on cleanup. Yet, by 1993 EPA had recovered only $829 million of the $4.3 billion in government expenditures that it had sought to collect from PRPs. And "by mid-1990, . . . after 10 years of program operation, only sixty-three of the more than twelve hundred national Priorities List sites had been cleaned up."

The opportunity costs engendered by adversarial and legalistic methods of regulation also impede the issuance and implementation of well-founded new regulations. Confronted with statutory demands for analytical perfection and with the prospect of lengthy appeals and judicial scrutiny of their decisions, OSHA and EPA officials delayed for years the promulgation of new regulations concerning workplace health hazards and toxic air pollutants while they struggled to find the money and the time to commission more research and conduct legally defensible cost-benefit analyses. And as described by Mashaw and Harfst, the National Traffic Safety Agency's motor vehicle safety rules were so often appealed to the courts and subjected to further demands for new tests and justifications that the agency partially retreated from issuing design standards altogether.

Divisiveness

One of adversarial legalism's more intangible costs is its corrosive effect on personal and institutional relationships. When a regulatory inspector and a regulated enterprise become locked in an adversarial posture, exchange of information and cooperation, so essential to effective regulation, are often reduced. Comparing U.S., British, and Australian nursing home regulation, Braithwaite observed, "American nursing homes have higher fire safety standards than Australian nursing homes, better food and nutrition standards than English nursing homes, . . . better care planning, and more varied activities." But overall, Braithwaite concluded, quality of care in the United States is worse, primarily because the highly prescriptive and legalistic American enforcement system elicits a defensive, legalistic approach to compliance rather than a fully cooperative response. Most disturbingly, he writes:

> Ask the complaints coordinator in an Australian state to tell you the worst abuse case they have known in the past year and most tell a story of a nasty shoving or bruising incident. To the follow-up question, "Haven't you had a worse case than that? What about someone punching or slapping a resident?" some answer, "No we haven't had a complaint like that since I started in the job." Ask the same question of people in a comparable position in the United States, and they often tell a story of the murder of a nursing home resident by a staff member. . . . They will tell a story of rape of an elderly woman or of stuffing a washcloth with feces on it in the mouth of a ninety year old woman. . . . In the United States, 197 individuals were convicted criminally in 1989 for abuse of nursing home residents; there have been no such criminal cases in Australia during the five years of our study.

More routinely, Braithwaite and colleagues found, legalistic and potentially punitive American nursing home regulation has encouraged a "ritualistic" bureaucratized attitude toward compliance, oriented to meeting the letter of the law rather than its ultimate purposes. After sitting in on meetings that included a facility, director of nursing, a dietician, and a quality assurance coordinator (a position required by law), Braithwaite observed, "The question that holds center stage during quality assurance meetings is not, 'What is the best way to design this program to deliver maximum improvement in quality of care?' It is, 'What is it that they [the regulators] want of us here? What is the minimum we have to do to satisfy the requirement of having a quality assurance program?' " Defensiveness is also manifested in a disturbingly high incidence of falsification of medical and other records in order to avoid violations. Finally, Braithwaite noted that legalistically enforced prescriptive regulations, which often govern "inputs" (facility design, staffing, programmed routines, and documentation) rather than goals, tend to discourage innovation:

> [I]f an Australian nursing home achieves good outcomes for residents with staffing levels that are below the industry average, or with professionally unqualified staff, regulators might applaud this as cost-efficient accomplishment of the outcomes. Notwithstanding the rhetoric of outcome-orientation, regulatory practice in the United States will punish nursing homes that skimp on staffing inputs or that fail to use staff with mandated professional qualifications, regardless of resident outcomes.

Similar observations pervade comparative studies of other regulatory programs. Comparing "Q Corp.'s" environmental compliance programs at its factories in the United States and Japan, Aoki, Kagan, and Axelrad say, "One can think of [environmental managers in the U.S. plant] as playing legal defense instead of playing environmental offense. Q Japan officials have more time to do the latter." They go on:

> Whereas Q Japan environmental officials express dismay that Q USA has actually violated the law on occasion, Q USA officials, while clearly committed to the goals of environmental protection, seem to regard occasional violations of particular regulatory rules as something close to inevitable and as something less than shameful. In the U.S., where legal penalties often are imposed for unintentional violations that do not entail serious harm, the social stigma attached to a regulatory "violation" seems less severe than in Japan, where sanctions are reserved for serious violations.
>
> In Japan, we conclude, the regulatory regime appears to have gathered greater "normative gravity," partly because Q Japan officials view it as comprehensible, reasonable and predictable. This appears to facilitate the internalization of regulatory norms by operating managers and workers. The fluctuating, polycentric character of the American regime, in contrast, seems to *impair* the law's normative gravity (although not its threat) and to make it more difficult for regulatory norms and the idea of perfect compliance to permeate the corporate culture and the planning process.

The defensiveness stimulated by adversarial legalism also impedes U.S. administrators' efforts to institutionalize more cooperative modes of regulation. One of the most heralded of such programs is EPA's "Project XL," announced in a 1995 Clinton administration document, *Reinventing Environmental Regulation*. It authorizes state regulatory agencies to conclude agreements with regulated businesses under which, in return for relief from highly prescriptive regulatory requirements, the enterprise institutes performance-oriented pollution reduction methods that promise "superior" environmental benefits. The enterprise also must make public detailed records of its actual environmental performance and update goals in light of experience. But progress in reaching Project XL agreements has been painfully slow. Although EPA set an initial goal of fifty projects, by the end of 1997 only seven had been finally approved, with twelve under development. The reason is that they take place in the shadow of adversarial legalism. Regulators must guard against the charge that they are casting aside the law to accommodate a polluter. Each of the scores of legal waivers for particular prescriptive regulations must be arduously negotiated. A negotiation between EPA and 3M Corporation broke down in part because "EPA could not provide 3M with satisfactory assurances that compliance with XL would immunize the company from civil liability for technical violations of existing statutes." Opposition from environmental advocacy groups, which often are reluctant to give up the power they gain from prescriptive rules and rights to litigate, almost scuttled EPA's showcase Project XL agreement with Intel.

Similarly, several American states have encouraged regulated companies to adopt programs of self-audits for compliance with environmental regulations by granting them immunity from prosecution if self-detected violations are promptly disclosed and corrected. But EPA has objected that such laws should not exempt the company from fines or *federal* prosecution in certain cases, and surveys suggest that prospects of criminal liability and private lawsuits have inhibited the expansion of corporate self-audit and disclosure programs. Large American companies thus have lagged well behind their counterparts in Europe and Japan in seeking certification of corporate environmental programs under the International Standards Organization's ISO 14000 program, which commits companies to certifiable environmental management and pollution reduction programs. The lag is at least partly due to the much more legalistic and threatening regulatory environment firms must deal with in the United States.

This is not to say that all efforts to institute more cooperative modes of regulation in the United States founder, for many successful examples do exist. Rather, the point is that a regulatory system structured by adversarial legalism makes it particularly difficult to institutionalize more informal cooperative methods, and that the defensiveness it engenders often keeps American regulation from reaching the gains that would flow from cooperation.

Compared to other economically advanced democracies, the United States has been remarkably successful in fostering vibrant financial markets, promoting innovation and entrepreneurial activity, facilitating industrial restructuring, and creating new jobs. However costly American social regulation may be, the country's economic record suggests that adversarial legalism's negative economic effects have not been so large as to squelch investment in the United States or to undermine the competitiveness of American business as a whole. It may even have some positive economic effects. Compared to the closed-door decision-making methods of many other nations, American adversarial legalism provides both domestic and foreign companies greater assurance that they are competing on a relatively level regulatory playing field and that they have legal recourse against official arbitrariness or favoritism. In a nation that distrusts both government and corporate power, some observers argue, adversarial legalism helps legitimate the regulatory process because it emphasizes legal accountability, transparency, and rights of public participation.

Nor should we overglamorize the regulatory systems of other countries. It would not be difficult for those knowledgeable about particular regulatory problems to point to instances or entire regulatory arenas in which American regulation is considerably more effective and efficient, or in which other countries' regulatory regimes are poorly enforced. That said, it does not follow that adversarial and legalistic regulation is optimal for the United States. Even in a successful economy, wasteful legally imposed expenditures and regulatory uncertainties are troublesome. The United States benefits from the enormous market it offers both American and foreign businesses; they cannot afford to abandon the United States even if its regulatory system is especially costly. But those "extra" costs, even if they do not sink a dynamic economy, are often very significant for particular firms and generally wealth-depleting for the society as a whole. Regulatory waste and inefficiency are just as undesirable in the economic realm as governmental waste and inefficiency are in military procurement or highway building.

Even more significant, perhaps, are the social and political costs of adversarial regulation. Legalistic enforcement may be necessary for some firms and for some departments in larger firms, but there is little hard evidence that American businesses, overall, are less cooperative than businesses in other economically advanced democracies. Indeed, lack of cooperation between regulators and regulated enterprises often appears to be a *consequence* of adversarial legalism. In its prescriptiveness, punitiveness, and formalization of business-government relationships, American adversarial legalism induces mutual resentment, defensiveness, and mistrust. It thereby discourages the kind of cooperation that is essential to the full achievement of regulatory goals, and it gives regulation a bad name, making it more difficult to adopt justifiable new regulatory programs and rules. That is its most serious consequence.

COMMENTS AND QUESTIONS

1. If adversarial legalism is as costly (in so many ways) as Kagan suggests, why do we continue to embrace it? Whose interests are served by the system as Kagan describes it?

2. In a review of Kagan's book, Frank Cross links adversarial legalism to the structure of politics created by the U.S. Constitution. Here is an excerpt:

> For economists, a key factor of the U.S. legal system involves the presence of "multiple vetoes," which is another way of expressing the system of checks and balances, and which is contrary to the consensual corporatist system. In a country with a parliamentary system of government and relatively little judicial review power, government action can be taken by a single branch of government. In contrast, in a country having a president, a legislature, and an active judiciary, the support of three different branches (or veto points) may be required for government action. It is "American lawyers" who "have mobilized actively, in a

century-long campaign, to differentiate American courts from party and executive control" and, in the process, have produced a "moderation of the state, or division of power." Adversarial legalism captures a powerful third veto point in the courts. While Professor Kagan laments the greater autonomy of the more powerful American judiciary, this is the very judicial independence that provides a check on the other branches of government. This is the "fragmented government" of which Professor Kagan complains.

To Professor Kagan, adversarial legalism obstructs the affirmative actions of government, for political reasons. He argues that the presence of its legal trumps (or multiple vetoes) complicates the "compromise so essential to effective governance." This sort of criticism begs the important question, though, in naively assuming that government will inevitably make the appropriate compromises desirable for the optimal society. It fails to consider the possibility that our governors will choose undesirable policy compromises, either out of error or self-interest. The legal trumps of adversarial legalism also block harmful government actions. It is not self-evident whether this is advantageous or disadvantageous. Professor Witold Henisz defines "political hazards" to business by "the extent to which a change in the preferences of any one actor may lead to a change in government policy" due to the absence of political constraints, such as the courts. Adversarial legalism may thus reduce political hazards. By blocking what Professor Kagan calls "socially constructive cooperation, governmental action," or essential compromise, adversarial legalism may improve the quality of government or at least protect individual rights placed in jeopardy by government action. The multiple vetoes not only make government's affirmative infringement of rights more difficult; they also add institutions that can create rights. . . .

Professor Kagan's lament over American adversarialism includes the observation that the rate of indictment of public officials has "swelled" over recent decades and suggests that this increase reflects a "growing use of criminal investigation of public officials as a mode of partisan struggle for political advantage." Alternatively, it might demonstrate the nation's ability to identify and punish public officials who take advantage of their position through criminality. A central purpose of courts is to provide an institution to check other branches of government, and this evidence is entirely consistent with their fulfillment of that purpose. . . .

Frank Cross, *America the Adversarial*,
89 Va. L. Rev. 189, 217–19 (2003)

If adversarial legalism is indeed connected to the basic structure of our government, can anything be done about it? In Cross's view, should anything be done about it?

3. In the next chapter, we turn to several reform proposals, all of which, in one way or another, attempt to soften the rigidity of the U.S. regulatory system and move it away from adversarial legalism. As you read the proposals, keep in mind Cross's observations about the relation between political structures and regulatory policy.

Proposals for Reform

15

In this chapter, we take on the basic challenge posed by the comparative materials of the last chapter and ask whether the adversarial legalism associated with the U.S. regulatory system should and/or can be softened or reformed. The proposals for general reforms discussed in this chapter are aimed at restructuring the processes or institutions that support the legalistic and rigid U.S. system that was revealed by our comparative analysis.

First, however, we want to briefly review the many regulatory reforms that have already been offered and analyzed in previous chapters. The regulatory approaches we have discussed have not always come labeled as "reforms," and so it is worthwhile here to think about the materials we have already discussed in light of their potential to offer avenues for change.

Looking back to chapter 2, the idea that the market might be the institution of first (and sometimes last) resort for dealing with risks to human health and life is in fact a basic argument in favor of large-scale deregulation—moving from government to markets as a means of controlling risk. We have since seen that the U.S. regulatory system has not rested with markets in its responses to risk and that vast regulatory regimes have been created to deal with this problem. Yet someone who took seriously the ideas explored in chapter 2 might undertake a significant restructuring and narrowing of the regulatory system in order to let markets lead the way in controlling risk.

Reform of the common-law tort system is another possibility we have discussed. The move from individual tort actions for injuries sustained in the workplace to the administrative system of workers' compensation, considered in chapter 6, is an important example. (For a recent proposal to create an administrative compensation remedy for environmental toxic torts, see Albert C. Lin, *Beyond Tort: Compensating Victims of Environmental Toxic Injury*, 78 S. Cal. L. Rev. 1439 (2005).) Efforts to reform the tort system have also moved in the other direction, away from easing burdens on compensation and toward increasing them. Indeed, in recent years the phrase "tort reform" has become synonymous with statutory changes designed to curb recovery in tort. Limits on punitive damage awards, caps on damages for pain and suffering, and adjustments to recovery-permitting legal doctrines have all surfaced as efforts to trim tort recoveries that many view as exorbitant and unfair. Courts have sometimes contributed to this effort by denying recovery forthrightly on the ground that tort claims can go too far as a matter of policy; this is one way to understand the Supreme Court's decision in *Buckley v. Metro-North*, presented in chapter 4.

The materials on the modern regulatory state also touched on a variety of reforms. The interest-group pluralism described by Richard Stewart (chapter 8) was itself a reform of the historical understanding of agency processes. As we will see in this chapter, current reformers believe the processes associated with interest-group pluralism—in particular, notice-and-comment rulemaking by administrative agencies—have become too rigid and legalistic, and they fix on more collaborative methods of decision making as potential solutions.

In chapter 9, we also encountered potential reforms to decision-making criteria, in particular, cost-benefit and cost-effectiveness analysis. And in chapters 10 and 11, we considered a wide array of regulatory instruments. Of these, as we will see in this chapter, the market-based instruments—such as disclosure requirements and trading schemes—are the most fashionable among academics today. Indeed, these are the types of regulatory instruments Richard Stewart associates with the "reconstitutive law" that he endorses in the first reading in this chapter.

Thus we have already canvassed a range of regulatory reforms. In this chapter, we revisit—and deepen—our discussion of some of those reforms (such as the market-based measures embraced by Stewart) and introduce several new reforms into the mix.

■ Madison's Nightmare
RICHARD B. STEWART
57 U. Chi. L. Rev. 335 (1990). Reprinted with permission of the University of Chicago Law Review

In the period 1965–1980, Congress adopted sweeping new environmental, health, safety, and antidiscrimination regulatory statutes. There are at present over sixty major federal programs regulating business and non-profit organizations. Congress dramatically increased funding for direct federal social insurance and assistance programs, many of which also apply to state and local governments. Congress also greatly increased federal funding of conditional grant programs to states and localities. They now impose over one thousand different sets of conditions and requirements on state and local governments. Nonprofit organizations such as universities and health care institutions that receive federal grants are also subject to these conditions. In many cases, these grants regulate not only the recipients' substantive policies, but their organizational structure, employment practices, and decision-making procedures as well. State and local governments submit to these requirements because of irresistible pressures from local interest group constituencies that stand to benefit from the federal funds.

On Madisonian premises, the growth of these federal programs should be welcomed as an authentic expression of the public interest and an appropriate consequence of the national government's superior performance in promoting that interest. The Founders, one could argue, clearly intended for a politics of the national good to override state and local measures. National regulatory and social programs can be understood as correctives for state and local neglect fostered by indifference, the local entrenchment of privilege, or the structural impediments in a federal system to decentralized regulation and redistribution.

These confident assumptions of latter-day champions of national control have, however, been badly shaken during the past decade. It is now widely understood that the processes through which national measures are adopted and enforced do not always ensure that assertions of national power serve the general interest. Instead, they can invite the very domination by faction that Madison so desired to prevent. This realization has been sharpened by the rise of public choice theory, which applies the methodology of economics to political conduct. Public choice theorists use a more detailed formulation of Madison's faction analysis to look beyond stated public interest goals and to focus on political incentives and their interplay with institutional arrangements. Genuine aspirations for social and economic progress may be subverted by institutional structures that fail to properly reconcile the incentives of the various decisionmakers.

Several factors explain the vulnerability of national policy to factional control. First, the strength of traditional territorially-based political parties has been sapped by the rise of a new political system, one based on the national media, mass mailings, and single issue political contributions. This system is dominated by nationally-organized economic and ideological interest groups of single issue rather that majoritarian politics.

Second, federal conditional grant programs, sometimes celebrated as a form of "cooperative federalism," are used to co-opt state and local interest groups and officials. The programs do so by exploiting such groups' dependency on federal monies to convert them into supporters of federal measures rather than defenders of state and local independence.

Third, the dominant reliance on legalistic "command and control" strategies to achieve national goals inevitably involves a substantial shift of decision-making power from Congress and the President to federal bureaucracies and courts, sidestepping the already weakened federalism and separation of powers safeguards against factions.

Command and control regulatory strategies attempt to achieve national goals by requiring or proscribing specific conduct on the part of regulated entities, such as the use of specific pollution control technologies, or the adoption of particular workplace safety measures. The rapid growth of federal controls has outstripped the capacity of Congress or the President to responsibly make the thousands of decisions required to dictate conduct throughout a vast, diverse, and dynamic nation. Such decisions are either delegated within Congress to subcommittees that are subject to only weak political accountability, or outside the legislative branch to federal bureaucracies and courts—whose political accountability is even weaker.

The exercise of administrative discretion is heavily influenced by organized economic and ideological interest groups, who offer political support, threaten political opposition, and deploy legal remedies to block or delay administrative actions. Since the 1960s, it has been popular wisdom that regulatory agencies are typically "captured" by the industries that they are supposed to regulate. But economic interests beyond the regulated entities have also played a major role in influencing agency decision-making. These include labor, government contractors, agricultural interests, and other client groups. In recent years, a variety of new ideological interest groups, including organizations championing the environment, consumers, religion, the handicapped, women, abortion rights, unborn children, and others, have arisen to join the "regulation game."

Rather than offsetting each other through mechanisms of countervailing power, as Madison envisaged, these groups have instead divided power among themselves. This parcelling of power has been accomplished though congressional delegations of authority to functionally specialized bureaucracies. Each of these new power centers is dominated by the officials of the agency in question and the small number of legislators and private groups interested in that agency's decisions.

Madison identified the problem of factional domination in territorially limited government. The growth of the national regulatory welfare state, however, has spawned a new form of factional domination. By an irony of inversion, Madison's centralizing solution to the problem of faction has produced Madison's Nightmare: a faction-ridden maze of fragmented and often irresponsible micro-politics within the government. The post–New Deal constitutional jurisprudence of majoritarian politics has helped produce this result, because the demands for national regulatory and spending programs have outstripped the capacity of the national legislative process to make decisions that are accountable and politically responsive to the general interest. This has subverted the very premises of Madisonian politics. . . .

The most promising solution to Madison's Nightmare is not indiscriminate devolution and deregulation. Neither is it a constitutional counterrevolution by the courts, nor stiffer judicial controls on administrators through administrative law. The best solution is to adopt new strategies for achieving national goals in lieu of the centralizing command and control techniques relied upon so heavily in recent decades.

The ultimate goal of national measures is to ensure that decisions by state and local governments, individuals, businesses, and nonprofit organizations promote national norms and goals. Command and control regulation attempts to achieve such harmonization by dictating the precise outcome of specific decisions within these various institutional systems. Rather than dictating conduct within other institutions, the national government can instead use more indirect methods to achieve "strategic coupling" of the institutions' decisions with national norms and goals. The laws governing these institutions can be reconstituted in order to steer the overall tendency of institutions' decisions in the desired direction without attempting to dictate particular outcomes in every situation. Reconstitutive law can in many areas replace command law as a means of promoting national goals. For example, the National Labor Relations Act transformed the structure of decision-making in labor relations from a model of private employer-employee contract to one of collective bargaining, reconstituting the labor market to emphasize the collective and inframarginal voice of workers, and collective decisions by employers, rather than relying on the signals given by marginal worker mobility. . . .

. . . [T]he current reliance on central administrative commands to promote occupational health and safety in the United States could be significantly reduced if measures were taken to promote greater efforts by employers and employees to address health and safety problems. Such measures could include disclosure of information about workplace hazards, joint employer-employee selection of occupational hazard officers, and steps to promote resolution of health and safety issues through collective bargaining. This approach would substitute flexibility and innovation for the current system of rigid and relatively ineffective central commands. . . .

What reason is there to expect that a new politics, one more favorable to re-constitutive strategies, will arise? It can hardly be expected that the factions that have entrenched themselves in the congressional and bureaucratic subsystems of centralized power will lightly yield place. Current conditions, however, seem favorable to the emergence of a new politics. The public has not abandoned its aversion to centralized controls—an aversion that propelled Ronald Reagan into the White House. The deregulatory and decentralizing initiatives of the Reagan presidency were a necessary and salutary check on the growth of Madison's Nightmare. Those initiatives that have succeeded enjoy continued support and are unlikely to be reversed to any great extent. But at the same time, the public is committed to national goals of social and economic justice, public health and safety, and the protection of the environment. Reconstitutive strategies can respond to these public sentiments and create a third course between indiscriminate deregulation and devolution on the one hand, and attempted government by central decree on the other.

Moreover, there are two powerful external constraints that will force the United States to develop less cumbersome, more cost-effective alternatives to the dominant command and control form of regulation. The first is the political constraint on increased federal spending. The current system of command regulation, which requires tremendous centralization of information and decision-making, is generally far more costly for the government to administer than alternatives that place greater reliance on market incentives. In addition, command and control regulation typically gives away valuable public resources and privileges for free, including use of the air and water to emit industrial residuals, radio and television frequencies, and airport landing slots. Regulatory programs that use market-based approaches are far more likely to generate appropriate revenues for the government.

The second invigorating constraint is international competitiveness. The command and control approach penalizes investment and innovation because of high compliance costs, the restrictions imposed by uniform, inflexible directives, and the delay and uncertainty created by protracted litigation and administrative licensing and standard-setting proceedings. As it strives to restore the international vitality of its key industries, the United States can no longer afford to maintain a regulatory system that puts it at a severe disadvantage in competing with other developed nations. Greater use of market-based and other reconstitutive strategies will be needed in order to reduce compliance burdens and encourage diversity, flexibility, and innovation on the part of businesses, consumers, nonprofit organizations, and state and local governments. Such strategies will permit the United States to meet social goals that it deservedly holds important, without compromising the nation's productivity and its economic standing in the world community.

COMMENTS AND QUESTIONS

1. What is "Madison's Nightmare," and why might "reconstitutive law" be a solution?

2. Is the inversion Stewart describes—the dominance of the national government by self-interested factions—inevitable? Why won't factions also dominate state governments if the states are given more authority to choose the means of achieving federally based ends?

3. We appear to be in the midst of a restructuring of the national constitutional system of the United States. Would term limits and a balanced budget amendment in themselves alleviate "Madison's Nightmare"? Might the courts properly rely on those amendments as a reason for reinterpreting *other* constitutional rules, such as the nondelegation doctrine or the apparent demise of limits on the national legislative power? (This is a theme associated with Bruce Ackerman, *We the People* (1991).)

4. The concept of reconstitutive law is most closely associated with the German sociologist Niklas Luhmann and his student, law professor Gunter Teubner. What aspects of current workplace safety and health regulation and environmental regulation could be described as illustrations of reconstitutive law? In light of what you have learned so far, do you believe that a complete regime of reconstitutive law would be a sound way of dealing with the issue of risk in the workplace and environment?

5. One reform proposal that might fit Stewart's vision of "reconstitutive law" involves encouraging firms to monitor their own compliance with regulatory requirements. This approach is described in the next article. Orts first describes environmental programs adopted by the European Union and then assesses the viability of such programs in the United States.

■ *Reflexive Environmental Law*
ERIC W. ORTS
89 Nw. U. L. Rev. 1227 (1995). Reprinted by special permission
of Northwestern University School of Law, Northwestern
University Law Review

. . . .

[The following discussion relates to the "environmental audit" program ("Eco-Management and Audit Scheme," or EMAS) of the European Union.]

5. Environmental Programs

A participating company must develop an environmental program for each site. The environmental program describes "the company's specific objectives and activities to ensure greater protection of the environment at a given site." Measures to be taken to achieve the company's environmental objectives are set forth in the company's environmental policy. Each site's environmental program must designate "responsibility for objectives at each function and level of the company" and state how those objectives will be achieved. Specialized programs are required for "new developments" and "new or modified products, services, or processes." Environmental management programs must also include appropriate deadlines for achieving environmental objectives. Each site's environmental program must aim to achieve "continuous improvement of environmental performance." This requirement raises difficult issues concerning how a company can measure environmental performance over time.

6. Environmental Management System

The environmental management system for each particular site includes "the organizational structure, responsibilities, practices, procedures, processes and resources for determining and implementing the [company's] environmental policy." The environmental management system therefore connects the detailed environmental programs drawn up for particular sites and the overall company policy that provides direction.

The EMAS regulation stipulates that the environmental management system must comply with detailed requirements set forth in an Annex to the regulation. These requirements include the following:

- Periodical review "at the highest appropriate management level."
- Designation of "key personnel" responsible for environmental performance.
- Education and training of "personnel, at all levels."
- Documenting and monitoring activities and results.
- Setting up procedures for "investigation and corrective action" in cases of "non-compliance."
- Establishing "internal and external" communication procedures concerning environmental practices.
- Establishing "operating procedures" designed to maintain "operational control."
- Keeping a register of "legislative, regulatory and other policy requirements."
- Keeping a register of "environmental effects" deemed "significant" at each participating site.

Although this is a very tall order, a number of large companies already have many of these kinds of procedures in place. Fitting them to the EMAS mold will probably pose no great difficulty. But for smaller businesses, the weight of these requirements may prove overwhelming. For this reason, the EMAS specifically encourages Member States to provide technical assistance to "small and medium-sized enterprises" and promises EU-level support. Even with some level of governmental financial help, however, small and medium-sized businesses will likely find themselves disadvantaged if and when the EMAS becomes widely subscribed.

In addition to the potential amount of bureaucratic red tape the EMAS could generate, a primary legal problem with this part of the regulation concerns what environmental effects are deemed "significant" enough to report and monitor at each site. As one commentator asks, does "significant" environmental effect mean, for instance, that the amount of carbon dioxide emitted by a site or a company should be considered in terms of its global impact? How exactly does a company determine what environmental effects are "significant"? There is no clear answer. One possibility is for a company to perform an environmental risk assessment, for which the technology is generally available. But even with the best science, judgment calls have to be made about how small a probability or effect will be judged insignificant.

7. Company Environmental Policy

At the initial stage of the environmental review, a company must adopt an environmental policy to govern its "overall aims and principles of action with respect to the environment." The company must periodically review and alter the policy in light of the performance of the company's environmental management system and programs. The "highest management level" must adopt the environmental policy, and it must be in writing. The policy must include a statement in favor of "compliance with all relevant regulatory requirements regarding the environment." It must also include "commitments aimed at the reasonable continuous improvement of environmental performance, with a view to reducing environmental impacts to levels not exceeding those corresponding to *economically viable application of best available technology."*

A debate emerged in the negotiation of the EMAS regulation concerning the italicized "best available technology" language. The original proposal would have held participating companies to a more exacting standard: assessment of environmental performance according to applicable legal standards and "best available pollution abatement technologies." The German government strongly backed this formulation, but the Council softened the language in the final version, which requires only "economically viable" technology, deferring to objecting states led by Great Britain. The more lenient result may have the virtue of encouraging more companies to opt in to the EMAS, but "economically viable" is subject to considerable interpretation. Who is to judge what technologies are economically viable, the participating companies themselves or their reviewing, independent "verifiers"?

The EMAS regulation also goes further, providing a statement of eleven basic principles of "good management practices" upon which a company must base its environmental policy. The principles are as follows:

1. A sense of responsibility for the environment amongst employees at all levels shall be fostered.
2. The environmental impact of all new activities, products and processes shall be assessed in advance.
3. The impact of current activities on the local environment shall be assessed and monitored, and any significant impact of these activities on the environment in general shall be examined.
4. Measures necessary to prevent or eliminate pollution, and where this is not feasible, to reduce pollutant emissions and waste generation to the minimum and to conserve resources shall be taken, taking account of possible clean technologies.
5. Measures necessary to prevent accidental emissions of materials or energy shall be taken.
6. Monitoring procedures shall be established and applied, to check compliance with the environmental policy and, where these procedures require measurement and testing, to establish and update records of the results.
7. Procedures and action to be pursued in the event of detection of non-compliance with its environmental policy, objectives or targets shall be established and updated.
8. Cooperation with the public authorities shall be ensured to establish and update contingency procedures to minimize the impact of any accidental discharges to the environment that nevertheless occur.
9. Information necessary to understand the environmental impact of the company's activities shall be provided to the public, and an open dialogue with the public should be pursued.
10. Appropriate advice shall be provided to customers on the relevant environmental aspects of the handling, use and disposal of products made by the company.
11. Provisions [*sic*—Precautions?] shall be taken to ensure that contractors working at the site on the company's behalf apply environmental standards equivalent to the company's own.

Once again, these principles are ambitious. They are also sometimes vague and even contradictory. For example, good management practice no. 5 seems radically overdrawn, committing a company to taking any "necessary" measures to prevent any accident from ever occurring. It also conflicts with good management practice no. 8, which requires contingency plans with public authorities in case an accident happens "nevertheless." In addition, good management practice no. 2's idea that all of a company's new activities, products, and processes must be "assessed in advance" for various environmental effects is overly ambitious and probably impossible. Nevertheless, assuming that verifiers and regulators will allow a company the elbow room needed to interpret these general policy prescriptions in terms of the concrete realities of a particular business, the formulation and periodic reevaluation of an environmental policy is a wise idea.

8. Internal Environmental Audits

Once a company has adopted an environmental policy, an environmental program for each registered site, and an environmental management system, the EMAS next provides for periodic internal environmental auditing. Auditing must examine both the specific sites registered and the environmental management system. The regulation allows "either auditors belonging to the company or external persons or organizations acting on its behalf" to conduct internal audits. In either case, the auditor-employees or the external auditors must be technically qualified. Internal auditors must also be "sufficiently independent of the activities they audit to make an objective and impartial judgment." For example, an auditor-employee could not be in charge of the site audited if the position involved a conflict between economic performance-based pay and professional auditing standards. A participating company, if it is large enough, may therefore consider setting up a separate auditing group within corporate headquarters, perhaps basing employee salaries on environmental performance. Smaller firms may have to employ outside auditors to assure objectivity.

Auditing must comport with international standards and procedures. The on-site auditing process includes interviews with personnel, inspection of the site, and review of written records and other data. The company must state in writing the specific objectives for each audit. Because both environmental management systems and compliance with environmental regulations must be evaluated, the EMAS regulation encompasses both "management audits" and "compliance audits" as they are known in the United States.

Each audit must cover a comprehensive number of issues. The internal auditors must produce a written report with "full, formal submission of the findings and conclusions of the audit," including a statement of "need for corrective action, where appropriate." They must communicate the findings and conclusions to "top company management," and an "audit follow-up" must assure any "appropriate corrective action."

With respect to frequency of audits, the EMAS provides that each site must be audited, or each "audit cycle" completed, at least every three years. Within the one to three year range, top management determines auditing frequency. The original proposal suggested a rule-of-thumb according to estimates of severity: one year for sites with "high environmental impact," two years for those with "moderate impact," and three years for "low impact" sites. Given the vagueness in this sort of formulation, however, the final version says simply that auditing frequency should depend on an assessment of the following four elements: nature, scale, and complexity of the activities; nature and scale of interaction with the environment; importance and urgency of the problems detected; and history of environmental problems. In addition, the regulation adds flexibility in determining frequency of auditing by giving a special committee authority to establish guidelines for this part of the regulation.

In summary, the nature of the auditing contemplated under the EMAS is exhaustive. Many industrial businesses already conduct rather extensive auditing, although it is not certain how many will wish to adhere to the structure and procedures of the EMAS. If the auditing provisions are interpreted flexibly and with an appreciation of differences among types of industries and companies, the EMAS stands a good chance of success. There is nothing in the regulation to indicate this kind of flexibility will not develop. After all, each company, not the government, chooses its own internal auditors. . . .

[In the next part of the discussion, Orts develops a proposal for the United States.]

7. Incentives to Participate

Without sufficient reason for businesses to sign up for a program that would expose them to public scrutiny and incur significant costs of developing environmental management and auditing processes, any voluntary EMAS system will fail. Therefore, a number of incentives should be built in to an American EMAS to encourage participation.

First, a voluntary American EMAS should protect the confidentiality of underlying auditing reports and self-critical review of environmental performance. The reflexive processes of environmental management and auditing must be open and genuinely self-critical. A defensive reflexion obsessed with the prevention of incriminating auditing documents will not achieve the desired kind of reform. Particularly in view of the tendency toward litigiousness in American society, legal protection of internal management and auditing processes is necessary.

A new federal evidentiary privilege of self-critical analysis for internal environmental management and auditing procedures would provide the needed protection and encourage participation. However, a self-critical analysis privilege should extend only to companies that sign up for the EMAS. Previous proposals have been made for a self-critical analysis privilege for compliance programs to be established in accordance with the federal sentencing guidelines. In addition, at least four states now recognize an evidentiary privilege for environmental audits under state statutes. These laws do nothing, however, to assure the public of the good faith of a company's environmental commitment. Public disclosure of environmental reports would help to close this gap in trust. A quid pro quo for public disclosure should be a self-evaluative privilege for the underlying information gathered through professional environmental management and auditing practices.

An exception to the evidentiary rule of privilege would have to apply to an EPA investigation concerning the accuracy of the information provided in the public environmental reports. The idea is to exempt a company from the dilemma of turning up adverse information about their environmental practices and subjecting themselves to civil and criminal liability if they enter into an environmental management and auditing program. For "good" environmental companies that opt in to an American EMAS, the underlying information should be confidential, except to the extent that the EPA needs to see the information to confirm the accuracy of public reports of environmental performance.

Providing for confidentiality of internal EMAS processes would free corporations to examine the real environmental problems they face without constantly worrying that their deliberations may one day end up in court. Confidentiality is essential to assuring a reasonable level of participation. Companies would especially welcome a confidentiality privilege in light of increasing governmental reliance on criminal penalties.

A second incentive that an American EMAS should provide involves a revision of governmental policies concerning the treatment of internal environmental auditing and management in investigations and prosecutions. For companies that opt in to an American EMAS—and only for those companies—the EPA and the Justice Department should state unequivocally that underlying auditing information will not be used against participating companies, with only very limited exceptions. A new federal self-evaluative environmental privilege would reduce the need for such policy statements. But because privileges are often waived inadvertently and because disputes can arise concerning whether particular material is covered by a privilege, additional concrete assurances in the form of policy statements would give companies another reason to participate.

Third, an American EMAS should recommend revisions of the new environmental sentencing guidelines for organizations to allow automatic credits for companies that opt in. This reform should continue existing incentives for companies to adopt environmental compliance programs without the disadvantages of defensive reflexion that currently weaken the approach. An American EMAS might even consider entirely exempting participating companies from criminal prosecution in exchange for possible criminal and civil liability under second-level of EMAS regulations concerning false, misleading, or omitted information in public environmental reports.

Finally, some sort of formal recognition of businesses participating in the program should be adopted, such as an EPA-certified "Green Business" decal. A marketable logo or emblem would help tap economic consumer interest. An American EMAS could perhaps be linked with private environmental labelling efforts. Already, one American private enterprise—to some extent a spin-off of Green Sea—has devised a "Green Audit" logo that suggests this possibility.... A formal Green Business or Green Audit decal provided under the auspices of an American EMAS would provide an additional incentive for companies to participate. A government-certified emblem or logo would increase public trust in the process. In addition, given the absence of a government-sponsored environmental labelling program in the United States, there seems to be no good reason to prevent a Green Business decal from being used in advertising and marketing. To deny this use, as does the European EMAS, is to deny a significant incentive for businesses to participate. With these kinds of incentives, an American EMAS would likely become widely established, especially among large industrial companies. Assuming the basic structure of the EMAS was flexible enough to accommodate existing environmental management and auditing systems, large companies would have little reason not to participate. Given the inevitable expenses involved, small companies may have more difficulty. As under the European EMAS, small businesses should be provided with technical and financial assistance. With meaningful incentives in place, and with technical and financial support available to small businesses, an American EMAS would be likely to entice broad-based participation over time. . . .

COMMENTS AND QUESTIONS

1. Orts calls his general strategy for reform "reflexive environmental law," which he says

    aims to enlist intermediate social institutions—between "the state" and "the market"—in the tasks of environmental protection. Social understanding must inform this focus on institutions. The basic idea is to encourage internal self-critical reflection within institutions about their environmental performance. The primary regulatory method employed by reflexive environmental law is therefore procedural; it aims to set up processes that encourage institutional self-reflective thinking and learning about environmental effects. Orts, 89 Nw. U. L. Rev. at 1254.

    How is this approach different from (and similar to) Stewart's reconstitutive law?

2. Would the environmental management and audit systems described by Orts soften the system of adversarial legalism described by Kagan (chapter 14)? If so, how?

3. The article that follows describes a workplace safety initiative that shares some similarities with Orts's "reflexive" approach to regulation.

■ *Interlocking Regulatory and Industrial Relations:*
  The Governance of Workplace Safety
  ORLY LOBEL
  57 Admin. L. Rev. 1071 (2005). © 2005 by the American Bar Association.
  Reprinted with permission

. . . .

In 1995, the Clinton Administration announced "the New OSHA" initiative, designed to enhance safety, trim paperwork, and fundamentally transform the agency. The initiative described OSHA as historically having been driven by statistics, rules, and a "one size fits all" approach to enforcement and inspection. The New OSHA plan, coupled with the more general Regulatory Reinvention Initiative, was designed to "cut obsolete regulations," to "reward results, not red tape," to create "grassroots partnerships" between regulator and regulated parties, and to "negotiate" rather than "dictate." The central piece of the New OSHA was the Cooperative Compliance Program (CCP), designed to induce dangerous workplaces to enter into partnership with OSHA under the threat of targeted enforcement in the case of refusal. Employers would be given a choice to cooperate with OSHA toward effective safety programs or be subject to traditional, yet upgraded, regulation and enforcement.

A. The Pilot: Maine 200

The CCP experiment that began in the mid-1990s in Maine, the state with the nation's highest accident rates at the time. Prior to the program, the Maine office had stepped up its enforcement activities. It began targeting large employers, conducting wall-to-wall inspections, citing serious violations, and imposing increased penalties. The worksites were large and the inspections were high profiled. The area director won OSHA achievement awards for the highest number of safety citations and the largest amounts of fines in the country. But despite these efforts, the Maine office was frustrated from the inability to change the safety patterns of a wide number of firms. The process was slow and in seven years, the office was able to complete inspections at only five plants. The office director identified over-regulation—under-regulation and over-enforcement—under-enforcement problems with his compliance officers' traditional interaction with industry. The director described four problems with the traditional enforcement method. The first problem was failure to *deter prior to inspection*. Inspections were not having a significant deterrent effect on the companies the office had not inspected. Despite state wide publicity about the targeting of large paper mill plants as the first priority of the office, the inspectors felt that firms did not make any visible efforts to correct obvious violations prior to inspections. This was particularly frustrating as the zealous director realized that his office did not have the resources to inspect all of Maine's high hazardous plants within his working lifetime. The second problem was the *failure to alter behavior after an inspection* had been completed. The compliance officers found repeat violations when they returned to sites several years after completing a thorough inspection. They felt that the alterations made at the firms that were inspected were merely "temporary fixes" rather than systemic long-term reforms. The third problem was that, under certain conditions, *citing for violations and large fines was counter productive*. There were firms who exemplified real intent and willingness to change and promote safety, correcting 95% of their safety violations. With those firms, repeatedly citing for the remaining violations through augmented fines was sending a message that "there is no pleasing OSHA." The fourth problem that the Maine office saw was the most disturbing. The compliance officers saw *a disconnect between compliance with safety regulations and the safety of workers*. Maine was imposing the most fines and still had the worst injury and illness rates in the country. At many plants, over fifty percent of injuries were related to soft tissue—sprains, strains, back injuries—from repetitive motions or strenuous physical work. Yet, OSHA did not have adequate regulations for these types of injuries. The enforcement process was not well suited for the prevention of accidents for which there was only a general duty and not specific standards. The Maine officers felt that they were "just spinning on our wheels." At the same time, worker compensation premiums under the state plan were skyrocketing and deterring businesses from operating in Maine.

In 1993, the Maine office invited the 200 workplaces that had the greatest number of claims for days lost at work due to injuries to participate in the new pilot program. The targeting was made possible through newly available data from Maine's workers' compensation system. The two hundred workplaces represented forty-five percent of the injuries at Maine, but only one percent of employers and thirty percent of workers. These firms were offered the choice to work cooperatively with the agency or to face increased enforcement. Workplaces that accepted the offer for cooperation were given assistance in developing effective safety programs and were given low priority of inspection. Almost all of the firms chose partnership. OSHA reviewed the management plans and monitored their implementation. Maine 200 was proclaimed as a great success, winning Ford Foundation and government awards for innovation. Employers self-identified more than 14 times as many hazards as could have been cited by OSHA and significantly lowered their injuries rates. Worker compensation claims in Maine during the first year of the implementation of the program dropped by thirty-five percent. In the following years, worker compensation claims continued to drop.

B. "Choose Your OSHA": Nationalizing the Cooperative Compliance Program

The championed success of Maine 200 led to the decision of the Clinton Administration to expand the initiative to other states. Under the direction of Vice President Al Gore, the administration made the Maine 200 a centerpiece of the National Performance Review initiative of reinventing government. The initiative sought to first implement the pilot in seven model areas and then continue its expansion, building on the lessons from the initial expansion. The program emphasized that compliance officers should focus on reducing injuries rather than "rack(ing) up their numbers of inspections, citations, and fines. Rather, they are supposed to focus on the underlying purpose of their agency. For many, this is a radical change from the traditional regulatory mentality."

In 1996, OSHA offices in 29 states had received headquarters' approval or were in the process of development of the Cooperative Compliance Program (CCP). Area offices sent letters inviting companies to participate in CCPs or be listed for increased enforcement. Covering approximately 12,500 relatively dangerous workplaces, the program would place each worksite on a "primary inspection list," and non-participation would result in a comprehensive inspection before the end of 1999. Participating companies would be placed on a secondary list of employers not to be subject to routine inspections. This would reduce the probability of inspection by 70 to 90 percent. OSHA's role would be to assist and provide information and consultation.

Companies were given sixty days to sign an employer participation contract. While the design details varied in different states, the main requirement of all CCPs was the development and implementation of a "comprehensive safety and health program" (CSHP). A CSHP includes planning on routine employer-conducted inspections of the workplace, investigations of "near-miss" incidents, and means by which employees can complain of unsafe practices and circumstances without fear of reprisal. Employers would be required to conduct comprehensive surveys identifying risks, and involving employees in the implementation of a safety and health program. An aspect of CSHP that was particularly contested by industry was that of addressing non-standardized issues, including problems associated with ergonomics, materials handling, bloodborne pathogens, confined spaces, and hazard communication. The directive stated that "[a]n effective [safety program] looks beyond specific requirements of law to address all hazards. It will seek to prevent injuries and illnesses, whether or not compliance is at issue." Industry argued that this was an attempt to introduce ergonomics standards through the backdoor....

C. APA Rule-Making and the Abandoned Program

The resistance by industry to the expansion of the Cooperative Compliance Program (CCP) culminated in a legal action by the U.S. Chamber of Commerce contesting the adoption of the program by OSHA. In 1999, the Federal Court of Appeals of the District of Columbia held that the CCP was not properly adopted by OSHA and invalidated the program. The court accepted the appellant's argument that the program should be regarded as a rule, which the agency should have adopted through notice and comment procedure under the Administrative Procedure Act. The court therefore invalidated the directive.

Two fundamental distinctions of administrative law were at the basis of the adjudicative debate. The APA expressly exempts "interpretive rules, general statements of policy, or rules of agency organization, procedure, or practice" from the requirements of notice and comment rulemaking. Thus, the first distinction is that between "rule" and "general policy." The second distinction is between "substantive/legislative rules" and "procedural/practice rules." The two latter categories in each pair are understood to be less significant in the action of public agencies. The APA exemptions classify what Congress believed are administrative actions that require public participation in their formulation and those that do not. Courts have construed the balance between rules and practices, as well as between substantive and procedural rule-making, as that between efficiency and public participation. These distinctions aim to strike a balance between the value of public participation in agency decision-making, which underlies the notice and comment requirement, and the agency's competing interest in "retain[ing] latitude in organizing [its] internal operations." An administrative agency can avoid the cumbersome and time-consuming mechanisms of notice and comment rule-making when it defines its general practices or makes a procedural rule. As a result, these doctrinal distinctions correlate with a practice of less structured participation and the informalization of the administrative process to allow certain types of discretionary activities and preclude others.

The CCP was issued by OSHA as a "directive" rather than a "rule." OSHA therefore claimed that the directive was a "general statement of policy," not subject to rule-making requirements. And indeed, as rule-making by administrative agencies has become increasingly formalized over the years, agencies have been expanding their "non-rule rulemaking," by issuing "interpretive rules," such as policy statements and good guidance. The courts have repeatedly held that agency instructions guidelines and manual books to agency officers are not legislative rules. However, here, the court held that the directive was a rule, as it generally affected the duties and rights of employers.

Alternatively, OSHA claimed that if the directive was a rule, it was a "procedural rule," exempt from APA notice and comment requirements. Under the APA, a "substantive rule" is a rule that holds a substantial impact upon private parties. By a substantive rule, the agency approves or disapproves of the behavior of the regulated parties. A "procedural rule" is one that does not itself alter rights or interests of parties, although it may alter the way in which parties present themselves to the agency. The ambiguities of the substantive/procedural rule distinction are particularly evident when we contrast the court's treatment of the integrated governance program with cases concerning conventional inspection programs. OSHA claimed that CCP was no more than "a formalized inspection plan." By contrast, the court described the directive as the "practical equivalent of a rule obliging employers to comply or to suffer the consequences." The court explained that in practical terms, the directive placed the burden of inspection upon those employers that failed to adopt a program and would have had a substantial impact upon all employers within its purview. The court reasoned that while it was true that the program did not "formally require anything: An employer is not subject to a legal penalty for failing to join the CCP," the practical effect was that some firms would be subject to higher scrutiny. Firms in selected high industries would be inspected unless they adopted comprehensive safety and health program designed to meet standards that, in some respects, exceeded those required by law. The stated purpose of the directive—that of leveraging OSHA's limited resources—could

> only mean that the agency is intentionally using the leverage it has by virtue solely of its power to inspect. The Directive is therefore the practical equivalent of a rule that obliges an employer to comply or to suffer the consequences; the voluntary form of the rule is but a veil for the threat it obscures.

> In stark contrast to this holding, courts have generally viewed regulations regarding the method of workplace inspections as procedural rules. Targeting calculations and inspection priorities are understood as not generating a "substantial impact on rights or interests of regulated parties." Therefore, OSHA's policies governing selection of employers have repeatedly been classified as procedural rules exempt from notice and comment requirements. . . .

> In contrast, the *Chamber of Commerce* court rejected the claims about procedural inspection and voluntary choice, stating that these were "two elements of the same rule." The fact that the CCP made "beyond compliance" requirements for those choosing partnership—that is, requirements to go beyond OSHA existing standards and make comprehensive changes addressing all hazards (including ergonomics)—was understood by the court as an indication for a substantive rule. The idea of complementarity is therefore critical in the court's decision. If regulatory and governance approaches are kept separate, then OSHA is safe to experiment with both targeted enforcement plans and voluntary programs. When, however, there is an attempt to integrate sticks and carrots, the agency must follow the requirements of rule-making.

D. Cooperation through Informality I: Invisible Governance

Following the *Chamber of Commerce* decision, OSHA could have decided to go back to the drawing board and convert the CCP directive into a rule, following notice and comment procedures, a process that could have taken several years to complete. Instead, the agency announced it would abandon the Cooperative Compliance Program and keep only the targeted inspection plan. To date, OSHA has no concrete plan to revive the CCP by a formal rule-making process. Rather, the agency has adopted the inspection plan through the same computation process it had devised for CCP and continues to expand its cooperative programs . . . on a purely voluntary basis.

Critically commenting on the court's decision to invalidate the CCP, the Kennedy School of Government scholar Malcom Sparrow writes: "Regulatory agencies are more likely to face legal challenge when they declare the basis for their exercise of discretion—however rational—than when they exercise their discretion in an arbitrary manner without declaring it."

Targeting decisions, including investigations, inspections, prosecutions, and negotiations, are inevitable choices of an administrative agency. They are also decisions that often bear more impact on the regulated entity than formal judgments through sanctions and adjudication. As Ed Rubin has commented, agencies "regularly negotiate, cajole, threaten, and plead with firms and individuals. . . . The kinds of controls that might alleviate some of the fairness concerns raised by these administrative processes are absent from the APA." Indeed, OSHA has discretion in its interaction with employers at all stages of the administrative process. First, the OSH Act includes a general duty clause as well as the requirement to comply with the promulgated OSHA standards. OSHA officers therefore exercise discretion when citing for violations beyond the specific standards promulgated by the agency. Second, inspection and investigation decisions themselves are regularly used as sanctions.

For example, OSHA has used the threat of inspection as a way to move from the individual worksite to corporate-wide cooperative compliance arrangements. Similarly, inspectors routinely offer to discontinue inspections, reduce penalties, and lengthen compliance schedules in return for a commitment to implement management plans, to audit all facilities, and to implement changes across all worksites, including sites that have not been inspected. Such settlements may include detailed requirements about non-standardized issues, including ergonomics, using the general duty clause. Thus, informally, OSHA has always routinely struck deals with employers. Particularly when employers cited for violations threaten to contest the citation, compliance officers negotiate lower fines in exchange for a myriad of promises. For example, agency officers regularly downgrade citations from "willful violations" to "unclassified." OSHA's field manual permits the "unclassified" designation when an employer is willing to correct unsafe conditions "but wishes to purge himself or herself of the adverse public perception attached to a willful violation." Increasingly, settlement agreements between OSHA and employers have expanded to include such procedural and substantive requirements that OSHA could not otherwise require using the OSH Act. For example, OSHA persuades employers to create a safety manager position within the firm that will be responsible for continuous supervision of the firm's worksites or to provide training to all its employees on a particular safety procedure.

Administrative law has yet to construct "a normative model that builds on best practices in an administrative world beset by inadequate budgets, legislative imperatives, and public resistance, as well as real scientific uncertainties." In particular, administrative law is just beginning to acknowledge cooperative relationships. Mostly, it has used them as proxies for differentiating between "good" and "bad" actors during sanctioned confrontations. The narrow focus on adversarialism in formal arrangements has produced both economic inefficiencies and democratic deficiencies: "The pathologies of adversarial legalism are of immense social importance, for they are both unpredictable and enormously debilitating. They engender costly "defensive medicine," deter the assertion of just claims and defenses, distort and delay the implementation of governmental programs, undermine faith in the justice system, and invite political overreaction."

As we have seen, as a practical matter, all of the elements of the CCP were actually available before and after OSHA developed the program. Today, OSHA uses the calculus it developed for CCP as a targeting system for inspections.... [C]ooperative programs are available for firms that wish to avoid routine inspections and are willing to implement internal safety plans. All of these have been possible without APA notice and comment procedures. Yet, when OSHA attempted to integrate cooperative governance choices into its core enforcement activities the administrative process proved burdensome. The obvious consequence is that instead of integrating sticks with carrots and effectively allocating scarce resources, the agency separates cooperative and sanctioned interactions with regulated parties into fragmented activities. Cooperation is made "purely voluntary," as demanded by industry interests. Enforcement activities offer no formal choice for targeted firms prior to inspection, but expand the practice of much choice at the stage of informal negotiations. The categories of "substantive rule-making"/ "procedure"/"practice" have failed to reflect these realities of the administrative process. Regulators use discretion, choice, and flexibility in their implementation activities. Agencies continue to employ a broad range of strategies in their interaction with regulated parties. Yet most of these strategies exist below the APA radar screen. Administrative strategies that are integrated and dynamic can better counter the weaknesses of both coercion and cooperation. Flexible regulatory relations that are articulated, formalized, and designed with clear risk calculations in mind can be more effective, transparent, and legitimate than using flexibility as an informal and unwritten practice. The novel aspect of a *governance* approach to regulation is therefore not the use of flexibility in the administrative process nor is it the existence of a range of cooperative and coercive approaches. The novelty is in the formalization and integration of partnership and flexibility as key components in the work of government.

COMMENTS AND QUESTIONS

1. If you were a member of the Chamber of Commerce, would you be happy with the ultimate outcome here? According to news reports, organized labor was uncomfortable with the CCP and preferred targeted enforcement.

2. In the past, the Department of Labor has suggested legislation that would require employers to include employees on labor-management safety committees with power to shut down operations that pose unreasonable health or safety risks. These committees would also have power to review the employer's health and safety plans, investigate individual accidents and overall injury and illness records, and make recommendations to the employer for changes. As Stewart suggested, these recommendations are often defended on the ground that they would improve the ability of United States firms to compete internationally. If so, why haven't firms adopted them voluntarily? (In fact, the proposals have been strongly resisted by business.)

3. The preceding materials show that there are real difficulties in eliciting the cooperation that is an important component of "reconstitutive" regulation. How, or under what circumstances, can those difficulties be overcome? The next readings propose different versions of collaborative decision making in

regulation. Consider how, or whether, they deal with the problems associated with instituting and implementing reconstitutive regulation.

■ *Collaborative Governance in the Administrative State*
JODY FREEMAN
45 UCLA L. Rev. 1 (1997). Reprinted with permission of Jody Freeman

. . . .

[This excerpt begins with a description of a regulatory negotiation ("reg neg") and then turns to broader issues.]

Fall Protection Negotiated Rule Making

In 1994, as part of the Occupational Safety and Health Administration's revision of safety standards for the construction industry, the agency initiated a negotiated rule making on subpart R of the regulation, which governed fall protection during the erection of steel structures. The OSHA convened the reg-neg in an attempt to update badly outdated fall protection standards in an area—steel erection—that the OSHA considers to be a particularly hazardous activity within an already hazardous industry. Members of the chartered committee, chosen by the OSHA from over sixty requests for membership, included representatives of labor, management, and state and federal agencies.

The negotiation initially focused on the height at which ironworkers would be "tied off"—that is, attached to a stable structure through a lanyard or safety belt. The OSHA proposed a height of six feet, whereas both management and labor representatives proposed that it be much higher in order to preserve worker mobility. Each of the parties was committed to different starting points, and it appeared that the purpose of the negotiation would be to bargain until the parties could arrive at a compromise number.

It also appeared that the participants had conceived of the problem they were trying to resolve as one of preventing workers from falling as they moved from one task to another through a series of risky states. This conception of the problem could be expected to generate a rule imposing different tie-off requirements for different activities that a worker might perform in the course of the same job. Parties would have to define what constitutes a particular activity (such as steel connecting), agree on the degree of risk, settle on a height at which to be tied off, and choose the device by which the tie-off would be accomplished. Indeed, participants actually approached the problem in this manner: they debated the costs and benefits of choosing certain heights at which to tie workers to the structure, and they considered the activities that would properly be included within the scope of the regulation. The parties exchanged information and corrected false assumptions. For example, one participant submitted a report indicating that most ironworker fatalities occur due to decking, not steel connecting as the committee had originally thought. Other participants, impressed with the data, agreed that steel connection required more fall protection.

In the course of the discussion over different heights, parties began to generate an enormous amount of information about the causes of accidents, and the focus gradually began to shift towards creating a safer work environment. The parties began to ask each other about their safety practices. They pointed to data that attributed a large percentage of falls to design or engineering flaws in the erected steel, to workers' refusals to comply with existing safety regulations, or to a lack of worker training. The Steel Coalition explained the link between safety and the production of steel by submitting data showing that contaminants from the manufacturing process make steel more slippery. One report, jointly produced by a labor and management team, suggested that being tied off was not the only way to prevent worker falls. Many participants reinforced this point by offering data on the best shoes to wear on various surfaces in order to prevent slips.

A representative from the Steel Decking Institute argued that given this information, imposing specific standards for each activity might engender a false sense of security, as tie-off rules could not substitute for safety practices. One member of the gallery observing the negotiations, a representative from the American Institute of Steel Erectors (AISE), suggested that the committee create a certification program under which companies would be certified for steel erection on the basis of a number of features, including worker training and safety precautions. His idea was that joint labor and management teams could demonstrate in a formal, certified plan, that they could safely erect buildings. The OSHA could perform the certification itself or authorize third parties to do so.

While the discussion on certification never proceeded very far, one can imagine a scheme in which certification might have become the basis for improving workplace safety without imposing specific tie-off rules....

And yet, despite the emergence of information about safety practices, the facilitator continued to press the importance of choosing heights at which to tie workers off. As the deadline for concluding the reg-neg approached, he distributed a split the difference compromise requiring steel connectors to be tied at fifteen feet, while allowing them the flexibility to detach themselves between fifteen and thirty feet. In the end, the consensus draft rule for subpart R that emerged from the negotiation consisted of a series of such compromises. Tie-off is required, for example, for steel connection and decking above two stories or thirty feet, whichever is lower.

Based on what actually happened in the reg-neg, and not on the latent ideas about certification, one could still make the case in favor of reg-neg over traditional notice and comment. Because the parties were forced to defend their positions face-to-face, they resisted being extreme or unrealistic. Sharing data improved the informational base of the rule making. Direct bargaining forced parties to make hard compromises over which heights were appropriate for which activities, a task that would have otherwise fallen to the agency. This produced a regulation better informed by the parties' views about the most dangerous activities and the best tie-off requirements. While one cannot be certain, the resulting rule is likely to be more implementable because labor and management had a direct hand in fashioning it. Negotiations were far from acrimonious, as they gave labor and management groups an opportunity to work together. The bargains struck do not appear to undermine the public interest in safety. Finally, because the rule was produced through consensus, it will likely be less vulnerable to challenge, potentially saving all sides the costs of financing prolonged litigation.

... [T]his analysis, while accurate, fails to adequately capture what transpired. The reg-neg's potential to illustrate collaborative governance appears in the revelations about safety and the possibilities for alternatives to a tie-off rule that emerged when information was pooled during discussions. By bringing parties together in advance of [a notice of proposed rulemaking], encouraging frank negotiation, and permitting parties a hand in structuring the process, the reg-neg provided a forum in which that information was more likely to emerge. In the relatively sterile and adversarial notice and comment process, there is virtually no opportunity to build on ideas and develop solutions as a group. Here, the parties to some extent reconceived the initial problem and jointly generated an unanticipated and implementable solution. They began to engage in problem solving. Safety plans would have been more adaptive than tie-off rules because they could be updated with new information about safety practices or worker training. The proposal might also have improved relationships between labor and management, whose representatives would jointly produce the safety plans. Finally, such collaboration would have created a new allocation of enforcement authority by inserting third-party certifiers between the agency and the regulated firms. The OSHA reg-neg was pregnant with the possibility of alternatives to traditional rules, produced in traditional notice and comment, and enforced by the agency in the traditional way. Nonetheless, much of that potential went unrealized. . . .

A. *Limited Scope*

Reg-negs often generate a great deal of wasted information because of the limited scope of a rule. If a discussion reveals that the "real" problem is in fact something other than what the parties originally envisioned, the negotiating committee may not feel free to pursue it. This prompted one observer to declare reg-neg "a great procedure to solve the wrong problem." There are both strategic and legal reasons why reg-negs are limited in scope at the outset. Agencies confine reg-negs to specific and well-defined problems on the theory that narrowly defined issues are easier for parties to resolve. . . . Moreover, advocates of reg-neg unanimously agree that deadlines are critical to their success.

Limited scope helps to explain why the certification idea was never seriously considered as a potential solution in the OSHA reg-neg. Tie-off heights were a familiar, accessible solution that easily fit within the negotiating committee's mandate. . . .

But, the impulse to limit the reg-neg's scope conflicts with the reality that problem solving requires an effort not to foreclose creative ideas or new conceptions of the issues to be negotiated. Only in the process of deliberation is the appropriate scope of a problem likely to emerge. In other words, the moment when scope issues arise in a negotiation is likely also to be the moment at which the key difficulty with the statute, the preexisting regulation, or the initial conception of the problem becomes clear. This is exactly what happened in the OSHA reg-neg. The discussion of safety practices revealed that a broader class of issues was responsible for fatalities and injuries. The parties who appreciated the import of the information proposed certification. And yet, without reconceiving the negotiating committee's authority, there was no way to devise a certification scheme. The OSHA intended subpart R of the regulation to cover only tie-off heights for predefined activities. The only way to continue the OSHA reg-neg without altering its scope was to relegate the important information to the margins and retreat to a discussion of heights. The perceived need to limit the scope coupled with the pressure to conclude the reg-neg by its deadline prompted the facilitator to maneuver the parties toward compromise....

IV. The Pursuit of Collaboration

A. Legitimacy

The above analysis [illustrates] the obstacles that stand in the way of pursuing collaboration more actively. Nonetheless, . . . reg-neg . . . ha[s] some potential to address the most significant weaknesses of the administrative process. None of the various stakeholders are likely to commit themselves to collaboration as a normative goal, however, without some reassurance that the model provides accountability. In other words, if collaborative governance can serve as an alternative to interest representation and either an alternative to, or an elaboration of, the civic republican commitment to deliberation, it is fair to ask whether it provides a satisfactory theory of administrative legitimacy. How can we be sure that the products of collaboration (the rules, the permits, the institutional arrangements) will be legitimate? . . .

1. Reasons for Concern

a. Collusion

Some critics worry that collaborative processes might be vehicles through which agencies, industry, and powerful public interest groups can collude to undermine the public interest. Rather than provide an alternative to interest representation, these processes might exacerbate all of its weaknesses. Like interest representation, collaboration relies on selecting participants as representatives of interest groups. By approaching policy making as negotiation, agencies may be tempted to broker deals among repeat players, without attention to the larger public interest. Moreover, offering interest groups direct access to decision making reproduces the same opportunity for log rolling that generates legislation in the first place; it merely grants groups who were unsuccessful at the legislative drafting stage new opportunities to influence public policy at the implementation stage. Worse yet, this access will inevitably weaken regulations because negotiations tend to favor powerful groups. Unless agencies can somehow level the bargaining power of all groups, consensus agreements will inevitably lower standards because of industry's resource advantage.

b. Subdelegation

The potential for collaboration to result in broad subdelegation of agency authority might also be viewed as problematic. Institutional arrangements that empower private groups to make public policy might be unconstitutional at worst, and corrode legitimacy at best. Critics would likely view any reliance on private entities as a manifestation of the administrative state's failures, rather than as a sign of its promise. In other words, the need to rely on public-private cooperation arises only because legislators delegate more and more responsibility to agencies, together with increasingly demanding analytic requirements such as cost-benefit and risk-assessment analysis, while denying them adequate resources to implement and enforce their mandates. Under such conditions, it is not surprising that agencies welcome opportunities to reallocate regulatory responsibility. The impetus to delegate policy making and implementation is not driven by a new collaborative ethic, critics would say, but rather by desperation.

c. Corporatism

Antipathy toward a greater or reconceived role for traditionally private groups in public policy making might also be rooted in an American intolerance for corporatism. Collaborative processes that rely on shared public-private responsibility for governance would seem to pose some of the dangers of corporatist regimes, including, "serious difficulties with the fixity of their interest categories and the vestedness of their constituent organizations." The selection of certain interests to participate in decision making will always potentially empower some groups at the expense of others and will establish selected players as authorities. This risk might be minimized in what David Johnson calls a "meso-corporatist" system, in which private groups have authority to participate with government in only limited arenas over a limited number of policy issues. Still, the risk of rigidity cannot be eliminated. Moreover, even marginally corporatist institutions can be seen as coopting political dissent by institutionalizing the role of disruptive social groups in policy making. By this I mean that providing access to groups who define themselves in terms of their outsider status might undermine their role as critics of the system. Some organizations will view the participation and responsibility that collaboration portends as ultimately disempowering.

d. Unfettered Agency Discretion

Even if the threats of subdelegation and corporatism are more imagined than real, collaboration poses another danger: it may augment unchecked agency discretion. The discussion of reg-neg . . . suggests that agencies should have broad enforcement discretion within which to facilitate agreements with stakeholder groups. Indeed, one could reasonably infer from that discussion that agencies and stakeholders ought to have broad enough discretion to reconsider the limits of statutes themselves, if the scope of the problem requires it. To some extent, the collaborative model presented here overlaps with recent appeals for "reflexive regulation" and "cooperative implementation," which call for increased reliance on private entities to regulate themselves. All of these proposals require that agencies enjoy broad enough enforcement discretion to waive existing requirements under some circumstances and to negotiate "individuated" agreements with firms that may depart from the letter of the law. . . .

■ **Administrative Democracy**
JERRY FRUG
40 U. Toronto L.J. 559 (1990). © 1990 University of Toronto Press Incorporated (www.utpjournals.com). Reprinted with permission

. . . .

One way to foster administrative democracy . . . might be to strengthen . . . existing attempts to establish democratic control of the government. For example, the number, membership, and power of citizen advisory committees could be expanded so that the committees could engage in government decision-making. One form this effort might take would be to create administrative boards of directors, altering the European notion of co-determination from a practice of joint decision-making by workers and management to a practice of joint decision-making by workers and members of the public. A model for such a board of directors can be found in the structure of the governing board of the Caja Laboral Popular, the central financial institution and major unifying ingredient in the network of worker-owned companies in Mondragon. One-third of the CLP board is elected democratically by the workers in the bank, and the remaining two-thirds is selected by the co-operatives whose interests the bank purports to serve. Administrative agencies could similarly be managed by boards of directors consisting of a majority of representatives of the public and a minority of representatives of the agency's employees. It is important both that members of the public be able to control the board's decision-making and that government employees be assured a voice in it. . . .

The creation of such a board would, however, significantly change the role of the politically appointed administrators who have the job of managing the full-time government work-force as representatives of the public. Under bureaucratic theory, these political appointees are the central figures linking civil service employees and the desires of the public; if democratically elected worker-representatives and members of the public constituted an agency's board of directors, the importance of politically appointed administrators would be considerably diminished. The administrators' effectiveness would come to depend on their ability to bring the two sets of representatives together. The task of "managing" the government to serve the public interest would become more than a job description; it would describe a process of face-to-face discussion with both the government workers and members of the public. Indeed, the more the board of directors gained the power of decision rather than simply the opportunity to offer advice—and the more it became representative of the public at large—the closer it would approach the "town meeting" model of decision-making, one based on direct discussion between members of the public and government employees.

A major problem with adopting such a co-determination structure for administrative democracy is the difficulty of finding an acceptable method of selecting public representatives. If representation on the boards of directors is based on a theory of interest group pluralism, as the other efforts designed to democratize the bureaucracy have been, the co-determination idea is likely to be frustrated by the same problems with interest group pluralist theory that have troubled these earlier initiatives. Uncertainty about whether the interest groups that participate in the bureaucratic process represent the public interest have led even defenders of interest group representation to oscillate between a desire to defer to collective decisions made by these groups (in order to promote democracy) and a desire to limit the groups' influence on bureaucratic decision-making (in order to avoid "capture" of the government by special interests). This kind of ambivalence will be even stronger if the powers exercised by the interest group representatives are increased in the way I have suggested. The ambivalence is unavoidable, however, as long as one continues to rely on group representatives rather than on the public as a whole to articulate the public interest.

A more radical strategy, therefore, would supplement (or replace) such a plan with mechanisms that allow the public at large to debate the recommendations of government employees and to reject them when they think it is appropriate to do so. It is not clear to me why many people seem to think that such a scheme is impossible. The reason cannot be that the general public is unable to make governmental decisions directly; the initiative and referendum, after all, are standard parts of American public life. Moreover, once it is recognized that administrative democracy envisions decentralization of power, it is clear that decision-making by the general public can be made not only by vote but also in a direct face-to-face discussion with other citizens and with government employees. Governance by assembly has re-curred throughout history. . . . One fear is that such an assembly will serve no useful purpose because experts ultimately will be able to control the decisions; an opposite fear is that assemblies actually will make decisions and therefore lead to mob rule. But neither the prospect that experts will retain too much power nor the prospect that they will retain too little is inevitable. While either fear could be realized, it is also possible that any new assembly, like others before it, could find a way to obtain the advantage of expertise without being overawed by it.

The critical question, in my view, is not whether a system of popular gover-nance is possible in modern society but how to implement it. Although in some cities the remnants of town meetings still exist and could be reinvigorated, in most cities new institutional structures would have to be created. One such structure might be built on the current practice of holding public hearings before bureau-cratic decisions are made. Currently, public hearings are advertised as open to the public and are designed to permit all interested citizens to participate in the ad-ministrative process. Of course, at present these hearings are well within the ex-pertise model of decision-making: they are intended to inform government experts, not to control them. One could, however, begin to certify to a public hearing the power to *decide* a specific issue. The issue selected would depend on the level of confidence in the democratic process; cautious reformers are more likely to fear that the meetings would be either poorly attended or "stacked" by interest groups than are those who are more willing to experiment with democratic forms. But since even now a vote on governmental issues is possible in an initiative or referendum, these meetings might turn out to be preferable; after all, they would allow public discussion of opposing sides, consultation with government officials, and an op-portunity to find compromise solutions. No doubt, given the current level of inexperience with public decision-making, a period of experimentation with any form of democratic decision-making would be essential; reinvigorated public hearings could not be organized to decide the full range of administrative matters overnight. But even the beginning of such a process would create—for many people for the first time in their lives—the experience of democratic decision-making: the experience of collectively deciding with members of their community (including strangers) issues of public policy. It would also introduce government officials to the practice (not just the formal invocation) of popular control. Re-invigorated public hearings could thus serve as vehicles to help us rethink and improve upon mechanisms to foster administrative democracy.

There is also an intermediate option between the interest group pluralist model and a fully democratic model of the relationship between political democracy and organizational democracy. One could create a citizen group of, say, one hundred people to serve for a stated period of time as public representatives in an admin-istrative agency; the group would have to be chosen by lot rather than by election or through interest group representation to ensure that its members were a mi-crocosm of the public at large. Once constituted, the group would be authorized to meet with an agency's employees, discuss the issues facing the agency, and, after the discussion, debate and decide how to proceed. As the rate of turnover of this citizen group grew and the number of agencies whose policies were governed by this process increased, the experience of democratic self-governance would become more widespread. One can envision this process as an expanded and modified form of the jury: as with jury service, citizens would be expected to devote a portion of their time to public policy decision-making. Moreover, like jurors, the public representatives would have the job of applying legal rules, and judges might retain the authority that they currently exercise in reviewing administrative decisions to ensure that the representatives keep within this mandate. Of course, for many people, this form of democratic control of administrative decision-making would raise the same fears of democracy as the proposal to change the nature of public hearings; for others, it is an unhappy compromise because only a limited number of members of the public would be involved. One could easily debate the proposal's desirability, but it certainly would be possible to implement it. . . .

Of course, adding these elements to the structure of the federal government will not ensure democratic control of its actions. The idea of "public" representation in government becomes more and more of an abstraction as the opportunity for widespread participation diminishes; democratic structures incorporated into the national government need to be regularly reconnected with local democracy to make their claimed "democratic" nature credible. Bob Reich describes one method of accomplishing this objective which was adopted by the United States Environmental Protection Agency, the agency empowered to promulgate national standards for emission of hazardous air pollutants. In 1982, the EPA had to decide whether American Smelting and Refining Company (Asarco), a major employer in the Tacoma, Washington, area, was within the statutory margin of safety for its emission of inorganic arsenic, a cancer-producing pollutant. Defining the required "margin of safety" was complex: the pollutant was admittedly a health hazard, but excessive controls would lead to the closing of the plant and thereby injure the area's economy.

> William Ruckelshaus, then Administrator of the EPA, decided that the citizens of the Tacoma area ought to wrestle with the problem. Accordingly, Ruckelshaus flew to Tacoma to announce a series of three public workshops to be held during the summer of 1983. Their purpose was to acquaint residents with the details of the pollution problem, help them prepare for subsequent formal hearings, and enable them to deliberate about what should be done. Two of the workshops were held in a local public high school in Tacoma; they attracted environmental groups, local citizen organizations, and a large number of smelter workers. The third workshop took place on Vashon Island, a residential area where the winds of Puget Sound carried many of Asarco's emissions; most of the attendees at this workshop were island homeowners. EPA officials began each workshop by explaining how the agency had estimated health risks from the factory and the likely effects of different levels of pollution control. They then divided the audience into three groups, and had agency officials and staff circulate among the groups to facilitate a more informal discussion.

The EPA's effort was highly controversial, but it suggests one way to involve the local public in a federal agency's decision-making. Although the public's role as envisioned by the EPA was simply advisory, even this role could well be influential—particularly if the federal agency itself were managed (as the EPA was not) by a board of directors consisting of a majority of public representatives. Moreover, there is no reason to assume that a public debate of this kind would be appropriate only in cases in which the effects of the decision were limited to a particular locality. Federal agencies could select representative localities—or pick localities by lot—to help resolve issues of national policy; juries, after all, are selected in a way that allows a random sample of the population to engage in public decision-making.

The public could also be incorporated into federal decision-making in another way. Many federal agencies (including the EPA) are now organized into district offices managed by a national headquarters in a top-down organizational structure, with little or no public involvement included at any level of decision-making. But district offices do not have to be operated in this hierarchical manner; they could instead become the vehicles for allowing public participation in federal agency decision-making. Each district office could, like local governments, include members of the public in its organizational structure, and the individual offices could be connected with each other in a manner analogous to the inter-city links described above. Regularly scheduled inter-district discussions—involving both public and employee representatives from district offices—could focus on agency policy and problems of implementation. As this structure developed, the power relationship between top officials in the central office and the people involved at the district level would begin to change: top officials would have to take seriously ideas developed on an inter-district basis rather than simply treat district employees as means to national ends. As with other democratic forms discussed earlier, there is no reason to assume that such a structure would transform an efficient organization into one that is unmanageable. On the contrary, worker and public involvement in decision-making might both improve national policies and help ensure that they have the support necessary to be implemented....

4. Bureaucratic Consciousness

As I hope I have demonstrated, there are a great many ways to increase democratic institutional mechanisms within our current system of government. How fast these changes could be made is a legitimate subject of debate. But implementing them would certainly transform the government bureaucracy. "Democracy" might not replace "bureaucracy," but the claim that bureaucratic form of government is inevitable would surely no longer seem credible.

What prevents us from making these changes? The answer, in my view, does not lie in our inability to create the necessary institutional mechanisms: suggestions such as those made above could be implemented if we wanted to do so. Nor does the answer lie in the charge that a government that included so many democratic institutions "wouldn't work." There is no uncontroversial definition of what "working" means. Indeed, there is an equally common charge that bureaucracy doesn't "work" either. Bureaucracy is the modern symbol not only of efficiency (as Weber suggested) but of incompetence—consider the powerfully negative associations with the word "bureaucrat" and the prevalence of the popular belief that public sector employees do not put much effort into their jobs. The notion of a smoothly operating bureaucracy is as much a utopian fantasy as the notion of a smoothly operating democracy. Why do we adopt a definition of "what works" that highlights the problems with democracy and minimizes the equally serious (although very different) problems with bureaucracy? Why do we accept the goals of one system and try to make the best of it and largely reject the promise offered by the other?

The answer, I think, lies in our distrust of democracy. If my suggestions of workplace democracy, popular control of the government, or decentralization are labelled "impossible," it is likely to be because it is so widely believed that people cannot govern themselves. Even if the size of an entity is small (as in a workplace or small town), even if the level of general education is high (as in most industrialized countries), even if solving the problem in question plainly requires the kind of judgment that expertise cannot possibly provide (as is true for most policy-making), democracy is commonly thought not to be an option. People are too lazy (or too busy), it is said; they won't participate. People are too stupid; they won't know what to do. Meetings will go on forever; no decisions will ever be made. Anyway, people want to have experts make decisions for them; they don't even want democracy. These anti-democratic sentiments, like countless others, are endlessly repeated, although they are rarely based on empirical evidence or a theoretical explanation of the reasons for different levels of popular participation. They are also not likely to be based on personal experience. They are often voiced by people who have had no personal experience in collective decision-making on an issue of public policy. These sentiments do not reflect an insight into "human nature" as is often claimed; they are instead a reflection of anti-democratic prejudice.

Anti-democratic prejudice shares many of the ingredients classically associated with other kinds of prejudice: the objects of prejudice are often depicted as lazy, ignorant, and needing to be kept in their place. Moreover, the assertions of anti-democratic prejudice mistake the nature of democracy. There is no single mode of decision, called "democracy," that specifies how much participation is required, how much time people need to spend in meetings, or the role of expertise in decision-making; there are countless ways to organize democratic forms of governance. The notion of democracy surely does not require everyone to decide everything in one big meeting. None of the suggestions offered above, for example, requires limitless participation or endless meetings. The amount of participation required depends on the democratic mechanism chosen, and there are many ways to organize discussions to budget people's time. It is wrong simply to assume that democratic participation will take more time than, say, bureaucratic infighting.

Moreover, democracy and expertise are not mutually inconsistent. Every form of government, whether democratic or authoritarian, has to obtain the benefit of knowledge and specialization. Expert knowledge plainly contributes to political decision-making; it is just no substitute for it. Hanna Pitkin and Sara Shumer have articulated why this is so:

> First off, stupidity knows no class. Maybe most people are foolish, but foolishness is found in all social strata. Education removes some kinds of ignorance, but may entrench or instill others. The cure is not to exclude some but to include as diverse a range of perspectives and experience as possible in political deliberation. Second, expertise cannot solve political problems. Contemporary politics is indeed full of technically complex topics, about which even the educated feel horribly ignorant. But on every politically significant

issue of this kind, the "experts" are divided; that is part of what makes the issue political. Though we may also feel at a loss to choose between them, leaving it to the experts is no solution at all. Finally, while various kinds of knowledge can be profoundly useful in political decisions, knowledge alone is never enough. The political question is what we are to *do*; knowledge can only tell us how things are, how they work, while a political resolution always depends on what we, as a community, want and think right. And those questions have no technical answer; they require collective deliberation and decision. The experts must become a part of, not an alternative to, the democratic political process.

Democratic systems, when they are successful, learn how to accommodate expertise: they neither automatically reject it nor automatically defer to it. At present, judges and politicians are the people with the most experience with this kind of engagement with experts; administrative democracy is an attempt to expand this kind of experience to the public at large.

Anti-democratic prejudice thrives in an environment in which experience with democracy is rare; it is re-created and reinforced in the process of accommodation to bureaucracy. Democratic theorists often insist that the experience of democracy creates a different kind of person—a different way of relating to others and even of being oneself. But the experience of bureaucracy nurtures a particular kind of person as well; it too fosters ways of relating to others and ways of being oneself. To survive in a world filled with bureaucratic institutions, we learn to defend our own assertion of expertise and our own deference to it. We assure ourselves that our power is legitimate—and that our powerlessness is legitimate as well. "Other people cannot be involved in our decisions," we claim; "they don't even want to be involved, and we can't be involved in their decisions either." Decision-making is thus allocated into a hierarchy of specialties, each filled with people chosen because of their technical competence. Indeed, people often treat the problem of choosing between democratic and bureaucratic forms of organization in this way. The issue is posed as a question that calls for a cost-benefit analysis or the correct allocation of different kinds of talent. To approach the issue in this way is the equivalent in thought of the bureaucratic form of organization: it calls for the application of expertise instead of politics, for an objective answer instead of discussion and compromise. Only under this approach could the question whether democracy is impossible be understood as answerable in an academic conference without the participation of anyone but scholars.

This kind of bureaucratic consciousness is a major impediment to fostering administrative democracy; it makes it hard to take the prospects of democracy seriously. Combating it is thus as important as institution building in overcoming the felt necessity of bureaucracy. Indeed, combating it is part of the process of institution-building. Suspicions about democracy, nurtured by the experience of bureaucracy, cannot be overcome simply as a matter of thought. They need to be confronted through experience with democracy. This is not to suggest that democratic experience is or ever will be unproblematic; neither democracy nor bureaucracy can be embraced in utopian terms. In building different kinds of institutions, we learn to confront different kinds of problems and in this way create a different sense of self. The end result of such a process cannot be known in advance; it depends on the institutions we build and how we learn to live with them. But if this is so, how do we decide what institutions to build? How do we decide if administrative democracy is a good idea? There are many ways to answer these questions. Surely one possible way to do so is to create democratic forms of organization that are empowered to analyse, debate, and decide them.

COMMENTS AND QUESTIONS

1. The preceding materials deal with small-scale or experimental uses of reconstitutive regulation. Can you identify the political conditions that make such uses possible? What are the political constraints on, and possibilities for, adopting reconstitutive regulation more broadly? Consider here what proponents of public choice analysis of choices of regulatory instruments might say—and what their critics would say—about those constraints and possibilities.

2. The most profound restructuring of the regulatory system in recent years has occurred through the activities of the Office of Information and Regulatory Affairs (OIRA), discussed in chapter 13. The basic idea behind OIRA's recent work has been that the regulatory system needs more centralized control and more use of expert-driven analytical frameworks such as cost-benefit analysis. How does this restructuring differ from the collaborative mechanisms Freeman and Frug describe? Can centralization and collaboration be reconciled? If so, how?

3. Stewart might be described as offering a centrist or center-right program of reconstitutive law. Freeman's program of collaborative governance might be similarly described. Frug's program is clearly more leftist. Could it be described as a reconstitutive law program? Among Stewart, Freeman, and Frug, who offers the more attractive program? How might Frug's recommendations be implemented in the contexts of workplace safety and health and environmental risk?

4. Much of this book has addressed the question of relative competencies, as between the public and "experts." After all we have read, whose side are you on? Do you have to choose? Do the reforms offered in this chapter offer a possible middle ground, in which we can draw on both perspectives?

Table of Cases

Principal cases appear in **bold**.

Index

fear of, 156, 169
of developing cancer, 132, 156, 169
of future illness, 132, 147, 156
of premature death, 147, 151–152
recovery for, 133, 150, 154, 160,
165, 170
Indian Gaming Regulatory Act, 369
Industrial revolution, 276
Industrial Workers of the World,
247, 276
Information, 69, 225, 551
acquisition by learning, 550–553,
595–597
asymmetry, 83
framing effects, 573–574, 594–595
limitations on ability to process, 550,
564–565
provision by markets, 548–549
Informational regulation, 531, 548–556,
561–562
and the First Amendment,
598–609
Proposition 65, 531, 563, 566
Informational remedies, 561
Injurious experience, 232
Injury
in-fact, 269
procedural, 269
Restatement definition of, 139, 144
Insecticides, 259–262
Insurance, 43, 225, 297–298, 301–304
Institutional choice, 683
Institutional competence
of administrative agencies,
214–219, 221
of the judiciary, 213
Interstate Commerce Commission, 415
Irreversibility, 208
"Ivey" memo, 112–113

Japan
criminal prosecution in, 764
environmental regulation in,
758–765, 774–777
law for the resolution of pollution
disputes, 761
Minamata, 758–760
Judicial review. *See also* Deference;
Standing
Arbitrary and capricious review,
438–449, 647

Administrative Procedures Act,
426–427
"hard look" vs. rational connection
review, 449
of administrative agency enforcement
actions, 745–749
of administrative agency procedure,
427–434
of administrative agency statutory
interpretation, 379–386. *See also*
Chevron
Jurisdiction, federal, 265

Kaldor-Hicks, 503
Kelman, Mark, 46, 686
Keynes, John Maynard, 684

Labor market
secondary vs. primary, 50–51
segmentation theory, 50
Landfills, 129, 166, 676
Latency period, 134–136, 310–311
Latin, Howard, 595–596
Law and Economics, 297
assumptions of, 49
Coase Theorem, 40–41
endowment effects, 588–589
equalizing differences, principle of, 51
ex ante perspective, 38
ex post perspective, 39
externalities, 464, 684
incentives, 39
Kaldor-Hicks, 503
law of demand, 39
margins, 39–41
moral hazard, 295–303
post-judgment bargaining, 41
transaction costs, 40–41, 83
Law, letter vs. spirit, 351. *See also*
Moral/formal distinction
Lawyers, role of, 237–238
Lead, 7
Legal ethics, 200
ABA Model Rules, 200–2001
confidentiality, 200
Legislation
rent-seeking, 693
supply and demand model of,
696–699
symbolic, 701